THE WESTERN HERITAGE

TEACHING AND LEARNING CLASSROOM EDITION

BRIEF FIFTH EDITION

COMBINED VOLUME

Donald Kagan
YALE UNIVERSITY

Steven Ozment
HARVARD UNIVERSITY

Frank M. Turner
YALE UNIVERSITY

PEARSON
Prentice Hall

Upper Saddle River, New Jersey 07458

Library of Congress Cataloging-in-Publication Data

Kagan, Donald.
  The western heritage / Donald Kagan, Steven Ozment, Frank M. Turner—Teaching and learning classroom ed., brief 5th ed.
    p. cm.
  "Combined volume."
  Includes bibliographical references and index.
  ISBN 0-13-221107-6
  1. Civilization, Western—History—Textbooks.   I. Ozment, Steven E.   II. Turner, Frank M. (Frank Miller), 1944-   III. Title.
  CB245K28 2006b
  909'.09821—dc22

                                                        2005036328

Vice President/Editorial Director: Charlyce Jones Owen
Executive Editor: Charles Cavaliere
Associate Editor: Emsal Hasan
Editorial Assistant: Maria Guarascio
Editor-in-Chief/Development: Rochelle Diogenes
Media Editor: Deborah O'Connell
**Vice President/Director of Production
  and Manufacturing:** Barbara Kittle
Senior Managing Editor: Joanne Riker
Production Liaison: Louise Rothman
Prepress and Manufacturing Manager: Nick Sklitsis
Prepress and Manufacturing Buyer: Benjamin Smith
Director of Marketing: Brandy Dawson
Assistant Marketing Manager: Andrea Messineo
Marketing Assistant: Jennifer Lang
Creative Design Director: Leslie Osher

Cover and Interior Design: Laura Gardner, Amy Rosen,
  Kathy Mrozek
Electronic Artist: Carey Davies
Cartographer: CartoGraphics
Director, Image Resource Center: Melinda Reo
Manager, Visual Research: Beth Brenzel
Cover Image Specialist: Karen Sanatar
Photo Researcher: Teri Stratford
Image Coordinator: Robert Farrell
Color Scanning Service: Joe Conti, Greg Harrison,
  Cory Skidds, Rob Uibelhoer, Ron Walko
**Composition and Full Service
  Project Management:** Caterina Melara/Prepare, Inc.
Printer/Binder: Courier Companies, Inc.
Cover Printer: Phoenix Color Corporation

Cover Art: Agnolo Bronzino, 1503-1572, Italian, *Eleanor (Medici) of Toledo with her son.* The Art Archive/Galleria degli Uffizi
  Florence/Dagli Orti (A). Ref: AA356740

Credits and acknowledgments borrowed from other sources and reproduced, with permission, in this textbook appear on
appropriate page within text or on page C-1.

Pearson Education LTD.   Pearson Education, Canada, Ltd
Pearson Education Australia PTY, Limited   Pearson Educación de Mexico, S.A. de C.V.
Pearson Education Singapore, Pte. Ltd   Pearson Education–Japan
Pearson Education North Asia Ltd   Pearson Education Malaysia, Pte. Ltd

10 9 8 7 6 5 4 3 2

ISBN 0-13-221107-6

3

Classical and Hellenistic Greece   56

Visualizing The Past

Goddesses and the Female Form in Ancient Art   86

4

Rome: From Republic to Empire   88

The Roman Empire   114

PART 2

THE MIDDLE AGES   144

Late Antiquity and the Early Middle Ages: Creating a New European Society and Culture (476–1000)   146

Visualizing The Past

PART 3

EUROPE IN TRANSITION 216

12

The Age of Religious Wars   290

13

European State Consolidation in the Seventeenth and Eighteenth Centuries   **312**

14

New Directions in Thought and Culture in the Sixteenth and Seventeenth Centuries   **340**

PART 4

ENLIGHTMENT AND REVOLUTION 404

The Age of Enlightenment: Eighteenth-Century Thought 406

The French Revolution 432

19

The Age of Napoleon and the Triumph of Romanticism   456

20

The Conservative Order and the Challenges of Reform (1815–1832)   482

21

Economic Advance and Social Unrest (1830–1850)   506

Visualizing The Past

PART 5

TOWARD THE MODERN WORLD   534

22

The Age of Nation-States   536

23

The Building of European Supremacy: Society and Politics to World War I   562

Visualizing The Past

24

The Birth of Modern European Thought 590

25

Imperialism, Alliances, and War 614

26 ★

Political Experiments of the 1920s   646

27

Europe and the Great Depression of the 1930s   668

Visualizing The Past

PART 6

GLOBAL CONFLICT, COLD WAR, AND NEW DIRECTIONS   688

World War II   **690**

29

The Cold War Era and the Emergence of a New Europe   **718**

30

The West at the Dawn of the Twenty-First Century   **746**

History's Voices

Encountering the Past

SPECIAL FEATURES

Maps

Visualizing the Past

PREFACE

he heritage of Western civilization remains a major point of departure for understanding the twenty-first century. The unprecedented globalization of daily life that is a hallmark of our era has occurred largely through the spread of Western influences. From the sixteenth century onward, the West has exerted vast influences throughout the globe for both good and ill, and today's global citizens continue to live in the wake of that impact. It is the goal of this book to introduce its readers to the Western heritage, so that they may be better informed and more culturally sensitive citizens of the emerging global age.

The attacks upon the mainland of the United States on September 11, 2001, and the subsequent American invasions of Afghanistan and Iraq have concentrated the attention of teachers, students, and informed citizens upon the heritage and future of Western civilization as have no other events since the end of World War II. Whereas previously, commentary about global civilization involved analysis of the spread of Western economic, technological, and political influences, we now must explain how the West has defined itself over many centuries and think about how the West will articulate its core values as it confronts new and daunting challenges. The events of recent years and the hostility that has arisen in many parts of the world to the power and influence of the West require new efforts both to understand how the West sees itself and how other parts of the world see the West.

Twenty years ago, the West still defined itself mainly in terms of the East–West tensions associated with the Cold War. The West is now in the process of defining itself in terms of global rivalries arising from conflict with political groups that are not identical with nation-states, groups that define themselves in terms of opposition to what they understand the West to be. Whether or not we are witnessing a clash of civilizations, as Samuel Huntington, the distinguished Harvard political scientist, contends, we have certainly entered a new era in which citizens of the West need to understand how their culture, values, economy, and political outlooks have emerged. They cannot leave it to those who would attack the West to define Western civilization or to articulate its values.

Since *The Western Heritage* first appeared, we have sought to provide our readers with a work that does justice to the richness and variety of Western civilization and its many complexities. We hope that such an understanding of the West will foster lively debate about its character, values, institutions, and global influence. Indeed, we believe such a critical outlook on their own culture has characterized the peoples of the West since the dawn of history. Through such debates we define ourselves and the values of our culture. Consequently, we welcome the debate and hope that *The Western Heritage*, Teaching and Learning Classroom Edition, can help foster an informed discussion through its history of the West's strengths and weaknesses, and the controversies surrounding Western history.

Human beings make, experience, and record their history. In this edition as in past editions, our goal has been to present Western civilization fairly, accurately, and in a way that does justice to that great variety of human enterprise. History has many facets, no one of which alone can account for the others. Any attempt to tell the story of the West from a single overarching perspective, no matter how timely, is bound to neglect or suppress some important parts of that story. Like all authors of introductory texts, we have had to make choices, but we have attempted to provide the broadest possible introduction to Western civilization. To that end, we hope that the many documents included in this book will allow the widest possible spectrum of people to relate their personal experiences over the centuries and will enable our readers to share that experience.

We also believe that any book addressing the experience of the West must also look beyond its historical European borders. Students reading this book come from a wide variety of cultures and experiences. They live in a world of highly interconnected economies and instant communication between cultures. In this emerging multicultural society it seems both appropriate and necessary to recognize how Western civilization has throughout its history interacted with other cultures, both influencing and being influenced by them. Examples of this two-way interaction, such as that with Islam, appear throughout the text.

GOALS OF THE TEXT

Our primary goal has been to present a strong, clear, narrative account of the central developments in Western history. We have also sought to call attention to certain critical themes:

- The capacity of Western civilization from the time of the Greeks to the present to transform itself through self-criticism.
- The development in the West of political freedom, constitutional government, and concern for the rule of law and individual rights.
- The shifting relations among religion, society, and the state.
- The development of science and technology and their expanding impact on Western thought, social institutions, and everyday life.
- The major religious and intellectual currents that have shaped Western culture.

We believe that these themes have been fundamental in Western civilization, shaping the past and exerting a continuing influence on the present.

Flexible Presentation   *The Western Heritage*, Teaching and Learning Classroom Edition, is designed to accommodate a variety of approaches to a course in Western civilization, allowing teachers to stress what is most important to them. Some teachers will ask students to read all the chapters. Others will select among them to reinforce assigned readings and lectures.

Integrated Social, Cultural, and Political History   *The Western Heritage*, Teaching and Learning Classroom Edition provides one of the richest accounts of the social history of the West available today, with strong coverage of family life, the changing roles of women, and the place of the family in relation to broader economic, political, and social developments. This coverage reflects the explosive growth in social historical research in the past three decades, which has enriched virtually all areas of historical study.

While strongly believing in the study of the social experience of the West, we also share the conviction that internal and external political events have shaped the Western experience in fundamental and powerful ways. The experiences of Europeans in the twentieth century under fascism, national socialism, and communism demonstrate that influence, as has, more recently, the collapse of communism in the former Soviet Union and eastern Europe. We have also been told repeatedly by teachers that no matter what their own historical specialization, they believe that a political narrative gives students an effective tool to begin to understand the past. Consequently, we have sought to integrate the political with the social, cultural, and intellectual.

No other survey text presents so full an account of the religious and intellectual development of the West. People may be political and social beings, but they are also reasoning and spiritual beings. What they think and believe are among the most important things we can know about them. Their ideas about God, society, law, gender, human nature, and the physical world have changed over the centuries and continue to change. We cannot fully grasp our own approach to the world without understanding the intellectual currents of the past and how they influenced our thoughts and conceptual categories.

Clarity and Accessibility   Good narrative history requires clear, vigorous prose. As in earlier editions, we have paid careful attention to our writing, subjecting every paragraph to critical scrutiny. Our goal was to make the history of the West accessible to students without compromising vocabulary or conceptual level. We hope this effort will benefit both teachers and students.

CHAPTER-BY-CHAPTER REVISIONS

Chapter 1   Increased coverage of Neolithic Europe, including an entire section on the "Ice man" found in the Alps. A major new section on the Persian Empire has also been added.

Chapter 6   Discussion of Late Antiquity now opens the chapter. Discussion of the Byzantine Empire has been expanded. Coverage of Islam and the early Islamic conquests has been increased.

Chapter 13   An entirely new chapter that examines European political history from the seventeenth to eighteenth centuries.

Chapter 18   Coverage of the French Revolution has been significantly revised and reorganized.

Chapter 25   Discussion of the New Imperialism has been significantly expanded, including a new section on the Scramble for Africa with case-study examinations of colonialism in Egypt, the Belgian Congo, and South Africa.

Chapter 27   New, fuller discussion of Keynesian economics.

Chapter 28   Revised and expanded section on the Holocaust and the destruction of Polish Jewry.

Chapter 29   Updated discussion of post–World War II European political history, especially as regards Russia, the European Union, and the invasions of Afghanistan and Iraq.

Chapter 30   Revised sections on immigration within Europe, Islam in Europe, and terrorism.

Recent Scholarship   As in previous editions, changes in this edition reflect our determination to incorporate the most recent developments in historical scholarship and the concerns of professional historians. Of particular interest are expanded discussions of cultural history, women's history, and the interaction between Islam and the West.

Maps and Illustrations   The entire map and photo program has been significantly revised. New maps include the Persian Empire, the slave trade, global migration in the nineteenth century, and the Holocaust. To help students understand the relationship between geography and history, approximately one-half of the maps include relief features. Up to two maps in each chapter feature interactive exercises on the Companion Website™ that accompanies the text. All maps have been carefully edited for accuracy. The text also contains abundant color and black and white illustrations, approximately one-third of which are new to this edition.

Pedagogical Features   This edition retains many of the pedagogical features of previous editions, while providing increased assessment opportunities.

- **NEW** • **Chapter Highlights** begin each chapter and provide a preview of the key developments and themes that are to follow.

- **Part Timelines** show the major events in social, political, and cultural history—side by side. Appropriate photographs enrich each timeline.

- **Chapter-Opening Questions**, organized by the main subtopics of each chapter, encourage careful consideration of important themes and developments. Each question is repeated at the appropriate place in the margin of the text.

- **Chronologies** within each chapter help students organize a time sequence for key events.

- **History's Voices**, including selections from sacred books, poems, philosophy, political manifestos, letters, and travel accounts, introduces students to the raw material of history, providing an intimate contact with the people of the past and their concerns. Questions accompanying the source documents direct students toward important, thought-provoking issues and help them relate the documents to the material in the text. They can be used to stimulate class discussion or as topics for essays and study groups.

- **Encountering the Past**   Each chapter includes an essay on a significant issue of everyday life or popular culture. These essays explore a variety of subjects including gladiatorial bouts and medieval games, midwivery, smoking in early modern Europe, and the politics of rock music in the late twentieth century. These thirty essays, each of which includes an illustration and study questions, expand *The Western Heritage* TLC Edition's rich coverage of social and cultural history. (See p. xxiii for a complete list of the "Encountering the Past" essays.)

- **Map Explorations** and **Critical-Thinking Questions** prompt students to engage with maps, often in an interactive fashion. Each Map Exploration is found on the Companion Website™ for the text.

- **Visualizing the Past** essays, found at the end of selected chapters, analyze important aspects of world history through photographs, fine art, sculpture, and woodcuts. Focus questions and a running narrative guide students though a careful examination of the historical issues raised by each topic in question. Two new "Visualizing the Past" essays have been added to this edition: "Imagining Women in the Eighteenth and Nineteenth Centuries," and "Identity and Nationalism in Contemporary Europe."

- **Chapter Review** questions help students focus on and interpret the broad themes of a chapter. These questions can be used for class discussion and essay topics.

- **Overview Tables** in each chapter summarize complex issues.

- **Quick Reviews,** found at key places in the margins of each chapter, encourage students to review important concepts.

- **Key Terms,** boldfaced in the text, are listed (with page reference) at the end of each chapter, and defined in the book's glossary.

 - **Documents CD-ROM,** containing over 200 documents in Western civilization, is bound with all new copies of the text. Relevant documents are listed at appropriate places in the margin of the text at the end of each chapter.

- **Study in Time,** a laminated six-panel timeline of Western history, provides a succinct overview of key developments in social, political, and cultural history in Western civilization from earliest times to the present.

A Note on Dates and Transliterations   This edition of *The Western Heritage* TLC Edition continues the practice of using B.C.E. (before the common era) and C.E. (common era) instead of B.C. (before Christ) and A.D. (anno Domini, the year of the Lord) to designate dates. We also follow the most accurate currently accepted English transliterations of Arabic words. For example, today *Koran* is being replaced by the more accurate *Qur'an*; similarly *Muhammad* is preferable to *Mohammed* and *Muslim* to *Moslem.*

ANCILLARY INSTRUCTIONAL MATERIALS

The Western Heritage TLC Edition is available with an extensive package of ancillary materials.

For the Instructor

- **Instructor's Resource Binder** This innovative, all-in-one resource organizes the *Instructor's Manual,* the Test-Item File, and the transparency pack by each chapter of *The Western Heritage,* TLC Edition to facilitate class preparation. The *Instructor's Resource Binder* also includes an **Instructor's Resource CD-ROM,** which contains all of the maps, graphs, and many of the illustrations from the text in easily downloadable electronic files.

- The *Instructor's Resource CD-ROM,* compatible with both Windows and Macintosh environments, provides instructors with such essential teaching tools as hundreds of digitized images and maps for classroom presentations, PowerPoint™ lectures, and other instructional material. The assets on the IRCD-ROM can be easily exported into online courses, such as WebCT and Blackboard.

- *Test Manager* is a computerized test management program for Windows and Macintosh environments. The program allows instructors to select items from the Test-Item File to create tests. It also allows online testing.

- The *Transparency Package* provides instructors with full-color transparency acetates of all the maps, charts, and graphs in the text for use in the classroom.

For the Student

- *History Notes* (Volumes I and II) provides practice tests, essay questions, and map exercises to help reinforce key concepts.

- *Documents* in *Western Civilization* (Volumes I and II) is a collection of 200 primary source documents in global history. Questions accompanying the documents can be used for discussion or as writing assignments.

- Produced in collaboration with Dorling Kindersley, the world's most respected cartography publisher, *The Prentice Hall Atlas of Western Civilization* includes approximately 100 maps fundamental to the study of western civilization—from early hominids to the twenty-first century.

- *Reading Critically About History* is a brief guide to reading effectively that provides students with helpful strategies for reading a history textbook.

- *Understanding and Answering Essay Questions* suggests helpful analytical tools for understanding different types of essay questions, and provides precise guidelines for preparing well-crafted essay answers.

- Prentice Hall is pleased to provide adopters of *The Western Heritage*, TLC Edition with an opportunity to receive significant discounts when copies of the text are bundled with Penguin Classics titles in history. Contact your local Prentice Hall representative for details.

MEDIA RESOURCES

Key Prentice Hall's Online Resource, **OneKey** lets instructors and students in to the best teaching and learning resources—all in one place. This all-inclusive online resource is designed to help you minimize class preparation and maximize teaching time. Conveniently organized by chapter, OneKey for *The Western Heritage*, TLC Edition, reinforces what students have learned in class and from the text. Among the student resources available for each chapter are: a complete media-rich e-book version of *The Western Heritage*, TLC Edition; quizzes organized by the main subtopics of each chapter; over 200 primary-source documents; and interactive map quizzes.

For instructors, OneKey includes images and maps From *The Western Heritage*, TLC Edition, instructional material, hundreds of primary-source documents, and PowerPoint™ presentations.

Prentice Hall One Search with Research Navigator: History 2005 This brief guide focuses on developing critical-thinking skills necessary for evaluating and using online sources. It provides a brief introduction to navigating the Internet with specific references to history Websites. It also provides an access code and instruction on using Research Navigator, a powerful research tool that provides entry to three exclusive databases of reliable source material: ContentSelect Academic Journal Database, the *New York Times* Search by Subject Archive, and Link Library.

The Companion Website with Grade Tracker™ *(www.prenhall.com/kagan3)* works in tandem with the text and features objectives, study questions, Web links to related Internet resources, document exercises, interactive maps, online essays on technology and global history, and map labeling exercises.

Western Civilization Document CD-ROM Bound into every new copy of this textbook is a free Western civilization Documents CD-ROM. This is a powerful resource for research and additional reading that contains more than 200 primary source documents central to Western history. Each document provides essay questions that are linked directly to a Website where short-essay answers can be submitted online or printed out. A complete list of documents on the CD-ROM is found at the end of the text.

ACKNOWLEDGMENTS

We are grateful to the scholars and teachers whose thoughtful and often detailed comments helped shape this revision:

Jennifer Wynot, Metropolitan State College of Denver
William B. Whisenhunt, College of DuPage
Jonathan Perry, University of Central Florida
David Hudson, California State University, Fresno
Wanda L. Scarbro, Pellissippi State Technical Community College
Lynn Lubamersky, Boise State University
Paul J. L. Hughes, Sussex County Community College
Patti Harrold, Edmond Memorial High School
Miriam Pelikan-Pittenger, University of Illinois at Urbana-Champaign

Steven Ozment would like to acknowledge the help of Adam Beaver and Elizabeth Russell. Frank Turner would like to acknowledge the aid of Magnus T. Bernhardsson. We are grateful for the fine editorial work of George Kosar (Tufts University and Harvard University) in preparing this new TLC edition. Finally, we would like to thank the dedicated people who helped produce this revision. Our acquisitions editor, Charles Cavaliere; our production liaison, Louise Rothman; Laura Gardner, who created the beautiful new design of this edition; Benjamin D. Smith, our manufacturing buyer; Caterina Melara, production editor; and Teri Stratford, photo researcher.

D.K.
S.O.
F.M.T.

DONALD KAGAN is Sterling Professor of History and Classics at Yale University, where he has taught since 1969. He received the A.B. degree in history from Brooklyn College, the M.A. in classics from Brown University, and the Ph.D. in history from Ohio State University. During 1958–1959 he studied at the American School of Classical Studies as a Fulbright Scholar. He has received three awards for undergraduate teaching at Cornell and Yale. He is the author of a history of Greek political thought, *The Great Dialogue* (1965); a four-volume history of the Peloponnesian war, *The Origins of the Peloponnesian War* (1969); *The Archidamian War* (1974); *The Peace of Nicias and the Sicilian Expedition* (1981); *The Fall of the Athenian Empire* (1987); and a biography of Pericles, *Pericles of Athens and the Birth of Democracy* (1991); *On the Origins of War* (1995) and *The Peloponnesian War* (2003). He is coauthor with Frederick W. Kagan of *While America Sleeps* (2000). With Brian Tierney and L. Pearce Williams, he is the editor of *Great Issues in Western Civilization*, a collection of readings. He was awarded the National Humanities Medal for 2002.

STEVEN OZMENT is McLean Professor of Ancient and Modern History at Harvard University. He has taught Western Civilization at Yale, Stanford, and Harvard. He is the author of eleven books. *The Age of Reform, 1250–1550* (1980) won the Schaff Prize and was nominated for the 1981 National Book Award. Five of his books have been selections of the History Book Club: *Magdalena and Balthasar: An Intimate Portrait of Life in Sixteenth Century Europe* (1986), *Three Behaim Boys: Growing Up in Early Modern Germany* (1990), *Protestants: The Birth of A Revolution* (1992), *The Burgermeister's Daughter: Scandal in a Sixteenth Century German Town* (1996), and *Flesh and Spirit: Private Life in Early*

Modern Germany (1999). His most recent publications are *Ancestors: The Loving Family of Old Europe* (2001), *A Mighty Fortress: A New History of the German People* (2004), and "Why We Study Western Civ," *The Public Interest* 158 (2005).

FRANK M. TURNER is John Hay Whitney Professor of History at Yale University and Director of the Beinecke Rare Book and Manuscript Library at Yale University, where he served as University Provost from 1988 to 1992. He received his B.A. degree at the College of William and Mary and his Ph.D. from Yale. He has received the Yale College Award for Distinguished Undergraduate Teaching. He has directed a National Endowment for the Humanities Summer Institute. His scholarly research has received the support of fellowships from the National Endowment for the Humanities and the Guggenheim Foundation and the Woodrow Wilson Center. He is the author of *Between Science and Religion: The Reaction to Scientific Naturalism in Late Victorian England* (1974); *The Greek Heritage in Victorian Britain* (1981), which received the British Council Prize of the Conference on British Studies and the Yale Press Governors Award; *Contesting Cultural Authority: Essays in Victorian Intellectual Life* (1993); and *John Henry Newman: The Challenge to Evangelical Religion* (2002). He has also contributed numerous articles to journals and has served on the editorial advisory boards of *The Journal of Modern History, Isis,* and *Victorian Studies.* He edited *The Idea of a University,* by John Henry Newman (1996) and *Reflections on the Revolution in France* by Edmund Burke (2003). Since 1996 he has served as a Trustee of Connecticut College. In 2003, Professor Turner was appointed Director of the Beinecke Rare Book and Manuscript Library at Yale University.

When writing history, historians use maps, tables, graphs, and visuals to help their readers understand the past. What follows is an explanation of how to use the historian's tools that are contained in this book.

TEXT

Whether it is a biography of Gandhi, an article on the Ottoman Empire, or a survey of Western civilization such as this one, the text is the historian's basic tool for discussing the past. Historians write about the past using narration and analysis. Narration is the story line of history. It describes what happened in the past, who did it, and where and when it occurred. Narration is also used to describe how people in the past lived, how they passed their daily lives and even, when the historical evidence makes it possible for us to know, what they thought, felt, feared, or desired. Using analysis, historians explain why they think events in the past happened the way they did and offer an explanation for the story of history. In this book, narration and analysis are interwoven in each chapter.

STUDY AIDS

A number of features in this book are designed to aid in the study of history. Each chapter begins with **Chapter Highlights**, mini-summaries that preview key themes and developments, and **Questions**, organized by the main subtopics of each chapter, which encourage careful consideration of important themes and developments. Each question is repeated at the appropriate place in the margin

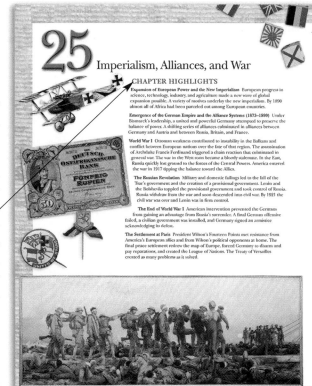

EXPANSION OF EUROPEAN POWER AND THE NEW IMPERIALISM

Europe's power was based on the progress it made during the nineteenth century in science, technology, industry, agriculture, transportation, communications, and military weaponry. These advancements enabled Europeans (and Americans) to impose their wills on peoples many times their number. The growth of nation-states, a Western phenomenon, also gave Europeans the means to exploit their advantages to maximum effect. Confidence in the superiority of their civilization made them energetic, self-righteous expansionists.

WHAT WAS the New Imperialism?

MAPS

Maps are important historical tools. They show how geography has affected history and concisely summarize complex relationships and events. Knowing how to read and interpret a map is important to understanding history. Map 12–1 from Chapter 12 shows the religious divisions of Europe in 1600. It has three features to help you read it: a **caption**, a **legend**, and a **scale**. The caption explains the geographical distribution of Christian communities in Europe.

The legend is situated on the bottom-left corner of the map. The legend provides information for what each colored area of the map represents. The yellow color represents Lutherans; purple represents Calvinists; the areas in light orange are Anglican communities; and, the territories in green are Catholic. The letters "L," "C," "A," and "R" represent minorities.

The scale, located on the top of the map, informs us that three-quarters of an inch equals 1000 miles (or about 1600 kilometers). With this information, estimates of distance between points on the map are easily made.

Finally, a **critical-thinking question** asks for careful consideration of the relationship between geography and history.

MAP EXPLORATION
Interactive map: To explore this map further, go to **http://www.prenhall.com/kagan3/map12.1**

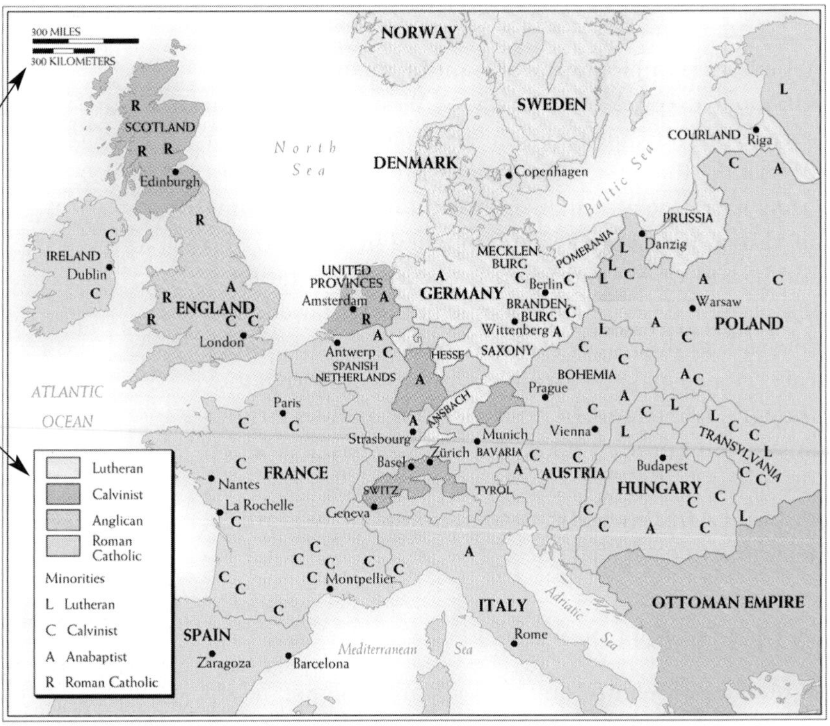

MAP 12–1

Religious Divisions about 1600   By 1600, few could seriously expect Christians to return to a uniform religious allegiance. In Spain and southern Italy, Catholicism remained relatively unchallenged, but note the existence elsewhere of large religious minorities, both Catholic and Protestant.

HOW WOULD you explain the division between Catholic and Protestant regions in Europe?

MAP EXPLORATIONS

Many of the maps in each chapter are provided in a useful interactive version on the text's Companion Website™. These maps are easily identified by a bar along the top (see example above) that reads **"Map Exploration."** An interactive version of Map 12–1 can be found at **www.prenhall.com/kagan3/map12.1.** The interactive version of this particular map provides an opportunity to move a timeline from left to right to see the spread of Muslim conquests.

ANALYZING VISUALS

Visual images embedded thoughout the text can provide as much insight into world history as can the written word. Within photographs and pieces of fine art lies emotional and historical meaning. Captions also provide valuable information, such as in the example on the left. When studying the image, consider questions such as: "Who are these people?"; "What are they doing?"; and "What can we learn from the way the people are dressed?" Such analysis allows for a fuller understanding of the way people lived in the past.

The English artist Francis Hayman in 1760 portrayed the victory in 1757 of Robert Clive over the Siraj-ud-daulah, the Mughal Nawab of Bengal, at Plassey. The victory brought English domination of the Indian subcontinent for almost two centuries. Note the manner in which this English artist clearly makes the victory one of the West over the East by contrasting the English horse and the Indian elephant and the contrasting dress of the protagonists. Clive had won the battle largely through bribing many of the Nawab's troops and potential allies.

The Granger Collection, New York

VISUALIZING THE PAST

These essays, found at the end of selected chapters, analyze important aspects of Western history through photographs, fine art, sculpture, and woodcuts. Focus questions and a running narrative guide students through a careful examination of the historical implications of each topic in question.

Visualizing The Past...

Imagining Women in the Eighteenth and Nineteenth Centuries

WHAT DOES the artistic depiction of women in the eighteenth and nineteenth centuries tell us about the ways in which Western artists have imagined the roles of women in modern society?

Although the roles of many women changed significantly in the eighteenth and nineteenth centuries, in part due to the new demands and opportunities brought about by industrialization, the themes of sexuality, docility, and maternal caring that characterized artists' imaginations of women in earlier eras also appear in the art of this period. Since most artists until the twentieth century were male, depictions of women and gender roles often derive from a male perspective on the *proper* roles of women in a society, and not necessarily on the reality of women's lives.

Thomas Gainsborough, *Robert Andrews and His Wife*, 1748.
Portraits, such as this one of the English landowner Robert Andrews and his wife, provide insights into the aristocratic and male dominance of landed society in the eighteenth century. The wife's seated posture next to her husband against the backdrop of his vast estate suggests the character of their legal relationship. Like the land, he controlled her property. She is as much one of his possessions as the rifle tucked beneath his arm and the dog at his feet.
Thomas Gainsborough, "Robert Andrews and His Wife". c. 1748-50. Oil on Canvas. 27 1/2" x 47" (69.7 x 119.3 cm). Photograph © Board of Trustees, National Gallery of Art, Washington, D.C.
▼

Encountering the Past

Each of these short essays examines a fascinating aspect of social or cultural history from the past.

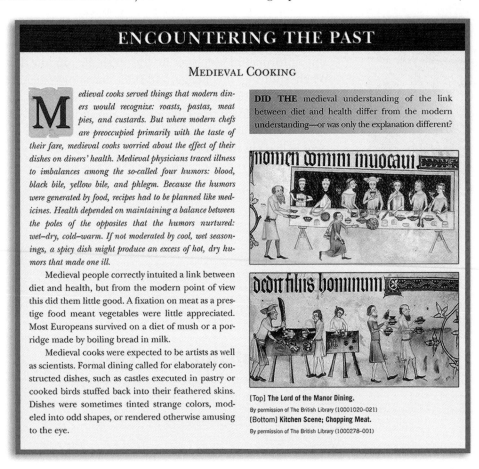

ENCOUNTERING THE PAST

MEDIEVAL COOKING

Medieval cooks served things that modern diners would recognize: roasts, pastas, meat pies, and custards. But where modern chefs are preoccupied primarily with the taste of their fare, medieval cooks worried about the effect of their dishes on diners' health. Medieval physicians traced illness to imbalances among the so-called four humors: blood, black bile, yellow bile, and phlegm. Because the humors were generated by food, recipes had to be planned like medicines. Health depended on maintaining a balance between the poles of the opposites that the humors nurtured: wet–dry, cold–warm. If not moderated by cool, wet seasonings, a spicy dish might produce an excess of hot, dry humors that made one ill.

Medieval people correctly intuited a link between diet and health, but from the modern point of view this did them little good. A fixation on meat as a prestige food meant vegetables were little appreciated. Most Europeans survived on a diet of mush or a porridge made by boiling bread in milk.

Medieval cooks were expected to be artists as well as scientists. Formal dining called for elaborately constructed dishes, such as castles executed in pastry or cooked birds stuffed back into their feathered skins. Dishes were sometimes tinted strange colors, modeled into odd shapes, or rendered otherwise amusing to the eye.

DID THE medieval understanding of the link between diet and health differ from the modern understanding—or was only the explanation different?

[Top] **The Lord of the Manor Dining.**
By permission of The British Library (10001020-021)
[Bottom] **Kitchen Scene; Chopping Meat.**
By permission of The British Library (1000278-001)

Overviews

The **Overview** tables in this text are a special feature designed to highlight and summarize important topics within a chapter. The Overview table shown here, for example, summarizes the developments in Science, Psychology, Sociology, and Fiction..

OVERVIEW   DEVELOPMENT IN SCIENCE, PSYCHOLOGY, SOCIOLOGY, AND FICTION

Discipline	Year	Development
Science	1830s	Comte's positivism says all knowledge should be knowledge common to the physical sciences
	1859	Darwin's theory of evolution by natural selection disputes creationism
	1895	Roentgen announces the discovery of X-rays
Psychology	1900	Freud, the founder of psychoanalysis, publishes *The Interpretation of Dreams*
	early 1900s	Jung, student of Freud, theorizes that the subconscious is inherited from ancestors
	mid-1900s	Horney and Klein attempt to establish a psychoanalytic basis for feminism
Sociology	1850s	Gobineau presents first arguments that race is the major determinant of

QUICK REVIEWS

Quick reviews, placed at key locations in the margins of each chapter, provide pinpoint summaries of important concepts.

> **QUICK REVIEW**
>
> **Anti-Clericalism**
> - Corruption and incompetence marred church administration
> - City governments took steps to improve the situation by endowing preacherships
> - Fifteenth century witnessed a growing sense that clerical privileges were undeserved

Significant Dates from the Period of the Protestant Reformation

1517	Luther posts ninety-five theses against indulgences
1519	Charles V becomes Holy Roman Emperor
1521	Diet of Worms condemns Luther
1524–1525	Peasants' Revolt in Germany
1527	The Schleitheim Confession of the Anabaptists
1529	Marburg Colloquy between Luther and Zwingli

CHRONOLOGIES

Each chapter includes **Chronologies** that list, in chronological order, key events discussed in the chapter. The chronology, shown here from Chapter 11, lists the dates of key events in the history of the Protestant Reformation. Chronologies provide a review of important events and their relationship to one another.

WESTERN CIVILIZATION DOCUMENT CD-ROM

Bound into every new copy of this textbook is a Western Civilization Document CD-ROM. This is a powerful resource for research and additional reading that contains more than 200 primary source documents central to Western history. Each document provides essay questions that are linked directly to a website where short-essay answers can be submitted online or printed out. Particularly relevant or interesting documents are called out at appropriate places in the margin of each chapter (see example). A complete list of documents on the CD-ROM is found at the end of the text.

11.2
Luther's *Ninety-Five Theses*

PRIMARY SOURCE DOCUMENTS

Historians find most of their information in written records, original documents that have survived from the past. These include government publications, letters, diaries, newspapers—whatever people wrote or printed, including many private documents never intended for publication. Each chapter in the book contains a feature called **History's Voices**—a selection from a primary source document. The example shown here is a commentary on nationalism in the nineteenth century. Each **History's Voices** begins with a brief introduction followed by questions on what the document reveals.

HISTORY'S VOICES

LORD ACTON CONDEMNS NATIONALISM

 he English historian Lord Acton (1834–1902) was an important observer of contemporary events, and he was one of the first commentators to recognize the political dangers posed by nationalism.

WHAT THREATS did Acton believe that nationalism posed?

By making the State and the nation commensurate with each other in theory, it [nationalism] reduces practically to a subject condition all other nationalities that may be within the boundary. It cannot admit them to an equality with the ruling nation which constitutes the State, because the State would then cease to be national, which would be a contradiction of the principle of its existence. According, therefore, to the degree of humanity and civilization in that dominant body which claims all the rights of the community, the inferior races are exterminated, or reduced to servitude, or outlawed, or put in a condition of dependence. . . .

A State which is incompetent to satisfy different races condemns itself; a State which labors to neutralize, to absorb, or to expel them, destroys its own vitality; a State which does not include them is destitute of the chief basis of self-government. The theory of nationality, therefore, is a retrograde step in history. . . .

[N]ationality does not aim either at liberty or prosperity, both of which it sacrifices to the imperative necessity of making the nation the mold and measure of the State. Its course will be marked with material as well as moral ruin, in order that a new invention may prevail over the works of God and the interests of mankind.

From John Emerich Edward Dalbert-Acton, *First Baron Acton, Essays in the History of Liberty,* ed. by J. Rufus Fears (Indianapolis: Liberty Classics, 1985), pp. 431–433.

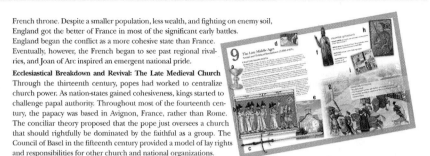

French throne. Despite a smaller population, less wealth, and fighting on enemy soil, England got the better of France in most of the significant early battles. England began the conflict as a more cohesive state than France. Eventually, however, the French began to see past regional rivalries, and Joan of Arc inspired an emergent national pride.

Ecclesiastical Breakdown and Revival: The Late Medieval Church Through the thirteenth century, popes had worked to centralize church power. As nation-states gained cohesiveness, kings started to challenge papal authority. Throughout most of the fourteenth century, the papacy was based in Avignon, France, rather than Rome. The conciliar theory proposed that the pope just oversees a church that should rightfully be dominated by the faithful as a group. The Council of Basel in the fifteenth century provided a model of lay rights and responsibilities for other church and national organizations.

Medieval Russia Kiev was the most important city in Russia around the turn of the millennium, so Prince Vladimir of Kiev's selection of Greek Orthodoxy as the state religion had ramifications that endure to the present. Starting in the eleventh century, Kiev lost its preeminence, and Russians split into three geographic and cultural groupings: the Great Russians, the White Russians, and the Little Russians or Ukrainians. In 1223, Ghengis Khan sent a Mongol (or Tatar) army into Russia. The Golden Horde brought much of Russia into the Mongol Empire. Mongol rule ended in 1480, by which time Moscow was the dominant city within Russia. In contrast to western Europe, where the nobility, the clergy, and the peasantry constituted distinct and easily identifiable groups in Russia the main social division was between freemen and slaves.

IMAGE KEY
for pages 218–219

a. Chalice, French, c.1325 (silver gilt)
b. Flagellants in the Netherlands town of Tournai (Doornik), 1349. Flagellants, known as the Brothers of the Cross, scourging themselves as they walk through the streets in order to free the world from the Black Death (Bubonic Plague)
c. Lugged Two-handed Sword, circa 1600
d. Detail from an illustrated manuscript of Boccaccio's "Decameron," physicians apply leeches to an emperor   Jean-Loup Charmet/Science Photo Library/Photo Researchers, Inc.
e. Exterior of a church, Novgorod, Russia
f. Statue of Pope Boniface VIII. Museo Civico, Bologna.   Scala/Art Resource. NY
g. Death of Wat Tyler (d. 1381) in front of Richard II, killed by Lord Mayor Walworth for wishing to abolish serfdom, by Jehan Froissart, (ca. 1460–80)
h. "Joan of Arc." Franco-Flemish miniature. Anonymous, 15h century. Archives Nationales, Paris, France. Photograph copyright Bridgeman-Giraudon/Art Resource, NY
i. A Caricature of physicians (early sixteenth century)

REVIEW QUESTIONS

1. What were the causes of the Black Death? Why did it spread so quickly? What were its effects on European society? How important do you think disease is in changing the course of history?

2. What were the causes of the Hundred Years' War? What advantages did each side have? Why were the French ultimately victorious?

3. What changes took place in the church and in its relationship to secular society between 1200 and 1450? How did it respond to political threats from increasingly powerful monarchs? How great an influence did the church have on secular events?

4. What is meant by the term "Avignon papacy"? What caused the Great Schism? How was it resolved? Why did kings in the late thirteenth and early fourteenth centuries have more power over the church than it had over them? What did kings hope to achieve through their struggles with the church?

5. How did the Kievan and medieval Russian states develop in terms of religion, politics, and social structure? What effect did Mongol rule have on Russian lands?

KEY TERMS

Avignon Papacy   (p. 230)   boyars   (p. 234)   Jacquerie   (p. 226)
Black Death   (p. 220)   Estates General   (p. 226)

 For additional study resources for this chapter, go to:
www.prenhall.com/kagan3/chapter9

SUMMARIES, REVIEW QUESTIONS, AND ADDITIONAL STUDY RESOURCES

At the end of each chapter a **summary** and **review questions** reconsider the main topics. An **Image Key** provides information about the illustrations that appear at the beginning of the chapter. The URL for the Companion Website™ is also found at the end of each chapter; this is an excellent resource for additional study aids. In addition, a laminated "Study in Time" chart is found at the front of the text and provides a succinct timeline of Western history.

GLOSSARY/KEY TERMS

Significant historical terms are called out in heavy type throughout the text, defined in the margin, and listed at the end of each chapter with appropriate page numbers. These are listed alphabetically and defined in a glossary at the end of the book.

EXPLORE THE POWER OF ONEKEY

OneKey is Prentice Hall's premium exclusive online resource for instructors and students. **OneKey** gives you access to the best online teaching and learning tools—all available 24/7. Harnessing the power of WebCT, Blackboard, and Course Compass , OneKey puts all of your resources in one place for maximum convenience, simplicity, and success.

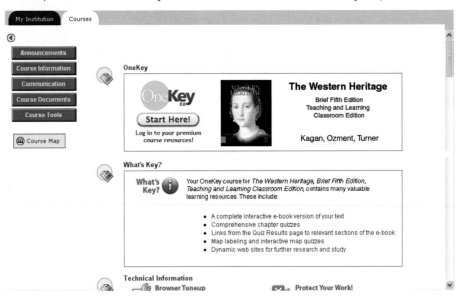

PRESENTATION RESOURCES FOR INSTRUCTORS

VISUALS

- Images
- Maps, Tables, Figures
- Map Outlines

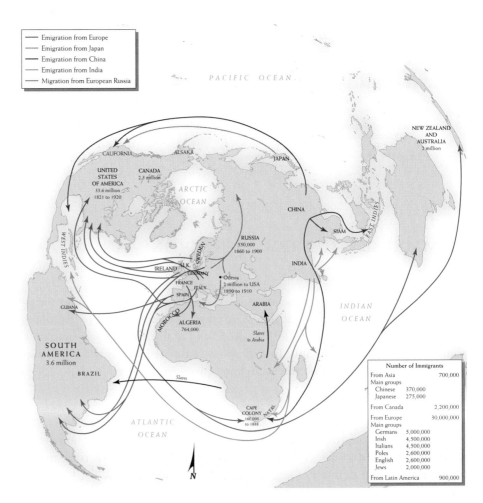

PowerPoint™ Presentations

- Lecture Aids—Visuals
- Lecture Aids—Text
- Lecture Aids—Lecture Outline

Changing Religious Life

✳ Religion in fifteenth-century life
- ◆ Clergy made up 6% to 8% of urban population
- ◆ Considerable political and religious power
- ◆ Monasteries were prominent and influential

✳ Religion in sixteenth-century life
- ◆ Numbers of clergy fell by 2/3
- ◆ Monasteries and nunneries nearly absent
- ◆ Worship conducted in the vernacular
- ◆ Clergy could marry, paid taxes

Animations and Activities

- Interactive Maps

Text

- Instructor's Manual

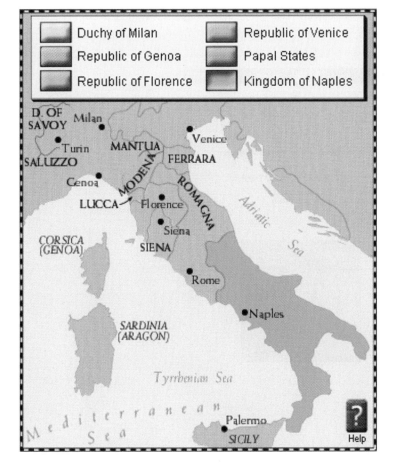

ASSESSMENT RESOURCES FOR STUDENTS

HOMEWORK

- Review Questions
- e-book

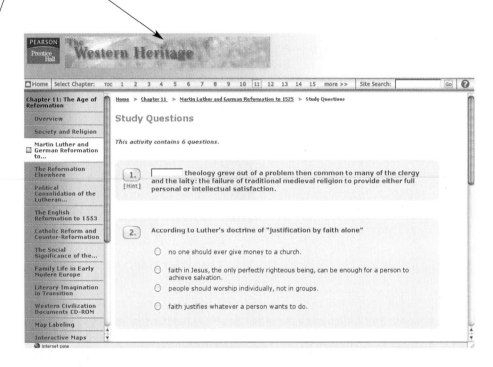

ADDITIONAL STUDENT RESOURCES

E-THEMES IN WORLD HISTORY

 RESEARCH NAVIGATOR

Take a tour at www.prenhall.com/onekey

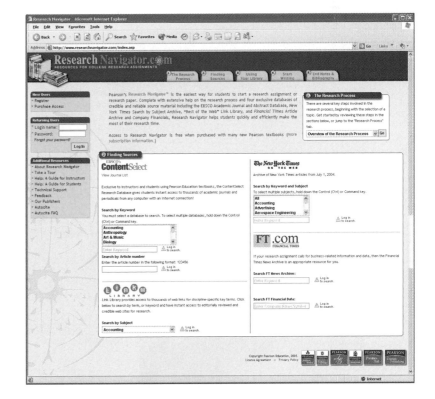

POLITICS & GOVERNMENT

ca. 3100–2700 B.C.E.	Egyptian Early Dynastic Period; unification of Upper and Lower Egypt
ca. 2800–2340 B.C.E.	Sumerian city-states' Early Dynastic period
2700–2200 B.C.E.	Egyptian Old Kingdom
ca. 2370 B.C.E.	Sargon established Akkadian Empire

2200–2052 B.C.E.	Egyptian First Intermediate Period
2052–1786 B.C.E.	Egyptian Middle Kingdom
1792–1750 B.C.E.	Reign of Hammurabi; height of Old Babylonian Kingdom; publication of Code of Hammurabi
1786–1575 B.C.E.	Egyptian Second Intermediate Period
ca. 1700 B.C.E.	Hyksos' Invasion of Egypt

▲ *Stele of Hammurabi*

◄ *Head of Sargon the Great*

SOCIETY & ECONOMY

ca. 1,000,000–10,000 B.C.E.	Paleolithic Age
ca. 8,000 B.C.E.	Earliest Neolithic settlements
ca. 3500 B.C.E.	Earliest Sumerian settlements
ca. 3000 B.C.E.	First urban settlements in Egypt and Mesopotamia; Bronze Age begins in Mesopotamia and Egypt
ca. 2900–1150 B.C.E.	Bronze Age Minoan society on Crete; Helladic society on Greek mainland

ca. 2000 B.C.E.	Hittites arrive in Asia Minor
ca. 1900 B.C.E.	Amorites in Babylonia

◄ *Venus of Willendorf*

RELIGION & CULTURE

ca. 30,000–6000 B.C.E.	Paleolithic art
ca. 3000 B.C.E.	Invention of writing
ca. 3000 B.C.E.	Temples to gods in Mesopotamia; development of ziggurat temple architecture
2700–2200 B.C.E.	Building of pyramids for Egyptian god-kings, development of hieroglyphic writing in Egypt

2200–1786 B.C.E.	Rise of Amon-Re as chief Egyptian god
ca. 1900 B.C.E.	Traditional date for Hebrew patriarch Abraham

▲ *Sumerian clay tablet*

◄ *Chauvet cave painting panel with horses*

ca. 1600 B.C.E. Fall of Old Babylonian Kingdom
1575–1087 B.C.E. Egyptian New Kingdom (or Empire)
ca. 1400–1200 B.C.E. Height of Hittite Empire
ca. 1400–1200 B.C.E. Height of Mycenaean power
1367–1350 B.C.E. Amunhotep IV (Akhenaten) in Egypt
ca. 1250 B.C.E. Sack of Troy (?)
1087–1030 B.C.E. Egyptian Post-Empire Period

Pharaoh Sety I ▶

ca. 1000–961 B.C.E. Reign of King David in Israel
ca. 961–922 B.C.E. Reign of King Solomon in Israel
ca. 1100–615 B.C.E. Assyrian Empire
ca. 800–400 B.C.E. Height of Etruscan culture in Italy
ca. 650 B.C.E. Spartan constitution formed
722 B.C.E. Israel (northern kingdom) falls to Assyrians
ca. 700–500 B.C.E. Rise and decline of tyranny in Greece
621 B.C.E. First written law code in Athens
612–539 B.C.E. Neo-Babylonian (Chaldean) Empire
594 B.C.E. Solon's constitutional reforms, Athens
586 B.C.E. Destruction of Jerusalem; fall of Judah (southern kingdom); Babylonian captivity
ca. 560–550 B.C.E. Peloponnesian League begins
559–530 B.C.E. Reign of Cyrus the Great in Persia
546 B.C.E. Persia conquers Lydian Empire of Croesus, including Greek cities of Asia Minor
539 B.C.E. Persia conquers Babylonia; temple at Jerusalem restored; exiles return from Babylonia
521–485 B.C.E. Reign of Darius in Persia
509 B.C.E. Kings expelled from Rome; Republic founded
508 B.C.E. Clisthenes founds Athenian democracy

▲ *The Capitoline Wolf*
The She–Wolf Suckling Romulus and Remus, late 15th–early 16th century. The National Gallery of Art, Washington DC, The Samuel H. Kress Collection. Photograph © Board of Trustees, National Gallery of Art, Washington, DC

▲ *Darius and Xerxes, detail, south wall of the treasury, Persepolis, Iran*

◀ *Queen Nefertiti*

ca. 1200 B.C.E. Hebrews arrive in Palestine

Homer, detail of statue ▶

ca. 1100–750 B.C.E. Greek "Dark Ages"
ca. 1000 B.C.E. Italic peoples enter Italy
ca. 800 B.C.E. Etruscans enter Italy
ca. 750–700 B.C.E. Rise of *polis* in Greece
ca. 750–600 B.C.E. Great age of Greek colonization
ca. 700 B.C.E. Invention of *hoplite* phalanx
ca. 600–550 B.C.E. Spartans adopt new communitarian social system
ca. 600–500 B.C.E. Athens develops commerce and a mixed economy

Female athlete ▶
of Sparta

1367–1360 B.C.E. Religious revolution led by Akhenaten makes Aton chief Egyptian god
1347–1339 B.C.E. Tutankhamun restores worship of Amon-Re

◀ *Tutankhamun and his queen*

ca. 750 B.C.E. Hebrew prophets teach monotheism
ca. 750 B.C.E. Traditional date for Homer
ca. 750 B.C.E. Greeks adapt Semitic script and invent the Greek alphabet
ca. 750–600 B.C.E. Panhellenic shrines established at Olympia, Delphi, Corinth, and Nemea; athletic festivals attached to them
ca. 700 B.C.E. Traditional date for Hesiod
ca. 675–500 B.C.E. Development of Greek lyric and elegiac poetry
ca. 570 B.C.E. Birth of Greek philosophy in Ionia
ca. 550 B.C.E. Oracle of Apollo at Delphi grows to great influence
ca. 550 B.C.E. Cult of Dionysus introduced to Athens
539 B.C.E. Restoration of temple in Jerusalem; return of exiles

Hercules taming ▶
Cerberus, Greek, 530 B.C.E.

PART ONE · THE FOUNDATIONS OF WESTERN CIVILIZATION IN THE ANCIENT WORLD

POLITICS & GOVERNMENT

490 B.C.E.	Battle of Marathon
485–465 B.C.E.	Reign of Xerxes in Persia
480–479 B.C.E.	Xerxes invades Greece
478–477 B.C.E.	Delian League founded
ca. 460–445 B.C.E.	First Peloponnesian War
450–449 B.C.E.	Laws of the Twelve Tables, Rome
431–404 B.C.E.	Great Peloponnesian War
404–403 B.C.E.	Thirty Tyrants rule at Athens
400–387 B.C.E.	Spartan war against Persia
398–360 B.C.E.	Reign of Agesilaus at Sparta
395–387 B.C.E.	Corinthian War
392 B.C.E.	Romans defeat Etruscans
378 B.C.E.	Second Athenian Confederation
371 B.C.E.	Thebans end Spartan hegemony
362 B.C.E.	Battle of Mantinea; end of Theban hegemony
338 B.C.E.	Philip of Macedon conquers Greece

Ancient Greek Athenian coin ▶

336–323 B.C.E.	Reign of Alexander III (the Great)
334 B.C.E.	Alexander invades Asia
330 B.C.E.	Fall of Persepolis; end Achaemenid rule in Persia
323–301 B.C.E.	Ptolemaic Kingdom (Egypt), Seleucid Kingdom (Syria), and Antigonid Dynasty (Macedon) founded
287 B.C.E.	Laws passed by Plebeian Assembly made binding on all Romans; end of Struggle of the Orders
264–241 B.C.E.	First Punic War
218–202 B.C.E.	Second Punic War
215–168 B.C.E.	Rome establishes rule over Hellenistic world
154–133 B.C.E.	Roman wars in Spain
133 B.C.E.	Tribunate of Tiberius Gracchus
123–122 B.C.E.	Tribunate of Gaius Gracchus
82 B.C.E.	Sulla assumes dictatorship
60 B.C.E.	First Triumvirate
46–44 B.C.E.	Caesar's dictatorship
43 B.C.E.	Second Triumvirate

▲ Painted relief from Ptolemaic temple

SOCIETY & ECONOMY

ca. 500–350 B.C.E.	Spartan population shrinks
ca. 500–350 B.C.E.	Rapid growth in overseas trade
477–431 B.C.E.	Vast growth in Athenian wealth
431–400 B.C.E.	Peloponnesian War casualties cause decline in size of lower class in Athens, with relative increase in importance of upper and middle classes

◀ Alexander the Great and Darius III

ca. 300 B.C.E.–150 C.E.	Growth of international trade and development of large cities in Hellenistic/Roman world
ca. 218–135 B.C.E.	Decline of family farm in Italy; growth of tenant farming and cattle ranching
ca. 150 B.C.E.	Growth of slavery as basis of economy in Roman Republic

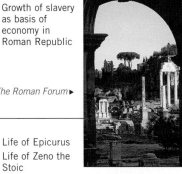

The Roman Forum ▶

RELIGION & CULTURE

ca. 500–400 B.C.E.	Great age of Athenian tragedy
469–399 B.C.E.	Life of Socrates
ca. 450–400 B.C.E.	Great influence of Sophists in Athens
ca. 450–385 B.C.E.	Great age of Athenian comedy
448–432 B.C.E.	Periclean building program on Athenian acropolis
429–347 B.C.E.	Life of Plato
ca. 425 B.C.E.	Herodotus' history of the Persian Wars
ca. 400 B.C.E.	Thucydides' history of the Peloponnesian War
ca. 400–325 B.C.E.	Life of Diogenes the Cynic
386 B.C.E.	Foundation of Plato's Academy
384–322 B.C.E.	Life of Aristotle
336 B.C.E.	Foundation of Aristotle's Lyceum

◀ Double bust of the Greek historians Herodotus and Thucydides

342–271 B.C.E.	Life of Epicurus
335–263 B.C.E.	Life of Zeno the Stoic
ca. 287–212 B.C.E.	Life of Archimedes of Syracuse
ca. 275 B.C.E.	Foundation of museum and library make Alexandria the center of Greek intellectual life
ca. 250 B.C.E.	Livius Andronicus translates the *Odyssey* into Latin
106–43 B.C.E.	Life of Cicero
ca. 99–55 B.C.E.	Life of Lucretius
86–35 B.C.E.	Life of Sallust
ca. 84–54 B.C.E.	Life of Catullus
70–19 B.C.E.	Life of Vergil
65–8 B.C.E.	Life of Horace
59 B.C.E.–17 C.E.	Life of Livy
43 B.C.E.–18 C.E.	Life of Ovid

Odysseus ▶ and Cyclops

31 B.C.E. Octavian and Agrippa defeat Anthony at Actium

27 B.C.E.–14 C.E. Reign of Augustus

14–68 C.E. Reigns of Julio-Claudian Emperors

69–96 C.E. Reigns of Flavian Emperors

96–180 C.E. Reigns of "Good Emperors"

180–192 C.E. Reign of Commodus

284–305 C.E. Reign of Diocletian; reform and division of Roman Empire

306–337 C.E. Reign of Constantine

330 C.E. Constantinople new capital of Roman Empire

361–363 C.E. Reign of Julian the Apostate

379–395 C.E. Reign of Theodosius

376 C.E. Visigoths enter Roman Empire

▲ Roman fleet of Octavian

◄ Roman amphitheatre

ca. 150–400 C.E. Decline of slavery and growth of tenant farming and serfdom in Roman Empire

ca. 250–400 C.E. *Coloni* (Roman tenant farmers) increasingly tied to the land

301 C.E. Edict of Maximum Prices at Rome

Caesar Augustus, ► Emperor of Rome

9 B.C.E. Ara Pacis dedicated at Rome

ca. 4 B.C.E. Birth of Jesus of Nazareth

ca. 30 C.E. Crucifixion of Jesus

64 C.E. Christians persecuted by Nero

66–135 C.E. Romans suppress rebellions of Jews

ca. 70–100 C.E. Gospels written

ca. 150 C.E. Ptolemy of Alexandria establishes canonical geocentric model of the universe

ca. 250–260 C.E. Severe persecutions by Decius and Valerian

303 C.E. Persecution of Christians by Diocletian

311 C.E. Galerius issues Edict of Toleration

312 C.E. Constantine converts to Christianity

325 C.E. Council of Nicaea

348–420 C.E. Life of St. Jerome

354–430 C.E. Life of St. Augustine

395 C.E. Christianity becomes official religion of Roman Empire

▲ Ara Pacis

Columns of Hellenistic gymnasium ►

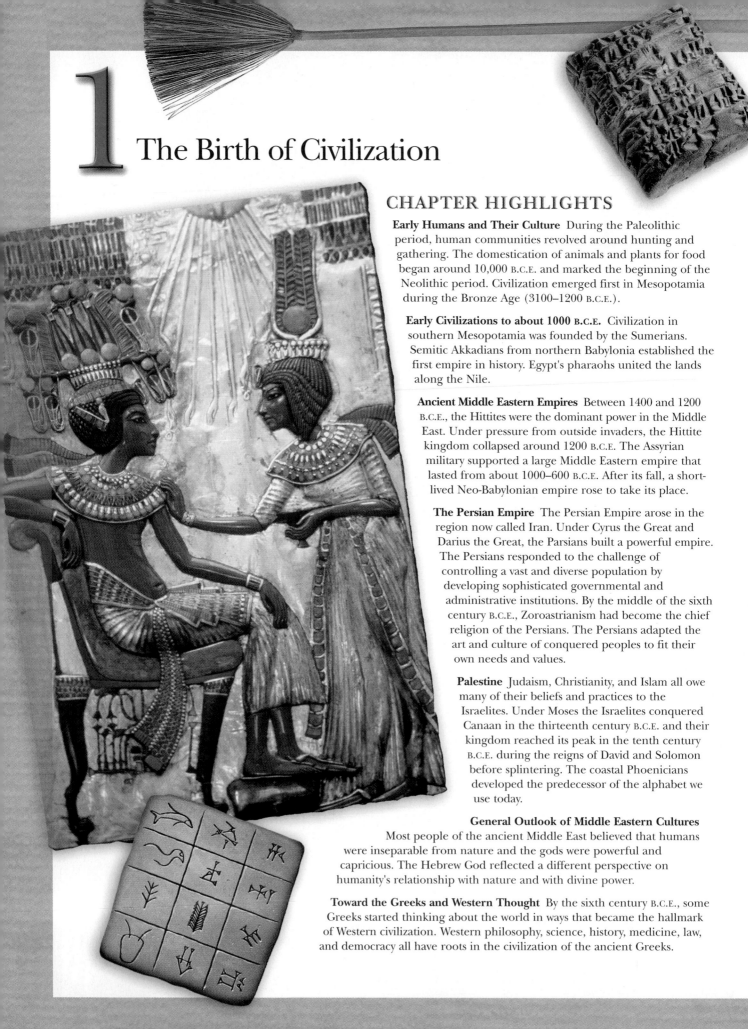

1 The Birth of Civilization

CHAPTER HIGHLIGHTS

Early Humans and Their Culture During the Paleolithic period, human communities revolved around hunting and gathering. The domestication of animals and plants for food began around 10,000 B.C.E. and marked the beginning of the Neolithic period. Civilization emerged first in Mesopotamia during the Bronze Age (3100–1200 B.C.E.).

Early Civilizations to about 1000 B.C.E. Civilization in southern Mesopotamia was founded by the Sumerians. Semitic Akkadians from northern Babylonia established the first empire in history. Egypt's pharaohs united the lands along the Nile.

Ancient Middle Eastern Empires Between 1400 and 1200 B.C.E., the Hittites were the dominant power in the Middle East. Under pressure from outside invaders, the Hittite kingdom collapsed around 1200 B.C.E. The Assyrian military supported a large Middle Eastern empire that lasted from about 1000–600 B.C.E. After its fall, a short-lived Neo-Babylonian empire rose to take its place.

The Persian Empire The Persian Empire arose in the region now called Iran. Under Cyrus the Great and Darius the Great, the Parsians built a powerful empire. The Persians responded to the challenge of controlling a vast and diverse population by developing sophisticated governmental and administrative institutions. By the middle of the sixth century B.C.E., Zoroastrianism had become the chief religion of the Persians. The Persians adapted the art and culture of conquered peoples to fit their own needs and values.

Palestine Judaism, Christianity, and Islam all owe many of their beliefs and practices to the Israelites. Under Moses the Israelites conquered Canaan in the thirteenth century B.C.E. and their kingdom reached its peak in the tenth century B.C.E. during the reigns of David and Solomon before splintering. The coastal Phoenicians developed the predecessor of the alphabet we use today.

General Outlook of Middle Eastern Cultures Most people of the ancient Middle East believed that humans were inseparable from nature and the gods were powerful and capricious. The Hebrew God reflected a different perspective on humanity's relationship with nature and with divine power.

Toward the Greeks and Western Thought By the sixth century B.C.E., some Greeks started thinking about the world in ways that became the hallmark of Western civilization. Western philosophy, science, history, medicine, law, and democracy all have roots in the civilization of the ancient Greeks.

CHAPTER QUESTIONS

HOW DID life in the Neolithic Age differ from the Paleolithic?

WHY DID the first cities develop?

WHAT WERE the great empires of the ancient Middle East?

HOW WAS Hebrew monotheism different from Mesopotamian and Egyptian polytheism?

WHAT WERE the Persian rulers' attitudes toward the cultures they ruled?

WHAT SOCIAL and political contrasts existed between ancient Middle Eastern and Greek civilizations?

CHAPTER OUTLINE

- Early Humans and Their Culture
- Early Civilizations to about 1000 B.C.E.
- Ancient Middle Eastern Empires
- The Persian Empire
- Palestine
- General Outlook of Middle Eastern Cultures
- Toward the Greeks and Western Thought

IMAGE KEY

for pages 4–5 is on page 30.

HOW DID life in the Neolithic

Age differ from the Paleolithic?

For hundreds of thousands of years, human beings lived by hunting and gathering what nature spontaneously provided. Only about 10,000 years ago did they begin to cultivate plants, domesticate animals, and settle in permanent communities. About 5,000 years ago, the Sumerians, who lived near the confluence of the Tigris and Euphrates Rivers (a region Greek geographers called "Mesopotamia," i.e., "between-rivers"), and the Egyptians, who dwelt in the Nile Valley, pioneered civilization. By the fourteenth century B.C.E.,[1] powerful empires had arisen and were struggling for dominance of the civilized world, but one of the region's smaller states probably had a greater influence on the course of Western civilization. The modern West's major religions (Judaism, Christianity, and Islam) are rooted in the traditions of ancient Israel.

EARLY HUMANS AND THEIR CULTURE

Scientists estimate that Earth may be 6 billion years old and its human inhabitants have been developing for 3 to 5 million years. Some 1 to 2 million years ago, erect tool-using beings spread from their probable place of origin in Africa to Europe and Asia. Our own species, ***Homo sapiens***, is about 200,000 years old, and fully modern humans have existed for about 90,000 years.

Humans are distinguished by a unique capacity to construct cultures. A **culture** may be defined as a way of life invented by a group and passed on by teaching. It includes both material things (tools, clothing, and shelter) and ideas, institutions, and beliefs. Because cultural behaviors are guided by learning rather than instinct, they can be altered at will to enable human beings to adapt rapidly to different environments and changing conditions.

THE PALEOLITHIC AGE

Anthropologists identify prehistoric human cultures by the styles of their most durable and plentiful artifacts—stone tools. The earliest period in cultural development—the **Paleolithic** (Greek for "old stone") Age—began with the first use of stone tools about a million years ago and continued until about 10,000 B.C.E. Throughout this immensely long era, people were nomadic hunters and gatherers who depended for their food on what nature spontaneously offered. An uncertain food supply and the inability of human beings to understand or control the mysterious forces that threatened their existence persuaded them that they occupied a world governed by superhuman powers. Cave art, ritual burial practices, and other evidences of religious or magical beliefs appeared during the Paleolithic era, and they bear witness to a suspicion as old as humanity itself that there is more to the world than meets the eye.

Human society in the Paleolithic Age was probably based on a division of labor by sex. Males ranged far afield on the hunt. Females, whose mobility was limited by the burdens of childbearing and nursing, gathered edibles of various kinds in the vicinity of a base camp. The knowledge that people acquired as hunters and gatherers eventually equipped them to develop agriculture and herding, and these food-producing technologies drastically changed the human lifestyle.

Homo sapiens   Our own species, which dates back roughly 200,000 years.

culture   Way of life invented by a group and passed on by teaching.

Paleolithic   Greek for "old stone"; the earliest period in cultural development that began with the first use of stone tools about a million years ago and continued until about 10,000 B.C.E.

---

[1]This book substitutes B.C.E. ("before the common era") and C.E. ("common era") for B.C. and A.D., and it uses the term "Middle East" in preference to "Near East."

THE NEOLITHIC AGE

About 10,000 years ago, people living in some parts of the Middle East made advances in the production of stone tools that marked the start of the **Neolithic** (i.e., "new stone") Age. But more significant than their tool-making technology was their shift from hunting and gathering to agriculture. They began to domesticate the wild species of sheep, goats, wheat, and barley that were native to the foothills of the region's mountains. Once domesticated, these species were transplanted to areas where they did not naturally occur.

Hunters and gatherers maintain their food supply by harvesting a district and then moving on, but farmers settle down next to the fields they cultivate. They establish villages, construct relatively permanent dwellings, and produce pottery in which to cook and store the grains they raise. The earliest Neolithic settlements featured small circular huts clustered around a central storehouse. Later Neolithic people built larger rectangular homes with private storage facilities and enclosures for livestock. The similarity in size and equipment of buildings suggests that a Neolithic village's residents differed little in wealth and social status. Although they engaged in some trade, their communities were largely self-sufficient.

The most exceptional of the known Neolithic settlements are Jericho (near the Dead Sea) and Çatal Hüyük (about 150 miles south of the capital of modern Turkey). Jericho was occupied as early as 12,000 B.C.E., and by 8000 B.C.E., it had a massive stone wall enclosing an area exceeding eight acres. (No other Neolithic site is known to have been fortified.) Çatal Hüyük was a somewhat later and larger community. It had a population well over 6,000. Its mud-brick dwellings were packed tightly together. There were no streets, and Çatal Hüyük's residents traveled across its buildings' roofs and used ladders to access their homes. Many interiors were elaborately decorated with sculptures and paintings that are assumed to have ritual significance.

Wherever agriculture and animal husbandry appeared, the relationship between human beings and nature changed forever. People began to try to control nature, not just respond to what it offered. This was a vital prerequisite for the development of civilization, but it was not without cost. Farmers had to work harder and longer than hunters and gatherers. They faced health threats from accumulating wastes. They had to figure out how to live together permanently in one place and cope with unprecedented population growth. The earliest Neolithic communities appeared in the Middle East about 8000 B.C.E., in China about 4000 B.C.E., and in India about 3600 B.C.E.

In 1991 a tourist discovered a frozen body in the Ötztal Tyrolean Alps on the Italian-Austrian border. The body turned out to be the oldest mummified human being yet discovered and sheds new light on the Neolithic period. Dated to 3300 B.C.E., it was the remains of a man between 25 and 35 years old, 5 feet 2 inches tall, weighing 110 pounds. He has been called Ötzi, the Ice Man from the place of his discovery. He had not led a peaceful life, for his nose was broken, several of his ribs were fractured, and an arrowhead in his shoulder suggests he bled to death in the ice and snow. Ötzi wore a fur robe of mountain animal skin, with a woven grass cape underneath and leather shoes stuffed with grass. He was heavily armed for his time, carrying a flint dagger and bow with arrows also tipped in flint. The blade of his axe was copper, indicating that metallurgy was already under way. His discovery vividly shows the beginning of the transition from the Stone Age to the Bronze Age.

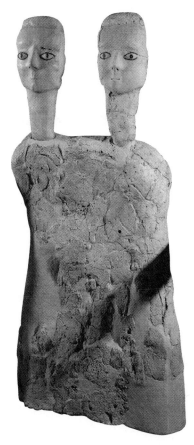

At Ain Ghazal, a Neolithic site in Jordan, several pits contained male and female statues made of clay modeled over a reed framework. Similar figures have been found at Jericho and other sites, all from the same period, about 8500–7000 B.C.E. They were probably used in religious rituals, perhaps connected with ancestor worship, as were plastered skulls, masks, carved heads, and other artifacts.

Archaeological Museum, Amman, Jordan, kingdom. Photograph © Erich Lessing, Art Resource, NY

Neolithic "New stone" age, dating back 10,000 years to when people living in some parts of the Middle East made advances in the production of stone tools and shifted from hunting and gathering to agriculture.

THE BRONZE AGE AND THE BIRTH OF CIVILIZATION

As Neolithic villages and herding cultures were spreading over much of the world, another major shift in human life styles began on the plains near the Tigris and Euphrates Rivers and in the valley of the Nile River. Villages grew to become towns and cities that dominated large areas. These new urban centers usually had some monumental buildings whose construction required the sustained effort of hundreds or thousands of people over many years. There is evidence of social stratification—of the emergence of classes distinguished by wealth, lineage, and religious and political authority. Writing was invented, probably to deal with the challenge of managing complex urban economies. Sophisticated works of art were created, and the first metal implements—made from bronze, an alloy of copper and tin—appeared. Although stone tools continued to be used, the increasing importance of metal ended the Stone Ages in the Middle East and inaugurated the **Bronze Age** (3100–1200 B.C.E.). The characteristics of Bronze Age cultures (i.e., urbanism; long-distance trade; writing systems; and accelerating technological, industrial, and social development) are regarded by historians as the hallmarks of **civilization**.

Ötzi is the nickname scientists have given to the remains of the oldest mummified human body yet discovered. This reconstruction shows his probable appearance and the clothing and weapons found on and with him.
Wieslav Smetek/Stern/Black Star

WHY DID the first cities develop?

Bronze Age (3100–1200 B.C.E.) Began with the increasing importance of metal that also ended the Stone Ages.

civilization Stage in the evolution of organized society that has among its characteristics urbanism, long-distance trade, writing systems, and accelerated technological and social development.

EARLY CIVILIZATIONS TO ABOUT 1000 B.C.E.

During the fourth millennium, populations of unprecedented density began to develop along Mesopotamia's Tigris and Euphrates Rivers and Egypt's Nile River. By about 3000 B.C.E., when the invention of writing began to produce the kinds of records that make the writing of history possible, urban life had spread throughout these regions and centralized states had begun to develop. Because city dwellers do not grow their own food, they need to establish some system to promote, collect, and disburse surpluses produced by rural farmers and herders. The arid climates of Mesopotamia and Egypt meant that farmers could meet the demands of urban populations for their products only with the help of extensive irrigation systems. Irrigation technology was more elaborate in Mesopotamia than in Egypt. In Egypt the Nile flooded at the right moment for cultivation, and irrigation simply involved channeling water to the fields. In Mesopotamia, however, the floods came at the wrong season. Dikes were needed to protect fields where crops were already growing and to store water for future use. The lifelines of Mesopotamian towns and villages were rivers, streams, and canals, and control of the water these channels supplied was a contentious issue that could lead to war. Mesopotamia was a flat plain. The terrain provided little protection from floods and allowed swollen rivers to carve

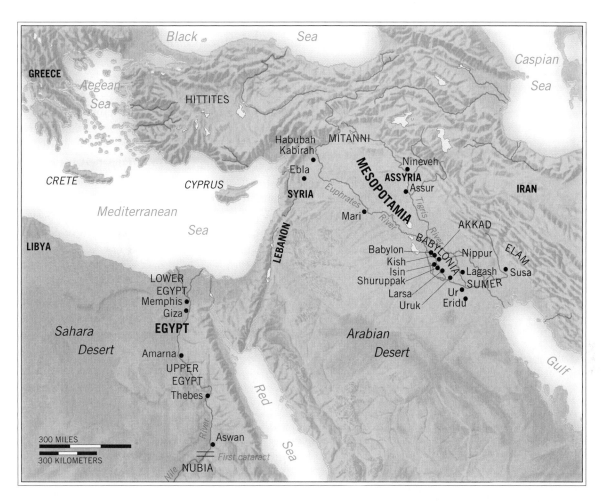

MAP 1–1
The Ancient Middle East   Two river valley civilizations thrived in the Ancient Middle East: Egypt, which was united into a single state, and Mesopotamia, which was long divided into a number of city-states.

BASED ON this map, what might explain why independent city-states were spread out in Mesopotamia while Egypt remained united in a single state?

new channels and change their courses. Cities were sometimes severely damaged or forced to relocate. At one time archaeologists assumed that the need to construct and manage irrigation systems caused the development of cities and centralized states, but they now know that large-scale irrigation appeared long after urban civilization was established. (See Map 1–1.)

MESOPOTAMIAN CIVILIZATION

Civilization seems to have made its first appearance in Babylonia, an arid portion of Mesopotamia that stretches from modern Baghdad to the Persian Gulf. The first cities appeared in Sumer, the southern half of Babylonia, during the fourth millennium B.C.E. The earliest urban center may have been at Uruk, a city that established outposts of its culture as far afield as Syria and southern Anatolia. During the Early Dynastic Period (i.e., 2800–2370 B.C.E.), Uruk was joined by a number of other city-states scattered along the banks of the Tigris and Euphrates. Competition for water and land led to wars among them.

The Victory Stele of Naram-Sin, the Akkadian ruler, commemorates the king's campaign (ca. 2230 B.C.E.) against the Lullubi, a people living in the northern Zagros Mountains, along the eastern frontier of Mesopotamia. Kings set up monuments like this one in the courtyards of temples to record their deeds. They were also left in remote corners of the empire to warn distant peoples of the death and enslavement awaiting the king's enemies (pink sandstone).

Louvre, Paris, France. The Bridgeman Art Library International Ltd.

1.5
Hammurabi's Law
Code

Leagues and alliances were formed, and the weaker cities became subject to kingdoms built by the stronger. Legend seats history's first monarchs in the city of Kish.

The Sumerian language is not related to any known language, and most of the Sumerians' neighbors spoke Semitic tongues (i.e., languages belonging to the same family as Hebrew and Arabic). Many of the Semitic peoples were influenced by Sumerian civilization and adapted the Sumerian writing system for their own use. Among these were the Akkadians, a people whose first king, Sargon, established his seat at Akkade (near Baghdad). Sargon built history's first empire by conquering all the Sumerian city-states and extending his authority into southwestern Iran and northern Syria. Memory of the dynasty's splendor led later Mesopotamians to think of the reign of Naram-Sin, his grandson, as the high point of their history.

External attack and internal weakness eventually combined to destroy the Akkadian state, but about 2125 B.C.E., the kings of the Third Dynasty of the ancient Sumerian city of Ur restored unity to a part of the old empire. Under the leadership of the Third Dynasty of Ur, Sumerian civilization had its final flowering. Great monuments were built, epic poems were composed to celebrate the deeds of ancient heroes, and thousands of surviving documents witness to the existence of a highly centralized administrative system. Ur survived, however, for little more than a century. An extended period of agricultural failure may have produced a famine that undercut its ability to defend itself. The Elamites invaded Sumer from the east, and the Amorites invaded from the north. They brought an end to Sumerian rule and eventually absorbed the Sumerian peoples. The Sumerian language survived but only as a learned tongue studied by priests and scholars—much like Latin in the modern West.

New Amorite dynasties seated themselves at Isin and Larsa, but they were soon brought under the control of a powerful dynasty that founded the famous city of Babylon. Babylon extended its control over most of Mesopotamia and reached its peak during the reign of Hammurabi (r. ca. 1792–1750 B.C.E.), a ruler who is best remembered for the collection of laws issued during his reign. Earlier kings had compiled lists of laws, but the so-called Code of Hammurabi is the earliest major collection to survive. It provides intimate insights into the values and institutions of an early civilization.

Amorite society consisted of nobles, commoners, and slaves, and each of these classes was treated differently by the law. Crimes against highly ranked individuals were punished more severely than those against inferior persons, but even the poor and humble had some protection under the law. The principle of justice was retribution: "an eye for an eye, a tooth for a tooth." Professionally trained judges decided cases on the basis of evidence and the testimony of witnesses. When that was unavailable, accused persons might be compelled to prove their innocence by taking sacred oaths or undergoing physical ordeals.

The Royal Standard of Ur, a mosaic that dates from about 2750 B.C.E., shows officials from the Sumerian city of Ur celebrating a military victory as animals are brought in to be slaughtered for a feast.

British Museum, London, UK/Bridgeman Art Library

Government   Monarchy was already established in Mesopotamia by the time that historical records began to accumulate. But different kinds of monarchies appeared in different times and places. Early Sumerian art depicts kings leading armies, executing captives, and making offerings to gods. In the northern district of Assyria, kings were the chief priests, but in the south, in Babylonia, kings and priests held separate offices. Kings often appointed their sons and daughters to priesthoods. Enheduanna, daughter of the Akkadian emperor Sargon, was one of these. Some of the hymns she composed have survived—making her history's first identifiable author.

Royal and priestly households were supported by income from large estates. Some of their land was worked by low-ranking laborers in exchange for food rations, and some was leased to citizen entrepreneurs who paid rent or farmed for a share of the crop. The palace and temple establishments also maintained large herds of animals to support, among other things, the manufacture of textiles on a large scale. Wool cloth was exported to pay for metals, for Mesopotamia lacked ore deposits. Not all the land was controlled by kings and priests. Some belonged to private individuals and was bought and sold freely.

Writing and Mathematics   The challenge of administrating a Sumerian city prompted the invention of the world's first system of writing. Modern scholars have named it **cuneiform** (from Latin *cuneus*, "wedge") after the wedge-shaped marks that the Sumerian scribe made by pressing a reed stylus into the common writing material, a clay tablet. Writing began with a few simple signs intended to remind readers of something they already knew. Gradually the system evolved to the point where it was possible to record language and use writing to communicate whatever could be thought. Sumerian scribes had to learn several thousand characters, some of which stood for words and

cuneiform   Developed by the Sumerians as the very first writing system ever used, it used several thousand characters, some of which stood for words and some for sounds.

Code of Hammurabi

Photo: Ch. Larrieu. Reunion des Muses Nationaux et Ecoli du Louvre, Paris/ Art Resource, NY

polytheists Name given to those who worship many gods and/or goddesses.

others for sounds. Because it took considerable time and training to learn how to write, the skill was restricted to a tiny elite whose services were much in demand.

Before 3000 B.C.E., no one seems to have conceived of numbers in the abstract—that is, apart from their use in counting specific things. Different numerals were employed for different kinds of things, and the same sign might mean, for example, either 10 or 18 depending on what was being counted. However, once numbers began to be thought of as entities in themselves, development was rapid. Sumerian mathematicians employed a sexagesimal system (i.e., based on the number 60) that survives today in our conventional 60-minute hour and 360-degree circle. Mathematics enabled the Mesopotamians to make progress in the study of astronomy that led to the development of accurate calendars.

Religion The Mesopotamians produced a large body of sacred literature, some of which influenced the composition of the Hebrew Bible. They were **polytheists**. That is, they worshiped many gods and goddesses, most of whom represented phenomena of nature (e.g., the powers behind storms, earthquakes, and fecundity). They assumed the gods, although immortal and much greater in power than themselves, had the same needs as they did. They believed the gods had created humanity to fulfill those needs—to do the work of raising food and housekeeping that the gods would otherwise have had to do for themselves. A temple was literally a god's home. The image of the deity that it housed was provided with meals, draped in clothing, offered entertainment, and honored with ritual and ceremony. It was equipped with a garden for the god's pleasure and a bed for his or her nightly repose. Deities had universal authority, but each major god and goddess also laid claim to a specific city. The greater temples in the Sumerian cities were erected on the tops of huge terraced mounds of mud-brick called *ziggurats*. Poets sometimes described these structures as mountains linking earth with heaven, but their precise purpose and symbolism remain uncertain.

The gods were grouped into families, and heaven was assumed to be organized much like a human community. Each deity had his or her own area of responsibility. It might involve the processes of nature or human skills and crafts. The great gods who dominated heaven, like the kings who governed human affairs, were too remote to be approached by common people. Ordinary men and women took their concerns to minor deities whom they hoped would intercede for them with higher ranking members of heaven's court. Intercession was needed, for the Mesopotamians had a keen sense of the fragility of human life. Religion provided them with their primary tools for coping with crises and uncertainties. (See "Encountering the Past: Divination in Ancient Mesopotamia.")

The Mesopotamians did not hold out any hope for a better life after death. Death doomed spirits to a glum existence in a dusty, dark netherworld where they suffered hunger and thirst unless their living relatives continued to supply them with offerings. There was no reward in death for those who had led virtuous lives and no punishment for the wicked. Everyone was equally miserable. Because the desperate spirits of the dead might escape confinement to haunt the living, families took the precaution of burying their dead with offerings and holding ceremonies from time to time to placate departed kin. At the funerals of some of the early rulers, large numbers of their servants were sacrificed to provide them with retinues in the underworld.

ENCOUNTERING THE PAST

DIVINATION IN ANCIENT MESOPOTAMIA

Mesopotamians believed the world was full of omens—events that, if properly interpreted, would enable them to predict the future. They did not view the future as a predestined, unalterable fate, but they assumed that if they knew what was going to happen, appropriate rituals and planning would enable them to head off unfavorable developments. Divination is the practice of foretelling the future by magical or occult means, and the Mesopotamians were pioneers of the art. One of the earliest and most trusted divination methods involved the examination of the entrails of the animals offered at religious sacrifices. Deformities of organs were believed to be warnings from the gods. Clay models were made of these organs, and together with a report of the events they were believed to have predicted, these models were preserved in a kind of reference library for temple diviners.

Animal sacrifice was expensive and used most commonly by the state. Ordinary Mesopotamians relied on more economical methods to obtain the information they needed to plan for their futures. The seers who served them examined patterns made by the smoke of burning incense or oil poured onto water. Chance remarks of strangers, facial features, dreams, and birth defects were all considered significant. The movements of the heavenly bodies were believed to be extremely portentous for events on earth. Mesopotamian faith in astrology had the positive effect of gathering data that led to advances in astronomy. Any divergence from what were considered normal forms or patterns was considered a portent of disaster and called for prayers and magic to ward off suspected dangers.

HOW DID the Mesopotamians try to predict the future, and what did they do with the information they obtained?

Ancient Mesopotamians used astrology to predict the future. This calendar from the city of Uruk dates from the first millennium B.C.E. and is based on careful observation of the heavens.

Astrological calendar. From Uruk, Mesopotamia. Babylonian, 1st mill. B.C.E. Museum of Oriental Antiquities, Istanbul, Turkey. Photograph © Erich Lessing/Art Resource, NY

Society   Hundreds of thousands of cuneiform texts, dating from the early third millennium to the third century B.C.E., provide us with a detailed picture of life in ancient Mesopotamia. Evidence from the reign of Hammurabi is particularly abundant. In addition to his famous law code, there are numerous administrative documents and royal and private letters. The amount of space given to various topics in Hammurabi's code suggests the issues that were of chief concern to his subjects.

The code's third largest category of laws deals with commerce. Regulations governing debts, rates of interest, security, default, and the conduct of professionals (e.g., contractors, surgeons, etc.) testify to the complexity of Babylonian economic life. The second largest group of laws relates to land tenure and suggests that individual landholders feared that powerful officials would try to take

OVERVIEW   MESOPOTAMIAN AND EGYPTIAN CIVILIZATIONS

	Mesopotamia	Egypt
Government	Different kinds of monarchies appeared in different times and places. Sumerian kings led armies; northern Assyrian kings were the chief priests; and, in the south, Babylonian kings and priests held separate offices.	*Nomarchs*, regional governors whose districts were called *nomes*, handled important local issues such as water management. However, old kingdom pharaohs held much of the power and resources.
Language and Literature	Sumerians developed the world's first system of writing, *cuneiform*. Sumerian scribes had to learn several thousand characters; some stood for words, others for sounds.	Writing first appears in Egypt about 3000 B.C.E. The impetus most likely derived from Mesopotamian *cuneiform*. This writing system, *hieroglyphs*, was highly sophisticated, involving hundreds of picture signs.
Religion	The Mesopotamians were *polytheists*, worshipping many gods and goddesses, most of whom represented phenomena of nature (storms, earthquakes, etc.). The gods were grouped into families, heaven being organized like a community.	Egyptians had three different myths to explain the origin of the world, and each featured a different creator-god. Gods were represented in both human and animal form. Egyptians placed great trust in magic, oracles, and amulets to ward off evil.
Society	Parents usually arranged marriages. A marriage started out monogamous, but husbands could take a second wife. Women could own their own property and do business on their own.	Women's prime roles were connected with the management of the household. They could not hold office, go to scribal schools, or become artisans. Royal women often wielded considerable influence. In art, royal and nonroyal women are usually shown smaller than the male figures.
Slavery	The two main forms of slavery were chattel and debt slavery. Chattel slaves were bought and had no legal rights. Debt slaves, more common than chattel slaves, could not be sold, but they could redeem their freedom by paying off the loan.	Slaves did not become numerous in Egypt until the Middle Kingdom (about 2000 B.C.E.). Black Africans and Asians were captured in war and brought back as slaves. Slaves could be freed, but manumission was rare.

their property from them. The largest collection of laws is devoted to family issues (e.g., marriage, inheritance, and adoption). Parents arranged marriages for their children. Grooms made payments for their brides and a bride's family provided her with a dowry. A marriage was expected to be monogamous unless it failed to produce offspring. A man whose wife proved to be barren could take a second wife to provide the children needed to care for them in their old age. Husbands were permitted extramarital affairs with concubines, slaves, and prostitutes, but wives were not granted comparable license. A married woman's place was assumed to be in the home, but she could own property and run her own business so long as she did not neglect her duty to her husband and family. A woman could initiate divorce, and she could reclaim her dowry so long as her husband could not convict her of any wrongdoing. Single women sometimes supported themselves as tavern owners, moneylenders, midwives, nurses, priestesses, or temple servants.

Slavery: Chattel Slaves and Debt Slaves   There were two kinds of slavery in ancient Mesopotamia: chattel slavery and debt slavery. Chattel slaves were pieces of property. They had no legal rights, for they were usually foreigners—prisoners of war or aliens bought from slave merchants. They were expensive luxuries and used primarily as domestic servants. Debt slavery was more common. Individuals could pledge themselves or members of their families as security for loans. Because interest rates were high, debtors ran the risk of defaulting on their loans. If that happened, they were enslaved to work off what they owed. However, they could not be sold, and they regained their freedom when they repaid their loan. As slaves, they could have businesses and property of their own and marry free persons.

Egyptian Civilization

While Mesopotamian civilization evolved along the banks of the Tigris and Euphrates Rivers, another great civilization developed in Egypt. It depended on the Nile, a river that flows from its source in central Africa some 4,000 miles north to the Mediterranean. The Nile divided Egypt into two geographically distinct districts: **Upper Egypt** (i.e., Egypt upstream), a narrow valley extending 650 miles from Aswan to the border of **Lower Egypt** (i.e., downstream Egypt), the Nile's 100-mile deep, triangularly shaped delta. Without the Nile, agriculture would have been impossible in Egypt's arid environment. Seasonal rains in central Africa caused the river to flood annually, saturating Egypt's fields and depositing a fresh layer of fertile silt just in time for the autumn planting season. As the waters retreated, farmers sowed their crops, and relatively simple irrigation techniques enabled them to maintain Egypt at a level of prosperity unmatched in the ancient world.

Egypt was a long, narrow country, but none of its people lived far from the Nile. The river tied them together, and by 3100 B.C.E., Upper and Lower Egypt were united under one government. While the Mesopotamian city-states warred among themselves and struggled with invaders, Egypt enjoyed remarkable stability and security. The cliffs and deserts that lined Egypt's borders protected it from invasion. The valley sheltered its people from the violent storms that swept the Mesopotamian plain, and the Nile's annual flooding was predictable and minimally destructive. The peace and order that characterized life in Egypt produced an optimistic outlook that contrasts markedly with the pessimistic tone of much Mesopotamian literature.

Ancient Greek historians grouped Egypt's rulers into thirty-one dynasties beginning with Menes, the king who united Upper and Lower Egypt, and ending with the death of Cleopatra (30 B.C.E.), the last member of a dynasty founded by one of Alexander the Great's Greek generals. Egypt was then absorbed into the Roman Empire and ruled by a Roman provincial governor. This 3,000-year-long era breaks down into three major periods of stability and creativity (the Old, Middle, and New Kingdoms) separated by relatively brief episodes of confusion (the Intermediate Periods).

The Old Kingdom (2700–2200 B.C.E.)   Egypt's first two dynasties (3100–2700 B.C.E., the Early Dynastic Period) unified the country and paved the way for the brilliant cultural achievements of the four dynasties that ruled the era called the Old Kingdom. The Old Kingdom produced many of the institutions, customs, and artistic styles that became the distinguishing features of ancient Egyptian civilization.

1.2
An Egyptian Hymn
to the Nile

QUICK REVIEW

Egypt and the Nile
- Egyptian civilization developed along the Nile
- Predictable annual floods aided agriculture
- The Nile tied the people of Egypt together

Upper Egypt   Narrow valley extending 650 miles from Aswan to the border of Lower Egypt.

Lower Egypt   The Nile's 100-mile deep, triangularly shaped delta.

The Book of the Dead. The Egyptians believed in the possibility of life after death through the god Osiris. Aspects of each person's life had to be tested by forty-two assessor-gods before the person could be presented to Osiris. In the scene from a papyrus manuscript of the *Book of the Dead*, the deceased and his wife (on the left) watch the scales of justice weighing his heart (on the left side of the scales) against the feather of truth. The jackal-headed god Anubis also watches the scales, and the ibis-headed god Thoth keeps the record.

British Museum, London, UK/The Bridgeman Art Library International Ltd.

pharaoh The god-kings of ancient Egypt.

nomes Egyptian districts ruled by regional governors who were called nomarchs.

The land and people of Egypt were the property of an absolute ruler who came to be called a **pharaoh** (i.e., master of "the great house"). The pharaoh was one of the gods on whom the safety and prosperity of Egypt depended. By building temples and honoring fellow gods with rituals and offerings the pharaoh maintained *maat*, the equilibrium of the universe. Pharaoh's word was law, and an elaborate bureaucracy of officials helped him (or her—a few women held the office) administer Egypt. Pharaoh's central government controlled granaries, land surveys, tax collections, and disbursements from the royal treasury. Egypt also had *nomarchs*, regional governors whose districts were called **nomes**. They handled important local issues such as water management.

The power and resources of the Old Kingdom pharaohs are clearly revealed by their most imposing and famous monuments, the pyramids. Djoser, a pharaoh of the Third Dynasty, inaugurated the construction of pyramids in Egypt. The architect who designed his tomb erected the world's first major masonry building— a solid six-layered "stepped" pyramid surrounded by an elaborate funeral complex. Snefru, founder of the Fourth Dynasty, built the first smooth-sided pyramid, and his son Khufu (Cheops, in Greek sources) commissioned the largest pyramid ever constructed. It rose on the desert plateau of Giza opposite the Old Kingdom's capital, Memphis, a city on the border between Upper and Lower Egypt. Khufu's appropriately named "Great Pyramid" covers 13.1 acres, originally soared to a height of 481 feet, and is composed of approximately 2.3 million blocks of stone (averaging 2.5 tons each). It is as remarkable for its precise engineering as its size. Khufu's successors built additional pyramids at Giza, and the pharaoh Khafre added the famous Sphinx, a huge version of the enigmatic half-lion, half-human creature that was a common subject for Egyptian sculptors. The pyramids and their temples were originally provided with lavish offerings to support the pharaoh in the afterlife, but they were stripped of their contents by ancient grave robbers. The only major artifacts the thieves missed were two full-sized wooden boats buried near the Giza pyramids. These were intended to convey the pharaoh on his journeys in the next world.

The First Intermediate Period and the Middle Kingdom (2200–1630 B.C.E.)
The Old Kingdom came apart when mounting political and economic difficulties gave the nomarchs and other royal officials opportunities to break free from the pharaoh's control. Central government faded, and confusion reigned throughout the First Intermediate Period (2200–2025 B.C.E.). Finally, Amunemhet I, a *vizier* (i.e., chief minister) to a dynasty of petty pharaohs seated in the Upper-Egyptian city of Thebes, reunited Egypt and inaugurated the era of the Middle Kingdom.

The First Intermediate Period may have done some lasting damage to the traditions that supported the pharaoh's authority, for the rulers of the Middle Kingdom were regarded as less remote and godlike than their predecessors. The nomarchs who served them had more autonomy, and to secure an uncontested succession to the throne pharaohs found it wise to establish their heirs as co-regents during their lifetimes. The literature of the era stressed the pharaoh's role as the shepherd of his people and the defender of the weak.

Egypt began to emerge from its isolation during the Middle Kingdom and to pay more attention to foreign affairs. The pharaohs pushed up the Nile into Nubia and built fortresses to guard the trade routes that brought African goods to Egypt. Syria and Palestine became areas of concern, and the government fortified the delta's borders to staunch the flow of migrants from the east.

The Second Intermediate Period and the New Kingdom (1630–1075 B.C.E.)   For unknown reasons the crown passed rapidly from hand to hand during the thirteenth dynasty, and the weaker pharaohs were challenged by rivals from the western delta. In the eastern delta, Asiatic migration continued until the region passed into the hands of people the Egyptians called Hyksos (i.e., "foreign chiefs"). Archaeological remains suggest these newcomers were probably Amorites. They occupied the delta and dominated the valley for about a century until Ahmose, first king of the eighteenth dynasty, drove them out and founded the New Kingdom.

The pharaohs of the New Kingdom had imperialistic aspirations. Their armies reached the Euphrates in the east and drove deep into Africa—extending Egyptian influence 1,300 miles south from Memphis. The Egyptian empire provided the pharaohs with unprecedented wealth and subjected them to numerous foreign influences. The result was the establishment in Thebes of a cosmopolitan court of extraordinary splendor and sophistication and the launching of a spate of monumental building projects throughout Egypt. The pharaohs of this era, hoping perhaps to safeguard the vast treasures they accumulated for the afterlife, ceased to erect pyramids that advertised the sites of their

Major Periods in Mesopotamian and Egyptian History

Mesopotamia

ca. 3500 B.C.E.	Cities appear
ca. 2800–2370 B.C.E.	First Dynasties
2370–2205 B.C.E.	Sargon's empire
2125–2027 B.C.E.	III Dynasty of Ur
1792–1750 B.C.E.	Reign of Hammurabi
ca. 1600 B.C.E.	Fall of Amoritic Babylon

Egypt

ca. 3100–2700 B.C.E.	Early Dynastic Period (dynasties I–II)
ca. 2700–2200 B.C.E.	The Old Kingdom (dynasties III–VI)
2200–2025 B.C.E.	I Intermediate Period (dynasties VII–XI)
2025–1630 B.C.E.	The Middle Kingdom (dynasties XII–XIII)
1630–1550 B.C.E.	II Intermediate Period (dynasties XIV–XVII)
1550–1075 B.C.E.	The New Kingdom (dynasties XVIII–XX)

graves and chose to be buried in cavelike tombs cut into the walls of the desolate "Valley of the Kings" near Thebes. Despite elaborate precautions, however, they failed to secure their final resting places. Only one pharaonic tomb (that of a young eighteenth dynasty ruler named Tutankhamun) escaped looting by ancient grave robbers. He was a fairly minor king who died prematurely and was buried in haste. His grave was doubtless less lavishly equipped than those of the more prominent pharaohs, but its treasures are truly awe inspiring.

Tutankhamun was succeeded by a line of solider-pharaohs who erected some of Egypt's most imposing monuments. They fought the Hittites, a powerful empire based in Asia Minor, for control of Syria and Palestine and fended off attacks on the delta from the Libyans and from the Sea Peoples who sailed the Mediterranean. An increasingly volatile international situation slowly eroded their position until, by 1075, Egypt was no longer an imperial power. Weakened by internal divisions, it succumbed to a succession of foreign conquerors—Assyrian, Persian, Greek, and ultimately Roman.

Language and Literature The Egyptians developed a writing system about 3000 B.C.E. They may have been inspired by Mesopotamia's example, but they invented their own techniques. The ancient Greeks called formal Egyptian writing **hieroglyphs** (i.e., "sacred carving"), for it was used to engrave holy texts on monuments. A cursive script that could be written much more rapidly and easily was used for ordinary everyday purposes. Egyptians wrote with pen and ink on sheets of paperlike material made from papyrus reeds. Texts were usually written on horizontal lines and read from right to left, but hieroglyphs were sometimes inscribed in horizontal columns. The hieroglyphic system was difficult to master, for its symbols could stand for syllables, words, or categories of speech.

The Egyptians produced a large and varied body of literature encompassing religious myths, entertaining stories, collections of proverbs, how-to advice for aspiring bureaucrats, love poems, personal letters, medical texts, astronomical observations, calendars, autobiographies, judicial records, and administrative documents. Curiously missing are any traces of epic poetry or of dramas, although the latter, at least, are known to have been performed as parts of cult rituals.

Religion: Gods, Temples, and the Afterlife The Egyptians were apparently untroubled by a lack of consistency in their religious beliefs. They had three different myths to explain the origin of the world, and each featured a different creator-god. Some gods had overlapping functions, and some were known by a variety of names. Gods were represented in both human and animal form and as hybrids—human bodies with animal heads. As in Mesopotamia, gods were believed literally to inhabit their temples, some of which were of staggering size. The sacred complex at Karnak (near Thebes) was under construction for over 2,000 years. The gods were served by armies of priests and priestesses, who were sustained by lavish temple endowments. Ordinary people did not worship in the great temples but on occasions when the images of the gods were brought out from their sanctuaries and exposed to public view.

The fact that Egypt's religion was extremely ancient and deeply rooted in the traditions of its people did not deter a pharaoh of the eighteenth dynasty from attempting to overhaul it. Amunhotep IV swept aside all the gods and declared exclusive allegiance to the Aten, a god symbolized by the disk of the sun. The old temples were closed, and the pharaoh and his queen, Nefertiti, were proclaimed sole mediators between the new god and the Egyptian people. To honor the Aten, Amunhotep changed his name to Akhenaten (i.e., "the effective spirit of the Aten")

hieroglyphs ("sacred carving") Greek name for Egyptian writing. The writing was often used to engrave holy texts on monuments.

and built a new capital called Akhetaten (i.e., "the horizon of the Aten") near Amarna north of Thebes. Akhenaten's religious reforms failed to take hold, and after his death the court returned to Thebes. Akhetaten was dismantled. The Aten cult was suppressed, and the worship of the former Theban sun-god, Amun, and Egypt's other deities was restored. The Aten was the only Egyptian god to be represented by an abstract symbol, not a human or animal image, and the art of the Amarna period also departed from the conventions of traditional Egyptian painting and sculpture. It was characterized by a unique expressionistic distortion of forms.

Most Egyptians worshiped at small local shrines, and many householders had private collections of sacred objects. Egyptians placed great trust in magic, oracles, and amulets to ward off evil and misfortune. Originally they assumed that only the pharaoh survived death to join the immortal gods, but gradually the belief spread that everyone who made the necessary preparations could enjoy this privilege. The spells needed to pass the various tests and fend off the

HISTORY'S VOICES

A HYMN OF ZOROASTER ABOUT THE TWO SPIRITS OF GOOD AND EVIL

Z*oroaster's reform made Ahura Mazda (the "Wise Lord") the supreme deity in the Iranian pantheon. The hymns, or Gathas, depict him as the greatest of the ahuras, the divinities associated with the good. This faith views the world through a moral dualism of good and evil, in which one has the freedom to choose the Truth or the Lie. The "Very Holy [Spirit]" chose Truth ("Righteousness"), and the "Evil [Spirit]" (Angra Mainyu, or Ahriman), chose the evil of "the Lie." Humans similarly can choose good or evil.*

WHAT LESSON or values does this passage teach?

(1) Then shall I speak, now give ear and hearken, both you who seek from near and you from far . . . (2) Then shall I speak of the two primal Spirits of existence, of whom the Very Holy thus spoke to the Evil One: "Neither our thoughts nor teachings nor wills, neither our choices nor words nor acts, not our inner selves nor our souls agree." (3) Then shall I speak of the foremost [doctrine] of this existence, which Mazda the Lord. He with knowledge, declared to me. Those of you who do not act upon this manthra, even as I shall think and speak it, for them there shall be woe at the end of life. (4) Then shall I speak of the best things of this existence. I know Mazda who created it in accord with truth to be the

Father of active Good Purpose. And his daughter is Devotion of good action. The all-seeing Lord is not to be deceived. (5) Then shall I speak of what the Most Holy One told me, the word to be listened to as best for men. Those who shall give for me hearkening and heed to Him, shall attain wholeness and immortality. Mazda is Lord through acts of the Good Spirit . . . (8) Him shall I seek to turn to us by praises of reverence, for truly I have now seen with my eyes [the House] of Good Purpose, and of good act and deed, having known through Truth Him who is Lord Mazda. Then let us lay up supplications to Him in the House of Song. (9) Him shall I seek to requite for us with good purpose, Him who left to our will [the choice between] holy and unholy. May Lord Mazda by His power make us active for prospering our cattle and men, through the fair affinity of good purpose with truth. (10) Him shall I seek to glorify for us with sacrifices of devotion, Him who is known in the soul as Lord Mazda; for He has promised by His truth and good purpose that there shall be wholeness and immortality within His kingdom (khshathra), strength and perpetuity within His house.

From Mary Boyce, ed. and trans., *Textual Sources for the Study of Zoroastrianism* (Manchester, U.K.: Manchester University Press, 1984), p. 36.

monsters of the underworld were contained in the *Book of the Dead*, a text often inscribed on tombs. The dead were assumed to want and need the same things as the living, and persons who could afford to do so loaded their tombs with provisions and equipment for life after death. It was the duty of their descendants to make periodic offerings at their tombs to replenish their supplies.

Women in Egyptian Society   The Egyptian woman's primary duty was the management of a household. She was not ordinarily admitted to scribal schools, artisan apprenticeships, or government offices, but she could own and manage property, sue for divorce, and claim the same legal protections as a man. Royal women were, of course, an exception. They often wielded considerable influence, and a few, such as Thutmosis I's daughter Hatshepsut, ruled Egypt either as regents for dependent males or in their own names. Women were common subjects for Egypt's artists, who depicted them making and receiving offerings and enjoying the pleasures of dining and hunting with their husbands.

Slaves   Slaves were not common in Egypt until the foreign campaigns of the pharaohs of the Middle Kingdom began to produce Nubian and Asian prisoners of war. The imperialistic ventures of the New Kingdom vastly increased the number of captives taken in battle and sometimes led to the enslavement of entire peoples.

Slaves were assigned all kinds of tasks. Some worked in the fields alongside the native peasants. Some were domestic servants. Some were trained as artisans. A few even exercised authority as policemen or soldiers. They could be freed, but manumission was rare. There were, however, no racial or other features that set them apart from the free population.

ANCIENT MIDDLE EASTERN EMPIRES

WHAT WERE the great empires of the ancient Middle East?

D uring the era of Egypt's New Kingdom, the Middle East witnessed the rise and fall of many states. The most significant were the empires founded by the Hittites and the Assyrians, but it should be noted, if only in passing, that a horde of other peoples—the Hurrians, Mitanni, Kassites, Canaanites, Phoenicians, Chaldaeans, and Israelites—also jockeyed for position. (See Map 1–2.)

THE HITTITES

The Hittites, who migrated into the Middle East from Europe in the sixteenth century B.C.E., were Indo-Europeans. That is, they spoke a language that belongs to the same family as Greek, Latin, and Indian Sanskrit. This distinguished them from the older residents of the Middle East, most of whom spoke Semitic languages. The Hittites built a strong centralized kingdom with its seat at Hattusas, a site near modern Ankara. Between 1400 and 1200 B.C.E., the Hittites extended their territory until they became the dominant power in the Middle East. They destroyed their neighbors, the Mitannians, and contested control of Syria and Palestine with Egypt. An indecisive battle in 1285 B.C.E. culminated in a truce between these two superpowers. They enjoyed fairly amicable relations until about 1200 B.C.E., when they were both threatened by invaders whom the Egyptians called the Sea Peoples. Egypt retreated to the safety of its valley, but the Hittite kingdom collapsed.

The Hittites assimilated many aspects of Mesopotamian culture and adapted cuneiform to write their language. Their political institutions, however, were their own. Hittite kings did not claim to be divine or even to be agents of the gods. The king was advised by a council of nobles who limited his power, and an

Statue of Hatshepsut

"Statue of Hatshepsut". Red Granite. Dynasty 18, 1490-1480 B.C. (Egyptian). The Metropolitan Museum of Art, Rogers Fund and Edward S. Harkness Gift, 1929. (29.3.1)

MAP EXPLORATION

Interactive map: To explore this map further, go to **http://www.prenhall.com/kagan3/map1.2**

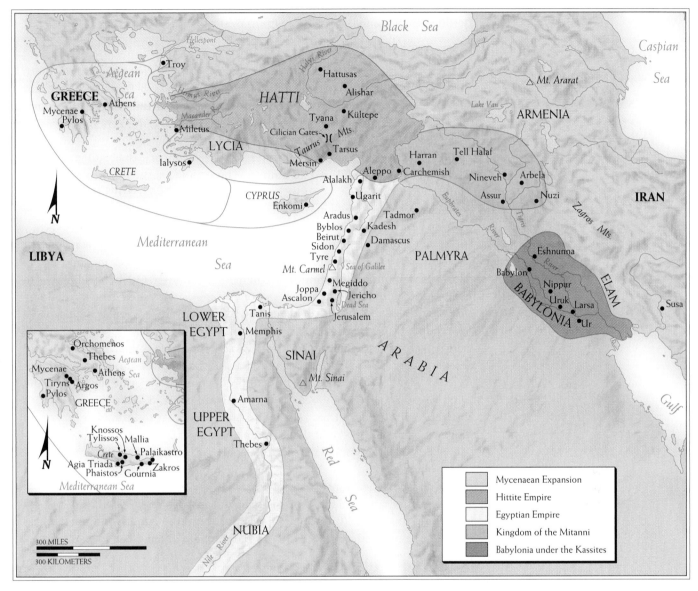

MAP 1–2

The Middle East and Greece CA. 1400 B.C.E.   About 1400 B.C.E., the Middle East was divided among four empires. Egypt extended south to Nubia and north through Palestine and Phoenicia. The Kassites ruled in Mesopotamia, the Hittites in Asia Minor, and the Mitanni in Assyrian lands. In the Aegean, the Mycenaean kingdoms were at their height.

BASED ON the locations of the various states that had risen by the fifteenth century B.C.E., what were these new states dependent on, geographically, to succeed?

heir's succession to the throne required ratification by the army. One thing that may have contributed to Hittite success was the invention in Asia Minor (prior to the rise of the Hittite kingdom) of techniques for smelting iron and forging it into weapons. Iron was more plentiful and, therefore, more economical than bronze, and its spreading use marked the beginning, about 1100 B.C.E., of a new era: the Iron Age. Clay tablets that survive from the Hittite archives have helped historians reconstruct the history of the Middle East, but they also contain the earliest information about the Greeks, the Hittites' western neighbors who were destined to play a major role in shaping Western civilization.

THE ASSYRIANS

The Assyrian homeland centered on Assur, a city on the Tigris River in northern Mesopotamia. The Assyrians had ancient trading ties with Babylonia, and they spoke a Semitic language related to Babylonian. During the fourteenth century B.C.E., Assyria expanded to the north and west. However, the general confusion that descended on the Middle East when Sumer collapsed at the end of the second millennium loosed an invasion by the Arameans that ended the first Assyrian attempt at building an empire. The Arameans spread throughout the Middle East from their point of origin in northern Syria, and their language, Aramaic, was spoken by some of the people who influenced the development of Judaism and Christianity.

About 1000 B.C.E., the Assyrians began to expand again, and by 665 B.C.E., they controlled Mesopotamia, southern Asia Minor, Syria, Palestine, and Egypt. They were famous for their innovative military technology and their willingness to commit atrocities to frighten their opponents into submission. The Assyrian empire was divided into provinces headed by military governors, and its subjects were kept in line by occupying armies. Pockets of potential resistance to Assyrian rule were sometimes broken up by evicting whole peoples from their homelands and resettling them in small groups scattered about the empire. Agricultural colonies were founded to bring unused land into production and provide supplies for the army. Great palaces were erected at Nineveh and Nimrud and ornamented with superb stone carvings in bas relief. They were designed to intimidate the vassal kings, who annually brought their tribute to the Assyrian capital.

The Assyrian empire may have become too large, given the communications available, to govern effectively, and squabbling among its leaders also set it up for disaster. The agents of its fall were the Medes, an Indo-European people settled in Iran, and the Babylonians (Chaldaeans). Overextended as it was, Assyria could not deal with both enemies at once, and the empire crumbled quickly. By 612 B.C.E., all the cities of the Assyrian homeland had been sacked.

THE NEO-BABYLONIANS

When the Medes failed to exploit the opportunity Assyria's fall gave them, the way was cleared for Babylon's king, Nebuchadnezzar, to build a Neo-Babylonian (or Chaldaean) empire. Babylon became the center of world trade, a city famous for its monuments and wonders. Nebuchadnezzar's empire was brilliant but unstable. Its throne passed rapidly through a number of hands, and its last heir so alienated his subjects that they failed to resist when Persia invaded Babylonia in 539 B.C.E. The city capitulated and survived to enjoy renewed prosperity within a new and more successful Persian Empire.

THE PERSIAN EMPIRE

WHAT WERE the Persian rulers' attitudes toward the cultures they ruled?

The great Persian Empire arose in the region now called Iran. The ancestors of its rulers spoke a language from the Aryan branch of the family of Indo-European languages, related to Greek and Latin. The most important collections of tribes among them were the Medes and the Persians, peoples

MAP EXPLORATION

Interactive map: To explore this map further, go to **http://www.prenhall.com/kagan3/map1.3**

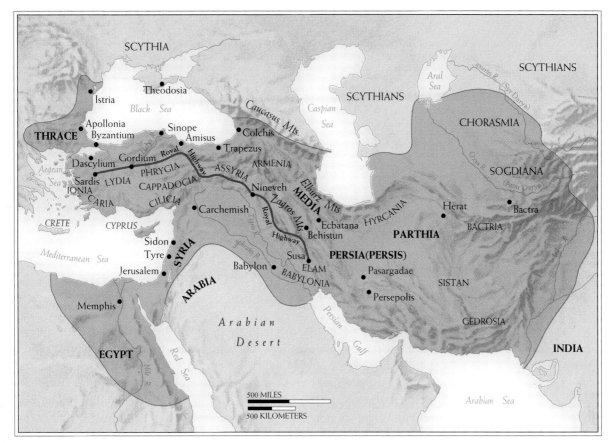

MAP 1–3

The Achaemenid Persian Empire   The empire created by Cyrus had reached its fullest extent under Darius when Persia attacked Greece in 490 B.C.E. It extended from India to the Aegean, and even into Europe, encompassing the lands formerly ruled by Egyptians, Hittites, Babylonians, and Assyrians.

so similar in language and customs that the Greeks used both names interchangeably. The Medes organized their tribes into a union and aggressively built a force that defeated the mighty Assyrian Empire in 612 B.C.E. The Persians were subordinate to the Medes until Cyrus II (called the Great) became King of the Persians (r. 559–530 B.C.E.), when the Persians began to dominate. About 550 B.C.E., Cyrus united the Medes and Persians under his own rule.

CYRUS THE GREAT

Cyrus quickly expanded his power, eventually extending it from the Aegean Sea to the Indus valley and modern Afghanistan. In the west, he decisively defeated King Croesus of Lydia in western Asia Minor, taking control of Croesus's capital city of Sardis and other Greek cities. At the same time Cyrus captured Babylon from an unpopular king, and was thus viewed as a liberator, not a conqueror. The cylinder that describes his version of events claims that the Babylonian god Marduk had "got him into his city Babylon without fighting or battle."

Unlike the harsh Babylonian and Assyrian conquerors who preceded him, Cyrus pursued a policy of toleration and restoration. He did not impose the

Darius. Persian nobles pay homage to King Darius in this relief from the treasury at the Persian capital of Persepolis. Darius is seated on the throne: his son and successor Xerxes stands behind him. Darius and Xerxes are carved in larger scale to indicate their royal status.

Courtesy of the Oriental Institute of the University of Chicago

Persian religion but claimed to rule by the favor of the Babylonian god. Instead of deporting defeated peoples and destroying cities, he allowed exiles to return and rebuilt cities. For example, upon his conquest of the Babylonian Empire, which included Palestine, Cyrus permitted the Hebrews, taken into captivity by King Nebuchadnezzar in 586 B.C.E., to return to their native land of Judah. Persian rule, however, was not entirely gentle; it demanded tribute and military service from its subjects, sometimes with brutal enforcement.

DARIUS THE GREAT

Cyrus's son Cambyses succeeded to the throne in 529 B.C.E. Cambyses conquered Egypt, establishing it as a satrapy (province) that extended to Lybia in the west and Ethiopia in the south. Civil war roiled much of the Persian Empire upon his death in 522 B.C.E. The following year Darius emerged as the new emperor. Found on a great rock hundreds of feet in the air near the mountains of Behistun, an inscription boasts of Darius's victories and the greatness of his rule. Discovered almost two thousand years later, it was carved in three languages, Babylonian, Old Persian, and Elamite, all in cuneiform script, thereby helping scholars to decipher all three languages. Darius's long and prosperous reign lasted until 486 B.C.E. and brought the Persian Empire to its greatest extent, with conquests in northern India, Scythian lands around the Black Sea, and Thrace and Macedonia on the fringes of the Greek mainland. In 499 B.C.E., the Ionian Greeks of western Asia Minor rebelled, launching wars between Greeks and Persians that would last for two decades.

GOVERNMENT AND ADMINISTRATION

Ahura Mazda   The chief deity of Zoroastrianism, the native religion of Persia. Ahura Mazda is the creator of the world, the source of light, and the embodiment of good.

The Persian Empire was a hereditary monarchy that claimed divine sanction from the god **Ahura Mazda**. The ruler, known as *Shahanshah*, "king of kings," in theory owned all the land and peoples in the empire as absolute monarch, and demanded tribute and service for the use of his property. In practice he depended on the advice and administrative service of aristocratic courtiers, ministers, and satraps (provincial governors), and was expected to rule justly, as Ahura Mazda's chosen representative. Still, the king ruled as a semidivine autocrat with the power of life and death over his subjects. The Greeks would see him as the model of a despot or tyrant who regarded his people as slaves.

The empire was divided into twenty-nine satrapies, ruled by satraps with considerable autonomy over civil and military affairs. The king exercised a degree of control through appointed provincial secretaries and military commanders, as well as inspectors who, as the "eyes and ears of the king," traveled throughout the empire. A system of excellent royal roads made these travels swifter and easier, as did a royal postal system that was a kind of "pony express" with men mounted on fast horses at stations along the way. The royal postal service traveled the 1500 miles from Sardis in Lydia to the Persian capital at Susa in less than two weeks; normally such a trip took three months. The Persians adopted Aramaic, the most common language of Middle Eastern commerce, as the imperial tongue, thereby simplifying civil and military administration.

Medes and Persians made up the core of the army and supplied the empire with its officers and imperial administrators. When needed, the army drafted large numbers of subject armies. A large Persian army, such as the one that invaded Greece in 480 B.C.E., included hundreds of thousands of non-Iranian soldiers organized by ethnic group, each dressed in its own uniforms, taking orders from Iranian officers.

RELIGION

Persia's religion was different from that of its neighbors and subjects. It derived from the Indo-European traditions of the Vedic religion that Aryan peoples brought into India about 1500 B.C.E. Its practice included animal sacrifices and a reverence for fire and, although polytheistic, unusually emphasized its chief god Ahura Mazda, the "Wise Lord."

Zarathustra, a Mede whom the Greeks called Zoroaster, changed the traditional Aryan worship sometime between 1000 B.C.E. and 600 B.C.E. This religious prophet and teacher made Ahura Mazda the only god, dismissing the others as demons not to be worshipped but fought. Polytheism and sacrifices were forbidden, and the old sacrificial fire was converted into a symbol of goodness and light. Zarathustra portrayed life as an unending struggle between two great forces, Ahura Mazda, the creator and only god, representing goodness and light, and Ahriman, a demon, representing darkness and evil. The good would be rewarded with glory, while the evil would be punished with suffering. (See "History's Voices: A Hymn of Zoroaster about the Two Spirits of Good and Evil.") By the middle of the sixth century B.C.E., Zoroastrianism had become the chief religion of the Persians. On the great inscribed monument at Behistun, Darius the Great praised the god of Zarathustra and his teachings: "On this account Ahura Mazda brought me help . . . because I was not wicked, nor was I a liar, nor was I a tyrant, neither I nor any of my line. I have ruled according to righteousness."

ART AND CULTURE

The Persians learned from and adapted much from the peoples they conquered. They adapted the **Aramaic** alphabet of the Semites to create a Persian alphabet and used the cuneiform symbols of Babylon to write the Old Persian language they spoke. They borrowed their calendar from Egypt. Persian art

Aramaic Semitic language spoken widely throughout the Middle East in antiquity.

and architecture also benefited from various talents and styles. Darius, for example, proudly described the varied sources of the construction of his palace at Susa:

> The cedar timber—a mountain by name Lebanon—from there it was brought . . . the yaka-timber was brought from Gandara and from Carmania. The gold was brought from Sardis and from Bactria . . . the precious stone lapis-lazuli and carnelian . . . was brought from Sogdiana. The . . . turquoise from Chorasmia. . . . The silver and ebony . . . from Egypt . . . the ornamentation from Ionia . . . the ivory . . . from Ethiopia and from Sind and from Arachosia. . . . The stone-cutters who wrought the stone, those were Ionians and Sardians. The goldsmiths . . . were Modes and Egyptians. The men who wrought the wood, those were Sardians and Egyptians. The men who wrought the baked brick, those were Babylonians. The men who adorned the wall, those were Medes and Egyptians.[1]

The Royal Palace at Persepolis, built by Darius and his successor Xerxes (r. 485–465 B.C.E.), is probably the most magnificent of Persian architectural remains. On a high foundation supported on all sides by a stone wall 20 or 30 feet high, the complex contained a Hall of a Hundred Columns where the kings carried out their official duties. The columns, grand stairway with carvings, and gateway with winged bulls reveal the grandeur of the ancient Persian Empire.

PALESTINE

HOW WAS Hebrew monotheism different from Mesopotamian and Egyptian polytheism?

Many large states flourished in the ancient Middle East, but none had as much influence on Western civilization as a tiny group of people who settled in Palestine about 1200 B.C.E. Three of the world's great religions (Judaism, Christianity, and Islam) trace their origins (at least in part) to this region and to the history of its inhabitants, the Israelites.

THE CANAANITES AND THE PHOENICIANS

Palestine's early settlers spoke Canaanite (a Semitic language), lived in walled cities, and earned their livings as farmers and seafarers. Their most influential cultural achievement was a highly simplified writing system. Instead of the hundreds of characters that were needed to write the cuneiform and hieroglyphic scripts, it used an alphabet of only twenty to thirty symbols. This made learning to read and write much easier, which promoted the spread of literacy.

The Israelite invaders who settled in Palestine about 1200 B.C.E. either forced the Canaanites of the interior region out or assimilated them. However, the Canaanites and Syrians who inhabited the northern coast hung on to their territory. They became the **Phoenicians**, a seafaring people who scattered trading colonies from one end of the Mediterranean to the other. The most famous of their colonial outposts was the city of Carthage (near modern Tunis in North Africa). Cultural influences accompanied the goods that flowed through the Phoenician trade network. The Phoenicians passed the alphabet to the Greeks, who handed it on to us.

Phoenicians Seafaring people (Canaanites and Syrians) who scattered trading colonies from one end of the Mediterranean to the other.

[1]T. Cuyler Young, Jr., "Iran, ancient," *Ecyclopedia Britannica Online.*

Exile of the Israelites. In 722 B.C.E. the northern part of Jewish Palestine, the kingdom of Israel, was conquered by the Assyrians. Its people were driven from their homeland and exiled all over the vast Assyrian Empire. This wall carving in low relief comes from the palace of the Assyrian king Sennacherib at Nineveh. It shows the Jews with their cattle and baggage going into exile.

Relief, Israel, 10th-6th Century: Judean exiles carrying provisions. Detail of the Assyrian conquest of the Jewish fortified town of Lachish (battle 701 BC). Part of a relief from the palace of Sennacherib at Niniveh, Mesopotamia (Iraq). British Museum, London, Great Britain. © Erich Lessing/Art Resource, NY.

THE ISRAELITES

Our knowledge of the Israelites derives primarily from their chief literary monument, the Bible. The Bible contains some historical narratives (as well as collections of laws, ritual instructions, wisdom, literature, poetry, and prophecy), but it was not meant to be read simply as objective history. Scholars have developed many strategies for extracting historical data from it, but their findings are tentative.

According to tradition, the Israelites or Hebrews (i.e., "wanderers") were the descendants of Abraham, a Semitic nomad whose family came from the region of Ur. He and his successors (the patriarchs) led their tribe into Palestine in the early second millennium and eventually on to Egypt. They may have entered Egypt during the period when the Hyksos, fellow Semites, ruled the delta. In the thirteenth century B.C.E., a man named Moses led them out of Egypt. They resumed wandering in the Sinai desert, but eventually breached the frontiers of Canaan and settled in Palestine's mountainous interior. Their scattered tribes made little progress until they united under the leadership of a king named David. He won control of most of Canaan and founded the city of Jerusalem. The Hebrew monarchy reached its peak in the tenth century B.C.E., during the reign of his son and heir Solomon. Following Solomon's death, the kingdom split in two. The northern section, Israel, was the larger and more advanced, but the southern portion, Judah, retained control over Jerusalem, the site of the Israelites' first temple.

In 722 B.C.E., Assyria conquered Israel, dispersed its people, and Israel's **ten lost tribes** disappeared from history. Judah survived as an independent kingdom until 586 B.C.E., when it was conquered by the Neo-Babylonian ruler Nebuchadnezzar II. He destroyed Jerusalem and its temple and resettled many of the people of Judah (i.e., Jews) in foreign lands. This period, known as "the Exile" or "Babylonian Captivity," did not last long. Babylon fell to Persia in

ten lost tribes   Israelites who were scattered and lost to history when the northern kingdom of Israel fell to the Assyrians in 722 B.C.E.

539 B.C.E., and the new emperor permitted some Jews to return to rebuild Jerusalem and its temple. In 70 C.E., the Romans once again destroyed Jerusalem and scattered its people, but in 1948 C.E., Jewish leaders regained control of Jerusalem and reestablished the state of Israel.

THE JEWISH RELIGION

The tiny nation of Israel would be of little interest to historians were it not for its religious significance. The ancient Jews believed they had been chosen by God for a unique religious mission. Their ancestor Abraham had made a covenant (i.e., a contract) with God. It committed God to preserving them, and them to the task of revealing God by remaining exclusively loyal to him and living according to his law. Their history was to be sacred history, a revelation of God's will for humankind.

Hebrew **monotheism**—faith in a single God, an all-powerful creator who loves humankind but demands righteous conduct—may be as old as Moses and certainly dates back to the preaching of the great biblical prophets of the eighth century B.C.E. The Jews did not imagine God to be a force of nature or a superhuman being, but a reality so transcendent it cannot be pictured in any way. Transcendence did not, however, imply distance from God, for the Jews believed God was intimately involved in their history. Like the teachings of Zarathustra (Zoroaster) in Iran, they assumed there was a link between ethics and religion. God was not content with sacrifices and worship; God judged people according to how they treated one another. The Hebrew prophets, who spoke for God, assured their followers that God dealt mercifully with repentant sinners, and the prophets explained the misfortunes that befell the Jews as just punishments for their failure to honor the terms of Abraham's covenant. Centuries of oppression ultimately convinced the Jews that God would have to intervene in history on their behalf if the promises to Abraham were to be fulfilled. They began to look for a special leader, a messiah (i.e., "annointed one"), whom God would empower to lead them to complete their mission in history. Christianity diverges from Judaism in maintaining that Jesus of Nazareth was that messiah.

GENERAL OUTLOOK OF MIDDLE EASTERN CULTURES

WHAT SOCIAL and political contrasts existed between ancient Middle Eastern and Greek civilizations?

*T*here were differences among the various cultures of the Middle East, but taken together they all diverge from the outlook of the Greeks, the ancient people who exerted the greatest influence on the Western tradition.

HUMANS AND NATURE

The peoples of the Middle East did not envision an absolute gulf between animate beings and inanimate objects. They believed all things are imbued with life and spirit and that the universe is an arena for a war of supernatural wills. Because nature seemed chaotic from the human perspective, it seemed to follow that the gods who governed the world must be capricious. The Babylonian creation myth claimed that the gods had created people for the sole purpose of serving them. Human life was, therefore, precarious, for the deities were interested only in themselves and paid scant attention to the wishes of their human servants. Even disasters, like wars, which might be explained as the products of human decisions, were assumed to be acts of the gods.

The helplessness of humankind in the face of irrational divine powers is the point of the story of a great primeval flood that is found in various forms in

monotheism   Having faith in a single God.

Babylonian, Egyptian, and Hebrew sources. In the Egyptian tale, the god Re, who created human beings, decides they are plotting against him, and Re sends the vicious goddess Sekhmet to destroy them. Humanity is saved only when Re has a last-minute, unexplained change of heart. In the Babylonian version of the story, it is the annoying noise made by an increasing human population that persuades the gods to destroy humanity. The species is saved when one man wins the favor of the god Enki, who helps him and his wife survive. In a world governed by such quixotic principles, human beings could not hope to understand and control events. At best, they might try to pit one mysterious force against another by means of magical spells.

HUMANS AND THE GODS, LAW, AND JUSTICE

Because the gods could destroy humankind—and might do so at any time for no apparent reason—people tried to win the gods' favor by offering prayer and sacrifice. There was, however, no guarantee of success, for gods were capricious beings who were not bound by reason or conscience.

In arenas that were more or less under human control, people attempted to establish more orderly and consistent principles to guide their lives. In the earliest civilized societies, rulers decreed laws to govern human relations, but effective laws are based on something more than a lawgiver's power to coerce obedience. The challenge for governments was to find justifications that would impart authority to laws. The Egyptians simply assumed that because the king was a god, he had the right to establish whatever rules seemed best to him at the moment. The Mesopotamians believed the gods commissioned their kings and gave them divine authority to keep order in the human herd. The Hebrews had a more subtle understanding of law. Their god was capable of destructive rages, but he was open to rational discussion and imposed certain moral standards on himself. In the biblical version of the flood story, God is wrathful but not arbitrary. His creatures deserve destruction as punishment for their sins. When God decides to save Noah, he does so because Noah is a good man who merits God's protection. The Hebrews believed God wanted human beings to live in just relationships with one another and that God was the leading advocate for human justice.

1.6
Laws of the
Hebrews

TOWARD THE GREEKS AND WESTERN THOUGHT

*M*any, if not most, Greeks in the ancient world must have thought about life in much the same way as their neighbors in the Middle East. Their gods resembled the arbitrary Mesopotamian deities; they trusted in magic and incantations to manage life's uncertainties; and they believed laws were to be obeyed simply because a power enforced them. The surprising thing is that some Greeks came to think differently about these things, and their strikingly original ideas charted a new path for the West.

In the sixth century B.C.E., thinkers who lived on the Aegean coast of Asia Minor began an intellectual revolution. Thales, the first Greek philosopher, urged his followers to try to explain natural events by referring them to other natural events and not to unknowable supernatural causes. His search for naturalistic explanations for phenomena launched Western science.

Rationalism of this kind characterized the approach major Greek thinkers took to exploring all kinds of issues. Xenophanes of Colophon, Thales's contemporary, pointed out that people had no grounds for imagining gods in human form. He argued that if oxen could draw pictures, they would sketch gods who looked like oxen. Comments like this might promote skepticism, but they also produced valuable insights. In the fifth century B.C.E., Thucydides of Athens wrote a history that made no reference to the gods and explained events as the result of human decisions and chance. Similarly, Hippocrates of Cos founded a school of medicine that diagnosed and treated disease without invoking the supernatural. The same lack of interest in divine causality characterized Greek attitudes toward law and justice.

IMAGE KEY

for pages 4–5

a. Cyprus papyrus d

b. An administrative document in Sumerian cuneiform

c. King Tut's Throne shows Tutankhamen and Queen

d. Tablet covered with cuneiform writing

e. Victory stele of Naram–Sin, King of Akkad, over the mountain-dwelling Lullubi, Mesopotamian, Akkadian Period, c. 2230 BC (pink sandstone). Louvre, Paris, France/The Bridgeman Art Library International Ltd.

f. "Seated Scribe" Dynasty 5, ca. 2510–2460 B.C.E. "Seated Scribe" from Saqqara, Egypt. 5th Dynasty, c. 2510-2460 B.C.E. Painted limestone, height 21' (53 cm). Musee du Louvre, Paris. Bridgeman-Giraudon/Art Resource, NY

g. Prehistorical grotto with many animal paintings, Vallon-pont-D'Arc, Ardeche, France

h. Detail. Relief: Eagle-headed winged being pollinating the sacred tree. From the Palace of Ashurnasirpal II (885–860 B.C.E.), King of Assyria The Metropolitan Museum of Art, Gift of John D. Rockefeller, Jr., 1932. (32.143.3) Photograph ©1983 The Metropolitan Museum of Art

i. Belly handled amphora, Kerameikos

j. Neolithic sculpture

k. The Royal Standard of Ur, a mosaic that dates from about 2750 B.C.E. British Museum, London, UK/Bridgeman Art Library

SUMMARY

Early Humans and Their Culture During the Paleolithic period, humans lived by hunting, fishing, and gathering food. They used tools, fire, and language; they believed in the supernatural. Around 10,000 B.C.E., humans started domesticating animals and plants for food. This Neolithic Revolution, which took place at different times in different parts of the world, was based on different crops in different environments. Civilization emerged, first in Mesopotamia, approximately during the Bronze Age, 3100 to 1200 B.C.E.

Early Civilizations to about 1000 B.C.E. Around 3000 B.C.E., civilizations along the Tigris and Euphrates Rivers in Mesopotamia, and the Nile River in Egypt, started to produce written records. Civilization in southern Mesopotamia was founded by Sumerians. Semitic Akkadians from northern Babylonia established the first empire in history; Sumerians returned to power in the Third Dynasty of Ur. Egypt's pharaohs united lands along the Nile. Hieroglyphs and tombs have left us an extensive record of life in ancient Egypt.

Ancient Middle Eastern Empires Between about 1400 B.C.E. and 500 B.C.E., new peoples and empires emerged in the Middle East. The Kassites and Mitannians were warrior peoples who ruled over the inhabitants of Babylonia and northern Syria/Mesopotamia, respectively. The Hittites based an empire in what is now Turkey. The Assyrian military supported a large Middle Eastern empire that lasted for almost half a millennium. Nebuchadnezzar overthrew the Assyrians and established a short-lived Neo-Babylonian dynasty.

The Persian Empire In the late sixth and early fifth centuries B.C.E., the Persian Empire reached the height of its power and geographical expansion under Cyrus the Great and Darius the Great. By assimilating cultures and peoples, the empire successfully combined a measure of autonomy among its twenty-nine satrapies (provinces) with a centralized authority based on the king's rule as a semidivine autocrat. Tolerance of other religions, use of the common language of Aramaic and existing writing systems, and an efficient communications system contributed to the Persians' imperial power. The Persian Empire was also built on the use of non-Persian soldiers and the art, architecture, and raw materials of its conquered lands.

Palestine Judaism, Christianity, and Islam all owe many of their beliefs and practices to the Israelites who settled in Palestine before 1200 B.C.E. Israelites under Moses conquered Canaan in the thirteenth century B.C.E., and their kingdom reached its peak in the tenth century B.C.E. in the reigns of David and Solomon before splintering. Polytheistic Canaanites had lived in Syria-Palestine and through the coastal Phoenicians gave the Greeks the predecessor of the alphabet we use today.

General Outlook of Middle Eastern Cultures Most people of the ancient Mideast believed humans were inseparable from nature, and the gods were powerful and capricious. The Hebrew God reflected a different perspective on humanity's relationship with nature and with divine power. All the ancient Middle Eastern attitudes toward religion, philosophy, science, and society in general differ markedly from what we will learn about the Greeks.

Toward the Greeks and Western Thought By the sixth century B.C.E., some Greeks started thinking about the world in ways that became the hallmark of Western civilization: They began to seek naturalistic, rational explanations for material phenomena and human behavior. Philosophy and science, as we understand them, could only develop once the Greeks had discarded supernatural explanations and reliance on divine intervention as ways of understanding the world. By the fifth century B.C.E., Greek thinkers had inaugurated the study of medicine and history, and by the fourth century B.C.E., Greek law and democracy had begun to evolve into forms recognizable to us.

REVIEW QUESTIONS

1. How was life during the Paleolithic Age different from life during the Neolithic Age? What advances account for the difference? Were these advances so significant that they warrant referring to the Neolithic as a revolutionary era?

2. What differences do you see in the political and intellectual outlooks of the Egyptian and Mesopotamian civilizations? How do their religious views compare? What influence did geography have on their religious outlooks?

3. What was significant about Cyrus the Great and Darius the Great? During their reigns, how did the Persians treat the cultures and peoples of subject lands?

4. What role did religious faith play in the political history of the Jews? Why did Middle Eastern civilizations regard the concept of Hebrew monotheism as a radical idea?

5. How did Greek thinkers diverge from the intellectual traditions of the Middle East? What new kinds of questions did Greeks ask?

KEY TERMS

Ahura Mazda (p. 24)	**hieroglyphs** (p. 18)	**Paleolithic** (p. 6)
Aramaic (p. 25)	*Homo sapiens* (p. 6)	**pharaoh** (p. 16)
Bronze Age (p. 8)	**Lower Egypt** (p. 15)	**Phoenicians** (p. 26)
civilization (p. 8)	**monotheism** (p. 28)	**polytheists** (p. 12)
culture (p. 6)	**Neolithic** (p. 7)	**ten lost tribes** (p. 27)
cuneiform (p. 11)	**nomes** (p. 16)	**Upper Egypt** (p. 15)

 For additional study resources for this chapter, go to:
www.prenhall.com/kagan3/chapter1

2 The Rise of Greek Civilization

CHAPTER HIGHLIGHTS

The Bronze Age on Crete and on the Mainland to about 1150 B.C.E. The Minoan civilization of Crete (2100–1150 B.C.E.) was built around the palaces of its kings. On the mainland, the Mycenaeans reached the height of their power between 1400 and 1200 B.C.E. Scholars have suggested a number of possible explanations for the fall of the Mycenaeans.

The Greek "Middle Ages" to about 750 B.C.E. The decline of the Mycenaeans led to a period of prolonged social and cultural decline and contributed to Greek migration around the Aegean. The *Iliad* and the *Odyssey* are our best sources of information about the Greek Dark Ages.

The *Polis* Greek social and political values are exemplified in the *polis*. *Polis* society was made possible by the *hoplite* phalanx. The power of kings and, later, the aristocrats was undermined by the emergence of these farmer-citizen-soldiers.

Expansion of the Greek World For about two centuries, starting around 750 B.C.E., the Greeks colonized widely throughout the Mediterranean world and trade became an increasingly important part of the Greek economy. By the end of the sixth century B.C.E., rule by tyrants had given way to new forms of government.

The Major States The two most powerful Greek *poleis* were Sparta and Athens. In the late sixth century B.C.E., Sparta was reorganized along military lines. By the fifth century B.C.E., democracy had taken root in Athens.

Life in Archaic Greece Social class shaped everyday life for the Ancient Greeks. The Greeks were polytheistic. Lyric poetry treated topics ranging from love to politics.

The Persian Wars In 490 B.C.E., the Persian emperor Darius launched an expedition to punish the Ionians for rebelling and the Athenians for supporting the rebels, an expedition that was defeated at Marathon. A Greek coalition turned back a much larger Persian invasion force between 481 and 479 B.C.E.

CHAPTER QUESTIONS

IN WHAT ways were the Minoan and Mycenaean civilizations different?

WHAT WERE the Greek Dark Ages?

DESCRIBE THE *polis* and how it affected society and government.

HOW and why did the Greeks colonize large parts of the Mediterranean?

HOW WERE the government and politics of Athens different from those of Sparta?

WHAT WAS the significance of the wars between the Greeks and the Persians?

CHAPTER OUTLINE

- The Bronze Age on Crete and on the Mainland to about 1150 B.C.E.
- The Greek "Middle Ages" to about 750 B.C.E.
- The *Polis*
- Expansion of the Greek World
- The Major States
- Life in Archaic Greece
- The Persian Wars

IMAGE KEY
for pages 32–33 is on page 54.

About 2000 B.C.E., Greek-speaking peoples settled the lands surrounding the Aegean Sea and established communities that made major contributions to the Western heritage. The Greeks' location at the eastern end of the Mediterranean put them in touch, early in their history, with Mesopotamia, Egypt, Asia Minor, and Syria-Palestine. The Greeks acknowledged debts to the cultures of these regions but were conscious (and proud) of the ways in which their way of life was unique.

IN WHAT ways were the Minoan and Mycenaean civilizations different?

THE BRONZE AGE ON CRETE AND ON THE MAINLAND TO ABOUT 1150 B.C.E.

ronze Age civilizations developed in three parts of the Aegean world: Crete, the smaller islands of the Aegean Sea, and the Greek mainland. Crete provided the bridge that linked these new cultural centers with the older civilizations of the Middle East.

THE MINOANS

Historians have named the Aegean's first civilization—the **Minoan** civilization of Crete—for Minos, a legendary king of the island. From 2100 to 1150 B.C.E. (the Middle and Late Minoan periods), Crete evolved a unique way of life. The palace sites that archaeologists have excavated at Phaestus, Haghia Triada, and especially Cnossus are its most striking remains. Cnossus was a labyrinth of rooms organized around great courtyards and rising in places to a height of four stories. The main and upper floors contained living quarters as well as workshops for making pottery and jewelry, and the cellars had elaborate storage facilities for oil and grain. There were richly decorated reception rooms and even bathrooms to which water was piped. Roofs were supported by columns of a unique design that tapered from broad capitals down to narrow bases. Murals depicting landscapes, seascapes, festivals, and sports in a unique style reflected Eastern influences.

Because Minoan palaces and settlements were wealthy, it is logical to assume they would have attracted raiders. It is surprising, therefore, that the great palace at Cnossos lacked defensive walls. Minoan command of the sea may have made the fortification of Crete unnecessary.

The Minoans wrote on clay tablets similar to those found in Mesopotamia. Many of the extant specimens were preserved accidentally when they were baked into tiles by a great fire that destroyed the palace at Cnossus. The Cnossus tablets are inscribed with three distinct kinds of writing: hieroglyphic (picture writing) and two different linear scripts (A and B). Only Linear B, which records an early form of Greek, has been deciphered.

The Linear B tablets found at Cnossus are pedestrian documents. Most are inventories, the working papers of the kind of elaborate bureaucracy that was characteristic of the ancient Middle Eastern monarchies. However, they raise an intriguing question. The Minoans were not Greeks, so why were records at Cnossus written in Greek?

THE MYCENAEANS

During the third millennium B.C.E. (the Early Helladic Period), the Greek mainland was occupied by people who, unlike the Greeks, were not Indo-Europeans. Some of the names they gave to places have survived, and these

This statuette of a female with a snake in each of her hands is thought to represent either the Minoan snake goddess herself or one of her priestesses performing a religious ritual. It was found on Crete and dates from around 1600 B.C.E.

Max Alexander/Dorling Kindersley © Archaeological Receipts Fund (TAP)

Minoan Civilization of Crete (2100–1150 B.C.E.), and the Aegean's first civilization, named for a legendary king on the island.

names do not fit the phonetic patterns of the Indo-European family of languages to which Greek belongs. Sometime after 2000 B.C.E., many of these Early Helladic sites were destroyed, abandoned, or occupied by a new people who were probably the Greeks. During the Late Helladic era (1580–1150 B.C.E.), the newcomers ruled the mainland and developed a civilization that historians have named **Mycenaean** for Mycenae, one of its cities. The Greek Linear B tablets found at Cnossus suggest that at the height of Mycenaean power (ca. 1400–1200 B.C.E.), the Mycenaeans conquered Crete. (See Map 2–1.)

The Mycenaean world contained a number of independent, powerful, and well-organized kingdoms. Their archaeological remains suggest a civilization that was influenced by, but very different from, that of Minoan Crete. The Mycenaeans appear to have been much more preoccupied with war than the Minoans were. The walls of Mycenaean palaces were decorated with scenes of battle and hunting, and Mycenaeans chose defensible sites for their cities. Military strife probably promoted the development of strong, centralized monarchies on the Greek mainland.

By 1500 B.C.E., Mycenaean kings were constructing monumental *tholos* tombs whose remains testify today to their wealth and power. Enormous blocks of dressed stones were used to construct great domed chambers that were buried beneath artificial mountains. The resources needed to finance such monuments probably came from raids and trade. Mycenaean ships visited the islands of the Aegean, the coast of Asia Minor, the cities of Syria, Egypt, and Crete, and ventured as far west as Italy and Sicily.

Chronology of the Rise of Greece

ca. 2900–1150 B.C.E.	Minoan period
ca. 1900 B.C.E.	Arrival of the Greeks on the mainland
ca. 1600–1150 B.C.E.	Mycenaean period
ca. 1250 B.C.E.	Sack of Troy
ca. 1200–1150 B.C.E.	Fall of the Mycenaean kingdoms
ca. 1150–750 B.C.E.	The Greek Dark Ages
ca. 750–500 B.C.E.	Greek colonial expansion
ca. 725 B.C.E.	Homer flourished
ca. 700 B.C.E.	Hesiod flourished
ca. 650 B.C.E.	Spartan constitution militarizes the state
546–510 B.C.E.	Athenian tyranny of Pisistratus and Hippias
508 B.C.E.	Clisthenes inaugurates Athenian democracy
499 B.C.E.	Miletus rebels against Persia
490 B.C.E.	Persian Wars: Darius
480–479 B.C.E.	Persian Wars: Xerxes

Mycenaean Civilization occupying mainland Greece during the Late Helladic era (1580–1150 B.C.E.).

The citadel of Mycenae, a major center of the Greek civilization of the Bronze Age, was built of enormously heavy stones. The lion gate at its entrance was built in the thirteenth century B.C.E.

Joe Cornish/Dorling Kindersley © Archaeological Receipts Fund (TAP)

MAP 2–1

The Aegean Area in the Bronze Age The Bronze Age in the Aegean area lasted from about 1900 to about 1100 B.C.E. Its culture on Crete is called Minoan and was at its height about 1900–1400 B.C.E. Bronze Age Helladic culture on the mainland flourished from about 1600–1200 B.C.E.

WHAT SOCIETAL differences between the Mycenaean civilization on mainland Greece and the Minoan civilization of Crete might be a direct result of the geographic differences between the two civilizations?

The Mycenaeans reached the height of their power between 1400 and 1200 B.C.E. They expanded their trade, established commercial colonies in the Middle East, and the scribes who compiled the Hittite and Egyptian archives began to take note of them. About 1250 B.C.E., the Mycenaeans probably sacked the city of Troy on the coast of northwestern Asia Minor. This campaign may have been the Mycenaeans' last great adventure, for by 1200 B.C.E., their world was in trouble, and by 1100 B.C.E., it was gone. Some memory of them survived, however, to give rise to the earliest monuments of Greek literature: Homer's epics, the *Iliad* and the *Odyssey*.

The Dorian Invasion   Many Mycenaean towns fell about 1200 B.C.E., but some flourished for another century, and the lives of a few never were disrupted. Greek legends suggest that the Peloponnesus (the southern Greek peninsula) may have been invaded by Dorians, a rude people from the north whose Greek dialect was different from that of the Mycenaeans. This may have set in motion a chain of events that undermined Mycenaean civilization. The rigid bureaucracies of the highly centralized Mycenaean kingdoms may have been too inflexible to adjust to the crisis, but it is impossible to say with any certainty what caused the turmoil that characterized the late Aegean Bronze Age.

The Greek "Middle Ages"
to about 750 B.C.E.

*T*he collapse of the Mycenaean kingdoms inaugurated a long period characterized by depopulation, impoverishment, and cultural decline in the Aegean region. Palaces and their staffs of literate bureaucrats were swept away, and the wealth and social order that made civilized life possible diminished.

Greek Migrations

The confusion that attended the Mycenaean decline caused many Greeks (including the Dorians who invaded the Peloponnesus) to relocate from the mainland to the Aegean islands and the coast of Asia Minor. Their resettlement turned the Aegean Sea into a Greek lake, but the disorder that attended the migrations hurt economic life and depressed cultures. Contacts among communities diminished, and people turned inward. No foreign power was poised to take advantage of the Aegean's situation, however, so the Greeks had a chance to recover and the freedom to evolve a new way of life. Little is known about this crucial era, for writing disappeared with the Mycenaean palaces and their scribes and was not reinvented until after 750 B.C.E. (when architecture, sculpture, and painting also resumed in the Greek world). For historians, therefore, this is a "dark age."

The Age of Homer

The *Iliad* and the *Odyssey* are our best sources of information about the Greek Dark Ages. They are the end products of a long tradition of oral poetry with roots in the Mycenaean era. For generations, bards passed on tales of the heroes who fought at Troy. They used rhythmic formulas to aid the accurate memorization of their verses, and this enabled some very old material to survive transmission over many generations. The poems were written down in the eighth century B.C.E. and attributed to an individual named Homer.

Although the poems narrate the adventures of Mycenaean heroes, the society they describe is not purely Mycenaean. Homer's warriors are not buried in *tholos* tombs but are cremated; they worship gods in temples, whereas no Mycenaean temples have been found; they have chariots but do not make much use of them in battle. These inconsistencies arise because Homer's epics combine memories of the ancient Mycenaeans with material drawn from the very different world in which the poets of the tenth and ninth centuries B.C.E. lived.

WHAT WERE the Greek Dark Ages?

2.2
Homer, from the *Iliad*

Iliad   Homer's poem narrates a dispute between Agamemnon the king and his warrior Achilles, whose honor is wounded and then avenged.

Odyssey   Homer's epic poem tells of the wanderings of the hero Odysseus.

This earliest depiction of the new method of warfare we call the hoplite phalanx appears on a wine jug known as the Chigi vase. It was made at Corinth in mainland Greece, around 650 B.C.E. It shows the two armies of heavily armed infantrymen in battle order ready to fight. The flute player set the beat for each army to keep in step and formation.

Hirmer Fotoarchiv, Munich, Germany

Black-Figure Hydria: Five Women Filling Hydriae in a Fountain House.

©2004 Museum of Fine Arts, Boston

arete   The highest virtue in Homeric society: the manliness, courage, and excellence that equipped a hero to acquire and defend honor.

Government and Society   The kings Homer describes had much less power than Mycenaean monarchs. Homeric kings had to arrive at decisions in consultation with their nobles, and these men felt free to debate vigorously and to oppose their king's wishes. In the *Iliad*, Achilles does not hesitate to accuse Agamemnon, the "most kingly" commander of the Trojan expedition, of having "a dog's face and a deer's heart." This was impolite but apparently it was not considered treasonous.

The right to speak before a royal council was limited to noblemen, but the common soldiers were not ignored. If a king planned a war or a major change of policy, he would call all his men together and explain his intentions. They could express approval or disapproval by shouting, but they could not debate or propose ideas of their own. The Greeks of the Dark Age seem, if only tentatively, to have experimented with popular government.

Homeric society was sharply divided into classes. A hereditary aristocracy presided over three kinds of commoners: *thetes*, landless laborers, and slaves. Individual *thetes* may have owned the land they worked, or their fields may have been the inalienable property of their family clans. The worst lot in life was that of the landless agricultural laborer. Slaves were attached to households that guaranteed them some protection and food, but free workers were desperately vulnerable. They were loners in a society in which the only safety lay in belonging to a group that looked out for its members. There were few slaves. Most were women who served as maids and concubines. Some male slaves worked as shepherds, but throughout Greek history most farmers were free men.

Homeric Values   The Homeric poems celebrated an aristocratic code that influenced all later Greek thinkers, for Greek education was based on Homer's works. The Greeks memorized Homer's texts and internalized respect for his values: physical prowess; courage; fierce protection of family, friends, and property; and, above all, defense of honor. The *Iliad* is the story of a dispute about honor. Agamemnon, the king who presides over the Greek army besieging Troy, wounds the honor of Achilles, his most important warrior. Achilles then refuses to fight and persuades the gods to avenge him by heaping defeat on the Greeks. When Achilles finally returns to the battlefield, he is brought back by a personal obligation to avenge the death of a friend, not by a sense of duty to his country.

The highest virtue in Homeric society was ***arete***—the manliness, courage, and excellence that equipped a hero to acquire and defend honor. Men demonstrated this quality by engaging in contests with worthy opponents. Homeric battles were usually single combats between matched competitors, and most Homeric festivals (even the funeral of Achilles' friend Patroclos, which ends the *Iliad*) featured athletic competitions.

Homer's view of life is summed up by the advice Achilles' father gave him when he left for the Trojan war: "Always be the best and distinguished above others." The father of another Homeric hero added a codicil to this prescription: "Do not bring shame on the family of your fathers." These admonitions articulated the ultimate concerns of the Homeric aristocrat: to enhance the honor of one's family by a personal demonstration of *arete*.

Women in Homeric Society   The male-oriented warrior society that Homer describes relegated women to domestic roles. Their chief functions were to bear and raise children and to manage and safeguard their husbands' estates when the men were called away to battle. A husband might have sexual adventures, but a wife was expected to be unswervingly faithful. Homer's ideal woman was Penelope, Odysseus's wife. Her husband disappears for twenty years, but she does not give him up for dead. She refuses the many suitors who seek her hand (and his estate) and lives in chaste seclusion with her maids. She fills her days with the labor that Greeks associated with women of all classes: spinning and weaving. Penelope's opposite, the epitome of female evil, was Agamemnon's wife, Clytemnestra. While her husband leads the war at Troy, she takes a lover, and the two of them assassinate Agamemnon when he returns home. Homer's upper-class females were free to come and go as they wished. They attended banquets with their husbands and conversed with other men. No such privileges were enjoyed by their aristocratic sisters in later periods in Greek history. These women were expected to confine themselves to special women's quarters in their family homes and to be as invisible as possible.

THE *POLIS*

C lassical Greek civilization is associated with the *polis* (plural *poleis*), a unique community that appeared during the Dark Ages. *Polis* is usually translated as "city-state," but that term implies too much and too little. All Greek *poleis* began as agricultural villages, and many never grew large enough to be considered cities. They were all states in the sense that they were self-governing, but a *polis* was more than a state—that is, more than a political institution. The citizens of a *polis* saw themselves as a kind of extended family—as descendants of a common legendary ancestor, people who shared religious cults and memberships in various hereditary subgroups, such as clans, tribes, and *phratries* (military fraternities).

In the fourth century B.C.E., hundreds of years after the *polis* became a fact of Greek life, the philosopher Aristotle devised a rationale for its existence. He said that the *polis* was simply a reflection of human nature. The human being is "an animal who lives in a *polis*," for the attributes that define humanity—the power of speech and the ability to distinguish right from wrong—emerge only when people live together.

THE DEVELOPMENT OF THE *POLIS*

Originally the word *polis* referred to a citadel, a defensible high ground to which the farmers of an area could retreat when attacked. (The most famous example is the **Acropolis** at the center of the city of Athens.) Unplanned towns tended to evolve spontaneously at such sites. Unlike the capitals of Mesopotamian city-states, the locations of Greek *poleis* were not determined by rivers and trade routes. Proximity to farmland and a natural fortress was the decisive factor. Spots well back from the coast were popular, for they minimized the danger of pirate raids. An *agora*—a place for markets and political assemblies—would be laid out in the shadow of the citadel to provide a center for community life.

Poleis probably appeared early in the eighth century B.C.E. and spread widely after 750 B.C.E. as the Greeks began to colonize the shores of the Mediterranean and Black Seas. Monarchy tended to disappear wherever *poleis* evolved. Sometimes vestigial kings survived to carry out ancient religious rites, but they had no

QUICK REVIEW

Women in a Warrior Society
- Women relegated to domestic roles
- Chief functions were to bear children and manage their husbands' estates
- Upper-class women had more freedom than later Greek women

2.1
Laws Relating to Women: Excerpts from the Gortyn Law Code

DESCRIBE THE *polis* and how it affected society and government.

Acropolis   At the center of the city of Athens, the most famous example of a citadel.

agora   Place for markets and political assemblies.

A large Spartan plate from the second quarter of the sixth century B.C.E.

Hirmer Fotoarchiv

political authority. A *polis* was often founded as a republic of aristocratic families, but over time political participation tended to be extended to commoners. About 750 B.C.E., coincident with the development of the *polis*, the Greeks reinvented writing. By adding symbols for vowels to the Phoenician writing system, they created the first complete alphabet. This made writing relatively easy to learn and empowered the ordinary man at a time when changes in military technology were also enhancing his importance.

THE *HOPLITE* PHALANX

Early Greek warfare was a disorganized free-for-all. Small troops of cavalry led by aristocratic "champions" cast spears at their enemies and then engaged individual opponents with swords at close quarters. Late in the eighth century B.C.E., a true infantry soldier called a **hoplite** began to dominate the battlefield. He was a heavily armed foot soldier, equipped with a spear and a large round shield (a *hoplon*). He fought in a tight formation called a **phalanx**, a company of men eight or more ranks deep. A phalanx that preserved its order on the field of battle could withstand cavalry charges and rout much larger armies consisting of less disciplined men. The phalanx reigned supreme in the ancient Mediterranean world until the more flexible Roman legion appeared.

A phalanx was effective only when all its members kept themselves in top physical condition, maintained their courage, and worked together as a team. *Hoplite* warfare favored brief violent battles that resolved disputes quickly with minimal risk to the property on which citizen families depended for their survival. Its goal was to kill or drive off an enemy, not enslave him or hold him for ransom.

Greeks had traditionally thought of war as an aristocratic profession, but in the era of the *hoplite* no *polis* could afford to limit recruitment to a small group of nobles. The strength of an infantry depended on numbers. Farmers working relatively small holdings had to join aristocrats in defending their cities, and because *hoplite* equipment was relatively inexpensive, they could afford to do so. Service in the army inevitably led to political enfranchisement, for a *polis* could not deny the men on whom it depended for protection the right to a share in its government.

EXPANSION OF THE GREEK WORLD

About the middle of the eighth century B.C.E., the Greeks launched a colonization movement that planted *poleis* from Spain to the Black Sea. The eastern end of the Mediterranean was already well populated, so they searched for sites in western regions that were still largely untouched by civilization. So many Greek colonies were established in southern Italy and Sicily that Italy's Latin-speaking Romans called this part of their world ***Magna Graecia***—"Great Greece." (See Map 2–2.)

THE GREEK COLONY

The pressures of overpopulation probably explain why thousands of Greeks left the cities of their birth to found new *poleis*. Emigration was difficult, but potentially rewarding. Colonies were carefully planned, and most had excellent prospects as centers of trade. Many copied the constitutions and the religious rites of the cities that founded them, but they were not controlled or exploited by their homeland. Colonies governed themselves. Although they usually maintained friendly relations with their mother-cities and each might ask the other for help, a city that tried to dominate its colonies risked provoking war.

HOW AND why did the Greeks colonize large parts of the Mediterranean?

hoplite A true infantry soldier that began to dominate the battlefield in the late eighth century B.C.E.

phalanx Tight military formation of men eight or more ranks deep.

Magna Graecia ("Great Greece") The areas in southern Italy and Sicily where many Greek colonies were established.

MAP EXPLORATION

Interactive map: To explore this map further, go to **http://www.prenhall.com/kagan3/map2.2**

MAP 2–2

Greek Colonization   The height of Greek colonization was between about 750 and 550 B.C.E. Greek colonies stretched from the Mediterranean coasts of Spain and Gaul (modern France) in the west to the Black Sea and Asia Minor in the east.

NOTE THE area of penetration in the various colonized areas on this map. How is this indicative of a colonization achieved mainly by means of the sea?

Colonization added greatly to the material and cultural resources of Greek civilization. Over 1,000 *poleis* were established. This helped the Greeks of the mainland maintain peace among themselves by providing outlets for excess population. It also heightened the Greeks' sense of their unique identity by bringing them into contact with different cultures. *Poleis* throughout the Mediterranean sent competitors and spectators to festivals such as the Olympic Games to keep alive their memory of their common heritage. (See "Encountering the Past: Greek Athletics.")

As the network of Greek colonies spread, life in the Greek homeland was transformed. Mainland farmers began to concentrate less on local consumption and more on producing specialized crops (e.g., olives and wine) for export to colonial markets. Demand also increased for manufactured goods such as pottery, tools, weapons, and fine metalwork. Expanding commercial opportunities enlarged the class of independent commoners, and their increasing prosperity led them to resent the aristocrats' traditional political privileges. This produced turmoil that enabled tyrants to seize control of some *poleis*.

THE TYRANTS (CA. 700–500 B.C.E.)

A tyrant, in the ancient Greek sense, was a ruler who ignored legal niceties and simply took over. Often he enjoyed popular support. A typical tyrant was an aristocrat who broke with his class and took control of a city by appealing to the masses of its poor and politically disenfranchised. He usually expelled his aristocratic opponents, distributed their land among his followers, and instituted economic programs that benefited the masses.

A tyrant's authority was backed by a personal bodyguard and troops of mercenary soldiers, but his rule was not inevitably oppressive. Tyrants preferred to concentrate on domestic development that would keep the people happy. Because aggression against a neighboring state required fielding a citizen army that might turn on its tyrant, tyrants preferred to avoid wars. They financed popular public works projects that provided employment for the poor, and they sponsored festivals and commissioned works of art that fostered civic pride.

Despite the positive effect tyranny had on the development of some *poleis*, tyrannies faded away during the sixth century B.C.E. Something about tyranny was inconsistent with the forces that created the *polis*. The institutions of a *polis* were shaped by the responsibility all its citizens bore for its defense. Because they shared this traditional responsibility of the military aristocracy, they felt entitled also to share the customary aristocratic political prerogatives. The rule of a

Panhellenic (All Greek) Sense of cultural identity that all Greeks felt in common with one other.

ENCOUNTERING THE PAST

GREEK ATHLETICS

Athletic contests were an integral part of Greek civilization throughout its entire history. They were much more than entertainments. They were religious festivals in which the Greeks celebrated the virtues and attitudes that they considered central to their way of life. International or **Panhellenic** ("all-Greek") contests were scheduled in alternating annual cycles. The most prestigious of these were the games that began to be celebrated in honor of Zeus at the southern mainland city of Olympia in 776 B.C.E.

The Greeks' primary interest was not team sports, but contests in which individuals could prove their superiority. Races of various lengths were the heart of Olympic competition, but there were also field events such as discus and javelin throws and combat sports such as wrestling and boxing. Only male athletes were admitted to the games, and by the fifth century B.C.E., all contestants (except those in a race in full armor) competed nude. The official prizes were simple wreaths, but *poleis* lavishly rewarded the native sons who brought home these tokens of victory.

WHY DID the Greeks prefer individual contests to team sports? What motivated them to train and compete?

A foot race, probably a sprint, at the Panathenaic Games in Athens, ca. 530 B.C.E.

Panathenaic Prize Amphora (Foot Race), Euphiletos Painter. Greek, Attic, ca. 530 B.C. Terracotta, 62.23 cm (Ht.) The Metropolitan Museum of Art, Rogers Fund, 1914. (14.130.12)

tyrant, no matter how beneficent, was unacceptable, for it was arbitrary and could not be held accountable. Tyranny did, however, contribute to the growth of popular government by breaking the monopoly aristocracies had on political power.

THE MAJOR STATES

*T*he many *poleis* were organized in many different ways. However, two cities were of such importance that they merit special attention: Sparta in the southern half of the Greek peninsula (the **Peloponnesus**) and Athens in the north.

SPARTA

A chain of events that began about 725 B.C.E. persuaded the Spartans to embrace a program of total military mobilization that created the most feared army in Greece. The Spartans conquered Messenia, their western neighbor. The acquisition of its land and enslavement of its people eased Sparta's economic problems but created a new threat to Spartan security. The Spartans found themselves outnumbered ten to one by **Helots**, their slaves. A slave revolt that nearly destroyed Sparta (ca. 650 B.C.E.) convinced the Spartans that they had to do everything possible to build up their army.

Spartan Society   The system the Spartans devised was designed to subordinate natural feelings of devotion to self and family to the needs of the state. The state required all its men to become superb soldiers. To this end, it persuaded them to sacrifice privacy and comfort and embrace a regimen of brutal physical conditioning and discipline. The Spartans allowed nothing to distract them from their goal of becoming the best warriors in the world. (See "History's Voices: Tyrtaeus on the Citizen Soldier.")

The Spartan *polis* controlled the life of each of its members from birth to death. Only infants whom officials of the state judged to be physically fit were allowed to live. At the age of seven boys left their mothers to begin training at military camps. They learned to fight, to endure privation, to bear physical pain, and to live off the land. At twenty they joined the army in the field, and they lived in barracks until the age of thirty. They were allowed to marry but not to enjoy the comforts of a home. Young Spartan husbands had to steal away from camp for conjugal visits with their wives. Only after a man acquired full citizen rights at the age of thirty could he set up a household. But even then he took his meals at a public mess with other members of his military unit. His sparse diet included little meat or wine, and he eschewed all luxuries. He was, however, financially secure, for he was supported by a grant from the state—a plot of land worked by Helots. He remained on active military duty until the age of sixty.

Females, like males, were trained to serve the Spartan state. Only fit female infants were raised, and young girls were given athletic training to strengthen them for childbearing. Because Spartan men were often absent from home or focused on military duties, Spartan women had much greater freedom and responsibility than other Greek females.

Spartan Government   The Spartan constitution mixed elements of monarchy, oligarchy, and democracy. Sparta had two royal families from which to choose its kings. The Spartan army was usually commanded by one of its kings

HOW WERE the government and politics of Athens different from those of Sparta?

2.4
Tyrtaeus, *The Spartan Code*

Peloponnesus   Southern half of the Greek peninsula.

Helots   Slaves to the Spartans that revolted and nearly destroyed Sparta in 650 B.C.E.

HISTORY'S VOICES

TYRTAEUS ON THE CITIZEN SOLDIER

he military organization of citizen soldiers for the defense of the polis *and the idea of the* polis *itself that permeated Greek political thought found echoes in Greek poetry. A major example is this part of a poem by Tyrtaeus, who wrote in Sparta about 625 B.C.E.*

WHY, according to Tyrtaeus, is the Spartan soldier right and wise to risk his life by showing courage in battle?

I would not say anything for a man nor take account
    of him
for any speed of his feet or wrestling skill he might have,
not if he had the size of a Cyclops and strength to go
    with it,
not if he could outrun Bóreas, the North Wind of
    Thrace,
not if he were more handsome and gracefully
    formed than Tithónos,
or had more riches than Midas had, or Kinyras too, not
    if he were more of a king than Tantalid Pelops,
or had the power of speech and persuasion Adrastos
    had,
not if he had all splendors except for a fighting spirit.
For no man ever proves himself a good man in war
    unless he can endure to face the blood and the
    slaughter,
go close against the enemy and fight with his hands.
Here is courage, mankind's finest possession, here is
the noblest prize that a young man can endeavor to
    win,
and it is a good thing his city and all the people
    share with him
when a man plants his feet and stands in the
    foremost spears
relentlessly, all thought of foul flight completely
    forgotten,
and has well trained his heart to be steadfast and to
    endure,
and with words encourages the man who is stationed
    beside him.
Here is a man who proves himself to be valiant in war.
With a sudden rush he turns to fight the rugged
    battalions

of the enemy, and sustains the beating waves of assault.
And he who so falls among the champions and loses
    his sweet life,
so blessing with honor his city, his father, and all his
    people,
with wounds in his chest, where the spear that he was
    facing has transfixed
that massive guard of his shield, and gave through
    his breastplate as well,
why, such a man is lamented alike by the young and
    the elders,
and all his city goes into mourning and grieves for
    his loss.
His tomb is pointed to with pride, and so are his
    children,
and his children's children, and afterward all the
    race that is his.
His shining glory is never forgotten, his name is
    remembered,
and he becomes an immortal, though he lies under
    the ground.
When one who was a brave man has been killed by
    the furious War God
standing his ground and fighting hard for his
    children and land.
But if he escapes the doom of death, the destroyer of
    bodies,
and wins his battle, and bright renown for the work
    of his spear,
all men give place to him alike, the youth and the
    elders,
and much joy comes his way before he goes down to
    the dead.
Aging he has reputation among his citizens. No one
tries to interfere with his honors or all he deserves,
all men withdraw before his presence, and yield their
    seats to him,
and youth, and the men of his age, and even those
    older than he.
Thus a man should endeavor to reach this high
    place of courage
with all his heart, and, so trying, never be backward
    in war.

Greek Lyrics, trans. by Richmond Lattimore (Chicago: University of Chicago Press. 1949, 1955, 1959), pp. 14–15.

when it was in the field, but kings did not govern Sparta. An oligarchic council of twenty-eight men (aged sixty or more and elected for life) devised policy and sat as a high court. All Spartan males over the age of thirty could take part in a democratic assembly that, in theory, had final authority. The assembly, however, could only consider proposals referred to it by the council. It was limited to ratifying decisions already taken or deciding between alternative proposals.

The administration of Sparta's government was the duty of a board of five *ephors*, executives elected annually by the assembly. They controlled foreign policy, oversaw the kings' management of campaigns, presided at the assembly, and policed the Helots.

The Peloponnesian League   Suppression of the Helots required all the energy Sparta had, and the Spartans did not want to overextend themselves by conquering and assimilating troublesome neighbors. They preferred to force these people into alliances that left them free internally but subservient to Sparta's foreign policy. Sparta eventually enrolled every southern Greek state except Argos in its Peloponnesian League and became the most powerful *polis* on the Greek mainland.

ATHENS

Athens evolved more slowly than Sparta. Because **Attica**, the region Athens dominated, was large by Greek standards (about 1,000 square miles), it was able to absorb a growing population without conquering its neighbors. But size slowed its consolidation as a *polis*, and its economic development was hampered by the fact that it was not situated on the trade routes most traveled during the eighth and seventh centuries B.C.E.

Political Tensions   In the seventh century B.C.E., aristocratic families held the most and the best land around Athens. They also dominated Attica by controlling the tribes, clans, and military fraternities that structured Athenian society. Athens's government was headed by the Council of the **Areopagus**, a group of nobles that annually chose the city's nine *archons*, the magistrates who administered the *polis*. There was no formal law, and leaders were guided primarily by custom and tradition.

Athens's political evolution was accelerated by an agrarian crisis that developed during the seventh century B.C.E. Many Athenians depended on small family farms that grew wheat, the staple of the ancient diet. Years of consistent cultivation diminished the fertility of their fields and the size of their harvests, but few could afford to shift to more profitable crops such as olives (pressed for oil) and grapes (for wine). A lot of capital was needed to bring a vineyard or olive grove into production. In bad years the poorer farmers were forced to borrow from their wealthier neighbors—mortgaging future crops and, therefore, their own labor (which was needed to raise these crops) as surety for their loans. This gradually reduced them to slavery, and some were even exported for sale outside Attica. The poor resented this and agitated for the abolition of debts and the redistribution of the land.

In 632 B.C.E., a nobleman named Cylon tried to exploit this situation to establish a tyranny. He failed, but his attempt frightened Athens's aristocratic leaders into taking steps to head off future coups. In 621 B.C.E., they commissioned a man named Draco to codify and publish Athens's laws. Draco decreed extremely hard punishments for crimes in hopes of deterring the blood feuds that resulted

Attica   Region (about 1,000 square miles) that Athens dominated.

Areopagus   Council heading Athens's government comprised of a group of nobles that annually chose the city's nine *archons*, the magistrates who administered the *polis*.

when victims sought revenge for wrongs done them. The establishment of a common standard of public justice for all Athenians was meant to dissuade individuals from taking things into their own hands.

In the year 594 B.C.E., the Athenians instituted a more radical reform. They empowered a single man, an *archon* named Solon, to reorganize the *polis* as he saw fit. Solon attacked agrarian problems by canceling debts and forbidding loans secured by the freedom of the borrower. He emancipated people who had been enslaved for debt and brought home many of the Athenians who had been sold abroad. Instead of alienating the rich by redistributing their land to the poor, however, he tried to expand Athens's economy to create different employment opportunities for the poor. He forbade the export of wheat (which might create shortages and drive up the price of the common person's food) but not olive oil (one of Attica's cash crops). He facilitated trade by conforming Athenian weights and measures to standards used by other commercial centers. And he developed industries by offering citizenship to foreign artisans who agreed to set up shop in Athens.

Solon also reformed Athenian political institutions. He divided Athens's citizens into four classes on the basis of wealth. Members of the two richest classes qualified for archonships and membership in the Council of the Areopagus. Men of the third class could serve as *hoplites* and be elected to a council of four hundred chosen by the citizens. Solon intended this council to serve as a check on the aristocratic Council of the Areopagus, and he gave it the power to decide the issues that were to be brought to the popular assembly, the political organization to which all adult male citizens belonged. The poorest class of Athenians, the *thetes*, voted in this assembly, participated in the election of *archons*, and sat on a new court that heard appeals from other jurisdictions. Women from citizen families were granted no role in the political process.

The Tyrannies   Because the beneficial effects of Solon's reforms were slow to be felt, tensions continued to mount in Athens. On several occasions rioting prevented the election of *archons*. A military hero named Pisistratus twice (in 560 B.C.E. and 556 B.C.E.) tried and failed to establish a tyranny, but his third attempt (in 546 B.C.E.) succeeded. Pisisitratus remained in power until his death in 527 B.C.E., and his son Hippias continued the tyranny until a competitor drove him from the city in 510 B.C.E.

Like the tyrants of other Greek cities, Pisistratus dominated his subjects by courting them. He sponsored public works programs, urban development, and civic festivals. He employed poets and artists to add luster to his court. And he secured his power by hiding it behind the facade of Solon's constitution. All the councils, assemblies, and courts continued to meet, and all the magistrates were elected. Pisistratus merely saw to it that his men won the key offices and dominated the important meetings. The constitutional cloak he spread over his tyranny won him a reputation as a popular, gentle ruler, but it also gave his subjects experience with (and a greater appetite for) self-government.

After Pisistratus's death, his elder son, Hippias, ruled Athens. Initially, he followed his father's example, but in 514 B.C.E., the murder of his brother, Hipparchus, led him to fear for his own safety and he began to impose harsh measures. His increasing unpopularity encouraged his enemies, and in 510 B.C.E., the Alcmaeonids, a noble family that had been exiled from Athens, persuaded the Spartans to overthrow Hippias. The Alcmaeonid leader, Clisthenes, then rallied the Athenians against the Spartans and established himself in control of Athens.

Democracy   Clisthenes weakened his aristocratic opponents by destroying the regional political machines that were the bases of their power. In 508 B.C.E., he divided Attica into small political units called *demes*. The *demes* were then grouped together to create the tribes that composed Athens's army and elected its government. Care was taken to make sure that each tribe was made up of *demes* from different parts of Attica. This prevented the wealthy aristocratic families, whose landed estates gave them control of large portions of the countryside, from dominating the new tribal organizations. Aristocrats now found themselves voting not with their economically dependent clients but with men who were strangers to them.

Clisthenes increased Solon's council from four hundred to five hundred members and gave it authority to receive foreign emissaries and manage some fiscal affairs. Its chief responsibility was to prepare legislative proposals for discussion by the popular assembly in which ultimate authority was vested. All adult male Athenians were members of this assembly and had the right to propose legislation and debate freely. Thanks to Solon, Pisistratus, and Clisthenes, Athens entered the fifth century B.C.E. well down the path to prosperity and democracy and prepared to claim a place among Greece's leading *poleis*.

QUICK REVIEW

Clisthene's Democracy

- Clisthenes sought to weaken his opponents by dividing Attica into *demes*
- Increased Solon's council from four to five hundred
- All adult male Athenians were members of the popular assembly

LIFE IN ARCHAIC GREECE

SOCIETY

Greek society's unique features began to become visible at the end of the Dark Ages. The vast majority of Greeks made their living from the land, but artisans and merchants acquired greater importance as contact with the non-Hellenic (non-Greek) world increased.

Farmers   Ordinary country folk rarely leave any record of their thoughts or activities, but the poet Hesiod (ca. 700 B.C.E.), who claimed in his *Works and Days* to be a small farmer, described what life was like for members of his class in ancient Greece. The crops farmers usually cultivated were barley, wheat, grapes for wine, olives for oil (for cooking, lighting, and lubrication), vegetables, beans, and fruit. Sheep and goats provided milk and cheese. Land that was fertile enough to grow fodder for cattle was needed to grow grain for human consumption, so supplies of meat were limited. Meat was most commonly eaten at religious festivals where worshipers shared the flesh of the animals sacrificed to the gods.

Hesiod had the help of oxen and mules and occasional hired laborers, but his life was one of continuous toil. The toughest season began with October's rains, the time for the first plowing. Plows were iron-tipped but light and fragile. Even with the aid of a team of animals it was difficult to break the sod. During autumn and winter, wood was cut and repairs were made to buildings and equipment. Vines needed attention in late winter. Grain was harvested in May. At the height of summer's heat there was time for a little rest, but in September grapes had to be harvested and pressed and the round of yearly tasks began again.

Hesiod says nothing about the pleasures and entertainments of ordinary people, but the fact that his poetry exists is witness to the presence in Greece of a more dynamic and confident rural population than we know of anywhere else in the ancient world.

Aristocrats Wealthy aristocrats worked their extensive lands with hired laborers, sharecroppers, and slaves. This gave them leisure for other kinds of activities. The centerpiece of aristocratic social life was the *symposium*, a men's drinking party. A *symposium* was sometimes only a pursuit of inebriation, but it could be more. It began with prayers and libations to the gods. There were usually games such as dice or *kottabos* (a contest in which wine was flicked from cups at a target). Sometimes dancing girls or flute girls offered entertainment. Guests also amused themselves by singing, reciting poetry, and engaging in philosophical discussions. These activities were often turned into contests, for aristocratic values put a premium on competition and the need to excel.

Athletics were fundamental to an aristocrat's education and lifestyle. Each *polis* maintained a *palaestra*, a place where the city's men gathered to train and compete. Races, wrestling, and field events were popular, but chariot races were the special preserve of the nobility. Only they could afford horses. Simple farmers led drab lives from the point of view of cultivated, leisured aristocrats.

RELIGION

Olympian Religion permeated every aspect of Greek life. The Greeks were polytheists whose official pantheon centered on twelve major deities, the residents of Mount Olympus. Zeus, a sky god, exercised patriarchal authority over the other gods. He had three sisters: Hera, who was also his wife; Hestia, goddess of the hearth; and Demeter, goddess of agriculture and marriage. Zeus's brother Poseidon was god of the seas and earthquakes. By various mates he had an assortment of children: Aphrodite, goddess of love and beauty; Apollo, god of the sun, music, poetry, and prophecy; Ares, god of strife; Artemis, goddess of the moon and the hunt; Athena, goddess of wisdom and the arts; Hephaestus, god of fire and metallurgy; and Hermes, a cunning messenger-god and patron of traders.

Gods were believed, apart from their superhuman strength and immortality, to resemble mortals. Zeus, the defender of justice, presided over the cosmos, but he and the other gods were not omnipotent. They operated within limits set by the Fates who personified the inviolable order of the universe. Olympian religion was shared by all the Greeks. Each *polis* honored one or more of the gods as its special guardian(s), but all of them supported shrines at Olympia (to Zeus), Delphi (to Apollo), Corinth (to Poseidon), and Nemea (also to Zeus). Each of these sanctuaries staged athletic festivals to which all Greeks were invited. Truces suspended wars so that everyone could safely participate.

In the sixth century B.C.E., the shrine of Apollo at Delphi became famous for its oracle, the most important of several that the Greeks looked to for guidance. Delphian Apollo endorsed the pursuit of self-knowledge and self-control. His mottos were "Know thyself" and "Nothing in excess!" *Hubris*, the arrogance produced by excessive wealth or good fortune, was believed to be the most dangerous of human failings. It caused moral blindness and tempted the gods to

symposium A men's drinking party at the center of aristocratic social life in archaic Greece.

hubris Arrogance produced by excessive wealth or good fortune.

take vengeance. The moral order the gods enforced was simple. Virtue consisted of paying one's debts, doing good to one's friends, and attacking one's enemies. Civic responsibility entailed honoring the state's deities, participating in political life, and serving in the army.

The Dionysian and Orphic Cults   The Olympian gods were the protectors of the state, not individuals. For their personal spiritual needs, Greeks turned to gods of a different kind. Countless lesser deities were associated with local shrines. Some of these gods were believed to have been men whose heroic deeds had won them divine status.

The worship of Dionysus, a fertility deity associated with the growing of grapes, was very popular—particularly with women. Dionysus was a god of drunkenness and sexual abandon. His female devotees (the *maenads*) cavorted by night and were reputed, when possessed by their god, to tear to pieces and devour any living creatures they encountered. The cult of Orpheus, a mythical poet, taught respect for life and offered the prospect of some kind of triumph over the grave—perhaps a transmigration of souls.

POETRY

A shift from epic to lyric poetry reflected the great changes that swept through the Greek world in the sixth century B.C.E. The poems of Sappho of Lesbos, Anacreon of Teos, and Simonides of Cos were intimately personal—often describing the pleasure and agony of love. Alcaeus of Mytilene, an aristocrat driven from his city by a tyrant, wrote bitter invectives. The most interesting poet of the century, at least from the political point of view, may be Theonis of Megara. He spoke for the aristocrats whose power over most *poleis* was waning. He insisted that only nobles could aspire to virtue, for only nobles possessed the crucial sense of honor. Honor, he claimed, could not be taught; it was innate, and noble families lost it if they debased their lines by marrying commoners. The political privileges of the nobility were reduced in most Greek states, but traditional assumptions of aristocratic superiority continued to influence important thinkers such as Plato.

This Attic cup from the fifth century B.C.E. shows the two great poets from the island of Lesbos, Sappho (center) and Alcaeus (far left).

Hirmer Fotoarchiv

THE PERSIAN WARS

*T*he Greeks' era of freedom from interference from the outside world came to an end in the middle of the sixth century B.C.E. First, the Greek settlements that had flourished on the coast of Asia Minor since the eleventh century B.C.E. came under the control of Croesus (ca. 560–546 B.C.E.), king of the Anatolian nation of Lydia. Then in 546 B.C.E., Lydia and its dependencies passed into the hands of the Persians.

WHAT WAS the significance of the wars between the Greeks and the Persians?

THE PERSIAN EMPIRE

The Persian Empire was created in a single generation by Cyrus the Great, founder of the Achaemenid dynasty. When Cyrus ascended the Persian throne in 559 B.C.E., Persia was a small kingdom well to the east of southern Mesopotamia. He steadily expanded his domain in all directions, conquered Babylon, and ultimately reached Asia Minor where he defeated Croesus and occupied Lydia. Most of the Greek cities of Asia Minor resisted the Persians, but by 540 B.C.E., they had all been subdued. (See Chapter 1.)

THE IONIAN REBELLION

The Greeks of **Ionia** (the western coast of Asia Minor) had become accustomed to democratic governments, and they were restive under Persian rule. The Persians, however, were clever empire builders. They appointed Greek tyrants to govern Greek cities. Because these native leaders usually ruled benignly and Persian tribute was not excessive, many Greeks were soon reconciled to life in Persia's empire. Neither the death of Cyrus in 530 B.C.E., nor the suicide of his successor Cambyses, nor the civil war that followed that event in 522–521 B.C.E. prompted the Greeks to revolt. In 521 B.C.E. when Darius became Great King (the Persian royal title), Ionia submitted to him as it had to his predecessors.

Aristagoras, an ambitious tyrant of Miletus, ended the era of peaceful cooperation between Ionia and Persia. In 499 B.C.E., he sought to escape punishment for having committed the Persians to an unsuccessful campaign against the island of Naxos by persuading the Ionian cities to join him in a rebellion. He courted support by helping overthrow unpopular fellow tyrants and by endorsing democratic constitutions for some cities. He also sought help from the mainland states. The Spartans declined to become involved. They had no ties with the Ionians, no interests in the region, and could not risk weakening their hold over their slaves by sending their army abroad.

The Athenians were more sympathetic toward Aristagoras. They were related to the Ionians, and they had reasons of their own to fear the Persians. Hippias, the deposed tyrant of Athens, had found refuge at Darius's court, and the Great King was willing to help Hippias regain control of Athens. The Persians also held both shores of the Hellespont, the narrow waterway that connected the Aegean with the Black Sea—the region from which Athens imported much of its grain.

In 498 B.C.E., an army of Ionians and Athenians sacked Sardis, the capital of Lydia and the seat of the Persian *satrap* (governor). The fall of Sardis encouraged others to join the rebellion, but the Greeks did not follow up their victory. Athens withdrew, and the Persians gradually recovered the ground they had lost. In 495 B.C.E., they defeated the Ionian fleet at Lade, and a year later they leveled Miletus.

THE WAR IN GREECE

In 490 B.C.E., Darius launched an expedition to punish the rebels and add the Aegean to his empire. He leveled the island *polis* of Naxos and then took another of Miletus's allies, Athens's neighbor Eretria. Despite the failure of these cities to withstand Darius's assault, the Athenians refused to negotiate surrender. With Miltiades, an Athenian with a personal grudge against the Persians, at their head, they marched out to Marathon, a plain north of Athens where the Persians had made their landing. There some 10,000 Athenians and neighboring Plataeans defeated two or three times their number, killing thousands of the enemy while losing only 192 of their own men.

A Persian victory at Marathon would have destroyed Athenian freedom and led to the conquest of all the mainland Greeks. The greatest achievements of Greek culture, most of which lay in the future, would never have occurred. But the Athenians won a decisive victory, instilling them with a sense of confidence and pride in their *polis*, their unique form of government, and themselves.

Ionia Western coast of Asia Minor.

OVERVIEW   THE GREEK WARS AGAINST PERSIA

560–546 B.C.E.	Greek cities of Asia Minor conquered by Croesus of Lydia
546 B.C.E.	Cyrus of Persia conquers Lydia and gains control of Greek cities
499–494 B.C.E.	Greek cities rebel (Ionian rebellion)
490 B.C.E.	Battle of Marathon
480–479 B.C.E.	Xerxes' invasion of Greece
480 B.C.E.	Battles of Thermopylae, Artemisium, and Salamis
479 B.C.E.	Battles of Plataea and Mycale

The Great Invasion Problems elsewhere in the Persian Empire prevented Darius from taking swift revenge for his loss at Marathon, and almost ten years elapsed before his successor, Xerxes, turned his attention to the Greeks. In 481 B.C.E., Xerxes assembled an army of at least 150,000 men and a navy of about 600 ships and set out for the Aegean.

By then Athens had changed significantly. Themistocles, the city's leading politician, had begun to turn the *polis* into a naval power. During his *archonship* in 493 B.C.E., Athens (an inland city) had constructed a fortified port on the Attic coast at Piraeus, and a decade later the income from a rich vein of silver discovered in the state mines funded the construction of an Athenian navy. By the time Xerxes set out, Athens had over two hundred ships. They proved to be the salvation of Greece.

Of the hundreds of Greek states, only thirty-one (led by Sparta, Athens, Corinth, and Aegina) were willing to commit to fighting the great Persian army that gathered south of the Hellespont in the spring of 480 B.C.E. Xerxes' strategy was to overwhelm the Greeks with superior numbers, but Themistocles perceived a weakness in the emperor's plan. The Persian army depended on the Persian fleet for its supplies. If Xerxes' ships were destroyed, his army would have to retreat. Themistocles, therefore, argued that the Greeks should wage the war at sea. Athens's allies saw things differently. They chose the Spartans, Greece's premier soldiers, as their leaders, and Sparta, which had no navy, fought on land.

The Spartans and their allies made a stand at Thermopylae. The Persian army had to stay near the coast to maintain contact with its fleet, and at Thermopylae the coastal passage was extremely narrow because mountains lay near the sea. It was possible for a small force to stop the Persians here by blocking a strip of beach at the foot of the mountains. The Greek army with which the Spartan king, Leonidas, hoped to hold this spot numbered only about 9,000—of which 300 were Spartans.

The Greeks were encouraged when storms wrecked a number of Persian ships. For two days the Greeks stood their ground and butchered the troops Xerxes threw at them. On the third day, however, a Greek traitor showed the Persians a trail through the mountains, and a company of Persians outflanked the Greek army and attacked it from the rear. Leonidas realized the situation was hopeless. He dismissed his Greek allies while it was still possible for them to retreat, but he and his three hundred Spartans chose to stay and to die fighting. The Persians slaughtered them to the last man, marched into Attica, and

MAP 2–3

The Persian Invasion of Greece This map traces the route taken by the Persian king Xerxes in his invasion of Greece in 480 B.C.E. The gray arrows show movements of Xerxes' army, the purple arrows show movements of his navy, and the green arrows show movements of the Greek army and navy.

ALTHOUGH Xerxes' army had superior numbers, how did Greece's geography favor the Greek cities over the Persians?

burned Athens. If an inscription discovered in 1959 is authentic, Themistocles had foreseen this possibility and evacuated the city while the Greek army was still at Thermopylae.

The fate of Greece was decided, as Themistocles predicted, by a sea battle. It was fought in the narrow straits between Attica and the island of Salamis. The Spartans wanted the Athenian fleet to move south to guard the coast of the Peloponnese while they attempted another stand on the isthmus of Corinth, but Themistocles threatened to abandon the war and use the fleet to carry the Athenians to new homes in Italy. When the Persians sailed into the straits of Salamis, the Athenians sank more than half of Xerxes' ships. The emperor then chose to return to Persia, but he left an army behind to continue the war under the command of a general named Mardonius.

Mardonius went into winter camp in central Greece, and Pausanias, the new Spartan leader, used the time to amass the largest army the Greeks had ever fielded. In the summer of 479 B.C.E., it decisively defeated the Persians at a battle near Plataea in Boeotia. At the same time, the Ionian Greeks persuaded the Greek fleet to take the offensive against a key Persian naval base at Mycale on the coast of Asia Minor. When Mycale fell, the Persians retreated from the Aegean and Ionia. Greece was safe, but no one knew for how long.

SUMMARY

The Bronze Age on Crete and on the Mainland to about 1150 B.C.E. During the Bronze Age, the Minoan and Mycenaean civilizations ruled over the Greek mainland and Aegean islands. The Minoan civilization on Crete is renowned for its beautiful palaces. They were the organizational center of Minoan society, and Minoan kings employed a large bureaucracy. The lack of defensive walls is a notable feature of Minoan settlements. On the Greek mainland, starting around 1600 B.C.E., the Mycenaean culture was warlike and ruled by strong kings. Mycenaeans traded widely. Historians and archaeologists have suggested various explanations for the fact that, by 1100 B.C.E., the Mycenaean culture had disappeared.

Greek "Middle Ages" to about 750 B.C.E. The Dorian invasion destroyed the Mycenaean palace culture. The Greek peoples spread around the Aegean. Trade diminished; writing and other arts disappeared. Oral poetry flourished, and Homer's *Iliad* and *Odyssey* provide both great stories and insights into life in the Greek "Dark Ages." The aristocratic values of the tenth and ninth centuries B.C.E. idealized the individual hero.

The *Polis* Greek social and political values are exemplified in the Greeks' characteristic form of community, the *polis*. All citizens in a *polis* were, in theory, related; in practice, they all participated in building a commom culture. Early *poleis* developed around 800 B.C.E. in locations that featured fertile farmland and, nearby, natural defensive positions. Later *poleis* always included an *agora*, a marketplace and civic center. *Polis* society was made possible by a new military technology, the *hoplite* phalanx. Group loyalty and individual bravery were both essential to the *hoplite* phalanx's success. The power of the kings and, later, the aristocrats was undermined by the emergence of the farmer-soldier-citizen in the *polis*. Eighth-century B.C.E. Greeks created the first complete alphabet.

Expansion of the Greek World For about two centuries starting around 750 B.C.E., the Greeks colonized widely throughout the Mediterranean world. Trade became an increasingly important part of the Greek economy. Expo-

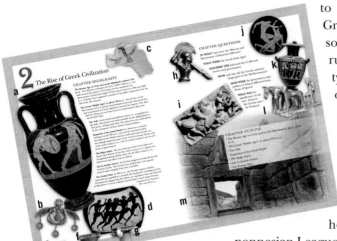

IMAGE KEY

for pages 32–33.

a. Greek vase, red-figured. Attic. ca. 480-470 B.C.E. Neck amphora, Nolan type. SIDE 1: "Greek warrior attacking a Persian." Said to be from Rhodes. Terracotta. H. 13-11/16 in. The Metropolitan Museum of Art, Rogers Fund, 1906. (06.1021.117) Photograph © The Metropolitan Museum of Art, Rogers Fund, 1903. (03.14.5) Photograph © 1986 The Metropolitan Museum of Art

b. Pendentive with Bees, ca. 1700-1400 B.C.E.

c. Dancing Lady, Palace of Knossos, Minoan, ca. 1500 B.C.E. (fresco painting)

d. Panathenaic Prize Amphora (Foot Race), Euphiletos Painter. Greek, Attic, ca. 530 B.C.E. Terracotta, 62.23 cm (Ht.) The Metropolitan Museum of Art, Rogers Fund, 1914. (14.130.12)

e., f., g. Three column capitals, two Doric and one Ionic, are displayed at the ancient site of Corinth

h. Warrior with spear and Beotian shield. Bronze statuette, ca. 500 B.C.E.

i. The "Alexander Sarcophagus" from the Phoenician royal necropolis at Sidon

j. Detail of Ancient Greek Cup with two athletes wrestling by Epictetos ca. 530 B.C.E.

k. Hydria (water jug). Greek, Archaic period, ca. 520 B.C.E. Athens, Attica, Greece, the Priam Painter. Ceramic, black-figure, H: 0.53 cm Diam (with handles): 0.37 cm. William Francis Warden Fund. © 2004 Museum of Fine Arts, Boston. Accession #61.195

l. Farmer plowing with oxen. First half 6th century B.C.E. Greek terracotta group from Thebes, Boetia. 11 x 22 cm. Inv.: CA 352. Photo: Herve Lewandownski. Louvre, Paris. Reunion des Musees Nationaux/Art Resource, NY

m. Lion Gate at Ancient Greek City of Mycenae

to other peoples and cultures fostered consciousness of Greek cultural identity and led to Panhellenic feelings. In some *poleis*, new social and economic conditions led to rule by tyrants. But by late in the sixth century B.C.E., tyrants had lost favor with the populace, and by the end of the century, they were gone.

The Major States The two most powerful Greek *poleis*, Sparta and Athens, developed differently. Starting around 725 B.C.E., Sparta gained land and power over the Messenians through warfare. Late in the sixth century B.C.E., Spartan society was reorganized along military lines to ensure that Sparta could continue its hold over Messenia. By 500 B.C.E., Sparta headed a Peloponnesian League, a mighty military alliance. In Athens, meanwhile, political and economic innovations included the publication of laws; by the fifth century B.C.E., prosperity and democracy had taken root in Athens.

Life in Archaic Greece Social class shaped everyday life for the ancient Greeks. Small farmers worked long, hard hours tending their crops. Members of the aristocracy enjoyed leisure activities that included attending *symposia*, sessions of drinking, conversation, entertainment, and games. Greeks were polytheistic, worshiping the Olympian gods and other deities through sacrifices and athletic contests. Lyric poetry treated topics ranging from love to politics.

The Persian Wars Cyrus the Great came to power in Persia in 559 B.C.E. and set about unifying and expanding his territory. For almost a century, starting around 550 B.C.E. and continuing into the mid–fifth century B.C.E., Greece faced intermittent military challenges from the Persian Empire. After Lydia came under Persian rule in 546 B.C.E., the Ionian Greeks sought military assistance from first the Spartans (who refused to get involved) and then the Athenians, who in 498 B.C.E. helped them in a short-lived revolt. Eventually the Persians withdrew from the Aegean Sea and Ionia.

REVIEW QUESTIONS

1. How were the Minoan and the Mycenaean civilizations similar? How were they different?

2. What was a *polis*? What role did geography play in its development? What contribution did it make to the development of Hellenic civilization?

3. How did the political, social, and economic institutions of Athens and Sparta compare around 500 B.C.E.? What explains Sparta's uniqueness? How did Athens make the transition from aristocracy to democracy?

4. Why did the Greeks and Persians go to war in 490 and 480 B.C.E.? Why were the Greeks victorious over the Persians?

KEY TERMS

Acropolis (p. 39)
agora (p. 39)
Areopagus (p. 45)
arete (p. 38)
Attica (p. 45)
Helots (p. 43)

hoplite (p. 40)
hubris (p. 48)
Iliad (p. 37)
Ionia (p. 50)
Magna Graecia (p. 40)
Minoan (p. 34)

Mycenaean (p. 35)
Odyssey (p. 37)
Panhellenic (All Greek) (p. 42)
Peloponnesus (p. 43)
phalanx (p. 40)
symposium (p. 48)

 For additional study resources for this chapter, go to:
www.prenhall.com/kagan3/chapter2

3
Classical and Hellenistic Greece

CHAPTER HIGHLIGHTS

Aftermath of Victory The unity the Greeks had shown while fighting against the Persians disintegrated. Athens and Sparta emerged as leaders of two spheres of influence.

The First Peloponnesian War: Athens Against Sparta The Peloponnesian Wars were the manifestation of conflict between Athens and Sparta. Initial Athenian victories gave way to Spartan advances and the first Peloponnesian War ended with the two sides agreeing to a thirty-year peace.

Classical Greece Athenian government was more democratic than any previous political system. All male citizens had important rights. The official status of women was severely circumscribed. Scholars debate the extent and importance of slavery to ancient Greek society.

The Great Peloponnesian War Between 435 and 404 B.C.E. Athens and Sparta fought for dominance in Greece. The war ended in 404 B.C.E. when Athens surrendered unconditionally to Sparta and its allies.

Competition for Leadership in the Fourth Century B.C.E. Missteps by Sparta led their allies, the Persians, to turn against them. Thebes and Athens enjoyed short-lived ascendancies, but in the second half of the century Greece descended into chaos.

The Culture of Classical Greece Classical Greece produced dramas, architecture, sculpture, and philosophical and historical works. Athenian culture was shaped by its religious and civic values and by sociopolitical changes brought about by the Peloponnesian War.

The Hellenistic World Greek culture mixed with Middle Eastern elements and spread throughout the eastern Mediterranean, Egypt, and far into Asia. This spread was facilitated by the conquests of Alexander the Great and by the kingdoms that were founded by his generals after his death.

Hellenistic Culture After the Macedonian conquest, Greeks turned from the political to the personal. In Athenian philosophy, the Epicureans and the Stoics gained prominence. Hellenistic styles in architecture and sculpture were diffused over a wide area. Mathematics and science blossomed.

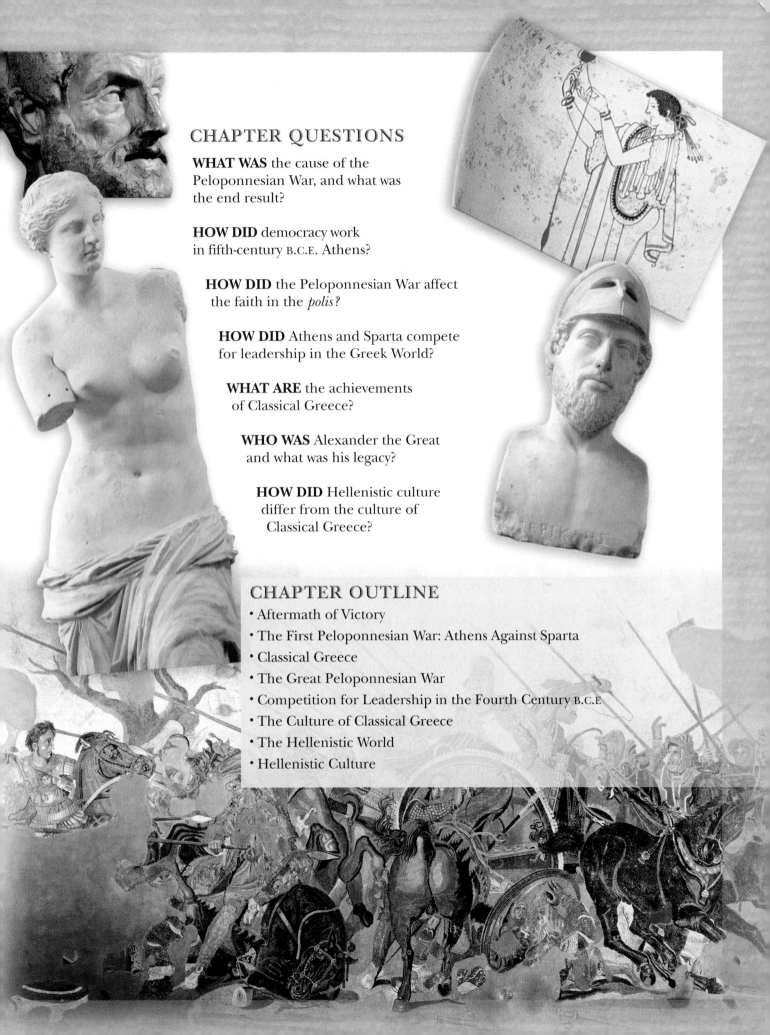

CHAPTER QUESTIONS

WHAT WAS the cause of the
Peloponnesian War, and what was
the end result?

HOW DID democracy work
in fifth-century B.C.E. Athens?

HOW DID the Peloponnesian War affect
the faith in the *polis*?

HOW DID Athens and Sparta compete
for leadership in the Greek World?

WHAT ARE the achievements
of Classical Greece?

WHO WAS Alexander the Great
and what was his legacy?

HOW DID Hellenistic culture
differ from the culture of
Classical Greece?

CHAPTER OUTLINE

- Aftermath of Victory
- The First Peloponnesian War: Athens Against Sparta
- Classical Greece
- The Great Peloponnesian War
- Competition for Leadership in the Fourth Century B.C.E.
- The Culture of Classical Greece
- The Hellenistic World
- Hellenistic Culture

IMAGE KEY
for pages 56–57 is on page 83.

The Greeks' victory over the Persians (489–479 B.C.E.) marked the start of an era of great achievement. Fear of another Persian incursion into the Aegean led the Greeks to contemplate some kind of arrangement for their joint defense. The Spartans refused to make commitments that would take them away from their homeland, but the Athenians were eager for leadership opportunities. They negotiated a military alliance called the Delian League. It laid the foundation for an Athenian Empire, and fear of Athenian expansion led other states to ally with Sparta. The Greek world was polarized and finally erupted in a self-destructive civil war. In 338 B.C.E., Philip of Macedon intervened, took control, and ended the era of the independent polis.

AFTERMATH OF VICTORY

The Greek *poleis* found it hard to cooperate, even when faced with invasion by the Persian emperors. Only two years after their victory in the Persian Wars, divisions among the Greeks were again causing them to fight among themselves.

THE DELIAN LEAGUE

The Spartans, who led the Greeks to victory against the Persian invaders of the Greek mainland, were not prepared to assume responsibility for defending the Aegean against the return of the Persians. Sparta could not risk stationing its troops far from home for long periods lest its slaves rebel. A *polis* with a navy was also better equipped to defend the Aegean than the Spartan army.

Athens was Greece's leading naval power, and Athens was an Ionian state with ties to the Greeks whom the Persians still threatened on the Aegean islands and the coast of Asia Minor. In the winter of 478–477 B.C.E., at a meeting on the sacred island of Delos, the Athenians joined other Greeks in a pact to continue the war with Persia. The purpose of their **Delian League** was to free Greeks still under Persian rule, to defend against a Persian return, and to obtain compensation for the war by raiding Persian lands.

The league drove back the Persians and cleared the Aegean of pirates. In 467 B.C.E., when it won a great victory over the Persians at the Eurymedon River in Asia Minor, some cities decided the alliance had served its purpose and tried to withdraw. However, Athens refused to let them go, and what had begun as a voluntary association of free states began to become an empire dominated by Athens.

THE RISE OF CIMON

Themistocles fell from power at the end of the Persian Wars, and for two decades Athens was led by Cimon, son of Miltiades, the general who triumphed at Marathon. At home, Cimon preserved a limited version of Clisthenes' democratic constitution. Abroad, he maintained pressure on Persia and cultivated friendly relations with Sparta.

THE FIRST PELOPONNESIAN WAR: ATHENS AGAINST SPARTA

In 465 B.C.E., the island of Thasos rebelled against the Delian League. During the two years it took to put down the revolt, Cimon was absent from Athens. When he returned, his political opponents tried to bring him down by charging him with taking bribes. He was acquitted, but a radically democratic faction headed by a man named Ephialtes (and his protégé, Pericles) continued to attack Cimon for his pro-Spartan, proaristocratic policies.

WHAT WAS the cause of the Peloponnesian War, and what was the end result?

Delian League Pact joined in 478 B.C.E. by Athenians and other Greeks to continue the war with Persia.

THE BREACH WITH SPARTA

The people of Thasos asked Sparta to help them break free from the Delian League, and Sparta agreed to invade Attica. However, an earthquake sparked a Helot revolt, and instead of attacking Athens, Sparta asked the Athenians for help. Cimon's mistake was to talk his fellow Athenians into sending it. When the Spartans changed their minds about letting an Athenian army into their land and ordered Cimon to retreat, the humiliated Athenians exiled Cimon (461 B.C.E.) and allied with Argos, Sparta's enemy. With Cimon gone, the way was clear for the radical democrats and Pericles to dominate Athenian politics.

THE DIVISION OF GREECE

Because Sparta had been willing to help Thasos break up the Delian League, Pericles was able to persuade the Athenians to support the city of Megara when it withdrew from Sparta's Peloponnesian League. Megara was also strategically important to Athens, for it commanded the road that linked Attica with the Peloponnesus. Sparta's vigorous objection led to the outbreak of the first of the **Peloponnesian Wars**. The Athenians maintained the upper hand until about 455 B.C.E., when they lost a fleet they had sent to Egypt to harass the Persians. Some members of Athens's empire seized the opportunity this gave them to rebel, and Athens had to disentangle itself from war with Sparta. A truce was arranged, and in 449 B.C.E., Athens made peace with Persia.

In 446 B.C.E., war again broke out between Sparta and Athens, but it was ended by negotiation. Sparta recognized the Athenian Empire and Athens promised to cease efforts to take over more of the Greek mainland. The two *poleis* also pledged to keep the peace for thirty years. Hostilities stopped, but the Greeks were effectively divided between Sparta, which dominated the Greek mainland, and Athens, which ruled the Aegean Sea.

CLASSICAL GREECE

THE ATHENIAN EMPIRE

The Athenians used the failure of their Egyptian campaign as an excuse to move the league's treasury from the island of Delos to the greater security of Athens, and they began to keep one-sixtieth of its annual revenues for themselves. By 445 B.C.E., only Chios, Lesbos, and Samos maintained a semblance of equality with Athens by contributing their own ships to the league's navy. All the other states paid tribute, a mark of servitude that some resented. The fading

HOW DID democracy work in fifth-century B.C.E. Athens?

Peloponnesian Wars Series of wars between Athens and Sparta beginning in 460 B.C.E.

An Athenian silver four-drachma coin (tetradrachm) from the fifth century B.C.E. (440–430 B.C.E.). On the front (a) is the profile of Athena and on the back (b) is her symbol of wisdom, the owl. The silver from which the coins were struck came chiefly from the state mines at Sunium in southern Attica.

Hirmer Fotoarchive

(a)

(b)

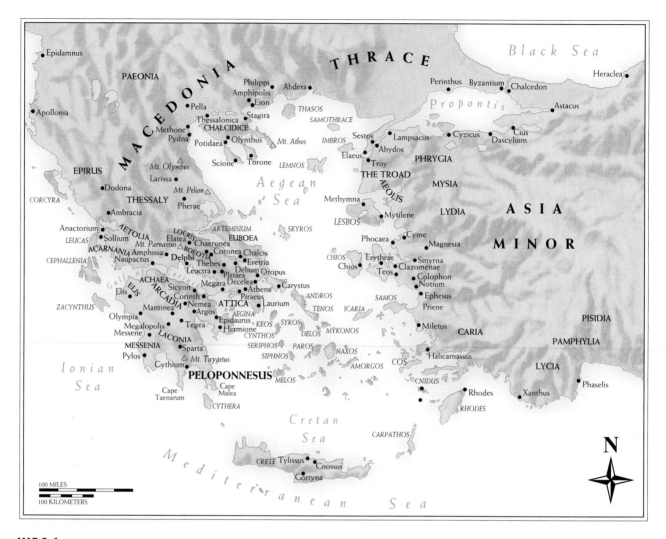

MAP 3–1

Classical Greece Greece in the Classical period (ca. 480–338 B.C.E.) centered on the Aegean Sea. Although there were important Greek settlements in Italy, Sicily, and all around the Black Sea, the area shown in this general reference map embraced the vast majority of Greek states

WHY WAS Athens not able to control its vast empire? What are some of the factors that led to its decline?

Persian threat had undercut the rationale for the league, but Athens profited too much from the Delian alliance to allow it to dissolve. Athenian dominance was also not universally unpopular. Athens supported democratic factions in its subject *poleis* and tried to behave more like a benevolent patron than an oppressor. (See Map 3–1.)

ATHENIAN DEMOCRACY

The people of Athens sensed no inconsistency in voting themselves more democratic privileges while they pursued an imperialistic foreign policy that diminished the freedoms of others. (See "Encountering the Past: The Panathenaic Festival.")

ENCOUNTERING THE PAST

THE PANATHENAIC FESTIVAL

Greek religious festivals celebrated both the gods and the poleis that the gods protected. One of the most famous and joyous of these occasions was the Panathenaia, Athens's commemoration of the birth of Athena, the city's patron deity. The Panathenaia was of ancient origin, but the wealth Athenians derived from their empire enabled them to stage the event with unparalleled magnificence in the mid-fifth century B.C.E. The festival was observed annually, but every fourth year a Great Panathenaia was scheduled and celebrated with special splendor.

The Panathenaia, like most Greek religious festivals, included athletic contests. The prizes were valuable, elaborately painted jars filled with olive oil (one of Athens's chief exports). There were competitions among *rhapsodes*, professional reciters of the *Iliad* and the *Odyssey*, and choruses of men and boys also sang and danced for prizes. The highlight of the occasion, however, was the procession that brought the gift of a brightly colored woolen robe to the image of the goddess in her temple on the Acropolis. This event is depicted by a frieze sculpted on the inner chamber of the Parthenon.

Although Athenian women usually avoided appearing in public, they played a major role in the Panathenaia. A group of priestesses and consecrated maidens spent a year weaving the goddess's robe, and they led the procession that conveyed it to her temple. The massive numbers of animals sacrificed to Athena provided a birthday feast for her worshipers. Because most Athenians rarely had an opportunity to eat fresh meat, the Panathenaia was an invitation to overindulgence. Several ancient sources refer to the (sometimes comical) consequences of crowds of people simultaneously gorging on meat.

HOW WERE religious and secular civic interests combined in the celebration of the Panathenaic festival?

Water-clock and Jury Ballots. Participants in an Athenian trial could speak for only a limited time. A water-clock (Clepsydra) like this kept the time. In front of it are two ballots used by the jurors to vote in favor of the plaintiff or the defendant.

Picture Desk/The Art Archive/Agora Museum Athens/Dagli Orti.

Democratic Legislation　Under Pericles' leadership, the Athenians suspended the traditional property qualification that allowed only wealthy individuals to run for high office. Men who could afford to equip themselves for service as *hoplites* qualified for election as *archons*. Pay was provided for jurors to make it possible for the poor to take time off from their jobs to serve. Circuit judges were sent into the countryside so the rural poor would have access to Athenian justice.

As democracy made citizenship an increasingly valuable commodity, the electorate guarded its privileges by limiting the number of voters. Citizenship was granted only to men who could prove their mothers as well as their fathers descended from citizen families. Every Greek *polis* (including the most democratic) denied participation in government to large segments of its population—resident aliens, women, and slaves.

Pericles (ca. 495-429 B.C.E.) was the leading statesman of Athens for much of the fifth century. This is a Roman copy in marble of the Greek bronze bust that was probably cast in the last decade of Pericles' life.

Library of Congress

3.5

Pericles' Funeral Oration by Thucydides

How Did the Democracy Work? Athenian democracy gave citizens extensive powers. Every decision of the state had to be approved by the popular assembly—by the voters themselves and not by some small group of elected representatives. Every judicial decision was subject to appeal to a popular court composed of not fewer than 51 and possibly as many as 1,501 citizens selected from the Athenian population at large. Many officials were chosen by casting lots, which eliminated considerations of class. Successful candidates for the chief offices— the imperial treasurers and the city's ten generals (who had political as well as military functions)—were usually wealthy aristocrats. But the voters could, in theory, elect anyone. All public officials had to submit to examination before taking office. They could be removed from office, and they had to account at the end of their term for the uses they had made of their authority. Because there was no standing army or police force, leaders lacked instruments they might have used to coerce or intimidate voters.

Pericles was elected to the generalship fifteen years in a row and thirty times in all, not because he was a dictator but because he was a persuasive speaker and a respected leader. On the few occasions when he lost the people's confidence, they did not hesitate to remove him from office. At the start of his career, Pericles was an imperialist. But after the defeat of the fleet Athens sent to Egypt and the city's failure to expand its territory on the mainland, he decided it was better to preserve the empire Athens already had and pursue peace with Sparta.

ATHENIAN WOMEN: LEGAL STATUS AND EVERYDAY LIFE

Greek society, like most others throughout history, was dominated by men, and democratic Athens was no exception. Women from citizen families were excluded from most aspects of public life. They could not debate, vote, or hold office and were subject all their lives to the authority of a masculine guardian— a father, a husband, or other male relative. Women married young, usually between the ages of twelve and eighteen, but men often did not marry until they were in their thirties. This meant that most men probably took brides much younger than themselves whom they treated like dependent children. Marriages were arranged, often without consulting the bride. Brides were given dowries, but they had no control over them or any other property. It was difficult for a woman to initiate divorce, for she had to find a male relative who agreed to take responsibility for her after the dissolution of her marriage.

The chief function of an Athenian woman from a citizen family was the production of male heirs to perpetuate her husband's *oikos* ("household"). A woman whose father died without leaving a male heir became an *epikleros*, an heiress. If she was married at the time, she had to separate from her husband and wed one of her father's relatives to bear a son who would reestablish her father's male line.

Because citizenship was inherited, the legitimacy of children was important. Athenian males consorted freely with prostitutes and concubines, but citizen women had no contact with any men but close relatives. They were confined to special women's quarters in their homes and spent their time raising children, cooking, weaving, and managing their households. Occasionally they emerged in

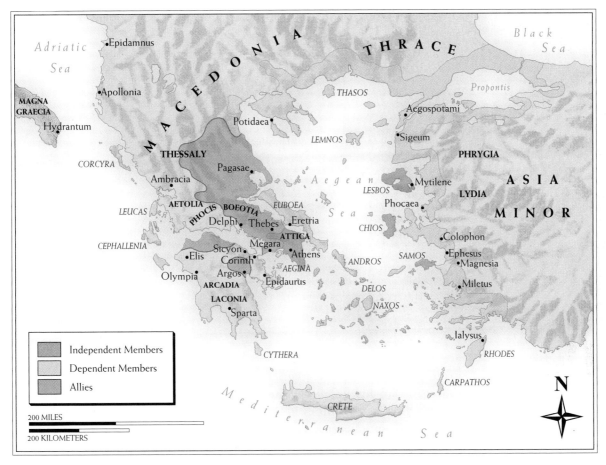

MAP 3–2
The Athenian Empire about 450 B.C.E.   The Athenian Empire at its fullest extent. We see Athens and the independent states that provided manned ships for the imperial fleet, but paid no tribute; dependent states that paid tribute; and states allied to, but not actually in, the empire.

WHY WOULD some of the weakest and most dependent Greek states be located in Asia Minor and Thrace?

public to take part in the state religion. But for the most part, they were expected to be invisible. In a frequently quoted speech, Pericles declared that "the greatest glory of women is to be least talked about by men, whether for good or bad."

Evidence from myths and from the works of the great Athenian dramatists (who often featured women in their plays) suggests that the roles played by Athenian women may have been more complex than their legal status implies. Only the rich could have afforded to lock their women up at home. The poor needed the labor of their women in fields and shops, and such women had to move about in public. Fetching water from the town wells and fountains was also women's work, and vase paintings and literature document the gathering of women at these places. Because historians disagree about the reliability of various sources, women's place in the Greek world remains a topic for debate.

An Exceptional Woman: Aspasia   Pericles' female companion, Aspasia, did not cultivate the invisibility that he said was "the greatest glory of women." She was a *hetaira*, an entertainer who came from Miletus (the city where Greek philosophy got its start). Highly intelligent and well educated, she could hold her own with thinkers such as Socrates. (Socrates' student, Plato, joked that she

QUICK REVIEW

Aspasia

- Pericles' female companion
- Highly intelligent and well educated
- Pericles discussed politics with her and respected her ideas

The Acropolis was both the religious and civic center of Athens. In its final form it is the work of Pericles and his successors in the late fifth century B.C.E. This photograph shows the Parthenon and to its left the Erechtheum.

Meredith Pillon, Greek National Tourism Organization

wrote Pericles' speeches.) Pericles clearly loved her. He divorced his wife, took her into his home, lavished affection on her, introduced her to his friends, discussed politics with her, and took her ideas seriously. Athens was scandalized—not because Pericles kept a woman, but because he treated one with such respect.

SLAVERY

Slavery always existed in Greece, but the earliest forms of bondage resembled serfdom more than chattel slavery. When the Spartans, for instance, conquered a people, they reduced them to the status of Helots, peasants who were bound to the land to work the farms that supported Sparta's citizen-soldiers. Until Solon put an end to the practice about 600 B.C.E., an Athenian citizen who defaulted on a debt was subject to temporary bondage or even sale into permanent slavery outside Attica.

Chattel slavery proper proliferated about 500 B.C.E. and remained important to Greek society thereafter. Most slaves of this kind were prisoners of war or persons abducted by pirates. The Greeks, like other ancient peoples, viewed foreigners as inferiors who were fit for slavery. Slaves were sometimes employed as shepherds, but Greek farms were often too small to afford more than one enslaved worker. As a rule, the landed estates of the upper classes were worked by free tenant farmers rather than slaves. Wealthy men usually invested in small scattered farms rather than the consolidated plantations associated with slave labor. Industries such as mining employed large numbers of slaves. Slaves also worked as craftsmen in almost every trade. Like slaves on small farms, these men and women labored alongside their masters. Householders used slaves for domestic help, and the state purchased slaves to serve as prison attendants, clerks, and secretaries.

Scholars debate the extent of slavery and its importance to ancient Greek society. Reliable statistics are hard to come by. Estimates of the number of slaves in Athens during the fifth and fourth centuries B.C.E. range from 20,000 to

100,000. If the truth is closer to the mean between these extremes, the city's 40,000 households owned about 60,000 slaves—or about two per family. Only a quarter to a third of free Athenians may have had slaves. This is comparable to the situation in the American South prior to the Civil War. Unlike the southern United States, however, the Athenian economy did not depend on a single cash crop produced by slave labor, and Greek slaves did not differ from their masters in skin color. (Slaves walked the streets of Athens with such ease as to offend class-conscious Athenians.) Americans also seldom emancipated slaves, but Greeks often did.

THE GREAT PELOPONNESIAN WAR

*T*he thirty years of peace that Sparta and Athens pledged to maintain in 445 B.C.E. ended prematurely. About 435 B.C.E., a dispute in a remote part of the Greek world escalated to become a war that shook the foundations of Greek civilization.

HOW DID the Peloponnesian War affect the faith in the *polis*?

CAUSES

The conflict began with a quarrel between Corinth and Corcyra, an island at the entrance to the Adriatic Sea. The Athenians decided to intervene to prevent Corinth, their commercial rival, from capturing Corcyra's large fleet. Corinth was understandably angered, and it appealed to Sparta, its ally, for help. At a meeting of the Peloponnesian League, which Sparta convened in the summer of 432 B.C.E., the Corinthians called for war with Athens, and the following spring (431 B.C.E.) the Spartans invaded Attica.

STRATEGIC STALEMATE

The Spartan strategy was traditional: invade the enemy's territory and by threatening the farms that supply their food, force them to accept battle with the Spartan infantry. Because the Spartans had the better army and outnumbered the Athenians by more than two to one, they were confident of victory.

Most *poleis* would probably have come to terms with Sparta, but Athens was in a unique position to resist. It had strong walls that Sparta could not breach, and it was connected to its port (the Piraeus) by the Long Walls, a kind of fortified highway. So long as the Athenians had their navy and their empire, they could ride out a siege by supplying themselves from the sea. By remaining secure behind their walls and ignoring the Spartan invasion, they could also show the world that Sparta's military might was useless against them. In the interim, the Athenian fleet could frighten Sparta's allies by raiding the Peloponnesian coast. Pericles believed this strategy would force the Peloponnesian League to recognize the hopelessness of the situation and sue for peace. The plan was brilliant but difficult to implement. The Athenians had to exercise great

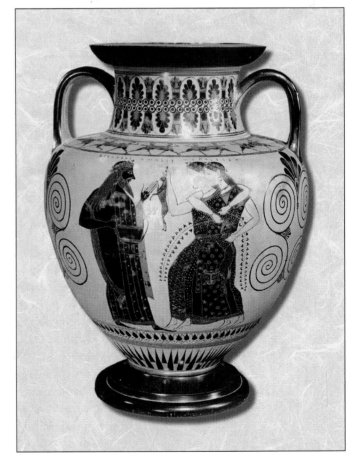

This storage jar *(amphora),* made about 540 B.C.E. is attributed to the anonymous Athenian master artist called the Amasis painter. It shows Dionysus, the god of wine, revelry, and fertility with two of his ecstatic female worshipers called maenads.

Cliché Bibliotheque Nationale de France—Paris

HISTORY'S VOICES

THUCYDIDES ON CIVIL WAR

I n 427 B.C.E., in the fifth year of the Peloponnesian War, a vicious and brutal civil war broke out on the island of Corcyra, an ally of Athens, between political factions—democrats who favored the Athenian alliance and oligarchs who preferred the Spartans. The historian Thucydides describes the affair and draws general conclusions from it about human behavior under extreme pressure.

ACCORDING TO Thucydides, how do the passions unleashed by such wars affect the behavior of individuals?

So bloody was the march of the revolution, and the impression which it made was the greater as it was one of the first to occur. Later on, one may say, the whole Hellenic world was convulsed; struggles being everywhere made by the popular chiefs to bring in the Athenians, and by the oligarchs to introduce the Lacedæmonians. In peace there would have been neither the pretext nor the wish to make such an invitation; but in war, with an alliance always at the command of either faction for the hurt of their adversaries and their own corresponding advantage, opportunities for bringing in the foreigner were never wanting to the revolutionary parties. The sufferings which revolution entailed upon the cities were many and terrible, such as have occurred and always will occur, as long as the nature of mankind remains the same; though in a severer or milder form, and varying in their symptoms, according to the variety of the particular cases. In peace and prosperity, states and individuals have better sentiments, because they do not find themselves suddenly confronted with imperious necessities; but war takes away the easy supply of daily wants, and so proves a rough master, that brings most men's characters to a level with their fortunes. Revolution thus ran its course from city to city, and the places which it arrived at last, from having heard what had been done before, carried to a still greater excess the refinement of their inventions, as manifested in the cunning of their enterprises and the atrocity of their reprisals. Words had to change their ordinary meaning and to take that which was now given them. Reckless audacity came to be considered the courage of a loyal ally; prudent hesitation, specious cowardice; moderation was held to be a cloak for unmanliness.

Thucydides, *The Peloponnesian War*, trans. by Richard Crawley (New York: Random House, 1951), p. 189.

self-control while Sparta destroyed their farms and taunted them. As citizens of a democracy, they could have changed their policies at any time, but Pericles' leadership helped them stay the course. In 429 B.C.E., however, plague swept the crowded city, Pericles died, and the politicians who succeeded him were less able men.

The Athenian electorate divided into two camps. One faction (led by a man named Nicias) wanted to continue Pericles' defensive strategy, but another (headed by a certain Cleon) proposed launching an offensive. In 425 B.C.E., when an Athenian naval expedition marooned and captured four hundred Spartans on an island on the coast of the Peloponnese, Athens passed up an opportunity to make peace. Sparta offered to end the war in exchange for the return of its men, but Cleon's party persuaded the Athenians to attempt some land battles.

The failure of two campaigns shook the Athenians' confidence in Cleon—particularly after the Spartan general, Brasidas, captured Amphipolis, an Aegean port that protected Athens's access to grain supplies. In 422 B.C.E., Cleon led an assault on Amphipolis in which he and Brasidas were killed, and the deaths of both leaders paved the way for a truce in the spring of 421 B.C.E. The struggle over Amphipolis had an additional outcome of a very different sort. An Athenian admiral named Thucydides was blamed for the loss of Amphipolis and punished with exile. He used his enforced leisure to write a masterful history of the war, which, as it turned out, was far from over.

THE FALL OF ATHENS

The Peace of Nicias, the agreement between Athens and Sparta, declared a truce that was supposed to last for fifty years, but neither side fulfilled all its treaty obligations. This meant that hostilities were likely break out again, but in 415 B.C.E. an ambitious young politician named Alcibiades persuaded the Athenians to squander their resources on a risky foreign adventure. Athens sent a huge expedition to Sicily and lost 200 ships and 4,500 men. When the subjects of the Athenian Empire seized the opportunity to rebel against a weakened Athens, Persia intervened to help the Greeks destroy themselves. It offered aid to Sparta.

The Athenians found the will to continue the fight, but their resources were no match for the support Spartans received from Persia. In 405 B.C.E., a Spartan fleet destroyed the Athenian ships that were guarding the city's grain-supply route. Lysander, the Spartan commander, cut off Athens's food supply and starved the city into submission (404 B.C.E.). Athens was stripped of its fleet and empire but allowed to survive.

COMPETITION FOR LEADERSHIP IN THE FOURTH CENTURY B.C.E.

HOW DID Athens and Sparta compete for leadership in the Greek world?

Sparta tried to take Athens' place as leader of the Greek world, but its limited manpower, restive slaves, conservative traditions, and indebtedness to Persia doomed its efforts to maintain order in the Aegean. The Greeks soon reverted to fighting among themselves.

THE HEGEMONY OF SPARTA

The Greeks grumbled when the Spartans repaid their debts to Persia by ceding Persia the cities of Ionia that the Greeks had liberated in the Persian Wars. Lysander made more enemies by trying to force the cities the Spartans had liberated from Athenian control into a new Spartan Empire. He overthrew democracies and installed oligarchies loyal to him in many Greek cities. He deployed Spartan garrisons to back up his puppet governments, and he exacted tributes that equaled those that Athens had demanded.

The oligarchs whom Lysander established in control of Athens following its surrender in 404 B.C.E. were so unpopular, they were called the Thirty Tyrants. Their oppression forced Athens's democratic leaders to flee to Thebes and begin to raise an army with which to retake the city. Sparta's cautious king, Pausanias, prevented an outbreak of fighting by recalling Lysander and allowing Athens to revert to democracy. So long as Athenian foreign policy remained under Spartan control, Sparta could afford to allow Athens to have any kind of government it wanted.

Persia might have been expected to take advantage of this confusion, but it was distracted by an internal power struggle. Following the death of the emperor Darius II in 405 B.C.E., a Persian prince named Cyrus tried to seize the Persian throne with the help of an army of Greek mercenaries. The Greeks routed the Persians. But when Cyrus died in battle in 401 B.C.E., they found themselves

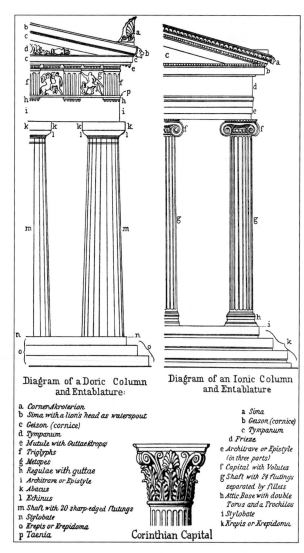

Diagram of a Doric Column and Entablature:

a Corner Akroterion
b Sima with a lion's head as waterspout
c Geison (cornice)
d Tympanum
e Mutule with Guttae (drops)
f Triglyphs
g Metopes
h Regulae with guttae
i Architrave or Epistyle
k Abacus
l Echinus
m Shaft with 20 sharp-edged flutings
n Stylobate
o Krepis or Krepidoma
p Taenia

Diagram of an Ionic Column and Entablature

a Sima
b Geison (cornice)
c Tympanum
d Frieze
e Architrave or Epistyle (in three parts)
f Capital with Volutes
g Shaft with 24 flutings separated by fillets
h Attic Base with double Torus and a Trochilos
i Stylobate
k Krepis or Krepidoma

Corinthian Capital

The three orders of Greek architecture, Doric, Ionic, and Corinthian, have had an enduring impact on Western architecture.

stranded without a leader or a purpose deep in enemy territory. They fought their way home, but the cities of Asia Minor that had supported Cyrus now faced the threat of Persian revenge.

In 396 B.C.E., when the Spartan king, Agesilaus, led an army out to defend his interests in Asia Minor, the Persians countered by offering aid to any Greek state that rebelled against Sparta. Thebes, Athens's neighbor, accepted, and in 395 B.C.E., it enlisted the cooperation of Argos, Corinth, and a resurgent Athens. The war that resulted forced the Spartans to retreat from Asia Minor, and in 394 B.C.E., the Persian fleet destroyed Sparta's navy. The Athenians seized the opportunity that Sparta's difficulties gave them to refortify their city, rebuild their navy, and recover some of their foreign possessions.

The Persians, who believed Athens was potentially a greater threat than Sparta, then agreed to aid Sparta so long as it confined its ambitions to the Greek mainland. In 382 B.C.E., Agesilaus seized Thebes in a surprise attack. However, an attempt to take Athens failed, and by 379 B.C.E., the Thebans had regained their independence. In 371 B.C.E., the great Theban general, Epaminondas, crushed the Spartan army at the battle of Leuctra. He followed this up by freeing the Helots and helping them organize to fight the Spartans. Deprived of land and slaves, Sparta's days as a major power came to an end.

THE HEGEMONY OF THEBES: THE SECOND ATHENIAN EMPIRE

Epaminondas's humiliation of Sparta opened the way for Thebes to become the dominant power in Greece. Thebes did take control of the Greek states north of Athens and west along the shores of the Corinthian Gulf, but Athens organized resistance to Theban expansion. In 362 B.C.E., Epaminondas routed Athens and its allies at the Battle of Mantinea, but he died in the fighting. The loss of the leader struck a fatal blow to Theban ambition.

In 378 B.C.E. (sixteen years before the Battle of Mantinea), a Second Athenian Confederation had been organized to oppose Spartan aggression in the Aegean. Although its constitution was designed to prevent Athens from exploiting this alliance as it had the Delian League, it was difficult for the members of the confederation to trust Athens. The collapse of Sparta and Thebes and the fading of the Persian threat persuaded some of them that the alliance had outlived its purpose. They rebelled, and by 355 B.C.E., Athens once again had lost an empire. It was also clear that despite two centuries of almost continuous warfare, the Greek world was still unstable.

WHAT ARE the achievements of Classical Greece?

THE CULTURE OF CLASSICAL GREECE

The Greeks' victories in the Persian Wars gave them tremendous self-confidence and unleashed a flood of creative activity that was rarely, if ever, matched anywhere at any time. The result was what has come to be called Western civilization's Classical Period.

THE FIFTH CENTURY B.C.E.

Much Classical art and architecture is characterized by calm and serenity, but a common theme of tension runs through the thought, art, literature, and lives of the Greeks of the Classical Period. This reflected the difficulty of reconciling private ambition with the restraints imposed by *polis* citizenship and the conflict between the Greeks' competitive drives and their belief that excessive striving led to disaster. The Greeks' faith in themselves was ratified by their victory over Persia, but they knew that they, like Xerxes, risked punishment if they went too far. As Athens and Sparta teetered on the brink of self-destructive war, Athenian playwrights explored the problem of striking the right balance between human ambition and divine justice.

Attic Tragedy   Greek plays were staged in groups at festivals honoring the god Dionysus. Each of the three playwrights whose work was chosen for presentation by the *archons* wrote three tragedies (which might or might not have a common subject) and a satyr play (a concluding comic choral dialogue with Dionysus). Each play was performed by no more than three actors, who were paid by the state, and a chorus of singers and dancers that was sponsored by a wealthy citizen. Plays were presented in the temple of Dionysus, a 30,000-seat amphitheater on the south side of the Acropolis. A jury of Athenians, chosen by lot, awarded prizes for the best author, actor, and sponsor.

Athenian playwrights used the theater to encourage the *polis*'s citizens to think deeply about the use they made of their power as voters in a democracy. A play might dramatize a contemporary or historical event, but authors usually preferred to retell a myth in a way that would illuminate current affairs. Aeschylus and Sophocles, who wrote our earliest extant plays, dealt with abstract ideas (religion, politics, and ethics). Euripides, a somewhat later poet, was more interested in exploring human psychology.

Old Comedy   Comedies were added to the Dionysian festival early in the fifth century B.C.E. The only complete comic plays to survive are those of Aristophanes (ca. 450–385 B.C.E), who wrote humorously about serious issues. He employed scathing invective and satire to lampoon his contemporaries—even powerful politicians such as Pericles and Cleon.

Architecture and Sculpture   Like the plays that members of Pericles' generation witnessed, the buildings their city erected reflect the creative tension of the Classical era. In 448 B.C.E., Pericles began to rebuild the Acropolis (using income from the Delian League). His plan included new temples and an imposing gateway for the sacred precinct. Pericles' intent was to create an environment in which the power and intellectual genius of Athens would become tangible experiences—making Athens, in his words, "the school of Hellas."

Philosophy   The art of the fifth century B.C.E. aimed at defining the essence of humanity and illustrating its place in the natural order. Similar concerns had

The Competition for Leadership of Greece

479 B.C.E.	Battles of Plataea and Mycale
478–477 B.C.E.	Formation of the Delian League
465–463 B.C.E.	Thasos attempts to leave the league
462 B.C.E.	Pericles begins to lead Athens
460–445 B.C.E.	First Peloponnesian War
454 B.C.E.	Athens is defeated in Egypt
449 B.C.E.	Athens makes peace with Persia
435 B.C.E.	Corinth attacks Corcyra
432–404 B.C.E.	Great Peloponnesian War
421 B.C.E.	Peace of Nicias
415–413 B.C.E.	Athens's Sicilian campaign
404 B.C.E.	Sparta defeats Athens
404–403 B.C.E.	Thirty Tyrants govern Athens
382 B.C.E.	Sparta seizes Thebes
378 B.C.E.	Second Athenian Confederation
371 B.C.E.	Thebes defeats Sparta at Leuctra
362 B.C.E.	End of Theban hegemony
338 B.C.E.	Philip of Macedon dominates Greece
336–323 B.C.E.	Reign of Alexander the Great

QUICK REVIEW

Athenian Drama

- Plays were staged in groups of three at festivals honoring the gods
- Plays were presented in the temple of Dionysus
- Playwrights used the theater to encourage citizens to think about the issues of the day

3.4
Drama: *Antigone* by Sophocles

prompted the invention of philosophy in the sixth century B.C.E. Thales, the first philosopher, wondered how a world filled with changing phenomena could hang together as a stable, coherent whole. He suggested that the changes we see taking place in the things around us are only alterations in the state of a single universal substance from which all these things are made. He believed this substance was water, for water is found in nature as a solid, a liquid, and a gas. Later thinkers proposed other universal substances, but some claimed Thales was naive in assuming that change and permanence could both exist in the same system.

Heraclitus said that permanence is an illusion produced by our inability to perceive changes that are very slow. Parmenides of Elea and his pupil Zeno countered that the concept of change is a logical absurdity, for it implies that something can arise from nothing. Empedocles of Acragas suggested a compromise between these opposing points of view. He said the world is composed of permanent elements (fire, water, earth, and air) whose combinations change. Similarly, Leucippus of Miletus and Democritus of Abdera imagined the world to be made up of innumerable tiny, indivisible particles (*atomoi*) that clump together and spin apart in the void of space. These philosophies all embraced materialism. That is, they claimed that spirit is simply a refined form of matter and that, therefore, physical laws can be discovered to explain even intellectual phenomena. Anaxagoras of Clazomenae, however, disagreed. He believed the universe was indeed composed of tiny fundamental particles ("seeds"), but he claimed it was controlled by another kind of reality—a rational force he called *nous* ("mind"). The debate between materialism and idealism that Greek thinkers such as these began has yet to be resolved.

Most philosophical speculations were too abstract to interest ordinary Greeks. However, the Sophists, a group of professional teachers who flourished in the mid–fifth century B.C.E., attracted a popular following by teaching a practical skill: rhetoric. The arts of persuasion were highly valued in democratic Athens, where public debates decided most important issues. Sophists refrained from speculations about the physical universe and concentrated their attention on rational critiques of beliefs and institutions. They were particularly interested in the impact that nature and custom had on human social behavior. The more traditional among them argued that society's laws were of divine origin and based in nature, but others dismissed laws as mere conventions—arbitrary arrangements people make so they can live together. The most extreme Sophists maintained that law is contrary to nature, for the weak use the law to restrain the strong—a reversal of the order of nature. Critias, an Athenian oligarch, even claimed the gods were nothing but inventions designed to deter people from doing what they want. Speculations such as these undermined the concept of justice on which the *polis* was founded, and the later giants of philosophy, Plato and Aristotle, worked hard to refute them.

History Herodotus—"the father of history"—was born shortly before the outbreak of the Persian Wars. In writing an account of those wars, he far exceeded attempts by earlier prose writers to describe and explain human actions. Although his *History* was completed about 425 B.C.E. and shows a few traces of Sophist influence, it is reminiscent of an earlier age. Herodotus accepted legendary material as fact (although not uncritically), and he believed in oracles and divine intervention. However, his recognition of the crucial role human intelligence plays in determining the course of events was in sync with the rational, scientific spirit of his day. He also acknowledged the importance of institutions. He credited Greece's victory over Persia to the love of liberty the *polis* instilled in its citizens.

Thucydides was born about 460 B.C.E. and died a few years after the end of the Peloponnesian War, the conflict whose history he devoted his life to describing. His thought was influenced by the rational skepticism of the Sophists of the late fifth century B.C.E., and he shared the scientific attitudes that characterized the work of contemporaries such as the physician Hippocrates of Cos. Thucydides took great pains to achieve factual accuracy, and he searched his evidence for significant patterns of human behavior. He hoped that by discovering these patterns people would be able to foresee events. Because human nature was, he believed, essentially unchanging, people ought to respond to similar circumstances in similar ways. Thucydides admitted, however, that the lessons of history were not always enough to guarantee success in dealing with the challenges we face. He believed an element of randomness (chance) affects human destiny.

THE FOURTH CENTURY B.C.E.

The Peloponnesian War diminished faith in the *polis* as an effective form of government. The Greeks of the fourth century B.C.E. may not fully have grasped what was happening, but they did sense threats to their traditional institutions. Some tried to revive the *polis*. Others looked for alternatives to it. Still others gave up on public life altogether.

Drama   The poetry of the fourth century B.C.E. reveals the disillusionment some Greeks felt with the *polis*. Poets switched their attention from politics and public

The theater at Epidaurus was built in the fourth century B.C.E. The city contained the Sanctuary of Asclepius, a god of healing, and drew many visitors who packed the theater at religious festivals.

Hirmer Fotoarchiv

The striding god from Artemisium is a bronze statue dating from about 460 B.C.E. It was found in the sea near Artemisium, the northern tip of the large Greek island of Euboea, and is now on display in the Athens archaeological museum. Exactly whom he represents is not known. Some have thought him to be Poseidon holding a trident; others believe he is Zeus hurling a thunderbolt. In either case, he is a splendid representative of the early Classical period of Greek sculpture.

National Archaeological Museum, Athens

events to the private concerns of ordinary people—family and the interior lives of individuals. Old Comedy had focused on matters of public policy, but Middle and New Comedy humorously depicted daily life and satirized domestic situations and personal relationships. The role of the chorus, a kind of symbol for the *polis* community in earlier theater, was much diminished. Menander (342–291 B.C.E.), the pioneer of New Comedy, wrote domestic tragicomedy: gentle spoofs of the foibles of ordinary people and the trials of thwarted lovers—the material of modern situation comedies.

Tragedy, which drew its inspiration from the robust political life of the *polis*, declined during the fourth century B.C.E. No plays from the period have survived. Theatrical producers must have sensed a decline in quality, for they began to revive the plays of the previous century. Euripides' tragedies, which had rarely won top honors when first produced, finally found their audiences. More than the other great Athenian playwrights, Euripides had explored the interior lives of individuals, and some of his late plays are more like fairy tales, fantasy adventures, or love stories than tragedies.

Sculpture The movement away from the grand, the ideal, and the general and toward the ordinary, the real, and the individual that we see in fourth-century B.C.E. literature is also apparent in sculpture. It explains the contrast between the work of Polycleitus (ca. 450–440 B.C.E.) and that of Praxiteles (ca. 340–330 B.C.E.) or Lysippus (ca. 330 B.C.E.).

PHILOSOPHY AND THE CRISIS OF THE *POLIS*

Socrates Socrates (469–399 B.C.E.) was one of the first Greek intellectuals to recognize the shortcomings of the *polis*. He seldom involved himself in Athenian political life, but he did not entirely reject the *polis* ideal. He did his duty as a citizen—serving in the army to defend his city, obeying its laws, and seeking a rational justification for its values.

Because Socrates wrote nothing, our knowledge of him depends on the reports of his disciples, Plato and Xenophon, and later commentators. In his youth Socrates supposedly studied the early philosophers who sought explanations for the phenomena of nature, but his interests soon shifted to the interior world—to the processes that govern thought and decision making. Unlike some Sophists, he believed in the existence of truth and the power of reason to discover it.

Socrates said that he hoped to discover truths by cross-examining people who were reputed to have them—that is, those who were confident in their ideas. His conversations with them always ended in the same way: by demonstrating that, except for some technical information and practical skills, people had few beliefs they could rationally support. It is not surprising that the Athenians whose opinions were shaken by his rigorous critiques accused him of undermining their confidence in values fundamental to the *polis*. Socrates also made no attempt to conceal his contempt for Athenian democracy, a political system that he said empowered the ignorant to make decisions about things they did not understand.

In 399 B.C.E., an Athens that was struggling to come to terms with its loss of the Peloponnesian War decided it could no longer tolerate Socrates. He was tried, convicted, and sentenced to die for undercutting the Athenian way of life.

OVERVIEW   THE THREE GREAT GREEK INTELLECTUALS

Socrates (469–399 B.C.E.)	One of the first Greek intellectuals to recognize the shortcomings of the *polis*. He believed in the existence of truth and the power of reason to discover it. He made no attempt to conceal his contempt for Athenian democracy—a political system that he said empowered the ignorant to make decisions about things they did not understand. Socrates was eventually tried and executed for undercutting the Athenian way of life.
Plato (429–347 B.C.E.)	The most important of Socrates' followers, he was the first to formulate a consistent worldview and a method for exploring all of life's fundamental questions. Like Socrates, Plato believed in the *polis* and saw it as consistent with humanity's social nature. He established the "Academy" in 386 B.C.E., a school for training statesmen and citizens. Plato believed power should be entrusted to philosophers only and that the *polis* could only be redeemed by improving its ability to produce good citizens.
Aristotle (384–322 B.C.E.)	The most prominent of Plato's students, he founded the Lyceum (the school of the Peripatetics). Unlike Plato's students at the Academy, Aristotle's students gathered, ordered, and analyzed data from all fields of knowledge. He wrote on logic, physics, astronomy, biology, ethics, rhetoric, literary criticism, and politics. Aristotle believed human beings are social creatures and that the *polis* was necessary to realize their potential. He also stated that a moderate constitution was necessary to create a state dominated by the middle class, not by the rich or the poor.

Having made its point, the city had no need to execute Socrates, and it gave him a chance to escape. Plato says, however, that Socrates refused to do so out of respect for the law. By taking this stand, Socrates proved he was not a Sophist or a skeptic whose only purpose was to foster doubt. He said the authority of the laws of the *polis*, which had protected him all his life, could not be denied simply because he now found the law inconvenient. Although he claimed never to have found the truth, by dying he witnessed to his faith in the existence of truth that transcends human conventions.

Plato   Plato (429–347 B.C.E.), the most important of Socrates' followers, is the prime example of the pupil who becomes greater than his master. Plato was the first systematic philosopher—the first to formulate a consistent worldview and a method for exploring all of life's fundamental questions. He was also a brilliant writer. His twenty-six philosophical discussions—most cast in the form of dialogues—are artistic masterpieces that make the analysis of complicated philosophical ideas dramatic and entertaining.

Plato was an Athenian aristocrat who initially planned a career in politics, but Socrates' execution discouraged him. He left Athens and moved to Sicily to serve as tutor and adviser to two of the tyrants of Syracuse, Dionysius I and II. Having been disillusioned by democracy, he pinned his hopes for the creation of ideal states on rationally disciplined tyrants—philosopher kings. When his Sicilian experiment failed, he returned to Athens and established a school for training statesmen and citizens. The "**Academy**," which he founded in 386 B.C.E., survived until a Christian emperor closed it in the sixth century C.E.

Like Socrates and unlike the radical Sophists, Plato believed in the *polis*. He saw it as consistent with humanity's social nature and believed it could be made into an instrument for creating good people. Socrates' insistence that virtue is a

Academy School founded by Plato in Athens to train statesmen and citizens.

kind of knowledge led Plato to reject democracy. The knowledge (*episteme*, "science") on which virtue is based was, he thought, beyond most people. Because only a few specially gifted and educated individuals could acquire it and because reason dictates that each person in society should do that to which he or she is best suited by nature, communities should entrust power only to philosophers. Only they are capable, in Plato's opinion, of subordinating private interests to those of the community. Only they could maintain harmony in a *polis* by eliminating the causes of strife: private property, family interests, and the personal ambitions that distract individuals from the public good.

Concern for the redemption of the *polis* was central to Plato's philosophy, and he believed the *polis* could only be redeemed and preserved by improving its ability to produce good citizens. That meant, of course, that he had to explore the nature of the kind of knowledge Socrates equated with goodness. Plato's attempt to work out a theory of knowledge led him into the realm of metaphysics and constituted what may be his most important contribution to the history of Western thought.

3.2
Aristotle,
Nichomachean Ethics

Aristotle The most prominent of Plato's students was Aristotle (384–322 B.C.E.). He was born at Stagirus in the Chalcidice, the son of a physician to the court of Macedon. After Plato's death he moved from Athens to Assos and Mytilene in Asia Minor, where he conducted research in marine biology. In 342 B.C.E., he accepted an appointment as tutor to Alexander, son of King Philip of Macedon, and in 336 B.C.E., he returned to Athens to found the **Lyceum**, or the school of the Peripatetics (from *Peripatos*, a covered walkway on its grounds). Following Alexander's death in 323 B.C.E., anti-Macedonian feeling swept Greece, and Aristotle decided to leave Athens. He died at Chalcis in Euboea a year later.

The program of the Lyceum was different from that of the Academy. Plato's students concentrated on mathematics, but Aristotle's gathered, ordered, and analyzed data from all fields of knowledge. The range of Aristotle's interests is astonishing. He wrote on logic, physics, astronomy, biology, ethics, rhetoric, literary criticism, and politics. He began the study of every subject the same way— by collecting data (physical or anecdotal, depending on the field). Data were then rationally analyzed to see if they revealed any general principles. Like Plato, Aristotle viewed things teleologically; that is, he explained them in terms of their ultimate ends or purposes. Plato claimed that the things of this world were governed by universal ideas or forms—transcendent realities that people could not directly experience. Aristotle, however, inferred the purposes of most things from our experiences of them. He believed matter strove to realize the form (i.e., the idea) that made it intelligible (i.e., defined it) to the human mind— that the world around us is constantly evolving from potentiality to actuality.

This metaphysical model is at the heart of Aristotle's thinking about the *polis*. He rejected the Sophists' claim that social life is made up of conventions that frustrate human nature. He believed human beings are social creatures and the *polis* was, therefore, necessary for the realization of their potential. The most important function of the *polis* was not economic or military. It was moral. The *polis* was the means to human fulfillment and happiness.

Aristotle was less interested in theorizing about the perfect state than in designing the best achievable state. To determine what this was, he studied the constitutions of 158 functioning *poleis*. (Only the *Constitution of the Athenians* has survived.) He concluded that moderation was the key attribute of the most successful constitutions. A moderate constitution created a state that was dominated by the middle class, not by the rich or the poor. A large middle class was essential for political

Lyceum School founded by Aristotle in Athens that focused on the gathering and analysis of data from all fields of knowledge.

stability, for the middle class, he claimed, is not tempted to the arrogance of the rich nor infected by the malice that resentment creates in the poor. Stable constitutions were also usually "mixed"—that is, they blended aspects of democracy and oligarchy.

All the political thinkers of the fourth century B.C.E. recognized the *polis* was in danger. Few, however, made such realistic proposals for its reform as Aristotle. It is ironic that his able defense of the *polis* ideal came on the eve of the *polis*'s demise.

THE HELLENISTIC WORLD

WHO WAS Alexander the Great and what was his legacy?

The term *Hellenistic* was coined in the nineteenth century to describe the period in Greek history that began when a Macedonian dynasty conquered both Greece and the Persian Empire. This blended aspects of Greek and Middle Eastern culture to create a new, cosmopolitan civilization.

THE MACEDONIAN CONQUEST

Macedon, the northernmost of the mainland Greek states, was a backward, semi-barbaric land by the standards of many Greeks. It had no *poleis* but was a kingdom ruled by a monarch who, like Homer's Agamemnon, had to contend with clans headed by powerful aristocratic families. Hampered by constant wars with raiders on its northern frontier, internal strife, weak institutions, and a poor economy, Macedon played no great part in Greek affairs until the fourth century B.C.E.

Philip of Macedon   Before Philip II (359–336 B.C.E.) inherited the Macedonian throne, he spent several years as a hostage in Thebes. This gave him an opportunity to study Greek politics and *hoplite* warfare under the tutelage of Epaminondas, the general who defeated Sparta. Philip's talent and training equipped him to forge Macedon into a true kingdom. He eliminated rivals to his power, pacified the tribes on Macedon's frontiers, and challenged Athenian dominance of the northern Aegean. The conquest of Amphipolis, the city Athens had lost to Sparta in the Peloponnesian War, gave him control of the gold and silver mines of nearby Mount Pangaeus, and he used this wealth to elevate the level of Macedonian culture. He founded cities and turned his army into the world's finest fighting force.

Hermes and Dionysus.

Praxiteles (c. 400-300 B.C.E.), "Hermes and Dionysius", c. 350-330 B.C.E. National Archeological Museum, Olympia. Scala/ Art Resource, NY

The Macedonian Army   Philip's army was more professional than the companies of amateur citizen-soldiers who defended most *poleis*. Philip recruited infantrymen from Macedon's sturdy farming class and feisty hill people and trained them in new combat techniques. He equipped them with pikes that were thirteen feet long. (The *hoplite*'s spear measured about nine feet.) This weapon allowed them to spread out and form a more open, flexible formation than the traditional phalanx. The Macedonian aristocrats who formed Philip's cavalry, the "Companions," lived with the king and were fiercely loyal to him. Philip also hired mercenaries who knew the latest tactics and were experienced with sophisticated siege machinery. Altogether, he could field an army of about 40,000 men.

The Invasion of Greece   Once Philip had Macedon firmly in hand, the Greeks gave Philip the excuse he needed to intervene in their affairs. The people of Thessaly asked Philip to assist them in a war with the Phocians. Philip won the war, occupied Thessaly, and marched on Thrace to take control of the Aegean's northern coast and the Hellespont.

These actions threatened the interests of Athens. Athens, however, was no longer the Athens of Pericles. It had a formidable fleet of three hundred ships, but its population was smaller than in the fifth century B.C.E. and it had no empire to help it fund a major war. The Athenians were, therefore, uncertain how to respond

Hellenistic   Term that describes the cosmopolitan civilization, established under the Macedonians, that combined aspects of Greek and Middle Eastern cultures.

to Philip. Eubulus, a financial official and conservative political leader, advocated a cautious policy of cooperation with Philip. He hoped that Philip's aims would prove to be limited and pose no real threat to Athens. Isocrates (436–338 B.C.E.), the head of an important rhetorical school, urged the Athenians to embrace Philip with enthusiasm. Isocrates believed that by uniting the Greeks and leading them into a war with Persia, Philip could solve the economic, social, and political problems that had mired the Greek world in poverty and civil strife ever since the Peloponnesian War. He was opposed by Demosthenes (384–322 B.C.E.), one of the greatest orators in Greek history. Demosthenes claimed Philip was a great danger to Greece, and he persuaded Athens to join Thebes in a war with Macedon. In 338 B.C.E., a cavalry charge led by Philip's eighteen-year-old son Alexander turned the tide in Macedon's favor at the Battle of Chaeronea and made Philip master of Greece.

The Macedonian Government of Greece   The Macedonian settlement of Greek affairs was not as harsh as many had feared. Macedonian garrisons were stationed throughout Greece to guard against rebellions, and Athens was spared on condition that it fall in with Philip's plans. In 338 B.C.E., Philip called representatives of the Greek states to Corinth where he announced the formation of the League of Corinth. The constitution of the new federation promised its members autonomy in local affairs, freedom from tribute and military occupation, and aid in suppressing piracy and civil war. It enabled the Greeks to submit to Macedonian dominance without loss of face. Their defeat at Chaeronea, however, effectively signaled the end of the independence of the *poleis.*

Philip had a reason for choosing Corinth as the site for the formation of a new panhellenic league. About 150 years earlier, the Greeks had gathered at Corinth to plan their strategy for the Persian Wars, and it was at Corinth, in 337 B.C.E., that Philip announced a new Persian War. He promised the Greeks that they could reclaim their past glory by joining him in invading the Persian Empire. They gathered in Macedon in the spring of 336 B.C.E., but on the eve of the campaign, Philip was assassinated.

ALEXANDER THE GREAT

The Conquest of the Persian Empire   Alexander III (356–323 B.C.E.), "the Great," was only twenty when he ascended his father's throne, but he had no hesitancy about implementing Philip's plan for invading Persia. The Persian Empire had enormous resources, but it was not an impossible target. Great size and the diversity of its population made it hard to control, and its rulers struggled with uprisings on their far-flung frontiers and intrigues within their courts. Like Macedon, Persia also had a new, untried king. But unlike Alexander, Darius III had a navy that controlled the sea, a huge army, and endless wealth.

In 334 B.C.E., Alexander crossed the Hellespont into Asia with an army of only about 30,000 infantry and 5,000 cavalry. He had little money and few ships. He could not risk heading inland until he had neutralized the Persian navy at his back, but he needed a quick victory to bolster the loyalty of his men and to obtain loot with which to pay them. Memnon, the commander of the Persian navy, proposed a plan that probably would have defeated Alexander. He urged his countrymen to retreat, avoid pitched battles, and scorch the earth to deprive the Greek invaders of supplies. The Persians, however, rejected his advice and gave Alexander exactly what he needed.

The Persians confronted Alexander at the Granicus River on the coast of Asia Minor. Alexander led a cavalry charge across the river and into the teeth of the enemy. He nearly lost his life, but his courage inspired his men to win a victory that opened all of Asia Minor to conquest by the Greeks. (See Map 3–3.)

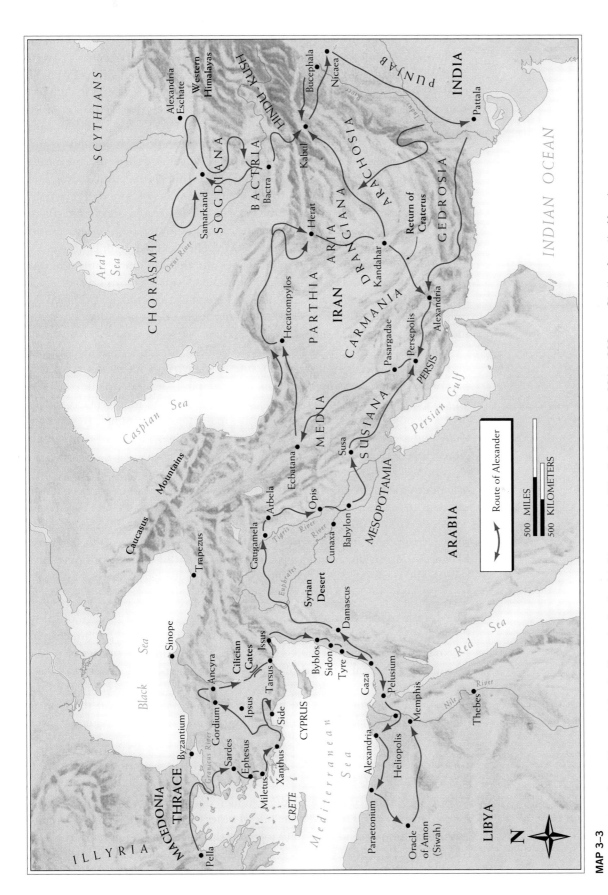

MAP 3–3

Alexander's Campaigns The route taken by Alexander the Great in his conquest of the Persian Empire, 334 to 323 B.C.E. Starting from the Macedonian capital at Pella, he reached the Indus Valley before being turned back by his own restive troops. He died of fever in Mesopotamia.

BEFORE CROSSING into Mesopotamia, what considerations determined Alexander's route? Was his aim merely to defeat the Persians?

In 333 B.C.E., Alexander crossed out of Asia Minor into Syria to meet the main Persian army and Darius. At Issus, Alexander led a cavalry charge that broke the Persian line, but instead of pursuing Darius as he retreated inland, Alexander continued south along the coast. He had to take all of Persia's ports to prevent the Persian navy from invading the Aegean and cutting him off from his homeland. When he arrived in Egypt, he was greeted as liberator and proclaimed pharaoh. Like all of Egypt's divine kings, he was declared a son of Re, the god who, as head of the Egyptian pantheon, the Greeks identified with Zeus.

In the spring of 331 B.C.E., Alexander marched into Mesopotamia to confront a huge army that Darius had amassed at Gaugamela (near the ancient Assyrian city of Nineveh). Once again the Persian line broke, and Darius fled. Alexander occupied Babylon, and in January 330 B.C.E., he entered Persepolis, the Persian capital. Acquisition of the Persian treasury ended Alexander's financial problems. The gold he showered on his troops put vast sums of money into circulation—an economic development whose effects were felt for centuries.

Alexander rested his men in Persepolis and then set out in pursuit of Darius. He failed to take the Persian king alive, however, for Darius's disillusioned men turned on him and killed him. Bessus, one of Darius's relatives, claimed the crown and retreated into the east. Alexander followed, routed what was left of the Persian army, and pushed on toward India.

Near Samarkand, in the land of the Scythians, Alexander founded Alexandria Eschate ("Farthest Alexandria"), one of many cities Alexander created as part of his plan for securing the future of his empire. Alexander planned to scatter Greeks throughout his new lands and encourage them to intermarry with its diverse peoples and accustom these people to the Greek way of life. To set an example, he took his first wife (a princess named Roxane, a native of a remote region called Bactria) and added 30,000 Persians to his army.

In 327 B.C.E., the Greeks crossed the Khyber Pass and entered the territory of modern Pakistan. Alexander forced Porus, its king, to submit, but by now it was clear to his men that the objectives of their campaign had changed. Alexander seemed intent on leading them literally to the ends of the earth, to the great river, Ocean, that Greek geographers believed encircled the world's landmass. Exhaustion drove them to mutiny and demand that he take them home for a rest. By the spring of 324 B.C.E., they were back in Babylon and celebrating, in true Macedonian style, with drunken sprees.

The Death of Alexander   By now Alexander had reached the age of thirty-three, and he was filled with plans for his future. In June 323 B.C.E., however, he succumbed to a fever and died. He immediately became the subject of myths, legends, romances, and historical controversies. Some people have seen him as a man of grand and noble vision who transcended Greek and Macedonian ethnocentrism and imagined a world in which everyone was united on the basis of their common humanity. Others have described him as a calculating despot, who was given to drunken brawls, brutality, and murder. The truth probably lies in some mixture of the two points of view.

THE SUCCESSORS

Nobody was prepared for Alexander's sudden death. He had no obvious successor, and it is doubtful that even he, one of history's greatest generals and administrative geniuses, could have held together the huge empire he had so quickly conquered. His nearest adult male relative, a weak-minded half brother, could not fill his shoes. Roxane, his queen, bore him a son soon after his death, but an infant heir could not preserve Alexander's legacy. The Macedonian generals, therefore, divided up responsibility for ruling the empire—allegedly, only until Alexander's son came of age. They were, however, soon at each other's throats, and in the battles that followed, all the members of the Macedonian royal house were eliminated. After the deaths of Roxane and her son in 310 B.C.E., the surviving generals declared themselves kings of the portions of the empire they ruled, and three major Macedonian dynasties emerged. Ptolemy I (ca. 367–283 B.C.E.) claimed Egypt and founded its thirty-first dynasty of pharaohs. (Egypt's famous queen Cleopatra, who died in 30 B.C.E., was the last of the Ptolemies.) The Seleucid dynasty established by Seleucus I (ca. 358–280 B.C.E.) ruled Mesopotamia and Syria, and Asia Minor and the Macedonian homeland passed to Antigonus I (382–301 B.C.E.) and his Antigonid dynasty.

For about seventy-five years after Alexander's death, the world economy expanded. The money that Alexander had loosed to circulate promoted economic activity, and the opening of huge new territories to Greek trade increased demand for Greek products and supplies of all kinds of goods. Hellenistic kings pursued enlightened economic policies that encouraged the growth of commerce. Emigration to the cities they founded eased problems of overpopulation on the Greek mainland and provided people with all kinds of opportunities.

The prosperity that resulted was not evenly distributed. Urban Greeks, Macedonians, and Hellenized natives—the upper and middle classes—lived comfortable, even luxurious, lives, while the standard of living for rural laborers declined. The independent small farmers who had built the early *poleis* disappeared. Arable land was consolidated into large plantations, and free farmers were reduced to the status of dependent peasants. During prosperous times their lot was bearable, but the costs of continuing wars and the effects of the inflation produced by the influx of Persian gold steadily eroded their position. Kings bore down heavily on the middle class, which shifted the burden to the peasants and the other laborers. These people responded by slowing their work and staging strikes. In parts of Greece, there were demands for the abolition of debt and the redistribution of land, and civil war returned.

Internal tensions and the strain of endemic warfare rendered the Hellenistic kingdoms vulnerable, and by the middle of the second century B.C.E., all of them, except for Egypt, had succumbed to conquest by the Italian city of Rome. Rome itself, however, was soon overtaken by the powerful new Greek civilization that had arisen in the wake of Alexander's conquests.

HELLENISTIC CULTURE

*A*lexander the Great's life marked a turning point in the history of Greek literature, philosophy, religion, and art. His empire and its successor kingdoms ended the role the *polis* had played in shaping Greek culture. Hellenistic cities were not free sovereign states but municipal towns submerged within great centrally managed empires.

As the freedoms characteristic of life in a *polis* faded, Greeks lost interest in politics. They abandoned public affairs and turned to the private practice of religion, philosophy, and magic for help in dealing with life's challenges. The confident humanism of the fifth century B.C.E. gave way to a kind of resignation to fate, a recognition of helplessness before forces too great for humans to comprehend.

HOW DID Hellenistic culture differ from the culture of Classical Greece?

One of the masterpieces of Hellenistic sculpture, the *Laocoön*. This is a Roman copy. According to legend, Laocoön was a priest who warned the Trojans not to take the Greeks' wooden horse within their city. This sculpture depicts his punishment. Great serpents sent by the goddess Athena, who was on the side of the Greeks, devoured Laocoön and his sons before the horrified people of Troy.

Musei Vaticani

PHILOSOPHY

Athens survived as the center of philosophical studies during the Hellenistic era. Plato's Academy and Aristotle's Lyceum continued to operate and were joined by the new schools of the Cynics, Epicureans, and Stoics.

The Lyceum drifted away from the scientific interests of its founder and turned to literary and historical studies. The Academy was even more radically transformed. Its critique of the weaknesses of all schools of thought led some of its members to embrace a philosophy called Skepticism—the doctrine that nothing could be truly known. Skeptics urged their students, in lieu of better options, to accept conventional morality and not to try to change the world.

Other followers of Socrates and Plato drew a more radical conclusion from the elusive nature of truth and the inevitability of human ignorance. Socrates had urged his students to behave ethically, but disdain the pursuit of wealth and power and prefer contemplation to an active political life. Diogenes of Sinope (ca. 400–325 B.C.E.), whom Plato described as Socrates gone mad, pushed the Socratic retreat from the world to an extreme. He dismissed the rules of civilized behavior as baseless conventions and insisted that happiness lay in giving in to nature's cruder impulses. He begged for his bread, wore rags, lived in a tub, performed intimate acts of personal hygiene in public, and ridiculed religious observances. Although the Cynics claimed to follow Socrates, they contradicted some of his core beliefs. Where Socrates had criticized but ultimately defended the *polis*, the Cynics abandoned it altogether. When Diogenes was asked about his citizenship, he answered he was *kosmopolites*, "a citizen of the world."

These views held little appeal for most of the middle-class city dwellers of the third century B.C.E. They wanted help in finding the kind of dignity and meaning that the duties of *polis* citizenship had given to the lives of their ancestors.

The Epicureans   Like many thinkers of his day, Epicurus of Athens (342–271 B.C.E.) doubted that human beings could obtain certain knowledge. Like the atomists, Democritus and Leucippus, he believed the world was nothing more than a swirl of physical particles continually falling through a void. Thought was only the stream of impressions these atoms left on human sense organs, and because atoms swerved in arbitrary, unpredictable ways, there was no such thing as a fixed, eternal truth. Philosophers, he argued, should abandon the pursuit of knowledge of the world and teach people how to cope with its reality. Epicurus believed that philosophy could free people from things like the fear of death by helping them understand that death was merely the dispersal of the atoms that compose the body and soul. Because nothing of themselves survived death to suffer pain, loss, or punishment, there was no reason to fear death. The proper pursuit of humankind, Epicurus argued, was pleasure—in the sense of *ataraxia*, a state of being undisturbed by any extreme feeling, either good or bad. The happiest people were those who withdrew from the world and eschewed the duties of family and public life. Epicurus's ideal was the genteel, disciplined selfishness of intellectual men of means. It was a dream not calculated to be widely attractive.

The Stoics   Soon after Epicurus began teaching in Athens, Zeno of Citium (335–263 B.C.E.) established the Stoic school (named for the *stoa poikile*, the Painted Portico in the Athenian marketplace where Zeno taught his disciples). Like the Epicureans, the Stoics sought the happiness of the individual, but Stoics, unlike Epicureans, believed happiness is to be found by embracing and not fleeing responsibility. Stoics claimed happiness is the sense of fulfillment that comes from living in harmony with nature. Nature, they argued, is governed by a divine *logos*, an eternal rational principle. Every human being has a spark of this divine "fire," which returns at death to its source. Contentment lies in realizing the essential rationality of existence and accepting one's place in the natural order. To live in accordance with natural law, however, a person has to understand which things in life are good and evil and which are morally "indifferent." Things such as prudence, justice, courage, and temperance are rational goods. Things such as folly, injustice, and cowardice are irrational evils. Some things— such as life, health, pleasure, beauty, strength, and wealth—are morally neutral. By themselves they do not produce either happiness or misery, but misery results if the soul, through attachment to them, suffers painful passion. The goal of life is *apatheia*, freedom from passion.

For the Stoics the world was a great *polis* in which all people were equally subject to the power of *logos*. The wise lived in accordance with this divine force and fatalistically accepted their places in the scheme of things. They dispassionately played out the roles they were assigned—be they kings or slaves. The Stoic way of life made sense to the subjects of well-ordered Hellenistic empires— societies that valued docile submission more highly than initiative and innovation.

Epicureans   People who believed the proper pursuit of humankind is undisturbed withdrawal from the world.

Stoics   People who sought freedom from passion and harmony with nature.

The Archimedes Palimpsest: A page from *On Floating Bodies.*

© Christie's images Inc.

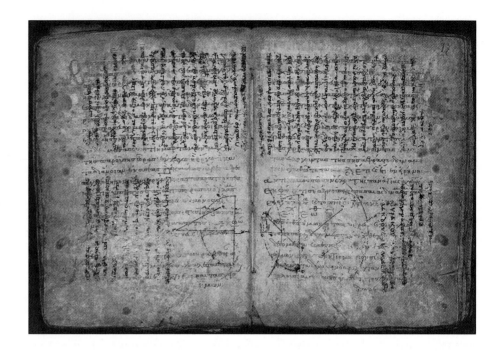

LITERATURE

Alexandria was the chief center of Hellenistic intellectual life in the third and second centuries B.C.E. Unlike the creative thinkers who participated in the government of the *poleis*, Alexandria's scholars were more preoccupied with the past than with current affairs. As subjects of great empires, they had little political influence. Alexandria owed its prominence to the "museum," a great research institute founded by the Ptolemies. Its library collected literature of all kinds and provided support for the specialists who edited and interpreted it. Much of their work was dry and petty, but they preserved the monuments of Classical literature.

ARCHITECTURE AND SCULPTURE

Hellenistic kings had great wealth and could afford to be lavish patrons of scholars, artists, and architects. They founded many cities and rebuilt old ones, usually on the efficient grid plan introduced in the fifth century B.C.E. by Hippodamus of Miletus. The famous artists who traveled the world, fulfilling royal commissions, created a kind of uniform international style. It abandoned the idealism that had been popular during the age of the *polis* in favor of a more emotional (sometimes sentimental) realism.

MATHEMATICS AND SCIENCE

Advances in mathematics and science were among the more original and significant achievements of the Hellenistic era. The scholars of Alexandria amassed the greater part of the scientific knowledge that was available to the West until the breakthroughs created by the scientific revolution of the sixteenth and seventeenth centuries C.E.

Euclid's *Elements* became the standard textbook for the study of plane and solid geometry in the third century B.C.E. and retained that post well into the modern era. Archimedes of Syracuse (ca. 287–212 B.C.E.) explained the principles of the lever in mechanics and invented hydrostatics. Heraclides of Pontus (ca. 390–310 B.C.E.) advanced a heliocentric theory of the universe that was fully developed by Aristarchus of Samos (ca. 310–230 B.C.E.). Unfortunately, however, because Hellenistic technology could not provide astronomical data to confirm their intuitions, their theories did not take hold. A geocentric model advanced by Hipparchus of Nicaea (born ca. 190 B.C.E.) and refined by a certain Ptolemy of Alexandria in the second century C.E. acquired currency and remained dominant until the work of Copernicus in the sixteenth century C.E. The scholars of the age knew the earth was round, and Eratosthenes of Cyrene (ca. 275–195 B.C.E.) calculated its circumference within about two hundred miles. His maps were more accurate than those available to Westerners during the Middle Ages.

SUMMARY

Aftermath of Victory The tenuous unity the Greeks had shown while fighting against the Persians disintegrated. Sparta and Athens emerged as leaders of two spheres of influence. Sparta was uninterested in continued aggression against Persia. The Athenians and the Ionians shared an interest in driving the Persians out of the Aegean region; with others, they formed the Delian League under Athenian leadership.

The First Peloponnesian War: Athens Against Sparta Pericles led a democratic, but aggressive Athens. The Peloponnesian Wars were the manifestation of the conflict between Sparta and Athens. After an initial victory, Athens seemed almost invincible, but soon military defeat abroad and rebellion at home weakened Athens so much that Sparta invaded. Pericles agreed to a 30-year peace, abandoning all Athenian possessions on the Greek mainland outside of Attica, but gaining Spartan recognition of the Athenian Empire.

Classical Greece Athenian government had become more democratic than any previous political system. All male citizens gained important rights, regardless of their property class. The official status of women was severely circumscribed, both in public and in private. Greek art, drama, and mythology suggest that women may have had more freedom and power than a strict reading of the documentary evidence would allow. Before around 500 B.C.E. there was little chattel slavery in Greece—although serfdom and bond slavery were more or less common in various times and places—but later war captives and other foreigners were held as chattel slaves. Slaves worked in agriculture, industry, and households, and served as shepherds, policemen, and secretaries. Most Athenians did not own any slaves, and those that did generally owned only a few.

The Great Peloponnesian War The Thirty Years' Peace of 445 B.C.E. lasted just over ten years, until a conflict between Corcyra and Corinth drew in their allies, Athens and Sparta, respectively. Sparta violated a clause of the peace that required arbitration of all disagreements between Athens and Sparta, and instead, in 431 B.C.E., invaded Attica. The outnumbered Athenians followed a daring strategy and won an important victory in 425 B.C.E. After a mix of victo-

IMAGE KEY
for pages 56–57.

a. Assortment of silver coins from ancient Greece
b. The Nike of Samothrace, goddess of victory.   Marble figure (190 B.C.E.) from Rhodos, Greece. Height 328 cm, MA 2369, Louvre, Dpt. des Antiquites Grecques/Romaines, Paris, France. Photograph © Erich Lessing/Art Resource, NY
c. The Archimedes Palimpsest
d. Ancient Greek Athenian coin
e. The Acropolis. This photograph shows the Parthenon and to its left the Erechtheum   Meredith Pillon/Greek National Tourism Organization
f. Aristotle (384-322 B.C.E.), Greek philosopher
g. Venus D'Milo statue
h. Battle between Alexander the Great and King Darius   House of the Faun, Pompeii VI 12, 2 Inv. 10020. Museo Archelogico Nazionale, Naples, Italy. Photograph © Erich Lessing/Art Resource, NY
i. Daily life on Greek Vases, woman spinning thread. Wine-jug, made in Athens, ca. 500-480 B.C.E. Copyright The British Museum
j. Bust of Pericles, Statesman of Greece   (495-429 BC) copy of a Greek original, Roman, 2nd century AD (marble). British Museum, London, UK/Index/ Bridgeman Art Library

ries and defeats, both sides signed the Peace of Nicias in 421 B.C.E. This peace, too, was short lived; this time the Athenians were the aggressors, against Sicily, in a disastrous 415 B.C.E. expedition that brought the Persians into the war on Sparta's side. The Athenians fought on, however, until 404 B.C.E., when they surrendered unconditionally.

Competition for Leadership in the Fourth Century B.C.E. After defeating Athens, Sparta had a golden opportunity to claim leadership, but Spartan arrogance—among other problems—caused their allies the Persians to turn against them. Theban victory at Leuctra in 371 B.C.E. brought an end to Spartan hegemony. But Theban dominance was short lived, ending in 362 B.C.E. in a defeat at the hands of the Athenians. Athens, however, repeated many of the same mistakes that had cost it allies in the Delian League, and by 355 B.C.E., Athens again had to abandon most of its empire. Greece descended into chaos.

The Culture of Classical Greece Classical Greece produced dramas, architecture and sculpture, and philosophical and historical works. The Golden Age of Athens, between the Persian and Peloponnesian wars, is epitomized by Attic tragedy, including the works of Aeschylus, Sophocles, and Euripedes. The buildings of the Acropolis are the product of Athenian religious and civic sensibility, and individual artistry and achievement. Philosophy continued to explore questions about the natural world. Herodotus and Thucydides wrote histories that are models of the genre. Sociopolitical changes brought about by the Peloponnesian War were reflected in drama and sculpture, especially in the philosophical traditions of Socrates, Plato, and Aristotle.

The Hellenistic World Greek culture mixed with Middle Eastern elements and spread throughout the eastern Mediterranean, Egypt, and far into Asia. This Hellenistic world was largely the result of military conquests by a short-lived, father-and-son Macedonian dynasty. Philip of Macedon introduced tactical innovations into the Macedonian army, and he coupled military force with diplomacy to conquer Greece. In 336 B.C.E., Philip was assassinated and succeeded by his son Alexander. Alexander lead his troops to victory in Persia, Egypt, Mesopotamia, and as far as what is now Pakistan. After his death, three of Alexander's generals founded significant dynasties that helped spread Hellenism in Egypt, Mesopotamia, and Asia Minor. Within Greece, class conflict and other internal divisions were exacerbated by the new wealth Alexander's conquests had brought to the region.

Hellenistic Culture The true *polis* was destroyed by the Macedonian invasion. Greeks turned from the political to the personal. In Athenian philosophy, the Epicureans (whose goal was hedonistic human happiness) and Stoics (who sought happiness through harmony and freedom from passion) gained prominence. Hellenistic Alexandria fostered literature and humanistic scholarship. Hellenistic styles in architecture and sculpture diffused over a wide area. Mathematics and science—especially astronomy—blossomed.

REVIEW QUESTIONS

1. What caused the Great Peloponnesian War? What strategies did Athens and Sparta hope would bring them victory? Why did Sparta win?

2. What were the tensions that characterized Greek life in the Classical Period, and how were they reflected in its art, literature, and philosophy? How does Hellenistic art differ from art of the Classical Period?

3. How and why did Philip II conquer Greece? Why was Athens unable to stop him? Was his success due to Macedon's strength or to the weaknesses of the Greek city-states?

4. What were the consequences of Alexander the Great's early death? What were his lasting achievements? Did he consciously promote Greek civilization, or was he only an egomaniac devoted to endless conquest?

5. What were the most significant elements that made up Hellenistic civilization and culture?

KEY TERMS

Academy   (p. 73)   **Hellenistic**   (p. 75)   **Peloponnesian Wars**   (p. 59)
Delian League   (p. 58)   **Lyceum**   (p. 74)   **Stoics**   (p. 81)
Epicureans   (p. 81)

 For additional study resources for this chapter, go to:
www.prenhall.com/kagan3/chapter3

Visualizing The Past...

Goddesses and the Female Form in Ancient Art

ANCIENT ARTISTS created images of women as often as men in their art, but there were key differences in how they depicted the female versus the male form. What were these differences, why did they come about, and what did they signify?

Artists celebrated gods and human men alike for their roles in society, as priests, warriors, or commoners. By contrast, from ancient times to the present, sexuality has been central to artistic conceptualizations of women and the female role in the divine and human realms. Earthly women and goddesses alike were usually drawn or sculpted nude, at least from the waist up, and, given the link between female sexuality and fertility, with breasts and hips prominent or even exaggerated. Goddesses in the ancient world tended to have a dual nature, of death and regeneration, and to be linked to symbols of earth, love, death, and war, and often also to mastery of snakes, a prominent symbol in many cultures of male fertility.

Innana-Ishtar, ca. 2025–1763 B.C.E., Babylonian goddess of love and death.
Innana-Ishtar has a lovely feminine form but talons instead of feet, denoting her dual nature. She bears the tail of her symbol, the lion, and has the wings of an owl, symbol of her mastery over death. Her helmet signifies her martial and ruling power. Like many female goddesses, she is an ambiguous figure whose female form is linked both to sexual desire and to death.

H. Lewandowski/Art Resource, NY ©Reunion des Musees Nationaux/Art Resource, NY

"Snake Goddess," Minoan, ca. 1650 B.C.E.
Strong cultural and economic ties linked Mediter-
ranean and Near Eastern cultures, as can be seen
in the similarities between this small statuette of a
Minoan goddess and the preceding image of
Innana-Ishtar. As was typical in Minoan and Greek
art, this goddess is nude only from the waist up.
Like Innana-Ishtar, however, her arms are raised
and she holds symbols of power, in this case snakes.
Photograph © Erich Lessing/Art Resource, NY

Coatlicue, Aztec mother goddess. ▶
Although she was a goddess
from the New World, and
depicted in a radically different
artistic tradition, Coatlicue, the
"goddess of the serpent skirt,"
shares with goddesses of
the Old World an emphasis on
mastery of male sexual power (her
serpent skirt), fertility and
motherhood (she was the
mother of the powerful Aztec
god Huitzilopochtli), and death
(she craved human sacrifices).
Mexican National Tourist Council

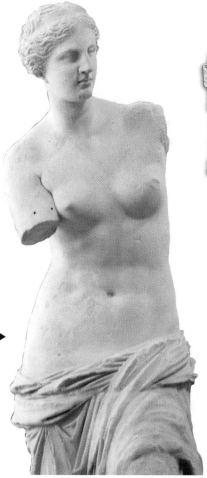

Venus D'Milo, statue, marble, 120–130 B.C.E. ▶
In this statue of Venus (Greek name: Aphrodite), the Roman goddess of love,
we again see the female figure nude to the waist and sexualized. Unlike the more
"masculine" Minerva (Greek name: Athena), goddess of wisdom born from the head
of the male god Jupiter (Greek name: Zeus), who was usually sculpted clothed
and helmeted, Venus personified love and sensuality. Like her counterparts
elsewhere in the world, she was also associated with strife and death, as her lover
was Mars (Greek name: Ares), god of war.
John Serafin/SBG.

4 Rome: From Republic to Empire

CHAPTER HIGHLIGHTS

Prehistoric Italy Bands of warring peoples speaking Italic languages invaded from across the Adriatic and along the northeastern coast starting around 1000 B.C.E. Their superior tools and craftsmanship helped them gain a dominant position in the lands they invaded.

The Etruscans Etruscan civilization emerged in Etruria around 800 B.C.E. Etruscan power peaked around 500 B.C.E. and declined rapidly under attack by the Gauls about 400 B.C.E.

Royal Rome During the sixth century B.C.E., under Etruscan rule, Rome developed political institutions that would endure for many centuries. The family was the center of Roman life. The two classes in royal Rome were the *patricians* and *plebeians*.

The Republic In 509 B.C.E., noble families revolted against the monarchy and created the Roman Republic. Plebeians chafed against the limits on their political participation, leading to the Struggle of the Orders. By the middle of the third century B.C.E., Rome controlled Italy. The Punic and Macedonian Wars contributed to Roman domination of the Mediterranean.

Civilization in the Early Roman Republic Greek thought and culture came to play an important role in Roman civilization. As Rome's conquests continued, slavery increased dramatically, leading to social, economic, and political problems.

Roman Imperialism: The Late Republic War, expansion, and the administration of the empire fundamentally altered Roman culture. Populist movements led by the Gracchi ended with their assassinations. Two ambitious generals, Marius and Sulla, competed for domination of the Republic.

The Fall of the Republic Crassus, Pompey, and Caesar formed the First Triumvirate to further their own private goals. Caesar's assassination led to civil war, ending with the defeat of his assassins and the ascendancy of Octavian.

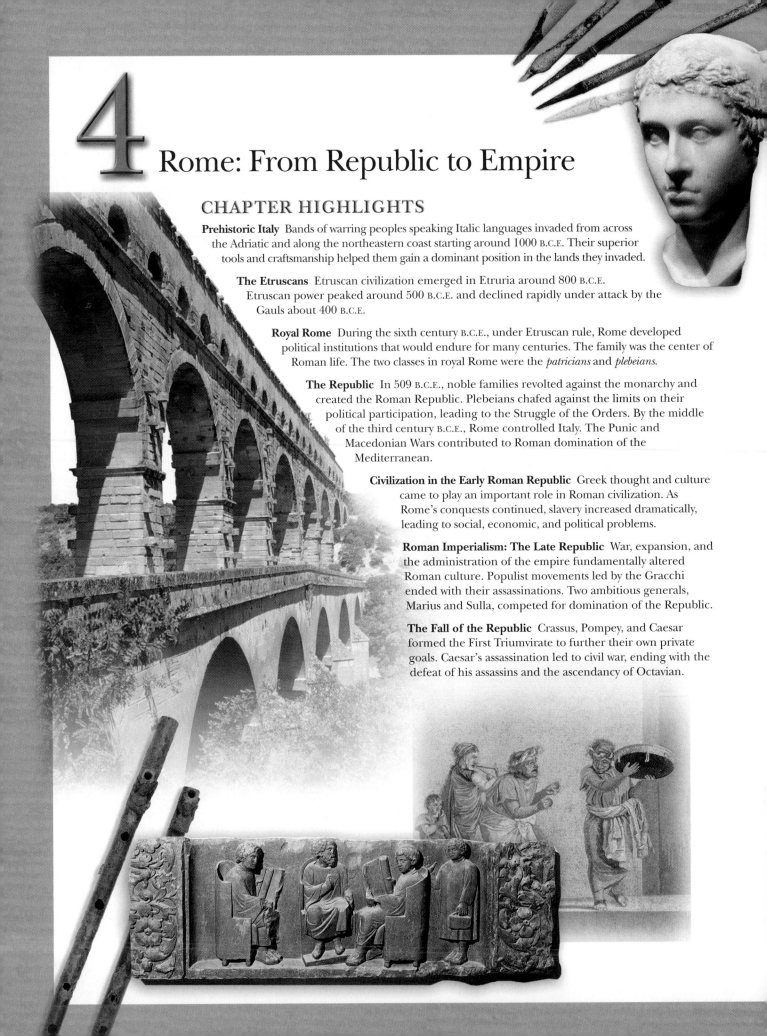

CHAPTER QUESTIONS

WHO WERE the Etruscans and how did they influence Rome?

WHAT ROLE did government, family, and women play in ancient Rome?

WHAT ROLE did consuls, the Senate, and the Assembly play in ancient Rome?

HOW DID contact with the Hellenistic world affect Rome?

HOW DID the expansion of Rome change the Republic?

WHAT EVENTS led to the fall of the Republic?

IMAGE KEY
for pages 88–89 is on page 111.

The Romans started with a small village in central Italy and went on to unite the peoples of the Western world and sustain the longest period of peace in Western history. By adapting Hellenistic culture and spreading it through their empire, they laid a universal Graeco-Roman foundation for Western civilization. The effects of their achievement are still being felt.

PREHISTORIC ITALY

Italy's cultural evolution began slowly. The Paleolithic era lingered in Italy until 2500 B.C.E., and Italy did not feel the effects of the Bronze Age until 1500 B.C.E. About 1000 B.C.E., the Umbrians, Sabines, Samnites, and Latins—immigrants from the east whose *Italic* languages gave the peninsula its name—pioneered Italy's Iron Age. By 800 B.C.E., they had occupied the highland pastures of the Apennines (the mountain range that runs the length of Italy) and had begun to challenge earlier settlers for control of the western coastal plains.

THE ETRUSCANS

WHO WERE the Etruscans and how did they influence Rome?

bout 800 B.C.E., a mysterious people whose language was not Italic appeared in Etruria (modern Tuscany) on a plain west of the Apennines between the Arno and Tiber Rivers. Although the origin of these "Etruscans" is unknown, aspects of their civilization suggest connections with Asia Minor and the Middle East.

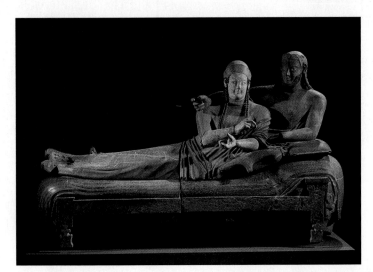

Much of what we know of the Etruscans comes from their funery art. This sculpture of an Etruscan couple is part of a sarcophagus.

Sarcophagus of a Couple. Etruscan, 6th BCE. Terracotta. H: 114 cm. Louvre, Paris, France. © Erich Lessing/Art Resource, NY

DOMINION

Etruscan communities were independent, self-governing city-states loosely linked in a religious confederation. Early monarchies were replaced in most cities by aristocratic councils and annually elected magistrates. The Etruscans were a militarized ruling class that subjugated various Italic peoples and took to the sea as traders and pirates. They competed successfully with the other maritime powers of the western Mediterranean, the Carthaginians of North Africa and Italy's Greek colonists.

During the seventh and sixth centuries B.C.E., Etruscan domination spread from Tuscany north to Italy's Po Valley, overseas to the islands of Corsica and Elba, and south into **Latium** (a region that included the small town of Rome) and Campania (a plain the Greeks of Naples colonized). The expansion of Etruscan influence was the work of independent warrior-chieftains whose unwillingness to work together constituted a fatal weakness. By 400 B.C.E., Celts from **Gaul** (modern France) had driven the Etruscans from the Po Valley, an area the Romans later called Cisalpine Gaul ("Gaul-this-side-of-the-Alps"), and the cities of Etruria gradually lost their independence. Etruscan ceased to be a living tongue, but Etruscan culture was not forgotten. It had a profound effect on Rome.

CULTURAL INFLUENCES

Roman religion bore the stamp of powerful Etruscan influences. The Romans, like the Etruscans, believed that innumerable supernatural beings had the power to intervene in human affairs, and the Romans assumed human survival depended on understanding and placating these spirits—many of whom were evil.

Latium   Region located in present-day Italy that included the small town of Rome.

Gaul   Area that is now modern France.

To divine the wills of the mysterious forces that surrounded them, the Romans relied on Etruscan methods for interpreting omens.

A major contrast between Greek and Roman society was the greater freedom that Roman women enjoyed, and this, too, was probably a result of Etruscan influences. Greek women were expected to be virtually invisible. They were confined to their homes and given little education. Etruscan women, however, appeared in public and many could read and write. They witnessed and took part in athletic contests. They joined their husbands and other males as guests at banquets. A common subject in Etruscan art is a representation of a husband and wife reclining together on a dining couch, a pose that implies a loving relationship. Etruscan tomb inscriptions also suggest that women had significant status, for they often mention the mother as well as the father of the deceased.

ROYAL ROME

Rome evolved from a collection of villages established by Latins and others on the southern bank of the Tiber River in the mid-eighth century B.C.E. It was fifteen miles inland from the sea at the point where the Tiber emerges from the foothills of the Apennines. Many trails converged here, for just southwest of Rome's Capitoline Hill an island made it fairly easy to cross the Tiber. Rome was well situated to become the center for Italy's inland communication and trade. (See Map 4–1.)

GOVERNMENT

Rome's potential did not begin to be realized until the sixth century B.C.E., when Etruscan kings established themselves in Rome and subdued most of Latium. Although one family monopolized the royal office, Roman kingship was technically elective. The Roman Senate, an aristocratic council, had to approve a candidate for the throne, and only the assembly of the Roman people could bestow on him his unique power—the *imperium*, the right to enforce commands by fines, arrests, and corporal and capital punishment. The king was Rome's chief priest, high judge, and supreme military leader.

According to legend, Rome's Senate originated when Romulus, Rome's founder, chose one hundred of Rome's leading men to advise him. The early Senate had no formal executive or legislative authority. It met only when the king convened it to ask for advice. In practice, however, the Senate was very influential. It was composed of the most powerful men in the state, men a king could not safely ignore.

The curiate assembly, an organization to which all citizens belonged, was the third organ of government. It met only when summoned by the king, and he set its

imperium   Right held by a Roman king to enforce commands by fines, arrests, and corporal and capital punishment.

WHAT ROLE did government, family, and women play in ancient Rome?

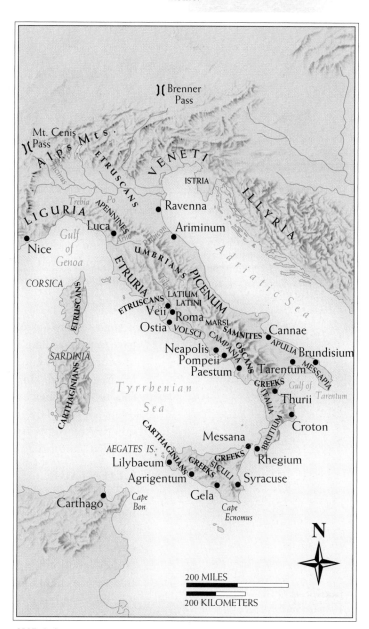

MAP 4–1
Ancient Italy   This map of ancient Italy and its neighbors before the expansion of Rome shows major cities and towns as well as several geographical regions and the locations of some of the Italic and non-Italic Peoples.

WHY, GEOGRAPHICALLY, was Rome ideal to become the center for Italy's inland communication and trade?

Busts of a Roman couple, from the period of the Republic. Although some have identified the individuals as Cato the Younger and his daughter Porcia, no solid evidence confirms this claim.

Bust of Cato and Porcia. Roman sculpture. Vatican Museums, Vatican State. Photograph ©Scala/ Art Resources, NY

agenda and decided who could address it. Its job was to hear and ratify the king's decrees. Romans voted, not as individuals, but as members of groups. Citizens were registered in thirty *curiae*, and each *curia* had a single vote that was cast according to the will of its majority.

THE FAMILY

Family organizations were the basic units of Roman society. The head of a family was its "king" in the sense that he held *imperium* over all its members. Like the king who presided over the state cult, a father supervised his family's religious rites. Like the king, he had the power to execute his dependents or sell them into slavery—even his adult sons. The male head of a household had less authority over his wife, for she was protected by her birth family. A husband could not divorce his wife unless she was convicted of serious offenses by a court of her male blood relatives. A Roman wife had authority as the administrator of her husband's household. She controlled access to its storerooms, kept its accounts, supervised its slaves, and reared its children. She was also a respected adviser to her husband on all matters affecting her family.

WOMEN

Roman society was male dominated and hierarchical. All adult women had to have male guardians to handle their legal affairs. Women could own and dispose of property and enter into contracts but only with the aid of these guardians. Marriages of two kinds transferred a woman from the *manus* ("hand") of her father to that of her husband. A third kind of marriage left a bride under her father's *manus*. This gave her more freedom from her husband and more inheritance rights from her father. To preserve the arrangement, she had to spend at least three consecutive nights a year outside her husband's home.

CLIENTAGE

The head of a wealthy family could extend its influence by providing patronage to dependents called clients. Roman clientage was a formal, legally recognized institution. A patron provided a client with physical and legal protection and economic assistance. A client might receive a grant of land, become a tenant farmer, labor on his patron's estates, or simply subsist on daily handouts of food. In return, a client fought for his patron, voted as his patron ordered, and did any jobs requested of him. Even members of the upper classes, when it served their ambitions, became clients of families whose political connections could further their careers.

PATRICIANS AND PLEBEIANS

From the start of Rome's history, Roman families were divided into two hereditary classes. The **patricians**, the upper class, originally monopolized all political authority. Only they could serve as priests, senators, and magistrates. The **plebeians**, the commoner class, may have sprung from families of small farmers,

patricians Upper class of Roman families that originally monopolized all political authority. Only they could serve as priests, senators, and magistrates.

plebeians Commoner class of Roman families, usually families of small farmers, laborers, and artisans who were early clients of the patricians.

laborers, and artisans who were early clients of the patricians. Wealth alone did not define the classes. Some plebeians were rich, and incompetence and bad luck sometimes impoverished patricians.

THE REPUBLIC

According to Roman tradition, in 509 B.C.E., an atrocity committed by a king's son sparked a revolt that drove the last Etruscan ruler from the city. The patricians then decided not to appoint another king but to establish a republic.

CONSTITUTION

The Consuls   The Roman Republic had an unwritten constitution that enshrined conservative traditions. In the beginning, it simply transferred the duties and trappings of monarchy to elected magistrates. Two patricians were annually chosen as **consuls** and vested with *imperium*. Like the former kings, they led the army, oversaw the state religion, and sat as judges. They even used the traditional symbols of royalty—purple robes, ivory chairs, and *lictors* (guards who accompanied them bearing *fasces*, bundles of rods wrapped around an axe to signify the power to discipline and execute). A consul was, however, not a king, for he held office for only a year and had an equal, a colleague who could prevent him from taking independent action. Consular *imperium* was also limited. Consuls could execute citizens who were serving with the army outside the city, but in Rome citizens had the right to appeal all cases involving capital punishment to the popular assembly.

The checks on the consular office discouraged initiative, swift action, and change. This was what a conservative, aristocratic republic wanted. But because a divided command could create serious problems for an army in the field, the Romans usually sent only one consul into battle or assigned consuls sole command on alternate days. If this did not work, the consuls could, with the advice of the Senate, step aside to clear the way for the appointment of a *dictator*. A dictator's term of office was limited to six months, but his *imperium* was valid everywhere and unlimited by any right of appeal.

These devices worked well enough for a small city-state whose wars were short skirmishes fought near home. But as Rome's wars grew longer and were fought farther afield, adjustments had to be made. In 325 B.C.E., it was decided to create **proconsulships** to extend the terms of consuls who had important work to

WHAT ROLE did consuls, the Senate, and the Assembly play in ancient Rome?

consuls   Elected magistrates from patrician families chosen annually to lead the army, oversee the state religion, and sit as judges.

proconsulships   Extension of terms for consuls who had important work to finish.

Lictors were attendants of the Roman magistrates who held the power of *imperium*, the right to command. In republican times these magistrates were the consuls, praetors, and proconsuls. The lictors were men from the lower classes—some were even former slaves. They constantly attended the magistrates when the latter appeared in public. The lictors cleared a magistrate's way in crowds, and summoned, arrested, and punished offenders for him. They also served as their magistrate's house guard.

Alinari Art Resource, NY

censors Men of unimpeachable reputation, chosen to carry the responsibility for enrolling, keeping track of, and determining the status and tax liability of each citizen.

tribunes Officials elected by the plebeian tribal assembly given the power to protect plebeians from abuse by patrician magistrates.

finish. This maintained continuity of command during a long war, but it created a way for a man to perpetuate himself in power.

Consuls were assisted by financial officers called *quaestors*, and a need for more military commanders led to the introduction of other aides called *praetors*. A *praetor*'s primary function was judicial, but he could also be granted a general's *imperium* and have his term of service in the field extended beyond a year. In the second half of the fifth century B.C.E., the consuls' responsibility for enrolling and keeping track of citizens was delegated to new officials, two **censors**. Because they determined the status and the tax liability of each citizen, they had to be men of unimpeachable reputation. They were usually senior senators who viewed the office as the pinnacle of their careers. By the fourth century B.C.E., censors had the right to expel from the Senate members whose conduct disgraced senatorial dignity.

The Senate and the Assembly The Senate was the only deliberative body continuously in session in the Roman Republic. Senators were prominent patricians, often leaders of clans and patrons with many clients. The Senate controlled the state's finances and foreign policy, and its advice was not lightly ignored by magistrates or the popular assemblies.

The *centuriate assembly*—the name for the Roman army when it was convened to deliberate rather than fight—was the early republic's most important popular assembly. It elected the consuls and several other magistrates, voted on bills the Senate put before it, made decisions of war and peace, and served as a court of appeal for citizens convicted of serious offenses. The centuriate assembly took its name from the *centuries*, the companies (theoretically of one hundred men) in which Roman men enrolled in the army and through which they voted. Because each soldier provided his own equipment, he was assigned to a century according to the kind of weapons and armor he could afford to buy. Each century cast a single vote, and votes were tallied beginning with the centuries that had the most expensive equipment, those of the cavalry and the first class of the infantry.

The Struggle of the Orders Plebeians were barred from all political and religious offices in the early days of the republic. They could not serve as judges. They did not even know the law, for the law was an oral tradition passed down in patrician families. Whenever Rome conquered new land, patrician leaders were often able to claim it for themselves. They dominated the assemblies and the Senate, and they preserved their privileges by refusing to marry outside their caste. This was deeply resented by wealthy plebeian families.

Tensions between patricians and plebeians fueled the "struggle of the orders," a fight for political, legal, and social equality that lasted for two hundred years. Plebeians had a strong position from which to negotiate, for plebeians made up a large part of the republic's army. When danger threatened, they simply withdrew from the city and refused to fight until the patricians granted them concessions.

The plebeians made progress one step at a time. They formed a political organization of their own, the plebeian *tribal assembly*, and elected **tribunes**, officials with the power to protect plebeians from abuse by patrician magistrates. Tribunes could veto any action of a magistrate or any bill in a Roman assembly or the Senate. To protect their rights, the plebeians also demanded that Rome's laws be fixed and published. In 450 B.C.E., the Twelve Tables, which codified Rome's harsh methods of enforcing justice, appeared. In 445 B.C.E., plebeians won the right to marry patricians, but they were still barred from some public offices. The consulship remained closed to plebeians until 367 B.C.E., but gradually all offices—even the dictatorship, the censorship, and the priesthoods—were opened to them. In 287 B.C.E., the plebeians completed their triumph by securing passage of a law that made decisions of the plebeian tribal assembly binding on all Romans.

The struggle of the orders did not turn Rome into a democracy. It simply cleared the way for wealthy plebeian families to enter politics and share the privileges of the patrician aristocracy. The *nobiles*, a small group of rich and powerful families of both patrician and plebeian rank, dominated Rome. Because there was no secret ballot, the numerous clients of the wealthy *nobiles* could easily be intimidated into voting as their patrons ordered. This created a way for the great families to build political machines that maintained their holds on the republic's offices. From 233 to 133 B.C.E., twenty-six families produced 80 percent of the consuls, and ten of those families accounted for almost 50 percent of the successful candidates. Because the politically dominant families were all represented in the Senate, the Senate became the republic's chief deliberative body. The product of the struggle of the orders was, therefore, a republican constitution that empowered a senatorial aristocracy. Most Romans accepted it, for it led Rome well in the wars that won Rome an empire.

THE CONQUEST OF ITALY

Not long after the birth of the republic in 509 B.C.E., a coalition of Romans, Latins, and Greeks defeated the Etruscans and drove them out of Latium. Rome's neighbor, the Etruscan city of Veii, continued to be a problem, but in 392 B.C.E., Rome destroyed Veii and doubled its size by annexing Veii's territory.

The Romans preferred to use inducements and threats to come to terms with their foes—to turn enemies into allies who then joined Rome's army. When land was conquered, it was sometimes redistributed to the Roman poor so they could afford to equip themselves for military service. This gave the poor a stake in the republic's success and helped reconcile them to its aristocratic regime. The poor were also pleased when the long campaign that was needed to subdue Etruscan Veii forced the Romans to begin paying men for military service. Without such assistance, the soldiers, many of whom were self-supporting farmers, could not have stayed in the field.

Gallic Invasion of Italy and Roman Reaction   Rome was not always victorious. In 387 B.C.E., Gauls marched south from the Po Valley, routed the Roman army, and burned the city. The Romans fled their homeland and had to pay the Gauls a ransom to get it back. They quickly recovered from this humiliation, but in 340 B.C.E., Rome's neighbors formed the Latin League, an alliance dedicated to resisting Roman dominance. In 338 B.C.E., Rome defeated the league and offered the Latins terms that set precedents leading to the unification of Italy.

Roman Policy Toward the Conquered   The Romans did not destroy any of the Latin cities. Some were given Roman citizenship. Others were granted municipal privileges: the right to govern themselves, to intermarry and trade with Romans, and to move to Rome and apply for citizenship. The treaties by which other states became allies of Rome differed from city to city. Some were given Latin rights of intermarriage and commerce with Romans; some were not. Land was taken from some but not from others. Allies did not pay taxes to Rome,

QUICK REVIEW

Roman Italy

• 392 B.C.E.: Rome destroys Veii and seizes its territory

• Rome tried to build constructive relationships with conquered Italian cities

• Colonies of veteran soldiers established on annexed land

but they supplied troops to serve in Rome's army under Roman officers, and they were forbidden to make private agreements among themselves.

The Romans planted colonies of veteran soldiers on some of the land they annexed. These men staffed a permanent garrison that deterred rebellion. A network of military roads began to be built to link the colonies with Rome. This enabled a Roman army swiftly to reinforce any colony that faced an uprising.

The Roman settlement of Latium illustrates the strategies that resulted in Roman dominance of Italy. The Romans employed both diplomacy and force to divide their opponents. They cultivated a reputation for rapid and harsh punishment of their enemies, but they were also generous to those who submitted. Loyal allies could improve their prospects and even achieve Roman citizenship. Rome's allies saw themselves as colleagues more than subjects, and most of them remained loyal to Rome even when put to severe tests.

Defeat of the Samnites   After Rome settled its difficulties with the Latins, it faced a series of wars with the tough mountain people of the southern Apennines, the Samnites. Some of Rome's allies defected to the Samnites, and the Samnites were also aided by various Etruscans and Gauls. But most of the allies remained loyal, and by 280 B.C.E., Rome had subdued the Samnites and won mastery of central Italy.

At this point, Rome's expanding territory brought it into direct contact with the Greek cities of southern Italy, and Rome's intervention in a quarrel between two of these cities led to a war with a Greek mercenary, Pyrrhus, king of Epirus. Pyrrhus, who was probably the best general of the day, defeated the Romans on several occasions but suffered so many casualties that he decided he could not afford to continue his campaign. Having won victories that were not worth their cost (what are now called "Pyrrhic victories"), he withdrew from Italy and left his Greek employers no choice but to join the Roman confederation. By 265 B.C.E., Rome dominated all of Italy south of the Po River, an area of 47,200 square miles, and its defeat of Pyrrhus had brought it recognition as a major power in the Hellenistic world.

Rome became a naval power late in its history, to defeat Carthage in the First Punic War (264–241 B.C.E.). This sculpture in low relief shows a Roman ship, propelled by oars, with both ram and soldiers, ready for either to ram or board an enemy.

A Roman warship. Direzione Generale Musei Vaticani

ROME AND CARTHAGE

Late in the ninth century B.C.E., the Phoenician city of Tyre had planted a colony called Carthage ("New City") on the coast of northern Africa near modern Tunis. In the sixth century B.C.E., the conquest of Tyre by the Assyrians freed the Carthaginians to build an empire of their own. Carthage had a superb harbor and rich lands worked by slave labor.

During the sixth century B.C.E., Carthage's domain expanded west along the coast of North Africa past Gibraltar and east into Libya. Parts of southern Spain, Sardinia, Corsica, Malta, the Balearic Islands, and western Sicily also came under Carthaginian control. The inhabitants of these lands paid tribute to

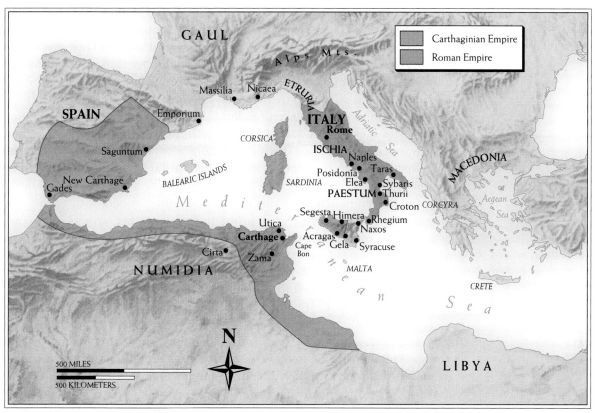

MAP 4–2

The Western Mediterranean Area During the Rise of Rome   This map illustrates the theater of conflict between the growing Roman dominions and those of Carthage in the third century B.C.E. The Carthaginian Empire stretched westward from the city (in modern Tunisia) along the North African coast and into southern Spain.

WHAT ECONOMIC and political effects did the Punic Wars have on Rome?

Carthage and were enlisted in the Carthaginian army and navy. Carthage claimed exclusive rights to trade in the western Mediterranean and warned other maritime powers to stay out of its waters. (See Map 4–2.)

Rome and Carthage became entangled when Hiero, tyrant of Syracuse, attacked the Sicilian city of Messana, a strategically important port that commanded the straits between Italy and Sicily. A band of Italian mercenaries, the Mamertines ("Sons of Mars"), had seized the city, and Hiero wanted to evict them. The Mamertines asked Carthage for help in fending him off, and Carthage agreed. But the Mamertines then tried to check Carthage by also inviting the Romans to send them aid. Rome realized that if it did not intervene, it was ceding control of the straits and possibly of Sicily to Carthage. Consequently, in 264 B.C.E., the assembly voted to send an army to Messana, a decision that led to three Punic Wars—conflicts that take their name from the Latin term for Carthaginian, *Puni* ("Phoenician").

The First Punic War (264–241 B.C.E.)   The Romans made no progress against Carthage until they built a fleet to blockade the Carthaginian ports at the western end of Sicily. Finally, in 241 B.C.E., the strain of what had become a war of attrition induced Carthage to capitulate. It surrendered Sicily and the islands between Italy and Sicily to Rome and agreed to pay a war indemnity. In 238 B.C.E., while Carthage

QUICK REVIEW

Path to War
- Carthage's power expanded throughout western Mediterranean in sixth century B.C.E.
- Carthage claimed exclusive rights to trade in the Mediterranean
- Conflict over Sicilian city of Messana sparked war

struggled to put down a revolt of mercenary soldiers whom it had failed to pay, Rome seized Sardinia and Corsica and demanded an additional indemnity. This was a provocative action that was to cost Rome a second war with Carthage.

It is hard to understand why Rome sought more territory, for the administration of lands outside of Italy created serious problems. Because the Romans did not feel it was possible to treat distant foreigners like they had treated their neighbors in Italy, they turned Sicily, Sardinia, and Corsica into the first provinces of a Roman empire. Provinces were held by occupying armies and ruled by military governors. This was an arrangement open to horrific abuse, for Rome made no arrangements to oversee the conduct of the men who ran its provinces. Provincials were neither Roman citizens nor allies; they were subjects who paid tribute in lieu of serving in the army. Rome collected this tribute by selling the right to gather money in the provinces to "tax farmers," entrepreneurs who were free to take as much as they could get from the defenseless provincials. Provincial governments promoted corruption that undermined the machinery of the Roman Republic.

While Rome struggled to adjust to its new situation, Hamilcar Barca, the Carthaginian governor of Spain (237–229 B.C.E.), put Carthage on the road to recovery. His plan was to develop Spain to make up for the lands Carthage had lost to Rome. Hasdrubal, Hamilcar's son-in-law and successor, continued his policies with such success that the Romans were alarmed. They responded by imposing a treaty that obligated Carthage not to expand north of Spain's Ebro River. Hasdrubal doubtless assumed that if Carthage accepted the Ebro as its northern frontier, Rome would grant Carthage a free hand in the south. He was wrong. Within a few years the Romans had violated the Ebro treaty (at least in spirit) by allying with Saguntum, a town one hundred miles south of the Ebro.

The Second Punic War (218–202 B.C.E.)   Hasdrubal was assassinated in 221 B.C.E., and the army chose Hannibal, the twenty-five-year-old son of Hamilcar Barca, to succeed him. Hannibal quickly consolidated his hold on Spain but avoided taking any action against Saguntum. However, when the Saguntines, encouraged by Rome's protection, began to stir up trouble for him, Hannibal captured the town. Rome then sent Carthage an ultimatum demanding Hannibal's surrender. Carthage refused, and Rome declared war (218 B.C.E.).

Although Rome had repeatedly provoked Carthage, it had taken no steps to prevent Carthage from rebuilding its empire and made no plans to defend itself against a Punic attack. Hannibal exacted a high price for these blunders. Rome expected to be able to fight Carthage on Carthaginian territory, but in the fall of 218 B.C.E., Hannibal crossed the Alps into Italy with an army the Gauls were eager to join. The Romans suffered the first of the many defeats he was to give them at the Ticinus River in the Po Valley. Not long thereafter he crushed the joint consular armies at the Trebia River, and in 217 B.C.E., he outmaneuvered and trapped another Roman army at Lake Trasimene. To take Rome, however, he had to persuade its allies to abandon it, and this most refused to do.

Sobered by their defeats, the Romans suspended consular government and chose a dictator, Quintus Fabius Maximus. Because time and supplies were on Rome's side, his plan was to avoid pitched battles and wear Hannibal's army down by harassing its flanks. In 216 B.C.E., Hannibal tempted the Romans to abandon this strategy by attacking a grain depot at Cannae in Apulia. They took the bait, met him on the field, and suffered the worst defeat in their history. Eighty thousand Roman soldiers were killed.

The disaster at Cannae shattered Rome's prestige, and many of the allies in southern Italy and the crucial port of Syracuse in Sicily went over to Hannibal. For the next decade, no Roman army dared confront Hannibal directly. Hannibal, however, had neither the numbers nor the supplies needed to besiege and starve walled cities into submission, and he did not have the equipment to storm them. So long as the Romans refused to fight, therefore, he could do little to bring the war to an end.

The Roman strategy for defeating Hannibal involved opening fronts outside of Italy. Publius Cornelius Scipio (237–183 B.C.E.), whose Carthaginian victories earned him the title "Africanus," undertook to conquer Spain to deprive Hannibal of reinforcements from that quarter. Scipio was not yet twenty-five, but he was almost as talented a general as Hannibal. Within a few years he had taken Spain and won the Senate's permission to invade Africa. In 204 B.C.E., Scipio bested the Carthaginian army in Africa, and this forced the city to order Hannibal to withdraw from Italy and come to the defense of his homeland. Hannibal had won every battle, but he had lost the war. His fatal error was to underestimate the determination of Rome and the loyalty of its allies. In 202 B.C.E., Hannibal and Scipio met at the Battle of Zama, and the day was decided by Scipio's generalship and the desertion of Hannibal's mercenaries. Carthage was allowed to survive, stripped of its lands and navy, and Rome emerged the undisputed ruler of the western Mediterranean.

THE REPUBLIC'S CONQUEST OF THE HELLENISTIC WORLD

The East   By the middle of the third century B.C.E., the three great Hellenistic kingdoms that dominated the eastern Mediterranean had achieved equilibrium. However, the balance of power among them was threatened by the plans that Philip V of Macedon (221–179 B.C.E.) and Antiochus III, the Seleucid ruler (223–187 B.C.E.), had to expand their domains. Philip had allied himself with Carthage during the Second Punic War, provoking Rome to stir up a conflict in Greece called the First Macedonian War (215–205 B.C.E.). Once the Second Punic War was over, Rome decided to make sure Macedon did not succeed Carthage as a threat to Italy. In 200 B.C.E., the Romans tried to intimidate Philip by ordering him to cease preying on the Greek cities, and two years later they demanded he withdraw from Greece entirely. Philip's refusal to comply provided Rome with justification for the Second Macedonian War. In 197 B.C.E., Flamininus, a gifted Roman general, defeated Philip at Cynoscephalae in Thessaly, and the following year (196 B.C.E.), Flamininus surprised the Greeks by restoring the autonomy of their city-states and pulling Rome's troops out of Greece.

Philip's retreat cleared the way for Antiochus to advance. On the pretext of freeing the Greeks from Roman domination, he invaded the Greek mainland. The Romans responded quickly, drove him from Greece, and, in 189 B.C.E., crushed his army at Magnesia in Asia Minor. Antiochus was forced to give up his war elephants and his navy and pay a huge indemnity. Although the Romans again annexed no territory, they treated Greece and Asia Minor as protectorates in whose affairs they could freely intervene.

In 179 B.C.E., Perseus succeeded Philip V as king of Macedon. His popularity with democratic, revolutionary

Significant Dates in Rome's Rise to Empire

509 B.C.E.	Republic founded
387 B.C.E.	Gauls sack Rome
338 B.C.E.	Rome defeats the Latin League
295 B.C.E.	Rome defeats the Samnites
287 B.C.E.	"Struggle of the Orders" ends
275 B.C.E.	Pyrrhus abandons Italy to Rome
264–241 B.C.E.	First Punic War
218–202 B.C.E.	Second Punic War
215–205 B.C.E.	First Macedonian War
200–197 B.C.E.	Second Macedonian War
189 B.C.E.	Rome defeats Antiochus
172–168 B.C.E.	Third Macedonian War
149–146 B.C.E.	Third Punic War
154–133 B.C.E.	Roman Wars in Spain

elements in the Greek cities convinced the Romans he was a threat to the stability of the Aegean. Following victory in a Third Macedonian War (172–168 B.C.E.), Rome dealt harshly with the Greeks. Macedon was divided into four separate republics. Their citizens were forbidden to intermarry or do business with each other, and leaders of anti-Roman factions in all the Greek cities were punished severely. Aemilius Paullus, the Roman general who defeated Perseus, brought so much booty home that Rome abolished some taxes. Romans were discovering that foreign campaigns could be profitable for the state, its soldiers, and its generals.

The West   Rome's worst abuses of power were directed not against the Greeks but against the people of the Iberian Peninsula whom the Romans considered barbarians. In 154 B.C.E., the natives of Iberia launched a fierce guerrilla campaign against their oppressors. By the time Scipio Aemilianus brought the war to a conclusion in 134 B.C.E. by taking the city of Numantia, Rome was having difficulty finding soldiers willing to go to Spain.

Although Carthage scrupulously observed the terms of its treaty with Rome and posed no threat to Rome, fear and hatred of Carthage were deeply ingrained in the Roman psyche. Cato, a prominent senator, is said to have ended all his speeches with a stern warning: "Besides, I think that Carthage must be destroyed." The Romans finally seized on a technical breach of the peace to declare war on Carthage, and in 146 B.C.E., Scipio Aemilianus destroyed the city. A province of Africa was then added to the five existing Roman provinces: Sicily, Sardinia-Corsica, Macedonia, Hither Spain, and Further Spain.

CIVILIZATION IN THE EARLY ROMAN REPUBLIC

HOW DID contact with the Hellenistic world affect Rome?

*T*he Roman attitude toward the Greeks ranged from admiration for their culture to contempt for their political squabbling and money grubbing. Conservatives such as Cato spoke contemptuously of the Greeks, but, as Roman life was transformed by association with the Greeks, even he learned Greek. The education of the Roman upper classes became bilingual, and young Roman nobles studied Greek rhetoric, literature, and philosophy. Greek refined the Latin language, and Greek literature provided the models that guided Latin authors.

RELIGION

The Romans equated their ancestral gods with similar Greek deities and worked Greek legends into their own mythology. But Roman religious traditions were little affected until the third century B.C.E., when new cults from the Middle East spread to Italy. In 205 B.C.E., the Senate endorsed worship of Cybele, the Great Mother goddess from Phrygia. Cybele's cult, however, involved rites that shocked and outraged conservative Romans, and the Senate soon reversed itself. For similar reasons, it banned the worship of Dionysus (Bacchus) in 186 B.C.E., and in 139 B.C.E., the Senate exiled Babylonian astrologers from Rome. (See "Encountering the Past: Roman Comedy.")

EDUCATION

In the early centuries of the Roman Republic, education was entirely the responsibility of the family. Fathers taught their sons vocational skills, moral rectitude, and respect for Roman tradition. (Daughters may not have been schooled in those days, but they were at a later period.) Boys learned to read, write, calculate, and farm. They memorized the laws of the Twelve Tables and legendary accounts of Rome's origin. They mastered the intricacies of religious rites, and they trained for military service.

ENCOUNTERING THE PAST

ROMAN COMEDY

I*n Rome, as in Greece, religious festivals were public entertainments involving gladiatorial contests, chariot races, and dramas. Initially, Roman audiences sat on hillsides and watched performances staged on temporary wooden platforms. Toward the end of the republican period, however, wealthy Romans began to donate permanent amphitheaters to their communities, and theaters spread to all the lands Rome ruled.*

Tragedies modeled on Greek examples were staged in Rome, but the works of the republic's best playwrights—Plautus (ca. 254–184 B.C.E.) and Terence (ca. 195–159 B.C.E.)—belong to the genre of Hellenistic New Comedy. The standard set for such plays was a city street where stock characters (clever slaves, dim-witted masters, young lovers, and shrewish women) enacted plots involving a tangle of mistaken identities, love affairs, and domestic disputes. The result was very similar to the situation comedies that are staples of modern television.

IS THERE any significance in the fact that the great plays that survive from the era of the Roman Republic are comedies, not tragedies?

This mosaic shows a scene from Roman comedy in which musicians played a significant role.

© Araldo de Luca/CORBIS

Hellenized Education   Contact with the Greeks of southern Italy in the third century B.C.E. produced momentous changes in Roman education. Greek teachers introduced the Romans to the study of language, literature, and philosophy—and to what the Romans called *humanitas*, the wide-ranging intellectual curiosity and habits of critical thinking that are the goals of liberal education.

Because Rome did not yet have much literature of its own, educated Romans learned Greek. Greek education centered on philosophy, but the practical Romans preferred rhetoric, the art of speaking and writing well. Rhetoric was of great use in political life and legal disputes. Some important Romans, such as Scipio Aemilianus (the destroyer of Carthage), enthusiastically advocated the study of Greek literature and philosophy. Scipio was the patron and friend of Polybius, a Greek who wrote a history of Rome's Punic wars. More conservative Romans, such as Cato the Elder, feared that Greek learning would weaken Roman moral fiber. The Senate occasionally expelled philosophers and teachers of rhetoric from Rome, but the Romans understood that if they were to deal with the Hellenistic Greeks, who were becoming their allies and subjects, they needed more sophisticated educations than those that had sufficed their simple agrarian ancestors.

humanitas   Wide-ranging intellectual curiosity and habits of critical thinking that are the goals of liberal education.

This carved relief from the second century C.E. shows a schoolmaster and his pupils. The pupil at the right is arriving late.

Rheinisches Landaesmuseum, Trier, Germany. Alinari/Art Resource, NY

In the late republic, Roman education, although still a family responsibility, became more formal and organized. Boys age seven to twelve attended elementary school in the care of a Greek slave called a *paedagogus* (pedagogue). He looked after them and helped them learn Greek by talking with them in his native language. They wrote on waxed tablets with styluses and learned to calculate using *calculi* (pebbles) and the abacus. From twelve to sixteen, they studied Greek and Latin literature with a *grammaticus*, who taught them dialectic, arithmetic, geometry, astronomy, music, and elements of rhetoric. Some young men sought advanced instruction in rhetoric, and a few, such as the great orator Cicero, traveled abroad to work with the great teachers of the Greek world.

Education for Women   Although evidence is limited, it suggests that upper-class girls received at least a basic education. They were probably taught at home by tutors and not sent out to school as was increasingly common for their brothers in the late republican period. Young women did not usually go on to study with philosophers and rhetoricians, for women were usually married by the age at which a man began this phase of his education. Still, some women did manage to continue their studies, and some became prose writers and poets. By the first century C.E., there were women in aristocratic circles who were famous or—as conservative males saw it—infamous for their learning.

SLAVERY

The Romans, like most ancient peoples, always had slaves. But the small farmers of early Rome owned few. Roman society only came to depend on slavery in the wake of Rome's conquests in the second century B.C.E. Between 264 B.C.E. and 133 B.C.E., the Romans enslaved some 250,000 prisoners of war. Children born to slaves further swelled the population of the unfree.

In Rome as in Greece, domestic slaves and those engaged in crafts and commerce could earn money of their own with which to purchase freedom. Emancipation was common, and it was not long before a considerable portion of the Roman population consisted of former slaves or their descendants. Some freedmen and their sons and grandsons earned fortunes and Roman citizenship. The importation of slaves from all over the Mediterranean world and their frequent emancipation made Rome an ethnically diverse place.

Rome's contribution to slavery was the invention of the plantation economy—huge commercial agricultural enterprises staffed by vast numbers of unfree workers. As the end of the republican era drew near, the number of slaves in Italy approached 2 to 3 million about 35 to 40 percent of the total population. Most labored on ***latifundia***, great estates that produced capital-intensive cash crops (wool, wine, olive oil, cattle) for the international market. *Latifundia* were designed to produce maximum profits. Because slaves were simply a means to that end, they were

latifundia   Great estates that produced capital-intensive cash crops for the international market.

HISTORY'S VOICES

ROME'S TREATMENT OF CONQUERED ITALIAN CITIES

Titus Livius (59 B.C.E.–17 C.E.), called Livy in English-speaking countries, wrote a history of Rome from its origins until his own time. In the following excerpt from it he describes the kind of settlement they imposed on various Italian cities after crushing their revolt in the years 340–338 B.C.E.

WHAT PRINCIPLES and purposes underlay Rome's treatment of the different cities?

The principal members of the senate applauded the consul's statement on the business on the whole; but said that, as the states were differently circumstanced, their plan might be readily adjusted and determined according to the desert of each, if they should put the question regarding each state specifically. The question was therefore so put regarding each separately and a decree passed. To the people of Lanuvium the right of citizenship was granted, and the exercise of their religious rights was restored to them with this provision, that the temple and grove of Juno Sospita should be common between the Lanuvian burghers and the Roman people. The peoples of Aricia, Nomentum, and Pedum were admitted into the number of citizens on the same terms as the Lanuvians. To the Tusculans the rights of citizenship which they already possessed were continued; no public penalty was imposed and the crime of rebellion was visited on its few instigators. On the people of Velitrae, Roman citizens of long standing, measures of great severity were inflicted because they had so often rebelled; their walls were razed, and their senate deported and ordered to dwell on the other side of the Tiber; any individual who should be caught on the hither side of the river should be fined one thousand asses, and the person who had apprehended him should not discharge his prisoner from confinement until the money was paid down. Into the lands of the senators colonists were sent; by their addition Velitrae recovered its former populous appearance.

Livy, *History of Rome*, trans. by D. Spillan et al. (New York: American Book Company, n.d.), Vol. 1, p. 561.

---

ruthlessly exploited—fed poorly, worked relentlessly, and discarded when they were no longer productive.

Harsh treatment spawned slave rebellions of a kind unknown in other ancient societies. A rebellion in Sicily in 134 B.C.E. kept that island in turmoil for over two years. In 73 B.C.E., a gladiator named Spartacus raised an army of 70,000 fugitive slaves that defeated several legions and overran all of southern Italy before it was finally crushed.

Slavery began to decline in the second century C.E. As Rome's empire ceased to expand and its wars produced fewer captives, the cost of slaves rose. General economic decline also forced many of the free poor to become *coloni*, tenant farmers who were bound to the lands they worked. By the time the Roman Empire fell, slaves had largely been replaced by laborers of a different kind in the West.

ROMAN IMPERIALISM: THE LATE REPUBLIC

Rome had no plan for building an empire. Much of its land was acquired as a by-product of wars that were undertaken for defensive purposes. The primary objective of Rome's foreign policy was to provide security for Rome on Rome's terms. Because these terms were often unacceptable to other peoples, conflicts arose; and, intentionally or not, Rome's domain expanded. (See Map 4–3.)

HOW DID the expansion of Rome change the Republic?

coloni Tenant farmers who were bound to the lands they worked.

MAP EXPLORATION

Interactive map: To explore this map further, go to **http://www.prenhall.com/kagan3/map4.3**

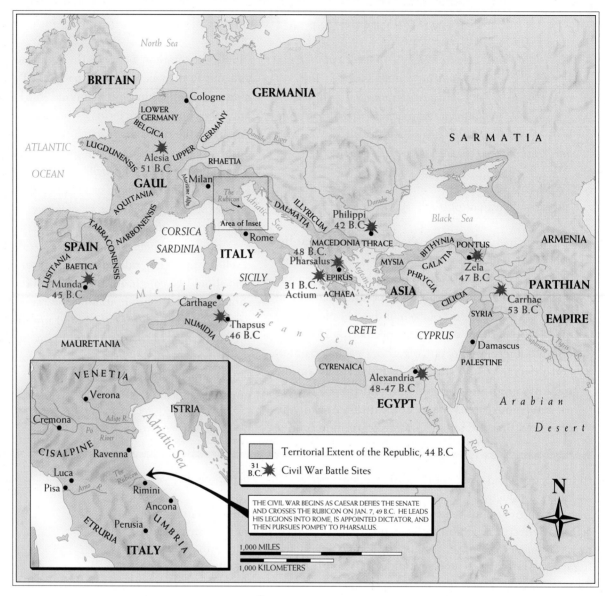

MAP 4–3
The Civil Wars of the Late Roman Republic   This map shows the extent of the territory controlled by Rome at the time of Caesar's death and the sites of the major battles of the civil wars of the late republic.

WHAT WAS the principal goal of Roman foreign policy during the period of the Roman Republic? How did this goal contribute to Roman expansion?

The burden of maintaining an empire undercut the republic the empire was built to protect. The republic was a government designed for a city-state. It could be adapted to rule Italy but not an empire that encircled the Mediterranean Sea.

THE AFTERMATH OF CONQUEST

Before the Punic Wars, most Italians owned their own farms and were largely self-sufficient. Some families had larger holdings than others, but they worked them with free laborers and, like their neighbors, grew grain for local consumption. The Punic Wars changed this. For fourteen years Hannibal marauded through Italy, doing terrible damage to its farms. Many veterans returned from the wars to find they did not have enough capital to get their devastated lands back into production. Some moved to Rome looking for work as day laborers. Others stayed in the country and became tenant farmers or hired hands. The farms they abandoned were taken over by the wealthy, who had the capital to convert them for the production of specialized crops for the world market. The upper classes had plenty of capital to invest in vineyards, olive orchards, and cattle ranches, for they monopolized political offices and, therefore, access to profitable provincial governorships. As the gap steadily widened between Rome's rich and poor, landed and landless, privileged and deprived, an increasingly tense situation developed that threatened to destabilize the republic.

THE GRACCHI

By the middle of the second century B.C.E., perceptive Roman nobles were aware that institutions fundamental to the republic were collapsing. The class of peasant farmers from which Rome recruited its soldiers was shrinking, and the patron-client organizations that ordered Roman society were weakening. Patrons found it hard to control rootless mobs of landless clients, and the introduction of the secret ballot in the 130s B.C.E. further diminished their declining ability to mobilize their political supporters.

Tiberius Gracchus   In 133 B.C.E., Tiberius Gracchus, a tribune, proposed land reform legislation that he claimed would solve these problems. He suggested reclaiming public land from the rich, who held it illegally, and redistributing it among the poor. Current occupants of this land were to be allowed to retain up to three hundred acres, but the state would take the rest and divide it up into plots for small-scale farmers. The men to whom these plots were given had to work them and were forbidden to sell them.

There was much opposition to Tiberius's proposal. Many wealthy senators would be hurt by its passage. Some worried about the precedent that would be set by interfering with property rights. Others feared the proposal would win Tiberius a popular following that would give him too much political power. When Tiberius put his land reform bill before the tribal assembly, he was not surprised, therefore, when one of his fellow tribunes, M. Octavius, vetoed it. Tiberius outmaneuvered Octavius by making a proposal that virtually eliminated the checks and balances of Rome's constitution. He urged the assembly to eliminate the veto that was blocking his popular legislation by voting Octavius out of office. This was an alarming development, for if the assembly could override the Senate and the veto of a tribune, Rome would cease to be an oligarchical republic and become a direct democracy like Athens.

This wall painting from the first century B.C.E. comes from the villa of Publius Fannius Synistor at Pompeii and shows a woman playing a cithera.

Fresco on lime plaster. H. 6 feet 1 1/2 inches W. 6 feet 1 1/2 inches (187 × 187 cm). The Metropolitan Museum of Art, Rogers Fund, 1903. (03.14.5) Photograph © 1986 The Metropolitan Museum of Art

4.4
Appian of Alexandria, *War, Slaves, and Land Reform: Tiberius Gracchus*

This statue of an unknown member of the Roman nobility from late in the first century illustrates a fundamental custom. He carries the images of two of his ancestors, probably his father and grandfather.

Marble. Musei Capitolini, Rome, Italy. Photograph ©Scala/Art Resource, NY

populares Politicians who followed Tiberius's example of politics and governing.

optimates ("the best men") Opponents of Tiberius and defenders of the traditional prerogatives of the Senate.

equestrians Men rich enough to qualify for cavalry service.

Having no hope of winning senatorial support, Tiberius drafted a second bill that was harsher than the first one he had proposed and, consequently, even more appealing to the masses. It contained a scheme for funding land redistribution. King Attalus of Pergamum had just died and left his kingdom to Rome, and Tiberius proposed using revenue from this source to finance implementation of land reform. This was a second assault on the constitution, for the Senate traditionally controlled Rome's finances and foreign affairs.

Tiberius knew he would be in personal danger once he lost the protection of his tribunal office, so he violated the republic's rules yet again by announcing he was going to run for reelection. By limiting its magistrates to single one-year terms, the republic prevented any individual from monopolizing a powerful office. If Tiberius changed the rules, he could conceivably have held the tribunate indefinitely and ruled Rome as a demagogue. Tiberius's enemies—seeing no legal recourse—resorted to illegal action. They killed Tiberius and some three hundred of his followers. The Senate beat back the threat to its rule but at the price of the first internal bloodshed in Rome's political history.

The tribunate of Tiberius Gracchus permanently changed the practice of politics in Rome. Heretofore, politics had been a struggle for honor and reputation among great families. Political rivalries rarely involved fundamental challenges to Rome's system of government. Tiberius, however, had shown how the tribunate could be used to evade senatorial dominance. Instead of courting a coalition of aristocratic supporters, he had cut out the aristocrats by appealing directly to the people with a popular issue. Politicians who followed his example came to be known as ***populares***, and their opponents, the defenders of the traditional prerogatives of the Senate, as ***optimates*** ("the best men"). These names did not signify the appearance of political parties with distinctive platforms. They only indicated alternative strategies for winning political power in Rome.

Gaius Gracchus In 123 B.C.E., ten years after Tiberius's death, Gaius Gracchus, his brother, became a tribune. Gaius kept himself in power by putting together packages of legislation that forced disparate groups of voters to support the whole in order to get the parts that benefited them. After Tiberius's murder, the Senate had placated the masses by allowing some land reform to begin, but without an enthusiastic backer the process had languished. Gaius renewed efforts to redistribute public land. He proposed new colonies, and he put through a law that stabilized the price of grain in Rome. Gaius undercut his opponents by pitting the republic's two wealthiest classes, the senators and the **equestrians** (men rich enough to qualify for cavalry service), against each other. In 129 B.C.E., Gaius won equestrian backing by passing a law that excluded senators from the juries that tried provincial governors. This prevented senators from sitting in judgment on themselves, but it did not improve the administration of the provinces. It meant that no senator could risk restraining the activities of the equestrian tax farmers in his province lest he find himself dragged before a court they controlled.

In 122 B.C.E., following reelection (which had become legal) to the tribunate, Gaius proposed legislation to right an injustice—and increase the number of his own supporters. He suggested extending citizenship to Rome's Italian allies. The allies had not received a fair share of the profits from the empire they had helped Rome win, and their resentment threatened to create serious problems for the republic. The Roman masses, however, did not want to dilute the power of their votes by creating more citizens. When they failed to support Gaius's bid for a third term in 121 B.C.E., the Senate seized its opportunity to murder him and some 3,000 of his followers. Force enabled the senatorial oligarchy to triumph once again over the *populares*, but the struggle was by no means over. Gaius's death simply convinced the *populares* that they had to find a way to match the Senate's violence, and a soldier named Marius showed them how.

MARIUS AND SULLA

In 111 B.C.E., a group of Italian businessmen in Numidia, a client kingdom in North Africa, were caught and killed in the crossfire of a dispute that had broken out over succession to the Numidian throne. The Roman electorate promptly declared war on Jugurtha, the Numidian prince whom it blamed for this insult to the republic's honor. The war dragged on longer than expected, and rumors circulated that Rome's generals were being bought off.

In 107 B.C.E., the assembly elected C. Marius (157–86 B.C.E.) to a consulship and (usurping the Senate's authority over foreign policy) commissioned him to end the Jugurthine War. Marius was not a member of the old Roman aristocracy, but a *novus homo*, a "new man" (the first in his family to hold a consulship). Marius quickly defeated Jugurtha, and the grateful Romans elected him to a second term to deal with another problem. In 105 B.C.E., two barbarian tribes, the Cimbri and the Teutones, had crushed a Roman army in the Rhone Valley. The long struggle needed to restore order in Gaul provided Marius with an excuse for holding five consecutive consulships.

Marius's military success owed much to the large armies he built, and the manpower for his armies was a product of his *populares* legislation. He persuaded the Romans to make it possible for poor men to have military careers by dropping the traditional property qualification for military service. Marius's army shifted the balance of power in Roman politics, for his soldiers were clients of their general. They were professionals paid by the state, and their continuing employment depended on his authority to use public money to reward them. Because a vote for him was a vote for themselves, they constituted a powerful political machine that kept him in office.

Marius's example inspired imitation. The most successful of his competitors was L. Cornelius Sulla (138–78 B.C.E.), an impoverished aristocrat who had served under Marius in the Jugurthine War. Sulla began his career by fighting in a war that Gaius Gracchus had tried to prevent. In 90 B.C.E. (about thirty years after Gaius Gracchus's death), Rome's Italian allies finally gave up hope of receiving fair treatment and formed an independent confederation of their own. Rome undercut their rebellion by offering citizenship to cities that remained loyal and to rebels who laid down their arms. Although all the allies eventually attained citizenship, hard fighting was still needed to put down the uprising.

Sulla's performance in the war brought him the consulship for 88 B.C.E. and command of a war against Mithridates, a native king who was threatening Roman interests in Asia Minor. Despite being seventy years old, Marius decided he wanted this assignment for himself and persuaded the assembly to rescind Sulla's commission. Sulla responded by marching on Rome with the army he had recruited for the Eastern campaign. Marius used the army to manipulate Rome politically, but Sulla was more direct. Sulla's command was restored, but after he left for the East, Marius and the consul Cinna occupied Rome with their armies.

Marius died soon after his election to a seventh consulship in 86 B.C.E., and Cinna inherited leadership of Marius's party. In 83 B.C.E., Sulla, who had forced Mithridates to retreat and agree to a truce, returned to Rome and drove Marius's followers from Italy.

Sulla claimed that to restore order he had to assume a dictatorship (a republican office). He wiped out his opponents by posting "proscription lists." Proscribed individuals were declared enemies of the state who were to be executed by anyone who found them. Their executioners were rewarded, and Sulla confiscated their property for redistribution among his followers. As many as 100,000 Romans may have died in Sulla's purge.

Sulla could have made himself the permanent ruler of Rome, but he opted to use his power to implement his conservative vision of the Roman Republic. He reaffirmed the Senate's political privileges and severely limited the tribunate, the office the Gracchi had used to undermine the Senate. In 79 B.C.E., Sulla declared his work complete and retired from public life. The political arrangements he had made proved much less durable than the lessons ambitious men drew from studying his rise to power.

THE FALL OF THE REPUBLIC

POMPEY, CRASSUS, CAESAR, AND CICERO

WHAT EVENTS led to the fall of the Republic?

Within a year of Sulla's death in 78 B.C.E., the Senate began to make exceptions to the very rules Sulla had designed to safeguard its power. It had no choice, for the only way to handle some crises was to create "special commands," which were special because they were free of the severe limitations imposed on constitutional magistracies. A general named Pompey (106–48 B.C.E.) built a remarkable career by advancing from one special command to another and largely ignoring elective offices.

Pompey emerged first in Roman politics as one of Sulla's supporters, and he made his reputation by helping track down and destroy the remnants of Marius's armies. In 73 B.C.E., the Senate commissioned him and Marcus Licinius Crassus, a wealthy senator, to put down the slave rebellion led by the gladiator, Spartacus. Crassus and Pompey then joined forces and used their influence to repeal most of Sulla's legislation. Ambitious generals understood how helpful demagogic tribunes could be in advancing their careers.

In 67 B.C.E., a special law aimed at the suppression of piracy gave Pompey *imperium* for three years over the entire Mediterranean and its coast inland for fifty miles. Pompey cleared the seas of pirates in a mere three months and then turned his attention to a second war that broke out with Mithridates. Pompey defeated Mithridates and then chose on his own initiative to push Rome's eastern frontier to the Euphrates River and the borders of Egypt.

Pompey returned to Rome in 62 B.C.E. By now he had more power than any Roman in history, and he could easily have emulated Sulla and established a dictatorship. Crassus was particularly worried, and he tried to protect himself by building alliances with leading politicians. The ablest of these was Gaius Julius Caesar (100–44 B.C.E.), a descendant of an old but obscure patrician family. Caesar was closely linked to the *populares*. Marius had married his aunt, and he had married Cinna's daughter. Both Crassus and Caesar knew that to survive in Roman politics, they had to build armies that could compete with Pompey's. To this end, Crassus funded the impoverished Caesar, and Caesar used his considerable rhetorical and political skills to advance their cause.

Cicero (106–43 B.C.E.), a "new man" from Marius's hometown of Arpinum, marshaled opposition to Crassus and Caesar. Although Cicero was an outsider to the senatorial aristocracy, he was a committed *optimates*. He thought he could engineer a "harmony of the orders" (the senators and the equestrians) that would consolidate the power of the propertied classes. The Senate backed him primarily to block the maneuvers of an extremist named Catiline. Cicero defeated Catiline for the consulship in 63 B.C.E., but Catiline refused to accept the verdict and made plans to seize control of Rome. Word leaked to Cicero, who exposed the plot in time for the Senate to rout Catiline and his men. This turn of events did not please Pompey.

4.6
Marcus Tullius Cicero:
The Laws

THE FIRST TRIUMVIRATE

Pompey landed at Brundisium in southern Italy near the end of 62 B.C.E. He had delayed coming home, hoping some crisis in Italy would justify returning with his army. Cicero's quick suppression of Catiline deprived him of a pretext, and Pompey had to disband his army to avoid the appearance of treason.

Pompey had achieved great things for Rome, and he expected the Senate to show its gratitude by deferring to him, ratifying the treaties he had negotiated in the East, and giving him land on which to retire his veterans. His requests were reasonable, and the Senate should have complied. However, it decided to delay in hopes of creating problems that would weaken Rome's strongman. The Senate's opposition drove Pompey into an alliance with his natural enemies, Crassus and Caesar. They formed the First Triumvirate, a private political arrangement that enabled them, by working together, to dominate the republic.

JULIUS CAESAR AND HIS GOVERNMENT OF ROME

With the aid of his colleagues, Caesar was elected to the consulship for 59 B.C.E., and he used the office to make sure each of the triumvirs got what he wanted. Pompey obtained land for his veterans and confirmation of his treaties. Crassus won tax concessions for the equestrians who were his chief backers. Caesar got a special military command that gave him a chance to rival Pompey. When Caesar's consulship ended, the triumvirs secured their gains by arranging for the election of friendly consuls and by forcing their leading opponents to leave Rome.

Caesar's special command gave him authority, for five years, over Cisalpine Gaul in the Po Valley and Narbonese Gaul on the far side of the Alps. With these provinces as his base, he set about conquering Gaul. He bought additional time in 56 B.C.E. by persuading Crassus and Pompey to renew the triumvirate, and by 50 B.C.E., Caesar had completed the work of pacifying Gaul as far north as the Lowlands and east to the Rhine River. In the process he had built a military machine that enabled him to rival Pompey.

As Caesar's term as governor of Gaul neared its end in 50 B.C.E., he searched for a way to retain an office that would allow him to keep his army. The triumvirate had dissolved in 53 B.C.E. when Crassus died leading an army into Parthia, the successor to the old Persian Empire, and the Senate had, in the intervening years, concluded that Pompey was a lesser threat than Caesar. It refused, therefore, to extend his term in Gaul and ordered him to lay down his command. Caesar knew this meant exile or death. Preferring treason, he ordered his legions to cross the Rubicon River, the boundary of his province, and march on Rome. This began a civil war from which Caesar emerged victorious in 45 B.C.E.

In theory, the Senate was to continue to play its traditional role in governing the republic, but Caesar's monopoly of military power made a sham of the

Senate's decrees. Caesar changed the character of the Senate by increasing its size and extending membership to Italians and Gauls as well as the sons of the old Roman families. In 46 B.C.E., the compliant Senate appointed Caesar dictator for ten years, and a year later it extended his term for life. Gaius Cassius Longinus and Marcus Junius Brutus concluded that Caesar was aiming at monarchy, and they persuaded about sixty of their fellow senators it was their patriotic duty to save the republic by murdering Caesar. The assassins struck during a meeting of the Senate on March 15, 44 B.C.E. They expected that once Caesar was dead the republic would automatically flourish, but they were wrong. Removing Caesar only cleared the way for renewed civil war—a thirteen-year conflict that ended the republican era and gave Rome an imperial form of government.

THE SECOND TRIUMVIRATE AND THE EMERGENCE OF OCTAVIAN

Caesar had adopted his grandnephew, an eighteen-year-old youth named Gaius Octavian (63 B.C.E.–14 C.E.). The Senate hoped to use the sickly, inexperienced young heir to block the rise of Rome's potential new strongman, Mark Antony. Mark Antony had been Caesar's second-in-command, and the troops automatically looked to him to lead them after Caesar's death. Mark Antony initially tried to steer a course between the Senate and Caesar's angry soldiers, but Octavian spoiled that plan. Despite his youth, Octavian won the consulship for 43 B.C.E., and then he called for war to avenge Caesar's death. Mark Antony and another of Caesar's officers, M. Aemilius Lepidus, knew this was what their armies expected Caesar's legitimate heirs to do, so they joined Octavian in establishing the Second Triumvirate. Unlike the first, this was a legal public arrangement, a joint dictatorship formed, ostensibly, for the purpose of restoring the republic.

In 42 B.C.E., the triumvirs defeated Brutus and Cassius at Philippi in Macedonia, and each of the victors rewarded himself with a command. The weakest member, Lepidus, was given Africa. Octavian took the West and its troubles: a war with one of Pompey's sons, the settlement of some 100,000 veterans, and the restoration of order in Italy. Antony received the most promising assignment: an Eastern command from which to launch an invasion of Parthia. A victorious Parthian campaign would have given Antony the resources and popularity he needed to sweep his fellow triumvirs aside.

The army Antony led into Parthia in 36 B.C.E. took heavy losses and was forced to retreat. This caused his soldiers to begin to doubt him, and it made him vulnerable to a propaganda campaign that Octavian had mounted. Octavian did a brilliant job of convincing the Romans that Antony was no longer responsible for himself—that passion had turned him into the helpless pawn of Egypt's queen, Cleopatra. By 32 B.C.E., all pretense of cooperation among the triumvirs had come to an end. Lepidus had already been shoved aside, and in 31 B.C.E., a minor naval skirmish at Actium off the western coast of Greece began Antony's precipitous fall from power.

Judging all to be lost, Antony and Cleopatra committed suicide. Their deaths ended the civil war and left Octavian, at the age of thirty-two, master of the Mediterranean world. His power was enormous, but so was the task before him. To restore peace and stability to Rome he needed to invent a form of government that could administer an empire without seeming to violate the republican traditions to which the Romans were still passionately devoted.

Portrait Head of Cleopatra VII.
©Sandro Vannini/CORBIS

SUMMARY

Prehistoric Italy The Neolithic era came late to Italy, around 2500 B.C.E., followed by the Bronze Age starting around 1500 B.C.E. Bands of warring peoples speaking Italic languages invaded from across the Adriatic and along the northeastern coast starting around 1000 B.C.E.; within two centuries they had occupied the Appenines and were challenging the earlier settlers on the western plains. Their tools and craftsmanship were better than those of Italy's earlier inhabitants. These peoples shaped Italy's history.

The Etruscans Etruscan civilization emerged in Etruria around 800 B.C.E. The Etruscans formed a military ruling class that held power over the native Italians. Etruscan religion exerted a strong influence throughout the region. Under Greek influence, the Etruscans started to worship human-shaped gods. Etruscan women had more visible roles than their Greek counterparts. Etruscans expanded their domains and controlled large holdings in Italy, Corsica, and Elba. Etruscan power had peaked by 500 B.C.E., then declined rapidly under attack by the Gauls around 400 B.C.E.

Royal Rome Rome's location on the Tiber River made it an important center for communication and trade. In the sixth century B.C.E., under the leadership of Etruscan kings, Rome developed political institutions that would endure through the Roman Republic, imperial Rome, and beyond. The kings of Rome held the power of *imperium,* but they were checked by the Senate and the curiate assembly. The family was the center of Roman life. Women and children had some protections. Upper-class women had positions of influence and respect greater than those available to Greek women. *Clientage* entailed mutual obligations between client and patron; the relationship was hereditary and sanctioned by religion. The two classes in royal Rome were *patricians,* a closed upper class that monopolized power, and the *plebeians,* who were originally poor but eventually came to include wealthy families unable to join the patrician class.

The Republic In 509 B.C.E., the noble families revolted successfully against the monarchy and created the Roman Republic. A limited form of the *imperium* was exercised by the consuls. Over the following centuries, the powers of the Senate increased substantially. Plebeians chafed against the limits on their political participation and other rights, leading to the Struggle of the Orders. By the middle of the third century B.C.E., Rome controlled the Italian peninsula. Conflict between Rome and Carthage in Sicily erupted in the First Punic War, through which Rome won control of Sicily. By mismanaging the peace, however, the Romans set the stage for the Second Punic War, in which Rome faced Hannibal. After winning every battle, Hannibal lost the war when the Roman general Scipio defeated the Carthaginians. Meanwhile, Rome had started meddling in Macedonian affairs, participating in the three Macedonian Wars. Rome's victory at the conclusion of the Third Macedonian War in 168 B.C.E. resulted in an uncharacteristically harsh peace.

IMAGE KEY
for pages 88–89

a. Pont du Gard, Nimes, Provence, France

b. Bronze flutes

c. Reed and bronze pens as well as bronze, iron and ivory styli

d. Cleopatra VII

e. Roman relief from Noviomagn Rheinisches Landesmuseum, Trier, Germany. Alinari/Art Resource, NY

f. Mosaic showing a scene from a Roman comedy

g. Bust of Cato and Porcia. Roman sculpture.   Vatican Museums, Vatican State. Photograph © Scala/Art Resource, NY

h. Lyre musical instrument, with tortoise shell for amplification

i. Roman lictors. Marble relief from Concordia. Mostra Augustea, Rome

j. Portland Vase, 3rd C. B.C.E. Cameo-cut glass   British Museum, London

k. "Family Group," traditionally called the "Family of Vunnerius Keramus." C. 25 C.E. Engraved gold leaf sealed between glass. D: 2 3/8" (6 cm). Museo Civico dell'Eta Cristiana, Brescia; Fotostudio Rapuzzi

l. Bust of Julius Caesar, 100-44 B.C.E. Roman statesman   Museo Archeologico Nazionale, Naples, Italy. Photograph © Scala/Art Resource, NY

Civilization in the Early Roman Republic Educated Romans were bilingual, in Latin and Greek; Greek mythology was incorporated into Roman religion; education became Hellenized, and Greeks took on significant roles in the formal educational system. Girls did not attend school, but among the upper classes they were tutored at home. Slavery increased dramatically as the Romans enslaved prisoners of war. Manumission was common, and former slaves enjoyed social and economic mobility. The development of the *latifundia* system of agriculture—basically, cash-crop plantations that depended on slave labor—fueled the growth of a harsher and more oppressive form of slavery, with the result that significant slave rebellions occurred. Slavery declined gradually; in agriculture, tenant farmers called *coloni* slowly filled the economic niche of slavery.

Roman Imperialism: The Late Republic War, expansion, and the administration of an empire fundamentally altered Roman culture. The availability of cheap land and labor sharpened class differences throughout Italy. Tiberius Gracchus's unconstitutional tactics in attempting to pass land reform legislation in 133 B.C.E. led eventually to a riot in which Tiberius and three hundred of his supporters were killed. Roman politics was changed forever. Fundamental issues were now clearly at stake. Tiberius's brother Gaius Gracchus assumed the tribunate in 123 B.C.E. and passed some populist reforms, but he too was assassinated. Soon senatorial privilege was challenged from abroad, through the Jugurthine War that began in 111 B.C.E. Two ambitious generals, Marius and Sulla, gained power through their victories. Later, fighting barbarian tribes to the north, Marius introduced innovations into the army that made soldiers more loyal to their general than to the state. All Italians gained citizenship after a revolt. Between 88 and 83 B.C.E., Marius and Sulla dragged the Romans into civil war in their competition for power; Sulla won, assassinated his opponents, and attempted to reform the constitution and government institutions.

The Fall of the Republic Soon after Sulla's death, Crassus and Pompey intimidated the Senate into granting them extraordinary powers. By 60 B.C.E., when Crassus, Pompey, and Caesar all found their ambitions thwarted by the Senate, they formed the First Triumvirate, an informal political alliance to further their own private goals. Caesar was elected consul in 59 B.C.E. and enacted the triumvirs' program. Through impressive military conquest and intense diplomacy Caesar held on to power until his assassination fifteen years later. Mark Antony and Gaius Octavius vied to succeed Caesar, although they joined with M. Aemilius Lepidus to form the Second Triumvirate to fight against Caesar's assassins in a civil war. After the triumvirate won, Octavian patronized the Roman arts and fostered the impression that Antony was a stooge of Cleopatra. When the power struggle between Octavian and Antony degenerated into battle, at Actium in 31 B.C.E., Octavian's forces won.

REVIEW QUESTIONS

1. How did the institutions of family and clientage and the establishment of patrician and plebeian classes contribute to the stability of the early Roman Republic? What was "the struggle of the orders"? What methods did plebeians use to get what they wanted?

2. Until 265 B.C.E., how and why did Rome expand its territory? How was Rome able to conquer and to control Italy? Why did Romans and Carthaginians clash in the First and Second Punic Wars? Could the wars have been avoided? What problems did the victory create for Rome?

3. What social, economic, and political problems faced Italy in the second century B.C.E.? How did Tiberius and Gaius Gracchus propose to solve them? What were the political implications of the Gracchan reform program? Why did reform fail?

4. What were the problems that plagued the Roman Republic in the last century B.C.E.? What caused these problems, and how did the Romans try to solve them? To what extent were ambitious, power-hungry generals responsible for the destruction of the republic?

KEY TERMS

censors (p. 94)

coloni (p. 103)

consuls (p. 93)

equestrians (p. 106)

Gaul (p. 90)

humanitas (p. 101)

imperium (p. 91)

latifundia (p. 102)

Latium (p. 90)

optimates (p. 106)

patricians (p. 92)

plebeians (p. 92)

populares (p. 106)

proconsulships (p. 93)

tribunes (p. 94)

 For additional study resources for this chapter, go to:
www.prenhall.com/kagan3/chapter4

5 The Roman Empire

CHAPTER HIGHLIGHTS

The Augustan Principate Octavian acted as the functional equivalent of a monarch. From 26 B.C.E. on he was referred to as Augustus. He made important governmental and economic reforms, professionalized the military, and acted as role model for traditional Roman values.

Civilization of the Ciceronian and Augustan Ages Roman culture flourished in the late republican and Augustan periods. Romans of this era made important contributions to history, poetry, law, and architecture.

Imperial Rome, 14–180 C.E. Military power was the basis of imperial rule. Vespasian's Flavian dynasty was followed by the five "good emperors." By the end of the second century C.E. a number of problems were converging to create a burgeoning crisis.

The Rise of Christianity Jesus of Nazareth gained a large following, especially among the poor. After his execution in 30 C.E., he was presented as the Son of God in the Gospels. Paul of Tarsus made the case that Christianity was a new and universal religion. By the end of the second century the Catholic Church had been institutionalized as the definer of Christian orthodoxy.

The Crisis of the Third Century External threats and internal weakness drew the empire into a downward spiral. The economy went into decline and social stratification increased. Invasions and anarchy characterized the century.

The Late Empire During the fourth and fifth centuries, the empire was reorganized and divided, and Christianity gained followers and power. By the end of the fourth century, the empire had been divided permanently.

Arts and Letters in the Late Empire Much of the art and literature of the late empire reflects the relationship between Christianity and pagan religions. The most significant of the period's Christian writers was Augustine who combined Christian faith and pagan (Classical) reason.

The Problem of the Decline and Fall of the Empire in the West Imperial government collapsed in the West in the fifth century in the face of Germanic invasions. Ever since, historians and commentators offered explanations for the fall of Rome. It can be argued, however, that the question should be, "How did the Roman Empire last as long as it did?"

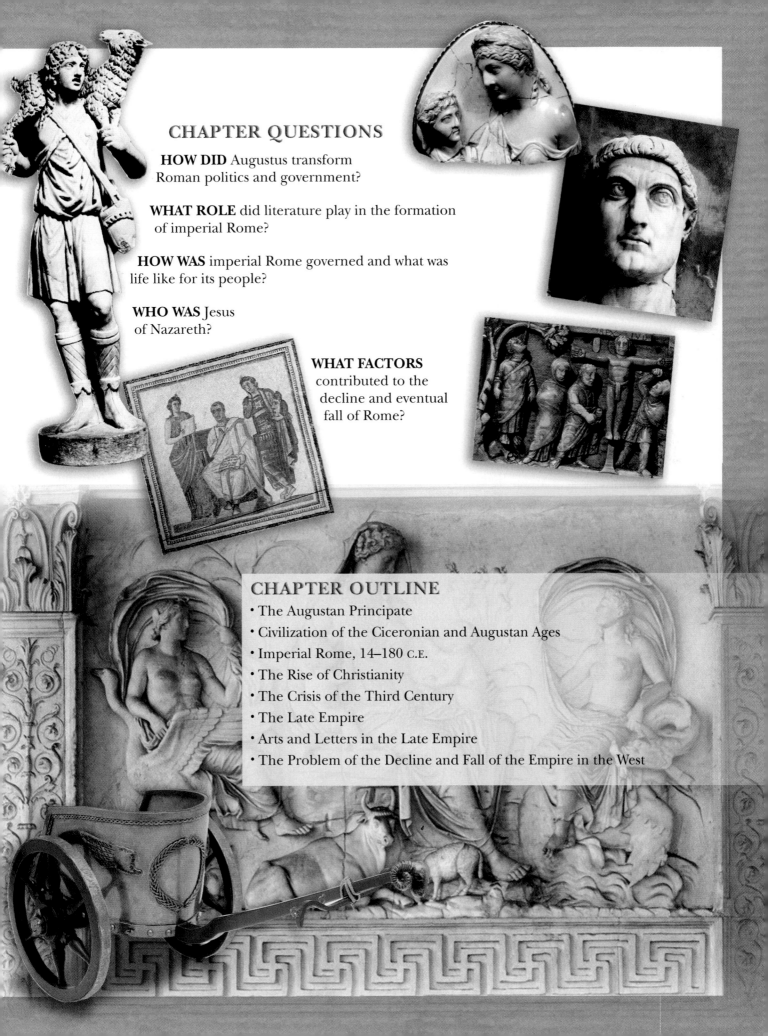

CHAPTER QUESTIONS

HOW DID Augustus transform Roman politics and government?

WHAT ROLE did literature play in the formation of imperial Rome?

HOW WAS imperial Rome governed and what was life like for its people?

WHO WAS Jesus of Nazareth?

WHAT FACTORS contributed to the decline and eventual fall of Rome?

CHAPTER OUTLINE

• The Augustan Principate
• Civilization of the Ciceronian and Augustan Ages
• Imperial Rome, 14–180 C.E.
• The Rise of Christianity
• The Crisis of the Third Century
• The Late Empire
• Arts and Letters in the Late Empire
• The Problem of the Decline and Fall of the Empire in the West

IMAGE KEY
for pages 114–115 is on page 141.

Octavian's victory over Mark Antony in 31 B.C.E. ended a century of civil strife that had begun with the murder of Tiberius Gracchus. Octavian (subsequently known as Augustus) stabilized Rome by establishing a monarchy hidden behind a republican facade. The unification of the Mediterranean world promoted peace and economic expansion. The spread of Latin and Greek as the empire's official languages promoted growth of a common Classical tradition that had a great influence on the development of a new religion that appeared in the first century C.E.: Christianity.

In the third century C.E., Rome's institutions began to fail, and its emperors resorted to drastic measures to try to maintain order. The result was growing centralization and militarization of an increasingly authoritarian government. A wave of invasions in the second half of the fifth century finally initiated the empire's collapse.

THE AUGUSTAN PRINCIPATE

HOW DID Augustus transform Roman politics and government?

The memory of Julius Caesar's fate was fresh in Octavian's mind in 31 B.C.E. as he pondered what to do with the empire he had won. He controlled all of Rome's armies. He had loyal, capable assistants, and the confiscation of Egypt's treasury provided him with ample capital. He had the means to be a strong ruler, but Caesar's fate had taught him the dangers of appearing to threaten the republican traditions to which the Romans were so passionately devoted.

Slowly Octavian pieced together a government that was acceptable to the Romans and capable of running an empire. Despite its republican trappings and an apparent deference to the Senate, it was a monarchy. Octavian disguised this fact by referring to himself as *princeps* ("first citizen") or **imperator** ("commander in chief"), but these titles soon acquired connotations of royalty that accurately reflected the power of his office.

During the civil war, Octavian's legal authority derived from the triumvirate, a joint dictatorship set up to restore the republic. In the years immediately following the civil war, Octavian held consecutive consulships. This was inconsistent with Roman tradition and looked like a stepping-stone to monarchy, so Octavian gradually worked out a more acceptable arrangement. At a dramatic Senate meeting held on January 13, 27 B.C.E., he offered to resign all his offices. The Senate, however, prevailed on him to retain a consulship and a few provincial governorships. This was a less radical step than it seems, for Octavian retained control of the borderland provinces (Spain, Gaul, and Syria) where twenty of Rome's twenty-six legions were stationed. The Senate, however, declared that the return of some provinces to its control marked the restoration of the republic, and it thanked Octavian by hailing him as **Augustus** ("revered"). Historians refer to him by this title from this point on in his career to indicate his role in establishing Rome's first truly imperial government, the *Principate*. In 23 B.C.E. Augustus made another republican gesture. He resigned the consulship. Henceforth his authority rested on two special powers: proconsular *imperium maius* (supreme military command) and the political privileges of an honorary tribune.

ADMINISTRATION

The Romans were willing to go along with Augustus, for they benefited from his administration. He weeded out inefficient and corrupt magistrates. He blocked ambitious politicians and generals who might otherwise have disturbed the peace. He eased tension among classes and between Romans and provincials.

imperator "Commander in chief."

Augustus ("revered") Name by which the Senate hailed Octavian for his restoration of the republic.

This scene from Augustus' Ara Pacis, the altar of Peace, in Rome shows the general Marcus Agrippa (63–12 B.C.E.) in procession with the imperial family. Agrippa was a powerful deputy, close friend, and son-in-law of Augustus. He was chiefly responsible for the victory over Mark Antony at the Battle of Actium in 31 B.C.E.

Museum of the Ara Pacis, Rome, Italy

And he fostered economic development. With his reign, a long era of stability—the *pax Romana* ("Roman peace")—began.

The Senate took over most of the political functions of the assemblies, but it became a less parochial institution. Augustus manipulated elections and saw to it that promising young men, whatever their origin, had opportunities to serve the state. Those who did well were rewarded with appointments to the Senate. This allowed equestrians and Italians who had no connection with the old Roman aristocracy to earn Senate membership, and it ensured a Senate composed of talented, experienced statesmen.

Augustus was careful to court Rome's politically volatile residents. He founded the city's first public fire department and police force. He organized grain distribution for the poor and set up an office to oversee the municipal water supply. The empire's rapidly expanding economy enabled him to fund a popular program of public works.

The provinces, too, benefited from Augustus's union of political and military power. For the first time, Rome had a central government that was able to oversee the conduct of the men who administered its provinces. Good governors were appointed. Those who abused their power were disciplined, and the provincials themselves were granted a greater degree of political autonomy.

THE ARMY AND DEFENSE

Augustus professionalized the military and reduced its numbers to about 300,000 men, a force barely adequate to hold the frontiers. The army consisted of legions recruited from Italians with citizenship and auxiliary companies composed of provincials. Soldiers enlisted for twenty-year terms. Pay was good, with occasional bonuses and the promise of a pension on retirement. Military units were permanently based in the provinces where they were likely to be needed, and their presence helped acquaint native peoples with Roman culture. Soldiers married local women and settled new towns. These developments helped provincials identify with the empire and commit to its defense.

Augustus's chief military worry was the stability of the empire's northern frontier. On this front, only a narrow strip of Roman territory protected Italy from invasion by German barbarians. Augustus decided, therefore, to push into Germany to establish a more defensible border, but in 9 C.E., a German chief named Herrmann (Arminius, in Latin) staged an ambush that obliterated three Roman legions. Their loss forced the aging Augustus to abandon his plan.

RELIGION AND MORALITY

Augustus tried to repair the damage that a century of strife had done to Rome's fundamental institutions. He devised a program to restore traditional values of family and religion. He passed laws to curb adultery and divorce and encourage early marriage and large families. His own austere behavior set a personal example for his subjects. He even banished his only child, a woman named Julia, to punish her flagrant immorality.

Augustus restored the dignity of formal Roman religion by building temples, reviving old cults, invigorating the priestly colleges, and banning the worship of some foreign gods. He did not accept divine honors during his lifetime, but, like his adoptive-father, Julius Caesar, he was deified after his death.

5.1
Augustus's Moral
Legislation:
Family Values

WHAT ROLE did literature play in the formation of imperial Rome?

CIVILIZATION OF THE CICERONIAN AND AUGUSTAN AGES

Roman civilization reached its pinnacle in the last century of the republic and during the Augustan Principate. Hellenistic Greek influences were strong, but the spirit and sometimes the form of Roman art and literature were unique.

THE LATE REPUBLIC

Cicero Cicero (106–43 B.C.E.), the most important literary figure of the late republic, wrote treatises on rhetoric, ethics, and politics, and he fostered Latin as a medium for philosophical disputation. The orations he delivered in Rome's law courts and the Senate and his private letters (many of which survive) are his most interesting works. They provide us with better insight into him than we have into any other figure from antiquity.

Cicero's thinking was pragmatic and conservative. He believed the world was governed by a divine natural law that human reason could comprehend and use to build civilized institutions. His respect for law, custom, and tradition as guarantors of stability and liberty led him to champion the Senate against *populares* leaders such as Mark Antony. When the Second Triumvirate seized power and began its purges, Antony marked Cicero for execution.

History Much of the work of the historians who wrote during the last century of the republic has been lost. A few pamphlets on the Jugurthine War and the Catilinarian conspiracy of 63 B.C.E. are all that survive from the pen of Sallust (86–35 B.C.E.), who was reputed to be the greatest historian of his generation. Julius Caesar wrote treatises on the Gallic and civil wars—military narratives intended for use as political propaganda. Their direct, simple, and vigorous style still makes them persuasive reading.

OVERVIEW   THE GREAT AUGUSTAN POETS

Vergil (70–19 B.C.E.)	The most important of the Augustan poets, Vergil wrote somewhat artificial pastoral idylls. Virgil transformed the early Greek poet's praise of simple labor into a hymn to the human enterprise—the civilizing of the world of nature. His most important poem, the *Aeneid*, celebrated Italy's traditional religious cults and institutions.
Horace (65–8 B.C.E.)	The son of a freedman, Horace was a highly skillful lyric poet. He produced a collection of genial, sometimes humorous poems called *Satires* and a number of *Odes*, songs that glorify the Augustan order. He skillfully adapted Latin to the forms of Greek verse.
Propertius (50–16 B.C.E.)	Propertius joined Vergil and Horace as a member of the poetic circle favored by Augustus's wealthy friend Maecenas. He wrote elegies that were renowned for their grace and wit.
Ovid (43 B.C.E.–18 C.E.)	Ovid was the only one of the great poets to run spectacularly afoul of Augustus. His poetic celebrations of the loose sexual mores of sophisticated Roman aristocrats did not serve the *princeps's* purpose. When Ovid published a poetic textbook on the art of seduction, *Ars Amatoria*, Augustus exiled him to a remote region of the empire.

Law Prior to the era of the Gracchi, Roman law evolved case by case from juridical decisions. However, contact with foreign peoples and the influence of Greek ideas forced a change. The edicts of *praetors* began to be added to the Roman legal code, and the decisions of the magistrates who dealt with foreigners spawned the idea of the ***jus gentium***—the law of all peoples as opposed to the law that reflected only Roman practice. In the first century B.C.E., Greek thought promoted the concept of the ***jus naturale***, a law of nature that enshrined the principles of divine reason that Cicero and the Stoics believed governed the universe.

Poetry Two of Rome's greatest poets, Lucretius (ca. 99–ca. 55 B.C.E.) and Catullus (ca. 84–ca. 54 B.C.E.), were Cicero's contemporaries. Each represented a different aspect of Rome's poetic tradition. Hellenistic literary theory maintained that poets ought to educate as well as entertain, and this was the intent of Lucretius's epic poem, *De Rerum Natura* (*On the Nature of Things*). Lucretius hoped to rescue his readers from superstitious fears by persuading them of the truth of philosophical materialism. If they understood they were temporary agglomerations of lumps of matter that dissolved utterly at death, they would cease to be anxious about suffering punishment, regret, or a sense of loss in an afterlife.

Catullus's poems were personal, even autobiographical, descriptions of the joys and pains of love. He hurled invective at powerful contemporaries such as Julius Caesar. He amused himself by composing witty exchanges with his acquaintances, but he was not interested in moral instruction. He celebrated himself—affirming one of the characteristics of Hellenistic art: the importance of the individual.

THE AGE OF AUGUSTUS

Augustus's era was the golden age of Roman literature. The power of the *princeps* set limits to freedom of expression, but he and his friends provided patronage for some of Rome's greatest writers. Although they often served his political agenda, they were not mere propagandists. They were sincerely grateful for what he was doing for Rome.

jus gentium Law of all peoples as opposed to the law that reflected only Roman practice.

jus naturale Law of nature that enshrined the principles of divine reason that Cicero and the Stoics believed governed the universe.

This mosaic found in Tunisia shows the poet Vergil reading from his *Aeneid* to the Muses of Epic and Tragedy.

Roger Wood/CORBIS/Bettmann

Vergil   The early works (*Eclogues* or *Bucolics*) of Vergil (70–19 B.C.E.), the most important of the Augustan poets, were somewhat artificial pastoral idylls. The subject for Vergil's *Georgics*, a reworking of Hesiod's *Works and Days*, may have been suggested to him by Maecenas, Augustus's chief cultural adviser. Vergil transformed the early Greek poet's praise of simple labor into a hymn to the heroic human enterprise—the civilizing of the world of nature.

Vergil's most important poem, the *Aeneid*, celebrated Italy's traditional religious cults and institutions. Augustus had rallied the Romans to his side during the civil war by persuading them that Mark Antony had succumbed to alien Eastern influences and only he, Augustus, could preserve Italy's culture. As *princeps*, therefore, he was committed to granting Italy special status within his empire, and in the *Aeneid* Vergil explained why Italy deserved preference. Vergil traced Roman ancestry to the basic myth of Hellenic civilization, the *Iliad's* account of the Trojan War. The *Aeneid's* hero, the Trojan prince Aeneas, is not motivated by Homeric lust for personal honor. He personifies Roman qualities: duty, responsibility, and patriotism—the civic virtues of men such as Augustus who maintain the peace and prosperity of the empire.

Horace   Horace (65–8 B.C.E.), the son of a freedman, was a highly skillful lyric poet. He produced a collection of genial, sometimes humorous poems called *Satires* and a number of *Odes*, songs that glorify the Augustan order. He skillfully adapted Latin to the forms of Greek verse.

Propertius   Sextus Propertius joined Vergil and Horace as a member of the poetic circle favored by Augustus's wealthy friend Maecenas. Propertius wrote elegies that were renowned for their grace and wit.

Ovid   Ovid (43 B.C.E.–18 C.E.) was the only one of the great poets to run spectacularly afoul of Augustus. Augustus wanted to inspire the Romans to return to the austere, family-centered values of their remote ancestors. Ovid's poetic celebrations of the loose sexual mores of sophisticated Roman aristocrats did not serve the *princeps's* purposes. When Ovid published a poetic textbook on the art of seduction, *Ars Amatoria*, Augustus exiled him to a remote region of the empire. Ovid tried, but failed, to recover favor by switching to less sensitive themes. His *Fasti* was a poetic essay on Roman religious festivals, and his most popular work, the *Metamorphoses*, was a charming survey of Greek mythology.

History   Augustus's interest in inspiring reverence for Roman tradition encouraged the writing of history, and his contemporary, Livy (59 B.C.E.–17 C.E.), devoted his life to writing a monumental survey of Roman history. Only a quarter of it survives, but the extant portions treat the important period from the legendary origins of Rome until 9 B.C.E. Livy based his history on secondary accounts and did little original research, but he was a gifted narrator. His sketches of historical figures have provided generations of teachers with materials for memorable lessons in patriotism and virtuous conduct.

Architecture and Sculpture   Augustus embarked on a building program designed to make Rome worthy of its history. He reconstructed the Campus Martius and the Roman Forum. He donated a new forum of his own to celebrate his victory in the civil war and erected a splendid temple to his patron god, Apollo, on Rome's Palatine Hill. Most of his new building conformed to the Greek Classical style, which emphasized serenity and order, and the same attributes are visible in the best surviving sculpture of his era.

IMPERIAL ROME, 14–180 C.E.

THE EMPERORS

Marcus Aurelius, Emperor of Rome from 161 to 180 C.E., was one of the five "good emperors" who brought a period of relative peace and prosperity to the empire. This is the only Roman bronze equestrian statue that has survived.

Capitoline Museums, Rome, Italy/Canali PhotoBank, Milan/Superstock

Because Augustus was ostensibly only the "first citizen" of a restored republic, he could not create a public process for choosing an heir to his power. He could only transfer it behind the scenes to his chief surviving male relative, his stepson Tiberius (r. 14–37 C.E.). Tiberius initially tried to follow Augustus's example and hide the monarchical nature of his authority. But as the Romans became accustomed to the new order, there was less reason to conceal its reality. The terms *imperator* and Caesar began to be used as titles for men whose connection with Julius Caesar's family positioned them to run the Roman world.

Tiberius was succeeded by his nephew, Gaius Caligula (r. 37–41 C.E.), who was widely thought to be insane. Vicious and cruel, Caligula spent large amounts of the state treasury and seized the property of wealthy Romans. In 41 C.E., the naked military basis of imperial rule was revealed when the Praetorian Guard, having assassinated Caligula, dragged his uncle, the lame, stammering, and frightened Claudius, from behind a curtain and made him emperor. Claudius left the throne to his stepson Nero (r. 54–68 C.E.), who so grossly mismanaged his affairs that he lost control of the army and committed suicide. Nero was the last member of the Julio-Claudian dynasty, the descendants of Augustus or Augustus's wife, Livia.

Following Nero's death power changed hands rapidly in 69 C.E., as a succession of Roman armies marched on Rome from the provinces. Vespasian (r. 69–79 C.E.), the fourth man to occupy the throne that year, restored order and founded the Flavian dynasty. Vespasian was the first emperor who had no connection with the old Roman nobility. He was a tough Italian soldier from the middle class. The sons who followed him to the throne, first Titus (r. 79–81 C.E.) and then Domitian (r. 81–96 C.E.), inherited his excellent administrative talents. Domitian, however, may have succumbed to paranoia, and his tyrannical behavior frightened his intimates into assassinating him.

Domitian had no close relative to succeed him, and those who killed him were not foolish enough to try to turn the clock back to the days of the republic. They appealed to the Senate to restore order by choosing a new emperor. The Senate elected one of its own, Nerva (r. 96–98 C.E.), the first of a line of dubbed "good emperors" that included Trajan (r. 98–117 C.E.), Hadrian (r. 117–138 C.E.), Antoninus Pius (r. 138–161 C.E.), and Marcus Aurelius (r. 161–180 C.E.). None of the first four men had a son to succeed him, so each followed Nerva's example and adopted an heir (who was usually an experienced adult). This system of succession was a fortunate historical accident, guaranteeing that worthy men were promoted to power. It provided a

HOW WAS imperial Rome governed and what was life like for its people?

century of peace and competent government that ended when Marcus Aurelius's unworthy son, Commodus (r. 180–192 C.E.), followed him to the throne.

THE ADMINISTRATION OF THE EMPIRE

Although some of the emperors tried to enlist the help of the senatorial class (as counselors, judges, and administrators) in running the empire, the imperial government was largely staffed by professionals. These career bureaucrats were usually an improvement over the amateurs who had annually rotated through the offices of the republic.

The provinces especially benefited, for the emperor controlled their governors and promoted their economies by integrating them into the commercial exchange system of a huge empire. Rome's leaders tried to unify the empire while simultaneously respecting local customs and differences. The *Romanitas* ("Romanness") they spread across the empire was more than superficial. By 212 C.E., citizenship had been extended to almost every inhabitant of the empire, and members of provincial families were becoming senators and emperors. (See Map 5–1.)

Local Municipalities   Administratively, the empire resembled a federation of cities and towns. The typical city had about 20,000 inhabitants. Only three or four had populations of more than 75,000. Rome, however, certainly had more than 500,000 residents—perhaps more than a million. The central government dealt with city governments and had little contact with people who lived in the countryside. Municipal charters placed great responsibility in the hands of local councils and magistrates, and men who filled these positions earned Roman citizenship. This integrated the upper classes of the provinces into the Roman system, spread Roman law and culture, and nurtured the loyalty of influential provincial families. Rome's policy of encouraging assimilation did not succeed everywhere. Jews refused to compromise with Roman customs on religious grounds, and when they rebelled in 66–70, 115–117, and 132–135 C.E., they were savagely suppressed. Egypt's peasants, who were exploited with exceptional ruthlessness, were also not offered opportunities to integrate.

The emperors took a broad view of their responsibility for the welfare of their subjects. Nerva conceived and Trajan launched the *alimenta*, a program of public assistance for children of indigent parents. More and more the emperors intervened when municipalities got into difficulties, sending imperial troubleshooters to deal with problems that were usually financial. As the central administration took on more and more functions, the autonomy of the municipalities declined and the provincial aristocracy began to view public service as a burden rather than an opportunity. The price paid for increased efficiency was a loss of vitality by the empire's local governments.

Foreign Policy   For the most part, Augustus's successors continued his foreign policy and focused primarily on defending the lands they already held. Trajan, however, took

Significant Dates from the Imperial Period

The Julio-Claudian Dynasty

27 B.C.E.–14 C.E.	Augustus
[ca. 4 B.C.E.–30 C.E.	Jesus of Nazareth]
14–37 C.E.	Tiberius
37–41 C.E.	Gaius "Caligula"
41–54 C.E.	Claudius
54–68 C.E.	Nero
[69 C.E.	"Year of the Four Emperors"]

The Flavian Dynasty

69–79 C.E.	Vespasian
79–81 C.E.	Titus
81–96 C.E.	Domitian
[ca. 70–100 C.E.	Composition of the Gospels]

The "Good Emperors"

96–98 C.E.	Nerva
98–117 C.E.	Trajan
117–138 C.E.	Hadrian
138–161 C.E.	Antoninus Pius
161–180 C.E.	Marcus Aurelius

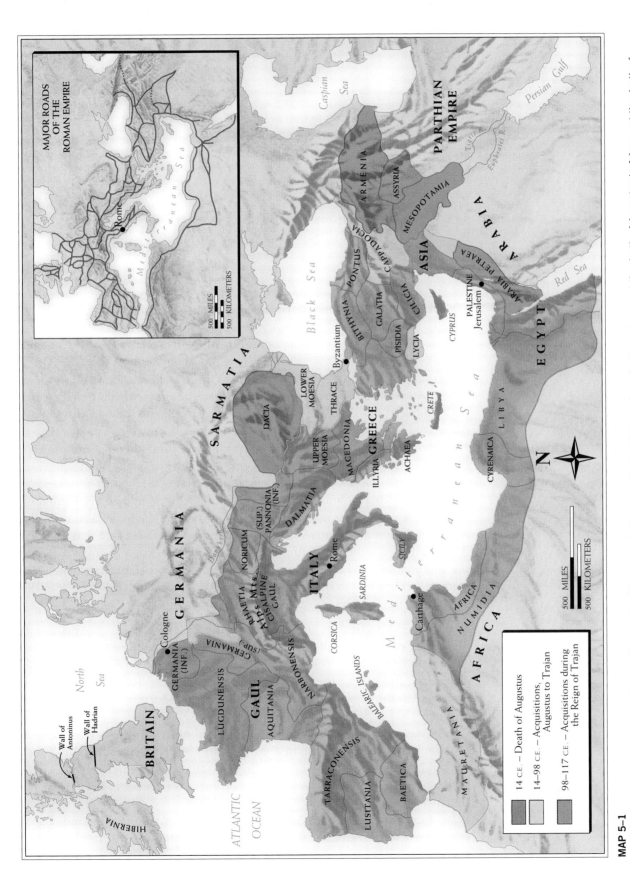

MAP 5–1

Provinces of the Roman Empire to 117 C.E. The growth of the empire to its greatest extent is here shown in three stages—at the death of Augustus in 14 C.E., at the death of Nerva in 98, and at the death of Trajan in 117. The division into provinces in 117. The insert shows the main roads that tied the far-flung empire together.

WHAT BOUNDARIES, both manmade and natural, did the Roman Empire have at each stage of its expansion?

Spoils from the temple in Jerusalem were carried in triumphal procession by Roman troops. This relief from Titus's arch of victory in the Roman Forum celebrates his capture of Jerusalem after a two-year siege. The Jews found it difficult to reconcile their religion with Roman rule and frequently rebelled.

Courtesy Davis Art Image

Imperial Roman cameo of Livia and Tiberius

©Burstein Collection/CORBIS

the offensive and added new territory to the empire. He crossed the Danube and added a province called Dacia (modern Romania) to the empire. His intent was probably to secure the frontier by occupying a wedge of territory between hostile barbarian tribes. Similar objectives may have motivated his invasion of the Parthian Empire (113–117 C.E.) and the creation of three additional eastern provinces: Armenia, Assyria, and Mesopotamia. It soon became apparent, however, that Trajan's conquests were overextending the empire, and Rome retreated from some of the land he had occupied.

Hadrian, Trajan's successor, concentrated on strengthening Rome's frontiers. Although the Romans rarely sought more territory, they often sent their armies beyond the borders of the empire to chastise and pacify troublesome neighbors. Hadrian diminished the need for such expeditions by hardening Rome's defenses. Where nature provided no protection, he built walls: a seventy-mile-long stone wall in the south of Scotland, and a wooden wall that spanned the space between the upper Rhine and Danube Rivers. Rome's retreat to defensive positions allowed the military initiative to pass to its barbarian neighbors. Marcus Aurelius had to spend most of his reign fending off their attacks in the east and on the Danube frontier.

Agriculture: The Decline of Slavery and the Rise of *Coloni* The defense of the empire's frontiers made enormous demands on its resources, but the effect was slow to be felt. Economic growth continued well into the reigns of the "good emperors." Internal peace and efficient administration benefited agriculture, trade, and industry, by making it easier to market products to more people over greater areas.

Some small farms survived, but more and more large estates, managed by absentee owners, dominated agriculture. At first, these estates were worked by slaves, but by the first century C.E., that had begun to change. Economic pressures forced many members of the lower classes to become *coloni* (tenant farmers) and replace slaves as the mainstay of agricultural labor. *Coloni* were sharecroppers who paid rent in cash, in labor, or in kind. Their movements were restricted, and they were ultimately tied to the land they worked.

WOMEN OF THE UPPER CLASSES

Upper-class Roman women of the late republican era were rich, educated, and politically influential. They preferred the form of marriage that left a wife free of her husband's *manus*. Divorce became common, and some women conducted their sexual lives as freely as men. Privileged women were reluctant to have children, and they employed contraception and abortion to avoid offspring. Augustus worried about falling birthrates in Italy and issued decrees intended to encourage procreation and protect the integrity of the family. His laws had little effect. Women defended their freedoms, and in the fourth century C.E., the emperor Diocletian granted them the right to conduct their own legal affairs rather than work through a fictive male guardian.

Several of the women who belonged to the imperial family exercised great political influence, if only unofficially. Augustus's wife and adviser Livia was honored with the title "Augusta" and survived him to influence the reign of his heir and her son, Tiberius. Claudius's wife, Messalina, tried to overthrow him, and Nero may have owed his ascension to the throne to the maneuvers of his mother, Agrippina.

LIFE IN IMPERIAL ROME: THE APARTMENT HOUSE

Crowding, noise, and bustle were inescapable features of urban life in the Roman Empire. In the city of Rome the rich lived in large, elegantly decorated single-storied homes built around courtyards. These occupied about a third of the city's space. Because public buildings (temples, markets, baths, theaters, and forums) took up another quarter, this forced the vast majority of Romans to squeeze into less than half the city's territory. Ordinary folks found housing in *insulae*, apartment houses that soared to five, six, or more stories. Shortage of space kept rents high, even though these buildings were as uncomfortable as they were dangerous. They had neither central heating nor plumbing. Water had to be carried upstairs from public fountains and sewage toted down (or dumped out a window). Smoky stoves provided heat, and torches, candles, and oil lamps offered light. All these open fires created a great risk of conflagration,

The largest city of the ancient region of Tripolitania, Leptis Magna was located 62 miles southeast of Tripoli on the Mediterranean coast of Libya in North Africa. In its heyday, it was one of the richest cities in the Roman Empire, and it contains some of the finest remains of Roman architecture. The city was lavishly rebuilt by the Emperor Septimius Severus (r. 193–211 C.E.), who was born at Leptis in 146 C.E.

Peter Wilson ©Dorling Kindersley

ENCOUNTERING THE PAST

CHARIOT RACING

Romans invested heavily in facilities for staging public entertainments, and among the earliest and most popular of these were race tracks. Romans were building race courses by the seventh and sixth centuries B.C.E. They called their tracks "circuses" ("circular") because of their curved layout. Rome's Circus Maximus ("Greatest Circus") was one of the earliest as well as the largest and most famous. It was used for a variety of events (riding exhibitions, wild animal hunts, etc.), but nothing rivaled the popularity of chariot racing.

The races staged in the Circus Maximus involved seven laps around the track, a distance of about 2.7 miles. As many as twelve chariots might compete at one time. Various numbers of horses could be used to pull a chariot, but the most common arrangement was the *quadriga*, the four-horse team. Short straightaways, sharp turns, and a crowded field made for a dangerous and, therefore, crowd-pleasing race. Raw speed was often less important than strength, courage, and endurance. Racing companies called *factiones* were formed to sponsor stables and professional riders. They were known by their colors.

The two first were the reds and the whites. They were eventually joined by the blues, greens, purples, and golds. Betting on the races was heavy, and factions went to extremes to win victories. Horses were drugged and drivers bribed—or murdered when they proved uncooperative.

WHY DID Roman politicians and emperors find it worth their while to spend lavishly on amusements like chariot races?

Romans bet heavily on the kind of chariot races shown on this low relief and were fanatically attached to their favorite riders and stables.

© Araldo de Luca/CORBIS

for *insulae* were cheaply built of flammable materials and kept in poor repair. Their collapse was not uncommon. Little wonder that the people of Rome spent most of their time out of doors.

THE CULTURE OF THE EARLY EMPIRE

Literature   The years between the death of Augustus and the reign of Marcus Aurelius (14–180 C.E.) are known as the Silver Age of Latin literature. The authors from this period are a bit more gloomy and pessimistic than the hopeful, optimistic Augustan poets. Their complaints and satirical comments reflect hostility to the power and excesses of the emperors, but to avoid irritating their rulers, they avoided commenting on contemporary affairs and events in recent history. Historical writing about remote periods was safe, as were scholarly studies, but the production of poetry declined. The third century C.E. saw a rise in demand for romances—entertaining, escapist literature that ignored reality.

Architecture   Advances in engineering enabled Rome's architects to design amazing buildings. The Flavian emperors commissioned Rome's immense free-standing amphitheater, the Colosseum, and the later emperors, Diocletian and Caracalla,

SER PENIVS

This mosaic shows a gladiator fighting a leopard. The Roman masses loved gladiatorial contests, which pitted man against man but also man against beast.

Scala/Art Resource, NY

funded construction of massive public baths. The Romans combined the post-and-lintel designs favored by the Greeks with the semicircular arch developed by the Etruscans, and they were the first to exploit the design potential of a Hellenistic invention: concrete. All these features appear in the Pantheon, which the emperor Hadrian erected in Rome (the only major Roman temple to survive intact into the modern era). They are also visible in multitudes of mundane but useful structures, such as bridges and aqueducts. (See "Encountering the Past: Chariot Racing.")

Society The Roman Empire reached its peak during the first two centuries C.E., but the increasing power of its government correlated with a tendency of its citizens to retreat from the public sphere into a world of private pursuits and distractions. In the first century C.E., members of the upper classes vied with one another for election to magistracies and for the honor of serving their communities. By the second century C.E., emperors were having to force unwilling citizens to accept public office. Reluctance to serve was understandable, for the central government held municipal leaders personally responsible for raising the taxes due from their towns. Wealthy men sometimes moved to the countryside to avoid political office, for an official's private property could be confiscated to make up for any shortfall in the taxes he was charged with collecting.

The empire's declining economy explains why the central government put so much pressure on officials of local governments. The end of the civil war and the influx of wealth looted from the East had helped the empire's economy to grow during the first century C.E., but the impact of these factors faded in the first half of the second century C.E. Population declined, but the costs of government continued to rise. Emperors tried to meet these costs by increasing taxes and debasing coinage, but these policies created difficulties that mounted until they threatened to overwhelm the empire.

THE RISE OF CHRISTIANITY

WHO WAS Jesus of Nazareth?

Among the significant developments of the early imperial centuries was the spread of the religion that was eventually to triumph over the West. There were significant odds against the success of Christianity. The faith originated among poor people in an unimportant, remote province of the empire. It had to compete with numerous cults and philosophies for converts, and it faced persecution by the imperial government.

JESUS OF NAZARETH

Christianity appeared in Judaea, a remote eastern province of the empire, in response to the life of an obscure Jew named Jesus from a village called Nazareth. Nothing is known about him apart from the information provided by the Christian scriptures (primarily the gospels of Matthew, Mark, Luke, and John). Mark's gospel, the earliest account of Jesus' ministry, was written about forty years after Jesus' death (ca. 70 C.E.), and it, like the other gospels, was not conceived as an objective historical narrative. Gospels are declarations of faith—proclamations of Jesus as the son of God who grants eternal life to those who believe in him.

Jesus was born during Augustus's reign, and his brief career as a preacher in the style of the Hebrew prophets came at about the midpoint of Tiberius's reign. Many of Jesus' Jewish contemporaries believed their prophets had predicted the coming of a **Messiah**, a redeemer who would vindicate their faith and establish the kingdom of God on earth. Jesus taught that the Messiah would not establish an earthly kingdom but would end the world as human beings know it at the Day of Judgment. God would then reward the righteous and punish the wicked. Jesus advised the faithful, who awaited the imminent apocalyptic event, to forget worldly ambitions and practice love, charity, and humility.

Jesus won a considerable following, but his criticism of the cultic practices associated with the temple in Jerusalem provoked the hostility of the Jewish religious authorities. The Roman governor of Judaea concluded that Jesus was a threat to peace and ordered his crucifixion (ca. 30 C.E.). Three days after his death, Jesus' followers claim he rose from the dead and that his resurrection revealed him to be the Messiah (or the equivalent Greek term, the *Christos*, the "anointed").

PAUL OF TARSUS

The most important missionary at work in the generation that founded the Christian church was a Jew named Paul (born Saul), a Roman citizen and native of the city of Tarsus in Asia Minor. Paul was originally a **Pharisee**, a member of a Jewish sect known for strict adherence to the Jewish law. He was an ardent opponent of Christianity who (ca. 35 C.E.) experienced a mysterious, precipitous conversion.

Jesus and his disciples were all Jews. Consequently, the early Christians had to consider the impact their new faith had on their relationship to Judaism. James, the brother of Jesus, led those who believed Christians should continue to adhere to Jewish law. The less conservative Hellenized Jews, who sided with Paul, saw Christianity as a new universal religion, and they argued that the imposition of the Jewish law—with its dietary prohibitions and painful rite of circumcision—would pose a needless obstacle to conversion.

Messiah Redeemer who would vindicate faith and establish the kingdom of God on earth.

Pharisee Member of a Jewish sect known for strict adherence to the Jewish law.

Paul's vigorous advocacy of a gentile mission made it possible for the Christian faith to spread beyond the confines of Judaism, and Paul, the church's first theologian, did much to define the content of that faith. Paul believed salvation could not be earned by affirming belief in doctrines and doing good deeds. True faith in Jesus as the Christ was a gift of God's grace, not an act of human will.

ORGANIZATION

The emphasis in Jesus' preaching on acts of love and charity focused the Christian community's attention on the needs of the weak, the sick, and the unprotected. Early Christianity was characterized by a warmth and a human appeal that contrasted markedly with the cold, impersonal pagan cults. The Christian message of salvation also confirmed the importance of each individual human soul to God, and this implied that all believers, no matter what their social class or gender, were spiritual equals. All these features of the faith helped it spread throughout the Roman Empire and beyond.

At first, Christianity appealed primarily to the urban poor, and its early rites were simple ceremonies congruent with the poverty of its people. Baptism by water brought converts into the community by cleansing them of original sin (the state of alienation from God into which they had been born). The central ritual of the church was a common meal, the *agape*, or "love feast," followed by a **eucharist** ("thanksgiving"), a celebration of the Lord's Supper in which bread and wine were blessed and consumed. Prayers, hymns, and readings from the scriptures were also part of worship.

The church's unique organization contributed to its success. Christian communities initially had little formal structure, but the need to support missionary preachers and charitable work prompted churches to elect officers: presbyters ("elders") and deacons ("servers"). By the second century C.E., converts had increased to the point where a city was likely to have many churches. This necessitated the appointment of a bishop (*episkopos*, "overseer") to coordinate their activities. Gradually, bishops acquired authority over the countryside as well as urban centers, and by convening councils of their peers they could resolve disputes and promote unity within the church. The quasi-monarchical power of a bishop led to the doctrine of **apostolic succession**, the claim that Jesus gave his disciples (the first bishops) special powers passed down from one generation of bishops to another. It is unlikely that Christianity could have survived the travails of its early years without the strong government provided by its bishops.

THE PERSECUTION OF CHRISTIANS

The Roman authorities could not at first distinguish Christians from Jews and, therefore, they gave Christians the same tolerance they extended to Jews. However, worrisome differences between the two faiths gradually became clear. Christians and Jews both incurred suspicion by denying the existence of the pagan gods and refusing to take part in the state cult of emperor worship. The Romans accepted this from the Jews, a people with ancient traditions who kept to themselves. Christians, however, were ardent missionaries dedicated to spreading their belief that the Roman world was about to be destroyed. They had a network of communities spread throughout the empire, and they were secretive about the rituals they practiced.

The emperor Claudius expelled Christians from the city of Rome, and Nero made them scapegoats for the great fire that destroyed Rome in 64 C.E. Generally, however, the Roman authorities did not initiate attacks on Christians.

This second-century statue in the Lateran Museum in Rome shows Jesus as the biblical Good Shepherd.

"The Good Shepherd", marble, Height: as restored cm 99, as perserved cm 55, head cm 15.5. Late 3rd century A.D. Vatican Museums, Lateran Museums, Pio-Christian Museum, Inv. 28590. Courtesy of the Vatican Museums

5.5
The Letter of Paul to the Romans

agape Common meal, or "love feast," that was the central ritual of the church in early Christianity.

eucharist ("thanksgiving") Celebration of the Lord's Supper in which bread and wine were blessed and consumed.

apostolic succession Special powers that were passed down from one generation of bishops to another.

HISTORY'S VOICES

CHRISTIANS IN THE ROMAN EMPIRE

*P*liny the Younger was governor of the Roman province of Bithynia in Asia Minor about 112 C.E. Confronted by problems caused by Christians, he wrote to the Emperor Trajan to report his policies and to ask for advice. The following exchange between governor and emperor provides evidence of the challenge Christianity posed to Rome and the Roman response.

WHAT PROCEDURES did Trajan recommend in dealing with the Christians?

To the Emperor Trajan

Having never been present at any trials of the Christians, I am unacquainted with the method and limits to be observed either in examining or punishing them.

In the meanwhile, the method I have observed towards those who have been denounced to me as Christians is this: I interrogated them whether they were Christians; if they confessed it, I repeated the question twice again, adding the threat of capital punishment; if they still persevered, I ordered them to be executed. For whatever the nature of their creed might be, I could at least feel no doubt that contumacy and inflexible obstinacy deserved chastisement. There were others also possessed with the same infatuation, but being citizens of Rome, I directed them to be carried thither. ...

Trajan to Pliny

The method you have pursued, my dear Pliny, in sifting the cases of those denounced to you as Christians is extremely proper. It is not possible to lay down any general rule which can be applied as the fixed standard in all cases of this nature. No search should be made for these people, when they are denounced and found guilty they must be punished; with the restriction, however, that when the party denies himself to be a Christian, and shall give proof that he is not (that is, by adoring our Gods he shall be pardoned on the ground of repentance even though he may have formerly incurred suspicion). Information without the accuser's name subscribed must not be admitted in evidence against anyone, as it is introducing a very dangerous precedent, and by no means agreeable to the spirit of the age.

Pliny the Younger, Letters, trans. by W. Melmoth, revised by W. M. Hutchinson (London: William Heinemann, Ltd, Cambridge, MA.: Harvard University Press, 1935), pp. 401, 403, 407.

(See "History's Voices: Christians in the Roman Empire.") Most of the persecutions during the church's first two centuries were the work of mobs, not governmental officials. Christians alarmed their pagan neighbors by ridiculing the ancient cults that protected the state. When misfortunes befell communities, it seemed logical that Christians were to blame for angering the gods. Persecution, however, strengthened the church by weeding out weaklings, uniting the faithful, and creating martyrs—the most persuasive witnesses to the power of Christian faith.

THE EMERGENCE OF CATHOLICISM

Internal disputes threatened the church as much as external persecution. The simple beliefs held by the great majority of Christians were open to a wide range of interpretations and left many questions unanswered. Consequently, arguments broke out about what constituted **orthodox** ("correct") faith, and minorities who disagreed with the **catholic** ("universal") majority were branded **heretics** ("takers" of contrary positions).

This porphyry sculpture on the corner of the church of San Marco in Venice shows Emperor Diocletian (r. 284–305 C.E.) and his three imperial colleagues. Dressed for battle, they clasp one another to express their mutual solidarity.

John Heseltine © Dorling Kindersley

To combat heresy, it was necessary to define orthodoxy. By the end of the second century C.E., the church had agreed on the core for the canon (the "standard"), the orthodox Christian scriptures: the Old Testament, the Gospels, and the Epistles of Paul. (Two more centuries passed before consensus was reached on the other items now found in the New Testament.) The church also drew up creeds, and bishops enforced conformity to these statements of faith. These measures ensured the clarity of doctrine, unity of purpose, and discipline needed for the church's survival.

ROME AS A CENTER OF THE EARLY CHURCH

At an early stage in the church's development, the bishops of the city of Rome began to lay claim to "primacy" (highest rank) among bishops. Rome was the capital of the empire, and it had the largest single Christian congregation of any city. Rome also claimed to be the place where Peter and Paul, the two most important leaders of the early church, were martyred. Peter, whom Rome claimed as its first bishop, was an especially significant figure, for a passage in the Gospel of Matthew (16:18) was interpreted as implying that Jesus had given Peter a unique commission. It quotes Jesus as responding to Peter's confession of faith by saying: "Thou art Peter [*Petros*, in Greek] and upon this rock [*petra*] I will build my church." The bishops of Rome claimed that this was Jesus' appointment of Peter as the head of the church, an office that passed to them as Peter's successors.

THE CRISIS OF THE THIRD CENTURY

Signs of serious trouble for the Roman Empire appeared during the reign of Commodus, the son and successor of Marcus Aurelius. Unlike the "good emperors," who were his predecessors, he was incompetent and autocratic.

BARBARIAN INVASIONS

The pressure on Rome's frontiers, which began to mount during the reign of Marcus Aurelius (d. 180 C.E.), reached massive proportions in the third century. In the East the empire was threatened by the Sassanians, an Iranian dynasty that replaced the Parthians in control of Persia in 224 C.E. The Sassanians raided deep into Roman provinces, and in 260 C.E. they captured and imprisoned the Roman emperor, Valerian.

On the empire's western and northern borders, an ever-increasing number of seminomadic German tribes posed a great danger. Although the Germans had been in contact with the Romans since the second century B.C.E., they had not been much affected by civilization. German males hunted, fought, and caroused. Their women and slaves did most of the farming and productive work. Tribes were led by the chiefs whom their warriors chose from a pool of candidates of royal lineage. A chief headed a *comitatus* ("fraternity"), a company of soldiers bound to him by personal oaths. These men were career raiders, and the wealthy Roman Empire was an irresistible target.

The Goths were the most aggressive of the Germans. By the third century C.E., they had wandered from the coast of the Baltic Sea, their original home, into southern Russia. They attacked Rome's Danube frontier, and about 250 C.E., they overran the empire's Balkan provinces. The threats posed by the Goths and the Sassanids forced the Romans to transfer men from their western to their eastern armies. This weakened the defenses of the West and made it easier for the tribes of the Franks and the Alemanni to cross the Rhine frontier.

Rome's internal weakness invited simultaneous attacks on multiple fronts. By the second century C.E., the Roman army was made up mostly of Romanized provincials, and the training, discipline, and professionalism of Rome's forces was declining. The situation was not improved when a manpower shortage that followed a devastating plague forced Marcus Aurelius to conscript slaves, gladiators, barbarians, and brigands.

Septimius Severus, who followed Marcus Aurelius's son Commodus to the throne (r. 193–211 C.E.), played a crucial role in transforming the character of the Roman army. Septimius was a usurper who owed his office to the support of his soldiers, many of whom were peasants from the less civilized provinces. He gave up all pretext of civilian authority and ruled as a military dictator.

ECONOMIC DIFFICULTIES

The role the army was coming to play in the empire was determined in part by Rome's financial difficulties (exacerbated by the barbarian attacks). To keep up with rising prices caused by inflation, Commodus had to raise the soldiers' pay and the Severan emperors had to double it. The cost to the imperial budget increased by as much as 25 percent, and emperors had to impose new taxes, debase their coinage, and even sell palace furniture to raise the funds they needed. Septimius also courted the soldiers by relaxing discipline and making military service the path to privileged social status.

As emperors devoted more of their attention and resources to the defense of the empire's frontiers, their ability to maintain internal order declined. Piracy, brigandage, and the neglect of roads and harbors hampered trade. Economic productivity diminished as taxation consumed the capital needed to fund economic activity. Efforts to stretch the money supply by debasing coinage produced inflation. The vitality of urban institutions declined as the upper classes fled the cities to escape taxation and the burdens of public office. Artisans began to close

In 305 C.E., Diocletian retired and compelled Maximian to do the same, but the hope for a smooth transition faded when Constantius died prematurely and his son, Constantine began a power struggle by claiming his father's throne. Constantine (r. 306–337 C.E.), who began the fight, ended it by defeating the last of five opponents in 324 C.E. He continued many of Diocletian's policies with two major exceptions. He ruled as sole emperor, and instead of trying to stamp out Christianity, as Diocletian had, Constantine became the church's patron.

Development of Autocracy   The crises facing the government encouraged a drift toward total military mobilization. Traditions of popular government were suppressed in the name of improving efficiency. Emperors ruled by decree, consulting only a few high officials whom they themselves appointed. They protected themselves from assassination by distancing themselves from their people. They surrounded themselves with elaborate courts and appeared in crowns and robes that proclaimed their exalted status. People prostrated themselves before them, kissed the hems of their purple garments, and addressed them as *dominus* ("lord"), a title that implied their authority was divinely based.

Constantine built a superb new city to serve as the empire's capital. Constantinople (modern Istanbul) was situated midway between the eastern and Danubian frontiers on the Bosporus in a Greek district called Byzantium. The city's dedication in 330 C.E. marked the start of a new empire, one that repudiated Rome's pagan and republican traditions and embraced Christianity and autocracy.

Constantinople's rulers protected themselves by creating separate civil and military bureaucracies for their empire. This made it difficult for someone to combine both kinds of power and mount a coup. An elaborate administrative hierarchy divided responsibility and prevented anyone from having much power, and society was kept under surveillance by a network of spies and secret police. Unfortunately, these arrangements invited corruption and promoted inefficiency.

The costs of a 400,000-man army, a vast civilian bureaucracy, an imperial court, and the splendid buildings the emperors continued to commission were more than the Roman world's weak economy could sustain. The fiscal policies that Diocletian introduced and Constantine continued only made things worse. In 301 C.E., Diocletian tried to halt inflation by issuing the Edict of Maximum Prices, but rather than selling their goods and services at the legally mandated prices, people simply began to trade on an underground black market. Diocletian dealt with declining agricultural productivity by herding peasants onto state plantations. This drove poor farmers, who could not survive on their own and who faced enslavement by their government, into the arms of the wealthy few who owned large rural estates. They became *coloni* and worked the land for these new masters in exchange for protection from the emperor and his tax collectors.

Division of the Empire   Constantine divided the empire among his three sons. Constantius II (r. 337–361 C.E.), the eldest, survived his brothers, reunited the empire, and bequeathed it to his cousin Julian (r. 361–363 C.E.). Julian "the Apostate" (as he was dubbed by Christian historians) is remembered primarily for attempting to revive Rome's pagan cults. His reign, however, was too short to permit his ideas to take root, and when he died in battle, the pagan renaissance died with him.

By the time a soldier named Valentinian (r. 364–375 C.E.) won the throne, there were so many trouble spots that the new emperor concluded he could not

QUICK REVIEW

Constantinople
- Dedicated by Constantine in 330 C.E.
- Situated on the Bosporus midway between eastern and Danube frontiers
- Marked the start of a new empire

defend his realm alone. He divided it and gave the eastern half to his brother Valens (r. 364–378 C.E.). Valentinian resided at Milan and spent his time defending the West against the German tribes of the Franks and Alemanni.

In the East, a group of Germans confronted Valens with a different kind of problem. In 376 C.E., the tribe of the Visigoths asked permission to enter the empire to escape the Huns, a fierce people who were migrating out of central Asia. Valens acquiesced but was unable to provide adequately for all the refugees who fled into the empire. When the desperate Goths began to plunder the Balkan provinces, Valens called out his army. He and his men confronted them near the city of Adrianople in 378 C.E. and were destroyed.

Control of the East then passed to an able general named Theodosius (r. 379–395 C.E.). He pacified the Goths and enlisted many of them in his army. After his western colleague died, Theodosius reunited the empire for what proved to be the last time.

The Rural West   The disintegration of the empire was encouraged not just by wars and politics, but by the diverging cultures of its eastern and western halves. The West, which had fewer and younger cities, was largely rural, and villas, fortified country estates, came to control much of its territory. As the rich abandoned urban life and moved to the country, they slipped from the control of the imperial authorities. The ability of the central government to provide essential services, such as the maintenance and policing of roads, declined. This handicapped commerce and made communications difficult. Standards of living fell, and regions became increasingly self-sufficient. By the fifth century C.E., the western empire had dissolved and been replaced by isolated estates. The rural aristocrats who owned the land dominated a population composed primarily of dependent laborers, and only the Christian church kept the memory of imperial unity alive.

The Byzantine East   The loss of the West strengthened the East by enabling Constantinople to concentrate on its own affairs. Constantinople diverted most of the barbarian invaders into the West and protected the ancient, thriving cities of the East. Central government continued to function, and a flourishing hybrid of Christian and Classical culture was born as the East entered the "Byzantine" phase in its civilization. For the next thousand years, Roman emperors reigned in Constantinople.

THE TRIUMPH OF CHRISTIANITY

Christianity's rise to become the Roman state religion was linked with political and cultural events that were transforming the empire in other ways. The traditional state cults were closely linked to the fading civic life of Rome's declining cities. Many people still adhered to the ancient rites, but the pagan deities seemed less and less effective as the problems of the fourth and fifth centuries C.E. mounted. Worshipers sought more powerful gods who offered them personal help in this world and immortality in the next. Many new religions appeared, and old ones were combined and reinterpreted. (See Map 5–3.)

Manichaeism, a religion founded by a Persian prophet in the third century C.E., offered early Christianity stiff competition. The Manichaeans interpreted human history as a war between forces of light and darkness, good and evil. They taught that the human body was a material prison for the element of light that was the human soul. To achieve salvation, individuals had to free the light by mastering the desires of the flesh. Manichaeans led ascetic lives, worshiped simply, and developed durable institutions. Their faith persisted into the Middle Ages.

Christianity drew much from the novel eastern cults with which it competed for converts. None, however, had its universal appeal, and none was as great a threat to it as the ancient philosophies and the state religion.

Imperial Persecution Rome's emperors largely ignored Christianity until the middle of the third century. As the empire's problems increased and Christians became more numerous and visible, this changed. A growing sense of insecurity made rulers less willing to tolerate dissent.

Serious trouble erupted for the church in 250 C.E., when an emperor named Decius (r. 249–251 C.E.), who was mired in a war with the Goths, ordered all citizens to sacrifice to the state gods. When Christians refused, Decius tried to purge them from the empire. Valerian (r. 253–260 C.E.) continued to persecute the church—partly out of desire to confiscate the wealth of rich Christians. Later emperors were, however, preoccupied by other more pressing matters, and persecution lapsed until the end of the century.

By Diocletian's day, both the numbers of Christians and hostility toward them had increased. Diocletian's plan for saving the empire demanded conformity to the imperial will, and in 303, he implemented the most serious and thorough of the attempts to obliterate the church. Persecution was, however, self-defeating. The government's extreme actions horrified many pagans, and the courageous demeanor of Christian martyrs aroused sympathy and made new converts.

In 311 C.E., Galerius, Diocletian's successor in the East and one of the most vigorous persecutors, was persuaded (perhaps by his wife) to issue an edict of toleration legitimating Christian worship. Constantine concurred, and a year later

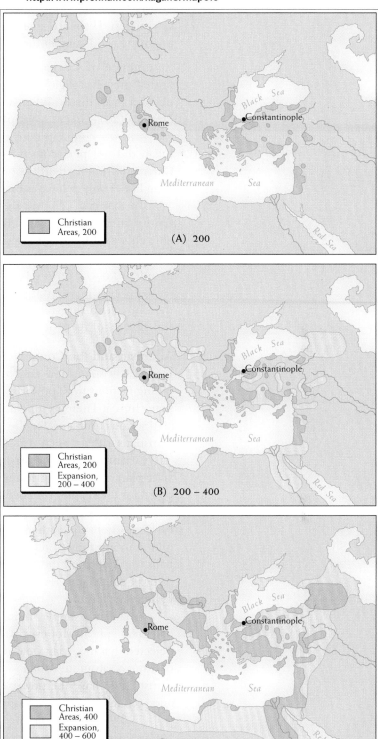

MAP 5–3

The Spread of Christianity   Christianity grew swiftly in the third, fourth, fifth, and sixth centuries—especially after the conversion of the emperors in the fourth century. By 600, on the eve of the birth of the new religion of Islam, Christianity was dominant throughout the Mediterranean world and most of western Europe.

HOW IMPORTANT was state acceptance of Christianity important to the religion's growth in the Roman Empire?

Constantine celebrated his conquest of the western empire by converting to Christianity. His patronage ensured the ultimate triumph of the church over its opponents and competitors.

Emergence of Christianity as the State Religion   Constantine's sons supported the new religion, but the succession of their cousin, Julian the Apostate, posed a brief threat. Julian was a Neoplatonist, a follower of the philosopher, Plotinus (205–270 C.E.). Neoplatonism combined rational speculation and mysticism and was contemptuous of Christianity's lack of intellectual sophistication. Julian did not persecute the church, but he withdrew its privileges, removed Christians from high offices, and introduced new forms of pagan worship. His reform lasted only as long as his brief reign.

In 394 C.E., Theodosius outlawed pagan rites and recognized Christianity as the sole legal religion of the empire. This solved some of the church's problems but created others. The church's growing prestige and influence threatened its spiritual fervor by attracting large numbers of people who converted for the wrong reasons. Dependence on state patronage also posed dangers. The strong eastern emperors subordinated the church to the state, and the collapse of the western empire deprived the church of its protector.

Arianism and the Council of Nicaea   Once the threat of persecution was removed, Christians were free to concentrate on their doctrinal disputes, and opposing factions were powerfully motivated to struggle for control of the wealthy state church. Their arguments spilled over into the streets, caused riots, and created serious problems for the state. Christians, as it turned out, could persecute Christians with as much zeal as pagan fanatics.

Arianism, the most disruptive of the doctrinal controversies, was sparked by an explanation that a priest named Arius of Alexandria (ca. 280–336 C.E.) proposed for the relationship between Christ, the Son, and God the Father. Arius insisted that Christ was the first of God the Father's creations and the being through whom the Father created all other things. For Arius, Jesus was neither fully man nor fully God but something in between. Arius was opposed by Christians who endorsed the doctrine of the Trinity, the belief that God is a unity of three equal persons (Father, Son, and Holy Spirit). Arius dismissed this as thinly veiled polytheism.

Arianism's simple, rational explanation of the central Christian mystery had great appeal. However, Athanasius (ca. 293–373 C.E.), bishop of Alexandria, objected that the Arian view of Christ destroyed Christ's effectiveness as an agent of human salvation. Athanasius noted that only a fully human and fully divine Christ could have the power to bridge the gap between humanity and divinity and reconcile sinners with God.

In 325 C.E., Constantine tried to resolve the issue by inviting all the Christian bishops to a meeting at Nicaea, a city near Constantinople. Athanasius's arguments prevailed and were enshrined in the council's Nicene Creed. This, however, did not stop the spread of Arianism. Some of the later emperors were Arians, and some of the most successful of the missionaries who worked among the Germans were Arians. Many of the German tribes embraced Arian Christianity before their entry into the empire. Christianity had the power to divide as well as to unite.

Arianism   Belief that Christ was the first of God the Father's creations and the being through whom the Father created all other things.

ARTS AND LETTERS IN THE LATE EMPIRE

*T*he art and literature of the late empire reflect the confluence of pagan and Christian ideas and the changing tastes of the Roman aristocracy, the ancient world's literary class. Much of the literature of the late empire is polemical, and much of its art is propagandist. The men who came to power as the empire declined were soldiers from the provinces whose roots were in the lower classes. By mastering and preserving Classical culture, these men hoped to stabilize their world and confirm their credentials as its rightful leaders.

Crucifixion, carving, c. 420 C.E. (ivory)
British Museum, London, UK/Bridgeman Art

THE PRESERVATION OF CLASSICAL CULTURE

Acquisition of Classical culture by the newly arrived ruling class was facilitated in several ways. Works by great authors were copied and circulated widely. Instead of being written on continuous rolls of papyrus or parchment, they were published in a more convenient new form as codices (bundles of pages stitched together like modern books). Scholars assisted novice readers by condensing long works and writing commentaries that explained difficult texts. Grammars for Greek and Latin also had to be created, for new languages were replacing the Classical tongues in many parts of the Roman world.

CHRISTIAN WRITERS

Original works by pagan writers of the late empire were neither numerous nor especially distinguished, but Christian literature abounded. Christian "apologists" used poetry and prose to explain Christian practices to pagans, and Christians wrote sermons, hymns, and biblical commentaries for their own use.

Several of Christianity's most influential scholars flourished during the waning years of the empire. Jerome (348–420 C.E.), who was thoroughly trained in Classical literature and rhetoric as well as Hebrew, created the **Vulgate**, the Latin translation of the Bible that became the standard text for the Catholic Church. Eusebius of Caesarea (ca. 260–ca. 340 C.E.) wrote an idealized biography of Constantine and an *Ecclesiastical History* that set forth a Christian view of history as a process whereby God's will is revealed. However, it is the work of Augustine (354–430 C.E.), bishop of Hippo in North Africa, that towers over all others and best illustrates the fruitfulness of the era's efforts to use the tools of Classical culture to explicate Christian faith.

Augustine was born at Carthage and trained as a teacher of rhetoric. His father was a pagan, but his mother was a Christian and hers was ultimately the stronger influence. He explored Manichaeism, skepticism, and Neoplatonism before he came to Christianity. But following his conversion, his Classical education in rhetoric and philosophy served him well. He became the most influential of the Latin theologians.

Augustine's belief that reason prepares people to accept what is revealed by faith helped him reconcile Christianity and Classical culture. His greatest works are *Confessions*, an autobiography that describes his journey to faith, and *The City of God*, a response to the pagan charge that a sack of Rome by the Visigoths in 410 C.E. took place because Rome abandoned its old gods. Augustine explained the course of history as a complex interaction of the secular, the "City of Man,"

Vulgate Latin translation of the Bible that became the standard text for the Catholic Church.

and the spiritual, the "City of God." The former was fated to be destroyed on the Day of Judgment, but Augustine saw no reason to assume that conditions would improve for human life before that. The fall of Rome was neither surprising nor all that significant, for all states, even a Christian Rome, were part of the City of Man. They were, therefore, corrupt and mortal. Only the City of God, the true church, was immortal, and it was untouched by earthly calamities.

THE PROBLEM OF THE DECLINE AND FALL OF THE EMPIRE IN THE WEST

Although Augustine doubted their transcendent significance, the events of the fifth century did change the course of Western civilization, and people have never ceased to speculate about reasons for the ancient world's collapse. Soil exhaustion, plague, climatic change, and even poisoning caused by lead water pipes have been proposed as contributing causes. Some scholars blame the institution of slavery for Rome's failure to make the advances in science and technology that might have solved its economic problems. Others claim that excessive governmental interference in the economic life of the empire was at fault—particularly insofar as this affected the fate of cities and the literate urban classes.

Although many of these things may have been contributing factors, there is a simpler explanation for Rome's failure. The growth of Rome's empire was fueled by conquests that fed on themselves. The resources from conquests funded additional conquests until the Romans overextended themselves. As pressure from outsiders grew, the Romans could not find the resources needed to fend off their enemies. To blame them for their failure to end slavery and bring on industrial and economic revolutions is fruitless, for we do not yet fully understand what caused those revolutions in the modern era. At the very least, the Romans deserve respect for their tenacity, for the real question we should ask about them may not be why their empire fell, but how it managed to last as long as it did.

SUMMARY

The Augustan Principate After defeating Mark Antony at Actium in 31 B.C.E., Octavian started transforming his rule into the functional equivalent of a monarchy. In 26 B.C.E., he made a show of giving up his powers, no doubt expecting the Senate to beg him to keep them, as it in fact did. From then on he was referred to as Augustus. He introduced administrative reforms, widened the talent pool from which senators were selected, and generally improved his subjects' standard of living. He professionalized the military and attempted to secure the northern frontier. He modeled austere morality and supported traditional Roman religion.

Civilization of the Ciceronian and Augustan Ages Roman culture flourished in the late republican period and in the Principate of Augustus. Hellenistic influences permeated the arts and literature, but the great works are clearly Roman in character. History, poetry, and law all found able practitioners in the late republic. Augustus simplified patronage for the arts. Augustan literature features

Civilization of the Ciceronian and Augustan Ages Roman culture flourished in the late republican period and in the Principate of Augustus. Hellenistic influences permeated the arts and literature, but the great works are clearly Roman in character. History, poetry, and law all found able practitioners in the late republic. Augustus simplified patronage for the arts. Augustan literature features some of the most recognizable names of the period: Vergil, Horace, Ovid, among others. Augustus also supported the visual arts; some of Rome's loveliest monuments were built under his reign.

Imperial Rome, 14–180 C.E. The monarchical, hereditary rule of Augustus's successors was based on undisguised military power. In 69 C.E., Vespasian, the first emperor who was not a descendant of Roman nobility, assumed the throne. His Flavian dynasty was followed by the five "good emperors." The provinces were generally peaceful during this period. Latin was spoken throughout the West; in the East, Greek was still the predominant language. Culturally, "Romanitas" spread throughout the cities and towns of the empire. The situation for Jews and for peasant farmers was not attractive. Border defenses, particularly in the north, were a recurring problem for the empire. Women's status improved. Many people lived in *insulae*, multistory apartment buildings that were cramped and uncomfortable. Latin literature experienced a "Silver Age" between 14 and 180 C.E., offering a more critical worldview than the works of the Augustan period. Architecture flourished. By the second century C.E., problems such as a decline in the vitality of local government, a stagnating economy, the expense of defense, and probably a mysterious decline in population were foreshadowing crises to come.

The Rise of Christianity Jesus of Nazareth was born in Judaea under the reign of Augustus. He gained a large following, particularly among the poor, with a message of a coming Day of Judgment and criticism of existing religious practices. Feared and misunderstood by the authorities, Jesus was crucified in Jerusalem, probably in 30 C.E. Written decades after his death, the Gospels present Jesus as the Son of God, a redeemer who was resurrected after death. The writings of Paul of Tarsus are especially important, since he makes the case that Christianity is a new and universal religion. The *agape* ("love feast") created a sense of solidarity across classes among early Christians, and it helped the religion spread throughout the Roman Empire and beyond. By the end of the second century C.E., the Catholic Church had been institutionalized as the definer of Christian orthodoxy.

The Crisis of the Third Century External military threats and internal social weakness interacted in a vicious circle. Commodus came to power in 180 C.E. When he was assassinated in 192 C.E., civil war again erupted and military strongman Septimius Severus emerged victorious. In the third century C.E., others invaded the outskirts of the empire. Repelling these challenges required more resources than the society could spare; labor shortages, inflation, and neglect of infrastructure such as roads weakened Rome's economy. Social stratification increased. Invasions and anarchy characterized the middle of the third century C.E.

IMAGE KEY

for pages 114–115.

a. Augustus of Primaporta, c.20 B.C.E., Roman art

b. Model of Colosseum

c. Clay plaque for roof showing emblem of 20th Roman Legion, a charging boar

d. Arch of Titus, C.E. 81, Relief: Spoils from temple in Jerusalem

e. "The Good Shepherd", Late 3rd century C.E.   Marble, Height: as restored cm 99, as perserved cm 55, head cm 15.5. Late 3rd century C.E. Vatican Musuems, Pio-Christian Museum, Inv. 28590. Courtesy of the Vatican Museums

f. The title of this mosaic in the Bardo Museum in Tunis, Tunisia is "Virgil writing the Aeniad, inspired by two muses," Cleo (left) is the muse of storytelling and Melpomene (right) is the muse of tragedy

g. Saturnia, Tellus, Goddess of Earth, Air and Water. Panel from the Ara Pacis. 13-9 B.C.E. Museum of the Ara Pacis, Rome.   Nimathallah/Art Resource, NY

h. Imperial Roman Cameo of Livia and Tiberius

i. Head of the emperor Constantine from a colossal statue nearly forty feet high located in his monumental basilica

j. Crucifixion, carving, c. 420 AD (ivory). Bristish Museum, London, UK/Bridgeman Art Library

and his co-emperor retired in 305 C.E. Diocletian and Constantine both ruled autocratically from Eastern cities. Diocletian tried to suppress Christianity, whereas Constantine supported it. Constantine's death was followed by yet another struggle for power. By the end of the fourth century, the empire had been divided permanently. Christianity's continued viability depended on its ability to cope with political interference and doctrinal disputes.

Arts and Letters in the Late Empire   Much of the art and literature of the late empire reflects the relationship between Christianity and pagan religions. The empire's new rulers came from the lower classes of the provinces; in their efforts to restore classical culture, they inevitably reshaped it. Christian writings were numerous, the most significant among them the works of Augustine in which he combined Christian faith and pagan (Classical) reason.

The Problem of the Decline and Fall of the Empire in the West   Imperial government fell in the West in the fifth century, in the face of barbarian invasions. Ever since, historians and commentators have offered explanations, many of which seem specious. Like the early-twentieth-century historian Edward Gibbon, the authors believe the question should be more properly framed as, "How did the Roman Empire last as long as it did?" rather than, "Why did the Roman Empire decline and fall?" The Roman Empire could not expand forever; without the infusion of new people and new wealth that territorial conquest provided, the Roman Empire could not survive.

REVIEW QUESTIONS

1. How did Augustus alter Rome's constitution and government? How did his innovations solve the problems that had plagued the republic? Why were the Romans willing to accept him?

2. How did the literature of the "Golden Age" differ from that of the "Silver Age"? What did poets contribute to the success of Augustus's reforms?

3. Why were Christians persecuted by the Roman authorities? What enabled them to acquire such an enormous following by the fourth century C.E.?

4. What were the political, social, and economic problems that beset Rome in the third and fourth centuries C.E.? How did Diocletian and Constantine deal with them? Were these men able to halt Rome's decline? Were there problems they could not solve?

KEY TERMS

agape   (p. 129)

apostolic succession   (p. 129)

Arianism   (p. 138)

Augustus   (p. 116)

catholic   (p. 130)

eucharist   (p. 129)

heretics   (p. 130)

imperator   (p. 116)

jus gentium   (p. 119)

jus naturale   (p. 119)

Messiah   (p. 128)

orthodox   (p. 130)

Pharisee   (p. 128)

tetrarchy   (p. 133)

Vulgate   (p. 139)

 For additional study resources for this chapter, go to:
www.prenhall.com/kagan3/chapter5

PART TWO · THE MIDDLE AGES

POLITICS & GOVERNMENT

330	Constantinople becomes new capital of Roman Empire
410	Visigoths sack Rome
451–453	Attila the Hun invades Italy
455	Vandals overrun Rome
476	Odovacer deposes the last Western emperor
489–493	Theodoric's Ostrogoth kingdom established in Italy

527–565	Reign of Justinian
568	Lombard invasion of Italy

Emperor Justinian ▶
Justinian, detail c. 547. Mosaic technique.
Canali Photobank, Capriolo, Italy

SOCIETY & ECONOMY

400	Cities and trade begin to decline in the West; Germanic (barbarian) tribes settle in the West

533–534	*Corpus juris civilis* compiled by Justinian

◀ *Interior of Hagia Sophia*

RELIGION & CULTURE

312	Constantine embraces Christianity
325	Council of Nicaea
380	Christianity becomes the official religion of the Roman Empire
413–426	Saint Augustine writes *City of God*
451	Council of Chalcedon
496	The Franks embrace Christianity

Abbey of ▶
Monte Cassino

529	Saint Benedict founds monastery at Monte Cassino
537	Byzantine Church of Hagia Sophia completed
590–604	Pope Gregory the Great
622	Muhammad's flight from Mecca (Hegira)

◀ *The Great Mosque in Mecca*

632–733	Muslim expansion and conquests
732	Charles Martel defeats Muslims at Poitiers
768–814	Reign of Charlemagne
843	Treaty of Verdun partitions Carolingian empire

▲ *Charlemagne on horseback*

◀ *Bust of Charlemagne*

918	Saxon Henry I becomes first non-Frankish king, as Saxons succeed Carolingians in Germany
987	Capetians succeed Carolingians in France
1066	Battle of Hastings (Norman Conquest of England)
1071	Seljuk Turks defeat Byzantine armies at Manzikert
1099	Jerusalem falls to Crusaders

▲ *Harold's crowning, The Bayeux Tapestry*

1152	Frederick I Barbarossa first Hohenstaufen emperor
1187	Saladin reconquers Jerusalem from West
1204	Fourth Crusade captures Constantinople
1214	Philip II Augustus defeats English and German armies at Bouvines
1215	Magna Carta
1240	Mongols dominate Russia
1250	Death of Frederick II (end of Hohenstaufen dynasty)
1257	German princes establish electoral college to elect emperor

▲ *Magna Carta*

632–733	Muslims disrupt western Mediterranean trade
700	Agrarian society centered around the manor predominates in the West
700–800	Moldboard plow and three field system in use
700	Islam enters its Golden Age
800	Byzantium enters its Golden Age
800	Introduction of collar harness
850	Muslims occupy parts of Spain
880s	Vikings penetrate central Europe

900	Introduction of the horseshoe
900–1100	Rise of towns, guilds, and urban culture in West
1086	*Domesday Book*

◀ *11th or 12th century horseshoe*

Cathedral facade, ▶ *Chartres, France*

| 1130 | Gothic architecture begins to displace Romanesque |
| 1200 | Shift from dues to rent tenancy on manors |

725–787	Iconoclastic Controversy in East
ca. 775	*Donation of Constantine*
782	Alcuin of York runs Charlemagne's palace school
800	Pope Leo crowns Charlemagne emperor

| 910 | Benedictine monastery of Cluny founded |

◀ *Abbey at Cluny*

1122	Concordat of Worms ends Investiture Controversy
1158	First European university founded in Bologna
1210	Franciscan order founded
1216	Dominican order founded
1265	Thomas Aquinas's *Summa Theologica* begun
ca. 1275	*Romance of the Rose*

◀ *Icon of the Virgin Episkepis*

980s	Orthodox Christianity penetrates Russia
1054	Schism between Eastern and Western churches
1075	Pope Gregory VII condemns lay investiture
1095	Pope Urban II preaches the First Crusade

St. Francis ▶

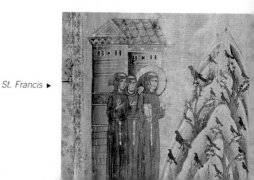

6 Late Antiquity and the Early Middle Ages
Creating a New European Society and Culture (476–1000)

CHAPTER HIGHLIGHTS

On the Eve of the Frankish Ascendancy Late antiquity, the centuries before and after the fall of Rome (476), was a vibrant period of self-discovery and self-definition for the peoples of the Mediterranean. The emergence of distinctive European, Byzantine, and Islamic civilizations took place against the backdrop of the collapse of the Roman Empire in the West.

The Byzantine Empire The eastern portion of the Roman Empire endured as the Byzantine Empire. It reached the peak of its power under Justinian in the mid–sixth century. Justinian codified Roman law and supported Orthodox Christianity. Constantinople was the economic, administrative, and cultural heart of the empire.

Islam and the Islamic World In the seventh century, Muhammad founded a new religion on the Arabian peninsula. By 750 the Islamic Empire stretched from Spain to India. The West profited from its contact with Islam.

Western Society and the Developing Christian Church As trade declined in the West, people migrated from cities to farmland. New social arrangements including serfdom, manorialism, and feudalism emerged. The Christian church played a key role in the emerging European civilization.

The Kingdom of the Franks Clovis founded the first Frankish dynasty, the Merovingians. The Carolingian dynasty made strategic alliances with the nobility and the Church. Under Charlemagne, the Franks built an impressive empire. The empire collapsed after his death in 814. During the ninth and tenth centuries, invasions by the Vikings and others ushered in a "dark age" for Europe.

Feudal Society The feudal system was built around the exchange of land, labor, and military protection. All participants in the feudal system constantly negotiated and competed for advantage. In time, feudalism contributed many of the political and legal institutions that developed into the modern nation-state.

CHAPTER QUESTIONS

HOW DID Germanic migrations contribute to the fall of the Roman Empire?

HOW DID the Byzantine Empire continue the legacy of Rome?

HOW DID Islamic culture influence the West?

HOW DID the developing Christian Church influence Western society during the early Middle Ages?

HOW DID the reign of Clovis differ from that of Charlemagne?

WHAT WERE the characteristics of a feudal society?

CHAPTER OUTLINE

• On the Eve of the Frankish Ascendancy
• The Byzantine Empire
• Islam and the Islamic World
• Western Society and the Developing Christian church
• The Kingdom of the Franks
• Feudal Society

IMAGE KEY

for pages 146–147 is on page 170.

HOW DID Germanic migrations contribute to the fall of the Roman Empire?

Scholars increasingly view the period between 250 C.E. and 800 C.E.—called Late Antiquity—as a single world, both cohesive and moving apart, bounded by the Roman and Sassanian (Persian) empires. The western and eastern (Byzantine) empires of Rome never succumbed culturally to barbarian and Muslim invaders. In the east, the Sassanians created a powerful empire and deeply penetrated Rome's provinces. By the mid–eighth century, Arab conquests extended Muslim influence from the Middle East to North Africa and Spain. In western Europe, Germanic heritage, Judeo-Christian religion, Roman language and law, and Greco-Byzantine administration and culture gradually combined to create a uniquely European way of life.

ON THE EVE OF THE FRANKISH ASCENDANCY

*T*he strategies devised to save the Roman Empire in the late third century succeeded only in influencing how it fell. Diocletian (r. 284–305) strengthened Rome's defenses by dividing his realm in half and appointing a co-emperor. As this arrangement became permanent, the halves of the empire embarked on different courses. Imperial rule faded from the West and grew increasingly autocratic in the East.

The empire was briefly reunited by Constantine the Great (r. 306–337), and in 324, he moved its capital to Constantinople. This "new Rome" on the border between Europe and Asia Minor flourished as old Rome declined. Rome was even superceded as an administrative center in the West by the city of Milan, which had better communications with the Rhine and Danube frontiers. In 402, even Milan was judged too exposed to barbarian invasions, and the western court relocated to Ravenna on the Adriatic coast. By then, the western empire's days were numbered, and Constantinople defended what was left of Roman prestige.

GERMANIC MIGRATIONS

The Germans who invaded the West were not strangers. Romans and Germans had traded and commingled for centuries, and some Germans even rose to command posts in the Roman army. However, in 376, the pace of German migration began to accelerate until it overwhelmed the western half of the empire. The process began in 376, when the eastern emperor Valens (r. 364–378) admitted the Visigoths ("West Goths") into the empire. They were fleeing the approach of the notoriously violent Huns of Mongolia. The Huns were a potential threat to Rome as well, and by enlisting the Visigoths as *foederati* (allied aliens resident within the empire), Valens hoped to strengthen the East's defenses. (See Map 6–1.)

The Visigoths entered the empire as impoverished refugees. Exploitation of their misery by Roman profiteers caused them to rebel, and in 378, at the Battle of Adrianople, they destroyed Valens and his army. Constantinople defended itself by persuading the Visigoths to invade Italy, and the western empire responded by withdrawing troops from its frontiers to defend Italy. This allowed other German tribes to cross the Rhine unopposed and wander virtually through the western provinces.

Although the largest German tribe probably numbered no more than 100,000 people, the much larger Roman population offered little resistance to the German migration. The western empire was badly overextended and weakened by decades of famine, pestilence, and overtaxation. Its government was also handicapped by internal power struggles.

MAP EXPLORATION

Interactive map: To explore this map further, go to **http://www.prehnall.com/kagan3/map6.1**

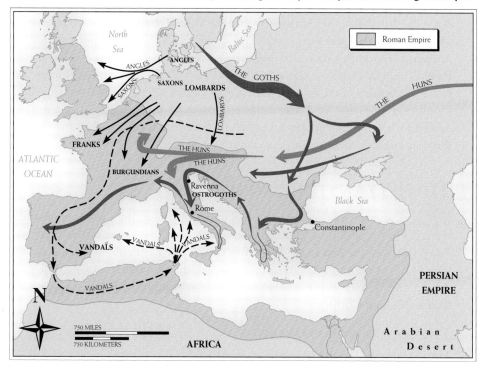

MAP 6–1

Barbarian Migrations into the West in the Fourth and Fifth Centuries   The forceful intrusion of Germanic and non-Germanic barbarians into the Roman Empire from the last quarter of the fourth century through the fifth century made for a constantly changing pattern of movement and relations. The map shows the major routes taken by the usually unwelcome newcomers and the areas most deeply affected by the main groups.

WHICH PART of the Empire was least affected by barbarian migrations?

NEW WESTERN MASTERS

In the early fifth century, Italy suffered a series of devastating blows. Led by a competent king named Alaric (ca. 370–410), the Visigoths sacked Rome in 410. In 452, the infamous Attila and the Huns invaded the peninsula, and in 455, the Vandals sacked Rome. By the mid–fifth century, barbarian chieftains had replaced Roman emperors throughout western Europe, and in 476 the barbarian general Odovacer (ca. 434–493) deposed the last of the West's figurehead emperors, Romulus Augustulus.

In 493, Constantinople's emperor Zeno (r. 474–491) sent the Ostrogoths ("East Goths") under their king Theodoric (ca. 454–526) west to reclaim Italy (nominally) for the eastern empire. By then, German tribes had thoroughly overrun the West. The Ostrogoths settled in Italy, the Franks in northern Gaul, the Burgundians in Provence, the Visigoths in southern Gaul and Spain, the Vandals in Africa and the western Mediterranean, and the Angles and Saxons in England.

The Germans did not reduce western Europe to savagery. They respected Roman culture and learned from their Roman subjects. Except in Britain and northern Gaul, vernacular Latin and Roman governmental institutions survived and blended with German customs. Only the Vandals and the Anglo-Saxons (and, after 466, the Visigoths) refused to keep the myth of the empire alive by professing titular obedience to Constantinople.

The Visigoths, the Ostrogoths, and the Vandals had converted to Christianity before entering the West, but the missionaries who worked among them were Arians (heretics who claimed Christ was a creature subordinate to God the Father). Their faith was an obstacle to relations with their orthodox Roman subjects. The leaders of the Franks wisely chose (about 500) to embrace the Catholic ("universal") version of Christianity endorsed by the bishops of Rome. This brought them popular support that helped them subdue rival tribes and become the dominant German power in western Europe.

THE BYZANTINE EMPIRE

*A*s western Europe succumbed to the Germans, the eastern empire also changed. It became the medieval Byzantine Empire, a term that came into use first in the West after the empire's collapse in 1453. From the date of its founding in 324 to its conquest by the Ottoman Turks in 1453, Constantinople remained the seat of the "Roman" emperor whose subjects were Greek-speaking Christians.

THE REIGN OF JUSTINIAN

The Byzantine Empire reached a territorial and cultural peak during the reign of the emperor Justinian (r. 527–565). At a time when urban life was disappearing from the West, Justinian's domain boasted over 1,500 cities. Constantinople, with about 350,000 residents, was the largest, but the eastern empire had provincial cities with populations of about 50,000. They were bustling centers of economic and intellectual activity. At Justinian's command, fortifications, churches, monasteries, and palaces arose across

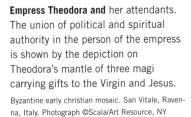

HOW DID the Byzantine Empire continue the legacy of Rome?

Empress Theodora and her attendants. The union of political and spiritual authority in the person of the empress is shown by the depiction on Theodora's mantle of three magi carrying gifts to the Virgin and Jesus.

Byzantine early christian mosaic. San Vitale, Ravenna, Italy. Photograph ©Scala/Art Resource, NY

the empire. Most famous and enduring is Constantinople's Church of Hagia Sophia (Holy Wisdom) completed in 537. Its key feature is a massive dome, 112 feet in diameter, and many windows and open spaces, which give the interior a remarkable airiness and luminosity.

Justinian's remarkable wife Theodora (d. 548) was his chief counselor. If the *Secret History* of Procopius, Justinian's court historian, is to be believed, Theodora was the daughter of a circus bear trainer and began her career as a prostitute. Her background may have given her a toughness that was useful to her husband. She was particularly helpful in dealing with the religious quarrels that threatened the unity of the empire. As emperor, Justinian professed orthodox Christianity, but Theodora's quiet support for the heretical **Monophysites** helped control a powerful popular movement. The Monophysites believed Jesus had a single nature (a composite of the human and divine), whereas the orthodox church claimed he had two distinct natures—one fully human and the other fully divine. The Monophysites were especially powerful in the eastern provinces of the empire. After Theodora's death, the imperial government tried to stamp them out. This was a mistake, for a few years later, when Persian and Arab armies invaded, the resentful Monophysites offered little resistance.

Law   Byzantine policy emphasized centralized governmental control and social conformity ("one God, one empire, one religion"). To achieve this, Justinian commissioned scholars to codify Roman law. The *Corpus Juris Civilis* (*Body of Civil Law*), which resulted, was issued in four parts: the *Code* revised imperial edicts dating back to the reign of Hadrian (117–138), the *Novellae* (*New Things*) contained Justinian's decrees, the *Digest* summarized opinions of famous legal experts, and the *Institutes* provided a textbook for training lawyers. The medieval West was governed by what is called common law, but from the late medieval Renaissance on, Justinian's Roman law transformed the administration of justice and promoted the centralization of governments across Europe.

Reconquest in the West   Justinian sought to reconquer the imperial provinces lost to the barbarians in the West. Beginning in 533, his armies overran the Vandal kingdom in North Africa and Sicily, the Ostrogothic kingdom in Italy, and part of Spain. The price of conquest was high: By Justinian's death, his empire was financially exhausted, and plague had ravaged Constantinople and must of the East. Byzantine rule survived in Sicily and parts of southern Italy until the eleventh century, but most of Justinian's Western and North African conquests were soon lost to Lombards and Muslim Arabs. (See Map 6–2.)

6.2
Corpus Juris Civilis: Prologue

Built during the reign of Justinian, Hagia Sophia (Church of the Holy Wisdom) is a masterpiece of Byzantine and world architecture. After the Turkish conquest of Costantinople in 1453, Hagia Sophia was transformed into a mosque with four minarets, still visible today.

Marvin Trachtenberg

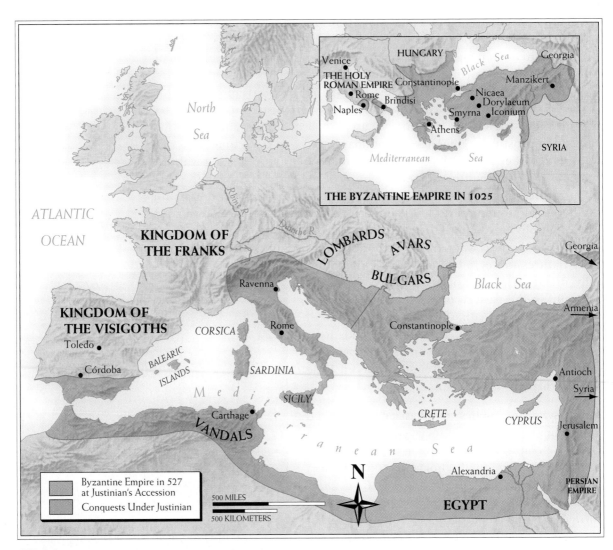

MAP 6–2

The Byzantine Empire at the Time of Justinian's Death Justinian reconquered lands in the West that once belonged to the Roman Empire. From 500 to 1100, the Byzantine Empire was the center of Christian civilization. The inset shows the empire in 1025, before its losses to the Seljuk Turks.

IN THE second half of the first millennium c.e., how did the power and influence of Rome and Constantinople compare?

THE SPREAD OF BYZANTINE CHRISTIANITY

In the late sixth and seventh centuries, nomadic, pagan tribes of Avars, Slavs, and Bulgars invaded and occupied the Balkan provinces of the eastern empire, more than once menacing Constantinople itself. Yet after almost two centuries of intermittent warfare, the Slavs and Bulgars eventually converted to Eastern Orthodoxy or Byzantine Christianity. In the ninth century the Slav Duke Rastislav of Moravia turned to Constantinople for help against Franks from the West, who had conquered the Avars and were attempting to convert his people to Roman Catholicism in Latin, a language they did not understand. In response, the emperor sent two learned missionaries to convert the Moravians: the priests, brothers, and future saints Constantine, later known as Cyril, and Methodius. They created a new, Greek-based alphabet, which permitted the Slavs to create their own written language, later known as Cyrillic after St. Cyril. That language gave the Christian gospels and Byzantine theology a lasting Slavic home. Known today as Old Church Slavonic, it was the international Slavic language through which Christianity penetrated eastern Europe.

PERSIANS AND MUSLIMS

During the reign of Emperor Heraclius (r. 610–641), the Byzantine Empire took a decidedly Eastern, as opposed to a Western Roman, direction. Heraclius spent his entire reign resisting Persian and Islamic invasions, the former successfully, the latter in vain. After 632, Islamic armies overran much of the empire, directly attacking Constantinople for the first time in the mid–670s. In the 700s the Byzantines repelled Arab armies and regained most of Asia Minor, having lost forever Syria, Egypt, and North Africa. This traumatic setback forced a change in provincial government, from governance by local elites to direct control by imperial generals, making possible a more disciplined and flexible use of military power. In the tenth century, the forces of Constantinople pushed back the Muslims in Armenia and northern Syria and conquered the Bulgar kingdom in the Balkans.

The empire's fortunes reversed in the eleventh century. After defeating the Byzantine army at Manzikert in Armenia in 1071, Muslim Seljuk Turks overran most of Asia Minor, from which the Byzantines had drawn most of their tax revenue and troops. The empire never fully recovered, although its end would not come until 1453, when the Seljuks' cousins, the Ottoman Turks, captured Constantinople. Threatened by the Turkish advance, the Byzantines called for Western aid, helping to spark the First Crusade. In 1204, the Fourth Crusade was diverted from Jerusalem to Constantinople, not to rescue the city, but rather to inflict more damage on it and the Byzantine Empire than all previous non-Christian invaders had done before. The Byzantines recovered their city in 1261, but their power and wealth were significantly reduced, tensions between Latin West and Greek East were even higher, and the Turks had become a constant threat.

ISLAM AND THE ISLAMIC WORLD

 new religion called **Islam** apeared in Arabia in the sixth century in response to the work of the Prophet Muhammad. It inspired a third medieval civilization and rapidly created one of history's greatest empires.

MUHAMMAD'S RELIGION

Muhammad (570–632) was orphaned at a young age and raised by various relatives. He had no fortune or powerful political connections. He worked on caravans as a merchant's assistant until, at the age of twenty-five, he married a wealthy widow. With her support, he became a kind of social activist fighting the increasing materialism of his contemporaries. When he was about forty, he had a religious experience, which he understood to be a visitation from the angel Gabriel. From time to time for the rest of his life, he was inspired to recite what his followers believed were literally God's words. Between 650 and 651, the revealed texts that God had chosen him to convey were collected in a sacred book, the **Qur'an** ("reciting"). At the heart of Muhammad's message was a call for all Arabs to submit to God's will as revealed through "the Prophet." The terms *Islam* and *Muslim* both imply submission or surrender.

Muhammad did not claim his message was new—only that it was final and definitive. What he taught was consistent with what the Jewish prophets, from Noah to Jesus, had taught. His unique mission was to be the last of the prophets. He claimed that after him God would send no more, but he also insisted "the Prophet" was only a

6.3
The Qur'an

HOW DID Islamic culture influence the West?

Islam   New religion appearing in Arabia in the sixth century in response to the work of the Prophet Muhammad.

Qur'an   Sacred book comprised of a collection of the revealed texts that God had chosen Muhammad to convey.

man. Like Judaism, Islam was to be a strictly monotheistic, theocentric religion that rejected Christianity's trinitarian view of God and its claim that Jesus was God incarnate.

Muhammad's faith in a single transcendent God set him at odds with his people. Muhammad was a native of Mecca, the site of the **Ka'ba**, one of Arabia's holiest shrines. (The Ka'ba was a simple rectangular building built to contain a sacred black stone and numerous holy images.) When Muhammad began to preach against the idols of the Ka'ba, he not only assaulted traditional Arab religion, he threatened Mecca's economy. Respect for the Ka'ba helped make Mecca a center for Arab trade. In 622, the Meccan authorities forced Muhammad and his followers to flee to Medina, an oasis 240 miles north of Mecca. This event, the *Hegira*, provides the pivotal date for the Islamic calendar, for it marks the founding of the first Muslim community.

Muhammad and his followers prospered in Medina by raiding the caravans that served Mecca. Converts accumulated until, by 624, he was powerful enough to persuade Mecca to submit to his authority. He returned in triumph and cleansed the Ka'ba of its idols, but he preserved the building as a shrine. Islam, like Christianity, eased life for its converts by making compromises with the pagan traditions they cherished.

Muhammad stressed practice more than doctrine, and, as Islam matured, its characteristic disciplines emerged: (1) honesty and modesty in all conduct, (2) absolute loyalty to the Islamic community, (3) abstinence from pork and alcohol, (4) prayer toward Mecca five times a day, (5) giving alms to support the poor and needy, (6) fasting during daylight hours for one month each year, and (7) making a pilgrimage to Mecca at least once in a lifetime. Muslim men were allowed as many as four wives—provided they treated them all justly and equally. A man could divorce a wife with a simple declaration of his intent. A wife could also initiate divorce, but this was a more complicated process. A wife was expected to be totally devoted to her husband, and only he was to see her face.

Islam had no priesthood. It was led by the *ulema* ("persons with correct knowledge"), a scholarly elite. The *ulema*'s authority derived from the reputations of its members for piety and learning. Their opinions had the force of legislation in Muslim society, and they ensured that Muslim governments adhered to the law of the Qur'an.

ISLAMIC DIVERSITY

Islam succeeded in unifying Arab tribes and various pagan peoples by appealing to the pride of groups that had been marginalized in a world dominated by Judaism and Christianity. Islam declared Muhammad to be history's most important figure and Muhammad's followers to be the people whom God had chosen to receive his definitive revelation.

Passionate faith in Muhammad did not, however, prevent divisions from emerging within Islam. Factions contested who had the best claim to the **caliphate**, the office of the leader of the Muslim community. Doctrinal differences also spawned controversies just as they did among Christians.

The most radical Muslims were the Kharijites, who seceded from the camp of the fourth caliph, Ali (r. 656–661). They accused Ali of sacrificing important principles for political advantage, and in 661, a Kharijite assassinated him. The Kharijites were "Puritans" who wanted to purge Islam of persons who did not meet their rigorous moral standards.

More influential was the **Shi'a**, the "party" of Ali. The Shi'a believed Ali and his descendants (by virtue of their kinship with the Prophet and the Prophet's

Ka'ba One of Arabia's holiest shrines located in Mecca, the birthplace of Muhammad.

Hegira Forced flight of Muhammad and his followers to Medina, 240 miles north of Mecca. This event marks the beginning of the Islamic calendar.

ulema ("Persons with correct knowledge") Scholarly elite leading Islam.

caliphate Office of the leader of the Muslim community.

Shi'a The "party" of Ali. They believed Ali and his descendants were Muhammad's only rightful successors.

own will) were Muhammad's only rightful successors. For the Shi'a, Ali's assassination represented a basic truth of devout Muslim life: a true *imam* ("ruler") and his followers must expect persecution. A theology of martyrdom is the mark of Shi'a teaching, and the Shi'a is still an embattled minority within Islam.

A third group, which has dominated Islam for most of its history, is composed of the *Sunnis* (followers of *sunna*, "tradition"). Sunnis emphasize loyalty to the fundamental principles of Islam and have spurned the exclusivity and purism that cause the Kharijites and the Shi'a to separate from the wider Muslim community.

ISLAMIC EMPIRES

Under Muhammad's first three successors—the caliphs Abu Bakr (r. 632–634), Umar (r. 634–644), and Uthman (r. 644–656)—Muslim armies swept throughout the southern and eastern Mediterranean, acquiring lands still held by Muslim states. Islam's capital moved from Mecca to the more centrally located Damascus, and by the eighth century, the caliphs of the Umayyad dynasty ruled an empire that stretched from Spain to India. In 750, the Abbasid family overthrew the Umayyads and moved the seat of the caliphate to Baghdad. Shortly thereafter, their huge empire began to break up, and rival caliphs appeared to contest their authority. (See Map 6–3.)

The Muslim conquerors profited from the fact that their Byzantine and Persian opponents had exhausted themselves in a long war. The Arabs struck just as the Byzantine emperor Heraclius forced the Persians to evacuate Egypt, Palestine, Syria, and Asia Minor, but before Heraclius died in 641, the Arabs had taken all these lands (except Asia Minor) from him. By 643, they had overrun what remained of the Persian Empire, and by the end of the century, the last Byzantine outpost in North Africa had fallen to them. The Muslim advance was facilitated by the fact that many of the inhabitants of the Byzantine lands the Muslims occupied were Semitic peoples with ethnic ties to the Arabs. Constantinople's efforts to stamp out all forms of Christianity that it regarded as heretical also led many of the Christians of Egypt and Syria to welcome the Islamic invaders as liberators.

Islam swept across North Africa and Spain, but its thrust into the European heart of Christendom was rebuffed in 732 by Charles Martel, ruler of the Franks. His defeat of an Arab raiding party at Poitiers (in central France) marked the point at which the Muslim advance in the West was halted and slowly began to reverse.

THE WESTERN DEBT TO ISLAMIC CULTURE

Christian Europe was hostile to Islam, but it profited a great deal from contact with the Muslim world. The works of the great scientists and philosophers of the Classical era were largely forgotten by Europeans until Arabs reintroduced them. Latin translations of Arabic translations of and commentaries on Greek originals revolutionized intellectual life in medieval Europe. As late as the sixteenth century, the

Muslims are enjoined to live by the divine law, or Shari'a, and have a right to have disputes settled by an arbiter of the Shari'a. Here we see a husband complaining about his wife before the state-appointed judge, or qadi. The wife, backed up by two other women, points an accusing finger at the husband. In such cases, the first duty of the qadi, who should be a learned person of faith, is to try to effect a reconciliation before the husband divorces his wife, or the wife herself seeks a divorce.

Bibliothèque Nationale de France, Paris

Sunnis Followers of the *sunna*, "tradition." They emphasize loyalty to the fundamental principles of Islam.

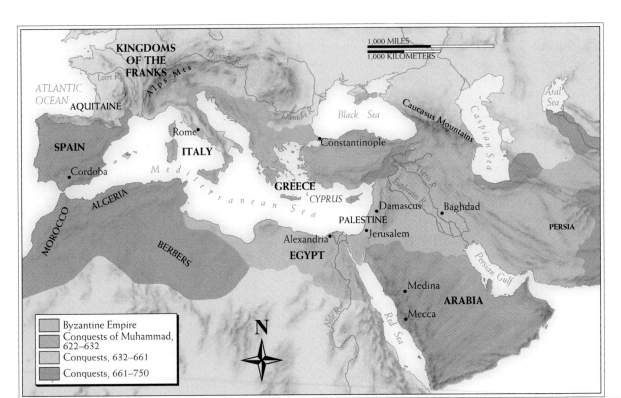

MAP 6–3

Muslim Conquests and Domination of the Mediterranean to about 750 C.E. Within 125 years of Muhammad's rise, Muslims came to dominate Spain and all areas south and east of the Mediterranean.

HOW WERE Muslims able to dominate much of the area east and south of the Mediterranean within 125 years of Muhammad's rise?

study of medicine in Europe relied primarily on the works of the ancient physicians Hippocrates and Galen, the Baghdad physician Al-Razi, and the Muslim philosophers Avicenna (980–1037) and Averröes (1126–1198), Islam's greatest authorities on Aristotle. Multilingual Jewish scholars helped make the translations that bridged the gap between the Muslim and Christian worlds. The medieval Arabs also gave the West one of its most popular books: *The Arabian Nights*, poetic folk tales that are still read and imitated in the West.

WESTERN SOCIETY AND THE DEVELOPING CHRISTIAN CHURCH

HOW DID the developing Christian Church influence Western society during the early Middle Ages?

Facing barbarian invasions from the north and east and a strong Islamic presence in the Mediterranean, the West found itself in decline in the fifth and sixth centuries. In the seventh century, the Byzantine emperors, their hands full with the Islamic threat in the East, were unable to assert themselves in the West. Mediterranean shipping declined, compelling urban populations to seek employment and protection in the countryside on the estates of landholders. In short, western Europeans were developing a distinctive culture of their own.

Amidst these social changes, the Christian church remained firmly entrenched and became increasingly powerful. Like the imperial Roman administration, its governing structure was centralized and hierarchical. As Roman governors withdrew, bishops and cathedral chapters filled the vacuum of authority: The local cathedral became the center of urban life, the local bishop the highest local authority, and in Rome, the pope took control as the western emperors gradually departed and died out. The Christian church became the best repository of Roman administrative skills and classical culture, even as its deep involvement in secular affairs cost the church some of its spiritual integrity. It was a potent civilizing and unifying force, with a religious message of providential purpose and individual worth that could give solace and meaning to life at its worst. The church's ritual of baptism and its creed, or statement of belief, unified people across the traditional barriers of social class, education, and gender.

MONASTIC CULTURE

The early medieval church drew much of its strength from its monasteries. The first monks were Christians who fled the cities of the Roman Empire to live as hermits in the wilderness. They could not accept the fact that Christian life became safe and easy after Constantine endorsed the church, for they believed faith required them to witness against the world. Because martyrdom by the state was no longer a choice, they opted for harsh environments and ascetic disciplines that made their lives a kind of living martyrdom. The sufferings they embraced as a witness to faith made them the church's new heroes.

Medieval Christians viewed monastic life—governed, as it was, by the biblical "counsels of perfection" (the practice of chastity, poverty, and obedience)—as humanity's highest calling. Monks—and eventually the secular, or parish, clergy whom popular opinion forced to adopt some monastic disciplines—were expected to meet higher spiritual standards than ordinary Christians. Consequently, clergy came to be respected as superior to laity, a belief that served the papacy well in struggles with secular rulers.

The monastic movement was inspired by the lives of hermits, such as Anthony of Egypt (ca. 251–356), but monks soon abandoned solitude and formed communal institutions. Anthony's contemporary and fellow countryman, Pachomius (ca. 286–346), founded a highly regimented community in which hundreds of monks lived in accordance with a strict code. The form of monasticism that spread throughout the East, however, followed rules laid down by Basil the Great (329–379). It urged monks to focus less on personal asceticism and more on caring for the needy outside their communities.

The monastic practices evolving in the East were introduced to the West by Athanasius (ca. 293–373) and Martin of Tours (ca. 315–ca. 399), but it was a rule (constitution) written in 529 by Benedict of Nursia (ca. 480–547) for a monastery he established at Monte Cassino near Naples, Italy, that set the standard for the West. The Benedictine Rule discouraged the kind of flamboyant asceticism popular in the East. It decreed a daily schedule that governed a monk's every activity. It provided for adequate food, some wine, serviceable clothing, proper amounts of sleep, and opportunities for relaxation. Time was set aside each day for prayer, communal worship, study, and the manual labor by which monks supported themselves. The objective was to create autonomous religious communities that were economically, spiritually, and intellectually self-sufficient. Benedictine monks did not, however, turn their backs on the world. They were chiefly responsible for the missionary work that converted England and Germany to Christianity, and they kept civilization alive in Europe during the darkest of the Dark Ages. (See "History's Voices: The Benedicture Order Sets Its Requirements for Entrance.")

7.2
Benedict of Nursia: *The Rule of St. Benedict*

HISTORY'S VOICES

THE BENEDICTINE ORDER SETS ITS REQUIREMENTS FOR ENTRANCE

*T*he religious life had great appeal in a time of political and social uncertainty. Entrance into a monastery was not, however, escapism. Much was demanded of the new monk, both during and after his probationary period, which is described here. Benedict's contribution was to prescribe a balanced blend of religious, physical, and intellectual activities within a well-structured community.

WHAT ARE Benedict's reasons for not allowing a monk to change his mind and leave the cloister, once vows have been taken?

When anyone is newly come for the reformation of his life, let him not be granted an easy entrance, but, as the Apostle says, "Test the spirits to see whether they are from God." If the newcomer, therefore, perseveres in his knocking, and if it is seen after four or five days that he bears patiently the harsh treatment offered him and the difficulty of admission, and that he persists in his petition, then let entrance be granted him, and let him stay in the guest house for a few days.

After that let him live in the novitiate, where the novices study, eat, and sleep. A senior shall be assigned to them who is skilled in winning souls, to watch over them with the utmost care. Let him examine whether the novice is truly seeking God, and whether he is zealous for the Work of God, for obedience and for humiliations. Let the novice be told all the hard and rugged ways by which the journey to God is made.

If he promises stability and perseverance, then at the end of two months let this Rule be read through to him, and let him be addressed thus: "Here is the law under which you wish to fight. If you can observe it, enter; if you cannot, you are free to depart." If he still stands firm, let him be taken to the above-mentioned novitiate and again tested in all patience. And after the lapse of six months let the Rule be read to him, that he may know on what he is entering. And if he still remains firm, after four months let the same Rule be read to him again.

Then, having deliberated with himself, if he promises to keep it in its entirety and to observe everything that is commanded him, let him be received into the community. But let him understand that, according to the law of the Rule, from that day forward he may not leave the monastery nor withdraw his neck from under the yoke of the Rule which he was free to refuse or to accept during that prolonged deliberation.

St. Benedict's Rule for Monasteries, trans. by Leonard J. Doyle (Collegeville, MN.: Liturgical Press, 1948), pp. 79–80.

THE DOCTRINE OF PAPAL PRIMACY

The eastern emperors treated the church like a department of state. They intervened in its theological debates and chose its leaders. After the fifth century, however, the bishop of Rome had no emperor to contend with. He could assert "papal primacy" and claim leadership of a church that had a right to be totally independent of the state.

Papal primacy became an issue as early as 381, when the ecumenical Council of Constantinople declared the patriarch of Constantinople to be first in rank after the bishop of Rome. Pope Damasus I (366–384) objected and claimed that the Roman see's unique "apostolic" status meant its bishop had no peer. He was heir to the legacy of the Apostle Peter, the "rock" on which Jesus said the church was built (Matthew 16:18). In 451, the Council of Chalcedon ignored this and recognized the Byzantine patriarch as having the same primacy over the East that Rome traditionally had over the West. Pope Leo I (440–461) declared his belief that his office was superior to that of all other bishops by assuming the ancient Roman title *pontifex maximus* ("supreme priest"). At the end of the fifth century, Pope Gelasius I (492–496) made an even more extreme claim. He decreed that papal authority was "more weighty" than that of secular governments, for the church was responsible for the most serious human concern, salvation.

Constantinople's power to influence the papacy faded in proportion to its declining fortunes in Italy. The emperor Justinian had driven the Ostrogoths out and returned Italy to Byzantine control, but late in the sixth century, Lombard tribes crossed the Alps and forced the Byzantines to retreat. Having no alternative, Pope Gregory I, "the Great" (590–604), ignored the eastern emperor and negotiated an independent peace treaty with the Lombards.

THE RELIGIOUS DIVISION OF CHRISTENDOM

In both East and West, religious belief alternately served and undermined imperial political unity. In 391, Christianity became the official faith of the Eastern empire, while all other religions and sects were deemed "demented and insane." Since the fifth century, the patriarch of Constantinople had blessed Byzantine emperors, attesting to the close ties between rulers and the Eastern Church. Between the fourth and sixth centuries, the patriarchs of Constantinople, Alexandria, Antioch, and Jerusalem received generous endowments of land and gold from rich, pious donors, empowering the church to act as the state's welfare agency. However, from time to time rulers supported Christian heresies, and Christianity was compelled to absorb and adapt to certain local pagan practices and beliefs.

The empire was also home, albeit inhospitably, to large numbers of Jews. Pagan Romans viewed Jews as narrow, dogmatic, and intolerant but tolerated Judaism as an ancient and acceptable form of worship. When Rome adopted Christianity, Jews retained this legal protection as long as they did not attempt to convert Christians, build new synagogues, or try to hold certain positions or enter some professions. Neither persuasion, such as tax breaks, nor coercion succeeded in converting the empire's Jews.

The differences between Eastern and Western Christianity grew to be no less irreconcilable than those between Christians and Jews. One issue even divided Justinian and his wife Theodora. The former was strictly orthodox in belief, but Theodora supported a divisive teaching that the Council of Chalcedon in 451 had condemned as heresy, namely, that Christ had a single, immortal nature and was not both eternal God and mortal man in one and the same person. The **Monophysites**—believers in the single nature—became a separate church in eastern lands, from Armenia to Egypt.

A similar dispute appeared in Eastern debates over the relationship among the members of the Trinity, specifically whether the Holy Spirit proceeded only from the Father, as the Nicene–Constantinopolitan Creed taught, or from the Father and the Son (*filioque* in Latin), an idea that became increasingly popular in the West and was eventually adopted by the Western church and inserted into its creed. Eastern theologians argued that adding filioque to the creed weakened a core Christian belief—the divine unity and dignity of all three persons of the Trinity.

Another major rift between the Christian East and West took place over the veneration of images in worship. In 726, Emperor Leo III (r. 717–741) forbade the use of images and icons that portrayed Christ, the Virgin Mary, and the saints. Veneration had been commonplace for centuries, therefore the decree came as a shock. The change in policy, called **iconoclasm**, probably had several

Monophysites   Believers in a single, immortal nature of Christ; not both eternal God and mortal man in one and the same person.

iconoclasm   Opposition to the use of images in Christian worship.

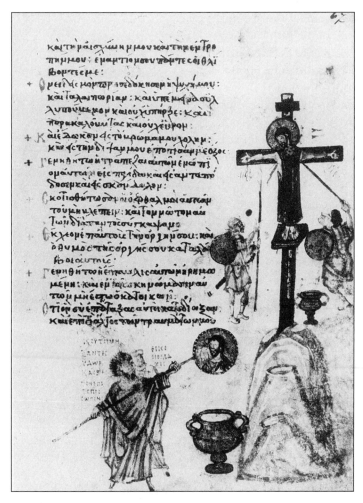

A ninth-century Byzantine manuscript shows an iconoclast whiting out an image of Christ. The Iconoclastic Controversy was an important factor in the division of Christendom into separate Latin and Greek branches.

State Historical Museum, Moscow

HOW DID the reign of Clovis differ from that of Charlemagne?

Caesaropapism Emperor acting as if he were pope as well as caesar.

motivations, in particular the emperor's wish to accommodate Muslim sensitivities while at war with the Arabs (Islam strictly forbade making images, deeming it the exclusive preserve of Allah). Leo's decree drove the popes closer to the Franks to seek protection from iconoclasm. In the end, veneration of images was eventually restored in the Eastern churches.

A third difference between East and West was the Eastern emperors' pretension to absolute sovereignty, both secular and religious. Expressing their sense of sacred mission, the emperors presented themselves in the trappings of holiness and directly interfered in matters of church and religions, what is called **Caesaropapism**, or the emperor acting as if he were pope as well as caesar. To a degree unknown in the West, Eastern emperors appointed and manipulated the clergy, convening church councils and enforcing church decrees. By comparison, the West nurtured a distinction between church and state that became visible in the eleventh century.

The Eastern church also rejected several disputed requirements of Roman Christianity. It denied the existence of Purgatory, permitted lay divorce and remarriage, allowed priests, but not bishops, to marry, and conducted religious services in the languages that people in a given locality actually spoke (the so-called "vernacular" languages) instead of Greek and Latin. In these matters Eastern Christians gained opportunities and rights that Christians in the West would not enjoy, and then only in part, until the Protestant Reformation in the sixteenth century. (See Chapter 11.)

Over time, these differences ultimately resulted in a schism between the two churches in 1054, when a Western envoy of the pope visited the Patriarch of Constantinople, hoping to overcome the differences. The patriarch was not welcoming, and after mutual recriminations, before leaving the city, the papal envoy left a bull of excommunication on the altar of Hagia Sophia. In response, the patriarch proclaimed Western popes to be heretics. Attempts to heal the schism have since been made, including an ecumenical gesture in 1965, but such official pronouncements have not overcome the many religious and cultural differences between Eastern and Western Christianity.

THE KINGDOM OF THE FRANKS

MEROVINGIANS AND CAROLINGIANS: FROM CLOVIS TO CHARLEMAGNE

A chieftain named Clovis (ca. 466?–511), from the tribe of the Franks, founded the German dynasty that first attempted to pull Europe back together. Clovis united the Salian and Ripuarian Franks, subdued the Burgundians and Visigoths, won the support of the native Gallo-Romans by converting to orthodox Christianity, and turned the Roman province of Gaul into France ("land of the Franks").

OVERVIEW

MAJOR POLITICAL AND RELIGIOUS DEVELOPMENTS OF THE EARLY MIDDLE AGES

313	Emperor Constantine issues the Edict of Milan
325	Council of Nicaea defines Christian doctrine
410	Rome invaded by Visigoths under Alaric
413–426	Saint Augustine writes *City of God*
451	Council of Chalcedon further defines Christian doctrine
451–453	Europe invaded by the Huns under Attila
476	Barbarian Odovacer deposes Western emperor and rules as king of the Romans
489–493	Theodoric establishes kingdom of Ostrogoths in Italy
529	Saint Benedict founds monastery at Monte Cassino
533	Justinian codifies Roman law
622	Muhammad's flight from Mecca (*Hegira*)
711	Muslim invasion of Spain
732	Charles Martel defeats Muslims between Poitiers and Tours
754	Pope Stephen II and Pepin III ally

Governing the Franks   Clovis and his descendants, the Merovingian kings, struggled with the perennial problem of medieval politics: balancing the claims of the "one" against those of the "many." As kings worked to centralize governments, powerful local magnates fought to preserve their regional autonomy. The result was a battle between the forces of societal unification and fragmentation.

The Merovingian kings tried to pull their kingdom together by making pacts with the landed nobility and utilizing a new kind of royal official, the count. Counts were assigned authority over districts in which they held no personal land. This made them easier to control than the local aristocrats who commanded the loyalty of the people living on their estates. As time passed, however, counts established hereditary claims to their offices and effectively asserted their independence. The unification of the Frankish state was further impeded by Frankish inheritance customs, which gave all a king's legitimate male heirs a right to a share in his kingdom.

By the seventh century, the Merovingian king was king in title only. Real executive authority had devolved on his chief minister, the "mayor of the palace." The family of Pepin I of Austrasia (d. 639) monopolized this office until 751, when his descendant, Pepin III (with the pope's support), deposed the last Merovingian. Pepin's ascension to the Frankish throne inaugurated the Carolingian dynasty.

Pepin III's kingdom rested on a firm foundation laid by his predecessor, Charles "Martel" ("Hammer"; d. 741). Charles built a powerful cavalry by granting **fiefs** or benefices ("lands") to men to fund their equipment and service. His army proved its worth at Poitiers in 732, when it stopped the Muslim advance and secured the Pyrenees Mountains as Christendom's western frontier. Much of

fiefs   ("Lands") Granted to cavalry men to fund their equipment and service.

the land that Martel distributed to his soldiers came from the church. The church needed the protection of the Franks, and it could not prevent the confiscation of property used to fund its defense. Eventually, however, the church was partially compensated for its losses.

Where the Merovingians had tried to weaken the aristocrats by raising landless men to power, the Carolingians forged an alliance with the landed aristocracy and staffed their government almost entirely from its ranks. By playing to strength rather than challenging it, the Carolingians secured their position—at least in the short run.

The Frankish Church The church played a major role in the Frankish government, for its monasteries were the intellectual centers of Carolingian society. The higher clergy were employed in tandem with counts as royal agents, and Christian missionaries helped pacify barbarian elements in new lands the Carolingians added to their domain. Conversion to orthodox Christianity was considered essential for the assimilation of new subjects.

The missions of the church and state tended to be confused when the king appointed Christian bishops to political offices, and the lines between the two institutions were also blurred by the arrangements that created the Carolingian dynasty. In 751, Pope Zacharias (741–752) sanctioned the deposition of the last of the Merovingian puppet kings and dispatched Boniface (ca. 680–754), an Anglo-Saxon missionary monk, to preside at Pepin III's coronation. As part of the ceremony, Boniface may have anointed Pepin, a ritual that gave the Carolingian monarchy a sacred character.

If the pope shared sacred authority with the Frankish king, the king returned the favor by bolstering the secular authority of the pope. In 753, Pepin took an army into Italy to help Zacharias's successor, Pope Stephen II (752–757), drive the Lombards back from Rome. In 755, the victorious Franks confirmed the pope as the secular ruler of central Italy, a region that came to be called the **Papal States**.

The Franks drew almost as slight a boundary between state and church as did the eastern emperors, and the papacy wanted to guard against domination of the church by its new German protector. About this time (750–800), a document called the *Donation of Constantine* appeared in the papal archives. It said that in gratitude for recovery from an illness Constantine had given the western half of his empire to the pope. This implied that the church had a certain precedence over the state in the West. The *Donation* was exposed as a forgery in the fifteenth century.

THE REIGN OF CHARLEMAGNE (768–814)

In 774, Charlemagne, the son of Pepin the Short, completed his father's work by conquering Italy's Lombards and assuming their crown. He devoted much of his reign to wars of conquest. The Saxons of northern Germany were brutally subdued. The Muslims were pushed a bit south of the Pyrenees, and the Avars (a tribe related to the Huns) were practically annihilated, bringing the Danubian plains into the Frankish orbit. By the time of Charlemagne's death (January 28, 814), he ruled modern France, Belgium, Holland, Switzerland, almost the whole of western Germany, much of Italy, a portion of Spain, and the island of Corsica. (See Map 6–4.)

The New Empire Charlemagne believed his huge domain merited his assumption of the imperial title, and he did all he could to bolster the legitimacy of his claim. Because ancient Roman and contemporary Byzantine emperors ruled from fixed capitals, he constructed a palace city at Aachen (Aix-la-Chapelle), and like a Byzantine emperor, he intervened in the affairs of the church.

QUICK REVIEW

Church and State
- Church played a large role in Frankish government
- Christian bishops became lords in service of the king
- Franks confirm pope as ruler of the Papal States in 755

Papal States Central part of Italy where Pope Stephen II became the secular ruler when confirmed by the Franks in 755.

MAP 6–4
The Empire of Charlemagne to 814   Building on the successes of his predecessors, Charlemagne greatly increased the Frankish domains. Such traditional enemies as the Saxons and the Lombards fell under his sway.

WHAT REASONS might Charlemagne have had for expanding the Frankish domains into the regions in which he did?

Charlemagne's imperial pretensions were confirmed on Christmas Day, 800, when Pope Leo III (795–816) crowned him emperor. The ceremony, which established a fateful link between Germany and Italy (the future **Holy Roman Empire**), was an attempt by the pope to gain some leverage over his powerful king. By arranging for the emperor to receive the crown from his hands, the pope set a precedent that was useful for the church in its future dealings with the state. At the time, however, Charlemagne's authority was in no way compromised. Even the eastern emperors reluctantly acknowledged his title.

Holy Roman Empire   The domain of the German monarchs who revived the use of the Roman imperial title during the Middle Ages.

6.7
The Book of Emperors and Kings: Charlemagne and Pope Leo III

QUICK REVIEW

Carolingian Administration
- 250 counts administred empire
- Counts tended to become despots in their own regions
- Charlemagne often appointed churchmen to government offices

The New Emperor At a height of six feet three and one-half inches (his remains were exhumed and measured in 1861), Charlemagne literally towered over his contemporaries. His personality matched his physique. He was vigorous, restless, and gregarious—ever ready for a hunt or for a swim with his friends in Aachen's hot springs. He was known for his practical jokes, lusty humor, and hospitality. Foreign diplomats flocked to his festive court to do him honor. The most splendid of their gifts was probably the war elephant that the caliph of Baghdad, Harun-al-Rashid, sent him in 802.

Charlemagne had five official wives (in succession), many mistresses and concubines, and numerous children. This connubial variety caused some political problems. Pepin, his oldest son by his first marriage, grew jealous of the attention he showed the sons of his second wife and launched an ill-fated rebellion against his father. It was put down, and he was confined to a monastery for the rest of his life.

Problems of Government Charlemagne employed about 250 counts in the administration of his empire. A count was usually a local magnate rich enough to support some soldiers of his own. Royal generosity persuaded him and his men to serve the king. A count defended territory, maintained order, collected dues, and administered justice in the king's name. The count's district law court (the *mallus*) delivered verdicts based less on evidence than on the reputations witnesses had for truthfulness. When witness testimony was insufficient, the court had recourse to duels or tests called *ordeals*. A defendant's hand might be immersed in boiling water and his innocence determined by the way his wounds healed. Or a suspect might be bound with ropes and thrown into a river or pond that had been blessed by a priest. If the water rejected him and he floated, he was assumed guilty. Once guilt was determined, the *mallus* ordered monetary compensation to be paid to injured parties. This settled grievances that otherwise might have sparked long bloody vendettas.

Charlemagne never solved the problem of adequately policing the men who served him. His counts, like their Merovingian predecessors, tended to become despots within their districts. Charlemagne issued *capitularies* (royal decrees) that defined the policies he wanted his administrators to follow. He sent envoys, the *missi dominici*, to check up on the counts and report back on their behavior. When the *missi*'s infrequent inspections had little effect, he appointed provincial governors (prefects, dukes, and margraves) to keep permanent watch over the counts. They, however, were no more trustworthy than the counts.

Charlemagne often appointed churchmen to government offices, for bishops were considered royal servants. This had little effect on the character of his administration, for the higher clergy shared the secular lifestyles and aspirations of the counts. They were generally indistinguishable from the lay nobility. To be a Christian at this difficult period in the history of Europe was largely a matter of submitting to rituals such as baptism and assenting to creeds. Both clergy and laity were too preoccupied with the struggle to survive to burden themselves with ethical scruples.

Alcuin and the Carolingian Renaissance Charlemagne tried to improve the government of his empire by providing educations for the aristocratic boys who were destined for offices in the church and state. He attracted scholars from Spain, Ireland, and England as well as his own lands to staff his palace school. Alcuin of York (735–804), an Anglo-Saxon educator, supervised the development of a curriculum dedicated to giving students a grounding in grammar, logic, rhetoric, and simple mathematics—the tools of the career bureaucrat.

Although the aspirations of Charlemagne's scholars were modest, they constituted a true renaissance—a "rebirth" of intellectual activity. Alcuin and his colleagues halted the deterioration of Latin (the only written language). They improved communications by standardizing the use of a new legible style of handwriting called Carolingian "minuscule." They collected, restored, and copied ancient manuscripts. Alcuin worked on the text of the Bible and produced editions of the works of Gregory the Great and Benedict's rule. They reformed the church's liturgy, and they elevated standards for the clergy.

BREAKUP OF THE CAROLINGIAN KINGDOM

As Charlemagne aged and his vigilance diminished, his empire became progressively ungovernable. In feudal society the strength of a man's commitment to his lord depended on how near or how far away his lord was. People obeyed local leaders more readily than distant kings. Poor communications meant that Charlemagne had to grant a great deal of autonomous authority to the men who held the far-flung regions of his empire for him, and their power diminished his. The noble tail tended to wag the royal dog.

Louis the Pious   Charlemagne began the process of persuading the Germans that, as subjects of a unified empire, they were more than followers of regional and tribal leaders. However, his successor, his only surviving son, Louis the Pious (r. 814–840), was unable to maintain the unity of the empire. Louis had three sons by his first wife, and according to Salic law (the law of the Salian Franks), each was entitled to a share of his estate. Louis tried to break with tradition by recognizing his eldest son, Lothar (d. 855), as co-regent and sole imperial heir (817). In 823, however, Louis's second wife bore him a fourth son, Charles "the Bald" (d. 877). To secure an inheritance for this boy, she urged her stepsons, Pepin and Louis the German, to rebel and force their father to revise his will. The pope backed them, and they defeated their father in a battle near Colmar in 833.

The Treaty of Verdun and Its Aftermath   Pepin's death in 838 cleared one contender from the field, and in 843 the Treaty of Verdun divided the Carolingian empire among the three remaining princes. Lothar inherited the empty honor of the imperial title and a region called Lotharingia (roughly modern Holland, Belgium, Switzerland, Alsace-Lorraine, and Italy). France fell to Charles the Bald, and Germany to Louis the German.

The Treaty of Verdun was only the start of the division of the Carolingian lands. When Lothar died in 855, his "middle kingdom" was split up among his three sons. The much larger eastern and western Frankish kingdoms of France and Germany then seized portions of Lothar's legacy, and Carolingian power in Italy evaporated. The pope tried to fill the political vacuum this created, but developments were afoot that were about to turn popes and kings into petty figures and deliver Europe into the hands of the feudal nobility.

Carolingian cavalry, from a ninth-century Swiss manuscript.
Mansell Collection/Timepix/Getty Images, Inc.

Major Developments of the Early Middle Ages

313	Emperor Constantine legalizes Christianity
ca. 251–356	Anthony of Egypt inspires the monastic movement
410	Visigoths sack the city of Rome
476	Deposition of Romulus Augustulus, last western Roman emperor
ca. 466–511	Clovis founds the Franks' Merovingian dynasty
527–565	Reign of Byzantine emperor Justinian
622	Muhammad's *Hegira*, the foundation of Islam
732	Charles Martel stops the Muslim advance at Tours
751	Pepin III founds the Carolingian dynasty
768–814	Reign of Charlemagne
ca. 875–950	Invasions, feudal fragmentation, and the Dark Ages

This **75-foot**-long Viking burial ship from the early ninth century is decorated with beastly figures. It bore a dead queen, her servant, and assorted sacrificed animals to the afterlife. The bodies of the passengers were confined within a burial cabin at mid-ship surrounded with a treasure trove of jewels and tapestries. © Museum of CulturalHistory-University of Oslo, Norway

The last quarter of the ninth and the first half of the tenth centuries can accurately be characterized as Europe's Dark Ages. The gains that had been made in restoring political and religious institutions were lost as Europe confronted a second wave of invasions. Vikings (Normans, or North-men) descended from Scandinavia. Magyars (Hungarians from the plains of Russia) charged up the Danube Valley, and Muslims based in Sicily and Africa raided Italy and southern France. Kings and centralized governments could not move quickly enough to defend large territories that were simultaneously attacked from multiple directions. As their subjects turned to local strongmen for protection, political fragmentation spread.

The Vikings posed the most serious threat. They raided Europe's coasts, and their shallow-draft ships navigated its rivers to reach targets deep inland. They moved rapidly and struck randomly, making it hard to devise a strategy to defend against them. Leaders built forts and castles to which their people could flee when danger threatened. Sometimes they bribed raiders to withdraw. France's king created a duchy of Normandy for one group of Vikings in the hope they would fight off others.

VIKINGS, MAGYARS, AND MUSLIMS

At this point in European history—the late 800s and early 900s—one may speak with particular justification of a "dark age." These years saw successive waves of Normans (North-men), or Vikings, from Scandinavia; Magyars, or Hungarians, the great horsemen from the eastern plains; and Muslims from the south. The Vikings both traded and raided, and in the 880s even penetrated to Aachen and besieged Paris. They made York, England, a major trading post and traveled to Newfoundland and perhaps even to New England. The Magyars swept into Western Europe from the eastern plains, while Muslims made incursions across the Mediterranean from North Africa. In the resulting turmoil, local populations in Europe became more dependent than ever on local strongmen for life, limb, and livelihood—the essential precondition for the maturation of feudal society.

FEUDAL SOCIETY

*T*he inability of their formal governments to protect them meant medieval people had to make the private arrangements characteristic of feudalism. As the weaker submitted to the stronger, the medieval world fragmented and reorganized.

Feudal society was held together by personal oaths—by pledges to serve someone in exchange for protection or maintenance. Men who were tapped as soldiers took oaths of vassalage that bound them to warlords who granted them fiefs. They became members of a professional military fraternity governed by a code of knightly conduct. In the absence of any other authority, they assumed the right to govern the people who lived on their lands, and their personal relationships were the primary things that structured society.

ORIGINS

Beginning in the sixth and seventh centuries, the weakness of the West's governments forced freemen, who could not fend for themselves, to seek alliances with more powerful neighbors. Those who entered into contractual relations that

WHAT WERE the characteristics of a feudal society?

made them dependent on others were called **vassal**, collectively as *vassi* ("those who serve"). Owners of large estates (lords) acquired as many vassals as they could afford to equip as soldiers for their private armies. At first, they maintained their vassals in their households. But as numbers of vassals grew, this became impractical. The collapse of the economy caused money to disappear from circulation, so the only way to pay vassals was to grant them the right to use a piece of their lord's land to maintain themselves. This grant was called a *fief* or *benefice*. Vassals lived on their fiefs and were responsible for the peasants who farmed them.

VASSALAGE AND THE FIEF

A vassal swore fealty to his lord. That meant he promised to serve his lord and to refrain from actions contrary to his lord's interests. His chief function was that of a knight. Bargaining determined the specific terms of his military service, but custom limited the number of days his lord could keep him in the field. (In France in the eleventh century, forty days was standard.) A vassal was also expected to attend his lord's court when summoned and to render his lord financial assistance at times of special need: (1) to ransom him from his enemies, (2) to outfit him for a major military campaign, and (3) to defray the costs of the festivities at the marriage of a daughter or the knighting of a son.

Louis the Pious extended vassalage beyond the lay nobility to the higher clergy. He required bishops and abbots to swear fealty and to accept their appointments on the same terms as the fiefs given knights. He formally "invested" clerics with the rings and staffs that symbolized their spiritual offices. This practice was offensive to the church, for it implied the subservience of the church to the state. In the late tenth and eleventh centuries, reform-minded clergy refused to submit to "lay investiture," but they never considered surrendering the grants of land that were the rewards for oaths of homage.

A lord was obliged to protect his vassal from physical harm, to stand as his advocate in court, and to provide for his maintenance by giving him a fief. In Carolingian times a fief varied in size from a small villa to several *mansi* (a unit of 25 to 48 acres). Royal vassals might receive fiefs of 30 to 200 *mansi*. Prizes of this size made vassalage acceptable to the highest classes in Carolingian society. In the short run, oaths of vassalage marshaled the nobility behind the king. But in the long run, grants of fiefs undercut royal power, for kings found it difficult or impossible to reclaim land once it was granted to a vassal.

DAILY LIFE AND RELIGION

The Humble Carolingian Manor   Early medieval Europe's chief economic institution was a communal farm called a **manor**. Medieval farmers often preferred to cluster in villages rather than to live on individual farms. This provided security, but it also enabled them to share labor and the costs of expensive plows and oxen. The residents of a manor farmed communally, but they did not divide their harvests equally. Each family on a manor had specific fields assigned to it and lived from what grew on its land.

The status of peasants was determined by the nature of their holdings. A freeman had allodial property (land free from the claims of an overlord). A man who surrendered his land to a lord in exchange for protection became a **serf**. He received land back from his lord, but with a new set of rights and obligations. He had a right to stay on the land in exchange for working his lord's *demesne*, the

A seventh-century portrayal of a vassal, who kneels before his lord and inserts his hands between those of his lord in a gesture of mutual loyalty: the vassal promising to obey and serve his lord, the lord promising to support and protect his vassal.

Spanish School (7th century). Lord and vassal, decorated page (vellum). Archivo de la Corona de Aragon, Barcelona, Spain. Index/bridgeman Art Library

vassal   A person granted an estate or cash payments in return for rendering services to a lord.

manor   Communal farm considered to be early medieval Europe's chief economic institution.

serf   Peasant bound to the land he worked.

fields on the manor that produced the crops meant for the lord's table. Peasants who brought little property with them when they entered a lord's service became unfree serfs. They were more vulnerable to a lord's demands, often spending up to three days a week working his fields. Peasants who had nothing to offer but labor had the lowest status and were the least protected from exploitation.

A new type of plow came into use during the Carolingian era. It was heavy enough to break up the dense, waterlogged soils of northern Europe and work land that had defeated Roman farmers. Unlike the ancient "scratch" plow (a pointed stick), it cut deeply and had a moldboard that turned the earth over and utilized more of its fertility. Ancient farmers used a two-field system of cultivation to maintain the fertility of their fields. That is, they divided their land in half, and alternatively planted one half and left the other fallow. (A fallow field was plowed but not planted.) Medieval farmers developed a **three-field system** that was more productive. In the fall, one field was planted with winter crops of wheat or rye, which were harvested in early summer. In late spring, a second field was planted with summer crops of oats, barley, lentils, and legumes, which were harvested in August or September. The third field was left fallow. This arrangement limited the amount of nonproductive plowing, used crop rotation to restore soil fertility, and provided backup crops should one harvest fail. (See "Encountering the Past: Medieval Cooking.")

The Cure of Carolingian Souls   The masses of ordinary people who were burdened, fearful, and devoid of the hope of improving their lots this side of eternity sought comfort and consolation in religion. Privilege rendered the upper classes no less pious. Charlemagne frequented the Church of Saint Mary in Aachen several times a day, and his will decreed that most of his estate be used to fund masses and prayers for his soul.

The lower clergy, the parish priests who served the people, were poorly prepared to provide spiritual leadership. Lords owned the churches on their lands and staffed them with priests recruited from their serfs. The church expected a lord to liberate a serf who was ordained to the priesthood, but many such priests said mass on Sunday and toiled as peasants during the rest of the week.

Because priests on most manors were no better educated than their congregations, religious instruction barely existed. For most people religion was more a matter of practice than doctrine. They baptized their children, attended mass, tried to learn to recite the Lord's Prayer and the Apostles' Creed, and received the last rites when death approached. They were in awe of sacred relics and the saints who they hoped would intercede for them with their divine overlord in the court of heaven. Simple faith had little need for understanding.

FRAGMENTATION AND DIVIDED LOYALTY

A vassal who had sufficient land could portion out his fief and create vassals of his own. It was also possible for a vassal to accept fiefs from more than one lord. The concept of the "liege lord," the master to whom a vassal owed primary duty, evolved in the ninth century. This helped avoid confusion, but it did not halt progressive fragmentation of land and loyalty.

Kings were weakened by the fact that vassals tended to establish rights to the fiefs they were granted. Ownership of a fief technically remained with the lord who granted it, but it was hard for a lord to prevent a vassal's heir from inheriting that fief. In the ninth century, the hereditary rights of vassals were legally recognized. This confirmed the nobility's hold on their fiefs and led to their gradual appropriation of much of the royal domain.

three-field system   Developed by medieval farmers, a system in which three fields were utilized during different growing seasons to limit the amount of nonproductive plowing and to restore soil fertility through crop rotation.

ENCOUNTERING THE PAST

MEDIEVAL COOKING

edieval cooks served things that modern diners would recognize: roasts, pastas, meat pies, and custards. But where modern chefs are preoccupied primarily with the taste of their fare, medieval cooks worried about the effect of their dishes on diners' health. Medieval physicians traced illness to imbalances among the so-called four humors: blood, black bile, yellow bile, and phlegm. Because the humors were generated by food, recipes had to be planned like medicines. Health depended on maintaining a balance between the poles of the opposites that the humors nurtured: wet–dry, cold–warm. If not moderated by cool, wet seasonings, a spicy dish might produce an excess of hot, dry humors that made one ill.

Medieval people correctly intuited a link between diet and health, but from the modern point of view this did them little good. A fixation on meat as a prestige food meant vegetables were little appreciated. Most Europeans survived on a diet of mush or a porridge made by boiling bread in milk.

Medieval cooks were expected to be artists as well as scientists. Formal dining called for elaborately constructed dishes, such as castles executed in pastry or cooked birds stuffed back into their feathered skins. Dishes were sometimes tinted strange colors, modeled into odd shapes, or rendered otherwise amusing to the eye.

DID THE medieval understanding of the link between diet and health differ from the modern understanding—or was only the explanation different?

[Top] **The Lord of the Manor Dining.**
By permission of The British Library (10001020–021)

[Bottom] **Kitchen Scene; Chopping Meat.**
By permission of The British Library (1000278–001)

Feudal ties were contractual relationships, but because few medieval laymen could read, contracts of vassalage had to be oral agreements. Specific ritual acts evolved to make the terms of what was being promised clear to everyone. A freeman became a vassal by an "act of commendation," by swearing an oath of fealty to a superior. In the mid–eighth century, the solemnity of the oath was enhanced by having the vassal swear with his hand on a sacred relic or a Bible. By the tenth and eleventh centuries, it had become customary for the vassal to take his oath with his hands cupped between those of his lord and for the two men to ratify their agreement with a kiss.

Despite feudalism's obvious vulnerability to abuse and confusion, the order it maintained made it possible for Europeans to rebuild their societies. The genius of feudal government lay in its adaptability. Contracts of different kinds could be made with almost anyone to serve almost any purpose. As lords and vassals fine-tuned their feudal arrangements, they reconstructed foundations for centralized government and for Europe's modern nation-states.

IMAGE KEY
for pages 146–147

a. Mohammed, Abu Bakr and Ali travel to the Ukaz Fair, from Siyar-i Nabi (Life of the Prophet) IV. 2, f. 132v.

b. Reproduction of St. Matthew and an Illuminated Initial Page from Codex 51, Latin Gospels, ca. 700–899

c. Reproduction of Crucifixion and Commencement of Penitentiale from Codex 1395, Latin Gospels 9th century

d., f., j. Tesserae—Brick tiles used to make mosaics found at Tockenham, UK

e. Saint Gregory the Great, shown here in a monastic scriptorium (an area devoted to copying and preserving books)   Kunsthistorisches Museum, Wien oder KHM, Wien

g. A Qadi hears a case   Bibliotheque Nationale de France, Paris

h. Coronation of Charlemagne at St. Peter's by Pope Leo III   Grandes Chroniques de France, fol. 106r. Musee Goya, Castres, France. Giraudon/Art Resource, NY

i. The Court of Empress Theodora. Byzantine early christian mosaic. San Vitale, Ravenna, Italy. Photograph © Scala/Art Resource, NY

k. Byzantine (476–1453). The inner compartment of the reliquary of the True Cross. Constantinople, c.960 C.E. Treasury, Cathedral, Limburg an der Lahn, Germany

l. "The Lord of the Manor dining"

SUMMARY

On the Eve of the Frankish Ascendancy In the late fourth century, the western empire was weakening, and the Visigoths were being forced out of their own home territories by invading Huns. The Visigoths defeated the Romans in the ensuing conflict. Soon other barbarians had established territories within the Western empire. By the mid–fifth century, Rome had been sacked repeatedly, and by the end of the century the Western empire was history. Roman culture endured, although it was transformed through its contact with the Germanic peoples. Christianity, too, endured and changed through cultural contact.

The Byzantine Empire The eastern portion of the Roman Empire endured as the Byzantine Empire. Although the empire lasted until Constantinople (the capital) fell to the Turks in 1453, it peaked under Justinian, in the mid–sixth century. Although Justinian and his wife, the empress Theodora, were both Christians, she was a believer in Monophysitism, a heresy that influenced the later course of the empire's history. Justinian codified Roman law, which was to prove influential in the West for centuries. Justinian supported Orthodox Christianity, although some of his successors supported other forms of Christianity. Constantinople and smaller urban centers formed the economic, administrative, and cultural backbone of the empire. The empire's eastern orientation increased under Heraclius in the early seventh century. In the early eighth century, Leo's Caesaropapism led him to attempt to ban the use of images in churches.

Islam and the Islamic World In the seventh century, Muhammad founded a new religion on the Arabian peninsula. In 624, Muhammad's Medina-based army conquered Mecca, and in the following years the basic rules of Islamic life were articulated. Islam expanded substantially, until by 750 the Islamic Empire stretched from Spain through North Africa, the southern and eastern Mediterranean, and eastward into India. But this was the peak of Muslim territorial expansion, and Islam did not spread farther than Spain into the remnants of the Western Roman Empire. The West profited from its contact with Islam, since much of the Arab world's technology and scholarship was superior to Europe's in the early Middle Ages.

Western Society and the Developing Christian Church As trade declined throughout the West, people migrated from cities to farmlands. New types of relationships between landowners and peasants emerged, including serfdom, the manorial system, and the feudal system. The Christian church provided a strong element of continuity with the educational and administrative achievements of the Roman Empire. Monastic culture took shape. Christianity was a potent unifying and civilizing force within the West, although it was also the source of a fundamental rift with the Eastern Empire. By the middle of the eighth century, the papacy in Rome faced military threats from the north and doctrinal threats from the East; Pope Stephen boldly initiated an alliance with the Franks that influenced history for the next millennium or more.

The Kingdom of the Franks Clovis founded the first Frankish dynasty, the Merovingians. Then the Carolingian dynasty made strategic alliances with the landed nobility and with the church. The most illustrious Carolingian ruler, Charlemagne, conquered additional lands and, on Christmas Day in 800 had himself crowned Holy Roman Emperor by Pope Leo III. His capital, Aachen was a center of scholarship and intelligent administration. The social organization of the manor and innovations such as new plows improved agricultural productivity. Soon after Charlemagne's death in 814, his empire disintegrated as it was divided up, messily, among his grandsons. The late ninth and early tenth centuries were truly "dark ages" in Europe: Both secular and church-based organizations were weak, and at the same time invaders such as the Vikings were attacking. Peasants sought security at almost any price, so the institution of feudalism spread and matured.

Feudal Society   The feudal system was built around the exchange of land, labor, and military protection. Vassals would swear fealty to a more powerful individual, in return for the promise of protection. Kings and nobles built their military strength by acquiring increasing numbers of vassals; as the system developed, benefices replaced residence in the lord's household, scutage replaced direct military service, and other innovations formalized and institutionalized the relationships of feudal society. All participants in the feudal system constantly negotiated and competed for advantage. Loyalties could become divided as vassals swore fealty to multiple lords, to gain multiple land holdings. Eventually, vassals could claim hereditary possession of the lands they worked, reducing their sense of obligation to lords. Nonetheless, feudalism provided a first glimpse of many of the political and legal institutions that developed into the modern nation-state.

REVIEW QUESTIONS

1. What changes took place in the Frankish kingdom between its foundation and the end of Charlemagne's reign? What were the characteristics of Charlemagne's government? Why did Charlemagne encourage learning at his court? Why did his empire break apart?

2. How and why was the history of the eastern half of the former Roman Empire so different from that of its western half? Did Justinian strengthen or weaken the Byzantine Empire? How does his reign compare to Charlemagne's?

3. What were the tenets of Islam? How were the Muslims able to build an empire so quickly? What contributions did the Muslims make to the development of Western Europe?

4. How and why did feudal society begin? What were the essential features of feudalism? Do you think modern society could slip back into a feudal pattern?

KEY TERMS

Caesaropapism   (p. 160)
caliphate   (p. 154)
fiefs   (p. 161)
Hegira   (p. 154)
Holy Roman Empire   (p. 163)
iconoclasm   (p. 159)

Islam   (p. 153)
Ka'ba   (p. 154)
manor   (p. 167)
Monophysites   (p. 159)
Papal States   (p. 162)
Qur'an   (p. 153)

serf   (p. 167)
Shi'a   (p. 154)
Sunnis   (p. 155)
three-field system   (p. 168)
ulema   (p. 154)
vassal   (p. 167)

   For additional study resources for this chapter, go to:
www.prenhall.com/kagan3/chapter6

7

The High Middle Ages
The Rise of European Empires and States (1000–1300)

CHAPTER HIGHLIGHTS

Otto I and the Revival of the Empire Otto I continued the program of unification and expansion begun by his father, Henry I. The Ottonian dynasty faltered in the early eleventh century because Otto I's successors paid little attention to events in Germany, and the church established an independent base of power for itself.

The Reviving Catholic Church The Catholic Church shed the secular control of the ninth and tenth centuries to become a powerful independent institution. The reform movement that began in the monastery of Cluny was endorsed by the papacy, creating conflict between the church and secular authorities. The Crusades led to increased trade and exposure of the West to the civilizations of the East. Pope Innocent III made broad claims about the extent of papal authority.

England and France: Hastings (1066) to Bouvines (1214) William, duke of Normandy, won the Battle of Hastings (1066) and was crowned king of England. William's grandson Henry married Eleanor of Aquitaine, creating the Angevin Empire. English barons forced King John to accept the Magna Carta in 1215. The Capetian kings concentrated on securing their territory and controlling the nobility. The French defeated a combined English and German force at Bouvines (1214).

France in the Thirteenth Century: The Reign of Louis IX Louis IX enjoyed almost fifty years as the ruler of a unified and secure France. He focused on domestic reform and the cultivation of culture and religion. He was less successful in foreign affairs, allowing the English to maintain their claims on various French lands, setting the stage for the next century's Hundred Years' War.

The Hohenstaufen Empire (1152–1272) The leaders of the Holy Roman Empire failed to develop a sustainable political structure. Throughout the Hohenstaufen dynasty, conflicts with the popes and designs to control Italy distracted Frederick I and his successors from consolidating their control at home. By the late thirteenth century, the Hohenstaufen had little real power and Germany was fragmented.

CHAPTER QUESTIONS

HOW WAS Otto able to secure the power of his Saxon dynasty?

WHAT WAS the Cluniac reform movement?

HOW DID England and France develop strong monarchies?

IN WHAT ways were the leadership of Henry II of England and Louis IX of France similar?

WHY WAS Germany not as stable as the twelfth- and thirteenth-century governments of England and France?

2. CLUNY (NO).

CHAPTER OUTLINE

IMAGE KEY
for pages 172–173 is on page 192.

Europe in the High Middle Ages (1000–1300) was characterized by political expansion and consolidation and by intellectual flowering and synthesis. This may indeed have been a more creative era than the Italian Renaissance or the German Reformation.

The borders of western Europe were secured against invaders, and Europeans, who had long been the prey of foreign powers, mounted a military and economic offensive against the East. By adapting feudal traditions, the rulers of England and France established nuclei for centrally governed nation-states. The parliaments and popular assemblies that emerged in some places enabled the propertied classes to exert some political influence. Germany and Italy, however, resisted the general trend toward political consolidation and remained fragmented until the nineteenth century.

The distinctive Western belief in the separation of church and state was established during the High Middle Ages. The popes acquired monarchical authority over the church and prevented it from being absorbed into Europe's emerging nation-states. Their methods, however, led to accusations that the papacy was diverting the church from its spiritual mission into the murky world of politics.

HOW WAS Otto able to secure the power of his Saxon dynasty?

OTTO I AND THE REVIVAL OF THE EMPIRE

*T*he fortunes of both the Holy Roman Empire and the papacy began to revive in the tenth century. Europe's Dark Age ended, and the most creative of the medieval eras began to unfold.

UNIFYING GERMANY

In 918, Henry I, "the Fowler," (d. 936) duke of Saxony, founded Germany's first non-Frankish dynasty and began to reverse the process of political fragmentation that had set in with the decline of the Carolingian Empire. He consolidated the duchies of Swabia, Bavaria, Saxony, Franconia, and Lotharingia and fended off invading Hungarians and Danes.

The state that Henry bequeathed to his son Otto I, "the Great," (r. 936–973) was the strongest kingdom in Europe, and Otto made it even greater. In 951, he invaded Italy and declared himself its king. In 955, he defeated the Hungarians at the Battle of Lechfeld and established secure frontiers for Germany and western Europe.

EMBRACING THE CHURCH

Otto secured the power of his Saxon dynasty by refusing to recognize the German duchies as independent hereditary states and treating them as subordinate parts of a unified kingdom. He curtailed the power of lay lords in his government by using bishops and abbots of monasteries as administrators of his lands. Clergy were more likely than laymen to favor strong royal government, and unlike laymen, they could not marry and produce sons with hereditary rights to the lands their fathers held from the king. The clergy were not concerned about potential conflicts between their spiritual and secular offices, and they eagerly embraced the wealth and power Otto offered them.

In 961, Otto helped Pope John XII (955–964) in a fight with an Italian nobleman, and on February 2, 962, the grateful pope revived the lapsed imperial title and bestowed it on Otto. The German king's intervention in Italian politics increased the power he was already exercising over the church. He appointed men to the major church offices and declared himself the protector of the Papal States. Pope John belatedly recognized the royal web in which he had become entangled. But when Otto discovered John was plotting against him, he ordered an ecclesiastical synod to depose the pope and to agree that no future pope take office without swearing allegiance to the emperor. Popes ruled at Otto's pleasure.

Otto's desire to found a Holy Roman Empire undercut the progress he had made toward the establishment of a German kingdom. Italy preoccupied his successors, Otto II (r. 973–983) and Otto III (r. 983–1002), and they allowed their German base to disintegrate. When the fledgling empire began to crumble in the first quarter of the eleventh century, the papacy seized the opportunity to reassert its independence.

THE REVIVING CATHOLIC CHURCH

While Otto was bringing the church under his control in Germany and Italy, a reform movement with a very different program was taking hold in France. Its goal was to liberate the clergy from the power of the feudal nobility.

THE CLUNY REFORM MOVEMENT

Since the last days of the Roman Empire, monks—the least worldly of the clergy—had been the church's most popular representatives. They were the best educated people in Europe. Their prayers and the sacred relics they guarded were believed to have a magical potency, and the religious ideals embodied in their way of life set the standard for all Christians.

In 910, William the Pious, duke of Aquitaine, endowed a new monastery at Cluny in south-central France. The church in William's day was in dire need of reform, and Cluny was intended as an experiment with a strategy for its renewal. The Cluniacs argued that so long as laymen had the power to use appointments to church offices to advance their personal political agendas and family interests, the church would suffer. It could realize its spiritual potential only if its leaders were chosen by the clergy themselves—by persons with genuine spiritual vocations. Cluny's patron granted its monks the right to choose their own leaders and manage their own affairs. As a result, Cluny quickly built a reputation for discipline and spiritual integrity.

The Cluniac movement spread from the monastery to all other parts of the church. The reformers argued that the **secular clergy** (those serving the *saeculum*, the "world") ought to imitate, insofar as possible, the ideal lifestyles of the **regular clergy** (those living under a *regula*, the rule of a monastic order). The higher clergy, who led the church, should also be free of feudal obligations and answerable only to an independent papacy.

The Cluniac reform spread to monasteries throughout France and Italy, until about 1,500 cloisters were affiliated with Cluny. Cluniacs pushed for changes that would benefit society at large as well as the church. In the late ninth and early tenth centuries, they tried to ease the suffering caused by the endemic warfare that plagued medieval society by promoting the "Peace of God" movement. Its decrees threatened soldiers who attacked noncombatants (women, peasants, merchants, and clergy) with excommunication. A subsequent "Truce of God" prohibited combat from Wednesday night to Monday morning and in all holy seasons.

Cluniac reformers advanced to high offices in the church, and Pope Leo IX (r. 1049–1054) appointed some to key administrative posts in Rome. They urged the pope to suppress *simony* (the sale of church offices) and to enforce celibacy among parish priests. The papacy itself, however, continued to be dominated by

WHAT WAS the Cluniac reform movement?

secular clergy   Those clergy serving the *saeculum*, the "world."

regular clergy   Those clergy living under a *regula*, the rule of a monastic order.

powerful laymen. Emperor Henry III of Germany (r. 1039–1056) deposed three popes, who were pawns of the Roman aristocracy, and put Leo himself on the papal throne.

Henry's heir, Henry IV (r. 1056–1106), was a minor when he came to the throne. The weakness of the boy-king's regents gave the popes an opportunity to establish some important precedents. Pope Stephen IX (r. 1057–1058) reigned without seeking imperial confirmation of his title, and in 1059, Pope Nicholas II (r. 1059–1061) decreed that a group of high church officials (the College of Cardinals) would henceforth have the right to elect the popes. The procedures developed (and which are still followed) were intended to prevent Italian noble families and German kings from foisting their own candidates onto the papal throne, but laymen continued to exert considerable indirect influence on the process of choosing popes.

THE INVESTITURE STRUGGLE: GREGORY VII AND HENRY IV

7.1
Gregory VII's Letter to the Bishop of Metz, 1081

The German monarchy did not react to the papacy's new policies until the reign of Pope Gregory VII (r. 1073–1085), a fierce advocate of Cluny's reforms. In 1075, Gregory condemned "lay investiture," the appointment of someone to a church office by a layman. The pope's decree attacked the foundations of imperial government. Since the days of Otto I, German kings had preferred to use bishops rather than lay nobles to administer state lands. If the king lost the right to appoint men to ecclesiastical office, he lost the power to choose the men who administered much of his land. By prohibiting lay investiture, the pope emphasized the spiritual nature of the episcopacy, but he failed to recognize the church's religious offices had long since become entwined with the state's secular offices.

Henry opposed Gregory's action on the grounds it violated well-founded tradition, but the pope had important allies. The German nobles were eager for opportunities to increase their independence by diminishing the power of their king. Things came to a head in 1076. Bishops loyal to Henry assembled at Worms in January of that year and repudiated the pope's authority. Gregory responded by excommunicating Henry and absolving his subjects from their oaths of allegiance to him. The German magnates seized on this as an excuse and began to organize a rebellion against Henry.

Henry seized the initiative by crossing the Alps in midwinter to reach Canossa, Italy, where Gregory was waiting for the passes to clear so he could join the rebels in Germany. Henry compelled Gregory to grant him absolution by reportedly doing penance barefoot in the snow for three days. Henry's maneuver deprived his nobles of their excuse for rebelling and turned them against Gregory. The king regrouped his forces, and in March 1080, Gregory excommunicated Henry once again. The German nobles, however, refused to rise to the bait a second time. Four years later Henry drove Gregory into exile and placed his own man, Clement III, on the papal throne.

The investiture controversy ended in 1122 with a compromise spelled out by the Concordat of Worms. Emperor Henry V (r. 1106–1125) agreed to cease investing bishops with the ring and staff that symbolized spiritual office. In return, Pope Calixtus II (1119–1124) recognized the emperor's right to be present at episcopal consecrations and to preside at the ceremonies that bestowed fiefs on bishops. The old church-state "back scratching" continued, but now on a basis that made the church look more independent. The papacy's attempt to weaken Germany's kings did little to liberate the church. When the power of monarchs declined, the strength of the feudal nobles increased, enabling them to dominate the clergy.

QUICK REVIEW

Investiture Struggle

- Investiture struggle centered on authority to appoint and control clergy
- Pope Gregory excommunicated Henry IV when he proclaimed his independence from papacy
- Crisis settled in 1122 with Concordat of Worms

A twelfth-century German manuscript portrays the struggle between Emperor Henry IV and Pope Gregory VII. In the top panel, Henry installs the puppet pope Clement III and drives Gregory from Rome. Below, Gregory dies in exile. The artist was a monk; his sympathies were with Gregory, not Henry.

Thuringer Universitäts- und Landesbiblithek Jena, Ms. Bos. q. 6, 79

THE CRUSADES

What the Cluny reform was to the clergy, the **Crusades** to the Holy Land were to the laity—that is, an outlet for the religious zeal and self-confidence that characterized Europe in the High Middle Ages. Late in the eleventh century, Alexius I Comnenus, emperor of Constantinople, asked the pope to help him recruit soldiers for a war he hoped would win back lands his predecessors had lost to the Seljuk Turks. At the council of Clermont in 1095, Pope Urban II turned Alexius's request into a call for a Crusade. (See "History's Voices: Pope Urban II (r. 1088–1099) Preaches the First Crusade.")

The First Crusade appealed to different people for different reasons. The pope's successful launch of a Crusade confirmed his status as Europe's spiritual leader and won him leverage in dealing with the Byzantine church. The departure of large numbers of quarrelsome warriors pacified Europe, and hordes of restless young knights were enthralled by the opportunities the Crusade offered for adventure and personal profit. Many Crusaders were the younger sons of noblemen who had no inheritances to look forward to. Given limited land and soaring population, they had little hope of obtaining fiefs at home.

Although motives were mixed, the First Crusade was a less mercenary and more genuinely pious venture than some of the later Crusades. Popes recruited Crusaders by promising those who died in battle a plenary indulgence—a complete remission of punishment for their sins and from all suffering in purgatory. The Crusade was a true Holy War, a passionate struggle to rescue the most sacred Christian shrines from the clutches of hated infidels. It was also the ultimate

Crusades Campaigns authorized by the church to combat heresies and rival faiths.

HISTORY'S VOICES

POPE URBAN II (R. 1088–1099) PREACHES THE FIRST CRUSADE

When Pope Urban II summoned the First Crusade in a sermon at the Council of Clermont on November 26, 1095, he painted a savage picture of the Muslims who controlled Jerusalem. Urban also promised the Crusaders, who responded by the tens of thousands, remission of their unrepented sins and assurance of heaven. Robert the Monk is one of four witnesses who has left us a summary of the sermon.

WHAT ARE the images of the enemy he creates and how accurate and fair are they?

From the confines of Jerusalem and the city of Constantinople a horrible tale has gone forth and very frequently has been brought to our ears, namely, that a race from the kingdom of the Persians [that is, the Seljuk Turks], an accursed race, a race utterly alienated from God, a generation forsooth which has not directed its heart and has not entrusted its spirit to God, has invaded the lands of those Christians and has depopulated them by the sword, pillage and fire; it has led away a part of the captives into its own country, and a part it has destroyed by cruel tortures; it has either entirely destroyed the churches of God or appropriated them for the rites of its own religion. They destroy the altars, after having defiled them with their uncleanness. They circumcise the Christians, and the blood of the circumcision they either spread upon the altars or pour into the vases of the baptismal font. When they wish to torture people by a base death, they perforate their navels, and dragging forth the extremity of the intestines, bind it to a stake; then with flogging they lead the victim around until the viscera having gushed forth, the victim falls prostrate upon the ground. Others they bind to a post and pierce with arrows. Others they compel to extend their necks and then, attacking them with naked swords, attempt to cut through the neck with a single blow. What shall I say of the abominable rape of the women? The kingdom of the Greeks is now dismembered by them and deprived of territory so vast in extent that it can not be traversed in a march of two months. On whom therefore is the labor of avenging these wrongs and of recovering this territory incumbent, if not upon you? ...

Jerusalem is the navel of the world; the land is fruitful above others, like another paradise of delights. This the Redeemer of the human race has made illustrious by His advent, has beautified by residence, has consecrated by suffering, has redeemed by death, has glorified by burial. This royal city, therefore, situated at the centre of the world, is now held captive by His enemies, and is in subjection to those who do not know God, to the worship of the heathens. She seeks therefore and desires to be liberated, and does not cease to implore you to come to her aid. From you especially she asks succor, because, as we have already said, God has conferred upon you above all nations great glory in arms.

Accordingly undertake this journey for the remission of your sins, with the assurance of the imperishable glory of the kingdom of heaven.

Translations and reprints from *Original Sources of European History*, Vol. I (Philadelphia: Department of History, University of Pennsylvania, 1910), pp. 5–7.

pilgrimage, and the desire to be part of it affected even those who did not leave home. They crusaded by massacring their Jewish neighbors.

The First Victory Three great armies (perhaps 100,000 men) gathered in France, Germany, and Italy and converged on Constantinople in 1097 by different routes. They were not the disciplined, professional force Alexius had hoped to enlist. He was suspicious of their motives, and the common people whom they pillaged along the route of their march hardly considered them models of faith. Nonetheless, the Crusaders succeeded where earlier Byzantine armies had

MAP EXPLORATION

Interactive map: To explore this map further, go to **http://www.prenhall.com/kagan3/map7.1**

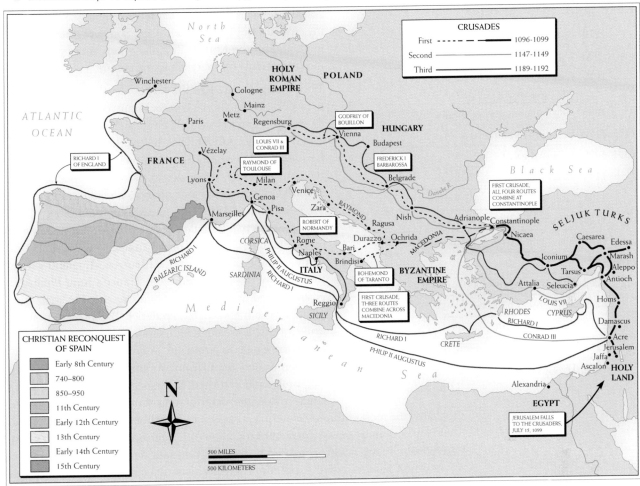

MAP 7–1

The Early Crusades   Routes and several leaders of the Crusades during the first century of the movement are shown. The names on this map do not exhaust the list of great nobles who went on the First Crusade. The even showier array of monarchs of the Second and Third Crusades still left the Crusades, on balance, ineffective in achieving their goals.

COMPARE AND contrast the scope and result of each of the first three Crusades. Overall, how successful were these Crusades?

failed. They defeated one Seljuk army after another, and, on July 15, 1099, they captured Jerusalem. They owed their success to the superior military technology Europeans had evolved and to the inability of the Muslim states to cooperate in mounting an effective resistance. (See Map 7–1.)

The Crusaders established feudal states (Edessa, Antioch, and Jerusalem) in the lands they conquered and proclaimed Godfrey of Bouillon first king of Jerusalem. Godfrey's realm was little more than a collection of European outposts in a hostile Muslim world. Its precarious situation became clear as the Muslims rallied to oppose the Christian "savages" who had invaded their lands. The Crusaders erected castles, hunkered down to live under conditions of perpetual

Significant Dates from the Period of the High Middle Ages

910	Cluniac reform begins
955	Otto I defeats Magyars
1059	College of Cardinals empowered to elect popes
1066	Norman conquest of England
1075–1122	Investiture Controversy
1095–1099	First Crusade
1144	Edessa falls; Second Crusade
1152	Hohenstaufen dynasty founded
1154	Plantagenet dynasty founded
1187	Jerusalem falls to Saladin
1189–1192	Third Crusade
1202	Fourth Crusade sacks Constantinople
1209	Albigensian Crusade
1210	Franciscan Order founded
1215	Fourth Lateran Council; Magna Carta
1250	Death of Fredrick II

siege, and became businessmen devoted to promoting trade between East and West. Orders of soldier-monks were established to protect and assist pilgrims to the Holy Lands, and the services they provided for travelers spawned banking and money-lending ventures. Some of the orders—most notably the Knights Templar—were among Europe's most powerful commercial organizations.

The Long-Term Results The Crusaders maintained their posts in the Middle East for about forty years, and then their grip began to loosen. Each setback prompted a call for a new Crusade. After Edessa fell to the Muslims in 1144, Bernard of Clairvaux (1091–1153), a prominent abbot and religious reformer, persuaded the king of France to lead a Second Crusade. It was an embarrassing failure. In October 1187, Saladin (r. 1138–1193), the Muslim ruler of Egypt and Syria, conquered Jerusalem, and Europe's most powerful monarchs enlisted in a Third Crusade (1189–1192). Germany's Emperor Frederick Barbarossa, England's King Richard "the Lion-Hearted," and France's King Philip Augustus all led armies to Jerusalem's rescue, but their campaign was a tragicomedy. Frederick Barbarossa drowned while fording a stream in Asia Minor. Richard and Philip Augustus drew near to Jerusalem. Intense personal rivalry, however, prevented them from working together, and Philip Augustus soon returned to France to prey on Richard's lands. When the deteriorating situation finally persuaded Richard (the most enthusiastic of the Crusaders) to head home, he was captured and held for ransom by the German emperor, Henry VI. England's bill for its king's Eastern adventure was greatly increased by the sum Germany demanded for his release.

The Crusades failed to achieve their political objectives, but their economic and cultural impact on Europe was significant. They stimulated trade between Europe and the Middle East, and the merchants of Venice, Pisa, and Genoa, who followed in the wake of the Crusaders, had more luck challenging Muslim domination at sea than the crusading armies did on land. As trade contacts proliferated, so did cultural exchanges.

THE PONTIFICATE OF INNOCENT III (R. 1198–1216)

The pope who inaugurated the Crusades hoped they would unite Europe behind the leader of its church. His successors shared the dream of winning some kind of authority over Europe's secular rulers, and none did more to make the dream a reality than Pope Innocent III.

The New Papal Monarchy Innocent greatly increased the flow of revenue to the church and used this wealth to create a papal monarchy that could compete with the power and organization of secular kingdoms. He collected an income tax of 2.5 percent from the clergy. Appointees to church offices paid *annates* (the equivalent of their first year's income). The pope demanded substantial fees for bestowing the *pallium*, the stole that symbolized an archbishop's authority. The papacy claimed the exclusive right to grant absolution for many kinds of sins (and to pocket the fees imposed as penances). Innocent also collected Peter's pence, a tax imposed on all but the poorest laymen.

Crusades in France and the East   The church's increasing wealth and secular influence was seen by some as a sign of its corruption and spiritual decline. Disillusionment with clerical greed prompted criticism that sometimes blossomed into heresy. When that happened, Innocent did not shrink from pitting Europeans against one another in Holy War.

In 1209, Innocent launched a Crusade to exterminate heretics called **Albigensians** (from the French town of Albi) or Cathars ("pure ones"). These people advocated a simple, pious way of life following the example set by Jesus and the Apostles, but they rejected key Christian doctrines. They denied that the wrathful god of the Old Testament, who created the sinful material world, was the same god as the heavenly Father to whom Jesus prayed. They saw history as a war between the god of flesh and the god of spirit, and their belief that the flesh was the source of the sins that imprisoned the spirit caused them to reject the Christian claim that God was incarnate in Jesus. The true church, they insisted, was a spiritual entity, not the materialistic institution headed by the pope. The more radical Cathars practiced strict asceticism and recommended celibacy, contraception, or abortion to prevent more immortal souls from being captured and imprisoned in sinful matter. Paradoxically, the Cathars' dualism could also lead to moral laxity. If flesh and spirit are totally separate realities, what the former does can have little impact on the latter.

The south of France, where the heresy spread, was a rich land, and knights from northern France seized on the pope's Crusade as an opportunity to dispossess their wealthy neighbors. Massacres and a campaign led by the French king, Louis VIII, in 1226 utterly devastated the prosperous Albigensian region. Pope Gregory IX (r. 1227–1241) followed up by sending the **Inquisition** to root out any heretics who remained. The Inquisition was a formal ecclesiastical court dedicated to discovering and punishing heresy. Bishops had used such courts in their dioceses since the mid–twelfth century, but Innocent III's Inquisition was a centralized organization that dispatched papal legates to preside at trials and executions throughout Europe.

In 1202, Innocent dispatched the Fourth Crusade. It was supposed to go to the Holy Lands, but it was diverted to an attack on Constantinople. Many of the approximately 30,000 Crusaders who gathered in Venice were poor soldiers of fortune who could not pay what the Venetians demanded for their transport. The Venetians persuaded them to work off their passage by conquering Zara, a Christian city that was one of Venice's commercial rivals. To the shock and anger of Pope Innocent III, the Crusaders obliged and then allowed Venice to lead them farther afield for an assault on Constantinople.

Once the Crusaders had taken Constantinople, the pope came to terms with them and shared the spoils. One of Innocent's confidants was appointed patriarch of Constantinople and charged with persuading the Greeks and the Slavs to submit to the authority of the pope. The Latins occupied Constantinople until 1261, when the Genoese, who envied Venice's coup, helped the exiled Byzantine emperor (Michael Paleologus) recapture the city. The Crusade and the subsequent half century of Latin mismanagement hardly helped reunite the church or strengthen the Christian position in the Middle East.

The Fourth Lateran Council   The culminating event of Innocent's papacy was the Fourth Lateran Council, which met in 1215 (a year before the pope's death). The doctrinal issues the meeting resolved and the disciplines it imposed were designed to enhance the authority of the church and its clergy. The council affirmed

Thirteenth-century statue of St. Maurice, patron saint of Magdeburg, Germany. An Egyptian Christian who commanded a Roman legion, St. Maurice was executed in 286 C.E. after refusing to worship the Roman gods. Portrayed as a white man for centuries, during the era of the Crusades, Maurice became a perfect talisman for Europeans venturing eastward.

Constantin Beyer

Albigensians   Heretical sect that advocated a simple, pious way of life following the example set by Jesus and the Apostles, but rejecting key Christian doctrines.

Inquisition   Formal ecclesiastical court dedicated to discovering and punishing heresy.

Dominicans (left), **and Franciscans** (right). Unlike the other religious orders, the Dominicans and Franciscans did not live in cloisters, but wandered about preaching and combating heresy. They depended for support on their own labor and the kindness of the laity.

Cliche Bibliothéque Nationale de France, Paris

the doctrine of **transubstantiation** as the explanation for the key Christian sacrament, the Eucharist. The doctrine states that at the moment of priestly consecration the bread and wine of the Lord's Supper become the body and blood of Christ. This was what many Christians had come to believe by the twelfth century, and it served the interests of the papacy. The power that clergy alone possessed to perform this miracle gave them precedence over the laity. The council further empowered the priesthood by formalizing the sacrament of penance and requiring every adult Christian to confess and commune at least annually (usually at Easter).

Franciscans and Dominicans   Piety and faith surged at the turn of the twelfth century, and new religious movements proliferated. Most advocated a life of poverty in imitation of Christ. Idealization of poverty was not heretical, but the criticism of the worldly clergy it implied caused groups such as the Waldensians, Beguines, and Beghards to be suspected of harboring heretical opinions.

Innocent created a safe outlet for the champions of poverty by licensing two new religious orders: the Franciscans and the Dominicans. These were orders of *friars* ("brothers"), who differed from traditional monks in that they refused to accept land and endowments and did not retreat into cloisters. They devoted themselves to preaching and caring for the poor and supported themselves by working and begging. The saintly behavior of these *mendicants* did much to restore respect for the church they served. The "Third orders" (tertiaries) they established allowed laypeople to affiliate with the movement and receive guidance that prevented their piety from drifting into heresy.

The Franciscan Order was founded in 1210 by Francis of Assisi (1182–1226), the son of a rich Italian cloth merchant. The Dominican Order (the Order of Preachers) was founded in 1216 by Dominic (1170–1221), a well-educated Spanish cleric. Both orders reported directly to the pope and not to the bishops of the dioceses in which they worked. They constituted a kind of army of dedicated servants that the central government of the church could dispatch on special missions.

Pope Gregory IX (1227–1241) canonized Francis only two years after Francis's death. However, the pope also diverted the Franciscans from the path Francis charted for them. He declared that absolute poverty was impractical and he announced the church would accept property and hold it in trust for the friars to fund their work. Most Franciscans accepted the pope's moderation of their lifestyle, but a radical branch, the Spiritual Franciscans, refused and were condemned by a pope in the fourteenth century.

transubstantiation   Christian doctrine which holds that, at the moment of priestly consecration, the bread and wine of the Lord's Supper become the body and blood of Christ.

The Dominicans specialized in combating heresy. They preached, staffed the offices of the Inquisition, taught at universities, and supervised convents of **Beguines** (sisterhoods of pious, self-supporting single women). They produced one of the greatest of medieval thinkers, Thomas Aquinas (d. 1274). His efforts to reconcile faith's revealed truths with human reason produced what the Catholic Church has acknowledged to be the definitive statement of its beliefs.

Beguines   Sisterhoods of pious, self-supporting single women.

ENGLAND AND FRANCE: HASTINGS (1066) TO BOUVINES (1214)

HOW DID England and France develop strong monarchies?

While struggles between popes and emperors were complicating the political development of Germany and Italy, England and France were evolving effective monarchies. There were, however, troublesome ties between these two kingdoms as between Germany and Italy.

The old Roman province of Britain became England ("Anglo-land") as Germans from the tribes of the Angles and Saxons took it over at the start of the Middle Ages. Edward the Confessor, the last of their kings, died childless in 1066, and a fight broke out for his throne. The Anglo-Saxons supported a native nobleman, Harold Godwinsson, but he was challenged by Edward's distant relative, Duke William of Normandy (d. 1087). The Normans invaded and obliterated the Anglo-Saxon army in a battle fought near Hastings on October 14, 1066. The victory made William king of England as well as duke of a major portion of northern France.

WILLIAM THE CONQUEROR

William constructed the most effective monarchy in Europe by judiciously combining continental feudalism and Anglo-Saxon custom. To discover precisely what he had won at Hastings, he carried out a county-by-county survey of its people, animals, and implements. The results were compiled as the *Domesday Book* (1080–1086), a virtually unique description of a medieval kingdom. William claimed all the land in England by right of conquest and compelled every landlord

The **Battle of Hastings**. Detail of the *Bayeux Tapestry*, c. 1073–83. Wool embroidery on linen, height 20" (50.7 cm).

Centre Guillaume le Conquérant. "Detail of the Bayeux Tapestry-XIth century" and "By special permission of City of Bayeux"

OVERVIEW — A COMPARISON OF LEADERS IN THE HIGH MIDDLE AGES

	England	France	Germany
Leader	Henry II	Louis IX	Frederick II
Reign	(1154–1189)	(1226–1270)	(1212–1250)
Accomplishments	Henry brought to the throne greatly expanded French holdings. The union with Eleanor created the Angevin (English–French) Empire. Henry conquered a part of Ireland and made the king of Scotland his vassal.	Louis IX embodied the medieval view of the perfect ruler. His greatest achievements lay at home. The French bureaucracy became an instrument of order and fair play in government under Louis. He abolished private wars and serfdom within his domain. Respected by the kings of Europe, Louis became an arbiter among the world's powers.	Within a year and a half of Frederick's crowing, the treacherous reign of Otto IV came to an end on the battlefields of Bouvines.
Failures	As Henry acquired new lands abroad, he became more autocratic at home. He tried to recapture the efficiency and stability of his grandfather's regime, but in the process steered the English monarchy toward an oppressive rule.	Had Louis ruthlessly confiscated English territories on the French coast, he might have lessened, if not averted altogether, the conflict underlying the Hundred Years' War.	During his reign, Frederick effectively turned dreams of a unified Germany into a nightmare of disunity. Living mostly outside of Germany during his rule, he did little to secure the rights of the emperor in Germany. Frederick's relations with the pope were equally disastrous, leading to his excommunication on four different occasions.

to take an oath of vassalage and to acknowledge his land was held as a fief from the king. Feudal nobles usually tried to weaken their kings, but the Norman nobles—having no support from their new Anglo-Saxon subjects—needed the help of a powerful leader. William's hand was further strengthened by the tax and court systems he found already in place in England, and he continued the Anglo-Saxon custom of parleying with the nobility before making major decisions. The tradition of consultation between the king and (at least some of) his subjects led ultimately to England's influential parliamentary system of government.

HENRY II

The strength of the English monarchy continued to grow under William's sons and heirs, William Rufus (r. 1087–1100) and Henry I (r. 1100–1135). But when Henry died leaving only a female heir, a civil war threatened near anarchy. In the end, the competing factions compromised and pledged their allegiance to

Henry II (r. 1154–1189), son of the duke of Anjou and Henry I's daughter Matilda. Henry's Plantagenet dynasty ruled England until the death of Richard III in 1485.

Henry, by inheritance and by marriage to Eleanor of Aquitaine (ca. 1122–1204), built the Angevin (from Anjou, his father's domain) Empire. In addition to England, he ruled much more of France than did the king of France, and he conquered part of Ireland and forced the king of Scotland to pledge homage. The French king did what he could to contain the English, but the French were not to evict the English from the Continent until the mid–fifteenth century.

ELEANOR OF AQUITAINE AND COURT CULTURE

Eleanor of Aquitaine had been married to King Louis VII of France before she wed Henry II of England, and she was a powerful influence on both their kingdoms. Women of Eleanor's generation began to venture into traditionally masculine fields, such as politics and business, and Eleanor led the way. She insisted on accompanying her first husband on the Second Crusade, and she stirred up so much trouble for her second husband that from 1179 until his death in 1189 he kept her under house arrest.

After her marriage to Henry, the court that Eleanor established in Angers (Anjou's chief town) became a major center of patronage for musicians and poets. Bernart de Ventadorn, one of the new troubadour poets, composed many of the popular love songs of the period in her honor. In 1170, Eleanor separated from Henry and moved to Poitiers to live with her daughter Marie, the countess of Champagne, another patroness of the arts. The court of Poitiers popularized an aristocratic entertainment to which modern scholars have given the name "courtly love." The troubadours who elaborated the rules of game contrasted carnal love with "courteous" love, a spiritual passion for a lady that ennobled her knightly lover. Chrétien de Troyes's stories of King Arthur and the Knights of the Round Table (and of Sir Lancelot's tragic, illicit love for Arthur's wife, Guinevere) are the most famous products of the movement.

POPULAR REBELLION AND MAGNA CARTA

Henry II believed the church should operate within parameters set by the state, and in 1164, his Constitutions of Clarendon spelled out new rules for the English clergy. Henry limited the right to appeal cases to the papal court, subjected clergy to the king's justice, and gave the king control over the election of bishops. Henry also bestowed the office of archbishop of Canterbury, the head of the English church, on his compliant chancellor Thomas à Becket (1118?–1170). Much to Henry's surprise, Becket opposed the Constitutions and mounted a furious campaign to force Henry to rescind them. In 1170, several of Henry's men assassinated the troublesome archbishop, and the church seized the opportunity to declare Becket a martyr and embarrass the king by canonizing him (1172). (See "Encountering the Past: Pilgrimage.")

Henry was followed on the throne by two of his sons: Richard the Lion-Hearted (r. 1189–1199) and John (r. 1199–1216). Neither was a success. Richard imposed ruinous taxation to fund the fruitless Third Crusade and died fighting to recover lands he lost to the French while he was in the Middle East. In 1209, Pope Innocent III excommunicated Richard's successor, John, in a dispute over the appointment of an archbishop for Canterbury. To extricate himself from a mess of his own making and to win support for a war with France, John surrendered to the pope and declared his kingdom a papal fief. John had lost most of England's territory on the continent, and the campaign he mounted in 1214 to win it back failed abysmally.

ENCOUNTERING THE PAST

PILGRIMAGE

Thomas à Becket's tomb at Canterbury quickly became one of the most frequented pilgrimage shrines in Europe. The perennially popular Canterbury Tales of Geoffrey Chaucer (ca. 1345–1400) provide a fictional account of one such trip. As Chaucer describes it, a medieval pilgrimage was both a spiritual and a social event. Because travel to distant shrines involved self-sacrifice (danger and expense), clergy often imposed pilgrimages as penances for sins. Pilgrims also set out on their own in the hope that contact with a saint's relics or the waters of a sacred well or spring would provide a miraculous cure for a bodily affliction. Parents even brought the corpses of dead infants to shrines to beg the saints to bring them back to life.

The most prestigious pilgrimages were those to the Holy Lands and to the graves of St. Peter in Rome and St. James at Compostela in northern Spain. Pilgrim traffic was so great that businesses sprang up along these routes to assist travelers. Transportation, shelter, emergency services, and even guidebooks were available. Pilgrims, particularly to distant locals, often traveled in groups, and an opportunity to share stories and adventures with others made for diverting entertainment. Travel then, as now, was highly educational.

WHY WERE pilgrimages so popular with medieval people?

A thirteenth-century stained glass window depicts pilgrims traveling to Canterbury Cathedral.
© Archivo Icongrafico, S.A./CORBIS

In 1215, John, facing rebellion by his disillusioned barons, agreed to limitations on his authority that were spelled out in a document called **Magna Carta** ("Great Charter"). Among the king's more significant concessions were promises not to arrest and hold people without giving reasons and not to impose new taxes without consulting representatives of the propertied classes. Magna Carta had little effect, for John repudiated it. But it kept alive traditions and precedents that came to undergird modern English law.

PHILIP II AUGUSTUS

In England during the High Middle Ages, the propertied classes struggled to prevent a strong monarchy from encroaching on their interests. The shoe was on the other foot in France, where kings confronted powerful subjects who opposed the growth of monarchy.

After the Carolingian line came to an end in France in 987, the nobles made the crown an elective office. They chose Hugh Capet, count of Paris, to be

Magna Carta ("Great Charter") Document spelling out limitations on royal authority agreed to by John in 1215. It created foundation for modern English law.

their king, and by repeatedly winning elections, his descendants created a Capetian dynasty. For the next two centuries, however, the great feudal princes were France's real rulers. The early Capetian kings were so weak that they were not even fully in control of their personal domain, the area around Paris and the region known as the Ile-de-France. By the time Philip II (r. 1180–1223) came to the throne, the Capetians had won recognition of their hereditary rights to the throne, and it was finally possible for them to assert their authority without the risk of being deposed. The Norman conquest of England in 1066 may actually have helped them, for it was in the self-interest of France's nobles to support them in their efforts to contain the far more powerful and threatening Plantagenet kings. The wealthy merchant class beginning to appear in France also favored a strong monarchy that could provide protection for commerce.

The king of England was, as duke of Normandy, a vassal of the French king. A skillful politician such as France's King Philip II Augustus (r. 1180–1223) was able to exploit the ambiguity of this relationship. Whenever his English rival failed to honor his obligations as a vassal, Philip could declare his fiefs forfeit and call on France's nobles for help in forcing the English king to give them up. Richard the Lion-Hearted and John both played into Philip's hands and allowed him to reclaim all the lands the English had occupied in France except for part of Aquitaine.

John of England tried to recover what he had lost by persuading the German emperor Otto IV (r. 1198–1215) to join him in invading France. A battle fought at Bouvines in Flanders on July 27, 1214, decided what was, in effect, Europe's first multinational war. Philip won, and his victory rallied his subjects in support of their monarchy. Otto IV fell from power, and John's subjects welcomed him home with the rebellion that culminated in Magna Carta.

FRANCE IN THE THIRTEENTH CENTURY: THE REIGN OF LOUIS IX

*T*he legitimacy of the Capetians' growing power appeared to be confirmed by the achievements and reputation of Philip's grandson, Louis IX (r. 1226–1270). Louis so embodied the medieval ideal of a king that he was canonized shortly after his death. Louis had ascetic tastes, and his ethical standards were far superior to those of his royal and papal contemporaries. He was approachable and had compassion for the poor, but he was also a decisive leader and an enthusiastic soldier.

GENEROSITY ABROAD

Some of Louis's decisions suggest naiveté or an overly scrupulous conscience. He could, for instance, have driven the English off the Continent, but he refused to take advantage of the English king's weakness. In 1259, he negotiated the Treaty of Paris, a generous compromise that ended a long-simmering dispute between England and France. Had he been more ruthless and seized the last English outposts in France, he might have prevented subsequent wars and spared Europe a great deal of bloodshed.

Louis did not take the opportunity that a long struggle between the papacy and the German emperor Frederick II gave him to intervene in Italy. After Frederick's death, however, Louis's brother, Charles of Anjou, did enter the fray on the pope's side. In exchange for Charles's help in destroying Frederick's heirs, the pope confirmed Charles in possession of a royal title and Frederick's kingdom of Naples and Sicily.

IN WHAT ways were the leadership of Henry II of England and Louis IX of France similar?

Choir (c. 1060–75) and nave (1095–1115), St.-Savin-sur-Gartempe, France.

CORBIS/Bettmann

WHY WAS Germany not as stable as the twelfth- and thirteenth-century governments of England and France?

ORDER AND EXCELLENCE AT HOME

Louis's greatest achievements were the improvements he made in France's government. The bureaucratic machinery he inherited from his predecessors had been developed so the king might more efficiently exploit his subjects. Louis used it to secure order and improve the administration of justice. He sent out *enquêteurs* (auditors) to monitor the *baillis* and *prévôts* whom Philip Augustus had created to handle local administration. He abolished private warfare among the nobles and serfdom within the royal domain. He gave his subjects the judicial right of appeal from local to higher courts, and he made the tax system more equitable.

The French people's enthusiasm for monarchy grew in proportion to the services they received from their king, and his increasing significance in their lives helped them develop a sense of national identity. Other things contributed to this. Louis's reign was the golden age of Scholasticism, a time when scholars such as the Dominican, Thomas Aquinas, and the Franciscan, Bonaventure, made the University of Paris Europe's intellectual center. France led Europe in monastic reform, codes of chivalry, and the arts of courtly love. Suger, abbot of St. Denis and adviser to Louis IX's great-grandfather, Louis VII, pioneered the development of the Gothic style in art and architecture that spread throughout the medieval world. France's enduring reputation as the leader of European culture dates to the reign of St. Louis.

Louis's virtues were those of a medieval king. He was fanatical about religion. He supported the work of the Inquisition, and he personally led the last two major Crusades for the Holy Land. Both were failures, but Louis's death of a fever during the second of his holy wars only confirmed his reputation for saintliness. The Capetians' production of a king of Louis's stature confirmed many of their subjects in the belief that God had given them a divine right to France's throne.

THE HOHENSTAUFEN EMPIRE (1152–1272)

During the twelfth and thirteenth centuries, while stable governments were evolving in England and France, the Holy Roman Empire (Germany, Burgundy, and northern Italy) took quite a different course. Political fragmentation triumphed over monarchical centralization and created a troublesome legacy that endured into modern times.

FREDERICK I BARBAROSSA

The Investiture Controversy (the popes' assault on the right of kings to appoint the higher clergy) weakened Germany's monarchs but strengthened its feudal barons. The power the king lost to influence appointments to church offices simply passed to the German princes.

Imperial authority revived with the accession to the throne of Frederick I Barbarossa (r. 1152–1190), founder of the Hohenstaufen dynasty. Frederick had some help in laying a foundation for a new empire. Disaffection with the incessant squabbling of the feudal princes was widespread, and resentment of the theocratic pretensions of the papacy was growing. Irnerius (d. 1125), a scholar at the University of Bologna, had also revived the study of Roman law (Justinian's

Code). This was useful to Frederick, for Roman law promoted the centralization of states and provided a secular justification for imperial power that minimized the importance of papal coronation.

From a base of operation in Switzerland, Frederick waged a relatively successful campaign to assert his authority over the German nobility. The balance tipped in his favor in 1180, when his strongest rival, Henry the Lion (d. 1195), duke of Saxony, was exiled to Normandy. Frederick never grew strong enough to intervene in the internal affairs of Germany's greater duchies, but he vigilantly enforced his rights as their feudal overlord. This kept the memory of royal authority alive until a king was able to risk a showdown with Germany's powerful magnates.

Italy was both the means and the obstacle to the realization of Frederick's dreams of empire. In 1155, Frederick defeated Arnold of Brescia (d. 1155), a revolutionary who had wrested control of Rome from the papacy, and returned the city to Pope Adrian IV (1154–1159). Frederick's reward was an imperial coronation that implied he had some rights in Italy.

The imperial assembly sanctioned Frederick's claims, but the city of Milan organized fierce resistance to his exercise of royal authority. At this crucial juncture, Alexander III (1159–1181) was elected pope. As a cardinal, the new pope had previously negotiated an alliance between the papacy and the Norman kingdom of Sicily. As a result, Frederick soon found himself at war with Milan, the pope, and the kingdom of Sicily. In 1167, the combined forces of the northern Italian cities drove him back into Germany, and almost a decade later (1176) an Italian army soundly defeated him at Legnano. In 1183, Frederick agreed to a peace that recognized the Lombard cities' right to self-rule.

HENRY VI AND THE SICILIAN CONNECTION

Frederick ended his reign stalemated in Germany and defeated in Italy. In the last years of his life, however, he created an opportunity for his dynasty to renew its fight for dominance over Italy. The Norman ruler of the kingdom of Sicily, William II (r. 1166–1189), asked Frederick for help in a war with Constantinople. They sealed their alliance in 1186 by a marriage between Frederick's son, the future Henry VI (r. 1190–1197), and Constance, heiress to Sicily.

Sicily was a fatal acquisition for the Hohenstaufen kings. It tempted them to neglect Germany to pursue projects in Italy. It alarmed the Italians and increased their determination to resist. And by forecasting Hohenstaufen encirclement (and absorption) of Rome, it convinced the papacy that its survival hinged on the empire's destruction.

When Henry VI came to the throne in 1190, he faced a multitude of enemies: nervous Lombard cities, a hostile papacy, independent German princes, and even the king of England. (Henry the Lion, the exiled duke of Saxony, involved Richard the Lion-Hearted in plots against the Hohenstaufens.) In 1194, Constance bore her husband a son (the future Frederick II), and Henry campaigned vigorously for recognition of the boy's hereditary right to the imperial throne. The German princes were reluctant to compromise their right to elect their kings, and the encircled papacy was determined to prevent anything that might secure Hohenstaufen power.

OTTO IV AND THE WELF INTERREGNUM

Henry died prematurely in September 1197, and his widow tried to save at least the throne of Sicily for her infant son by arranging for him to become a ward of the papacy. The boy's uncle, Philip of Swabia, claimed the title of king in Germany,

QUICK REVIEW

Frederick I Barbarossa (r. 1152–1190)

- Founder of the Hohenstaufen dynasty
- From base in Switzerland waged war to control the German nobility
- Efforts to conquer Italy ended in defeat at Legnano in 1176

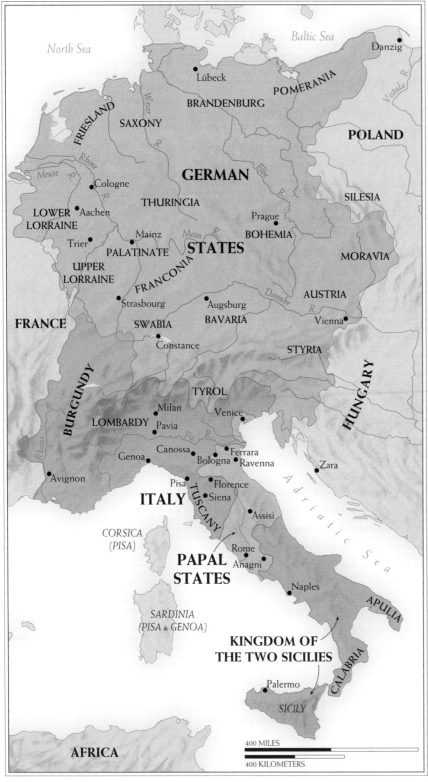

MAP 7–2

Germany and Italy in the Middle Ages Medieval Germany and Italy were divided lands. The Holy Roman Empire (Germany) embraced hundreds of independent territories that the emperor ruled only in name. The papacy controlled the Rome area and tried to enforce its will on Romagna. Under the Hohenstaufens (mid–twelfth to mid–thirteenth century), internal German divisions and papal conflict reached new heights; German rulers sought to extend their power to southern Italy and Sicily.

HOW DID Roman emperors, German rulers, and the papacy all vie for power in Germany and Italy in the Middle Ages?

but the Welf family, the Hohenstaufens' traditional German enemies, backed a rival—Otto of Brunswick, the son of the troublesome Henry the Lion. Richard of England supported Otto; the French supported the Hohenstaufens; and the papacy switched its allegiance back and forth to prevent anyone from becoming strong enough to threaten Rome. The result was anarchy and civil war.

After Philip's death in 1208, Otto's faction elected him king in Germany and Pope Innocent III (1198–1215) crowned him emperor. Four months after the coronation, the pope decided this had been a mistake. Otto attacked Sicily, a move that implied he had aspirations to conquer Italy and Rome. The pope excommunicated Otto and raised up Prince Frederick as a rival candidate for Germany's throne. (See Map 7–2.)

FREDERICK II

Pope Innocent's ward, the Hohenstaufen prince Frederick, was now of age, and unlike Otto he had a hereditary claim to the German crown. In December 1212, the pope, Philip Augustus of France, and Otto's German enemies arranged for Frederick II to be crowned king in the German city of Mainz. Philip Augustus's victory over Otto and John of England at the Battle of Bouvines in 1214 ended Otto's career and cleared the way for Frederick to mount the imperial throne in Charlemagne's city of Aachen (1215). The young ruler's allies probably expected him to be their puppet. If so, they were soon disabused of that notion.

Frederick had grown up in Sicily, and he had little interest in Germany. He spent only nine of the thirty-eight years of his reign there, and he wanted only one thing from the German princes: a secure hold on the imperial title for himself and his sons. To win this, he was willing to grant Germany's nobles virtual independence. Frederick's policy doomed hopes for the development of a centralized monarchy in Germany and condemned the country to six centuries of chaotic disunity.

Frederick's policy with respect to the papacy was equally disastrous. The popes excommunicated Frederick four times and came to view him as the Antichrist, the biblical beast of the Apocalypse whose persecution of the faithful will signal the end of the world. Frederick's chief political objective was to win control of Lombardy, unite it with his Sicilian kingdom, and surround Rome. The popes were desperate to prevent this.

Pope Innocent IV (1243–1254) organized and led the German princes against Frederick, and German and Italian resistance kept Frederick on the defensive throughout his last years. In the end, the popes won the fight, but their victory was Pyrrhic. The struggle forced Innocent to immerse the church ever more deeply in European politics. The wholesale secularization of the papacy increased criticism of the church by religious reformers and the patriotic champions of national monarchies.

Frederick died in 1250, and hopes for an effective German monarchy died with him. The German nobles repudiated the theory that succession to their throne was hereditary, and in 1257 they formed an electoral college that claimed the right to bestow the imperial title. This made it very likely they could control the kings they created.

Frederick's legitimate heir was a young grandson called Conradin, but the only adult defender of the Hohenstaufen legacy was an illegitimate son named Manfred. Manfred fought hard to save some of his father's lands, but he was defeated in 1266. In 1286, Charles of Anjou, the adventurous brother of the saintly Louis IX, killed Conradin and took possession of southern Italy and Sicily. Germany, at least for the moment, ceased to be a problem for Italy, but Italy was not free from the threat of external interference. The French and, to a lesser extent, the English saw Germany's retreat as an opportunity for them to meddle in Italy's affairs.

SUMMARY

Otto I and the Revival of the Empire In 918, Henry I became the first Saxon king of Germany; eighteen years later his son Otto I took power, continuing his program of unification and expansion. He invaded Italy in 951, and proclaimed himself king. By the end of his reign, Otto the Great had even established authority over the Papal States and the pope himself. The Ottonian dynasty faltered in the early eleventh century, however, because Otto I's successors did not pay enough attention to events in Germany, and the church established an independent base of power for itself. By contrast, during this same period the Capetian kings in France focused on their home turf and built the basis for enduring royal power.

The Reviving Catholic Church The Catholic Church shed the secular control of the ninth and tenth centuries to emerge as a powerful independent institution. The reform movement based at the French monastery in Cluny spread throughout Europe and was endorsed by the pope. In 1075, Pope Gregory VII outlawed lay investiture of the clergy; this led to a battle of wills between popes and emperors, until the 1122 Concordat of Worms formalized a new relationship between church and state. Meanwhile, the Crusades provided an outlet

IMAGE KEY
for pages 172–173

a. Virgin and Child wood sculpture from Auvergne region, France. Late 12th century.   Oak with Polycromy, H: 31: (78.7 cm).The Metropolitan Museum of Art, New York. Gift of J. Pierpont Morgan, 1916 (16.32.194). Photograph © 1999. The Metropolitan Museum of Art

b. William haranguing his troops for combat with the English army. Detail from the Bayeux tapestry, scene 51. Musee de la Tapisserie, Bayeaux, France. Photograph © Bridgeman–Giraudon/Art Resource, NY

c. Round stained glass window

d. Medieval monk's habit

e. Emperor Otto receives the homage of the nations. Gospels of Emperor Otto (II or III), also called "Registrum Gregorii." Ottonian art, 10th   Photograph © Erich Lessing/Art Resource, NY

f. Friedrich I Barbarossa depicted as crusader. Miniature of 1188, engraved from the original in the Vatican Library, Rome

g. Capture of Antioch, 1098, Le Miroir Historical by Vincent de Beauvais; XV century.   Musee Conde Chantilly. E. T. Archive, London

h. King Louis IX (1266–1270) giving justice   From "Justiniani in Fortiatum," fol. 34. France, 14th c. Biblioteca Real, El Escorial, Madrid, Spain. Photograph © Bridgeman-Giraudon / Art Resource, NY

i. A drawing of the Romanesque abbey church of Cluny, France, built between 1080 and 1225

j. Henry II of England

k. Romanesque Chapel at east end of Abbey in Conques, France

for popular religious zeal. Repeated Christian expeditions to the Holy Lands did not do much to encourage Muslim respect for Europeans, but the Crusades did stimulate trade and expose the West to the civilizations of the East. Around 1200, Pope Innocent III asserted increased papal power, suppressed internal dissent, clarified church doctrine, and sanctioned two new monastic orders: the Franciscans and the Dominicans.

England and France: Hastings (1066) to Bouvines (1214)
William, the duke of Normandy, won the Battle of Hastings in 1066, and soon was crowned king of England. Building on Anglo-Saxon traditions, he created a strong monarchy that used parleying to channel communications between the king and other leaders. William's grandson Henry married Eleanor of Aquitaine, creating the Angevin Empire. Later kings of England became more oppressive, raised taxes, and caused other problems, until English barons revolted and forced King John to recognize the Magna Carta in 1215. In roughly this same period in France, the Capetian kings first concentrated on securing their territory, then on exercising authority over the nobility. By 1214, in the battle at Bouvines against a combined English and German force, the French were able to defeat their opponents.

France in the Thirteenth Century: The Reign of Louis IX In the middle of the thirteenth century, Louis IX enjoyed almost fifty years as the ruler of a unified and secure France. He was able to focus his energies on domestic reform and the cultivation of culture and religion. He improved the justice system and presided over the emergence of Paris as the intellectual capital of Europe. He was fiercely religious, sponsoring the French Inquisition and leading two Crusades. In his dealings with foreigners, especially the English, he might be accused of naiveté; he failed to press his advantage at the Treaty of Paris in 1259 and allowed the English to maintain their claims on various French lands, thereby setting the stage for the Hundred Years' War in the next century.

The Hohenstaufen Empire (1152–1272) While stable governments that balanced central authority with the local needs of the populace were developing in England and France, the leaders of the Holy Roman Empire were squandering their opportunities to develop a sustainable political structure, a failure that would have negative repercussions through centuries of German history. Throughout the Hohenstaufen dynasty, conflicts with the popes and imperial schemes to control Italian lands distracted Frederick I Barbarossa and his successors from the task of maintaining the allegiance of the nobility and keeping their territory unified. By the late thirteenth century, the Hohenstaufen dynasty had lost all meaningful power and Germany was fragmented.

REVIEW QUESTIONS

1. How did the Saxon king Otto I rebuild the German Empire and use the church to achieve his political goals? How did his program fit with the aspirations of the Cluny reform movement? What was at stake for each of the disputants in the Investiture Controversy? Who won?

2. What developments in western and eastern Europe led to the start of the crusading movement? How did the Crusades to the Holy Lands affect Europe and the Muslim world?

3. Why were France and England able to coalesce into reasonably strong states, but not Germany?

KEY TERMS

Albigensians (p. 181)   **Inquisition** (p. 181)   **secular clergy** (p. 175)

Beguines (p. 183)   **Magna Carta** (p. 186)   **transubstantiation** (p. 182)

Crusades (p. 177)   **regular clergy** (p. 175)

 For additional study resources for this chapter, go to:
www.prenhall.com/kagan3/chapter7

8 Medieval Society Hierarchies, Towns, Universities, and Families (1000–1300)

CHAPTER HIGHLIGHTS

The Traditional Order of Life The nobility were warriors who lived off the labor of others and resided in mansions or castles in the countryside. The clergy constituted a noticeable portion of the medieval population. The agrarian peasantry was the largest and most important social group.

Towns and Townspeople Towns grew in size and significance during this period. Townspeople and kings often made alliances with towns gaining rights and status at the expense of the nobility. Cities, particularly in France and Germany, were centers of Europe's Jewish population.

Schools and Universities In the twelfth century, European scholars, with the critical help of Islamic translators, rediscovered classical scholarship. The flood of new information led to a cultural renaissance and the creation of the university. Scholastics used logic and rational analysis in an attempt to harmonize Christian doctrine and classical sources. Scholasticism had critics and some scholastics challenged church teachings on logical grounds.

Women in Medieval Society Scholarly theories about femininity were at odds with the reality of the lives of medieval women. Medieval women had limited rights. Noble women ran their households. Many women chose to live as nuns. Most women, however, in addition to their duties as wives and mothers, worked in a variety of trades and professions.

The Lives of Children A sizable portion of children died before the age of five. Children worked as soon as they were able and adults saw their greatest responsibility as equipping children for useful employment. Nonetheless, medieval people saw childhood as a distinct and special stage of life.

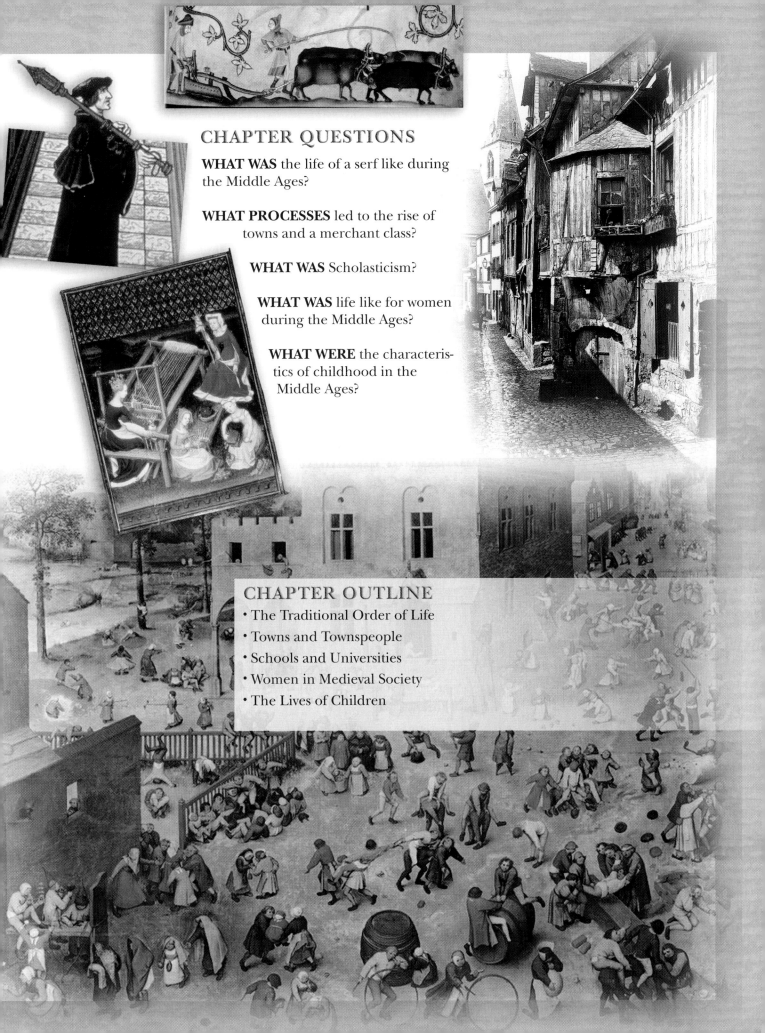

CHAPTER QUESTIONS

WHAT WAS the life of a serf like during the Middle Ages?

WHAT PROCESSES led to the rise of towns and a merchant class?

WHAT WAS Scholasticism?

WHAT WAS life like for women during the Middle Ages?

WHAT WERE the characteristics of childhood in the Middle Ages?

CHAPTER OUTLINE

· The Traditional Order of Life
· Towns and Townspeople
· Schools and Universities
· Women in Medieval Society
· The Lives of Children

IMAGE KEY

Image Key for pages 194–195 is on page 212.

From the tenth to the twelfth centuries, increasing political stability helped Europe advance on multiple fronts. Agricultural production increased, population exploded, and trade and urban life revived. Crusades multiplied contacts with foreign lands that stimulated both economic and cultural development. A new merchant class, the ancestors of modern capitalists, appeared to serve the West's growing markets, and an urban proletariat developed.

Muslim intellectuals guided Europe's scholars in the rediscovery of Classical literature, and an explosion of information led to the rise of the university. Literacy increased among the laity and a renaissance in art and thought blossomed in the twelfth century. The creative vigor that surged through Europe in the High Middle Ages became tangible in the awesome Gothic churches that were the supreme products of medieval art and science.

WHAT WAS the life of a serf like during the Middle Ages?

THE TRADITIONAL ORDER OF LIFE

Medieval political theorists claimed that the maintenance of human communities required three essential services and God had made each one the responsibility of a separate class of people: knights provided protection, clergy interceded with prayer, and peasants and village artisans produced food and supplies. The revival of towns and trade in the eleventh century created a fourth class composed of merchants. Its members were thought of as a "middle class." They were economically productive like peasants, but they did not work the land. They had wealth like nobles and clergy, but they were not part of the political power structure. They did not fit neatly into the old social order, and the pressure they exerted ultimately caused it to collapse.

NOBLES

Nobles were distinguished by the fact that they owned significant amounts of land and exercised authority over other people. They did not farm or trade, but many had ancestors who had done these things. Late medieval society boasted both a higher and a lower nobility. The higher consisted of great landowners and territorial magnates, and the lower was populated by petty knights with fiefs, newly rich merchants who bought country estates, and prosperous farmers who rose from serfdom. Nobles were lords of manors who neither tilled the soil nor engaged in commerce—work that was beneath the dignity of an aristocrat.

Warriors European warfare had changed dramatically with the appearance of the stirrup in the eighth century. Stirrups gave riders secure seats on their mounts and thereby enabled them to strike blows at their enemies without lofting themselves off their horses. The stirrup gave cavalry the power to rout the infantry that had dominated battle in the ancient world. However, cavalry equipment and training were expensive, and lords who wanted to employ cavalrymen had to divide up their lands to create fiefs to support them. Thus the use of arms came to be associated with ownership of land and military service with nobility.

The code by which medieval nobles lived stressed the importance of physical strength, reputation, and aggressive behavior. Nobles welcomed war as an opportunity to increase their fortunes by plunder and to win respect by acts of courage. Peace threatened economic stagnation and boredom for nobles but held out the promise of prosperity for peasants and townspeople. Consequently, the interests of the medieval social classes conflicted, and the nobles dismissed the commoners' love of peace as cowardice.

The Joys and Pains of the Medieval Joust. This scene from a manuscript from c. 1300–1349 idealizes medieval noblewomen and the medieval joust. Revived in the late Middle Ages, jousts were frequently held in peacetime. They kept the warring skills of noblemen sharp and became popular entertainment. Only the nobility were legally allowed to joust, but over time, uncommon wealth enabled a persistent commoner to qualify.

University of Heidelberg

The quasi-sacramental ceremony that bestowed knighthood marked a man's entrance into the noble class. A candidate for knighthood first took a bath as a sign of ritual purification. He then confessed, communed, and stood a night-long prayer vigil. At his dubbing ("striking") ceremony, a priest blessed his standard, lance, and sword and girded him with the weapons he was to use in the defense of the church and the service of his lord. A senior knight then struck him on the shoulders with a sword and raised him to a status as sacred in its way as clerical ordination.

In the twelfth century, knighthood was legally restricted to men of high birth. The closing of the ranks of the nobility was a reaction to the growing wealth and power of the social-climbing commercial classes. Kings, however, reserved the right to bestow knighthood on anyone, and by selling titles to wealthy merchants (an important source of royal revenue) they kept an avenue of social mobility open.

Way of Life   Noblemen honed their military skills by hunting and taking part in tournaments. Their passion for hunting was so great that they forbade commoners to take game from the forests. Peasants resented being deprived of this source of free food, and anger at the nobility's hunting monopoly was one of many grievances that motivated peasant uprisings in the late medieval period.

Tournaments sowed seeds of social disruption of a different kind, for they tended to get out of hand. Serious bloodshed could lead to calls for vengeance and turned mock battles into real wars. The church opposed tournaments because of their promotion of violence and association with pagan revelry, and kings and princes finally agreed that tournaments were a threat to public order. Henry II of England proscribed tournaments in the twelfth century, but they continued in France until the mid–sixteenth century. (See "Encountering the Past: Warrior Games.")

During the twelfth century, distinctive standards for courtesy ("conduct at court") appeared to regulate the behavior of the nobility. Thanks to the influence of powerful women such as Henry II's queen, Eleanor of Aquitaine, knowledge of court etiquette became almost as important for a nobleman's advancement as battlefield expertise. The new codes required the knight to be both a courageous athlete and a cultivated gentleman. He was supposed to be strong in battle, but clean, well dressed, and sufficiently literate to compose lyric poems in honor of his lady. The woman who inspired his raptures was usually another man's wife. His songs might flirt with frank eroticism, but courtly love was supposed to be an ennobling experience that did not sink to the level of sexual seduction. Some poets warned that illicit carnal love led to suffering, and the courtly love movement may actually have been an attempt to curtail the notorious philandering of the noble classes.

Social Divisions   Medieval society was hierarchical, and status within the nobility was a function of how much authority one had over others. Lords with many vassals obviously outranked those with fewer, but shifts in wealth and power in the late Middle Ages drastically restructured the noble class. Climatic changes depressed the agricultural economy that was the source of the landed nobility's wealth, and famines and plagues caused massive demographic dislocations. Changing military tactics rendered noble cavalry nearly obsolete, and the influence of wealthy townsmen increased as they helped kings establish more effective control of the nobility. After the fourteenth century, a fortune counted more than a family tree as a qualification for social advancement.

ENCOUNTERING THE PAST

WARRIOR GAMES

The cultural environment surrounding the medieval nobility—poetry, songs, arts, and entertainments—glorified war. This was consistent with the interests of a warrior class whose men spent their lives fighting and training for battle. A young nobleman might receive his first horse and dagger at the age of two. By the time he turned fourteen, he was ready to handle adult weapons.

Tournaments (mock combats) provided him with both practical training and diversion. They proved so popular with all members of society that they survived as pastimes even after changes in warfare diminished the need for a knight's traditional skills.

The military preoccupations of the knights influenced the behavior of other members of medieval society. Aristocratic women hunted but were limited to the role of spectators at entertainments such as tournaments. Some clergy were famous sportsmen and warriors, but, like women, their taste for violence was usually satisfied vicariously by rooting for champions at tournaments and by playing chess, backgammon, and competitive games such as "Tick, Tack, Toe." Commoners attended tournaments and developed similar warlike games and sports of their own. The equivalent of a tournament for men and boys of the lower classes was a rough ball game—an early version of rugby, soccer, or football. Medieval people were ingenious at inventing diversions for their idle hours, as Pieter Breughel's painting, *Children's Games* (1560), documents. It depicts boys and girls engaged in seventy-eight different activities.

WHY DID the medieval nobility play warlike games? How did these influence the behavior of other members of society?

Breughel, *Children's Games.* Pieter the Elder Breughel (1525–1569), "Children's Games," 1560. Oil on oakwood, 118 × 161 cm. Kunsthistoriches Museum, Vienna, Austria.
Photo copyright Erich Lessing/Art Resource, NY

CLERGY

Clergy, unlike nobles and peasants, were ranked more by training and ordination than by birth. People of talent could climb the clerical hierarchy no matter what their origins. The church, therefore, offered gifted commoners their best opportunity for social mobility.

Secular and Regular Clerics   There were two clerical vocations: secular and regular. The **secular clergy** lived and worked among the laity in the *saeculum* ("world"). The most prestigious of secular clergy were the wealthy cardinals, archbishops, and bishops (men often, but not always, of noble birth). Next in rank were the urban priests, the cathedral canons, and the court clerks. At the bottom of the clerical hierarchy was the humble parish priest, who was neither financially nor intellectually superior to the laypeople he served. Until the eleventh century, parish priests routinely lived with women in relationships akin to marriage and

secular clergy   Clergy, such as bishops and priests, who lived and worked among the laity in the *saeculum* ("world").

stretched their meager incomes by working as teachers, artisans, and farmers. These customs were accepted and even defended by their parishioners.

Regular clergy were monks and nuns (although, strictly speaking, women were not accorded clerical status) who lived under the *regula* ("rule") of a cloister. They retreated from the world and adopted rigorous ascetic disciplines in the belief they were following the example set by Christ's life of poverty and self-sacrifice. Their devotion to what their contemporaries regarded as the ideal Christian way of life earned them respect and influence. The regular clergy were, however, never completely cut off from the secular world. They maintained contact with the laity as dispensers of charity, as instructors in schools, and as preachers and confessors who assisted in parish work. The intellectual gifts and educations of some monks fit them for service as secretaries and private confessors for kings and queens. Nunneries produced famous female scholars, and monasticism inspired many of the religious and social reform movements of the medieval era.

The Benedictine rule had been adopted by most Western monasteries by the end of the Carolingian era, but during the High Middle Ages many new orders appeared. The monastic rule devised by Saint Benedict emphasized the pursuit of economic self-sufficiency through hard physical labor more than rigorous ascetic discipline. Thanks, however, to generations of bequests and careful husbandry of resources, many Benedictine houses, like the famous Cluny, grew wealthy and self-preoccupied. Benedictine monks did little manual labor and spent their time chanting ever more elaborate liturgies in their ever more elegantly appointed sanctuaries. The new orders rejected this Benedictine "luxury" and sought to return to the ideals of Christlike poverty and simplicity that had characterized the monastic movement in the beginning.

The Carthusians, whose order was founded in 1084, were the strictest of the new monks. They lived apart from one another as hermits, fasted three days a week, observed long periods of silence, and disciplined their flesh by acts of self-flagellation.

The Cistercians, whose order was established in 1098 at Cîteaux in Burgundy, set out to restore what they believed was the original intent of the Benedictine rule. They condemned materialism and stressed cultivation of the inner life. To avoid contamination by the secular world and the temptations of wealth, they located their houses in remote wilderness areas where they faced a struggle to survive.

The monastic ideal was so popular in the eleventh century that many secular clergy (and some laypersons) tried to merge the spiritual disciplines of the cloister with traditional pastoral duties. The Canons Regular were groups of secular clergy who lived according to a rule credited to the fifth-century saint Augustine of Hippo, who stayed in the world to serve the laity. The mendicant friars (most notably, the Dominicans and Franciscans who appeared early in the thirteenth century) also combined the secular and regular clerical professions. During the late thirteenth and fourteenth centuries, satellite convents known as Beguine houses sprang up to accommodate unmarried women who for reasons of class or wealth were not admitted to traditional nunneries. (One hundred of these organizations appeared in the city of Cologne between 1250 and 1350.) The Franciscans and Dominicans often assumed responsibility for directing the Beguine houses and making sure their spiritual enthusiasm did not erupt into heresy.

Prominence of the Clergy   The clergy were far more numerous in the Middle Ages than they are today. By the fourteenth century, 1.5 percent of Europe's population may have been clergy. Like the nobility, they usually lived on the labor of

Lovers playing chess on an ivory mirror back, ca. 1300.

The Bridgeman Art Library International

regular clergy   Monks and nuns who lived under the *regula* ("rule") of a cloister.

others. The church was a major landowner and had a huge income from rents and fees. The great fortunes claimed by monastic communities and high prelates brought them immense secular power.

Respect for clergy as members of society's "first estate" derived from their role as mediators between God and humankind. When the priest celebrated the Eucharist, he brought the very Son of God down to earth in tangible form. The priest alone had the power to extend God's forgiveness to sinners or to block their access to it by imposing excommunication (decrees that cut sinners off from the sacraments, the only means for their salvation).

Because a priest was the agent of a heavenly authority far superior to that of any earthly magistrate, it was considered inappropriate for him to be subservient to the laymen who governed the state. Clergy, therefore, had special privileges and immunities. They were not to be taxed by secular governments without approval from the church. Clerical crimes were under the jurisdiction of special ecclesiastical tribunals, not the secular courts. The churches and monasteries where clergy worked were also deemed to be outside the legal jurisdiction of the state. People who took refuge in them received asylum and could not be apprehended by officials of secular governments.

By the late Middle Ages, laypeople had come to resent the special privileges of the clergy, and the anticlerical sentiment that was mounting among them contributed to the success of the Protestant Reformation in the sixteenth century. Protestant theologians challenged medieval tradition by claiming that clergy and laity had equal spiritual standing before God.

Peasants

The largest and lowest class in medieval society was the one on whose labor the welfare of all the others depended: the agrarian peasantry. The fundamental institutions of medieval rural life are called *manors*. For the early Franks, manors were plots of twelve to seventy-five acres of land that were assigned a man by his tribe or clan. As others joined him on his land, he became the lord of the manor and assumed leadership of a self-sufficient community. A manor was not necessarily the same as a village, for a given village might be home to peasant workers who belonged to different manors.

The Duties of Tenancy   The lord of a manor demanded a certain amount of produce and various services from the peasants who worked his land, but he left them free to divide the labor this entailed among themselves. Anything they produced above and beyond what they owed him they could keep. No set rules governed the size of a manor or the number of manors a lord could hold.

There were two kinds of manors: servile and free. The tenants (serfs) of free manors were descendants of Roman *coloni*, free persons who had traded their land and freedom for a guarantee of protection by their lord. Tenancy obligations on free manors were limited because the property their members brought to the manor gave them some leverage in negotiating the terms for their service on the manor. Tenants of servile manors were initially more vulnerable to the whims of their landlords, but time tended to obscure differences between the two types of manors. In many regions, self-governing communities of free peasants, who acknowledged no lord, could also be found.

The lord was the supreme authority on his manor. Serfs had to cultivate his *demesne* (the land producing his income) and reap his harvest before attending to their own fields. He could impress his tenants into labor gangs for special projects or lead them out as foot soldiers when he went to war. He could extort additional

8.1
Manorial Court Records

manor   A self-sufficient rural community that was a fundamental institution of medieval life.

income from them in several ways. He owned and leased some of the instruments and facilities they needed to raise and process food, and he maintained profitable monopolies called **banalities** (e.g., the right to demand that his tenants pay to grind all their grain in his mill and bake all their bread in his oven). The lord also collected an inheritance tax from a serf's heir (usually the best animal from the deceased's estate). A serf who wished to travel or to marry outside his manor also had to obtain his lord's permission (and usually pay a fee).

The Life of a Serf   Burdened as a serf's life was, it was superior to chattel slavery. Serfs had their own dwellings and modest strips of land. They managed their own labor. They could sell any surpluses they produced for their own profit. They were free to choose their own spouses from the manor community. Their marriages were protected by the church. Their property passed to their children, and they could not be sold away from their land.

In this eleventh-century manuscript, peasants harvest grain, trim vines, and plow fields behind yoked oxen.

Giraudon/Art Resource, NY

Serfs seldom ventured far from the villages where they were born. The single village church that was available to them limited their religious options. However, the poverty of religious instruction meant that their beliefs and practices were by no means unambiguously Christian. There were social and economic distinctions among them, but the common struggle for survival forced them to work together. The ratio of seed to grain yield was poor throughout the Middle Ages. About two bushels of seed had to be sown to produce six to ten bushels of grain—in good years. There was rarely an abundance of bread and ale, the staple peasant foods. Europeans did not discover two of the crops on which the modern West depends, potatoes and corn (maize), until the sixteenth century. Pork was the major source of animal protein, for pigs, unlike cattle, could forage for themselves in the forests. As winter set in, excess plow animals were slaughtered and their meat dried or salted. Life hinged on grain crops. When they failed or fell short, there was no other resource that could be tapped to stave off famine.

Changes in the Manor   Technological advances such as the horse collar (ca. 800), the horseshoe (ca. 900), and the three-field system of crop rotation improved agricultural productivity. The stimulation of demand from the new markets that were created as towns proliferated during the High Middle Ages prompted peasant farmers to bring more land into production. These things produced surplus income that serfs used to buy their freedom from the obligation of feudal labor service. Once towns revived trade and restored a money-based economy, lords also found it more profitable to lease their lands to free entrepreneurial tenant farmers than to work them with unwilling serfs. As the medieval era waned, therefore, the manor and serfdom gave way to the independent single-family farm, but that did not mean peasants were not necessarily better off materially. In hard times serfs might expect assistance from their lords, for lords had to preserve the labor force that worked their manors. Free rent-paying farmers, however, had to take care of themselves.

The expanding economy and rising standards of living that characterized the High Middle Ages affected landed aristocrats as well as servile workers.

banalities   Monopolies maintained by landowners giving them the right to demand that tenants pay to grind all their grain in the landowner's mill and bake all their bread in his oven.

The incomes that lords drew from their manors were fixed by tradition, but the costs of their lifestyle were not. It became progressively difficult for them to make ends meet, and in the mid–fourteenth century, nobles in England and France tried to increase taxes on peasants and to limit laborers' ability to bargain for higher wages. This prompted revolts that were brutally crushed, but which suggested that traditional medieval society was breaking up.

TOWNS AND TOWNSPEOPLE

WHAT PROCESSES led to the rise of towns and a merchant class?

*I*n the eleventh and twelfth centuries, only about 5 percent of Europeans lived in towns, and most urban communities were small. Of Germany's 3,000 towns, 2,800 had populations under 1,000. Only 15 exceeded 10,000, and the largest (Cologne) had a mere 30,000. London was the only English city greater than 10,000. Paris was bigger than London, but not by much. Italy boasted Europe's greatest towns. Florence and Milan approached 100,000.

THE CHARTERING OF TOWNS

Despite their small size, towns were, in the Middle Ages as now, where the action was. The secular and ecclesiastical lords who dominated the medieval landscape often welcomed the growth of towns on their estates, for they wanted the products (and opportunities for levying taxes) that urban traders provided. New towns tended to be dominated by the feudal magnates who controlled the region in which they were built, but most won their independence by purchasing a charter from their lord. A charter spelled out privileges that granted the residents of a town much greater freedom than rural workers enjoyed. Freedom was a requirement of life for men and women who lived by invention and audacious commercial enterprise.

Towns hastened the disintegration of feudal society by providing serfs who wanted to escape manorial life with a place to go. It was tempting to flee, for the economy of a flourishing town offered individuals who mastered crafts and worked hard good prospects for improving their social standing. The mere possibility that a lord's serfs might migrate to a town, however, improved the lot of the peasants who stayed in the countryside as well as those who actually made the move. A lord who wanted to keep his labor force on his land had to offer them favorable terms.

THE RISE OF MERCHANTS

The first merchants were probably enterprising serfs or outcasts who found no place in the feudal system. Having no protector and no legal standing, they had to provide for themselves. They organized armed caravans, bought goods as cheaply as possible in one place, and then took them to another where they hoped to be able to sell them for a profit. Our modern urban lifestyle springs from the greed and daring of these rough-hewn men.

Merchants were considered an oddity, for they did not fit into the three classes (noble, clergy, and peasant) that theoretically constituted feudal society. As late as the fifteenth century, nobles still snubbed the urban patriciate (the hereditary ruling class that arose in some cities). Over time, however, the politically powerful grew to respect the merchants as much as the powerless aspired to imitate them, for wherever merchants were, wealth accumulated.

CHALLENGING THE OLD LORDS

As traders settled down and established towns, they grew in wealth and numbers and began to challenge the feudal authorities. In the eleventh century, they began to form merchant guilds (unions, protective associations) to oppose restrictions

MAP EXPLORATION

Interactive map: To explore this map further, go to **http://www.prenhall.com/kagan3/map8.1**

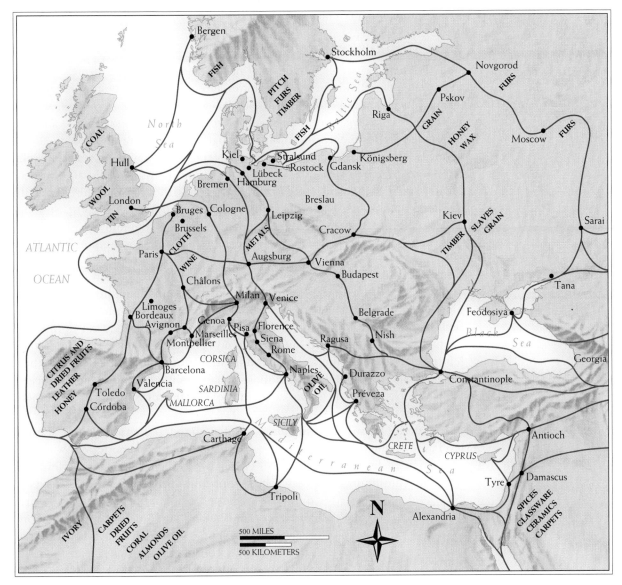

MAP 8–1
Some Medieval Trade Routes and Regional Products   The map shows some of the channels that came to be used in interregional commerce and what was traded in a particular region.

GIVEN THE KINDS of items traded, was international trade essential or peripheral to the lives of medieval people?

that hampered the flow of goods. Guilds of craftsmen appeared in the twelfth century, and all these organizations of commoners had as their objective the transformation of a social order that the feudal classes assumed to be natural and static.

Merchants opposed the fortress mentality that had prompted the division of the countryside into a plethora of tiny feudal jurisdictions. They wanted to end the myriad tolls and tariffs demanded by the petty lords through whose fiefs their caravans traveled. They favored governments that could enforce simple, uniform laws throughout large areas. City dwellers also wanted to wrest control of their communities away from the feudal nobility and improve security by reversing the political fragmentation that feudalism encouraged. For similar reasons, the church and Europe's kings were willing to join townspeople in efforts to bring the feudal nobility under control.

NEW MODELS OF GOVERNMENT

By 1100, the older noble families that had tried to dominate Europe's growing towns had merged with their communities' most prosperous commoner families. The rich began to work together to establish and control the town councils that became the chief organs of municipal government. Small artisans and craftsmen responded by forming associations and fighting for representation on these councils. The oppressed and economically exploited urban poor were generally left out of the power structure. This was dangerous because medieval townspeople were politically volatile. As citizens, not subjects, they believed they were entitled to certain rights. When necessary, they rioted to make this point. So long, however, as there was enough social mobility in urban communities to offer the poor hope, they had a stake in the system and were willing to support it.

Social Tensions   Despite democratic tendencies, townspeople were very conscious of class distinctions. The wealthiest urban groups aped the lifestyle of the old landed nobility. They acquired coats of arms, bought country estates, and built castles. Once the heads of great business enterprises had set up lines of communication and worked out banking procedures for transferring funds, they left traveling to underlings and settled down to run their companies from their rural mansions. The migration of these social-climbing entrepreneurs and capitalists to the countryside was an economic loss for the towns that had given them their starts.

A desire for social distinction was not confined to the rich. People at every level were tempted to imitate the dress and habits of their superiors. Towns tried to restrain costly competition of this kind by decreeing appropriate levels of dress and consumption for each social group and vocation. Conspicuous expenditure was regarded as a kind of indecent exposure, and it was punished by "sumptuary" laws (regulations that punished people who tried to live beyond what the community considered appropriate to their station). These rules were intended to maintain order by keeping each person in his or her proper place.

The need for laws to limit competition among classes hints at the tensions that strained medieval urban communities. Towns were collections of self-centered groups that had to live in close proximity to one another. Conflict among these factions particularly the haves and the have-nots was inevitable. The poorest workers in the export trades (usually the weavers and wool combers) were clearly inferior to independent artisans and small shopkeepers. In turn, the interests of these craftsmen differed from those of the great merchants. The latter imported foreign goods to compete with the things the former produced locally. Theoretically, poor men could work their way up this hierarchy, and some lucky ones

Skilled workers were an integral component of the commerce of medieval towns. This scene shows the manufacture of cannons in a foundry in Florence.

Scala/Art Resource, NY

actually did so. Until they reached a fairly high plateau, however, they were excluded from membership on the town council, and full citizenship came to be reserved for property-owning families of long standing. Urban self-government tended, therefore, to become progressively inbred and aristocratic.

Artisans assumed that by working together they could increase their political clout. The guilds they formed for this purpose benefited the "masters" who organized them but at a significant cost to others. Guilds used their power on town councils to establish monopolies—to win exclusive rights to deal in goods for the local market. They protected that market by ensuring that those who served it produced acceptable products at fair prices, but they discouraged improvements in techniques of production for fear this would give the inventors advantages over others. Once there were enough producers in town, a guild also avoided saturating its market by refusing to license new shops. This infuriated the journeymen who trained in guild shops, for it reduced the likelihood they would ever be able to set up in business for themselves. It condemned them to the status of politically disenfranchised workers who had no hope of advancement. The protectionism practiced by the guild-dominated urban governments of the Middle Ages created a true proletariat and ultimately depressed the economy for everyone.

TOWNS AND KINGS

A natural alliance developed between towns and the kings who were struggling to construct central governments for nation-states. Kings staffed their administrations with urban bureaucrats and lawyers familiar with Roman law, the tool for designing kingdoms. Towns provided the money that kings needed to hire professional agents and soldiers and free themselves from dependence on the feudal nobility. Towns, in short, had the human, financial, and technological resources to empower kings.

Towns wanted kings to establish effective monarchies, for royal governments that controlled large territories provided the best support for commerce. A strong king could control the local despots whose tolls and petty wars disrupted trade, and kings, unlike local magnates, tended to keep their distance and allow towns considerable autonomy. In addition to protection, monarchies also issued standardized currencies that made buying and selling much easier.

The relationship between kings and towns fluctuated with the fate of monarchical development in each part of Europe. In France, where the Capetian dynasty flourished, towns were integrated into royal government. In England, towns supported the barons against unpopular kings (such as John) but cooperated with the efforts of more effective monarchs to subdue the nobility. In Germany, where the feudal magnates triumphed over kings, towns came under the control of territorial princes. Italy, by comparison, offered towns quite different opportunities. Italy had no native royal family for towns to support against the nobility. Italy's townspeople also shared the nobility's opposition to the political ambitions of German kings and Roman popes. The two classes, therefore, worked together, and as their leaders intermarried, towns extended their authority into the countryside and began to resemble the ancient world's city-states.

Between the eleventh and fourteenth centuries, towns enjoyed considerable autonomy and once again became the centers of Western civilization. As centralized monarchies began to take hold in the fourteenth century, kings were able to assert increasing authority over towns and the church. By the seventeenth century, few towns had escaped integration into the larger purposes of the state.

QUICK REVIEW

Basis of the Alliance
- Towns were a source of human, financial, and technological resources for kings
- Effective royal government created the best environment for commerce
- Monarchies issued standardized currencies that facilitated buying and selling

JEWS IN CHRISTIAN SOCIETY

Medieval Europe's Jews could not take Christian oaths of homage. They were, therefore, excluded from feudal land tenure and forced to earn their livings from trade. They congregated in towns and (for both protection and the practice of their religion) formed tight separate communities. The church forbade them to employ Christians, and the lack of contacts between Christians and Jews promoted mutual suspicion. Ignorance of Jewish practices, resentment of the wealth acquired by some Jews, and a popular tendency to hold the Jews responsible for Christ's crucifixion fueled baseless rumors of Jewish schemes to undermine Christian society. These sparked periodic outbreaks of mob violence against Jews and the imposition of fines or sentences of exile on whole communities of Jews by governmental authorities.

SCHOOLS AND UNIVERSITIES

WHAT WAS Scholasticism?

*I*n the twelfth century, European scholars discovered Aristotle's treatises on logic, the writings of Euclid and Ptolemy, Roman law, and the basic works of Greek physicians and Arab mathematicians. Islamic scholars living in Spain were chiefly responsible for the translations and commentaries that made these ancient texts accessible to Europeans. The flood of new information created a cultural renaissance and a new kind of center for intellectual activity, the university.

UNIVERSITY OF BOLOGNA

All that the term *university* initially implied was a corporation of individuals working together for their mutual benefit. The new schools that sprang up in the twelfth century attracted students and teachers from great distances. Many were foreigners who had no civil rights in the towns where they worked. Their vulnerability to exploitation and abuse by landlords and civic authorities led them to organize (like members of an urban craft guild) to protect themselves. When their scholars' guild acquired legal recognition, a university was born.

The university in the Italian city of Bologna was the first of the great medieval schools to receive such recognition. Emperor Frederick Barbarossa issued it a charter in 1158, and it became a model for schools in Italy, Spain, and southern France. Bologna was a guild of students, who unionized to ensure that landlords and tavern owners charged them fair prices and teachers gave them excellent instruction. The students hired professors, set pay scales, and assigned lecture topics. Instructors who did not live up to their expectations were boycotted, and they countered price-gouging townspeople by threatening to move the university and the profitable business it generated to another town.

Bologna was Europe's premier center for advanced studies in law. In the late eleventh century, Europeans discovered the *Corpus Juris Civilis*, the collection of ancient Roman laws made by the Byzantine emperor Justinian in the sixth century. In the early twelfth century, Irnerius of Bologna began to show how Roman law could be used to create *glosses* (commentaries) that clarified existing European laws. Around 1140 in Bologna, a monk named Gratian wrote the text that became standard for studying the church's canon law: *Concordance of Discordant Canons*, or simply *Decretum*.

Students were not the only scholars to form guilds to protect their interests. Their teachers, or *masters*, did so as well, and faculty guilds dominated the uni-

OVERVIEW   TWO SCHOOLS OF THE HIGH MIDDLE AGES

University of Bologna	• Chartered in 1158
	• First of the great medieval schools to acquire recognition as a university
	• Students hired professors, set pay scales, and assigned lecture topics
	• Europe's premier center for advanced studies in law
University of Paris	• Chartered in 1200
	• Provided the model for the schools of northern Europe
	• Students given protections and privileges exceeding those of other citizens
	• Teachers were required to be examined thoroughly before being licensed
	• Twenty or more years were needed to earn a doctorate in theology

versities of northern Europe. Paris was preeminent among them. Masters' guilds held a monopoly on teaching, and tests for admission to these guilds set standards for certification of teachers. The licenses to teach that medieval guilds awarded were the predecessors of modern academic degrees.

CATHEDRAL SCHOOLS

Students usually entered the university between the ages of twelve and fifteen. Because all books and all instruction were in Latin, they were expected to arrive knowing how to read and speak that language. The first four years of their course of study were devoted to the *trivium* (grammar, rhetoric, and logic), which polished their Latin and earned them a bachelor's degree. A master's degree entailed an additional three or four years of work on the *quadrivium* (arithmetic, geometry, astronomy, and music). This was primarily the study of ancient texts dealing with mathematics, natural science, and philosophy. Doctoral degrees were available in a few fields such as law, medicine, and theology. Twenty or more years were needed to earn a doctorate in theology at the University of Paris.

The university's curriculum centered on the liberal arts programs that early medieval cathedral and monastery schools had created to train clergy. These were the only schools that existed during the early medieval centuries, and clergy were the only people whose vocations required literacy. But by the late eleventh century, students who wanted to become notaries or merchants—not clergy—began to frequent the church's schools. In 1179, a papal decree ordered cathedrals to provide teachers gratis for laity who wanted to learn. By the thirteenth century, the demand for literate men to staff the urban and territorial governments and merchant firms gave rise to schools offering secular vocational education. (See "History's Voices: Student Life at the University of Paris.")

Medieval school scene
German Information Center

UNIVERSITY OF PARIS

The University of Paris, which provided the model for the schools of northern Europe, evolved, in part, from the school maintained by Paris's Cathedral of Notre Dame. King Philip Augustus and Pope Innocent III chartered it in 1200 and gave its students protections and privileges exceeding those of ordinary citizens. Only in self-defense, for instance, was a citizen permitted to strike a student,

HISTORY'S VOICES

STUDENT LIFE AT THE UNIVERSITY OF PARIS

As the following account by Jacques de Vitry makes clear, not all students at the University of Paris in the thirteenth century were there to gain knowledge. Students fought constantly and subjected each other to ethnic insults and slurs.

WAS THE RIVALRY among faculty members as intense as that among students?

Almost all the students at Paris, foreigners and natives, did absolutely nothing except learn or hear something new. Some studied merely to acquire knowledge, which is curiosity; others to acquire fame, which is vanity; others still for the sake of gain, which is cupidity and the vice of simony. Very few studied for their own edification, or that of others. They wrangled and disputed not merely about the various sects or about some discussions; but the differences between the countries also caused dissensions, hatreds and virulent animosities among them, and they impudently uttered all kinds of affronts and insults against one another.

They affirmed that the English were drunkards and had tails; the sons of France proud, effeminate and carefully adorned like women. They said that the Germans were furious and obscene at their feasts; the Normans, vain and boastful; the Poitevins, traitors and always adventurers. The Burgundians they con-

sidered vulgar and stupid. The Bretons were reputed to be fickle and changeable, and were often reproached for the death of Arthur. The Lombards were called avaricious, vicious and cowardly; the Romans, seditious, turbulent and slanderous; the Sicilians, tyrannical and cruel; the inhabitants of Brabant, men of blood, incendiaries, brigands, and ravishers; the Flemish, fickle, prodigal, gluttonous, yielding as butter, and slothful. After such insults from words they often came to blows.

I will not speak of those logicians [professors of logic and dialectic] before whose eyes flitted constantly "the lice of Egypt," that is to say, all the sophistical subtleties, so that no one could comprehend their eloquent discourses in which, as says Isaiah, "there is no wisdom." As to the doctors of theology, "seated in Moses' seat." they were swollen with learning, but their charity was not edifying. Teaching and not practicing, they have "become as sounding brass or a tinkling cymbal," or like a canal of stone, always dry, which ought to carry water to "the bed of spices." They not only hated one another, but by their flatteries they enticed away the students of others; each one seeking his own glory, but caring not a whit about the welfare of souls.

Translations and reprints from the *Original Sources of European History*, Vol. 2 (Philadelphia: Department of History, University of Pennsylvania, 1902), pp. 19–20.

and all citizens were required to testify against anyone who was seen to abuse a student. University regulations required that teachers be examined thoroughly before being licensed to teach. French law, in short, recognized students as a valuable and vulnerable resource.

Paris originated the college or house system. The first colleges were charitable hospices set up to provide room and board for poor students who would not otherwise be able to afford to study. The university discovered these institutions were useful for maintaining discipline among its students, and it encouraged all its students to enroll in them. (Today, the University of Paris is popularly known by the name of its most famous college, the Sorbonne, founded about 1257 by a royal chaplain named Robert de Sorbon.) Endowed colleges changed the nature of the university. The first universities had no buildings of their own and relied on rented or borrowed space. They were mobile institutions that could easily relocate if need be. College buildings, however, rooted universities in place, and this reduced their leverage in negotiating with townspeople. The acquisition of physical facilities made it difficult for universities to threaten to move if the towns in which they were located failed to meet their demands.

THE CURRICULUM

The early cathedral and monastery schools provided a limited education consisting primarily of (Latin) grammar, rhetoric, and some elementary geometry and astronomy. The standard texts were the grammars of Donatus and Priscian, Augustine's *On Christian Doctrine*, Cassiodorus's *On Divine and Secular Learning*, Boethius's treatises on arithmetic and music, and a few of Aristotle's essays on logic. The books that Europeans obtained from the Muslim world in the early twelfth century vastly expanded Europe's libraries and provided materials for more elaborate programs of study at universities. The most revolutionary of the new texts were works by Aristotle that had previously been unknown in Europe. They had passed into general circulation by the mid–thirteenth century and inspired **Scholasticism**, the method of study associated with the medieval university.

In the High Middle Ages, scholars assumed truth was not something one had to discover for oneself. Truth was already enshrined in the works of the great authorities of the past—men such as Aristotle and the fathers of the church. Teachers did not prepare students to strive independently for new information, but only to comprehend and absorb what they found in ancient sources. They used logic and dialectic (rational analysis) to harmonize, not critique, the accepted truths of tradition. Dialectic, the art of discovering a truth by finding contradictions in arguments against it, reigned supreme in all disciplines. Medieval students did not observe phenomena for themselves. They read the authoritative texts in their fields, summarized them, disputed the pros and cons of various interpretations, and drew conclusions based on logical cogency.

All books were written out by hand, for printing with moveable type was not invented until the fifteenth century. Books were expensive, and few students could afford to purchase personal copies of the texts they studied. Most learned by listening to lectures and discussions and memorizing what they heard. The goal of an education was to equip a scholar with the rhetorical skills needed to construct subtle logical arguments and win debates. This required a person to become a walking encyclopedia filled with information that could be regurgitated as needed.

PHILOSOPHY AND THEOLOGY

Scholastics quarreled over the proper relationship between philosophy, by which they meant almost exclusively the writings of Aristotle, and theology, which they believed to be a "science" based on divine revelation. In Christian eyes, Aristotle's writings contained heresy; for example, Aristotle taught the eternality of the world, which called into question the Judeo-Christian teaching in the book of Genesis that God created the world in time. Church authorities wanted the works of Aristotle and other ancient authorities to be submissive handmaidens to Christian truth.

ABELARD

When philosophers and theologians applied the logic and metaphysics of Aristotle to the interpretation of Christian revelation, many believed it posed a mortal threat to biblical truth and church authority. Peter Abelard (1079–1142), the first European scholar to gain a large student audience, and possibly the brightest

In this engraving, a teacher at the University of Paris leads fellow scholars in a discussion. As shown here, all of the students wore the scholar's cap and gown.

CORBIS/Bettmann

8.4
St. Thomas Aquinas: *The Summa Against the Gentiles (Summa Contra Gentiles, 1259–1264)*

Scholasticism   Method of study associated with the medieval university.

logician and dialectician of the high Middle Ages, gained great notoriety for such wrongful interpretation of the Scriptures. He boldly subjected church teaching to Aristotelian logic and dialectic, making him many powerful enemies at a time when there was no tenure to protect genius and free speech in schools and universities. Accused of multiple transgressions of church doctrine, he ended his life in a monastery and wrote an autobiography about the calamitous results of his teachings and behavior.

Abelard's critics especially condemned him for his subjective interpretations of Scripture. His ethical teachings questioned vital theological issues like the nature of the Holy Trinity and Christ's crucifixion. He stressed Christians' intent over their deeds, asserting that the motives of the doer made an act good or evil, not the act itself. Inner feelings were thus more important for receiving divine forgiveness than the church's sacrament of penance administered by a priest.

In Paris, Abelard gave his powerful enemies an opportunity to strike him down when he seduced Heloise, a bright, seventeen-year-old niece of a powerful canon (cathedral priest) who had hired him to be her tutor in his home. Their passionate affair ended in scandal, with Heloise pregnant and Abelard, being a university teacher, required to be single and celibate. They wed secretly and placed their illegitimate child with Abelard's sister to raise. The enraged uncle exposed their secret marriage and hired men to castrate Abelard. Heloise entered a convent, where she lived another twenty years and gained renown for positive efforts to reform cloister rules. Abelard became a self-condemning recluse, with his works officially condemned. Their story powerfully reveals both public and private life in the Middle Ages.

WOMEN IN MEDIEVAL SOCIETY

WHAT WAS life like for women during the Middle Ages?

Scholarly theories about femininity were at odds with the reality of the lives of medieval women. Studies of the Bible and Graeco-Roman medical, philosophical, and legal texts convinced medieval theologians that women were physically, mentally, and morally inferior to men. The Bible clearly taught that a female is a "weaker vessel" who requires protection and guidance from a male. It ordered wives to submit to their husbands—even, medieval authorities assumed, to the point of accepting beatings for conduct that displeased their husbands. As celibates, Christian clergy viewed marriage as a debased condition and honored virgins and chaste widows more highly than wives.

Contrary forces shaped roles for women in medieval society. The church reinforced traditional negative assumptions about women, but insisted on the female's spiritual equality with the male. The learned churchman Peter Lombard argued, for instance, that the fact that God took Eve from Adam's side meant woman was neither to rule nor be ruled but to be a partner with her husband in a marriage characterized by mutual aid and trust. In chivalric romances, in courtly love literature, and in the cult of the Virgin Mary that swept Europe in the twelfth and thirteenth centuries, female traits of gentleness, compassion, and grace were seen as essential correctives for the rougher male virtues. Women were put on pedestals and worshiped as men's superiors in the arts of self-control and civilized conduct.

Women in German tribes had been treated better than those in civilized Rome, and this helped create some rights for medieval women. In ancient Rome, women had married in their early teens and usually wed men who were much older than themselves. German women, however, married later in life and took husbands of their same age. German grooms endowed their brides with property

A fourteenth-century English manuscript shows women at their daily tasks: carrying jugs of milk from the sheep pen, feeding the chickens, carding and spinning wool.

of their own to support them if they were widowed, and the Germanic law codes recognized the right of women to inherit, administer, dispose of, and bequeath family property and personal possessions. German women could also prosecute men in court for bodily injury and rape.

Polygyny, concubinage, and casual divorce were all part of German tradition, but in the ninth century, the church persuaded the Carolingian rulers that monogamous marriage should be official policy. This was both a gain and a loss for women. On the one hand, the choice of a wife became a very serious matter, and wives gained greater dignity and legal security. But on the other hand, a woman's burden as household manager and bearer of children greatly increased. Where previously several women shared responsibility for running a nobleman's estate and providing heirs to continue his line, all these duties now came to rest on the shoulders of one woman. Mortality rates for Frankish women rose following the ninth century, and their average life spans decreased.

Life Choices   The demands medieval society placed on wives explain why the cloister had so much appeal for women. Few women, however, had the option of choosing the celibate life. Nuns were required to make sizable donations to their cloisters, and only a few upper-class women could afford the price of admission. There may have been no more than 3,500 nuns in all of England at the end of the Middle Ages. Monasteries did, however, offer women unique opportunities to obtain educations and exercise political influence and leadership.

Most medieval women were neither administrators of aristocratic households nor nuns. They were women who, in addition to their duties as wives and mothers, were members of a community's work force. They could not attend the universities and were, therefore, excluded from the learned professions of scholarship, medicine, and law. They were, however, admitted to craft and trade guilds. Between the ages of ten and fifteen, middle-class girls, like boys, served apprenticeships. When they married, they might become assistants and partners in their husband's line of work, or operate a bakery, brewery, or other business of their own. Medieval women worked in virtually every field from butcher to goldsmith. They were especially prominent in the food and clothing industries and domestic service. Some earned the rank of master in guilds, but employment opportunities for women were more restricted than those for men. Women were paid about 25 percent less than men for comparable work. Some urban women had opportunities to attend school and learn to read and write their vernacular tongues. Peasant women, however, labored beside their men in the fields and had no opportunities for self-improvement.

WHAT WERE the characteristics of childhood in the Middle Ages?

IMAGE KEY
for pages 194–195

a. Limbourg Brothers (15th c.). The Month of September. Grape Harvest. Chateau de Saumur. From the Tres Riches Heures du Duc de Berry. Ms.65/1284,fol.9v. Musee Conde, Chantilly, France. Photograph © Bridgeman–Giraudon/Art Resource, NY

b. 14th century key for locking up money

c. Cloisonné and gold medallion crafted by Georgian artists for a Byzantine icon frame, ca. 1100, showing Jesus Christ

d. A lady and her knight going hunting

e. Plowing with oxen from Luttrel Psalter English Manuscript ca. 1340

f. A University of Paris teacher, engraving ca. 1400

g. "Story of Gaia," Women in the Role of Men's work. De Claris Mulieribus, Giovanni Boccaccio (1313–1375). Fr. 12420, f. 71   © Art Resource, NY

h. "Children's Games", Pieter the Elder Brueghel (b.1525–1569),1560. Oil on oakwood, 118 x 161 cm. Kunsthistorisches Museum, Vienna, Austria. Photo copyright Erich Lessing/Art Resource, NY

i. The Rue du Matelas, a French street in Rouen, Normandy, was preserved intact from the Middle Ages to World War II   Getty Images, Inc.–Liaison.

THE LIVES OF CHILDREN

With children, as with women, image and reality diverged in medieval society. The Romans regulated family size by exposing unwanted children, but they showered affection on the offspring they chose to raise. The Germans, by contrast, had large families but paid little attention to their children. In German law, the *wergild*—the compensatory fine paid as recompense for an injury—was much lower for a child's loss than an adult's.

Although the church condemned infanticide, it continued throughout the Middle Ages. This might suggest children were held in low esteem, and the fact that medieval artists depicted children as small adults has suggested to some historians that medieval people did not regard childhood as a distinct period of life requiring special treatment. Given that 30 to 50 percent of children died before the age of five, these historians speculate that medieval parents minimized emotional trauma by not becoming attached to their offspring. However, high rates of infant and child mortality may just as well have made children all the more precious to their parents. The many kinds of children's toys and pieces of child-rearing equipment (e.g., walkers and potty chairs) that existed in the Middle Ages suggest people paid a great deal of attention to children. Medieval medical texts also offered advice on postnatal care and treatments for childhood diseases. They cautioned against abuse and recommended moderation in discipline. The church urged parents to love their children as Mary loved Jesus, and in medieval art and literature parents are depicted as grieving as much over the loss of a child as families would today.

Childhood was brief in the Middle Ages, and young children were introduced early to adult responsibilities. Peasant children joined their parents in the fields as soon as they could physically manage some labor. The urban working class sent children as young as eight away from home to begin apprenticeships. The church allowed boys to marry at fourteen and girls at twelve. The pressure put on children to mature and learn may have been a sign of concern for them, for no parental responsibility was deemed greater than that of equipping a child for useful employment.

SUMMARY

The Traditional Order of Life The nobility were warriors who lived off the labor of others and resided in mansions or castles in the countryside. The clergy constituted a noticeable portion of the medieval population. The "regular" clergy, who lived separately from the world, and the "secular" clergy, who lived among the laity, had their own hierarchies and responsibilities. The agrarian peasantry were the largest and most significant group. During the Middle Ages, families were the basic socioeconomic unit.

Towns and Townspeople Towns grew in size and significance. The nobility and upper clergy's newfound taste for fancy manufactured goods was an early impetus for the growth of towns. Ironically, as towns grew and artisans and traders gained status, it was generally the nobility that suffered. Throughout Europe, it was common for townspeople and kings to form alliances that impinged on the traditional powers of the nobility. Especially in France and Germany, cities also attracted large numbers of Jews.

Schools and Universities Starting in Bologna in 1158, Western universities taught the *trivium* (language arts) and the *quadrivium* (math). Scholasticism, the favored method of study, relied on logic, memorization, argumentation, and recitation. Most of the content of the instruction came from Latin translations of Greek and Arabic texts. Because education had been limited previously to mostly theological instruction for clerical students, and given the pervasiveness of religion in everyday life, it is not surprising that some of the writings of the ancient philosophers studied by university students—especially the writings of Aristotle—were controversial.

Women in Medieval Society The male Christian clergy portrayed women in the Middle Ages as having two options: subjugated housewife or confined nun. The vast majority of them, in fact, worked in a range of trades, although they were concentrated in the food and clothing industries. Nuns avoided the problems associated with pregnancy and could attain some power. Aristocratic women could manage large households.

The Lives of Children Most historians have probably misunderstood the lives of children in the Middle Ages. Children had a 30 to 50 percent chance of dying before they turned five, so some historians have suggested that parents would not risk making a big emotional investment in young children. Children worked as soon as they were able and are depicted in medieval art as "little adults," so some historians have wondered whether people in the Middle Ages had an understanding of childhood as a distinct phase of life, with its own needs. But medieval medical and clerical authorities did, in fact, write about childhood as a special stage in life, and evidence indicates that parents and society at large cherished their babies and children.

REVIEW QUESTIONS

1. How did the responsibilities of the nobility differ from those of the clergy and peasantry during the High Middle Ages? What led to the revival of trade and the growth of towns in the twelfth century? How did towns change medieval society?

2. What were the strengths and weaknesses of the educations provided by medieval universities? How would you evaluate the standard curriculum?

3. How would you define Scholasticism? What was the Scholastic program and method of study? Who were the main critics of Scholasticism, and what were their complaints?

4. Do Germanic law and Roman law reflect different understandings of the position of women in society? How did options and responsibilities differ for women in each of the social classes? What are the theories concerning the concept of childhood in the Middle Ages?

KEY TERMS

banalities (p. 201)   **regular clergy** (p. 199)   **Scholasticism** (p. 209)
manor (p. 200)   **secular clergy** (p. 198)

 For additional study resources for this chapter, go to:
www.prenhall.com/kagan3/chapter8

Visualizing The Past...
The Divine in the Middle Ages

HOW DID artists of different religions depict the divine? How did their differing conceptions of the divine, and rules within religions about how, and whether, the divine should be depicted, shape religious art?

The Middle Ages witnessed the creation of a new world religion, Islam, and the expansion and consolidation of others, including, in the West, Christianity and Judaism. Each of these religions fostered forms of religious art suited to its conception of the divine. Religious and secular leaders alike commissioned the art as objects or focuses of worship, teaching tools, and decorations. Secular leaders enhanced their status by associating themselves with the divine through patronage of religious art.

Jonah Eaten by the Whale, from a Hebrew Bible, 1299 (Vellum) by Joseph Asarfati (fl. 1299)

Although Jewish tradition prohibits creating any sort of image of God, European Jewish illuminated manuscripts did depict the human form, and thus like the Christian illuminated manuscripts they closely resembled, were filled with images of scenes from the Torah and Jewish history. Hebrew writing also developed into an elaborately beautiful calligraphy. Many of these Jewish medieval illuminated manuscripts were, like their Christian counterparts, commissioned by wealthy and influential leaders of Jewish communities in Europe.

Instituto da Biblioteca Nacional, Lisbon, Portugal/Bridgeman Art Library

This is a page from a vellum medieval Qur'an with a rosette in the margin, by the medieval Islamic school. Islam follows the Jewish tradition in prohibiting images of God (Allah). Because Islam also prohibits depicting the human form (although some Islamic artists did produce images of people and animals), as this picture shows, Islamic art tended to be highly abstract, and Islamic writing itself became an art form of great beauty and refinement.

The Bridgeman Art Library International Ltd. Musee Conde, Chantilly, France/Bridgeman Art Library

This cloisonné and gold medallion crafted by Georgian artists for a Byzantine icon frame, ca. 1100 C.E., shows Jesus Christ. His divinity is communicated by his halo, and his wisdom as a human teacher by the book he carries. By the Middle Ages, the Byzantine world had produced many icons, and the defeat in the ninth century of the iconoclasts, who opposed the creation of religious images for fear that ordinary people would worship them, ensured that religious art replete with images of God, Jesus, and the saints would dominate medieval Christian art throughout Europe.

Art Resource, NY ©Giraudon/Art Resource, NY

"The Virgin of Paris," Anonymous Early fourteenth century, Notre Dame, Paris. This sculpture communicates another important way in which medieval Christians envisioned God, as the infant Jesus in the arms of his mother, Mary, to whom Catholics prayed to intercede for them with her son. In this image, an excellent example of northern Gothic sculpture, Mary also personifies the Catholic Church, "mother" of the faithful, and Our Lady of France.

Art Resource, NY
©Giraudon/Art Resource, NY

PART THREE EUROPE IN TRANSITION

POLITICS & GOVERNMENT

1309–1377	Pope resides in Avignon
1337–1453	Hundred Years' War
1356	*Golden Bull* creates German electoral college

1415–1433	Hussite revolt in Bohemia
1428–1519	Aztecs expand in central Mexico
1429	Joan of Arc leads French to victory in Orléans
1434	Medici rule begins in Florence
1455–1485	Wars of the Roses in England
1469	Marriage of Ferdinand and Isabella
1487	Henry Tudor creates Court of Star Chamber

▲ *Palace of Popes*

▲ *Joan of Arc*

SOCIETY & ECONOMY

1315–1317	Greatest famine of the Middle Ages
1347–1350	Black Death peaks
1358	*Jacquerie* shakes France
1378	Ciompi Revolt in Florence
1381	English peasants' revolt

1450	Johann Gutenberg invents printing with movable type
1492	Christopher Columbus encounters the Americas
1498	Vasco da Gama reaches India

RELIGION & CULTURE

◄ *Two scenes from English peasant revolt of 1381*

1414–1417	The Council of Constance
1425–1450	Lorenzo Valla exposes the *Donation of Constantine*
1450	Thomas à Kempis, *Imitation of Christ*
1492	Expulsion of Jews from Spain

1300–1325	Dante Alighieri writes *Divine Comedy*
1302	Boniface VIII issues bull *Unam Sanctam*
1350	Boccaccio, *Decameron*
1375–1527	The Renaissance in Italy
1378–1417	The Great Schism
1380–1395	Chaucer writes *Canterbury Tales*
1390–1430	Christine de Pisan writes in defense of women

Canterbury Cathedral ▶

1500–1600

1519	Charles V crowned Holy Roman Emperor
1530	*Augsburg Confession* defines Lutheranism
1547	Ivan the Terrible becomes tsar of Russia
1555	*Peace of Augsburg* recognizes the legal principle, *cuius regio, eius religio*
1558–1603	Reign of Elizabeth I of England
1572	Saint Bartholomew's Day Massacre
1588	English defeat of Spanish Armada
1598	Edict of Nantes gives Huguenots religious and civil rights

▲ *Ferdinand Magellan's ship, Vittoria*

1519	Hernan Cortes lands in Mexico
1519–1522	Ferdinand Magellan circumnavigates the Earth
1525	German Peasants' Revolt
1532–1533	Francisco Pizarro conquers the Incas
1540	Spanish open silver mines in Peru, Bolivia, and Mexico
1550–1600	The great witch panics

◄ *Elizabeth I, The Armada Portrait*

1513	Niccolo Machiavelli, *The Prince*
1516	Erasmus compiles a Greek New Testament
1516	Thomas More, *Utopia*
1517	Martin Luther's Ninety-five theses
1534	Henry VIII declared head of English Church
1540	Jesuit order founded
1541	John Calvin becomes Geneva's reformer
1543	Copernicus, *On the Revolutions of the Heavenly Spheres*
1545–1563	Council of Trent
1549	English *Book of Common Prayer*

1600–1700

1624–1642	Era of Richelieu in France
1629–1640	Charles I's years of personal rule
1640	Long Parliament convenes
1642	Outbreak of civil war in England
1643–1661	Cardinal Mazarin regent for Louis XIV
1648	Peace of Westphalia
1649–1652	The *Fronde* in France
1649	Charles I executed
1660	Charles II restored to the English throne
1661–1715	Louis XIV's years of personal rule
1682–1725	Reign of Peter the Great
1685	James II becomes king of England
	Louis XIV revokes Edict of Nantes
1688	"Glorious Revolution" in Britain

▲ *Cardinal Richelieu*

1600–1700	Period of greatest Dutch economic prosperity
1600–early 1700s	Spain maintains commercial monopoly in Latin America
1607	English settle Jamestown, Virginia
1608	French settle Quebec
1618–1648	Thirty Years' War devastates German economy
1619	African slaves first bought at Jamestown, Virginia
1650s–1670s	Commercial rivalry between Dutch and English
1661–1683	Colbert seeks to stimulate French economic growth
1690	Paris Foundling Hospital established

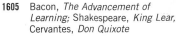

Jamestown, Virginia ►

1605	Bacon, *The Advancement of Learning*; Shakespeare, *King Lear*, Cervantes, *Don Quixote*
1609	Kepler, *The New Astronomy*
1611	King James Version of the English Bible
1632	Galileo, *Dialogue on the Two Chief Systems of the World*
1637	Descartes, *Discourse on Method*
1651	Hobbes, *Leviathan*
1687	Newton, *Principia Mathematica*
1689	English Toleration Act
1690	Locke, *Essay Concerning Human Understanding*

▲ *First page of Hobbes' Leviathan, 1651*

1700–1789

1700–1721	Great Northern War between Sweden and Russia
1701–1714	War of Spanish Succession
1713	Treaty of Utrecht
1720–1740	Age of Walpole in England and Fleury in France
1740	Maria Theresa succeeds to the Habsburg throne
1740–1748	War of the Austrian Succession
1756–1763	Seven Years' War
1767	Legislative Commission in Russia
1772	First Partition of Poland
1776	American Declaration of Independence
1778	France aids the American colonies

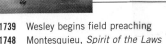

Declaration of Independence ►

1715–1763	Era of major colonial rivalry in the Caribbean
1719	Mississippi Bubble in France
1733	James Kay's flying shuttle
1750s	Agricultural Revolution in Britain
1750–1840	Growth of new cities
1763	Britain becomes dominant in India
1763–1789	Enlightened absolutist rulers seek to spur economic growth
1765	James Hargreaves's spinning jenny
1769	Richard Arkwright's waterframe
1773–1775	Pugachev's Rebellion

1739	Wesley begins field preaching
1748	Montesquieu, *Spirit of the Laws*
1750	Rousseau, *Discourse on the Moral Effects of the Arts and Sciences*
1751	First volume Diderot's *Encyclopedia*
1762	Rousseau, *Social Contract* and *Émile*
1763	Voltaire, *Treatise on Tolerance*
1774	Goethe, *Sorrow of Young Werther*
1776	Smith, *Wealth of Nations*
1781	Kant, *Critique of Pure Reason*
	Joseph II adopts policy of toleration in Austria

Portraits of ►
Encyclopedists

9 The Late Middle Ages
Social and Political Breakdown (1300–1453)

CHAPTER HIGHLIGHTS

The Black Death Between 1348 and the early fifteenth century, close to 40 percent of the population of Western Europe was killed by the Black Death. The fear inspired by the disease, and by the responses to it, influenced European attitudes and religious beliefs for centuries. The sharp drop in population caused by the plague had profound social, economic, and political consequences, creating new challenges and opportunities for Europeans.

The Hundred Years' War and the Rise of National Sentiment The direct cause of the Hundred Years' War was the controversy over the succession to the French throne. England began the conflict as a more cohesive state than France. However, over the course of the conflict, the French developed an emerging sense of national unity.

Ecclesiastical Breakdown and Revival: The Late Medieval Church Throughout the thirteenth century, popes had worked to centralize church power. As nation-states gained cohesiveness, kings began to challenge papal authority. For most of the fourteenth century, the papacy was based in Avignon. Discontent with the clergy was expressed in popular movements like those led by John Wycliffe and John Huss. Opposition to the Avignon papacy led to the Great Schism (1378–1417) and the Conciliar Movement.

Medieval Russia Starting in the eleventh century, Kiev began to lose its prominence as Russia's most important city. As Kiev declined, Russia split into three geographic and cultural groupings: the Great Russians, the White Russians, and the Little Russians or Ukrainians. In 1223 Ghengis Khan led the Mongol conquest of Russia. Mongol rule came to an end in 1480, by which time Moscow had become Russia's political and religious capital. In Russia the main social division was between freemen and slaves.

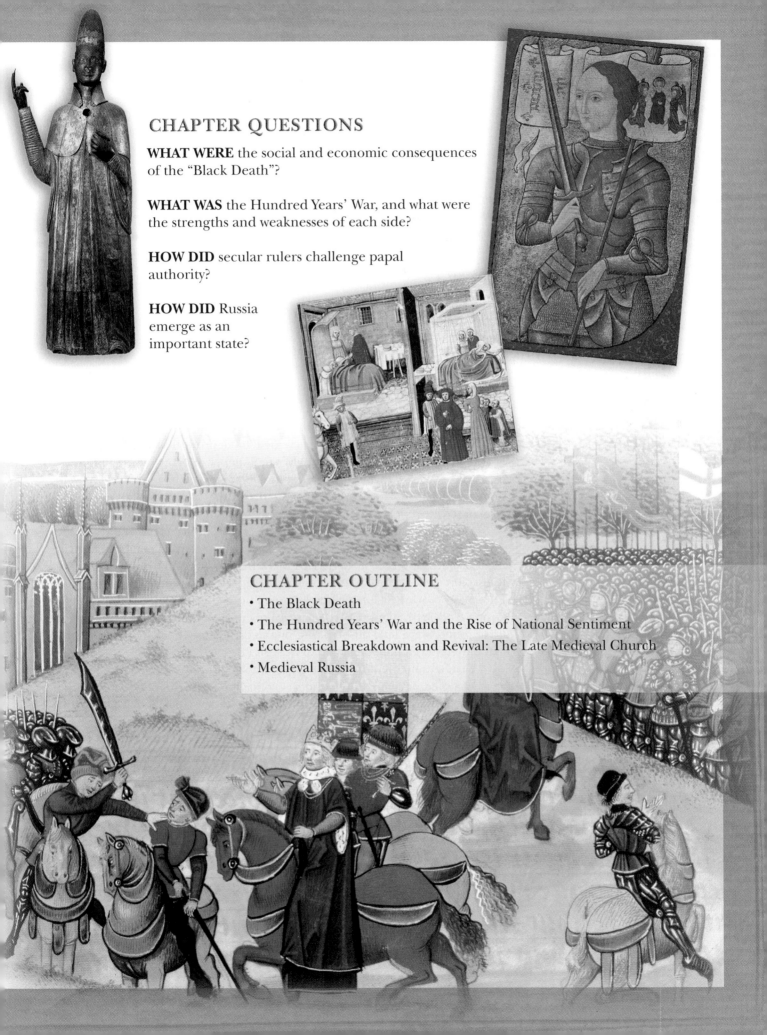

CHAPTER QUESTIONS

WHAT WERE the social and economic consequences of the "Black Death"?

WHAT WAS the Hundred Years' War, and what were the strengths and weaknesses of each side?

HOW DID secular rulers challenge papal authority?

HOW DID Russia emerge as an important state?

CHAPTER OUTLINE

IMAGE KEY
Image Key for pages 218–219 is on page 235.

The West endured so many calamities as the Middle Ages drew to a close that European civilization seemed in imminent danger of collapse. From 1337 to 1453, France and England were locked in a bloody conflict called the Hundred Years' War. Between 1347 and 1350, a devastating plague swept through Europe and carried off a third of its population. In 1378, a quarrel between competing candidates for the papacy began a schism that kept the church divided for thirty-nine years. In 1453, the Turks overran Constantinople and charged up the Danube valley toward the heart of Europe.

These crises were accompanied by intellectual developments that undercut many of the assumptions about faith, life, and the social order that had comforted earlier generations. Some philosophers concluded that human reason is much more limited in scope than the Scholastics had realized. Feudal institutions, which had been assumed to be divinely ordained, were assaulted by kings who aspired to absolute monarchy. Competing claims to authority were made by kings and popes, and both of these leaders were challenged by political theorists who argued that subjects had the right to hold rulers accountable for how they used their power.

WHAT WERE the social and economic consequences of the "Black Death"?

9.1
The Flagellants

THE BLACK DEATH

PRECONDITIONS AND CAUSES

European society in the late Middle Ages was still thoroughly agrarian. Nine-tenths of the population worked the land. The three-field system of seasonal planting and crop rotation had increased food production, but population growth kept pace with the food supply. The number of people living in Europe doubled between 1000 and 1300, until the point was reached where there were more mouths than could be fed. At least once during the average European life span of thirty-five years, an individual could expect to suffer extreme hunger.

Between 1315 and 1317, crop failures produced the worst famines of the Middle Ages. Starvation undermined health and increased vulnerability to a virulent plague that struck in 1347. This **Black Death** (so called because of the way it discolored the bodies of its victims) followed the trade routes from Asia into Europe. Appearing first in Sicily, it entered Europe through the ports of Venice, Genoa, and Pisa. Some places, such as Bohemia, where there were no major trade routes, were little affected, but by the early fifteenth century, the plague may have reduced the population of western Europe by two-fifths.

Flea bites injected the plague bacilli into an individual's bloodstream, and a victim's sneezes could also spread the contagion. Medieval physicians had no understanding of these processes and could offer no explanation, defense, or cure. (See "Encountering the Past: Medieval Medicine.") Consequently, the plague inspired deep pessimism, panicky superstition, and an obsession with death and dying. Amulets and folk remedies abounded. Some people put their trust in a temperate, disciplined regimen. Others, fearing that death was near, threw themselves into the pursuit of pleasure. Troops of flagellants, religious fanatics who did penance by whipping themselves, paraded through the countryside stirring up mass panic. Groundless rumors that unpopular minorities (particularly the Jews) were spreading the disease sparked bloody purges.

SOCIAL AND ECONOMIC CONSEQUENCES

Farms Decline   The plague was most virulent in places where people lived close together. Whole villages and urban districts were sometimes wiped out. This reduced the labor force and created a demand for workers that drove up wages. Agricultural profits diminished because consumers were fewer, and prices rose for luxury and manufactured goods (the products of skilled artisans who had become scarce).

Black Death   Virulent plague that struck in Sicily in 1347 and spread through Europe. It discolored the bodies of its victims. By the early fifteenth century, the plague may have reduced the population of western Europe by two-fifths.

MAP EXPLORATION

Interactive map: To explore this map further, go to **http://www.prenhall.com/kagan3/map9.1**

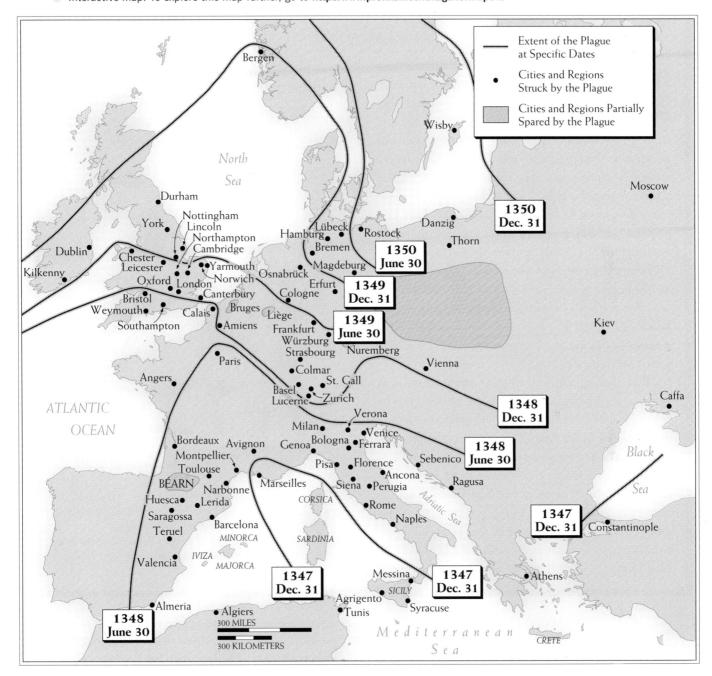

MAP 9–1

Spread of the Black Death   Apparently introduced by seaborne rats from Black Sea areas where plague-infested rodents had long been known, the Black Death brought huge human, social, and economic consequences. One of the lower estimates of Europeans dying is 25 million. The map charts the plague's spread in the mid–fourteenth century. Generally following trade routes, the plague reached Scandinavia by 1350, and some believe it then went on to Iceland and even Greenland. Areas off the main trade routes were largely spared.

WHAT DOES the spread of the plague indicate about the networks of trade routes and economic development in Europe in the mid-fourteenth century?

ENCOUNTERING THE PAST

MEDIEVAL MEDICINE

Medieval medicine was a mix of practices ranging from diet, exercise regimens, and medicines to prayer, magical amulets, and incantations. Celestial forces (the stars and planets) were assumed to influence human physical and mental states, and physicians turned to astrology for help in explaining illnesses and devising treatments. In a world where lives tended to be short and suffering difficult to ease, people were desperate for cures and willing to take advice from any source. The wealthy sought help from university-trained physicians. These men were the most prestigious, if not inevitably the most effective, healers. They relied on diet and medication to treat internal illnesses. Apothecaries supplied their patients with medicinal herbs, and surgeons performed any physical operations they prescribed. Some surgeons had university educations, but many were humble barbers who learned their trade as apprentices.

Bloodletting was prescribed as a treatment for illness and a preservative of health, for medical theory held that illness was a result of an imbalance of humors (fluids) in the body. Greek science maintained there were four elements (earth, air, fire, and water), each associated with a quality (hot, cold, moist, and dry). The mix of these in the body determined its condition, and treatment called for draining off excesses or shifting humors to different locations in the body. Physicians commonly diagnosed problems by examining urine and blood and checking pulses.

The urine flask was the medieval equivalent of the stethoscope—the badge of the physician.

WHAT KIND of medical help was available to medieval people?

A caricature of physicians (early sixteenth century). A physician carries a uroscope (for collecting and examining urine); discolored urine signaled an immediate need for bleeding. The physician/surgeon wears surgical shoes and his assistant carries a flail—a comment on the risks of medical services.
Hacker Art Books Inc.

Serfs began to abandon farming for more lucrative jobs in towns. All of these economic developments hurt the privileged classes, whose incomes derived in large part from landed estates. To keep workers on their manors, landowners had to offer them better deals and lower the rents their peasants paid. The clergy were insulated from some of the problems that afflicted the secular nobility. As a great landholder, the church suffered economic losses, but these were offset by an increased demand for masses for the dead and by a flood of gifts and bequests.

Some landowners tried to recoup their losses by converting arable land to sheep pasture. Herding required far fewer expensive laborers than did grain cultivation. Nobles also used their monopoly of political power to reverse their declining fortunes. They passed laws freezing wages at low levels and ordering peasants to stay on the land. Resentment of this legislation fueled France's Jacquerie and England's Peasants' Revolt.

OVERVIEW   EFFECTS OF THE BLACK DEATH

Social	Rumors abounded that unpopular minorities were spreading the disease. Serfs began to abandon farming for more lucrative jobs in towns.
Economic	Agricultural profits diminished because consumers were fewer. Prices rose for luxury and manufactured goods as artisans became scarce.
Cultural	Churches saw increased demand for masses for the dead. Deep pessimism, superstition, and obsession with death were inspired.
Political	Nobles used their monopoly of political power to reverse declining fortunes. Laws passed freezing low wages and ordering peasants to stay on the land.

Cities Rebound Although the plague hit urban populations especially hard, cities ultimately profited from its effects. The omnipresence of death whetted the appetite for pleasure and for the luxuries produced by cities. Initially the demand for manufactured goods could not be met, for the first wave of plague drastically diminished a supply of artisans that the guilds had purposefully kept low. This caused the prices of manufactured and luxury items to rise to new heights. As wealth poured into cities, the shrunken population reduced demand for agricultural products. Falling prices made food cheaper and lowered the cost of living for urban dwellers. The forces that enriched townspeople impoverished the landed nobility. City dwellers began to buy up manors whose value had diminished. This extended the power of the town into the countryside and began to blend the rural gentry with the urban patriciate.

The rapidly changing economic conditions the plague created were not an unmixed blessing for towns, for they increased tensions that had long seethed within urban communities. The merchant classes found it difficult to maintain their traditional dominance over the prospering artisans' guilds. The guilds used their growing political clout to enact restrictive legislation that protected local industries. Master artisans kept demand for their products high by limiting the number of shops licensed to share their market. This frustrated many journeymen who were eager to set up in business for themselves, and it created strife within the guilds.

This Burgundian manuscript, c. 1470, depicts a bath said to be fit for a cardinal or king, seen standing at the door. The couple on the left, behind a closable curtain, suggests a house of prostitution, while on the right the men and their younger, good-looking, bejeweled partners appear not to be husbands and wives.

AGK London Ltd.

THE HUNDRED YEARS' WAR AND THE RISE OF NATIONAL SENTIMENT

*L*ate medieval rulers headed what were still feudal governments but grander in scale and more sophisticated than those of their predecessors. The Norman kings of England and the Capetian kings of France centralized royal power by fine-tuning feudal relationships. They stressed the duties of lesser magnates to greater ones and insisted on the unquestioning loyalty of all vassals to the king. They struck up alliances with powerful factions (among the nobles, clergy, and townspeople) within their domains. This fostered a sense of "national" consciousness that equipped both kingdoms for war on an unprecedented scale.

WHAT WAS the Hundred Years' War, and what were the strengths and weaknesses of each side?

Edward III pays homage to his feudal lord Philip VI of France. Legally, Edward was a vassal of the king of France.

Archives Snark International/Art Resource, NY

CAUSES OF THE WAR

A disputed claim to the French throne provided justification for the events that led to the outbreak of the Hundred Years' War in May 1337. In 1328, the death of Charles IV of France extinguished the senior branch of the Capetian royal house. Edward III (r. 1327–1377), king of England, claimed France's throne by right of his mother, Charles IV's sister. The French barons, however, had no intention of turning themselves over to England's king. They pledged their allegiance to a cadet branch of the Capetian house, to Charles IV's cousin, Philip VI, duke of Valois (r. 1328–1350). (This began the Valois dynasty that ruled France into the sixteenth century.)

England and France had long been on a collision course, and the English king's claim to the French throne provided an excuse for war that had multiple causes. Since the days of the Norman conquest, the king of England had held fiefs on the Continent as a vassal of the king of France. English possession of French land hampered attempts by the French kings to centralize the government of their nation. England and France also had competing economic interests in Flanders and on the high seas. The Hundred Years' War was a struggle for national identity and sovereignty as much as for territory.

French Weakness France should have had no difficulty in winning the war. It had three times the population of England, far greater resources, and the advantage of fighting on its own soil. Yet, until 1415, all the major battles were stunning victories for the English.

Internal disunity prevented France from marshaling all its forces against the English, and powerful feudal traditions slowed France's adaptation to novel military strategies that the English employed. England's infantry was more disciplined than France's, and English archers wielded a formidable weapon, the longbow. A longbowman could fire six arrows a minute and pierce the armor of a knight at two hundred yards.

PROGRESS OF THE WAR

The war unfolded in three stages.

The Conflict During the Reign of Edward III The first steps toward war were taken when Edward forbade shipment of the English wool that fed the Flemish cloth-making industry. His intent was to encourage Flanders to repudiate its feudal ties with Philip VI. In 1340, the Flemish cities decided their economic interests lay with England, and they acknowledged Edward's claim to be king of France and over-lord of Flanders. On June 23 of that year, Edward defeated the French fleet in the Bay of Sluys, the first great battle of the war. (See Map 9–2.)

In 1346, Edward invaded Normandy. A series of easy raids was capped by a major battle at Crécy. England's bowmen tipped the balance in Edward's favor at Crécy, but Edward lacked the manpower to exploit his victory. He seized the port of Calais and returned to England. Exhaustion and the onset of plague forced a truce. There was no further action until 1356, when the English won their greatest victory. Near Poitiers, they routed France's feudal levies and captured the French king, John II "the Good", r. 1350–1364. The loss of king and vassals caused a breakdown of government in France.

Power shifted momentarily to the **Estates General**, an assembly of representatives from France's propertied classes. The powerful merchants of Paris, led by Etienne Marcel, demanded rights similar to those that Magna Carta had promised to the English privileged classes. The Estates General was, however, too divided to provide effective government. Leaders of the far-flung regions of a large nation such as France were strangers to one another, and they found it difficult to communicate and agree on plans of action.

MAP 9–2

The Hundred Years' War   The Hundred Years' War went on intermittently from the late 1330s until 1453. These maps show the remarkable English territorial gains up to the sudden and decisive turning of the tide of battle in favor of the French by the forces of Joan of Arc in 1429.

USING THE map as a reference, what were the major English victories or French weaknesses that led to England's significant influence in France by 1429?

MAP EXPLORATION

Interactive map: To explore this map further, go to **http://www.prenhall.com/kagan3/map9.2**

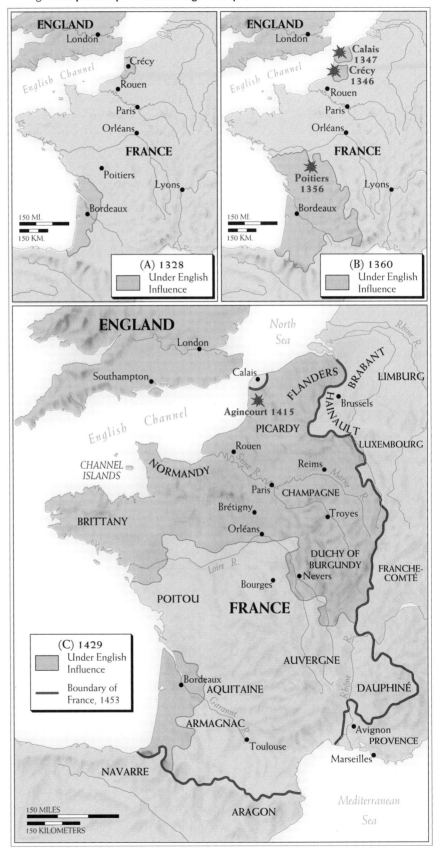

The French privileged classes avoided taxation and foisted the costs of the war with England onto the backs of peasants. Beginning in 1358, the desperate peasants waged a series of bloody rebellions called the **Jacquerie** (from "Jacques Bonhomme," a peasant caricature). The nobles restored order by matching the rebels atrocity for atrocity.

On May 9, 1360, England compelled France to accept terms spelled out in the Peace of Brétigny. Edward renounced his claim to the French throne, but he demanded an end to his vassalage to the king of France and confirmation of his sovereignty over the lands he held in France (Gascony, Guyenne, Poitou, and Calais). France was also required to pay a ransom of 3 million gold crowns for King John's return. The treaty was unrealistic, and sober observers on both sides knew the peace it brought could not last. Within a few years France had reopened hostilities, and by the time of Edward's death in 1377, the English occupied only a few coastal enclaves and the territory around Bordeaux.

French Defeat and the Treaty of Troyes Late in Edward's reign, England began to have problems at home that caused it to lose interest in its war with France. Edward's grandson and successor, Richard II (r. 1377–1399), faced a popular uprising similar to the Jacquerie. In June 1381, John Ball, a priest, and Wat Tyler, a journeyman, led a mob in an assault on London. The "Peasants' Revolt" was put down, but it left scars that took decades to heal.

Richard's autocratic behavior turned his nobles against him, and he was forced to abdicate the throne in favor of his cousin, Henry IV. Henry's son and heir, Henry V (r. 1413–1422), revived the war with France as a strategy for rallying his people to support the new royal line. His moment was well chosen, for the French nobility had split into warring factions that refused to cooperate in defending their country. At the Battle of Agincourt in Normandy (1415), Henry defeated the army of the Armagnacs. This shocked their opponents, the party of the duke of Burgundy, and led to efforts to heal the breach that had divided France's forces. Hope for cooperation was shattered, however, in September 1419, when the duke of Burgundy was assassinated by an Armagnac. Burgundy's son and heir then avenged his father's death by helping the English invade Armagnac territory. Henry took Paris, captured the French king, Charles VI, and married Charles's daughter. In 1420, the Treaty of Troyes disinherited the French king's son and proclaimed Henry V heir to the French throne. When Henry and Charles died within months of one another in 1422, Henry's infant son, Henry VI, was declared king of both France and England.

Joan of Arc and the War's Conclusion Charles VI's son, the future Charles VII, escaped the English and asserted his right to his father's throne. His eventual victory owed much to a remarkable young peasant woman from Domrémy, Joan of Arc (1412–1431). In March 1429, Joan appeared at Charles's court-in-exile and informed him God had commissioned her to rescue the city of Orléans from the English armies that were besieging it. The king was skeptical, but he was willing to try anything to reverse France's fortunes.

Circumstances worked to Joan's advantage. By the time she arrived, the siege of Orléans had gone on for six months. The exhausted English troops were already contemplating withdrawal when Joan arrived with a fresh French army. The English retreat from Orléans was followed by a succession of victories popularly attributed to Joan. She deserved credit—if not for military genius, for an ability to inspire her men

Estates General Assembly of representatives from France's propertied classes.

Jacquerie (From "Jacques Bonhomme," a peasant caricature) Name given to the series of bloody rebellions that desperate French peasants waged beginning in 1358.

A contemporary portrait of Joan of Arc (1412–1431) in the National Archives in Paris.

Anonymous, 15th century. "Joan of Arc." Franco-Flemish miniature. Archives Nationales, Paris, France. Photograph copyright Bridgeman-Giraudon/Art Resource, NY

HISTORY'S VOICES

JOAN OF ARC REFUSES TO RECANT HER BELIEFS

J oan of Arc, threatened with torture, refused to recant her beliefs and instead defended the instructions she had received from the voices that spoke to her. Here is a part of her self-defense from the contemporary trial record.

WHY WAS Joan deemed "heretical" and not "insane" when she acknowleged hearing voices?

On Wednesday, May 9th of the same year [1431], Joan was brought into the great tower of the castle of Rouen before us the said judges and in the presence of the reverend father, lord abbot of St. Cormeille de Compiegne, of masters Jean de Châtillon and Guillaume Erart, doctors of sacred theology, of André Margucric and Nicolas de Venderos, archdeacons of the church of Rouen, of William Haiton, bachelor of theology, Aubert Morel, licentiate in canon law, Nicolas Loiscleur, canon of the cathedral of Rouen, and master Jean Massieu.

And Joan was required and admonished to speak the truth on many different points contained in her trial which she had denied or to which she had given false replies, whereas we possessed certain information, proofs, and vehement presumptions upon them. Many of the points were read and explained to her,

and she was told that if she did not confess them truthfully she would be put to the torture, the instruments of which were shown to her all ready in the tower. There were also present by our instruction men ready to put her to the torture in order to restore her to the way and knowledge of truth, and by this means to procure the salvation of her body and soul which by her lying inventions she exposed to such grave perils.

To which the said Joan answered in this manner: "Truly if you were to tear me limb from limb and separate my soul from my body, I would not tell you anything more and if I did say anything, I should afterwards declare that you had compelled me to say it by force." Then she said that on Holy Cross Day last she received comfort from St. Gabriel, she firmly believes it was St. Gabriel. She knew by her voices whether she should submit to the Church, since the clergy were pressing her hard to submit. Her voices told her that if she desired Our Lord to aid her, she must wait upon Him in all her doings. She said that Our Lord has always been the master of her doings, and the Enemy never had power over them. She asked her voices if she would be burned and they answered that she must wait upon God, and He would aid her.

The Trial of Jeanne D'Arc, trans. by W. P. Barrett (New York: Gotham House, 1932), pp. 303, 304.

---

with self-confidence and enthusiasm for a common cause. Within a few months of the liberation of Orléans, Charles VII had recovered the city of Rheims and been anointed king in its cathedral (the traditional place for French coronations).

Charles showed little gratitude to his unconventional female ally and abandoned her after the Burgundians captured her in May 1430. The Burgundians and the English tried to demoralize their opponents by discrediting Joan. They accused her of heresy and turned her over to the Inquisition for trial. After ten weeks of brutal interrogation, the "Maid of Orléans" was executed as a relapsed heretic (May 30, 1431). Twenty-five years later (1456), Charles reopened her case and had her cleared of all charges, but she was not canonized as Saint Joan until 1920.

Once France was united behind Charles VII, the English had no hope of clinging to their continental possessions. In 1435, the duke of Burgundy recognized the inevitable, abandoned the English, and came to terms with Charles. By the time the war ended in 1453, England held only a little territory around the port of Calais.

QUICK REVIEW

Joan of Arc (1412–1431)

- March 1429: Joan appears at Charles' court-in-exile
- Joan inspires French to a string of victories starting with Orléans
- Captured by the Burgundians in May 1430 and executed by the English as a heretic in May 1431

The long struggle that ended in England's decisive separation from France determined the destiny of both countries. The Hundred Years' War awakened French nationalism and hastened France's transition from a feudal monarchy to a powerfully centralized state. In England, however, the loss of the war and continental empire diminished faith in the government and led to domestic upheaval.

ECCLESIASTICAL BREAKDOWN AND REVIVAL: THE LATE MEDIEVAL CHURCH

HOW DID secular rulers challenge papal authority?

Kings seized the opportunities that the rising power of the towns and the declining status of the feudal nobility gave them to centralize governments and economies. The church might have vigorously opposed their promotion of national sentiments, but it faltered just as the new monarchies began to flex their muscles. The plague had weakened the church by killing large numbers of clergy, but the church's major problems were of its own creation.

THE THIRTEENTH-CENTURY PAPACY

In the latter half of the thirteenth century, the papacy appeared to be in a strong position. Frederick II had been vanquished. Imperial pressure on Rome had been removed. The saintly French king, Louis IX, enthusiastically supported the church. In 1274, the Eastern orthodox clergy even accepted reunion with Rome in a bid to persuade the Latin West to aid Constantinople against the Turks.

Papal power reached its medieval pinnacle during the reign of Pope Innocent III (r. 1198–1216), but even then there were signs of trouble. Innocent's creation of a centralized papal monarchy with a clearly defined political mission had increased the church's secular power but diminished its spiritual authority. The thirteenth-century papacy created laws to govern the conduct of Europe's Christians and enforced its legislation in its own courts. It employed a highly efficient bureaucracy and was preoccupied with finances and the pursuit of secular power. The papacy grew strong by focusing more on its own needs than on those of the church at large.

Many contemporary observers noted how far the papacy had drifted from the simplicity and otherworldliness of the Christian leaders described in the New Testament. Some even began to make a distinction between the papal monarchy and the "true" church.

Political Fragmentation The papacy's position in Italy was paradoxically undermined by the success of its campaign against the Hohenstaufen emperors. As external threats from Germany retreated, political intrigues swept the Italian states. In the turmoil that resulted, the papacy became just another prize up for grabs.

Pope Gregory X (r. 1271–1276) had tried to ensure free papal elections by ordering sequestration for the cardinals whenever they were faced with choosing a successor to the papal throne. Physical isolation was supposed to prevent outsiders from promoting candidates

Significant Dates from the Period of the Late Middle Ages

1309–1377	Avignon Papacy
1340	Sluys, first major battle of Hundred Years' War
1346	Battle of Crécy and seizure of Calais
1347	Black Death strikes
1356	Battle of Poitiers
1358	Jacquerie disrupts France
1360	Peace of Brétigny
1378–1417	Great Schism
1381	English Peasants' Revolt
1414–1417	Council of Constance
1415	Battle of Agincourt
1420	Treaty of Troyes
1431	Joan of Arc executed as a heretic
1431–1449	Council of Basel
1453	End of Hundred Years' War

simply to advance political agendas, but this was a weak safeguard for the highly politicized College of Cardinals. Infighting was so great that from 1292 to 1294 the college was unable to elect a pope. In frustration, the cardinals finally chose a compromise candidate, a saintly but inept Calabrian hermit who took the name Celestine V. Celestine shocked Europe by abdicating after only a few weeks in office, and his death, which soon followed, led to rumors he had been murdered to clear his successor's title. The worldly wisdom of the new pope, Boniface VIII (r. 1294–1303), contrasted vividly with Celestine's naive innocence.

BONIFACE VIII AND PHILIP THE FAIR

Germany had been defeated, but in England and France, Boniface faced rising monarchies. France's Philip IV "the Fair" (r. 1285–1314), was a ruthless politician who taught Boniface that the power the pope had presumably inherited from Innocent III was more illusion than reality.

The Royal Challenge to Papal Authority   If Edward I (r. 1272–1307) of England had been able to resolve his problems with Scotland, the Hundred Years' War might have been underway by the time Boniface ascended the papal throne. France and England were both mobilizing resources for a war they considered inevitable, and their preparations created a problem for Boniface. Despite the fact that Pope Innocent III had decreed in 1215 that rulers had no right to tax the clergy without papal approval, both kings were levying extraordinary taxes on their clergy. This forced Boniface to take a stand, and on February 5, 1296, he issued the bull *Clericis Laicos* to caution the kings they had no jurisdiction over the church.

Edward retaliated by denying the clergy and their property the protection of the state's courts. Philip deprived the papacy of the bulk of its income by forbidding the export of money from France to Rome. Boniface had no choice but to come to terms, and he issued a second bull that conceded the right of a king to tax clergy "during an emergency." He also courted Philip by agreeing to canonize Philip's grandfather, Louis IX.

For much of his reign, Boniface was besieged by powerful enemies in Italy. The Colonnas (rivals of Boniface's family, the Gaetani) joined the radical Spiritual Franciscans in a campaign to invalidate Boniface's election. They alleged that Boniface had forced his predecessor from office, murdered him, and won the papacy by bribing the cardinals. Boniface defended himself effectively, and he was greatly encouraged by the response to his proclamation of 1300 as a "Jubilee year." Tens of thousands of pilgrims flocked to Rome to take advantage of the special opportunity this created to be absolved of their sins, and the pope interpreted the crowds as a show of popular support for his administration.

The Jubilee emboldened Boniface to imitate Innocent III and exercise a leadership role in international politics. The support he offered the Scots infuriated Edward, but his most serious difficulties were with Philip. Philip arrested Boniface's Parisian legate, Bishop Bernard Saisset of Pamiers, and convicted him in the royal courts of heresy and treason. The king then demanded that Boniface recognize the legitimacy of the proceedings. To do so, however, would have been to relinquish the pope's jurisdiction over the French clergy. Boniface, therefore, demanded Saisset's unconditional release and revoked his previous concessions on the matter of clerical taxation. In December 1301, Boniface sent Philip the bull *Ausculta Fili* (*Listen, My Son*), which baldly stated the papacy's claim that "God has set popes over kings and kingdoms."

Philip responded with a ruthless attack on the papacy's claim to temporal authority, and on November 18, 1302, Boniface released another bull, *Unam*

QUICK REVIEW

The Hundred Years' War and the Papacy

- Both Edward I and Philip the Fair taxed their clergy to raise funds for coming war
- Boniface's efforts to stop taxation of clergy were met with retaliation by both monarchs
- Boniface was forced to back down

Pope Boniface VIII (r. 1294–1303), depicted here, opposed the taxation of the clergy by the kings of France and England and issued one of the strongest declarations of papal authority over rulers, the bull *Unam Sanctam*. This statue is in the Museo Civico, Bologna, Italy.

Statue of Pope Boniface VIII. Museo Civico, Bologna. Scala/Art Resource, NY

Sanctam. It insisted that the temporal authority of kings was "subject" to the spiritual power of the church. Philip announced this was a declaration of war. His chief minister, Guillaume de Nogaret, informed the French clergy that the pope was a criminal and common heretic, and the French army invaded Italy and captured the pope in residence in Anagni. Boniface was nearly killed before the people of Anagni rescued him. The French retreated, and the aged pontiff returned to Rome, where he died two months later.

Boniface's successor, Benedict XI (r. 1303–1304), excommunicated Nogaret. He was, however, in no position to retaliate against the French king, and his successor, Clement V (r. 1305–1314), himself a Frenchman, utterly capitulated. He lifted Nogaret's excommunication and declared that *Unam Sanctam* was not intended to diminish royal authority in any way. He also cleared the way for Philip to confiscate the wealth of the Knights Templar by yielding to the king's demand that the Crusading order be condemned for heresy and dissolved. France's victory was crowned in 1309 by Clement's decision to move the papal court to Avignon—supposedly for safety and convenience. Avignon was an independent town on land that belonged to the pope, but it was in the southeast corner of territory that was culturally French. The papacy remained in Avignon for almost seventy years.

THE AVIGNON PAPACY (1309–1377)

During Clement V's pontificate, Frenchmen flooded into the College of Cardinals, and he and successive Avignon popes appeared—even when they were not—to be dominated by the French king. Cut off in Avignon from their Roman estates, the popes had to find new sources of income, and their ingenuity and success earned them unfortunate reputations for greed and materialism. Clement V increased papal taxation of the clergy. Clement VI (r. 1342–1352) began selling indulgences (releases from penance for sin). The doctrine of purgatory (a place where souls ultimately destined for heaven atoned for venial sins) developed as part of this campaign. By the fifteenth century, the church was urging the living to buy reduced sentences in purgatory for deceased loved ones.

Pope John XXII By the time Pope John XXII (r. 1316–1334) ascended the throne, the popes were well enough established in Avignon to reenter the field of international politics. A quarrel that erupted between the pope and the German emperor, Louis IV, launched an important debate about the nature of legitimate authority.

John had backed a candidate who lost the imperial election to Louis, and the pope obstinately and without legal justification refused to confirm Louis's title. Louis retaliated by accusing John of heresy and declaring him deposed in favor of an antipope. Two outstanding pamphleteers made the case for the king: William of Ockham (d. 1349), whom John excommunicated in 1328, and Marsilius of Padua (ca. 1290–1342), whose teaching John declared heretical in 1327.

William of Ockham was a brilliant logician and critic of philosophical realism, the theory that abstract terms (*church*, for instance) refer to transcendent entities that have some sort of real existence. Ockham was a nominalist who believed such words are only names the human mind invented for its own convenience. Ockham argued that the real church is the historical human community, not some supernatural entity and the pope is only one of its members. As such, he has no special powers of infallibility. The church is best guided, Ockham argued, not by popes but by scripture and by councils representing all the Christian faithful.

Avignon Papacy Period from 1309 to 1377 when the papal court was situated in Avignon, France, and gained a reputation for greed and worldly corruption.

In *Defender of Peace* (1324), Marsilius of Padua argued that the jurisdiction of the clergy was limited to the spiritual realm and that—the punishment for spiritual transgressions being a matter for the next life and not this one—the clergy had no legitimate coercive authority over the laity. An exception might be made only if a secular ruler declared a divine law a law of the state, for it was the state's exclusive, God-given right to use force to maintain social order. A true pope would, like the Apostles in the New Testament, eschew all earthly pomp and power and lead only by spiritual example.

National Opposition to the Avignon Papacy   John's successor, Benedict XII (r. 1334–1342), began construction of a lavish palace at Avignon, and his high-living French successor, Clement VI (r. 1342–1352), presided over a splendid, worldly court. His cardinals grew rich serving as lobbyists for various secular patrons, and the papacy's fiscal tentacles spread farther and farther afield.

Secular governments reacted to these developments by passing laws that restricted papal jurisdiction and taxation. The English had no intention of supporting a papacy they believed was the puppet of their French enemy. The French insisted on their "Gallican liberties," a well-founded tradition that granted the king extensive authority over ecclesiastical appointments and taxation. German and Swiss cities also took steps to limit and even revoke well-established clerical privileges and immunities.

John Wycliffe and John Huss   Mass discontent with the worldly clergy and the politicized papacy generated lay popular movements that were highly critical of the church and traditional religious practices. The Lollards in England and the Hussites in Bohemia were the most significant. The Lollards drew their inspiration from John Wycliffe (d. 1384)—as did John Huss (d. 1415), the martyr whose death launched the successful Hussite revolt against papal authority.

9.2
Propositions of Wycliffe Condemned at London, 1382, and the Council of Constance, 1415

Wycliffe, an Oxford theologian, was a major defender of the rights of kings against the secular pretensions of popes. Wycliffe strongly supported the steps that the English monarchy took (beginning about 1350) to curtail the power of the Avignon papacy over the church in England. Like the original Franciscans, he believed clergy ought to embrace poverty and be content with basic food and clothing. His arguments were popular with secular governments, for they justified the state's confiscation of ecclesiastical property.

Wycliffe maintained that because all authority comes from God, only leaders who live pious lives (as God requires) can claim legitimacy. He believed faithful laypeople have the right to pass judgment on corrupt ecclesiastics and take the lead in reforming the church. Wycliffe anticipated some positions that Protestants would eventually take. He challenged papal infallibility, the doctrine of transubstantiation that gave the priesthood power over the laity, and church policies that restricted the laity's access to the Scriptures. Opposition to the Avignon papacy persuaded the English king to protect him, even though the argument he made for repudiating corrupt clergy could just as easily be used to justify rebellion against a secular ruler. The subjects of any leader who behaved badly could argue he had forfeited his mandate from God.

The Lollards who embraced Wycliffe's ideas preached in the vernacular, disseminated translations of the Scriptures, and championed clerical poverty. So long as they restricted themselves to religion, the English authorities tolerated them. But after the Peasants' Revolt of 1381, the government became suspicious of the egalitarian implications of Wycliffe's works. In 1401, Lollardy was declared a capital offense.

Heresy was not so easily suppressed in Bohemia, for government was weaker there than in England. The University of Prague, founded in 1348, became a center

A portrayal of John Huss as he was led to the stake at Constance. After his execution, his bones and ashes were scattered in the Rhine River to prevent his followers from claiming them as relics. This pen-and-ink drawing is from Ulrich von Richenthal's *Chronicle of the Council of Constance* (ca. 1450).

CORBIS/Bettmann

for Czech nationalists who opposed the increasing prominence of Germans in Bohemia. In 1403, John Huss, a student of Wycliffe's thought, became rector of the university and began a religious reform movement that was also a defense of Czech identity. The reformers used vernacular translations of the Bible and rejected practices (particularly some associated with the Eucharist) that smacked of superstition. Like the Lollards, they believed a sinful priest had no power to perform a valid sacrament, and they denied that clergy were spiritually superior to laity. Medieval Catholic custom reserved the cup at communion to the priest. The Hussites, however, thought this smacked of clerical privilege, and they gave the people the consecrated wine as well as the bread. Opposition to priestly claims to special powers also led the Hussites to reject the doctrine of transubstantiation.

Huss was excommunicated in 1410, and in 1414, he successfully petitioned for a hearing before an international church council convening in Constance, Switzerland. Although the Holy Roman Emperor Sigismund guaranteed Huss safe conduct, he was imprisoned, tried, and burned at the stake for heresy in 1415. The reaction in Bohemia to his execution and that of his colleague, Jerome of Prague, a few months later was fierce. The Taborites, a militant branch of the Hussites, took up arms under John Ziska and declared their intention to turn Bohemia into a state that incorporated Huss's religious and social ideals. Within a decade, they had won control of the Bohemian church.

THE GREAT SCHISM (1378–1417) AND THE CONCILIAR MOVEMENT TO 1449

In January 1377, Pope Gregory XI (r. 1370–1378) yielded to international pressure and announced the papacy would leave Avignon and return to Rome. Europe rejoiced—prematurely, as it turned out—at the end of the church's "Babylonian Captivity" (the exile of the ancient Israelites from their homeland).

Urban VI and Clement VII   Gregory died soon after returning to Rome, and the cardinals elected an Italian archbishop, Pope Urban VI (r. 1378–1389). When Urban announced his intention to reform the Curia (the church's central administration), the cardinals, most of whom were French, sensed a challenge to their power and insisted on returning the papacy to their base of operation in Avignon. Five months after Urban's enthronement, a group of thirteen cardinals declared Urban's election invalid. It had, they said, been forced on them by the Roman mob. They then proceeded to elect a "true" pope, Clement VII (r. 1378–1397), a cousin of the French king. Urban denied their allegations and appointed new cardinals to replace them in his college.

Europe, confronted with two papal courts, distributed its support along political lines: England and its allies (the Holy Roman Empire, Hungary, Bohemia, and Poland) acknowledged Urban VI, whereas France and those in its orbit (Naples, Scotland, Castile, and Aragon) supported Clement VII. (Today, the Roman Catholic Church accepts the Roman line of popes as the legitimate one.)

The schism threatened the survival of the church in its traditional form, and there were many reasons to end it as quickly as possible. The easiest solution would have been for one or both of the popes to resign, but neither was willing to sacrifice himself for the common good.

Conciliar Theory of Church Government   Europe's leaders, seeing no other option, finally decided an ecumenical church council had to be convened to end the schism. Only a pope, however, could call a legitimate council, and none of the popes wanted to summon a council that intended to depose him. Because a pope's authority derived directly from God and not from his people, it was also uncertain that a council had authority to depose a pope.

Scholars called *conciliarists* developed the arguments needed to legitimate the council. In the process, they radically altered medieval assumptions about the nature of authority and created a rationale for popular government. The conciliarists defined the church as the community of all Christian peoples. Because the papacy had been established by God to care for the people's church, a pope was, the conciliarists argued, ultimately accountable to the people whose well-being it was his job to protect. If he failed in his mission, his people had a natural right to depose him to save their church.

The Council of Pisa (1409–1410)   In 1409, thirty-one years after the schism began, cardinals from both Rome and Avignon tried to resolve the schism themselves. They met in Pisa, deposed their respective popes, and united in support of a new one. To their consternation, the popes in Rome and Avignon ignored them and appointed new colleges of cardinals. The attempt to end the schism had succeeded only in creating a third pope.

The Council of Constance (1414–1417)   Emperor Sigismund finally prevailed on John XXIII, the Pisan pope, to summon a council to meet in the Swiss city of Constance in 1414. Europe's kings agreed to cooperate, which deprived the competing popes of the support they needed to continue their fight. The three popes either resigned or were deposed, and the cardinals at the council chose a new pope whom everyone agreed to accept, Martin V (r. 1417–1431). The council also issued a decree (*Sacrosancta*) stating that councils, not popes, were the ultimate source of authority in the church, and it established a schedule for convening future councils at regular intervals.

The Council of Basel (r. 1431–1449)   Conciliar power peaked when a council meeting at Basel entered into negotiations with Bohemia's Hussites, whom the pope regarded as heretics. In November 1433, it granted the Bohemians jurisdiction over their church similar to that held by the French and English. The Hussites also won the right to a unique liturgy and disciplinary system that put clergy and laity on the same footing.

In 1438, the pope upstaged the council and restored the prestige of his office by negotiating a reunion with the Eastern church. The agreement signed in Florence in 1439 was short lived, but it marked the point at which support for conciliarism began to fade. The council of Basel disbanded in 1449, and a decade later the papal bull *Execrabilis* (1460) condemned conciliarism. The movement had, however, achieved several things. By giving secular governments greater authority over religious matters, it helped establish national or territorial churches. It also popularized the tenet that the role of the leader of an institution is to care for the well-being of its members. This idea had wide-ranging ramifications for the governments of states as well as the church.

MEDIEVAL RUSSIA

*P*rince Vladimir (r. 980–1015) received delegations at his court in Kiev representing the Muslim, Roman Catholic, Hebrew, and Greek Orthodox faiths. He then reviewed what each camp had to offer and chose the Greek option. His decision determined Russia's religion and strengthened commercial ties between Russia and the Byzantine Empire.

QUICK REVIEW

Church Councils

• Council of Pisa (1409–1410): Attempt to resolve schism ended in creating a third pope

• Council of Constance (1414–1417): Three popes resigned or were deposed and Martin V was chosen as new pope

• Council of Basel (1431–1449): Entered into negotiations with the Hussites

Justice in the late Middle Ages. Depicted are the most common forms of corporal and capital punishment in Europe in the late Middle Ages and the Renaissance. At top: burning, hanging, drowning. At center: blinding, quartering, the wheel, cutting of hair (a mark of great shame for a freeman). At bottom: thrashing, decapitation, amputation of hand (for thieves).
Herzog August Bibliothek

HOW DID Russia emerge as an important state?

POLITICS AND SOCIETY

Vladimir's successor, Yaroslav the Wise (r. 1016–1054), turned Kiev into a magnificent political and cultural center that rivaled Constantinople. After his death, however, rival princes split the Russian people into three groups (the Great Russians, the White Russians, and the Little Russians or Ukrainians), and a diminished Kiev became simply one principality among many.

The governments of the Russian states combined monarchy (a prince), aristocracy (a council of noblemen), and democracy (a popular assembly composed of all adult males). The broadest social division was between freemen and slaves. Freemen included clergy, army officers, **boyars** (wealthy landowners), townsmen, and peasants. Slaves were mostly prisoners of war, and debtors working off their debts formed a large semifree group.

MONGOL RULE (1243–1480)

In the thirteenth century, Mongols (or Tatars) swept over China, much of the Islamic world, and Russia. The armies of Ghengis Khan (1155–1227) invaded Russia in 1223, and Kiev fell to the Mongol general Batu Khan in 1240. A division of the Mongol Empire, the *Golden Horde* (a name derived from the Tatar words for the color of Batu Khan's tent), established a capital on the lower Volga River and exacted tribute from the Russian cities. The Mongols converted to Islam, and their Eastern culture pulled the Russians away from the European West. Some Russian women began to wear veils and to seclude themselves, but the Mongols interfered little with the political institutions and religion of their Russian subjects. The order they maintained and the trade links they established improved economic prospects for most Russians. The princes of Moscow grew wealthy by assisting their Mongol masters with the collection of tribute. As Mongol rule weakened, Moscow's power increased, and its rulers embarked on a project called "the gathering of the Russian Land." It aimed at expanding the territory under Moscow's control by all possible means: purchase, colonization, and conquest.

In 1380, Grand Duke Dimitri of Moscow (r. 1350–1389) gave the Tatar forces a defeat that precipitated the decline of Mongol hegemony. Another century passed before Ivan III, "the Great" (d. 1505) brought all of northern Russia under Moscow's control and ended Mongol rule (1480). By the last quarter of the fourteenth century, Moscow had become Russia's political and religious capital, and after Constantinople fell to the Turks in 1453, it declared itself the "third Rome" and the guardian of Orthodox civilization.

SUMMARY

The Black Death Between 1347 and the early fifteenth century, close to 40 percent of the population of western Europe was killed by the Black Death. People had no idea what the bubonic plague was, how it was transmitted, or how to treat the sick. The fear inspired by the disease itself, and by the responses to it, influenced European attitudes and religious beliefs for centuries. The sharp reduction in population changed fundamental social, economic, and political patterns. Increased demand and reduced supply of luxury goods brought more power and wealth to cities and to skilled artisans; the landed nobility suffered economically as demand for food diminished.

The Hundred Years' War and the Rise of National Sentiment The so-called Hundred Years' War between England and France actually lasted for more than a century, from 1337 to 1453, although there were long intervals of peace during this period. The direct cause of the war was controversy over the succession to the

boyars   Wealthy landowners among the freemen in late medieval Russia.

French throne. Despite a smaller population, less wealth, and fighting on enemy soil, England got the better of France in most of the significant early battles. England began the conflict as a more cohesive state than France. Eventually, however, the French began to see past regional rivalries, and Joan of Arc inspired an emergent national pride.

Ecclesiastical Breakdown and Revival: The Late Medieval Church
Through the thirteenth century, popes had worked to centralize church power. As nation-states gained cohesiveness, kings started to challenge papal authority. Throughout most of the fourteenth century, the papacy was based in Avignon, France, rather than Rome. The conciliar theory proposed that the pope just oversees a church that should rightfully be dominated by the faithful as a group. The Council of Basel in the fifteenth century provided a model of lay rights and responsibilities for other church and national organizations.

Medieval Russia Kiev was the most important city in Russia around the turn of the millennium, so Prince Vladimir of Kiev's selection of Greek Orthodoxy as the state religion had ramifications that endure to the present. Starting in the eleventh century, Kiev lost its preeminence, and Russians split into three geographic and cultural groupings: the Great Russians, the White Russians, and the Little Russians or Ukrainians. In 1223, Ghengis Khan sent a Mongol (or Tatar) army into Russia. The Golden Horde brought much of Russia into the Mongol Empire. Mongol rule ended in 1480, by which time Moscow was the dominant city within Russia. In contrast to western Europe, where the nobility, the clergy, and the peasantry constituted distinct and easily identifiable groups in Russia the main social division was between freemen and slaves.

REVIEW QUESTIONS

1. What were the causes of the Black Death? Why did it spread so quickly? What were its effects on European society? How important do you think disease is in changing the course of history?

2. What were the causes of the Hundred Years' War? What advantages did each side have? Why were the French ultimately victorious?

3. What changes took place in the church and in its relationship to secular society between 1200 and 1450? How did it respond to political threats from increasingly powerful monarchs? How great an influence did the church have on secular events?

4. What is meant by the term "Avignon papacy"? What caused the Great Schism? How was it resolved? Why did kings in the late thirteenth and early fourteenth centuries have more power over the church than it had over them? What did kings hope to achieve through their struggles with the church?

5. How did the Kievan and medieval Russian states develop in terms of religion, politics, and social structure? What effect did Mongol rule have on Russian lands?

IMAGE KEY
for pages 218–219

a. Chalice, French, c.1325 (silver gilt)

b. Flagellants in the Netherlands town of Tournai (Doornik), 1349. Flagellants, known as the Brothers of the Cross, scourging themselves as they walk through the streets in order to free the world from the Black Death (Bubonic Plague)

c. Lugged Two-handed Sword, circa 1600

d. Detail from an illustrated manuscript of Boccaccio's "Decameron," physicians apply leeches to an emperor   Jean-Loup Charmet/Science Photo Library/Photo Researchers, Inc.

e. Exterior of a church, Novgorod, Russia

f. Statue of Pope Boniface VIII. Museo Civico, Bologna.   Scala/Art Resource, NY

g. Death of Wat Tyler (d. 1381) in front of Richard II, killed by Lord Mayor Walworth for wishing to abolish serfdom, by Jehan Froissart, (ca. 1460–80)

h. "Joan of Arc." Franco-Flemish miniature. Anonymous, 15h century. Archives Nationales, Paris, France. Photograph copyright Bridgeman-Giraudon/Art Resource, NY

i. A Caricature of physicians (early sixteenth century)

KEY TERMS

Avignon Papacy   (p. 230)   **boyars**   (p. 234)   **Jacquerie**   (p. 226)
Black Death   (p. 220)   **Estates General**   (p. 226)

 For additional study resources for this chapter, go to:
www.prenhall.com/kagan3/chapter9

10 Renaissance and Discovery

CHAPTER HIGHLIGHTS

The Renaissance in Italy (1375–1527) The Renaissance was a period of transition between the medieval and modern worlds and a time of unprecedented cultural creativity. Italian city-states, fueled by their expanding trade networks, were great incubators for artistic expression, political innovation, and humanistic study.

Italy's Political Decline: The French Invasions (1494–1527) In the late fifteenth century, the balance of power between Italian city-states began to destabilize. The French king, Charles VIII invaded Italy and conquered Florence. A quarter century of military conflicts left Italy weak and politically fragmented.

Revival of Monarchy in Northern Europe Sovereign monarchies emerged in France, Spain, and England in the late fifteenth century. In France, Charles VII and, later Louis XI, expanded French territory, built trade and industry, and curbed the power of the nobility. In Spain, Isabella and Ferdinand created a united Spain that played a leading role in sixteenth-century European expansion. In England, Henry VII founded the Tudor dynasty and found ways to rule without consulting Parliament. The Holy Roman Empire failed to develop a strong centralized monarchy.

The Northern Renaissance The Renaissance spread from Italy to northern Europe. Northern humanists were interested in religious reforms and spreading humanism to a large audience, a task made easier by the invention of movable-type printing. In Germany, England, and France humanism laid the groundwork for the Reformation.

Voyages of Discovery and the New Empire in the West In the fifteenth century Europeans began a process of global expansion. Spain established an empire in Latin America, introducing Catholicism, new forms of social, political, and economic organization to the region, along with diseases to which the local population had no resistance. Spain's empire brought new ideas and products to Europe and led to inflation.

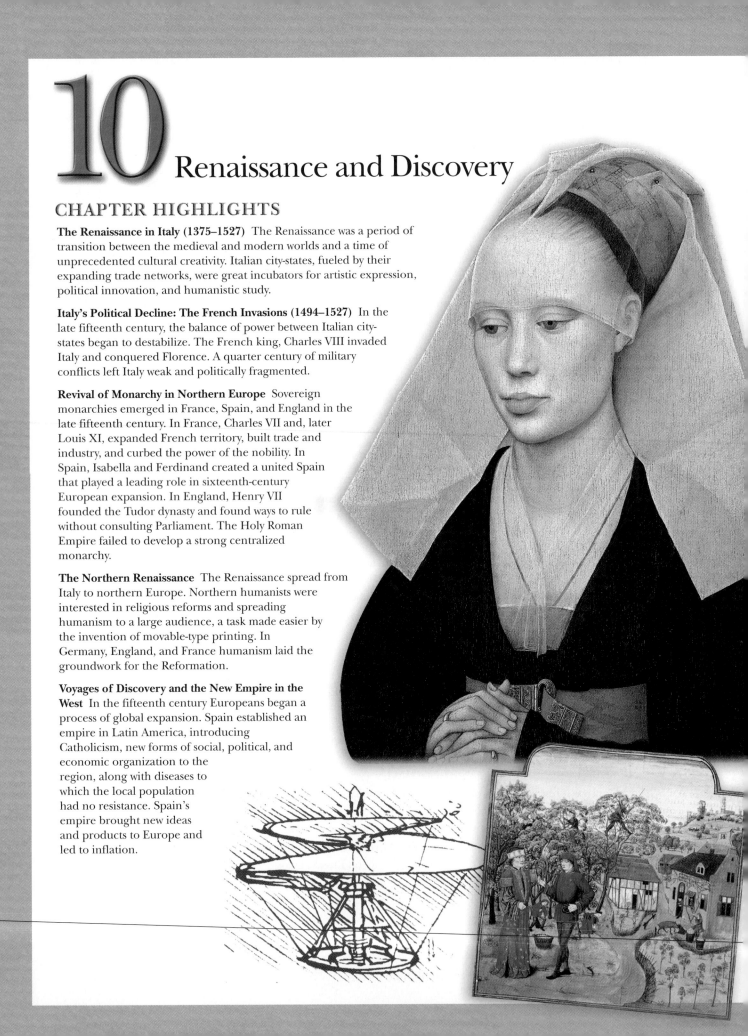

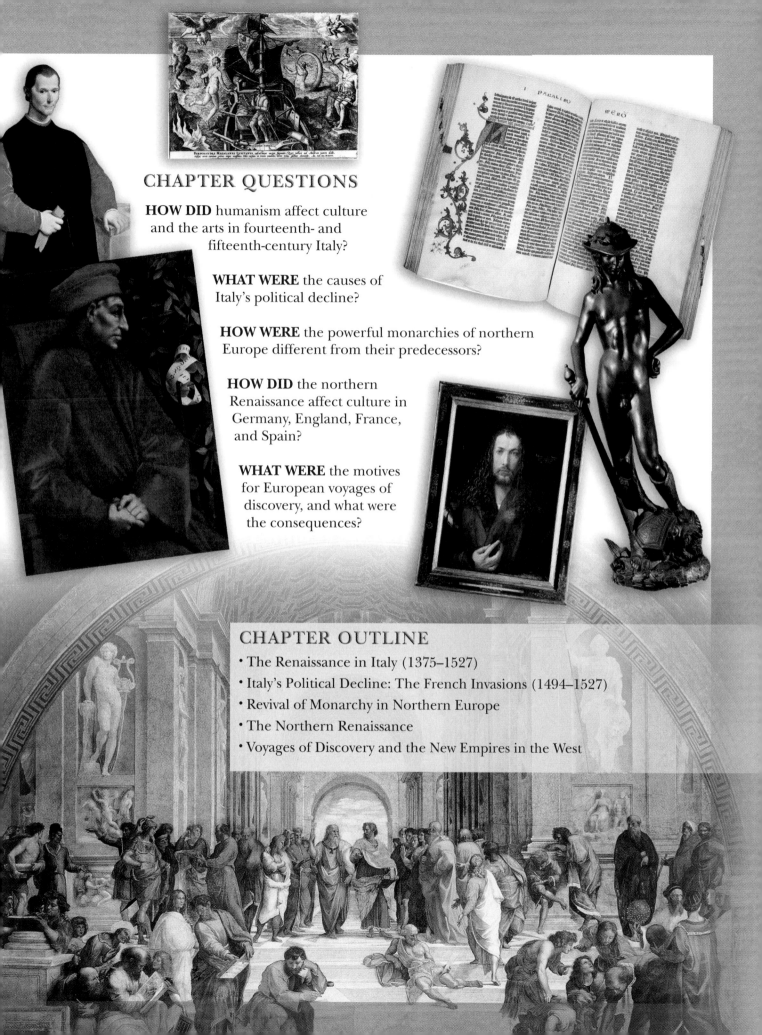

CHAPTER QUESTIONS

HOW DID humanism affect culture and the arts in fourteenth- and fifteenth-century Italy?

WHAT WERE the causes of Italy's political decline?

HOW WERE the powerful monarchies of northern Europe different from their predecessors?

HOW DID the northern Renaissance affect culture in Germany, England, France, and Spain?

WHAT WERE the motives for European voyages of discovery, and what were the consequences?

CHAPTER OUTLINE

• The Renaissance in Italy (1375–1527)
• Italy's Political Decline: The French Invasions (1494–1527)
• Revival of Monarchy in Northern Europe
• The Northern Renaissance
• Voyages of Discovery and the New Empires in the West

IMAGE KEY

Image Key for pages 236–237 is on page 260.

The late medieval period was an era of creative disruption. The social order that had persisted in Europe for a thousand years failed, but Europe did not decline. It merely changed direction. By the late fifteenth century, its population had nearly recovered from the losses inflicted by the plagues, famines, and wars of the fourteenth century. Able rulers were establishing stable, centralized governments, and Italy's city-states were doing especially well. Italy's strategic location enabled it to dominate world trade, which still centered on the Mediterranean. Italy's commercial wealth gave its leaders means to provide patronage for education and the arts and fund the famous Italian Renaissance.

Renaissance scholars, the humanists, revived the study of classical Greek and Latin languages and literature. They reformed education and, thanks to the invention of the printing press, became the first scholars able to reach out to the general public. In their eagerness to educate ordinary men and women, they championed the use of vernacular languages as vehicles for art and serious thought.

During the late fifteenth and the sixteenth centuries, powerful nations arose in western Europe and sponsored voyages of exploration that spread Europe's influence around the globe. The colonies they planted and empires they built yielded a flood of gold, information, and new materials that transformed the Western way of life.

THE RENAISSANCE IN ITALY (1375–1527)

HOW DID humanism affect culture and the arts in fourteenth- and fifteenth-century Italy?

The Renaissance began the transition from the medieval to the modern worlds. Medieval Europe was a fragmented feudal society with a marginal agrarian economy. Intellectually, it was dominated by the church. Renaissance Europe, after the fourteenth century, was characterized by political centralization, awareness of national identities, capitalistic urban economies, and an increasingly secular culture. These changes appeared first in Italy.

THE ITALIAN CITY-STATE

Italy's location had always given it cultural and commercial advantages over the rest of Europe. Italy dominated the Mediterranean Sea, the center of international trade, and the wealth and stimulating foreign influences that flowed through Italy promoted the growth of a unique urban culture. During the thirteenth and fourteenth centuries, Italy's towns extended their authority over the countryside and became city-states. (See Map 10–1.)

Growth of City-States The destiny of Italy's cities was shaped by endemic warfare between Guelf (pro-papal) and Ghibelline (pro-imperial) factions. If either the pope or the emperor had enjoyed a free hand in Italy, he might have brought its cities under control. Instead, each man tried to undercut the other, and the cities were the winners. They escaped dominance by kings and popes, took charge of the regions in which they were located, and became self-governing city-states. The five greatest were the duchy of Milan, the republics of Florence and Venice, the Papal States, and the kingdom of Naples.

Florentine women doing needlework, spinning, and weaving. These activities took up much of a woman's time and contributed to the elegance of dress for which Florentine men and women were famed.

Palazzo Schifanoia, Ferrara/Alinari Art Resource, NY

Social Class and Conflict Competition among leaders, political factions, and social classes contributed to instability in Italy's city-states and led, by the fifteenth century, to despots assuming power in most of them. Venice was a notable exception; it remained an oligarchic republic governed by a small group of merchant families.

Florence offers a more typical example of the evolution of a Renaissance city. Four groups jockeyed for advantage in Florence: the old rich (the *grandi*, the noble and established families that traditionally led); an emerging merchant class (wealthy capitalists and bankers—the *popolo grosso*, "fat people"); the middle-burgher ranks (guild masters, shop owners, and professionals); and the *popolo minuto* (the "little people"). In 1457, about one-third of the residents of Florence were listed as paupers—as having no wealth.

Despotism and Diplomacy In 1378, the economic dislocation caused by the Black Death prompted the Ciompi Revolt, a great uprising of the Florentine poor. Stability was not fully restored until Cosimo de' Medici (1389–1464), the richest man in Florence, took charge in 1434. Cosimo de' Medici was an astute statesman. He controlled the city from behind the scenes by skillfully manipulating its constitution and influencing elections. Florence was governed by the *Signoria*, a council of six (later, eight) men elected from the most powerful guilds. Cosimo's influence with the electoral committee ensured that his men dominated the *Signoria*, and his grandson, Lorenzo the Magnificent (1449–1492; r. 1478–1492), established a virtually totalitarian government. He was, however, careful to court popular support.

Despotism was less subtle elsewhere. Whenever internal fighting and foreign intrigue threatened to paralyze a city's government, its warring factions would agree to appoint a *podestà*. He was a neutral outsider, a hired strongman charged to do whatever was necessary to maintain law and order and foster a good climate for business. Because a despot could not depend on everyone's cooperation, he policed and protected his town with a mercenary army hired from military brokers called ***condottieri***. The *podestà's* job was hazardous. He might be dismissed by the oligarchy that hired him or assassinated by factions he offended. The potential spoils of his career were, however, worth the risk because a *podestà* might establish a dynasty. The Visconti family that ruled Milan after 1278 and the Sforza family that followed them in 1450 both had *podestà* founders.

The kind of government that maintained discipline in an Italian city seemed to have little effect on the climate it offered for intellectual and artistic activity. Despots promoted Renaissance culture as enthusiastically as republicans, and spiritually minded popes were no less generous than worldly vicars of Christ.

 MAP EXPLORATION
Interactive map: To explore this map further, go to
http://www.prenhall.com/kagan3/map10.1

MAP 10–1

Renaissance Italy   The city-states of Renaissance Italy were self-contained principalities whose internal strife was monitored by their despots and whose external aggression was long successfully controlled by treaty.

HOW DID city-states help shape the political climate of Renaissance Italy?

condottieri Military brokers from whom one could hire a mercenary army.

HUMANISM

Leonardo Bruni (1374–1444), a Florentine, was the first to describe the scholarship of the Renaissance as ***studia humanitas*** or **humanism**. Modern authorities do not agree on how to define humanism. Some claim it is an un-Christian philosophy emphasizing human dignity, individualism, and secular values. There were, however, Christian humanists who defended faith from attack by extreme rationalists. Humanism, for many of its Renaissance proponents, may have been less a philosophical position than an educational program. It championed the study of Latin and Greek classics and Christian church fathers as an end in itself and as a guide to reforming society. The first humanists were orators and poets, specialists in rhetoric. Some taught at universities, but many worked as secretaries, speech writers, and diplomats at princely and papal courts.

Italy's humanists were not the first Europeans to take an interest in the study of classical and Christian antiquities. There had been a Carolingian renaissance in the ninth century, and another was led by the cathedral school of Chartres in the twelfth century. The University of Paris was transformed by the study of Aristotle in the thirteenth century, and the works of Augustine of Hippo reinvigorated intellectual life in the fourteenth century. These scholarly revivals pale, however, in comparison with Italy's Renaissance.

The medieval Scholastics were governed by an evolving tradition that was created as they summarized and reconciled the views of respected commentators on the subjects they studied. Renaissance humanists swept aside layers of interpretation and went directly to original sources. They avidly searched out forgotten manuscripts to recover all that remained of ancient Greek and Latin literature, edited what they found, and made it generally available. They so assimilated the classics and so identified with the ancients that they came to think of the immediate past as a hiatus, a "dark middle age" during which civilization languished awaiting its rebirth in their own day.

10.1
Petrarch: Rules for the Ruler

Petrarch, Dante, and Boccaccio Francesco Petrarch (1304–1374), "the father of humanism," modeled his writing on the works of the giants of Roman literature. His *Letters to the Ancient Dead* was an imagined correspondence with Cicero, Livy, Vergil, and Horace. His epic poem *Africa* (a tribute to the Roman general Scipio Africanus) was conceived as a continuation of Vergil's *Aeneid*, and his biographies of famous Romans, *Lives of Illustrious Men*, were modeled on Plutarch's essays. Petrarch's most popular work, however, was not an imitation of the classics. It was a collection of highly introspective Italian love sonnets, which he addressed to a married woman named Laura. Like a medieval courtly lover, he worshiped her from afar.

Classical and Christian values coexist in Petrarch's work. He dismissed Scholasticism as sterile and useless, but he wrote tracts refuting Aristotelian arguments that undercut faith in personal immortality. His acceptance of many traditional medieval Christian beliefs is also apparent in the set of imaginary dialogues with the fifth-century saint, Augustine of Hippo, which he composed.

Petrarch's point of view was, however, more secular than that of his famous near contemporary, Dante Alighieri (1265–1321). Dante's *Vita Nuova* and *Divine Comedy* rank with Petrarch's sonnets as cornerstones of the new vernacular literature associated with the Renaissance, but they are also expressions of medieval piety. Petrarch's student, Giovanni Boccaccio (1313–1375), created bridges of another kind between medieval literature and humanism. His best known work, *Decameron*, is a collection of one hundred tales (many re-

***studia humanitas* (humanism)**
Scholarship of the Renaissance that championed the study of Latin and Greek classics and Christian church fathers as an end in itself and as a guide to reforming society. Some claim it is an un-Christian philosophy emphasizing human dignity, individualism, and secular values.

told from medieval sources), but he was famous in his own day for an encyclopedia of Greek and Roman mythology.

Educational Reforms and Goals   Humanists were activists. They believed the intensive study of the ancients would cure the ills that plagued contemporary society by teaching the practice of virtue. Humanist learning was intended to ennoble people by promoting the free use of their gifts of mind and body.

Traditional methods of education had to be reformed to nurture the kind of well-rounded people the humanists wanted to produce. The rediscovery in 1416 of the complete text of Quintilian's *Education of the Orator* provided them with a classical guide for the revision of curricula. Vittorino da Feltre (d. 1446) described the goals and methods of the reform. He advised students to master difficult works by Pliny, Ptolemy, Terence, Plautus, Livy, and Plutarch, but also to undergo vigorous physical training. Humanist learning was not confined to the classroom. Baldassare Castiglione's (1478–1529) influential *Book of the Courtier*, a practical guide for conduct at the court of Urbino, urged its readers to combine the study of ancient languages and history with the practice of athletic, military, and musical skills. Castiglione also warned that a true courtier needed more than good manners and accomplishments. He required exemplary moral character.

Women, most notably Christine de Pisan (1363?–1434), profited from educational reform and helped guide it. Christine's father was physician and astrologer to the court of King Charles V of France. At the French court she received as fine an education as any man and became an expert in classical, French, and Italian languages and literature. Married at fifteen and widowed with three children at twenty-seven, she turned to writing lyric poetry to support herself. Her works were soon being read at all the European courts. Her most famous book, *The Treasure of the City of Ladies*, chronicles the accomplishments of the great women of history.

The Florentine "Academy" and the Revival of Platonism   Italy's Renaissance differed from earlier revivals of interest in the past in its passionate devotion to Greek literature, particularly the works of Plato. In 1397, Florence invited a Byzantine scholar, Manuel Chrysoloras, to come to Italy and open a school offering training in Greek. More Greek scholars (bringing more manuscripts) arrived in 1439 to attend the Council of Ferrara-Florence and negotiate a reunion of the Greek and Latin churches. More Greeks arrived in 1453 as refugees following the Turkish conquest of Constantinople.

The Scholastics' enthusiasm for Aristotle led to a preoccupation with logic and science. The humanists' love of Plato promoted an interest in poetry and mysticism. Platonism's appeal lay in its flattering view of human nature and the fact that it could be more easily reconciled with Christianity than Aristotelianism. Platonism posited the existence of a realm of eternal ideas that were the prototypes for the imperfect, perishable things of this world. Plato claimed that human beings had an innate knowledge of mathematical truths and moral standards that proved they were rooted in the eternal.

Cosimo de' Medici (1389–1464) encouraged the study of Plato and the Neoplatonic philosophers by founding the Platonic Academy, a gathering of influential Florentine humanists headed first by Marsilio Ficino (1433–1499) and

Christine de Pisan, who has the modern reputation of being the first European feminist, presents her internationally famous book, *The Treasure of the City of Ladies*, also known as *The Book of Three Virtues*, to Isabella of Bavaria amid her ladies in waiting.

Historical Picture Archive/CORBIS/Bettmann

later by Pico della Mirandola (1463–1494). The Platonism to which the Florentine scholars introduced Europe was more confident about the potential of human nature than medieval Christianity. Pico's *Oration on the Dignity of Man* boldly articulated the Renaissance's humanistic faith. Published in Rome in December 1486, the *Oration* was a preface to a collection of nine hundred theses that Pico proposed for a public debate. It lauded human beings as the only creatures endowed with the freedom to create themselves—to become angels or pigs.

Critical Work of the Humanists: Lorenzo Valla   The humanists' careful study of classical languages sometimes had unexpected consequences. Lorenzo Valla (1406–1457), a papal secretary who wrote the era's standard text on Latin philology (*Elegances of the Latin Language*), published a devastating critique of *The Donation of Constantine*. Since the eighth century, popes had used the *Donation* to bolster their claim to authority over emperors, but Valla proved on linguistic grounds the document was a forgery that could not have dated from the era of the emperor Constantine. He also pointed out errors in the Vulgate, the church's authorized Latin Bible.

Civic Humanism   Although some humanists were clubbish snobs whose narrow, antiquarian interests appealed only to an intellectual elite, others advocated a "civil humanism," an educational program designed to foster virtue and equip people for public service. They entered politics, employed their artistic and literary skills to promote their cities, urged scholars to use the vernacular so ordinary people could profit from their work, and wrote histories of contemporary events.

RENAISSANCE ART

The Renaissance (like the later religious movement, the Reformation) reversed the medieval tendency to value the clerical lifestyle more highly than that of the laity. Its affirmation of secular values and purely human pursuits led to significant adjustments in medieval Christian attitudes. Europe's increasing "this-worldliness" also owed something to the crises within the papacy that diminished the medieval church's power and prestige. The new attitudes were consistent, as well, with the rise of patriotic nationalism, the increasing prominence of laypersons in governmental bureaucracies, and the rapid growth of educational opportunities for the laity in the late medieval period.

The new perspective on life can be perceived in the painting and sculpture of the "high," or mature, Renaissance (the late fifteenth and early sixteenth centuries). Whereas medieval art was abstract and formulaic, Renaissance art described the natural world and expressed human emotions. Its rational (mathematical) organization and its focus on symmetry and proportionality reflect the humanistic faith in a harmonious, intelligible universe.

Artists developed techniques during the fifteenth century that allowed them to do new things. Slow-drying oil-based paints, new methods of drafting, the use of *chiaroscuro* (shading to enhance naturalness), linear perspective, the adjustment of the size of figures to create the illusion of depth—all promoted greater realism. Whereas two-dimensional Byzantine and Gothic paintings were intended to be read like pages in a book, Renaissance paintings were windows on a three-dimensional world filled with life. (See "Encountering the Past: The Garden.")

Giotto (1266–1336), the father of Renaissance painting, was the first to intuit what could be done with the new techniques. He dealt with serious religious themes, but his work was less abstract and more naturalistic than that of a medieval painter. The Black Death of 1340 slowed the development of art, but Giotto's ideas were taken up in the fifteenth century by the painter Masaccio (1401–1428)

Vitruvian Man, by Leonardo da Vinci, c. 1490. Like most Ranaissance artists, Leonardo sought to portray human beauty and perfection. This sketch is named after the first-century C.E. Roman architect Marcus Pollio Vitruvius, who used squares and circles to demonstrate the human body's symmetry and proportionality.

ENCOUNTERING THE PAST

THE GARDEN

Gardens were sources of both necessities and pleasures for the people of the Middle Ages and the Renaissance, and every household from the grandest to the humblest had one. In addition to their practical functions, gardens had religious and social associations. They were enclosed behind walls, fences, or hedges to protect their contents, and they served as private retreats in a world that offered little shelter for privacy. They called to mind the Garden of Eden and the more sensuous pleasures of the garden described in the Bible's Song of Songs (4:12). They were symbols of paradise and reminders of the temptations that led to Adam's fall.

Wealthy people had gardens (adorned with grottoes and fountains) that were designed primarily for pleasure. They provided ideal settings for the romantic trysts of courtly lovers. Even great houses, however, like the cottages of the poor, also had gardens devoted to much more utilitarian purposes. A medieval/Renaissance household depended on its garden for much of its food and medicine. The fruit it produced was mainly used to concoct sweet drinks, and it was the source of the limited range of vegetables medieval people consumed: cabbage, lentils, peas, beans, onions, leeks, beets, and parsnips. The herbs and flowers from gardens were highly prized as flavorings for a diet heavy on bland, starchy foods. They were also the era's most effective medicines.

A wealthy man oversees apple picking at harvest time in a fifteenth-century French orchard. In the town below, individual house gardens can be seen. Protective fences, made of woven sticks, keep out predatory animals.

By permission of The British Library

and the sculptor Donatello (1386–1466). The heights were reached by the great masters of the High Renaissance: Leonardo da Vinci (1452–1519), Raphael (1483–1520), and Michelangelo Buonarroti (1475–1564).

Leonardo da Vinci   Leonardo came closer than anyone to achieving the Renaissance ideal of universal competence. He was one of the greatest painters of all time—as his famous portrait, the *Mona Lisa*, demonstrates. He also had one of the great scientific minds of his age. He was in demand as a military engineer. He did significant descriptive work in botany. He defied the church by dissecting corpses to study human anatomy, and he filled sketch books with designs for such modern machines as airplanes and submarines. He had so many ideas it was difficult for him to concentrate long on any one of them.

Raphael   Raphael, an unusually sensitive man, was loved for both his work and his kindly personality. He is best known for his tender depictions of madonnas. Art historians consider his fresco *The School of Athens*, a group portrait of the great Western philosophers, a perfect example of Renaissance technique.

Combining the painterly qualities of all the Renaissance masters, Raphael created scenes of tender beauty and subjects sublime in both flesh and spirit.

Musee du Louvre, Paris/Giraudon, Paris/SuperStock

mannerism Reaction against the simplicity, symmetry, and idealism of High Renaissance art. It made room for the strange, even the abnormal, and gave free reign to the subjectivity of the artist. The name reflects a tendency by artists to employ "mannered" ("affected") techniques—distortions that expressed individual perceptions and feelings.

WHAT WERE the causes of Italy's political decline?

Michelangelo   Michelangelo, like Leonardo, excelled in several fields. His *David*, an eighteen-foot-high sculpture of a biblical hero in the guise of a Greek god, splendidly illustrates the Renaissance artist's devotion to harmony, symmetry, and proportion—and to the glorification of the human form. Four different popes commissioned works from Michelangelo. The most famous are the frescoes that Pope Julius II (r. 1503–1513) ordered for the Vatican's Sistine Chapel. They originally covered 10,000 square feet and featured 343 figures—most of which Michelangelo executed himself with minimal help from his assistants. It took him four years to complete the extraordinarily original images, some of which have become the best known icons of the Christian faith.

Michelangelo lived to be nearly ninety, and his later works illustrate the passing of the High Renaissance and the advent of a new style called **mannerism**. Mannerism was a reaction against the simplicity, symmetry, and idealism of High Renaissance art. It made room for the strange, even the abnormal, and gave free reign to the subjectivity of the artist. The name reflects a tendency by artists to employ "mannered" ("affected") techniques—distortions that expressed individual perceptions and feelings. The Venetian Tintoretto (d. 1594) and the Spanish El Greco (d. 1614) represent mannerism at its best.

SLAVERY IN THE RENAISSANCE

The vision of innate human nobility that inspired the Renaissance's artists and thinkers was marred by what modern observers would consider a major inconsistency. Slavery flourished in Italy as extravagantly as art and culture. Spaniards began to sell Muslim war captives to wealthy Italians as early as the twelfth century. Slaves were usually employed as domestic servants, but the slave-based sugarcane plantations that the Venetians established on Cyprus and Crete during the High Middle Ages provided the model for later New World slavery.

The demand for slaves soared after the Black Death (1348–1350) reduced the supply of laborers throughout western Europe. A strong young slave cost the equivalent of the wages paid a free servant over several years. Given the prospect of a lifetime of free service, however, slaves were a good bargain. If need be, their owners could also recover their capital by reselling them, for legally they were private property. Most well-to-do Italian households had slaves, and even the clergy owned them.

Slavery was not based on any concept of race, and peoples from Africa, the Balkans, Constantinople, Cyprus, Crete, and the lands surrounding the Black Sea were enslaved. As in ancient Greece and Rome, slaves of the Renaissance era were often integrated into households like family members. Some female slaves became mothers of their masters' children, and quite a few of these children were adopted and raised as legitimate heirs. It was in owners' self-interest to protect their investments by keeping their slaves healthy and happy, but slaves were uprooted, resentful people who posed a threat to social stability.

ITALY'S POLITICAL DECLINE: THE FRENCH INVASIONS (1494–1527)

Italy's ability to defend itself from foreign invasion depended on the ability of its independent city-states to work together. During the last half of the fifteenth century, the Treaty of Lodi (1454–1455) allied Milan and Naples (traditional enemies) with Florence against Venice and the Papal States and created a balance of power that helped stabilize Italy internally. The peace established by the Treaty of Lodi ended in 1494 when Naples, Florence, and Pope Alexander VI joined forces to oppose Milan. The despot who ruled Milan, Ludovico il Moro, appealed to France for help. France had ruled Naples from 1266 to 1435, and its young king, Charles VIII (r. 1483–1498), was eager to win it back.

CHARLES VIII'S MARCH THROUGH ITALY

Charles responded to Ludovico's call with lightning speed. It took him only five months to cross the Alps (August 1494) and drive through the territory of Florence and the Papal States to Naples. When Piero de' Medici, Florence's ruler, tried to placate the French king by ceding him the city of Pisa and other Florentine possessions, the radical preacher Girolamo Savonarola (1452–1498) rallied the angry Florentines, and they drove Piero into exile. Savonarola claimed that France's invasion was God's punishment for Florence's sins, and he persuaded the Florentines to do penance by submitting to Charles and paying him a ransom to spare their city. Savonarola dominated Florence for four years, but the Florentines eventually tired of his puritanical tyranny and executed him (May 1498).

Charles's advance into Italy alarmed Spain's Ferdinand of Aragon. He viewed an axis of Franco-Italian states as a threat to his homeland, and he proposed an alliance of Aragon, Venice, the Papal States, and the Emperor Maximilian I against the French. When Milan, which had come to regret inviting the French into Italy, joined Ferdinand's League of Venice, Charles was forced to retreat.

POPE ALEXANDER VI AND THE BORGIA FAMILY

An alliance between Louis XII (r. 1498–1515), Charles's successor, and Pope Alexander VI (r. 1492–1503) allowed the French to return to Italy. Alexander, a member of the infamous Borgia family, may have been the church's most corrupt pope. His intent was to create a hereditary duchy for his son Cesare by using the power of the papacy to recover Romagna, a district on the Adriatic coast northeast of Rome that had broken free from the Papal States while the papacy was headquartered in Avignon. Venice's opposition to this scheme caused the pope to break with the League of Venice and side with France.

France, with papal assistance, conquered Milan, and the pope's reward was the hand of the sister of the king of Navarre for his son and the promise of French military aid in Romagna. In 1500, Louis and Ferdinand of Aragon agreed on a division of the Kingdom of Naples, and the pope and Cesare completed the conquest of Romagna.

POPE JULIUS II

Julius II (r. 1503–1513), the "warrior pope," suppressed the Borgias and reclaimed Romagna for the papacy. Julius's reign marked the pinnacle of the Renaissance papacy's military prowess and convoluted diplomatic maneuvers. Once he had established firm control over Romagna (1509) and the Papal States, he set about ridding Italy of his former allies, the French. To this end, he formed a second Holy League with Ferdinand of Aragon and Venice in October 1511. Emperor Maximilian I and the Swiss also signed on, and by 1512, the alliance had forced the French to retreat.

Significant Dates from the Italian Renaissance (1375–1527)

1434	Medici rule established in Florence
1454–1455	Treaty of Lodi
1494	Charles VIII of France invades Italy
1495	League of Venice
1499	Louis XII invades Italy
1500	The Borgias conquer Romagna
1512–1513	The Holy League defeats the French
1515	Francis I invades Italy
1527	Sack of Rome by imperial soldiers

QUICK REVIEW

The Warrior Pope

- Julius II's (r. 1503–1513) reign marked the pinnacle of the papacy's military prowess

- After securing Romagna and the Papal States, he set about pushing the French out of Italy

- Julius formed a Holy League with Ferdinand of Aragon and Venice in 1511 for this purpose

The French were, however, nothing if not persistent. Louis's successor, Francis I (r. 1515–1547), invaded Italy yet again and dealt a severe blow to the Holy League by defeating the Swiss at Marignano in September 1515. The Habsburg emperor then stepped into the breach and launched the first of four Habsburg-Valois wars—none of which France won.

Francis had better luck in dealing with the pope. In August 1516, the pope agreed to the Concordat of Bologna. He ceded Francis control over the French clergy in exchange for the right to continue to collect certain fees from the French clergy and France's support for the pope's campaign to repudiate conciliarism. By virtually nationalizing the French Catholic church, the Concordat ensured that France's kings would have nothing to gain by embracing the Reformation that was soon to sweep Germany and Switzerland.

10.2
Machiavelli: From the
Discourses

NICCOLÒ MACHIAVELLI

As the armies of France, Spain, and Germany made a shambles of Italy, Niccolò Machiavelli (1469–1527), a Florentine scholar, struggled to make sense of the tragedies befalling his homeland. Italy's experience persuaded him that political ends—the maintenance of peace and order—are justified by any means.

Machiavelli's humanist education had included a close, if somewhat romanticized, study of the history of ancient Rome. He was impressed by the apparent ability of the Romans to act decisively and heroically for the good of their country, and he lamented the absence of such traits among his compatriots. He believed that if Italians ceased their feuding and worked together, they could defend their country from invaders. Machiavelli was devoted to republican ideals, but political realities convinced him that only a strongman could rescue the Italians from the consequences of their shortsighted behavior. The salvation of Italy required, he believed, a cunning dictator who was willing to use "Machiavellian" techniques to manipulate his people.

Machiavelli may have intended *The Prince*, which he wrote in 1513, to be a satire on politics, not a serious justification for despotism. However, he seems to have been in earnest when he defended fraud and brutality as necessary means to the higher end of unifying Italy. Machiavelli hoped the Medici family might produce the leader Italy needed. In 1513, its members controlled both the papacy (Leo X, r. 1513–1521) and Florence. *The Prince* was dedicated to Lorenzo de' Medici, duke of Urbino and grandson of Lorenzo the Magnificent. The Medicis, however, failed to rise to the challenge Machiavelli set them, and in the year he died (1527), a second Medici pope, Clement VII (r. 1523–1534), watched helplessly as the army of Emperor Charles V sacked Rome—an event that some scholars see as marking the end of the Renaissance. (See "History's Voices: Machiavelli Discusses the Most Important Trait for a Ruler.")

Santi di Tito's portrait of Machiavelli, perhaps the most famous Italian political theorist, who advised Renaissance princes to practice artful deception and inspire fear in their subjects if they wished to be successful.

Scala/Art Resource, NY

HOW WERE the powerful monarchies of northern Europe different from their predecessors?

REVIVAL OF MONARCHY IN NORTHERN EUROPE

Medieval monarchies tended to be weak, for various factions jockeyed for advantage within them. Vassals sought maximum independence from their lords, and nobles, clergy, and townsmen joined forces in representative assemblies (such as the English Parliament, the French Estates General, the German Diet, and the Spanish *Cortés*) to moderate royal authority. By 1450, however, kings had won the upper hand in many parts of Europe and true sovereigns were establishing themselves in control of national monarchies.

HISTORY'S VOICES

MACHIAVELLI DISCUSSES THE MOST IMPORTANT TRAIT FOR A RULER

achiavelli believed that the most important personality trait of a successful ruler was the ability to instill fear in his subjects.

HOW WOULD you describe Machiavelli's views about the nature and characteristics of man?

Here the question arises: whether it is better to be loved than feared or feared than loved. The answer is that it would be desirable to be both but, since that is difficult, it is much safer to be feared than to be loved, if one must choose. For on men in general this observation may be made: they are ungrateful, fickle, and deceitful, eager to avoid dangers, and avid for gain, and while you are useful to them they are all with you, offering you their blood, their property, their lives, and their sons so long as danger is remote, as we noted above, but when it approaches, they turn on you. Any prince, trusting only in their words and having no other preparations made, will fall to his rain, for friendships that are bought at a price and not by greatness and nobility of soul are paid for indeed, but they are not owned and cannot be called upon in time of need. Men have less hesitation in offending a man who is loved than one who is feared, for love is held by a bond of obligation which, as men are wicked, is broken whenever personal advantage suggests it, but fear is accompanied by the dread of punishment which never relaxes.

Niccolò Machiavelli, *The Prince* (1513), trans. and ed. by Thomas G. Bergin (New York: Appleton-Century- Crofts. NY. 1947). p. 48.

Towns were crucial in effecting this political transition. Townspeople made feudalism anachronistic by taking over many of the functions of the feudal nobility. They helped kings reclaim the powers of taxation, war making, and law enforcement that feudalism had delegated to semiautonomous vassals. As these vassals ceded these functions to centralized governments, the people who lived on their fiefs began to look beyond them to their monarch and to develop "national" consciousness. The hereditary nobility cultivated a local power base, but the loyalty of a monarch's professional civil servants (such as the Spanish *corregidores*, the English justices of the peace, and the French bailiffs) was to the state.

The machinery of bureaucratic government gave kings the instruments they needed to enforce their decrees directly and to bypass feudal councils and representative assemblies. Ferdinand and Isabella, who ruled Spain at the end of the fifteenth century, rarely called the *Cortés* into session. The French Estates General did not meet from 1484 to 1560. And after 1485, when England's Parliament granted Henry VII (r. 1485–1509) the right to collect the customs revenues he needed to cover the costs of government, the king summoned no more parliaments.

By the fifteenth century, monarchs had also begun to create standing armies that ended the feudal nobility's traditional military monopoly. Professional soldiers who fought for pay and booty were more efficient than feudal vassals who fought for honor's sake. Changing weaponry and tactics (artillery, for instance) also shifted the emphasis on the battlefield away from the noble cavalry and to the common man's infantry. The strength of infantry derives from numbers, and monarchs wanted large armies. Professional soldiers tend to mutiny, however, if payrolls are not met. Royal governments had, therefore, to find sources of income to meet the rising costs of warfare in the fifteenth and sixteenth centuries. Efforts to expand royal revenues were hampered by the upper classes' attitude toward taxation.

Feudal tradition held that the king should meet the costs of his government, as his vassals did, from the income of his personal estates. Nobles considered taxation demeaning, and their fierce resistance tempted kings to take the easier route of shifting the tax burden to their less powerful and far less wealthy subjects.

Monarchs had several sources of income. They collected rents from the royal domain. They levied national taxes on basic food and clothing. France, for instance, had a tax on salt, and Spain had a 10 percent sales tax. Rulers could also, with the approval of parliamentary bodies (in which the lower classes had no representation), levy direct taxes on the peasantry. The French monarch collected such a tax, the *taille*, and set new rates for it annually. Governments sometimes sold public offices, issued high-interest bonds, and leaned heavily on bankers for loans. A king's most powerful subjects were often also his creditors.

FRANCE

Charles VII (r. 1422–1461) was a king made great by those who served him. His ministers created a permanent professional army, which Joan of Arc inspired to drive the English out of France. An enterprising merchant banker, Jacques Coeur, served the king as a kind of finance minister and strengthened France's economy, diplomatic corps, and central administration. These tools helped Charles's son, the ruthless Louis XI (r. 1461–1483), turn France into a great power.

The rise of France in the fifteenth century followed the defeat of two opponents: the king of England and the duke of Burgundy. The Hundred Years' War ended the threat England posed to France, but at the war's end the duchy of Burgundy, England's sometime ally, was Europe's strongest state. Its ruler, Charles the Bold, intended to use his considerable military might to link up his scattered possessions and form a "middle kingdom" between France and Germany. A coalition of continental powers formed to block him, and after his death in battle in 1477, the dream of a Burgundian empire faded.

Louis XI and the Habsburg emperor, Maximilian I, divided up Burgundy's lands. The Habsburgs got the better parts, but Burgundy's fall left Louis XI free to concentrate on France's internal affairs. He fostered trade and industry, disciplined the feudal nobility, and ended his reign with a kingdom almost twice the size of the one with which he had started.

The dream of conquering Italy distracted Louis's successors from focusing, as he had, on the consolidation of royal power in France. The long series of losing wars they fought with the Habsburgs left their country, by the mid–sixteenth century, almost as divided internally as it had been during the Hundred Years' War.

SPAIN

In 1469, the marriage of Isabella, queen of Castile (r. 1474–1504), and Ferdinand, king of Aragon (r. 1479–1516), laid a foundation for a monarchy ruling most of the Iberian peninsula. Castile was the richer and more populous of the two kingdoms, having about 5 million inhabitants to Aragon's 1 million. Castile also had a lucrative, centrally managed sheep-farming industry run by a state-backed agency called the *Mesta*.

The two Spanish kingdoms were united by the royal marriage, but each retained its own government agencies, laws, armies, coinage, taxation, and cultural traditions. Ferdinand and Isabella were, however, able to do together what neither could do alone: bring the nobility under control, secure the borders of their realms, launch wars of conquest, and enforce a common Christian faith among all their subjects. In 1492, they conquered Granada, the last Muslim state on the

Iberian peninsula. Naples became a Spanish possession in 1504, and by 1512, Ferdinand had completed the conquest of Aragon's northern neighbor, the kingdom of Navarre.

Ferdinand and Isabella relied on the *Hermandad*, a league of cities and towns, for help in subduing the powerful landowners who dominated the countryside. Townspeople replaced nobles within the royal administration, and the monarchy circumscribed the power of the nobility by exerting its authority over wealthy chivalric orders.

Spain had long been remarkable among European lands as a place where Islam, Judaism, and Christianity managed to coexist—and sometimes cooperate. Ferdinand and Isabella, however, sought to unify their country by imposing a state-controlled Christian church on all their subjects, and they greatly strengthened the Inquisition (the ecclesiastical court that tried cases of heresy) to enforce religious conformity in Spain. In 1479, the Inquisition's director, Isabella's confessor, Tomás de Torquemada (d. 1498), assumed responsibility for policing the activities of the forced converts—the *conversos* (former Jews) and the *Moriscos* (Muslims). In 1492, the Jews who refused to convert were exiled and their properties confiscated by the crown. In 1502, the same fate befell the Moors of Granada. Rigorous enforcement of orthodoxy kept Spain a loyal Catholic country and made it a base of operations for the Counter-Reformation, the Catholic Church's program for regaining ground lost to the Protestant Reformation in the sixteenth century.

The marriages arranged for Ferdinand and Isabella's children were part of a grand plan to surround and contain France, and they shaped Europe's political destiny for a century. In 1496, Ferdinand and Isabella's eldest daughter and heir, Joanna ("the Mad") wed Archduke Philip, the son of the Habsburg emperor, Maximilian I. Charles V, the child of this union, inherited Spain, Flanders-Burgundy, and the Habsburgs' central European domain. His election as Holy Roman Emperor in 1519 gave him some authority over Germany and Italy as well—creating an empire almost as large as Charlemagne's. Ferdinand and Isabella's second daughter, Catherine of Aragon, wed Arthur, heir to England's king, Henry VII. Following Arthur's early death, she married his brother and became the first of King Henry VIII's six wives. The Spanish portion of Charles's legacy also included the lands in the Western Hemisphere that the Genoese explorer, Christopher Columbus (1451–1506), had claimed for his sponsors, Ferdinand and Isabella. Mexico and Peru yielded a flood of gold and silver that helped Spain dominate Europe during the sixteenth century.

ENGLAND

The last half of the fifteenth century was an especially difficult period for the English. In the wake of England's loss of the Hundred Years' War, a fight broke out between two branches of its royal family, the House of York and the House of Lancaster. This began a thirty-year-long dynastic struggle called the Wars of the Roses. (York's heraldic emblem was a white rose and Lancaster's a red rose.) From 1455 to 1485, England was in a state of turmoil.

The war began when Henry VI (r. 1422–1461), a weak king from the Lancastrian house, was challenged by his more competent cousin, the duke of York. In 1461, the duke of York's son seized power as Edward IV (r. 1461–1483). Although his reign was interrupted (1470–1471) by a short-lived restoration of Henry VI, Edward recovered the throne and did much to restore the power and wealth of the monarchy. Edward's brother, Richard III (r. 1483–1485), usurped

QUICK REVIEW

Unification of Spain

- Aragon and Castile unified by marriage of Ferdinand and Isabella
- 1492: The last Muslim state in the Iberian peninsula, Granada, falls
- Ferdinand and Isabella sought to create religious uniformity in their lands by force

the throne from Edward's young heirs, and he was, in turn, overthrown by Henry Tudor, a distant relation who had inherited the leadership of the Lancastrian faction. Henry's victory terminated the medieval Plantagenet line and launched the Tudor dynasty. Shakespeare's powerful play *Richard III*, which depicts Richard as an unprincipled villain, reflects the influence of Tudor propaganda.

Henry VII (Henry Tudor, r. 1485–1509) wed Edward IV's daughter, Elizabeth of York, and her bloodline provided added legitimacy for the Tudor dynasty. In 1487, Henry further secured the monarchy, winning Parliament's sanction for the establishment of the Court of Star Chamber. This court had jurisdiction over cases involving noblemen, and the king found it a useful instrument for intimidating the English nobles and forcing them to submit to his control. Henry construed legal precedents to the advantage of the crown, and he found excuses for confiscating so much property that he did not have to convene Parliament to raise the money he needed to govern. Thanks in part to Henry, Queen Elizabeth I, his granddaughter, was among early modern Europe's most effective rulers.

THE HOLY ROMAN EMPIRE

Germany and Italy were exceptions to the general trend toward political centralization that swept Europe during the last half of the fifteenth century. Germany's rulers often reverted to the ancient practice of partitioning their lands among all their male heirs, and by the end of the Middle Ages, Germany was divided into some three hundred autonomous entities. The powerlessness of its fragmented governments helps explain the success of the revolution that produced the Protestant Reformation.

In 1356, the Holy Roman Emperor and the major German territorial rulers agreed on arrangements that helped stabilize Germany. The emperor's **Golden Bull** limited participation in the election of emperors to a college of seven "electors": the archbishops of Mainz, Trier, and Cologne, the duke of Saxony, the margrave of Brandenburg, the count of Palatine, and the king of Bohemia. It acknowledged that the emperor reigned more than ruled. (The extent of his powers, especially over the seven electors, was to be renegotiated with each imperial election.) In the fifteenth century, a national convention (the imperial diet, or *Reichstag*) began to meet on a regular basis. It provided opportunities for the seven electors, the nonelectoral princes, and Germany's sixty-five imperial free cities to debate and agree on common policies.

In 1495, the diet won concessions from Maximilian I (r. 1493–1519) that brought more order to a disorderly country. It banned private warfare, established a court (the *Reichskammergericht*) to enforce peace, and appointed an imperial Council of Regency (the *Reichsregiment*) to coordinate the development of policy. Although these reforms were helpful, they fell far short of the creation of a centralized state. The territorial princes were virtually sovereign rulers in their domains throughout the sixteenth and seventeenth centuries.

Golden Bull Arrangements agreed to by the Holy Roman Emperor and the major German territorial rulers in 1356 that helped stabilize Germany.

HOW DID the northern Renaissance affect culture in Germany, England, France, and Spain?

THE NORTHERN RENAISSANCE

Renaissance humanism nourished interest in religious and educational reforms, and an environment favorable to change evolved as knowledge of the works of Italy's humanists spread throughout Europe. The Brothers of the Common Life, an influential lay religious movement in the Netherlands, founded schools that became important centers of humanist scholarship in northern Europe.

The northern humanists developed an identity of their own. They tended to come from more diverse social backgrounds and to be more interested in religious reform than their Italian colleagues. They were also more willing to write for lay audiences. This was to have significant consequences, for a printing press with movable type appeared in the mid–fifteenth century. For the first time in history, the press enabled intellectual elites to argue their cases before the public and spark mass movements.

THE PRINTING PRESS

Since the days of Charlemagne, Europe's rulers had understood the importance of schools and literacy. Effective government required a staff of officials who could read, think critically, keep records, and write accurate reports. During the late Middle Ages, the number of universities in Europe tripled from twenty to sixty, and these schools spread literacy far beyond the ranks of the clergy.

However, it was not only schools that made literacy a more common skill. Late medieval inventions made writing materials more affordable. In the early Middle Ages, scribes copied out books longhand on expensive sheets of leather called *vellum.* Books were extremely costly. A complete text of the Bible, for instance, required 170 calfskins or 300 sheepskins. A block of wood was sometimes carved and inked to produce a single-sheet woodcut print—a kind of medieval poster.

In the mid–fifteenth century, the growing demand for books prompted Johann Gutenberg (d. 1468) of Mainz to invent printing with movable type. This and the development of a process for manufacturing inexpensive paper dramatically reduced costs of production and vastly multiplied the number of books. Booksellers were soon making books and pamphlets (on subjects ranging from theology to farming and child rearing) available to the public in all price ranges. The new technology generated a great demand, and the number of presses exploded. By 1500 (about fifty years after Gutenberg opened his shop), printers were operating in over two hundred of Europe's cities.

Spreading literacy equipped more and more people with an enhanced sense of self-esteem and a critical frame of mind. The print revolution gave everyone access to standardized texts, and access to a common fund of information made anyone who could read an authority. Ordinary men and women became less credulous and docile than their ancestors, but print also gave their rulers a powerful tool for manipulating them.

ERASMUS

The career of Desiderius Erasmus (ca. 1466–1536), the most famous of the northern humanists, illustrates the impact of the printing press. Erasmus was both an educational and a religious reformer—one of many loyal Catholics who advocated religious reform before the Protestant Reformation erupted.

Erasmus was a prolific writer who supplemented his income as a tutor. For his students he wrote a popular collection of short Latin dialogues called *Colloquies.* They provided people with inspiring examples of how to live as well as models of how to speak, and thus they promoted both reform and literacy. Erasmus's interest in religious reform prompted him to expand their subsequent editions to include anticlerical dialogues and satires of religious superstitions. He offered more helpful, practical advice in a popular collection of proverbs entitled *Adages.* It went through many editions and expanded from 800 examples to over 5,000. It is the source of common expressions such as "Leave no stone unturned," and "Where there is smoke, there is fire."

Albrecht Dürer (1471–1528). "Portrait of the Moorish Woman Katharina." Drawing. Uffizi Florence, Italy.

Photograph ©Foto Marburg/Art Resource, NY

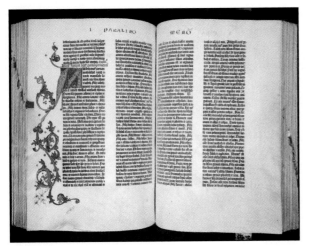

The printing press made possible the diffusion of Renaissance learning. No book stimulated more at this time than did the Bible. With Gutenberg's publication of a printed Bible in 1454, scholars gained access to a dependable, standardized text, so Scripture could be discussed and debated as never before.

This item is reproduced by permission of The Huntington Library, San Marino, California

Erasmus advocated a life that combined the classical ideals of humanity and civic virtue with the Christian virtues of love and piety. He believed disciplined study of the classics and the Bible would reform individuals and society, and he opposed anyone, Catholic or Protestant, who let doctrine and disputation take precedence over pious humility and the practice of Christian principles. He characterized his position as the *philosophia Christi* (philosophy of Christ): simple, ethical piety modeled on Christ's life.

Erasmus used his knowledge of classical languages to produce an improved text of the Bible based on the best manuscript sources available to him. His Greek edition of the New Testament in 1516 became the basis for the publication of a more accurate Latin Vulgate in 1519. He believed that a pure, unadulterated scriptural text was the best guide for reforming contemporary society, but church authorities were unsettled by the so-called improvements he made to their traditional Bible (and by his popular satires of the clergy). At one point in the mid–sixteenth century, the church placed all of Erasmus's works on a list of books that Catholics were not supposed to read. Luther, the Protestant leader, also condemned some of Erasmus's views. Both his friends and foes, however, used the scholarly tools he forged to promote reform.

HUMANISM AND REFORM

Humanism encouraged educational and religious reforms, but with different results in different parts of Europe.

Germany   Italian learning was introduced to German intellectual circles by Rudolf Agricola (1443–1485). Conrad Celtis (d. 1508), the first German poet laureate, and Ulrich von Hutten (1488–1523), a knight, gave German humanism a nationalistic tinge that promoted hostility to non-German (especially Roman) cultures. Hutten attacked indulgences, published an edition of Valla's exposé of the *Donation of Constantine*, and was killed taking part in a revolt of the German knights against their princes.

The so-called Reuchlin affair helped create common ground for reform-minded German humanists. About 1506, the Dominican friars of Cologne and a man named Pfefferkorn—a convert to Christianity from Judaism—inaugurated a campaign to suppress Jewish literature. Pfefferkorn attacked Johann Reuchlin (1455–1522), a respected scholar who was Europe's foremost Christian authority on Judaism. Reuchlin was the first Christian to compile a reliable Hebrew grammar, and he was personally attracted to Jewish mysticism. Concern for academic freedom (not Judaism) prompted many German humanists to come to Reuchlin's defense, and the controversy produced one of the great books of the period, the *Letters of Obscure Men* (1515), a merciless satire of monks and Scholastics. It also predisposed humanists to support Martin Luther in 1517, when some of the same people who attacked Reuchlin attacked Luther.

England   English scholars and merchants and touring Italian prelates introduced humanism to England. Erasmus lectured at Cambridge and made a close friend of Thomas More (1478–1535), the most famous of the English humanists. More's *Utopia* (1516), a critique of contemporary values, ranks with the plays of Shakespeare as one of the most read pieces of English literature from the sixteenth century. *Utopia* described an imaginary society that overcame social and political injustice by holding all property and goods in common and requiring all persons to earn their bread by their own labor.

OVERVIEW   HUMANISM AND REFORM

Germany	• Rudolf Agricola, the father of German humanism, brought Italian learning to Germany.
	• German humanism was given a nationalist coloring hostile to non-German cultures.
	• The Reuchlin affair caused the unification of reform-minded German humanists.
	• When Martin Luther came under attack in 1517, many German humanists rushed to his side.
England	• Thomas More is the best known English humanist.
	• More's *Utopia* depicted a tolerant, just society that held property and goods in common.
	• Humanism in England played a key role in preparing the way for the English Reformation.
France	• Guillaume Budé and Jacques Lefèvre d'Etaples were the leaders of French humanism.
	• Lefèvre's works exemplified the new critical scholarship and influenced Martin Luther.
	• A new generation was cultivated by Marguerite d'Angoulême.
	• The future Protestant reformer John Calvin was a product of this native reform circle.
Spain	• Unlike the other countries, in Spain humanism entered the service of the Catholic Church.
	• Francisco Jiménez de Cisneros was the key figure in Spanish humanism.
	• In Jiménez's *Complutensian Polygot Bible*, Hebrew, Greek, and Latin appeared together.
	• This with church reform helped keep Spain strictly Catholic in the Age of Reformation.

Humanism in England, as in Germany, paved the way for the Protestant Reformation, but some humanists, such as More and Erasmus, remained steadfastly loyal to the Roman Catholic Church. More, one of Henry VIII's chief councillors, resigned his office and was executed in July 1535 for refusing to accept the king's decision to divorce Catherine of Aragon and break with the papacy.

France France's invasions of Italy led to Italy's humanism invading France. Guillaume Budé (1468–1540), an accomplished Greek scholar, and Jacques Lefévre d'Etaples (1454–1536), a biblical authority, led the movement. Lefèvre's work exemplified the kind of critical scholarship that stimulated Martin Luther's thinking and brought on the Reformation. Marguerite d'Angoulême (1492–1549), sister of King Francis I, queen of Navarre, and a noted spiritual writer, provided patronage for a generation of young reform-minded French humanists. The Protestant reformer, John Calvin, was among them.

Spain In Spain, humanism served to strengthen the Catholic faith more than challenge it. The country's leading humanist was Francisco Jiménez de Cisneros (1437–1517), confessor to Queen Isabella and, after 1508, the Grand Inquisitor and Spain's chief defender of orthodoxy. In 1509, he founded the University of Alcalé near Madrid. He sponsored printing of a Greek edition of the New Testament, and he translated religious tracts that were used to reform clerical life and train the clergy to guide the pious practices of the laity. His greatest achievement was the *Complutensian Polyglot Bible*, a six-volume edition of the Hebrew, Greek, and Latin texts of the Bible in parallel columns.

WHAT WERE the motives for
European voyages of discovery,
and what were the consequences?

VOYAGES OF DISCOVERY AND THE NEW EMPIRE IN THE WEST

*T*he discovery of the Americas dramatically expanded the geographical and intellectual horizons of Europeans. Commercial supremacy progressively shifted from the Mediterranean and Baltic Seas to the Atlantic seaboard, while knowledge of the New World's inhabitants and the exploitation of its mineral and human wealth set new cultural and economic forces in motion throughout western Europe.

THE PORTUGUESE CHART THE COURSE

In 1415 Prince Henry "the Navigator" (1394–1460), brother of the king of Portugal, captured the North African Muslim city of Ceuta, thus beginning the Portuguese exploration of the African coast. His and subsequent quests had aims that were religious—converting Muslims and pagans to Christianity—and mercenary—trading in gold, spices, and slaves. By the century's end, the Portuguese had found a sea route around Africa to Asia's spice markets. The pepper and cloves obtained from this trade preserved and enhanced the dull European diet, and in the fifty years before 1500, Portuguese ships delivered 150,000 slaves to Europe.

Prior to this sea route, Europeans could only get spices through the Venetians, who traded with Muslim merchants in Egypt and the Ottoman Empire. By sailing directly to Asia, the Portuguese beat this powerful monopoly, but the first voyages were slow and tentative: with each attempt to round the next cape, sailors feared that winds would not return them to land. Each navigational step down the African coast became a victory and a lesson, giving the crews the skills they needed to cross the oceans to the Americas and East Asia.

In addition to mercantile advantage, the explorations raised hope of Christian victories against the Muslims, along with mass conversions. In 1455, a self-interested pope granted the Portuguese voyagers all the spoils of war—land, goods, and slaves—from the West African coast to the Indies in East Asia.

Bartholomew Dias (ca. 1450–1500) pioneered the eastern Portuguese Empire in 1487 after safely rounding the Cape of Good Hope at the tip of Africa. In 1498, Vasco da Gama (1469–1525) reached India, returning to Portugal with a cargo of spices worth sixty times the cost of the voyage. The Portuguese would later establish Indian colonies, directly challenging the Arab and Venetian spice trade.

The Spanish aimed to find a shorter route to the East Indies by sailing westward across the Atlantic. Instead, Christopher Columbus (1451–1506) discovered the Americas.

THE SPANISH VOYAGES OF COLUMBUS

Thirty-three days after departing the Canary Islands on October 12, 1492, Columbus landed in San Salvador (Watlings Island) in the eastern Bahamas. He mistook his first landfall as an island of Japan—understandable, since Columbus had been relying in part on Martin Behaim's map of the presumed world, in which only ocean and Cipangu (Japan) divided the Europe's west coast and Asia's east coast. Only in 1498, while on his third voyage to the Caribbean, did Columbus realize he had not reached Japan and China.

Naked, friendly natives—Taino Indians—met Columbus and his crew. They amazed him with their generosity, as they freely gave his men all the corn, yams,

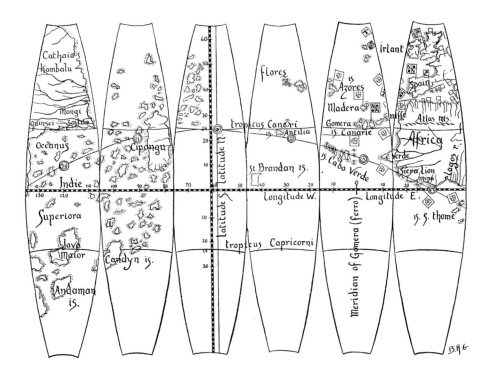

and sexual favors they desired. He also observed how easily the Spanish could enslave them. Believing he had landed in the East Indies, Columbus called these people Indians, a name that stuck with Europeans.

Subsequently, Amerigo Vespucci (1451–1512), after whom America is named, and Ferdinand Magellan (1480–1521) explored the South American coastline, confirming that Columbus had indeed discovered an entirely unknown continent. Magellan was continuing the search for a westward route to the Indies, and sailed around South America to the Philippines. Although killed there in a skirmish, his squadron sailed on to Spain and became the first sailors to circumnavigate the globe.

INTENDED AND UNINTENDED CONSEQUENCES

Columbus's first voyage marked the beginning of more than three centuries of a vast Spanish empire in the Americas. The Christian wars of Aragon and Castile against Islamic Moors in Spain had ended in 1492, yet the zeal for conquering and converting non-Christians persisted, helping to turn voyages of discovery into expeditions of conquest.

The voyages created Europe's largest and longest-surviving trading bloc and spurred colonial ventures from other European countries. Wealth from America financed Spain's religious and political wars in Europe and fueled a Europe-wide economic expansion. Europeans introduced many new fruits, vegetables, and animals into the Americas, and brought American species back home. Diseases were exchanged, too: Vast numbers of Native Americans died from measles and smallpox epidemics, while Europeans died from a form of syphilis that may have come from America. For the Native Americans, the voyages of discovery began a long history of conquest, disease, and slave labor. Spanish rule left a lasting imprint of Roman Catholicism, economic dependency, and hierarchical social structure, all still visible today. (See Map 10–2.)

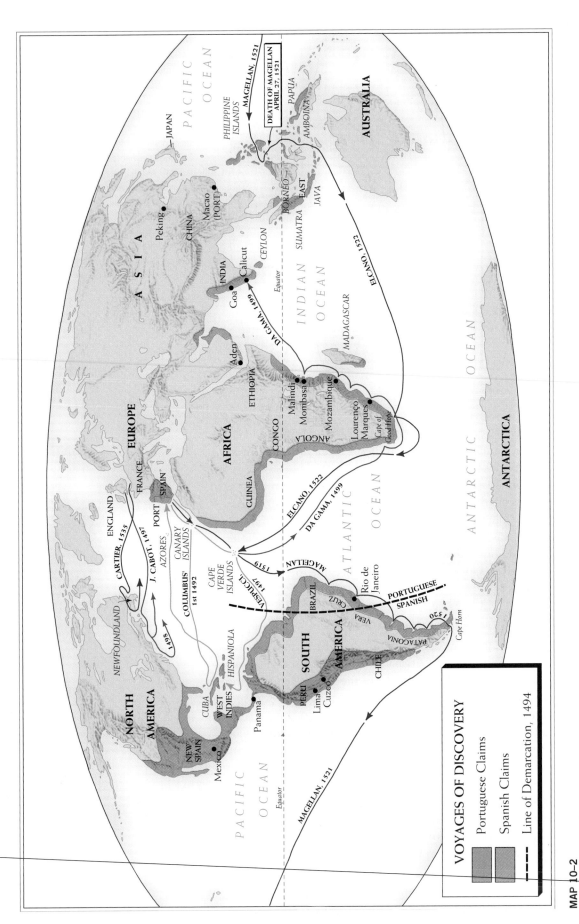

MAP 10–2

European Voyages of Discovery and the Colonial Claims of Spain and Portugal in the Fifteenth and Sixteenth Centuries
The map depicts Europe's global expansion in the fifteenth and sixteenth centuries.

WHAT REASONS did European explorers have for their many voyages of discovery?

THE SPANISH EMPIRE IN THE NEW WORLD

The Aztecs   When the first Spanish explorers arrived, Mesoamerica was dominated by the Aztecs and Andean America by the Incas. The forebears of the Aztecs settled the Valley of Mexico early in the twelfth century, and in 1428, one of their chiefs, Itzcoatl, inaugurated an era of rapid conquest that built an Aztec Empire ruled from the city of Tenochtitlán (Mexico City). The Aztecs extorted heavy tribute from the peoples they subjugated, for their religion held that their gods must literally be fed on human blood. The thousands of captives they claimed for sacrifice each year spread fear and resentment among their subject peoples.

In 1519, Hernán Cortés landed on the coast of Mexico with a mere five hundred men. Montezuma, the Aztec ruler, may initially have believed Cortés was the Aztec god Quetzalcoatl, who had departed centuries earlier but promised to return. Montezuma tried to appease Cortés with gold, but this only stimulated the Spaniards' appetites. Cortés's forces marched on Tenochtitlán and captured Montezuma, who died under unexplained circumstances. The Aztecs rose up and nearly wiped the Spaniards out, but Cortés returned, and in 1521, he defeated the last Aztec ruler, Cuauhtemoc (ca. 1495–1525). He razed Tenochtitlán and built a new capital on its site to govern a territory he called "New Spain."

The Incas   The Incas of the highlands of Peru rapidly expanded the territory under their control in the fifteenth century, and by the time the Spaniards arrived, the Incas ruled an empire that rivaled that of the Chinese and the Ottoman Turks. Instead of tribute, they exacted military service and labor on public works projects from their subjects.

In 1531, Cortés's example prompted Francisco Pizarro to land on the western coast of South America and invade the Inca Empire. He had only two hundred men, but guns, swords, and horses gave them a great advantage over the Incas. Pizarro lured the Inca chief Atahualpa to a conference where he seized him and killed hundreds of his followers. Atahualpa paid a huge ransom in gold, but in 1533, Pizarro executed him. Insurrections by the natives and squabbles among the Spaniards prolonged the struggle to impose royal control over the sprawling Inca territories until the late 1560s.

The conquests of Mexico and Peru are among the most brutal episodes in modern world history. Small numbers of European invaders subdued large strong empires in a remarkably brief period of time. They owed much of their success to the diseases they inadvertently spread to the Americas. Illnesses to which Europeans had evolved defenses devastated Native Americans, who had quite different immune systems. In addition to the wholesale loss of life, whole civilizations and much of the evidence of their histories and achievements were also destroyed. Native American cultures endured, but they had to change to accommodate European dominance. The Spanish conquest began the process that turned South America into Latin America.

THE CHURCH IN SPANISH AMERICA

Many of the priests who accompanied Spain's invading armies were imbued with the social and religious ideals of humanism. They were eager to convert the Native Americans to the "philosophy of Christ" and to civilization as Europeans knew it. Conquest created opportunities for missionary work, but some priests objected to the treatment given subjugated native peoples. Bartolomé de Las

10.4
Bartholomé de La Casas: "*Amerindians and The Garden of Eden*"

Casas (1474–1566), a Dominican friar, wrote an exposé of the situation that prompted the Spanish government to issue some reforming regulations. Las Casas's work also become the source of the "Black Legend," a tradition that has exaggerated Spanish cruelty and soft-pedaled such things as Aztec human sacrifice.

The church in Spanish America quickly became one of the chief props for colonialism. It prospered, like the Spanish laity, by exploiting the resources and peoples of the New World. As a great landowner, it ceased to voice objections to any but the most extreme modes of Spanish economic dominance, and by the time the colonial era came to an end in the late eighteenth century, the church had become one of the most conservative forces in Latin America.

THE ECONOMY OF EXPLOITATION

The Americas were quickly drawn into the Atlantic economy and the world of competitive European commercialism. For the native peoples of Latin America—and later the blacks of Africa—that meant various forms of forced labor. The colonial economy of Latin America had three components: mining, agriculture, and shipping.

Mining   The early **conquistadores** ("conquerors") were primarily interested in finding gold, but by the middle of the sixteenth century, silver mining had become the major source of metallic wealth. The chief mining centers were Potosí in Peru and various smaller sites in northern Mexico. The Spanish crown received one-fifth (the *quinto*) of all mining revenues and held a monopoly on the production and sale of the mercury used to process silver. Mining by forced native labor for the benefit of Spaniards epitomized the extractive economy that was fundamental to colonial life.

Agriculture   Slavery and the importation of black Africans was introduced to the Americas on sugar plantations in the West Indies (Cuba, Hispaniola, Puerto Rico, and other islands). It was an extension of a system of forced labor that the Spanish and the Portuguese had previously used in Europe.

The agricultural institution that characterized most Spanish colonies was not a slave-based plantation but a large landed estate called a **hacienda**. Its owners were either *peninsulares*, individuals born in Spain, or *creoles*, persons of Spanish descent born in America. Some kind of formal servitude bound the people who worked a hacienda to its owners, and they were usually bound to the land and prevented from moving from the service of one master to another.

Labor Servitude   The Spaniards developed several strategies for exploiting the labor of the native Indians. The earliest was the *encomienda*, a legal grant of the right to the labor of a specific number of Indians for a particular period of time. Spain's monarchs were suspicious of this arrangement, for they feared the holders of *encomienda* might establish a powerful, independent aristocracy in the New World. The *encomienda* was gradually phased out in favor of the *repartimiento*, a kind of tax paid in labor. It required all adult male Indians to devote a certain number of working days annually to Spanish economic enterprises. *Repartimiento* duty was often extremely harsh. The temptation was to work men who were obligated only for a limited term of service literally to death, for they were due to be replaced anyway. Eventually a shortage of workers and the crown's opposition to extreme kinds of forced labor led to employment of free laborers. The freedom of Indian workers was, however, more apparent than real. They had to purchase

conquistadores
"Conquerors"

hacienda Large landed estate that characterized most Spanish colonies.

encomienda Legal grant of the right to the labor of a specific number of Indians for a particular period of time. This was used as a Spanish strategy for exploiting the labor of the natives.

the goods they needed from the land and mine owners who employed them, and this led to debt *peonage*—a lifetime struggle to pay off an ever-mounting obligation.

Deaths in combat, by forced labor, and from European diseases had devastating demographic consequences for Indian communities. Within a generation of the conquest, the Indian population of New Spain (Mexico) shrank from 25 million to 2 million.

THE IMPACT ON EUROPE

The loss of life and destruction of cultures in the New World was a mixed blessing for the Old World. The bullion that flowed into Europe through Spain vastly increased the amount of money in circulation and fueled an inflation rate of 2 percent a year. In Spain prices doubled by 1550 and quadrupled by 1600. In Luther's Wittenberg, the cost of basic food and clothing increased almost 100 percent between 1519 and 1540. Wages and rents, in contrast, lagged well behind the rise in prices.

The new money enabled governments and private entrepreneurs to sponsor basic research and industrial expansion. The economic thinking of the age favored the creation of monopolies, the charging of high interest for loans, and the free and efficient accumulation of wealth. The late fifteenth and the sixteenth centuries saw the maturation of this type of capitalism and its attendant social problems. Owners of the means of production were ever more clearly separated from the workers who produced. The new wealth raised expectations among the poor and encouraged reactionary behavior by the rich.

The revolutionary passions that found expression in the Reformation were fed by resentment of the social distinctions that were becoming increasingly visible and even by the discoveries of explorers like Columbus. Europeans learned there was much more to the world than their ancestors had imagined. This emboldened them to criticize traditional institutions and sparked their appetite for innovations—especially those that promised freedom and a chance at a better life.

Armored Spanish soldiers, under the command of Pedro de Alvarado (d. 1541) and bearing crossbows, engage unprotected and crudely armed Aztecs, who are nonetheless portrayed as larger than life by Spanish artist Diego Duran (sixteenth century).

Codex Duran: Pedro de Alvarado (c. 1485–1541), companion-at-arms of Hernando Cortés (1845–1547) besieged by Aztec warriors (vellum) by Diego Duran (16th Century), Codex Duran, Historia De Las Indias (16th century). Biblioteca Nacional, Madrid, Spain. The Bridgeman Art Library International Ltd.

SUMMARY

The Renaissance in Italy (1375–1527) The Renaissance first appeared in Italy and thrived from 1375 to 1527. This period, a transition between the medieval and modern worlds, was a time of unprecedented cultural creativity. Italian city-states, with their extensive trade networks and their competition with one another, were great incubators for artistic expression, political innovation, and humanistic studies. The significance of "humanism" is debated by scholars today, but for Renaissance Italians humanism implied studies of Classical languages and arts that offered moral preparation for a life of virtuous action. Authors and artists, including Petrarch, Dante, Boccaccio, Leonardo da Vinci, Raphael, and Michelangelo, exemplify the values of Renaissance humanism.

IMAGE KEY

for pages 236–237

a. Rogier van der Weyden (Netherlandish, 1399.1400-1464), "Portrait of a Lady". 1460.   370 x .270 (14 1/16 x 10 5/8); framed: .609 x .533 x .114 (24 x 21 x 4 1/2). Photo: Bob Grove. Andrew W. Mellon Collection. Photograph © Board of Trustees, National Gallery of Art, Washington, D.C.

b. Plan by Leonardo da Vinci for a flying machine

c. 15th century French orchard

d. Santi di Tito (1536-1603), "Portrait of Niccolo Machiavelli (1469–1527)." Italian philosopher and writer. Palazzo Vecchio, Firenze

e. Cosimo de' Medici (1389–1464) Jacopo Pontormo (1494–1556), "Cosimo de' Medici the Elder, Pater Patriae," (1389–1464). Oil on wood, 87 x 65 cm. Inv. 3574. Uffize, Florence. Photograph © Erich Lessing/Art Resource, NY

f. School of Athens, from the Stanza della Segnatura, 1510–11 (fresco) by Raphael (Raffaello Sanzio of Urbino) (1483–1520)

g. Ferdinandes Magalanes Lusitanus (Magellan)

h. Bible. 1450–55

i. Donatello (1386–1466), "David" (Frontal view)   Museo Nazionale del Bargello, Florence. Nimatallah/Art Resource, NY

j. Albrecht Dürer (1471–1528), "Self-portrait at age 28 with fur coat" 1500.   Oil on wood, 67 x 49 cm. Alte Pinakothek, Munich, Germany. Photograph ©Scala/Art Resource, NY

Italy's Political Decline: The French Invasions (1494–1527) In the late fifteenth century, the balance of power among Italian city-states that had been enforced by the Treaty of Lodi started to unravel. In 1495, at the invitation of the Milanese leader Ludovico il Moro, French king Charles VIII invaded Italy and conquered Florence. This invasion triggered several rounds of diplomacy, alliance making, and strategic marriages involving families of popes, the leaders of Italian city-states, French kings, and the rulers of Aragon and Brittany, among others. A quarter century of military conflicts led to political fragmentation and military weakness in Italy. In 1513, Niccolò Machiavelli wrote *The Prince*, in which he argued that only a strong and cunning dictator could unify Italy.

Revival of Monarchy in Northern Europe Sovereign monarchies, in which kings and their appointed agents—usually townspeople, not nobility—control national policies on taxation, warfare, and law enforcement, emerged in France, Spain, and England in the late fifteenth century. In France, Charles VII and, later, Louis XI were able to capitalize on the French victories over England and Burgundy, to expand French territory, build trade and industry, and suspend the Estates General. In Spain, Isabella of Castile and Ferdinand of Aragon married in 1469, and they proceeded to impose state control on religion, arrange marriages for their children that would shape future European history, and sponsor global exploration. In England, Henry VII founded the Tudor dynasty and found ways to govern without consulting Parliament. The Holy Roman Empire (Germany) was northern Europe's chief example of a country that failed to develop a strong centralized monarchy.

The Northern Renaissance The Renaissance spread from Italy to northern Europe through traders and merchants, students, religious practitioners, and others. Northern humanists, however, were more interested in religious reforms and in spreading humanism to a broad audience than Italian humanists had been. Gutenberg's invention of the moveable-type printing press facilitated the wide dissemination of texts. Erasmus exemplified northern humanists' interest in reform of the Catholic Church. In Germany, England, and France, humanism laid the groundwork for the Reformation, but in Spain, the humanist movement, like most other aspects of culture, was controlled by Ferdinand and Isabella, and therefore did not challenge the church.

Voyages of Discovery and the New Empire in the West In the fifteenth century, Europeans began the process of expansion that eventually led to European control over huge regions of the globe. Searching for gold, spices, and later, slaves, the Portuguese, Spanish, and others established maritime trade routes to the coasts of Africa, India, and the Americas. Spain established an empire in what became Latin America, introducing Catholicism, new forms of social, political, and economic organization—including servitude—and diseases to which the indigenous peoples had no resistance. Mexico lost approximately 92 percent of its population within a generation after the Spanish conquest. Spain's empire brought new ideas and products to Europe and led to inflation.

REVIEW QUESTIONS

1. How would you define Renaissance humanism? In what ways was the Renaissance a break with the Middle Ages? Who were the leading literary and artistic figures of the Italian Renaissance? What defined them as people of the Renaissance?

2. What was the purpose and outcome of the French invasion of Italy in 1494? Given the cultural productivity of Renaissance Italy, is it a valid assumption that creative work thrives best in periods of calm and peace?

3. How did the northern Renaissance differ from the Italian Renaissance? In what ways was Erasmus the embodiment of the northern Renaissance?

4. What prompted the voyages of discovery? How did the Spanish establish their empire in the Americas? What did native peoples experience during and after the conquest?

KEY TERMS

condottieri   (p. 239)

conquistadores   (p. 258)

encomienda   (p. 258)

Golden Bull   (p. 250)

hacienda   (p. 258)

mannerism   (p. 244)

studia humanitas **(humanism)**
(p. 240)

   For additional study resources for this chapter, go to:
www.prenhall.com/kagan3/chapter10

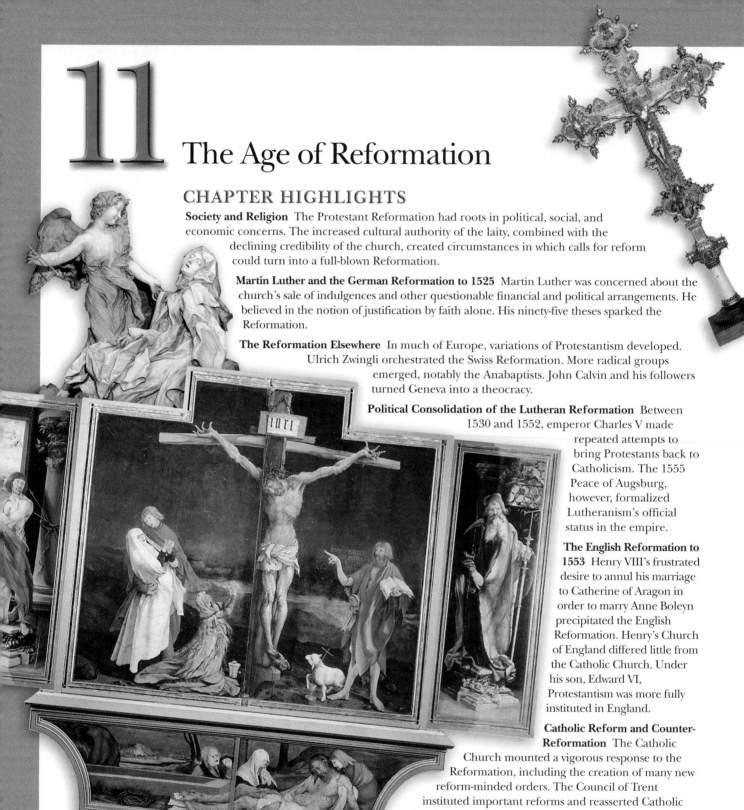

11

The Age of Reformation

CHAPTER HIGHLIGHTS

Society and Religion The Protestant Reformation had roots in political, social, and economic concerns. The increased cultural authority of the laity, combined with the declining credibility of the church, created circumstances in which calls for reform could turn into a full-blown Reformation.

Martin Luther and the German Reformation to 1525 Martin Luther was concerned about the church's sale of indulgences and other questionable financial and political arrangements. He believed in the notion of justification by faith alone. His ninety-five theses sparked the Reformation.

The Reformation Elsewhere In much of Europe, variations of Protestantism developed. Ulrich Zwingli orchestrated the Swiss Reformation. More radical groups emerged, notably the Anabaptists. John Calvin and his followers turned Geneva into a theocracy.

Political Consolidation of the Lutheran Reformation Between 1530 and 1552, emperor Charles V made repeated attempts to bring Protestants back to Catholicism. The 1555 Peace of Augsburg, however, formalized Lutheranism's official status in the empire.

The English Reformation to 1553 Henry VIII's frustrated desire to annul his marriage to Catherine of Aragon in order to marry Anne Boleyn precipitated the English Reformation. Henry's Church of England differed little from the Catholic Church. Under his son, Edward VI, Protestantism was more fully instituted in England.

Catholic Reform and Counter-Reformation The Catholic Church mounted a vigorous response to the Reformation, including the creation of many new reform-minded orders. The Council of Trent instituted important reforms and reasserted Catholic doctrine.

The Social Significance of the Reformation in Western Europe The Reformation revolutionized religious practice and institutions in the areas where it took strongest root. Protestant reformers helped disseminate humanism along with new visions of the nature of marriage and family.

Family Life in Early Modern Europe Marriage occurred later in life in the early modern period. Parents were involved in arranging their children's marriages. A nuclear family with two to four children was the norm. Parents demonstrated their love of their children and marriage partners in ways that reflected the realities of early modern life.

Literary Imagination in Transition Cervantes lived and worked in Catholic Spain. Shakespeare was a product of Protestant England. Their writings reflect the different conditions and concerns of their respective countries.

CHAPTER QUESTIONS

WHAT WAS the social and religious background of the Reformation?

WHY DID Martin Luther challenge the church?

WHERE DID other reform movements develop and how were they different from Luther's?

WHAT WERE the political ramifications of the Reformation?

HOW WAS the English Reformation more political than theological?

WHAT WAS the Counter-Reformation?

WHAT WAS the social significance of the Reformation and how did it affect family life?

WHAT WAS family life like in early modern Europe?

HOW WAS the transformation from medieval to modern reflected in the works of the great literary figures of the era?

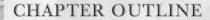

CHAPTER OUTLINE

- Society and Religion
- Martin Luther and the German Reformation to 1525
- The Reformation Elsewhere
- Political Consolidation of the Lutheran Reformation
- The English Reformation to 1553
- Catholic Reform and Counter-Reformation
- The Social Significance of the Reformation in Western Europe
- Family Life in Early Modern Europe
- Literary Imagination in Transition

IMAGE KEY
Image Key for pages 262–263 is on page 288.

WHAT WAS the social and religious background of the Reformation?

In the second decade of the sixteenth century, a powerful religious movement began in northern Germany. Reformers, attacking what they believed to be superstitions and abuses of authority, rebelled against the medieval church. The Protestant Reformation that resulted from their efforts opposed aspects of the Renaissance—especially the optimistic view of human nature that humanist scholars derived from classical literature. The reformers did, however, embrace some Renaissance ideas, particularly educational reforms and training in ancient languages that equipped scholars to go to the original sources of important texts. Protestant challenges to Catholic practices were based on appeals to the Hebrew and Greek Scriptures.

SOCIETY AND RELIGION

A struggle between the rulers who were centralizing governments of nation-states and the towns and regions that were fighting to preserve their autonomy set the stage for the Reformation. During the fourteenth century, the king's law began (almost everywhere) to supersede local law and custom. Many townspeople and village folk saw rebellion against the church as a part of a wider fight to limit encroachment on their liberties.

The Reformation began in the free cities of Germany and Switzerland. There were about sixty-five of these, and most developed Protestant movements even if they did not ultimately become Protestant towns. In their efforts to defend themselves against intervention in their affairs by princes, cities were hampered by deep internal social and political divisions. Some factions favored the Reformation more than others. Guilds whose members were prospering and rising in social status were often in the forefront of the Reformation, but less distinguished groups were also attracted to the Protestant revolt. People who felt pushed around by either local or distant authorities tended, at least initially, to develop Protestant sympathies. The peasants on the land responded as much as the townsfolk, for their freedoms, too, were eroded by princely governments.

Many converts to Protestantism saw religion and politics as two sides of the same coin. When Protestant preachers scorned the authority of ecclesiastical landlords and ridiculed papal laws as arbitrary human inventions, they touched political as well as religious nerves. An attack on the legitimacy of the one kind of authority translated easily into a critique of the other.

POPULAR RELIGIOUS MOVEMENTS AND CRITICISM OF THE CHURCH

The Protestant Reformation was partially a response to the crises in leadership that the church suffered in the late Middle Ages: the papacy's "exile" in Avignon, the Great Schism, the conciliar movement, and the flagrant worldliness of the Renaissance popes. These troubling developments prompted many clergy and laity to become increasingly critical of traditional teachings and spiritual practices. They prompted calls for reform and widespread religious experimentation.

The laity were less subservient to the clergy in the late medieval period than in earlier eras. Urban residents had opportunities for travel (as merchants, pilgrims, soldiers, and explorers) that increased their understanding of the wider world and politics. The establishment of postal systems and printing presses made more information available to them. Easier access to books and libraries improved their literacy rates, and humanist educational reforms encouraged them to take more responsibility for themselves.

The lay religious movements that preceded the Reformation were all inspired by an ideal of apostolic poverty. They urged all Christians (and especially clergy) to model their lives on the example Jesus and his disciples set in the Gospels. They wanted a more egalitarian church that gave a voice to its members, and they wanted a more spiritual church that emulated the simplicity of the church described in the New Testament.

The Modern Devotion   One of the most constructive lay religious movements of the period was led by the Brothers of the Common Life. They exemplified the "Modern Devotion," a religious discipline inaugurated by Gerard Groote (1340–1384), that spread through northern Europe from its base in the Netherlands. The brothers brought clergy and laity together in quasi-monastic communities. Lay members did not take formal vows, wear religious dress, or abandon their secular vocations, but they shared a common life that stressed individual piety and practical religion. Thomas à Kempis (d. 1471) captured the spirit of the movement in a perennially popular devotional tract, the *Imitation of Christ.* This guide to the inner life was intended for monks and nuns, but it spoke to laity who sought spiritual growth through the practice of ascetic disciplines.

The Brothers of the Common Life flourished at a time when the laity's appetite for good preaching and religious instruction was increasing. The brothers helped meet this need by running schools, working as copyists, sponsoring publications, and running hospices for poor students. The noted humanists Erasmus and Reuchlin began their training with the brothers.

The Modern Devotion has been credited with inspiring humanist, Protestant, and Catholic reformers, but it was actually a very conservative movement. By integrating traditional clerical doctrines and values with an active common life, the brothers met the need of late medieval people for a more personal religion and a better informed faith. The Modern Devotion helped ordinary men and women develop fuller religious lives without turning their backs on the world.

Lay Control over Religious Life   The medieval papacy's successful campaign to wrest control of appointments to church offices from the laity did not improve the church's administration. Popes sold ecclesiastical posts to the highest bidders. The purchasers collected the income from the offices they bought, but they did not personally have to carry out the duties attached to those offices. They hired inexpensive (often poorly trained and motivated) substitutes to do their work while they resided elsewhere. Rare was the late medieval German town that did not complain about clerical malfeasance or dereliction of duty.

City governments sometimes took the initiative and tried to improve religious life in their communities by endowing preacherships. These positions supported well-educated spiritual leaders whose preaching and pastoral care were far superior to the perfunctory services offered by other clergy. These prominent urban pulpits became platforms for Protestant reformers.

As holy places, medieval churches and monasteries were exempted from secular taxes and laws. Holy persons (clergy) were also not expected to do "dirty jobs" (such as military service, compulsory labor, standing watch at city gates, and other obligations of citizenship). Nor was it thought right that any of the laity should sit in judgment over God's priestly intermediaries. On the eve of the Reformation, however, a growing sense that clerical privileges were undeserved was leading secular governments to curtail them.

Long before 1520, when Luther published a famous summary of economic grievances (*Address to the Christian Nobility of the German Nation*), communities

Martin Schongauer (c. 1430-1491), a German engraver, portrays the devil's temptation of St. Anthony in the wilderness as a robust physical attack by demons rather than the traditional melancholic introspection.

National Gallery of Art, Washington D.C.

11.1
Erasmus: A Diatribe Against the Pope

QUICK REVIEW

Anti-Clericalism

- Corruption and incompetence marred church administration
- City governments took steps to improve the situation by endowing preacherships
- Fifteenth century witnessed a growing sense that clerical privileges were undeserved

were protesting the financial abuses of the medieval church—particularly the sale of indulgences (papal letters that released sinners from time in purgatory). Rulers and magistrates who received a share of the profits usually did not object, but it was a different matter when local revenues were siphoned off for projects far from home. The state did not join the campaign against the church's financial exactions until its rulers recognized how they might profit from religion. The appeal of Protestantism for some rulers was the rationale it provided for disbanding monasteries and confiscating church property.

WHY DID Martin Luther challenge the church?

Martin Luther and the German Reformation to 1525

The kings of France and England were strong enough to limit papal taxation and jurisdiction within their homelands, but Germany lacked the political unity needed to enforce "national" religious policies. The restraints that England and France imposed on the church on a universal level were enacted locally and piecemeal in Germany whenever popular resentment of ecclesiastical abuses boiled over. By 1517, mass discontent was pervasive enough to win Martin Luther a widespread, sympathetic audience.

Luther (1483–1546) was the son of a successful Thüringian miner. He received his early education in a school run by the Brothers of the Common Life, and in 1501, he attended the University of Erfurt. After receiving his master of arts degree in 1505, Luther did what his parents wished and registered with the law faculty, but he never began the study of law. On July 17, 1505, he disappointed his family by entering a monastery in Erfurt (the Order of the Hermits of Saint Augustine). A terrifying lightning storm had prompted him to promise Saint Anne, the patron of travelers in distress, that he would enter a cloister if she saved his life. There was, however, more to his decision than this. Behind it lay many years of personal spiritual struggle.

Luther led a conventional monastic life and was ordained to the priesthood in 1507. In 1510, he went to Rome on business for his order and saw firsthand some of the abuses that were discrediting the church. In 1511, he moved to the Augustinian monastery in Wittenberg. A year later, he earned his doctorate in theology from Wittenberg's university and joined its faculty.

Justification by Faith Alone

Reformation theology was a response to the fact that many of the laity and clergy were ceasing to find traditional medieval religious beliefs and practices personally satisfying. Luther was especially plagued by his inability to achieve the righteousness that medieval theology taught that God required for salvation. The sacrament of penance failed to console Luther and give him hope, for the church seemed to demand of him a perfection he knew neither he nor any other human being could achieve.

The study of St. Paul's letters finally brought Luther an insight into the process of salvation that quieted his fears. Luther concluded from his reading of the Scriptures that the righteousness that God demanded did not consist of good works and participation in rituals. It was a gift God gives to those who believe and trust in Jesus Christ—who alone is perfectly righteous. Believers in Christ, Luther claimed, stood before God clothed in Christ's righteousness. They were justified solely by faith in him and not by their own actions.

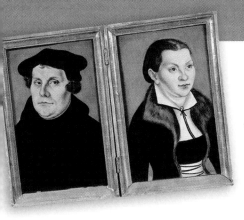

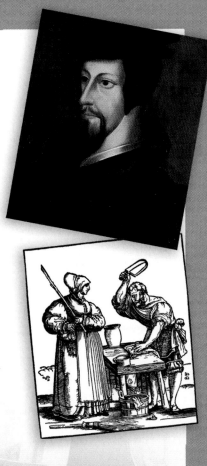

CHAPTER QUESTIONS

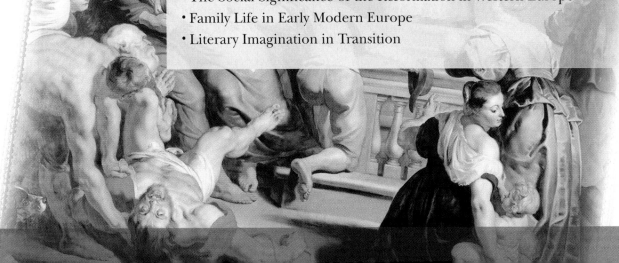

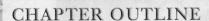

THE ATTACK ON INDULGENCES

Luther's doctrine of justification by faith was incompatible with the church's practice of issuing indulgences, for an **indulgence** was a remission of the obligation to perform a "work of satisfaction" for a sin. The medieval church taught that after priests absolved penitents of guilt, penitents still had to pay penalties for their sins. They could discharge their penalties in this life by prayers, fasting, almsgiving, retreats, and pilgrimages. If their works of satisfaction were insufficient at the time of their deaths, they would continue to suffer for them in purgatory.

Indulgences had originally been devised for Crusaders whose deaths in battle with the enemies of the church deprived them of an opportunity to do penance for their sins. Gradually, the church extended indulgences to others who were anxious about the consequences of neglected penances and unrepented sins. In 1343, Pope Clement VI (r. 1342–1352) declared the existence of a "treasury of merit," an infinite reservoir of credit that the saints and Christ had earned that the pope could appropriate for use by lesser Christians. Papal "letters of indulgence" were drafts on this treasury to cover the works of satisfaction owed by penitents. In 1476, Pope Sixtus IV (r. 1471–1484) greatly expanded the market for these letters by proclaiming the church's power to grant indulgences not only to the living but also to souls in purgatory.

Originally, indulgences had been granted only for major services to the church, but by Luther's day their price had been significantly discounted to encourage mass marketing. In 1517, Pope Leo X (r. 1513–1521) revived a special Jubilee indulgence for sale to raise funds for rebuilding Saint Peter's in Rome. Archbishop Albrecht of Mainz welcomed the opportunity it provided him. He was in debt to the Fugger bank of Augsburg for a loan he had taken out to pay the pope for permission to ignore church law and simultaneously occupy the archbishoprics of Mainz and Magdeburg and the bishopric of Halberstadt. Albrecht agreed to promote the sale of the Jubilee indulgence in Germany for a share of the proceeds, and John Tetzel (d. 1519), a popular preacher, was given the job of drumming up business in Luther's neighborhood.

According to tradition, Luther posted his ninety-five theses opposing the sale of indulgences on the door of Castle Church in Wittenberg on October 31, 1517. Luther was especially disturbed by Tetzel's insinuation that indulgences remitted sins and released the dead from punishment in purgatory. Luther believed Tetzel's claims went far beyond traditional practice and made salvation something that could be bought and sold.

ELECTION OF CHARLES V

The ninety-five theses made Luther famous overnight and prompted official proceedings against him. In April 1518, he was summoned to appear before the general chapter of his order in Heidelberg, and the following October he was called to Augsburg to be examined by the papal legate and general of the Dominican Order, Cardinal Cajetan. At that point the Holy Roman Emperor, Maximilian I, died (January 12, 1519), and attention was diverted from Luther to the election of a new emperor.

Maximilian's nineteen-year-old grandson, Charles V, was chosen to succeed him, but the electors exacted a price for their votes. They forced Charles to agree

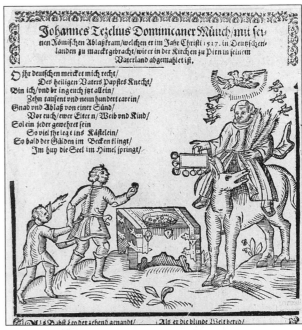

A contemporary caricature depicts John Tetzel, the famous indulgence preacher. The last lines of the jingle read: "As soon as gold in the basin rings, right then the soul to Heaven springs." It was Tetzel's preaching that spurred Luther to publish his ninety-five theses.

Courtesy Stiftung Luthergedenkstaten in Sachsen-Anhalt/Lutherhalle, Wittenberg

11.2
Luther's *Ninety-Five Theses*

indulgence Remission of the obligation to perform a "work of satisfaction" for a sin.

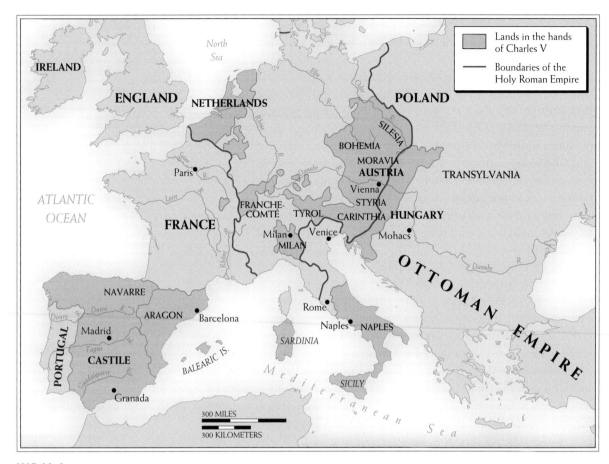

MAP 11–1

The Empire of Charles V Dynastic marriages and simple chance concentrated into Charles's hands rule over the lands shown here, plus Spain's overseas possessions. Crowns and titles rained down on him; his election in 1519 as emperor gave him new distractions and responsibilities.

WERE THE acquisitions of large portions of Europe more of a burden than a privilege for Charles V?

to consult with the imperial diet on all major domestic and foreign issues. This prevented Charles from taking unilateral action in Germany—something for which Luther was soon to be thankful. (See Map 11–1.)

LUTHER'S EXCOMMUNICATION AND THE DIET OF WORMS

While the imperial election was being held, Luther went to Leipzig to debate John Eck, a professor from Ingolstadt (June 27, 1519). Luther used the occasion to question the infallibility of the pope and the inerrancy of church councils and, for the first time, to suggest the Scriptures should be regarded as the sole authority governing faith.

In 1520, Luther explained his position in three famous pamphlets. *Address to the Christian Nobility of the German Nation* urged the German princes forcefully to reform the Roman Catholic Church and curtail its political and economic power. *The Babylonian Captivity of the Church* examined the sacraments and concluded that only two of the church's seven (baptism and the Eucharist) were authentic. The pamphlet also claimed that the Scriptures, decrees of church councils, and decisions of secular princes were superior to the authority of a pope. *Freedom of a Christian* eloquently argued the case for Luther's key theological insight, that salvation came from faith not works.

On June 15, 1520, a papal bull, *Exsurge Domine*, condemned Luther for heresy and gave him sixty days to retract his opinions. The final bull of excommunication, *Decet Pontificem Romanum*, was issued on January 3, 1521. In April of that year, Luther appeared before the imperial diet and the newly elected Charles V in the city of Worms. Luther refused the diet's order to recant, for such an act, he claimed, would violate Scripture, reason, and conscience. On May 26, 1521, Luther was placed under the imperial ban, which made his heresy a crime punishable by the state. Friends protected him and hid him in Wartburg Castle. He spent about a year (April 1521 to March 1522) in seclusion and devoted his time to the creation of one of the essential tools of the Reformation: a German translation of Erasmus's Greek text of the New Testament.

IMPERIAL DISTRACTIONS: FRANCE AND THE TURKS

Charles V was too preoccupied with military ventures to pay much attention to the Reformation that erupted in Wittenberg in the wake of Luther's trial. France was invading Italy to drive a wedge between parts of this empire, and the Ottoman Turks were threatening it in the East. Charles needed friendly relations with the German princes in order to recruit German troops for his armies.

In 1526, the Turks overran Hungary at the Battle of Mohacs, and in western Europe the French organized the League of Cognac to prepare for the second of the four Habsburg-Valois wars (1521–1559). Busy as Charles was meeting these challenges, he had little time for Germany. At the Diet of Speyer in 1526, he granted each German prince the right to deal as he saw fit with the situation Luther was creating. This cleared the way for the Reformation to put down roots in places where princes sympathized with it, and it established a tradition of princely control over religion that was enshrined in law by the Peace of Augsburg in 1555.

HOW THE REFORMATION SPREAD

In the 1520s and 1530s, leadership of the Reformation passed from theologians and pamphleteers to magistrates and princes. City governments acted on the proposals of Protestant preachers and their growing flocks, and as they mandated reforms, religious practices ceased to be a matter of slogans and became laws binding on all of a town's residents. Like urban magistrates, some regional princes (notably, the elector of Saxony and the prince of Hesse) implemented the reform in large states. They saw political and economic advantages in overthrowing the Roman Catholic Church and urged their colleagues in other states to join them. Powerful alliances were negotiated, and Protestant leaders prepared for war with their Catholic emperor.

THE PEASANTS' REVOLT

In its first decade, the Protestant movement suffered more from internal division than from imperial resistance. By 1525, Luther had become as controversial a figure in Germany as the pope, and

AETHERNA IPSE SVAE MENTIS SIMVLACHRA LVTHERVS EXPRIMIT · AT VVLTVS CERA LVCAE OCCIDVOS · M · D · X X ·

In 1520, Luther's first portrait, shown here, depicted him as a tough, steely eyed monk. Afraid that this portrayal might convey defiance rather than reform to Emperor Charles V, Elector Frederick the Wise of Saxony, Luther's protector, ordered court painter Lucas Cranach to soften the image. The result was a Luther placed within a traditional monk's niche reading an open Bible, a reformer, unlike the one depicted here, who was prepared to listen as well as to instruct.

Martin Luther as a monk, 1521. © Foto Marburg/Art Resource, NY

A handwritten manuscript depicts the Execution of Jaklein Rohrbach. The sixteenth-century German radical burns at a stake inside a ring of fire.

Courtesy of the Library of Congress

many of his early supporters had broken with him. Germany's peasants, who had welcomed Luther as an ally, had a particular reason for losing faith in him. Since the late fifteenth century, their leaders had been struggling to prevent the territorial princes from ignoring traditional limits and imposing oppressive regulations and taxes. Many peasants assumed Luther's defense of Christian freedom and criticism of monastic landowners implied his support for their cause. Luther and his followers sympathized with the peasants, but Lutherans were not social revolutionaries. Luther's freedom of the Christian individual was an inner experience of release from guilt and anxiety for one's soul. It did not entail restructuring society by violent revolution. When the peasants rebelled against their masters in 1524, Luther condemned them in the strongest possible terms and urged the princes to crush the revolt. Possibly as many as 100,000 peasants died in the struggle. Had Luther supported the Peasants' Revolt, he would not only have misrepresented his own teaching, he would probably have ended any chance for his reform to survive beyond the 1520s.

THE REFORMATION ELSEWHERE

WHERE DID other reform movements develop and how were they different from Luther's?

*L*uther's revolt against the church was the first, but similar reform movements soon developed independently in France and Switzerland.

ZWINGLI AND THE SWISS REFORMATION

Switzerland, like Germany, offered the kind of politically diverse environment in which rebellion had a good chance to succeed. It was a loose confederacy of thirteen autonomous cantons (states). Some (particularly, Zurich, Bern, Basel, and Schaffhausen) became Protestant. Some (especially in the heartland around Lucerne) remained Catholic, and a few sought a compromise.

Two developments prepared the ground for the Swiss Reformation. The first was the growth of national feeling that sprang from opposition to the practice of impressing Swiss soldiers into mercenary service outside their homeland. The second was the interest in church reform that was stimulated by the famous church councils that met in the Swiss cities of Constance (1414–1417) and Basel (1431–1449).

The Reformation in Zurich Ulrich Zwingli (1484–1531), the leader of the Swiss Reformation, credited Erasmus and humanism for sparking his interest in reform. He also served as chaplain to Swiss soldiers in Italy in 1515, an experience that made him an ardent opponent of mercenary service. By 1518, he was publicly objecting to the sale of indulgences and denouncing some traditional religious practices as superstitions.

In 1519, Zwingli applied for the post of people's priest in Zurich's main church. His fitness was questioned because he acknowledged having had an affair with a barber's daughter. Many of his contemporaries, however, sympathized with clergy who found celibacy more than they could bear, and Zwingli defended himself forthrightly. Later he led a fight to abolish clerical celibacy and grant clergy the right to marry.

Zwingli's post as the people's priest in Zurich gave him a pulpit from which to campaign for reform, and on January 29, 1523, the Zurich town government decided to implement his ideas. The standard Zwingli proposed for judging religious practice was simple. Whatever lacked literal support in Scripture was to be neither believed nor done. This conviction caused him, like Luther, to question many aspects of medieval Catholicism: fasting, transubstantiation, the worship of

HISTORY'S VOICES

ZWINGLI LISTS THE ERRORS OF THE ROMAN CHURCH

Prior to the first Zurich Disputation (1523), which effectively introduced the Protestant Reformation in Zurich, the reformer Zwingli wrote the Sixty-Seven Articles, which summarized for public disputation his criticisms of the Roman Church. Here are some of them.

TO ZWINGLI, what is the source of divine authority and who in the church has power?

All who consider other teachings equal to or higher than the Gospel err, and they do not know what the Gospel is.

In the faith rests our salvation, and in unbelief our damnation; for all truth is clear in Christ.

In the Gospel one learns that human doctrines and decrees do not aid in salvation.

That Christ, having sacrificed himself once, is to eternity a certain and valid sacrifice for the sins of all faithful, wherfrom it follows that the Mass is not a sacrifice, but is a remembrance of the sacrifice and assurance of the salvation which Christ has given us.

That God desires to give us all things in his name, whence it follows that outside of this life we need no [intercession of the saints or any] mediator except himself.

That no Christian is bound to do those things which God has not decreed, therefore one may eat at all times all food, where from one learns that the decree about cheese and butter is a Roman swindle.

That no special person can impose the ban upon anyone, but the Church, that is, the congregation of those among whom the one to be banned dwells, together with their watchman, i.e. the pastor.

All that the spiritual so-called state [i.e., the papal church] claims to have of power and protection belongs to the lay [i.e., the secular magistracy], if they wish to be Christians.

Greater offence I know not than that one does not allow priests to have wives, but permits them to hire prostitutes.

Christ has borne all our pains and labor. Hence whoever assigns to works of penance what belongs to Christ errs and slanders God.

The true divine Scriptures know naught about purgatory after this life.

The Scriptures know no priests except those who proclaim the word of God.

Ulrich Zwingli (1484–1531): Selected Works, ed. by Samuel M. Jackson (Philadelphia: University of Pennsylvania Press, 1972), pp. 111–117.

saints, pilgrimages, purgatory, clerical celibacy, and some of the sacraments. The rigor with which the Swiss purged their church of these practices led eventually to the so-called puritan element in Protestantism. (See "History's Voices: Zwingli Lists the Errors of the Roman Church.")

The Marburg Colloquy Landgrave Philip of Hesse (1504–1567) believed Protestants had to cooperate if they hoped to fend off attacks from Catholics, and he tried to unite the Swiss and German reformations. He arranged for Luther and Zwingli to meet in his castle at Marburg in early October 1529, but theological disagreements over the nature of Christ's presence in the Eucharist drove a permanent wedge between the two leaders. Luther dismissed Zwingli as a dangerous fanatic, and Zwingli charged that Luther was irrationally in thrall to medieval ideas. The disagreement at Marburg splintered the Protestant movement. Cooperation between the two sides did not cease entirely, but the followers of Luther and Zwingli published separate creeds and formed separate defense leagues.

Swiss Civil Wars   Protestants and Catholics divided up the Swiss cantons and wars erupted among them. There were two major battles—both at Kappel (one in June 1529, the other in October 1531). The first was a Protestant victory that forced the Catholic cantons to repudiate their foreign alliances and recognize the rights of Protestants. The second battle cost Zwingli his life, but the treaty that ended the fighting confirmed the right of each canton to determine its own religion. Heinrich Bullinger (1504–1575), Zwingli's protégé, assumed leadership of the Swiss Reformation, and under his direction, Protestantism came to be accepted as an established religion in Switzerland.

ANABAPTISTS AND RADICAL PROTESTANTS

Some people were discontented by what they regarded as the failure of the Lutheran and Zwinglian reformations to elevate standards of ethical conduct and by the slow pace of change the two factions effected in society's institutions. Protestants who wanted a more rapid and thorough restoration of the "primitive Christianity" described in the New Testament accused the leading reformers of going only halfway. They struck out on their own and formed more radical Protestant organizations. The most important of these were called **Anabaptists** ("rebaptizers") by their enemies. The name derived from their rejection of infant baptism and their insistence on baptizing adult converts who had been baptized as infants.

Conrad Grebel (1498–1526) inaugurated the Anabaptist movement by performing the first baptism of a previously baptized adult in Zurich in January 1525. A few years earlier (in October 1523), Grebel's passion for biblical literalism had caused him to break with Zwingli, his mentor. He opposed Zwingli's decision to respect the town government's plea to proceed slowly in altering religious practices. In 1527, Grebel's followers, the Swiss Brethren, published a statement of their beliefs, the *Schleitheim Confession*. They endorsed adult baptism, opposed the swearing of oaths, pledged themselves to pacifism, and refused to recognize the authority of secular governments. Anabaptists literally withdrew from society to be free to live as they believed the first Christians had lived. States interpreted this as an attack on society's fundamental bonds.

The Anabaptist Reign in Münster   Lutherans and Zwinglians joined Catholics in persecuting the Anabaptists. In 1529, rebaptism became a capital offense throughout the Holy Roman Empire, and from 1525 to 1618 between 1,000 and 5,000 people were executed for undergoing rebaptism.

Brutal punishments for nonconformists increased after a group of Anabaptist extremists took over the German city of Münster in 1534. Anabaptist converts won control of Münster's town government and used their authority to compel Lutherans and Catholics to convert or emigrate. They turned Münster into an Old Testament theocracy run by charismatic prophets who shocked their contemporaries by reviving the ancient Hebrew practice of polygamy. Outraged Protestants and Catholics fought side by side to reconquer Münster, and the bodies of its Anabaptist leaders were hung up in public as a warning to others who might be tempted to push religious reform beyond socially acceptable limits.

After this bloody episode, the Anabaptists reasserted their commitment to pacifism and attempted to maintain low profiles. Their movement found more moderate leaders and survived largely in rural districts. It is represented today by the Mennonites (followers of Menno Simons, 1496–1561) and the Amish.

Anabaptists ("rebaptizers") The most important of several groups of Protestants forming more radical organizations that sought a more rapid and thorough restoration of the "primitive Christianity" described in the New Testament.

Other Nonconformists   The Anabaptists were not the only Protestant radicals. The Reformation also produced the Spiritualists—extreme individualists who believed the only religious authority was the guidance of God's spirit in each person's heart. Thomas Müntzer (d. 1525), an early convert to Lutheranism and a leader of a peasants' revolt, belonged to this camp, as did Sebastian Franck (d. 1541), a freelance critic of all dogmatic religion, and Caspar Schwenckfeld (d. 1561), a prolific author for whom the tiny Schwenckfeldian denomination is named.

At the other extreme, the Reformation's critique of religious superstition turned some Protestants into rationalists. They preached a commonsense, rational religion that focused primarily on ethics. Some, like the Spanish reformer Michael Servetus (1511–1553), were Antitrinitarians. Servetus sought refuge from Catholic persecution in Geneva, but its Protestant government executed him for his rejection of the doctrine of the Trinity. In Italy, the reformers Lelio (d. 1562) and Faustus Sozzini (d. 1604) founded a humanistic faith called Socinianism. It opposed all the emerging Protestant orthodoxies and advocated religious toleration.

JOHN CALVIN AND THE GENEVAN REFORMATION

In the second half of the sixteenth century, Calvinism replaced Lutheranism as the dominant Protestant force in Europe. Calvinists believed strongly in predestination, but they also believed Christians were called to reorder society in accordance with God's plan. They were zealous reformers who used the machinery of government to compel men and women to live according to codes of conduct they believed were set forth in the Scriptures.

Calvinism's founder, John Calvin (1509–1564), was the son of a well-to-do secretary to the bishop of Noyon in Picardy. The church benefices the boy was given at age twelve paid for the excellent education he received at Parisian colleges and the law school in Orléans. Young Calvin was drawn to the writings of Catholic humanists such as Jacques Lefèvre d'Etaples and Marguerite d'Angoulême, the queen of Navarre. Calvin eventually concluded that these people were ineffectual agents for reform, but they helped awaken his interest in reform movements.

Calvin described his conversion to Protestantism (which probably occurred in the spring of 1534) as God's making his "long stubborn heart … teachable." In May 1534, he took the decisive step of surrendering the church benefices that provided his income and declared his support for the Reformation.

Political Revolt and Religious Reform in Geneva   In Luther's Saxony, religious reform paved the way for political revolution. In Calvin's Geneva, political revolution awakened the appetite for religious reform.

In 1527, the city-states of Fribourg and Bern helped the Genevans drive out their resident prince-bishop and win their independence from the House of Savoy. Late in 1533, Bern sent the Protestant reformers Guillaume Farel (1489–1565) and Antoine Froment (1508–1581) to Geneva to advise the city's new governing councils. In the summer of 1535—and following much internal turmoil—the Genevans discontinued the Catholic mass and various other religious practices.

On May 21, 1536, Geneva officially endorsed the Reformation, and in July of that year Calvin came to Geneva. He fled France to avoid persecution for his religious beliefs and had intended to seek refuge in Strasbourg. The third Habsburg-Valois war forced him to detour to Geneva, where Farel persuaded him to stay. Before a year had passed, Calvin had drawn up articles for the governance of Geneva's new church as well as a catechism to guide its people. Both were presented for approval to the city councils in early 1537. The strong measures they proposed for policing the moral conduct of the Genevans led to accusations that the reformers wanted to establish a "new papacy." Opponents within Geneva and elsewhere objected to any attempt to impose a new orthodoxy, and Bern, which had adopted a more moderate Protestant reform, persuaded the Genevans to retain some of the ceremonies and holidays that Calvin and Farel wanted to eliminate. In February 1538, the four syndics (the leading city magistrates) turned against the reformers and drove them out.

Calvin went to Strasbourg to became pastor to a group of French exiles. While in Strasbourg, he wrote a second edition of his masterful *Institutes of the Christian Religion*. Many scholars consider this the definitive theological explication of Protestant faith. Calvin also married, took part in ecumenical discussions, and learned important lessons in practical politics from the Strasbourg reformer Martin Bucer.

Calvin's Geneva   In 1540, Geneva elected syndics who wanted to establish their city's independence from Bern. They believed Calvin would be a valuable ally and invited him to return. Within months of his arrival in September 1540, the city implemented new ecclesiastical ordinances, and its civil magistrates promised to work with its clergy to maintain a high standard of discipline among its residents.

Calvin created four kinds of officials to oversee the practice of religion in Geneva: (1) five presiding pastors; (2) teachers and doctors charged with religious instruction; (3) twelve elders, laymen chosen by and from the Genevan councils to "oversee the life of everybody"; and (4) deacons, laymen who managed the church's charitable disbursements. Calvin believed a Christian city could not tolerate any conduct that was displeasing to God. A strong church government was needed, therefore, to maintain the highest moral standards in the community. This responsibility was assigned to the consistory, a committee composed of the elders and the pastors of the church and chaired by one of the four syndics. It meted out punishments for a broad range of moral and religious transgressions—everything from missing church services (a fine of 3 sous) to fornication (six days on bread and water and a fine of 60 sous). The making of statements critical of Calvin and the consistory was listed among the sins meriting punishment. Calvin branded his opponents wanton "Libertines" and showed them little mercy. His most prominent victim was Michael Servetus, the Antitrinitarian he burned at the stake.

By 1555, the city's syndics were all solidly behind Calvin, and he began to attract disciples from across Europe. Geneva welcomed the thousands of Protestants who were driven out of France, England, and Scotland, and at one point more than a third of the population of the city consisted of refugees (over 5,000 of them). They were utterly loyal to Calvin, for in their experience Geneva was Europe's only "free" city. Whenever they were allowed to return to their homes, they took their ardent Calvinism with them.

WHAT WERE the political ramifications of the Reformation?

POLITICAL CONSOLIDATION OF THE LUTHERAN REFORMATION

y 1530, the Reformation had become irreversible, but it took several decades for that fact to be accepted throughout Europe.

THE EXPANSION OF THE REFORMATION

Emperor Charles V spent most of his reign in Spain and Italy, but in 1530, he came to Germany to preside over a diet at Augsburg. The purpose of the meeting was to resolve the religious conflicts begun by Luther's break with the papacy in 1520. Charles ended the meeting by bluntly ordering all Lutherans to return to the Catholic faith. The Reformation was, however, too far advanced by then to be halted by such a peremptory gesture. The emperor's mandate served only to bring the Lutherans together in a defensive alliance, the Schmalkaldic League. The league endorsed the **Augsburg Confession**, a moderate Protestant creed that Charles had rejected at the diet, and in 1538, Luther issued a more strongly worded declaration of theological principles, the *Schmalkaldic Articles*. Lutheran states replaced the bishops who had previously administered their churches with regional consistories (courts staffed by theologians and lawyers). The outbreak of new hostilities with the French and the Turks prevented Charles from doing much about these developments, and the league's leaders, Landgrave Philip of Hesse and Elector John Frederick of Saxony, were able to hold him at bay while Lutheranism spread.

Christian II (r. 1513–1523) introduced Lutheranism to Denmark, where it became the state religion. In 1527, Sweden's king Gustavus Vasa (r. 1523–1560) and his nobles embraced the reform and the opportunity it gave them to confiscate the church's property. Poland, having no centralized government to enforce conformity, became a model of religious pluralism and toleration. In the second half of the sixteenth century, it provided refuge for Lutherans, Anabaptists, Calvinists, and even Antitrinitarians.

REACTION AND RESOLUTION: THE PEACE OF AUGSBURG

In 1547, the armies of Charles V crushed the Schmalkaldic League, and the emperor issued the Augsburg Interim. It ordered Protestants to return to Catholic beliefs and practices but made a few concessions to Protestant tastes. Clerical marriage was permitted in individual cases that received papal approval, and laity were allowed to receive both the bread and the wine at communion. Many Protestant leaders chose exile rather than comply with the terms of the Interim, and the Reformation was too entrenched by 1547 to be ended by brute force and imperial fiat.

Maurice of Saxony, whom Charles V hand-picked to replace Elector John Frederick as ruler of Saxony, recognized the inevitable and shifted his allegiance to the Protestants. Charles, wearied by three decades of war, also gave up the struggle to restore Europe's religious unity. In 1552, he reinstated John Frederick and Philip of Hesse and issued the Peace of Passau, which granted Lutherans religious freedom. The Peace of Augsburg in September 1555 made the religious division of Christendom permanent by endorsing the principle of *cuius regio, eius religio*—the right of a ruler to choose the religion for his people. Subjects who disagreed with their ruler's choice were expected to move to a place where their faith was legal, for it was assumed a state would not be politically stable unless all its citizens conformed to the same religion.

THE ENGLISH REFORMATION TO 1553

*T*he king of England was the only major European monarch to break with the papacy, but England's Reformation owed more to politics than theology.

THE PRECONDITIONS OF REFORM

England had a long history of asserting the crown's right to limit papal intervention in English affairs. Edward I (d. 1307) successfully opposed Pope Boniface VIII's attempt to deny kings the right to tax their clergy. In the mid–fourteenth

HOW WAS the English Reformation more political than theological?

Augsburg Confession
Moderate Protestant creed endorsed by the Schmalkaldic League (a defensive alliance of Lutherans).

Hans Holbein the Younger (1497–1543) was the most famous portrait painter of the Reformation. Here he portrays a seemingly almighty Henry VIII.

National Gallery of Ancient Art, Rome, Italy/Canali PhotoBank, Milan/SuperStock

century, the English Parliament passed the first Statutes of Provisors and Praemunire. These curtailed the right of the pope to appoint candidates to church offices in England, limited the amount of money that could be sent out of England to Rome, and restricted the number of court cases that could be appealed to Rome from English jurisdictions.

In the late Middle Ages, the critiques of papal and priestly authority by Wycliffe and the Lollards spread proto-Protestant ideas at every level in English society. In the early 1520s, advocates of reform began to smuggle Lutheran writings into England. An English-language New Testament, translated by William Tyndale (ca. 1492–1536) and printed in Cologne and Worms, was circulating by 1526. Access to a Bible in the language of the people became the centerpiece of the English Reformation.

THE KING'S AFFAIR

Henry VIII (r. 1509–1547), the king who severed England's ties with the papacy, initially opposed the Reformation. When Luther's ideas first began to circulate, Henry's advisers, Cardinal Thomas Wolsey (ca. 1475–1530) and Sir Thomas More (1478–1535), urged him to rush to the pope's defense. Henry declared his Catholic convictions by publishing a treatise justifying the seven sacraments. It earned him a contemptuous response from Luther and the grant of a title ("Defender of the Faith") from Pope Leo X.

It was the king's unhappy marriage, not his theology, that allowed the Reformation to take root in English soil. In 1509, Henry had preserved an alliance with Spain by wedding his brother's widow, Catherine of Aragon (d. 1536), daughter of Ferdinand and Isabella and aunt of Emperor Charles V. The marriage had required a papal dispensation, for a biblical passage (Leviticus 18:16, 20:21) implied it was incestuous. By 1527, the union had produced miscarriages and stillbirths and only one surviving child, a daughter named Mary. Henry feared that civil war would erupt if he left his throne to a daughter (as it had on the one other occasion in England's history when this was tried). Eagerness for a younger wife who might bear him a son convinced the king his marriage had been cursed for violating God's law. Catherine, however, staunchly refused to cooperate in dissolving their bond.

By 1527, Henry's affections had been captured by Anne Boleyn, one of the aging Catherine's youthful ladies in waiting. To wed her he needed a papal annulment of his marriage to Catherine. It would have been difficult for the pope to justify the annulment of a marriage that had been approved by a papal dispensation, and the political situation made it impossible. The soldiers of the Holy Roman Empire had recently mutinied and sacked Rome, and Pope Clement VII was a virtual prisoner of Catherine's nephew, Charles V.

Henry assigned the task of negotiating the annulment to Cardinal Wolsey, his Lord Chancellor. After two years of profitless diplomatic maneuvering, Henry concluded that Wolsey had failed and dismissed him in disgrace (1529). Two men with Lutheran sympathies, Thomas Cranmer (1489–1556) and Thomas Cromwell (1485–1540), succeeded Wolsey as the king's advisers, and they proposed a different course. Why not, they asked, free England from the interference of foreigners in its affairs and simply declare its king supreme over its church as he was over its state?

QUICK REVIEW

Legal Break with Rome

- 1531: Convocation recognizes Henry VIII as head of the church in England
- 1532: Parliament gives the king jurisdiction over the clergy and canon law
- 1534: Parliament ends all payments to Rome and gives king jurisdiction over ecclesiastical appointments

THE "REFORMATION PARLIAMENT"

In 1529, a Parliament that was to sit for seven years began to chip away at the power of the pope over the English church. In January 1531, Convocation (a legislative assembly representing the English clergy) recognized Henry as head of the church in England "as far as the law of Christ allows." In 1532, Parliament passed a decree (the Submission of the Clergy) that gave the king jurisdiction over the clergy and canon law. Another act (the Conditional Restraint of Annates) recognized the king's power to withhold the payment of dues traditionally owed the pope.

In January 1533, Thomas Cranmer secretly wed Henry to the pregnant Anne Boleyn. In February 1533, Parliament's Act for the Restraint of Appeals forbade appeals from the king's courts to those of the pope. In March 1533, Cranmer became archbishop of Canterbury and used his authority as England's primate (highest ranking clergyman) to declare the king had never been validly married to Catherine. In 1534, Parliament ended all payments by the English clergy and laity to Rome and gave Henry jurisdiction over ecclesiastical appointments. The Act of Succession in the same year declared Anne Boleyn's children legitimate heirs to the throne, and the **Act of Supremacy** proclaimed Henry "the only supreme head on earth of the Church of England." In 1536, the first Act for Dissolution of Monasteries closed the smaller houses, and three years later all English monasteries were disbanded and their endowments confiscated by the king.

Not all of Henry's subjects approved of the nationalization of their church, but Henry encouraged compliance by making examples of two of his most prominent critics. He executed Thomas More, his former chancellor, and John Fisher, bishop of Rochester, for refusing to accept the Act of Succession and the Act of Supremacy.

WIVES OF HENRY VIII

Henry was a more successful politician than husband. In 1536, he charged Anne Boleyn, who had disappointed him by bearing him a second daughter (Elizabeth), with treason and adultery and beheaded her. Henry married four more times. His third wife, Jane Seymour, died in 1537, shortly after giving birth to the long-desired male heir, Edward VI. Henry then wed Anne of Cleves as part of a plan that Cromwell promoted to forge an alliance among Protestant princes. Neither the alliance nor Anne—whom Henry thought bore a remarkable resemblance to a horse—proved worth the trouble. The marriage was annulled by Parliament, and Cromwell was executed. Catherine Howard, Henry's fifth wife, was beheaded for adultery in 1542. His last wife, Catherine Parr, was a patron of humanists and reformers. Henry was her third husband, and she survived him to marry a fourth time.

THE KING'S RELIGIOUS CONSERVATISM

Henry was far bolder in politics than in piety. Except for breaking with Rome and using an English Bible, Henry did not want the English church to depart from its traditional faith and practice. The Ten Articles he issued in 1536 to summarize his position made only slight concessions to Protestant tenets. In 1539, the king tried to stem a rising tide of support for Protestantism by publishing the Six Articles. They reaffirmed transubstantiation, denied the Eucharistic cup to the laity, preserved mandatory celibacy for the clergy, authorized private masses, and ordered the continuation of auricular confession. England had to wait for Henry to die before it could become a genuinely Protestant country.

Act of Supremacy   Act of 1534 proclaiming Henry VIII "the only supreme head on earth of the Church of England."

THE PROTESTANT REFORMATION UNDER EDWARD VI

Henry's son, Edward VI (r. 1547–1553), was only ten years old at the time of his succession. The regents chosen to educate him imbued him with Protestant ideas, and he even corresponded with John Calvin. Edward's pro-Protestant government repealed Henry's Six Articles and laws against heresy, and it sanctioned clerical marriage and lay communion with both cup and bread. In 1547, the *chantries*, endowments supporting priests who said masses for the dead, were dissolved. In 1549, the Act of Uniformity imposed Thomas Cranmer's *Book of Common Prayer* on all English churches, and a year later images and altars were ordered removed from those churches.

In 1552, the Second Act of Uniformity revised the *Book of Common Prayer*. Thomas Cranmer wrote a forty-two-article creed that endorsed the Protestant doctrines of justification by faith and supremacy of Holy Scripture. It recognized only two sacraments and rejected the doctrine of transubstantiation (while still affirming the real presence of Christ in the Eucharistic elements).

The turn toward Protestantism that took place during Edward's reign was reversed by his heir, Catherine of Aragon's fervently Catholic daughter, Mary. In 1553, Mary succeeded her teenaged half brother and made it her mission, as queen, to restore England to the Catholic community. Despite a bloody persecution of Protestants, she failed to undo the work her father and brother had begun. When she died childless in 1558, her half sister, Anne Boleyn's daughter Elizabeth (d. 1603), inherited her throne. Elizabeth's policy favored compromise and the establishment of a nationalized, but only moderately Protestant, church in England.

CATHOLIC REFORM AND COUNTER-REFORMATION

WHAT WAS the Counter-Reformation?

*B*efore Luther spoke out, some Catholics were already calling for the reform of their church. Popes, however, were suspicious of proposals for change, for they remembered how the councils of Constance and Basel had attacked the traditions on which papal authority rested.

SOURCES OF CATHOLIC REFORM

In 1517, the Oratory of Divine Love was founded in Rome. Consistent with the principles of the New Devotion, the Oratory brought together learned laity and clergy who were deeply committed to the cultivation of inner piety, Christian living, and reform.

There was no lack of fervor among Catholics in the sixteenth century, and it produced recruits for many new religious orders. The Theatines (founded in 1524) groomed devout, reform-minded leaders for the higher levels of the church hierarchy. The Capuchins (established in 1528) returned to the ideals of Francis of Assisi and ministered to the poor. The Somaschi (in the mid-1520s) and the Barnabites (in 1530) dedicated themselves to caring for the residents of war-torn areas of Italy. The Ursulines (founded in 1535) provided education for girls from all social classes. The Oratorians (established in 1575) produced religious literature and church music. The great hymnist and musician Giovanni Palestrina (1526–1594) was one of them. In addition to new orders, older ones were renewed by the inspiration of the Spanish mystics, Teresa of Avila (1515–1582) and John of the Cross (1542–1591).

IGNATIUS OF LOYOLA AND THE JESUITS

The most influential of the new orders, the Society of Jesus, was organized in the 1530s by Ignatius of Loyola (1491–1556). Ignatius, a dashing courtier and *caballero*, began his spiritual pilgrimage in 1521 when he was seriously wounded in battle. He passed a lengthy and painful convalescence reading Christian classics and studying the techniques the church's saints used for overcoming mental anguish and pain. A dramatic conversion experience determined him to do whatever was necessary to become a "soldier of Christ." Ignatius's personal spiritual struggle convinced him that, through study and discipline, a person could create a new self, and he wrote a devotional guide (*Spiritual Exercises*) to teach others what he had learned about the quest for spiritual self-mastery.

The Protestant reformers of Ignatius's day made a virtue of challenging the authority of the traditional church. Ignatius, however, urged his followers to humble themselves and submit to the church. They were to cultivate self-control, enthusiasm for traditional spirituality, mysticism, and a willingness to subordinate personal goals to those of their church. Within a century, Ignatius's original ten "Jesuits" had become an order numbering 15,000. As soldiers of the papacy, they assumed responsibility for the church's most difficult jobs. They won back Austria, Bavaria, and the Rhineland from the Protestants and staffed the missions that followed Europe's explorers to India, Japan, and the Americas.

THE COUNCIL OF TRENT (1545–1563)

Pope Paul III (r. 1534–1549) ultimately yielded to pressure from Emperor Charles V and called a council to address the crisis created by the Reformation. The pope appointed Caspar Contarini (1483–1542), a member of the Oratory of Divine Love, chair of the commission that prepared for the council. Contarini was such an enthusiastic reformer that he was branded a "semi-Lutheran," and the report he presented to the pope in February 1537 was so blunt an indictment of the papal curia that Protestants circulated it to justify their break with the papacy.

The opening of the council, which met in Trent in northern Italy, was delayed until 1545, and it continued for eighteen years (1545–1563). War, plague, and politics caused long gaps between sessions. Unlike the late medieval councils, Trent was strictly under papal control and dominated by Italian clergy. Only high-ranking churchmen could vote. Theologians from the universities, the lower clergy, and the laity had no voice in the council's decisions.

The council focused on the restoration of internal church discipline. It curtailed the selling of church offices and other religious goods. It ordered bishops who resided outside their dioceses to go home and to work to elevate the conduct of their priests. Bishops were enjoined to preach and to conduct frequent tours of inspection of the clergy. Trent also tried to increase respect for the parish priest by requiring him to be neatly dressed, better educated, strictly celibate, and active among his parishioners. Trent called for the construction of a seminary in each diocese to provide educational opportunities for priests.

Trent made no doctrinal concessions to Protestantism. On the contrary, it ringingly affirmed most of the things to which Protestants objected: scholastic education; the importance of good works for salvation; the authority of tradition; the seven sacraments; transubstantiation; the withholding of the Eucharistic cup from the laity; clerical celibacy; purgatory; indulgences; and the veneration of saints, relics, and sacred images.

Trent did not set out to heal the rifts that had developed within Christendom but to strengthen the Roman Catholic Church in opposition to Protestantism.

11.6
The Catholic Response:
The Council of Trent

MAP EXPLORATION

Interactive map: To explore this map further, go to **http://www.prenhall.com/kagan3/map11.2**

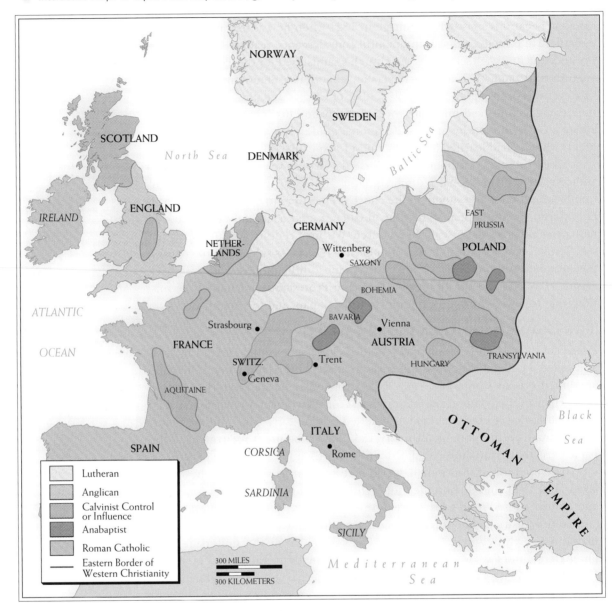

MAP 11–2

The Religious Situation about 1560 By 1560, Luther, Zwingli, and Loyola were dead, Calvin was near the end of his life, the English break from Rome was complete, and the last session of the Council of Trent was about to assemble. This map shows the "religious geography" of western Europe at the time.

HOW WOULD you characterize Christianity in western Europe at this time? Which reform movements seem to have had the most success?

Some secular rulers were initially leery of Trent's assertion of papal authority, but they were reassured as the new legislation took hold and parish life revived under the guidance of a devout and better trained clergy. The religious polarization of Europe that Trent encouraged was, however, a source for worry. (See Map 11–2.)

THE SOCIAL SIGNIFICANCE OF THE REFORMATION IN WESTERN EUROPE

*L*uther, Zwingli, and Calvin believed Christians should not separate them-selves from the world but take up their duties as citizens of the state. They have been called "magisterial reformers," meaning not only that they were leaders of major movements but that they were willing to use the mag-istrate's sword to advance their causes.

Some modern observers condemn this as a compromise of religious princi-ples, but the reformers did not see it that way. They knew their reform programs had to deal with the realities of their world. They were so sensitive to what they believed was politically and socially possible that some scholars claim they fought to preserve the status quo. De-spite their innate political conservatism, however, they ef-fected radical changes in traditional religious practices and some social institutions.

THE REVOLUTION IN RELIGIOUS PRACTICES AND INSTITUTIONS

Religion in Fifteenth-Century Life   On the eve of the Reformation, the clergy and other religious accounted for 6 to 8 percent of the inhabitants of the central European cities that were about to become Protestant. They exer-cised both spiritual authority and considerable political power. They legislated, taxed, tried cases in special church courts, and enforced discipline with threats of excommu-nication. About one-third of the year was given over to re-ligious observances, and the church calendar regulated daily life. Monasteries had great influence. They educated the children of prominent citizens and enjoyed the pa-tronage of powerful aristocratic families. Business boomed at religious shrines, where pilgrims gathered by the hun-dreds or thousands. Begging friars constantly worked the streets, and several times each year special preachers ap-peared to sell letters of indulgence.

The conduct of the religious professionals was a source of concern. Clergy were sworn to celibacy, but many had concubines and children. Society's reaction to this situation was mixed, and the church tolerated it—if appropriate fines were paid as penances. There were com-plaints about the clergy's exemption from taxation and immunity from prosecution in civil courts, and people grumbled when nonresidents collected the income from church offices and either neglected or assigned the work of those offices to others.

Religion in Sixteenth-Century Life   The Reformation made few changes in the politics or class structures of cities. The same aristocratic families continued to govern, and the same people were rich and poor. The Reforma-tion did, however, profoundly alter the lives of clergy.

Significant Dates from the Period of the Protestant Reformation

1517	Luther posts ninety-five theses against indulgences
1519	Charles V becomes Holy Roman Emperor
1521	Diet of Worms condemns Luther
1524–1525	Peasants' Revolt in Germany
1527	The Schleitheim Confession of the Anabaptists
1529	Marburg Colloquy between Luther and Zwingli
1529	England's Reformation Parliament convenes
1531	Formation of Protestant Schmalkaldic League
1533	Henry VIII weds Anne Boleyn
1534	England's Act of Supremacy
1534–1535	Anabaptists take over Münster
1536	Calvin arrives in Geneva
1540	Jesuits, founded by Ignatius of Loyola, recognized as order by pope
1546	Luther dies
1547	Armies of Charles V crush Schmalkaldic League
1547–1553	Edward VI, king of England
1555	Peace of Augsburg
1553–1558	Mary Tudor, queen of England
1545–1563	Council of Trent
1558–1603	Elizabeth I, queen of England; the Anglican settlement

Their numbers fell by two-thirds. One-third of parish churches and of religious holidays disappeared. Monasteries and nunneries were closed or turned into hospices and schools. Worship services were conducted in the vernacular, not Latin. Sometimes the walls of sanctuaries were stripped bare and whitewashed.

The Reformation also had an impact on the lives of the laity. They were no longer obliged to observe any fasts. Local shrines honoring saints, relics, and images were closed down, and punishments were decreed for venerating such things. Copies of Luther's translation of the New Testament or excerpts from it proliferated in private hands. Instead of controlling access to the Bible, Protestant clergy urged the laity to study it. Protestant clergy married, paid taxes, and could be prosecuted in civil courts. Laity as well as clergy served on the committees that supervised the morals of Protestant communities, and secular magistrates had the last word whenever there were disputes.

Not all Protestant clergy were happy about sharing power with the laity, and some laity complained about "new papists"—Protestant preachers who tried to exercise the same authority over their lives that the Catholic clergy had claimed. Some laity could be just as reactionary as some clergy. Over half of the initial converts to Protestantism returned to the Catholic fold before the end of the sixteenth century.

THE REFORMATION AND EDUCATION

The humanist curriculum emphasized language skills and the importance of consulting original sources. This was an ideal program of study for Protestants, who acknowledged no authority higher than that of Scripture. Reformers' views on doctrine and human nature often differed from those of the humanists, but they shared with the humanists a belief in the unity of wisdom and the importance of rhetorical eloquence and the active life. The Reformation's endorsement of humanist education had significant cultural impact.

In 1518, Philip Melanchthon (1497–1560), a young professor of Greek, joined Luther at the University of Wittenberg and delivered an inaugural address (*On Improving the Studies of the Young*) attacking scholasticism and defending classical studies. Melanchthon and Luther completely restructured Wittenberg's curriculum. New chairs of Greek and Hebrew were created. Canon law and commentaries on Lombard's *Sentences* were dropped. Straightforward historical and textual analysis replaced lectures consisting of scholastic glosses and commentaries on Aristotle's works. Candidates for theological degrees defended their theses by exegetical analyses of biblical passages and not by citations from the "authorities." Luther and Melanchthon also pressed for universal compulsory education so that both boys and girls could at least learn to read the Bible in vernacular translation.

The university that developed in Geneva from an academy founded by John Calvin and his successor, Theodore Beza, developed a program similar to Wittenberg's. The many refugees who flocked to Geneva came under its influence and spread its educational reforms when they returned to France, Scotland, and England, or established homes in the New World.

The focus of humanist education may have narrowed as Protestants took it over, but humanist culture and learning profited from the Reformation. By the seventeenth century, a working knowledge of Greek and Hebrew was commonplace in educated circles, and Protestant schools preserved many of the pedagogical achievements of humanism and transmitted them to the modern world. (See "Encountering the Past: Table Manners.")

ENCOUNTERING THE PAST

TABLE MANNERS

Humanists believed that education ought to mix pleasure with discipline. The family meal was, therefore, a suitable occasion for instructing the young in the lessons of life. Learning required neatness, order, respect, and attentiveness—traits that Hans Sachs, a sixteenth-century father, wanted his children to learn at his table.

HOW DO table manners prepare a child for life?

Listen you children who are going to table.

Wash your hands and cut your nails.

Do not sit at the head of the table;

This is reserved for the father of the house.

Do not commence eating until a blessing has been said.

…permit the eldest to begin first.

Proceed in a disciplined manner.

Do not snort or smack like a pig.

Do not reach violently for bread….

Do not stir food around on your plate or linger over it….

Rushing through your meal is bad manners.

Do not reach for more food while your mouth is still full,

Nor talk with your mouth full….

Chew your food with your mouth closed.

Do not lick the corners of your mouth like a dog….

Do not belch or cry out….

Do not stare at a person as if you were watching him eat.

Do not elbow the person sitting next to you….

Do not rock back and forth on the bench, lest you let loose a stink….

If sexual play occurs at table, pretend you do not see it….

Do not pick your nose….

Let no one wipe his mouth on the table cloth….

Silently praise and thank God for the food he has graciously provided.

Translation by S. Ozment from S. Ozment, *When Fathers Ruled: Family Life in Reformation Europe* (Cambridge, MA: Harvard University Press, 1983), 142–143.

A Family Meal. In Max Geisberg, *The German Single-Leaf Woodcuts*, ill: *1500–1550*, rev. and ed. by W. L. Strauss (New York, Hacker Art Books, 1974).

Used by permission of Hacker Art Books

THE REFORMATION AND THE CHANGING ROLE OF WOMEN

The Protestant reformers rejected ascetic disciplines as vain attempts to earn salvation. They urged clergy to marry to dispel the belief that the lives of clergy were spiritually more meritorious than those of laity. This created a more positive attitude toward sexuality that improved views of women.

Medieval thinkers tended to look down on sexually active women (as following the path of Eve) and exalt virgins (imitators of Jesus' mother, Mary). Protestants, however, saw women as worthy in their own right and honored their roles as wives and mothers as biblical vocations. Reformers acknowledged the contributions their wives made to their ministries. They viewed husband and wife as co-workers in the family, and they regarded the family as a sacred, God-ordained institution. Protestant marriage was, however, not a sacrament. Divorce was possible, and women had the right to leave husbands who flagrantly violated marriage contracts. From a modern perspective, Protestant women were still subservient to men, but they were accorded new respect and given greater legal protection.

Protestants promoted literacy among women, for they expected women to study the Bible to learn how to function as pious housewives. Female authors contributed to the literature of the Reformation, and some of them made much of the biblical passages that suggested women were equal to men before God. This encouraged serious thought about women's roles that inched society marginally closer to female emancipation.

WHAT WAS family life like in early modern Europe?

FAMILY LIFE IN EARLY MODERN EUROPE

During the sixteenth and seventeenth centuries, customs associated with marriage and family life changed in many ways, but this was only partially due to the Reformation.

LATER MARRIAGES

Men and women of the Reformation era tended to wait longer before marrying than their medieval ancestors had. The church-sanctioned minimum age for marriage remained fourteen for men and twelve for women, and betrothal could occur at these young ages if parents approved. Grooms, however, were usually in their mid-to-late twenties rather than their late teens and early twenties. Brides wed in their early-to-mid twenties rather than their teens. These later marriages reflected the difficulty couples had in amassing enough capital to establish independent households. Increasing family size and population during the fifteenth and early sixteenth centuries led to property being divided among more heirs. Smaller shares meant couples had to work longer to prepare materially for marriage. Up to 20 percent of sixteenth-century women may not have married. Their lot was often to suffer increasing impoverishment as they aged without the support of husband or children.

ARRANGED MARRIAGES

Marriages tended to be arranged in the sense that the male heads of the families to which the potential bride and groom belonged usually met to consider the prospect of marriage before admitting their children to the discussion. It was rare, however, for the man and woman involved not to know each other or have no prior relationship. Children had a legal right to resist an unwanted marriage, and a forced marriage was, by definition, invalid. The best marriage was one desired by both parties and approved by their families.

The custom of marrying later in life meant the average length of marriages decreased and the rate of remarriage increased. Older women were more likely to die bearing children, and as the rapid growth of orphanages and foundling homes between 1600 and 1800 testifies, delayed marriage exposed more of them to the problems created by out-of-wedlock pregnancies.

FAMILY SIZE

The early modern family was conjugal or nuclear. It consisted of a father and a mother and an average of two to four surviving children. Pregnancies might occur about every two years. About one-third of the children born died by age five, and one-half were dead by age twenty. Rare was the family at any social level

 THE REFORMATION AND THE CHANGING ROLE OF WOMEN

Education	• Encouraged female literacy in the vernacular
	• Women found biblical passages that suggested they were equal to men
	• Women became independent authors
Later Marriages	• Men and women tended to wait until their mid-to-late twenties to marry
	• Later marriages meant marriages of shorter duration
	• Remarriage was now more common for men who lost wives in childbearing
Arranged Marriages	• Bride and groom often knew each other in advance of marriage
	• Emotional feeling for one another was increasingly respected by parents
	• Forced marriages were, by definition, invalid and often failed
Family Size	• Large households consisted of in-laws, servants, laborers, and boarders
	• The average husband and wife had seven or eight children but most families experienced infant mortality and child death
Wet Nursing	• Church and physicians condemned the use of wet nurses
	• Upper-class women viewed the use of wet nurses as a symbol of high rank
	• The practice increased the rate of infant mortality

that did not suffer the loss of children. Martin Luther fathered six children, two of whom died—one at eight months and another at thirteen years.

BIRTH CONTROL

Birth control methods of limited effectiveness (acidic ointments, sponges, and coitus interruptus, for example) have been available since antiquity. The church's growing condemnation of contraception in the thirteenth and fourteenth centuries suggests its use was increasing. Thomas Aquinas justified the church's position by arguing that a natural act, such as sex, was moral only when it served the end for which it was created—in this case, the production of children.

WET NURSING

Theologians and physicians both condemned the widespread custom of turning newborn infants over to wet nurses. A wet nurse was usually a poor woman who was paid to suckle a wealthier woman's child. Wet nursing often exposed infants to greater risks from disease and neglect, but nursing a child was a chore many upper-class women found distasteful. Husbands also disliked it, for the church forbade sexual intercourse while a woman was lactating on the theory that sexual activity spoiled a woman's milk. Nursing also depresses a woman's ovulation cycles, and some women may have prolonged nursing to fend off another pregnancy. For wealthy burghers and noblemen who wanted an abundance of male heirs, the time their wives spent nursing was time wasted.

LOVING FAMILIES?

In addition to wet nursing, other practices of early modern families seem cold and unloving from our perspective. A child who spent the first year of life living away from home with a wet nurse might, between the ages of nine and fourteen, find herself or himself sent away from home again for an apprenticeship or employment. Husbands were often much older than wives. This may have hampered their intellectual intimacy. Widowed individuals sometimes remarried very quickly.

Expressions of love and affection are, however, as relative to time and culture as other behaviors. Given the context, a kindness in one historical period can seem a cruelty in another. Conditions made single life difficult in the sixteenth century and necessitated rapid remarriage. Children who began their apprenticeships at an early age had an advantage in a competitive economic environment that offered limited educational opportunities. No persuasive evidence indicates that people of the Reformation era were less capable of loving one another than modern people are.

LITERARY IMAGINATION IN TRANSITION

HOW WAS the transition from medieval to modern reflected in the works of the great literary figures of the era?

*A*s Europe approached the seventeenth century, it was no longer medieval but neither was it yet modern. The great literary figures of the era produced transitional works that combined traditional values and fresh perspectives on human life.

MIGUEL DE CERVANTES SAAVEDRA: REJECTION OF IDEALISM

There was religious reform in Spain but no Protestant Reformation. The state used the Inquisition to enforce religious conformity in Spain, and the religion of which the state approved was the mystical, ascetic Christianity of the early Middle Ages. For centuries, Spain had been a nation of crusaders, and the union of Catholic piety and secular power, characteristic of crusades, imbued Spain's culture with tinges of medieval chivalry. The novels and plays of the period are almost all devoted to stories in which the virtues of honor and loyalty are tested.

Miguel de Cervantes Saavedra (1547–1616), generally described as Spain's greatest writer, was fascinated by the strengths and weaknesses of religious idealism. Cervantes was self-educated. He read widely and immersed himself in the "school of life." As a youth, he lived for a while in Rome working for a Spanish cardinal. He entered the army and was decorated for gallantry in the Battle of Lepanto (1571). He was later captured by pirates and spent five years as a slave in Algiers. Back in Spain, his work as a tax collector inadvertently set him on the path to literary repute. In prison in 1603 for padding his accounts, he began to write his great book, *Don Quixote*.

Cervantes set out to satirize the chivalric romances popular in Spain in his day, but he developed an affection for Don Quixote, the deluded knight whose story his novel tells. *Don Quixote* is superficially satirical. It asks serious questions about what gives meaning to human lives. Don Quixote is a none-too-stable, middle-aged man driven mad by reading too many chivalric romances. He aspires to become the knight of his own imagination and sets out on a quest for opportunities to prove himself. As a courtly lover, he dedicates himself to the service of Dulcinea, a quite unworthy peasant girl whom he mistakes for a refined, noble lady. Sancho Panza, a clever, worldly wise peasant, accompanies him as his squire and watches with bemused skepticism as the Don repeatedly makes a fool of himself. The story ends tragically when a well-meaning friend restores Don Quixote's reason by defeating him in battle and forcing him to renounce his quest for knighthood. Stripped of the delusion that gave meaning to his life, the Don returns to his village to die a shamed and brokenhearted old man. *Don Quixote* places the modern realism of Sancho Panza beside the old-fashioned religious idealism of the Don and comes to the conclusion that both are essential elements in fully developed humanity.

WILLIAM SHAKESPEARE: DRAMATIST OF THE AGE

Little is known about William Shakespeare (1564–1616), the greatest playwright in the English language. He married young (at age eighteen), and by 1585, he and his wife, Anne Hathaway, had three children. He may have worked for a time as a schoolteacher. The wide but erratic knowledge of history and classical literature that informs his plays suggests he was not schooled as a professional scholar.

Once he could afford it, Shakespeare chose to live the life of a country gentleman. He entered eagerly into the commercialism and the bawdy pleasures of the Elizabethan Age, and his work shows no trace of Puritan anxiety about worldliness. He was radical in neither politics nor religion, and his few allusions to Puritans are more critical than complimentary. By modern standards he was a political conservative, accepting the social rankings and the power structure of his day and demonstrating unquestioned patriotism.

Shakespeare knew every aspect of life in the theater. He was playwright, actor, and owner-producer. He wrote and performed for an important company of actors, the King's Men, and, between 1590 and 1610, many of his plays were staged at Elizabeth's court. French drama in Shakespeare's day closely imitated classical models, but the Elizabethan audience that Shakespeare strove to please welcomed a mixture of styles. Shakespeare drew inspiration from the past and from his contemporaries, and his work combined aspects of classical drama, medieval morality plays, and current Italian short stories.

Shakespeare's most original tragedy may be *Romeo and Juliet* (1597). His four greatest were written in close succession: *Hamlet* (1603), *Othello* (1604), *King Lear* (1605), and *Macbeth* (1606). He also wrote comedies and plays based on historical events. The latter reflect propaganda that served the interests of the Tudor monarchy, but almost all of Shakespeare's plays have demonstrated a remarkable ability to transcend the limits of the world for which they were written. Their keen analyses of motivation, stirring evocation of emotion, and stunning language keep them alive and still filling theaters.

SUMMARY

Society and Religion The Protestant Reformation had roots in political, social, and economic concerns. The emergence of centralizing national governments was challenging local custom and authority through much of Europe; in Germany and Switzerland, the free imperial cities were important early hotbeds of Protestantism. Often, groups (such as guilds) or regions in which people felt controlled by authority figures were particularly receptive to Protestantism. Laypeople were gaining power to criticize, and attempt to reform, the church, both because they were gaining cultural authority in general and because the church's crises had cost it so much credibility.

Martin Luther and the German Reformation to 1525 Martin Luther, like many other Germans, was concerned about the church's sale of indulgences and other financial and political arrangements. An ordained priest with a doctorate in theology, he developed the doctrine of justification by faith alone, which

IMAGE KEY
for pages 262–263

a. The Ecstasy of Saint Teresa de Avila
   by Gianlorenzo Bernini

b. Isenheim altarpiece, c. 1513-1515.
   Mathias Grunewald,
   1470/80–1528, German

c. 15th Century Italian Silver Cross

d. Gemalde von Lucas Cranach d. A.,
   1529, "Dr. Martin Luther und seine
   Ehefrau Katharina von Bora."
   (Martin Luther and his wife
   Katharina von Bora)

e. Henry VIII, 16th century, Hans the
   younger Holbein—C.1497–1543,
   German

f. Painting, Flemish, 17th century
   Peter Paul Rubens (1577-1640)
   "The Miracle of Saint Ignace
   Loyola"

g. A portrait of the young John Calvin
   Bibliotheque Publique et Universitaire,
   Geneva

h. "The Subservient Husband" by
   Hans Schaufelein

offers salvation to believers in Christ. In 1517, Luther posted ninety-five theses against indulgence on the door of a church in Wittenberg. This sparked the Reformation. In the following years, Luther developed and publicized his theology; he was excommunicated in 1521. German humanists, peasants, and others supported Luther and his ideas, although Luther urged princes to suppress the peasants' revolt of 1524–1525.

The Reformation Elsewhere In Switzerland, France, and elsewhere in Europe, variations of Protestantism developed. In the 1520s, Ulrich Zwingli orchestrated the Swiss Reformation, from his post as the people's priest in the main church of Zurich. Zwingli believed a literal reading of Scripture should guide Christian beliefs and practices. More radical groups emerged, including Anabaptists, who believed baptism should only be performed on adults, who were capable of choosing their religion. John Calvin and his followers wanted to transform society morally, starting in Geneva in 1540. In the second half of the sixteenth century, Calvinism displaced Lutheranism as Europe's dominant form of Protestantism.

Political Consolidation of the Lutheran Reformation Between 1530 and 1552, the emperor Charles V made repeated attempts to persuade or force Protestants to revert to Catholicism. The 1555 Peace of Augsburg formalized Lutheranism's official status in the empire. Lutheranism also became the official state religion in Denmark and Sweden. Calvinists and Anabaptists, among others, were still excluded from official recognition throughout Europe.

The English Reformation to 1553 King Henry VIII's marital history had dramatic consequences for England's religion: because Henry wanted to marry Anne Boleyn, and because Pope Clement VII would not annul Henry's marriage to Catherine of Aragon, Parliament decreed that the king, not the pope, was the "supreme head on earth of the Church of England." But, by the 1530s, many of Henry's subjects were far more sympathetic to Protestantism than the king himself was; Henry's Church of England differed little from the Catholic Church. Only under the reign of his son, Edward VI, was Protestantism really instituted in England.

Catholic Reform and Counter-Reformation Protestants were not the only critics of the Catholic Church. Although the popes resisted reform, many new reform-oriented orders were established in the sixteenth century. Ignatius of Loyola founded what became one of the most significant of these orders, the Jesuits, who stressed a powerful combination of discipline and traditional spirituality. Between 1545 and 1563, a council of the church met at Trent to reassert Catholic doctrine. As a result of the Council of Trent, internal church discipline was reformed, but doctrine became even more strongly traditional and scholastic in orientation. Improvements in the education and behavior of local clergy helped revive parish life.

The Social Significance of the Reformation in Western Europe Although the Reformation was politically conservative, it revolutionized religious practice and institutions in part of Europe. In cities that became Protestant, many aspects of life were transformed. The numbers of clergy in these cities declined by two-thirds, one-third of all churches were closed, there were one-third fewer religious holidays, and most cloisters were closed. Some changes did not endure: more than half the original converts to Protestantism returned to the Catholic Church by the end of the sixteenth century. Protestant reformers helped disseminate humanist learning and culture. The ideal of the companionate marriage and other Protestant views helped improve the status of women.

Family Life in Early Modern Europe   Marriage occurred at a later age in the sixteenth through eighteenth centuries than it had previously in Europe and England. One reason for this shift was that, in a time of population growth, it took couples longer to accumulate the capital needed to raise a family. Parents were involved in arranging their children's marriages, although the couple's own wishes also carried significant weight. Generally, two to four children survived to adulthood in the European nuclear family. Birth control was not very effective; wet nursing was controversial. Although they sometimes exhibited it in ways that may seem strange to us, early modern parents almost certainly loved their children, and probably also each other.

Literary Imagination in Transition   Miguel de Cervantes Saavedra and William Shakespeare are among the most renowned authors of this period. Cervantes lived and worked in Catholic Spain; Shakespeare was a product of Protestant England. Their writings reflect their very different situations and interests. Cervantes's most famous work, *Don Quixote*, pays homage to the tradition of chivalric romance. Shakespeare's dramas cover a wide range of topics, including history; his universal themes and brilliant technique explain his enduring popularity.

REVIEW QUESTIONS

1. What were the main problems of the church that contributed to the Protestant Reformation? On what did Luther and Zwingli agree? On what did they disagree? What about Luther and Calvin?

2. What was the Catholic Reformation? What were the major reforms instituted by the Council of Trent? Did the Protestant Reformation have a healthy effect on the Catholic Church?

3. Why did Henry VIII break with the Catholic Church? Did he establish a truly Protestant religion in England? What problems did his successors face as a result of his religious policies?

4. What impact did the Reformation have on women in the sixteenth and seventeenth centuries? What new factors and pressures affected relations between men and women, family size, and child care during this period?

KEY TERMS

Act of Supremacy   (p. 277)   **Augsburg Confession**   (p. 275)   **indulgence**   (p. 267)
Anabaptists   (p. 272)

   For additional study resources for this chapter, go to:
www.prenhall.com/kagan3/chapter11

12 The Age of Religious Wars

CHAPTER HIGHLIGHTS

Renewed Religious Struggle After the 1555 Peace of Augsburg, religious strife in Europe centered on the conflict between Calvinism and Catholicism. In time, some intellectuals, and a very few political leaders, came to support religious toleration.

The French Wars of Religion (1562–1598) The rulers of France tried to suppress the France's Huguenots. Conflict between Catholic and Protestant elites led to bloodshed and civil war. In 1593 Henry IV renounced Protestantism and, in 1598, issued the Edict of Nantes.

Imperial Spain and the Reign of Philip II (r. 1556–1598) Philip II controlled vast territories, many people, and much wealth. During the first half of his reign, Philip focused his attention on the demographic and economic changes within his realm, conflict with the Turks, and the annexation of Portugal. The second half of his reign was dominated by the failed effort to hold on to control of the Netherlands.

England and Spain (1553–1603) Under Mary I, England returned to Catholicism and Protestants were persecuted. Over the course of her long reign, Mary's successor, Elizabeth I, steered a middle course in all areas, most notably religion, where she created a moderate Anglican church.

The Thirty Years' War (1618–1648) Germany's political fragmentation set the stage for the Thirty Years' War. The war had four distinct periods: the Bohemian period (1618–1625), the Danish period (1625–1629), the Swedish period (1630–1635), and the French period (1635–1648). The war was brought to an end by the 1648 Treaty of Westphalia.

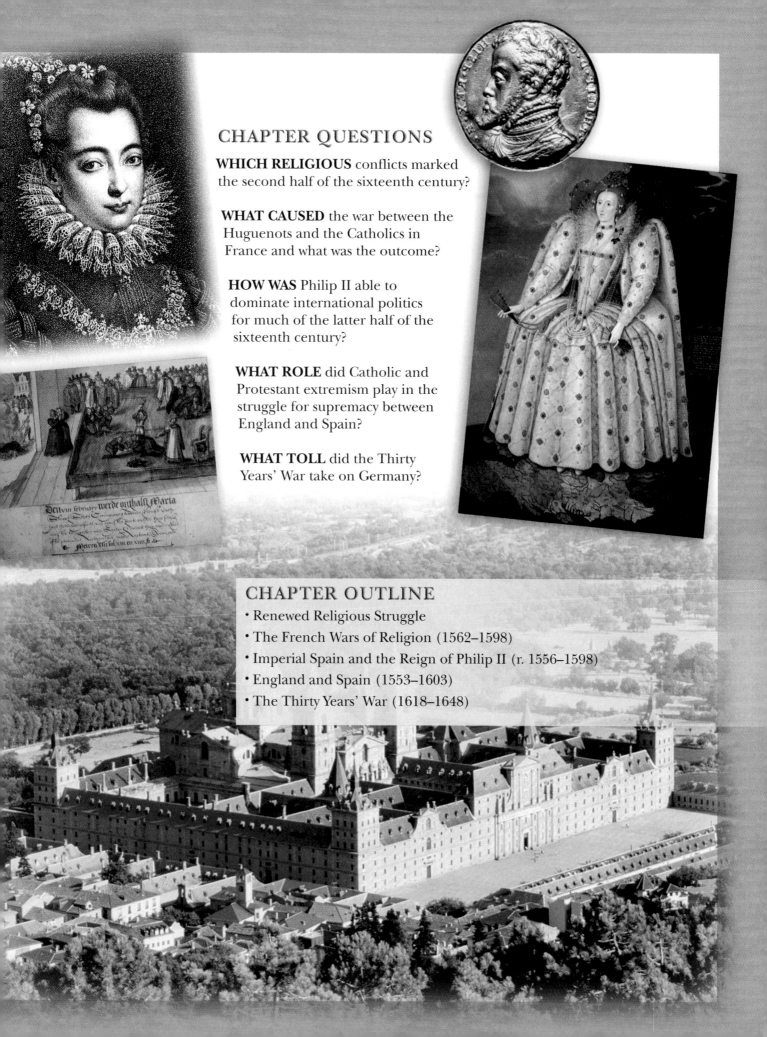

CHAPTER QUESTIONS

WHICH RELIGIOUS conflicts marked the second half of the sixteenth century?

WHAT CAUSED the war between the Huguenots and the Catholics in France and what was the outcome?

HOW WAS Philip II able to dominate international politics for much of the latter half of the sixteenth century?

WHAT ROLE did Catholic and Protestant extremism play in the struggle for supremacy between England and Spain?

WHAT TOLL did the Thirty Years' War take on Germany?

CHAPTER OUTLINE

- Renewed Religious Struggle
- The French Wars of Religion (1562–1598)
- Imperial Spain and the Reign of Philip II (r. 1556–1598)
- England and Spain (1553–1603)
- The Thirty Years' War (1618–1648)

IMAGE KEY
Image Key for pages 290–291 is on page 310.

WHICH RELIGIOUS conflicts marked the second half of the sixteenth century?

Political rivalries and religious conflicts combined to make the late sixteenth and the early seventeenth centuries an "age of religious wars." The era was plagued by civil conflicts within nations and by battles among nations. Catholic and Protestant factions contended within France, the Netherlands, and England. The Catholic monarchies of France and Spain attacked the Protestant regimes in England and the Netherlands. Ultimately, every major nation in Europe was drawn into a conflict that devastated Germany: the Thirty Years' War (1618–1648).

RENEWED RELIGIOUS STRUGGLE

During the first half of the sixteenth century, religious war was confined to parts of central Europe where Lutherans fought for recognition. In the second half of the sixteenth century, the primary arena for hostilities shifted to western Europe (France, the Netherlands, England, and Scotland) where Calvinists struggled for their cause.

The Peace of Augsburg (1555) ended the first phase of the war in central Europe by granting each ruler of a region within the Holy Roman Empire the right to determine the religion of his subjects. The only kind of Protestantism that Augsburg recognized, however, was Lutheranism. Lutherans and Catholics joined forces to suppress Anabaptists and other sectarians, and Calvinists were not yet numerous enough to attract attention.

By the time the Council of Trent adjourned in 1563, the **Counter-Reformation** had reinvigorated the Roman Catholic Church, and the Jesuits were spearheading an offensive to recover regions lost to Protestantism. John Calvin, who died in 1564, made Geneva both a refuge for Protestants fleeing persecution and a school to train them to meet the Catholic challenge.

Counter-Reformation A reorganization of the Catholic Church that equipped it to meet the challenges posed by the Protestant Reformation.

Genevan Calvinism and post-Trent Catholicism were equally dogmatic and aggressive and mutually incompatible. Calvinism mandated a presbyterian organization that distributed authority over the church among local boards of lay and clerical *presbyters* (elders) representing individual congregations. The administration of the Roman Catholic Church was, by contrast, a centralized hierarchy under the absolute control of the pope. The pope and bishops ruled supreme without the necessity of consulting the laity. Calvinism attracted people who favored the decentralization and distribution of political power and who opposed authoritarian rule, whereas Catholicism was preferred by advocates of absolute monarchy—by those who favored "one king, one law, one faith."

Contrast between an eighteenth-century Catholic baroque church in Ottobeuren, Bavaria and a seventeenth-century Calvinist plain church in the Palatinate. The ornamental Catholic church inspires worshipers to self-transcendence, while the undecorated Protestant church focuses attention on God's word.

(Left) Art Resource, NY (Right) German National Museum, Nuremberg, Germany

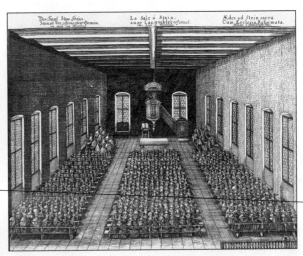

1559	Treaty of Cateau-Cambrésis ends Habsburg-Valois wars
1559	Francis II succeeds to French throne under regency of his mother, Catherine de Médicis
1562	Protestant worshipers massacred at Vassy in Champagne by the duke of Guise
1572	The Saint Bartholomew's Day Massacre leaves thousands of Protestants dead
1589	Assassination of Henry III brings the Huguenot Henry of Navarre to throne as Henry IV
1593	Henry IV embraces Catholicism
1598	Henry IV grants Huguenots religious and civil freedoms in the Edict of Nantes
1610	Henry IV assassinated

As religious wars engulfed Europe, intellectuals perceived the wisdom of religious pluralism and toleration. Skepticism, relativism, and individualism in matters of faith increasingly came to be seen as virtues. Valentin Weigel (1533–1588), a Lutheran who surveyed a half century of religious strife in Germany, spoke for many when he advised people to look within themselves for religious truth and not to churches and creeds.

Politicians were slower than intellectuals to embrace principles of toleration, but the ones who did succeeded best at keeping religious tension under control. These so-called *politiques* (pragmatic monarchs such as Elizabeth I of England) preserved order by endorsing moderation and compromise. Rulers who took religion with utmost seriousness (Mary I of England, Philip II of Spain, and England's Oliver Cromwell, for example) failed to maintain stability.

THE FRENCH WARS OF RELIGION (1562–1598)

In the 1520s, Lutheran ideas began to circulate in Paris and to excite the suspicions of the French government. French Protestants were dubbed **Huguenots** after Besançon Hugues, the leader of the revolt that won Geneva its freedom at that time.

In 1525, Emperor Charles V captured King Francis I of France at the Battle of Pavia in Italy. The French authorities then began to persecute Protestants in the hope that by cooperating with Charles's anti-Protestant campaign they might win favorable terms for the king's release. A second crackdown followed a decade later in reaction to Protestant groups that (on October 18, 1534) plastered Paris and other cities with anti-Catholic placards. The government's actions persuaded some French reformers (John Calvin among them) to flee their homeland.

The Habsburg-Valois wars between France and the Holy Roman Empire ended with the Treaty of Cateau-Cambrésis in 1559. The treaty marked a shift in the European balance of power that favored Habsburg Spain, and it was followed by the outbreak of civil war in France.

In 1559, France's king Henry II (r. 1547–1559) was mortally wounded in a tournament, and his sickly fifteen-year-old son, Francis II, ascended the throne.

WHAT CAUSED the war between the Huguenots and the Catholics in France and what was the outcome?

politique Ruler or person in a position of power who puts the success and well-being of his or her state above all else.

Huguenots French Protestants, named after Besançon Hugues, the leader of the revolt that won Geneva its freedom at that time.

Catherine de Médicis (1519–1589) exercised power in France during the reigns of her three sons Francis II (r. 1559–1560), Charles IX (r. 1560–1574), and Henry III (r. 1574–1589).

Liaison Agency, Inc.

The queen mother, Catherine de Médicis (1519–1589), headed a regency government for her son, and its weakness tempted three powerful families to make bids for power. The Bourbons dominated southern and western portions of France. The Montmorency-Chatillons were strong in the center, and the base for the Guises was in the east.

The Guises initially enjoyed most influence with the young king. Duke Francis of Guise had commanded Henry II's army. His brothers, Charles and Louis, were both cardinals, and King Francis married their niece, Mary Stuart, Queen of Scotland. The Guises were militant, reactionary Catholics. France's Protestants rallied in support of their opponents, the Bourbon prince of Condé, Louis I (d. 1569), and the Montmorency-Chatillons admiral, Gaspard de Coligny (1519–1572).

APPEAL OF CALVINISM

French Calvinism drew its recruits primarily from ambitious aristocrats and discontented townspeople. By 1561, there were more than 2,000 Huguenot congregations in France, but Huguenots accounted for only about one-fifteenth of France's population. They were in the majority in only two regions (Dauphiné and Languedoc). However, they controlled important districts and were heavily represented among the more powerful classes in French society. Over two-fifths of the country's aristocrats became Huguenots. Many saw Protestantism as a route to greater authority over their domains. They hoped it would lead to France endorsing a principle of territorial sovereignty for magnates akin to the arrangements the imperial diet negotiated in the Peace of Augsburg.

The military forces led by Condé and Coligny gradually merged with the Huguenot churches, for they had much to gain from one another. Calvinism provided both a theological justification and a practical motive for opposing the Catholic monarchy. Calvinism needed military support if it hoped to become a viable religion in France, but the confluence of secular and sacred motives raised doubts about the religious sincerity of some Huguenot leaders. Religious conviction was neither the only nor always the main reason for their conversion to Protestantism.

CATHERINE DE MÉDICIS AND THE GUISES

Francis II died in 1560, but his mother, Catherine de Médicis, continued to rule France as regent for his heir, her second son, Charles IX (r. 1560–1574). Catherine's overriding concern was to preserve the prerogatives of the monarchy. To balance the power of the Guises, she sought allies among the Protestants. In 1562, she issued the January Edict, a decree that granted Protestants the right to hold public worship services in the countryside and private meetings in towns. Royal efforts to encourage toleration ended abruptly, however, when in March 1562, the duke of Guise massacred a Protestant congregation at Vassy. Had Condé and the Huguenot armies rushed immediately to the queen's side after this attack, they might have secured an alliance with Catherine, who feared the powerful Guises. But the Protestant leaders hesitated, and the Guises won control of the young king and his mother.

The Peace of Saint-Germain-en-Laye   The duke of Guise was assassinated during the initial phase of the French religious wars (April 1562 to March 1563). Hostilities flared up again in 1567–1568, and the bloodiest phase in the conflict raged from September 1568 to August 1570. Huguenot leadership passed to Coligny, a fine military strategist, and in 1570, he negotiated the Peace of Saint-Germain-en-Laye. The crown acknowledged the power of the Protestant nobles by granting them religious freedom within their territories and the right to fortify their cities.

Queen Catherine tried to protect the throne by balancing the fanatical Huguenot and Guise extremes. She, however, favored Catholicism and tolerated Protestants only to counter Guise domination of the monarchy. After the Peace of Saint-Germain-en-Laye strengthened the Huguenots, Catherine switched sides and began to plot with the Guises to prevent the Protestants from winning over her son. Catherine had reason to fear Coligny, for he was on the verge of persuading the young king to invade the Netherlands to help the Dutch Protestants against their Catholic Habsburg ruler. This would have set France on a collision course with Spain, Europe's strongest state, and likely disaster.

The Saint Bartholomew's Day Massacre   On August 18, 1572, the French nobility gathered in Paris for the wedding of the king's sister, Marguerite of Valois, to Henry of Navarre, a Huguenot leader. Four days later, an attempt was made on Coligny's life. Catherine had apparently been party to a plot by the Guises to eliminate Coligny, and when it failed, she panicked. She feared both the king's reaction to her complicity with the Guises and what the Huguenots and Coligny might do in seeking revenge. In desperation, she convinced Charles that a Huguenot coup was afoot and only the swift execution of the Protestant leaders could save the crown.

On Saint Bartholomew's Day, August 24, 1572, Coligny and 3,000 fellow Huguenots were ambushed in Paris and butchered. Within three days, an estimated 20,000 Huguenots died, the victims of coordinated attacks throughout France. Protestants everywhere were horrified, whereas Pope Gregory XIII and Philip II of Spain greeted the news with special religious celebrations.

Catholics came to regret the slaughter of the Huguenots, for Saint Bartholomew's Day changed the nature of all the struggles between Protestants and Catholics. The disastrous outcome of France's religious squabbling convinced Protestants in many lands that they were engaged in an international fight to the death with an adversary whose cruelty justified any means of resistance.

Protestant Resistance Theory   At the start of the Reformation, Protestants tried to honor the Scripture that admonishes subjects to obey the rulers God gives them (Romans 13:1). Only after Charles V ordered Protestants to return to the Catholic faith (1530) did Luther grudgingly approve opposition to the emperor. Calvin, secure in his control of Geneva, condemned rebellion against lawfully constituted governments. He, however, also taught that the lower magistrates of those governments had the duty to oppose higher officials if these officials abused their authority. John Knox, a Scot driven into exile by the Catholic regent for Scotland, Mary of Guise, was strongly motivated by his personal experiences to develop a Calvinist rationale for revolution. Knox's *First Blast of the Trumpet Against the Terrible Regiment of Women* (1558) declared that the removal of a heathen (Catholic) tyrant was not only permissible but a Christian duty. The Saint Bartholomew's Day Massacre brought other Calvinists around to his point of view. François Hotman's *Franco-Gallia* (1573) argued that the Estates General, France's representative assembly, was the country's highest authority and empowered to authorize resistance to the crown. Theodore Beza's *On the Right of Magistrates over Their Subjects* (1574) justified the overthrow of tyrants by lower authorities, and Philippe du Plessis Mornay's *Defense of Liberty Against*

HISTORY'S VOICES

THEODORE BEZA DEFENDS THE RIGHT TO RESIST TYRANNY

uther and other Protestants, although accused by Catholics of fomenting social division and revolution, had defended strict obedience to established political authority. After the 1572 St. Bartholomew's Day Massacre however, many Protestants urged resistance to tyranny. In 1574, Theodore Beza pointed out the duties of rulers to their subjects and explained circumstances that justified resistance to authority.

TO BEZA, what are the obligations of rulers? What are the rights of subjects?

It is apparent that there is a mutual obligation between the king and the officers of a kingdom; that the government of the kingdom is not in the hands of the king in its entirety, but only the sovereign degree; that each of the officers has a share in accord with his degree; and that there are definite conditions on either side. If these conditions are not observed by the inferior officers, it is the part of the sovereign to dismiss and punish them. . . . If the king, hereditary or elective, clearly goes back on the conditions without which he would not have been recognized and acknowledged, can there be any doubt that the lesser

magistrates of the kingdom, of the cities, and of the provinces, the administration of which they have received from the sovereignty itself, are free of their oath, at least to the extent that they are entitled to resist flagrant oppression of the realm which they swore to defend and protect according to their office and their particular jurisdiction? . . .

We must now speak of the third class of subjects, which though admittedly subject to the sovereign in a certain respect, is, in another respect, and in cases of necessity the protector of the rights of the sovereignty itself, and is established to hold the sovereign to his duty, and even, if need be, to constrain and punish him. . . . The people is prior to all the magistrates, and does not exist for them, but they for it. . . . Whenever law and equity prevailed, nations neither created nor accepted kings except upon definite conditions. From this it follows that when kings flagrantly violate these terms, these who have the power to give them their authority have no less power to deprive them of it.

Constitutionalism and Resistance in the Sixteenth Century: Three Treatises by Hotman, Beza, and Mornay, trans. and ed. by Julian H. Franklin (New York: Pegasus, 1969), pp. 111–114.

Tyrants (1579) urged princes, nobles, and magistrates to cooperate in rooting out tyranny wherever it appeared. (See "History's Voices: Theodore Beza Defends the Right to Resist Tyranny.")

THE RISE TO POWER OF HENRY OF NAVARRE

Henry III (r. 1574–1589), the last of Henry II's sons to wear the French crown, was caught between the vengeful Huguenots and the Catholic League, an alliance of radicals that Henry of Guise formed in 1576. Like his mother Catherine, Henry sought a middle course and appealed to the moderate Catholics and Huguenots, who valued political stability more than religious unity. The terms Henry offered in the Peace of Beaulieu (May 1576) promised the Huguenots almost complete religious and civil freedom, but the Catholic League (which had Spain's backing) was able to force Henry to reverse himself. In October 1577, the Edict of Poitiers again restricted Huguenot worship to specifically designated areas.

By the mid–1580s, Henry II was desperate to escape domination by the Catholic League, and in 1588 (on the "Day of the Barricades"), he launched a surprise attack to try to rout the league. It failed, and the king fled. But the timely arrival of the news that the English had given Spain a major defeat emboldened him to order the assassinations of both the duke and the cardinal of Guise. These murders enraged the Catholic League, which was led by another Guise brother, Duke Charles of Mayenne. In April 1589, the king was driven to seek an alliance with the Protestant leader, Henry of Navarre, the Bourbon heir to the throne. As the two Henrys prepared to attack the Guise stronghold in Paris, a fanatical Jacobin friar assassinated Henry III, the Valois king, and cleared the way for Henry of Navarre to become Henry IV (r. 1589–1610), France's first Bourbon monarch. Pope Sixtus V and King Philip II of Spain were aghast at the prospect of France suddenly becoming a Protestant nation. Philip sent troops to support the Catholic League and to claim the throne of France for his daughter, Isabella, Henry II's granddaughter.

Henry IV of France (r. 1589–1610) on horseback, painted in 1594.

Reunion des Musees Nationaux, Art Resource, NY

Spain's intervention rallied the people of France to Henry IV's side and strengthened his hold on the crown. Henry was a popular man who had the wit and charm to neutralize any enemy in a face-to-face meeting. He was also a *politique,* a leader who considered religion less important than peace. Henry reasoned that because most of his subjects were Catholics, he could best rule (and protect Protestants) as a Catholic. Consequently, on July 25, 1593, he converted to Catholicism—allegedly quipping, "Paris is worth a mass." The Huguenots were horrified. Pope Clement VIII was skeptical, but most of the French were relieved. They had had enough of war.

THE EDICT OF NANTES

On April 13, 1598, Henry's Edict of Nantes ended the civil wars of religion, and on May 2, 1598, the Treaty of Vervins made peace between France and Spain. The Edict of Nantes confirmed a promise of toleration that Henry IV had made the Huguenots (who now numbered well over a million) at the start of his reign. It designated certain towns and territories within France as places where Huguenots could openly worship, hold public offices, enter universities, and maintain forts. Nantes, however, was more a truce than a peace. It came close to creating states within the state, and it turned a hot war into a cold one that claimed Henry as a victim. In May 1610, he was assassinated by a Catholic fanatic.

11.5
The Edict of Nantes

IMPERIAL SPAIN AND THE REIGN OF PHILIP II (R. 1556–1598)

PILLARS OF SPANISH POWER

Philip II of Spain dominated international politics for much of the latter half of the sixteenth century. Bitter experience had led his father, Charles V, to conclude that the Habsburg family lands were too extensive to be governed by one man. He, therefore, divided them between his son and his brother. Philip inherited the intensely Catholic and militarily supreme western half. The eastern portion (Austria, Bohemia, and Hungary) and the imperial title went to Philip's uncle, Ferdinand I.

HOW WAS Philip II able to dominate international politics for much of the latter half of the sixteenth century?

Philip was a reclusive man who preferred to rule as the remote executive manager of a great national bureaucracy. His character is reflected in the unique residence he built outside Madrid, the Escorial. A combination palace, church, tomb, and monastery, it was a home for a monkish king. Philip was a learned and pious Catholic, a regal ascetic with a powerful sense of duty. He may even have arranged the death of his son Don Carlos (1568), when he concluded the prince was too mad and treacherous to be entrusted with the power of the crown.

New World Riches   Philip's home base, Castile, was populous and prosperous, and the wealth of the New World that flowed through the port of Seville gave him ample funds to finance wars and international intrigues. Despite the floods of bullion, however, Philip's expenses exceeded his income. Near the end of his reign he destroyed one of Europe's great banking families, the Fuggers of Augsburg, by defaulting on his loans.

The American wealth that flowed through Spain had a dramatic impact on Europe. Increased prosperity supported population growth. By the early seventeenth century, the towns of France, England, and the Netherlands had tripled and quadrupled in size, and Europe's population had reached about 100 million. More people with more currency to spend meant more competition for food and jobs, which caused prices to double and triple. Inflation proceeded steadily at the rate of 2 percent per year while wages stagnated. This was especially true in Spain, where the new wealth was concentrated in the hands of a few. Nowhere did the underprivileged suffer more than in Castile. Philip's peasants, the backbone of his empire, were the most heavily taxed people in Europe.

Supremacy in the Mediterranean   At the start of Philip's reign, a struggle with the Turks demanded all his attention. During the 1560s, the Turks had advanced deep into Austria, and their fleets had spread out across the Mediterranean. Between 1568 and 1570, armies under Philip's half brother, Don John of Austria, the illegitimate son of Charles V, suppressed and dispersed the Moors in Granada. In May 1571, Spain, Venice, and the pope formed the Holy League and dispatched Don John to counter Turkish maneuvers in the Mediterranean. On October 7, 1571, Don John's fleet engaged the Ottoman navy off Lepanto in the Gulf of Corinth and won the greatest naval battle of the sixteenth century. Thirty thousand Turks died, and over one-third of the Turkish fleet was sunk or captured. Spain dominated the Mediterranean—at least for the moment.

In 1580, Philip further improved his position by annexing Portugal. The Portuguese fleet augmented Philip's navy, and he added the Portuguese colonies in Africa, India, and the Americas to his empire.

THE REVOLT IN THE NETHERLANDS

Philip had far less success in northern Europe than in the Mediterranean. A rebellion in the Netherlands, the richest district in Europe, set in motion a chain of events that ended Spain's dream of world dominion. The Netherlands was governed for Philip by his half sister, Margaret of Parma, and a council headed by Cardinal Granvelle (1517–1586). Granvelle hoped to check the spread of Protestantism in the Netherlands by promoting church reform. He also wanted to limit the liberties of the seventeen Netherlands provinces and establish a centralized royal government directed from Madrid. The merchant towns of the Netherlands were, however, accustomed to considerable independence, and many, such as magnificent Antwerp, had become Calvinist strongholds. Two members of the governing council opposed their Spanish overlords: the Count of Egmont (1522–1568) and the Prince of Orange, William of Nassau (1533–1584), or "William the Silent" (so called because of his small circle of confidants).

William of Orange was a *politique* who considered the political autonomy and well-being of the Netherlands to be more important than allegiance to religious creeds. In 1561, he, a Catholic, married Anne of Saxony, the daughter of the Lutheran elector Maurice and the granddaughter of the late landgrave Philip of Hesse. He converted to Lutheranism six years later, and he became a Calvinist following the Saint Bartholomew's Day Massacre in 1572.

In 1561, Cardinal Granvelle began an ecclesiastical reorganization of the Netherlands that was intended to tighten the Catholic hierarchy's control over the country and to accelerate its assimilation as a Spanish dependency. Orange and Egmont, with the support of the Dutch nobility, engineered Granvelle's removal from office in 1564. The aristocrats who took Granvelle's place were, however, inept governors, and popular unrest mounted.

In 1564, Philip unwisely insisted the decrees of the Council of Trent be enforced throughout the Netherlands. Opposition materialized under the leadership of William of Orange's younger brother, Louis of Nassau, who had been raised a Lutheran. The Calvinist-inclined lesser nobility and townspeople joined him in drawing up the *Compromise*, a solemn pledge to oppose Trent and the Inquisition. In 1566 (after Margaret's government spurned the protesters as "beggars"), the Calvinists rioted, and Louis appealed to France's Huguenots and Germany's Lutherans for aid. Rebellion against the Spanish regency seemed about to erupt.

The Duke of Alba   A revolt failed to materialize, for the Netherlands' higher nobility were repelled by the behavior of Calvinist extremists and refused to support them. Philip sent an army of 10,000 men under the command of the duke of Alba to restore order and make an example of the would-be revolutionaries. Power to govern the Netherlands was delegated to a special tribunal, the Council of Troubles (as Spain called it) or the Council of Blood (as it was known among the Netherlanders). The new government inaugurated a reign of terror. It executed the counts of Egmont and Horn and several thousand suspected heretics, and it imposed high taxes to force the Netherlanders to pay the cost of Spain's occupation of their country. Tens of thousands of refugees fled the Netherlands during Alba's cruel six-year rule, and the duke came to be more hated than Granvelle or the radical Calvinists.

Resistance and Unification   William of Orange, who spent these turbulent years as an exile in Germany, emerged as the leader of an independence movement. Orange was the *stadholder* (governor) of Holland, Zeeland, and Utrecht, and these northern, Calvinist-inclined provinces provided his base. In the Netherlands, as elsewhere, the fight for political independence was linked with the struggle for religious liberty.

The uprising in the Netherlands was a true popular revolt that enlisted all kinds of people. William even backed the raids of the "Sea Beggars," an international group of anti-Spanish exiles and criminals who were brazen pirates. In 1572, the Beggars captured Brill and other seaports in Zeeland and Holland and incited the native population to join the rebellion. Resistance spread steadily southward. In 1574, the people of Leiden heroically withstood a long Spanish siege, and the Dutch opened the dikes and flooded their country to repulse the hated Spanish. The faltering Alba had by then ceded power to Don Luis de Requesens.

NOT LONGE TIME SINCE I SAWE A COWE.
DID FLAVNDERS REPRESENTE
VPON WHOSE BACKE KINGE PHILIP RODE
AS BEING MALÉCONTNT.

THE QVEENE OF ENGLAND GIVING HAY
WHEARE ON THE COW DID FEEDE.
A? ONE THAT WAS HER GREATEST HELPE.
IN HER DISTRESSE AND NEEDE.

THE PRINCE OF ORANGE MILKT THE CO
AND MADE HIS PVRSE THE PAYLE.
THE COW DID SHYT IN MONSIEURS HAND
WHILE HIE DID HOLD HER TAYLE.

The Milch Cow, a sixteenth-century satirical painting depicting the Netherlands as a cow in whom all the great powers of Europe have an interest. Elizabeth of England is feeding her (England had long-standing commercial ties with Flanders); Philip II of Spain is attempting to ride her (Spain was trying to reassert its control over the entire area); William of Orange is trying to milk her (he was the leader of the anti-Spanish rebellion); and the king of France holds her tail (France hoped to profit from the rebellion at Spain's expense).

Rijksmuseum, Amsterdam

The greatest atrocity of the war followed Requesens's death in 1576. Leaderless and unpaid, Spanish mercenaries ran amok in Antwerp on November 4, 1576. By the time order was restored, 7,000 people lay dead in the streets. This spate of violence (the so-called Spanish Fury) did more to unify the Netherlanders than all previous appeals to religion and patriotism. The ten predominantly Catholic southern provinces (roughly modern Belgium) joined the seven largely Protestant northern provinces (the modern Netherlands) in opposing Spain.

The Netherlanders resolved religious differences by agreeing to territorial arrangements similar to those that the Peace of Augsburg mandated for the Holy Roman Empire in 1555, and the Pacification of Ghent declared the Netherlands unified on November 8, 1576. In January 1577, the last four provinces joined the Union of Brussels, and for the next two years the Spanish faced a united, determined Netherlands.

In November 1576, Don John, the victor over the Turks at Lepanto, took command of Spain's land forces and promptly suffered his first defeat. In February 1577, he signed the Perpetual Edict, a humiliating treaty that required him to withdraw all Spanish troops from the Netherlands within twenty days. The Spanish were, however, nothing if not persistent. The nobility's fear of Calvinist extremism undermined the Union of Brussels, and Don John and Alessandro Farnese of Parma, the regent Margaret's son, reestablished Spanish control in the southern provinces. In January 1579, these provinces formed the Union of Arras and made peace with Spain. The northern provinces responded by organizing the Union of Utrecht.

Netherlands' Independence   Philip tried to break the back of the Netherlands' resistance by declaring William of Orange an outlaw and placing a bounty of 25,000 crowns on his head. This, however, only stiffened the resistance of the northern provinces, and Orange, in the *Apology,* a famous speech he delivered before the Estates General of Holland in December 1580, denounced Philip as a heathen tyrant who had no claim on the Netherlands.

On July 22, 1581, most of the northern provinces belonging to the Union of Utrecht formally repudiated Philip's authority and pledged allegiance to the duke of Alençon, Catherine de Médicis's youngest son. Alençon was seen as a compromise between the extremes of Spanish Catholicism and Calvinism, and he was expected to aspire to nothing more than titular authority over the provinces. In 1583, however, when it became clear that he aspired to much more than that, he was deposed and sent back to France.

William of Orange was assassinated in July 1584, and his son, Maurice (1567–1625), succeeded him as leader of the Dutch resistance. Fortunately for him and his cause, Philip II was by then overextending himself. By meddling in the affairs of France and England, he stretched his resources, and after England defeated his great Armada in 1588, his empire began to fray. By 1593, the northern provinces had driven all of Spain's soldiers out, and in 1596, France and England formally recognized the independence of these provinces. They concluded peace with Spain in 1609 and received international recognition in the Peace of Westphalia in 1648.

ENGLAND AND SPAIN (1553–1603)

MARY I

As it became clear that Henry VIII's son, Edward VI (d. 1553), would not live to sire children of his own, he tried to protect the Reformation in England by disinheriting his Catholic half sister, Mary Tudor (r. 1553–1558). His Protestant cousin, Lady Jane Grey, was named as his heir, but the people of England rallied to Mary, and Jane lost her head as well as the crown.

Queen Mary exceeded the worst fears of the Protestants. Her Parliaments repealed Edward's Protestant statutes, and she restored many Catholic practices. She executed the Protestant leaders who had served her brother (John Hooper, Hugh Latimer, and Thomas Cranmer), and she convicted 287 individuals of heresy and burned them at the stake. Many Protestants avoided martyrdom by fleeing to the Continent. These "Marian exiles" settled in Germany and Switzerland, where they established communities, wrote tracts urging armed resistance, and waited for the time when a Protestant counteroffensive could be launched in their homeland. Many returned to England more radical than when they had left.

In 1554, Mary displeased her subjects by marrying Prince Philip—later to become King Philip II—of Spain. She favored him because Spain headed the militant Catholic offensive against Protestantism, and Mary wanted to return England to the Catholic fold. Many of Mary's subjects feared the marriage would produce a child who, as heir to both England and Spain, would absorb England into Spain's great empire. The marriage was, however, unproductive, and Mary died knowing that her half sister, Elizabeth, the daughter of her father's first Protestant marriage, would claim the throne.

ELIZABETH I

Elizabeth I (r. 1558–1603), the daughter of Henry VIII and Anne Boleyn, was perhaps the most astute politician of the sixteenth century, and with the help of a shrewd adviser, Sir William Cecil (1520–1598), she built a strong monarchy. Between 1559 and 1563, she and Cecil guided a religious settlement through Parliament. It merged a centralized episcopal system of administration for the church (which the queen controlled) with broadly defined Protestant doctrine and traditional Catholic ritual. The Anglican church it created avoided inflexible religious extremes and spared England (at least for the time being) the religious conflicts that were bloodying continental nations. (See "Encountering the Past: Going to the Theater.")

Catholic and Protestant Extremists Religious compromises were unacceptable to zealots of both persuasions, and subversive groups worked to undermine Elizabeth. At the time of her coronation, most of her subjects were Catholics, and the radicals among them (aided by the Jesuits) plotted to replace her with

WHAT ROLE did Catholic and Protestant extremism play in the struggle for supremacy between England and Spain?

Portrait of Mary I (r. 1553–1558), Queen of England. By Sir Anthony Mor (Antonio Moro) (1517/20–1576/7), Prado, Madrid. 1554 (panel).

The Bridgeman Art Library International

ENCOUNTERING THE PAST

GOING TO THE THEATER

T*he Elizabethan era was a Golden Age for English theater. During the late Middle Ages, troupes of players had toured the countryside performing morality plays. The church often sponsored these companies, for plays offered religious education and moral instruction as well as entertainment. The rural theater was nothing more than a circular field ringed with mounds of earth on which spectators sat. Four tents were pitched at the points of the compass to give actors opportunities to enter and exit the action as the plot required.*

During the fifteenth century, players began to stage their productions in the courtyards of urban inns. Inns were renovated to provide permanent stages and more complex sets. The enclosed space also made it possible to limit the audience to paying customers and to turn theater into a profitable business enterprise. The urban setting altered the content as well as the staging of plays. The allegorical moralizing of the medieval country theater was replaced by a more ribald, worldly entertainment, and the inn setting provided the workmen and young women who comprised much of the audience with rooms to which to retreat for performances of their own.

London's theater world matured in the late sixteenth and early seventeenth centuries in the work of Shakespeare and his contemporaries. Special theaters (notably The Rose and The Globe, for which Shakespeare wrote) were built in the 1590s on the south bank of the river Thames. Plays were hugely popular with Londoners. Women were excluded from the stage, so all parts were acted by men and boys. Audiences (particularly in "the pit," the ground floor) were rowdy. They responded to the witty repartee and bawdy action on stage and overindulged in the food and drink sold during the performance.

HOW DID medieval theater differ from the theater of Elizabeth's era?

A seventeenth-century sketch of the Swan Theatre, which stood near Shakespeare's Globe Theatre on the south bank of the Thames.
Private Collection. The Bridgeman Art Library

Scotland's Catholic queen, Mary Stuart. Unlike Elizabeth, whose father had declared her illegitimate, Mary Stuart had an unblemished claim to the throne inherited from her grandmother, Henry VIII's sister. Elizabeth responded swiftly to Catholic assassination plots but rarely let emotion override her political instincts. Despite proven cases of Catholic treason and even attempted regicide, she executed fewer Catholics during her forty-five years on the throne than Mary Tudor had executed Protestants during her brief five-year reign.

Elizabeth dealt cautiously with England's "Puritans," Protestants who wanted to "purify" the church of every vestige of "popery." The Puritans had two major grievances. They despised the Church of England's retention of Catholic ceremony and vestments, for these things made it appear that no Reformation had taken place. They also wanted to end the system of episcopal government, which gave the queen a kind of papal authority over the church.

The more extreme Puritans, the **Congregationalists**, believed every congregation ought to be autonomous, a law unto itself controlled by neither bishops nor presbyterian assemblies. Most sixteenth-century Puritans, however, were **Presbyterians**. That is, they favored a national church of semiautonomous congregations governed by representative presbyteries (the model Calvin had established in Geneva). Neither of these options was acceptable to the queen, for the episcopal hierarchy was the instrument through which she controlled the church. The Conventicle Act of 1593 gave Puritan "separatists" the option of either conforming to the practices of the Church of England or facing exile or death.

Deterioration of Relations with Spain   Despite the sincere desire of both Philip II and Elizabeth I to avoid direct confrontation, events led inexorably to war between England and Spain. In 1567, when the Spanish duke of Alba marched his army into the Netherlands, many in England assumed that Spain intended to use the Netherlands as a base for an invasion of England. In 1570, Pope Pius V (r. 1566–1572) confirmed their fears by branding Elizabeth a heretic and proposing a military expedition to recover England for Catholicism.

In 1571, Don John's demonstration of Spain's awesome sea power at the Battle of Lepanto prompted England and France to sign a mutual defense pact. England also took to the sea. Throughout the 1570s, Elizabeth's privateers, John Hawkins (1532–1595) and Sir Francis Drake (1545–1596), preyed on Spanish shipping in the Americas, and Drake's circumnavigation of the globe (1577–1580) forecast England's ascendancy on the high seas.

The Saint Bartholomew's Day Massacre forced Elizabeth to change her foreign policy. Protestants in France and the Netherlands appealed to her for protection, and in 1585, she sent English soldiers to the Netherlands. Funds she had previously funneled covertly to Henry of Navarre, the Protestant leader in France, now flowed openly. These developments strained relations between England and Spain, but the event that precipitated war was Elizabeth's decision to execute Mary, Queen of Scots (1542–1587).

Mary, Queen of Scots   Mary Stuart, the daughter of King James V of Scotland and Mary of Guise, had left Scotland for France at the age of six. She was raised in France to prepare her for the role as the wife of its king, Francis II. The death of her young husband in 1561 sent Mary back to Scotland to rule a land she barely knew.

A year before Mary returned to Scotland, the Scots had embraced a fervent Protestant Reformation. Mary had grown up at France's Catholic court, and she had no sympathy with Scotland's new religion—especially its dour morality. She wanted her Scottish court to mirror the gaiety and sophistication of Paris. John Knox, the leader of Scotland's Reformation, objected strenuously to the queen's

An idealized likeness of Elizabeth Tudor when she was a princess, attributed to Flemish court painter L. B. Teerling, ca. 1551. The painting shows her blazing red hair and alludes to her learning by the addition of books.

Unknown, formerly attributed to William Scrots. Elizabeth I, when Princess (1533–1603). The Royal Collection © 2005, Her Majesty Queen Elizabeth II.

12.2
Elizabeth's Act of Uniformity

Congregationalists   The more extreme Puritans who believed every congregation ought to be autonomous, a law unto itself controlled by neither bishops nor presbyterian assemblies.

Presbyterians   Puritans who favored a national church of semiautonomous congregations governed by representative presbyteries.

continuing to practice her Catholic faith even in private, for Scottish law made this a capital offense. Queen Elizabeth personally despised Knox, but she encouraged his defense of Protestantism. It served her foreign policy by making it difficult for Mary to persuade the Scots to cooperate with France against England.

In 1568, a scandal cost Mary her throne. Mary had married Lord Darnley, a youth with connections to the royal houses of both England and Scotland. She had a son by him (the James who was eventually to inherit the crowns of both Scotland and England). Darnley, however, proved an impossible husband, and Mary reputedly took the earl of Bothwell as her lover. He, in turn, allegedly murdered Darnley, abducted Mary, and married her. This amounted to usurpation of the throne, and the outraged Scots forced Mary to abdicate in favor of her infant son.

Mary fled Scotland and unwisely sought refuge from her cousin Elizabeth in England. Mary was a threat to Elizabeth, for Catholics considered Mary the rightful heir to the English throne. Elizabeth placed Mary under house arrest and held her captive for nineteen years. In 1583, Elizabeth's vigilant secretary, Sir Francis Walsingham, discovered that the Spanish ambassador, Bernardino de Mendoza, was scheming to unseat Elizabeth. In 1586, Walsingham exposed still another Spanish plot, and this time he had proof of Mary's involvement. Elizabeth was loath to execute Mary. She feared that such an act would diminish the aura of divine right that was one of the props of monarchy, and she knew it would raise a storm of protest among Catholics. In the end, however, she concluded she had no choice, and Mary was beheaded on February 18, 1587. Mary's death dashed Catholic hopes for a bloodless reconversion of England and persuaded Philip II that the time had come for a military assault on the Protestant nation.

The Armada Spain's preparations for war were interrupted in the spring of 1587 by raids Sir Francis Drake led on the port city of Cádiz and the coast of Portugal. These attacks forced Philip to postpone his invasion of England, but on May 30, 1588, the Armada (130 ships and 25,000 men) set sail. The expedition's commander, the duke of Medina-Sidonia, soon found himself in trouble. The barges that were to transport his soldiers from their galleons onto England's shores were late in leaving Calais and Dunkirk for their rendezvous with the fleet. While the Spanish vessels waited, an "English wind" sprang up and helped the swifter English and Dutch ships scatter the Spanish forces.

Spain never fully recovered from the Armada's loss, and by the time of Philip's death (September 13, 1598), it was experiencing reversals on multiple fronts. Philip's successors, Philip III (r. 1598–1621), Philip IV (r. 1621–1665), and Charles II (r. 1665–1700), were all inadequate men. Spain's decline allowed France to emerge as the leading continental power, while the Dutch and English nibbled away at Spain's empire.

When Elizabeth died on March 23, 1603, she left behind a strong nation poised on the brink of acquiring a global empire. Because she had never married (choosing instead to use the hope of winning her hand as a tool for English diplomacy), her death ended the Tudor dynasty. Ironically, her heir was Mary's son, James VI of Scotland (James I of England).

THE THIRTY YEARS' WAR (1618–1648)

The Thirty Years' War in the Holy Roman Empire was the last and the most destructive of the wars of religion. The passions it raised escalated to the point where the combatants seemed willing to sacrifice everything in pursuit of victories that were increasingly less worth winning. Virtually every major European

QUICK REVIEW

The Spanish Armada

- Assembled for invasion of Protestant England

- Attacks by Sir Francis Drake in 1587 forced Philip to postpone invasion

- Failure of Armada in May 1588 dealt a severe blow to Spain's military power

WHAT TOLL did the Thirty Years' War take on Germany?

state was drawn into the conflict. When the hostilities ended in 1648, the agreements among the victors drew the map of northern Europe much as it appears today.

PRECONDITIONS FOR WAR

Fragmented Germany   In the second half of the sixteenth century, Germany was a collection of about 360 autonomous political entities: secular principalities (duchies, landgraviates, and marches), ecclesiastical principalities (archbishoprics, bishoprics, and abbeys), free cities, and regions dominated by knights with castles. The Peace of Augsburg (1555) had granted each a degree of sovereignty within its borders. This made trade and travel difficult, for each levied its own tolls and tariffs and coined its own money. Many little states also had pretensions that exceeded their powers.

During the Thirty Years' War, Germany—Europe's crossroads—became Europe's stomping ground. The great conflict had many causes, but chief among them was the threat that the unification of Germany posed to the balance of power in Europe. Protestants suspected a conspiracy by the papacy and the Holy Roman Empire to work together to reimpose Catholic dominance first in Germany and then in the rest of Europe. The imperial diet, which was controlled by Germany's territorial leaders, was leery of any attempt to consolidate the empire, for this threatened its members' liberties. Some urged allies outside of Germany to help them fend off attempts by the emperor to strengthen his authority over them. Many governments had a variety of reasons for being alarmed at the prospect of a united Germany controlled by a Catholic emperor.

Religious Division   By 1600, there may have been slightly more Protestants than Catholics in the Holy Roman Empire. The territorial principle proclaimed by the Peace of Augsburg in 1555 was intended to freeze Lutherans and Catholics in place by forcing each territory to declare its faith, but as time passed, there were unsettling shifts of jurisdiction. As Lutherans gained ground in some Catholic areas and Catholics in a few places designated as Lutheran, tensions increased. Catholic rulers, who were in a weakened position after the Reformation, resented the concessions they had had to make to Protestants, and they insisted the ecclesiastical property administered by clergy who converted be returned to Catholic control. Protestants, however, were often unwilling to comply. The situation was further complicated by divisions within the Protestant camp between liberal and conservative Lutherans and between Lutherans and Calvinists. (See Map 12–1.)

Calvinism was not recognized as a legal religious option by the Peace of Augsburg, but it won a foothold in the empire when Frederick III (r. 1559–1576), elector Palatine, declared it the official religion of his domain. Heidelberg, his capital, became the German "Geneva"—the staging area for Calvinist penetration of the empire. Lutherans came to fear Calvinists almost as much as they did Catholics, for the bold missionary forays of the Palatine Calvinists threatened the stability that the Peace of Augsburg had brought the empire. Lutherans were also offended by blunt Calvinist criticism of Lutheran doctrines (particularly the Lutheran belief in Christ's real presence in the Eucharist).

The Jesuits joined the Calvinists in undermining the Peace of Augsburg. Catholic Bavaria, led by Duke Maximilian and supported by Spain, did for the Counter-Reformation what the Palatinate did for Calvinism. Jesuit missionaries, operating from Bavaria, returned major cities (notably, Strasbourg and Osnabrück) to the Catholic fold. In 1609, Maximilian organized a Catholic League to counter a Protestant alliance formed in the same year by the Calvinist elector Palatine, Frederick IV (r. 1583–1610). The army the league assembled under the command of Count Johann von Tilly tipped Germany into war.

MAP EXPLORATION
Interactive map: To explore this map further, go to **http://www.prenhall.com/kagan3/map12.1**

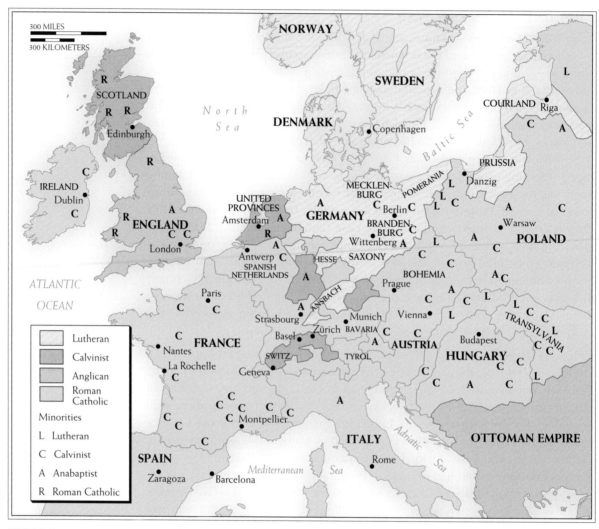

MAP 12–1

Religious Divisions about 1600 By 1600, few could seriously expect Christians to return to a uniform religious allegiance. In Spain and southern Italy, Catholicism remained relatively unchallenged, but note the existence elsewhere of large religious minorities, both Catholic and Protestant.

HOW WOULD you explain the division between Catholic and Protestant regions in Europe?

FOUR PERIODS OF WAR

The Bohemian Period (1618–1625) The war broke out in Bohemia following the ascent to the Bohemian throne in 1618 of Ferdinand, the Habsburg archduke of Styria and heir to the empire. Ferdinand, who had been educated by Jesuits, was determined to restore Catholicism to the Habsburg lands. No sooner had he become king of Bohemia than he revoked the religious liberties that had been granted to Bohemia's Protestants. The Protestant nobility responded in May 1618 by literally throwing his regents out a window (the "defenestration of Prague"). A year later, when Ferdinand (II) became Holy Roman Emperor, the Bohemians repudiated him in favor of the Calvinist elector Palatine, Frederick V (r. 1616–1623).

The Bohemian revolt triggered an international war. Ferdinand was supported by Spain, Maximilian of Bavaria, and the Lutheran elector of Saxony, John George I (r. 1611–1656). He saw the war as an opportunity to expand his domains at the expense of his fellow Protestant, the Calvinist elector Palatine. Johann von Tilly, who commanded Ferdinand's armies, routed Frederick V's troops in 1620, and by 1622, Ferdinand had subdued Bohemia and conquered the Palatinate. As the remnants of Frederick's army retreated north, Duke Maximilian of Bavaria followed, claiming land as he went.

Bohemian protesters throw three of Emperor Ferdinand II's agents out of windows at Hradschin Castle in Prague to protest his revocation of Protestant freedoms.

Art Resource, NY

The Danish Period (1625–1629) Maximilian's successful forays into northwestern Germany raised the alarming prospect of German unification. This prompted England, France, and the Netherlands to urge Christian IV (r. 1588–1648), the Lutheran king of Denmark and duke of the German duchy of Holstein, to go to the rescue of Germany's Protestants. Duke Maximilian, however, quickly forced him to retreat.

Emperor Ferdinand, who felt threatened by Maximilian's growing power, turned the conduct of the war over to Albrecht of Wallenstein (1583–1634), a mercenary he had employed against the Bohemians. Wallenstein was a brilliant military strategist, ruthless, and a law unto himself, but by 1629, he had so effectively broken the back of Protestant resistance that Ferdinand issued the Edict of Restitution. It outlawed Calvinism and ordered the Lutherans to return to Catholic ownership all the church lands they had acquired since 1552. This entailed the surrender of sixteen bishoprics and twenty-eight cities and towns, and it had the unintended effect of reigniting resistance to the Habsburgs.

The Swedish Period (1630–1635) Gustavus Adolphus of Sweden (r. 1611–1632), a pious Lutheran monarch and a military genius, took up the gauntlet for Protestantism. He was handsomely bankrolled by two very interested bystanders—the Dutch (long-standing opponents of the Habsburgs) and the French. Cardinal Richelieu, chief adviser to the Catholic king of France, was eager to prevent a powerful Habsburg Empire from materializing on France's border.

The Swedish king suddenly reversed the course of the war by winning a stunning victory at Breitenfeld in 1630. The battle was significant, but far from decisive, and the Protestant cause faltered when Gustavus Adolphus died battling Wallenstein's forces at Lützen in November 1632. Two years later, Ferdinand arranged for Wallenstein, who was outliving his usefulness, to be assassinated, and he negotiated a truce with the German Protestants (the Peace of Prague, 1635). The Swedes, however, refused to compromise with the Catholic emperor, and support from France and the Netherlands helped them renew hostilities.

The Swedish-French Period (1635–1648) The French openly entered the war in 1635 and prolonged it for thirteen more years. French, Swedish, and Spanish soldiers looted the length and breadth of Germany while the Germans, too disunited to put up much resistance, simply looked on and suffered. By the

MAP EXPLORATION

Interactive map: To explore this map further, go to **http://www.prenhall.com/kagan3/map12.2**

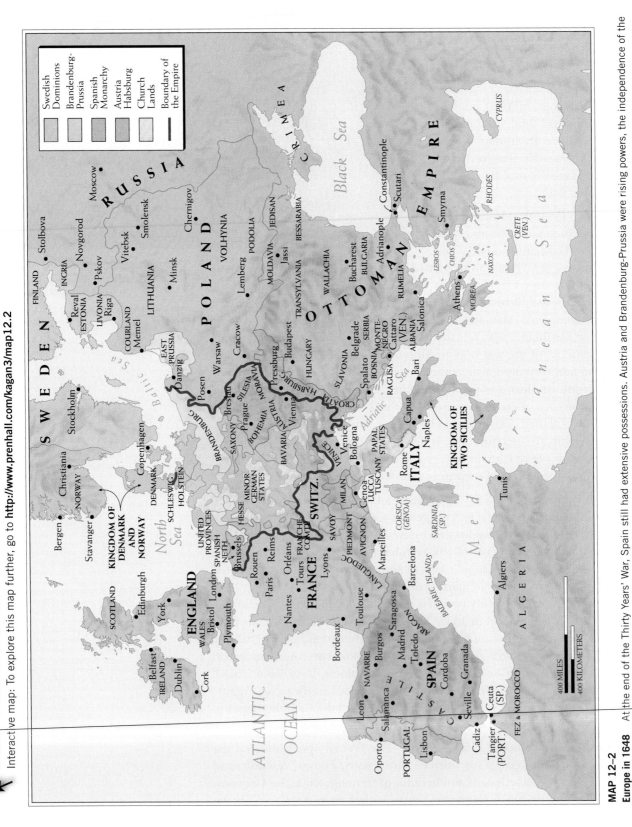

MAP 12–2

Europe in 1648 At the end of the Thirty Years' War, Spain still had extensive possessions. Austria and Brandenburg-Prussia were rising powers, the independence of the United Provinces and Switzerland was recognized, and Sweden had footholds in northern Germany.

WHAT DOES this map indicate about the German lands and the Holy Roman Empire in 1648?

time peace talks began in the Westphalian cities of Münster and Osnabrück in 1644, Germany's population may have been reduced by a third. It was the worst catastrophe suffered by a European state since the Black Death of the fourteenth century.

THE TREATY OF WESTPHALIA

The Treaty of Westphalia ended hostilities in 1648 by ensuring the continued fragmentation of Germany. The territorial principle proclaimed by the Peace of Augsburg in 1555 was reasserted, and rulers were confirmed in their right to determine the religions of their subjects. Calvinism was added to the list of legal religious options, and the German princes won recognition of their independence. Bavaria was elevated to the rank of an elector state, and Brandenburg-Prussia emerged as the most powerful north German principality. The Swiss Confederacy and the United Provinces of Holland were recognized as sovereign states, and France acquired considerable territory. (See Map 12–2.)

War between France and Spain continued outside the empire until 1659, when the French forced the Spanish to accept the humiliating Treaty of the Pyrenees. Germany's fragmentation and Spain's humbling left France the dominant power in Europe. The roots of the competitive nationalisms that have loomed so large in the history of the modern world are to be found in the religious conflicts of the seventeenth century.

12.4
The Peace of
Westphalia, 1648

SUMMARY

Renewed Religious Struggle The Peace of Augsburg recognized Lutheranism as a legal religion in the Holy Roman Empire in 1555. For the remainder of the sixteenth century, religious strife centered on the conflict between Calvinism and Catholicism. Calvinism and Catholicism both were dogmatic, aggressive, and irreconcilable. Even the art and architecture of the Catholic Counter-Reformation, with its baroque energy, stands in marked contrast to Protestant restraint. Slowly some intellectuals—and a very few political leaders—came to adopt a more skeptical, tolerant view of religion, but in the meantime the Thirty Years' War between 1618 and 1648 drew every nation of Europe into some degree of religious conflict.

The French Wars of Religion (1562–1598) The rulers of France repeatedly cracked down on France's Protestant Huguenots. After the death of King Henry II, the French monarchy was weak. Although Calvinists made up only a small part of the population, France's Calvinists included much of the aristocracy. Catherine de Médicis attempted with some success to play Catholics and Huguenots off against each other. In 1593, a few years after the Bourbon Huguenot Henry of Navarre took the French throne, Henry renounced his Protestantism in favor of Catholicism; his 1598 Edict of Nantes sanctioned minority religious rights within Catholic France.

Imperial Spain and the Reign of Philip II (r. 1556–1598) Philip II, who ruled Spain through most of the second half of the sixteenth century, controlled vast territories, many people, and much wealth. For the first twenty-five years or so of Philip's reign, his attention was focused on the demographic and economic changes within his kingdom, defense against the Turks in the Mediterranean,

IMAGE KEY

for pages 290–291

a. Artwork of a 17th century musket made of wood and metal finishing

b. The massacre of Protestants at Vassy, France, by order of Francois de Lorraine, Duc de Guise, on 1 March 1562; colored engraving, French, 17th century. Geoff Dann © Dorling Kindersley, courtesy of the Wallace Collection, London.

c. French closed helmet, 1575

d. A 16th century sword

e. A 16th century sword hilt

f. Catherine de Médicis (1519–1589)

g. A portrayal of the execution of Mary, Queen of Scots. Unknown Dutch Artist

h. Spain, Madrid, San Lorenzo del Escorial, high view over monastery

i. Gold medal of King Philip II of Spain and Queen Mary I of England, 1554

j. Elizabeth I (1558-1603) of England in 1592   By courtesy of the national Portrait Gallery, London

and the annexation of Portugal (which led to control over Portugal's wealthy colonies). The second half of his reign was overshadowed by unrest and, eventually, defeat in the Netherlands.

England and Spain (1553–1603) Catholic Mary I ruled England for five bloody years. Many Protestants were martyred or exiled during her reign. She married Spain's Prince Philip. Her half sister, Elizabeth I, succeeded her and ruled for most of the second half of the sixteenth century (r. 1558–1603). Elizabeth was probably the most successful European leader of her time. She steered a middle course between extremes in all areas, most notably religion, where she created the moderate Anglican church. She took firm measures against extremist Puritans (with the Conventicle Act), against would-be assassins (she executed Mary Queen of Scots for plotting against her), and Spain (the English navy defeated Spain's Armada in 1588).

The Thirty Years' War (1618–1648) Germany's political fragmentation, and conflict throughout Europe among Lutherans, Catholics, and Calvinists, set the stage for the Thirty Years' War. This devastating conflict drew in all the major lands of Europe before it was over; it has shaped the map of Europe up to the present. There were four distinct phases to the war, named after the region that was most actively involved in fighting at that time: the Bohemian period (1618–1625), the Danish period (1625–1629), the Swedish period (1630–1635), and the Swedish-French period (1635–1648). Finally, the 1648 Treaty of Westphalia put an end to hostilities and, among other provisions, reasserted the right of each ruler to determine the religion in his or her land.

REVIEW QUESTIONS

1. What part did politics play in the religious positions adopted by France's leaders? How did the French monarchy decide which side to favor? What led to the infamous Saint Bartholomew's Day Massacre? What resulted from it?

2. How did Spain acquire the dominant position in Europe in the sixteenth century? What were its strengths and weaknesses as a nation? What were Philip II's goals? Which did he fail to achieve? Why?

3. What changes occurred in the religious policies of England's government in the process of establishing the Anglican church? What were Mary I's political objectives? What was Elizabeth I's "settlement"? How was it imposed on England? Who were her opponents? What were their criticisms of her?

4. Why was the Thirty Years' War fought? Could matters have been resolved without war? To what extent did politics determine the outcome of the war? What were the terms and objectives of the Treaty of Westphalia?

KEY TERMS

Congregationalists   (p. 303)   **Huguenots**   (p. 293)   **Presbyterians**   (p. 303)
Counter-Reformation   (p. 292)   *politique*   (p. 293)

   For additional study resources for this chapter, go to:
www.prenhall.com/kagan3/chapter12

13 European State Consolidation in the Seventeenth and Eighteenth Centuries

CHAPTER HIGHLIGHTS

The Netherlands: Golden Age to Decline The United Netherlands enjoyed a Golden Age in the seventeenth century and was more urbanized than any other area in Europe. Dutch agriculture and financial systems were the models for the rest of Europe. After the death of William of Orange in 1702, the Netherlands entered a period of stagnation and decline.

Two Models of European Political Development England and France developed forms of government that served as models for other European nations. In England, elites forced the monarch to defer to the wishes of Parliament. In France, elites tied their own interests to the power and person of the monarch.

Constitutional Crisis and Settlement in Stuart England Conflict between the king and Parliament led to civil war and the execution of Charles I. From 1649 until the restoration of Charles II in 1660, England was officially ruled by Parliament. In 1688, James II was deposed and replaced with William and Mary in the "Glorious Revolution." Under the leadership of Sir Robert Walpole (1676–1745), Britain enjoyed increased stability and power.

Rise of Absolute Monarchy in France: The World of Louis XIV Louis XIII and his chief advisor Cardinal Richelieu concentrated on centralizing power in the hands of the monarch. Louis XIV's attitudes were shaped by his experience of the *Fronde*. Louis XIV believed he ruled by divine right. His palace at Versailles contributed to the subjugation of the nobility. His near constant wars placed France in grave fiscal danger.

Central and Eastern Europe A weak, elective monarchy and an ineffectual legislative body undermined effective government in Poland. The expansion of the Habsburg Empire was not matched by increased political unity and the empire grew increasingly fragile. In Prussia, militaristic monarchs reformed the state in ways that increased the power and prestige of Prussia's military.

Russia Enters the European Political Arena Under the Romanovs, Russia took its place as a major European power in the seventeenth century. The Russian nobility retained considerable power until Peter the Great assumed personal rule in 1689. Peter was determined to westernize Russia and increase the nation's military strength. When he died in 1725, however, he had failed to appoint a successor and power reverted to nobles and soldiers.

The Ottoman Empire The Ottoman Empire dominated the Muslim world after 1516. However, social and political hurdles blocked innovation and seventeenth-century military defeats marked the beginning of the end for the Empire.

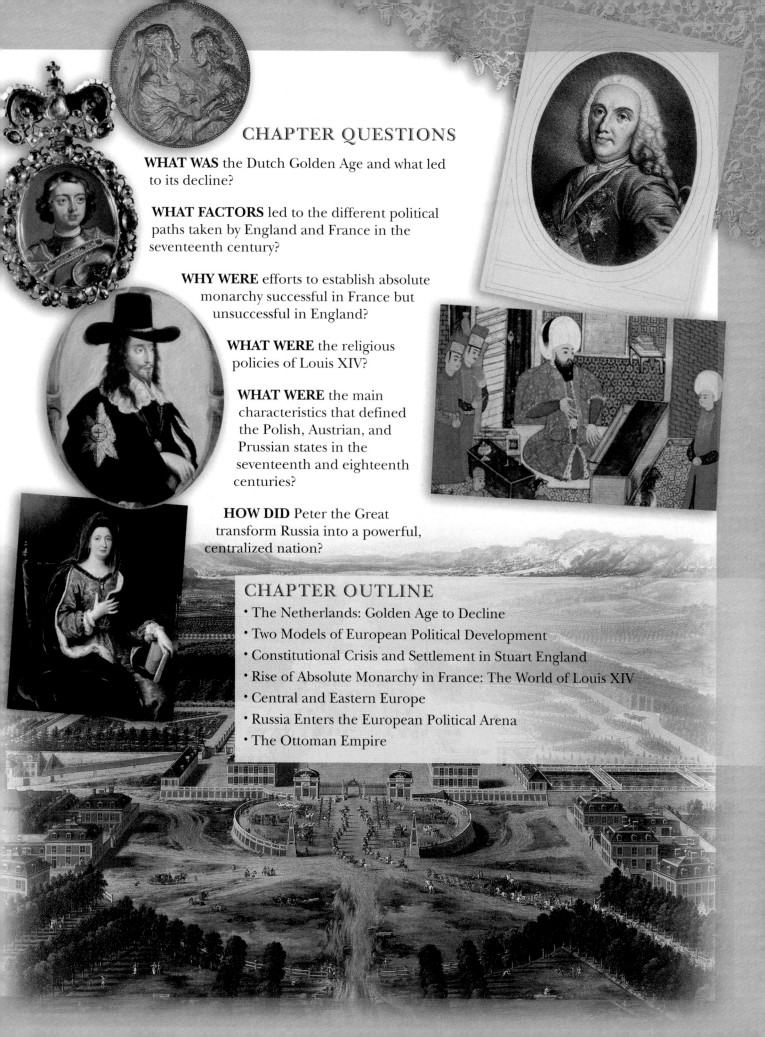

CHAPTER QUESTIONS

WHAT WAS the Dutch Golden Age and what led to its decline?

WHAT FACTORS led to the different political paths taken by England and France in the seventeenth century?

WHY WERE efforts to establish absolute monarchy successful in France but unsuccessful in England?

WHAT WERE the religious policies of Louis XIV?

WHAT WERE the main characteristics that defined the Polish, Austrian, and Prussian states in the seventeenth and eighteenth centuries?

HOW DID Peter the Great transform Russia into a powerful, centralized nation?

CHAPTER OUTLINE

- The Netherlands: Golden Age to Decline
- Two Models of European Political Development
- Constitutional Crisis and Settlement in Stuart England
- Rise of Absolute Monarchy in France: The World of Louis XIV
- Central and Eastern Europe
- Russia Enters the European Political Arena
- The Ottoman Empire

IMAGE KEY

Image Key for pages 312–313 is on page 337.

WHAT WAS the Dutch Golden Age and what led to its decline?

Between the early seventeenth and mid–twentieth centuries, no region so dominated other parts of the world politically, militarily, and economically as Europe. Such had not been the case before this period, nor would it be so after World War II. This era of European dominance coincided with a shift of power with Europe itself from the Mediterranean—in particular, Spain and Portugal—to the states of northern Europe.

By the mid–1700s, five states—Great Britain, France, Austria, Prussia, and Russia—organized themselves politically and came to dominate Europe, and later, large areas of the world through military might and economic strength. These states arose at the expense of Spain, Portugal, the United Provinces of the Netherlands, Poland, Sweden, the Ottoman Empire, and the Holy Roman Empire.

THE NETHERLANDS: GOLDEN AGE TO DECLINE

The United Provinces of the Netherlands was the only genuinely new state to appear in Europe during the early modern period. Resistance to Spanish domination brought its seven component districts together in 1572, and its sovereignty as an independent state was internationally recognized in 1648.

The Netherlands was a republic governed by the States General, an assembly representing its provinces. Whenever a situation demanded a powerful executive, the Dutch would choose a leader from the noble House of Orange. The threat posed by Louis XIV of France brought William III, the *stadtholder* of Holland, to power. William, with his wife Mary, also ascended England's throne. After his death in 1702 and the conclusion of peace with France in 1714, the Dutch republic was restored.

The Netherlands officially embraced the (Calvinist) Reform faith, but allegiance to a state church was not enforced. The Dutch enjoyed a reputation for tolerance, and the Netherlands provided a refuge for Jews driven out of other countries. Religious tolerance spared the Netherlands the internal strife that plagued so many other European states.

URBAN PROSPERITY

The technologically advanced fleet of the Dutch East India Company, shown here at anchor in Amsterdam, linked the Netherlands' economy with that of southeast Asia.

Andries van Eertvelt (1590–1652), "The Return to Amsterdam of the Fleet of the Dutch East India Company in 1599." Oil on copper. Johnny van Haeften Gallery, London, UK. The Bridgeman Art Library

The Dutch were regarded as remarkable by their contemporaries as much for their prosperity as their spirit of tolerance. While other states squandered resources on religious wars, the Dutch invested theirs in economic development. They transformed agriculture, promoted trade and finance, and built an overseas empire. The Netherlands became the most urbanized region in Europe, and the percentage of its population that lived in cities was not equaled by other countries until the industrial era.

The concentration of the Dutch in cities was made possible by agricultural innovations copied throughout Europe. During the seventeenth century, Dutch farmers reclaimed a great deal of land from the sea. The cheap grain that Dutch traders imported from the Baltic to feed their people freed Dutch farmers to devote their land to profitable cash crops (dairy products, meat, and tulip bulbs). Dutch fishing fleets supplied much of the herring (the major source of inexpensive protein) consumed on the Continent, and Dutch mills provided textiles to many parts of Europe. Dutch ships moved much of the trade of Europe, and shipbuilding itself was a highly lucrative industry for the Netherlands. Profits from all these enterprises provided capital for banks, and the Dutch created the most advanced financial system of their day. Shareholders funded ventures such as the Dutch East Indies Company, which took control of the East Asian spice trade away from the Portuguese. The Netherlands retained colonies in Indonesia until World War II.

ECONOMIC DECLINE

For a variety of reasons, the Dutch economy began to weaken in the eighteenth century. After William III's death in 1702, the provinces blocked the rise of another *stadtholder,* and their government suffered from the lack of a strong executive. The fishing industry declined. Dutch manufacturing began to stagnate, and the Dutch lost the technological lead in shipbuilding. As countries began to construct their own vessels rather than relying on Dutch ships to carry their goods, naval supremacy began to pass to England. Weak political leadership handicapped efforts to confront these challenges, but the Netherlands retained considerable influence thanks to its banks and stock exchange.

TWO MODELS OF EUROPEAN POLITICAL DEVELOPMENT

*I*n the second half of the sixteenth century, changing military technology sharply increased the cost of warfare and forced governments to look for new sources of revenue. Monarchs who, like France's kings, found sources of income that were not controlled by nobles or by assemblies representing their wealthy subjects achieved absolute power. In places such as England, where rulers had insufficient funds and limited powers of taxation, kings had to negotiate political policies with the groups on which they depended for financial support, and royal authority was compromised.

The contrast between the French and English political systems (between royal **absolutism** and **parliamentary monarchy**) was visible by the end of the seventeenth century, but not in 1603 when England's Elizabeth I died. The much revered queen had broad support, and Parliaments met during her reign only to approve taxes. The Stuart kings who succeeded to her throne had a different experience. Their fiscal and religious policies alienated their nation's propertied classes and united them against the crown.

Elizabeth's contemporary, Henry IV (r. 1589–1610) of France, presided over a divided nation that was only beginning to emerge from the turmoil of religious war. His successor, Louis XIII (r. 1610–1643), asserted more of the crown's authority, and in the second half of the seventeenth century, Louis XIV brought the French nobles under control. The aristocratic *Parlement* of Paris won the right to register royal decrees before they officially became law, and the king allowed regional *parlements* considerable latitude to deal with local issues. However, the nobles lost interest in turning the Estates General into something comparable to England's Parliament, for they saw a strong monarchy as a source of rich patronage and a guardian of their privileged place in society. Once the king won control over taxation, there was little reason for the Estates General to meet, and no sessions were called between 1614 and 1789 (the eve of the French Revolution).

WHAT FACTORS led to the different political paths taken by England and France in the seventeenth century?

absolutism   Government by a ruler with absolute authority.

parliamentary monarchy English rule by a monarch with some parliamentary guidance or input.

parlements   Regional courts allowed considerable latitude by Louis XIV to deal with local issues.

WHAT WERE the conflicts between Parliament and the monarchy over taxation and religion in early Stuart England?

CONSTITUTIONAL CRISIS AND SETTLEMENT IN STUART ENGLAND

JAMES I

When the childless Elizabeth died in 1603, the heir to her throne was James VI of Scotland, the son of Mary Stuart, Queen of Scots, and the grandnephew of Henry VIII. No one disputed his coronation as James I of England, but his prospects for a successful reign were not good. As a Scot, he was an outsider who had no native constituency to help him deal with England's religious factions or raise the funds needed to pay his kingdom's substantial debts. James was also an advocate of the divine right of kings. He had even written a book on the subject: *A Trew Law of Free Monarchies* (1598). His understanding of monarchy set him on a collision course with English tradition.

England's Parliament, the country's chief check on royal power, met only when the monarch summoned it to authorize tax levies. James figured out ways to fund his government without calling Parliament. Relying on the authority of ill-defined privileges that he alleged were royal prerogatives, he created new customs duties called *impositions*. Members of Parliament resented these, but they preferred to wrangle and negotiate behind the scenes rather than risk serious confrontation.

Religious problems added to the political tensions of James's reign. **Puritans** within the Church of England had hoped James's upbringing as a Scottish Presbyterian would dispose him to support their program for reforming the English church. They wanted to eliminate elaborate priestly rituals and end government of the church by bishops. They favored simple services of worship and congregations run by presbyters elected by the people. James, however, had no intention of turning his national church into a model of representative government—a political system he rejected as an infringement on the divine right of kings. In January 1604, James responded to a list of Puritan grievances (the Millenary Petition) by pledging to maintain and even strengthen the Anglican episcopacy. As he explained, "A Scottish presbytery agreeth as well with monarchy as God and the devil. No bishops, no king." James did, however, yield to the Protestant demand for the use of vernacular Scriptures, and he established a commission to make a new translation. In 1611, the eloquent Authorized (King James) Version of the Bible appeared.

James had no sympathy with English Puritanism's implicit moral agenda. He viewed recreations and sports, which the Puritans condemned, as innocent activities that were good for people. He also believed Puritan rigidity about such things discouraged Roman Catholics from converting to the Church of England. Consequently, in 1618, James tried to force a change by ordering the clergy to read his *Book of Sports*—a royal decree legalizing the playing of games on Sunday—from their pulpits. They refused, and he backed down. Religion even touched on issues of sports and smoking. (See "Encountering the Past: Early Controversy over Tobacco and Smoking.")

James's lifestyle was as offensive to Puritans as his policies, for scandal and corruption made the royal court infamous. The king was powerfully influenced by a few court favorites. One of these, the duke of Buckingham, was rumored to be James's homosexual lover. Buckingham controlled access to the king and openly sold peerages and titles to the highest bidders.

Disappointment and disgust with James led some Puritans voluntarily to leave England for the New World. In 1620, Puritan separatists founded Plymouth

Puritans English Protestants who wanted simpler forms of church ceremony and strictness and gravity in personal behavior.

ENCOUNTERING THE PAST

EARLY CONTROVERSY OVER TOBACCO AND SMOKING

King James defended sports from the Puritan charge that all amusements were sinful when enjoyed on the Sabbath, but the king did not favor all popular pleasures. He was ardently opposed to tobacco, one of the novelties that Europeans discovered in the Americas. Tobacco smoking excited opposition almost from the start. Spanish missionaries associated it with pagan religious practices. Sir Francis Bacon (1561–1626) noted it was addictive, and it was condemned by both Christian and Muslim clerics. None of this, however, impeded the spreading use of the pipe.

In 1604, James published a work that left smokers in no doubt as to his opinion of them and their practice. In *A Counterblast to Tobacco* he wrote, "Have you not reason then to be ashamed, and to forbear this filthy novelty…? In your abuse thereof sinning against God, harming yourselves in person … [with a] custom loathsome to the eye, hateful to the nose, harmful to the brain, dangerous to the lungs, and the black stinking fume thereof, nearest resembling the horrible Stygian smoke of the pit that is bottomless." [*A Counterblast to Tobacco* (1604), reprinted by the Rodale Press, London, 1954, p. 36.] James tried to stem the use of tobacco by heavily taxing it. When this had the result of encouraging smugglers, James lowered the tax. That, however, produced a stream of revenue that became increasingly important to his government. In 1614, he made the importation of tobacco a royal monopoly, and by 1619, Virginia was shipping 40,000 pounds of tobacco to England annually. James's government, like modern ones, put itself in the odd position of depending on taxes imposed to stop the practice that produced those taxes.

Practically from the moment of its introduction into Europe tobacco smoking was controversial. Here a court jester is portrayed as exhaling rabbits from a pipe as three pipe-smoking gentlemen look on.

© Christel Gerstenberg/CORBIS

Colony in Cape Cod Bay. Later in the same decade another larger and better financed group founded the Massachusetts Bay Colony.

James's conduct of foreign affairs roused as much opposition as his domestic policies. James preferred peace to war, for he knew wars would generate debts and debts would make him dependent on Parliament. In 1604, he negotiated a peace with Spain that was long overdue, but some of his subjects saw it as an indication of their king's pro-Catholic sentiments. Their suspicions increased when James tried (unsuccessfully) to relax the penal laws against Catholics. His reasonable hesitation to send English troops to aid German Protestants at the start of the Thirty Years' War offered further confirmation of their fears—as did his plan to wed his heir to the Infanta, the daughter of the king of Spain.

As James aged and his health failed, the reins of his government passed to his son Charles (and to Buckingham). Parliamentary opposition and Protestant sentiment combined to defeat his pro-Spanish foreign policy. The marriage alliance was rejected, and in 1624, shortly before James's death, Parliament pushed England into a war with Spain.

OVERVIEW — TWO MODELS OF GOVERNMENT

	France's Absolutism	England's Parliamentary Monarchy
religious factors	Louis XIV, with the support of Catholics, crushed Protestantism for religious uniformity.	A strong Protestant religious movement known as Puritanism limited the monarchy.
institutional differences	Opposition to the monarchy lacked a tradition of liberties, representation, or bargaining tools.	Parliament was to be consulted, and it appealed to concepts of liberty when conflicts arose.
economic policies	Louis XIV made French nobility dependent on his good will by supporting their status.	Political groups invoked traditional liberties to resist the monarchy's economic intrusions.
the role of personalities	Louis XIV had guidance from Cardinals Mazarin and Richelieu, training him to be hardworking.	The four Stuart monarchs, acting on whims, had trouble simply making people trust them.

QUICK REVIEW

Charles I (r. 1625 – 1649)

- 1629: Charles dissolves Parliament in face of criticism of his policies
- Unable to wage foreign wars without funds granted by Parliament
- 1640: Efforts to enforce religious conformity within England and Scotland force Charles to reconvene Parliament

CHARLES I

Parliament favored war with Spain, but distrust of Buckingham undercut its willingness to finance the venture. This forced Charles I (r. 1625–1649), with the help of the unpopular Buckingham, to find novel ways to raise the money he needed. He imposed tariffs and import duties without consulting Parliament, restored discontinued taxes, and subjected people of property (under threat of imprisonment) to the "forced loan" (a levy that the government was, in theory, supposed to refund someday). Soldiers in transit to war zones were also quartered in English homes.

By the time Parliament met in 1628, its members were furious. They refused to acquiesce to the king's request for funds unless he agreed to abide by terms they set forth in a Petition of Right. They demanded that he cease to force loans and collect taxes Parliament had not ratified. They insisted he not imprison citizens without due cause, and they wanted an end to the billeting of troops in private homes. Charles acquiesced to these demands, but Parliament did not trust him to keep his word. The next year after further disputes, Charles dissolved Parliament and did not recall it until 1640.

Without funds from Parliament, Charles could not wage foreign wars. When he made peace with France in 1629 and Spain in 1630, however, some of his subjects accused him of wanting to strengthen his ties with Roman Catholic nations. To allow Charles to rule without having to negotiate with Parliament for money, the king's minister, Thomas Wentworth, earl of Strafford (after 1640), imposed strict efficiency and administrative centralization in the government and exploited every fund-raising device, enforcing previously neglected laws and extending existing taxes into new areas.

Charles might have avoided calling another Parliament if he had maintained the tolerant religious policies of his father. Instead, he made the mistake of trying to impose religious conformity within England and Scotland. Charles favored Anglo-Catholicism, a state church with a powerful episcopacy and plenty of pomp and ceremony. In 1637, William Laud (1573–1645), his religious adviser and archbishop of Canterbury (after 1633), supported his decision to impose the English episcopal system and prayer book on Scotland. This drove the Scots to rebel and forced Charles to convene Parliament.

The members of Parliament were in the peculiar position of wanting to oppose their king's policies while crushing the rebellion against him. Led by John Pym (1584–1643), they refused to discuss funding for the war until Charles agreed to redress their grievances. The angry king responded by dissolving what came, for obvious reasons, to be known as the Short Parliament (April–May 1640). A few months later, the Presbyterian Scots invaded England, defeated an English army at Newburn, and left Charles no choice but to recall Parliament for what proved to be a long, fateful session.

The Long Parliament and Civil War   The aptly named Long Parliament met from 1640 to 1660. It enjoyed support from many important factions. It represented the landowners and the merchant classes who resented the king's financial exactions and paternalistic rule, and many of its members were Puritans who disliked Charles's religious policies.

The House of Commons began by impeaching the king's chief advisers, the earl of Strafford and Archbishop Laud. (Strafford was executed for treason in 1641 and Laud in 1645.) Parliament then abolished the courts that had enforced royal policy and prohibited the levying of new taxes without its consent. It announced it could not be dissolved without its own consent and that no more than three years could elapse between its meetings.

Parliament, however, was sharply divided over religion. All the Puritans—the Presbyterian moderates and the extremist Independents—wanted to abolish the episcopal system and end use of the *Book of Common Prayer*. Many conservatives in both houses of Parliament did not want any changes in England's church at all. These divisions intensified in October 1641, when a rebellion in Ireland compelled the king to ask Parliament for more money for his army. Pym and his followers argued that Charles could not be trusted and that Parliament itself should take command of England's military.

On December 1, 1641, Parliament presented Charles with the Grand Remonstrance, a summary of over two hundred grievances against the crown. In January 1642, Charles responded by invading Parliament to arrest Pym and other leaders, but they escaped. The House of Commons authorized Parliament to raise its own army. The king withdrew from London, and for the next four years (1642–1646) civil war engulfed England, with the King's supporters known as Cavaliers and the parliamentary opposition as Roundheads.

OLIVER CROMWELL AND THE PURITAN REPUBLIC

Two things contributed to Parliament's victory. The first was an alliance with Scotland in 1643 that committed Parliament to a presbyterian system of church government. The second was the reorganization of the parliamentary army under Oliver Cromwell (1599–1658), a middle-aged country squire who favored the Independents. He and his "godly men" wanted neither the king's episcopal system nor Scotland's presbyterian organization. The only state church they supported was one that granted freedom of worship to Protestant dissenters.

Defeated by June 1645, for the next several years Charles tried to exploit the divisions within Parliament, but members who might have been sympathetic to the monarch were expelled from Parliament in December 1648. On January 30, 1649, after trial by a special court, Parliament executed the king and abolished the monarchy, the House of Lords, and the Anglican church. The civil war had become a political revolution that turned England into a Puritan Republic.

From 1649 to 1660, England was officially governed by Parliament, but Cromwell was in firm control. The military achievements of the Republic were

King CHARLES the FIRST in the HOUSE of COMMONS, demanding the FIVE impeached MEMBERS to be delivered up to his AUTHORITY.

One of the key moments in the conflict between Charles I and Parliament occurred in January 1642 when Charles personally arrived at the House of Commons intent on arresting five members who had been responsible for for opposing him. They had already escaped. Thereafter Charles departed London to raise his army. The event was subsequently often portrayed in English art. The present illustration is from an eighteenth-century engraving.

The Granger Collection, New York

QUICK REVIEW

The Long Parliament (1640–1660)

- Enjoyed wide support
- Members united in desire to curb power of monarchy but divided on issue of religious reform
- Request by king for more money in October 1641 intensified divisions

Oliver Cromwell's New Model Army defeated the royalists in the English Civil War. After the execution of Charles I in 1649, Cromwell dominated the short-lived English republic, conquered Ireland and Scotland, and ruled as Lord Protector from 1653 until his death in 1658.

Stock Montage, Inc./Historical Pictures Collection

impressive. Cromwell conquered Ireland and Scotland and united the countries that now compose Great Britain. Cromwell was, however, a better general than a politician. In 1653, when the House of Commons entertained a motion to disband his expensive army of 50,000 men, he disbanded Parliament.

Thereafter Cromwell ruled as Lord Protector according to a written constitution (the Instrument of Government) that created a military dictatorship. It had minimal popular support. Commerce suffered, and people chafed under Cromwell's rigorous enforcement of Puritan codes of conduct. The Lord Protector was as intolerant of Anglicans as the king had been of Puritans. (See "History's Voices: John Milton Defends Freedom to Print Books.") By the time he died in 1658, a majority of the English were ready to end experimentation and return to traditional institutions of government. In 1660, the exiled Charles II (r. 1660–1685), son of Charles I, was invited home to restore the Stuart monarchy.

CHARLES II AND THE RESTORATION OF THE MONARCHY

Charles II, a man of considerable charm and political skill, ascended the throne amid great rejoicing, and England returned to the institutions it had rejected in 1642: a hereditary monarchy that was not required to consult with Parliament, and an Anglican church with bishops and an official prayer book. Charles's secret Catholic sympathies led him to favor religious toleration, which offered Catholics as much safety as they could hope for in England. Few in Parliament, however, believed the state could risk giving free rein to religious diversity. Between 1661 and 1665, Parliament enacted the Clarendon Code, which excluded Roman Catholics, Presbyterians, and Independents from religious and political offices. Penalties were imposed for attending non-Anglican worship services.

Charles's foreign policy centered on a series of naval wars with Holland. In 1670, Charles allied with the French, who were also at war with Holland, and received French aid to underwrite the cost of his campaign. In exchange for a substantial subsidy from France's King Louis XIV, Charles secretly pledged to announce, at some propitious moment, his conversion to Catholicism. The time to fulfill that promise never came.

In 1672, Charles tried to rally his English subjects in support of the war with Holland (and to show good faith with Louis XIV) by issuing the Declaration of Indulgence, which suspended the laws against Roman Catholics and Protestant nonconformists. Parliament, however, opposed the king's efforts to promote religious tolerance, and it forced Charles to rescind the declaration by refusing to grant him money for the war. Parliament also passed the Test Act, which barred Roman Catholics from office by requiring royal officials to swear oaths repudiating the doctrine of transubstantiation. The Test Act was aimed in large measure at the king's brother, James, duke of York, heir to Charles's throne and a devout convert to Catholicism.

In 1678, a notorious liar, Titus Oates, accused Charles's Catholic wife of plotting with Jesuits and Irishmen to kill her husband and bring his Catholic brother to the throne. Oates's alleged "Popish Plot" whipped Parliament into a state of hysteria. Several people were executed, and a faction in Parliament, the Whigs, nearly won passage for a bill excluding James from the succession.

HISTORY'S VOICES

JOHN MILTON DEFENDS FREEDOM TO PRINT BOOKS

*S*ome Puritans worried that Parliaments might govern as tyrannically as kings. Parliament's imposition of strict censorship during the English Civil War prompted John Milton, the poet who wrote Paradise Lost, to compose an essay ("Areopagitica," 1644) in defense of freedom of the press.

WHY DOES Milton think it may be more harmful to attack a book than to attack a person? Is he right?

I deny not but that it is of greatest concern in the Church and Commonwealth to have a vigilant eye how books demean themselves as well as men; and thereafter to confine, imprison, and do sharpest justice on them as [if they were criminals]; for books are not absolutely dead things, but do contain a progeny of life in them to be as active as that soul was whose progeny they are; nay, they do preserve as in a vial the purest efficacy and extraction of that living intellect that bred them. ... He who kills a man kills a reasonable creature, God's Image; but he who destroys a good book, kills reason itself, kills the Image of God, as it were. ... Many a man lives [as] a burden to the Earth; but a good book is the precious life-blood of a master spirit, embalmed and treasured up on purpose to a life beyond life. It is true, no age can restore a life, whereof, perhaps there is no great loss; and revolutions of ages do not oft recover the loss of a rejected truth, for the want of which whole nations fare the worse. We should be wary, therefore, what persecution we raise against the living labours of public men, how we spill that seasoned life of man preserved and stored up in books; since we see a kind of homicide may be thus committed, sometimes a martyrdom, and if it extends to the whole impression, a kind of massacre, whereof the execution ends not in the slaying of an elemental life, but strikes at that ethereal ... essence, the breath of reason itself; slays an immortality rather than a life.

From J. A. St. John, ed., *The Prose Works of John Milton* (London: H. G. Bohn, 1843–1853), 2:8–9.

Chronically short of money and having little hope of persuading Parliament to grant him what he wanted, Charles increased customs duties, extracted more financial aid from Louis XIV, and avoided convening a Parliament after 1681. By the time he died in 1685 (after making a deathbed conversion to Catholicism), he had cowed his opponents and positioned James II, his successor, to call a Parliament filled with royal friends.

THE "GLORIOUS REVOLUTION"

James II (r. 1685–1688) did not know how to use his opportunities. He alienated Parliament by insisting on the repeal of the Test Act. When Parliament balked, he dissolved it and flaunted the Test Act by openly appointing known Catholics to high offices. In 1687, he issued a Declaration of Indulgence that suspended religious tests and permitted free worship.

A birth galvanized James's enemies into action. They had hoped he would die without a male heir and the throne would pass to Mary, his eldest daughter. She was a Protestant and the wife of William III of Orange, *stadtholder* of the Protestant Netherlands, great-grandson of William the Silent, and the leader of the European states that were threatened by Louis XIV's military ventures. On June 20, 1688, James's second wife alarmed England's Protestants by giving birth to a son, a Catholic heir to their throne. Within days of the boy's birth, Whig and

QUICK REVIEW

James II (r. 1685–1688)

• Policy of toleration of Catholicism alienated Parliament

• June 20, 1688: Birth of son alarms opponents

• James forced to leave England and William and Mary of Orange invited to become new monarchs

Tory members of Parliament had agreed to invite William and Mary to invade England and establish a monarchy that would preserve "traditional liberties."

William of Orange's army landed in England in November 1688, and James, receiving no support from his subjects, was forced to flee to France. Parliament then carried out a bloodless **"Glorious Revolution"** by declaring the throne vacant and proclaiming William and Mary its heirs. The new monarchs, in their turn, issued a Bill of Rights that limited their power and protected the civil liberties of England's privileged classes. Henceforth, England's rulers would be subject to law and would govern with the consent of a Parliament that convened in regular sessions and not only when summoned by the crown. The Bill of Rights prohibited Roman Catholics from occupying the English throne, but the Toleration Act of 1689 legalized all forms of Protestantism (except those that denied the Trinity). Roman Catholicism was outlawed.

In 1701, the Act of Settlement closed the "century of strife" (as the seventeenth century came to be known in England) by decreeing that the English crown would pass to the Protestant House of Hanover in Germany if none of the children of Queen Anne (r. 1702–1714), the last of the Stuart monarchs, survived her. Anne did outlive her children, and in 1714, the elector of Hanover became King George I of England—the third foreigner to occupy England's throne in just over a century.

THE AGE OF WALPOLE

Despite surviving a challenge to the throne in 1715, George I's reign remained politically unstable until Sir Robert Walpole (1676–1745) took over the helm of government. Walpole, regarded as the first prime minister of Great Britain, owed his power to royal support, his ability to handle the House of Commons, and his control of government patronage. He maintained peace abroad, promoted the status quo at home, and presided over an expansion of foreign trade. The central government did not interfere with the local power of nobles and other landowners, who consequently cooperated by serving as administrators, judges, and military commanders, and also collected and paid taxes.

The power of British monarchs and their ministers had real limits. Members of Parliament maintained independent views, and Britain enjoyed freedom of speech, freedom of association, and religious toleration. British political life became the model for all progressive Europeans who questioned the development of absolutism on the Continent.

15.1
Richelieu: Controlling the Nobility

WHY WERE efforts to establish absolute monarchy successful in France but unsuccessful in England?

"Glorious Revolution"
Parliament's bloodless 1688 declaration of a vacant throne and proclamation that William and Mary were its heirs.

RISE OF ABSOLUTE MONARCHY IN FRANCE: THE WORLD OF LOUIS XIV

*H*istorians once portrayed Louis XIV's reign (r. 1643–1715) as a time when the French monarchy exerted far-reaching, direct control of the nation at all levels. A somewhat different picture has now emerged.

The French monarchy only gradually achieved the firm authority for which it became renowned in the late seventeenth century. Two powerful chief ministers, Cardinal Richelieu (1585–1642), under Louis XIII (r. 1610–1643), and then Cardinal Mazarin (1602–1661), laid the groundwork for Louis XIV's absolutism. They attempted to impose direct royal administration on France, and Richelieu circumscribed many of the political privileges that French Protestants had gained under the Edict of Nantes (1598). These policies provoked widespread rebellions among French nobles between 1649 and 1652. Though unsuccessful, these rebellions, known as the ***Fronde*** (after the slingshots used by street boys) convinced Louis XIV and his advisors that, even as they concentrated unprecedented authority in the monarchy, they needed to assure nobles and other wealthy groups of their social standing and influence on the local level.

YEARS OF PERSONAL RULE

Upon Mazarin's death in 1661, Louis XIV assumed personal control of the government at the age of twenty-three. With no chief minister to resist, rebellious nobles would now be challenging the king directly. Devoting enormous personal energy to his political tasks, Louis ruled through councils that controlled foreign affairs, the army, domestic administration, and economic regulations. He depended on families with long histories in royal service, and also promoted figures just rising in the social structure, thus ensuring their loyalty to the crown, not to local power bases.

Louis made sure that the nobility and other social groups benefited from the growth of his own authority. He limited the national, but not local influence of noble institutions, and never tried to abolish them. He conferred with regional judicial bodies, called *parlements,* before making rulings that would affect them. Although he curtailed the power of the Parlement of Paris in 1673, even this act had the support of many regional *parlements* and other authorities that had long resented its power.

VERSAILLES

Louis and his advisors became masters of propaganda and political image creation. By manipulating symbols, Louis never missed an opportunity to impress the grandeur of his crown on the French people, most especially on the French nobility. For example, when the *dauphin* (the heir to the French throne) was born in 1662, Louis appeared for the celebration dressed as a Roman emperor.

Gold fleur-de-lis with gold crown.

Neil Lukas ©Dorling Kindersley, Courtesy of l'Etablissement Public du Musee et du Domaine National de Versailles

Fronde Widespread rebellions in France between 1649 and 1652 (named after a slingshot used by street ruffians) aimed at reversing the drift toward absolute monarchy and preserving local autonomy.

Versailles, as painted in 1668 by Pierre Patel the Elder (1605–1676). The central building is the hunting lodge built by Louis XIII earlier in the century. Louis XIV added the wings, the gardens, and the forecourt.

Pierre Patel, *Perspective View of Versailles,* Chateau de Versailles et de Trianon, Versailles, France. Copyright Giraudon/Art Resource, NY

The palace of Versailles was the central element of the monarchy's image. Built between 1676 and 1708 on the outskirts of Paris, Versailles became Louis's permanent residence after 1682. Designed and decorated to proclaim the glory of the Sun King, as Louis was known, it had magnificent fountains and gardens, housed thousands of the more important nobles and officials, and had stables that could hold 12,000 horses.

By ruling personally, Louis became the chief source of favors and patronage in France. Court life was organized around every aspect of his own daily routine. Moments near the king—such as the chance to hold Louis's night candle as he went to bed—were important to most court nobles because they were effectively excluded from the real business of government. Many bobles depleted their resources to remain in residence at Versailles, or depended on royal patronage to reside there. Some nobles, of course, avoided Versailles, managing their own estates. Yet even here Louis's support of France's traditional social structure and noble privileges strengthened his reign.

KING BY DIVINE RIGHT

An important source for Louis's concept of royal authority was his devout tutor, the political theorist Bishop Jacques-Bénigne Bossuet (1627–1704). Bossuet defended what he called the "**divine right of kings**" and cited examples of Old Testament rulers divinely appointed by and answerable only to God. Medieval popes had insisted that only God could judge a pope; so Bossuet argued that only God—not mere nobles, nor parliaments—could judge a king. Such assumptions lay behind Louis XIV's alleged declaration: "*L'etat, c' ést moi*" ("I am the state").

Despite these claims, Louis's rule did not exert the oppressive control over the daily lives of his subjects that police states would do in the nineteenth and twentieth centuries. His absolutism functioned in the making of war and peace, the regulation of religion, and the oversight of economic activity. Local institutions and elites retained their social and financial privileges. Unlike the Stuart kings of England, Louis prevented noble interference to his authority on the national level.

LOUIS'S EARLY WARS

By the late 1660s, France was superior to any other European nation in population, administrative bureaucracy, army, and national unity. Because of the economic policies of his minister Jean-Baptiste Colbert (1619–1683), Louis could afford to raise and maintain a large, powerful army. His enemies claimed that Louis wished to dominate all of Europe, but it would appear that his chief military and foreign policy goal was to secure France's international boundaries—especially along the Spanish Netherlands, the Franche-Comté, Alsace, and Lorraine, traditional areas from which foreign armies had invaded France. Nevertheless, Louis's pursuit of French interests threatened and terrified neighboring states and led them to form coalitions against France.

Louis's early wars included conflicts with Spain and the United Netherlands. The first was the War of the Devolution, in which Louis contended that inheritance of the Spanish Netherlands should have "devolved" upon his first wife, Marie Thérèse. In 1667, Louis's armies invaded Flanders and the Franche-Comté, but was repulsed by England, Sweden, and the United Provinces. The next year, under the Treaty of Aix-la-Chapelle, Louis gained control of some towns on the Netherlands border. Louis invaded the Netherlands again in 1672, but was met by an alliance that included the Prince of Orange, the future

"divine right of kings" The belief that God appoints kings and that kings are accountable only to God for how they use their power.

William III of England, the Holy Roman Emperor, Spain, Lorraine, and Brandenburg. The Peace of Nijmwegen in 1678 and 1679 ended the war inconclusively, but France gained more territory, including the Franche-Comté.

LOUIS'S REPRESSIVE RELIGIOUS POLICIES

Louis believed that political unity and stability required religious conformity. To that end he repressed both Roman Catholics and Protestants.

Suppression of the Jansenists   The French had long guarded their ecclesiastical independence or "Gallican Liberties" from papal authority in Rome, but after King Henry IV converted to Roman Catholicism in 1593, Jesuit influence in France grew. The Jesuit religious order, fiercely loyal to Papal authority, monopolized the education of French upper-class men, even serving as confessors to Henry IV, Louis XIII, and Louis XIV.

In the 1630s, a Roman Catholic religious movement known as **Jansenism**, named after the Flemish theologian and bishop of Ypres Cornelius Jansen (d. 1638), arose in opposition to Jesuit theology and political influence. Influenced by the teachings of St. Augustine (354–430), the serious and uncompromising Jansenists opposed Jesuit teachings about grace and salvation. They believed that original sin had so corrupted humankind that individuals could do nothing good nor secure their own salvation without divine grace.

The Jansenists, whose theology resembled Calvinism, were known to live extremely pious and morally austere lives. Though firm Roman Catholics, they resembled English Puritans. Jansenism spread among prominent families in Paris and became associated with opposition to royal authority. Some Jansenist families had been involved in the Fronde.

In 1653, Pope Innocent X declared heretical five Jansenist theological propositions on grace and salvation and banned a book by Jansen that attacked Jesuit teachings. In 1713, Pope Clement XI issued another official condemnation of Jansenism. Louis XIV supported these papal decisions, but in so doing, turned his back on the long tradition of protecting **Gallican Liberties** of the French Church. This had long-term political significance, for it fostered a core of opposition to royal authority. During the eighteenth century, French judicial bodies, such as the Parlement of Paris, reasserted their authority and held in common with Jansenists resistance to the Monarchy's power and what eighteenth-century public opinion saw as the corruption of the French royal court.

Revocation of the Edict of Nantes   After the Edict of Nantes in 1598, relations between the Catholic majority and Protestant minority remained hostile. French Huguenots numbered about 1.75 million out of a total population of approximately 18 million, but their numbers were declining. The French Catholic church had long supported their persecution as both pious and patriotic. After the Peace of Nijmwegen, persecution of Protestants intensified. Influenced by his mistress and eventually second wife Madame de Maintenon (1635–1719), a deeply pious Catholic who drew Louis toward a much more devout religious observance, the king launched a methodical campaign against

Pierre Mignard "Portrait of Françoise d'Aubigne marquise de Maíntenon (1635–1719), mistress and second wife of Louis XIV," by Pierre Mignard (1612–1695)

Oil on canvas, 128 x 97 cm. Inv.: MV 3637. Chateaux de Versailles et de Trianon, Versailles. Bridgeman-Giraudon/Art Resource, NY

Jansenism   Appearing in the 1630s, it followed the teachings of St. Augustine, who stressed the role divine grace played in human salvation.

Gallican Liberties   The French Roman Catholic Church's ecclesiastical independence of papal authority in Rome.

the Huguenots. Intending to unify France religiously, Louis hounded Huguenots out of public life, banning them from government office and certain professions. In October 1685, Louis revoked the Edict of Nantes. Under the religious repression that followed. Protestant churches and schools were closed, nonconverting laity were forced to be galley slaves, and Protestant children were baptized by Catholic priests.

The revocation was a major blunder. Henceforth, Protestants across Europe considered Louis a fanatic who must be resisted at all costs. More than a quarter million people, many highly skilled, left France and formed new communities in England, Germany, Holland, and the New World. France became a symbol of religious repression in contrast to England's reputation for moderate, if not complete, religious toleration.

LOUIS'S LATER WARS

The League of Augsburg and the Nine Years' War After the Treaty of Nijmwegen in 1678–1679, Louis maintained his army at full strength and restlessly probed beyond his borders. New defensive coalitions formed against him, one of which, the League of Augsburg, supported by Habsburg emperor Leopold I (r. 1658–1705), included England, Spain, Sweden, the United Provinces, and the major German states. The League and France battled each other for nine years, while England and France struggled to control North America. The Peace of Ryswick ended the war in 1697, securing Holland's borders and thwarting Louis's expansion into Germany.

War of the Spanish Succession The last Habsburg king of Spain, Charles II (r. 1665–1700), died in 1700 without direct heirs. He left his entire inheritance to Louis's grandson Philip of Anjou, who became Philip V of Spain (r. 1700–1746). Spain and the trade with its American empire appeared to have fallen to France, prompting England, Holland, and the Holy Roman Empire to form the Grand Alliance in 1701 to preserve the existing balance of power. The Alliance also wanted to secure Flanders permanently as a barrier between Holland and France and gain a fair share of the Spanish inheritance for the emperor (who was a Habsburg). Louis increased the stakes by recognizing the Stuart claim to the English throne.

The War of the Spanish Succession, which lasted from 1701 to 1714, enveloped western Europe, and marked the first time Louis went to war with inadequate finances, a poorly equipped army, and mediocre generals. The English, in contrast, had advanced weaponry (flintlock rifles, paper cartridges, and ring bayonets) and superior, more maneuverable tactics. John Churchill, the Duke of Marlborough (1650–1722) scored successes in every major engagement, although French arms triumphed in Spain. By 1714, Philip V remained king of Spain, England had become a Mediterranean power by securing Gibraltar and the island of Minorca, and Louis had recognized the right of the House of Hanover to the English throne.

FRANCE AFTER LOUIS XIV

Despite France's military reverses, it remained a great power. Although less strong in 1715 than in 1680, it still had the largest European population, an advanced, if troubled, economy, and Louis's administrative structure. Moreover, all the major states of Europe were drained by war. Louis XIV was succeeded by his five-year-old great-grandson Louis XV (r. 1715–1774). The boy's uncle, the duke of Orléans,

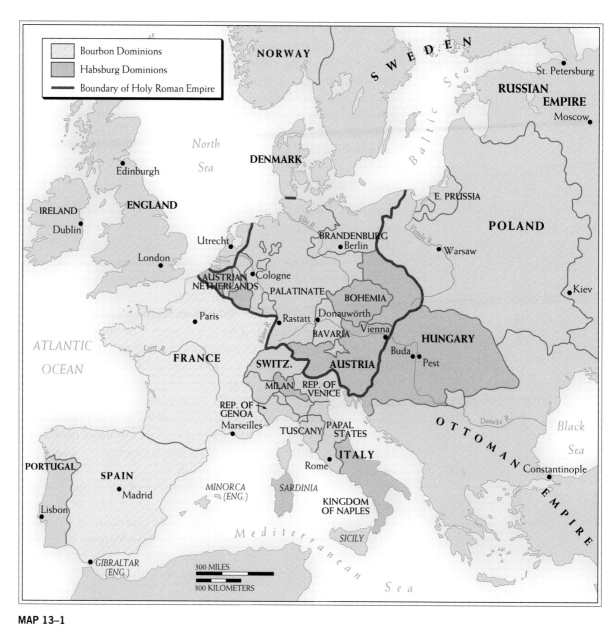

MAP 13–1

Europe in 1714   The War of the Spanish Succession ended a year before the death of Louis XIV. The Bourbons had secured the Spanish throne, but Spain had forteited its possessions in Flanders and Italy.

HOW DID the territorial makeup of Europe change during the long reign of Louis XIV?

presided over a regency that lasted until 1720 and that was marked by financial and moral scandals, which further undermined the monarchy's faltering prestige.

John Law and the Mississippi Bubble   The duke of Orléans was a gambler, and for a time he entrusted the kingdom's financial management to John Law (1671–1729), a Scottish mathematician and fellow gambler. With the regent's permission, Law established a bank in Paris that, by issuing paper money, Law believed would stimulate France's economic recovery. Law then organized the Mississippi Company, which had a monopoly on trading privileges with the French colony of Louisiana in North America, and which took over management of the French national debt.

Law's scheme backfired, harming France economically and bringing disgrace on the government. In exchange for government bonds, which had fallen sharply in value, the Mississippi Company issued shares of its own stock. In 1719 the stock's price rose handsomely. Smart investors netted profits by selling their stock in exchange for paper money at Law's bank, and then sought to trade it for gold. The bank, however, lacked enough gold to redeem all the paper money. By 1720, all gold payments in France were halted. The burst of the so-called Mississippi Bubble forced Law to flee the country. Although the Mississippi Company was later reorganized and functioned profitably, fear of paper money and speculation marked French life for decades.

Renewed Authority of the *Parlements*   The duke of Orléans made a second decision that diminished the monarchy's power. Attempting to draw the French nobility once again into the decision-making processes of government, he set up a system of councils on which nobles were to serve along with bureaucrats. The experiment failed, for the years of idle noble domestication at Versailles had removed from the nobility both the talent and desire to govern.

The nobles, however, did not surrender their ancient ambition to assert their rights, privileges, and local influence over those of the monarchy. Their most effective instrument was the *parlements*, or courts dominated by the nobility. Different from the English Parliament, these French courts did not legislate; instead they had power to recognize or not to recognize the legality of an act or law promulgated by the monarch. Reversing Louis XIV's policy, the duke of Orléans reinstituted the *parlements'* full power to allow or disallow laws. In the eighteenth century, these courts became natural centers for aristocratic and popular resistance to royal authority. Thus, they—not the monarch—would come to be seen as more nearly representing the nation.

By 1726, the general political direction of the nation had come under the authority of Cardinal Fleury (1653–1743), who sought to maintain the monarchy's authority (for example, by continuing repression of Jansenists) and to preserve the French nobility's local interests. Like Walpole in Britain, he pursued economic prosperity at home and peace abroad. Also like Walpole, after 1740, Fleury could not prevent France from entering a worldwide colonial conflict. (See Chapter 16.)

CENTRAL AND EASTERN EUROPE

WHAT WERE the main characteristics that defined the Polish, Austrian, and Prussian states in the seventeenth and eighteenth centuries?

Central and eastern Europe was economically much less advanced than western Europe. Except for the Baltic ports, its economy was agrarian. It had fewer cities, many more large estates worked by serfs, and no overseas empires. Its political authorities were weak because the almost constant warfare of the seventeenth century encouraged temporary and shifting loyalties among princes and aristocracies.

In the late 1600s, three strong dynasties, whose rulers aspired to the absolutism then being constructed in France, emerged in central and eastern Europe and would dominate the region until the end of World War I in 1918. The Austrian Habsburgs began to consolidate power outside Germany, while Prussia under the Hohenzollern dynasty emerged among the north German states. Most important, Russia under the Romanov dynasty at the opening of the eighteenth century became a major military and naval power. By contrast, in the eighteenth century Poland failed to establish a viable centralized government.

POLAND: ABSENCE OF STRONG CENTRAL AUTHORITY

In no other part of Europe was the failure to maintain a competitive political position so complete as in Poland. The fault lay with the Polish nobility, who blocked every attempt to establish an effective central government. The Polish monarchy was elective, and rivalries among the noble families prevented them from choosing one of their own as king. Most of Poland's monarchs, therefore, were outsiders and puppets of foreign powers. The Polish nobles belonged to a central legislative body called the **Sejm**, or diet. It specifically excluded representatives from corporate bodies, such as towns, and was virtually powerless. A practice known as *liberum veto* allowed any one of its members unilaterally to disband its meetings. The need to achieve unanimous agreement before taking any action made it extremely difficult for the diet to do much. Government as it was developing elsewhere in Europe simply was not tolerated in Poland, and during the last half of the eighteenth century, Poland temporarily disappeared from the map of Europe.

THE HABSBURG EMPIRE AND THE PRAGMATIC SANCTION

The close of the Thirty Years' War marked a fundamental turning point in the history of the Austrian Habsburgs. They had hoped, in alliance with their Spanish cousins, to bring Germany under their control and back to the Catholic fold. They failed, and with the decline of Spanish power, were on their own.

After 1648, Habsburg influence grew in three areas. The dynasty still had a firm hold on the title of Holy Roman Emperor, but the power of this crown depended less on the force of arms than on the cooperation it could elicit from the various political bodies in the empire, which included large German states (such as Saxony, Hanover, Bavaria, and Brandenburg), as well as scores of cities, bishoprics, principalities, and territories. The Habsburgs also consolidated power outside the empire, in Bohemia, Moravia, Silesia, Hungary, Croatia, and Transylvania. Lastly, under the Treaty of Rastadt in 1714, they claimed the former Spanish Netherlands and Lombardy in northern Italy. Thereafter, Habsburg power and influence would be based primarily on the territories outside of Germany. (See Map 13–2.)

The diversity of the Habsburgs' empire limited its ability to unify. In each of the many territories, the Habsburgs ruled by virtue of a different title—king, archduke, duke—and needed the cooperation of the local nobility, which was not always forthcoming. Various languages, customs, and faiths hindered political unification, and most of the governmental bodies dealt with only a portion of the Habsburg holdings.

Despite these internal difficulties, Leopold I (r. 1658–1705) managed to resist the aggression of the Ottoman Empire in the south and of Louis XIV in the west. He achieved sovereignty over Hungary in 1699 and took control of much of the Balkan Peninsula and western Romania, including access to the Adriatic and Mediterranean seas through the port of Trieste. Joseph I (r. 1705–1711) continued Leopold's policies.

Charles VI (r. 1711–1740) succeeded Joseph and added a new problem to the chronic one of territorial diversity. Charles had no male heir and only a very weak precedent for a female ruler of the Habsburg domains. He feared a breakup of the empire after his death—the fate that had befallen the Spanish Habsburgs in 1700. Therefore he devoted most of his reign to seeking the approval of his family, the estates of his realms, and the major foreign powers for a document called **Pragmatic Sanction**, which provided the legal basis for a single line of Habsburg inheritance through his daughter Maria Theresa (r. 1740–1780). He did indeed

Sejm   Central legislative body to which the Polish nobles belonged.

Pragmatic Sanction   Document recognizing Charles VI's daughter Maria Theresa as his heir.

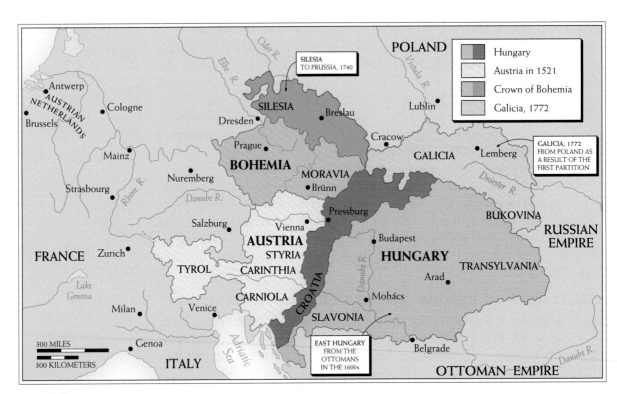

MAP 13–2

The Austrian Habsburg Empire, 1521–1772   The empire had three main units—Austria, Bohemia, and Hungary. Expansion was mainly eastward: eastern Hungary from the Ottomans (seventeenth century) and Galicia from Poland (1772). Meantime, Silesia was lost after 1740, but the Habsburgs remained Holy Roman Emperors.

WHY WAS expansion of the Austrian Hasburg Empire mostly eastward?

secure the legal unity of the empire, but had to make various concessions to nobles and other rules. Maria Theresa inherited the line of succession, but had neither a strong army nor a full treasury. This invited foreign aggression, and within two months of Charles VI's death, Frederick II of Prussia invaded the Habsburg province of Silesia in eastern Germany.

PRUSSIA AND THE HOHENZOLLERNS

The rise of Prussia occurred within the German power vacuum created by the Peace of Westphalia of 1648. The Hohenzollern family, which had ruled Brandenburg since 1417, inherited a series of disconnected German lands, including Cleves, Mark, Ravensburg, and East Prussia. Although their territories lacked good natural resources, by the late 1600s, within the Holy Roman Empire the Hohenzollern holdings rivaled only those of the Habsburgs.

The person who began to forge these areas into a modern state was Frederick William (r. 1640–1688), who became known as the Great Elector. He established himself and his successors as the central uniting power by breaking the medieval parliaments or estates, organizing a royal bureaucracy, and building a strong army. He collected taxes by force, using the money to build an army, which allowed him to enforce his will without the approval of the nobility.

To obtain the support and obedience of the **Junkers**, or German noble landlords, the Elector allowed them to have almost complete control over the serfs on their estates. Frederick William co-opted potential noble opponents by choosing Junkers as administrators and army officers, with the tax burden falling

Junkers (Prussian nobles) They were allowed to demand absolute obedience from the serfs on their estates in exchange for their support of the Hohenzollerns.

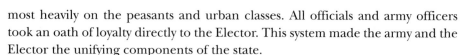

most heavily on the peasants and urban classes. All officials and army officers took an oath of loyalty directly to the Elector. This system made the army and the Elector the unifying components of the state.

Despite Frederick William's accomplishments, the house of Hohenzollern did not possess a crown. The Great Elector's son, Frederick I (r. 1688–1713) achieved this status during the War of the Spanish Succession by putting his army at the disposal of the Habsburg Holy Roman Emperor Leopold I, who permitted Frederick to assume the title of "King of Prussia" in 1701.

His successor, Frederick William I (r. 1713–1740), was one of the most effective Hohenzollern rulers. He instilled military priorities and values throughout Prussian government, society, and daily life, and increased the Prussian army's size from about 39,000 in 1713 to over 80,000 in 1740. This made the army Europe's third or fourth largest, even though Prussia's population, in contrast, ranked thirteenth in size. Laws, customs, and royal attention made the officer corps the highest social class of the state, attracting the sons of Junkers to military service. The army, *Junker* nobility, and monarchy were thus forged into a single political entity. It has often been said that whereas other states possessed armies, the Prussian army possessed its state.

Frederick William I built the best army in Europe, but he also avoided conflict. The army was a symbol of Prussian power and unity, not an instrument for foreign adventures. However, on succeeding to the throne, his son Federick II (Frederick the Great, r. 1740–1786) almost immediately invaded Silesia, thereby upsetting the Pragmatic Sanction and crystallizing the Austrian-Prussian rivalry for control of Germany.

RUSSIA ENTERS THE EUROPEAN POLITICAL ARENA

*T*he rise of Prussia and the consolidation of the Austrian Habsburg domains doubtless seemed to many at the time only one more shift in the old game of German politics. Russia's entrance into the European political arena was, however, something wholly new. Russia had long been considered a part of Europe only by courtesy. Hemmed in by Sweden on the Baltic and by the Ottoman Empire on the Black Sea, it had no warm-water ports. Its chief outlet to the West (the port of Archangel on the White Sea) was closed by ice during part of the year. Russia was a land of vast but unexploited potential.

THE ROMANOV DYNASTY

The reign of Ivan IV, "the Terrible," (1533–1584) was followed by a period of anarchy and civil war. In 1613, an assembly of nobles tried to end the confusion of this "Time of Troubles" by uniting in support of Michael Romanov (r. 1613–1654). His dynasty remained in power in Russia until 1917.

Michael Romanov and his two successors. Alexis I (r. 1654–1676) and Theodore III (r. 1676–1682), maintained order, but their country was weak and poor. Its government was dominated by an entrenched hereditary nobility (the *boyars*), and it was only barely able to meet the challenges posed by peasant revolts and raids by Cossacks (horsemen who lived on the steppe frontier). The *streltsy*, Moscow's garrison, was also prone to mutiny.

PETER THE GREAT

In 1682, the *streltsy* decided a bloodily disputed succession by placing two boys on Russia's shaky throne: Peter I, "the Great" (r. 1682–1725) and Ivan V. The boys' elder sister, Sophia, served as their regent until Peter overthrew her in 1689.

Peter the Great (r. 1682–1725), seeking to make Russia a military power, reorganized the country's political and economic structures. His reign saw Russia enter fully into European power politics.

The Apotheosis of Tsar Peter the Great 1672–1725 "by unknown artist, 1710. Historical Museum, Moscow, Russia E.T. Archive

He ruled thereafter, although theoretically sharing power with his co-tsar the sickly Ivan's death in 1696.

Like Louis XIV of France, who, as a boy, experienced the upheaval of the *fronde*, Peter resolved to establish an overwhelmingly powerful monarchy, and he turned to the West for help in doing this. Products and workers from the West had filtered into Russia, and Europe's culture, particularly its military science, intrigued Peter. In 1697, Peter made a famous tour of Europe. For convenience, he traveled officially incognito rather than as a head of state. (This minimized the ceremonial functions that diplomatic courtesy would otherwise have required.) The European leaders he visited regarded their almost seven-foot-tall guest as crude, but Peter was thoroughly at home in their shipyards and munitions factories. These places offered him what he had come to find.

Peter returned to Moscow determined to westernize Russia. He set himself four objectives and pursued them ruthlessly. He tamed the *boyars* and the *streltsy*. He brought the church under royal control. He reorganized governmental administration, and he promoted economic development. His goal was to increase Russia's military power and strengthen its monarchy.

Taming the *Streltsy* and *Boyars*

As Peter was returning to Russia in 1698, the *streltsy* rebelled. Peter violently suppressed the revolt by torturing and executing about a thousand men and exhibiting their corpses as a warning to future dissidents. Peter then set about building a new military. He drafted an unprecedented 130,000 soldiers, and by the end of his reign he had a well-disciplined army of 300,000.

Peter also launched a campaign to wean the *boyar* nobility from Russian customs that Europeans ridiculed. He personally shaved their long beards and sheared off the dangling sleeves of their shirts and coats. His tendency to make major policy decisions without consulting the *boyars* offended them and prompted them to plot against him. He controlled them by playing factions off against each other.

Developing a Navy

Peter built Russia's first navy, and it greatly increased his country's visibility on the world stage. In the mid-1690s, he constructed a fleet with which to challenge the Ottomans, and in 1696, he detached the Black Sea port of Azov from the Ottoman Empire. A major reason for his subsequent tour of Europe was to learn how to build warships that would win him a foothold on the Baltic. His chief competitor on this front was Sweden.

Russian Expansion in the Baltic: The Great Northern War

Sweden's reward for being on the winning side in the Thirty Years' War was control of the Baltic Sea, and it was able, for a time, to deny Russia a port and permit Poland and Germany access only on its terms. Sweden's economy was, however, not equal to its military ambitions. In 1700, Peter began the Great Northern War (1700–1721), a campaign to win Russia a foothold on the Baltic coast. His opponent, King Charles XII (r. 1697–1718) of Sweden, initially succeeded in stopping him, but Russia's superior resources gradually won Peter the upper hand. The Peace of Nystad, which ended the war, confirmed Peter's conquest of Estonia, Livonia, and part of Finland and gave Russia ice-free ports and permanent access to western Europe.

FOUNDING ST. PETERSBURG

In 1703, Peter began construction of St. Petersburg, a new capital for Russia on the Gulf of Finland. In imitation of Louis XIV, he built palaces in the style of Versailles and compelled the *boyar* nobles to construct townhouses and gather about him in the new city. St. Petersburg was, however, more than a seat for an imperial court. It was a western European city transplanted to the Russian environment, and it indicated the seriousness of Peter's intent to westernize his homeland. Many of his subjects resented it as a symbol of autocracy and an attack on their native culture.

THE CASE OF PETER'S SON ALEKSEI

Peter feared that opposition to him would coalesce into support for his son, Aleksei. Aleksei was not particularly intelligent or ambitious, and Peter openly berated him for his shortcomings and quarreled with him. Resentment of his father may have driven him to compromise himself. In 1716, while the Great Northern War was still raging, Aleksei made a secret journey to Vienna to meet with the Habsburg emperor, Charles VI. The two men (probably with Sweden's encouragement) discussed conspiring against Peter, but nothing materialized. When Aleksei returned to Russia in 1718, his father opened an inquiry into his conduct and that of various nobles and members of the Senate. A six-month-long investigation led to Aleksei's condemnation, and he died under mysterious circumstances on June 26, 1718.

REFORMS OF PETER THE GREAT'S FINAL YEARS

Aleksei's case was more than a family dispute. It taught Peter that opposition to him was more widespread than he had realized. The tsar understood he could not simply exterminate his many opponents, as he had the *streltsy*. Instead, he implemented administrative reforms designed to bring the nobles and the church under closer control of persons he trusted.

Administrative Colleges   In 1717, Peter reorganized his administration to enhance his personal authority and fight corruption. He adopted a Swedish model—a system of eight *colleges,* or bureaus, charged with managing tax collection, foreign relations, war, and the economy. Peter staffed these colleges with persons of proven loyalty and each was advised by a foreign expert. The colleges moderated the influence of the Senate, in which Aleksei had sympathizers.

Table of Ranks   In 1722, Peter drew the nobles into state service by issuing a **Table of Ranks**. It made rank in the bureaucracy or military, not lineage, the determinant of an individual's social status. Earlier tsars had sometimes conferred

Events and Reigns

1533–1584	Ivan the Terrible
1584–1613	Time of Troubles
1613	Michael Romanov becomes tsar
1640–1688	Frederick William, the Great Elector
1643–1715	Louis XIV, the Sun King
1648	Independence of the Netherlands recognized
1682–1725	Peter the Great
1683	Turkish siege of Vienna
1688–1713	Frederick I of Prussia
1697	Peter the Great's European tour
1700–1721	The Great Northern War
1703	Saint Petersburg founded
1711–1740	The Great Northern War
1703	Saint Petersburg founded
1711–1740	Charles VI, the Pragmatic Sanction
1713	War of the Spanish Succession ends
1713–1740	Frederick William I of Prussia
1714	George I founds England's Hanoverian dynasty
1715	Louis XV becomes king of France
1720–1741	Robert Walpole dominates British politics
1726–1743	Cardinal Fleury
1727	George II
1740	Maria Theresa succeeds to the Habsburg throne
1740	Frederick II invades Silesia

15.6
Peter the Great:
Correspondence
with His Son

Table of Ranks   Issued by Peter the Great to draw nobles into state service, it made rank in the bureaucracy or military, not lineage, the determinant of an individual's social status.

nobility as a reward for service, but Peter envisioned pulling all the nobles into government service. The tsars, however, never won the kind of loyalty from Russia's nobles that the Junkers felt for their Prussian ruler.

Achieving Secular Control of the Church Peter moved to suppress the independence of the Russian Orthodox Church, where some bishops and clergy had displayed sympathy for the tsar's son. In 1721, Peter abolished the office of patriarch and put the church under the control of a government department, the *Holy Synod*. It was staffed by several bishops and chaired by a layman, the *procurator general*. A Lutheran model guided the reorganization of the church—the most radical transformation of a traditional institution undertaken by Peter.

Peter had not, by the time of his death in 1725, decided on a successor, and a disputed succession gave the soldiers and nobles the opportunity they needed to reassert their influence. For the next thirty years, they decided who ruled Russia. Peter laid foundations for a modern state, but not stable one.

SWEDEN: THE AMBITIONS OF CHARLES XII

Sweden had seized the opportunity of the Thirty Years' War to make a bid for empire. During the seventeenth century, it controlled the Baltic, and Russia and Germany had access to that sea only on Sweden's terms. Sweden's economy was not strong enough, however, to underwrite its political ambitions.

In 1697, the headstrong and possibly insane Charles XII (r. 1697–1718) ascended Sweden's throne. Three years later the Great Northern War (1700–1721) began as Russia made a bid to win a base on the Baltic. Charles XII fought vigorously, but he mismanaged the campaign. After an initial victory and a distracting foray into Poland, he invaded Russia. His army bogged down in the brutal environment of winter and suffered decisive defeat at Poltava in 1709. The war ended in 1721, when Sweden ran out of resources. Russia occupied a large section of the eastern Baltic coast and broke Sweden's hold on the sea. After Charles's death, the Swedish nobles limited the power of the monarchy, and Sweden abandoned foreign adventures.

THE OTTOMAN EMPIRE

WHAT WAS the attitude of the Ottoman rulers toward religion in their empire and how was this reflected in their policies?

The **Ottoman Empire** was the largest and most stable state to appear in and near Europe Turks who conquered Constantinople and ended the Byzantine Empire in 1453. By the early seventeenth century, only the emperor of China had a larger territory and larger cities under his sway than the Ottoman sultan. (See Map 13–3.)

RELIGIOUS TOLERATION AND OTTOMAN GOVERNMENT

In 1516, the Ottomans took control of the sacred cities of Mecca, Medina, and Jerusalem and became the dominant power in the Muslim world. Their empire was diverse ethnically, linguistically, and religiously, and it offered more religious freedom than could be found anywhere in Europe. Thousands of Jews found refuge in Ottoman lands after they were evicted from Spain at the end of the fifteenth century, and the empire had a significant number of Christian subjects. The empire was governed through units called **millets** (communities of the officially recognized religions). The millet to which people belonged (not the territory they inhabited) determined which laws applied to them. *Dhimmis* (members of legal non-Islamic groups) managed their own community affairs through their religious leaders, but they paid a special tax, could not serve in the army or the administrative hierarchy of the empire, and were compelled in various ways

Ottoman Empire The authority Instanbul's Ottoman Turkish sultan exercised over the Balkans, the Middle East, and North Africa from the end of the Middle Ages to World War I.

millets Communities of the officially recognized religions that governed portions of the Ottoman Empire.

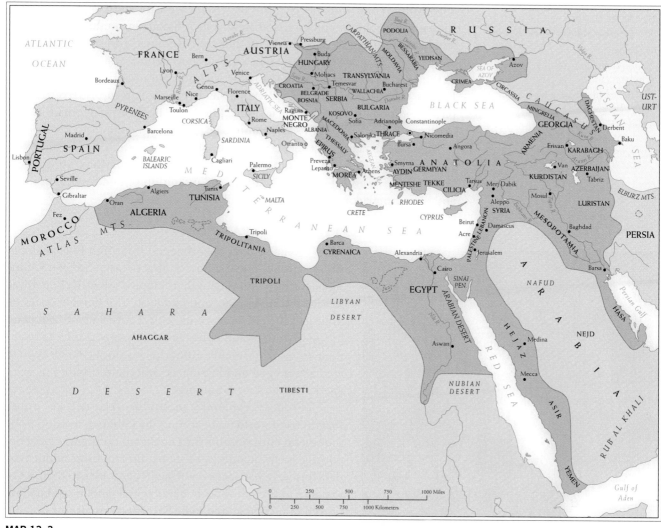

MAP 13–3

The Ottoman Empire in the Late Seventeenth Century   By the 1680s the Ottoman Empire had reached its maximum extent, but the Ottoman failure to capture Vienna in 1683 marked the beginning of a long and inexorable decline that ended with the empire's collapse after World War I.

FROM THE late 1600s until 1918, which non-Turkish peoples would rise up against Turkish rule in the Ottoman Empire?

to acknowledge their inferiority to Muslims. The Ottomans discouraged Muslims from mixing with *dhimmis,* and this prevented Muslims from acquiring the valuable skills and learning that these people possessed.

The sultan tried to prevent the rise of aristocratic competitors for his office by drawing his soldiers and administrators from groups that were expected to be especially loyal to him. Until the end of the seventeenth century, the Ottomans, utilizing a practice called *devshirme,* recruited their elite troops from Christian communities. By separating young Christian boys from their homelands and converting them to Islam, the sultan created a group of rootless men who were totally dependent on him. The most famous unit of the Ottoman infantry, the *Janissaries,* was formed in this way. The practice had the effect of excluding native Islamic peoples from the military and administrative structures of the empire. The thousands of men who filled influential government posts were largely recruited from the outer reaches of the empire. Technically they were the sultan's slaves, but their power made them the envy of many free subjects.

QUICK REVIEW

The *Ulama*

- *Ulama:* Dominant group of Muslim scholars
- Sultan and his advisors consulted with *Ulama*
- *Ulama* advised against modernization and adoption of European ideas

The Role of the *Ulama* A group of Muslim scholars, the *Ulama*, dominated the empire's schools and courts as well as its religious institutions. The sultan and his administrators consulted with them to ensure that government policy accorded with Islamic law and the Qur'an, and they, in turn, supported the sultan as the chief protector of *Shar'ia* (Islamic law) and Sunni Islam. At a time when Europe was modernizing, the *Ulama* persuaded the sultan to preserve the empire's traditional way of life. As a result, Muslim civilization, which had helped medieval Europe rebuild its civilization, began to stagnate and to fall behind Europe—particularly in science and technology. The Ottomans attempted to catch up in the eighteenth century by importing European advisers, but the conservative *Ulama* and the lack of cultural grounding prevented foreign customs and ideas from taking root in Muslim soil.

THE END OF OTTOMAN EXPANSION

Devshirme. An Ottoman portrayal of the *Devshirme*. This miniature painting from about 1558 depicts the recruiting of young Christian children for the Sultan's elite Janissary corps.

Arifi, "Suleymanname," Topkapi Palace Museum. II 1517, fol. 31b, photograph courtesy of Talat Halman

The Ottomans made their deepest foray into European territory in 1683. Their failure on that occasion to take Vienna signaled the beginning of their empire's slow decline. Rivalries within the military and administrative bureaucracies diminished the efficiency of its central government, and elites in the provinces and cities seized the opportunity to assert themselves. The sultan's authority was not so much repudiated as renegotiated by subjects who paid tribute but exercised considerable autonomy.

European explorers, meanwhile, charted sea routes that diverted world trade around the Ottoman territories. By the seventeenth century, the Dutch and Portuguese were importing great quantities of items directly from South Asia that formerly had passed through (and enriched) the Ottoman Empire. European naval power and weaponry improved at a comparable rate. The effects of all this became apparent in the 1690s, when war broke out between the Ottomans and a European league (Austria, Venice, Malta, Poland, Tuscany, and Russia). In 1699, the Ottomans were forced to retreat from Hungary, and Russia then began to challenge their hold on the northern shores of the Black Sea. A gulf steadily widened between the Ottomans and the Europeans, the former continuing to think of themselves as culturally superior and the latter regarding them as a declining, backward-looking people.

SUMMARY

The Netherlands Golden Age to Decline By the mid-eighteenth century, Britain and France had emerged as the dominant powers in western Europe and Spain had lost influence. The United Netherlands had enjoyed a Golden Age in the seventeenth century, and it was more urbanized than any other area of Europe. Dutch agriculture and financial systems were models for the rest of Europe, and the Dutch were the leading traders of Europe. After the death of William of Orange in 1702, the loose republican system that had given the Netherlands valuable flexibility turned into a handicap in the absence of leadership.

Two Models of European Political Development In the seventeenth century, England and France developed two different forms of government that served as models for other European countries in the eighteenth century. In England, nobles and the wealthy were politically active and had a tradition of broad liberties, representation, and bargaining with the monarch through Parliament. The English nobility felt little admiration or affection for the Stuart monarchs. In France, members of the French nobility believed the strength of Louis XIV served their personal interests as well as those of the king. This led to the so-called absolutism of the French monarchy, which became the country's sole significant national institution.

Constitutional Crisis and Settlement in Stuart England In the first half of the seventeenth century, many of the English suspected that their leaders were Catholic sympathizers. Oliver Cromwell led opposition in a civil war from 1642 to 1646, and then ruled until 1658. In 1660, the Stuart monarchy was restored under Charles II. His relationship with Parliament was testy. His brother and successor, the Catholic James II, was not as astute as Charles II. In 1688, members of Parliament invited William III of Orange to invade England and take the throne. After the success of the "Glorious Revolution," in 1689 William and Mary recognized a Bill of Rights, limiting the monarchy's powers, guaranteeing civil liberties to some, formalizing Parliament's role, and barring Catholics from the throne. The 1689 Toleration Act allowed Protestants freedom to worship, but denied Catholics similar privileges. The monarchy in Great Britain passed to the house of Hanover, and George I sought support from the Whigs. Robert Walpole functioned as George's prime minister. Parliament checked royal influence, and provided strong central political authority. Britain's economy was strong, and political life was remarkably free.

Rise of Absolute Monarchy in France: The World of Louis XIV Louis XIV's monarchy gathered unprecedented power on the national level in the area of foreign and military affairs, domestic administration, and economic regulation. At the same time, Louis was careful to allow nobles to retain their local power and privileges. He ensured loyalty to the crown by employing nobles in his administration, and crafted a political image as the "Sun King" based at Versailles. At this palace, Louis built a system of patronage that effectively excluded many nobles from government, even as it occupied them in ritual and ceremony all designed to promote Louis's personal rule and divine right monarchy. Louis's armies instilled fear in its neighbors, prompting several alliances to be formed against France throughout his reign. He repressed the anti-Jesuit Jansenists and revoked the Edict of Nantes, which had ensured toleration of French Protestants. These policies reinforced Europe's image of Louis as a repressive fanatic and sowed the seeds of domestic opposition to the monarchy, not only among Jansenist sympathizers, but also in noble and judicial bodies. The Habsburg Empire expanded so much that by the eighteenth and nineteenth centuries, Habsburg power and influence were based more on territories outside of Germany than within. Political unity was in short supply. The Hohenzollerns created a Prussian army that, according to an axiom, possessed the nation, rather than the other way around.

IMAGE KEY
for pages 312–313

a. Gold Fleur De Lys with Gold Crown. Neil Lukas © Dorling Kindersley, Courtesy of l'Etablissement Public du Musee et du Domaine National de Versailles.

b. Hyacinthe Rigaud (1659–1743), "Portrait of Louis XIV"   Louvre, Paris, France. Photograph copyright Bridgeman-Giraudon/Art Resource, NY

c., i. A pair of mid-17th century point de France lappets, lace. c. 1650

d. Jean Warin III (1604–1672). Foundation medal of Val-de-Grace. Verso: Anne of Austria her son Louis XIV. Bronze medaillon. 1638.   Musee de la Ville de Paris, Musee Carnavalet, Paris. Bridgeman-Giraudon/Art Resource, NY

e. Portrait of Peter the Great in a gold frame with a crown on top, artist unknown

f. Detail, "An Eyewitness Representation of the Execution of King Charles I (1600–49) of England, 1649 (oil on canvas) by Weesop (fl. 1641–49).   Private Collection/Bridgeman Art Library, London

g. Pierre Mignard (1612–1695), "Portrait of Francoise d'Aubigne, marquise de Maintenon (1635-1719), mistress and second wife of Louis XIV", c. 1694.   Oil on canvas, 128 x 97 cm. Inv.: MV 3637. Chateaux de Versailles et de Trianon, Versailles. Bridgeman-Giraudon/Art Resource, NY

h. Pierre Patel, "Perspective View of Versailles." Chateaux de Versailles et de Trianon, Versailles, France.   Photo © Bridgeman-Giraudon/Art Resource, NY

j. Portrait of Philip V

k. Suleyman I (Kanuni); Shehzade by Talikizade Suphi.   Folio 79a of the Talikizade Shehnamesi, Library of the Topkapi Palace Museum, A3592, photograph courtesy of Talat Halman

Central and Eastern Europe The economies and political structures of central and eastern Europe were weaker than those of the west. Late in the seventeenth century, Poland could not develop a strong central authority, while Austria, Prussia, and Russia emerged as political and military powers.

Russia Enters the European Political Arena In the seventeenth century, Russia became one of the nations of Europe, and the Romanov dynasty was founded. Russia's old nobility. the *boyars,* retained considerable authority until Peter (later Peter the Great) assumed personal rule in 1689. Peter was zealous in his efforts to westernize Russia, to curb the power of the *boyars* and Moscow garrison guards (the *streltsy*), and to increase the nation's military strength. He was remarkably successful in most of his efforts. His critical failure was that, when he died in 1725, he had not appointed as successor; for decades after his death, power reverted to nobles and soldiers.

The Ottoman Empire The Ottoman Empire conquered Constantinople and ended the Byzantine Empire in 1453, and dominated the Muslim world after 1516. The Ottomans' empire was diverse ethnically, linguistically, and religiously, and offered more religious freedom than could be found anywhere in Europe. Social and political structures prevented leading families from interacting meaningfully with the ruling elite, which limited the infusion of new ideas and personalities into government. Military defeats in the late seventeenth century marked the beginning of the end for the Ottoman Empire.

REVIEW QUESTIONS

1. Why did Britain and France remain leading powers while the United Netherlands declined? How did the structure of British government change under the political leadership of Walpole?

2. What similarities and differences do you see between the systems of government and religious policies in place in England and France at the end of the seventeenth century? What accounts for the path each nation took?

3. Why did the English king and Parliament come into conflict in the 1640s? What was the "Glorious Revolution"? How did England in 1700 differ from England in 1600?

4. How did Louis XIV consolidate his monarchy? How successful was his foreign policy? What were the domestic and international consequences of his religious policies?

5. How did Peter the Great's plan for building a greater Russia compare with the conduct of the Ottoman leaders who allowed their empire to decline?

6. How was the Hohenzollern family able to forge a conglomerate of diverse land holdings into the state of Prussia? How do the Hohenzollerns and the Habsburgs compare in the ways they dealt with the problems that confronted their domains?

7. What sorts of political and diplomatic problems did questions about successions to thrones create for various states between 1685 and 1740?

KEY TERMS

absolutism   (p. 315)

"divine right of kings"   (p. 324)

Fronde   (p. 323)

Gallican Liberties   (p. 325)

"Glorious Revolution"   (p. 322)

Jansenism   (p. 325)

Junkers   (p. 330)

millets   (p. 334)

Ottoman Empire   (p. 334)

parlements   (p. 315)

parliamentary monarchy   (p. 315)

Pragmatic Sanction   (p. 329)

Puritans   (p. 316)

Sejm   (p. 329)

Table of Ranks   (p. 333)

 For additional study resources for this chapter, go to:
www.prenhall.com/kagan3/chapter13

14 New Directions in Thought and Culture in the Sixteenth and Seventeenth Centuries

CHAPTER HIGHLIGHTS

The Scientific Revolution Copernicus proposed a heliocentric model of the universe. Kepler used data collected b[...] show that the planets have elliptical orbits. Galileo was a strong advocate of the heliocentric model and a believer i[...] rationality of nature. Newton derived laws of motion and the theory of universal gravitation.

Philosophy Responds to Changing Science Philosophers were profoundly influenced by the scientific revolution. Bacon, Descartes, Hobbes, and Locke all articulated philosophies influenced by the models suggested by the new science.

The New Institutions of Expanding Natural Knowledge The expansion of natural knowledge changed existing centers of learning and led to the creation of new "institutions of sharing." Scientific societies encouraged the exchange of ideas.

Women in the World of the Scientific Revolution Women were more often the subject of study and description than participants in early modern science. However, some noblewomen and female artisans were able to overcome the obstacles placed in their way and contribute to the scientific revolution.

The New Science and Religious Faith The new science challenged religion. Most natural philosophers worked hard to reconcile their work with mainstream religious views. Galileo's condemnation was an exception to the rule of accommodation between science and religion.

Continuing Superstition Throughout the seventeenth century, most Europeans believed in some form of magic. Witch hunts soared in the late sixteenth and early seventeenth centuries. Scholars have proposed a number of possible explanations for the rise and fall of witchcraft prosecutions during this period.

Baroque Art Depictions were naturalistic rather than idealized and sought to involve the observer on an emotional level through dramatic portrayals and contrast of light and darkness.

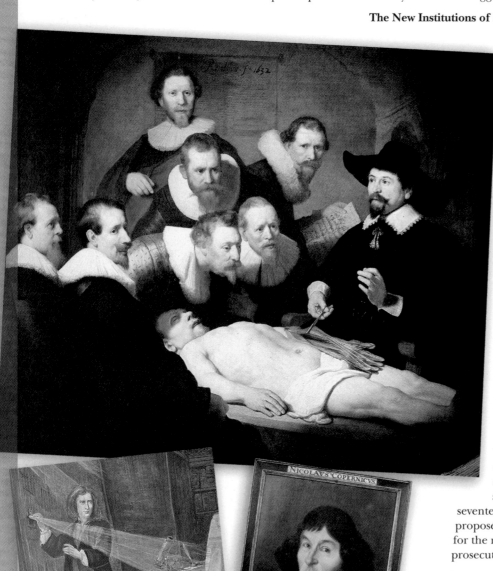

CHAPTER QUESTIONS

WHAT WAS the Scientific Revolution?

WHAT IMPACT did the new science have on philosophy?

WHICH NEW scholarly associations were established to foster scientific research?

WHAT ROLE did women play in the scientific revolution?

HOW DID the new science challenge traditional understandings of religion?

WHAT FORMS did superstition take in response to science in the sixteenth and seventeenth centuries?

HOW DID baroque art serve both religious and secular ends?

G. Galilei.

CHAPTER OUTLINE

- The Scientific Revolution
- Philosophy Responds to Changing Science
- The New Institutions of Expanding Natural Knowledge
- Women in the World of the Scientific Revolution
- The New Science and Religious Faith
- Continuing Superstition
- Baroque Art

IMAGE KEY

Image Key for pages 340–341 is on page 356.

WHAT WAS the scientific revolution?

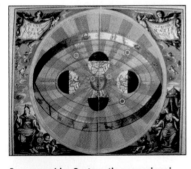

Scenographia: Systematis copernicani
Astrological Chart, ca. 1543.

British Library, London, UK/Bridgeman Art Library

scientific revolution The emergence in the sixteenth century of rational and empirical methods of research that challenged traditional thought and promoted the rise of science and technology.

During the sixteenth and seventeenth centuries, science created a new view of the universe that challenged many previously held beliefs. Earth moved from the center of the universe and became only one of several planets orbiting a sun that was only one of countless stars. This new cosmology forced people to rethink humanity's place in the larger scheme of things. The new scientific ideas came into apparent conflict with traditional religion and raised doubts about the grounds for faith and morality. Europeans discovered the world was a much more complex place than their ancestors had imagined. The telescope opened the heavens to them while the microscope disclosed the existence of a realm of microorganisms. A spate of scientific discoveries added to the intellectual dislocation already created by the Reformation and contact with the New World.

THE SCIENTIFIC REVOLUTION

The intellectual breakthroughs of the sixteenth and seventeenth centuries are said to constitute a **scientific revolution**, but that metaphor may be misleading if it implies a rapid, widespread transformation of culture. The development of science was a slow process that never involved more than a few hundred people, and these pioneers called themselves "natural philosophers," not scientists (a term that originated in the 1830s). Progress in science also owed much to the inventiveness of artisans and craftspeople as well as a few brilliant minds. Some individuals worked at universities or had the patronage of kings, but many pursued their studies informally from their homes or private workshops. It was not until the second half of the seventeenth century that learned societies and academies were established to promote research.

Despite this rather casual approach to scientific work, by the end of the seventeenth century the new ideas and research methods that were emerging were so impressive that they were setting the standard for testing the validity of all knowledge in the West. Science was achieving the cultural supremacy over other forms of intellectual activity that it still enjoys, and it was becoming a major defining characteristic of modern Western civilization. The discipline that did most to initiate these developments was astronomy.

NICOLAUS COPERNICUS REJECTS AN EARTH-CENTERED UNIVERSE

Nicolaus Copernicus (1473–1543), a respected Italian-educated Polish astronomer, had a reputation as a fairly conventional thinker until he published *On the Revolutions of the Heavenly Spheres* (1543). The book did not create a revolution, but it laid the groundwork for one by providing Copernicus's successors with material for critiquing the widely accepted view of Earth's place in the universe.

The Ptolemaic System The maps of the universe in use in Copernicus's day were variants of one found in the ancient Greek astronomer Ptolemy's *Almagest* (ca. 150 C.E.). They assumed Earth was the center point of a ball-shaped universe composed of concentric layers of rotating crystalline spheres to which the heavenly bodies were attached. Beyond these spheres lay the realm of God and the angels. Ptolemy's model was based on assumptions about the laws of physics made by the Greek philosopher Aristotle. Earth was at the center of the universe because it was presumed to be the heaviest of objects. Rest was thought to be the natural state of all objects. Therefore, an explanation had to be found for the motion of the heavenly bodies. They were said to be attached to invisible rotating spheres, each moved by the one above it. At the highest level, the "prime mover" imparted motion to the system. Christians equated Aristotle's "prime mover" with God.

Medieval astronomers were aware of problems with the **Ptolemaic system**. Chief among these was the fact that the planets did not appear to move in circular orbits. Sometimes they actually seemed to go backward. Ptolemy and his disciples explained this by proposing the existence of *epicycles*—that is, planets moving in short circular cycles that travel the orbits of much larger cycles. This accounted fairly well for what astronomers observed, but it was a very cluttered model for the universe.

Copernicus's Universe   Copernicus's *On the Revolutions of the Heavenly Spheres* was not meant to refute Ptolemy's model but to propose a refinement that would provide a more elegant solution to some of the mathematical problems it created. Copernicus suggested that if Earth was assumed to rotate about the sun in a circular orbit, the epicycles could be eliminated or reduced in size, and the apparent retrograde motion of the planets could be explained as an illusion created by viewing other planets from a planet that was itself in motion. Except for modifying Earth's position, Copernicus retained most of the other assumptions of Ptolemaic astronomy, and his system was no better than older ones at predicting movements of the planets. The Copernican model of the universe was, therefore, slow to attract adherents, and the initial importance of his work lay in the encouragement it gave people to think in new ways about scientific problems.

TYCHO BRAHE AND JOHANNES KEPLER MAKE NEW SCIENTIFIC OBSERVATIONS

Tycho Brahe (1546–1601), a Danish astronomer, spent most of his life trying to refute Copernicus and defend a revised version of Ptolemy's Earth-centered model for the universe. He thought the moon and the sun revolved around Earth and the other planets revolved around the sun. To make his case, Brahe collected the most accurate astronomical data that had ever been acquired by observation with the naked eye.

When Brahe died, his astronomical tables passed to Johannes Kepler (1571–1630), a German astronomer and a convinced Copernican. After much work, Kepler discovered that if the planets were assumed to move in elliptical, not circular, orbits, Brahe's data supported the Copernican theory that Earth revolved about the sun. Kepler published his findings in *The New Astronomy* (1609), but their acceptance was hampered by the fact that no one could explain why planets were locked in orbits of any shape rather than spinning out into space. That remained a mystery until Isaac Newton proposed his theory of universal gravitation.

GALILEO GALILEI ARGUES FOR A UNIVERSE OF MATHEMATICAL LAWS

By Kepler's day, little was known about the universe that could not have been known to Ptolemy, for all data had been gathered with the naked eye. In the year Kepler published his work, however, an Italian scientist, Galileo Galilei (1564–1642), turned a Dutch invention called a telescope on the heavens and saw things that had never been seen before. Unknown stars appeared, mountains were seen on the moon, spots passed across the face of the sun, and moons were discovered orbiting the planet Jupiter. Galileo argued that a Copernican model of the universe provided the simplest explanation for what the telescope revealed.

Galileo did not pursue science in the seclusion of an ivory tower. He worked at the court of the Medici Grand Duke of Tuscany, and his livelihood depended on promoting his discoveries in ways that enhanced his patron's reputation. Galileo, therefore, publicized his findings in literate treatises that were accessible to a wide audience. This made him appear to be the leading advocate for the Copernican

Ptolemaic system   Astronomical theory, named after Greek astronomer Ptolemy, that assumed Earth was the center point of a ball-shaped universe composed of concentric layers of rotating crystalline spheres to which the heavenly bodies were attached.

Sir Isaac Newton's experiments dealing with light passing through a prism became a model for writers praising the experimental method.

CORBIS/Bettmann

model of the universe and caused problems for him with the Roman Catholic Church (discussed later).

Galileo did more than popularize Copernicanism. He fostered belief in a universe governed by rational laws stated in mathematical formulas. The mathematical regularity that Copernicus saw in the heavens, Galileo believed, was characteristic of all nature. This conviction encouraged scientists to look for explanations for things by focusing primarily on phenomena that could be quantified. They sought mathematical models to account for qualities such as color, beauty, and taste—and even to explain social relationships and political systems. When viewed from such a perspective, nature appeared to be a cold, mechanistic system, and only things that could be measured mathematically seemed real or significant. This attitude portended a major intellectual shift for Western civilization.

ISAAC NEWTON DISCOVERS THE LAWS OF GRAVITATION

The puzzle that Copernicus, Kepler, and Galileo left unsolved was why the heavenly bodies moved in the orderly fashion described by the new astronomy. It was the mystery that lay behind the laws of planetary motion that led Isaac Newton (1642–1727), an English mathematician, to make the discoveries that established a new understanding of physics—one that worked well as a basis for scientific research for over two centuries.

In 1687, Newton published *The Mathematical Principles of Natural Philosophy* (or *Principia Mathematica*). He shared Galileo's faith that reality could be described mathematically, and he was influenced by Galileo's theory of inertia. Earlier scientists had assumed that rest (motionlessness) was an object's natural state and movement had to be explained. Galileo suggested that what physicists ought to ask is not why there is motion instead of rest, but why there is a change in an existing state—either stillness or movement.

Newton theorized that the revolutions of the heavenly bodies were controlled by gravity, a pull that every physical object exerts on the objects around it. The strength of this force is proportional to the mass and proximity of each object, and the order that exists among the planets can be explained as the balance they have achieved among their mutual attractions. Newton demonstrated the effects of gravity mathematically, but he did not attempt to explain what gravity itself is.

Newton believed that mathematics held the key to understanding nature, but, like other advocates of the new science, he also believed the ultimate test of a theory was its ability to explain empirical data and observation. The worth of a hypothesis depended on its ability to describe what could be observed. Science began and ended with empirical observation of what was actually in nature, not with a rational argument about what ought to be there. Religious dogma, therefore, could not dictate conclusions to science.

WHAT IMPACT did the new science have on philosophy?

PHILOSOPHY RESPONDS TO CHANGING SCIENCE

The progress of science prompted major rethinking of the Western philosophical tradition. The religious assumptions that guided the thought of the medieval Scholastics were abandoned in favor of mathematics and mechanical metaphors. The universe was envisioned as a kind of gigantic clock. This dispelled much of the mystery of existence and reduced God to the role of an observer—a great mechanic who had constructed the machinery of the universe but who did not participate in its operation. Philosophers had previously assumed an understanding of the natural order would reveal divine mysteries and yield transcendent insights, but now they concluded that knowledge of nature revealed nothing beyond itself. Such knowledge might lead to physical improvements for living beings, but it could not disclose a divine purpose for life.

FRANCIS BACON: THE EMPIRICAL METHOD

Francis Bacon (1561–1626), the English lawyer, statesman, and author who is often honored as the father of the scientific method of research, was not a scientist. He contributed to science by fostering an intellectual climate conducive to its growth. In books such as *The Advancement of Learning* (1605), the *Novum Organum* (1620), and the *New Atlantis* (1627), Bacon attacked medieval Scholasticism's reverence for authority (its belief that truth had already been discovered or revealed and only needed to be explicated). He urged his contemporaries to strike out on their own and search for a new understanding of nature. Bacon was a leader among the writers who shifted the attention of European intellectuals from defending tradition to promoting innovation and change.

Bacon believed knowledge was not just an end in itself but should improve the human condition. He claimed Scholasticism had nothing useful to contribute, for its practitioners only rearranged old ideas. Real progress required that thinkers go back and reexamine the foundations of their thought. If they relied on empirical observation more than logical speculation, Bacon promised they would discover things that would open new possibilities for humankind.

Bacon's rejection of past methods of inquiry sprang from his awareness that the world was becoming a much more complicated place than it had been for his medieval forebears. Like Columbus (and partially because of him), Bacon claimed a new route to intellectual discovery had to be charted. The lands new to Europeans that were being explored around the globe were opening new vistas for the Western mind. Most people in Bacon's day assumed the best era in human history lay in antiquity, but Bacon disagreed. He anticipated a future of material improvement and better government achieved by empirical examination of natural phenomena.

RENÉ DESCARTES: THE METHOD OF RATIONAL DEDUCTION

René Descartes (1596–1650), the gifted French mathematician who invented analytic geometry, popularized a scientific method that emphasized deduction, and thinkers all over Europe eagerly applied his techniques to all kinds of subject matters. Descartes's *Discourse on Method* (1637) proposed a technique for putting all human thought on a secure mathematical footing. In order to arrive at truth, Descartes said it was necessary for us to doubt all our ideas except those that were clear and distinct. An idea was worthy of trust not because some authority vouched for it but because the ever rational mind intuited its validity. Descartes began his search for truth by seeing if he had any ideas he could not doubt (any

Sir Francis Bacon (1561–1626), champion of the inductive method of gaining knowledge.

By courtesy of the National Portrait Gallery, London

13.1
Francis Bacon: from *First Book of Aphorisms*

QUICK REVIEW

The Empirical Method

- Francis Bacon believed Scholasticism did nothing more than arrange old ideas
- Thinkers should reexamine the foundations of their thought
- Reliance on empirical evidence would yield the best results

Queen Christina of Sweden (r. 1632–1654), shown here with the French philosopher and scientist René Descartes, was one of many women from the elite classes interested in the new science. In 1649 she invited Descartes to live at her court in Stockholm, but he died a few months after moving to Sweden.

Pierre-Louis the Younger Dumesnil (1698–1781), "Christina of Sweden (1626–89) and her Court: detail of the Queen and Rene Descartes (1596–1650) at the Table." Oil on canvas. Chateau de Versailles, France/Bridgeman Art Library

13.4
Thomas Hobbes: Chapter XIII from *Leviathan*

ideas that were self-substantiating). He concluded it was not possible to question his own act of thinking without first assuming he existed. To doubt doubting, one could not doubt the existence of the doubter. With this clear and distinct idea as his premise, Descartes was able to construct arguments deducing the existence of God and a real world external to the human mind.

Descartes divided existing things into two basic categories: things in thought and things in space. Thinking was a characteristic of the mind and extension (occupying space) of the body. Because space is mathematically measurable, mathematical laws govern the world of extension. Its laws are discoverable by reason, for mathematical truths form coherent systems in which each part can be deduced from some other part. Spirits, divinities, and immaterial things have no place in the world of extension, which belongs exclusively to scientists. They explain it by using mathematics and rational inference to discover the mechanical properties of matter.

Natural scientists eventually abandoned Descartes's deductive method for induction, the process of generalizing from discrete bits of empirical data to formulate a hypothesis (and then devising an experiment to test that hypothesis). Deduction, however, remained popular with people who pondered subjects for which little empirical data was available (political theory, psychology, ethics, and theology).

THOMAS HOBBES: APOLOGIST FOR ABSOLUTISM

The new scientific attitudes greatly altered thinking about politics, as is apparent in the work of Thomas Hobbes (1588–1679), the most original political philosopher of the seventeenth century. Hobbes was an urbane, much-traveled man and an enthusiastic supporter of the new scientific movement. He visited Paris and made Descartes's acquaintance. He spent time in Italy with Galileo, and he was interested in the work of William Harvey (1578–1657), the man who first recognized that blood circulates through the human body. Hobbes was also a superb classicist. He made the first English translation of Thucydides' *History of the Peloponnesian War*, and his dark view of human nature probably owed something to Thucydides.

The turmoil of the English Civil War colored Hobbes's thinking about politics. *Leviathan*, the famous book he published in 1651, offered a thoroughly materialistic, mechanistic explanation for human behavior (and brutality). Hobbes claimed that all mental states derive from sensation and all motivations are egoistical. The driving force behind human life is the quest to increase pleasure and minimize pain. Human beings, Hobbes said, have no spiritual ends and serve no great moral purpose. They simply strive to meet the needs of daily life, and this is why they form governments. A sovereign commonwealth is all that prevents a society of egotists from tearing itself apart.

Hobbes used a mythical description of human origins to illustrate his political philosophy. He claimed that nature inclines people to a "perpetual and restless desire" for power. In the state of nature (before civilization intervenes),

The famous title page illustration for Hobbes's *Leviathan*. The ruler is pictured as absolute lord of his lands, but note that the ruler incorporates the mass of individuals whose self-interests are best served by their willing consent to accept him and cooperate with him.

Rare Books Division. The New York Public Library, Astor, Lenox and Tilden Foundations

all people want and have a right to everything. This breeds enmity, competition, diffidence, and perpetual quarreling: "a war of every man against every man." Philosophers and theologians have often imagined the original human condition as a lost paradise, but Hobbes saw it as a corrupt, chaotic battleground that drove people, who were desperate for order, to organize societies. Unlike Aristotle and Christian thinkers such as Thomas Aquinas, Hobbes did not believe human beings were naturally sociable. He claimed they were self-centered beasts who were utterly without discipline unless it was imposed on them by force.

People escape their terrible natural state, Hobbes said, by making a social contract that obligates them to live in a commonwealth ruled by law. A desire for "commodious living" and a fear of death drives them to accept the constraints of communal life. The social contract obliges every person, for the sake of peace and security, to agree to set aside his or her right to all things and be content with as much liberty against others as he or she would allow others against himself or herself. Because words and promises are insufficient to guarantee this agreement, the social contract authorizes the coercive use of force to compel compliance.

England's Civil War convinced Hobbes that the dangers of anarchy were greater than those of tyranny. This being so, he concluded that rulers should have unlimited power. He did not think it mattered much what form a government took (monarchy or democracy) so long as there could be no challenge to its power. There is little room in Hobbes's political philosophy for protests motivated by an individual's conscience, for Hobbes insisted that suppression of a few individuals was preferable to the suffering the outbreak of civil war imposed on everyone. Both Catholics and Puritans objected to his subordination of spiritual authority to a secular sovereign, but he maintained that only a single, uncontested head of state could preserve order.

JOHN LOCKE: DEFENDER OF MODERATE LIBERTY AND TOLERATION

The most influential critic of the kind of political absolutism Hobbes favored was another Englishman, John Locke (1632–1704). Locke's sympathies were with the leaders of popular revolutions. His father fought with the parliamentary army during the English Civil War, and in 1682, Locke himself joined a rebellion led by Anthony Ashley Cooper, the earl of Shaftesbury, against Charles II. Its failure forced him to seek asylum in Holland.

Locke's two *Treatises of Government* were written after Charles II restored the English monarchy. The first was a devastating critique of the traditional argument for royal absolutism that equated states with families and rulers with the heads of patriarchal households. Locke argued that both fathers and rulers are bound by the law of nature that creates everyone equal and independent. In his *Second Treatise of Government,* he made the case for government's obligation to be responsive to the wishes of the governed. He disagreed with Hobbes's assumption that people are driven only by passion and selfish interests, and he noted they are also endowed by nature with reason and goodwill. They are able to cooperate and live together in peace on their own, and Locke claimed it is the desire to facilitate social life that leads them to establish governments. Governments are based on social contracts that are meant to protect human liberty, not restrain it. If rulers fail to honor the terms of such contracts, subjects have a right to replace them.

Locke believed governments should limit themselves to protecting property and should not interfere in the religious lives of their citizens. His *Letter Concerning Toleration* (1689) argued that each individual is responsible for working out his or her own salvation. Differences of opinion are likely, but unanimity cannot be imposed, for faith is a matter of conscience. Locke denied religious liberty to two groups—to atheists on the ground that their oaths (lacking divine sanction) could not be trusted, and to Roman Catholics on the ground they were pledged to serve a foreign prince (the pope).

Of all Locke's works, his *Essay Concerning Human Understanding* (1690) attracted the most immediate attention from his contemporaries, for it offered a scientific explanation for human psychology. Locke claimed the mind of a newborn is a blank tablet on which nothing is yet inscribed. No knowledge is innate. All ideas come from sensory experience. All human beings are, therefore, products of their environments, and they can be reformed and perfected by transforming the world that shapes them. Locke claimed that religious knowledge is acquired like other kinds of knowledge. Reliable spiritual information comes, however, only from studying the Scriptures and observing the natural order. Private revelations lead to fanaticism and superstition.

WHICH NEW scholarly associations were established to foster scientific research?

THE NEW INSTITUTIONS OF EXPANDING NATURAL KNOWLEDGE

Medieval scholars assumed that learning was a process of recovering what had already been discovered by ancient authorities (such as Aristotle) or revealed to the authors of the Bible and the founders of the church. Even the Protestant reformers saw themselves only as restoring the original Christian message and not as discovering something new in it. As science took root, however, confidence grew that genuinely new discoveries about nature and humanity were possible. Learning implied progress and a growing fund of information.

Of all Locke's works, his *Essay Concerning Human Understanding* (1690) attracted the most immediate attention from his contemporaries, for it offered a scientific explanation for human psychology. Locke claimed the mind of a newborn is a blank tablet on which nothing is yet inscribed. No knowledge is innate. All ideas come from sensory experience. All human beings are, therefore, products of their environments, and they can be reformed and perfected by transforming the world that shapes them. Locke claimed that religious knowledge is acquired like other kinds of knowledge. Reliable spiritual information comes, however, only from studying the Scriptures and observing the natural order. Private revelations lead to fanaticism and superstition.

Colbert was Louis XIV's most influential minister. He sought to expand the economic life of France and to associate the monarchy with the emerging new science from which he hoped might flow new inventions and productive technology. Here he is portrayed presenting members of the French Academy of Science to the monarch on the founding of the French Academy.

Henri Testelin (1616-1695), (after Le Brun). Minister of Finance Colbert presenting the members of the Royal Academy of Science (founded in 1667) to Louis XIV. Study for a tapestry. Photo: Gerard Blot. Chateau de Versailles et de Trianon, Versailles, France. Reunion des Musees Nationaux/Art Resource, NY

THE NEW INSTITUTIONS OF EXPANDING NATURAL KNOWLEDGE

Medieval scholars assumed that learning was a process of recovering what had already been discovered by ancient authorities (such as Aristotle) or revealed to the authors of the Bible and the founders of the church. Even the Protestant reformers saw themselves only as restoring the original Christian message and not as discovering something new in it. As science took root, however, confidence grew that genuinely new discoveries about nature and humanity were possible. Learning implied progress and a growing fund of information.

Science fostered a kind of intellectual faith that had wide-ranging social implications. Advocates of the new science were highly critical of Europe's universities, where traditional scholastic and Aristotelian modes of thought were deeply entrenched. This was not always fair, for the new ideas penetrated the universities, and a few natural philosophers (notably Newton) held university chairs. The slowness of the schools to assimilate scientific advances, however, persuaded scientists they had to establish different kinds of institutions to advance their work.

The most prominent of the new scholarly associations was the Royal Society of London. It was founded in 1660 to promote research and the sharing of scientific information. Similar organizations on both the local and national level sprang up in most European countries. Members of these societies met to hear papers and witness experiments. Many society "fellows" were men of high social standing, and their reputations lent credibility to reports of scientific discoveries. Their polite exchange of ideas also helped promote a culture of civility that elevated science above the kinds of religious and political squabbles that tore communities apart.

Members of these societies were drawn from the intellectual elite, but their interests led them to cooperate with laborers, craftspersons, and sailors whose skills, work experience, and travels made them invaluable sources of aid and information. Learned societies were eager to demonstrate what science could do to solve practical problems, advance the aims of government, and grow economies. Persons who had ideas for improving navigation, agriculture, engineering, and military technology turned to the societies for support, and the societies sponsored practical inventions, urged religious toleration, and promoted political liberty. They were the harbingers of a new and optimistic confidence in the future.

WHAT ROLE did women play in the scientific revolution?

QUICK REVIEW

Women and Science

- Significant obstacles stood in the way of women doing scientific work

- A few elite women, notably Margaret Cavendish, were allowed to make contributions

- Women from the artisan classes had more opportunities than other women

Women from the artisan classes had more opportunities to pursue science than other females, for they were trained to work in their families' businesses. Several German astronomers were assisted by their wives and daughters, and some of these women (most notably Maria Cunitz, Elisabetha Hevelius, and Maria Winkelmann) wrote books or made discoveries on their own. After the death of her astronomer husband in 1710, Maria Winkelmann (the discoverer of a comet) applied to the Berlin Academy of Sciences for permission to continue her husband's work. She was denied because of her gender. Years later she tried to return to the academy as an assistant to her son, but she was forced out and had to abandon astronomy.

In the 1730s, the French philosopher Voltaire drew on the mathematical expertise of Emilie du Châtelet for help in writing a book on Newton, but few women were admitted to the fields of science and medicine before the late nineteenth century. Some psychologists even argued that differences between male and female brains made women incapable of scientific work. The pursuit of natural knowledge was said to be a male vocation.

THE NEW SCIENCE AND RELIGIOUS FAITH

HOW DID the new science challenge traditional understandings of religion?

13.6
Rethinking the Bible: Galileo Confronts his Critics

The new science challenged traditional understandings of religion on at least three fronts. Biblical descriptions of the heavens disagreed with scientific discoveries. Scientists threatened to undermine the authority of clergymen, and science tended to promote an exclusively materialistic view of the universe.

THE CASE OF GALILEO

The Roman Catholic Church was going through a particularly difficult period in its history when, in 1633, it took the infamous step of condemning the Copernican theory and Galileo. The Council of Trent asserted the church alone had the authority to interpret the Bible, and to counter Protestant accusations that Catholicism had strayed from the Scriptures, the church's interpretations had become narrowly literal. Galileo's views on biblical interpretation, which he published in 1615 (*Letter to the Grand Duchess Christina*), sounded suspiciously Protestant to some Catholic leaders, and the astronomer's discoveries seemed to support the Copernican view of the universe, which the church had officially condemned as unbiblical in 1616.

Galileo apparently won the church's permission to write about Copernicanism so long as he did not assert its truthfulness but only entertained it as a theoretical possibility. In 1623, the newly elected Pope Urban VIII, who was an acquaintance of Galileo's, allowed him to publish his research. The result was a book, *Dialogue on the Two Chief World Systems* (1632), which clearly implied the correctness of the Copernican model of the heavens. The pope felt betrayed and mocked by Galileo's work and condemned him for breaking his promise to the church. Galileo was forced to repudiate his theories, and he spent the last nine years of his life under house arrest. The incident troubled the relationship between science and Catholic faith for a very long time. In 1992, the church finally admitted that errors had been made by Pope Urban's advisers.

Margaret Cavendish, who wrote widely on scientific subjects, was the most accomplished woman associated with the new science in seventeenth-century England.

ImageWorks/Mary Evans Picture Library Ltd.

OVERVIEW   MAJOR WORKS OF THE SCIENTIFIC REVOLUTION

Year	Work	Author
1543	*On the Revolutions of the Heavenly Spheres*	Copernicus
1605	*The Advancement of Learning*	Bacon
1609	*The New Astronomy*	Kepler
1610	*The Starry Messenger*	Galileo
1620	*Novum Organum*	Bacon
1632	*Dialogue on the Two Chief World Systems*	Galileo
1637	*Discourse on Method*	Descartes
1651	*Leviathan*	Hobbes
1687	*Principia Mathematica*	Newton
1689	*Letter Concerning Toleration*	Locke
1690	*An Essay Concerning Human Understanding*	Locke
1690	*Treatises of Government*	Locke

BLAISE PASCAL: REASON AND FAITH

Blaise Pascal (1623–1662), a French mathematician and physical scientist, made the most famous attempt to reconcile faith with the new science. Pascal was a deeply religious man who turned his back on wealth and chose a life of austerity. He, however, opposed both religious dogmatism and the skepticism of atheists and rationalists. He was drawn to Jansenism, the French Catholic movement that was based on the Augustinian teaching that grace alone brings salvation and knowledge of God. He was never able to integrate his insights into a fully developed system, but he published a collection of provocative reflections on the human condition entitled *Pensées*.

Pascal believed reason could reveal humanity's utter corruption, but that it was too weak to comprehend life's fundamental mysteries. They belonged to the realm of religion, and religion operated beyond reason. It involved a "leap of faith," absolute trust in divine grace. Pascal proposed an ingenious "wager" to demonstrate the unreasonableness of skepticism. He noted it is a better bet to believe that God exists than to doubt. If God does exist, the believer wins everything. If it turns out God does not exist, the believer has not lost much by believing. Furthermore, Pascal argued that, whether God exists or not, religious faith is still valuable in and of itself, for it motivates self-discipline and strengthens moral character. Pascal urged people to pursue self-awareness through "learned ignorance" (contemplation of the implications of human limits). This, he hoped, would counter what he saw as the false optimism of the new scientific rationalism.

THE ENGLISH APPROACH TO SCIENCE AND RELIGION

Francis Bacon tried to reconcile religion and science by suggesting divine revelation could come through both the Bible and the study of nature. Because both were created by God, it followed logically, he said, that the truths each disclosed would ultimately be discovered to constitute one consistent whole.

The mechanistic view of the universe that the new science supported convinced Newton and many others that nature's rational order implied reason was a characteristic of nature's Creator. To study nature was to study the Creator and to move by stages from knowledge of phenomena to an understanding of their ultimate cause. This faith underlay *physico-theology*, a popular ideology that appealed to Europeans who were tiring of wars of religion. It held out the hope that science might end such conflicts by developing a new understanding of God on which all parties could agree. Faith in a rational God had the additional appeal of encouraging faith in human rationality and humanity's ability to overcome the errors of its past. The new way of life that was emerging in response to the new science was increasingly justified as part of a divine plan. It seemed obvious that because God had given human beings reason and placed them in a rational world, it was their duty to master it. The pursuit of scientific and economic progress were religious missions.

CONTINUING SUPERSTITION

Despite the optimistic confidence some European intellectuals had in the ultimate triumph of reason, many of their sixteenth- and seventeenth-century contemporaries continued to believe in magic and the occult. Almost all Europeans believed to some degree in the devil and the power of his demons.

WHAT FORMS did superstition take in response to science in the sixteenth and seventeenth centuries?

WITCH-HUNTS AND PANIC

The trust in traditional certainties that began to fade in the late Middle Ages inspired some people to look for ways to ground truth in reason and science, but there was a darker alternative. Many people responded to the era's intellectual challenges with fear and suspicion, and their desperate search for security sent them across the line that divides religion from superstition. This was as true for the learned as for the less educated. Between 1400 and 1700, from 70,000 to 100,000 people were sentenced to death in the West for practicing *malificium* (harmful magic) and diabolical witchcraft. Between episodes of persecuting their neighbors, witches were said to fly off to conventions called *sabbats* where they engaged in sexual orgies with the devil and practiced every imaginable indecency. The Reformation contributed to this development by emphasizing the power of demons and the devil while eliminating many of the traditional sacraments and rituals that had once offered a defense against these powers of darkness.

VILLAGE ORIGINS

Belief in witchcraft pervaded both elite and mass cultures, but it was deeply rooted in rural areas. Village societies have customarily dealt with the threats and terrors of life by turning for help to "cunning folk," to people who are believed to have special powers to avert or mitigate natural disasters and ease problems caused by disease and infertility. The witch cultures of medieval and early modern village societies may also have been a form of peasant self-assertion. They subverted oppressive urban Christianity authorities by perpetuating ancient, pre-Christian religious practices.

Because a reputation for possession of magical powers gave a person standing in a village society, such powers tended to be claimed by people who were most in need of influence—the elderly, the impoverished, and single or widowed women. Should any of their neighbors claim, however, that they used their powers for evil rather than good, they were also the members of society least able to defend themselves. (See "History's Voices: Why More Women Than Men Are Witches.")

HISTORY'S VOICES

WHY MORE WOMEN THAN MEN ARE WITCHES

I n 1486, two Dominican monks, Heinrich Krämer and Jacob Sprenger, published The Hammer of Witches, *a guide to the detection and punishment of witches that was sanctioned by Pope Innocent VIII. It is a classic expression of misogyny.*

WHAT PROOF do the authors offer that women are more prone to witchcraft than men? What kinds of evidence do they regard as convincing?

Why are there more superstitious women than men? The first [reason] is that women are more credulous. ... The second reason is that women are naturally more impressionable and ready to receive the influence of a disembodied spirit. ... The third reason is that they have slippery tongues...; and since they are weak, they find an easy and secret manner of vindicating themselves by witchcraft. ... [Therefore] since women are feebler both in mind and body, it is not surprising that they should come more under the spell of witchcraft. ...

But the natural reason [for woman's proclivity to witchcraft] is that she is more carnal than a man, as is clear from her many carnal abominations. And it should be noted that there was a defect in the formation of the first woman, since she was formed from a bent rib. ... And since through this defect she is an imperfect animal, she always deceives. ...

As to her other mental quality, her natural will, when she hates someone whom she formerly loved, then she seethes with anger and impatience in her whole soul. ...

Just as through the first defect in their intelligence women are more prone [than men] to abjure the faith, so through their second defect of inordinate affections and passions they search for, brood over, and inflict various vengeances, either by witchcraft or by some other means. Wherefore it is no wonder that so great a number of witches exists in this sex. ... Blessed be the Highest who has so far preserved the male sex from so great a crime.

From *Malleus Maleficarum,* trans. by Montague Summers (Bungay, Suffolk, U.K.: John Rodker, 1928), pp. 41–47. Reprinted by permission.

INFLUENCE OF THE CLERGY

The widespread faith in magic that was the essential precondition for the great witch-hunts of the sixteenth and seventeenth centuries was not confined to ordinary people. It was shared by intellectuals and the Christian clergy whose sacramental powers had something in common with magic. The church invoked fear of demons and the devil to persuade people to accept its discipline, and priests claimed the power to exorcise demons.

Inasmuch as magical power was not human in origin, theologians reasoned it had to come either from God or from the devil. In the thirteenth century, the church declared that its priests alone were entitled to exercise supernatural powers. It followed, therefore, that all other wonder workers had to have acquired their magical potency through pacts with the devil. The church sincerely believed it was its duty to root out the servants of the devil, but such work was also self-serving. By destroying the "cunning folk," the church cleansed villages of the people who competed with its priests for spiritual authority.

WHO WERE THE WITCHES?

Roughly 80 percent of the victims of witch-hunts were women, most of whom were single and between forty-five and sixty years of age. It is possible that persecution of witches provided a male-dominated society with a means for ridding itself

Three witches charged with practicing harmful magic are burned alive in Baden in southwest Germany. On the left, two of them are feasting with demons at a *sabbat.*

Bildarchiv Preussischer Kulturbesitz

of unconventional women who were not under some man's control. Or it may simply be that older single women were attacked not because of their gender but because they were perceived to be, with other poor people, burdens on society. Some female professions, such as midwifery and nursing, exposed women to suspicion of malfeasance by associating them with mysterious deaths. (See "Encountering the Past: Midwives.") Economic need may also have driven more women than men to risk claiming powers to heal and cast spells.

END OF THE WITCH-HUNTS

The great witch panics occurred in the second half of the sixteenth and early seventeenth centuries. They were, in part, a response to the suffering caused by the religious divisions and wars that were ravaging Europe. Increasing levels of violence exacerbated fear and hatred and inspired a search for scapegoats on which to vent these emotions. Witch-hunts also helped the authorities of church and state enforce conformity and eliminate dissidents.

By the end of the seventeenth century, some people began to fear things were getting out of hand, and the witch trials ceased when it became evident that witch hunting was destabilizing society, not establishing order. The emergence of the new scientific worldview also undercut belief in witches, and the improvements science brought to fields like medicine gave people greater confidence in their ability to solve their problems without resorting to the supernatural. The Reformation may also have helped end the witch craze by declaring God's absolute sovereignty and ridiculing the sacramental magic of the old church. For Protestants, God's freely offered grace, not magic, was the only defense against the power of evil.

BAROQUE ART

HOW DID baroque art serve both religious and secular ends?

The term *baroque* denotes a variety of related styles associated with seventeenth-century painting, sculpture, and architecture. Baroque painters depicted their subjects in a thoroughly naturalistic, rather than idealized, manner; this focus paralleled the interest in natural knowledge that was associated with the new science and deeper understanding of human anatomy. Baroque painters such as Michelangelo Caravaggio (1573–1610) showed sharp contrasts of light and darkness. Baroque painting and sculpture is dramatic and theatrical, drawing the observer into emotional involvement with the subject.

Baroque art served both religious and secular ends. Especially in Roman Catholic countries, baroque painters often portrayed Biblical scenes as a form of religious instruction. Artists also used this style to depict everyday life in realistic detail. Dutch painters, for example, portrayed elaborate foodstuffs, while artists such as Louis LeNain (ca. 1593–1648) painted scenes of French peasant life.

Rightly or wrongly, baroque art became associated with Roman Catholicism and absolutist politics. The style first emerged in papal Rome, where Gian Lorenzo Bernini's great Tabernacle—situated under the dome of St. Peter's basilica, above the space where St. Peter is said to be buried—is the most famous example, along with the two vast colonnades outside the church. Bernini also created the dramatic sculpture of the Spanish mystic St. Teresa of Avila (1515–1582), depicting her in religious ecstasy.

baroque Artistic and architectural Styles that were naturalistic rather than idealized to involve observer on an emotional level through dramatic portrayals.

ENCOUNTERING THE PAST

MIDWIVES

Although women were excluded from formal medical training until well into the nineteenth century, the delivery of children was largely left to professional women called midwives. Midwifery was a trade often pursued by elderly or widowed women of the lower social classes. They underwent years of apprenticeship, but were not permitted to organize themselves into guilds. They were licensed by civil and church authorities who were invariably men. Sometimes upper-class women were appointed to supervise them.

A reputation for respectability and discretion was essential for a midwife, for she witnessed some of life's most private moments and was privy to the intimate affairs of families. Her character was also assumed to have an effect on the outcome of a birth. A bad character was said to produce stillbirths and imperfectly formed infants. Carelessness or incompetence could, of course, void her license.

Midwives had religious and civic duties associated with births. In emergencies they could baptize failing infants. They registered births, and they were required to report to the authorities any suspicion of abortion or infanticide. A trusted midwife might also be called on to testify to a child's legitimacy.

Male physicians began to replace midwives in the eighteenth century, and civil authorities increasingly required persons who assisted at births to have a formal medical training that was not available to women. Midwives, however, never ceased to serve the poor and rural populations of Europe.

WHY WAS midwifery long considered a female activity? Why did men eventually take charge of supervising the birthing process?

Until well into the eighteenth century, midwives oversaw the delivery of most children in Europe.
© CORBIS

In the secular world, England's Charles I (r. 1625–1649) ruled as a near-absolute monarch without Parliament. He employed the Roman Catholic Flemish artist Peter Paul Rubens (1577–1640), the leading religious painter of the Catholic Reformation, to decorate the Banqueting Hall's ceiling at his London palace in honor of his father, James I (r. 1603–1625). As a result, Puritans were suspicious of the king's Catholic sympathies, and not by coincidence was Charles I led to his execution in 1649 through the Banqueting Hall. In France, the interior of Louis XIV's palace at Versailles was decorated with vast, dramatic paintings of Louis as the Sun King. The Hall of Mirrors, gardens, and fountains reflected the power of the king. Monarchs across Europe imitated Louis's ostentatious displays and hoped to replicate his absolutist power.

IMAGE KEY

for pages 340–341

a. Rembrandt van Rijn (1606–1669). "The Anatomy Lesson of Dr. Tulp." Mauritshuis, The Hague, The Netherlands.   Scala/Art Resource, NY

b. Newton analyzing the ray of light. Engraving by Loudan

c. Portrait of Astronomer Copernicus ca. 16th century

d. Newton's First Telescope

e. Margaret Cavendish, Duchess of Newcastle, writer

f. Scenographia: Systematis Copernicani Astrological Chart, c. 1543, devised by Nicolaus Copernicus (1473–1543)

g. Detail of "Tycho Brahe's Observatory on Ven" by Joan Blaeu ca. 2003 Ven, Denmark

h. Sir Francis Bacon (1561–1626), champion of the inductive method of gaining knowledge.   National Portrait Gallery, London

i. Portrait of the Italian Astronomer Galileo Galilei (1564–1642)

j. Three witches suspected of practicing harmful magic are burned alive on a pyre

Catholic countries, baroque painters often portrayed Biblical scenes as a form of religious instruction. Artists also used this style to depict everyday life in realistic detail. Dutch painters, for example, portrayed elaborate foodstuffs, while artists such as Louis LeNain (ca. 1593–1648) painted scenes of French peasant life.

Rightly or wrongly, baroque art became associated with Roman Catholicism and absolutist politics. The style first emerged in papal Rome, where Gian Lorenzo Bernini's great Tabernacle—situated under the dome of St. Peter's basilica, above the space where St. Peter is said to be buried—is the most famous example, along with the two vast colonnades outside the church. Bernini also created the dramatic sculpture of the Spanish mystic St. Teresa of Avila (1515–1582), depicting her in religious ecstasy.

In the secular world, England's Charles I (r. 1625–1649) ruled as a near-absolute monarch without Parliament. He employed the Roman Catholic Flemish artist Peter Paul Rubens (1577–1640), the leading religious painter of the Catholic Reformation, to decorate the Banqueting Hall's ceiling at his London palace in honor of his father, James I (r. 1603–1625). As a result, Puritans were suspicious of the king's Catholic sympathies, and not by coincidence was Charles I led to his execution in 1649 through the Banqueting Hall. In France, the interior of Louis XIV's palace at Versailles was decorated with vast, dramatic paintings of Louis as the Sun King. The Hall of Mirrors, gardens, and fountains reflected the power of the king. Monarchs across Europe imitated Louis's ostentatious displays and hoped to replicate his absolutist power.

SUMMARY

The Scientific Revolution What we now call "science" emerged as a field of inquiry in the seventeenth century as "natural philosophy." Copernicus, hoping to simplify Ptolemy's geocentric system, had tentatively proposed in the sixteenth century that the sun might be the center of circular planetary motion. Brahe disagreed and performed extensive observations attempting to support the geocentric model. Brahe's assistant Kepler used Brahe's data to propose, in a 1609 book, that the sun was at the center of elliptical planetary orbits. Also in 1609, Galileo was the first to study astronomy through a telescope. Galileo became a strong advocate for the heliocentric universe and popularized the idea that the universe is rational and subject to the laws of mathematics. Finally, Newton combined mathematical modeling and scientific observation to derive his famous laws of motion and theory of universal gravitation.

Philosophy Responds to Changing Science Scientists of the seventeenth century were called natural philosophers, and there was some overlap between philosophers and natural philosophers. For this reason, and because of the challenges to traditional thinking posed by scientific work in this period, philosophers were profoundly influenced by the scientific revolution. Galileo's mathematical modeling of the physical world translated into a mechanistic worldview that was widespread among philosophers. Bacon, Descartes, Hobbes, and Locke all articulated philosophies that took aspects of the new science into account and

church, however, was a dramatic exception to the general rule of accommodation between science and religion.

Continuing Superstition Through the seventeenth century, most Europeans believed in some form of magic and in the power of demons. "Magic," in the form of transubstantiation, was indeed at the heart of Christian ritual. Although such beliefs had been present for centuries, witch-hunts and panics soared in the late sixteenth and early seventeenth centuries. Possible explanations for this phenomenon include the impact of wars and upheaval, spiritual insecurity in the aftermath of the Reformation, and villagers' sublimated hostility toward urban leaders. There are also a variety of possible explanations for why witch-hunts died out in the seventeenth century.

Baroque Art In the seventeenth century, styles of painting, sculpture, and architecture collectively known as *baroque* came to prominence across Europe. Baroque depictions were naturalistic rather than idealized, and sought to involve the observer on an emotional level through dramatic portrayals and contrasts of light and darkness. Catholic baroque art and architecture aimed to instruct and impress. Secular artists depicted everyday life, but also created grandiose monuments to political absolutism, such as Louis XIV's palace at Versailles.

REVIEW QUESTIONS

1. What contributions to the scientific revolution were made by Copernicus, Brahe, Kepler, Galileo, and Newton? Was the scientific revolution truly a revolution? Which has a greater impact on history, political or intellectual revolution?

2. How do the political philosophies of Hobbes and Locke compare? How did each view human nature? Would you rather live under a government designed by Hobbes or by Locke? Why?

3. What prevented women from playing a greater role in the development of the new science? How did family connections enable some women to contribute to the advance of natural philosophy?

4. What things account for the church's condemnation of Galileo? How did Pascal try to reconcile faith and reason? How do you explain the fact that witchcraft and witch-hunts flourished during an age of scientific enlightenment?

5. What purposes and goals did baroque painting, sculpture, and architecture serve in the religious and secular spheres?

KEY TERMS

baroque (p. 354)   Ptolemaic system (p. 343)   scientific revolution (p. 342)

  For additional study resources for this chapter, go to:
www.prenhall.com/kagan3/chapter14

Visualizing The Past...

Science, Art, and the Printing Press in Early Modern Europe

WHAT ROLE did art play in disseminating the discoveries of the scientific revolution? Why was the printing press especially important in this process?

O ne of the most important developments in the early modern period of European history (1450–1750) was the scientific revolution. Europeans, having finally absorbed the science of the ancient Greeks, lost to them until the close of the Middle Ages, were now ready to move beyond that legacy and, through exploration and experimentation, to make new scientific discoveries.

A new medium in Europe, the printing press, a machine Europeans developed in the fifteenth century, based on ideas originating in China, became the primary means of disseminating the new science. Images were as important as text in this process, and lavishly illusurated scientific works made scientific knowledge accessible to greater numbers of people than ever before. Science became a popular theme for European books and works of art.

This image is the title page to the sixteenth-century *Nova Reperta*, by Flemish artist Joannes Stradanus. *Nova Reperta* was a set of drawings celebrating the explosion of scientific discoveries, new technology, and new geographical discoveries of the sixteenth century. In this image we see depicted cartography and geography symbolized by the map of the New World, and gun powder, and the printing press.

The Newberry Library. Title page, *Nova Reperta*, 16th century engraving.
Photo courtesy of John M. Wing Foundation, The Newberry Library, Chicago

▼

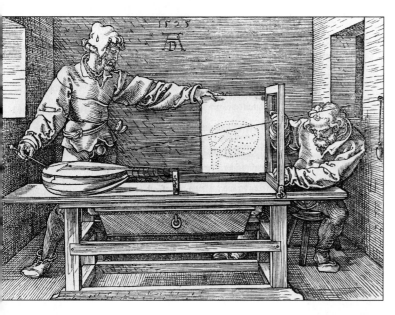

▲ **Engraving and woodcuts** became an especially important art form in the early modern period because they could be reproduced easily in books. Albrecht Dürer (1471–1528), one of the greatest artists of the Renaissance, was especially skilled at these art forms. Here we see a Dürer woodcut from the 1525 work *The Artist's Treatise on Geometry,* illustrating an artist using the technique of perspective to draw a lute.

Albrecht Durer, German, (1471–1528). *Artist Drawing a Lute,* demonstration of perspective from "The Artist's Treatise on Geometry," 1525, Woodcut. The Metropolitan Museum of Art, Harris Brisbane Dick Fund, 1941. (41,48.3)

This oil painting, Jan Vermeer's *The Astronomer,* is an excellent example of Dutch realism of the seventeenth century. Vermeer (1632–1675) painted many works for wealthy bourgeois households in Holland. What is interesting here is that the subject, an astronomer examining a globe of the heavens, would have attracted Vermeer's bourgeois clients. Science had become a central aspect of the cultural world and identity of ordinary Europeans by the second half of the seventeenth century. ▼

Jan Vermeer Van Delft (1632–1675). *The Astronomer.* Oil on canvas, 1668, 51.5 × 45.5 cm. RF 1983–28. The Louvre, Dpt. des Peintures, Paris, France, Photograph ©Erich Lessing/Art Resource, NY

▲ **Medicine also advanced** in the early modern period. One of the greatest physicians of the era was the Flemish doctor Andreas Vesalius. This image is an engraving, "De Humani corporis Fabrica," from Book II of Vesalius's *The Seven Books on the Structure of the Human Body (De humani corporis fabrica libri septem).* This landmark medical text used the artistic techniques developed in the Renaissance to depict the human form. It illustrated with great accuracy the human muscular system, in a format, the printed book, available to a relatively wide audience.

Andreas Vesalius (1514–1564), "Plate 25 from 'De Humani Corporis Fabrica,' Book II." Engraving. Courtesy of the New York Academy of Medicine Library

15 Society and Economy Under the Old Regime in the Eighteenth Century

CHAPTER HIGHLIGHTS

Major Features of Life in the Old Regime
European economies were dominated by agriculture. Society was oriented more toward the past than the future. Rights accrued not to individuals, but to groups.

The Aristocracy The nobility made up between 1 and 5 percent of the population in most European countries. Their income came largely from land ownership. Throughout Europe, nobles tried to preserve noble exclusivity, to resist the power of monarchies, and to improve their financial status.

The Land and Its Tillers Land cultivation was the primary task of Europe's peasants and serfs. Landowners' power increased the farther east one went in Europe. Peasants frequently resorted to violent uprising to express their discontent.

Family Structures and the Family Economy
In northwestern Europe, households were usually made up of a nuclear family and its servants. Eastern European households were larger and usually multigenerational. Everyone who could work contributed their labor to the support of the family unit.

The Revolution in Agriculture Europe's population increased rapidly in the eighteenth century. Increasing population led to greater demand and higher prices for wheat and bread. Landlords began to treat agriculture as a commercial operation. In Eastern Europe, economic and social barriers discouraged agricultural innovation.

The Industrial Revolution of the Eighteenth Century Europe's economy was transformed by industrialization. The Industrial Revolution was first felt in textile production. As work was reorganized to accommodate industrialization, labor was increasingly segregated on the basis of gender.

The Growth of Cities Cities grew substantially between 1500 and 1800. Social class shaped city dwellers' experience of urban life.

The Jewish Population: The Age of the Ghetto Jews were segregated and discriminated against throughout Europe. Most Jews lived in Eastern Europe and most were poor. Jews were sometimes subject to violence and forced conversion to Christianity.

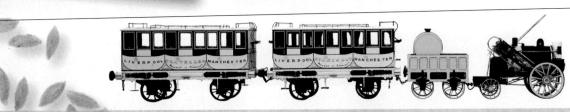

CHAPTER QUESTIONS

WHAT WERE the patterns of life in the Old Regime?

WHAT WERE the varieties of aristocratic privilege?

HOW WERE peasants and serfs tied to the land in eighteenth-century Europe?

HOW WAS family life structured in preindustrial Europe?

HOW WAS agriculture revolutionized in the eighteenth century?

WHAT WAS the Industrial Revolution?

WHAT PROBLEMS arose as a result of the growth of cities?

HOW DID the suppression of Jews in European cities lead to the formation of ghettos?

CHAPTER OUTLINE

- Major Features of Life in the Old Regime
- The Aristocracy
- The Land and Its Tillers
- Family Structures and the Family Economy
- The Revolution in Agriculture
- The Industrial Revolution of the Eighteenth Century
- The Growth of Cities
- The Jewish Population: The Age of the Ghetto

IMAGE KEY

Image Key for pages 360–361 is on page 382.

*The French Revolution of 1789 was a turning point in European history. The era that led up to it—the ancien régime (**Old Regime**)—was characterized by absolutist monarchies and agrarian economies that suffered chronic scarcity of food. Tradition, hierarchy, corporateness, and privilege were dominant features of the era. Men and women saw themselves less as individuals than as members of groups. The social order seemed fixed and rigid, but there was some change. Population grew, and standards of living improved. As farming was slowly commercialized, food became more abundant, and as the Industrial Revolution took hold, consumer goods became more plentiful. The spirit of rationality that had fostered the scientific revolution of the seventeenth century thrived in the eighteenth, the "Age of Reason" or the "Enlightenment." In many ways, the Old Regime nourished the changes that terminated its way of life.*

WHAT WERE the patterns of life in the Old Regime?

MAJOR FEATURES OF LIFE IN THE OLD REGIME

MAINTENANCE OF TRADITION

Prerevolutionary Europe was dominated by aristocratic elites with numerous inherited privileges and by established churches that were allied with the aristocracy and the state. At the other end of the social scale were an urban labor force (usually controlled by guilds) and a rural peasantry (burdened by high taxes and feudal obligations). Most people believed the past was the best guide for the future and innovation was undesirable (especially if it altered social relationships). When people agitated for change, they claimed not to want a new order but only restoration of traditional custom. Nobles tried to keep kings from interfering with their power over local government, and peasants fought to preserve manorial privileges (access to common lands, courts, and grievance procedures).

HIERARCHY AND PRIVILEGE

The traditional order that everyone claimed to be defending was the medieval social hierarchy. Distinctions of rank and degree not only persisted during the eighteenth century, they became more rigid. People were not treated as individuals. Their rights were determined by the "communities" (villages, municipalities, noble families, professions, guilds, universities, or parishes) to which they belonged. Each of these categories had a characteristic set of privileges: a license to practice a trade or educate children for a particular occupation, entitlement to a certain kind of income, or exemption from taxation or from some form of punishment for crime. The economies of most countries were as tradition bound as their social systems. Everything depended on the quality and quantity of the grain harvest. Britain, where there was some early industrial development, was an exception.

WHAT WERE the varieties of aristocratic privilege?

Old Regime Eighteenth-century era marked by absolutist monarchies, agrarian economies, tradition, hierarchy, corporateness, and privilege.

THE ARISTOCRACY

The eighteenth century was the great age of the aristocracy. In most countries, aristocrats accounted for only 1 to 5 percent of the population, but they were the wealthiest and most influential of the social classes. Land remained the most respectable of investments, but over the century, aristocrats tended to diversify their holdings. Their chief interests were the management of their estates and dominance of local government. They were represented in their homeland's parliament, estate, or diet, and they spent time at their ruler's

The foundation of aristocratic life was the possession of land. English aristocrats and large landowners controlled local government as well as the English Parliament. This painting of Robert Andrews and his wife by Thomas Gainsborough (1728–1788) shows an aristocratic couple on their estate. The gun and the hunting dog in this portrait suggest the importance landowners assigned to the virtually exclusive hunting privileges they enjoyed on their land.

© National Gallery, London

court. Their lives defined high culture and set standards of artistic taste and polite behavior for the rest of society. Codes of aristocratic conduct differed from place to place, but aristocratic status always entailed inherited privilege.

VARIETIES OF ARISTOCRATIC PRIVILEGE

British Nobility   Great Britain had the smallest, wealthiest, best defined, and most socially responsible aristocracy. It numbered about four hundred families, the male heads of which sat in Parliament's House of Lords. The aristocracy also used patronage and local influence to dominate elections to the Commons. British nobles, however, had few exemptions from taxation or legal privileges. The landowners who levied taxes in Parliament also paid them.

Direct and indirect control of local government gave noble families immense influence, which they augmented by entering business and the professions. The landed estates from which British aristocrats drew rents ranged from a few thousand to 50,000 acres and accounted for about one-fourth of the country's arable land. Nobles also invested in commerce, canals, urban real estate, mines, and industries. Because family titles and estates passed intact to the eldest son in an aristocratic family, his younger brothers had to find careers in business, the army, the professions, and the church. Thus most positions of leadership in society were occupied by men with noble connections.

French Nobility   The class structures of large continental nations such as France were more complex than those of Britain. France had approximately 400,000 nobles divided into two groups: nobles of the sword and nobles of the robe. The former derived their status from military service; the latter purchased their titles or earned them by serving the government. Nobles were further distinguished between those who attended the royal court at Versailles and those who did not. The court nobility reaped immense wealth from government posts and monopolized appointments to the church and the military officer corps. The provincial nobility (the *hobereaux*) could not compete, and they were often little better off than wealthy peasants. Hereditary privilege of one kind or another, however, distinguished an aristocrat from everyone else in French society.

Nobles collected many feudal dues from the tenants on their estates, and they enjoyed exclusive hunting and fishing rights. They paid a kind of income tax, the *vingtième* ("twentieth"), but they were exempt from many other social burdens. They did not pay the *taille* (the levy on land that was the basic tax of the Old Regime), and they could not be drafted for the *corvées* (the forced labor on public works required of peasants).

Eastern European Nobilities   The structures of aristocratic society east of the Elbe River were more complicated and repressive, for in these regions nobility was often tied to military service. Poland had thousands of nobles (*szlachta*). They were relatively poor, but after 1741, they were exempt from taxes and until 1768 they had absolute power over their serfs. The country's few wealthy aristocrats dominated its fragile government.

In Austria and Hungary, nobles enjoyed various degrees of exemption from taxation, and their manorial courts exercised judicial authority over the peasantry. A few aristocrats (particularly Hungary's Prince Esterhazy, who owned 10 million acres of land) were extraordinarily rich.

Frederick the Great elevated the status of Prussia's Junker nobles by recruiting officers for his army almost entirely from the Junker class. Prussia's bureaucracy was, like its army, headed by nobles, and in Prussia, as elsewhere in eastern Europe, nobles had extensive power over the serfs who lived on their estates.

Russia reinvented its aristocracy in the eighteenth century. Peter the Great (r. 1682–1725) tried to unite and dominate the aristocracy by linking noble status and state service. Nobles, however, resisted royal demands for compulsory service. In 1736, Empress Anna (r. 1730–1740) limited the term for such service to twenty-five years, and in 1762, Peter III (r. 1762) exempted the greater nobles from service. In 1785, Catherine the Great (r. 1762–1796) legally defined the rights of the nobility in exchange for the assurance that nobles would voluntarily serve the state. The wives and children of Russian aristocrats shared their noble status. Their privileges and their property rights were protected by law. They had immense power over their serfs, and they were exempted from personal taxes.

ARISTOCRATIC RESURGENCE

As the eighteenth century unfolded, nobles throughout Europe concluded that the growth of national monarchies was threatening the privileges that defined their caste, and they took steps to defend themselves. The so-called **aristocratic resurgence** had several objectives. It maintained the exclusiveness of noble rank by making it difficult to obtain. It reserved all powerful posts in the army officer corps, the state bureaucracy, government ministries, and the church to nobles. It used institutions dominated by aristocrats (the British Parliament, the French *parlements*, and the diets of Germany and the Habsburg Empire) to limit royal power. It protected nobles from taxation, and it increased their power over the peasantry.

THE LAND AND ITS TILLERS

HOW WERE peasants and serfs tied to the land in eighteenth-century Europe?

Land was the economic basis of eighteenth-century life. Well over three-fourths of all Europeans lived in the country, and few people ever traveled more than a few miles from their birthplaces. Except for the wealthier landowners, most people who lived on the land were poor and vulnerable to exploitation.

aristocratic resurgence
Eighteenth-century resurgence of nobles that mantained the exclusiveness of noble rank, made it difficult to obtain, reserved powerful posts to nobles, and protected nobles from taxation.

PEASANTS AND SERFS

Europe's rural classes were subject to different degrees of social dependency. Tenants on estates in England and most French farmers were legally free, but serfdom survived in Germany, Austria, and Russia. Everywhere, however, the class that owned the land dominated the class that tilled it.

Obligations of Peasants   The power of landlords increased across Europe from west to east. There were some serfs in eastern France, but most French peasants owned a bit of land. Few possessed enough to support their families, and most had to rent more from a lord. They remained subject to feudal obligations, such as *banalités* (requirements to use their lord's mill to grind their grain and his oven to bake their bread—for a fee) and the *corvée*.

In Prussia and the Habsburg Empire, despite attempts by monarchs late in the century to enact reforms, landlords enjoyed almost total control over serfs. In the parts of southeastern Europe dominated by the Ottoman Empire, peasants were technically free but were, in practice, dependent on their lords. An estate's owner was often an absentee landlord whose property was managed by an overseer. During the seventeenth and eighteenth centuries, these estates came increasingly to be run as commercial enterprises specializing in cash crops. Scarcity of labor did more than legislation to improve the peasant's lot, for oppressed peasants would migrate to the landlords who offered them the best conditions. The political disorder that spread through the Balkan peninsula in the seventeenth century, however, forced peasants to turn to their landlords for protection from bandits and rebels. As in medieval times, the local manor house became the peasants' refuge. Landlords also controlled peasants by providing housing, tools, and seed grain. Despite legal freedoms, Balkan peasants became thoroughly dependent on their landlords.

Russian serfdom was the worst of all. Russian nobles, who reckoned their wealth by the number of "souls" (male serfs) they owned rather than by the acreage they possessed, treated serfs as commodities. Landlords could demand six days of labor a week from their serfs, and they had the right to punish them as they saw fit. Serfs had no legal protections, and little distinguished a Russian serf from a slave.

Peasant Rebellions   The tsars contributed to the degradation of Russia's serfs. Peter the Great gave whole villages to favored nobles, and Catherine the Great confirmed the authority of the nobles over their serfs in exchange for the nobles' political cooperation. Between 1762 and 1769, abuse of serfs spawned over fifty peasant revolts in Russia, including Pugachev's Rebellion (1773–1775), the largest peasant uprising of the eighteenth century. It was brutally put down and doomed any attempt to improve the condition of serfs for at least a generation. Smaller revolts occurred in Bohemia in 1775, in Transylvania in 1784, in Moravia in 1786, and in Austria in 1789. With the exception of England, there were almost no rural rebellions in western Europe.

Peasant rebellions were conservative movements. Wrath was directed more against property than persons and aimed at defending traditional customs against practices peasants viewed as innovations or abuses (for example, increased feudal dues, changes in methods of payment or land use, corrupt officials, or brutal overseers). No one advocated a radical change to a class-based society as traditionally structured.

FAMILY STRUCTURES AND THE FAMILY ECONOMY

HOUSEHOLDS

In preindustrial Europe, the family household was the basic unit of production and consumption. Because few shops or farms employed many people who were not relatives of their owners, the structure of the family determined the structure of the economy.

Emelyan Pugachev (1726–1775) led the largest peasant revolt in Russian history. In this contemporary propaganda picture he is shown in chains. An inscription in Russian and German was printed below the picture decrying the evils of revolution and insurrection.

Bildarchiv Preussischer Kulturbesitz

QUICK REVIEW

Eastern European Peasants
- Power of landlords increased across Europe from west to east
- Reform efforts by Prussian and Habsburg monarchs were failures
- Russian serfs endured the worst conditions

HOW WAS family life structured in preindustrial Europe?

Northwestern Europe Families were structured differently in different parts of Europe. People in northwestern Europe favored nuclear families: husband, wife, younger children, and servants. Households were small, averaging five or six members. High mortality, late marriage, and short life spans meant that three generations seldom lived together. Children left home in their early teens to enter the work force—usually as servants living and working in another household. A child of a skilled artisan might remain with a parent to learn a skill, but only rarely would more than one child do so. Children's labor was more remunerative outside the home.

The word *servant* in this context may be misleading, for it does not refer to someone who provides personal services for the wealthy. A servant in preindustrial Europe was a person hired to work for a household in exchange for room, board, and wages. The servant was usually young and by no means socially inferior to his or her employer. Normally the servant was an integral part of the household and ate with the family. Young people spent a number of years in service (often as many as eight or ten) to acquire training and to accumulate the savings they needed to strike out on their own.

When young men and women married, they did not return with their spouses to the parental household to become part of an extended family. They established separate, independent homes of their own. It took them time to amass the capital this required. Consequently, they married late (men after age twenty-six and women after twenty-three). They usually had children as soon after marriage as possible. Premarital sexual relations were common and brides were often pregnant. Births out of wedlock, however, were rare.

Eastern Europe In eastern Europe, households tended to be at least twice as large as in western Europe, for young married couples moved in with their parents. This allowed them to marry at a much younger age than in the West (usually before twenty). It was not unusual, especially among Russian serfs, for wives to be older than their husbands and for three or four generations of a family to live together.

Landholding patterns in eastern Europe influenced family organization, as did lords who wanted to ensure adequate labor forces for their estates. In Poland, for example, a landlord could forbid his serfs to marry someone from another estate, and he could force the widowed to remarry. Polish landlords preferred not to hire free laborers (western Europe's "servants"), which removed a source of employment that would have enabled people to accumulate the capital they needed to set up independent households. In Russia, landlords ordered serf families to arrange early marriages for their children and to find mates for them within their home villages. Large households containing people of different ages decreased the likelihood that a death or serious illness would cause the household to cease to function and cultivate the land assigned it.

Throughout Europe, almost everyone lived in a household, for it was virtually impossible for individuals to produce everything they needed for themselves. People who were not part of a household were viewed with suspicion. Some were criminals and others were beggars who constituted a drain on community resources.

THE FAMILY ECONOMY

Frequent poor harvests and economic slumps prevented most households from accumulating a surplus to fall back on. Everyone in a household, therefore, worked and contributed all he or she produced to sustain the household.

Few families in western Europe had farms large enough to support them, so some of their members usually worked elsewhere and sent wages home. Fathers of peasant families often became migrant workers and left the burden of tilling the family farm to their wives and younger children.

Skilled urban artisans relied on family economies as much as rural peasants did. The father of the household was usually its chief craftsman. He might employ one or more servants but would expect his children to work also. He usually trained his eldest child in his trade. His wife often sold his wares or opened a small shop of her own. Wives of merchants might run their husbands' businesses, especially when their husbands were traveling. If business was poor, family members would take outside employment to support not only themselves but the family unit.

In western Europe, the death of a father could mean disaster for a household, for its survival often depended on his land or skills. Sometimes a widow or children were able to take over a farm or business, but widows generally kept their households from foundering by quickly remarrying. High mortality rates meant that many households were composed of a mix of spouses and children, the survivors of the breakups of earlier families. Households often simply dissolved. Widows who could not remarry or support themselves became dependent on charity or on relatives. Their children either entered the work force at an unusually early age or resorted to crime and begging.

The large multigenerational households characteristic of the family economy of eastern Europe provided greater security for individuals. There were, however, fewer artisan and merchant households and far less freedom of movement in the East than in the West.

During the seventeenth century the French Le Nain brothers painted scenes of French peasant life. Although the images softened many of the harsh realities of peasant existence, the clothing and the interiors were based on actual models and convey the character of the life of better off French peasants whose lives would have continued very much the same into the eighteenth century.

Erich Lessing/Art Resource, NY

WOMEN AND THE FAMILY ECONOMY

Except for aristocrats and members of religious orders, few women could support themselves. Thus marriage was an economic necessity for most women. A woman helped maintain her parents' household until she devised a means of getting a household of her own. The bearing and rearing of children were her chief means to this end.

By the age of seven, a girl would have begun to work and contribute to the support of her household. She remained in her parents' home until her labor elsewhere promised to be more remunerative to her family. An artisan's daughter who was learning and practicing a valuable skill might stay with her parents until marriage, but a farm girl, whose tasks could be assumed by her parents and brothers, usually left home between the ages of twelve and fourteen. She might find employment on another farm, but more often she would move to a nearby town and become a servant. A young woman's chief goal was to accumulate sufficient capital for a dowry. Marriage was a joint economic undertaking. Both the bride and the groom contributed capital toward the establishment of their new household, and it might take a young woman ten years or more to save a dowry.

Once married, a woman's chief concern was not homemaking or child rearing but coping with economic pressures. She and her husband engaged in a

During the eighteenth century farm women normally worked in the home and performed such tasks as churning butter as well as caring for children. As time passed, tasks such as making butter were mechanized and women were displaced from such work.

Francis Wheatley (RA) (1747–1801), "Morning,", signed and dated 1799, oil on canvas, 17$\frac{1}{2}$ H × 21$\frac{1}{2}$ H in. (44.5 × 54.5 cm). Yale Center for British Art, Paul Mellon Collection, USA/Bridgeman Art Library (B1977.14.120)

constant struggle to ensure an adequate food supply for their household. Couples practiced birth control to limit family size, and infants were often turned over to wet nurses so their mothers could return to work.

A married woman's work was often affected by her husband's occupation. In the few peasant households that had enough land to support themselves, wives were their husbands' chief assistants. In most cases, however, men had to find outside employment to supplement the income from their land, and women had to assume primary responsibility for plowing, planting, and harvesting. An artisan's or merchant's wife would usually be involved in her husband's trade or manufacturing enterprise. If her husband died, she might take over the family business or hire an artisan to work under her management. Despite the economic necessity that women contribute to the support of their families, many occupations and professions were closed to them because of their gender. At every level of society women had fewer opportunities for education than men. They usually received lower wages than men for the same work, and as mechanization of agriculture and the textile industry set in during the eighteenth century, men monopolized many jobs and employment opportunities for women diminished.

CHILDREN AND THE FAMILY ECONOMY

For all women, childbirth was a time of fear and personal vulnerability. Contagious diseases endangered both mother and child and midwives were not always skillful. Most mothers and newborn infants faced the challenges of immense poverty and wretched housing. Some women nursed their own infants, but many surrendered them at birth to wet nurses who took them away and kept them for months or years. Convenience encouraged this practice among the wealthy, but economic necessity dictated it for the poor. The demands of the family economy did not give a woman the freedom to devote herself entirely to rearing a child.

The birth of a child was not always welcome, particularly if its mother was unwed or it imposed an additional economic burden on an already hard-pressed household. Records indicate a correlation between rising food prices and numbers of abandoned children. Unwanted births sometimes prompted infanticide, but during the eighteenth century society's sense of responsibility for abandoned children increased and expressed itself in the growing size and number of foundling hospitals. In the early part of the century, about 1,700 children were being admitted to the Paris Foundling Hospital annually, but in 1772 (the peak year), the orphanage accepted 7,676 children. Not enough institutions were available to care for all who were in need, and some hospitals used lotteries to decide which children to admit. Parents who had to abandon a baby would sometimes leave personal tokens with it, hoping they might someday be able to identify and reclaim it. Leaving a child at a foundling hospital did not guarantee its survival. Only about 10 percent of children lived to age ten in Paris's hospitals.

The modern awareness of the importance of childhood can be traced to the eighteenth century. The era gave unprecedented attention to the education of children. However, despite improving literacy rates and the increasing demands of a job market that valued literacy, most eighteenth-century Europeans were unable to read and write. Not until the late nineteenth century, when nations realized the importance of a trained citizenry, did formal schooling become a routine childhood experience.

THE REVOLUTION IN AGRICULTURE

The chief concern of traditional peasant society was to ensure the food supply. The tillers of the soil usually resisted change. Traditional methods of cultivation had been proven to work, and experiments entailed risks that few wanted to take. (See "History's Voices: Turgot Describes French Landholding.") Failure of a harvest was often more than a hardship. It resulted in death by starvation. Even small increases in the cost of food could exert heavy pressure on peasant or artisan families.

As the eighteenth century progressed, population growth slowly but steadily drove up the price of bread, the staple food of the poor. Inflation hurt consumers, urban laborers, and peasants with small farms, but rising grain prices benefited landowners and the wealthier peasants who had surplus grain to sell. A profitable market encouraged landlords to experiment with techniques to increase yields, and this began an *Agricultural Revolution.* The new methods devised to commercialize farming frightened the peasants, for they altered the traditional means of production on which the rural poor had always depended for their survival. The tenants of estates sometimes rose up to challenge their entrepreneurial landlords, and the politically dominant landed aristocracy responded by sending in soldiers to compel their compliance.

New Crops and New Methods   The Low Countries were uniquely motivated by growing population and land shortages to search for ways to improve agricultural production. During the sixteenth and seventeenth centuries, Dutch agriculturalists improved methods for building dikes and draining land, and they experimented with new crops that increased the supply of animal fodder and restored the soil.

In the eighteenth century, English landlords took the lead in commercializing agriculture. They adapted ideas from the Low Countries and introduced some new farming methods. They invented iron plows that worked the soil to a greater depth and machines that planted wheat by drilling rather than wasteful casting. They developed fertilizers that made sandy soil productive and replaced fallow-field farming with a system of crop rotation (utilizing wheat, turnips, barley, and clover). This provided fodder to feed more animals through the winter and ensure a year-round supply of meat. Larger herds also increased the manure available to fertilize grain fields.

Enclosure Replaces Open-Field Method   Many of the era's agricultural innovations were incompatible with the way land had traditionally been used in England. Most farming had been done by small cultivators, each of whom tilled his own strips of land scattered about the fields belonging to his village. Much of the land was left fallow and unproductive each year in order to maintain its fertility. Animals grazed on common land in the summer and on the stubble of the harvest in the winter. Methods of cultivation had to be agreed upon by the whole community. This need for consensus discouraged innovation and favored the poorer farmers who needed the common land and stubble fields to maintain

HOW WAS agriculture revolutionized in the eighteenth century?

HISTORY'S VOICES

TURGOT DESCRIBES FRENCH LANDHOLDING

Until the nineteenth century, economic growth and political stability depended largely on agricultural production. During the eighteenth century, many observers became keenly aware that different kinds of landholding led to different attitudes toward work and to different levels of production. Robert Jacques Turgot (1727–1781), who later became finance minister of France, analyzed these differences in an effort to reform French agriculture.

WHY DOES Turgot favor those farmers who can make investments in the land they rent from a proprietor?

1. What really distinguishes the area of large-scale farming from the areas of small-scale production is that in the former areas the proprietors find farmers who provide them with a permanent revenue from the land and who buy from them the right to cultivate it for a certain number of years. These farmers undertake all the expenses of cultivation, the ploughing, the sowing and the stocking of the farm with cattle, animals and tools. They are really agricultural entrepreneurs, who possess, like the entrepreneurs in all other branches of commerce, considerable funds, which they employ in the cultivation of land. ...

   They have not only the brawn but also the wealth to devote to agriculture. They have to work, but unlike workers, they do not have to earn their living by the sweat of their brow, but by the lucrative employment of their capital, just as the ship owners of Nantes and Bordeaux employ theirs in maritime commerce.

2. *Métayer* System The areas of small-scale farming, that is to say at least four-sevenths of the kingdom, are those where there are no agricultural entrepreneurs, where a proprietor who wishes to develop his land cannot find anyone to cultivate it except wretched peasants who have no resources other than their labor, where he is obliged to make, at his own expense, all the advances necessary for tillage, beasts, tools, sowing, even to the extent of advancing to his *métayer* the wherewithal to feed himself until the first harvest, where consequently a proprietor who did not have any property other than his estate would be obliged to allow it to lie fallow.

   After having deducted the costs of sowing and feudal dues with which the property is burdened, the proprietor shares with the *métayer* what remains of the profits, in accordance with the agreement they have concluded. The proprietor runs all the risks of harvest failure and any loss of cattle: he is the real entrepreneur. The *métayer* is nothing more than a mere workman, a farm hand to whom the proprietor surrenders a share of his profits instead of paying wages. But in his work the proprietor enjoys none of the advantages of the farmer who, working on his own behalf, works carefully and diligently; the proprietor is obliged to entrust all his advances to a man who may be negligent or a scoundrel and is answerable for nothing.

3. This *métayer*, accustomed to the most miserable existence and without the hope and even the desire to obtain a better living for himself, cultivates badly and neglects to employ the land for valuable and profitable production; by preference he occupies himself in cultivating those things whose growth is less troublesome and which provide him with more foodstuffs, such as buckwheat and chestnuts which do not require any attention. He does not worry very much about his livelihood; he knows that if the harvest fails, his master will be obliged to feed him in order not to see his land neglected.

A. M. R. Turgot, *Œuvres, et documents les concernant*, ed. by F. Schelle, 5 vols. (Paris, 1914), vol. II, pp. 448–450, as quoted and translated in S. Pollard and C. Holmes, eds., *Documents of European Economic History*, vol. I (London: Edward Arnold, 1968), pp. 38–39.

their animals. Traditional methods of farming were intended to produce a steady, but not growing, supply of food.

In 1700, approximately half the arable land in England was worked in this way. During the second half of the century, however, the rising price of wheat encouraged landlords to consolidate or "enclose" their lands so they could cultivate them more efficiently. Enclosure promoted rational, commercially productive land use, but it entailed the fencing of common lands, reclaiming untilled waste, and combining strips into block fields—all of which disturbed the structures of rural society and prompted riots.

Many English farmers either owned the strips of land they worked or rented them with traditional rights that amounted to ownership. The great landlords, therefore, had to resort to parliamentary acts to legalize the enclosure of the land their families had long leased to their tenant farmers. Between 1761 and 1792, almost 500,000 acres were enclosed through acts of Parliament, and in 1801, a general enclosure act streamlined the process. The enclosures expanded commercial farming, encouraged innovation, and increased food production. However, they also disrupted traditional communities. Some people were forced off the land, but enclosure did not depopulate the countryside. In some counties population increased as additional land was brought into production and demand grew for services subsidiary to farming. The enclosure movement did not create a labor force for the British Industrial Revolution by displacing farm workers, but it did demonstrate the entrepreneurial, capitalistic spirit that encouraged industrialization in England.

As commercialization of agriculture slowly spread from Britain across the Continent, the paternal relationship that had long existed between the governing and governed classes was strained. Landlords had always looked after the welfare of the lower orders by accepting price controls or waiving rents during depressed periods, but a new emphasis on maximizing profits caused them to abandon the peasants to the mercy of the marketplace.

Limited Improvements in Eastern Europe The Agricultural Revolution had its greatest impact west of the Elbe. Few farming improvements were made in Prussia, Austria, Poland, and Russia, for the relationship between serf and lord discouraged innovation. Landlords or their agents managed farming, and they tried to increase their incomes by making their serfs work harder, not more productively. The chief strategy for increasing production was to bring previously untilled lands under the plow. The only change in agriculture that improved nutrition was the introduction of new crops: maize and the potato.

POPULATION EXPANSION

The population explosion with which the world contends today began in the eighteenth century. Previously, whenever Europe experienced dramatic increases in population, plagues, wars, or famine restored the balance. Beginning in the second quarter of the eighteenth century, however, population began to increase despite these calamities. In 1700, Europe's population (excluding the European provinces of the Ottoman Empire) was between 100 million and 120 million. By 1800, there were almost 190 million Europeans, and by 1850, 260 million. The population of England and Wales rose from 6 million in 1750 to over 10 million in 1800. France grew from 18 million in 1715 to approximately 26 million in 1789. Russia's population increased from 19 million in 1722 to 29 million in 1766. Such extraordinary sustained growth put new demands on all resources and considerable pressure on social institutions.

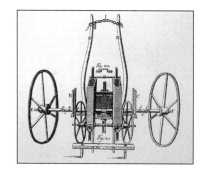

This seed drill, devised by the English agricultural innovator Jethro Tull (1674-1741), increased wheat crops by planting seed deep in the soil rather than just casting it randomly on the surface.

Image Works/Mary Evans Picture Library Ltd.

Population expanded across the Continent in both rural and urban districts, but no one is certain why. The death rate declined, owing to the relatively few wars and epidemics that raged during the eighteenth century. Hygiene and sanitation improved, but the most important factor may have been changes in the food supply. Grain production expanded, and, more important, the potato began to be cultivated. The potato was a New World vegetable that came into widespread European production during the eighteenth century. It was a significant new product, for a single acre of land could produce enough potatoes to feed a peasant family for an entire year. More food meant that more children survived to adulthood to rear children of their own.

The impact of the population explosion can hardly be overestimated. It increased demands for food, goods, labor, and services. It provided a larger pool of workers. It forced revisions in traditional modes of production and lifestyles. It prompted migration as economies were reorganized, and it spread social and political discontent. The world of the Old Regime literally outgrew its traditional bounds.

THE INDUSTRIAL REVOLUTION OF THE EIGHTEENTH CENTURY

WHAT WAS the Industrial Revolution?

The industrialization of Europe's economy (in which Britain led the way) began in the second half of the eighteenth century and grew, in the early nineteenth century, into a full-fledged **Industrial Revolution**. Industrialization increased humanity's control over the forces of nature. It met existing consumer demands by producing more goods and services. It created markets for new products. It raised standards of living. It ended the widespread poverty that Europeans had always taken for granted, and it inaugurated an era of unprecedented, sustained economic growth. Previously, periods of growth had alternated with periods of stagnation, but since the late eighteenth century, the expansion of the Western economy has been relatively uninterrupted. The process of industrializing has, however, exacted a high social cost. New means of production demanded new skills, new discipline in work, and a large labor force. By the middle of the nineteenth century, it was also apparent that industrialization was causing problems with the environment.

A REVOLUTION IN CONSUMPTION

The most visible aspects of the Industrial Revolution were the invention of machinery, the establishment of factories, and the creation of a new kind of work force. Less tangible changes in attitudes and expectations lay behind these developments. An unprecedented demand for the relatively humble goods of everyday life developed in the early eighteenth century. Designers, inventors, and manufacturers fed a growing market for clothing, buttons, toys, china, furniture, rugs, kitchen utensils, candlesticks, brassware, silverware, pewterware, glassware, watches, jewelry, soap, beer, wines, and foodstuffs. As each consumer expectation was met, a new one took its place, and the surging market drove the development of an ever more productive industrialized economy.

Several things promoted the growth of a consumer-driven economy. During the seventeenth century, the Dutch had enjoyed enormous prosperity and pioneered a society centered on consumption. As increasing numbers of people acquired more disposable income in the eighteenth century (possibly because of the improvements taking place in agriculture), they were able to buy more consumer goods. Europe's economy began to grow not only by exporting things, but by feeding a stronger domestic market.

Industrial Revolution Term coined by early nineteenth-century observers to describe the changes that the spreading use of powered machinery made in society and economics.

OVERVIEW	MAJOR INVENTIONS IN THE TEXTILE-MANUFACTURING REVOLUTION
1733	James Kay's flying shuttle
1765	James Hargreaves's spinning jenny (patented 1770)
1769	James Watt's steam engine patent
1769	Richard Arkwright's water frame patent
1787	Edmund Cartwright's power loom

These developments were not entirely spontaneous. Entrepreneurs resorted to new marketing methods to persuade people that they needed or wanted the new consumer goods. The strategy employed by the porcelain manufacturer Josiah Wedgwood (1730–1795) was typical. He first produced luxury goods that appealed to the royal family and the aristocracy. Once their patronage built his reputation, he began to make less expensive versions of his tableware for middle-class customers. He advertised, opened showrooms, and sent out traveling salesmen with samples and catalogs. He discovered there was no limit to the market for consumer goods that could be created by pandering to the desire of the masses to emulate their social superiors. Manufacturers soon realized that by changing styles they could further increase demand, for the desire to have the latest in fashions and inventions prompted people to return to the market again and again.

Increasing consumption steadily blurred the edges of social distinctions. As people saw what others were consuming, human nature led them to imitate their neighbors. Fashion publications made all levels of society aware of new styles that could be quickly and inexpensively copied. Even servants began to dress well if not luxuriously. New foods and beverages created a demand for new kinds of dishes with which to serve them. New modes of leisure necessitated new items for their enjoyment. New standards for polite living were described in print and quickly and widely disseminated. People began to define their status by the quality and quantity of the goods they consumed.

The consumer economy has always had its critics. Yet ever-increasing consumption has become a hallmark of modern life. It would be difficult to overestimate the importance of the desire for consumer goods and an increasing material standard of living in modern societies. Availability of consumer goods has become the chief indicator of a nation's prosperity, and the lack of these things (as much as the absence of civil liberties) lies behind the social tensions that currently plague many countries.

INDUSTRIAL LEADERSHIP OF GREAT BRITAIN

Great Britain inaugurated the Industrial Revolution and remained Europe's industrial leader into the mid–nineteenth century. Several things encouraged Britain's industrialization. Chief among them were an increasing domestic demand for goods and the markets that existed in Britain's North American colonies. England took the lead in promoting the consumer society. Newspapers thrived in Britain and provided advertising that spurred consumer demand. London was the largest city in Europe in the eighteenth century, and it set international standards for fashion and taste. The structure of British society allowed

QUICK REVIEW

Josiah Wedgwood (1730–1795)

- Started as producer of luxury goods
- Once established, produced less expensive items for middle-class customers
- Took advantage of middle-class desire to emulate social superiors

ordinary people to ape the lifestyles of the upper classes, and the British were the first to develop the love affair with changing fashions that fuels insatiable appetites for novelties.

Britain's economic development was also encouraged by the fact that it was the single largest free-trade area in Europe. It had an excellent infrastructure of roads and waterways, and it was endowed with natural resources—fertile soil, coal, and iron ore. It was politically stable, and the property rights of its citizens were secure. Sound systems of banking and credit maintained a stable climate for investment. Taxes were high, but collection was efficient and fair. Parliament regulated taxation so all social classes and regions paid comparable dues. British society was also relatively open. The aristocracy admitted entrepreneurs who amassed large fortunes, and all persons of wealth enjoyed a degree of social prominence and political influence.

NEW METHODS OF TEXTILE PRODUCTION

Textile manufacturers spearheaded the Industrial Revolution—a movement that began in the countryside, not in urban areas. Eighteenth-century society was primarily agricultural, and the peasant family was the basic unit of economic production. Peasants were primarily agricultural workers, but they combined farming with other kinds of labor. They tilled the land in spring and summer and spun thread or wove textiles in the winter. Urban merchants obtained their wares by means of what is called the *putting-out* or **domestic system of textile production**. They bought wool or other unfinished fiber for distribution to peasant workers. These people took it home, spun it into thread, wove it into cloth, and returned the finished product to the merchants for sale. Spinning wheels and hand looms were standard equipment in thousands of peasant cottages from Ireland to Austria. Sometimes peasants owned these tools, but by the middle of the century the merchant capitalist usually provided both raw material and implements. Textiles remained part of the family economy in Britain and on the Continent well into the nineteenth century, but by the middle of the eighteenth century, the demand for cotton cloth was already outstripping home production. Market pressures encouraged the invention of machines that transformed the cloth industry.

The Spinning Jenny   Thanks to the invention of the flying shuttle in the 1730s, weavers had the technical capacity to produce enough cotton fabric to meet market demand. It was not until 1765, however, when James Hargreaves (d. 1778) invented the **spinning jenny**, that spinners began to be able to provide weavers with adequate supplies of thread. Hargreaves's machine spun sixteen spindles of thread simultaneously. By the close of the century, capacity had increased to 120 spindles.

The Water Frame   The spinning jenny ended the imbalance between the productive capacity of spinners and weavers, but it was still a machine intended for use in a cottage. The invention that moved cotton textile manufacture from the home to the factory was the **water frame**. In 1769, Richard Arkwright (1732–1792) patented a water-powered device that produced a 100 percent cotton fabric rather than the standard earlier blend of cotton and linen. When Arkwright lost his patent rights, other manufacturers hastened to appropriate his invention. Domestic hand production decreased as factories sprang up in the countryside near the streams that provided waterpower for machines. Cotton output increased by 800 percent between 1780 and 1800. By 1815, cotton

16.5
The Creation
of the Steam Loom

domestic system of textile production   Means by which urban merchants obtained their wares. They bought wool or other unfinished fiber for distribution to peasant workers who took it home, spun it into thread, wove it into cloth, and returned the finished product to the merchants for sale.

spinning jenny   Invented by James Hargreaves in 1765, this machine spun sixteen spindles of thread simultaneously.

water frame   Invented in 1769 by Richard Arkwright, this water-powered device produced a 100 percent cotton fabric rather than the standard earlier blend of cotton and linen.

represented 40 percent of the value of British domestic exports, and by 1830, it had surpassed 50 percent.

The Industrial Revolution had commenced in earnest by the 1780s, but its full economic and social ramifications were not felt until the early nineteenth century. Industry expanded and incorporated new inventions slowly. Although Edmund Cartwright (1743–1822), for instance, invented the power loom in the late 1780s, the number of power-loom weavers did not surpass hand-loom weavers in Britain until the 1830s. The fact that the first cotton mills used water-power, were located in the country, and rarely employed more than two dozen workers meant the social ramifications of industrialism were also slow to appear. Not until late in the century, after James Watt (1736–1819) perfected the steam engine (1769) and adapted it to textile machinery, could factories be located in cities. The steam engine linked urbanization and industrialization.

THE STEAM ENGINE

The steam engine gave people—for the first time in history—a steady, practically unlimited source of inanimate power that facilitated the industrialization of almost all production. Unlike engines driven by water, wind, animals, and people, the coal or wood-fed steam engine was portable, dependable, and inexhaustible. Its potential uses were legion.

Thomas Newcomen had invented the first engine using steam power early in the eighteenth century. It was driven by injecting steam into a cylinder to push up a piston that fell back when the steam condensed. The machine was heavy and energy inefficient, but it was widely used in Britain to pump water out of coal and tin mines. During the 1760s, James Watt, a Scottish engineer, experimented with the Newcomen machine and achieved much greater efficiency by separating the condenser from the piston and the cylinder. His design, however, required precisely tooled metalwork, a technical liability that Matthew Boulton, a successful toy and button maker, and John Wilkinson, a cannon manufacturer, helped him overcome. In 1776, a Watt steam engine found its first commercial application: pumping water from mines in Cornwall.

Watt retained exclusive patent rights to the steam engine until 1800. His reluctance to alter his invention slowed the development of applications for it, but Boulton finally persuaded him to adapt steam engines so that they could be used for running cotton mills as well as pumping. By the early nineteenth century, the steam engine had become the prime mover in every industry and had also begun to transform transportation.

IRON PRODUCTION

Techniques for manufacturing high-quality iron are basic to modern industrial development, for iron is the chief material used in all heavy industry and transportation. In the early eighteenth century, British ironmakers produced somewhat less than 25,000 tons annually because technical problems limited their output. They used charcoal to smelt ore. Charcoal, which came from Britain's diminishing forests, was expensive, and it was hard to use it to maintain ideal temperatures. The blasts of air needed to generate the intense heats of smelters were also difficult to produce. Iron production soared after the steam engine solved the latter problem, and smiths discovered that coke, a charcoal-like derivative of Britain's abundant coal, could fuel their blast furnaces. The steam engine had the felicitous effect of improving the production of iron and increasing demand for it.

In 1784, Henry Cort (1740–1800) introduced a new "puddling" process (a method for melting and stirring ore). Cort's technique improved iron's quality by removing more of the slag (the mix of impurities) that bubbles to the top of a pot of molten ore. Cort also developed a rolling mill that formed molten metal into continuous bars, rails, or sheets. Metal had previously been shaped by pounding, but the mill yielded a better, more versatile, and less costly product. By the early nineteenth century, Britain was producing over a million tons of iron annually.

THE IMPACT OF THE AGRICULTURAL AND INDUSTRIAL REVOLUTIONS ON WORKING WOMEN

Women had always been part of Europe's labor force, but the Agricultural and Industrial Revolutions limited their options for employment. Peasant women worked the land with men and often managed industries related to farming (for example, dairy production or brewing). When increasing commercialization and mechanization began to transform farming, men and machines took over many tasks that had previously been assigned to women. Women naturally opposed changes that deprived them of the opportunity to earn a living from the land, and many proponents of the new agricultural techniques viewed women as impediments to reform.

A similar development took place in the textile industry. The spinning of thread had been a female occupation from time immemorial, but the development of large spinning jennies in factory settings made this a job for men. When women found employment in textile factories, they were assigned duties that required less skill and received lower pay than the work available to men. Many women turned to cottage industries and supported themselves by producing items (such as buttons, knitted items, baskets, gloves, etc.) that could be made at home. This work was very poorly paid, and the poverty that sometimes forced these women into crime and prostitution damaged the reputations of working women in general.

The only alternative employment available to many women was domestic service in the homes of landed or commercial families. Service was the largest female profession in the nineteenth century. It was respectable but did not provide women with opportunities to develop the skills they needed to enter the technologically advanced fields of factory manufacturing or transportation. Many people assumed women were incapable of being trained for industrial work.

By the end of the eighteenth century, the work and workplaces of men and women were becoming separate and distinct. Women's work—whether in cottage industries or domestic service—was associated with the home and men's with the factory. Europeans also began to assume that a woman worked only to supplement the income of a male who was chiefly responsible for her support. This provided justification for paying female workers less than males and for imposing restrictions on their employment in factories. The belief spread that women belonged in domestic settings and were to be discouraged from seeking factory work—something inherently unsuitable for members of their sex.

WHAT PROBLEMS arose as a result of the growth of cities?

THE GROWTH OF CITIES

Remarkable changes occurred in urban areas between 1500 and 1800. In 1500, there were only 156 cities in Europe (excluding Hungary and Russia) with populations reaching or exceeding 10,000. Only four of these (Paris, Milan, Venice, and Naples) were larger than 100,000. By 1800, there were about 363 cities of 10,000 or more inhabitants, and seventeen had populations topping 100,000. The percentage of Europeans living in urban areas had risen from about 5 percent to 9 percent, and northern Europe had surpassed southern Europe in urban concentration.

PATTERNS OF PREINDUSTRIAL URBANIZATION

Towns grew particularly rapidly in the eighteenth century. London, which had about 700,000 inhabitants in 1700, reached almost a million by 1800. By then, Paris had over 500,000 inhabitants. Berlin's population tripled during the century, reaching 170,000. Warsaw had almost 120,000 in 1794, and Saint Petersburg, which did not exist until 1703, numbered over 250,000 inhabitants at the end of the century. Despite this growth, probably somewhat less than 20 percent of the population of England and Britain lived in cities, and a town of 10,000 was much more common than a giant urban center.

Growth of Capitals and Ports   The cities that grew most vigorously between 1600 and 1750 were the capitals and ports that profited from the development of the monarchical state and the burgeoning of its bureaucracies, armies, courts, and support personnel. The growth of ports reflected Europe's expanding overseas trade (particularly the Atlantic route).

Except for Manchester in England and Lyons in France, most great urban conglomerates in this era (1600–1750) were not centers of industrial manufacturing. Rural labor was cheaper than urban labor, and expansion of the putting-out system transferred much of the production characteristic of medieval cities to the countryside. Consequently, cities with populations of fewer than 40,000 inhabitants declined.

In the middle of the eighteenth century, the growth of existing large cities slowed, new cities appeared, and smaller cities expanded. There are several explanations for this. There was the general overall population increase. The early Industrial Revolution was a rural phenomenon that fostered the growth of smaller towns. Factory organization created some concentrations of population in new places, and the increasing prosperity of European agriculture, like industrialization, promoted urban development.

URBAN CLASSES

A town's rich and poor residents were visibly segregated. The moneyed classes lived in fashionable townhouses bordering urban parks. The poor often congregated along rivers. The lesser merchants and craftsmen lived above their shops, and whole families might share a single room. There was little clear water and sanitary facilities that are now taken for granted were unknown. (See "Encountering the Past: Water, Washing, and Bathing.") Cattle, pigs, goats, and other animals wandered the streets. All the contemporary descriptions of Europe's eighteenth-century cities emphasize the grace and beauty of the homes of the wealthy and the dirt and stench that prevailed elsewhere. Conditions other than those created by the factories of the Industrial Revolution turned cities into hellholes for the poor and the dispossessed.

Poverty was usually worse in the countryside, but its effects (crime, prostitution, vagrancy, begging, and alcoholism) were more visible in cities. So were its punishments. Public tortures and executions of criminals were frequent spectacles in every European town. Many a young person left the countryside in search of a better life in town only to find degradation and death. The harsh reality of the drama of London's streets at midcentury has been graphically recorded by a keen observer, the artist William Hogarth (1697–1764).

ENCOUNTERING THE PAST

WATER, WASHING, AND BATHING

C*lear water was scarce in Europe until the end of the nineteenth century. Households that did not have wells drew their water from streams, rivers, and public wells or fountains. Governments did nothing to assure the purity of a resource whose importance was less appreciated than it is today. Where the average American now uses about 210 liters of water per day, an individual in the eighteenth century may have needed only about 7.5 liters.*

Public bathhouses were common during the Middle Ages. Bodily cleanliness was associated with spiritual purity, and aristocrats and townspeople bathed frequently. In the late medieval period, however, physicians began to argue that bathing was unhealthy. They reasoned that it opened the pores of the skin and allowed *miasma* (bad air) to infect the body with disease. Until the end of the eighteenth century, medical texts advised people to wash only the parts of the body that are publicly visible (hands, face, neck, and feet). Clean clothing was, however, considered indispensable. A switch from wool to linen garments, which began in the sixteenth century, made laundering easier, and social mores of the Renaissance-Reformation era placed a great deal of emphasis on the quality and appearance of one's clothing. Consequently, garments were washed much more frequently than bodies.

Attitudes began to change again toward the middle of the eighteenth century. Bathing was once more seen as healthful (particularly as the germ theory of disease received acceptance). Public baths reappeared in the nineteenth century, and great engineering projects were undertaken to provide urban dwellers with sewage disposal and clean water (see Chapter 23).

WHAT CAUSED bathing customs to fluctuate from age to age?

In the eighteenth century, washing linen clothing by hand was a major task of women servants.

J. B. S. Chardin, "The Washerwoman". Nationalmuseum med Prins Eugens Waldemarsudde. Photo: The National Museum of Fine Art

The Upper Classes The pinnacle of the urban social scale was occupied by a small group of nobles, major merchants, bankers, financiers, clergy, and government officials. These men (and they were always men) controlled their towns. Rights of self-government enshrined in a royal charter usually gave an urban corporation or town council authority to choose a town's leaders. The town councils of a few continental cities were dominated by artisan guilds, but it was more common for towns to be run by self-perpetuating oligarchies of nobles and wealthy merchants.

The Middle Class A city's most dynamic inhabitants were the members of its middle class, the *bourgeoisie*—the lesser merchants, tradesmen, bankers, and professional people. The middle class was much less clearly defined than the aristocracy, for it was not a single, cohesive entity. Different groups occupied the middle of the social scale, and some were at odds with others. Professionals, for instance, tended to look down on those who were engaged in commerce. Less wealthy bourgeoisie envied richer colleagues, and the rich aspired to mix with the nobility.

Middle-class people did not derive their incomes from the land. They were the agents and beneficiaries of their era's expanding commerce. They concentrated on amassing capital and using it to improve their social standing. They saw themselves as energetic, productive workers who supported reform, change, and legislation fostering economic development. They were both contemptuous and envious of the "idle" aristocrats whose manners they imitated. They led the development of the consumer society. As owners of factories and of wholesale and retail businesses, they produced and sold goods for a consumer market in which they were the primary customers. They did not enjoy the titles and social prestige of the nobility, but they could emulate the material comfort and elegance of the aristocratic lifestyle.

The middle class and the aristocracy had a complicated relationship. Nobles, especially in England and France, augmented the fortunes they inherited by profits from commercial ventures. They managed their estates in a businesslike fashion and funded entrepreneurial enterprises. Wealthy members of the middle class sought respectability by purchasing landed estates (the traditional aristocratic investment). Despite diverging behaviors, the two groups were often at odds over the issue of sharing power. Nobles felt threatened by the upward social mobility of the bourgeoisie, and they defended themselves by using their control of governments to frustrate the schemes of traders, bankers, manufacturers, and lawyers.

The urban middle class envied the nobility, but it feared the lower orders. The poor were a potentially violent element in society, a threat to the property of others, and—as objects of charity—drains on community resources.

Artisans   The lower classes were both varied and numerous. Shopkeepers, artisans, and wage earners constituted the single largest group in any city. They had their own culture, values, and institutions, and, like rural peasants, they tended to be conservative defenders of local traditions. They were economically vulnerable, but they had enough wealth to contribute to the revolution in consumption. They could buy more goods than the poor of earlier generations, and they tended to copy the middle class's pattern of consumption.

The lives of artisans and shopkeepers centered on their workplaces and their residential neighborhoods. They often lived near or in their places of employment. Their workshops often employed fewer than a half dozen people. The medieval guild system continued, but it was losing much of its power. Guilds were suspicious of change and innovation. Their strategy for preserving the jobs of their members was to reduce competition by limiting the number of people who could enter their trade. A guild was an artisan's chief protector in the newly evolving commercial economy, and guilds, like other medieval institutions, remained strong in central Europe.

16.2
Life in the Eighteenth Century: An Artisan's Journey

THE URBAN RIOT

The conservative outlook of the artisan class shaped its concept of social and economic justice. The poor accepted grim situations that were long established and seemed, therefore, inevitable. But they opposed any change that threatened to increase their burdens and reduce their already scant opportunities.

Fluctuations in the price of bread, the staple food of the poor, often sparked urban disorder. The poor, having no voice in town governments, often staged riots to command the attention of the authorities. Fear of provoking a riot

This engraving illustrates a metalworking shop such as might have been found in almost any town of significance in Europe. Most of the people employed in the shop probably belonged to the same family. Note that two women are also working. The wife may very well have been the person in charge of keeping the accounts of the business. The two younger boys might be children of the owner or apprentices in the trade, or both.

The Granger Collection

that would damage property was the chief restraint on the greed of merchants. Bread riots were not the irrational acts of desperate people. They were customary behaviors that helped regulate the Old Regime's economy of scarcity and maintain acceptable "just prices" for essential items.

Riots of many kinds were common in the eighteenth century, for they were the only way in which the many people who were excluded from the political processes could make their wills known. Religious bigotry incited some rioting, but violence was more often directed against property than people. Rioters were usually not riffraff but small shopkeepers, freeholders, craftsmen, and wage earners. Their intent was not to overthrow the social order but to restore a traditional right or practice they feared was endangered.

During the last half of the eighteenth century, politicians often manipulated urban riots for private ends. The angry crowds that tore up the streets of towns could become tools of warring factions within the upper classes. Paris's aristocratic *Parlement* often urged the Parisians to riot to strengthen its hand in dealing with the monarchy. In Great Britain in 1792 the government incited mobs to attack supporters of the French Revolution.

THE JEWISH POPULATION: THE AGE OF THE GHETTO

HOW DID the suppression of Jews in European cities lead to the formation of ghettos?

*J*ewish communities in Amsterdam and other western European cities produced famous intellectuals in the eighteenth century, but the vast majority of Europe's Jews lived in eastern Europe. Fewer than 100,000 lived in Germany, approximately 40,000 in France, and only about 10,000 in either England or Holland. About 3 million could be found in Poland, Lithuania, and the Ukraine.

In most countries, unless governments specifically granted them privileges, Jews did not enjoy the same rights as Christians. They were treated as resident aliens who could be evicted at any moment. They lived apart from Christians in **ghettos**. In cities these were separate districts, and in the countryside they were entire villages. Poland's Jewish communities were virtually self-governing for much of the century, but everywhere Jews struggled under the burden of discriminatory legislation. They were often prevented from owning land and were,

ghettos Separate districts in cities and entire villages in the countryside where Jews lived apart from Christians in eighteenth-century Europe.

therefore, forced to make their livings by trade and commerce. During the seventeenth century, a few became bankers rich enough to help governments finance wars. The loans they made to monarchs were often not repaid, but these "court Jews" became famous for their financial acumen and influence. They formed a tiny network of closely intermarried, exclusive families whose situations were hardly characteristic of those facing the vast majority of Jews.

Most of Europe's Jews lived in poverty. They occupied the most undesirable sections of cities or poor rural villages, and they worked at the lowest occupations. Their religious beliefs, rituals, and the laws of most countries kept them separated from their Christian neighbors and relegated them to positions of social inferiority. Those who converted to Christianity were welcomed, if not always warmly, into gentile society. Until the last two decades of the eighteenth century, those who remained loyal to their faith suffered discrimination and persecution. They were barred from some professions, restricted in their freedom of movement, deprived of political representation and protection under the law, subjected to exile and confiscation of their property, and generally regarded as lesser beings. Force was sometimes used to persuade them to convert, or their children were taken away from them for Christian indoctrination. The Jews of the Old Regime knew that at any moment their gentile neighbors could turn on them. The end of the era, however, brought major improvements in their lives.

During the Old Regime, European Jews were separated from non-Jews, typically in districts known as ghettos. Relegated to the least desirable section of a city or to rural villages, most lived in poverty. This watercolor painting depicts a street in Kazimlesz, the Jewish quarter of Cracow, Poland.

Judaica Collection, Max Berger, Vienna, Austria, Photograph © Erich Lessing/Art Resource, NY

SUMMARY

Major Features of Life in the Old Regime Many aspects of life in the 18th century still followed traditional patterns. European economies were dominated by agriculture; nothing mattered more to most individuals—or their governments—than the grain harvest. Society was more oriented toward the past than the future. Rights accrued not to individuals, but to groups. Nobles and peasants lobbied for the restoration of customary rights, and some cities still enforced sumptuary laws regulating which groups of people could wear what kinds of clothing.

The Aristocracy The aristocratic resurgence that took place across Europe was a noteworthy feature of 18th century European social history. The nobility made up between 1 percent and 5 percent of the population in most European countries. They were wealthy and powerful; their income came largely from land ownership. In England especially, they also invested in various ventures, including industries. Other aristocratic characteristics varied from country to country, but nobles throughout Europe all tried to preserve noble exclusivity, to resist the growing power of the monarchies, and to improve their financial status.

The Land and Its Tillers Land was the basis of noble wealth, and its cultivation was the task of the huge class of peasants and serfs. Landowners controlled local government and the courts; continental Europe's tax burden fell on those who

IMAGE KEY

for pages 360–361

a. "The Iron Forge," 1772 (oil on canvas) by Joseph Wright of Derby (1734–97). Broadlands Trust, Hampshire, UK/Bridgeman Art Library, London

b. J. B. S. Chardin, "The Washerwoman"

c. Grains of Wild Einkorn

d. A reproduction of Stephenson's Rocket, 1830s first class carriage from the Liverpool and Manchester line, and a tender that holds coal and barrel for water

e. Detail, Francis Wheatley (RA) (1747–1801) "Noon," signed and dated 1799 Oil on canvas, 17 1/2 x 21 1/2 in. (44.5 x 54.5 cm), Yale Center for British Art, Paul Mellon Collection, USA/Bridgeman Art Library. (B1977.14.119)

f. Butter Churn

g. Detail, Jean-Baptiste-Simeon Chardin "The Governess" (#6432) National Gallery of Canada, Ottawa

h. Joseph Vernet, "Construction of a Road". Louvre, Paris, France. Bridgeman-Giraudon/Art Resource, NY

i. Anonymous. Meissen Ceramic: The Charlottenburg Concerto, c. 1760

j. Judaica Collection Max Berger, Vienna, Austria Photograph ©Erich Lessing/Art Resource, NY

tilled the soil. Landowners' power increased the farther east one went in Europe. In Prussia, Austria, and Russia, a serf's life was nothing but a commodity to an aristocrat. Peasants revolted violently and repeatedly. English game laws, which prohibited hunting by anyone other than large landowners, were an example of aristocratic domination of rural life—although they failed to prevent poaching.

Family Structures and the Family Economy The "family economy" was the norm throughout Europe before the Industrial Revolution. In northwestern Europe, the "household" was generally a nuclear family and its servants. Premarital sex was common, and people married in their twenties, usually after spending several years earning wages. Eastern European "households" were larger, with more than nine members of three generations living together. Landowners in eastern Europe discouraged families from separating into multiple households. Everyone worked, who could, with the goal of supporting the family unit. The death of the father could easily spell disaster for the family. Women's economic contributions to the household were more important than their reproductive capacities. Women and babies experienced high mortality rates, and many infants were abandoned for economic reasons.

The Revolution in Agriculture Europe's population in 1750 was between 100 and 120 million people; by 1800, there were almost 190 million, and by 1850, there were 260 million. Historians have proposed many explanations for this population growth. One factor was the introduction of the potato from America. Increasing population led to increasing demand and prices for wheat and bread. This hurt peasants but helped larger landowners. Landlords began to treat crop cultivation as a commercial operation and introduced new techniques that increased crop yields. The economic and social organization of farming also changed: the enclosure movement in England rationalized the use of land and saw higher productivity. Governments sided with landowners, and serf revolts were suppressed. In eastern Europe, land ownership and social structures were less encouraging of agricultural innovation.

The Industrial Revolution of the Eighteenth Century Europe's economy of scarcity was replaced by a demand-driven cycle of growth. Advertising and social emulation fueled consumer demand. In Great Britain political and economic factors were also favorable for innovation. The domestic system of textile production was the first area of industry to be transformed, through the invention of the spinning jenny in 1765, the water frame in 1769, and the power loom in the late 1780s. The 1769 steam engine was applied to industries ranging from mining to textiles to transportation. Iron became the backbone of industrial machinery. As work was reorganized to accommodate the new machines, labor was increasingly segregated by gender, and women's work was systematically devalued.

The Growth of Cities Many cities grew substantially between 1500 and 1800. Between 1600 and 1750, capital cities and ports grew most vigorously; most smaller cities actually lost population. After 1750, smaller cities began to grow more rapidly than larger ones, and entirely new cities emerged. City dwellers led radically different lives, depending on their social class. The upper classes lived quite comfortably and often controlled city government. The middle class had aspirations and fears that led them to support reform, change, and economic growth. Artisans, the largest group, were generally conservative. Bread riots were sparked by artisans who believed merchants were not charging "just" prices; other forms of riots could be fueled by religious prejudice or political agendas.

The Jewish Population: The Age of the Ghetto Jews were segregated and discriminated against on religious grounds throughout Europe. The vast majority of Jews lived in eastern Europe, particularly Poland, Lithuania, and the Ukraine. In most countries Jews were treated as resident aliens, without political or civil rights and socially inferior; only in England was it possible for Jews to mingle with mainstream society. This was the age of the ghetto, or separate community, which were either distinct districts within cities or separate Jewish villages in rural areas. Most Jews were poor; one exceptional category was the so-called court Jews, who helped finance royal projects (usually wars). Jews, especially children, were sometimes forcibly converted to Christianity, and they were sometimes killed for their religious beliefs.

REVIEW QUESTIONS

1. How did the situation of the English aristocracy differ from that of the French? What kind of privileges distinguished European aristocrats from other social groups?

2. What was the family economy? How did households in northwestern Europe differ from those in eastern Europe? In what ways were the lives of women constrained by the family economy?

3. What caused the Agricultural Revolution? To what extent did the English aristocracy contribute to it? What explains the growth of Europe's population in the eighteenth century? How did population growth change consumption?

4. What caused the Industrial Revolution of the eighteenth century? Why did Great Britain take the lead in the Industrial Revolution? What was city life like during the eighteenth century? How did the lifestyle of the upper class differ from that of the middle and lower classes? What were some of the causes of urban riots?

KEY TERMS

aristocratic resurgence   (p. 364)
domestic system of textile production   (p. 374)

ghettos   (p. 380)
Industrial Revolution   (p. 372)
Old Regime   (p. 362)

spinning jenny   (p. 374)
water frame   (p. 374)

 For additional study resources for this chapter, go to:
www.prenhall.com/kagan3/chapter15

16 The Transatlantic Economy, Trade Wars, and Colonial Rebellion

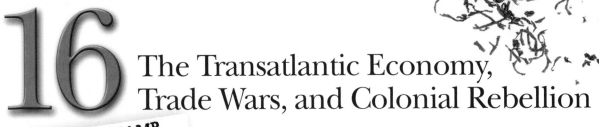

This is the Place to affix the STAMP.

CHAPTER HIGHLIGHTS

Periods of European Overseas Empires There have been four stages of European relations with the wider world, starting with exploration in the sixteenth century and ending with decolonization in the twentieth century. This chapter focuses on the second stage, one characterized by rivalries between mercantile empires.

Mercantile Empires Mercantilists assumed that the growth of one nation came at the expense of another and that countries should seek to monopolize trade with their colonies. Colonial rivalries sometimes grew into conflicts between European nations.

The Spanish Colonial System Spain attempted to control trade with its colonies by restricting the ports to which Spanish ships could sail. Spanish colonial administration concentrated power in the crown. Philip V tried to implement French administrative techniques in the Spanish colonies. Charles III tried to use imperial reform and liberalization of trade to improve Spain's economy.

Black African Slavery, the Plantation System, and the Atlantic Economy The heavy reliance of the plantation economy on slavery made it unique. The racist element in the justification of slavery in the Americas left a legacy that is with us today. The volume and economic impact of the slave trade shaped the histories of both Europe and the Americas.

Mid-Eighteenth-Century Wars The mid-eighteenth-century European state system encouraged warfare. Many European wars spilled over into the colonies.

The American Revolution and Europe British efforts to tax American colonists led to resistance and conflict. In 1776, the Continental Congress declared the colonies' independence. America's victory in the Revolutionary War was ratified by the Treaty of Paris. Revolutionaries developed new ideas and models for advocates of government based on popular consent.

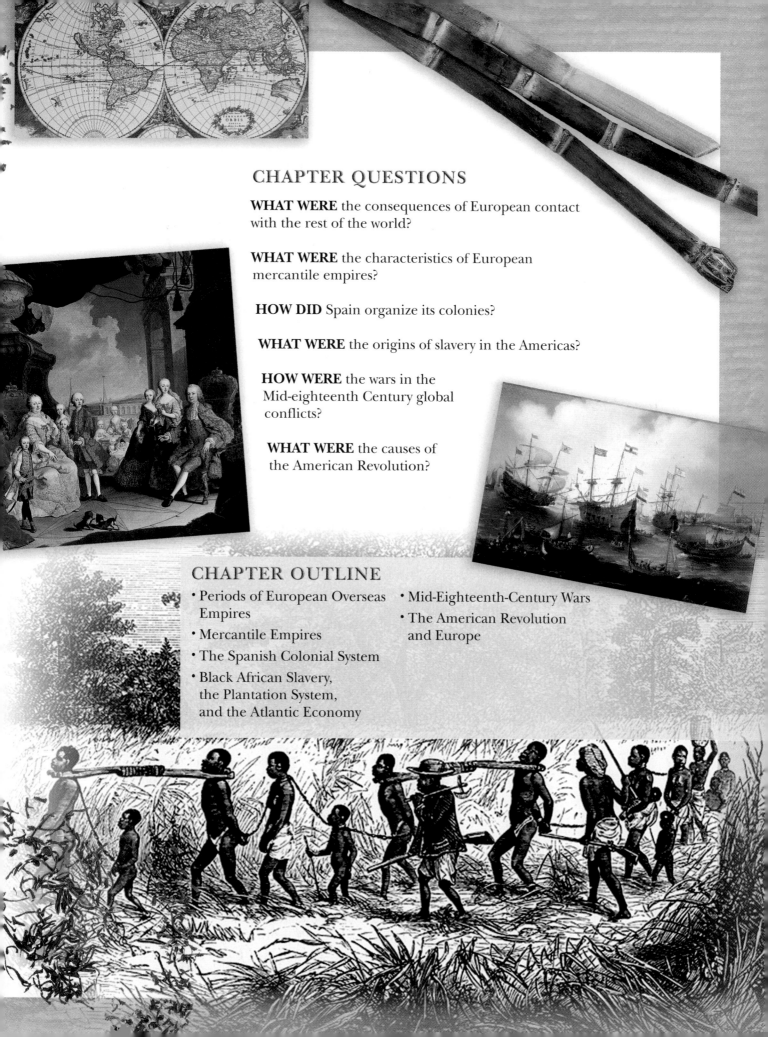

CHAPTER QUESTIONS

WHAT WERE the consequences of European contact with the rest of the world?

WHAT WERE the characteristics of European mercantile empires?

HOW DID Spain organize its colonies?

WHAT WERE the origins of slavery in the Americas?

HOW WERE the wars in the Mid-eighteenth Century global conflicts?

WHAT WERE the causes of the American Revolution?

CHAPTER OUTLINE

- Periods of European Overseas Empires
- Mercantile Empires
- The Spanish Colonial System
- Black African Slavery, the Plantation System, and the Atlantic Economy
- Mid-Eighteenth-Century Wars
- The American Revolution and Europe

IMAGE KEY

Image Key for pages 384–385 is on page 402.

During the eighteenth century, Europeans began to make wars on a global scale. Austria and Prussia struggled in central Europe, and Great Britain and France competed for colonies abroad. The result was a new balance of power on the Continent and on the high seas. Prussia became one of Europe's leading nations and Great Britain won a world empire. Wars forced European states to subordinate financial planning to military policy and led to economic decisions that had far-reaching political consequences. These included the American Revolution, the development of enlightened absolutist monarchies, a financial crisis for the French monarchy, and reform of Spain's American empire.

PERIODS OF EUROPEAN OVERSEAS EMPIRES

WHAT WERE the consequences of European contact with the rest of the world?

Europe's relations with the wider world have gone through four stages. The first—the age of exploration, conquest, and settlement of the New World—was over by the end of the seventeenth century.

The second, which ended about 1820, was characterized by rivalries among the mercantile empires of Spain, France, and Great Britain that spawned naval wars linked to combat on the European continent. This was also the era of the largest forced migration in history—the shipment of African slaves to the Americas. The Atlantic economy and American cultures that developed during this period were created by Europeans and Africans. They pushed Native Americans to the margins of society and ultimately freed themselves (both the British colonies of North America and the Spanish colonies of Central and South America) from European control.

During the third stage of Europe's interaction with the non-European world (the nineteenth century), European states built and administered empires in Africa and Asia. In some places European elites ruled indigenous peoples. In others (Australia, New Zealand, and South Africa) European settlers replaced them.

The fourth stage in Europe's overseas adventures featured the dismantling of Europe's colonial empires. The process of "decolonization," which began in the mid–twentieth century, ceded political independence to former colonies, but Europe continues to wrestle with a troubling legacy. For four-and-a-half centuries, the relatively small continent of Europe dominated much of the world. Europeans owed their ascendancy not to any innate cultural superiority but to technological advances that gave them greater military power. They, however, often treated other peoples as natural inferiors.

MERCANTILE EMPIRES

WHAT WERE the characteristics of European mercantile empires?

The empires European nations built in the eighteenth century were viewed as commercial enterprises, not places for the resettlement of Europeans. These empires were held together by navies that protected merchant shipping.

In 1713, the Treaty of Utrecht defined the boundaries of Europe's various empires. Except for Brazil (which was Portuguese), Spain claimed all of mainland South America, the islands of Cuba, Puerto Rico, half of Hispaniola, and the North American territories of Florida, Mexico, California, and the Southwest. The British held the North Atlantic seaboard, Nova Scotia, Newfoundland, Jamaica, Barbados, and a few trading stations on the Indian subcontinent. The French occupied the valleys of the Saint Lawrence, the Ohio, and the Mississippi Rivers; the West Indian islands of Saint Domingue (Hispaniola), Guadeloupe, and Martinique; and stations in India. The Dutch controlled Surinam (Dutch Guiana) in South America, various posts in Ceylon and Bengal, and trade with

mercantilism Economic theory in which governments heavily regulated trade and promoted empires in order to increase national wealth.

Java (Indonesia). All these nations also claimed numerous smaller islands in the Caribbean.

MERCANTILIST GOALS

Critics have coined the term *mercantilism* to describe the economic theories that drove Europe's quest for empires. Mercantilists believed bullion was the measure of a country's wealth, and they advocated courses of action that encouraged its accumulation. The goal was to maintain an excess of exports over imports, for a favorable trade balance siphoned gold and silver away from trading partners. Mercantilists assumed the world's resources were limited and one nation's economy could grow only at the expense of others.

The economic well-being of the home country was the primary goal of the mercantilist system. It was taken for granted that a colony was the inferior partner in its relationship with its European sponsor. Colonies were established to provide markets and natural resources to support industries in the home country. The home country furnished its colonies with military security and political administration. Colonies were expected to remain subordinate and trade only with their homelands. Each country maintained monopolistic control of its colonies' commerce by means of navigation laws, tariffs, and regulations that prohibited trade with other colonies and European states.

Mercantilism worked better in theory than practice, for it was at odds with economic realities and human nature. Colonial and home markets failed to mesh. Spain could not produce sufficient goods for all of South America, and manufacturing in Britain's North American colonies competed with factories in England. It was also impossible to prevent trade among colonies belonging to different countries. English colonists, for instance, could buy sugar more cheaply from the French West Indies than from English suppliers, and efforts to prevent them simply encouraged smuggling and ultimately goaded them to rebel.

FRENCH-BRITISH RIVALRY

The French and British colonists of North America quarreled endlessly. Both groups coveted the lower Saint Lawrence River valley, upper New England, and the Ohio River valley. They fought over fishing rights and the fur trade and made competing alliances with Native American tribes. However, competition among European nations for American territory focused primarily on the West Indies. The tobacco, cotton, indigo, coffee, and, above all, the sugar produced on these islands made them the jewels of empire.

France and England also confronted each other on the Indian subcontinent. Both countries granted exclusive rights to trade with India to monopolistic corporations—England's East India Company and France's Compagnie des Indes. India had the potential to become a huge market for European goods and to provide Europeans access to China. The European trading posts in India, the *factories*, initially held licenses from various Indian governments, but in the middle of the eighteenth century, the political situation changed. The governments of a number of Indian states weakened, and the leaders of the French

During the seventeenth and eighteenth centuries, European maritime nations established overseas empires and set up trading monopolies within them in an effort to magnify their economic strength. As this painting of the Old Custom House Quay in London suggests, trade from these empires and the tariffs imposed on it were expected to generate revenue for the home country. But behind many of the goods carried in the great sailing ships in the harbor and landed on these docks lay the labor of African slaves working on the plantations of North and South America.

Samuel Scott, *Old Custom House Quay* Collection. V & A Images. The Victoria and Albert Museum, London

QUICK REVIEW

Sites of Rivalry

- North America: Colonists quarrel over land and trade rights
- Indian subcontinent: French and British companies compete for trade rights
- French and European companies took control of local governments in India

and English trading companies—Joseph Dupleix (1697–1763) and Robert Clive (1725–1774), respectively—seized the opportunity to expand their privileges. Each company began, in effect, to take control of parts of India and to try to check the growth of its competitor. The other major European power in the Far East was the Netherlands. It, however, concentrated its attentions on Indonesia.

THE SPANISH COLONIAL SYSTEM

HOW DID Spain organize its colonies?

The primary purpose of the Spanish Empire until the mid–eighteenth century was to supply Spain with precious metals from the New World.

COLONIAL GOVERNMENT

Queen Isabella of Castile (r. 1474–1504) had commissioned Columbus, and the crown of Castile linked the New World with Spain. There were few limitations on the Spanish monarch's powers, but Spain's administration of its empire was more rigid in theory than in practice. Spain governed America through a Council of the Indies, which, in conjunction with the crown, legislated for the colonies and nominated the viceroys of New Spain (Mexico) and Peru. Virtually all political power flowed from the top down. Each of the viceroyalties was divided into judicial councils, or *audiencias*. There were also various kinds of local officers, the most important of whom were the *corregidores,* the chairs of municipal councils. The system provided the monarchy with vast opportunities for patronage, which was usually bestowed on persons born in Spain.

TRADE REGULATION

The government of Spain's colonies was designed to serve Spain's commercial interests. The Casa de Contratación (House of Trade) in Seville regulated all commerce with the New World, and Cádiz was the only port authorized for use by ships trading with America. A complicated system of fleets operating from Seville guarded Spain's trade monopoly. Each year, the *flota* (a fleet of commercial vessels belonging to Seville's merchants and escorted by warships) carried merchandise from Spain to a few specified ports in America. The ships were then reloaded with silver and gold bullion for the return voyage, and after wintering in fortified Caribbean ports, they sailed back to Spain. Spanish colonists were forbidden to trade directly with each other and to develop their own shipping and commerce. Foreign merchants were also denied access to Spain's colonies.

COLONIAL REFORM UNDER THE SPANISH BOURBON MONARCHS

A crucial change in the Spanish colonial system took place after the War of the Spanish Succession (1701–1714) brought a French Bourbon prince to Spain's throne. Philip V (r. 1700–1746) and his successors tried to improve Spain's economy and its international prestige by strengthening the empire's trade monopoly. The *flota* system had never worked perfectly and it had been allowed to decay under the last of Spain's Habsburg kings. The coastal patrol vessels that Philip dispatched to suppress smuggling in American waters engaged English ships and provoked war between Spain and England in 1739. In the same year, Philip tightened his grip on the Americas by establishing the viceroyalty of New Granada (modern Venezuela, Colombia, and Ecuador).

The European wars that raged during the reign of Philip's successor, Ferdinand VI (r. 1746–1759), disclosed the vulnerability of Spain's empire to naval penetration. After Spain acknowledged defeat in 1763, Charles III (r. 1759–1788) tried to save the empire by implementing administrative reforms. He increased the power of royal ministers and diminished the authority of the Council of the Indies and the Casa de Contratación. In 1765, he abolished the monopolies of Seville and Cádiz and permitted other Spanish cities to trade with America. He also opened more South American and Caribbean ports to trade and authorized some commercial exchanges among colonial ports. In 1776, he organized a fourth viceroyalty, the Rio de la Plata (modern Argentina, Uruguay, Paraguay, and Bolivia). Charles III compensated for the revenue lost through relaxing control of trade by increasing the efficiency of tax collection and eliminating bureaucratic corruption. This duty was assigned to the office of *intendent,* the kind of agency Louis XIV had found to be a useful instrument of absolutism. (See Map 16–1.)

The Bourbon reforms expanded and diversified Spain's trade but hastened the end of its empire. Charles dispatched more Spaniards to the New World as government officials and merchants and allowed these *peninsulares* (persons born in Spain) more control over the colonies. They administered the colonies for the benefit of Spain and made the *creoles* (persons born in the colonies) feel like second-class subjects. Resentment built, and in the early nineteenth century wars of independence erupted.

BLACK AFRICAN SLAVERY, THE PLANTATION SYSTEM, AND THE ATLANTIC ECONOMY

WHAT WERE the origins of slavery in the Americas?

Slavery had existed in European societies since ancient times, and its morality was not questioned until the eighteenth century. Portugal turned to Africa as a source of slaves after the Ottoman Empire, in the second half of the fifteenth century, prohibited the exportation of white slaves from its territory. The northern European economy had little use for slaves, however, and Europe's few black slaves were exotic ornaments—personal servants found primarily at royal courts and in wealthy homes. The rise of a plantation economy in the New World transformed slavery. Large-scale economic enterprises based on slave labor appeared first in the West Indies and the Spanish and Portuguese settlements in South America and then in British colonies along the southern Atlantic seaboard of North America. They drew Africans into the Western experience as never before.

THE AFRICAN PRESENCE IN THE AMERICAS

The Europeans who pioneered settlements in the New World faced a severe labor shortage. They had no intention of undertaking manual labor themselves, and the ravages of the new diseases they brought to the Americas quickly and severely diminished the native population. The Spanish and Portugese turned to Africa to replenish their work forces, and the English who settled portions of North America where plantation farming was profitable eventually followed their example.

The major sources of supply were the slave markets of Central West Africa, where an extensive slave trade had thrived for centuries. The identity of the African peoples who were enslaved changed from decade to decade depending on which internal wars were producing the captives that were sent to market. Europeans did not bring slavery to Africa but profited greatly from the African custom of condemning defeated enemies to servitude.

MAP 16–1

Viceroyalties in Latin America in 1780   The late-eighteenth-century viceroyalites in Latin America display the effort of the Spanish Bourbon monarchy to establish more direct control of the colonies. They sought this control through the introduction of more royal officials and by establishing more governmental districts.

GIVEN THE SIZE of the Spanish viceroyalties, how effectively do you think Spain was in controlling its Latin American territories and trade?

The West Indies, Brazil, and Sugar   Citizens of the United States date the beginning of slavery in their country to 1619, when a Dutch ship first brought African slaves to Jamestown, Virginia. Slaves had already been traded in the West Indies and South America for over a hundred years, and by the late sixteenth century, the number of Africans in these parts of the Americas often equaled or surpassed the number of Europeans. Both peoples obviously contributed to the new cultures that were springing up in the Americas.

The enslaved population diminished in much of Spanish South America during the late seventeenth century, but it expanded in Brazil and the Caribbean as the sugar industry thrived. By the end of the seventeenth century, the Caribbean was the world center for supplying an ever-growing consumer demand for sugar. (See "Encountering the Past: Sugar Enters the Western Diet.") During the eighteenth century, coffee and tobacco plantations and Brazil's gold mines also helped to drive up prices and increase volume on the slave market. In the early years of that century, the West Indies alone imported an average of 20,000 Africans annually. Demand remained high, for overwork, disease, and malnutrition kept the fertility rate of enslaved populations low. Slave communities tended always to have large numbers of new arrivals who infused new elements into emerging African-American cultures.

The Silver Mines of Potosí. Worked by conscripted Indian laborers under extremely harsh conditions, these mines provided Spain with a vast treasure in silver.

Hulton/Hulton Archive/Getty Images

SLAVERY AND THE TRANSATLANTIC ECONOMY

Different nations dominated the slave trade at different times. The Portuguese and Spanish led during the sixteenth century. The Dutch edged ahead of them in the seventeenth, and thereafter the English, and to a lesser extent the French, handled most of the traffic.

Slavery was an integral part of the transatlantic economy. European goods were carried to Africa to be exchanged for slaves. Slaves were taken to the Americas to be traded for agricultural products and raw materials that were shipped back to European markets. Even North American colonies that participated only marginally in the slave trade profited from it indirectly by supplying other kinds of goods to the West Indies. The slaves that fed this trade were by-products of civil wars in the Kongo and the widespread internal political turmoil that plagued Africa during the eighteenth century. Sometimes African leaders financed arms purchases for their wars by conducting raids to garner captives for sale to Europeans.

This eighteenth-century print shows bound African captives being forced to a slaving port. It was largely African middlemen who captured slaves in the interior and marched them to the coast.

North Wind Picture Archives

THE EXPERIENCE OF SLAVERY

The slave trade was as inhumane as it was profitable. The Spanish, Portuguese, Dutch, French, and English all assisted in the forcible transport of perhaps as many as 9 million black Africans to the New World. During the first four centuries of settlement, far more black slaves came involuntarily to the New World than free Europeans came voluntarily. The conditions under which the Africans crossed the Atlantic were unspeakably wretched. They were packed into the holds of vessels

ENCOUNTERING THE PAST

SUGAR ENTERS THE WESTERN DIET

Sugarcane requires tropical temperatures and abundant rainfall. It could not be cultivated in Europe, and, prior to the discovery of the Americas, European consumers had to import it from Arab lands at great expense. It was a luxury item that few could afford.

Columbus quickly recognized the Caribbean's potential as a sugar-producing region, and he carried cane to the New World in 1493. Within a decade slaves were being used to grow it on Santo Domingo. Demand for sugar grew steadily until, by the eighteenth century, the small Caribbean islands that produced it (with slave labor) had become the most valuable real estate on earth. North American colonies imported large amounts of sugar to make rum, and it became Britain's largest colonial import. The market for it accelerated as Europeans acquired a taste for other tropical products—coffee, tea, and chocolate. Enormous quantities of these stimulants (all sweetened with sugar) were consumed in the seventeenth and eighteenth centuries.

As production increased, prices fell, but demand never slackened. The greater availability of a former luxury item persuaded people they were improving their living standards by consuming more and more of it. During the nineteenth century, the custom developed in Western countries to end meals with desserts—foods sweetened with sugar.

WHY DID demand for sugar steadily accelerate in Western societies from the sixteenth century to the present?

Sugar was both raised and processed on plantations such as this one in Brazil.
© Hulton-Deutsch Collection/CORBIS

like goods, not passengers. Their food was bad. Disease ran rampant among them, and huge numbers died on the crossing. The trade thrived, however, for it was cheaper to import new slaves than to create living conditions that would allow children born in slavery to grow to adulthood. Mortality rates for slaves on plantations were such that more and more Africans had to be enslaved simply to keep the labor force at a consistent level.

Transportation and sale broke up traditional family structures, which slaves found difficult to reestablish. More males than females were imported, and slave populations developed internal divisions. The most valuable slaves were those who had been enslaved for several years or who were descendants of earlier generations of slaves. They were assumed to be more accustomed to and accepting of their lot in life than newcomers. New slaves were "seasoned" in the West Indies for sale to North American plantations. The process involved assigning them new names, teaching them new work skills, and equipping them with some knowledge of a European language.

Language and Culture Plantations were situated in relatively isolated rural settings, but slaves on neighboring plantations had opportunities to contact one another and sustain some elements of their native cultures. From the West Indies southward, African languages tended to be spoken by more people than the European colonial tongues. The regional dialects that gradually developed combined African and European languages.

Slaves on large plantations organized themselves into "nations" on the basis of language. They shared similar, although not identical, ties with various regions in West Africa and probably felt a greater solidarity in the Americas than they would have had they still been in Africa. The nations helped some slaves preserve aspects of their ancestral religions, one of which was Islam. The nations appointed leaders and established governments to provide their members with assistance, and the languages they preserved proved useful when slaves wished to communicate things they did not want their masters to understand—particularly when revolts were being organized.

Slaves on the plantations of the American South were the chattel property of their masters and their lives were grim. Some artists sought to disguise this harsh reality by depicting the lighter moments of slave society, as in this scene of slaves dancing.
Getty Images Inc.—Hulton Archive Photos

Daily Life   Conditions of life for slaves on plantations differed from colony to colony. Slaves in Portuguese areas had the least legal protection. In the Spanish colonies, the church tried to provide some help for black slaves, but it was more interested in Native Americans. In the seventeenth century, laws governing slavery were enacted in the British and the French colonies, but they provided only the most limited protection. Their chief purpose was to head off the slave revolts all slave owners feared. Slave masters could whip slaves and inflict exceedingly harsh corporal punishment. Slaves were forbidden to gather in large groups lest they plot against their masters. The marriages of slaves were usually not recognized, and the children of slaves inherited the servile status of their parents. Slave families could be separated by their owners, and investment in their welfare (in their food and shelter) was proportional to the market value of their labor. It was usually cheaper to replace them than to maintain them. Some scholars have pointed out that slaves lived better in some areas than others, but all slaves led difficult lives under conditions that did not vary significantly.

    17.2
Demands from a Slave Rebellion

Conversion to Christianity   The Africans who were transported to the Americas were, like the Native Americans, mostly converted to Christianity. In the Spanish, French, and Portuguese domains, they became Roman Catholics; in the English colonies, Protestants. Although some aspects of African cultures survived in muted forms, religious conversion was part of a process that imposed a crushing set of European values on non-Europeans.

European Racial Attitudes   Many Europeans considered Africans savages and looked down on them because they were slaves. Many Western cultures attached negative connotations to blackness and this promoted a racism used to justify slavery. Racial arguments legitimating slavery became more insistent in the nineteenth century, but the fact that slaves could be differentiated physically from the rest of the population was fundamental to the maintenance of slavery and to the creation of the racial prejudices that plague the modern West.

QUICK REVIEW

Slaves' Lives
- Conditions on plantations varied from colony to colony
- Slave masters had all but unlimited power over slaves
- Many African slaves converted to Christianity

The American societies that were totally dependent on slave labor and racial differences were something new in both European and world history. Every nation where this form of plantation slavery once existed still struggles with its long-term effects.

MID-EIGHTEENTH-CENTURY WARS

HOW WERE the wars in the mid-eighteenth century global conflicts?

Europe tended toward instability in the mid-eighteenth century, for the statesmen of the era viewed warfare as the accepted means for building a nation. No country believed that it was its duty to prevent war or maintain peace. Wars were fought by professional military men. Because civilians were rarely drawn into them, a fear that a war might spark a domestic, political, or social upheaval seldom restrained a ruler. Peace was viewed as an opportunity to prepare for inevitable battles over territory and trade monopolies. The great rivalries of the age played out in two arenas: the overseas empires, and central and eastern Europe.

THE WAR OF JENKINS'S EAR

The challenge that English smugglers, shippers, and pirates mounted to Spain's monopoly of West Indian trade came to a head in the late 1730s. The Treaty of Utrecht (1713) granted Great Britain two privileges that gave its traders and smugglers entry to the markets of the Spanish Empire. One was a thirty-year *asiento* (contract) to furnish slaves to the Spanish, and the other was the right to send one ship a year to the trading fair at Portobello, a major Caribbean seaport on the Panamanian coast. When the British took advantage of these arrangements to send additional vessels to resupply, under cover of darkness, the one that was authorized to trade in Portobello, the Spanish government began to board English vessels looking for contraband.

During one such boarding operation in 1731 there was a fight, and a Spaniard cut off the ear of an English captain named Robert Jenkins. Jenkins preserved his severed ear in a jar of brandy, and in 1738, he exhibited it before the British Parliament as an illustration of the atrocities that British merchants in the West Indies were alleged to suffer at the hands of the Spanish. Sir Robert Walpole (1676–1745), the British prime minister, succumbed to the demands of powerful commercial interests and, late in 1739, he declared war on Spain. Continental European politics turned this, a seemingly minor skirmish, into a series of wars that lasted until 1815.

THE WAR OF THE AUSTRIAN SUCCESSION (1740–1748)

Maria Theresa Preserves the Habsburg Empire   In December 1740, Frederick II, the new ruler of Prussia, took advantage of the death of the Habsburg emperor, Charles VI, to annex the Austrian province of Silesia. His move upset the continental balance of power as established by the Treaty of Utrecht, and it could have triggered the collapse of the Habsburg Empire by encouraging other states to prey on its lands. The great achievement of Maria Theresa, the twenty-three-year-old woman who inherited Charles's throne, was not the reconquest of Silesia, which eluded her, but the preservation of her empire.

Maria Theresa's youth and heroism won her some support, but so did the privileges she granted the nobility. She preserved the Habsburg Empire by sacrificing the power of its central government. Hungary, for instance, remained loyal, because its Magyar nobles were promised considerable autonomy—the kind of promise that was made when emperors were weak and ignored when they were strong.

OVERVIEW   EIGHTEENTH-CENTURY CONFLICTS

Date	War	Participants	Factors
1739	The War of Jenkins's Ear	Great Britain vs. Spain	Sparked by British captain Robert Jenkins's account of atrocities inflicted on British merchants by Spaniards
1740–1748	The War of the Austrian Succession	Prussia and France vs. Austria and Great Britain	France and Great Britain were dragged into this war after Prussia seized an Austrian province
1756–1763	The Seven Years' War	France and Austria vs. Prussia	Prussia was aided financially by Great Britain in this war that continued in America between France and Britain
1776–1783	The American Revolution	Great Britain vs. Colonial America	Fought for American independence from Great Britain; France and Spain joined the colonists before war's end

France Draws Great Britain into the War   French intervention in the war between Prussia and Austria brought Britain and Spain into the conflict. France's long-standing hostility to the Habsburgs persuaded Louis XV's elderly first minister, Cardinal Fleury (1653–1743), to support Prussia against Austria. This proved to be a fateful decision, for France's aid helped Prussia consolidate a powerful German state that was one day to endanger France.

Great Britain entered the war to prevent France from taking the Low Countries away from Austria, and in 1744, France backed Spain against Britain in the New World. As the war spread beyond the Continent, it taxed everyone's resources, and in 1748, the combatants declared a stalemate. The Treaty of Aix-la-Chapelle restored peace in Europe but not America. Clashes between French and English settlers in the Ohio River valley and upper New England (America's French and Indian War) continued.

THE "DIPLOMATIC REVOLUTION" OF 1756

A dramatic shift of alliances set the stage for the next war. Frederick II feared that Russia had designs on Prussian territory, and he hoped to head off invasion by winning a promise of support from Great Britain. The Convention of Westminster, which the two powers signed in 1756, was intended to prevent foreign troops from entering the Germanies, but it alarmed Maria Theresa. Great Britain, which had been Austria's ally since the days of Louis XIV, appeared to have joined forces with Prussia, Austria's chief enemy. However, Prince Wenzel Anton Kaunitz (1711–1794), the empress's foreign minister, saw an opportunity for Austria in the fact that France did not want to be caught between Prussia and Britain. Kaunitz persuaded France to join Austria in dismembering Prussia, and in a stunning reversal of foreign policy, France committed itself to promoting the expansion of Austria's power in central Europe.

THE SEVEN YEARS' WAR (1756–1763)

Frederick the Great Opens Hostilities   In August 1756, Frederick II invaded Saxony to prevent it from joining the Franco-Austrian alliance against Prussia, and his attack hastened the thing it was intended to prevent. Within a few months, France and Austria had persuaded Sweden, Russia, and many small German states

The English artist Francis Hayman in 1760 portrayed the victory in 1757 of Robert Clive over the Siraj-ud-daulah, the Mughal Nawab of Bengal, at Plassey. The victory brought English domination of the Indian subcontinent for almost two centuries. Note the manner in which this English artist clearly makes the victory one of the West over the East by contrasting the English horse and the Indian elephant and the contrasting dress of the protagonists. Clive had won the battle largely through bribing many of the Nawab's troops and potential allies.

The Granger Collection, New York

QUICK REVIEW

Treaty of Paris (1763)

• Ended the Seven Years' War

• Britain gave France generous terms

• War launched Britain as a global power

---

to unite in opposition to Prussia, and the Seven Years' War was underway. Frederick's stubborn defense of his kingdom earned him the title "the Great," but fortitude alone did not save Prussia. Britain furnished considerable financial aid, and Russia withdrew from the conflict when Empress Elizabeth died in 1762. The Treaty of Hubertusburg ended the conflict in 1763 with no significant changes in prewar borders.

William Pitt's Strategy for Winning North America

While Frederick the Great was establishing Prussia as a major power, William Pitt the Elder (1708–1778) was plotting a successful strategy for strengthening Prussia's ally, Great Britain. Pitt early in his career had opposed involving Britain with the Continent, but he reversed himself in 1757 by sending huge financial subsidies to Frederick the Great. His plan was to use the German conflict to divert French resources and attention from the colonial struggle. He later boasted of having won America on the plains of Germany.

North America was Pitt's real interest, and thanks to him, the English acquired control of everything east of the Mississippi. He persuaded the American colonies to work together (as never before) and attacked French Canada with an army of 40,000 men, an army of unprecedented size for a colonial war. France could not equal England's resources, and in September 1759, Britain's general James Wolfe defeated France's lieutenant general Louis Joseph de Montcalm on the Plains of Abraham by Quebec City.

Pitt aspired to more than the conquest of French Canada. British fleets won control of islands in the French West Indies and of the sugar production that Britain needed to finance its wars. The British also took the slave trade from the French. Between 1755 and 1760, the value of French colonial commerce fell by over 80 percent. In India in 1757, the British commander, Robert Clive, routed the French at the Battle of Plassey and opened the way for the conquest of Bengal and all India. No European power had ever before enjoyed such military success on a global scale.

The Treaty of Paris of 1763

By 1763, when the Treaty of Paris ended the war, Pitt was no longer secretary of state. George III (r. 1760–1820) had replaced him with the earl of Bute (1713–1792), and Bute offered the French generous terms. Britain took all of Canada, the Ohio River valley, and the eastern half of the Mississippi River valley, but it returned to France Pondicherry and Chandernagore in India and the West Indian sugar islands of Guadeloupe and Martinique.

The battles of the Seven Years' War, which had been scattered about the globe, transformed relations among nations. Prussia kept Silesia and reduced the Habsburg Holy Roman Empire to an empty shell depending largely on Hungary. France ceased to be a great colonial power. The Spanish Empire, although still intact, was being infiltrated by the British. The British East India Company was imposing its authority on the decaying indigenous governments of India, and in North America the English were reorganizing the former French territories.

The war had launched Great Britain on its long career as a world power, but the financial burden of the campaign astounded contemporaries. Britain's search for revenue to pay off its war debts and rebuild its armies had far-ranging consequences—particularly for the British colonies of North America.

THE AMERICAN REVOLUTION AND EUROPE

WHAT WERE the causes of the American Revolution?

A merica's revolution was closely tied to events on the European continent. Taxes that Britain imposed on its colonies to pay for the Seven Years' War helped to provoke it. It became part of a larger and longer conflict between Britain and France, and it increased the financial and political difficulties of the French monarchy that led to France's revolution.

RESISTANCE TO THE IMPERIAL SEARCH FOR REVENUE

The Treaty of Paris acknowledged the existence of a British empire that, at the time (1763), had yet to be organized administratively. To win the wars that built the empire, Britain's citizens had accepted a high rate of taxation and acquired a huge national debt. Britain's American colonies had been major beneficiaries of the conflict. Therefore, Parliament concluded they should bear a greater share of its costs. (See Map 16–2.)

The British drive for revenue commenced in 1764 with the passage of the Sugar Act by the ministry of George Grenville (1712–1770). The act was designed to increase revenue from the colonies' imports by more rigorously collecting what was actually a lower tax. A year later, Parliament passed the Stamp Act, a tax on legal documents and such things as newspapers. From the British point of view, these taxes were legal because they were approved by Parliament, and they were just because the money they raised was to be spent in the colonies. Americans, however, claimed that because they were not represented in Parliament, only their colonial legislatures had the right to tax them. They also saw British control of colonial finances as a threat to the power of colonial governments.

In October 1765, a Stamp Act Congress met in America to draft a protest to the crown, and groups with names like "the Sons of Liberty" encouraged resistance. Parliament responded to the colonists' threat to boycott British imports by repealing the Stamp Act (1766), but it passed the Declaratory Act affirming its power to legislate for the colonies. The crisis set the pattern for the next ten years. Parliament would pass a law. The Americans would oppose it with reasoned arguments, economic pressure, and violence. The British would repeal the legislation, and the process

 MAP EXPLORATION

Interactive map: To explore this map further, go to
http://www.prenhall.com/kagan3/map16.2

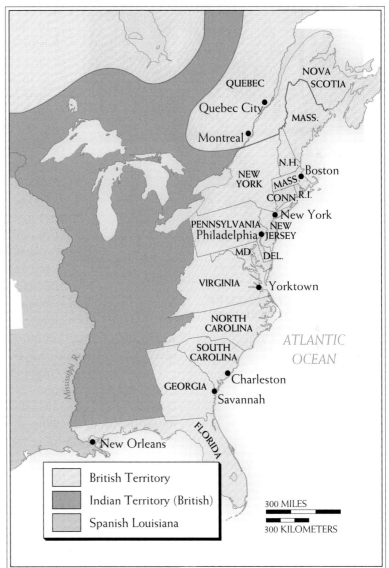

MAP 16–2

North America in 1763   In the year of the victory over France, the English colonies lay along the Atlantic seaboard. The difficulties of organizing authority over the previous French territory in Canada and west of the Appalachian Mountains would contribute to the coming of the American Revolution.

HOW COSTLY would it seem to conquer and control the territory encompassing the British colonies, former French Canada, and land east of the Mississippi River?

The BOSTONIAN'S Paying the EXCISE-MAN, or TARRING & FEATHERING

Plate 1.

Many Americans fiercely objected to the British Parliament's attempts to tax the colonies. This print of a British tax collector being tarred and feathered warned officials of what could happen to them if they tried to collect these taxes.

Philip Dawe (ca.1750–1785), "The Bostonians paying the Excise-Man or Tarring & Feathering." London, 1774. Colored Engraving. The Gilder Lehman Collection on deposit at the Pierpont Morgan Library. GL 4961.01. Photography: Joseph Zehavi. The Pierpont Morgan Library/ Art Resource, NY

Intolerable Acts   Series of laws passed by Parliament in 1774 that closed the port of Boston, reorganized the government of Massachusetts, quartered soldiers in private homes, and transferred trials of customs officials accused of crimes to England.

would begin again. Each time, tempers became more frayed and positions more irreconcilable.

THE CRISIS AND INDEPENDENCE

In 1767, Charles Townshend (1725–1767), the British finance minister, persuaded Parliament to pass a series of revenue acts relating to colonial imports. When the colonists again resisted, the ministry sent over its own customs agents to collect the taxes—and it protected those it stationed in Boston with British troops. Tensions escalated, and in March 1770, the soldiers fired on a mob. Five people died in the "Boston Massacre." In the same year, Parliament repealed all of the new taxes except one on tea.

In May 1773, Parliament passed a new law relating to the sale of tea. It lowered the price of tea by allowing the East India Company to ship tea directly to the American colonies. However, it also imposed a new tax on tea without the colonists' consent. Colonists in some cities refused to allow the tea to be unloaded; in Boston, a shipload of tea was thrown into the harbor.

The British ministry of Lord North (1732–1792) then set out to establish Parliament's authority over the colonies once and for all. During 1774, Parliament passed a series of laws that Americans dubbed the **Intolerable Acts**. The acts closed the port of Boston, reorganized the government of Massachusetts, quartered soldiers in private homes, and transferred trials of customs officials accused of crimes to England. The Quebec Act (also 1774), which extended the boundaries of Quebec to include the Ohio River valley, offered yet more provocation. It looked like an attempt to halt the spread of American concepts of liberty at the Appalachian Mountains.

Americans who opposed Britain's policies formed committees and established lines of communication throughout the colonies. They helped the colonists understand that they shared common problems—an essential precondition for unified action. In September 1774, the First Continental Congress convened in Philadelphia. Its initial purpose was to persuade Parliament to give up direct supervision of the colonies, but that proved impossible.

In April 1775, the battles of Lexington and Concord were fought. In May, a Second Continental Congress met, and in June, the colonists were defeated at Bunker Hill. The Congress still hoped to conciliate Britain, but necessity forced it to organize a government for the colonies. By August, King George III had declared the colonies in rebellion. During the ensuing winter, the circulation of *Common Sense,* a pamphlet by Thomas Paine (1737–1809), helped create consensus on the necessity of separating from Great Britain.

The Continental Congress commissioned an army and navy. In April 1776, it opened American ports to trade with all nations, and on July 4, 1776, it adopted the Declaration of Independence. Early in 1778, Benjamin Franklin (1706–1790) persuaded France to support the rebellion, and in 1779, the Spanish came to the aid of the colonies. The American Revolution widened into a European conflict that continued until George Washington defeated Lord Cornwallis at Yorktown in 1781. In 1783, the Treaty of Paris recognized Britain's thirteen former colonies as the United States of America.

AMERICAN POLITICAL IDEAS

The political ideas that led up to the American Revolution were rooted in arguments that seventeenth-century English aristocrats used to counter the claims of the Stuart kings to absolute authority. The colonists believed the English Revolution of 1688 had established fundamental liberties that belonged to all English people—those in the colonies as well as the homeland. This Whig political philosophy owed much to the writings of John Locke, but Locke's work was only part of colonial America's ideological heritage from England. Throughout the eighteenth century, a succession of political writers in Britain, the Commonwealthmen, had kept alive the radical republican ideals of the Puritan revolution. These men—especially John Trenchard and Thomas Gordon, author of *Cato's Letters*—were motivated by opposition to the governments of Sir Robert Walpole and his successors. They regarded much parliamentary taxation as nothing more than a method to finance political corruption, and they viewed standing armies as instruments of tyranny.

The Commonwealthmen were largely ignored in Great Britain, for most Britons thought theirs was the freest government in the world. Three thousand miles away in the colonies, however, the security of British liberty was less certain. Events that coincided with the start of George III's reign convinced many colonists that there was substance to the Commonwealthmen's dire warnings.

EVENTS IN GREAT BRITAIN

George III (r. 1760–1820) believed his two predecessors had been dominated by a few powerful Whig families and the ministries they controlled. He was determined, therefore, to assert his independence by choosing his own ministers and imposing his will on Parliament. He used royal patronage to buy influence with the House of Commons, and between 1761 and 1770, he tried one minister after another. Each failed to win sufficient support from the factions in the House of Commons. In 1770, the king finally found in Lord North a first minister who could handle the reins of government, and North remained in office until 1782. The Whigs denounced the king's efforts to curb the power of certain aristocrats as tyranny. George III certainly wanted to strengthen the monarchy, but he was no tyrant.

The Challenge of John Wilkes   In 1763, the various factions that opposed the king coalesced around John Wilkes (1725–1797), a London political radical, member of Parliament, and publisher of a newspaper called *The North Briton*. Wilkes used his paper to attack Lord Bute, the king's first minister, for his handling of peace negotiations with France. Bute had him arrested, but Wilkes's privileges as a member of Parliament won his release. The courts ruled that the vague warrant by which he had been arrested was illegal. The House of Commons, however, convicted him of libel and expelled him. Wilkes fled the country and was outlawed, but many saw him as a victim of political persecution.

In 1768, Wilkes returned to England and was reelected to Parliament. The House of Commons, however, bowed to the wishes of the king and refused to seat him. Although he won three subsequent elections, the House

17.7
John Adams: *Thoughts on Government*

Significant Dates from the Eighteenth Century

1713	Treaty of Utrecht
1739	War of Jenkins's Ear
1740–1748	War of the Austrian Succession
1756–1763	Seven Years' War
1763	John Wilkes challenges the British monarchy
1764	Sugar Act
1765	Stamp Act
1770	Boston Massacre
1773	Boston Tea Party
1774	First Continental Congress
1776–1783	War of the American Revolution

ignored the verdict of the electorate and seated a rival government-supported candidate. Shopkeepers, artisans, and small property owners took to the streets to support Wilkes, and aristocrats who wanted to humiliate the king also backed him. Wilkes maintained that his was the cause of English liberty, and his supporters adopted the slogan, "Wilkes and Liberty." Wilkes became lord mayor of London and was finally seated by Parliament in 1774.

The American colonists followed these developments closely, for they seemed to confirm the colonists' suspicion that the king and Parliament were conspiring against English liberty. The Wilkes affair highlighted the arbitrary power of the monarch, the corruption of the House of Commons, and the contempt of both for the electorate. These aspects of tyranny seemed, to the colonists, to be at the heart of their struggles with England.

Movement for Parliamentary Reform   The British ministry understood its American troubles were related to domestic political problems. Most residents of the British Isles could (like the colonists) have objected to being taxed without representation, for most of them were no more represented in the House of Commons than were the Americans. The Wilkes affair made it clear that many in England were prepared to challenge the king and the largely self-selected aristocratic Parliament. Wilkes's appeal to public opinion against the legally constituted political authorities and his followers' use of mass demonstrations even showed how a popular reform movement might function.

The American colonists gave Europe's leaders their clearest lesson in how restive subjects might successfully oppose tyranny. The Americans established revolutionary, but orderly, political bodies that functioned outside the existing governmental framework. They based the legitimacy of their congresses and conventions not on ancient political traditions but on a new idea: the consent of the governed.

The Yorkshire Association Movement   The American Revolution led to calls for parliamentary reform in Britain, and the reformers used the American strategy of working through extralegal associations. In northern England in 1778, Christopher Wyvil (1740–1822), a landowner and retired clergyman, initiated the Yorkshire Association Movement. Yorkshire's men of property held a mass meeting to demand moderate changes in the corrupt system of parliamentary elections. Similar groups soon appeared elsewhere and began to propose additional reforms affecting the entire government. (See "History's Voices: Major Cartwright Calls for the Reform of Parliament.") The movement faded in the early 1780s, for its leaders were reluctant to follow the example set by Wilkes and the American rebels and appeal to the masses for support.

Parliament was, however, influenced by the Association Movement. In April 1780, the Commons advocated a reduction in the power of the crown. In 1782, Parliament implemented an "economical" reform, which abolished some sources of royal patronage, and in 1783, Parliament forced Lord North to form a ministry with Charles James Fox (1749–1806), a longtime critic of the king. In the same year, the king turned to William Pitt the Younger (1759–1806) for help in creating a more pliable House of Commons. During the election of 1784, Pitt used immense amounts of royal patronage to fill the House of Commons with men friendly to the king. Efforts to reform Parliament faded, and by the mid–1780s, the king's political dominance had been restored. Its resurgence was, however, short lived. George III succumbed to mental illness, and the regency that had to be established to govern for him could not aggressively exercise royal authority.

HISTORY'S VOICES

MAJOR CARTWRIGHT CALLS FOR THE REFORM OF PARLIAMENT

During the American Revolution there were many calls in England to reform Parliament. In this pamphlet of 1777, Major John Cartwright demands that many more English citizens be allowed to vote for members of the House of Commons. He also heaps contempt on the opponents of reform.

HOW DOES Cartwright believe Britain has been deprived of its liberties?

Suffering as we do, from a deep parliamentary corruption, it is no time to tamper with silly correctives, and trifle away the life of public freedom: but we must go to the bottom of the stinking sore and cleanse it thoroughly: we must once more infuse into the constitution the vivifying spirit of liberty and expel the very last dregs of this poison. *Annual parliaments* with an *equal representation of the commons* are the only specifics in this case: and they would effect a radical cure. That a house of commons, formed as ours is, should maintain septennial elections [i.e., elections every seven years], and laugh at every other idea is no wonder. The wonder is, that the British nation which, but the other day, was the greatest nation on earth, should be so easily laughed out of its liberties. ...

Those who now claim the *exclusive* right of sending to parliament the 513 representatives for about six million souls (amongst whom are one million five hundred thousand males, *competent as electors*) consist of about two hundred and fourteen thousand persons; and 254 of these representatives are elected by 5,723. ... Their pretended rights are many of them, derived from *royal favour*; some from ancient usage and prescription; and some indeed from act of parliament; but neither the most authentic acts of royalty, nor precedent, nor prescription, nor even parliament can establish any flagrant injustice; much less can they strip one million two hundred and eighty-six thousand of an inalienable right, to vest it in a number amounting to only one-seventh of that multitude. ...

John Cartwright, *Legislative Rights of the Commonality Vindicated*, as cited in S. Maccoby, *The English Radical Tradition, 1763–1914* (London: Adam and Charles Black, 1966), pp. 32–33.

BROADER IMPACT OF THE AMERICAN REVOLUTION

As the crisis with Britain unfolded during the 1760s and 1770s, the American colonists first believed they were fighting to preserve traditional English liberties against a tyrannical king and corrupt Parliament. In the end, however, they developed a different concept of liberty. They created a nation in which popular consent (sovereignty) rather than divine law, natural law, tradition, or the will of kings was the highest legal authority. The state constitutions, Articles of Confederation, and federal Constitution (1788) they drafted showed Europeans there could be government without kings and nobles. Their novel political system could not be ignored.

Americans embraced democratic ideals, but they did not create a thoroughly democratic society. The equality of white male citizens—both before the law and in society—was endorsed. All white males were promised a chance to improve their social standing and economic lot by hard work and individual enterprise, and they alone were enfranchised. Slaves were not freed. Nor were the issues of women's rights and those of Native Americans addressed. Still, the American colonists of the eighteenth century produced a freer society than any the world had yet seen. Their revolution was a genuinely radical movement, whose influence would spread and inspire Europeans to question their traditional modes of government.

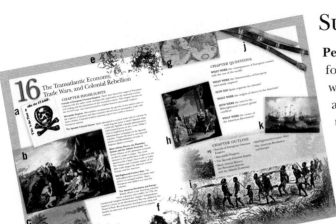

IMAGE KEY
for pages 384–385

a. Stamp Act cartoon

b. General James Wolfe (1727–1759), the British officer who captured Louisbourg and Quebec during the French and Indian War dies in battle on the Plains of Abraham above Quebec

c. Sugar Plantation

d. A luxury merchant ship © National Maritime Museum, London

e., f. A variety of tea leaves

g. Four-Hemisphere World Map. Elaborate allegorical and mythological decorations surround a map showing the Western, Northern, Eastern, and Southern Hemispheres. 1680

h. Martin van Meytens: "Kaiserin Maria Theresia mit ihrer Familie auf der Schloßterasse von Schobrunn." Kunsthistorisches Museum, Vienna, Austria

i. "To be sold as slaves." A slave coffle in an eighteenth-century print

j. Several sugarcane stems

k. Detail, Andries van Eertvelt (1590-1652), "The Return to Amsterdam of the Fleet of the Dutch East India Company in 1599."   Oil on copper. Johnny van Haeften Gallery, London, UK. The Bridgeman Art Library

SUMMARY

Periods of European Overseas Empires There have been four stages in Europe's interactions with the rest of the world: (1) by the end of the seventeenth century, discovery and settlement of the New World, introduction of the transatlantic plantation economy, and market penetration of Southeast Asia; (2) by the 1820s, mercantile empires, with resulting competition among European powers, and independence in most of the Americas; (3) in the nineteenth century, formal empires ruled directly by Europe; and (4) by the late twentieth century, decolonization. Prior to colonial independence, Europeans generally treated indigenous peoples as inferior. Ships and guns gave Europeans insurmountable advantages. This chapter covers the mercantile period.

Mercantile Empires Mercantilism, an economic theory based on the economy of scarcity, assumed the growth of one nation came at the expense of another. The goal of the mercantile system was for each European power to monopolize trade with its colonies, with the profits—in the form of gold and silver bullion—enriching each ruling country. Colonial rivalries could grow into conflicts between European nations. French-British rivalry was intense in the West Indies and in India. Dutch power in what is now Indonesia was acknowledged by other Europeans.

The Spanish Colonial System Spain attempted to impose control on trade with the colonies by restricting the American ports to which Spanish ships could sail. Smugglers, however, always found ways to carry out their work. The political system under which the Spanish colonies were administered concentrated power in the crown; local officials were appointed through royal patronage. In 1700, when the French Bourbon king Philip V took the Spanish throne, he tried to introduce effective French administrative techniques to Spain's empire. Spain was defeated in Europe's mid-eighteenth-century wars, and Charles III tried to use imperial reform and colonial trade liberalization to bolster Spain's economy. He was successful initially, but he stoked resentments that would erupt into colonial rebellion.

Black African Slavery, the Plantation System, and the Atlantic Economy The transatlantic plantation economy created social, political, and production systems unlike any others in world history. Although slavery was practiced in many other times and places, the extent to which the plantation economy depended on slave labor made it unique. The racist element in the justification for the trade in black African human beings left a cultural legacy that is still with us. The sheer volume and economic impact of the slave trade itself, and the goods produced by slave labor, make slavery one of the most important elements in the history of the Americas, and an important factor in the histories of Europe and of Africa as well.

Mid-Eighteenth-Century Wars The mid-eighteenth-century European state system encouraged warfare. Monarchs thought they could use war to further their own ends without risking the lives of their subjects or the stability of their societies. Overseas empires and central and eastern Europe saw repeated international rivalries. The 1739 British-Spanish conflict, the War of Jenkins's Ear, began a period of European warfare that lasted until 1815. Prussia, Austria, France, and other European nations fought wars that spilled over into colonial conflicts. Maria Theresa preserved the Habsburg Empire, at the cost of power sharing with the nobility and with the Hungarian Magyars. Frederick II saved Prussia, becoming "Frederick the Great." Britain's William Pitt the Elder set his country on the path to a global dominance it would enjoy for the next century and a half by deploying troops into colonial battlefields.

The American Revolution and Europe The Treaty of Paris of 1763 left Britain with the problems of financing its empire and administering vast new North American territories. Starting in 1764, Britain passed a series of taxes on the American colonies that it intended to collect more aggressively. In each case, American resistance led Britain to rescind most of the legislation. Tensions increased. In 1776, the colonists' Continental Congress declared independence from Britain. France and Spain entered the war as American allies, and the Americans' victory was ratified by the 1783 Treaty of Paris. Through this period, Britain's King George III alienated Whigs and convinced radical political theorists that he wanted to impose tyranny. The writings and examples offered by John Wilkes in Britain, and the revolutionaries in America, provided a new vocabulary for advocates of liberty and new models for free sovereign government.

REVIEW QUESTIONS

1. What were the main points of conflict between Britain and France in North America, the West Indies, and India? How was the Spanish colonial empire in the Americas organized and managed?

2. What was the nature of slavery in the Americas? How was it integrated into the economies of the Americas, Europe, and Africa? What was the plantation system?

3. What were the results of the Seven Years' War? Which countries emerged in a stronger position? Why?

4. To what extent were the colonists who began the American Revolution influenced by European ideas and political developments? What influence did their actions and arguments have on Europe?

KEY TERMS

Intolerable Acts   (p. 398)   **mercantilism**   (p. 387)

   For additional study resources for this chapter, go to:
www.prenhall.com/kagan3/chapter16

PART FOUR   ENLIGHTMENT AND REVOLUTION

POLITICS & GOVERNMENT

1713	Treaty of Utrecht
1713–1740	Frederick William I builds Prussian military
1720–1740	Walpole in England, Fleury in France
1739	War of Jenkins's Ear
1740	Maria Theresa succeeds to Habsburg throne
1740–1748	War of the Austrian Succession
1756–1763	Seven Years' War
1767	Legislative Commission in Russia
1772	First Partition of Poland
1775–1783	American Revolution
1785	Catherine the Great of Russia issues Charter of Nobility

Versailles Palace, ▶ France

1789	Gathering of the Estates General at Versailles; fall of the Bastille; Declaration of the Rights of Man and Citizen
1791	French monarchy abolished
1793	Louis XVI executed; Second Partition of Poland
1793–1794	Reign of Terror
1795	Third Partition of Poland

◀ The Boston Massacre

SOCIETY & ECONOMY

1715–1763	Colonial rivalry in the Caribbean
1733	James Kay's flying shuttle
1750s	Agricultural Revolution in Britain
1750–1840	Growth of new cities
1763	British establish dominance in India
1763–1789	Enlightened absolutist rulers seek to spur economic growth
1765	James Hargreaves's spinning jenny

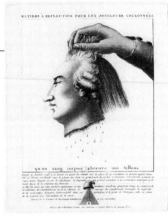

Hargreaves's Spinning Jenny ▶

▲ Execution of Louis XVI

1769	Richard Arkwright's waterframe
1773–1775	Pugachev's Rebellion
1780	Gordon riots in London
1787	Edmund Cartwright's power loom

1789–1802	Revolutionary legislation restructures French political and economic life

RELIGION & CULTURE

1721	Montesquieu, *Persian Letters*
1733	Voltaire, *Letters on the English*
1738	Voltaire, *Elements of the Philosophy of Newton*
1739	Wesley begins field preaching
1748	Hume, *Inquiry into Human Nature*
1748	Montesquieu, *Spirit of the Laws*
1750	Rousseau, *Discourse on the Moral Effects of the Arts and Sciences*
1751	First volume of Diderot's *Encyclopedia*
1762	Rousseau, *Social Contract* and *Émile*
1763	Voltaire, *Treatise on Tolerance*
1774	Goethe, *Sorrows of Young Werther*
1776	Smith, *Wealth of Nations*
1779	Lessing, *Nathan the Wise*
1781	Joseph II adopts toleration in Austria
1781	Kant, *Critique of Pure Reason*

◀ Voltaire

1789	Blake, *Songs of Innocence*
1790	Civil Constitution of the Clergy; Burke, *Reflections on the Revolution in France*
1792	Wollstonecraft, *Vindication of the Rights of Woman*
1793	France proclaims Cult of Reason

1795	The Directory established in France
1799	Napoleon named First Consul in France
1803	War resumes between Britain and France
1804	Napoleonic Code; Napoleon crowned emperor
1805	Third Coalition formed against France; battles of Trafalgar and Austerlitz
1806	Napoleon establishes the Continental System
1807	Treaty of Tilsit between France and Russia
1808	Spanish resistance to Napoleon stiffens
1812	Napoleon invades Russia, meets defeat
1814	Napoleon abdicates; Congress of Vienna opens; Louis XVIII restored in France

1815	Napoleon defeated at Waterloo
1819	Carlsbad Decrees in Germanies; Peterloo Massacre and the Six Acts, Britain
1820	Spanish Revolution begins
1821	Greek Revolution begins
1823	France intervenes in Spanish Revolution
1825	Decembrist Revolt in Russia
1829	Catholic Emancipation Act in Great Britain
1830	Revolution in France, Belgium, and Poland; Serbia gains independence
1832	Great Reform Bill in Britain
1848	Revolutions sweep across Europe

▲ *Power-Looms in an English Mill*

| 1794–1824 | Wars of independence in Latin America break the colonial system |
| 1810 | Abolition of serfdom in Prussia |

▲ *Napoleon Bonaparte*

1800–1850	British industrial dominance
1825	Stockton and Darlington Railway opens
1828–1850	First European police departments
1830–1850	Railway building in western Europe
1833	English Factory Act to protect children
1834	German *Zollverein* established
1842	Chadwick, *Report on the Sanitary Condition of the Labouring Population*
1846	Corn Laws repealed in Britain
1847	Ten Hour Act passed in Britain
1848	Serfdom abolished in Austria and Hungary

Queen Victoria's ▶
railway carriage

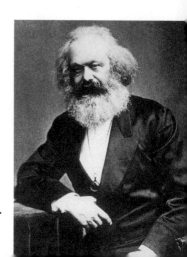

◀ *Georg Wilhelm Friedrich Hegel*

1794	France proclaims Cult of the Supreme Being
1798	Wordsworth and Coleridge, *Lyrical Ballads;* Malthus, *Essay on the Principle of Population*
1799	Schleiermacher, *Speeches on Religion to Its Cultured Despisers*
1802	Chateaubriand, *Genius of Christianity*
1802	Napoleon, Concordat with the Papacy
1806	Hegel, *Phenomenology of Mind*
1807	Fichte, *Addresses to the German Nation*
1808	Goethe, Faust, Part I
1812	Byron, *Childe Harold's Pilgrimage*

1817	Ricardo, *Principles of Political Economy*
1819	Byron, *Don Juan*
1829	Catholic Emancipation Act in Great Britain
1830–1842	Comte, *The Positive Philosophy*
1830	Lyell, *Principles of Geology*
1833	Russia begins "Official Nationality" policy
1835	Strauss, *Life of Jesus*
1840	Villermé, *Catalogue of the Physical and Moral State of Workers*
1843	Kierkegaard, *Fear and Trembling*
1848	Marx and Engels, *Communist Manifesto*

Karl Marx ▶

17 The Age of Enlightenment
Eighteenth-Century Thought

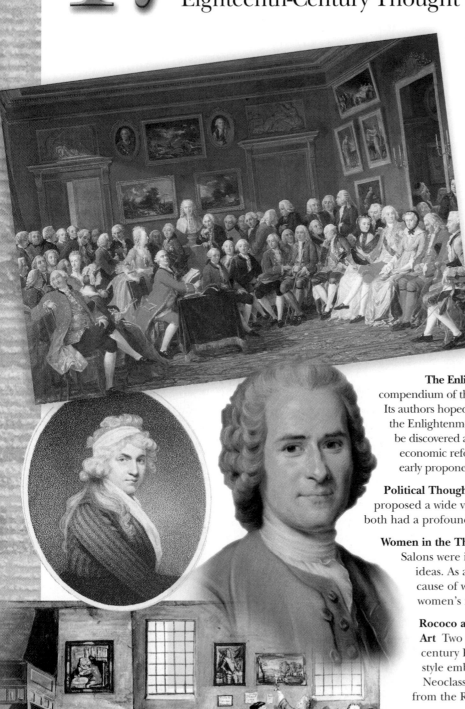

CHAPTER HIGHLIGHTS

Formative Influences on the Enlightenment
The ideas of the Enlightenment were based on the Newtonian worldview, Locke's psychology, Britain's wealth and stability, French reform, and the emerging print culture. Literary culture was generally divided between high and low.

The *Philosophes* The *philosophes* believed that wide-ranging reforms could produce better societies. The *philosophes* were not an organized group and did not agree on all issues. They all believed, however, in the centrality of reason to reform.

The Enlightenment and Religion While many *philosophes* were hostile to the church, most did not oppose religion itself. Deists believed that God set the universe in motion according to natural laws and then left it alone. *Philosophes* valued religious toleration but did not always practice it.

The Enlightenment and Society The *Encyclopedia* was a compendium of the *philosophes'* opinions on a wide variety of issues. Its authors hoped to secularize learning and spread the ideas of the Enlightenment. The *philosophes* believed that social laws could be discovered and that society could be improved. Many French economic reformers were physiocrats. Adam Smith was an early proponent of laissez-faire economic policies.

Political Thought and the *Philosophes* The French *philosophes* proposed a wide variety of reforms. Montesquieu and Rousseau both had a profound impact on future political thought.

Women in the Thought and Practice of the Enlightenment
Salons were instrumental in spreading Enlightenment ideas. As a group, the *philosophes* did little to advance the cause of women's rights. Mary Wollstonecraft placed women's rights within the Enlightenment agenda.

Rococo and Neoclassical Styles in Eighteenth-Century Art Two contrasting styles dominated eighteenth-century European art and architecture. The Rococo style embraced lavish, often lighthearted, decoration. Neoclassicism embodied a return to models drawn from the Renaissance and the ancient world.

Enlightened Absolutism Many *philosophes* were monarchists. Frederick II of Prussia, Joseph II of Austria, and Catherine the Great of Russia all incorporated Enlightenment ideas in their policies and positions. In the late eighteenth century, all three of these countries became increasingly conservative and politically repressive, a process accelerated by the French Revolution.

CHAPTER QUESTIONS

WHAT WAS the intellectual and social background of the Enlightenment?

WHO WERE the *philosophes?*

HOW DID the *philosophes* affect religious thought?

HOW DID the Enlightenment affect European society?

HOW DID *philosophes* affect political thought?

WHAT ROLE did women play in the Enlightenment?

HOW DID Rococo and neoclassicism styles reflect and contribute to the prevailing trends of the age?

WHAT WAS enlightened absolutism?

CHAPTER OUTLINE

- Formative Influences on the Enlightenment
- The *Philosophes*
- The Enlightenment and Religion
- The Enlightenment and Society

- Political Thought of the *Philosophes*
- Women in the Thought and Practice of the Enlightenment
- Rococo and Neoclassical Styles in Eighteenth-Century Art
- Enlightened Absolutism

IMAGE KEY

Image Key for pages 406–407 is on page 430.

WHAT WAS the intellectual and social background of the Enlightenment?

18.1
John Locke: Chapter 1 from *Essay Concerning Human Understanding*

tabula rasa   (a blank page) John Locke's *An Essay Concerning Human Understanding* (1690) theorized that at birth the human mind is a tabula rasa.

The modern world's faith in the possibility and desirability of change is a key intellectual inheritance from the eighteenth century's self-proclaimed Enlightenment. The leaders of the movement were convinced that human reason could comprehend the processes of nature and manipulate them to create a better world. They believed the rational order that the Scientific Revolution had discovered in the physical universe should also exist in human societies. They insisted that all traditional beliefs and institutions be exposed to rational critique, which would inevitably inspire innovation and improvement. Some of the era's monarchs caught the spirit of the age and used the power of "enlightened absolutism" to implement rational plans for reordering their subjects' lives.

FORMATIVE INFLUENCES ON THE ENLIGHTENMENT

Newtonian science, the political example set by Great Britain's stability and prosperity, France's need for reform, and the communications made possible by the rise of the so-called *print culture* were the chief factors that promoted the Enlightenment.

IDEAS OF NEWTON AND LOCKE

Isaac Newton (1642–1727) and John Locke (1632–1704) were the forerunners of the Enlightenment. Newton's theory of gravitation brought a long scientific search to a triumphant conclusion by answering questions that had been raised by the discoveries of Copernicus, Kepler, and Galileo. It provided a coherent, unified explanation for astronomical phenomena and the laws of physics. Newton was a sincere Christian, but he rejected supernaturalism and insisted the human mind could discover truth without the help of revelation. All people needed to do, he believed, was to formulate rational theories and test them by empirical observation.

The implication of Newton's work was that the universe operated like a machine, and some of his contemporaries believed mechanical explanations could also be found for human nature and society. John Locke's *An Essay Concerning Human Understanding* (1690) theorized that at birth the human mind is a **tabula rasa**, a blank page. Personality is created as the senses imprint this page with experience of the external world. Human nature is, Locke claimed, the product of environment and can, therefore, be engineered by shaping the environment that shapes it. Locke's psychology rejected the Christian doctrine that people are permanently flawed by sin and in need of divine grace to change their lives. He insisted that rational means were at hand for people to redesign themselves.

THE EXAMPLE OF BRITISH TOLERATION AND STABILITY

Newton and Locke offered a rationale and methods for reforming society, and the success of their homeland, Great Britain (the stable kingdom that developed after the Glorious Revolution of 1688), provided motivation and encouragement. Enlightened programs seemed to work in Great Britain to everyone's benefit. All religions except Unitarianism and Roman Catholicism were officially tolerated, and dissidents, if not approved of, were not actually persecuted. Speech and press were relatively free. The monarch's power was limited, for Parliament exercised sovereignty. Courts protected citizens from arbitrary action by government officials. The country's army was small, and economic activity was far less regulated than in France and other continental states. Reformers pointed out that these liberal policies, far from courting disorder, nurtured a loyal, prosperous citizenry. They may have idealized the English situation, but England's subjects enjoyed more freedoms than any of their contemporaries on the Continent.

THE EMERGENCE OF A PRINT CULTURE

The printing press contributed greatly to the success of the Protestant Reformation, but the Enlightenment was the first major movement in European history to flourish in a cultural environment created by the printed word. Books were costly, but the information they contained could be widely

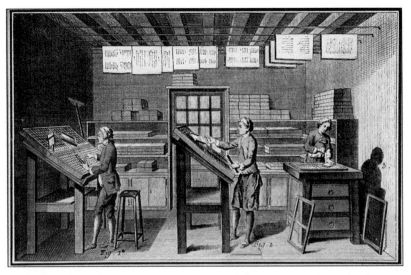

Printing shops were the productive centers for the books and newspapers that spread the ideas of the Enlightenment.

The Granger Collection

disseminated by private and public libraries and inexpensive newspapers and journals. The volume of printed material increased dramatically during the eighteenth century, and print became (and remained) the chief vehicle for the communication of ideas until the invention of the electronic media of our own day.

The growing audience for the printed word affected the choice of issues discussed in print. During the Middle Ages, the clergy were the dominant literate class, and most literature dealt with religion. As ordinary men and women learned to read, however, their secular and material interests began to be explored in print. In the seventeenth century, half the books published in Paris had religious themes; by the 1780s, only 10 percent still did.

Increasingly, members of the aristocracy and the middle class were expected to be familiar with books and secular ideas. Periodicals such as Joseph Addison and Richard Steele's *The Spectator* (founded in 1711) provided vehicles for communicating with a wide public. Secret societies, such as the movement of Freemasons that began in Britain at this time, promoted reading and debate, and people gathered in private homes or met in places such as coffeehouses for serious discussions. (See "Encountering the Past: Coffeehouses and Enlightenment.")

The expanding market for printed matter made it possible for writers, for the first time, to earn a living from the sale of their work. Print made authorship an occupation and authors celebrities. Parisian ladies sought out popular writers as honored guests for parties in their fashionable salons, and some authors (notably Alexander Pope and Voltaire) earned fortunes. There was, however, both a high and a low literary culture. The most successful authors addressed themselves to, and were accepted into, the upper levels of society, but others eked out precarious livings on whatever newspapers or journals would pay them for their pages. There were many hacks, who blamed their lack of success on society. They often took Enlightenment ideas to radical extremes and transmitted them in an embittered fashion to a lower-class audience.

The spread of printed materials created a new and increasingly influential social force: public opinion. Nothing like it seems to have existed before the middle of the eighteenth century. A book or newspaper could persuade thousands to a single point of view, and authors were accountable only to the readers to whom they marketed their works. Their ability to channel information to the public meant governments could no longer freely operate in secret or disregard the opinions of their subjects. Continental European governments sensed the

ENCOUNTERING THE PAST

COFFEEHOUSES AND ENLIGHTENMENT

Europe's first coffee imports came from the Ottoman Empire, where coffee drinking was encouraged by the Islamic prohibition of alcohol. Venice, which had close commercial ties with the Ottomans, opened the first European coffeehouse in the 1640s. By the middle of the eighteenth century, thousands of similar facilities were scattered across Europe.

Because no alcohol was served, behavior in a coffeehouse tended to be better than in a tavern, and coffeehouses provided social contexts for discussions of current events and serious issues. Proprietors of coffeehouses attracted customers by furnishing copies of newspapers and journals. Some even sponsored lectures on such topics as Newtonian physics or the relationship between science and religion. Respectable women did not frequent coffeehouses, but men of many different professional backgrounds and varying interests did. The coffeehouse provided a common meeting ground for persons interested in debating ideas and hearing the latest news and rumors from courts and governments. Although the discussion in such places often centered on issues of political liberty and freedom of thought, the great quantities of coffee and sugar their customers consumed were produced by the slaves who labored on Caribbean and Brazilian plantations.

HOW DID the coffeehouse work with the print culture to create an informed public?

Business, science, religion, and politics were discussed in London coffeehouses such as this.

political power of the new print culture and realized the threat it posed to their authority. They censored books and newspapers and imprisoned authors who offended them. The spread of the print culture revealed the power and importance of freedom of the press as an instrument for maintaining political accountability.

THE *PHILOSOPHES*

WHO WERE the *philosophes*?

The writers who created the Enlightenment were called *philosophes*—activist philosophers who advocated the use of reason and common sense to reform institutions and social conduct. They forged a new attitude that viewed change positively rather than as a threat to traditional beliefs and institutions.

A few of the philosophes were university professors, but most were free agents who could be found in London coffeehouses, Edinburgh pubs, the salons of fashionable Parisian ladies, the country houses of reform-minded nobles, and the courts of monarchs. They were not part of an organized movement and did not all advocate the same things. The chief bond among them was a common de-

philosophes Activist philosophers (creators of the Enlightenment) who advocated the use of reason and common sense to reform institutions and social conduct.

sire to reform intellectual attitudes, society, and government in ways that enhanced liberty. They were intellectuals, but intellectuals who were interested in practical projects that would transform daily life.

Many of the philosophes were born into the middle class, whence they drew the bulk of their readership. Members of the middle class had sufficient income and leisure to buy, read, and discuss the philosophes' works. Although the writers of the Enlightenment did not consciously champion the goals or causes of the middle class, they did create an intellectual ferment that undermined traditional institutions the middle class found restrictive. They taught middle-class readers how to pose pointed, critical questions, and they supported the developments that were enlarging the middle class by promoting the phenomenal economic growth that took place during the eighteenth century.

VOLTAIRE—FIRST AMONG THE *PHILOSOPHES*

Françoise-Marie Arouet, or Voltaire (1694–1778), was by far the most influential of the philosophes. His essays, histories, plays, stories, and letters made him the literary dictator of Europe. Voltaire was a Frenchman with a taste for sarcasm and a gift for satirical social criticism that were not appreciated by the government of his homeland. After a period of imprisonment in France, he spent some time in England, a country whose tolerant attitudes, moderate politics, and prosperity he admired. He contrasted England's institutions with those of France (much to England's advantage) and popularized the scientific work of Isaac Newton. He later established his home near Geneva—just across the border from France (and beyond the reach of its royal authorities).

Voltaire's most popular work is probably *Candide* (1759), an attack on war, religious persecution, and unwarranted (as he saw it) optimism about the human condition. Like most *philosophes*, Voltaire believed society could and should be improved, but he was not confident that reforms could be sustained. The Enlightenment is associated with optimistic attitudes, but its sunny outlook radiated more hopefulness than certainty.

Statue of Voltaire by Jean-Antoine Houdon (Theatre Francais, Paris).

Musee Lambinet, Versailles/Giraudon/Art Resource, NY

THE ENLIGHTENMENT AND RELIGION

Many philosophes believed Europe's churches were the chief impediment to the betterment and happiness of its people. They condemned almost all varieties of Christianity and especially Roman Catholicism, for they thought piety and religious authoritarianism hindered scientific study and the pursuit of a life guided by reason. Both Protestants and Catholics accepted the doctrine of original sin, which held that human nature was fundamentally flawed and could not be corrected. Both faiths taught that people could not better themselves; improvement was possible only if God bestowed the gift of grace on them. Both shifted their followers' focus from reforming this world to preparing for the world to come. The philosophes marshaled a great deal of historical evidence to support their argument that churches promoted intolerance and bigotry and that quarrels over obscure points of doctrine turned religious enthusiasts into torturers and warmongers.

HOW DID the *philosophes* affect religious thought?

The philosophes' critique of religion was an assault on some of Europe's most significant institutions. The churches were essential to the power structure of the Old Regime. They owned large amounts of land. The higher clergy were sons of aristocratic families active in politics. Acceptance of a country's favored religion was often a requirement for admission to its political life and full protection under its laws. Clergy branded disobedience to government authorities a sin against God and provided intellectual justification for maintaining the social and political status quo.

DEISM

The *philosophes* were not opposed to all religion. What they wanted was rational religion, a faith without fanaticism and intolerance that acknowledged the sovereign authority of reason. The *philosophes'* theology is called **deism** to distinguish it from faiths based on revelation, such as Judaism, Christianity, and Islam. John Toland, author of *Christianity Not Mysterious* (1696), was one of the pioneers of deism. He and later deists claimed religion was not a supernatural phenomenon based on mystical communications, but it was also not atheism. Deists insisted the existence of God and the precepts of God's will could be discovered by empirical observation of natural phenomena. An ordered universe implied the existence of a rational Creator, and a rational Creator would want the creatures to whom he gave reason to use it. Reason dictates that good be rewarded and evil punished, else morality makes no sense. Because this is not always the case in this life, the deists claimed that justice necessitates a life after death when appropriate rewards and punishments are meted out. Deism viewed God less as a presiding monarch than as a divine watchmaker. He built the cosmic machine and set it in motion, but he did not intervene in its operation. Newton, the deists' hero, disagreed with them on this point. He clung to the traditional belief that God interfered with the natural order to produce miracles.

Because deism was empirically based, tolerant, reasonable, and capable of encouraging virtuous living, the deists promoted it as a replacement for traditional Christianity. It would, they expected, end fanaticism, persecution, and sectarian rivalry and eliminate the clergy (whom deists blamed for fomenting much of the strife that plagued European societies). Once people realized each rational individual could arrive at the essentials of religion (knowledge of God's existence and the necessity of moral conduct) by him or herself, there would be no need for clergy and no reason to prefer one of the world's traditional religions to another. Many could be respected as embodying different elements of divine truth in different ways.

TOLERATION

The *philosophes*, whose homelands were just emerging from Europe's wars of religion, insisted that commitment to religious toleration was an essential precondition for the conduct of a virtuous life. They took it as self-evident that life on earth and human relationships should not be subordinated to religion but that secular values and considerations were more important than religious ones. In 1763, a controversial trial and brutal execution of a Huguenot named Jean Calas inspired Voltaire to pen a *Treatise on Tolerance*. Voltaire claimed the case proved the need for rational reforms that would enable the judicial process to counter Catholic and Protestant fanaticism. In 1779, Gotthold Lessing's influential play, *Nathan the Wise*, went so far as to insist that toleration be extended to all faiths, not just varieties of Christianity.

deism The *philosophes'* theology. A rational religion, a faith without fanaticism and intolerance that acknowledged the sovereign authority of reason.

RADICAL ENLIGHTENMENT CRITICISM OF CHRISTIANITY

Some *philosophes* were not content with proposing rational religion as an alternative to revelation-based faith. They took the offensive against traditional beliefs. Voltaire's *Philosophical Dictionary* (1764) pointed out inconsistencies in the biblical texts and humorously described the immoral behavior of various biblical figures. The Scottish philosopher David Hume (1711–1776), in *Inquiry into Human Nature* (1748), argued that there is no empirical evidence for the miracles central to Christian faith. In *The Decline and Fall of the Roman Empire* (1776), the English historian Edward Gibbon (1737–1794) traced the rise of Christianity to natural causes, not divine intervention. A few *philosophes* came close to advocating atheism and materialism, but theirs was a minority opinion. Most sought not the abolition of religion but its transformation into a humane force that encouraged virtuous living. As the title of a book by the German philosopher Immanuel Kant put it, they sought *Religion Within the Limits of Reason Alone.*

Dutch Jewish philosopher Baruch Spinoza.
Library of Congress

JEWISH THINKERS IN THE AGE OF ENLIGHTENMENT

Despite their pleas for toleration, the philosophes' critiques of religion often led them to attack Judaism more vehemently than Christianity. Some declared Judaism to be a more primitive faith than Christianity, and they were openly contemptuous of much of the material in the Hebrew Scriptures. The Enlightenment, therefore, could pose obstacles for Jews who struggled to come to terms with Europe's dominant Christian culture. Two Jewish intellectuals, however, made major contributions to the era's discussion of the issue of religious toleration: Baruch Spinoza (1632–1677), who lived in the Netherlands, and Moses Mendelsohn (1729–1786), a German.

Spinoza was powerfully influenced by the scientific revolution, and like his contemporary, Descartes, he believed all traditional beliefs should be subjected to rational critique and reformulation. He claimed that a thoroughly natural explanation could be found for the origin of religion and that Scripture should be subjected to the same kinds of rational interpretation as other ancient texts. In his most famous book, *Ethics,* he so closely identified God with nature that there was little distinction between them. This eliminated the need for revelation, for it implied that the scientific study of natural phenomena yielded knowledge of God. Spinoza recognized no reality beyond the natural order. Because nature is governed by the mechanistic laws of physics, he, therefore, seemed to leave no room for free will, human moral responsibility, and the survival of an individual soul after death. Both Jews and Christians accused him of being an atheist, and at the age of twenty-four his synagogue excommunicated him. The *philosophes* hailed him as a martyr to the cause of reason, and his situation enabled them to hold Judaism in contempt while also advocating more freedom for Jews to participate in European society.

Moses Mendelsohn sought to find a way for Jews to join the European mainstream without having to abandon Judaism. His most influential book, *Jerusalem, or, On Ecclesiastical Power and Judaism* (1783), made a case for religious diversity and urged governments to maintain neutrality on religious issues. He described Judaism as just one of many paths leading to knowledge of God. He argued that although different groups of believers found different sets of rituals and laws conducive to promoting ethical behavior (the chief purpose of religion, according to the

QUICK REVIEW

Baruch Spinoza (1632–1677)

- Dutch Jewish thinker who was influenced by the scientific revolution
- Closely identified God and nature
- Recognized no reality beyond the natural order

Topkapi Palace, Istanbul. Inside the imperial harem, a sanctuary from the outside world, this elegant room was used to entertain the sultan, who watched the proceedings from his large throne.

Tony Souter © Dorling Kindersley

philosophes), this was no reason to deny civil rights to some of them. Not only should different faiths tolerate each other in the civil community, but each should tolerate a wide diversity of opinions within its own ranks and rely on the fundamental rationality of human beings to work things out.

ISLAM IN ENLIGHTENMENT THOUGHT

There were few Muslims in Europe outside the Balkan peninsula. Europeans' knowledge of the faith came primarily from books that were, with rare exceptions, hostile to Islam and misleading. Islam was seen as a heretical rival to Christianity, a false religion that promoted carnality and worshiped a false prophet. The Qur'an does describe heaven as a place of sensuous delights, and Islamic law authorizes polygamy. But Islam is decidedly not "Muhammadanism"— the worship of Muhammad. It dismisses as blasphemy any claim that Muhammad was divine.

Several university chairs for the study of Arabic were established in the seventeenth century, but better knowledge of Islamic sources did not produce more sympathetic scholarship. Well-informed reference works and histories began to appear at the end of the seventeenth century and the first English translation of the Qur'an in 1734. However, Islam continued to be represented as a faith that virtually embodied fanaticism.

Philosophes both damned and praised Islam. Some, like Voltaire, saw it as an example of the kind of fanaticism they so opposed in Christianity. The deist John Toland contended that Islam was actually a form of Christianity that derived from early Christian writings. The historian Edward Gibbon (1737–1794) contrasted Christianity's role in bringing down the Roman Empire with Islam's success at conquering and ruling a vast territory. Some commentators noted with approval the Qur'an's emphasis on charitable work and Islam's historical record of tolerance for other faiths. Expressions of empathy for Islam were, however, few. One of the best informed among them was a woman, Lady Mary Wortley Montague (1689–1762), wife of England's ambassador to the Ottoman court (1716–1718). She found much to praise in Ottoman society—the practice of vaccination against smallpox, magnificent architecture, and even the freedoms enjoyed by upper-class Turkish women. Her published work, *Turkish Embassy Letters*, maintained that a great deal of what was believed in Europe about Islam was simply wrong.

Muslims, for their part, showed little interest in western Europe. Few traveled there, and Ottoman scholars paid scant attention to the work of their European colleagues. The Islamic religious establishment insisted that God's revelations to Muhammad superceded Christianity and that, therefore, the Islamic world had nothing to learn from Christian Europe.

HOW DID the Enlightenment affect European society?

18.4
The *Encyclopédie*

THE ENLIGHTENMENT AND SOCIETY

THE *ENCYCLOPEDIA*

In the middle of the eighteenth century, one of the greatest monuments of the Enlightenment began to appear, the *Encyclopedia* edited by Denis Diderot (1713–1784) and Jean le Rond d'Alembert (1717–1783). The first of its seventeen volumes of text and eleven volumes of plates (illustrations) was issued in 1751 and the last in 1772. About 16,000 copies of various editions were sold before 1789.

All the major French philosophes were invited to contribute to the *Encyclopedia,* and more than a hundred authors collaborated on its production.

It brought together the most advanced ideas of its day—critiques of religion, government, and philosophy—and made a collective plea for reform. This annoyed French officials, and they attempted to censor it and halt its publication. Contributors to the *Encyclopedia*, however, learned to avoid censure by hiding controversial ideas in obscure articles or by cloaking them with irony.

The project was intended to secularize learning and undermine intellectual assumptions that lingered from the Middle Ages and the Reformation. Articles on politics, ethics, and society ignored divine law and concentrated on practical issues that affect human well-being. Classical antiquity more than Christianity shaped the ideas advanced by the *Encyclopedia*. Its authors implied that improvements in the human condition depended not on pleasing God or following divine commandments but on developing the earth's resources and living at peace with neighbors. The *Encyclopedia* spread abroad the Enlightenment's confidence that the good life was to be achieved by applying reason to human relationships.

BECCARIA AND REFORM OF CRIMINAL LAW

The *philosophes* believed a rational examination of society would reveal laws for human relationships similar to those that governed natural phenomena. Although the term did not appear until later, the idea of *social science* originated with the Enlightenment. *Philosophes* hoped that by discovering the laws that made societies function they could stamp out crime and cruelty. Like most people, however, the *philosophes* had blind spots. Their reform proposals assumed a world dominated by males and focused mostly on men. With few exceptions, they showed little interest in bettering woman's lot.

A utilitarian philosophy that sought to maximize happiness in this life was characteristic of most of the Enlightenment programs for social reform. The work of Cesare Beccaria (1738–1794), author of *On Crimes and Punishments* (1764), was typical. Beccaria argued that crimes should be thought of as transgressions of the laws of nature and not of someone's concept of God's will. The purpose of law, Beccaria maintained, was not to impose a divinely mandated standard of conduct but to secure the greatest happiness for the greatest number of people. The intent of punishment should be deterrence, not vengeance—which meant both torture and capital punishment should be outlawed.

THE PHYSIOCRATS AND ECONOMIC FREEDOM

Mercantilist principles, which recommended the use of legislation to protect a country's trade from foreign competition, informed the economic policies of most eighteenth-century European nations. However, many *philosophes* (most notably France's *physiocrats*) opposed mercantilism. Their leaders, François Quesnay (1694–1774) and Pierre Dupont de Nemours (1739–1817), argued that a government's intervention in a state's economy should be limited to protecting property and ensuring the rights of owners to use it freely. Their Enlightenment faith in rational efficiency prevented them from endorsing the radical individualism this seemed to imply. They supported, for instance, the consolidation of small peasant holdings into large, scientifically managed farms.

Denis Diderot was the heroic editor of the *Encylopedia,* published in seventeen volumes of text and eleven volumes of prints between 1751 and 1772. Through its pages many of the chief ideas of the Enlightenment reached a broad audience of readers.

Réunion des Musées Nationaux/Art Resource, NY

18.7
Adam Smith: Division
of Labor

ADAM SMITH ON ECONOMIC GROWTH AND SOCIAL PROGRESS

Adam Smith's *Inquiry into the Nature and Causes of the Wealth of Nations* (1776) was the Enlightenment's most important contribution to the field of economics. Smith believed economies should be left alone to function according to nature's laws. He urged the abolition of mercantilism's navigation acts, bounties, tariffs, trade monopolies, and regulations governing labor and manufacturing. Mercantilists insisted these policies increased the wealth of one state by confiscating the riches of others, but Smith claimed their real effect was to hinder economic growth for everyone.

The mercantilists assumed that the earth's resources were limited and a country could acquire wealth only at the expense of others. Smith challenged this dogma. He insisted the resources of nature were boundless and existed to be exploited for the enrichment of humankind. Poverty could be abolished, he maintained, if individuals were freed to pursue their self-interest. Smith believed each person would find a way to prosper if he or she had a free hand to serve the needs of others in an open market. Freedom would stimulate innovation and create an economy that expanded and provided greater resources for everyone. Although Smith is often labeled a **laissez-faire** economist, he was not opposed to all government intervention in economic activity. The state, he believed, should provide schools, armies, navies, and roads, and it should fund commercial ventures that were desirable but beyond the means of private enterprise.

When Smith wrote, the population of the world was smaller, its people poorer, and the quantity of undeveloped resources per capita much greater than now. For Smith and his contemporaries in the eighteenth century, improvement of the human condition seemed to demand and to justify uninhibited exploitation of nature. Only recently has concern for the environment forced a rethinking of this position.

Smith's *The Wealth of Nations* helped ground another assumption that later generations of Europeans came to question. Smith theorized that all societies pass through four stages of economic development, each associated with a level of civilization. Nomadic hunters and gatherers are the most barbarous. Herding societies are somewhat more civilized (for they at least recognize the concept of private property). Farmers are superior to herders, but civilization is fully realized only by commercial societies that practice extensive manufacture and trade. The *four-stage theory* provided Europeans with a scale by which to rate the progress of all other peoples on earth. Because it maintained that the European form of commercial life was the highest manifestation of civilization, it encouraged Europeans to look down on everyone else and to assume it was their mission to "civilize" the world by imposing Europe's values and institutions everywhere. This was an excellent justification for colonial exploitation.

POLITICAL THOUGHT OF THE *PHILOSOPHES*

*M*ost *philosophes* found something to criticize in the political institutions of their homelands, but the French were particularly motivated. The most important political debates of the Enlightenment took place in France, but they produced no consensus. The French *philosophes* advocated everything from reformed aristocracy, to democracy, to absolute monarchy.

HOW DID the *philosophes* affect political thought?

laissez-faire Policy of noninterference, especially the policy of government noninterference in economic affairs or business.

MONTESQUIEU AND *SPIRIT OF THE LAWS*

Charles Louis de Secondat, Baron de Montesquieu (1689–1755), was a lawyer, a noble of the robe, a member of a provincial *parlement*, and a fellow of the Bordeaux Academy of Science. Although he was comfortably ensconced within the bosom of the French establishment, he favored reform. In 1721, he denounced the cruelty and irrationality of European society in *The Persian Letters*, a collection of satirical epistles purportedly written by two Persian tourists to explain European behavior to their friends at home.

In 1748, he published *Spirit of the Laws*, perhaps the single most influential book of the century. To research it, Montesquieu used the empirical methods of the new science. He compared the political institutions of both ancient and modern states and concluded from his study that no single set of laws could apply to all peoples at all times and in all places. Numerous variables had to be taken into account to determine the best political system for a particular country. Size, population, social and religious customs, economic structures, traditions, and climate all helped determine whether a land should have a monarchy, a republic, or something else. Montesquieu anticipated by a century the discipline now known as *sociology*.

Montesquieu believed France would be best served by a limited monarchy, a government in which groups of citizens had rights that curtailed the power of their ruler. He pointed to the *parlements*, the aristocratic courts, as an example of the kind of political associations he thought could protect the rights of Frenchmen. By championing these aristocratic bodies, he seemed to endorse political conservativism, but he chose them because he considered them the most effective available instruments for reforming a monarchy whose authority had become oppressive and inefficient.

One of Montesquieu's most influential ideas was that power ought to be divided among separate branches of a government. He drew this insight from Britain, where executive authority was vested in a king, legislative power in Parliament, and judicial oversight in a system of independent courts. Montesquieu assumed that any two of these branches could check the actions of the third and this would prevent any one of them from ever becoming oppressive. He failed, however, to understand how patronage and electoral corruption functioned to deliver Britain's government into the hands of a few powerful aristocrats. He was also unaware of emerging developments that would subordinate the British monarch to Parliament.

Montesquieu's description of the British system was not accurate, but he did suggest how constitutional limits might be placed on monarchs by independent legislatures. Having set out to defend the French aristocracy, Montesquieu ended by inspiring the formation of liberal democracies.

ROUSSEAU: A RADICAL CRITIQUE OF MODERN SOCIETY

Jean-Jacques Rousseau (1712–1778) was a troubled genius who was at odds with the other *philosophes*. They assumed all that was needed to make people happy and life worth living was to produce more goods and consume more of the fruits of the earth. Rousseau raised challenging questions about the meaning of life and the role of consumption.

Rousseau despised societies that valued commerce and industry as the most important human activities. His *Discourse on the Moral Effects of the Arts and Sciences* (1750) charged Europe's materialistic civilization with having corrupted human nature, and his *Discourse on the Origin of Inequality* (1755) traced society's problems to the tendency of commerce to produce an uneven distribution of property.

OVERVIEW — MAJOR WORKS OF THE ENLIGHTENMENT AND THEIR PUBLICATION DATES

Date	Work	Author
1670	*Theologico-Political Treatise*	Spinoza
1677	*Ethics*	Spinoza
1687	*Principia Mathematica*	Newton
1690	*Essay Concerning Human Understanding*	Locke
1696	*Christianity Not Mysterious*	Toland
1721	*Persian Letters*	Montesquieu
1733	*Letters on the English*	Voltaire
1738	*Elements of the Philosophy of Newton*	Voltaire
1748	*Spirit of the Laws*	Montesquieu
1748	*Inquiry into Human Nature*	Hume
1750	*Discourse on the Moral Effects of the Arts and Sciences*	Rousseau
1751	*Encyclopedia* (Vol. 1)	Edited by Diderot
1755	*Discourse on the Origin of Inequality*	Rousseau
1759	*Candide*	Voltaire
1762	*Social Contract* and *Emile*	Rousseau
1763	*Treatise on Tolerance*	Voltaire
1764	*Philosophical Dictionary*	Voltaire
1764	*On Crimes and Punishments*	Beccaria
1776	*Decline and Fall of the Roman Empire*	Gibbon
1776	*Wealth of Nations*	Smith
1779	*Nathan the Wise*	Lessing
1783	*Jerusalem, or, On Ecclesiastical Power and Judaism*	Mendelsohn
1792	*Vindication of the Rights of Woman*	Wollstonecraft
1793	*Religion Within the Limits of Reason Alone*	Kant

Rousseau did not limit his critiques to economics. He also assaulted popular political ideas. Most eighteenth-century political theorists assumed society was merely a collection of individuals, each of whom was motivated by personal, self-centered goals. They believed the best way to improve society was to liberate these individuals from undue restraint by government. Rousseau picked up the stick from the other end. In *The Social Contract* (1762) he argued that society is more important than its individual members, for it determines their options. Only a relationship to a larger community creates the moral environment in which individuals are capable of significant action. The true task of a reformer, therefore, is to create the kind of community that inculcates people with the highest level of morality.

A society that was an aggregate of competing individuals, who each sought selfish independence, was not, in Rousseau's opinion, an ideal community. He envisioned a world in which individuals found personal freedom by serving group interests. He thought the ends of the individual and the group could be reconciled if freedom was conceived as obedience to democratically enacted laws that represented the general will. Rousseau believed the will of the majority of informed citizens was always right and always consistent with real freedom. This faith led him to the notorious conclusion that some people have to be forced to be free. Rousseau's ideal state was a direct democracy that collectively suppressed dissidents.

Because Rousseau rejected the eighteenth-century cult of the individual and the fruits of selfishness, his impact on his contemporaries was slight. Too many people were either making or hoping to make money to appreciate his criticism of commercial values. Rousseau proved, however, to be one of the Enlightenment figures to whose thought later generations returned. He inspired many of the leaders of the French Revolution, and he influenced most of the writers of the nineteenth and twentieth centuries who were critical of the general tenor and direction of Western societies.

ENLIGHTENED CRITICS OF EUROPEAN EMPIRE

Most European thinkers associated with the Enlightenment favored the extension of European empires across the world. Although some commentators criticized European civilization and excessive economic regulation of the empires, on the whole, most believed European civilization to be superior to be superior to that of other cultures. However, a few Enlightenment voices—most notably Denis Diderot, Immanuel Kant, and Johann Gottlieb Herder—criticized European empires on moral grounds, especially the conquest of the Americas, the treatment of Native Americans, and the enslavement of Africans on the two American continents. (See "History's Voices: Denis Diderot Condemns European Empires.")

Three ideas in particular provided the grounds for this criticism. Kant, Diderot, and Herder argued for a form of shared humanity that the sixteenth-century conquerors had ignored. To these thinkers, no single definition of human nature could be made, and all peoples, whatever their appearance, deserved respect simply because they were human. In addition, some writers argued that non-European cultures should be respected and understood rather than destroyed. Herder, for example, contended that Europe did not have the sole standard for culture. This outlook, which would later be known as cultural relativism, accepted that different societies could develop as humans in culturally different ways. Another related idea asserted that each culture possessed its own intrinsic value that made simple comparisons impossible. These ideas, however, remained isolated from Enlightenment thought and would not be strongly revived until the close of the nineteenth century.

WOMEN IN THE THOUGHT AND PRACTICE OF THE ENLIGHTENMENT

WHAT ROLE did women play in the Enlightenment?

Aristocratic women, especially in France, hosted gatherings in their salons (drawing rooms) that were crucial to the careers of philosophes. Politically well-connected women, such as Madame Geoffrin, Mademoiselle de

HISTORY'S VOICES

DENIS DIDEROT CONDEMNS EUROPEAN EMPIRES

*S*ome of the writings of Denis Diderot, who is most famous as the editor of the Encyclopedia, *were published without being directly attributed to him. Among these were his criticisms of the European colonial empires that had arisen since the Spanish encounter with the New World. Diderot particularly condemned the inhumane treatment of the native populations of the Americas, the greed all Europeans displayed, and the various forms of forced labor.*

WHAT IS the basis for Diderot's view that Europeans have behaved tyrannically?

Let the European nations make their own judgment and give themselves the name they deserve. ... Their explorers arrive in a region of the New World unoccupied by anyone from the Old World, and immediately bury a small strip of metal on which they have engraved these words: *This country belongs to us.* And why does it belong to you?

...You have no right to the natural products of the country where you land, and you claim a right over your fellow men. Instead of recognizing this man as a brother you only see him as a slave, a beast of burden. Oh my fellow citizens! You think like that and you behave like that; and you have ideas of justice, a morality, a holy religion ... in common with those whom you treat so tryannically. This reproach should especially be addressed to the Spaniards.

* * *

Beyond the Equator a man is neither English, Dutch, French, Spanish, nor Portuguese. He retains only those principles and prejudices of his native country which justify or excuse his conduct. He crawls when he is weak; he is violent when strong; he is in a hurry to acquire, in a hurry to enjoy, and capable of every crime which will lead him most quickly to his goals. He is a domestic tiger returning to the forest; the thirst for blood takes hold of him once more. This is how all the Europeans, every one of them, indistinctly, have appeared in the countries of the New World. There they have assumed a common frenzy—the thirst for gold.

* * *

The Spaniard, the first to be thrown up by the waves onto the shores of the New World, thought he had no duty to people who did not share his color, customs, or religion. He saw in them only tools for his greed, and he clapped them in irons. These weak men, not used to work, soon died in the foul air of the mines, or in other occupations which were virtually as lethal. Then people called for slaves from Africa. Their number has gone up as more land has been cultivated. The Portuguese, Dutch, English, French, Danes, all the nations, free or subjected, have without remorse sought to increase their fortune in the sweat, blood and despair of these unfortunates. What a horrible system!

Denis Diderot, *Political Writings*, John Hope Mason and Robert Wokler. eds., (Cambridge: Cambridge University Press, 1998) pp. 177, 178, 186.

Lespinasse, and Madame de Tencin, helped *philosophes* make useful contacts. Association with a fashionable salon enhanced a *philosophe*'s social status and added luster to his ideas and sales to his books. A powerful patroness might also provide him with money and protection from persecution. Madame de Pompadour, the mistress of Louis XV, countered attacks on *philosophes* and helped defeat efforts to censor the *Encyclopedia*.

Despite their ties with learned women, few *philosophes* could be called feminists. Many advocated broader educations for women and rejected the ascetic view of sexuality that was part of the traditional religious training given girls. Montesquieu's *The Persian Letters*, for instance, devoted considerable space to condemning the restrictions European society placed on women. Montesquieu denied that women are naturally inferior to men, and he urged expansion of their social roles. However, although his *Spirit of the Laws* supported the right of divorce and opposed laws that oppressed women, it recommended a dominant position for husbands in marriage and upheld the ideal of chastity for women.

The *Encyclopedia* suggested some ways to improve women's lives, but women's issues did not appear on its reform agenda. The Encyclopedists were almost all male, and most of the articles that discussed women emphasized their physical weakness and inferiority (liabilities usually attributed to menstruation and child-bearing). Women were invariably viewed in the context of the family—in roles as daughters, wives, and mothers. Child rearing was said to be their chief occupation. The sexual double standard was never questioned, and some of the *Encyclopedia*'s contributors opposed social equality for women. The *Encyclopedia*'s articles convey the impression that women were reared to be frivolous and indifferent to serious issues, but the *Encyclopedia*'s illustrations show many women engaged in important economic activity. Many of these were working-class women, a group largely ignored in the *Encyclopedia*'s articles.

Rousseau, the most radical of the Enlightenment's political theorists, held extremely conservative opinions on gender. His novel *Emile* (1762) stressed the differences between males and females and recommended that women's educations center on duties relating to the bearing and rearing of children. Rousseau wanted to exclude women from public affairs and confine them to the home. He considered women to be inferior to men in every respect except the capacity for feeling and loving. He claimed their chief duty was to make themselves pleasing to men.

In spite of these views and his ill treatment of the many women who bore his many children, Rousseau won a vast female following. Women responded to his appreciation of their feelings and his proclamation of the importance of their vocations as wives and mothers. He accorded them a degree of dignity in the domestic sphere that they were denied in public life. The praise he showered on female nurturing motivated thousands of upper-class women to lay claim to a significant social role by breast-feeding their children rather than putting them out to wet nurses.

In 1792, *A Vindication of the Rights of Woman*, by Mary Wollstonecraft (1759–1797), indicted Rousseau and the philosophes for failing to follow through on the Enlightenment's commitment to the rational reform of society. Wollstonecraft (who, like so many women of her day, died of puerperal fever) argued that to confine women to the home because of their supposed physical limitations was to condemn them to sexual slavery and make them victims of male tyranny. She insisted that denying women good educations impeded the progress of all humanity. Wollstonecraft broadened the reform agenda of the Enlightenment by demanding for women the freedom that the *philosophes* had, for more than a century, been claiming for men.

Mary Wollstonecraft in *A Vindication of the Rights of Woman* defended equality of women with men on the grounds of men and women sharing the capacity of human reason.

CORBIS/Bettmann

ROCOCO AND NEOCLASSICAL STYLES IN EIGHTEENTH-CENTURY ART

Two contrasting styles dominated eighteenth-century European art and architecture. The **Rococo** style embraced lavish, often lighthearted decoration with an emphasis on pastel colors and the play of light. **Neoclassicism** embodied a return to figurative and architectural models drawn from the Renaissance and the ancient world. The Rococo became associated with Old

HOW DID Rococo and Neoclassicism styles reflect and contribute to the prevailing trends of the age?

Rococo   Style that embraced lavish, often lighthearted decoration with an emphasis on pastel colors and the play of light.

Neoclassicism   Style that embodied a return to figurative and architectural models drawn from the Renaissance and the ancient world.

The color, the light, and the elaborate decorative details associated with rococo style are splendidly exemplified in the Imperial Hall (*Kaisarsaal*) built in Würzburg, Bavaria, according to the design of Balthasar Neumann (1687–1753).

Dorothea Zwicker-Berberich / Art Resource, NY

Regime aristocracies, while Neoclassicism recalled republican values that implicitly criticized the Old Regime and that, late in the century, the French Revolution and Napoleon embraced.

The Rococo style originated in France after Louis XIV's death in 1715, when aristocrats spent less time at Versailles and more time in Paris, where they built houses known as *hôtels*. Compensating for the relatively small scale of these mansions, designers used light colors to make interiors seem brighter and more spacious. In such aristocratic settings, with art that emphasized leisure, romance, and seduction, fashionable Parisian hostesses held salons attended by *philosophes*. Paintings included scenes of elegant parties in lush gardens and, in the case of *Pilgrimage to Isle of Cithera* by Jean-Antoine Watteau (1684–1721), young lovers. Other artists such as Francois Boucher (1700–1770) and Jean-Honoré Fragonard (1732–1806) produced works of female nudes and men and women in sexually suggestive poses.

Rococo also became known as the Style of Louis XV and was associated the monarchy, court, and aristocracy with frivolity and decadence. The style spread across Europe for use in the design of public buildings and churches. The Imperial Hall (*Kaisarsall*) in Würzburg, Bavaria, for example, boasted an elaborate design by Balthasar Neumann (1687–1753), with ceilings from Greek mythology painted by the Venetian Gian Battista Tiepolo (1696–1770). Although many aristocrats were hardworking and disciplined, the Rococo style increased popular hostility toward Old Regime political and social elites.

The rise of Neoclassicism constituted a return to themes, topics, and styles drawn from antiquity and the Renaissance. In his works *Thoughts on the Imitation of Greek Works in Painting and Sculpture* and *The History of Ancient Art*, Johann Joachim Winckelmann (1717–1768) contrasted this ancient approach with Rococo's superficiality. The simultaneous rediscovery and partial excavation of the ancient Roman cities of Pompeii and Herculaneum further spurred interest in antiquity. Artists and aristocrats visited Rome on what was called the "Grand Tour," and brought back to their European homes works of art and the desire to commission paintings, sculptures, and buildings in the Neoclassical style.

Neoclassical art was didactic rather than emotional or playful. Its subject matter was usually concerned with public life and illustrated a moral theme, instead of intimate family life and leisure activity favored by Rococo artists. Neoclassical painters depicted scenes of heroism and self-sacrifice from ancient history. For example, Jacques-Louis David (1748–1825) emphasized the corruption of the French monarchical government in his *Oath of the Horatii* of 1784. The painting, derived from the ancient Roman historian Livy, shows soldiers taking an oath to die for the Roman Republic, and portrays separate spheres for men and women—the latter watching on in emotion as the former demonstrate their duty to the civic life of the republic.

Enlightenment thinkers themselves became the subjects of Neoclassical artists. The French sculptor Jean Antoine Houdon (1741–1828) portrayed the *philosophes* Voltaire and Rousseau as well as the Americans Benjamin Franklin (1706–1790) and Thomas Jefferson (1743–1826). Certain Neoclassical religious structures were later transformed into monuments to the Enlightenment and Revolution. For example, construction of the Pantheon in Paris began in 1758 as a Jesuit church modeled after its Roman namesake. During the French Revolution, the government turned it into a national monument, interring in it the remains of Voltaire in 1791 and of Rousseau in 1794.

The Pantheon in Paris (construction commencing 1758) embodied the neoclassical style used for a Jesuit church. After the French Revolution it became a national monument where famous figures of the Enlightenment and Revolution were buried. The bodies of both Voltaire and Rousseau were transferred there during the 1790s.

Jacques German Soufflot (1713–1780), Facade of the Pantheon (formerly Church of Ste. Genevieve), 1757. Pantheon, Paris, France. © Bridgeman Giraudon/Art Resource, NY

ENLIGHTENED ABSOLUTISM

Most of the *philosophes* rejected Montesquieu's reformed aristocracy and Rousseau's direct democracy as unrealistic. They believed it was necessary to work with the established monarchies. Voltaire, Diderot, and others wanted not to limit the power of kings, but to use it to rationalize social structures and liberate intellectual life. *Philosophes* were not opposed to power so long as they guided the powerful. Many *philosophes* praised the *enlightened absolutism* of Frederick II of Prussia, Joseph II of Austria, and Catherine II of Russia as the ideal political system, for the rigorously centralized governments they led gave them the power to implement reforms with maximum efficiency.

The Enlightenment's intellectuals often overestimated their ability to shape public policy. Monarchs such as Frederick II and Catherine II corresponded with *philosophes*, hosted them at court, and made a show of referring to their ideas. Enlightened absolutists were, however, motivated by more than a philosophe's zeal for humanitarian reform. They were interested in economic and social reform programs that promised to increase their military strength. Many of the enlightened reforms endorsed by the monarchs of Russia, Prussia, and Austria were designed to increase royal revenues and solidify states. They were rational reforms driven by a militarism that the *philosophes* considered irrational.

FREDERICK THE GREAT OF PRUSSIA

More than any other ruler of the age, Frederick the Great of Prussia embodied enlightened absolutism. Building on the work of his Hohenzollern predecessors, he forged a state that commanded the loyalty of the military, the *junker* nobility,

WHAT WAS enlightened absolutism?

the Lutheran clergy, a bureaucracy recruited from an educated middle class, and university professors. With an authoritative Prussian monarchy, a strong military, and loyal subjects, Frederick had the confidence to discuss more openly and even to institute Enlightenment ideas. In contrast to France, Prussian subjects sympathetic to the Enlightenment tended to support the state rather than criticize it.

Promotion Through Merit   Frederick frequently described himself as "the first servant of the State," contending that his own personal and dynastic interests should always be subordinate to the good of his subjects. He protected the Prussian nobility's local social and political interests, but also required nobles to earn positions in the bureaucracy through merit. By 1770, a Prussian Civil Service Commission oversaw the education and examinations required for all major government appointments, making it clear that merit rather than privilege of birth would determine who served the Prussian state.

The few persons whom Frederick ennobled earned their titles by merit. State service required education, therefore nobles attended universities and studied with middle-class Prussians who were training to be clergy or bureaucrats. As a result, Prussia did not experience the conflicts between monarchy and aristocracy that troubled other European states. Also, Prussian professors praised and supported Frederick, who participated in intellectual life and offered professors wide latitude to discuss new ideas. Across the professions, Prussians shared moderate exposure to Enlightenment ideas and were loyal to the state.

Religious Toleration   Frederick made religious toleration a core part of state policies by continuing the Hohenzollern toleration of skilled foreign workers, such as Catholics and Jews, who settled in predominantly Lutheran Prussia. After conquering Silesia in the 1740s, he protected the Catholics of that province. He even was willing to build mosques for Turks if they were to settle in Prussia. His religious toleration won strong support from *philosophes* such as Immanuel Kant and Moses Mendelsohn. Nevertheless, Frederick tended to appoint Protestants to most key positions in the bureaucracy and army.

Administrative and Economic Reforms   Like other enlightened monarchs, Frederick undertook a new codification of Prussian law, which was completed after his death. His aim was to extend and strengthen royal power, but also to rationalize the existing legal system and make it more efficient. His legal reforms eliminated regional peculiarities, reduced aristocratic influence, and also abolished torture and limited the number of capital crimes.

After the mid–century wars, which had inflicted considerable economic damage on Prussia, Frederick used the power of the state to foster economic growth. He sought to develop agriculture by draining swamps, introducing new crops such as potatoes and turnips, and encouraging—or sometimes compelling—peasants to migrate. Frederick also established a land-mortgage credit association to help landowners finance agricultural improvements. Despite these efforts, most Prussians—that is, peasants and townspeople—suffered under a heavy tax burden, while nobles enjoyed royal protection.

JOSEPH II OF AUSTRIA

No eighteenth-century monarch so embodied rational, impersonal force as Joseph II of Austria (r. 1765–1790), Maria Theresa's son and co-ruler (1765–1780). He was an austere, humorless man who prided himself on an ascetic lifestyle and a passionless, rational approach to life. Despite his cold personality, Joseph II sincerely wanted to improve the lot of his people and was, unlike his colleagues who ruled Prussia and Russia, neither a political opportunist nor a cynic. Despite his good intentions, however, the reforms he autocratically decreed spawned rebellions by both aristocrats and peasants.

Centralization of Authority   The empire the Austrian Habsburgs headed was the most diverse of Europe's great eighteenth-century states. Its subjects spoke many languages and had few cultural ties to unite them The throne could not depend on the aristocracy for much support, for the War of the Austrian Succession (1740–1748) had compelled Maria Theresa to grant her nobles (especially in Hungary) extensive freedoms.

Maria Theresa strengthened the power of the crown outside of Hungary by increasing the size of the empire's administrative bureaucracy. Her efficient tax agents collected from the clergy as well as the nobles in Austria and Bohemia. She appointed councils to handle various kinds of problems, and she brought education under state control to ensure her government a sufficient supply of trained officials. Her concern for schools extended to increasing opportunities for primary education at the local level. She also tried to protect peasants and serfs by using the royal bureaucracy to enforce limits on the amount of labor noble landowners could demand from their tenants. Her concern was not solely humanitarian. She wanted to preserve the pool of manpower from which she drew her soldiers.

Joseph II followed the path blazed by his mother. He was, however, even more determined to have his way, and his reforms were more wide ranging. Joseph planned to expand the Habsburg domain at the expense of Poland, Bavaria, and the Ottoman Empire, but his chief concern was to increase his authority over the lands he already ruled. His strategy was to reduce the pluralism that characterized his empire by imposing central authority in places that Maria Theresa had wisely chosen to ignore. In particular, Joseph sought to rein in the Hungarian nobility. To avoid having to guarantee their existing privileges or promise them new ones, he refused to be separately crowned as king of Hungary at his coronation. He reorganized local governments in Hungary to increase the authority of his officials and required the use of German in all transactions. The Magyar nobility protested vigorously, and in 1790, Joseph backed down.

Ecclesiastical Policies   Joseph also sought to force the church to submit to royal absolutism. The Habsburgs were the most important dynasty to champion Roman Catholicism after the Reformation. Maria Theresa had adamantly opposed religious toleration. She refused, however, to allow the church to limit her authority, and she adopted the enlightened policy of discouraging the more extreme forms of Catholic popular piety (such as flagellation as penance for sin).

Joseph II was a practicing Catholic, but enlightenment and pragmatism persuaded him of the virtues of toleration. In October 1781, he issued a Toleration Patent (decree) that extended freedom of worship to Lutherans, Calvinists, and Greek Orthodox. These groups were allowed to establish places of worship, sponsor schools, enter skilled trades, and hold academic appointments and positions in public service. Later, Joseph relieved the Jews of certain taxes and symbols of personal degradation and granted them the right of private worship. This benefited the Jews but fell short of granting them equality with other Habsburg subjects.

Joseph brought various Roman Catholic institutions under direct royal control. He forbade communication between his bishops and the pope. He dissolved and confiscated the endowments of more than six hundred monasteries that failed to demonstrate their utility to society by running schools or hospitals.

He used the funds he confiscated from the monks to create new parishes in places where there were shortages of priests. He accused the established seminaries of training priests who were too loyal to the pope and showed too little concern for their parishioners, and he replaced these schools with eight new seminaries with curricula emphasizing parish duties. *Josephinism,* the emperor's ecclesiastical policy, subjected the Roman Catholic Church to state control and made its priests state employees.

Economic and Agrarian Reform   Like Frederick of Prussia, Joseph tried to use powers of government to promote economic expansion. He abolished many internal tariffs and encouraged road building and the improvement of river transport. He inspected farms and factories. He reconstructed the judicial system to make laws more uniform and rational. He set up national courts with power over the local courts of landlords. All of this was intended to unify the state and increase the taxes paid to the imperial treasury.

During the course of Joseph's reign, a series of reforms relating to serfdom altered the structure of rural society. Joseph did not abolish the power of landlords over their peasants, but he did try to reduce it and make it accountable to royal officials. He ended serfdom as a legally recognized servile condition. He granted peasants a wide array of personal freedoms (rights to marry, to engage in skilled work, and to have their children trained for trades—all without permission from their landlords). He reformed the procedures of the manorial courts and created avenues for appeal to royal officials. He encouraged landlords to change land leases to make it easier for peasants to inherit them or to transfer them to other tenants. The intent of his reforms was to make the peasants more productive and industrious farmers by reducing their traditional burdens.

In 1789, near the end of his reign, Joseph proposed a new and daring system of taxation. He cancelled aristocratic exemptions from taxation and decreed that all landed proprietors be taxed regardless of social status. No longer were the peasants alone to bear the burden of supporting the state. The *robot* (the forced labor required of peasants) was commuted to a monetary payment, shared between the landlord and the state.

The nobles blocked implementation of Joseph's tax reforms, and his death in 1790 ended efforts to enforce them. His tax policies and earlier reform proposals had the unwelcome effect of spreading turmoil throughout the Habsburg realm. Disputes over the interpretation of the new rights granted to the peasants prompted them to rebel, and the Magyars forced Joseph to rescind his moves to centralize Hungary's government. When Joseph's brother, Leopold II (r. 1790–1792), inherited the throne, he had to repeal the most controversial of Joseph's decrees. He retained Joseph's religious policies and pursued political centralization to the extent he thought possible, but expediency and conviction forced him to restore many of the nobility's privileges.

CATHERINE THE GREAT OF RUSSIA

Joseph II took the claims of royalty to autocratic authority literally and never grasped the practical necessity of forging political constituencies to support his reforms. Catherine II (r. 1762–1796), a German princess who became empress of Russia, understood only too well the fragility of her Romanov dynasty's authority. Tsar Peter the Great (d. 1725) had exercised vast power, but after his death the court nobles and soldiers, who controlled the succession to the throne, chose rulers who dissipated the power of the monarchy. Peter was succeeded by his wife, Catherine I

(r. 1725–1727), and then his grandson, Peter II (r. 1727–1730). The crown then devolved on Anna, his niece. Ivan VI, who was less than a year old, became nominal tsar in 1740, until Peter's daughter, Elizabeth, took control in 1741. Political and romantic intrigues made a shambles of her court, and at her death in 1762 she was succeeded by a nephew, Peter III, whose mental stability was doubtful. He exempted the nobles from compulsory military service and precipitously reversed Russia's foreign policy in the Seven Years' War. Adolescent hero worship for Frederick the Great prompted him to refuse to continue cooperating with Austria and France in efforts to contain Prussia. That decision may have saved Prussia, but it did Russia no good. Peter's one accomplishment was his marriage in 1745 to a young German princess from Anhalt Zerbst, Russia's future empress, Catherine the Great.

For almost twenty years, Catherine endured a precarious, miserable life at her mother-in-law's court. She was, however, a shrewd woman who honed her survival skills by studying a palace that seethed with rumors, intrigue, and conspiracy. She befriended important nobles and read widely in the works of the *philosophes*. Her demented husband inspired neither affection nor respect, and a few months after his accession as tsar, she acquiesced to his murder and seized his throne (1762).

Catherine's study of the Enlightenment and the culture of western Europe made her aware of how backward Russia was and gave her ideas for reforms that would turn her country into a great power. She understood that reform would not succeed without widespread support and that she—a foreign woman who had usurped the throne in a palace coup—was not strong enough to act unilaterally.

In 1767, Catherine formed a Legislative Commission and charged it with responsibility for proposing changes in Russian law and government. The empress provided her commissioners, who represented various sectors of Russian society, with a set of *Instructions* drawn from the political works of the philosophes. A year later, Catherine dismissed the commission before several of its key committees reported, but its members had not wasted their time. The commission had gathered vast amounts of information about local administration and economic life, and the upshot of discussions among the commissioners was that few Russians saw any alternative to autocratic monarchy. Their consensus provided support for Catherine's exercise of enlightened absolutism.

Limited Administrative Reform   Catherine's reforms made a virtue of necessity. She knew the Moscow nobles and the military men who had given her the throne could take it away. She also knew she had too few educated subjects to staff an independent bureaucracy and her treasury could not sustain the cost of an army. Catherine, therefore, had no choice but to rely on the nobles for help in running and defending her empire. In 1777, she reorganized local governments to solve problems discovered by the Legislative Commission, and she appointed nobles to most of the offices that dealt with local administration. In 1785, she issued a Charter of the Nobility that secured many of the rights and privileges of the aristocracy.

Economic Growth   Catherine followed the example of Peter the Great in promoting economic development. She removed internal barriers to trade and greatly increased exports of grain, flax, furs, and naval stores. She protected the small Russian urban middle class, which was vital to trade, and befriended and corresponded with philosophes to promote Russia's image in western Europe as a progressive nation.

Territorial Expansion   Catherine's program for the development of Russia, like Peter the Great's, called for the acquisition of warm-water ports through which Russia could maintain uninterrupted contact with Europe. The ports she wanted belonged to the Turks. In 1769, the Ottoman Empire obliged her by declaring war on Russia, and Russia occupied the Ottoman provinces on the Danube River and the Crimean coast of the Black Sea. In 1774, the Treaty of Kuchuk-Kainardji ended hostilities by granting Russia access to the Black Sea, navigation rights on that sea, and free passage through the Bosporus to the Mediterranean. The province of the Crimea became an independent state, which Catherine easily annexed in 1783. (See Map 17–1.)

The Partition of Poland   Russia's expansion along the Danube River was most unwelcome to Austria, for Austria had hoped to move into the same region. Russia's aggression also alarmed the Ottoman Empire, and it appealed for help to Frederick the Great of Prussia. Frederick found a way to turn the situation to his own advantage while preserving peace among the central European powers. He proposed that Russia relinquish its Danubian provinces and Austria and Prussia compensate Russia by helping it annex a large part of Poland. Prussia claimed a stretch of Polish land between East Prussia and Prussia proper that linked together some of Frederick's scattered possessions, and Austria took Galicia and other parts of Poland.

The Polish aristocracy had blocked the development of a strong centralized monarchy in Poland, and they lacked the leadership they needed to defend themselves. In September 1772, they were compelled to accept the loss of nearly a third of their territory. This humiliation inspired a burst of patriotic feeling, and an attempt was made to create a stronger government in what was left of Poland. This was, however, too little too late. The partition of Poland clearly demonstrated that without a strong monarchy, bureaucratic administration, and army, no state could hope to compete in Europe.

Russia and Prussia partitioned Poland again in 1793. In 1795, when they did so for the third time, Poland disappeared from the map of Europe for more than a century. Each time the great powers carved up Poland, they contended they did so to preserve peace in Europe. They argued that squabbles among the Poles threatened to spread to neighboring states and spark a general war. In reality, Poland's political weakness made it an irresistible target for plunderers, who would not have hesitated to attack one another had the need to cooperate in dismembering Poland not been so rewarding.

THE END OF THE EIGHTEENTH CENTURY IN CENTRAL AND EASTERN EUROPE

As the eighteenth century waned, enlightened absolutism became increasingly conservative and repressive. Frederick the Great retreated from public life as he aged and allowed the Prussian aristocracy to take over important military and admin-

MAP EXPLORATION
To explore this interactive map, go to
http://www.prehnall.com/kagan3/map17.1

MAP 17–1
Expansion of Russia, 1689–1796   The overriding territorial aim of the two most powerful Russian monarchs of the eighteenth century, Peter the Great (in the first quarter of the century) and Catherine the Great (in the last half of the century) was to secure navigable outlets to the sea in both the north and the south for Russia's vast empire; hence Peter's push to the Baltic Sea and Catherine's to the Black Sea. Russia also expanded into Central Asia and Siberia during this time period.

WHICH EMPIRE came into direct conflict with Russian expansion?

istrative functions. A reaction to Enlightenment ideas also set in among Prussia's intellectuals. The Habsburg government responded to the Austrian nobility's calls for an end to Joseph II's reform programs by resorting to censorship and to intimidation by a secret police. In Russia, Catherine the Great never fully recovered from the fear of social upheaval raised by the Pugachev peasant rebellion (1771–1775), and when the French Revolution broke out in 1789, the nervous empress censored books based on Enlightenment thought and sent offending authors into exile in Siberia. By the close of the century, fear of and hostility to change permeated the ruling classes of central and eastern Europe, and monarchs who had pursued enlightened absolutism increasingly repudiated the humanity and liberalism of the Enlightenment.

SUMMARY

Formative Influences on the Enlightenment The ideas of the Enlightenment were based on the Newtonian worldview, Locke's psychology, Britain's wealth and stability, French reform, and the emerging print culture in Europe. The print culture facilitated increasing secularism, made writing an economically viable profession, and allowed the emergence of collective public opinion. Literary culture was generally divided between high and low.

The *Philosophes* The writers and critics of the eighteenth century who believed religion, politics, society, and the economy could be reformed to better support human liberty—the *philosophes*—included Montesquieu, Diderot, Rousseau, Hume, and Kant. Voltaire was the most influential, and his satire *Candide* reflects the *philosophes'* concerns and general attitudes. They were not an organized group, and they did not agree on all issues, but they all sought to use reason and common sense to improve institutions and social practices. The commercial and professional classes read and discussed the philosophes' works.

The Enlightenment and Religion Many eighteenth-century *philosophes* were hostile to the church and religious institutions in general. They did not, however, in general oppose religion itself. Deism was a movement that understood religion as something natural and rational, with God as the "divine watchmaker" who had created the universe, set it in motion according to certain laws, and then left it alone. Deists believed the existence of God could be proved empirically, and they believed in life after death, when virtue would be rewarded and sin punished. *Philosophes* valued religious toleration, although they did not always practice it. Jewish thinkers—particularly Spinoza and Mendelsohn—both contributed to, and responded to, the ideas of the Enlightenment. Enlightenment thinkers had less direct contact with Islam, and most sources of information about Islam available in the West were hostile.

The Enlightenment and Society In an effort to secularize learning, *philosophes* compiled the *Encyclopedia,* a twenty-eight-volume compendium of the views of most of France's leading *philosophes* on subjects ranging from religion to canal building. The *Encyclopedia* was completed in 1772 and had sold between 14,000 and 16,000 copies before 1789. It helped spread Enlightenment ideas throughout Europe. The *philosophes* wanted to apply their ideas because they believed that human relationships obeyed rational laws through empirical examination and reason, that social laws could be learned, and that society could be improved. They criticized mercantilism and hoped to reform prisons and legal

IMAGE KEY

for pages 406–407

a. Anicet Charles G. Lemonnier (1743–1824), "The Soiree at the House of Madame Geoffrin." Chateaux de Malmaison et Bois-Preau, Rueil-Malmaison. Bridgeman-Giraudon/Art Resource, NY

b. Portrait of author Mary Wollstonecraft

c. London Coffee House Permission of the Trustees of the British Museum

d. Portrait of Jean Jacques Rousseau (1712–1778), by Maurice Quentin de la Tour, made around 1740

e. Catherine II of Russia (1729–96)

f. Baruch Spinoza

g. The composing room of a print shop: engraving for Denis Diderot's Encyclopedie, ou Dictionnaire Raisonne des Sciences, des Arts et des Metiers, Paris, 175

h. Illustration of Embroidery Tools and Techniques

i. Denis Diderot

punishments. Many French economic reformers were physiocrats, who believed government's primary role was to provide only the protections necessary to allow owners to use their property to best advantage. Adam Smith's 1776 *Inquiry into the Nature and Causes of the Wealth of Nations* is described as the founding document for laissez-faire economic policy. One unsophisticated concept embedded in his work, the "four-stage theory" of social development, would have long-term consequences in relationships between the West and other cultures. The philosophes had other weak spots, most notably their tendency to equate "human" with "male."

Political Thought of the *Philosophes* The French *philosophes* were the most discontented of a discontented lot. France's problems gave the philosophes more to criticize there than elsewhere in Europe at the time. The French *philosophes* proposed a wide array of reforms. Montesquieu and Rousseau both had a substantial influence on future political developments, and they represent two very different perspectives. Montesquieu admired the British constitution and thought many of its features could be introduced into a French monarchical system in which the aristocracy played a significant role. Rousseau was a radical, who raised the fundamental question of what constitutes the good life. He believed society was more important than the individual, because only within a properly functioning society could an individual live a moral life. A few thinkers criticized European treatment of and attitudes toward native peoples living in European empires, especially in the Americas, but such views would not gain significant public resonance until the end of the nineteenth century.

Women in the Thought and Practice of the Enlightenment The salons of French women were instrumental in spreading the ideas of the *philosophes,* but most of the *philosophes* were at best weak advocates of reforms that would help women. Some *philosophes* advocated improvements in education for women. But many *philosophes*—even the otherwise radical Rousseau!—had very traditional ideas about gender roles, and endorsed the double standard that frowned on female sexual expression. The beliefs that women were physiologically inferior to men and women's activities and aspirations should be limited to the domestic sphere, were widely endorsed by *philosophes*. Late in the eighteenth century, Mary Wollstonecraft's *A Vindication of the Rights of Women* placed women's rights within the Enlightenment agenda.

Rococo and Neoclassical Styles in Eighteenth-Century Art In the early eighteenth century, the Rococo style of art and architecture flourished in the private estates of monarchs and aristocrats and also in public buildings, both secular and religious. Rococo expressed frivolity, sensuality, and ornamentation that, by representing political and social elites of the Old Regime, eventually helped to increase popular hostility toward the decadence and corruption among the privileged strata of society. In the second half of the century, Rococo gave way to Neoclassicism, which embodied a didactic and disciplined attitude that hearkened back to the Renaissance and antiquity. Neoclassical works were concerned with public life and moral questions about civic virtue and self-sacrifice. Its works of art and architecture became identified with Enlightenment thought and criticism of the Old Regime, and eventually with the French Revolution.

Enlightened Absolutism Many *philosophes* were fundamentally monarchists, although they believed monarchies should be reformed. Voltaire, Diderot, and the physiocrats advocated rationalization of monarchies. In the last third of the eighteenth century, enlightened absolutism emerged under Frederick II of Prussia, Joseph II of Austria, and Catherine II of Russia. These rulers differed from the *philosophes* in their attitudes toward war, which the *philosophes* rejected as irrational. Frederick the Great tried to improve Prussian agriculture and the economy, with limited success. He widened religious toleration, codified Prussian law, and described himself as "the first servant of the State." Joseph II of Austria was unsuccessful in many of his reform efforts, and his successor repealed many of them. Catherine the Great empowered the local nobility and had some success in growing Russia's economy. She expanded Russian territory through various means including the partition of Poland. Late in the eighteenth century, all three of these regimes became increasingly conservative and politically repressive. After the French Revolution, central and eastern Europe's ruling classes began to resist change and oppose Enlightenment values.

REVIEW QUESTIONS

1. What were the major formative influences on the *philosophes*? Why did the *philosophes* consider organized religion their greatest enemy? What were the basic tenets of deism? What were the attitudes of the philosophes toward women?

2. How did the arguments of the mercantilists differ from the theories developed by Adam Smith in *The Wealth of Nations*? How did each side in this debate view the earth's resources?

3. What political views were held by Montesquieu and Rousseau? Was Rousseau a child of the Enlightenment, or was he its opponent? Which did Rousseau value more, the individual or society?

4. What were the main Enlightenment attitudes about women? What was the significance of Mary Wollstonecraft?

5. How did the eighteenth-century styles of Rococo and Neoclassicism reflect and contribute to the prevailing political and social trends of the age?

6. Were the enlightened monarchs true believers in the ideals of the *philosophes* or was their "enlightenment" merely a pose or veneer? Was their power really absolute?

KEY TERMS

deism (p. 412)	*philosophes* (p. 410)	**Rococo** (p. 421)
laissez-faire (p. 416)	**tabula rasa** (p. 408)	**Neoclassicism** (p. 421)

 For additional study resources for this chapter, go to:
www.prenhall.com/kagan3/chapter17

18 The French Revolution

CHAPTER HIGHLIGHTS

The Crisis of the French Monarchy The cost of the Seven Years' War and French participation in the American Revolution exacerbated French fiscal problems. The monarchy's need for cash created an opportunity for the nobility to gain concessions, including the reconvening of the Estates General.

The Revolution of 1789 Unhappy with procedures in the Estates General, on June 20, 1789, the Third Estate split off and formed the National Assembly. On July 14, a mob stormed the Bastille. In the countryside, the Great Fear intensified peasant uprisings. These events accelerated the move toward constitutional monarchy.

The Reconstruction of France The National Constituent Assembly reorganized France as a constitutional monarchy with a rational administration, an unregulated economy, and a state-controlled church. The reconstructed country was not, however, stable.

The End of the Monarchy: A Second Revolution The emergence of the Jacobins and the *sans-culottes* signaled the radicalization of the revolution. On January 21, 1793, Louis XVI was executed.

Europe at War with the Revolution European governments adopted repressive policies in response to France's ideas and military actions. Political freedoms were repressed in Britain, and Poland was partitioned twice. By April 1793, Austria, Prussia, Britain, Spain, Sardinia, and Holland had formed the First Coalition, an alliance to protect member countries from the revolution.

The Reign of Terror In 1793 mobilization for war touched every aspect of French life. France created Europe's first citizen army. Robespierre led a Reign of Terror against perceived enemies of the revolution. In July of 1794, Robespierre himself was executed.

The Thermidorian Reaction The Thermidorian Reaction was a tempering of the revolution. Many of the policies of the previous years were rolled back. A new constitution created an executive Directory. The ineptness of the Directory and ongoing wars with Austria and Britain created an opportunity for Napoleon Bonaparte to rise to power.

CHAPTER QUESTIONS

HOW DID the financial weakness of the French monarchy lay the foundations of revolution in 1789?

WHAT IS the Declaration of the Rights of Man and Citizen?

HOW DID the National Constituent Assembly reorganize France?

HOW DID the French monarchy come to an end?

HOW DID Europe respond to the French Revolution?

WHAT WAS the Reign of Terror?

WHAT COURSE did the French Revolution take after 1794?

CHAPTER OUTLINE

- The Crisis of the French Monarchy
- The Revolution of 1789
- The Reconstruction of France
- The End of the Monarchy: A Second Revolution

- Europe at War with the Revolution
- The Reign of Terror
- The Thermidorian Reaction

IMAGE KEY
Image Key for pages 432–433 is on page 454.

HOW DID the financial weakness of the French monarchy lay the foundations of revolution in 1789?

In 1789, the long-festering conflict between the French monarchy and aristocracy turned into a revolution that overturned the political and social order of France. Amidst the turmoil, small-town lawyers, artisans, and others of low birth exercised more control over events than kings and nobles. Neither France nor Europe would ever be the same.

THE CRISIS OF THE FRENCH MONARCHY

The French Revolution shattered many of the political, social, and ecclesiastical structures of Europe. However, none of the revolutionary changes would have occurred had the monarchy not reached a state of financial crisis so serious that it could not function within the limits of existing political institutions. By the late 1780s, the French royal government could not collect sufficient taxes to finance itself. This led to a deadlock that forced Louis XVI and his ministers to summon the Estates General, which had not met since 1614. This gathering would give rise to a new set of issues and problems that would lead to the revolution itself.

THE MONARCHY SEEKS NEW TAXES

The French monarchy emerged from the Seven Years' War (1756–1763) deeply in debt and unable thereafter to put its finances on a sound basis. French support of the American revolt against Great Britain further deepened this financial crisis. Paradoxically, France was a rich nation with an improverished government: Its debt was not disproportionate to that of other European states, but the royal government could not tap the nation's wealth through taxes to service and repay the debt.

French absolutism had always involved ongoing negotiation between the monarchy and local aristocratic interests, but this process had become more difficult after the death of Louis XIV (r. 1643–1715), when the aristocracy sought to reclaim parts of the influence it had lost, particularly through the *parlements*.

To resolve its financial difficulties, the French monarchy would have had to bring the aristocracy under tighter control, but each royal minister who tried to devise a scheme for taxing the nobles was blocked by opposition from courtiers and the *parlements*. Both Louis XV (r. 1715–1774) and Louis XVI (r. 1774–1792) lacked the strength of character to wage a determined campaign. They hesitated, retreated, and lied.

In 1770, Louis XV's chancellor, René Maupeou (1714–1792), pushed him to take drastic action. Maupeou abolished the *parlements*, dispersed their members to different parts of the country, and began to reorganize France's administration to make it more efficient. Louis's death in 1774 contributed to the failure of Maupeou's program more than aristocratic resistance, for the new king, Louis XVI, tried to win popular support by restoring the *parlements*. Although totally dominated by aristocrats, the *parlements* represented themselves as the champions of liberty against an oppressive monarchy and appear to have enjoyed popular support. The nobles, inspired by Enlightenment writers such as Montesquieu, wanted to regain the role in government they had enjoyed before Louis XIV established absolute monarchy in the previous century. The king's fiscal problems gave them the leverage they needed.

Well meaning but weak and vacilating, Louis XVI (r. 1774–1792) stumbled from concession to concession until he finally lost all power to save his throne.

Joseph Siffred Duplessis, *Louis XVI*. Versailles, France, Giraudon/Art Resource, NY

The monarchy was unable to rally public opinion to its side because it had lost much of its moral authority. Louis XV's sexually scandalous life was known throughout France. Marie Antoinette (1755–1793), the wife of Louis XVI, rightly or wrongly gained a reputation for sexual misconduct and personal extravagance. Louis XVI's morally upright conduct could not outweigh the monarchy's reputation for scandal. Furthermore, the royal family continued to live at Versailles, rarely mixing with the aristocracy who, unlike in the days of Louis XIV, more often lived in Paris or on their own estates. The French monarchy, unlike Frederick II of Prussia, Joseph II of Austria, or George III of Great Britain, did not have a public image of devotion to the state and to the improvement of the nation.

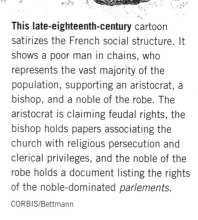

Necker's Report   France's plan to humiliate Great Britain by underwriting the American Revolution was a political triumph and a fiscal disaster. In 1781, Jacques Necker (1732–1804), a Swiss banker who became France's director-general of finances, published a budget intended to quiet the nation's fears. He claimed that when the expenditures for the American war were discounted, the budget was in surplus, and he pointed out that a large portion of the state's income went to pay pensions for aristocrats and court favorites. His exposé mobilized furious courtiers, and they drove him from office. His dubious budget claims survived, however, and were used to challenge later government officials when they insisted there was a need to raise taxes.

This late-eighteenth-century cartoon satirizes the French social structure. It shows a poor man in chains, who represents the vast majority of the population, supporting an aristocrat, a bishop, and a noble of the robe. The aristocrat is claiming feudal rights, the bishop holds papers associating the church with religious persecution and clerical privileges, and the noble of the robe holds a document listing the rights of the noble-dominated *parlements*.

CORBIS/Bettmann

CALONNE'S REFORM PLAN AND THE ASSEMBLY OF NOTABLES

The monarchy hobbled along until 1786, when Charles Alexandre de Calonne (1734–1802), the minister of finance, proposed another reform. He hoped to promote economic growth by encouraging internal trade, lowering some taxes, and transforming peasants' services to money payments. Calonne's most significant proposal was a new tax on land to be paid by all landowners, regardless of social class. Calonne intended to set up local assemblies to approve these taxes, and voting power in them was to depend on how much land one owned rather than one's social status. The new assemblies were designed to undermine the *parlements* on which the political influence of the aristocracy was based.

In 1787, Calonne sought backing for his plan by convening an Assembly of Notables representing the higher-ranking aristocrats and clergy. Although the creditors were at the door and the treasury was nearly empty, the assembly adamantly refused to cooperate with Calonne. Instead, it called for the reappointment of the optimistic Necker, and it insisted it had no power to consent to new taxes. That authority, it said, was vested in the Estates General, a medieval institution that had not met since 1614. In its traditional form, the Estates General was a tool that empowered the aristocracy and clergy.

DEADLOCK AND THE CALLING OF THE ESTATES GENERAL

Louis XVI yielded and replaced Calonne with Etienne Charles Loménie de Brienne (1727–1794), archbishop of Toulouse and Calonne's chief opponent in the Assembly of Notables. Once Brienne took office, he found, to his astonishment, that the situation was as bad as Calonne had said it was, and Brienne became a supporter of the land tax. The *Parlement* of Paris blocked action by again insisting that only the Estates General had the authority to approve such an innovation. In desperation, Brienne appealed to the Assembly of the Clergy for help in meeting a payment on the national debt. The clergy not only refused; they reduced the contributions they had been making to the government.

As pressures on the government mounted, from both the Notables and the *parlements* and estates of the provinces, the king agreed to convene an Estates General in 1789. Brienne resigned, and Necker returned to office. In the country of its origin, royal absolutism had been defeated, and political reform of some kind was now inevitable.

THE REVOLUTION OF 1789

THE ESTATES GENERAL BECOMES THE NATIONAL ASSEMBLY

WHAT IS the Declaration of the Rights of Man and Citizen?

Three groups were represented in the Estates General. The First Estate was the clergy; the Second, the nobility; and the Third, everyone else. In reality, the **Third Estate** represented members of the commercial and professional middle classes. The Estates General was composed entirely of men of property, but this did not ensure cooperation among its members. The estates had different interests over which they clashed from the start.

Debate over Organization and Voting A debate about the organization of the Estates General split the aristocracy and the Third Estate before the meeting convened. The aristocrats first demanded an equal number of representatives for each estate. Then, in September 1788, the *Parlement* of Paris ruled that each estate, not each delegate, should have one vote. This was a strategy for maintaining aristocratic dominance, for the First and Second Estates were likely to work together and consistently outvote the Third Estate. Members of the Third Estate charged the aristocrats, who were accusing the king of trampling on French liberties, of hypocrisy, and the meeting convened in an atmosphere of suspicion and resentment.

Doubling the Third The royal council decided the Third Estate would be its best ally in the fight for fiscal reform. Therefore, in December 1788, it granted the Third Estate twice as many representatives as the nobles and clergy. This meant the Third Estate could dominate the Estates General if votes were individually counted. It was correctly assumed that some liberal nobles and clergy would support the Third Estate, for all the estates had some interests in common. The king had not yet decided the crucial issue of how votes would be taken when the Estates General gathered at Versailles in May 1789.

The *Cahiers de Doléances* The men who assembled at Versailles presented the king with a list of grievances (*cahiers de doléances*) compiled by the citizens who had elected them. The voters were upset about government waste, indirect taxes, church taxes, corrupt clergy, and the hunting rights of the aristocracy. They wanted periodic meetings of the Estates General, more equitable taxes, more local control, unified weights and measures, a free press, and equality of rights among all the king's subjects. Although conflict prevailed between the three orders, the *cahiers* indicated broad agreement across estates on the need for major reforms. (See "History's Voices: The Third Estate of a French City Petitions the King.")

Third Estate Members of the commercial and professional middle classes, or everyone but the clergy (the First Estate) and the nobility (the Second Estate).

OVERVIEW   THE ESTATES GENERAL BECOMES THE NATIONAL ASSEMBLY

Debate over organization and voting	• Public debate over proper organization • Spokespeople denounced the claims of the aristocracy • Resistance of nobility confirmed suspicions of Third Estate members
Doubling the Third	• Council announces Third Estate would elect more representatives • Doubling meant Third Estate could dominate the Estates General • Liberal nobles and clergy supported the Third Estate
The *Cahiers de Doléances*	• Lists of grievances brought to the royal palace by representatives • Documents recorded government waste, indirect taxes, and corruption • Demand was for equality of rights among the king's subjects
The Third Estate creates the National Assembly	• Third Estate refused to sit as a separate order as the king desired • For several weeks there was a standoff • Clergy and nobles joined Third Estate, becoming National Assembly
The Tennis Court Oath	• National Assembly took oath to sit until they gave France a constitution • The king eventually stipulated and requested the Estates to join them • Henceforth, monarchy could govern only in cooperation with Assembly

The Third Estate Creates the National Assembly   Unresolved procedural problems prevented the Estates General from immediately taking up issues of substance, and things ground to a halt when the Third Estate refused to obey the king and convene as a separate group. On June 1, the Third Estate took things into its own hands and invited the clergy and the nobles to join it in dissolving the Estates General and setting up a new legislative body. On June 17, the Third Estate declared itself the National Assembly, and two days later the Second Estate, by a narrow margin, voted to join the assembly.

The Tennis Court Oath   On June 20, members of the National Assembly took an oath not to disperse until they had given France a constitution. This significant step is called the Tennis Court Oath, for the assembly, having been accidentally locked out of its intended meeting place, convened in a nearby tennis court. Louis XVI ordered the assembly to desist, but within a few days it had recruited the majority of the clergy and a large group of nobles. On June 27, the king capitulated and formally requested the First and Second Estates to meet with the National Assembly and to vote by head rather than by estate. The National Assembly (renamed the National Constituent Assembly) brought together men from all three estates who shared hopes for liberal reform. They succeeded in their campaign to end government by privileged hereditary orders but at the cost of a revolution that continued for over a century.

FALL OF THE BASTILLE

Many members of the National Constituent Assembly wanted to establish a constitutional monarchy, but they were thwarted by Louis's refusal to cooperate. The king's decision to oppose the diverse groups converging against him only served to unite them and spur on the revolution he tried to halt. The king's wife, Marie

QUICK REVIEW

National Assembly
• June 17, 1789: Third Estate declares itself National Assembly
• Tennis Court Oath: pledge to sit until France had a constitution
• June 27, 1789: king capitulates to National Assembly

HISTORY'S VOICES

THE THIRD ESTATE OF A FRENCH CITY PETITIONS THE KING

*T*he cahiers de doléances *were the lists of griev-ances brought to Versailles in 1789 by members of the Estates General. This particular* cahier, *typical of many, originated in Dourdan, a city in central France, and reflects the complaints of the Third Estate.*

WHICH OF THE following petitions relate to political rights and which to economic equality? The slogan most associated with the French Revolution was "Liberty, Equality, Fraternity." Which of these petitions represents each of these values?

The order of the Third Estate of the City … of Dourdan … supplicates [the king] to accept the grievances, complaints, and remonstrances which it is permitted to bring to the foot of the throne, and to see therein only the expression of its zeal and the homage of its obedience.

It wishes:

1. That his subjects of the Third Estate, equal by such status to all other citizens, present themselves before the common father without other distinction which might degrade them.

2. That all the orders, already united by duty and common desire contribute equally to the needs of the State, also deliberate in common concerning its needs.

3. That no citizen lose his liberty except according to law: that, consequently, no one be arrested by virtue of special orders, or, if imperative circumstances necessitate such orders, that the prisoner be handed over to regular courts of justice within forty-eight hours at the latest. …

12. That every tax, direct or indirect, be granted only for a limited time, and that every collection beyond such term be regarded as peculation, and punished as such. …

15. That every personal tax be abolished; that thus the *capitation* [a poll tax] and the *taille* [tax from which nobility and clergy were exempt] and its accessories be merged with the *vingtièmes* [an income tax] in a tax on land and real or nominal property.

16. That such tax be borne equally, without distinction, by all classes of citizens and by all kinds of property, even feudal … rights.

17. That the tax substituted for the *corvée* be borne by all classes of citizens equally and without distinction. That said tax, at present beyond the capacity of those who pay it and the needs to which it is destined, be reduced by at least one-half.

John Hall Stewart, *A Documentary Survey of the French Revolution* (New York: Macmillan, 1951), pp. 76–77.

Antoinette, his brothers, and the most conservative nobles urged him to use force to break up the National Constituent Assembly. He tried to intimidate it by mustering royal troops in the vicinity of Versailles and Paris, and on July 11, he signaled his intent to ignore the assembly by abruptly dismissing Necker, the minister of finance, without informing the assembly.

The mustering of royal troops spread fear through Paris, which numbered more than 600,000 people and was the scene of recent bread riots. The Parisians had met to elect representatives to the Third Estate, and they had continued to meet after the elections were over. In June they had even formed a citizen militia. Louis's dismissal of Necker convinced the Parisians that the king intended to attack Paris and the National Constituent Assembly.

On July 14, somewhat more than 800 mostly working-class people marched to the Bastille (a fortress in Paris) to demand weapons for the city's militia. The governor of the Bastille lost control of the situation, and his troops fired into the

QUICK REVIEW

July 14, 1789

- June 1789: fear of attack by king spread throughout Paris
- July 14: 800 mostly working-class people march on the Bastille to demand weapons for the city's militia
- Bastille was stormed after soldiers fired on crowd

crowd. Ninety-eight people died, and many others were wounded. The enraged crowd stormed the fortress, gained entrance, released seven prisoners, and killed the governor and some of his soldiers.

On July 15, the militia of Paris—calling itself the National Guard—offered its command to a hero of the American Revolution, the Marquis de Lafayette (1757–1834). He suggested the guard's insignia: red and blue stripes (the colors of Paris) separated by a white stripe (the emblem of the king). This pattern became the *cockade*, the badge that signified the revolution and became France's flag.

The attack on the Bastille was the first of many acts by the people of Paris that determined the course of the revolution. As word of the Bastille's fall spread, mobs in the provincial cities took to the streets and assaulted other governmental institutions. The National Constituent Assembly could not control all the forces that wanted to have a hand in shaping France's destiny, and even the king bowed to the force of events. He donned a revolutionary cockade, went to Paris, authorized its National Guard, and recognized the electors' organization as the city's legitimate government. The citizens of Paris had become a separate and independent political force with which other groups would have to negotiate.

THE "GREAT FEAR" AND THE NIGHT OF AUGUST 4

The disturbances in Paris spawned a rumor that royal troops were being sent to occupy the countryside. This multiplied the few scattered peasant revolts that had also erupted that spring until a "Great Fear" swept the countryside. Mobs burned chateaux, destroyed public records and documents, and declared an end to feudal dues. The peasants seized stores of scarce foods and reclaimed land that they had lost during the last quarter century to the "aristocratic resurgence."

On the night of August 4, 1789, aristocrats in the National Constituent Assembly made a gesture they hoped would calm the peasant rebels and restore order to the countryside. Liberal nobles and clergy renounced their feudal rights, dues, and tithes, and their emotional speeches inspired other members of the assembly to divest themselves of their privileges. In a sense, these men gave up what they had already lost and what they could not have regained without civil war. Most also had enough political influence to see to it that they were compensated for what they were giving up. Nonetheless, their act of renunciation put all French citizens on the same legal footing and paved the way for reconstruction of French law and society.

The rioters who stormed through city streets and roamed the countryside had more on their minds than the political issues being debated at Versailles. Harvests in 1787 and 1788 had been poor, and the winter of 1788–1789 had been unusually cold. Wages had not kept pace with rising food prices (which were, in 1789, higher than they had been for almost a century). Many people were suffering severely from hunger.

The political, social, and economic grievances that were building throughout the country threatened a cataclysmic revolution, and the National Constituent Assembly used the fear created by the popular uprisings to intimidate the king and the conservative aristocrats. However, the assembly failed to speak with one voice. Quarrels erupted among factions, and the contenders turned to the masses for support. The shopkeepers and artisans were best organized to respond, and they exacted a price for their cooperation.

THE DECLARATION OF THE RIGHTS OF MAN AND CITIZEN

On August 27, 1789, the National Constituent Assembly approved the Declaration of the Rights of Man and Citizen, a statement of the political principles that would guide the writing of a new constitution. It affirmed that all men were born

19.2

"The Declaration of the Rights of Man and Citizen"

The women of Paris marched to Versailles on October 5, 1789. The following day the royal family was forced to return to Paris with them. Henceforth, the French government would function under the constant threat of mob violence.

France, 18th c., *To Versailles, to Versailles.* The women of Paris going to Versailles, 7 October 1789. Musée de la Ville de Paris, Musée Carnavalet, Paris, France. Giraudon/Art Resource. NY

free and equal with inalienable rights to liberty, property, and personal security. Governments, it said, existed to protect those rights, and governments ought to guarantee all their citizens equal protection before the law and equal opportunity to serve in public office (commensurate, of course, with each individual's ability). The declaration affirmed due process of law, freedom of religion, and presumption of innocence until proof of guilt. It stated that taxes should be apportioned according to ability to pay and that property was a right ordained by God. The declaration was an indictment of the abuses of absolutist monarchy and a death certificate for the Old Regime.

The document's ideas were framed in universal language that would readily apply across national borders. Its concepts of civic equality and popular sovereignty would respectively challenge legal and social inequalities in Europe and assert that governments must be responsible to the governed.

The declaration's proclamation of the rights of men did not include women. Many of the Enlightenment's political theorists believed men and women occupied separate (if complementary) spheres in society. Men were said to be suited for public service (citizenship) and women for domestic duties (motherhood and homemaking). Nonetheless, in the charged atmosphere of the summer of 1789, many French women hoped a new constitution would improve their legal situation—particularly with respect to property, inheritance rights, family, and divorce. Some believed the declaration might eventually extend full citizenship to women. Those hopes would be disappointed.

THE PARISIAN WOMEN'S MARCH ON VERSAILLES

When Louis XVI was slow to ratify the declaration and the aristocrats' renunciation of their feudal privileges, rumors spread that the king was again contemplating military action. On October 5, a crowd of about 7,000 Parisian women (armed with pikes, guns, swords, and knives) marched to Versailles to demand relief from a bread shortage. They intimidated Louis, and he agreed to sanction the decrees of the assembly. The Parisians, however, did not trust him, and they insisted the royal family move to Paris so its conduct could be monitored. Having no option, Louis's carriage followed the crowd into the city to the palace of the Tuileries on October 6, 1789. The women's march was the first mass insurrection to use the language of popular sovereignty against a monarch.

THE RECONSTRUCTION OF FRANCE

he National Constituent Assembly followed the royal family to Paris, and the situation remained relatively peaceful until the summer of 1792. The assembly decided to establish a constitutional monarchy that rationalized administration, left trade free and unregulated, protected rights of private property, and limited the power of clergy. The aristocracy and the middle-class elite were united in support of equality before the law, but the assembly was not in favor of social equality and radical democracy. It wanted to leave control of the nation in the hands of men of property.

HOW DID the National Constituent Assembly reorganize France?

POLITICAL REORGANIZATION

The Constitution, which the assembly issued in 1791, established a unicameral Legislative Assembly as the chief political authority for the nation. It granted the monarch a veto that could delay, but not halt, legislation, and it set up an elaborate system of indirect election intended to minimize pressure on the government from the masses.

Active and Passive Citizens   France's citizens were divided into two categories: active and passive. Active citizens were men who paid annual taxes equal to three days of local labor wages. Only they could vote to elect the electors who elected the members of the legislature. Higher property qualifications were set for service as an elector and as a member of the legislature, so that only about 50,000 of France's 25 million people qualified for office. These constitutional arrangements made wealth rather than birth the basis of political power, and they made no distinctions among forms of wealth (aristocratic landed estates or commercial businesses). They recognized the changes that were taking place in French society by giving newly emerging economic interests a voice in government, but no women were enfranchised.

Olympe de Gouges's Declaration of the Rights of Woman   Some women objected to the exclusion of their gender from politics. In 1791, Olympe de Gouges, a butcher's daughter from Montauban, published a Declaration of the Rights of Woman. It added the word *woman* to each clause in the Declaration of the Rights of Man and Citizen that mentioned men and demanded that women be regarded as citizens in their own right and not simply as dependents of citizen families. Olympe de Gouges wanted property rights and improved education for women and equality between wives and husbands in marriage. She also wanted the law to compel men to recognize the paternity of all their children.

By issuing a list of rights for men, the National Assembly had established a set of principles against which its own conduct could be measured. Those to whom it had not extended liberty asked why they had been shut out and warned that the revolution would not be complete until they too were included.

Departments Replace Provinces   The National Constituent Assembly (consistent with the principles of Enlightenment science) decreed a rational reorganization of France's government and judiciary. It eliminated provinces that conformed to medieval baronies and divided the country into eighty-three *départements* of approximately equal size (subdivided into districts, cantons, and communes). These were named for rivers, mountains, or other geographical features. (See Map 18-1.) A uniform court system (staffed by elected judges and prosecutors) replaced the various seigneurial courts and *parlements*. Legal procedures were simplified, and the most degrading punishments were eliminated.

19.2
"Declaration of the Rights of Women and the Female Citizen"

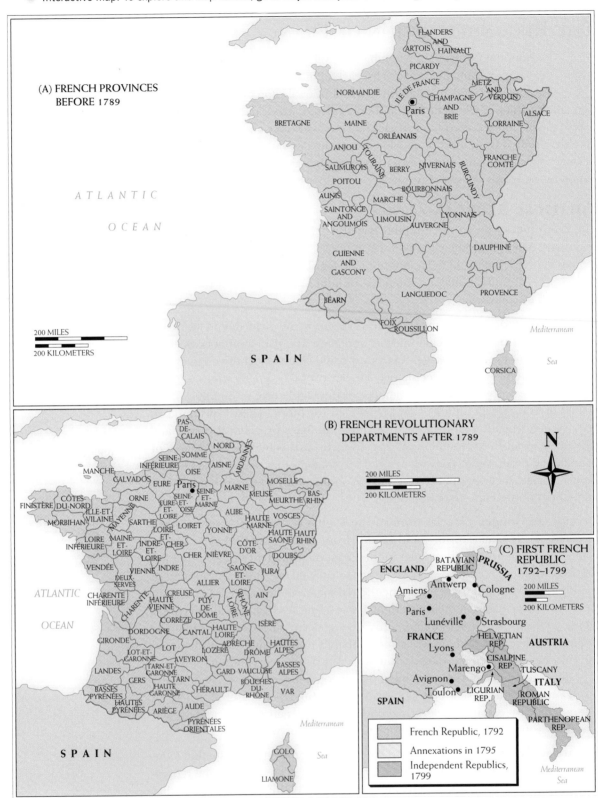

MAP 18–1

French Provinces and the Republic   In 1789, the National Constituent Assembly redrew the map of France. The ancient provinces (A) were replaced with a large number of new, smaller departments (B). This redrawing of the map was part of the assembly's effort to impose greater administrative rationality in France. The borders of the republic (C) changed as the French army conquered new territory.

WHAT DO the revolutionary departments suggest about prevailing attitudes toward administrative governance after 1789?

ECONOMIC POLICY

The National Constituent Assembly embraced the economic policies proposed by Louis XVI's reformist ministers. This chiefly amounted to removing restraints on commerce by doing such actions as suppressing guilds and liberating the grain trade. Enlightenment enthusiasm for rationalism also led the assembly to endorse the metric system as France's standard for weights and measures. (See "Encountering the Past: The Metric System.")

ENCOUNTERING THE PAST

THE METRIC SYSTEM

France's revolutionaries hoped to realize the Enlightenment dream of dispelling superstition and obscurity by establishing the reign of science in all things. One of the revolution's lasting achievements was to simplify commercial transactions by eliminating the numerous local systems of weights and measures that had sprung up during the Middle Ages. There were political as well as economic motives for promoting the use of a common standard of measurement throughout the country. It symbolized France's existence as a single "indivisible" republic.

The metric (from *meter*) system, which the assembly adopted (and is widely used today), was based on the work of astronomers. The revolutionaries wanted nature to establish the basic unit of measurement, and they chose the height of the arch of meridians (the highest point reached by the sun around the earth) in the latitude of Paris as their reference point. The meter was defined as one ten-millionth of one-quarter of that meridian. All other measurements of length were defined as decimal fractions or multiples of the meter. The gram, the standard for measuring weights, was decreed to be the weight of a cube of pure water measuring 0.01 meter on each side. Each measurement of weight was a decimal fraction or multiple of the gram.

Scientists quickly took to the new system, but the public resisted and clung to familiar weights and measures. Not until 1840 did political pressure, rationality, and convenience succeed in establishing use of the metric system throughout France. By the end of the nineteenth century, most of continental Europe had adopted it and it had been introduced to Latin America. It spread throughout Asia and Africa in the twentieth century. Today, English-speaking countries constitute the primary exceptions to its use. Scientists, engineers, and physicians employ it, but many people in the United States and Great Britain, despite encouragement, have declined to follow suit.

HOW WAS the metric system consistent with the principles of the Enlightenment? Why has its use spread so widely?

Jean-Baptiste Delambre (1749–1822) was one of the French astronomers whose measurements of the arch of meridians formed the basis for establishing the length of the meter.

Image Works/Mary Evans Picture Library Ltd.

Workers' Organizations Forbidden   The assembly's determination to create a "natural" economy freed from all artificial restraints led it to oppose attempts by workers to organize for their own protection. On June 14, 1791, it enacted the Chapelier Law, which forbade workers' associations (unions). The revolution left peasants and workers to the mercy of a largely unregulated marketplace.

Confiscation of Church Lands   The assembly inherited the job of doing something about the financial crisis that had forced Louis XVI to convene its predecessor, the Estates General. The assembly did not, as governments sometimes had in the past, simply repudiate the royal debt. (The debt was owed to bankers, merchants, and commercial traders who had influence with the assembly.) It chose instead to replace old, much-resented indirect taxes with new taxes on land. When these yielded insufficient revenue, the assembly took what may well have been its most decisive action. It confiscated and sold off the property belonging to the country's Roman Catholic Church. This put so much wealth into circulation that it ignited inflation. It also invited religious schism and civil war.

The *Assignats*   In December 1789, the assembly authorized the issuance of *assignats*, government bonds whose value was backed up by the revenue to be generated from the sale of church property. Initially a limit was set on the number of *assignats* to be sold, but the public's eagerness to buy them tempted the assembly to print enough of them to liquidate the national debt. This created a large body of bondholders with personal stakes in the survival of the revolutionary government, but within a few months the value of their *assignats* began to fall, and rising inflation further stressed the urban poor.

THE CIVIL CONSTITUTION OF THE CLERGY

The confiscation of church lands necessitated reorganization of the church. In July 1790, the assembly (without consulting the pope or the French clergy) issued the Civil Constitution of the Clergy. This imposed state control on the Roman Catholic Church in France. The number of bishoprics was reduced from 135 to 83 to make the dioceses of religious administrators conform with the new *départements* of civil government. Priests and bishops became salaried employees of the state and were to be elected like other state officials.

The Civil Constitution of the Clergy was a major blunder. The French clergy vigorously opposed it, and their opposition provoked the assembly to demand that all clergy take an oath of loyalty to the state. Only seven bishops and about half the clergy complied. Those who refused were removed from their ecclesiastical offices. In February 1791, the pope condemned not only the Civil Constitution of the Clergy but also the Declaration of the Rights of Man and Citizen, and the Roman Catholic Church launched an offensive against liberalism and revolution that continued throughout the nineteenth century. Many French people found themselves in the position of having to choose between their faith and their loyalty to the revolution.

COUNTERREVOLUTIONARY ACTIVITY

The revolution had other enemies besides the pope and devout Catholics. Many aristocrats (known as the **émigrés**) fled to countries on France's borders and set up bases for counterrevolutionary activities. The king's younger brother, the count of Artois (1757–1836), was among them, and in 1791, he and the queen persuaded Louis XVI to attempt to flee France.

QUICK REVIEW

National Constituent Assembly Policies

- National Constituent Assembly embraced economic policies of Louis XVI's reformist ministers
- Forbid formation of workers' organizations
- Confiscated and sold church lands

émigrés   French aristocrats and enemies of the revolution who fled to countries on France's borders and set up bases for counterrevolutionary activities.

Flight to Varennes   On the night of June 20, 1791, Louis and his immediate family donned disguises and set out for Metz. At Varennes the king was recognized and prevented from going farther. A company of soldiers brought the royal family back to Paris on June 24. The leaders of the National Constituent Assembly, who hoped to preserve support for establishing a constitutional monarchy, claimed the king had not fled but been abducted. This public fiction failed, however, to cloak the fact that the nation's most prominent counterrevolutionary occupied its throne.

Declaration of Pillnitz   Two months later, Marie Antoinette's brother, Leopold II of Austria, and Prussia's King Frederick William II issued the Declaration of Pillnitz. It stated that both rulers were prepared to intervene to protect the royal family and to preserve the French monarchy if the major European nations supported them. This provision rendered the declaration meaningless, for Great Britain would never have endorsed their efforts. To do so would have been to upset the continental balance of power. France's revolutionaries concluded, however, that they were surrounded by hostile monarchists, and their anger increased the precariousness of the royal family's situation.

The *assignats* were government bonds that were backed by confiscated church lands. They circulated as money. When the government printed too many of them, inflation resulted and their value fell.

Bildarchiv Preussischer Kulturbesitz

THE END OF THE MONARCHY: A SECOND REVOLUTION

HOW DID the French monarchy come to an end?

The National Constituent Assembly completed the work of establishing a constitutional monarchy and dissolved itself in September 1791. One of its last acts was to declare all its members ineligible for election to the Legislative Assembly that took its place. This new assembly, which convened on October 1, faced immense problems relating to the Civil Constitution of the Clergy, the king's flight, and the Declaration of Pillnitz.

Factionalism plagued the Legislative Assembly throughout its short life (1791–1792). Much of this stemmed from the activities of clubs that deputies from the Third Estate had established (while the Estates General was still in session) to bring together persons with similar political philosophies.

EMERGENCE OF THE JACOBINS

The **Jacobins** were the best organized of the political clubs. They took their name from the Dominican (Jacobin) monastery in Paris where their leaders met, but they had a network of local clubs established in the provinces. The Jacobins embraced the most radical of the Enlightenment's political theories, and they wanted a republic, not a constitutional monarchy. The events of the summer of 1791, which had diminished support for the monarchy, strengthened their hand.

A group of Jacobins—the Girondists (from the department of the Gironde that many of them represented) or Brissotins (from their spokesman in 1792, Jacques-Pierre Brissot)—assumed leadership of the Legislative Assembly and took the offensive against the forces of counterrevolution. They ordered the émigrés to return or suffer confiscation of their property, and they threatened the clergy who refused to support the Civil Constitution with loss of their state pensions. The king vetoed these acts, but he did not oppose the Girondists when they, on April 20, 1792, persuaded the Legislative Assembly to declare war on Austria and Prussia.

Jacobins   The best organized of the political clubs, they embraced the most radical of the Enlightenment's political theories, and they wanted a republic, not a constitutional monarchy.

The Girondists believed the war would solidify domestic support for the revolution and make the revolution more radical. Louis XVI, for his part, hoped war would rally the country behind him, its chief executive. He may also have felt he had nothing to lose, for defeat of the revolutionary armies would have cleared the way for foreign intervention and restoration of the Old Regime.

The war was to disappoint the king and delight the Girondists, for it began a second, more radical revolution that replaced the constitutional monarchy with a republic. The government had to mobilize all its resources to defend France, and its need for support persuaded it to lend a sympathetic ear to appeals for rights from groups that had previously been ignored. As early as March 1792, a group of women led by Pauline Léon petitioned the Legislative Assembly for the right to bear arms and to fight for the revolution. Once the war began, a number of French women enlisted in the army and served with distinction.

The war at first went badly, and Prussian threats of dire consequences if the royal family was harmed only increased suspicion of the king's loyalty. On August 10, 1792, a large crowd of Parisians invaded the Tuileries palace and forced Louis XVI and Marie Antoinette to take refuge in the Legislative Assembly. The crowd fought with the king's Swiss guards, and several hundred of the soldiers and a large number of Parisians were killed. Once order was restored, the assembly imprisoned the royal family in comfortable quarters and prohibited the king from exercising his political functions. The constitutional monarchy shunted its monarch aside.

THE CONVENTION AND THE ROLE OF THE *SANS-CULOTTES*

In July radicals from the working class had designated Paris a commune and turned the city's government over to a committee representing the municipal wards. Two months later the Paris Commune ordered the **September Massacres**. Some of the approximately twelve hundred people whom it executed were aristocrats or priests, but the majority were common criminals who, because they were being held in the city's jails, were assumed to be counterrevolutionaries. News of this event and of the imprisonment of the royal family spread rapidly across Europe, rousing new hostility toward the revolutionary government.

The Paris Commune compelled the Legislative Assembly to institute universal male suffrage and call an election for a new assembly to write a democratic constitution. The newly elected body, called the **Convention** (after the American Constitutional Convention of 1787), met on September 21, 1792, a day after the French army halted the Prussian advance at the Battle of Valmy in eastern France. The triumph of democratic forces on the domestic front was confirmed by victory on the battlefield, and the Convention's first act was to declare France a republic—a nation governed by an elected assembly without a king.

Goals of the *Sans-culottes*   The second revolution was the work of two groups: a faction of Jacobins who were more radical than the Girondists, and Parisians called *sans-culottes*. The term means "without breeches," and it referred to long trousers that working men wore in place of the knee breeches sported by aristocratic courtiers. The *sans-culottes* were shopkeepers, artisans, wage earners, and factory workers who had been ignored by the Old Regime and victimized by the economic policies of the National Constituent Assembly. The revolutionary government needed their help to win its war, and between the summers of 1792 and 1794, they were the dominating force that set the course of the revolution.

The *sans-culottes* knew what they wanted: immediate relief from food shortages, government-imposed price controls, and an end to social inequality. They

September Massacres   The execution ordered by the Paris Commune of approximately 1,200 aristocrats, priests, and common criminals who, because they were being held in city jails, were assumed to be counterrevolutionaries.

Convention   The newly elected French body that met on September 21, 1792, whose first act was to declare France a republic—a nation governed by an elected assembly without a king.

sans-culottes   Parisians (shopkeepers, artisans, wage earners, and factory workers who had been ignored by the Old Regime) who, along with radical Jacobins, began the second revolution in France.

were intensely hostile to aristocrats and suspected the original leaders of the revolution of aspiring to become a new aristocracy. Their campaign against inequality did not, however, imply the abolition of private property. They envisioned a nation of small property owners who all enjoyed the same political rights. They were antimonarchical and distrustful of representative government.

The Policies of the Jacobins The goals of the *sans-culottes* were not entirely compatible with those of the Jacobins, who favored representative government and an unregulated economy. After Louis XVI's flight to Varennes, however, the more extreme Jacobins (called "the Mountain" from their seats at the top of the assembly hall) sided with leaders of the Parisian *sans-culottes*. They subordinated other concerns to enlisting support for the war and ending the monarchy.

Execution of Louis XVI In December 1792, Louis XVI was charged with conspiring against the liberty and security of France. The Girondists tried to spare his life, but the Mountain won his conviction. Louis was stripped of his title, and on January 21, 1793, "Citizen Capet" (as he was renamed after the founder of his dynasty) was beheaded.

The execution of the king increased pressure on the government. The Prussians renewed their offensive and drove the French out of Belgium. Every major European power declared its opposition to the revolution, and the Convention declared war on Great Britain, Holland, and Spain. In March 1793, a royalist revolt erupted in western France and began to spread. These developments convinced the Mountain that the Girondists, who had taken the country into the war, were incapable of defending it.

Execution of Louis XVI. On January 21, 1793, the Convention executed Louis XVI.
Cliché Bibliotheque Nationale de France, Paris

EUROPE AT WAR WITH THE REVOLUTION

Not all Europeans were initially opposed to the French Revolution. Some reformers believed the revolution would demonstrate how rational methods could successfully reorganize corrupt, inefficient states. Some foreign rulers hoped the revolution would preoccupy France and distract it from international affairs for years. By 1792, however, the European monarchies were fully alert to the dangers posed by the spread of French political ideas. The Declaration of the Rights of Man and Citizen was a highly exportable document, and one government after another instituted repressive domestic policies to contain its revolutionary ideology.

HOW DID Europe respond to the French Revolution?

EDMUND BURKE ATTACKS THE REVOLUTION

In 1790, Edmund Burke (1729–1799), a British statesman, outlined the position that was to be taken by Europe's emerging conservative political parties in *Reflections on the Revolution in France*. He claimed that Enlightenment rationalism was not a realistic instrument for reform, and he predicted disaster for any government that failed to recognize the historical realities of its homeland's political evolution or failed to accommodate the complexities of human social relationships. The efforts of inexperienced people to govern France would, he claimed, result in turmoil, and events unfolded much as he predicted. Burke's ideas came to have many admirers. In direct response to Burke, Thomas Paine, the hero of the American Revolution, composed *The Rights of Man* to defend the revolutionary principles. His volume sold more copies at the time, but Burke's work exercised more influence in the long run.

SUPPRESSION OF REFORM IN BRITAIN

Prime Minister William Pitt the Younger (1759–1806) had been a supporter of moderate reform of Parliament during the 1780s, but he eventually came to oppose reform and popular political movements. His government suppressed the London Corresponding Society, a working-class organization that advocated reform, and drove the chemist Joseph Priestley (1733–1804), a radical political thinker, out of the country. Early in 1793, Pitt secured parliamentary approval for suspension of habeas corpus and broadened the definition of treason to include not just actions but writings of which the government disapproved. Pitt had less success curbing freedom of the press, but any group that opposed him risked being indicted for sedition.

THE SECOND AND THIRD PARTITIONS OF POLAND, 1793, 1795

The final two partitions of Poland by Austria, Prussia, and Russia, following on the first partition in 1772, occurred directly because of fears by the eastern powers that French revolutionary principles were establishing themselves in Poland. The first partition had spurred reforms among Polish leaders to create a stronger state. In 1791, a group of nobles known as the Polish Patriots issued a new constitution that made the monarchy elective rather than hereditary, provided real executive authority to the monarch and his council, established a new bicameral diet, and eliminated the *liberum veto*—the Polish tradition that had given power to any diet member to disband the Polish assembly and that had been the cause of most diets being broken up in the preceding century. The Polish government also adopted equality before the law and religious toleration.

Although Frederick William II of Prussia (r. 1786–1797) at first defended this new constitutional order, eventually the rivalries of Poland's neighbors led to its destruction as a state. In 1792 the Russian army defeated Polish forces led by Tadeusz Kosciuszko (1746–1817), a veteran of the American Revolution. Subsequently, Prussian troops occupied parts of Poland, and in 1793, Frederick William II and Catherine the Great of Russia agreed to a second partition of Poland. The reformed constitution was abolished and a new Polish government created under Russia's influence.

In 1794, a mutiny by Polish officers against Russian dominance led to a rebellion under Kosciuszko's leadership. The language and symbols of the French Revolution appeared in Polish cities, but by year's end, Russia, Prussia, and Austria had defeated the Poles and proceeded in the following year to dissolve Poland in a third partition.

WAR WITH EUROPE

France's invasion and reorganization of the Austrian Netherlands roused the other European powers to hostile action, and heads of state were further alarmed, in November 1792, when the Convention announced it would aid all peoples everywhere who wanted to cast off the burdens of aristocracy and monarchy. The British, whose commerce was directly threatened, were on the point of declaring war on France when the Convention beat them to it (February 1793). By the time the Jacobins took charge of France's government in April 1793, France was at war with Austria, Prussia, Great Britain, Spain, Sardinia, and Holland.

THE REIGN OF TERROR

The task of mobilizing their country for war in 1793 changed the way the French revolutionaries thought about themselves. They were engaged, they believed, not in a struggle over territorial borders but in the defense of a bold new ideology: a republican political and social order that the world was determined to destroy. To protect the revolution, the government employed extreme measures and unleashed what is known as the **Reign of Terror**.

THE REPUBLIC DEFENDED

France's revolutionary government was dominated by powerful committees. Their efforts to mobilize the country for the military defense of revolutionary liberty resulted, ironically, in the suppression of many of those liberties and bloody purges directed at suspected internal enemies of the revolution.

The Committee of Public Safety   In April 1793, the Convention vested executive authority in a Committee of General Security and a Committee of Public Safety. The second of these was chaired by Jacques Danton (1759–1794), Maximilien Robespierre (1758–1794), and Lazare Carnot (1753–1823). It gradually supplanted its companion and acquired almost dictatorial power. Its leaders were committed republicans, who believed it was their duty to save the revolution from mortal enemies at home and abroad. To that end, they found it expedient to court the *sans-culottes* of Paris and to suppress many of the rights the revolution claimed to protect. Chief among these was the right to life. France's precarious international situation intensified anxiety about national security and prompted a rigorous search for internal enemies that quickly got out of hand.

The *Levée en Masse*   In early June (1793) the Parisian *sans-culottes* invaded the Convention, expelled the Girondists, and established the radical Mountain in control. On June 22, the Convention approved a fully democratic constitution but delayed its implementation until the end of the war. On August 23, Carnot issued a ***levée en masse***, an order for total military mobilization of both men and property, and on September 17, the ceiling on prices that the *sans-culottes* demanded was instituted. Never before had Europe seen a country organized in this way—nor one defended by a citizen army.

In the autumn of 1793, the most infamous phase in the history of the revolution began. The new republic unleashed the Reign of Terror, a spate of self-inflicted, quasi-judicial bloodletting that continued until midsummer 1794. The spectacle did nothing to persuade other European states that they could risk reform and revolution, and it can be understood only in the context of a foreign war and an overheated political situation in which the *sans-culottes* pressed the Convention for a rapid transformation of society.

THE "REPUBLIC OF VIRTUE" AND ROBESPIERRE'S JUSTIFICATION OF TERROR

The threat of foreign armies closing in on France made it easy to dispense with legal due process, but the revolution's leaders did not see their actions simply as expedients required by war. They believed they had created something new in world history, a "republic of virtue" where concern for the common good had replaced aristocratic corruption. Every aspect of society was now to be transformed for the benefit of the masses. Streets were renamed to memorialize the egalitarian vocabulary of the revolution. People affected a new republican style of dress patterned after the ordinary clothing of the *sans-culottes* or the imagined garb of the Roman republic.

WHAT WAS the Reign of Terror?

19.4
Robespierre: Justification of Terror

Reign of Terror   Extreme measures employed by the French government in an effort to protect the revolution.

levée en masse   Order for total military mobilization of both men and property.

Maximilien Robespierre (1758–1794) emerged as the most powerful revolutionary figure in 1793 and 1794, dominating the Committee of Public Safety. He considered the Terror essential for the success of the revolution.

Musée des Beaux-Arts, Lille, Bridgeman-Giraudon/Art Resource, NY

Plays whose themes were not sufficiently republican were suppressed, and special efforts were made to fight crimes such as prostitution that were supposedly characteristic of aristocratic societies. The core republican virtue was the elevation of public over private good, and it was in the name of the public good that the Committee of Public Safety instituted the terror.

Robespierre was the dominant member of the Committee of Public Safety. He was a complex individual. Controversial in his day and in ours, he was selfless and utterly committed to republican ideals, but he was also a shrewd politician. The Parisian *sans-culottes* provided the base of his support, but he did not alter his dress or conduct to toady to them. For him, the "republic of virtue" entailed renunciation of efforts to make selfish gains from political office. This was a noble thought, but his confidence in his own selflessness enabled him to overlook issues of morality and view the Terror as nothing more than an instrument of swift, republican justice. He and his supporters were the first in the long line of secular ideologues (both on the left and the right) who, in the name of humanity, have caused much suffering in Europe during the past two centuries.

REPRESSION OF THE SOCIETY OF REVOLUTIONARY REPUBLICAN WOMEN

Women were excluded from formal participation in republican politics, but some of them set up institutions of their own and went in pursuit of the internal enemies of the revolution. The Society of Revolutionary Republican Women, which Pauline Léon and Claire Lacombe founded in May 1793, filled the galleries of the Convention with women who came to hear the debates and cheer their favorite speakers. They pushed a radical political agenda: stricter controls on the price of food and other commodities, persecution of food hoarders, and the indictment of working women who were judged to be insufficiently revolutionary.

By October 1793, the Convention had begun to fear the turmoil these women were creating, and it suppressed their organization. The deputies justified their action in Rousseauian terms—arguing that women were, by nature, domestic creatures who had no place in the public realm that belonged to men. Olympe de Gouges, author of the Declaration of the Rights of Woman, objected, and when she spoke out against the Terror and accused certain Jacobins of corruption, she was guillotined (November 1793). Legislation was then passed to exclude women from military service and shut them out of the galleries of the Convention. In the republic of virtue, men were to handle the responsibilities of citizenship while women tended to their homes.

DE-CHRISTIANIZATION

The republic of virtue's most dramatic effort to break with a past it regarded as corrupt was its decision to de-Christianize France. In October 1793, the Convention issued a new calendar that chose the day on which the Republic was established, not the birth of Christ, as history's pivot point. The year was divided into twelve months of thirty days each with names (Thermidor, Floreal, etc.) derived from the seasons. Every tenth day, rather than every seventh, was a holiday. In November the Convention declared the Cathedral of Notre Dame in Paris a "Temple of Reason," and officers were dispatched to the provinces to close churches, persecute believers, and sometimes force priests to marry. This roused much opposition and drove a wedge between the provinces and the revolutionary government in Paris. In May 1794, the government abandoned the worship of reason as too abstract an idea for the masses, and it endorsed the "Cult of the Supreme Being." This was a deistic civic religion, the purpose of which was to promote morality.

The Festival of the Supreme Being, which took place in June 1794, inaugurated Robespierre's new civic religion. Its climax occurred when a statue of Atheism was burned and another statue of Wisdom rose from the ashes.

Pierre-Antoine Demachy, *Festival of the Supreme Being at the Champ de Mars on June 8. 1794.* Musée de la Ville de Paris, Musée Carnavalet, Paris, France. Bridgeman-Giraudon/Art Resource, NY

REVOLUTIONARY TRIBUNALS

During the summer of 1793, the Convention established tribunals to search out and try the enemies of the republic. Much hinged on the definition of *enemy*, which shifted as the months passed. The term eventually came to include some staunch republicans who made the mistake of opposing the will of the dominant faction in the revolutionary government.

The first victims of the terror were Marie Antoinette, other members of the royal family, and some aristocrats, who were executed in October 1793. Certain Girondist politicians were next. By the early months of 1794, the search for enemies of the revolution had spread to the provinces and had begun to involve members of every social class—including the *sans-culottes*. Thousands died.

THE END OF THE TERROR

Revolutionaries Turn Against Themselves   Late in the winter of 1794, Robespierre began to manipulate the Terror to remove persons who threatened him—both radicals and conservatives. On March 24, he executed some leaders of the *enragés, sans-culottes* extremists who were pressing for more price regulation, social equalization, and de-Christianization. Robespierre then accused some conservative republicans of a lack of commitment to the war, of profiting, and of rejecting the link between politics and moral virtue. On June 10, he secured passage of the Law of 22 Prairial, which increased the murderous efficiency of the tribunals by permitting them to convict suspects without hearing substantial evidence.

Fall of Robespierre   On July 26, Robespierre made an ill-tempered speech in the Convention, declaring that unnamed leaders of the government were conspiring against the revolution. This vague but potent threat caused the members of the Convention, who feared becoming his next victims, to act on their instinct for self-preservation. The next day, the ninth of the month of Thermidor, they shouted him down when he rose to make another speech. That night they arrested him, and the following day (July 28, 1794) he was executed. Robespierre had destroyed his rivals without creating any supporters of his own.

THE THERMIDORIAN REACTION

By the late summer of 1794, uprisings in the provinces had been crushed, and the foreign war was also going well. A growing sense of security and a spreading conviction that the revolution had consumed enough of its children brought the Terror to an end. The largest number of its over 25,000 victims had been peasants and *sans-culottes*.

WHAT COURSE did the French Revolution take after 1794?

The French Revolution

1789

May 5	The Estates General opens at Versailles
June 17	The National Assembly is declared
June 20	The Tennis Court Oath
July 14	Fall of the Bastille
August 4	Surrender of feudal rights
August 27	Declaration of the Rights of Man and Citizen
October 5	Parisian women march on Versailles

1790

July 14	Louis XVI accepts constitutional monarchy

1791

June 20	The royal family attempts to flee
October 1	Formation of the Legislative Assembly

1792

April 20	France declares war on Austria
September 2	The September Massacres
September 21	The Convention meets; monarchy is abolished

1793

January 21	Louis XVI is executed
February 1	France declares war on Great Britain
April	Formation of the Committee of Public Safety
June 22	Adoption of the Constitution of 1793
August 23	*Levée en Masse* proclaimed
October 16	Marie Antoinette is executed
November 10	The Cult of Reason and the revolutionary calendar

1794

March 24	Execution of leaders of the *sans-culottes*
May 7	Cult of the Supreme Being proclaimed
June 10	The Law of 22 Prairial is adopted
July 27	Ninth of Thermidor, the fall of Robespierre

1795

August 22	Constitution of the Year III and the Directory

Thermidorian Reaction
Tempering of revolutionary fervor that led to the establishment of a new constitutional regime.

A tempering of revolutionary fervor—the **Thermidorian Reaction**—had set in by July 1794, and it led to the establishment of a new constitutional regime. Wealthy middle-class and professional people replaced the *sans-culottes* as the dominant influence on politics. The Convention allowed the Girondists who had been in prison or hiding to retake their seats, and there was a general amnesty for political prisoners. The power of the Committee of Public Safety was greatly reduced, and the notorious Law of 22 Prairial was repealed. The Paris Commune was outlawed, and some of its leaders and some Convention deputies were executed. A bloody reaction (the "white terror") set in as persons who had been involved in the Reign of Terror were attacked and often murdered. The Jacobin Club was closed, and Jacobins were executed with no more due process than they had extended to their victims. Some of this was spontaneous mob action, but some was approved by the Convention.

The republic of virtue succumbed, if not to vice, at least to pleasure. Well-to-do people gave up the affectation of dressing like the poor. Theaters presented new plays. Prostitutes returned to the streets. Families of victims of the Terror gave parties in which they appeared with shaved necks (like prisoners prepared for the guillotine) banded by blood-red ribbons. Catholic worship services were again legalized, and there was a marked resurgence of Catholic piety. The Thermidorians had had enough of proposals for political and social reform. They wanted the stability of traditional institutions and a return to prerevolutionary family life—an objective that cost French women whatever new liberties they had obtained.

ESTABLISHMENT OF THE DIRECTORY

The fully democratic constitution adopted in 1793 had never gone into effect, and the Convention now replaced it with the Constitution of the Year III. This provided for a bicameral legislature: a Council of Elders composed of married or widowed men over forty years of age, and a Council of Five Hundred whose members were married or single males who were at least thirty years old. A five-person Directory chosen by the Elders from a list submitted by the Council of Five Hundred provided executive leadership. Only civilians who met certain property qualifications could vote, but all soldiers were enfranchised.

By 1795, permanent changes had taken place in France, and the Directory sought only to moderate, not reverse, the revolution. Assumptions of civic equality had replaced traditional distinctions of rank and birth, and social status was determined more by property than blood. Some people who had never been allowed political power now had it—at least to a limited degree. The principle of representative government had been established, but it was not yet clear who would be permitted representation. The post-Thermidorian course of the French Revolution was a victory for people of property, and the largest new propertied class to emerge from the revolutionary turmoil was the peasantry. The destruction of aristocratic privilege allowed the small farmers to claim the land they worked without assuming the burden (imposed on peasants who were liberated elsewhere) of paying compensation to its previous owners.

REMOVAL OF THE *SANS-CULOTTES* FROM POLITICAL LIFE

With the war effort succeeding, the Convention severed its ties with the *sans-culottes,* repealed the price controls they had demanded, and returned to an unregulated economy. This led, in the winter of 1794–1795, to the worst food shortages of the revolutionary era. Royalist agents tried to take advantage of the discontent to turn the people against the Convention, and on October 5, 1795 (13 Vendémiaire), rioting erupted in Paris. The Directory dispatched a general named Napoleon Bonaparte (1769–1821) to disperse the crowd with cannon.

In March 1795, the Convention concluded peace with Prussia and Spain and took steps to prevent either extreme democrats or royalists from winning seats in the Council of Five Hundred. The Directory then again beat back the radicals by executing Gracchus Babeuf (1760–1797), the leader of a "Conspiracy of Equals" that advocated radical democracy and greater equality of property. The Directory lacked a broad base of support, but it survived because no one wanted to overturn the government while France was at war with Austria and Great Britain. The Directory's dependence on (and vulnerability to) its army was, however, to have profound consequences for France and the Western world.

SUMMARY

The Crisis of the French Monarchy The cost of the Seven Years' War had caused a financial crisis for all Europe's monarchies. France's financial situation was exacerbated by the expenses incurred in joining the colonists' side in the American Revolutionary War. The government needed to raise new taxes; new taxes had to be approved by the nobility. France's noble class had been trying to reassert power ever since the end of Louis XIV's reign. The monarch's need for cash presented a perfect opportunity for the aristocrats to gain concessions from the king. Through various negotiations and standoffs, the aristocracy forced Louis XVI to reconvene the Estates General, which had not met since 1614.

The Revolution of 1789 The 1789 calling of the Estates General and the events that followed have shaped the meanings of nation, state, and citizenship ever since. The royal council doubled the third estate, potentially strengthening the hand of the bourgeoisie and the nobility. On June 20, 1789, as delegates to the Estates General were attempting to resolve procedural questions, the Third Estate launched the National Assembly. On July 14, 1789, a mob stormed the Bastille and injected a populist, urban element into the political drama. In the countryside, the "Great Fear" intensified ongoing peasant disturbances aimed at limiting aristocratic privilege; on August 4, 1789, nobles and liberals in the National Constituent Assembly renounced their privileges. From then on, all French men were subject to the same laws. On August 27, 1789, the Assembly issued the Declaration of the Rights of Man and Citizen. Again, women were not portrayed as holding political rights. On October 5, 1789, Parisian women marched on Versailles and forced Louis XVI to move to Paris.

The Reconstruction of France The National Constituent Assembly reorganized France as a constitutional monarchy, with a rational administration, an unregulated economy, and a state-controlled church. Property, in all its forms, was protected, and

wealth—rather than bloodlines and titles—determined power. The Assembly divided the citizenry into "active" (propertied males) and "passive" (everyone else) elements. Olympe de Gouges protested with her "Declaration of the Rights of Woman." Local and judicial administration was reorganized, and workers' organizations were banned. Most significantly in the long term, the Assembly confiscated all land and property of the Roman Catholic Church in France, in order to pay the royal debt. Under the Civil Constitution of the Clergy, the Roman Catholic Church was brought under the direct control of the French state. These moves against the church created massive opposition. The royal family attempted to flee France. The National Constituent Assembly closed in September 1791, having transformed the nation. The newly reconstructed nation was not stable, however.

The End of the Monarchy: A Second Revolution The short-lived (1791–1792) Legislative Assembly was factionalized. Jacobins had lobbied for a republic during the National Constituent Assembly. A faction within the Jacobin faction, the Girondists, took the leadership of the Legislative Assembly. On April 20, 1792, the Legislative Assembly declared war on Austria. The Girondists hoped war would suppress the counterrevolution within France; Louis XVI also supported war with Austria, hoping war would strengthen the monarchy. Instead, the *sans-culottes* seized control. In August 1792, a Parisian mob forced the royal family to take refuge in the Legislative Assembly; from then on, Louis XVI was unable to function as a monarch. The Paris Commune executed 1,200 prisoners in the September Massacres, and on September 21, 1792, the Convention met to write a democratic constitution for a French republic. Radical Jacobins within the Convention who collaborated with the *sans-culottes* constituted the "Mountain." In February 1793, the Convention declared war on Great Britain, Holland, and Spain; in March, the Vendée in France erupted in a royalist revolt.

Europe at War with the Revolution British statesman Edmund Burke, in his 1790 *Reflections on the Revolution in France,* was the first observer to articulate theoretical criticisms of the French Revolution and to predict further turmoil as a result of the revolution. European governments adopted repressive policies in response to France's ideas and military actions. In response to Polish reforms inspired by the Revolution, Austria, Prussia, and Russia partitioned Poland out of existence. William Pitt the Younger suppressed political freedoms in Great Britain. By April 1793, the governments of all the countries with which France was at war—Austria, Prussia, Great Britain, Spain, Sardinia, and Holland—formed the First Coalition, an alliance to protect their social structures, political systems, and economic interests from the aggression of the revolution.

The Reign of Terror In 1793, mobilization for war touched almost every aspect of French life. The Committee of General Security and the Committee of Public Safety were formed in April 1793 to facilitate the war effort. In August, the entire nation was requisitioned into national service; France had Europe's first citizen army. At about the same time, the Reign of Terror began. Robespierre and others in the Convention believed they were creating a "republic of virtue." The Convention established revolutionary tribunals in the summer of 1793; the Terror's first victims were Marie Antoinette and other members of the royal family. The Society of Revolutionary Women were among the first groups to be suppressed; Olympe de Gouges was guillotined in November 1793. Also in November 1793, the Convention attempted to de-Christianize France. Robespierre opposed this move, fearing it would lead to a backlash. In May 1794, he established the "Cult of the Supreme Being," a deistic cult over which he presided. Executions increased in 1794, as Robespierre turned on his political enemies, and a new law permitted convictions even in the absence of substantial evidence. Finally, on July 27, 1794, Robespierre himself was arrested. He was executed the next day, and the Terror died out soon thereafter.

The Thermidorian Reaction   The Thermidorian Reaction represented a tempering of the revolution. Propertied middle-class and professional people replaced the *sans-culottes* as the most influential group. The "white terror" turned violence against some of those responsible for the Terror. Catholicism revived throughout the country. Some progressive social legislation was repealed; women had, if anything, fewer rights than they had in 1789. The Constitution of the Year III created a bicameral legislature, under a five-man executive Directory, all limited to property-holding men. Voting was also limited to property holders and—significantly—soldiers. As the power of the *sans-culottes* waned, they and royalists revolted in Paris in October 1795. Napoleon Bonaparte was the general in charge of putting down their insurrection. Gracchus Babeuf led the equally unsuccessful Conspiracy of Equals in the spring of 1796, arguing for more radical democracy and resulting in his execution. The wars with Prussia and Spain ended in 1795, but France remained at war with Austria and Great Britain. In the absence of broad public support, the Directory came to rely on the army for stability.

REVIEW QUESTIONS

1. How did the financial weaknesses of the French monarchy pave the way for the revolution of 1789? What role did Louis XVI play in the French Revolution? Would a constitutional monarchy have succeeded, or did the revolution ultimately have little to do with the competence of the monarch?

2. How was the Estates General transformed into the National Assembly? Which social and political values associated with the Enlightenment are reflected in the Declaration of the Rights of Man and Citizen? Why has the Civil Constitution of the Clergy been called the greatest blunder of the National Assembly?

3. Why were some political factions dissatisfied with the constitutional settlement of 1791? Who were the *sans-culottes*? How did they acquire political influence? What drew the *sans-culottes* and the Jacobins together? What ended their cooperation?

4. Why did France go to war with Austria in 1792? What were the benefits and drawbacks for France of fighting an external war while in the midst of a domestic political revolution? What were the causes of the Terror? In what ways did the French Revolution both live up to and betray its motto: "liberty, equality and fraternity"?

KEY TERMS

Convention   (p. 446)
émigreés   (p. 444)
Jacobins   (p. 445)

levée en masse   (p. 449)
Reign of Terror   (p. 449)
sans-culottes   (p. 446)

September Massacres   (p. 446)
Thermidorian Reaction   (p. 452)
Third Estate   (p. 436)

    For additional study resources for this chapter, go to:
www.prenhall.com/kagan3/chapter18

19 The Age of Napoleon and the Triumph of Romanticism

CHAPTER HIGHLIGHTS

The Rise of Napoleon Bonaparte In 1799, taking advantage of the weakness of the Directory, Napoleon made himself First Counsul. His use of dictatorial power foreshadowed the policies of twentieth-century dictators.

The Consulate in France (1799–1804) Napoleon's Consulate seemed to bring the stability and moderation the bourgeoisie and peasants desired. He steadily increased his power and crowned himself emperor in 1804.

Napoleon's Empire (1804–1814) Between 1804 and 1815 Napoleon conquered most of Europe. Britain was Napoleon's most powerful and persistent opponent.

European Response to the Empire Opposition to Napoleon fanned the flames of nationalism. Napoleon's invasion of Russia spelled the beginning of the end of his domination. He was forced into exile in the spring of 1814.

The Congress of Vienna and the European Settlement The 1815 Congress of Vienna redrew the map of Europe. Napoleon's escape from exile ended with his final defeat at Waterloo in June 1815.

The Romantic Movement Romanticism was a reaction against the Enlightenment. Romantics emphasized the aspects of human experience that lie outside the realm of reason.

Romantic Questioning of the Supremacy of Reason Rousseau and Kant laid the intellectual foundations of Romanticism. Rousseau believed that civilization was a corrupting influence. Kant argued for the subjectivity of human knowledge.

Romantic Literature Romantic literature stressed imaginative elements and was not bound by formal rules. English and German romantics produced some of the seminal works of the movement.

Romantic Art Romantic artists often featured scenes from the Middle Ages. For them, the Middle Ages represented the social stability and religious reverence that was disappearing from their own era. Romantic artists also sought to portray nature in all of its majestic power.

Religion in the Romantic Period Romantics stressed the emotional connection between the individual and the divine. Methodism developed in England in response to deism and rationalism in the Church of England.

Romantic Views of Nationalism and History Romanticism glorified individuals and individual cultures. The sensibilities of the romantic movement modified European views of Islam and the Arab world, while still preserving some traditional negative attitudes.

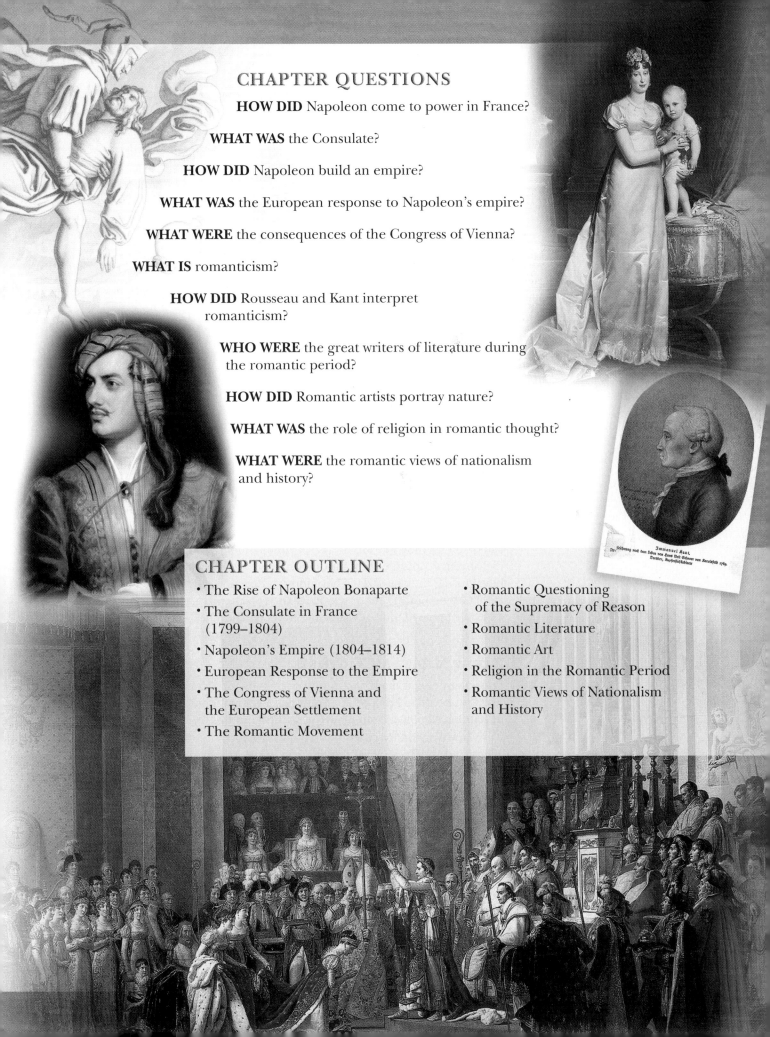

CHAPTER QUESTIONS

HOW DID Napoleon come to power in France?

WHAT WAS the Consulate?

HOW DID Napoleon build an empire?

WHAT WAS the European response to Napoleon's empire?

WHAT WERE the consequences of the Congress of Vienna?

WHAT IS romanticism?

HOW DID Rousseau and Kant interpret romanticism?

WHO WERE the great writers of literature during the romantic period?

HOW DID Romantic artists portray nature?

WHAT WAS the role of religion in romantic thought?

WHAT WERE the romantic views of nationalism and history?

CHAPTER OUTLINE

- The Rise of Napoleon Bonaparte
- The Consulate in France (1799–1804)
- Napoleon's Empire (1804–1814)
- European Response to the Empire
- The Congress of Vienna and the European Settlement
- The Romantic Movement
- Romantic Questioning of the Supremacy of Reason
- Romantic Literature
- Romantic Art
- Religion in the Romantic Period
- Romantic Views of Nationalism and History

IMAGE KEY

Image Key for pages 456–457 is on page 479.

HOW DID Napoleon come to power in France?

By the late 1790s, many French people—especially property owners, who now included the peasantry—were longing for more political stability than the Directory seemed able to provide. The army, an institution associated with the values and successes of the revolution, offered the best hope for securing the nation. The most political of its generals was Napoleon Bonaparte. Once in power, he consolidated many of the achievements of the revolution. Ultimately, however, he overthrew the republic, declared himself emperor, and embarked on a mission of conquest that continued for over a decade. France's military offensive overturned Europe's old political and social order and fostered fierce nationalism among the French and the countries that allied to defeat Napoleon.

The Napoleonic period saw the flowering of the romantic era in European cultural history. Some romantic ideas (nationalism, for example) sprang from the French Revolution, but the revolutionaries had opposed others (respect for history and religion most specifically).

THE RISE OF NAPOLEON BONAPARTE

The chief danger to the Directory came from royalists. Royalists believed the restoration of the Bourbon monarchy offered the best hope for restoring stability to France, and in the spring elections of 1797, supporters of constitutional monarchy won the majority of offices. On 18 Fructidor (September 4, 1797) the Directory staged a coup d'état to preserve the republic. They seized control of the legislature, imposed censorship, exiled some of their opponents, and asked Napoleon Bonaparte, the soldier who had put down the riots spawned by the Thermidorian Reaction, to protect them once again.

Napoleon Bonaparte was born in 1769 on the Mediterranean island of Corsica. France's annexation of Corsica a year earlier made it possible for him to go to French schools and obtain a commission as a French artillery officer (1785). Napoleon's family was impoverished minor nobility, but he was a fiery Jacobin and strong supporter of the revolution. His radical background was a career liability during the era of the Thermidorian Reaction, but he won the trust of the Directory by putting down the Parisian mob that threatened it on October 5, 1795. As a reward, he was promoted to brigadier general and given a command in Italy.

EARLY MILITARY VICTORIES

Prussia and Spain made peace with France in 1795, but Britain and Austria refused to accede to France's annexation of Belgium. France put pressure on them by sending Napoleon into Italy to evict the Austrians from the provinces of Lombardy and Venetia. Napoleon won a quick victory and, on his own initiative, he negotiated the Treaty of Campo Formio with Austria. Austria ended hostilities and acknowledged France's domination of Italy and Switzerland.

Napoleon did not think it was possible to invade Britain from France. He proposed instead to undermine Britain by weakening its hold on its empire. His plan was to take Egypt from the Ottomans and use it as a base to drive the British fleet from the Mediterranean and cut Britain's communications with India. Napoleon overran Egypt without difficulty, but he was stranded there when the British admiral, Horatio Nelson (1758–1805), destroyed the French fleet at Abukir on August 1, 1798. The primary effect of his campaign was to alarm Russia, Austria, and the Ottomans and drive them into an alliance with Britain (the Second Coalition). By 1799, France was facing invasion and the Ottoman Empire, having previously lost the Crimea to Russia, began to contemplate reforms in hopes of resisting further European encroachments on its territory.

THE CONSTITUTION OF THE YEAR VIII

As confidence in the Directory faded, one of the Directors (the Abbé Siéyès) plotted to establish a new government with an executive that was strong enough to ignore the whims of the electorate. This gave Napoleon an opportunity, for military support was essential to any coup's success. The general deserted his doomed army in Egypt, which was soon occupied by Britain, and returned to France. Some people thought he deserved a court-martial, but Siéyès needed the help Napoleon offered. On 19 Brumaire (November 10, 1799), Napoleon's troops dispersed the legislature and cleared the way for Siéyès's faction to implement a new constitution.

In this early-nineteenth-century cartoon, England, personified by a caricature of William Pitt, and France, personified by a caricature of Napoleon, are carving out their areas of interest around the globe.

Bildarchiv Preussischer Kulturbesitz

Siéyès intended to vest executive authority in three consuls. (Their title was intended to invite comparison with the Roman Republic.) Napoleon, however, swept him aside and in December (1799) issued the Constitution of the Year VIII. Behind a screen of democratic and republican gestures, it vested total authority in a magistrate called the First Consul—a post Napoleon claimed for himself. Napoleon anticipated the dictators of the twentieth century by combining military force, revolutionary rhetoric, and appeals to nationalism to mobilize his country for imperialistic conquests.

THE CONSULATE IN FRANCE (1799–1804)

WHAT WAS the Consulate?

*T*he French Revolution ended with Napoleon's **Consulate**. From the perspective of most members of the Third Estate, it had achieved its goals. Hereditary privilege was abolished. Obstacles to the careers of professionals and merchants had been removed. The peasants were satisfied with the land they had acquired and the termination of their feudal dues. The politically influential propertied classes were profoundly conservative, and they did not want to imperil their new privileges or share them with the lower social orders. They overwhelmingly approved Napoleon's constitution in a national plebiscite, for they believed he would provide the best defense for the status quo.

SUPPRESSING FOREIGN ENEMIES AND DOMESTIC OPPOSITION

Napoleon pleased his supporters by making peace with France's enemies. Russia had already left the Second Coalition, and in 1800, a French victory at Marengo, Italy, induced Austria to end hostilities. Britain, having been abandoned by its allies, came to terms with Napoleon in 1802 (the Treaty of Amiens). (See "Encountering the Past: Sailors and Canned Food.")

Having secured his country from external threats, Napoleon set about restoring its internal order. He stamped out a royalist rebellion in the west and,

Consulate   A republican facade for one-man government by Napoleon.

ENCOUNTERING THE PAST

SAILORS AND CANNED FOOD

N ew technologies often emerge during wartime, and in 1803, Napoleon's navy carried out the first experiments with something that has become a staple of modern life: canned food. Earlier methods of food preservation (drying, salting, pickling, smoking, fermenting, or condensing) altered taste and destroyed nutrients. Navies were hampered by the fact that sailors who spent a long time at sea on a diet of bread and salted meat developed scurvy and other illnesses caused by malnutrition. If fleets were to undertake longer tours of duty at sea and armies campaign where they could not live off the land, some way had to be found to supply them with more healthy food.

In the 1790s, the French government offered a prize for anyone who could invent a superior method for preserving food. The challenge was met by Nicholas Appert, a Parisian chef, who invented canning. Appert did not know of the existence of the microbes that spoil food, but he stumbled across a process that worked by destroying them. He sealed food in glass jars filled with water or sauce and cooked these jars in a hot water bath. The result was food that did not deteriorate and kept its taste and nutrients. Sailors on several of Napoleon's ships were the first (in 1803) to test Appert's new products.

In 1810, Appert published information about his process, and by 1813, an English company was canning food in tins (which were cheaper and more durable than glass jars). By the middle of the nineteenth century, canned goods had entered the diets of millions of people in western Europe and North America.

WHAT MOTIVATED the work that went into the discovery of the canning process?

Nicholas Appert (1749–1841) invented canning as a way of preserving food nutritiously. Canned food could be transported over long distances without spoiling.

Private Collection/Bridgeman Art Library

for the first time in years, brought Brittany and the Vendée under the control of the central government. He courted his enemies, issued a general amnesty, and provided employment for people of all political persuasions. He found offices for those who had led the Reign of Terror, those who had fled it, those who favored constitutional monarchy, and those who had been agents of the Old Regime. Napoleon valued loyalty to his person above ideology, and his tightly centralized government (and secret police) efficiently eliminated all opposition.

Napoleon seized every opportunity to strengthen his regime. In 1804, his soldiers even violated the sovereignty of the German state of Baden by invading it to capture the Bourbon duke of Enghien. The duke was accused of leading a royalist plot and put to death even though Napoleon knew him to be innocent. The episode turned other countries against France, and Charles Maurice de

The coronation of Napoleon, December 2, 1804, as painted by Jacques-Louis David. Having first crowned himself, the emperor is shown about to place the crown on the head of Josephine. Napoleon instructed David to paint Pope Pius VII with his hand raised in blessing.

Jacques Louis David (1748–1825), "Consecration of the Emperor Napoleon I and Coronation of Empress Josephine," 1806-07. Louvre, Paris. Bridgeman-Giraudon/Art Resource, NY

Talleyrand-Périgord (1754–1838), Napoleon's foreign minister, later branded it "worse than a crime—a blunder."

CONCORDAT WITH THE ROMAN CATHOLIC CHURCH

Religion created problems for Napoleon's government. Some of the Roman Catholic clergy were counterrevolutionaries, and many pious laypeople were unhappy with the secularism the revolution had promoted. Napoleon understood religion's value as an instrument of social control, and he wanted to harness it for use by the state. In 1801, he shocked his anticlerical supporters by concluding a concordat with Pope Pius VII. By acknowledging "Catholicism to be the religion of the great majority of French citizens," the agreement restored the official status of the Roman Catholic Church, but Napoleon did not grant the church any power or independence. Its clergy had to swear oaths of loyalty to the state. The state appointed its bishops, paid their salaries, and provided financial support for one priest in each of its parishes. In exchange, the church gave up claims to the property it had lost to the revolution. In 1802, a document called the Organic Articles declared the state supreme over the church, and privileges granted to Protestants and Jews further moderated the influence of Roman Catholicism in France.

THE NAPOLEONIC CODE

In 1802, a plebiscite granted Napoleon the office of consul for life. He then revised the constitution to enhance his authority and recodified French law to strengthen central government. The Civil Code of 1804 (the so-called Napoleonic Code) was designed to safeguard property and the established social order. It confirmed the abolition of privileges based on birth. It forbade the selling of state offices and endorsed appointment based on merit. It took a conservative approach to labor and family issues. It forbade workers' organizations and gave fathers extensive power over their children—and husbands over their wives. It rejected primogeniture in favor of a system of inheritance that distributed estates among all a decedent's children, including females. It required married women to gain the consent of their husbands before disposing of property, and it made divorce more difficult for women than for men. The Napoleonic Code superseded a patchwork of earlier legal customs that differed from region to region, and this made it more difficult for women to protect their interests. They could no longer, as some had previously, exploit confusions within the law.

ESTABLISHING A DYNASTY

In 1804, a failed assassination attempt provided Napoleon with a rationale for ending the republic and establishing an empire. He argued that as emperor he could found a dynasty, and the hereditary rights of his descendants would guarantee continuity of government and make assassination pointless. This necessitated yet another constitution, which received overwhelming ratification by a plebiscite. Napoleon invited the pope to the cathedral of Notre Dame to witness his coronation, but not to crown him. Emperor Napoleon I placed the crown on his own head.

HOW DID Napoleon build an empire?

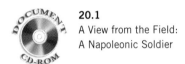

20.1
A View from the Field:
A Napoleonic Soldier

NAPOLEON'S EMPIRE (1804–1814)

Between 1804, when he was crowned emperor, and 1815, when he was defeated at Waterloo, Napoleon conquered most of Europe. His campaigns astonished the world, redrew political borders, and unleashed the powerful forces of nationalism. Napoleon's success derived in part from his control of the resources of a country that had been militarily mobilized by revolution. He could muster about 700,000 soldiers at a time, risk as many as 100,000 in a single battle, endure heavy losses, and return to fight again. No single opponent could match his resources. Even coalitions failed to equal him, until Napoleon made some fatal mistakes.

CONQUERING AN EMPIRE

The Peace of Amiens, which France and Great Britain concluded in 1802, was merely a truce, for France's neighbors were suspicious of—and opposed to—Napoleon's ambitions. When he sent an army to recover Haiti from rebels who had seized it, the British assumed this was the beginning of a campaign to win back France's American empire. His interventions in the Dutch Republic, Italy, and Switzerland, and the opportunity the Treaty of Campo Formio gave him to diminish Austria's influence and dominate western Germany's petty states spread anxiety among the European powers.

British Naval Supremacy   Britain declared war on France in May 1803. William Pitt the Younger returned as prime minister in 1804 and organized the Third Coalition. Once again, Russia and Austria joined Britain in opposing France, and on October 21, 1805, a great naval victory raised the allies' hopes. Horatio, Lord Nelson, a British admiral, destroyed the combined French and Spanish fleets at the Battle of Trafalgar. The victory cost Nelson his life, but it guaranteed that France could not invade Britain and gave Britain control of the sea for the rest of the war.

Napoleonic Victories in Central Europe   The allies had less to rejoice at on land. Before Trafalgar, Napoleon had marched down the Danube River and engaged the Austrians. In mid-October, he defeated a large Austrian army at Ulm and proceeded to occupy Vienna. On December 2, 1805, in perhaps his greatest victory, he routed a combined Austrian and Russian army at Austerlitz. Austria then agreed (in the Treaty of Pressburg) to withdraw from Italy and leave Napoleon in control of the peninsula north of Rome. In July 1806, Napoleon established the Confederation of the Rhine

OVERVIEW   NAPOLEON AND THE CONTINENTAL SYSTEM

1806	Napoleon establishes the Continental System, prohibiting all trade with England
1807	The peace conference at Tilsit results in Russia joining the Continental System and becoming an ally of Napoleon
1809 and 1810	Napoleon at the peak of his power
1810	Russia withdraws from the Continental System and resumes relations with Britain; Napoleon plans to crush Russia militarily
1812	Napoleon invades Russia; the Russians adopt a scorched earth policy and burn Moscow; the thwarted Napoleon deserts his dwindling army and rushes back to Paris

and removed most of the western German principalities from the Habsburgs' Holy Roman Empire. Francis II of Austria conceded the end of the old empire and henceforth styled himself "Emperor of Austria."

At this point, Prussia, which had remained neutral, declared war on France, but Napoleon crushed the Prussians in famous encounters at Jena and Auerstädt (October 14, 1806). Two weeks later he entered Berlin. On June 13, 1807, he defeated the Russians at Friedland and moved on to Königsberg, the capital of East Prussia.

Treaty of Tilsit   Tsar Alexander I (r. 1801–1825) could not risk another defeat, and on July 7, 1807, he sued for peace. The Treaty of Tilsit confirmed France's conquests, but Alexander managed to save his Prussian ally from extinction—but at the cost of the loss of half its territory.

Napoleon disposed of the lands he conquered as if they were his family's private property. He surrounded his French empire with satellite states governed by his relatives. His stepson governed Italy. Three of his brothers and his brother-in-law became kings. (Only his brother Lucien, whose wife Napoleon disliked, was denied a kingdom.) Napoleon's aggrandizement of his family was unpopular and provided a focus for organizing opposition to his imperial pretensions.

THE CONTINENTAL SYSTEM

The Treaty of Tilsit left Britain the only remaining major power still opposed to France. Napoleon could not compete militarily with the British navy, but he was able to threaten his opponent with economic warfare. The Berlin and Milan decrees, which he issued in 1806 and 1807, closed all continental ports to British commerce—both those he controlled directly and those of the remaining neutral states that could not risk offending him. This "Continental System" was intended to cripple the British economy, cause domestic unrest, and prompt a revolution that would overthrow the British government. It backfired, however. It hurt the European states more than Britain, whose economy was sustained by access to growing markets in the Americas and the eastern Mediterranean. (See Map 19–1.)

Napoleon refused to compensate for the loss of foreign trade by establishing free trade within his empire and imposed tariffs favoring France. This reduced the willingness of merchants to cooperate with the boycott of Britain and encouraged smuggling. It was in part to prevent smuggling that Napoleon invaded Spain in 1808 and began the campaign that led to his ruin.

QUICK REVIEW

The Continental System
- Treaty of Tilsit left Britain as sole power opposing France
- Napoleon tried to cripple Britain's economy by closing continental ports to British commerce
- Policy created resentment in Europe

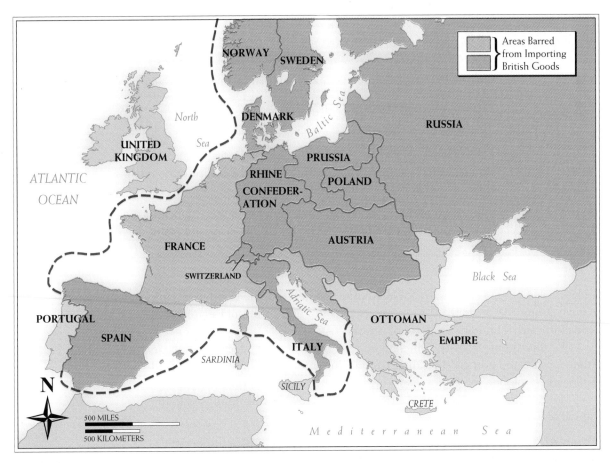

MAP 19–1

The Continental System, 1806–1810 Napoleon hoped to cut off all British trade with the European continent and thereby drive the British from the war. The areas in peach indicate the French Empire. These lands, along with the Grand Empire and Napoleon's allies (in blue) made up the Continental System.

DID THE Continental System deprive Britain of all its overseas trade? Did it guarantee free trade within continental Europe?

EUROPEAN RESPONSE TO THE EMPIRE

WHAT WAS the European response to Napoleon's empire?

Napoleon's conquests spread Enlightenment reforms and the ideals of France's revolution. Wherever he ruled, the Napoleonic Code was imposed, hereditary social distinctions were abolished, feudal dues disappeared, peasants were freed from serfdom, the guilds and oligarchies that had long dominated urban life were deprived of power, churches were subordinated to the state, and policies of religious toleration replaced church monopolies. It was clear, however, that Napoleon's policies were intended first and foremost to promote his own glory and enrich France. It was not long, therefore, before the peoples he had conquered became restive.

GERMAN NATIONALISM AND PRUSSIAN REFORM

Napoleon's wars had a major impact on Germany. The great German intellectuals of the Enlightenment (Immanuel Kant, Friedrich von Schiller, and Gotthold Lessing) had been neither politically active nor nationalistic. Germany, of course, had never been a united country with a clear sense of national identity.

Nationalism was a new idea. It flourished with the romantic movement that sprang up in Germany in the early nineteenth century.

In the beginning, German nationalists simply celebrated the uniqueness of German culture, which they said sprang from the special history of the German people. Napoleon's humiliation of Prussia at Jena in 1806, however, changed their thinking, and they began to view nationalism as a safeguard for German culture. They warned that conquest by France endangered the independence and achievements of German-speaking peoples, and they claimed that Germans had to unite if they hoped to survive the French onslaught. France had become powerful by appealing to the patriotism of its people, and the German nationalists hoped something similar would guarantee a future for Germany.

After Tilsit, only a remnant of Prussia was free to indulge patriotic feelings. Other German states were either under Napoleon's thumb or actively collaborating with him. Their nationalists, therefore, fled to Prussia, where they called for German unification and reform. These ideas were anathema to the Junker nobility and Prussia's ruler, Frederick William III, but the losses at Jena gave them no option but to reform and reorganize. Baron von Stein (1757–1831) and Count von Hardenberg (1750–1822) headed efforts to rebuild Prussia. Neither man wanted to reduce the monarch's autocratic power or weaken the Junkers who staffed the state bureaucracy and the army officer corps. Their plan was to fight France by becoming what it had become—a democracy led by a strong monarchy. To this end, Stein abolished serfdom and ended the Junker monopoly of land ownership. The Junkers, however, resisted the clean sweep of medieval customs that took place in western Germany's principalities. Prussian peasants were allowed to leave the land if they chose, but those who stayed continued to owe manorial labor. The end of serfdom was politically progressive, but it did nothing to solve social and economic problems created by a population explosion that was enlarging the country's landless work force.

Prussia's loss at Jena made it clear that an army composed of serfs and mercenaries and commanded by a hereditary nobility could not equal France's companies of free patriots led by officers chosen for merit. Prussia's reformers tried to remedy this situation by abolishing inhumane discipline, nurturing patriotism, giving merit promotions, admitting commoners to the officer corps, and establishing war colleges to modernize strategy and tactics. These measures helped restore the Prussian military, but Napoleon tried to impede its growth by limiting Prussia to 42,000 active troops. The Prussians evaded the ceiling he imposed by raising a new group of "active" recruits each year and shifting soldiers who completed their training to the reserves. After Napoleon's retreat in 1813, Prussia imposed universal conscription, and by 1814, it had an army of 270,000 men.

THE WARS OF LIBERATION

Spain   Resentment of French occupation was stronger in Spain than elsewhere in Europe. In 1807, a French army was allowed to enter the Iberian Peninsula to help Spain put pressure on Portugal, England's ally. The army stayed in Spain to protect lines of supply, and in 1808, Napoleon deposed the Spanish Bourbon dynasty and made his brother Joseph king of Spain. Subsequent attacks on the privileges of the church increased public outrage, and the peasants, urged on by the lower clergy and the monks, rose in rebellion.

Napoleon faced a new kind of warfare in Spain. Instead of massed armies, small guerrilla bands cut his communication lines, killed stragglers from his forces, destroyed isolated garrisons, and disappeared into the mountains before he could respond. The British eventually sent an army commanded by the future

Goya y Lucientes, Francisco de Goya, recorded Napoleon's troops executing Spanish guerrilla fighters who had rebelled against the French occupation in The Third of May, 1808.

Francisco de Goya, "Los fusilamientos del 3 de Mayo 1808." 1814. Oil on canvas, 8.6× 11.4. © Museo Nacional del Prado, Madrid

duke of Wellington, Sir Arthur Wellesley (1769–1852), to aid the Spanish insurgents. This began a long campaign that drained French soldiers from other fronts and contributed to Napoleon's eventual defeat.

Austria France's troubles in Spain tempted Austria to renew the war and avenge German losses at Austerlitz. This proved to be a serious miscalculation. The help Austria counted on from German princes did not materialize, and Napoleon's difficulties elsewhere were not as great as the Austrians had assumed. Napoleon again defeated the Austrians (at the Battle of Wagram) and forced them, by the Peace of Schönbrunn, to surrender territory containing over 3.5 million people. Among the spoils Napoleon claimed was Marie Louise, the Austrian emperor's daughter. Napoleon's forty-six-year-old wife, Josephine de Beauharnais, had borne him no children, and he was determined to found a dynasty. By divorcing Josephine and marrying the eighteen-year-old Habsburg princess, he hoped to produce offspring with ties to the most regal lineage in Europe.

THE INVASION OF RUSSIA

The Franco-Russian alliance concluded at Tilsit was unpopular with Russia's nobles. They disliked France's liberal politics, and Napoleon's Continental System interfered with their timber sales to Britain. Tsar Alexander I also had a long list of grievances against Napoleon. Russia received no help from France in its struggle with the Ottoman Empire, and following the Battle of Wagram, Napoleon annoyed the tsar by creating a French satellite state (the Grand Duchy of Warsaw) on Russia's doorstep. Napoleon violated the Treaty of Tilsit by annexing Holland, and his recognition of the French marshal Bernadotte as King Charles XIV of Sweden and his marriage to Marie Louise of Austria suggested that someone had to do something to curb his ambition. Russia withdrew from the Continental System at the end of 1810 and prepared for war. (See Map 19–2.)

Napoleon mobilized 600,000 soldiers to crush Russia's army of 160,000 men. His preferred strategy was a short campaign determined by a decisive battle, but the Russians deprived him of that option. Knowing it was foolish to risk confronting his superior numbers, they "scorched the earth" and retreated. This deprived the invader of opportunities to forage for food and supplies. Napoleon's so-called Grand Army was unable to live off the land as it progressed, and it could not maintain

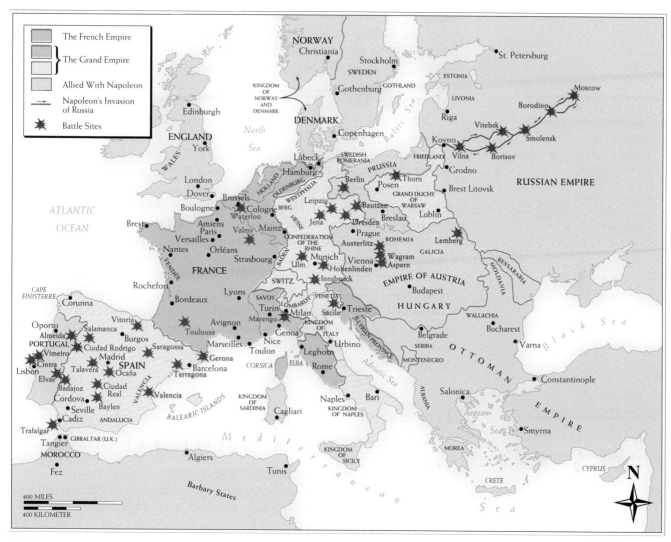

MAP 19–2

Napoleonic Europe in Late 1812   By mid-1812 the areas shown in peach were incorporated into France, and most of the rest of Europe was directly controlled by or allied with Napoleon. But Russia had withdrawn from the failing Continental System, and the decline of Napoleon was about to begin.

WHICH AREAS in Europe were most problematic for Napoleon?

supply lines that lengthened as it was drawn ever more deeply into Russia. Napoleon's advisers urged him to give up the venture, but he was afraid an admission of failure would undermine his hold on his empire. He staked his future on the gamble that the Russians would give him battle rather than abandon Moscow.

In September 1812, public opinion forced the canny Russian commander, General Kutuzov, to halt the retreat and give Napoleon battle. Napoleon fought his bloodiest engagement at Borodino, not far west of Moscow. The French lost 30,000 men and the Russians almost 60,000. Because the Russian army was not destroyed, however, and continued its retreat, Napoleon gained nothing from his victory. The Russians set fire to Moscow and left Napoleon to face a fierce winter far from home with a diminished army and few supplies.

Napoleon made several overtures to Alexander offering to negotiate a peace, but the tsar ignored him. In October what was left of the Grand Army

WHAT WERE the consequences of the Congress of Vienna?

began a long retreat from Moscow, and by December plots against Napoleon were blossoming in France. The emperor left the remnants of his army to struggle home while he hastened ahead to Paris. Only 100,000 of the Grand Army's 600,000 soldiers survived to describe their ordeal.

EUROPEAN COALITION

Napoleon weathered the crisis the disaster created. He put down his opponents in Paris and raised another 350,000 soldiers. Neither the Prussians, the Austrians, nor the Russians were eager to continue fighting, and Prince Klemens von Metternich (1773–1859), Austria's foreign minister, wanted Napoleon to survive with enough power to prevent Russia from dominating Europe. Napoleon, however, refused their offers of compromise. He feared that his self-made dynasty, which lacked the support of history and tradition, would not survive if it showed any sign of weakness.

The last and most powerful coalition against Napoleon formed in 1813. The Russians, with British funding, mounted an offensive and joined forces with the armies of Prussia and Austria. Britain's Wellington, meanwhile, invaded France from Spain. Napoleon's newly rebuilt army was inexperienced and poorly equipped, and his exhausted generals were losing confidence in him. Napoleon himself was worn out and sick. He managed one more victory at Dresden, but in October he was beaten by the allied forces at Leipzig ("the Battle of the Nations"). When Paris fell at the end of March 1814, Napoleon abdicated and went into exile on the island of Elba off the coast of northern Italy.

THE CONGRESS OF VIENNA AND THE EUROPEAN SETTLEMENT

Before Paris fell, the British foreign secretary, Robert Stewart, Viscount Castlereagh (1769–1822), negotiated an agreement with his country's allies. The Treaty of Chaumont (March 9, 1814) restored the Bourbons to the French throne and returned France to the borders it had in 1792. Britain, Austria, Russia, and Prussia also established the Quadruple Alliance, a twenty-year commitment to keep peace in Europe. Remaining problems (and there were many) were to be ironed out at a conference to be held in Vienna. Fear of Napoleon had held the victorious coalition of his enemies together, and as soon as he was gone, differences developed among them.

TERRITORIAL ADJUSTMENTS

The Congress of Vienna met from September 1814 until November 1815. The great powers found it easy to agree on what should be done about France. None of them wanted a single state to dominate Europe, and all were determined that France should not attempt to do so again. France, for a while, welcomed the restoration of its Bourbon monarchy, and most of its citizens considered the restoration of its former boundaries a fair settlement.

The powers erected barriers to block future attempts to expand French territory. It established a kingdom of the Netherlands (including Belgium) on France's northern frontier, and combined Genoa and Piedmont in the south. Austria resumed control of parts of northern Italy, and Prussia claimed land along the Rhine River east of France. Most of Napoleon's arrangements in the rest of Germany were not altered. The congress firmly endorsed the authority of legitimate monarchies and condemned the French Revolution's republican and democratic ideologies. (See Map 19–3.)

MAP EXPLORATION

Interactive map: To explore this map further, go to **http://www.prenhall.com/kagan3/map19.3**

MAP 19–3

Europe 1815, After the Congress of Vienna   The Congress of Vienna achieved the post-Napoleonic territorial adjustments shown on the map. The most notable arrangements dealt with areas along France's borders (the Netherlands, Prussia, Switzerland, and Piedmont) and in Poland and northern Italy.

IN THE European Settlement of 1815, did any single power dominate Europe?

The most difficult challenge that faced the Congress of Vienna was the reorganization of eastern Europe. Alexander I of Russia wanted all of Poland. Prussia was willing to give it to him if it received all of Saxony. Austria, however, refused to surrender its share of Poland, and it did not want Prussia to grow and Russia to penetrate deeper into central Europe. The congress came to a standstill, and a new war might have developed had Talleyrand, France's representative and Napoleon's ex-foreign minister, not suggested a way out. He proposed that France join Britain and Austria in opposing Alexander. When news of a secret treaty among these powers leaked out, the tsar backed down. He agreed to accept a

Significant Dates from the Era of Napoleonic Europe

1797	The Treaty of Campo Formio
1798	Nelson defeats the French navy
1799	The Consulate is established in France
1801	Concordat between France and the papacy
1802	Treaty of Amiens
1803	War renewed between France and Britain
1804	Execution of the Duke of Enghien
	Napoleonic Civil Code issued
	Napoleon crowned emperor
1805	Nelson wins at Trafalgar (October 21)
	Battle of Austerlitz (December 2)
1806	Battle of Jena
	Continental System imposed (November 21)
1807	Treaty of Tilsit
1808	Spain revolts against Napoleon
1809	Battle of Wagram
	Napoleon marries Marie Louise of Austria
1810	Russia leaves the Continental System
1812	Invasion of Russia, battle at Borodino
1813	Leipzig ("Battle of the Nations")
1814	Treaty of Chaumont and the Quadruple Alliance
	Congress of Vienna convenes (September)
1815	Napoleon returns from Elba (March 1)
	Battle of Waterloo (June 18)
	Holy Alliance formed (September 26)
	Quadruple Alliance renewed (November 20)
1821	Napoleon dies on Saint Helena

smaller share of Poland, and Frederick William III of Prussia received only a part of Saxony. Talleyrand's strategy restored France's status as one of Europe's great powers by showing that France still wielded significant influence in international politics.

THE HUNDRED DAYS AND THE QUADRUPLE ALLIANCE

News that the allies in Vienna were squabbling among themselves encouraged Napoleon to escape from Elba, and on March 1, 1815, he landed in France. The French army was loyal to him, and many French people—believing he would better protect their interests than the Bourbon monarch—welcomed his return to power. Napoleon promised a liberal constitution and a peaceful foreign policy, but the allied nations were not convinced. They declared him an outlaw (a new possibility under international law) and mobilized armies to crush him. On June 18, 1815, Wellington, aided by the Prussians under Field Marshal von Blücher, defeated Napoleon at Waterloo, Belgium. Napoleon again abdicated and was exiled to Saint Helena, a tiny Atlantic island off the coast of Africa. He died there in 1821.

The Hundred Days, as the period of Napoleon's return is called, frightened the great powers into imposing harsher terms on France. These included minor territorial losses, a war indemnity, and an army of occupation. Tsar Alexander, whose thinking was influenced by a mystical religious faith, proposed that Europe's monarchs form a "Holy Alliance"—a common front maintained by commitment to Christian principles. Austria and Prussia signed on; but Castlereagh, who thought the idea absurd, declined for England. The Holy Alliance was soon associated with extreme political reaction, and the maintenance of peace in Europe became the task of a renewed Quadruple Alliance of England, Austria, Prussia, and Russia (November 20, 1815).

The settlements negotiated at the Congress of Vienna allowed Europe to avoid general war for a hundred years. Europe's leaders had learned from past failures that the purpose of a treaty should not be to exploit victory but to secure peace. Their goal was not to punish France but to make arrangements that would ensure future stability. This necessitated the creation of a balance of power among states and a process for negotiating adjustments as changing conditions dictated. Politicians rejected the simplistic argument that a country's strength required a trade surplus—the assumption a state could prosper only at the expense of others. They began instead to pursue general growth in agriculture, commerce, and industry in the belief this would benefit everyone.

The diplomats at Vienna have been criticized for failing to recognize the great nationalistic and democratic movements that were to erupt during the course of the nineteenth century. Their chief concern, however, was to cure past ills. To anticipate problems that had yet to manifest themselves, they would have had to have had more insight than is humanly possible.

LE CONGRÈS.

In this political cartoon of the Congress of Vienna, Talleyrand simply watches which way the wind is blowing, Castlereagh hesitates, while the monarchs of Russia, Prussia, and Austria form the dance of the Holy Alliance. The king of Saxony holds on to his crown and the republic of Geneva pays homage to the kingdom of Sardinia.

Bildarchiv Preussischer Kulturbesitz

THE ROMANTIC MOVEMENT

While the French Revolution and Napoleon's reign were unfolding, an important new intellectual movement called **romanticism** spread throughout Europe. It was a reaction against the rationalism and scientism of the Enlightenment. Romantics insisted on the importance of human feelings, intuition, and imagination as supplements for reason in the human quest to understand the world. Many encouraged a revival of Christianity and of the art, literature, and architecture of Europe's Christian Middle Ages. They were fascinated by folklore, folk songs, and fairy tales, and they took dreams, hallucinations, and sleepwalking seriously as phenomena that pointed to a world that lay beyond the reach of empirical observation, sensory data, and discursive reasoning.

ROMANTIC QUESTIONING OF THE SUPREMACY OF REASON

The romantic movement drew on the individualism fostered by the Renaissance and Reformation Protestantism, and the emotionalism associated with religious pietism, sentimental novels, and German poetry of the so-called *Sturm and Drang* era. Two writers closely associated with the Enlightenment, Jean-Jacques Rousseau and Immanuel Kant, also encouraged it by questioning the sufficiency of the *philosophes'* rationalism.

ROUSSEAU AND EDUCATION

Although sharing in the reformist spirit of the Enlightenment, Jean-Jacques Rousseau opposed many of its assumptions. Romantic writers were especially drawn to his claim that society and wealth corrupted human nature. Rousseau's novel *Emile* (1762) set forth his theories about human development. It describes stages in the human maturation process and urges that children be allowed to grow freely and individually—learning by trial and error what reality is and how best to deal with it. The proper role of parents and teachers, Rousseau argued, was to provide the basic necessities of life and ward off manifest harm. Beyond that adults should stay out of the way and let nature take its course. Rousseau

WHAT IS romanticism?

HOW DID Rousseau and Kant interpret romanticism?

20.5
Jean-Jacques Rousseau: from *Emile*

romanticism   Reaction against the rationalism and scientism of the Enlightenment, insisting on the importance of human feelings, intuition, and imagination as supplements for reason in the human quest to understand the world.

Sturm and Drang   ("Storm and Stress") Movement in German romantic literature that emphasized feeling and emotion.

insisted that a child's feelings as well as its reason should be allowed to flourish, and he claimed that his method of unguided education would bring about a new social order dictated by the needs of nature and undistorted by human artifice. The romantics drew two lessons from Rousseau: Individual uniqueness is to be respected, and the individual, nature, and society are organically interrelated.

KANT AND REASON

Immanuel Kant (1724–1804) wrote the two greatest philosophical works of the late eighteenth century: *The Critique of Pure Reason* (1781) and *The Critique of Practical Reason* (1788). They were products of an ambitious attempt to reconcile the rationalism of the Enlightenment with belief in human freedom, immortality, and the existence of God.

Kant rejected the opinion shared by Locke and others that knowledge derives solely from sensory experience. He claimed that the human mind is not a mirror that passively reflects the world around it. The mind actively imposes itself on the world of sensory experience and shapes its perceptions of that world using tools it generates for itself. He called these tools "forms of sensibility" and "categories of understanding." In other words, he believed the mind perceives the world as it does because of its methods of perception. Human knowledge is not the product of an active world imposing itself on a passive mind but of an interaction between sensory experience and a creative intellect.

Kant differentiated between "pure reason," which deals with the phenomenal world of sensory experience, and "practical reason," which intuits a "noumenal" world of ethics and aesthetics. The portion of reality accessible to pure reason was, he thought, quite limited. It could not provide evidence to support belief in transcendental ideas—such as God, eternal life, and ultimate rewards and punishments for personal conduct. These truths belong to the realm of practical reason.

Kant thought all human beings possess an innate sense of moral duty, which he called a **categorical imperative**, an inner command to act in every situation as one would have other people act in that same situation. Kant saw the existence of this imperative (conscience) as proof that nature has endowed us with personal freedom. If we were not free, conscience would have no purpose, for we would not be able to let it guide our actions. This insight gave Kant a starting point for exploring transcendental realities. Whether the romantics called it "practical reason," "imagination," "intuition," or "feeling," they shared Kant's belief that human understanding is a creative act, not just the passive reception of sensory data that Hobbes, Locke, and Hume had imagined. Most romantics assumed that poets and artists possess this creative ability in particular abundance.

ROMANTIC LITERATURE

The term *romantic* was used in England and France as early as the seventeenth century to describe literature that was judged to be unrealistic, sentimental, or excessively fanciful. In both England and Germany, all literature that violated classical norms and gave free play to the imagination was considered romantic. Most folk tales and much of the art of medieval Europe fell into this category. In the early nineteenth century, August Wilhelm von Schlegel (*Lectures on Dramatic Art and Literature, 1809–1811*) began to use *romantic* as a term of praise rather than approbation. For him it signified an exciting alternative to the predictable, lifeless work of authors who merely imitated classical

WHO WERE the great writers of literature during the romantic period?

categorical imperative Kant's view that all human beings possess an innate sense of moral duty, an inner command to act in every situation as one would have other people act in that same situation.

HISTORY'S VOICES

MADAME DE STAËL DESCRIBES THE NEW ROMANTIC LITERATURE OF GERMANY

Madame de Staël was the daughter of Louis XVI's finance minister, Jacques Necker. She visited Germany and read widely in the literature of Germany's emerging romantic movement. Her book, Concerning Germany *(1813), offered a wide-ranging commentary on contemporary German culture. Her work helped introduce romanticism to French- and English-speaking Europeans.*

HOW DOES Madame de Staël think that classical literature compares with the work of the romantics?

The word *romantic* has been lately introduced in Germany, to designate that kind of poetry which is derived from the songs of the Troubadours; that which owes its birth to the union of chivalry and Christianity. ...

Some French critics have asserted that German literature is still in its infancy; this opinion is entirely false: men who are best skilled in the knowledge of languages, and the works of the ancients, are certainly not ignorant of the defects and advantages attached to the species of literature which they either adopt or reject; but their character, their habits, and their modes of reasoning, have led them to prefer that which is founded on the recollection of chivalry, on the wonders of the middle ages, to that which has for its basis the mythology of the Greeks. The literature of romance is alone capable of further improvement, because, being rooted in our own soil, that alone can continue to grow and acquire fresh life: it expresses our religion; it recalls our history; its origin is ancient, although not of classical antiquity. ...

The new school maintains the same system in the fine arts as in literature, and affirms that Christianity is the source of all modern genius; the writers of this school also characterize, in a new manner, all that in Gothic architecture agrees with the religious sentiments of Christians. It does not follow however, from this, that the moderns can and ought to construct Gothic churches; ... it is only of consequence to us, in the present silence of genius, to lay aside the contempt which has been thrown on all the conceptions of the middle ages.

From Madame de Staël, *Concerning Germany* (London: John Murray, 1814) as quoted in Howard H. Hugo, ed., *The Romantic Reader* (New York: Viking, 1957), pp. 64–66.

---

models. He associated Dante, Petrarch, Boccaccio, Shakespeare, the Arthurian legends, Cervantes, and Calderón with romanticism.

The romantic movement peaked in Germany and England before Madame de Staël (1766–1817) and Victor Hugo (1802–1885) made it a major force in France. So respected was the classical tradition in France that no French writer openly claimed to be a romantic until 1816. The first was Henri Beyle (1783–1842) who wrote very successful novels under the pseudonym Stendhal. (See "History's Voices: Madame de Staël Describes the New Romantic Literature of Germany.")

THE ENGLISH ROMANTIC WRITERS

Lockean psychology, which viewed the mind as a passive receptor of sensory data, explained poetry as a mechanical exercise of "wit" following prescribed rules. The English romantics disagreed. They saw poetry as proof of the mind's ability to create truth and not merely respond to stimuli. Far from being idle play, it was the highest of human acts, the fulfillment of humanity's unique ability to transcend the level on which other sentient beings operate.

20.6
Samuel Taylor Coleridge:
from *Aids to Reflection*

QUICK REVIEW

William Wordsworth (1770–1850)

- Found inspiration in nature
- Believed that children existed in a more perfect spiritual state
- Believed that as people age they lose contact with natural and spiritual world

---

Coleridge Samuel Taylor Coleridge (1772–1834) was the master of Gothic poems of the supernatural. His "Rime of the Ancient Mariner" tells the story of a sailor cursed for killing an albatross (a symbol for crimes against nature and God). The poem explores guilt, punishment, and the redemptive possibilities of humility and penance. In the end, the mariner grasps the unity and beauty of all things, repents, and is delivered from the curse of having the dead albatross hung around his neck.

Wordsworth Coleridge and his closest friend, William Wordsworth (1770–1850), published a manifesto (*Lyrical Ballads*) that urged poets to free themselves from the rules endorsed by eighteenth-century critics. Wordsworth's "Ode on Intimations of Immortality" (1803), which he wrote to console Coleridge during a personal crisis, is among his most important later works. It deals with the loss of poetic vision. Nature, which Wordsworth had worshiped, had ceased to communicate with him, and he feared it might never speak again. He had lost what he believed all human beings necessarily lose as they mature—their childlike vision and inborn intimacy with spiritual reality. Both Wordsworth and Coleridge viewed childhood as a glorious period of creative imagination. Wordsworth believed the soul exists before birth in a celestial state and that children, being close to this experience of the eternal and still undistracted by knowledge of the world, recollect the supernatural much more easily than adults. Age and urban life corrupt and deaden the adult imagination, making inner feelings and the beauty of nature seem less important. Wordsworth's autobiographical description of his intellectual development—a book-length poem, *The Prelude* (1850)—illustrated his point.

Lord Byron Most of Britain's romantic writers distrusted and disliked the greatest rebel their movement produced: Lord Byron (1788–1824). Outside England, however, his rejection of tradition, his advocacy of the freedom of the individual, and his unconventional love life won him the reputation of being the virtual embodiment of the "new person" of the age of the French Revolution. Byron had little sympathy for theories about imagination, and he was outrageously skeptical and mocking even of his own beliefs. In the poem *Childe Harold's Pilgrimage* (1812), he created a caricature of the melancholy romantic hero. His *Don Juan* (1819) employed ribald humor, described nature's cruelty as well as its beauty, and expressed an unfashionable admiration for urban life.

THE GERMAN ROMANTIC WRITERS

Almost all the major German romantics wrote both novels and poetry. Their novels tended to be sentimental, and they often borrowed material from medieval romances. The characters they created functioned as symbols, not descriptions of real individuals, and they avoided purely naturalistic description. The first German romantic novel was Ludwig Tieck's *William Lovell* (1793–1795), the story of a young man who lives for love and imagination and avoids the cold rationality that leads others to unbelief, misanthropy, and egoism. In the end, Lovell is ruined when two women, whom he naively loves, infect him with philosophy, materialism, and skepticism.

Schlegel *Lucinde* (1799), by Friedrich Schlegel (1767–1845), demonstrates how the romantics dealt with the social issues of their day. The novel attacked the assumption that women could be nothing more than lovers and domestics. Lucinde is the hero's perfect companion (and unsurpassed sexual partner). The book was considered shocking for its frank discussion of sex and its description of Lucinde as the equal of its male protagonist.

Goethe   Towering above all other German writers is Johann Wolfgang von Goethe (1749–1832), a romantic and a critic of the excesses of romanticism. A novel, *The Sorrows of Young Werther* (1774), first brought him to the public's attention. It purported to be an exchange of letters documenting the sentimental feelings of a young man in love with someone else's wife. When their correspondence ends, grief drives Werther to suicide. The book was much admired because of its insistence on the importance of feeling and its call for people to transcend the conventions of polite society.

Goethe's masterpiece is *Faust*, a long dramatic poem. In Part I (1808), Faust, a world-weary scholar, promises his soul to the devil in exchange for knowledge. Faust seduces and abandons a young woman named Gretchen. When she dies, disgraced on earth but judged worthy of heaven, he struggles with grief and guilt. In Part II of the poem (completed in the year of Goethe's death, 1832), Faust has strange adventures with witches and mythological beings, but in the end he finds peace, understanding, and salvation by dedicating his life to the improvement of humankind.

ROMANTIC ART

The art of the Romantic Era, like its poetry and philosophy, stood largely in reaction to that of the eighteenth century. Whereas the Rococo artists had looked to Renaissance models, and Neoclassical painters to the art of the ancient world, Romantic painters often portrayed scenes from medieval life. For them, the Middle Ages represented the social stability and religious reverence that was disappearing from their own era.

THE CULT OF THE MIDDLE AGES AND NEO-GOTHICISM

Like many early Romantic artists, the English landscape painter John Constable (1776–1837) was politically conservative. In *Salisbury Cathedral, from the Meadows*, he portrayed a stable world in which neither political turmoil nor industrial development challenged the traditional dominance of the church and the landed classes. The works of both nature and humankind—in this case, majestic old trees and a medieval cathedral—present a powerful sense of enduring order. In a similar manner, Constable and other English conservatives viewed the church and the British constitution as intimately related and part of the traditional order that must resist political radicalism. Constable and other Romantics tended to idealize rural life, which they believed was connected to the medieval past and was opposed to the increasingly urban, industrializing, commercial society that was developing around them.

This **neo-gothic** revival took place in architecture as well. Many medieval cathedrals were restored in this era, and new churches were modeled on forerunners from the Middle Ages. The British Houses of Parliament, built in 1836–1837, are a famous example of this revival, but many other new structures took medieval designs, including town halls, schools, railroad stations, and aristocratic country houses. The single most remarkable neo-gothic building was the castle of Neuschwanstein constructed between 1869 and 1886 on a mountain in southern Germany by King Ludwig II of Bavaria (r. 1864–1886).

NATURE AND THE SUBLIME

Beyond their attraction to history, Romantic artists also sought to portray nature in all of its majestic power. Like Romantic poets, they were drawn to the mysterious and unruly side of nature rather than the rational Newtonian

HOW DID Romantic artists portray nature?

neo-gothic   Style that idealized nature and portrayed it in all its power.

Caspar David Friedrich's *The Polar Sea* illustrated the power of nature to diminish the creations of humankind as seen in the wrecked ship on the right of the painting.

Kunsthalle, Hamburg, Germany/A.K.G., Berlin/ SuperStock

order that had prevailed during the Enlightenment. Painters would travel to remote areas such as the Scottish Highlands, the Welsh mountains, or the Swiss Alps to portray the sublime—that is, to depict subjects from nature that aroused strong emotions such as fear, dread, and awe. In this view, Romantics saw the forces of nature as able to overwhelm the smallness of mankind. For example, in his 1824 painting *The Polar Sea*, German artist Caspar David Friedrich (1774–1840) showed a ship trapped by a vast polar ice field. Other artists illustrated human beings shrouded in the darkness of a moonlit night.

Romantic artists portrayed industrial, man-made forces as well. *Rain, Steam and Speed—The Great Western Railway*, painted in 1844 by Joseph Mallord William Turner (1775–1851) depicted a railway engine barreling through an enveloping storm. Both Turner's and Friedrich's paintings symbolize the contradictory forces of nature and of man-made industry, which could challenge each other in power, awe, and mystery.

RELIGION IN THE ROMANTIC PERIOD

WHAT WAS the role of religion in romantic thought?

Medieval religion centered on the church. The Reformation based faith on the authority of the Bible, and Enlightenment thinkers tried to derive religion from reason and nature. For the romantics, however, it sprang from deep inner emotion.

METHODISM

Methodism Movement begun in England by John Wesley, an Oxford-educated Anglican priest, the first major religion to embody romanticism. It emphasized religion as a "method" for living more than a set of doctrines.

Methodism, a movement begun in England by John Wesley (1703–1791), an Oxford-educated Anglican priest, was the first major religion to embody romanticism. Wesley emphasized religion as a "method" for living more than a set of doctrines. In 1735, he came to America as a missionary and made the acquaintance of the Moravians, a sect of German pietists. Their unquestioning trust in God struck him as a faith much stronger than his own, but in 1739, he had a quiet conversion experience that assured him of his salvation and sent him forth to preach a message of simple trust. Thousands of humble people responded to his call for inward, heartfelt faith and a striving for moral perfection, and by the late eighteenth century, Methodism had spread widely in Britain and America.

NEW DIRECTIONS IN CONTINENTAL RELIGION

Methodism viewed emotional experience as fundamental to Christian conversion and worship, and after Wesley's day religious revivals became highly emotional. Similar religious impulses were also at work on the Continent. A strong Roman Catholic revival in France followed the Thermidorian Reaction, and Viscount Frangois Reni de Chateaubriand (1768–1848) argued in *The Genius of Christianity* (1802) that the essence of religion was "passion." Friedrich Schleiermacher (1768–1834), a Protestant theologian, agreed, and in *Speeches on Religion to Its Cultured Despisers* (1799) he defined religion as a feeling of absolute dependence on an infinite reality.

John Wesley (1703–1791) was the founder of Methodism. He emphasized the role of emotional experience in Christian conversion.

CORBIS/Bettmann

ROMANTIC VIEWS OF NATIONALISM AND HISTORY

WHAT WERE the romantic views of nationalism and history?

Romanticism, in all its forms, glorified individuality (in cultures as well as human beings), and German idealism provided this aspect of romanticism with a philosophic underpinning. Idealism held that the world was a projection of the subjective ego of the individual. J. G. Fichte (1762–1814) compared the individual human ego to the absolute creative power that underlies all things. The world is what it is, he argued, because certain human beings (such as Napoleon) have conceived of it in a particular way and imposed their wills on it.

HERDER AND CULTURE

Johann Gottfried Herder (1744–1803), who resented the preponderance of French culture in Germany, led Germans on a search for the roots of their identity as a "folk" (an ethnic people). Herder urged Germans to collect the songs and sayings of what might today might be called their popular culture. The best example of this sort of thing is the famous collection of fairy tales amassed by the Grimm brothers, Jakob (1785–1863) and Wilhelm (1786–1859). Herder believed language and culture are expressions of a people's unique character, and he opposed the Enlightenment's attempt to impose universal, rational institutions. His emphasis on the value of uniqueness revived the study of history and ultimately stimulated Europe's interest in world cultures, comparative literature and religions, and philology.

HEGEL AND HISTORY

Georg Wilhelm Friedrich Hegel (1770–1831), one of the most difficult and important philosophers in the history of Western civilization, exerted a powerful romantic influence on the writing of history. He claimed that a historical period

When Napoleon invaded Egypt in 1799, he met stiff resistance. On July 25, however, the French won a decisive victory. This painting of that battle by Baron Antoine Gros (1771–1835) emphasizes French heroism and Muslim defeat. Such an outlook was typical of European views of Arabs and the Islamic world.

Antoine Jean Gros (1771–1835).detail, "Battle of Aboukir, July 25,1799", c. 1806. Oil on canvas. Chateau de Versailles et de Trianon, Versailles, France. Bridgeman-Giraudon/Art Resource, NY

is shaped by the ideas accepted by the people who live it. History, therefore, evolves like ideas evolve—through a process of contradiction and resolution. The ideas that hold sway over a given generation constitute a *thesis*. An *antithesis* appears when this set of beliefs is challenged by conflicting ideas, and ultimately, a *synthesis*, a new consensus, emerges. This then becomes a new thesis, and the cycle begins all over again. Because each stage in the process is necessary to the one that follows it, Hegel maintained that all periods of history are of equal value and all cultures are important. Each contributes to the clash of ideas by which humankind evolves.

ISLAM, THE MIDDLE EAST, AND ROMANTICISM

The sensibilities of the romantic movement modified European views of Islam and the Arab world while simultaneously preserving some traditional negative attitudes. A reinvigorated and highly emotional Christianity embraced the old belief that the church faced an inevitable enemy in Islam. The medieval crusades fired the imaginations of romantic artists, poets, and novelists, and the word *crusade* even crept into the rhetoric of nineteenth-century politicians. The romantics' nationalism further encouraged opposition to the Ottoman Empire and Islam. A revolution in which the Greeks struggled to free themselves from what was alleged to be Ottoman despotism (see Chapter 20) was heartily endorsed by some of the most famous romantics.

Some aspects of the romantic movement promoted more generous views of the Islamic world. The romantics valued literature from different cultures and were much attracted to such eastern works as *The Thousand and One Nights*, the first translation of which (a French version) appeared in 1778. Romantic historians acknowledged the importance of Arab contributions to the course of civilization. Herder praised Muhammad for converting his people to monotheism. Thomas Carlyle (1795–1881) saw Muhammad as a hero of faith, one of the great religious leaders of history whose deep subjective experience of God enabled him to mediate a sense of the divine to others. Hegel agreed that Islam had been significant, but he argued it had played its part and was no longer of much importance. This fit with the European inclination to underestimate Islam and dismiss it as a spent historical force.

Napoleon's Egyptian expedition (1798) did much to revive Europe's interest in the Middle East, for his was the first European invasion of the Middle East since the last of the medieval crusades. Napoleon did not intend a war against Islam, and his expedition included scholars of Arabic and Islamic culture who, he hoped, would help him establish good relations with the Egyptians. The discovery of the famous Rosetta Stone, which provided the key to the translation of ancient hieroglyphic writing, and the twenty-three volume *Description of Egypt* that Napoleon's scholars published focused Europe's attention on Egypt, but primarily on the ancient phase in its civilization. Islam was seen as a small, if important, part of a much larger story whose outline reflected European priorities. European travelers followed in the wake of Napoleon's invasion, and Middle Eastern motifs spread through Western culture. In Washington, D.C., Americans even chose the Egyptian obelisk as the model for a monument honoring George Washington.

SUMMARY

The Rise of Napoleon Bonaparte In France in 1799, Napoleon Bonaparte made himself First Consul. He had taken advantage of the Directory's weaknesses, his own past military successes, and the naivete of politicians who thought Napoleon could be used as a figurehead, to grant himself powers comparable to those of Roman emperors. The way he used this power foreshadowed the dictators of the twentieth century: he used military force, camouflaged by talk of revolution and nationalism, to instigate imperialist aggression that served to strengthen his hold on power.

The Consulate in France (1799–1804) The French Revolution ended with Napoleon's Consulate; the bourgeoisie and the peasants were satisfied. Napoleon seemed to offer stability, and the voters approved his constitution in a plebiscite. Napoleon signed treaties that brought peace to Europe and maneuvered to build coalitions and crush dissent at home. He concluded a concordat with the pope in 1801, which ratified the status quo but allowed Napoleon to replace clergy throughout France. Napoleon continued to increase his power and initiated codification of French law (the Napoleonic Code), which mostly endorsed changes that had been effected by the revolution while incrementally enhancing the state's power. By 1804, Napoleon was ready to crown himself emperor, making himself Napoleon I.

Napoleon's Empire (1804–1814) Between 1804 and 1815, Napoleon conquered most of Europe, dismantling remnants of the Old Regime along the way. The revolution had mobilized France, and Napoleon took advantage of the fact that he could field more troops at once than any other military leader. Napoleon's greatest victory was probably his 1805 defeat of combined Austrian and Russian forces at Austerlitz. He occupied Vienna, reorganized Germany, caused the dissolution of the Holy Roman Empire, and reduced Prussia by half. Only Britain could compete with France. Napoleon's chief defeat had come in 1805 at the hands of Lord Nelson, at the Battle of Trafalgar. Napoleon attempted to weaken Britain through trade embargoes, but this turned out to hurt the Continental System more than it hurt Britain.

European Response to the Empire Opposition to Napoleon fanned the flames of nationalism. Following his victory over the Prussians at Jena in 1806, nationalists called for Germany's unification. When he deposed the Bourbon monarchs of Spain in favor of his brother, the Spaniards rebelled. Austria's declaration of war on France gave him an opportunity to occupy Austrian territory, and in 1810, Russia's withdrawal from the Continental System prompted him to march on Moscow. The Russian winter forced him to retreat, and in October 1813, a powerful coalition defeated him. In the spring of 1814, he went into exile on the island of Elba.

The Congress of Vienna and the European Settlement In 1815 the Congress of Vienna broke new ground in international law by concluding treaties among states that prevented war in Europe for a century. France was reduced in size and its Bourbon dynasty restored. State boundaries were adjusted around France and in eastern Europe to enhance security. Napoleon attempted a comeback while the Congress was still debating these arrangements, but a

IMAGE KEY
for pages 456–457

a. Jean Auguste Dominique Ingres (1780–1867), "Napoleon on His Imperial Throne", 1806. Oil on canvas, 259 x 162 cm. Musee des Beaux-Arts, Rennes. Photograph © Erich Lessing/Art Resource, NY

b. An aquatint print by C. Moret of Andrea Appiami's portrait of the young Napoleon, ca. 1825

c. The participants at the 1815 Congress of Vienna dancing in a French cartoon

d. Chair with arms in the form of swans. One of four, designed for the Empress Josephine. Jacob-Desmalter (1770–1841). Réunion des Musées Nationaux/Art Resource, NY

e. Scene from Goethe's "Faust," ca. 1825

f. Lord Byron. (1788–1824) oil on canvas by Tomas Phillips

g. Jacques Louis David (1748–1825), "Consecration of the Emperor Napoleon I and Coronation of Empress Josephine," 1806–07. Louvre, Paris. Bridgeman-Giraudon/Art Resource, NY

h. Napoleon's second wife, Marie Louise, who bore him a son "Marie Louise (1791–1847) and the King of Rome" (1811–32) (oil on canvas) by Francois Pascal Simon Gerard, Baron (1770–1837). Chateau de Versailles, France/Lauros/Giraudon/Bridgeman Art Library, London/Giraudon

i. Profile portrait of German philosopher Immanuel Kant (1724–1804). Drawn from life by Hans Veit Schnorr in 1789

British and Prussian force defeated him at Waterloo in June 1815, and he was exiled once again—this time to the island of Saint Helena.

The Romantic Movement Romanticism was an intellectual movement that emerged throughout Europe during the period of the French Revolution and Napoleonic rule. In a reaction against the Enlightenment, romanticism emphasized the value of intuition, spirituality, folklore, dreams, and other forms of human experience that lie beyond the realm of reason.

Romantic Questioning of the Supremacy of Reason Romanticism's intellectual foundations were laid largely by Jean-Jacques Rousseau and Immanuel Kant. Rousseau's belief that human nature is corrupted by society and by material prosperity, and his interest in childhood, was reflected in the romantic movement's efforts to reform education and family life. Kant argued for the subjectivity of human knowledge. He theorized that because humans share an innate understanding of the categorical imperative, morality must be something independent of sensory experience.

Romantic Literature "Romantic literature" meant slightly different things in different countries and periods. In general, it meant literature that stressed the imaginative elements and was not bound by formal rules. Romantic literature peaked in England and Germany before France. English romantics such as Coleridge and Wordsworth excelled in poetry that dealt with themes including morality, mortality, and creativity. German romantics also wrote a great deal of poetry, but most of the major German romantic authors wrote at least one novel. Goethe was the greatest German writer of the era, although he was a more complicated figure than the label "romantic" suggests. *Faust* was his seminal work.

Romantic Art The art of the Romantic Period, like its poetry and philosophy, reacted against the orderly, secular views of the Enlightenment that confidently sought to improve the world. Romantic artists looked to the Middle Ages for inspiration to capture the qualities of what they viewed as a more enduring order that emphasized social stability, religious reverence, the pastoral countryside, and nature in all its majestic and awesome force. The art of this era both feared and was impressed by the tremendous power of the industrializing world.

Religion in the Romantic Period Romanticism in religion stressed the individual's heartfelt response to the divine. Methodism developed in England in the eighteenth century as a reaction against deism and rationalism in the Church of England. Methodists believe in Christian perfectibility in this life; the enthusiastic emotional experience is part of Christian conversion. In France, Chateaubriand argued that passion is at the heart of religion. Schleiermacher described religion as a feeling of dependence on an infinite being.

Romantic Views of Nationalism and History Romanticism glorified both individuals and individual cultures. The German philosophy of idealism helped explain the relationship between the acts of strong individuals and the shaping of history. German romantics also encouraged the study of folk culture. The German philosopher G. W. F. Hegel explained history in terms of the evolution of the prevailing ideas of a time and place. Europe's interest in the Arab world was revived by current events such as Napoleon's invasion of Egypt. The new European scholarship on Islam, however, perpetuated old Western stereotypes.

REVIEW QUESTIONS

1. How did Napoleon rise to power? What were the stages by which he eventually made himself emperor? What were his major domestic achievements? Did his rule more nearly fulfill or betray the ideals of the French Revolution?

2. How did Napoleon acquire and rule his empire? Why did he invade Russia? Why did his campaign fail? Was he a military genius, or did his successes owe more to the ineptitude of his opponents?

3. Who were the principal personalities at the Congress of Vienna? What were the most significant problems they addressed? What was the long-term significance of the Congress?

4. How does the role romantic writers assigned to feelings compare with the role Enlightenment writers claimed for reason? What questions did Rousseau and Kant raise about reason? How did the romantic understanding of religion differ from Reformation Protestantism and Enlightenment deism? What was the importance of history to the romantics? What inspired Romantic artists?

KEY TERMS

categorical imperative   (p. 472)   **Methodism**   (p. 476)   *Sturm and Drang*   (p. 471)
Consulate   (p. 459)   **romanticism**   (p. 471)   **neo-gothic**   (p. 475)

  For additional study resources for this chapter, go to:
www.prenhall.com/kagan3/chapter19

20 The Conservative Order and the Challenges of Reform (1815–1832)

CHAPTER HIGHLIGHTS

The Challenges of Nationalism and Liberalism Secular ideologies including nationalism and liberalism gained currency in the nineteenth century. As a practical matter, nationalism and liberalism were often linked, even though the goals of nationalists and liberals were often at odds.

Conservative Governments: The Domestic Political Order The conservative political program was a response to nationalism and liberalism. Burke and Hegel were the most important conservative theorists. Conflicts between conservatives on the one hand, and liberals and nationalists on the other, threatened Europe's post-1815 stability.

The Conservative International Order The Concert of Europe was created at the Congress of Vienna as a tool for the maintenance of international peace. The 1820 revolution in Spain was suppressed, but Greece and Serbia became independent nations.

The Wars of Independence in Latin America The Napoleonic era marked the end of Europe's domination of Latin America. Between 1804 and 1824, France was driven from Haiti, Portugal lost control of Brazil, and Spain was forced to withdraw from all of its American empire except Cuba and Puerto Rico. In general, on the South American continent the Creole elite led the movements against Spain and Portugal. The Creoles were determined that political independence from Spain and Portugal would not cause social disruption or the loss of their own privileges.

The Conservative Order Shaken in Europe Starting in the mid-1820s, political discontent led to upheaval across Europe. In Russia, the Decembrist Revolt was ruthlessly suppressed. In France, the Bourbon dynasty was overthrown and Louis Philippe took power. Belgium gained independence. Britain's Great Reform Bill widened the franchise and brought more people into the political system.

CHAPTER QUESTIONS

WHAT IS nationalism?

WHAT IS conservatism?

WHAT WAS the Concert of Europe?

WHAT SPARKED the wars of independence in Latin America?

HOW DID Russia, France, and Britain respond to challenges to the conservative order?

CHAPTER OUTLINE

- The Challenges of Nationalism and Liberalism
- Conservative Governments: The Domestic Political Order
- The Conservative International Order
- The Wars of Independence in Latin America
- The Conservative Order Shaken in Europe

IMAGE KEY
Image Key for pages 482–483 is on page 504.

Reactionary movements that favored monarchy and aristocracy dominated European politics for the decade following the Congress of Vienna. However, nationalism and liberalism, two new ideologies, challenged the traditional understanding of the state as nothing more than a collection of properties belonging to a royal dynasty. Nationalists claimed that ethnicity was the true basis for statehood, and they wanted to redraw the map of Europe to reflect boundaries among ethnic groups. Liberals challenged the traditional order in a different way. They wanted governments to implement moderate political reforms and establish freer economic markets.

WHAT IS nationalism?

THE CHALLENGES OF NATIONALISM AND LIBERALISM

The nineteenth century was the great age of "-isms": liberalism, nationalism, republicanism, socialism, and communism. These secular ideologies captured the imaginations of both intellectuals and the masses and mobilized opposition to the political and social status quo.

THE EMERGENCE OF NATIONALISM

Nationalism was the most powerful of the political ideologies of the nineteenth and early twentieth centuries. Nationalism is the belief that a people who share an ethnic identity (language, culture, and history) should also be recognized as having a right to a government and political identity of their own.

Opposition to the Vienna Settlement Early-nineteenth-century nationalists opposed the principle upheld by the Congress of Vienna that it was not the ethnicity of subjects but the rights of rulers that established a basis for political unity. Nationalists resisted states such as the Austrian and Russian empires that combined peoples of many different languages and cultures. Implicit in the rhetoric of nationalism was an assertion of popular sovereignty—of the belief that the identity of a people is the sole basis for political legitimacy. This, of course, raised the troubling issue of the status of minorities in regions ruled by a different ethnic majority.

Creating Nations During the first half of the nineteenth century, small intellectual elites promoted nationalism in various parts of Europe by generating enthusiasm for the study of its regional cultures. Scholars wrote histories of their homelands and collected folk literatures. The schoolteachers, who spread the fruits of this work abroad, nurtured the development of national languages and identities and marshaled the support of the masses for the nationalist political movements that flourished in the second half of the century.

Nationalists put a great deal of emphasis on the language used in schools and government offices. France and Italy replaced local dialects in their schools with official versions of the national language. In parts of Scandinavia and eastern Europe, nationalists tried to resurrect earlier, "purer" versions of a national language. These tongues were often the inventions of modern linguists, but they served to bring people together. Standardization of speech was further aided by the increasing availability of printed materials (books, journals, magazines, and newspapers) that fixed language in a permanent form. A national printed language augmented local dialects in many communities and was accepted as the preferred instrument for serious thought and political debate. Europe developed far more linguistic uniformity than it had ever had, but there was still a great deal of variety. By 1850, less than half the people of France spoke official French.

nationalism The belief that the people who share an ethnic identity (language, culture, and history) should also be recognized as having a right to a government and political identity of their own.

Meaning of Nationhood   Nationalists explained nationhood, and argued for it, in different ways. Their greatest difficulty was deciding which ethnic groups had the right to be considered nations with claims to territory and political autonomy. In practice, recognition as a nation has usually been based on possession of a population large enough to support a viable economy, a history of significant cultural association, an educated elite that promotes a national language, and a capacity to defend oneself or conquer others. Small ethnic groups that have tried but failed to meet these criteria have been a source of much unrest.

Regions of Nationalistic Pressure   Europe dealt with nationalistic upheavals on six fronts during the nineteenth century. England's decision in 1800 to govern Ireland directly created an "Irish problem" that continues to complicate British politics to this day. German nationalists, who wanted to unite all German-speaking peoples, opposed the Austrian Empire and pitted Prussia and Austria against each other. Italian nationalists tried to drive the Austrians off the Italian peninsula. Polish nationalists struggled to free their land from Russian domination. A host of eastern European groups—Hungarians, Czechs, Slovenes, and others—sought legal privileges within the Austrian Empire or freedom from it, and in southeastern Europe, Serbs, Greeks, Albanians, Romanians, and Bulgarians fought the Ottoman and Russian Empires. Nationalist activities ebbed and flowed in each of these areas, and their rulers often assumed they needed only to ride things out and stability would return. However, during the course of the century, nationalists changed Europe's map and political culture.

EARLY-NINETEENTH-CENTURY POLITICAL LIBERALISM

The word *liberal*, as applied to politics, entered the West's vocabulary in the nineteenth century. Its meaning has changed over the years, and its current use in America has little or nothing to do with what it originally signified.

Political Goals   The liberal political program derived from the Enlightenment, from England's institutions, and from the so-called principles of 1789 embodied in France's Declaration of the Rights of Man and Citizen. Liberals favored equality before the law for all citizens, religious toleration, and freedom of the press. They wanted constitutional political machinery that would prevent governments from arbitrarily using their powers against the persons or property of individuals. They tended to believe that government derives its legitimacy from the freely given consent of the governed as expressed through elected, representative, or parliamentary bodies. (See "History's Voices: Benjamin Constant Discusses Modern Liberty.") And they insisted that ministers of state ultimately be responsible to the representatives of the people, not to a monarch.

The aspirations of liberal reformers were limited. Their primary desire was to see constitutional governments established throughout Europe. There were none in 1815, and conservatives distrusted constitutions. They associated them with the upheaval that followed the French Revolution, and they did not believe all the political arrangements a people might need could be prescribed by a document.

Liberals tended to be educated, prosperous people who had been blocked in some way from participating in politics. They were often academics, members of the professions, or people involved in the increasingly important commercial and manufacturing segments of the economy. The monarchical, aristocratic regimes that the Congress of Vienna restored often failed to recognize the increasing importance of these people, and governments failed to accommodate their economic, professional, and social aspirations.

QUICK REVIEW

Liberal Political Program

- Derived from principles embodied in the Declaration of the Rights of Man and Citizen
- Favored equality before the law, religious toleration, and freedom of the press
- Wanted to see constitutional governments established throughout Europe

HISTORY'S VOICES

BENJAMIN CONSTANT DISCUSSES MODERN LIBERTY

I n 1819, the French liberal theorist Benjamin Constant (1767–1830) delivered lectures on the character of ancient and modern liberty. In this passage, he emphasizes the close relationship of modern liberty to economic freedom and a free private life. He then ties the desire for a free private life to the need for a representative government. Modern life did not leave people enough time to make the political commitment that the ancient Greek polis had required. His argument also provides a foundation for rejecting direct democracy, which he and other liberals associated with the Reign of Terror and with Napoleon's plebiscites.

ACCORDING TO CONSTANT, what is liberty to the modern citizen? How does he defend a representative government?

[Modern liberty] is, for each individual, the right not to be subjected to anything but the law, not to be arrested, or detained, or put to death, or mistreated in any manner, as a result of the arbitrary will of one or several individuals. It is each man's right to express his opinions, to choose and exercise his profession, to dispose of his property and even abuse it, to come and go without obtaining permission and without having to give an account of either his motives or his itinerary. It is the right to associate with other individuals, either to confer about mutual interests or profess the cult that he and his associates prefer or simply to fill his days and hours in the manner most conforming to his inclinations and fantasies. Finally, it is each man's right to exert influence on the administration of government, either through the election of some or all of its public functionaries, or through remonstrances, petitions, and demands which authorities are more or less obliged to take into account. …

Just as the liberty we now require is distinct from that of the ancients, so this new liberty itself requires an organization different from that suitable for ancient liberty. For the latter, the more time and energy a man consecrated to the exercise of his political rights, the more free he believed himself to be. Given the type of liberty to which we are now susceptible, the more the exercise of our political rights leaves us time for our private interests, the more precious we find liberty to be. From this … stems the necessity of the representative system. The representative system is nothing else than an organization through which a nation unloads on several individuals what it cannot and will not do for itself. Poor men handle their own affairs; rich men hire managers. This is the story of ancient and modern nations. The representative system is the power of attorney given to certain men by the mass of the people who want their interests defended but who nevertheless do not always have the time to defend these interests themselves.

Benjamin Constant, "Ancient and Modern Liberty," as translated and quoted in Stephen Holmes, *Benjamin Constant and the Making of Modern Liberalism* (New Haven, CT: Yale University Press, 1984), pp. 66, 74.

Liberals wanted to open politics to wider participation, but they did not advocate democracy. They sought greater representation for the propertied classes, and second only to their hostility for aristocrats was their contempt for the poor. Liberals wanted to redefine the eighteenth century's concept of aristocratic privilege by substituting wealth for birth as the determinate of the rights to which an individual was entitled. This created a gap between them and the rural and urban working classes that was to have important consequences.

Economic Goals   The economic policies of nineteenth-century liberals erected another barrier between them and working people. The commercial classes embraced the theories of Adam Smith, the Enlightenment economist who urged the abolition of the trade restraints enacted by mercantilists and the regulated economies managed by absolutist monarchs. Liberals wanted to manufacture and sell goods freely, and they opposed paternalistic governments and guilds that regulated wages and labor practices. For them, labor was simply a commodity to be bought and sold at whatever price it would bring on the free market. They believed that if people were free to exploit the opportunities they had to enrich themselves, the result would be more and cheaper goods and services for everyone.

Relationship of Nationalism to Liberalism   The liberals' reform programs varied according to where they lived. In Great Britain and France, liberals wanted to protect civil liberties, define the respective powers of monarch and elected representative body, and expand the electorate (but avoid democracy). In German-speaking regions of Europe, monarchs and aristocrats offered German liberals fewer opportunities to participate in government. The aristocratic landowning class staffed government bureaucracies and army officer corps and looked down on the small commercial, industrial middle class that had no role to play in government. Most German liberals wanted to unify Germany and believed that either the Austrian or Prussian monarchies would be best agents for this purpose. Consequently, they were more tolerant of strong state and monarchical power than other liberals. They deferred hopes for a freer social and political order until after unification.

There was no logical link between liberalism and nationalism. Indeed, nationalists sometimes opposed liberal reforms. Some nationalists wanted their own ethnic group to dominate the other peoples resident in their homelands, and some refused to cooperate with groups they regarded as cultural inferiors or historical enemies. Liberalism and nationalism could, however, complement each other, for people who were fighting for representative government, civil liberties, and economic freedom in one nation readily identified with those engaged in similar struggles elsewhere.

CONSERVATIVE GOVERNMENTS: THE DOMESTIC POLITICAL ORDER

espite the challenges mounted by liberalism and nationalism, conservative institutions had remarkable durability. Their influence did not fade until after World War I.

CONSERVATIVE OUTLOOKS

Conservatism promoted legitimate monarchies, landed aristocracies, and established churches. Historically, these groups had often been competitors for power, but the upheavals of the French Revolution and the Napoleonic era turned them (sometimes reluctantly) into friends.

The fate of Louis XVI convinced most monarchs that it was safe to share political power only with aristocrats, the very wealthiest members of the middle class, and some professionals. These people generally profited from the status quo and feared that their property and influence would be endangered by genuinely representative government. Most clergy also assumed it was their duty to defend traditional institutions against the critical rationalism unleashed by the Enlightenment.

The conservative factions in society retained their customary arrogance. However, they lost the confidence on which it had been grounded, for they knew they could be driven from power. They understood that revolution in one country could spill over into another, and they were determined, therefore, to deal firmly with every potential source of unrest.

WHAT IS conservatism?

conservatism   Form of political thought that, in mid-nineteenth-century Europe, promoted legitimate monarchies, landed aristocracies, and established churches.

Prince Klemens von Metternich
(1773–1859) epitomized nineteenth-
century conservatism.

Sir Thomas Lawrence (1769-1830) "Clemens
Lothar Wenzel, Prince Metternich" (1773-1859),
RCIN 404948, OM 905 WC 206. The Royal Col-
lection © 2005, Her Majesty Queen Elizabeth II

QUICK REVIEW

Threats to Habsburg Empire

• Nationalism

• Liberal political reforms

• Ethnic divisions

Considerable unrest was generated by the difficulty of reorganizing societies that had been militarily mobilized for a quarter century. It was hard to refit
them for an era of peace. Economies that had been fueled by war had to be restructured. Employment had to be found for former soldiers and sailors, and
young people faced futures that were no longer structured by military priorities.
Conservative governments varied in the extent of the repressive measures they
used to deal with the domestic unrest this situation produced.

LIBERALISM AND NATIONALISM RESISTED IN AUSTRIA AND THE GERMANIES

Prince Metternich (1773–1859), a devoted servant of the Habsburg emperor of
Austria, epitomized conservatism more than any other early-nineteenth-century
statesman. He and Britain's Viscount Castlereagh (1769–1822) were the architects of the agreements ratified at the Congress of Vienna.

Dynastic Integrity of the Habsburg Empire The Congress of Vienna replaced the defunct Holy Roman Empire with a German Confederation consisting of thirty-nine more or less autonomous states under Austrian
leadership. Austria was determined to prevent the development of constitutional governments in these states, for the Habsburgs feared they would lead
to the German Confederation becoming a German national state. The Habsburg Empire was more threatened by liberalism and nationalism than most
political entities, for it was nothing but a collection of diverse ethnic groups.
The only thing that held it together was the fact that each of these groups
recognized the emperor as its hereditary ruler. Metternich feared that representative government would lead to internal squabbling among the component parts of the empire and this would paralyze Austria and diminish its
international influence.

Defeat of Prussian Reform Prussia joined Austria in holding the line against
nationalism and liberalism. In 1815, Frederick William III (r. 1797–1840) was carried away by the excitement that followed the "War of Liberation" (Germany's
final struggle with Napoleon) and promised Prussia a constitutional government. In 1817, he created a new Council of State that improved administrative efficiency, but he did not issue a constitution. In 1819, a major
disagreement over the reorganization of the army prompted the resignation
of the king's reform-minded ministers, and they were replaced with hardened conservatives. In 1823, Frederick William III established eight provincial assemblies to serve as advisory bodies. They were dominated by Junkers
and strengthened the old links among crown, army, and landholders in
Prussia—a conservative alliance opposed to German nationalism.

Student Nationalism and the Carlsbad Decrees In bids to broaden their
bases of support, the rulers of three southern German states (Baden, Bavaria, and
Württemberg) issued constitutions following the events of 1815. None recognized
popular sovereignty, and all defined political rights as gifts from a monarch. Many
young Germans, whose nationalism was inflamed by opposition to Napoleon,
were unhappy with this. The best organized youth were the university students.
Their *Burschenschaften* (student associations) had many social functions, one of
which was to subordinate provincial loyalties to enthusiasm for a united Germany.

In 1817, a student club in Jena organized a celebration of the fourth
anniversary of the Battle of Leipzig and the tercentenary of the posting of
Luther's Ninety-Five Theses. More than five hundred people gathered for

ENCOUNTERING THE PAST

DUELING IN GERMANY

Dueling clubs were prestigious student organizations in the German universities of the nineteenth century. Europe's aristocracy had deep roots in the military, and dueling had long been the preferred method for resolving disputes among "gentlemen" (members of the upper class). The injury and loss of life this occasioned had prompted most western European governments to outlaw dueling by the mid-nineteenth century, but the conservative aristocratic-military class that dominated Germany kept it alive. Dueling was technically against the law, but it was socially acceptable and considered a test of manhood that elevated the status of those who practiced it.

Duels were a part of aristocratic life, and respect for the aristocracy was so great in Germany that any man who fought a duel elevated his social standing. The universities, whose students were drawn from the upper middle class and the aristocracy, congregated men for whom dueling was considered a form of character building. Duels elsewhere were usually fought with pistols, but students fenced with sabers. They seldom killed one another, but their weapons inflicted facial wounds—producing scars that served a man as a badge of honor for a lifetime. The fad for dueling persisted into the era of World War I, but it faded following the defeat of Germany's militaristic establishment in 1918.

WHAT CAN you conclude about the politics of Germany in the nineteenth century from the fact that dueling became an avenue to social mobility?

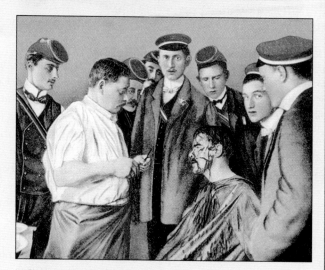

While fellow dueling-club members look on, a German student slashed in a duel is treated by a surgeon.

Image Works/Mary Evans Picture Library Ltd.

---

bonfires, songs, and processions. Because some professed republicans were involved, the event made the government nervous. Two years later the authorities' fears were confirmed when a *Burschenschaft* member, Karl Sand (d. 1820), assassinated a conservative dramatist, August von Kotzebue (1761–1819). Sand was executed, and some nationalists proclaimed him a martyr. At this point, Metternich decided that student clubs and other liberal associations had to be suppressed.

In July 1819, Metternich persuaded the German states to endorse the Carlsbad Decrees. These dissolved the *Burschenschaften* and provided for university inspectors and press censors. The next year, the German Confederation promulgated the Final Act. It limited the subjects that could be discussed in the constitutional chambers of Bavaria, Württemberg, and Baden, and affirmed a monarch's right to resist the demands of constitutionalists. For many years thereafter, the secret police of the various German states harassed anyone who sought even moderate social or political change. (See "Encountering the Past: Dueling in Germany.")

In May 1820, Karl Sand, a German student and a member of a *Burschenschaft*, was executed for his murder of the conservative playwright August von Kotzebue the previous year. In the eyes of many young German nationalists, Sand was a political martyr.

Bildarchiv Preussischer Kulturbesitz

POSTWAR REPRESSION IN GREAT BRITAIN

Britain enacted its most repressive political policies during the years 1819 and 1820, a period of economic hardship. Poor harvests and spreading unemployment as men were discharged from the army and navy in the wake of the Napoleonic wars created serious problems for the government.

Lord Liverpool's Ministry and Popular Unrest

The Tory ministry of Lord Liverpool (1770–1828) was unprepared to deal with the challenges that faced it. It concentrated on protecting the wealthy, and its legislation signaled the abandonment of the British ruling class's traditional sense of paternalistic responsibility for the poor. In 1799, the Combination Acts had outlawed labor unions, and during the Napoleonic wars Britain's government had ended protection for wages. In 1815, Parliament passed a Corn Law that maintained high prices for domestically produced grain by imposing duties on imports. The next year, Parliament replaced income taxes with sales taxes, which weighed much more heavily on the poor than on the rich. Many of the well-off also called for the abolition of the poor law, which provided aid for the destitute and unemployed. It is hardly surprising that the lower social orders began to call for reform of Parliament. Mass meetings were held, reform clubs were organized, and radical newspapers sprang up.

Government ministers viewed the organizers of the protest as demagogues who wanted to seduce the people from allegiance to their natural leaders. Memories of *sans-culottes* crowds hanging French aristocrats from lampposts were still vivid, and Britain's governing class had no intention of letting the rabble get out of hand. In December 1816, an unruly mass meeting at Spa Fields near London gave Parliament an excuse to pass the Coercion Act (March 1817). It temporarily suspended habeas corpus and expanded existing laws condemning seditious gatherings.

"Peterloo" and the Six Acts

Threats of repression and improved harvests produced a period of calm, but by 1819 restiveness was returning. Well-organized mass meetings in the industrialized north of England called for reform, and on August 16, 1819, one of these—a large gathering in Manchester at Saint Peter's Fields—ended disastrously. Troops sent to ensure order panicked the crowd, and at least eleven people were killed and scores injured. In a mocking reference to Wellington's victory at Waterloo, the event was dubbed the Peterloo massacre.

The responsibility for Peterloo lay with the local Manchester officials. Lord Liverpool's cabinet felt, however, that it had to support these authorities and the time had come for decisive action. It incarcerated radicals, and in December 1819, a few months after the German Carlsbad Decrees, it passed the Six Acts. These acts (1) forbade large unauthorized, public meetings, (2) raised the fines for seditious libel, (3) speeded up the trials of political agitators, (4) increased newspaper taxes, (5) prohibited the training of armed groups, and (6) allowed local officials to search homes in certain counties.

BOURBON RESTORATION IN FRANCE

Napoleon's abdication in 1814 opened the way for a restoration of the Bourbon monarchy that had been unseated by the revolution. The new king, Louis XVIII

(r. 1814–1824), was Louis XVI's brother. (Louis XVI's son, Louis XVII, had died uncrowned in prison.) Twenty years in exile had made Louis XVIII a political realist. He knew France had changed irreversibly and he could not turn back the clock. Consequently, he agreed to be a constitutional monarch under a constitution of his own making.

The Charter   Louis XVIII's constitution was called the Charter. It combined hereditary monarchy and representative government provided by a bicameral legislature. The monarch appointed the upper house. Members of the lower house (the Chamber of Deputies) were elected, but only men with substantial property were qualified to vote. The Charter ratified most of the rights enumerated in the Declaration of the Rights of Man and Citizen. It declared Roman Catholicism France's official religion, but it promised toleration for other faiths. Significantly, the Charter also promised not to challenge the property rights of people who held land that the revolution had confiscated from aristocrats and the church. Louis XVIII hoped this would encourage the large number of people who had benefited materially from the revolution to accept his regime.

Ultraroyalism   Louis XVIII's conciliatory mood was not shared by many of his royalist supporters. Their families had suffered from the revolution, and their leader, the count of Artois (1757–1836), demanded revenge. After Napoleon's defeat at Waterloo, royalists in the south and west of France launched the White Terror, an attack on the supporters of the revolution and Napoleon. The king could do little or nothing to halt the bloodshed, and the Chamber of Deputies, the elected house, was so extreme in its royalist sentiment that it had no wish to do so. So many of those elected in 1816 were so dangerously reactionary that the king dissolved the chamber and called for another election.

Years of give and take, during which liberals made moderate advances, ended with the assassination, in February 1820, of the duke of Berri, Artois's son and second in line after his father to Louis's throne. The ultraroyalists persuaded Louis that liberal politicians were to blame, and the king enacted repressive measures. Electoral laws were revised to give wealthy men two votes. The press was censored, rules protecting people from arbitrary arrest were relaxed, and in 1821, the government gave Roman Catholic bishops charge of secondary education in France. The monarchy's constitutional aura faded as liberals were driven out of politics.

THE CONSERVATIVE INTERNATIONAL ORDER

The Congress of Vienna closed with an understanding that the major powers (Russia, Austria, Prussia, and Great Britain) would hold postwar meetings to consult on matters affecting Europe as a whole. This agreement, the Concert of Europe, aimed at coordinating foreign policies and preventing any nation from acting without the assent of the others. The Concert of Europe was intended to protect a balance of power that was threatened by Russia's military might and the potential for renewed aggression by France.

THE CONGRESS SYSTEM

The first Concert of Europe meeting convened at Aix-la-Chapelle in 1818. The four major powers agreed to remove their troops from France and restore France's standing among European nations. Britain, however, rejected a proposal by Tsar Alexander I (r. 1801–1825) that the Quadruple Alliance promise to

WHAT WAS the Concert of Europe?

preserve all the borders and governments that then existed in Europe. Debate of the wisdom of such a policy remained academic until 1820, when revolution erupted in southern Europe.

THE SPANISH REVOLUTION OF 1820

After Napoleon's fall, Ferdinand VII (r. 1814–1833), heir to the Spanish branch of the Bourbon dynasty, ascended Spain's throne. He had promised to issue a written constitution, but once he was in power, he ignored his pledge, dissolved Spain's parliament (the *Cortés*), and ruled alone. In 1820, a military unit that was to be sent to suppress revolution in Spain's Latin American colonies rebelled and frightened Ferdinand into accepting a constitution. About the same time, a revolt in Naples forced the king of the Two Sicilies to endorse a constitution, and there were similar, but unsuccessful, uprisings elsewhere in Italy.

Metternich wanted to intervene, for he feared that disturbances in Italy might spread into the Habsburg lands. Britain, however, opposed joint intervention by the major powers in either Italy or Spain. When the Congress of Troppau met in late October 1820, Tsar Alexander persuaded the members of the Holy Alliance (Austria and Prussia) to endorse the Protocol of Troppau—a declaration of the right of stable governments to intervene to restore order in countries threatened by revolution. The decision to authorize Austrian intervention in Italy was, however, delayed until the Congress of Laibach met in January 1821. Austrian troops then marched into Naples and restored monarchy and nonconstitutional government to the Two Sicilies. Metternich hoped to win local support for this move by making improvements to governmental administration.

The final postwar congress took place in October 1822 at Verona. Once again Britain balked at authorizing joint action to deal with the situation in Spain. Its new foreign minister, George Canning (1770–1827), favored minimizing Britain's involvement in the affairs of the Continent. Austria, Prussia, and Russia, however, agreed to allow the French to send an army into Spain in April 1823, and the Spanish revolution was suppressed within a few months. The purge of liberals that followed was one of the century's bloodiest manifestations of reactionary politics.

What did not happen in Spain was as significant for the new international order as what did take place there. France's intervention was not seen as justification for expanding France's territory or power. All the interventions of the period were intended simply to maintain the stable international order established at Vienna.

The Spanish situation gave George Canning an opportunity to advance Britain's commercial interests. He prevented Europe's reactionary governments from intervening in the affairs of the Latin American colonies that had rebelled against Spain. Canning exploited their revolutions to break Spain's colonial monopoly and win Britain access to Latin American trade. Britain supported the Monroe Doctrine of 1823, which declared U.S. opposition to European intervention in the Americas for the same reason. Thanks to Canning, Britain dominated Latin American commerce for the rest of the century.

REVOLT AGAINST OTTOMAN RULE

The Greek Revolution of 1821   While conservative governments were being restored in Italy and Spain, a famous revolution erupted in Greece. It attracted the support of illustrious liberal literary figures who saw their hopes crushed elsewhere in Europe. They hoped Greece's revolt heralded the return of democracy to the land that gave it birth. Philhellenic societies flourished in most countries, and Lord Byron, one of the era's famous poets, died in Greece fighting for the cause of liberty in 1824.

The Greeks were struggling to break loose from the Ottoman Empire, and in the Enlightenment context their campaign was viewed as a fight to overthrow oriental despotism and establish Western freedoms. In more practical terms, the slow deterioration of the Ottoman Empire posed a real threat to the international balance of power. Most of Europe's great nations had designs on Ottoman territory in the eastern Mediterranean. Russia and Austria wanted parts of the Balkans. France and Britain wanted commercial privileges within the empire and control of key naval stations in the Mediterranean. Christians of all nations wanted access to the shrines in the Holy Land.

For several years, conservative governments' ingrained opposition to rebellions and nationalistic movements delayed direct intervention in Greek affairs by European nations. Ultimately, however, Britain, France, and Russia decided that Greek independence would serve their strategic interests without threatening their domestic stability, and in 1827, they issued the Treaty of London. It demanded that the Ottomans grant Greece its independence, and its signatories sent a joint fleet to support the Greek revolt. In 1829, Russia conquered and annexed the Ottoman territory now known as Romania, and the Treaty of Adrianople, which ended that campaign, also stipulated that the Ottomans allow Britain, France, and Russia to decide Greece's future. In 1830, a second Treaty of London declared Greece an independent kingdom, and two years later Greece's throne was bestowed on Otto I (r. 1832–1862), son of the king of Bavaria.

Serbian Independence   The year 1830 saw the establishment of a second independent state on the Balkan peninsula. Serbia had sought independence from the Ottoman Empire since the late eighteenth century. From 1804 to 1813, a remarkable soldier, Karageorge (1762–1817), waged a guerrilla war, which, although unsuccessful, publicized the Serbian cause and built a sense of national identity. In 1816, another leader, Milos (1780–1860), won greater autonomy for part of Serbian territory, and in 1830, the Ottoman sultan granted independence to Serbia. By the late 1830s, the major powers had recognized the new Serbian nation.

The political structure of Serbia remained in doubt for many years. Milos became its hereditary prince and persuaded the Ottomans to extend its borders in 1833. The new boundaries held until 1878, but Serbia's continuing agitation for land created problems with Austria. Questions about the status of minorities, particularly Muslims, also generated internal tension. In the 1820s, Slavic Russia, separated from Serbia by Austrian territory, declared itself the protector of Slavic Serbia. In 1856, the great powers established a collective protectorate over Serbia, but Russia still claimed a special relationship with the Serbs.

An English poet appears as an Albanian. The famous English poet, George Gordon, Lord Byron (1788–1824) was one of many European liberals who went to Greece to aid the cause of its independence. He died there of fever in 1824.

The Granger Collection, New York

THE WARS OF INDEPENDENCE IN LATIN AMERICA

WHAT SPARKED the wars of independence in Latin America?

The wars of the French Revolution and, more particularly, those of Napoleon sparked movements throughout Latin America for independence from European domination. In less than two decades, from 1804 to 1824, France was driven from Haiti, Portugal lost control of Brazil, and Spain

Toussaint L'Ouverture (1746–1803) began the revolt that led to Haitian independence in 1804.

Stock Montage

was forced to withdraw from all of its American empire except Cuba and Puerto Rico. Three centuries of Iberian colonial government over the South American continent ended. The period of transatlantic history from the American Revolution to the Latin American Wars of Independence constituted the first era of decolonization from European rule.

REVOLUTION IN HAITI

Between 1791 and 1804, the French colony of Haiti achieved independence. This revolution had trans-Atlantic significance because it was sparked by the French Revolution. Moreover, it demonstrated that slaves of African origins could lead a revolt against white masters and mulatto freemen. This example would terrify slaveholders throughout the Americas for years.

In 1791, the French National Assembly decreed that free property-owning mulattos on Haiti should enjoy the same rights as white plantation owners. The Colonial Assembly in Haiti resisted these orders, but in the same year, a full-fledged slave rebellion—the result of a secret conspiracy among slaves—shook the island. François-Dominique Toussaint L'Ouverture (ca. 1743–1803), a former slave, led the rebellion, which involved enormous violence and loss of life on both sides. Slaves sided with an invading French force, and in 1793, the French abolished slavery in Haiti. Spain and Great Britain, hoping to extend their influence in the Caribbean and to take advantage of Haiti's rich sugar-producing lands, tried to intervene. In the end, Toussaint L'Ouverture took over Haiti, imposed an authoritarian constitution, and made himself Governor-General for life.

The French government distrusted L'Ouverture and feared that his example would undermine French authority elsewhere. In 1802, Napoleon sent an army to Haiti, captured him, and sent him back to France, where he died in prison in 1803. Other Haitian military leaders such as Jean-Jacques Dessalines (1758–1806) continued to resist, and Napoleon, at war again with Britain in 1803, decided to abandon his American empire, selling Louisiana to the United States and withdrawing his forces from Haiti.

WARS OF INDEPENDENCE ON THE SOUTH AMERICAN CONTINENT

Haiti's Revolution, as a popular uprising of a repressed social group, proved to be an exception. In general, on the South American continent, the **Creole** elite—merchants, landowners, and professional people of Spanish descent—led the movements against Spain and Portugal. Few Native Americans, black people, mestizos, mulattos, or slaves became involved in these movements or benefited from the end of Iberian rule. Like the American revolutionaries in the southern British colonies (who wanted to achieve independence and keep their slaves), and like the French revolutionaries (who wanted to depose the king but not extend liberty to the working class), the Creoles wanted independence without loss of their privileges.

Creole Discontent Creole discontent had many sources. Latin American merchants wanted freer trade within their region and with North America and Europe, and they wanted an end to commercial regulations that favored their European motherlands. Creoles in Spanish districts deeply resented the fa-

Creole Merchants, landowners, and professional people of Spanish descent.

Date	Nation	Leader/s
1804	Haiti	Toussaint L'Ouverture and Jean-Jacques Dessalines
1820	Peru	José de San Martín
1821	New Spain	Miguel Hidalgo and José María Morelos
1821	Venezuela	Simón Bolívar

voritism the Spanish government showed to *peninsulares* (whites born in Spain) when making appointments to offices in the colonial governments, the church, and the army.

The Creoles drew inspiration for their revolutions from the works of the Enlightenment philosophes, from the American Revolution, and from Napoleon's toppling of the monarchies of Portugal in 1807 and of Spain in 1808. The Portuguese royal family fled to Brazil and set up a government in exile. Spain's Bourbon monarchy, however, disappeared, and the Creole elite feared that Napoleon's puppet monarchy in Spain would drain them of money to fund France's wars. Between 1808 and 1810, therefore, various Creole *juntas* (political committees) assumed responsibility for governing different parts of Latin America, and Spain was never able to restore its authority over the continent.

San Martín in Rio de la Plata   Vast size, geographical barriers, regional differences, and the absence of an integrated economy caused different parts of Latin America to take different routes to independence. The first region to assert itself was the Rio de la Plata, modern Argentina, where the revolt centered on Buenos Aires. In 1810, the revolutionary junta not only repudiated Spanish authority for itself but sent armies to liberate Paraguay and Uruguay. They were defeated, but Spain still lost control of the region. Paraguay asserted its independence, and Brazil absorbed Uruguay.

The Buenos Aires government also sought to liberate Peru, the most loyal royalist stronghold on the Continent. José de San Martín (1778–1850), a prominent leader of the Rio de la Plata revolt, assembled a disciplined army and led it on a daring march over the Andes Mountains. By early 1817, he had occupied Santiago, Chile, where a local rebel, Bernardo O'Higgins (1778–1842), had established himself as dictator. San Martín then built a navy at Santiago and launched it against Peru in 1820. A year later, the royalist forces retreated from Lima, and José de San Martín became Protector of Peru.

Simón Bolívar's Liberation of Venezuela   What San Martín did for the south, Simón Bolívar (1783–1830) did for the north. In 1810, Bolívar, the son of wealthy aristocrats, helped organize a republican junta in Caracas, Venezuela. Civil war erupted, and from 1811 to 1814 the fledgling republic was assaulted by royalists from one side and slaves and *llaneros* (cowboys) from the other. Bolívar was forced into exile, but in 1816, the president of Haiti helped him renew his fight for a republican Venezuela. He captured Bogota, capital of New Granada

Simón Bolívar was the liberator of much of Latin America. He inclined toward a policy of political liberalism.

© Christie's Images/CORBIS

21.4
Simón Bolívar's Political Ideas

(a viceroyalty that encompassed modern Colombia, Bolivia, and Ecuador), and used it as a base for war in Venezuela. By the summer of 1821, he had taken Caracas and been named president.

A year later, Bolívar and San Martín cooperated in liberating Quito, the capital of Ecuador. San Martín opposed Bolívar's republicanism and urged the establishment of monarchies in Latin America. San Martín, however, soon gave up the struggle, retired from public life, and exiled himself to Europe. Without his guidance, the political situation in Peru deteriorated, and in 1823, Bolívar marched in and took control. On December 9, 1824, at the Battle of Ayacucho, he gave the royalist forces the defeat that ended their campaign to retain an empire in America for Spain.

INDEPENDENCE IN NEW SPAIN

21.1
"Sentiments of a Nation": A Mexican Call for Independence

The campaign for independence in New Spain (the viceroyalty that encompassed modern Mexico, Texas, California, and the southwestern United States) illustrates the conservative nature of the Latin American revolutions. The local junta that here, as elsewhere, began the revolt quickly lost the initiative. A Creole priest, Miguel Hidalgo y Costilla (1753–1811), proposed a program of sweeping social reform and incited the Indians of his parish to rise up. They and other repressed groups (namely, black and mestizo urban and rural workers) responded enthusiastically to his call, and soon Father Hidalgo had an army of 80,000. They captured several major cities and marched on Mexico City itself. In July 1811, Hidalgo was captured and executed, and leadership of his movement passed to José María Morelos y Pavón (1765–1815), a mestizo priest who was far more radical than Hidalgo. He called for land reform and an end to forced labor. He kept the revolt alive for four more years, but in 1815, he, too, was captured and executed.

The revolt had the effect of uniting Mexico's conservatives, both Creole and Spanish, for both opposed any developments that might reduce their privileges. When Spain's newly restored Bourbon monarch, Ferdinand VII, was forced to accept a liberal constitution, the conservative Mexican leaders feared he might impose liberal reforms on them, and they rebelled to defend their conservative government. In 1821, a former royalist general, Augustín de Iturbide (1783–1824), proclaimed Mexico's independence and declared himself its emperor. His regime was short lived, but it established the enemies of social reform in control of an independent Mexico.

BRAZILIAN INDEPENDENCE

Brazil's independence came relatively simply and peacefully. In 1807, the Portuguese royal family and several thousand government officials and members of the court took refuge from Napoleon in Brazil. Their arrival turned Rio de Janeiro into a royal capital. The prince regent, João, addressed local grievances and in 1815 declared Brazil a kingdom independent of Portugal. In 1820, a revolution in Portugal allowed João VI (r. 1816–1824) to return to Lisbon, and he left his son, Dom Pedro, behind as regent for Brazil. In 1822, Dom Pedro blocked attempts by a revolutionary government in Portugal to regain control of its former colony by proclaiming himself emperor of Brazil. Unlike most other Latin American nations, Brazil won its independence without an internal fight that disrupted established institutions. This was a mixed blessing. Wars of independence encouraged the abolition of slavery elsewhere in Latin America, but not in Brazil. (See Map 20–1.)

MAP 20–1

Latin America In 1830   By 1830 most of Latin America had been liberated from Europe. This map shows the initial borders of the states of the region with the dates of their independence. The United Provinces of La Plata formed the nucleus of what later became Argentina.

WHAT CAUSED the spread of independence throughout Latin America in the first quarter of the nineteenth century?

HOW DID Russia, France, and Britain respond to challenges to the conservative order?

THE CONSERVATIVE ORDER SHAKEN IN EUROPE

During the first half of the 1820s, Europe's conservative governments successfully resisted the forces of liberalism. The only exceptions were the Greek revolution and the Latin American Wars of Independence, and these occurred on the periphery of the European world. In the middle of the 1820s, however, things changed, and conservative regimes began to be assaulted by new waves of discontent. Russia responded with suppression, France with revolution, and Britain with accommodation.

RUSSIA: THE DECEMBRIST REVOLT OF 1825

Unrest in the Army As the Russian army pursued Napoleon across Europe and occupied France, some of its aristocratic officers became aware of how backward their homeland was. Many of them had been exposed to the ideals of the French Revolution and the political theories of the Enlightenment, but the reformist sympathies they developed were not shared by their tsar. Alexander I took the lead in suppressing liberalism and nationalism both at home and abroad, and while he lived, it was impossible to challenge tsarist autocracy.

Politically engaged officers avoided the tsar's surveillance by forming secret societies to discuss reform, but no coherent program emerged from their meetings. The so-called Southern Society advocated representative government and the abolition of serfdom. The more moderate Northern Society also favored abolition of serfdom, but it wanted constitutional monarchy and protection for the aristocracy. Both, however, agreed that Russia's government had to change, and they worked together to plan a coup that was to be launched in 1826.

Dynastic Crisis Alexander I suddenly and unexpectedly died in late November 1825. He left no direct heir, and a peculiar dispute broke out over the succession. His brother Constantine, who would have been next in line for the throne, had disqualified himself by marrying a woman who was not of royal blood, and Constantine did not want the crown. Alexander had left secret instructions naming a younger brother, Nicholas (r. 1825–1855), as the new tsar, but Nicholas was not confident about the legality of this arrangement. He claimed that Constantine was tsar, and Constantine countered by insisting the crown belonged to Nicholas. This muddle continued for about three weeks, until the army's leadership alerted Nicholas to conspiracy within the officer corps. Much to the relief of the exasperated Constantine, Nicholas overcame his scruples and mounted the throne.

A number of junior officers had plotted to rally their men to the cause of reform, and on December 26, 1825, when the army was to take its oath of allegiance to its new tsar, the Moscow regiment (whose officers, surprisingly, were not members of one of the secret societies) refused. They called for a constitution and the coronation of Constantine, who was personally more popular than Nicholas and politically less conservative. Nicholas responded by ordering the cavalry and artillery to attack the insurgents, and more than sixty people were killed. Nicholas then appointed and presided over a commission that was charged with investigating the Decembrist Revolt and the army's secret societies. Five plotters were executed and more than a hundred exiled to Siberia. The Decembrist Revolt failed, but Russia's small clique of liberals venerated the martyrs it produced for a century.

The Autocracy of Nicholas I   Although Nicholas was neither an ignorant nor a bigoted reactionary, he feared that any tinkering with Russia's traditional institutions—even serfdom, which he admitted to be an evil—might cause the country's nobles to overthrow the monarchy. Consequently, he opposed reform and became the most extreme of nineteenth-century autocrats. He established a large force of secret police, imposed censorship, and did little to ensure the efficiency and honesty of his administration. The only reform he carried out was a codification of Russian law (1833).

Official Nationality   Nicholas tried to undercut calls for reform by sponsoring an educational program called Official Nationality. Its slogan, which was repeated again and again in government documents, newspapers, journals, and schoolbooks, was "Orthodoxy, Autocracy, and Nationalism." Official Nationality recognized the Russian Orthodox faith as the foundation for morality, education, and intellectual life in Russia. It called on the church, which controlled Russia's schools, to teach young people to accept their places in life and spurn dreams of social mobility. The autocracy of the tsar, Official Nationality claimed, was the only thing strong enough to hold the huge Russian state together and guarantee its prosperity and influence. Official Nationality also glorified nationalism and told the Russian people that their religion, language, and customs embodied unique wisdom that protected them from the moral corruption and political turmoil of the West.

Revolt and Repression in Poland   Poland had remained under Russian domination after the Congress of Vienna, but the tsar had granted it a constitutional government. Alexander I and his successor Nicholas appointed their brother, the Grand Duke Constantine (1779–1831), governor of Poland. Both tsars frequently infringed on Poland's constitution and quarreled with the Polish Diet, but this arrangement lasted through the 1820s.

 MAP EXPLORATION
Interactive map: To explore this map further, go to
http://www.prenhall.com/kagan3/map20.2

MAP 20–2
Centers of Revolution, 1820–1831   The conservative order imposed by the great powers in post-Napoleonic Europe was challenged by various uprisings and revolutions, beginning in 1820–1821 in Spain, Naples, and Greece and spreading to Russia, Poland, France, and Belgium later in the decade.

WHICH COUNTRIES were spared uprisings in this period?

In late November 1830, news of recent revolutions in France and Belgium reached Poland and inspired a small insurrection in Warsaw. The disturbance spread throughout the country, and on December 18, the Polish Diet declared the revolt to be a nationalist movement. When the Diet voted to repudiate Nicholas's authority over Poland, the tsar sent troops to suppress the uprising, and in February 1832, his Organic Statute declared Poland an integral part of the Russian Empire. The Polish uprising confirmed all of Nicholas's worst fears and persuaded him to become the *gendarme* of Europe, a monarch ever ready to provide troops for the suppression of liberal and nationalist movements.

REVOLUTION IN FRANCE (1830)

Poland's revolt was one of several disturbances inspired by the overthrow of France's Bourbon dynasty in July 1830.

The Reactionary Policies of Charles X   Charles X (r. 1824–1830), Louis XVIII's brother and successor, was a firm believer in the divine right of kings. His first action as king was to order France's Chamber of Deputies to indemnify the aristocrats who had lost lands during the revolution. He raised the money that was needed by lowering the rate of interest the government paid on its bonds. This alienated members of the middle class who held those bonds. Charles also restored primogeniture as a legally mandated system of inheritance, and he declared sacrilege against the Roman Catholic Church a crime punishable by imprisonment or death.

In the elections of 1827, liberals, whom the king's actions had angered, won enough seats in the Chamber of Deputies to force him to compromise. He appointed a less conservative ministry. Laws restraining the press and imposing government domination on education were eased. Liberals, however, wanted more (a genuinely constitutional regime), and in 1829, the king decided it was useless to try to reach accommodation with them. He replaced his moderate ministers with ultraroyalists headed by the Prince de Polignac (1780–1847).

The July Revolution   In 1830, Charles X called new elections and the liberals scored a stunning victory. Instead of trying to work with the new Chamber of Deputies, the king set out to destroy it. In June 1830, Polignac dispatched a naval expedition to Algeria, and reports of its victory (the foundation for France's North African empire) reached Paris on July 9. Charles X hoped the public's euphoria would provide him with sufficient support to stage a coup d'état. On July 25, 1830, he issued the Four Ordinances. They limited freedom of the press, dissolved the recently elected Chamber of Deputies, restricted the franchise to the wealthiest people in the country, and called new elections that, given the restricted franchise, promised a royalist outcome.

Reaction was swift and decisive. Liberal newspapers called on the nation to reject the monarch's actions, and Parisian workers, who were suffering from a downturn in the economy, took to the streets. The king sent in his troops. More than 1,800 people were killed, but Charles failed to regain control of Paris. On August 2, he accepted defeat, abdicated, and went into exile. The Chamber of Deputies named a new ministry, composed of constitutional monarchists, and ended the Bourbon dynasty by transferring the crown to Louis Philippe (r. 1830–1848), the liberal duke of Orléans.

Monarchy under Louis Philippe   Serious political and social tension confronted the new monarchy. The Revolution of 1830 might have failed if Charles X had deployed enough troops to maintain order in Paris. Also, if the aristocratic and middle-class liberals, who favored constitutional monarchy, had not acted quickly, the workers of Paris might have tried to form a republic. Liberals, however, feared popular revolution and did not want another *sans-culottes* regime. France's hard-pressed laborers and its prosperous middle class had worked together to win the Revolution of 1830, but these groups had different agendas that made it hard for them to stay united.

Politically, the so-called July Monarchy was more liberal than the Bourbon monarchy of the restoration era. It recognized constitutional government as the right of the French people, not just a concession from their king. It declared Catholicism the religion of the majority but not the official religion. It abolished censorship. It broadened the franchise a bit, and it obligated the king to work with the Chamber of Deputies.

On July 5, 1830, French forces captured Algiers, which France would continue to rule until 1962. Note how this drawing contrasts the power and modernity of the French conquerors with the almost medieval appearance of the Algerian defenses.

Getty Images, Inc. - Liaison

Socially, however, the new order the Revolution of 1830 created was quite conservative. The hereditary peerage was abolished in 1831. However, the power of the landed oligarchy was not touched, and the government soon distinguished itself for corruption. In 1830, the Paris workers had called for protection of jobs, better wages, and the preservation of the traditional crafts, but the monarchy showed scant interest in the plight of the lower classes. The kind of economic regulation the poor favored was inconsistent with the political liberalism of Louis Philippe's government. It viewed the working classes primarily as a source of trouble.

Late in 1831, troops had to be called out to suppress a workers' revolt in the city of Lyons, and in July 1832, a funeral for a popular Napoleonic general sparked another uprising in Paris. The government again deployed its soldiers, and over eight hundred people were killed or wounded. In 1834, it crushed a large strike by silk workers in Lyons. This kind of harsh suppression temporarily silenced dissidents, but France was to have no lasting peace until it established a government that addressed its social and economic problems.

Louis Philippe's government fully exploited the opportunity that Charles X's conquest of the city of Algiers gave it to build a North African empire. It dismantled Algeria's Ottoman administration and pushed deep into the interior of the country. By dint of constant warfare with Arab tribesmen, the French invaders came to dominate a land larger than France itself. Close commercial ties with France and the settlement of many French people in Algeria led France's government, by the late nineteenth century, to regard Algeria not as a colony but, despite its Muslim population, as a part of France. This had serious consequences for France when, after World War II, a pro-independence movement developed among Muslim Algerians.

BELGIUM BECOMES INDEPENDENT (1830)

The skirmish that established France's July Monarchy ignited revolutionary fires in neighboring Belgium. In 1815, the Congress of Vienna had joined Belgium, the former Austrian Netherlands, to the kingdom of Holland and tried to combine two countries that differed in language, religion, and economy. The Belgian upper classes were never reconciled to the arrangement, and on August 25, 1830, a disturbance that erupted in Brussels (after performance of an opera with

a revolutionary theme) prompted them to take action. The city's authorities and propertied classes formed a provisional government of their own and set about restoring order. When attempts at compromise with the Dutch government failed, William of Holland (r. 1815–1840) invaded. By November 1830, he had been defeated, and a few months later a national congress ratified a liberal constitution for Belgium.

The revolution in Belgium upset the boundaries established by the Congress of Vienna, but the major powers were not inclined to intervene. Russia, Austria, Prussia, and other German states were busy suppressing a number of disturbances elsewhere. France favored an independent Belgium (which France expected to dominate), and Britain was prepared to tolerate a liberal Belgium so long as it was not the pawn of another nation. In December 1830, Lord Palmerston (1784–1865), the British foreign minister, gathered representatives of the great powers in London and persuaded them to recognize Belgium as an independent, neutral state. In July 1831, the Belgians crowned Leopold of Saxe-Coburg (r. 1831–1865) their king. Belgium's neutrality, which was established by the Convention of 1839, was respected until the early twentieth century. Its violation by Germany brought Britain into World War I.

THE GREAT REFORM BILL IN BRITAIN (1832)

George IV's death in 1830 and the accession of a new king, William IV (r. 1830–1837), necessitated the calling of a parliamentary election for the summer in which France's July Revolution took place. The new House of Commons that then assembled was the first to propose major reform of Parliament, but it does not seem to have been influenced by events in France. The Great Reform Bill (1832) was the result of an accommodation between the forces of conservatism and reform that was unique to Britain.

Political and Economic Reform   The inclination to accommodate, which was a characteristic of British politics, had several sources. The commercial and industrial classes were larger in Britain than in other countries, and every British government recognized that the nation's prosperity depended on protecting the economic interests of those classes. Britain's aristocratic Whig liberals believed in constitutional liberty and advocated reform by a succession of moderate steps, not revolution. Britain also had a long tradition, backed by law and public opinion, of respect for civil liberties.

Catholic Emancipation Act   Repressive conservative government reached a peak in Britain with Lord Liverpool's notorious Six Acts (1819). In 1820, however, the Tory minister shuffled his cabinet and created a government more disposed to accommodating change. It expanded economic freedoms and repealed some restraints on labor organizations.

England's relationship with Ireland occasioned another change. In 1800, fear that Irish nationalists might rebel (as they had in 1798) and offer Ireland to

Significant Dates from the Era of Political Reaction and Reform

1814	Louis XVIII, Bourbon monarchy restored in France
1815	Holy Alliance (Russia, Austria, and Prussia) Quadruple Alliance (Russia, Austria, Prussia, and Britain)
1819	Carlsbad Decrees Peterloo Massacre The Six Acts passed in Great Britain
1820	Spanish revolution
1821	Greek revolution
1823	France intervenes to crush the Spanish revolution
1824	Charles X becomes king in France
1825	Decembrist Revolt in Russia
1829	Catholic Emancipation Act passed in Great Britain
1830	Charles X abdicates; Louis Philippe proclaimed king Belgian revolution Polish revolt
1832	Great Reform Bill passed in Great Britain

Napoleon as a base for a French invasion of England, induced Parliament to pass the Act of Union. Ireland was granted a hundred seats in the House of Commons, but only Irish Protestants were permitted to stand for election. During the 1820s, Irish nationalists organized the Catholic Association to agitate for Catholic emancipation, and in 1828, they challenged the law by electing one of their leaders, Daniel O'Connell (1775–1847), to a parliamentary seat he could not legally occupy. To head off civil war, the British ministry (led by the duke of Wellington and Robert Peel) persuaded Parliament to pass the Catholic Emancipation Act (1829) and seat Catholics. This act, with an earlier repeal of restrictions against Protestant nonconformists (1828), ended the Anglican church's control of access to British political life.

Catholic emancipation was a liberal measure passed for a conservative purpose: the preservation of order in Ireland. It alienated many of Wellington's Anglican Tory supporters and split the Tory Party. When an election in 1830 seated a Parliament disposed to reform, Wellington's ministry fell, and King William IV asked Earl Grey (1764–1845), leader of the Whigs, to form the next government.

Legislating Change   The Whig ministry quickly sent the House of Commons a major reform bill. It proposed extending the franchise and replacing "rotten" boroughs with new districts that increased representation for cities and manufacturing areas. When the House of Commons rejected the bill, Grey called for a new election (1831). The new Commons passed the bill, but when the House of Lords refused to concur, mass protest meetings and riots spread throughout the country. William IV pressured the Lords into backing down by agreeing to create enough new peers to give a third reform bill a majority in their house. It became law in 1832.

The Great Reform Bill expanded the size of the English electorate, but it did not create a democracy. It increased the number of voters by about 50 percent, but it maintained the property qualification for the franchise. It ignored women, and some members of the working class actually lost the right to vote. What the bill achieved was representation in the House of a wider variety of propertied people. This reconciled previously unrepresented economic interests to the political institutions of the country, and by admitting people who wanted change to the legislative process, it undercut the need for revolution in Britain.

Beginning in the 1820s Daniel O'Connell revolutionized the organization of Irish politics. He created a grassroots organization and collected funds to finance Irish nationalist activities. He was also known as one of the great public speakers of his generation. Here he is portrayed addressing a political gathering in County Meath, Ireland.

Getty Images Inc.—Hulton Archive Photos

SUMMARY

The Challenges of Nationalism and Liberalism   Secular ideologies including nationalism, liberalism, republicanism, socialism, and communism gained currency in nineteenth-century Europe. Nationalists opposed multinational states that were held together only by the legitimacy of their rulers, such as the Austrian and Russian empires. The widespread existence of minority enclaves presented a practical problem for nineteenth century nationalists. Nations were often created in the nineteenth century through the work of intellectual elites who used the

IMAGE KEY

for pages 482–483

a. Soviet stamp showing Decembrist leaders

b. Eugene Delacroix (1798–1863), "Liberty Leading the People", 1830. Oil on canvas, 260 x 325 cm - RF 129. Louvre - Department des Peintures, Paris, France. Photograph © Erich Lessing/Art Resource, NY

c. Detail, General Jose de San Martin, (Miniature), 1818, by Jose Gil de Castro, Chilian, (1786–1850)

d. Polish Insurgents, 1831

e. Fez © Stockbyte

f. Francisco de Goya, "Los fusilamientos del 3 de Mayo, 1808" 1814. Oil on canvas, 8'6" x 11'4". © Museo Nacional del Prado, Madrid

g. Head and shoulders portrait of Francois Dominique Toussaint L'Ouverture (1743–1803), general and liberator of Haiti

h. Aleksei Venetisianov, "Harvesting: Summer", 1827 Tretiakov Gallery

i. Pistol 1830-60's

j. Sir Thomas Lawrence (1769–1830) "Clemens Lothar Wenzel, Prince Metternich (1773–1859)", RCIN 404948, OM 905 WC 206. The Royal Collection © 2005, Her Majesty Queen Elizabeth II

culture and schools to standardize a language and narrate a shared history. Nationalism was particularly fervent, and often politically disruptive, in nineteenth-century Ireland, Germany, Italy, Poland, eastern Europe, and the Balkans. Liberalism sought a political framework that institutionalized the "principles of 1789." Liberals were generally well educated and relatively wealthy; they did not trust the working class and did not want full democracy. They believed free trade would facilitate material progress. As a practical matter, nationalism and liberalism were often linked, although in some situations the goals of nationalists and liberals were directly contradictory.

Conservative Governments: The Domestic Political Order

Conservatism established itself as a coherent political program in Europe in response to nationalism and liberalism. Burke and Hegel were the most important conservative theorists, but conservatism was very much a product of local conditions. Throughout Europe, the peace after 1815 presented problems. In Austria, Prince Metternich was the Continent's mastermind of conservatism. Austria found nationalism and liberalism particularly threatening. Metternich dominated the German Confederation, in which he limited the spread of constitutionalism. Student movements were suppressed. In Great Britain, popular unrest was also suppressed. The Bourbon king Louis XVIII ascended the French throne. He was aware of the balancing act that his position required. Louis XVIII's moderation came to an end in 1820, however, when an heir to the throne was assassinated and ultraroyalists persuaded the king to break with liberal politicians.

The Conservative International Order The Concert of Europe was a device created at the Congress of Vienna whereby the major powers would meet from time to time to attempt to maintain international peace. It was unprecedented and surprisingly successful. The Spanish revolution of 1820 was consequential for Latin America, and, coupled with revolts in Italy, led Metternich to lobby the other powers for more active intervention in troubled regions. Greece and Serbia successfully revolted against the Ottoman Empire early in the nineteenth century. Independence movements throughout Latin America took various forms but had similar results. Between 1804 and 1824, Haiti won independence from France, Portugal lost control of Brazil, and Spain lost all of its American empire except for Cuba and Puerto Rico. Creoles in the American colonies generally retained their social and economic privileges. The wars of independence depleted the colonial economies, and the states created in the former Spanish Empire were weak. Overseas trade diminished.

The Wars of Independence in Latin America The Napoleonic era marked the end of Europe's long domination of Latin America. A slave revolt, begun in 1794, won Haiti its independence. The Haitian slave revolt haunted the Creoles, who were growing discontented. Between 1808 and 1810, various Creole juntas governed different parts of Latin America, and Spain was never able to restore its authority over the continent. Different parts of Latin American took different paths toward independence. José de San Martín assembled an army and liberated Peru. In the north, Simón Bolívar began the fight that led to a republican Venezuela. Miguel Hidalgo y Costilla and José María Morelos y Pavón, both priests, were involved in early attempts for an independent New Spain, but failed. Brazil's independence came relatively simply and peacefully. The prince regent, João, addressed local grievances and in 1815 declared Brazil a kingdom independent of Portugal. Latin America emerged from its wars for independence economically exhausted and politically unstable.

The Conservative Order Shaken in Europe Starting in the mid-1920s, political discontent led to suppression in Russia, revolution in France, independence in Belgium, and accommodation in Britain. The death of Tsar Alexander I in 1825 sparked a succession crisis, which led to the Decembrist Revolt of reform-minded army officers. The revolt was harshly suppressed; the Decembrists came to be seen by later reformers as political martyrs. Nicholas I feared reform at home and revolt abroad, so he ruled autocratically. In France, the Bourbon dynasty was overthrown in July 1830, after Charles X had attempted to concentrate political power in the monarchy. Louis Philippe's July Monarchy was politically liberal and socially conservative. Belgium revolted against the Dutch in 1830 and became a constitutional monarchy. In Britain, the Great Reform Bill widened the franchise and gave a broader section of Britain's population a stake in the existing political system.

REVIEW QUESTIONS

1. What is nationalism? What parts of Europe saw significant nationalist movements between 1815 and 1830? Which of these movements succeeded and which failed?

3. Which institutions and groups supported the conservative governments in Europe? What were the main threats to these governments?

3. What were the tenets of liberalism? What effects did liberalism have on political developments during the early nineteenth century? What relationship does liberalism have to nationalism?

4. What political changes took place in Latin America between 1804 and 1824? What were the main reasons for Creole discontent with Spanish rule? To what extent were Creole leaders influenced by Enlightenment political philosophy? Who were the major leaders in the fight for Latin American independence? Why did they succeed?

5. What kind of constitution was decreed for the restored monarchy in France? What were the causes of the Revolution of 1830? How do you explain the fact that although prior to 1820 Britain was moving down the same reactionary road as the other major European powers, events arrived at a different outcome in Britain?

KEY TERMS

conservatism   (p. 487)   **Creole**   (p. 494)   **nationalism**   (p. 484)

 For additional study resources for this chapter, go to:
www.prenhall.com/kagan3/chapter20

21 Economic Advance and Social Unrest (1830-1850)

CHAPTER HIGHLIGHTS

Toward an Industrial Society Britain took the lead in the Industrial Revolution. Textiles were the first industrialized industry. By the 1830s, Belgium, France, and Germany were industrializing rapidly. Population growth and urbanization continued to accelerate. Railroads, canals, and roads facilitated the movement of people and goods.

The Labor Force The early nineteenth-century labor force was extremely diverse. Industrialization threatened to make the skills of artisans obsolete. All workers faced the possibility of unemployment with no social safety net. British Chartists fought for political reform.

Family Structures and the Industrial Revolution Industrialization transformed the European family. By the 1830s, work was increasingly segregated on the basis of gender and age. Child labor laws improved children's working conditions, but further separated them from their families.

Women in the Early Industrial Revolution In the 1820s, factory work was widely available to women, but women were paid less than their male counterparts. Women who worked in factories were generally young and single, or widowed. Domestic cottage industries employed many women throughout Europe. Marriage and family life were reshaped by industrialization.

Problems of Crime and Order Fear of rising crime led to prison reform and the creation of new police systems. In the 1840s, the British and the French created institutions designed to rehabilitate, rather than punish, criminals.

Classical Economics Classical economists believed free enterprise was the best path to economic growth. The middle class supported policies derived from classical economics. Malthus and Ricardo argued that raising workers' wages was counterproductive. Bentham's ideas influenced British public policy.

Early Socialism Socialists claimed that societies should be conceived of as humane communities, not aggregates of autonomous individuals. Utopian socialists developed plans for the creation of ideal societies. Anarchists opposed any cooperation with industry or government. Marx proposed a new model of historical development built around the notion of class conflict.

1848: Year of Revolutions Revolutions occured throughout Europe in 1848. In France, the Habsburg Empire, Italy, and Germany, liberals and nationalists rose up, only to be turned back by the forces of conservativism.

CHAPTER QUESTIONS

HOW DID industrialization spread across Europe?

HOW DID industrialization change the European labor force?

HOW DID industrialization affect European families?

WHAT ROLE did women play in the Industrial Revolution?

HOW DID the establishment of police forces and the reform of prisons change society?

WHAT IS classical economics?

WHAT IS socialism?

WHY DID a series of revolutions erupt across Europe in 1848?

CHAPTER OUTLINE

- Toward an Industrial Society
- The Labor Force
- Family Structures and the Industrial Revolution
- Women in the Early Industrial Revolution
- Problems of Crime and Order
- Classical Economics
- Early Socialism
- 1848: Year of Revolutions

IMAGE KEY

Image Key for pages 506–507 is on page 529.

HOW DID industrialization spread across Europe?

QUICK REVIEW

Britain's Advantages

• Natural resources, investment capital, technology, and an adequate food supply

• Relatively mobile society

• Strong foreign and domestic markets

By 1830, Great Britain had become an industrialized nation, and the rest of Europe was also soon to resound with the pounding of machinery and the grinding of railway engines. Between 1825 and 1850, while the groups that opposed industrialism made their final protests, intellectuals articulated major creeds that both supported and criticized the emerging society. These were years of uncertainty, a period of self-conscious transition leading to an unknown future. They culminated in 1848 with a continentwide outbreak of revolution.

TOWARD AN INDUSTRIAL SOCIETY

Industrialism and the urban growth that accompanied it played as great a part in overturning the Old Regime as the political upheavals of the French Revolution. The slow but steady conversion of Europe's economy to industrial manufacturing during the first half of the nineteenth century transformed society. Unprecedented numbers of people migrated to cities to find work in the new factories and, as a consequence, to face situations that radically altered their lives.

The Industrial Revolution began in Great Britain in the eighteenth century and was pioneered by textile manufacturing. Natural resources, investment capital, technology, adequate food supply, a relatively mobile society, and strong foreign and domestic markets promoted the development of Britain's productive capacity. Britain also profited from the fact that for two decades the French Revolution and the Napoleonic wars disrupted economic activity on the Continent and weakened France as a competitor for Atlantic trade. The United States and Canada were rich markets for British goods. The Latin American Wars of Independence opened South America to British merchants, and Britain's bases in India expanded trade with southern Asia. British banks similarly dominated the international financial markets.

The wealth that Britain acquired through such industries as textile weaving, ironmaking, shipbuilding, and china production was invested in the development of global networks that enabled Britain to dominate the world economy in the nineteenth century. British textile mills, for example, imported cotton produced by slaves in the southern United States, turned it into finished cloth, and sold that cloth in India—and at each stage in the process, the exchanges moved along sea-lanes protected by the British navy.

By the 1830s, Belgium, France, and Germany had begun to imitate Britain. They had a growing number of steam engines in use, and they were substituting coke for charcoal in iron and steel production. Both these innovations stimulated mining in the coal fields of the Ruhr and the Saar basins, but large districts of concentrated manufacturing, comparable to the British Midlands, did not yet exist. There were some pockets of production in cities, but most manufacturing still took place in rural districts where new machines were integrated into the existing system of domestic production. By midcentury, peasants and urban artisans still had more political influence than factory workers.

London's Crystal Palace during the International Exhibition of 1851.

Victoria & Albert Museum, London Great Britain/Art Resource, NY

POPULATION AND MIGRATION

As industrialization spread, the population explosion that began in the eighteenth century continued. Between 1831 and 1851, France grew from 32 million to 35 million; Germany, from 26 million to 33 million; and Britain, from 16 million to 20 million. Increasingly, Europeans clustered in urban environments. By midcentury, half the population of England and Wales and a quarter of the

ENCOUNTERING THE PAST

THE POTATO AND THE GREAT HUNGER IN IRELAND

T*he potato was introduced to Europe from South America in the seventeenth century. It grew better than grain in parts of Europe that had cool, wet climates, and in these places it became the staple crop. On less than an acre of land, an Irish peasant could raise enough potatoes to feed eleven people for a year—and pay his rent (few owned their land). Reliance on a single food source is risky, however, for if that source fails, starvation threatens.*

WHY WAS the failure of a single crop such a disaster for Ireland? What long-range effect did it have on Ireland?

In 1845, a mysterious fungus blighted potato fields across Ireland, and half the crop was lost. In 1846, it reappeared and destroyed the entire harvest. The situation improved in 1847, but the blight struck again with devastating effects in 1848. The failure of the Irish potato crop was the worst natural disaster to strike Europe in the nineteenth century, and it created social catastrophe. Landlords drove peasants who could not pay their rent from the land, and the British government, which ruled Ireland, provided little aid.

Tens of thousands died, and many other thousands sought to escape "The Great Hunger" by emigrating to the United States and Britain. As a result, the population of Ireland began to fall. It stood at 8,197,000 in 1841. By 1901, it had declined to 4,459,000, and today Ireland is the only European country to have fewer inhabitants than it had in the nineteenth century.

So many people starved in the Irish famine that the workhouses could not shelter them all.

Private Collection/Bridgeman Art Library

---

population of France and Germany lived in cities. Eastern Europe, however, remained overwhelmingly rural and little industrialized.

Urban infrastructures were overwhelmed by the hordes that flocked to cities. Housing, water, sewers, food supplies, and lighting could not be improved quickly enough to deal with migration from the countryside. Indescribably filthy slums sprang up, and disease (especially cholera) ravaged communities. Crime became a way of life for some, and human misery and degradation seemed to contemporary observers to have no bounds.

The situation in the countryside was scarcely better. Liberal reformers had hoped the changes in land ownership that followed the French Revolution and the emancipation of serfs in Prussia, Austria, and Russia would turn peasants into progressive, industrious farmers. However, anxiety about holding on to their land made them cautious and conservative. Also, few had enough land to support themselves in an increasingly commercialized agrarian economy, and few had capital to invest to make their farms more productive. The emancipations of serfs did little for agrarian economies, but they assisted industrialization by freeing a labor force to move between country and town as needed. The pace of industrialization lagged wherever such migration was discouraged (primarily in Germany, eastern Europe, and Russia).

By midcentury, the revolution in landholding had improved agricultural production, but it had also driven many small farmers from the countryside into cities. Many others chose to emigrate, for Europe continued to be haunted by the specter of poor harvests. The century's worst agricultural disaster was the famine Ireland endured from 1845 to 1847. A disease that blighted the nation's potato crop caused about 500,000 Irish peasants to starve to death and hundreds of thousands to flee abroad. (See "Encountering the Past: The Potato and the Great Hunger in Ireland.")

RAILWAYS

George Stephenson (1781–1848) invented the locomotive in 1814, but the "Rocket," his improved design shown here, did not win out over other competitors until 1829. In the following two decades the spread of railways transformed the economy of western Europe.

Image Works/Mary Evans Picture Library Ltd.

HOW DID industrialization change the European labor force?

Industrial development in the 1830s and 1840s was encouraged by the construction of Europe's railway system. The Stockton and Darlington Line opened in England in 1825. The first French company began to operate in 1832. (Serious expansion of France's rail system waited, however, until the 1840s.) Belgium and Germany had begun to run trains by 1835. By midcentury, Britain had 9,797 kilometers of track; France, 2,915; and Germany, 5,856. (See Map 21–1.)

Railways epitomized the character of the industrial economy of the second quarter of the nineteenth century. This was an economy that stressed investment in capital goods (like railroads) more than consumer goods. Building railways stimulated industrialization in several ways. Trains were the most dramatic of the many applications of the steam engine. Railroad construction projects sharply increased demand for iron, steel, and skilled laborers. This demand encouraged expansion of manufacturing capacity at forges—thus making more iron and steel available for ships and machines. The capital industries also produced immense fortunes, and as these were invested in other enterprises, industrialism grew on itself.

THE LABOR FORCE

*T*he emphasis on capital goods rather than consumer production meant there was little for the working class to purchase with the wages it earned in the new industries. The early-nineteenth-century labor force was extremely diverse: factory workers, urban artisans, cottage industry craftspeople, household servants, miners, rural peddlers, farm workers, and railroad navvies. Some workers were reasonably well off, enjoying steady employment and decent wages. Others constituted a class of "laboring poor," people who had jobs that paid little more than subsistence wages. Some of these—particularly the women and children who worked naked in the mines of Wales—endured conditions that shocked Europe when they were described by a parliamentary report in the early 1840s.

During the first half of the century, the only manufacturing industry that was thoroughly mechanized and concentrated in factories was textiles. Factory workers were greatly outnumbered by artisans, but industrialization threatened to make the skills of many artisans useless and to deprive them of control over

MAP EXPLORATION

Interactive map: To explore this map further, go to **http://www.prenhall.com/kagan3/map21.1**

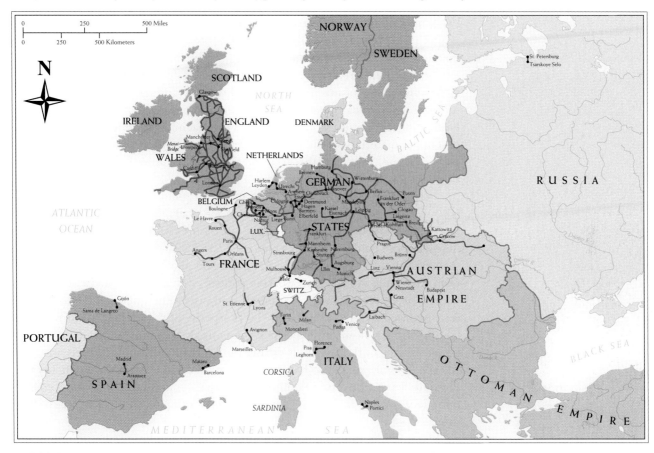

MAP 21–1

European Railroads in 1850   At midcentury Britain had the most extensive rail network and the most industrialized economy in Europe, but rail lines were expanding rapidly in France, the German states, and Austria. Southern and eastern Europe had few railways and the Ottoman Empire had none.

WHAT EFFECT did railroads have on the European work force?

their trades. All workers faced the possibility of unemployment with little or no provision for their security, and all sensed the dissolution of social ties that had been maintained by custom and community.

THE EMERGENCE OF A WAGE LABOR FORCE

During the nineteenth century, both artisans and factory workers experienced *proletarianization*. That is, as the factory system spread, they lost ownership of their means of production (equipment) and their control over their trades and became wage earners. People with capital constructed factories and purchased what was needed to run them: machinery, raw materials, and labor. Inventions, such as mechanical printing presses, also took over the work of artisans.

Factory workers, unlike self-employed artisans, had to submit to a new kind of discipline, for the needs of machines took precedence over those of their human operators. This was unpopular and difficult to enforce, and threats and punishments had to be used to compel laborers to match the pace and consistent performance of the cables, wheels, and pistons of the mechanisms with which

QUICK REVIEW

Factory Work

- Proletarianization: workers' loss of ownership of the means of production

- Factory work demanded submission to new kind of work discipline

- Factory workers were better off than the hand-loom workers who competed with them

they worked. Factory conditions were difficult, but workers in textile factories were better off than workers who tried to compete with them outside the factory system. English hand-loom weavers who worked in their homes slipped into ever-deepening poverty as they struggled to match the output of power looms.

Urban artisans were proletarianized more slowly than factory workers, and machinery was only one of the factors that contributed to their transformation. Factories actually created new opportunities for some artisans. The construction and maintenance of machines increased demand for skilled metalworkers. The erection of factories and expansion of cities to house factory work forces benefited the building trades, and lower prices for machine-made textiles reduced the cost of raw materials for the tailors and hatters from whom urban artisans bought their clothing. The chief threat to the skills and livelihood of these workers was the way the factory system reorganized production.

In the eighteenth century, the medieval guild system still governed Europe's urban workplaces. A master (guild member) owned a workshop and the larger pieces of equipment. He trained apprentices who, when they became journeymen, were paid wages with which they purchased their own tools. Ultimately, they expected to be admitted to the guild and allowed to set up shops of their own. The guild system gave workers control over labor recruitment, training, pace of production, quality of product, and price. The guild functioned to protect the integrity of the craft and the prosperity of the craftsmen. In the nineteenth century, however, it became increasingly difficult for guilds to control trades. France outlawed guilds during the French Revolution, and elsewhere in Europe, liberals worked to ban labor and guild organizations on the theory that they interfered with a free economy. Guild masters also faced increasing competition as machine production invaded craft-dominated industries. Many workshops responded by trying to improve efficiency. They instituted what the French called *confection,* the production of standard sizes and styles rather than special orders for individual customers. This promoted division of labor, for each of a shop's artisans produced only a part of a more or less uniform final product. He or she needed less skill to do this work and was, therefore, less well paid.

Masters also tried to increase production and reduce costs by lowering wages paid for piecework. Their employees fought back with work stoppages and strikes, but a flow of immigration from the countryside guaranteed a surplus of desperate people who would work for lower wages or under poorer conditions than traditional artisans. This made it difficult for urban journeymen to ascend the ladder and become masters with their own shops. More and more of them spent their lives as wage laborers whose skills were bought and sold according to their fluctuating value in the marketplace.

WORKING-CLASS POLITICAL ACTION: THE EXAMPLE OF BRITISH CHARTISM

In the 1830s, artisans, who were proud of their skills and frustrated by their diminishing opportunities for advancement, began to organize movements to protect their social and economic interests. By the middle of the century, they had become the most radical element in the European working class.

In 1836, William Lovett (1800–1877), a London artisan, formed the London Working Men's Association. In 1838, his organization issued the Charter, a proposal for political reform (**Chartism**) featuring the so-called Six Points: universal male suffrage, annual election of the House of Commons, the secret ballot, equal electoral districts, abolition of property qualifications for members of

Chartism   The London Working Men's Association's 1838 proposal for political reform featuring the Six Points.

Parliament, and payment of salaries to members of the House of Commons. For more than a decade, the Chartists fought for the adoption of their program. On three occasions the Charter was presented to Parliament. Petitions with millions of signatures were sent to the House of Commons. Strikes were called, and a newspaper, *The Northern Star,* was published—all to no avail.

The Chartists had more success dealing with local governments, but Chartism failed to cohere as a national movement. It split between those who favored violence and those who wanted to use peaceful tactics to enact reform. Rising prosperity in the wake of a depression in the late 1830s and early 1840s also led many working people to lose interest in the issues Chartism advocated. Nevertheless, as the first large-scale political movement organized by the working class, Chartism provided an inspiration and organizational model for workers throughout Europe who wanted to improve their situation.

FAMILY STRUCTURES AND THE INDUSTRIAL REVOLUTION

HOW DID industrialization affect European families?

*T*he European working-class family of the early industrial age is difficult to describe in general terms, for industrialism developed at different rates across the Continent. More is known about the family in Great Britain in this period than elsewhere, and many British developments foreshadowed those in other countries.

THE FAMILY IN THE EARLY FACTORY SYSTEM

Before England's revolution in textile production in the late eighteenth century, textile manufacturing was part of the family economy. Father and mother worked with their children as a family unit in a domestic setting. They trained and disciplined their children at home, and their family and work lives were closely intertwined. Early inventions, such as the spinning jenny, did not alter the situation, for these machines could be used at home.

It was the mechanization of weaving that caused major changes. A father who became a machine weaver labored in a factory, and his work was taken out of his home. Still, the adoption of machinery and factory production did not immediately transform the working-class family, for early English factories allowed fathers to preserve aspects of their traditional family role. Men employed their wives and children as their assistants and transferred parental training and discipline from the home to the factory. This, however, did not forestall changes in family life caused by the discipline required for factory work.

The major shift in Britain's family and factory structures occurred between the mid–1820s and mid–1830s as spinning and weaving were brought under one roof in larger factories. Improvements in machines expanded the role of relatively unskilled attendants and diminished demand for skilled artisans. Machine tending became the work of children and unmarried women, for they accepted lower wages than men and were less likely to form labor organizations.

22.2
Child Labor Inquiry

Concern for Child Labor   The children who labored in factories were usually the offspring of impoverished hand-loom weavers. Skilled adult male factory workers earned enough to support their families and to keep their wives at home and send their children to school. The familial links that had organized the work force in the British textile factory for over a quarter century faded as the women and children who worked in factories came to be supervised by men who were not their relatives.

Once parents ceased to be present and, therefore, able to watch over their children in factories, the public became concerned for the child laborer. In 1833, the English Factory Act forbade the employment of children under age nine, limited children below the age of thirteen to a nine-hour workday, and required that these children be given two hours of education a day at company expense. The effect of such reform legislation was to further divide work from home life. Adult males and older teenagers worked twelve-hour days, and younger children worked in relays of four or six hours. This diminished parent–child contact and shifted responsibility to schools for some of the nurturing and training that traditionally had been provided by the family. The English Factory Act inspired some British laborers to demand shorter workdays for adults as well as children. No longer having a relationship with their children at work, they wanted more time to spend with them at home. Parliament mandated a ten-hour workday in 1847.

Changing Economic Role for the Family   By the middle of the 1840s, men of the working class in the British textile industry had evolved distinct roles as breadwinners, fathers, and husbands. What took place in Britain was paralleled elsewhere as industrial capitalism and public education spread. The European family ceased to be a unit of production and consumption and became only a consumer. The family did not stop performing as an economic unit, but its members shared wages from different sources rather than work in a home or factory. Sharing wages rather than labor affected the strength of family bonds. Children could find work far from home, for wages could be sent over long distances.

WOMEN IN THE EARLY INDUSTRIAL REVOLUTION

WHAT ROLE did women play in the Industrial Revolution?

*T*he concerns reformers raised about working conditions for women arose in part from a spreading societal conviction that woman's place was in the home, not the factory or even the field.

OPPORTUNITIES AND EXPLOITATION IN EMPLOYMENT

The industrial economy had an immense impact on the lives of women. By taking virtually all productive work out of the home and allowing many families to live on the wages of a male spouse, it altered thinking about gender. It associated women with domestic duties (housekeeping, food preparation, child rearing and nurturing, and household management) and defined men as breadwinners. The division of labor into separate spheres for males and females that had previously characterized the lives of only a minority (the small middle class and the gentry) spread, during the nineteenth century, to the working class.

Women in Factories   Jobs given to women in factories required less skill than the work assigned to men, and they were more poorly paid. Paradoxically, factories created new employment opportunities for women but lowered the level of their skills. The women who sought factory work were single girls or widows. When a woman married—and certainly when she had a child—she was expected to give up her job. Employers did not want to accommodate her needs as a wife and mother, and society expected her husband to support her. The loss of her husband—her provider—sent her back into the factory work force.

Work on the Land and in the Home   In France, the largest group of employed women were workers on the land. In England, the majority of female laborers were domestic servants. All were poorly paid, relatively unskilled, and subjected to harsh working conditions. Desperation and need drove some to prostitution. The situation was not new, but what was new was the number of women who found themselves in positions of vulnerability.

CHANGING EXPECTATIONS IN WORKING-CLASS MARRIAGE

Many of the practices associated with the traditional family economy survived into the industrial era. Most women expected to marry as soon as possible, and they sought employment so they could earn dowries. A girl born in the country often migrated to a nearby town or city for a job as a domestic, sometimes with a relative. If she became a factory worker, she might live in a supervised dormitory. Factory owners established these institutions to recruit young workers from families that feared for their safety.

Female workers in nineteenth-century cities faced challenges known to few women of earlier generations. Movement to cities and entrance into the wage economy gave them more freedom in the choice of marriage partners. Family ties were weaker, and parents made fewer arranged marriages. There were more available young men in cities than in villages, but their increased ability to move about and change jobs made their relationships with women more fleeting. Cohabitation during courtship seems to have been common, and the number of illegitimate births increased. Marriage might improve a woman's situation economically, but if her husband became ill, died, or deserted her, she had to return to the labor market and face stiffer competition from younger women.

Industrialization undercut the traditional understanding of marriage as an economic partnership and created a new set of gender relationships. By separating the workplace from the home, industrialization made it difficult for women to combine domestic duties with paid employment. When married women worked, it was usually because of dire family necessity. Children were more likely to be sent out to work than their mothers (who stayed home to care for younger siblings). As they came to be thought of as economic assets for their parents, wives were encouraged to bear more of them.

The domestic duties of working-class women were unpaid but essential to their family's wage-based economy. While members of a family labored in factories, someone had to maintain the home front. The separation of home life from the workplace made homemaking a distinct occupation of major economic importance. A female homemaker was primarily responsible for the purchases that provided her family's food and maintained its shelter. Thus she often took charge of its finances—managing dispersal of the wages earned by its other members.

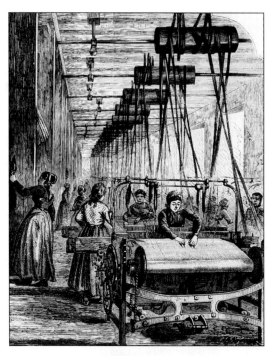

As textile production became increasingly automated in the nineteenth century, textile factories required fewer skilled workers and more unskilled attendants. To fill these unskilled positions, factory owners turned increasingly to unmarried women and widows who worked for lower wages than men and were less likely to form labor organizations.

Bildarchiv Preussischer Kulturbesitz

PROBLEMS OF CRIME AND ORDER

The revolutions Europe had witnessed at the turn of the century made its propertied classes anxious about social upheaval at a time when industrialization and urbanization were dislocating many communities. Thousands of people migrated from the countryside to the towns and cities, where they found poverty, disillusionment, and frustration. For the first sixty years of the nineteenth century, crime increased slowly but steadily.

HOW DID the establishment of police forces and the reform of prisons change society?

QUICK REVIEW

Modern Police

- First appeared in early nineteenth century
- A permanent security force separate from an army
- Salaried civilian professionals

London policeman. Professional police forces did not exist before the early nineteenth century. The London police force was created in 1828.

Peter Newark's Pictures

NEW POLICE FORCES

The ruling classes developed two strategies for containing crime: improved policing and prison reform. Police first appeared in the early nineteenth century as Europeans began to conceive of a permanent security force separate from an army. Police are salaried civilian professionals who are trained and charged with enforcing the law, keeping order, protecting property and lives, investigating crime, and apprehending offenders. Their function is partly preemptive. They prevent crime merely by being visible—for which purpose they are provided with easily recognizable uniforms. Theoretically, they have no involvement with politics.

Police forces differed from one country to another in the nineteenth century, but they were fundamental to the maintenance of order wherever they appeared. Professional police began to be employed in Paris in 1828, and that same year, Britain's Parliament authorized police for London's streets. The London police came to be called "bobbies" after Sir Robert Peel (1788–1850), the sponsor of the bill that created them. Police on the Continent bore arms, but those in Britain did not.

PRISON REFORM

Before the nineteenth century, Europe had several kinds of prisons: local jails, state prisons (such as Paris's Bastille), and prison ships. Some Mediterranean countries forced prisoners to work out their terms of incarceration as rowers on galleys. All prisoners lived under wretched conditions. Men, women, and children were housed together. Those who had committed minor offenses were mixed with those guilty of the most serious crimes. Late in the eighteenth century, the British government began to exile serious offenders to foreign colonies (notably, in Australia). This continued until objections from the colonies ended the practice in the middle of the nineteenth century. Britain then established institutions to house long-term prisoners.

Reformers, such as John Howard (1726–1790) and Elizabeth Fry (1780–1845) in England and Charles Lucas (1803–1889) in France, exposed the horrendous conditions in prisons and demanded improvements. There was little sympathy for criminals, however, and little support for taxes to construct prisons. Governments were, therefore, slow to respond, but in the 1840s, both the French and the English launched bold initiatives. On the theory that criminal acts were produced by character flaws, reformers tried to design modes of imprisonment that would correct the criminal psyche. The result was an exceedingly repressive system.

The most popular experiments spread to Europe from the United States. They involved separating prisoners from each other in individual cells. In the Auburn system (named for a prison in New York State), prisoners were confined alone during the night but worked together during the day. The Philadelphia system kept prisoners rigorously isolated at all times. In the Pentonville Prison near London, no prisoner was ever allowed to speak to or even see another one. Each wore a mask when in the prison yard, and each had a separate stall in the chapel. The point of the system was to turn the prisoner's mind in on itself and to force it to confront its criminal tendencies. The intense isolation often triggered mental collapse.

Prisoners were supposed to be trained in a trade or skill while in prison so they could emerge as reformed, productive citizens. Those who failed rehabilitation were dealt with harshly. In 1885, the French government began to send repeat serious offenders to places such as the infamous Devil's Island off the coast of South America. The intent was to excise from society criminal elements that could not be saved.

OVERVIEW   MAJOR WORKS OF ECONOMIC AND POLITICAL COMMENTARY

Year	Work	Author
1776	*The Wealth of Nations*	Adam Smith
1798	*Essay on the Principle of Population*	Thomas Malthus
1817	*Principles of Political Economy*	David Ricardo
1839	*The Organization of Labor*	Louis Blanc
1845	*The Condition of the Working Class in England*	Friedrich Engels
1848	*The Communist Manifesto*	Karl Marx and Friedrich Engels

CLASSICAL ECONOMICS

Nineteenth-century attitudes toward commerce were shaped by the "classical economists," disciples of Adam Smith who believed competitive free enterprise led to economic growth. They distrusted government intervention in economic processes, and their laissez-faire theory maintained that government's functions ought to be limited to maintaining a sound currency, enforcing contracts, protecting property, and keeping tariffs and taxes low. In their ideal society individual producers were totally free to compete for customers in the marketplace.

MALTHUS ON POPULATION

Classical economic theory, as developed by Thomas Malthus (1766–1834) and David Ricardo (1772–1823), maintained that improvements in the condition of the working class were impossible. Malthus's *Essay on the Principle of Population* (1798) claimed that population must eventually outstrip the supply of food, for population grows geometrically and food production arithmetically. If wages are raised, this only speeds up the process by encouraging workers to have more children. The only hope for bettering the lot of the poor, Malthus believed, lay in persuading the working class to have fewer children and to spend its money on consumer goods. Employers welcomed Malthus's theories as justifications for low wages and opposition to trade unionization.

RICARDO ON WAGES

David Ricardo's *Principles of Political Economy* (1817) derived an "Iron Law of Wages" from Malthus's work. He argued that if raising wages leads, as Malthus claimed, to a higher birthrate, overpopulation leads to lower wages. As the excess children of the poor enter the labor market, they increase competition for jobs, which allows employers to lower wages. As wages fall, working people respond by having fewer children. This produces a labor shortage that causes wages to rise again. The cycle operates, in the long run, to keep wages at a minimum level.

GOVERNMENT POLICIES BASED ON CLASSICAL ECONOMICS

The major classical economists were British, and their work meshed with the political theories of the British philosopher Jeremy Bentham (1748–1832). Bentham urged governments to formulate policies on the basis of a rational standard he called the "principle of utility." **Utilitarianism** maintained that people should always

WHAT IS classical economics?

22.6
Improving the Poor?

Utilitarianism Maintained that people should always pursue the course that promotes the greatest happiness for the greatest number.

pursue the course that promotes the greatest happiness for the greatest number. In *Fragment on Government* (1776) and *The Principles of Morals and Legislation* (1789), he argued that the application of the principle of utility would eliminate the influence of special interests and the legal clutter that obstructs justice. In 1834, Bentham's ideas and those of classical economists persuaded the House of Commons to pass a new Poor Law. It was premised on the idea that people who did not work were lazy and needed to be motivated to embrace self-discipline and hard labor. The Poor Law Commission disbursed poor relief through a system of workhouses, where living conditions were intentionally very unpleasant.

Classical economic theory also prompted the British government to repeal the Corn Laws in 1846. For years, an Anti–Corn Law League, representing manufacturers, had tried to persuade the government to abolish tariffs protecting the domestic price of grain. That, they argued, would lower food prices. If food was less expensive, they could cut wages for their workers, reduce the cost for British manufactured goods, and enhance Britain's competitive position in the world market. The need for grain imports to counteract the effects of the Irish potato famine also encouraged Parliament to act, and its repeal of the Corn Laws inaugurated an era of free trade that lasted until late in the century.

EARLY SOCIALISM

*T*he socialist movement (either in the form of communism or social democracy) was one of the major political forces in twentieth-century Europe, but 150 years ago it had no significant following. Early socialists often favored industrialization because of its ability to expand production, but they did not believe the free market could adequately manage the production and distribution of goods. They believed unregulated industries were characterized by mismanagement, and the result was low wages, poor product distribution, and widespread suffering. Socialists claimed that societies ought to be conceived as humane communities, not aggregates of atomistic, selfish individuals.

UTOPIAN SOCIALISM

Early critics of industrialism were dubbed **utopian socialists** by their opponents, for their visionary programs often involved plans to establish ideal societies based on noncapitalistic values. Almost all such proposals involved radical changes in traditional attitudes toward sexuality and the family. People who sympathized with their economic ideas were often alienated by their advocacy of free love and open family relationships.

Saint-Simonianism   Count Claude Henri de Saint-Simon (1760–1825) was the earliest of the socialist pioneers. A liberal French aristocrat, he fought in the American Revolution and welcomed the French Revolution. By Napoleon's day, he had become a writer and social critic. Saint-Simon claimed a truly modern society would be characterized by consistently rational management. His ideal government resembled a board of directors charged with responsibility for harmonizing the conduct of individuals and groups. His faith in expert management made him the ideological father of technocracy. He claimed the skillful management of wealth and not its simple redistribution was the route to alleviating poverty and suffering.

Owenism   Socialism's first major advocate in Britain was a self-made industrialist, Robert Owen (1771–1858). (Owen was a partner in one of Britain's largest mills, a cotton factory in New Lanark, Scotland.) Owen believed in the environmentalist

---

WHAT IS socialism?

utopian socialists   Early critics of industrialism whose visionary programs often involved plans to establish ideal societies based on noncapitalistic values.

Mᴿ OWEN'S INSTITUTION, NEW LANARK.
(Quadrille Dancing.)

Robert Owen, the Scottish industrialist and early socialist, created an ideal industrial community at New Lanark, Scotland. He believed deeply in the power of education and saw that the children of workmen received sound educations.

Eileen Tweedy/Picture Desk, Inc./Kobal Collection

principles of Enlightenment psychology. That is, he thought human characters could be improved by improving their surroundings. He also maintained that a company could provide humane working conditions and still be profitable.

Owen tested his theories at his own factory. He provided his workers with good housing, abundant opportunities for recreation, and schools for their children. He was a notorious freethinker on matters of religion and sex, but he made a place for their churches. He offered workers incentives to encourage productivity, and they vindicated his faith in them by making a fine profit for his company.

Visitors flocked from all over Europe to see what Owen had accomplished through enlightened management, and he penned numerous articles, pamphlets, and letters to influential people to plead for organizational reform of industrial manufacturing. He eventually sold his factory, and during the 1820s, he toured the United States and established an experimental model community at New Harmony, Indiana. It failed, but he was not discouraged. He returned to Britain and took up the cause of the Grand National Union, a plan to unify all the British trade unions. It collapsed in the early 1830s.

Fourierism   Charles Fourier (1772–1837), a Frenchman, held beliefs similar to Owen's, but he had less financial success and attracted less public attention. Fourier believed the industrial order erred by ignoring the emotional side of human nature, the innate human desire for things in which to take delight. He advocated the construction of communities called *phalanxes,* whose liberated customs would dispel the dullness of factory life.

Fourier envisioned agrarian rather than industrial production as a basis for his phalanxes. Sexual activity among their members was to be relatively free, and marriage was to be delayed until later in life. Fourier said no one should be required to perform the same job for an entire day—that people would be happier and more productive if they moved from one task to another. His discussion of the problem of boredom highlighted one of the key difficulties facing workers in modern industrialized economies.

QUICK REVIEW

Charles Fourier (1772–1837)

- Believed that industrial order ignored the emotional side of human nature
- Advocated the construction of communities called *phalanxes*
- Envisioned agrarian production as the basis of *phalanxes*

Saint-Simon, Owen, and Fourier turned to governments for help in implementing their proposals, but they failed to appreciate how difficult it is politically to bring about radical social transformations. Other socialist reformers paid more attention to practical politics. In 1839, Louis Blanc (1811–1882), in the publication *The Organization of Labor,* called for an end to competition but not for a wholly new social order. He believed giving votes to workers would empower them to reform the system through the political process. A state controlled by its working class would, he believed, sponsor workshops to employ the poor, and such shops might eventually replace private enterprise and reorganize industry to ensure universal employment. If the state was their employer, enfranchised workers could keep their employer true to the cause of improving conditions for labor.

ANARCHISM

A few of the social critics of the 1840s were **anarchists** who opposed any cooperation with industry or government. Some believed violence and terrorism were needed to force society to change; others trusted to more peaceful means.

Terrorism's major advocate, Auguste Blanqui (1805–1881), wanted to abolish both capitalism and the state. His vision for a new society was vague, but his strategy for achieving it was clear. It foreshadowed Lenin's program for Russia's revolution—develop a vanguard of professional revolutionaries to wage war on capitalism. The peaceful wing of anarchism is represented by Pierre Joseph Proudhon (1809–1865), author of *What Is Property?* (1840). He believed a system of small businesses peacefully cooperating and exchanging goods could make the state redundant. Proudhon's influence made the French labor movement less political than workers' movements in Britain and Germany.

MARXISM

European socialism is often seen as developing naturally or necessarily into **Marxism**, but nothing could be further from the truth. At midcentury the opinions of Karl Marx (1818–1883) were simply one ingredient among many in the heady mixture of ideas discussed by critics of emerging industrial capitalist society. Marxism differed from its competitors primarily in its claim to a scientific foundation and in its insistence on reform through revolution. Marx set the rise of industrialized societies in the context of a theory about the processes of historical development and drew sweeping political conclusions from the model he erected.

Karl Marx was the son of a German-Jewish family that converted to Lutheranism. At the University of Berlin, he absorbed Hegelian philosophy and extremist politics. He became the editor of a radical newspaper, the *Rheinische Zeitung,* and his political views prompted the conservative government of his homeland to exile him. He moved to Paris, then to Brussels, and finally (after 1849) to London.

Partnership with Engels In 1844, Marx met Friedrich Engels (1820–1895), another young middle-class German, but one with a wealthy father who owned a textile factory in Manchester, England. In 1845, Engels published *The Condition of the Working Class in England,* a devastating picture of industrial life. Late in 1847, Engels and Marx were asked to write a pamphlet explaining the philosophy of a newly organized (and short-lived) secret society called the Communist League. The league called itself *communist* because the term was more radical than *socialist.* Communism implied the outright abolition of private property rather than socialism's less thorough redistributive economics. The *Communist Manifesto* was only about fifty pages long, but it was to become the most influential

anarchists Those who opposed any cooperation with industry or government.

Marxism Socialist movement begun by Karl Marx in the mid–nineteenth century that differed from competing socialist views primarily in its claim to a scientific foundation and in its insistence on reform through revolution.

political document in modern European history (See "History's Voices: Karl Marx and Friedrich Engels Describe the Class Struggle".) The recent collapse of the Soviet Union and the communist governments of eastern Europe make it difficult for many people now to grasp the power that Marx's vision had for so many for so long.

Sources of Marx's Ideas   Marx drew his theories from German Hegelianism, French socialism, and British classical economics. Hegel had explained progress as the result of a historical process in which a thesis and an antithesis clash until they are resolved at a higher level by synthesis. What Hegel saw in the history of thought, Marx saw in the history of societies. That is, he claimed that conflicts between dominant and subordinate groups lead to the rise of a new dominant group, which then becomes the source of new discontents and conflicts that lead to yet further development.

The socialists alerted Marx to the significance of property distribution in the formation of classes, and the classical economists provided the analytical tools with which he carried out an empirical, scientific examination of industrial capitalist society. Marx concluded that the new industrial work force, the proletariat, was the most potent element in contemporary history, and he equated the fate of the working class with the fate of humanity itself. He argued that a universal utopian society would emerge as the proletariat succeeded in liberating itself from bondage to the capitalist mode of industrial production.

Revolution Through Class Conflict   In *The Communist Manifesto*, Marx and Engels contended that reason provides a simple explanation for the whole of human history: History, they claimed, is fundamentally the story of humankind's struggle with the physical world to obtain what it needs to survive, and the institutions, values, and ideas of a society are a function of the economy that sustains it. History is driven by a conflict between the classes who own and control the means of production and the classes who work for them. Conflict between these groups is not an accidental by-product of mismanagement or bad intentions. It is inherent in their relationship. Consequently, piecemeal reforms cannot eliminate social and economic evils. That requires a radical transformation of society, and Marx and Engels believed the natural development of capitalism would inevitably bring about a revolution that achieves the transition to the higher communist order.

Marx and Engels claimed that class conflict had become, early in the nineteenth century, a simplified struggle between the bourgeoisie and the proletariat—between the middle class and the workers. The nature of capitalism ensured that the struggle would intensify, for capitalist competition and large-scale industrial production would steadily increase the size of the unpropertied proletariat by forcing more and more of the smaller producers into its ranks. As business structures grew larger, competitive pressures would reduce the middle class and generate a larger and more miserable proletariat. Eventually suffering would drive the workers, Marx contended, to foment revolution and overthrow the few remaining owners of the means of production. Then for a time, the workers would manage the means of production by means of a dictatorship of the proletariat. This would eventually give way to a propertyless, classless communist society—the end product of the Hegelian dialectic process that governed history. Although the class conflict that would bring the proletariat to power resembled earlier social clashes, Marxists claimed it differed from them in a significant way.

Karl Marx's socialist philosophy eventually triumphed over most alternative versions of socialism in Europe, but his monumental work became subject to varying interpretations, criticism, and revisions that continue to this day.

Bildarchiv Preussischer Kulturbesitz

HISTORY'S VOICES

KARL MARX AND FRIEDRICH ENGELS DESCRIBE THE CLASS STRUGGLE

*I*n The Communist Manifesto *(1848), arguably the most influential political pamphlet of modern European history, Karl Marx and Friedrich Engels portrayed human history as developing through a series of economic class struggles that, in the contemporary world, occurred between the bourgeoisie, or capital-owning class, and the proletariat, or workers. The result was to be the final class conflict of history because, as Marx and Engels argued, the proletariat, unlike any previous group seeking to establish its liberty, was so large that its victory was also the victory of humanity itself.*

WHOM DO Marx and Engels portray as the previous enemies of the bourgeoisie? How did bourgeois economic development and dominance lead to a society based on the "cash nexus"?

The history of all hitherto existing society is the history of class struggles. …

Our epoch, the epoch of the bourgeoisie, possesses, however, this distinctive feature: it has simplified the class antagonisms. Society as a whole is more and more splitting up into two great hostile camps, into two great classes directly facing each other: Bourgeoisie and Proletariat. …

Each step in the development of the bourgeoisie was accompanied by a corresponding political advance of that class. …

The bourgeoisie, wherever it has gotten the upper hand, has put an end to all feudal, patriarchal, idyllic relations. It has pitilessly torn asunder the motley feudal ties that bound man to his "natural superiors," and has left remaining no other nexus between man and man than naked self-interest, than callous "cash payment."…

The proletariat goes through various stages of development. With its birth begins its struggle with the bourgeoisie. …

But with the development of industry the proletariat not only increases in number; it becomes concentrated in greater masses, its strength grows, and it feels that strength more. The various interests and conditions of life within the ranks of the proletariat are more and more equalized, in proportion as machinery obliterates all distinctions of labour, and nearly everywhere reduces wages to the same low level. …

The bourgeoisie finds itself involved in a constant battle. …

Of all the classes that stand face to face with the bourgeoisie today, the proletariat alone is a really revolutionary class. …

All previous historical movements were movements of minorities, or in the interest of minorities. The proletarian movement is the self-conscious, independent movement of the immense majority, in the interest of the immense majority. …

The advance of industry, whose involuntary promoter is the bourgeoisie, replaces the isolation of the labourers, due to competition, by their revolutionary combination, due to association. The development of Modern Industry, therefore, cuts from under its feet the very foundation on which the bourgeoisie produces and appropriates products. What the bourgeoisie, therefore, produces, above all, is its own grave-diggers. Its fall and the victory of the proletariat are equally inevitable. …

The proletarians have nothing to lose but their chains. They have a world to win.

Karl Marx and Friedrich Engels, *The Communist Manifesto,* in Lawrence H. Simon, ed., Karl Marx, *Selected Writings* (Indianapolis: Hackett Publishing Company, Inc, 1994), pp. 158, 159, 160, 161, 165, 166–167, 168, 169, 186.

The victorious proletariat, by its very nature as a huge majority, could not become a new oppressor class. Having no significant group to oppress, it would automatically seek the good of all.

Marx's prediction of the collapse of capitalism in the later part of the nineteenth century proved to be wrong. The middle class did not become proletarianized, as Marx had expected, for more and more people benefited from the capitalist industrial system and entered the middle class. Nonetheless, Marxist doctrines thrived, for their utopian vision appeared to be based on the empirical evidence of hard economic fact. People of the late nineteenth century were fascinated by all things scientific, and the scientific aura of Marxism enhanced its credibility. Within a generation, Marxism had captured the imagination of many socialists and large segments of the working class.

1848: YEAR OF REVOLUTIONS

A series of revolutions erupted across the Continent in 1848. They had no single cause, but the conditions that won them support were the same in many places: severe food shortages, economic depression, widespread unemployment, overburdened poor relief systems, wretched urban living conditions, and increasing frustration and discontent among the artisan and laboring classes.

The people who pushed for reform in 1848 were not workers but political liberals from the middle classes who wanted more civil liberties, better representative government, and an unregulated economy. Although they preferred to pursue their objectives by peaceful means, they pressured governments by appealing for support from the urban working classes. The workers had little interest in the liberal political agenda. They wanted improved working and economic conditions, and they were prepared to use violence to get them. Everywhere but in France the revolutionaries also appealed to nationalism.

The 1848 revolutions were stunning, for Europe had never known so many major upheavals in a single year. (See Map 21–2.) Without exception, however, the revolutions failed because their supporters fragmented. Nationalistic groups turned against each other, and differences in goals divided middle-class revolutionaries from their working-class compatriots.

FRANCE: THE SECOND REPUBLIC AND LOUIS NAPOLEON

Once again the Parisians were the first to ignite the tinder of revolution. France's economy sagged in 1846 and 1847, and the regime of Louis Philippe and his minister Guizot seemed adept only at corruption. The monarchy's liberal opponents organized a series of banquets to rally support for increasing the political privileges of the middle class, and angry workers were eager to back any movement critical of the government. When the king tried to silence his opponents by forbidding the political banquets (February 21, 1848), a crowd of disgruntled Parisian workers took to the streets. The government quickly lost control, and within a few days Louis Philippe had abdicated and fled to England (February 24, 1848).

The National Assembly and Paris Workers Liberals, led by the poet Alphonse de Lamartine (1790–1869), set up a provisional government to organize an election for a new National Assembly that was to write a republican constitution. Various Parisian working-class groups wanted a social as well as a political revolution and demanded posts in the cabinet for their leader, Louis Blanc, and two of his compatriots. These men forced the government to fund public works and relief programs.

On April 23, an election based on universal male suffrage chose the new National Assembly. Moderates and conservatives won most of the seats, for electors in the provinces were not as inclined to radical socialist reform as the workers of Paris. However, when the new government began to trim back public works

WHY DID a series of revolutions erupt across Europe in 1848?

MAP 21–2

Centers of Revolution in 1848–1849 The revolution that toppled the July monarchy in Paris in 1848 soon spread to Austria and many of the German and Italian states. Yet by the end of 1849, most of these uprisings had been suppressed.

WHY WOULD Austria and Germany have provided fertile grounds for the spread of a revolutionary movement that began in France?

projects and relief programs, crowds of unemployed Parisians rioted. Late in June, they began to barricade some city streets, and the authorities ordered General Cavaignac (1802–1857) to bring troops in from the conservative countryside to restore order. Over four hundred people were killed in two days of combat, and 3,000 more were hunted down in subsequent street fighting.

Emergence of Louis Napoleon The so-called June Days ended the drive for social revolution and confirmed the dominance in French politics of men who primarily wanted security for property. The conservatives were further strengthened when, late in 1848, Louis Napoleon Bonaparte (1808–1873), nephew of the former emperor, won election to the presidency. The voters associated the name Bonaparte with stability and greatness.

The election of the "Little Napoleon" doomed the Second Republic, for Louis Napoleon was dedicated to the pursuit of personal fame, not republican ideals. He was the first of the modern dictators, a man who ruled by manipulating unstable political situations and exploiting the insecurity of the masses. He opposed the National Assembly, claiming that he, not it, represented the will of the nation. When the assembly refused to amend the constitution to allow him to run for reelection, he dispatched soldiers to disperse it—on December 2, 1851, the anniversary of his uncle's victory at Austerlitz. Over two hundred people died resisting his coup, and more than 26,000 were arrested. About 10,000 of these were transported to Algeria. A plebiscite held on December 21, 1851, revealed that only about 600,000 voters objected to what Louis Napoleon had done. A year later, another plebiscite approved his decision to proclaim himself Emperor Napoleon III. For the second time in just over fifty years, France had swung from republicanism to Caesarism.

French Women in 1848 Following the collapse of the July Monarchy and Louis Philippe's abdication, numerous political clubs sprang up. Some, particularly in Paris, mobilized women to work for women's rights. A radical group called the *Vesuvians* (after Italy's volcano) demanded full equality with men in the home, the right of women to serve in the military, and similar dress for both sexes. Feminism of this kind remained a politically naive fringe phenomenon, but a more conservative women's movement won some support in the National Assembly. It defended itself against the charge that feminists wanted to destroy marriage by lauding the importance of the traditional family and motherhood.

Some Parisian feminists moved quickly to use the freedoms the liberals' victory made available to them. They founded a daily newspaper, the *Voix des femmes* (*The Women's Voice*), and used it to demand that special attention be given to women's interests. It pointed out that reforms that improved things for men did not inevitably benefit women. A society with the same name as the newspaper was established to work with male political groups. It cleverly appealed to conservatives by basing its case for women's rights on the importance of strong families. Because motherhood and child rearing were so crucial to society, the *Voix des femmes* argued that women needed educations, employment, economic security, civil and property rights, and the vote.

Feminists met the same fate as the workers who helped launch the revolution of 1848: total defeat. Women were hurt along with men when the conservative National Assembly cut back relief and public works projects. A subsequent crackdown on political clubs destroyed the organizations through which they worked for reform, and they were soon specifically forbidden to take part in any clubs of a political nature. The *Voix des femmes* tried to skirt this law by creating labor organizations for working-class women, but two leaders of this movement, Jeanne Deroin (d. 1894) and Pauline Roland (1805–1852), were arrested, tried, imprisoned, and exiled. By the time of Louis Napoleon's triumph in 1852, the feminist movement that had sprung up in 1848 had been eradicated.

THE HABSBURG EMPIRE: NATIONALISM RESISTED

France's revolution of 1848 shook the Habsburg domains, where the frustrations of liberals and nationalists were building to dangerous levels. The imperial regime was suddenly confronted by simultaneous revolts in Vienna, Prague, Hungary, and Italy, and its stability was adversely affected by additional disturbances that broke out in Germany.

The Vienna Uprising   The Habsburg troubles began on March 3, 1848, when Louis Kossuth (1802–1894), a Magyar nationalist and member of the Hungarian Diet, called for the independence of Hungary. His speeches inspired students to riot in Vienna, and the imperial army failed to restore order. Metternich resigned and fled the country, leaving his feeble-minded emperor, Ferdinand (r. 1835–1848), to try to calm the situation by promising a moderately liberal constitution. Radicals among the students were not satisfied with this and formed democratic clubs to press for more. On May 17, the emperor and his court fled to Innsbruck and surrendered Vienna to a committee of about two hundred members. Its chief concern was to address the plight of Viennese workers.

What the Habsburg government feared most was not an urban worker rebellion but an uprising of serfs. There had already been isolated instances of serfs invading manor houses and burning records. Almost immediately following the Vienna revolt, the imperial government emancipated serfs in much of Austria, and the Hungarian Diet also abolished serfdom in March 1848. This headed off the most serious potential threat to order in the empire, and the end of serfdom was one important, permanent achievement of the revolutions of 1848.

Louis Kossuth, a Magyar nationalist, shown here seeking to raise troops to fight for Hungarian independence during the revolutionary disturbances of 1848.

Bildarchiv Preussischer Kulturbesitz

The Magyar Revolt   The Vienna revolt encouraged dissident Hungarians to take action. The Magyar leaders were primarily liberals backed by nobles who wanted to protect their aristocratic privileges against infringement by the Habsburg monarchy. The Hungarian Diet's reform program was spelled out in the March Laws. It demanded equality of religion, jury trials, the election of a lower chamber, a relatively free press, and payment of taxes by the nobility. Emperor Ferdinand had little choice but to acquiesce.

The Magyars also wanted a nearly autonomous Hungarian state within the Habsburg domains. The partially independent nation they established annexed Transylvania, Croatia, and neighboring parts of the Habsburg Empire. However, the Romanians, Croatians, and Serbs who came under its control resisted its program of Magyarization (particularly its efforts to compel use of the Hungarian language). The minority populations concluded that their chances for ethnic survival would be better under a Habsburg government, and in late March, the Viennese authorities sent Count Joseph Jellachich (1801–1859) to aid the rebels who were rebelling against the Hungarian rebels. By early September 1848, he was leading an invasion force into Hungary that was strongly supported by the opponents of Magyarization.

Czech Nationalism   In the middle of March 1848, with Vienna and Budapest in revolt, Czech nationalists demanded that Bohemia and Moravia be recognized as an autonomous Slavic state within the empire. This ignited conflict between the Czechs and the Germans who also inhabited these regions.

The Czechs invited representatives of the Slavic peoples (Poles, Ruthenians, Czechs, Slovaks, Croats, Slovenes, and Serbs) to meet in Prague early in June. Francis Palacky (1798–1876), leader of this first Pan-Slavic Congress, issued a manifesto calling for the equality of Slavs within the Habsburg Empire and protesting the repression of the Slavic peoples who were under Habsburg, Hungarian, German, and Ottoman domination. The document envisioned a vast Slavic state or federation extending from Poland south and eastward through Ukraine. Such an entity never came into being, but the dream of a unified, independent Slavic people served some political leaders as a useful tool. Russia invoked Pan-Slavism to win the support of nationalist minorities in eastern Europe and the Balkans and to bring pressure to bear on Austria and Germany.

On June 12, the day the Pan-Slavic Congress closed, an insurrection erupted in Prague, but by June 17, General Prince Alfred Windischgraetz (1787–1862) had put it down. The middle class favored suppression of the radicals, and German residents supported efforts to smother Czech nationalism. A policy of "dividing and conquering" worked to end the revolt.

Rebellion in Northern Italy   In addition to the Hungarian and Czech revolts, the Habsburgs faced war in northern Italy. On March 18, 1848, a revolution began in Milan that quickly forced General Count Joseph Wenzel Radetzky (1766–1858), the Austrian commander, to withdraw from the city. King Charles Albert of Piedmont (r. 1831–1849), ruler of Lombardy (the province of which Milan is the capital), offered aid to the rebels, but in July Radetzky reappeared with more troops, defeated him, and suppressed the revolution.

Meanwhile, a newly elected assembly in Vienna was struggling to write a constitution while dealing with radicals who pressed for ever more concessions. When another insurrection broke out in October, the imperial government responded with force. It bombarded Vienna and sent in an army to crush the revolt. On December 2, Emperor Ferdinand, now clearly too feeble to govern, abdicated in favor of a young nephew, Francis Joseph (r. 1848–1916). A little more than a month later, Austrian troops occupied Budapest, and by March they had imposed military rule in Hungary. The Magyar nobles attempted one last rebellion, but in August, the Austrian army—reinforced by 200,000 soldiers whom Tsar Nicholas I of Russia (r. 1825–1855) was happy to lend—crushed the Hungarians. The Habsburg Empire survived the grave internal challenges of 1848 thanks to divisions among its enemies and its willingness to use military force.

ITALY: REPUBLICANISM DEFEATED

The brief Piedmont-Austrian war of 1848 was only the first stage in the Italian revolution. After the Austrians defeated Charles Albert of Piedmont, Italy's nationalists pinned their hopes for the unification of their country on their liberal pope, Pius IX (r. 1846–1878). Unfortunately, however, political radicalism got out of control in Rome. On November 15, 1848, a democratic extremist assassinated Count Pelligrino Rossi (1787–1848), the liberal minister of the Papal States. The next day, popular demonstrations forced the pope to appoint a radical ministry, and shortly thereafter the pope fled to Naples. In February 1849, the radicals declared Rome a republic, and nationalists from all over Italy—most prominently, Giuseppe Mazzini (1805–1872) and Giuseppe Garibaldi (1807–1882)—flocked to the city hoping to use it as a base of operations for a war to unite Italy.

In March 1849, radicals in Piedmont forced Charles Albert to renew war with Austria, and his prompt defeat led him to abdicate in favor of his son Victor Emmanuel II (r. 1849–1878). Piedmont's surrender meant the Roman Republic was left on its own to face France, a major opponent. France wanted to prevent the rise of a strong nation on its southern border, and in early June 1849, 10,000 French soldiers laid siege to Rome. The Roman Republic collapsed, and on July 3, the French occupied Rome. They remained in Italy to protect the pope until 1870. These events ended Pius IX's flirtation with liberalism and turned him into an archconservative. Italy's nationalists had, therefore, to look for another leader behind whom to rally in a fight to unify their homeland.

GERMANY: LIBERALISM FRUSTRATED

Revolutionary contagion spread rapidly through the German states of Württemberg, Saxony, Hanover, and Bavaria. The rebels wanted liberal governments and

The Revolutionary Crisis of 1848 to 1851

1848

February 22–24	Abdication of Louis Philippe
March 3	Kossuth demands freedom for Hungary
March 13	Revolution in Vienna
March 15	Habsburg emperor accepts the March Laws
March 18	Frederick William IV promises a constitution; Revolution in Milan
March 22	Piedmont declares war on Austria
April 23	Election of the French National Assembly
May 17	Emperor Ferdinand flees Vienna
May 18	Frankfurt Parliament gathers
June 2	Pan-Slavic Congress convenes in Prague
July 24	Austria defeats Piedmont
September 17	General Jellachich invades Hungary
October 31	General Windischgraetz pacifies Vienna
November 16	Revolution in Rome
November 25	Pope Pius IX flees Rome
December 2	Francis Joseph becomes Habsburg emperor
December 10	Louis Napoleon and the Second French Republic

1849

January 5	General Windischgraetz occupies Budapest
February 2	The Roman Republic proclaimed
March 12	War resumes between Piedmont and Austria
March 23	Piedmont is defeated, Victor Emmanuel II crowned
March 28	German crown offered to Frederick William IV
June 18	Frankfurt Parliament dispersed
July 3	Collapse of the Roman Republic
August 9–13	Austria defeats Hungarian forces

1851

December 2	Coup d'état of Louis Napoleon

greater national unity for Germany. The most serious disturbances were, however, in Prussia.

Revolution in Prussia Frederick William IV (r. 1840–1861) preferred to believe foreign agitators were to blame for riots that erupted in Berlin on March 15, 1848, and he refused to deploy his troops against his subjects. His government's failure to overcome its own internal divisions and restore order led the king to agree to convene a constituent assembly to write a Prussian constitution. He also implied he would support German unification.

Frederick William IV appointed a cabinet headed by David Hansemann (1790–1864), a respected moderate liberal. However, it could not work with the radical democrats seated in the constituent assembly. The frustrated king then tried replacing his liberal ministry with a conservative one and, in April 1849, he dissolved the assembly and proclaimed a constitution of his own. All adult males were given the vote, but they were divided into three classes (according to the taxes they paid) and limited to voting for representatives from their class. This meant the major taxpayers (about 5 percent of the population) elected about one-third of the Parliament. The ministry reported to the king alone, and the Prussian army swore direct loyalty to him.

The Frankfurt Parliament On May 18, 1848, representatives from all the German states gathered in Saint Paul's Church in Frankfurt to reorganize the German Confederation. The Frankfurt Parliament intended to write a moderately liberal constitution for a united Germany, but the assembly's liberalism alienated conservatives and members of the working class. Conservatives resented any challenge to the existing political order, and workers and artisans disliked liberalism's commitment to free trade and hostility to the protections the guild system offered labor. German conservatives were able to exploit the split that developed between liberals and workers at Frankfurt for the rest of the century.

Discussions of the issue of Germany unification also broke down at the Frankfurt Parliament, for members could not agree on whether to include Austria in a united Germany. The *kleindeutsch* (small German) faction prevailed over the *grossdeutsch* (large German) party when Austria rejected the whole notion of unification. The numerous nationalities within the Habsburg Empire feared that unification would lead to German domination.

Austria's opposition to unification strengthened support for Prussian leadership of Germany. On March 27, 1849, the parliament produced a constitution and offered the crown of a united Germany to Frederick William IV of Prussia. He rejected the offer, asserting that kings ruled by the grace of God, not parliaments. His refusal caused the Frankfurt Parliament to collapse and gave German liberals a blow from which they never recovered. In the end, all the various revolutions of 1848 did was to extend the franchise in some of the German states and establish some conservative constitutions.

SUMMARY

Toward an Industrial Society Multiple factors helped make Britain the early leader in the Industrial Revolution. Textiles were the first industrialized industry. Belgium, France, and Germany were industrializing rapidly by the 1830s. Population growth and urbanization continued; many cities were unable to accommodate the new influx of residents, so slums grew and crime increased.

Most peasants had become landowners, but many lacked the capital to use their land effectively. The ease with which people could leave rural land varied, with migration generally more difficult in eastern parts of Europe. Railroads, canals, and improved roads facilitated movement. Many railways were built in the 1830s and 1840s, reflecting this period's emphasis on capital production rather than consumer production.

The Labor Force   The labor experience varied, according to industry and location. In the first half of the nineteenth century, only textile manufacture was fully mechanized and factory based. Skilled artisans made up far more of the nonagricultural work force than factory workers. Both, however, were proletarianized. Textile workers who resisted factory production were slowly impoverished. Urban artisans were slowly proletarianized, as labor and guild organizations were suppressed for political reasons, and craftwork was standardized for economic reasons. British Chartists provided a model for a large-scale working-class political movement.

Family Structures and the Industrial Revolution   Industrialization transformed the family from being the chief unit of both production and consumption, to being the chief unit of consumption alone. This occurred slowly and was not completed throughout Europe before the end of the nineteenth century. Early textile factories, in the 1820s, often employed whole families as a unit. By the 1830s, work associated with textile machinery had largely been split into skilled work, performed by men who were relatively well paid, and unskilled work, performed by poorly paid unmarried women and the children of poor weavers. Child labor and education laws improved children's working conditions but further separated them from their families.

Women in the Early Industrial Revolution   With industrialization, the gender division of labor spread to the working class. In the 1820s, factory work for women became more widely available, but paid less. Wages for men in factories were often enough to support a family; in families where that was not the case, children were more likely to enter the work force than were wives. Therefore, the women who worked in factories were generally young and single, or widowed. By midcentury, more than half of all working women were still working someplace other than factories; in England, the largest group of working women was domestic servants; in France, they worked in agriculture. Domestic cottage industries employed many women throughout Europe. In virtually all cases, however, women were poorly paid. Marriage and family life changed too, although slowly. Women's domestic work became more sharply defined.

Problems of Crime and Order   Revolutions, industrialization, and urbanization all contributed to a fear of crime. In cities, crime did increase in the early to mid-nineteenth century. To assuage the fears of the propertied elite, prisons were reformed, and police systems were instituted or improved. The existence of a paid, professional, nonpolitical group of law enforcement officers, distinct from the army, was a new development in ninetenth-century Europe. By the end of the century, most Europeans of all classes viewed police favorably. Forms of punishment for criminals had varied and included sentencing

IMAGE KEY
for pages 506–507

a. A Liverpool and Manchester train ticket from 1830

b. Ana Ipatescu at Head of first group of revolutionaries in Transvylvania against Russia, 1848

c. Postcard of the townscape of the Burton breweries

d. Separate Cell in Pentonville Prison, from *The Criminal Prisons of London and Scenes of Prison Life by Henry Mayhew* (1812–87) and John Binny, 1862 (engraving)

e., i. Tubers, leaves, and flowers from potato plant

f. Revolution in Germany, 1848

g. Berlin street scene

h. Prisoners working on a treadmill

j. Karl Marx

k. George Stephenson's locomotive "Rocket"

l. London Metropolitan Police Sergeant of 1865; painted by Bryan Fosten

convicts to naval galleys and transportation to Australia. Prison reform efforts were hampered by public hostility toward criminals. In the 1840s, the British and the French instituted reforms based on rehabilitation. Experimental prisons based on models used in the United States, in which prisoners were separated from each other, were tried in England and France.

Classical Economics Laissez-faire economic theories predominated in this period. Classical economists believed competitive free enterprise was the best path to economic growth. The state should protect the nation's economic structure and foreign trade through military power. The middle class approved of these economists' views. Malthus argued that food supply could not grow as quickly as population; if working-class wages were raised, working-class families would have more children, worsening the situation. Ricardo postulated the "iron law of wages," linking wages and fertility in an even more deterministic and pessimistic way than Malthus. In France, the July monarchy embarked on building projects that provided jobs and wealth for the middle class, but did little to help the poor. In Germany, internal trade barriers were lowered, but direction of economic development continued. In Britain, Bentham's attempts to codify utilitarianism increased the influence of classical economic theory. In 1834, Bentham's followers passed a new Poor Law that funneled all poor relief through degrading workhouses, designed to motivate the poor. In 1846, the Corn Laws were repealed, allowing manufacturers to lower wages.

Early Socialism Socialists believed society could and should be organized as a community. They rejected the classical economists' claim that the free market was the best system. The earliest socialists tended to advocate some form of sexual liberation alongside their critique of the market economy, which cost them credibility. Saint-Simon in France advocated rational management; after his death, Saint-Simonian societies carried on discussions of economics and sexual politics. Owen combined a wholesome environment for employees with a healthy profit for himself at his factory. Later he established the community of New Harmony, Indiana, then returned to Britain and organized the Grand National Union. In the 1840s, anarchists rejected industry and government. Blanqui called for professional revolutionaries. Marxism gained dominance over other socialist theories largely because of Marx's extensive use of historical examples in his writing. Marx believed revolution, not reform, was inevitable. Although some of his predictions had already been disproved by the mid-nineteenth century, his theories proved themselves to be enormously appealing and influential.

1848: Year of Revolutions Revolutions occurred throughout Europe in 1848. All essentially ended in failure. During the revolutions, middle-class liberals, who wanted more representative government, civil liberty, and minimal economic regulations, joined forces with the urban working class, which sought improved working and economic conditions. Nationalists generally hoped to use the revolutions to further their own ends. Conservatives fought back, however, and the middle-class/working-class alliance faltered after the political liberals got what they wanted and refused to support working-class social demands. In France, king Louis Philippe abdicated in February 1848; in the new National Assembly, moderates and conservatives quickly displaced Paris radicals. Napoleon's nephew, Louis Napoleon Bonaparte, was elected president in December, and in 1852 he proclaimed himself emperor. Between 1848 and 1852, French women were politically active, but they were suppressed again after 1852. In the Habsburg Empire, Hungary called for independence in March 1848. Serfs were emancipated in Austria and Hungary. The Slavs held their first Pan-Slavic Congress in the summer. Northern Italy revolted against the Habsburgs, but was quickly suppressed. In late 1848 and early 1849, revolt spread throughout Italy, and the French sent troops to protect the pope until 1870. In Prussia, Frederick William IV went along with liberal demands while it suited him, then imposed his own reforms on the state. In Germany, attempts to revise the German Confederation failed and led to a long-standing division between German liberals and the working class.

REVIEW QUESTIONS

1. What inventions were particularly important in the development of industrialism? What changes did industrialism make in society? What is meant by "the proletarianization of workers"? In what ways did the industrial economy change the working-class family?

2. How did the police change in the nineteenth century? Why were new systems of enforcement instituted? In what ways were prisons improved? How do you account for the reform movement that led to the improvements?

3. How would you define *socialism?* Were Karl Marx's ideas different from those of the socialists?

4. Why did revolutions break out in so many places in 1848? Were circumstances essentially the same or were they different in the various countries? Why did the revolutions fail? What roles did liberals and nationalists play in them? Did they always agree?

KEY TERMS

anarchists (p. 520)   **Marxism** (p. 520)   utopian socialists (p. 518)
Chartism (p. 512)   **Utilitarianism** (p. 517)

 For additional study resources for this chapter, go to:
www.prenhall.com/kagan3/chapter21

Visualizing The Past...

Imagining Women in the Eighteenth and Nineteenth Centuries

WHAT DOES the artistic depiction of women in the eighteenth and nineteenth centuries tell us about the ways in which Western artists have imagined the roles of women in modern society?

Although the roles of many women changed significantly in the eighteenth and nineteenth centuries, in part due to the new demands and opportunities brought about by industrialization, the themes of sexuality, docility, and maternal caring that characterized artists' imaginations of women in earlier eras also appear in the art of this period. Since most artists until the twentieth century were male, depictions of women and gender roles often derive from a male perspective on the *proper* roles of women in a society, and not necessarily on the reality of women's lives.

Thomas Gainsborough, *Robert Andrews and His Wife*, 1748.
Portraits, such this one of the English landowner Robert Andrews and his wife, provide insights into the aristocratic and male dominance of landed society in the eighteenth century. The wife's seated posture next to her husband against the backdrop of his vast estate suggests the character of their legal relationship. Like the land, he controlled her property. She is as much one of his possessions as the rifle tucked beneath his arm and the dog at his feet.

Thomas Gainsborough, "Robert Andrews and His Wife". c. 1748-50. Oil on Canvas. 27 1/2" x 47" (69.7 x 119.3 cm). © National Gallery, London. Reproduced courtesy of the Trustees

▼

Jacques Louis David, *The Oath of the Horatii*, 1784. Jacques Louis David, the leading Neoclassical painter of his day, used themes from the supposedly morally austere and virtuous ancient Roman Republic to comment on the decadence and corruption of contemporary France. The Horatii, depicted on the left, take an oath from their father to protect the Roman Republic against its enemies, even if this means sacrificing their lives. One of these enemies is romantically involved with one of the sisters in the right of the painting. Patriotism must be upheld over other relationships. The sharp division of the painting, with a male world on the left and a female world on the right, illustrates how eighteenth-century republican thinkers, such as Rousseau, excluded women from civic life. The sisters and mother of the Horatii weep in a separate part of the scene, providing a sharp contrast between male civic virtue and female emotional frailty.

Jacques-Louis David (1748-1825), "The Oath of the Horatii," 1784. Oil on canvas, approx. 11 x 14 ft. (3.30 x 4.25m) Musee du Louvre, Paris, France. Bridgeman - Giraudon/Art Resource, NY

Eugene Delacroix, *The Women of Algiers in Their Harem*, 1834.

Delacroix, the leading French Romantic painter, spent six months in North Africa in 1832. In the painting shown here Delacroix depicts a common theme in eighteenth and nineteenth-century depictions of the "Orient": the position of women in Islamic society in general, and the harem in particular. Western commentators often described Islamic society as barbaric because of its perceived marginalization and exploitation of women. Note the passivity of the light-skinned women in contrast to the dominant pose of the black servant.

Eugene Delacroix (1798-1863). "Algerian Women in Their Apartment". Oil on Canvas. Louvre, Paris, France. Reunion des Musees Nationaux/Art Resource, NY

This postcard from late nineteenth-century New Zealand depicts a group of people bathing on the seaside. Here we see another recurring theme in modern images of gender: women as wives and mothers. The point here is that the beach and, by implication New Zealand itself, which many Europeans still viewed as an exotic and somewhat dangerous destination, was safe and "family-friendly." The wilderness of New Zealand, once home to the dangerous Maori, has now been tamed by European gentility and domesticity, so that it has become a suitable destination even for European women and children. © Dorling Kindersley

Devonport Beach. Auckland, N.Z.-717.

PART FIVE · TOWARD THE MODERN WORLD

POLITICS & GOVERNMENT

1851	Louis Napoleon seizes power in France
1854–1856	Crimean War
1861	Proclamation of the Kingdom of Italy
1862	Bismarck becomes prime minister of Prussia
1864	First International founded
1867	Austro-Hungarian Dual Monarchy founded
1868	Gladstone becomes British prime minister
1869	Suez Canal completed
1870	Franco-Prussian War; French Republic proclaimed
1871	German Empire proclaimed; Paris Commune
1874	Disraeli becomes British prime minister
1875	Britain gains control of Suez
1880s	Britain establishes protectorate in Egypt
1881	People's Will assassinates Alexander II; Three Emperors' League is renewed
1882	Italy, Germany, Austria form Triple Alliance
1884–1885	Germany forms African protectorates
1888	William II becomes German emperor

1894	Dreyfus convicted in France; Nicholas II becomes tsar of Russia
1898	Germany begins to build a battleship navy
1902	British Labour Party formed
1903	Bolshevik-Menshevik split
1904	Britain and France in Entente Cordiale

◄ *NASA photo of Suez Canal*

SOCIETY & ECONOMY

1850–1910	Height of European outward migration
1853–1870	Haussmann redesigns Paris
1857	Bessemer steelmaking process
1861	Serfdom abolished in Russia
1870	Education Act and first Irish Land Act, Britain
1875	Public Health and Artisan Dwelling Acts, Britain
1881	Second Irish Land Act
1886	Daimler invents internal combustion engine

1890s	Oil begins to have impact on world economy
1894	Union of German Women's Organizations founded
1895	Diesel engine invented
1897	German and Czech language equality in Austrian Empire; Russia mandates eleven-and-a-half hour workday
1901	National Council of French Women founded

The construction ►
of the Eiffel Tower

RELIGION & CULTURE

1850–1880	Jewish emancipation in much of Europe
1853–1854	Gobineau, *Essay on the Inequality of the Human Races*
1857	Flaubert, *Madame Bovary*
1859	Darwin, *On the Origin of Species*
1864	Pius IX, *Syllabus of Errors*
1867	Mill, *The Subjection of Women*
1869	Disestablishment of the Irish Church
1871	Darwin, *The Descent of Man;* Religious tests abolished at Oxford and Cambridge
1872	Nietzsche, *The Birth of Tragedy*
1873–1876	Bismarck's *Kulturkampf*
1879	Ibsen, *A Doll's House*
1880s	Growing anti-Semitism in Europe
1880	Zola, *Nana*
1883	Mach, *The Science of Mechanics*
1883	Nietzsche, *Thus Spake Zarathustra*

1892	Ibsen, *The Master Builder*
1893	Shaw, *Mrs. Warren's Profession*
1896	Herzl, *The Jewish State*
1899	Bernstein, *Evolutionary Socialism*
1900	Freud, *The Interpretation of Dreams;* Key, *The Century of the Child*
1902	Lenin, *What Is to Be Done?*

◄ *Charles Darwin*

1905 Revolution in Saint Petersburg suppressed; first Moroccan Crisis

1906 Dreyfus conviction set aside

1908–1909 Bosnian crisis

1911 Second Moroccan crisis

1912 Third Irish Home Rule Bill passed

1912–1913 First and Second Balkan Wars

1914–1918 World War I

1917 Russian Revolution; Bolsheviks seize power

◄ Bolshevik uprising

1919 Paris Peace Conference; Weimar constitution proclaimed in Germany

1922 Mussolini takes power in Italy

1923 France invades the Ruhr; Hitler's Beer Hall *Putsch;* first Labour government in Britain

1924 Death of Lenin

1925 Locarno Agreements

1931 National Government formed in Great Britain

1933 Hitler appointed chancellor of Germany

1935 Nuremburg Laws; Italy invades Ethiopia

1936 Popular Front in France; purge trials in the Soviet Union; Spanish Civil War begins

1938 Munich Conference; *Kristallnacht* in Germany

1939 Germany invades Poland, starts World War II

Mussolini ►

◄ Lenin

◄ Wright brothers at Kitty Hawk, NC

1903 Third Irish Land Act; British Women's Social and Political Union founded; Wright brothers fly the first airplane

1906 Land redemption payments canceled for Russian peasants

1907 Women vote on national issues in Norway

1918 Vote granted to some British women

1920s Worldwide commodity crisis

1921 Soviet Union begins New Economic Policy

1922 French Senate rejects vote for women

1923 Rampant inflation in Germany

1926 General strike in Great Britain

1928 Britain extends full franchise to women

1928–1933 First Five-Year Plan and agricultural collectivization in the Soviet Union

1929 Wall Street crash

1932 Lausanne Conference ends German reparations

mid-1930s Nazis stimulate German economy through public works and defense spending

◄ Poster advocating votes for Women

▲ Stock market crash Wall Street, NY

1903 Shaw, *Man and Superman*

1905 Weber, *The Protestant Ethic and the Spirit of Capitalism;* Termination of the Napoleonic Concordat in France

1907 Bergson, *Creative Evolution*

1908 Sorel, *Reflections on Violence*

1910 Pope Pius X requires anti-Modernist oath

1914 Joyce, *Portrait of the Artist as a Young Man*

Adolf Hitler ►

1919 Barth, *Commentary on the Epistle to the Romans*

1920 Keynes, *Economic Consequences of the Peace*

1922 Joyce, *Ulysses*

1924 Hitler, *Mein Kampf*

1925 Woolf, *Mrs. Dalloway*

1927 Heidegger, *Being and Time;* Mann, *Buddenbrooks*

1927 Woolf, *To the Lighthouse;* Mann, *Magic Mountain*

1929 Woolf, *A Room of One's Own*

1936 Keynes, *General Theory of Employment, Interest, and Money*

1937 Orwell, *Road to Wigan Pier*

1938 Sartre, *Nausea*

Virginia Woolf ►

22 The Age of Nation-States

CHAPTER HIGHLIGHTS

The Crimean War (1854–1856) Russia's attempts to expand its influence over the Ottoman Empire led to war in the Crimea with Britain and France. Ineptness on all sides contributed to the carnage. Russia lost territory and status after its defeat.

Reforms in the Ottoman Empire During the Tanzimat era, the Ottoman Empire underwent significant reforms. The empire was not, however, able to gain strength or stability. In the late 1870s, the Ottomans lost most of their European holdings. The empire collapsed after World War I.

Italian Unification Romantic nationalists had long wanted to unify Italy's many small principalities. Unification was achieved, however, under the leadership of Count Camillo Cavour, the moderately liberal prime minister of Piedmont. Cavour wanted to limit unification to northern Italy, but Garibaldi's campaign forced him to complete the unification of the peninsula.

German Unification The unification of Germany was the most important political development in Europe in the second half of the nineteenth century. Bismarck used a series of wars to secure Prussian domination of a united Germany.

France: From Liberal Empire to the Third Republic Between 1851 and 1860, Napoleon III led an authoritarian regime. Reversals in foreign policy in the late 1850s forced him to adopt more liberal policies. Defeat in the Franco-Prussian War led to the short-lived Paris Commune in 1871 and the creation of the Third Republic in 1875. The Third Republic's greatest trauma was the Dreyfus affair.

The Habsburg Empire Austrian power was undermined by its loss of Russia as an ally and military defeats at the hands of France and Prussia. In 1867, Emperor Francis Joseph compromised with the Magyars and created the dual monarchy of Austria-Hungary. Nationalist unrest in Austria-Hungary posed problems for Europe as a whole.

Russia: Emancipation and Revolutionary Stirrings Alexander II's efforts to impose reform from the top down resulted in the emancipation of the serfs in 1861, but little real change in the lives of Russia's peasants. After the Polish uprising of 1863, he turned increasingly repressive. Calls for radical change continued and Alexander II was assassinated in 1881. Alexander III reversed his father's reforms.

Great Britain: Toward Democracy Great Britain symbolized the confident liberal state. Britain was not without its difficulties and domestic conflicts, but it seemed able to deal with them through its existing political institutions. The general prosperity of the third quarter of the century mitigated the social hostility of the 1840s. All classes shared a belief in competition and individualism.

CHAPTER QUESTIONS

WHY WAS the Crimean War fought?

HOW DID the Ottoman Empire attempt to reform itself?

HOW DID Italy achieve unification?

HOW DID Germany unify?

WHAT EVENT led to the establishment of a Third Republic in France?

WHAT PROBLEMS did the Habsburg Empire face?

WHAT REFORMS did Alexander II institute in Russia?

HOW DID liberal democracy develop in Great Britain?

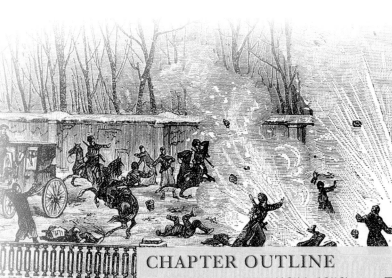

CHAPTER OUTLINE

- The Crimean War (1854–1856)
- Reforms in the Ottoman Empire
- Italian Unification
- German Unification
- France: From Liberal Empire to the Third Republic
- The Habsburg Empire
- Russia: Emancipation and Revolutionary Stirrings
- Great Britain: Toward Democracy

IMAGE KEY

Image Key for pages 536–537 is on page 558.

Although the revolutions of 1848 collapsed and authoritarian regimes spread across Europe in the early 1850s, many of the objectives of early-nineteenth-century liberals and nationalists had been achieved by 1875. Italy and Germany were each unified under constitutional monarchies. The Habsburg emperor accepted a constitution that recognized the liberties of the Magyars of Hungary. Russia's tsar emancipated the serfs. France again became a republic. Liberalism (even democracy) flourished in Great Britain, and the Ottoman Empire tried out major reforms. Paradoxically, most of this liberal agenda was enacted while conservatives were in power.

THE CRIMEAN WAR (1854–1856)

WHY WAS the Crimean War fought?

The impetus for the political reorganization of Europe in the mid-nineteenth century was the Crimean War (1854–1856), a product of Russia's long-standing desire to profit at the expense of the Ottoman Empire. Since the reign of Catherine the Great, the empire had granted Russia protective oversight of its Orthodox Christian subjects. France served a similar function for its Roman Catholics, and Russia was angered in 1851 when the Ottoman sultan granted control of some of Palestine's holy places to the French. In 1853, the Russians—claiming a duty to protect Orthodox Christians—occupied the Ottoman provinces of Moldavia and Wallachia (modern Romania), and the Ottoman Empire responded by declaring war on Russia.

Russia hoped to precipitate the breakup of the Ottoman Empire, an event from which it expected to profit greatly. France and Britain were equally willing to exploit Ottoman weakness, but they did not want Russia to expand and interfere with their naval and commercial interests in the eastern Mediterranean. On March 28, 1854, they allied with the Ottomans and declared war on Russia. The conflict was ineptly conducted on both sides, and the poorly equipped and led armies bogged down along the Crimean coast of the Black Sea. The Russian fortress of Sevastopol finally fell to the allies in September 1855, but by then the

This painting by Elizabeth Thompson, Lady Butler, portrays the comradeship and suffering of ordinary troops. Completed in 1874 and purchased by Queen Victoria, Butler's work reflects the public's awareness of the horrors of war and the mismanagement by discredited aristocratic army officers.

Lady Elizabeth Thompson Butler (1846–1933), "The Roll Call: Calling the Roll after an Engagement, Crimea (unframed)." The Royal Collection © 2005, Her Majesty Queen Elizabeth II. Photo by SC

OVERVIEW   REFORMS AND ATTEMPTS AT REFORM IN THE OTTOMAN EMPIRE

Year	Reform	Intention of Reform
1839	*Hatt-i Sharif of Gülhane*	A decree calling for reform measures.
1856	*Hatt-i Hümayun*	Rights of non-Muslims were spelled out. It put Jews and Christians on equal footing with Muslims for military service, school admission, and political offices.
1908	*Young Turks*	A military revolution brought up this group of reformist officers. Their decision to ally the empire with the Central Powers led to its defeat.

European public was aware of the suffering the mismanaged campaign had caused. The Crimean War was the first to be covered by war correspondents and photographers.

Peace Settlement and Long-Term Results In March 1856, Russia yielded and by the terms of the Treaty of Paris agreed to surrender territory near the mouth of the Danube River, to recognize the neutrality of the Black Sea, and to renounce its role as protector of the Ottoman Empire's Orthodox Christians. Austria had already forced Russia out of Moldavia and Walachia, the Ottoman provinces it had occupied at the start of the war. Russia's losses dispersed the aura of invincibility it had acquired by defeating Napoleon.

Also shattered was the Concert of Europe, the agreement that the great powers would cooperate to maintain the balance of power established by the Congress of Vienna. The suppression of the 1848 uprisings had diminished European governments' fears of revolution and made them more willing to embark on aggressive foreign policies. This promoted political instability and led to risky foreign adventures that reshaped Europe. The Ottomans, too, grasped the volatility of the situation and undertook reform.

REFORMS IN THE OTTOMAN EMPIRE

Napoleon's invasion of Egypt in 1798–1799 alerted the Ottoman Empire to its weakness, and in 1839, imperial bureaucrats who had studied in Europe persuaded the sultan to issue a reform decree, the *Hatt-i Sharif of Gülhane*. Their intent was to reconstruct the Ottoman government and military along European lines. The reforms attempted between 1839 and 1876, the era of *Tanzimat* (reorganization), were not arbitrary exercises of the sultan's power. They were the work of administrative councils influenced by liberal principles. They freed the economy, ended tax farming, fought corruption, and extended civic equality to all the empire's subjects regardless of their religion. In 1856, the rights of non-Muslims were explicitly spelled out in a reform decree called the *Hatt-i Hümayun*. It put Jews and Christians on an equal footing with Muslims for military service and admission to state schools and political offices. It also abolished torture and extended greater property rights to foreigners. Christian missionaries, many of whom were Americans, established Western-style schools and spread the use of printing presses.

HOW DID the Ottoman Empire attempt to reform itself?

The sultan's government hoped liberal reforms would increase its support and counter the divisive effects of the nationalism that was springing up in various parts of the empire. Its intent was to secularize society by treating all its citizens as imperial subjects, not members of distinct religious communities. Reforms, however, were difficult to implement. Some local rulers were virtually independent of Istanbul, and crippling power struggles broke out in the capital. These tensions and growing nationalism in various regions countered the reformers' efforts to stabilize and strengthen the empire. Many Ottomans also opposed abandoning traditional Islamic institutions.

Wars erupted in the Balkans in the late 1870s, and the empire lost most of its European territory to independence movements or the Austrians and Russians. These setbacks prompted calls for more rapid reform, and an attempt was made to modernize the economy and the military. In 1876, the sultan issued a constitution that established a parliament composed of an elected chamber of deputies and an appointed senate. It had little power, however, and was dismissed by a subsequent sultan. A military revolution in 1908 eventually brought a group of reformist officers, the *Young Turks*, to the fore. They were in charge when World War I broke out, and their decision to ally the empire with the Central Powers led to its defeat and collapse.

ITALIAN UNIFICATION

HOW DID Italy achieve unification?

Nationalists had long wanted to fuse the small principalities of the Italian peninsula into a single state. During the first half of the nineteenth century, however, there was no consensus about how this should be done.

ROMANTIC REPUBLICANS

After the Congress of Vienna, *romantic republicans* took the lead in rallying nationalistic sentiment. They organized secret societies throughout Italy and declared the unification of Italy to be a divine mission, a duty to God and to humanity. They were not effective.

In 1831, Giuseppe Mazzini (1805–1872), Europe's most important nationalist leader, founded the Young Italy Society. It was dedicated to driving Austria from the peninsula and establishing an Italian republic. During the 1830s and 1840s, Mazzini and his fellow republican, Giuseppe Garibaldi (1807–1882), led insurrections. Both were involved in the ill-fated Roman Republic of 1849, and throughout the 1850s they conducted what amounted to guerrilla warfare. They spent much time in exile campaigning for their cause throughout Europe and in the United States.

More moderate Italians favored an end to Austrian domination but did not want a republic. They considered the papacy as a vehicle for unification, but Pius IX's disastrous experience with the Roman Republic in 1849 made that impossible. Camillo Cavour (1810–1861), the prime minister of Piedmont, conceived a more workable plan. By skillfully combining military force and secret diplomacy, he united Italy under the authority of a constitutional monarchy.

CAVOUR'S POLICY

Piedmont in northwestern Italy was the most independent of Italy's states. The Congress of Vienna had established it as a buffer between the French and the Austrians, and in 1848 and 1849 its king, Charles Albert, went to war with Austria. Defeat

QUICK REVIEW

Romantic Republicans

- Giuseppe Mazzini (1805–1872)
- Giuseppe Garibaldi (1807–1882)
- Campaigned for Italian unification in the 1830s, 40s, and 50s

prompted him to abdicate in favor of his son, Victor Emmanuel II (r. 1849–1878), and in 1852, the new king appointed Count Camillo Cavour prime minister.

Cavour entered politics as a conservative but gradually moved toward a moderately liberal position. He was a practical man whose beliefs were formed by the Enlightenment, classical economics, and utilitarianism. He made a fortune investing in railroads, improving the cultivation of his estates, and editing a newspaper. He had no respect for Mazzini's romantic ideals or for republicanism. He believed economic progress in Italy required the country's unification and that material benefits, not fuzzy romantic yearnings, would bring Italians together. He promoted free trade, railway construction, credit expansion, and modernization of agriculture, and he tried to win the support of nationalists of every stripe by founding the Nationalist Society. The chapters it established throughout Italy worked to encourage the Italians to unite under the leadership of Piedmont. Cavour also solicited help from France.

Giuseppe Garibaldi, the charismatic leader, can be seen on the right urging on his troops in the rout of Neapolitan forces at Calatafimi, Sicily, in 1860.

Bildarchiv Preubischer Kulturbesitz

French Sympathies   In 1855, Piedmont provided France and Britain with 10,000 troops to help the allies in the Crimean War, and this won Cavour a seat at the Paris peace conference. He used the conference as a forum for discussing Italian unification. He received no firm commitments, but he impressed important diplomats and won Napoleon III's sympathy. His strategy was to court international support by depicting Piedmont as a moderate liberal alternative to Mazzini's republicanism on one hand and reactionary absolutism on the other.

In January 1858, an attempt on the life of Napoleon III by an Italian assassin motivated the French emperor to focus his attention on the Italian issue. He liked the idea of continuing his famous uncle's efforts to liberate Italy, and he wanted Piedmont as an ally against Austria. In July 1858, Cavour and Napoleon III met at Plombières, France, and agreed to provoke a war in Italy that would give them a chance to defeat Austria. Piedmont offered to cede French-speaking Nice and Savoy to France in exchange for its help.

War with Austria   Austria objected when Piedmont mobilized its army early in 1859, and Piedmont claimed this as a provocation for war. France joined in, and Austria was defeated at Magenta on June 4 and at Solferino on June 24. These victories encouraged revolutionaries, who wanted union with Piedmont, to seize control in Tuscany, Modena, Parma, and the Romagna provinces of the Papal States. Napoleon III viewed this development with alarm, and he made a separate peace with Austria. Cavour felt betrayed, but Austria had been driven from most of northern Italy, and Piedmont was able to annex Lombardy. Soon Parma, Modena, Tuscany, and the Romagna voted to unite with Piedmont.

Garibaldi's Campaign   At this point, the activities of the romantic republicans compelled Cavour to complete the unification of Italy. In May 1860, Garibaldi landed in Sicily with more than a thousand soldiers, captured Palermo, and prepared to invade the mainland. By September he was in control of the kingdom of Naples. Garibaldi wanted to establish an Italian republic, but Cavour forestalled him by sending Piedmontese troops into southern Italy. They occupied the

QUICK REVIEW

Keys to Italian Unification
- Piedmont's leadership under Count Camillo Cavour
- French assistance
- Victory in war with Austria
- Success of Garibaldi's campaign in the south

remaining Papal States, with the exception of the area around Rome. The French preserved this for the pope. Faced with the choice of sacrificing either republicanism or hope for national unity, Garibaldi unhappily accepted Piedmontese domination. Late in 1860, Naples and Sicily voted to join the Italian kingdom. In response to France's help and Napoleon III's concern over the new large nation-state on his borders, Piedmont ceded Savoy and Nice to France, where much of the population spoke French. (See Map 22–1.)

THE NEW ITALIAN STATE

Victor Emmanuel II was proclaimed king of Italy in March 1861, and three months later Cavour died. This was unfortunate, for the new state needed the skills of a consummate diplomat. Italy had been more conquered than united. Republicans resented Piedmont's treatment of Garibaldi, and clerical factions were offended by its occupation of the Papal States. Furthermore, Italy's north and south were somewhat incompatible. The north was industrializing and developing links to the rest of Europe, but the south was rural, poor, and backward. The peasants and large landowners of the south had little in common with the urban working class that dominated the north. The southerners took up arms and resisted the imposition of a Piedmontese-style administration until 1866.

The Piedmont monarchy's political institutions could not adequately govern Italy. Piedmont's constitution of 1848 had established a conservative constitutional monarchy with a two-chambered parliament: a senate appointed by the king and a chamber of deputies elected on a narrow franchise. Parliament had little power, for the nation's ministers reported only to the king. Parliament's leaders were content to avoid serious issues and perpetuate themselves in office by *transformismo*—by using bribes to "transform" enemies into friends. Italian politics became a byword for corruption.

Many Italians felt their nation would not be complete until it acquired Venetia and Rome. The kingdom won the former in 1866 by supporting Prussia in the Austro-Prussian War, and in 1870, when the Franco-Prussian War forced the French to withdraw the troops guarding the papacy, the Italian state annexed Rome and declared it the nation's capital. The papacy preserved the independence of the Vatican, but it was not until 1929 that the Lateran Accord established friendly relations between the pope and the Italian state.

By 1870, all the territory that was popularly thought of as Italian belonged to Italy except the Austrian-controlled province of Trent and city of Trieste. A patriotic desire to win control of these lands, *Italia Irredenta* ("Unredeemed Italy"), helped persuade the Italians to side with the Allies against Austria and Germany in World War I.

GERMAN UNIFICATION

The most important political development in Europe between 1848 and 1914 was the unification of Germany. This had been the dream of liberals for two generations, but it was the outcome of moves conservatives made to outflank liberals.

Although the major German states were linked by trade agreements and railways, their unification seemed a remote possibility throughout the 1850s. Liberal nationalists were in retreat after the suppression of the revolts of 1848 and 1849. Frederick William IV of Prussia had given up thoughts of leading a unification movement, and Austria opposed any political changes that might lessen its influence.

HOW DID Germany unify?

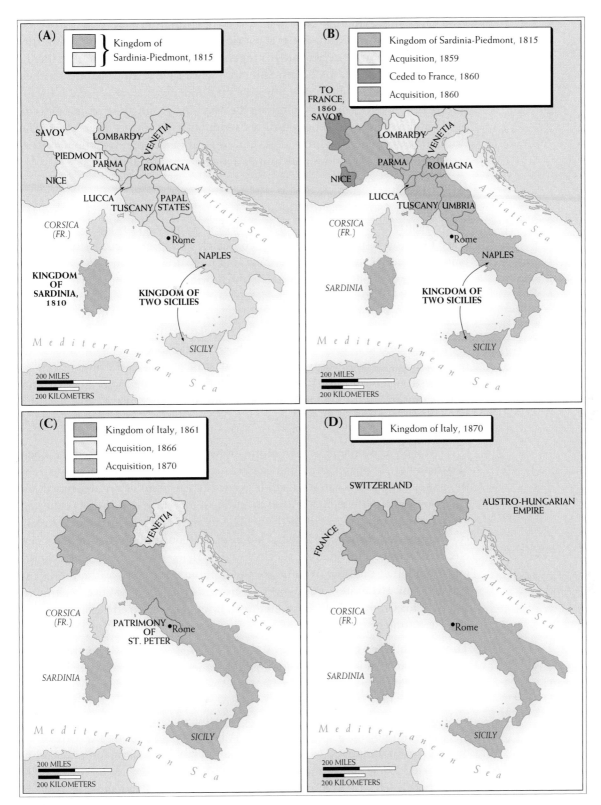

MAP 22–1

The Unification of Italy   Beginning with the association of Sardinia and Piedmont by the Congress of Vienna in 1815, unification was achieved through the expansion of Piedmont between 1859 and 1870. Both Cavour's statesmanship and the campaigns of ardent nationalists played large roles.

WHY WAS it so difficult to unify Italy?

In 1858, a change in Prussia's internal situation suddenly improved prospects for unification. King Frederick William IV was declared insane, and his brother William became his regent and finally his successor. William I (r. 1861–1888) was less an idealist and more a Prussian patriot than his brother. Consistent with his Hohenzollern dynasty's tradition, his first concern was for his troops. In 1860, he proposed enlarging the army, increasing the number of its officers, and extending the period of conscription from two to three years. The Prussian Parliament's liberal leaders, however, refused to approve the necessary taxes, and for two years monarch and Parliament were deadlocked.

BISMARCK

In September 1862, William I turned for help to the person who, more than any other single individual, determined the course of Europe's history for the next thirty years: Otto von Bismarck (1815–1898). Bismarck came from Junker stock. He attended university, joined a *Burschenschaft*, and took an interest in German unification. During the 1840s, he was elected to the provincial diet. From 1851 to 1859, he served as the Prussian delegate to the Frankfurt Diet of the German Confederation. He then became Prussia's ambassador to Russia, and he had just been named its ambassador to France when William I decided to make him Prussia's prime minister.

Over the years, Bismarck, who had been so reactionary as to alarm his king, mellowed into a conservative. He opposed parliamentary government but favored a strong constitutional monarchy. He understood the importance to a nation of a secure industrial base, and he was, above all, a pragmatic politician who believed change was wrought more by power and action than by debate and search for consensus.

As soon as Bismarck became prime minister in 1862, he attacked the liberal parliament. He maintained that the Prussian constitution gave the monarchy the power to impose whatever taxes it needed to carry out its regular functions. He ignored the parliament's refusal to authorize new taxes and simply collected what was required to expand the army. The military and administrative bureaucracy supported Bismarck's interpretation of the constitution, but in 1863 new elections sustained the liberal majority in the parliament. Bismarck had to find a way to undercut the liberals while soliciting popular support for the monarchy and the army. His strategy was to propose using Prussia's conservative institutions as a basis for German unification. In effect, Bismarck embraced German nationalism as a strategy to enable Prussian conservatives to outflank Prussian liberals.

The Danish War (1864)   Bismarck took a *kleindeutsch* (small German) position on unification; that is, he believed it would be easier for Prussia to dominate a Germany that did not include Austria. Because Austria was not likely to favor such an arrangement, Bismarck's strategy was to provoke and win a war with Austria. A quarrel between Denmark and the German Confederation gave him his opportunity.

The two northern duchies of Schleswig-Holstein had long been ruled by, but not part of, Denmark. Holstein's population was more German than Danish, and it belonged to the German Confederation. When the Danish parliament annexed both duchies in 1863, the smaller states of the German Confederation objected and clamored for war. Bismarck proposed that Prussia and Austria cooperate in resolving the situation, and Denmark was easily defeated. In August 1865, the Convention of Gastein declared that Austria would administer Holstein and Prussia, Schleswig. Meanwhile, Bismarck had gained Russia's friendship by supporting its suppression of a revolt in Poland. He had persuaded Napoleon III to remain neutral in the event that war broke out between Prussia and Austria, and in April 1866, he concluded a treaty with Italy that promised Italy control over Venetia if it joined Prussia in attacking Austria.

The Austro-Prussian War (1866)   Austrian and Prussian forces clashed frequently in Schleswig and Holstein, for Bismarck ordered his men to provoke the Austrians by being as obnoxious as possible. On June 1, 1866, when Austria asked the German Confederation to intervene, Bismarck claimed this violated Prussia's treaties with Austria. He launched the Seven Weeks' War and decisively defeated Austria at Königgrätz in Bohemia. The only territory the subsequent Treaty of Prague forced Austria to surrender was Venetia, but loss of the war deprived the Habsburgs of the role they had previously played in German affairs. Prussia emerged as the only major power among the German states.

The North German Confederation   In 1867, Prussia annexed the German states that had supported Austria in the war (Hanover, Hesse, Nassau, and Frankfurt) and united all of Germany north of the Main River. The states retained powers of local government, but their armies were placed under federal control. Prussia's king assumed the presidency of a German federation that was to be governed by a bicameral legislature. Representatives appointed by state governments sat in one house (the *Bundesrat*) and the members of the other (the *Reichstag*) were elected by universal male suffrage.

The constitution of the North German Confederation (which in 1871 became the constitution of the German Empire) looked more liberal than it was. The popularly elected *Reichstag* had little power. Government ministers reported only to the monarch, and only the king's chancellor could initiate legislation. Bismarck, in effect, imposed a military monarchy on Germany. His liberal opponents acquiesced because, in the end, their desire for national unity proved greater than their devotion to liberal principles. (See Map 22–2.)

THE FRANCO-PRUSSIAN WAR AND THE GERMAN EMPIRE (1870–1871)

Events in Spain gave Bismarck an excuse to bring the south German states into Prussia's confederation. In 1868, the Spaniards deposed their corrupt Bourbon queen, Isabella II (r. 1833–1868), and two years later they offered their throne to Prince Leopold of Hohenzollern-Sigmaringen, a Catholic cousin of Prussia's William I. Leopold's father, however, was afraid France would attack Prussia to prevent the Hohenzollerns from establishing themselves in Spain, and he renounced his son's candidacy. William I was relieved he had not had, as the French urged, to order Leopold to refuse Spain's offer.

The matter might have rested there had it not been for French impetuosity and Bismarck's guile. On July 13, the French government instructed its ambassador to Prussia, Count Vincent Benedetti (1817–1900), to ask William I for assurances he would tolerate no future Spanish candidacy for Leopold. The king refused and sent Bismarck, who was in Berlin, a telegram describing the meeting. Bismarck, who wanted war with France in order to bring the remaining German states into the Prussian federation, used the king's telegram to incite the war the king hoped to avoid. He released an edited version of the dispatch that made it appear William I had insulted the French ambassador.

Everything developed as Bismarck expected. France was goaded into declaring war on July 19, and once the conflict began, the south German states rallied to Prussia's side. On September 1, at the Battle of Sedan, the Germans defeated the French and captured Napoleon III. They laid siege to Paris in late September. The city capitulated on January 28, 1871, but by then the formation

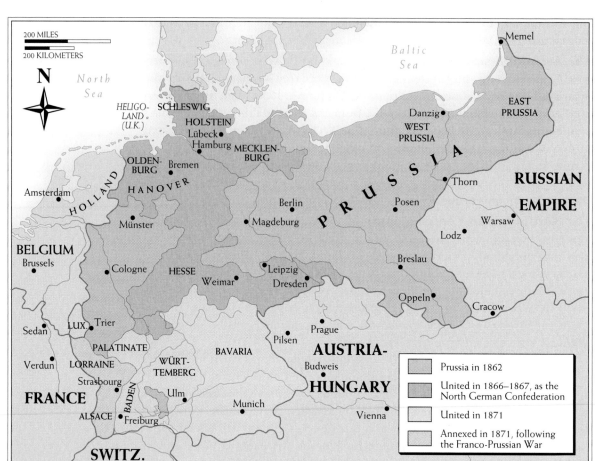

MAP 22–2

The Unification of Germany Under Bismarck's leadership, and with the strong support of its royal house, Prussia used diplomatic and military means, on both the German and international stages, to forcibly unify the German states into a strong national entity.

WHICH NEIGHBORING countries were most directly affected by German unification?

of a German Empire had been announced to the world in the Hall of Mirrors at the Palace of Versailles. France sued for peace and ceded control over Alsace and part of Lorraine to Germany.

German unification changed the face of Europe by creating a powerful new state that was far stronger than Prussia had been alone. France, having been humiliated under the leadership of a monarch, returned to republican government. The beleaguered Habsburgs hastened to come to terms with their unruly Magyar subjects, and liberals everywhere were alarmed. Conservative politics now had the backing of the Continent's strongest state.

France: From Liberal Empire to the Third Republic

WHAT EVENT led to the establishment of a Third Republic in France?

Historians divide the reign of Emperor Napoleon III (r. 1851–1870) into halves to mark a shift that took place in the year 1860 from authoritarian to more liberal government. Initially, Napoleon III controlled the legislature, censored the press, and harassed political dissidents. He

The Prussian victory at the battle of Sedan in September 1870 brought about the collapse of the regime of Louis Napoleon in France and sealed the Prussian accomplishment of the unification of Germany. In this contemporary photograph the Prussian infantry is making an advance.

Getty Images Inc.—Hulton Archive Photos

depended for support on the army, the Catholic clergy, property owners, and businessmen, and these people wanted a government strong enough to guarantee security for private property, the papacy, and commerce.

Late in the 1850s, Napoleon III suffered reverses in foreign affairs that forced him to change his domestic policy. His influence on Italy faded as that country consolidated behind the leadership of Piedmont. He also had little choice but to stand by and watch while Prussia reorganized Germany. He was further humiliated when he intervened militarily in the Spanish colonial empire to help seat the Archduke Maximilian of Austria (r. 1864–1867) on Mexico's throne and Maximilian was quickly overthrown and executed.

To shore up support at home for a government weakened by these foreign policy failures, Napoleon III began to make liberal concessions. In 1860, he granted the legislature greater freedom of debate. He concluded a free trade treaty with Britain. He relaxed the laws limiting the press and forbidding labor unions. In 1870, he accepted a ministry formed by moderates in the legislature, and he approved a liberal constitution that made ministers of state responsible to the legislature.

Napoleon III's decision to declare war on Prussia in 1870 was his last attempt to redeem his foreign policy and generate popular support for his Second Empire, but the Franco-Prussian War had quite a different outcome. The Prussians captured Napoleon at the Battle of Sedan (September 1, 1870), and when this news reached Paris, the French government repudiated the monarchy and proclaimed a republic. A Government of National Defense was organized while the Prussians besieged Paris, and most of France was ready to sue for peace long before Paris surrendered in January 1871.

THE PARIS COMMUNE

A new French National Assembly was elected in February 1871, and it accepted Prussia's terms. The Treaty of Frankfurt obligated France to pay a large indemnity, to permit occupation by Prussian troops until the indemnity was paid, and to surrender Alsace and part of Lorraine. Napoleon III was exiled to England and died there in 1873.

Many Parisians, who had suffered during the Prussian siege of their city, felt betrayed by the National Assembly's capitulation. On March 28, 1871, they organized the Paris Commune, a municipal government that undertook to administer

Paris separately from the rest of France. The National Assembly promptly surrounded Paris with its own army and ordered bombardment of the city (May 8). On the day on which the assembly signed the treaty with Prussia (May 21), its soldiers broke through Paris's defenses. About 20,000 Parisians were killed before order was restored.

The short-lived Paris Commune quickly became a legend. Marxists claimed it was a genuine proletarian government suppressed by the bourgeoisie, but they were wrong. The goal of the commune was not a worker's republic but a nation of relatively independent democratic enclaves. The commune's suppression was not the triumph of the middle class over the lower class. It was a victory of centralized national government over an alternative form of political organization. In Italy and Germany, armies pulled nations together; in France, an army prevented a nation from coming apart.

THE THIRD REPUBLIC

The National Assembly backed into a republican form of government against its will. Its monarchist majority was divided between support for the House of Bourbon and the House of Orléans. This problem could have been resolved by elevating the Bourbon claimant, the count of Chambord, to the throne. He had no children and was willing to declare the Orléanist candidate his heir. Chambord, however, refused to be king if France retained the tricolor flag of the revolution. Negotiations stalemated at that point, for restoration of the Bourbon flag was too reactionary even for the most conservative of the monarchists.

In 1873, France completed payment of the indemnity it owed Prussia, and Prussia withdrew its soldiers from France. The president of the assembly, Marshal MacMahon (1808–1893), favored restoration of the monarchy, but the quarrel over the choice of a king continued. Finally, in 1875, the frustrated National Assembly established a republican government featuring a chamber of deputies (elected by universal male suffrage), a senate (chosen indirectly), and a president (elected by the two legislative houses). This Third Republic proved to be more durable than many expected. It defended itself against a faction, headed by General George Boulanger (1837–1891), that wanted a stronger executive authority, and it survived a number of scandals.

THE DREYFUS AFFAIR

The Third Republic's greatest trauma was the Dreyfus affair. On December 22, 1894, a French military court found Captain Alfred Dreyfus (1859–1935) guilty of passing information to the German army. After he was sent to the notorious prison on Devil's Island, however, secrets continued to flow to the Germans. In 1896, a new head of French counterintelligence reopened the case and found that evidence against Dreyfus had been forged. Suspicion centered on a different officer, whom a military court quickly acquitted.

Dreyfus was Jewish, and the near-hysterical public debate over his case revealed the extent of French anti-Semitism. The army, the French Catholic Church, conservative politicians, and some newspapers vehemently contended that Dreyfus was guilty. In 1898, the novelist Emile Zola countered with a newspaper article: *J'accuse* (*I Accuse*). He contended that the army had consciously denied due process to Dreyfus and had plotted to suppress or forge evidence. The government's response was to convict Zola of libel and sentence him to a year in prison. Zola fled to England, but the political left (liberals, radicals, and socialists) took up Dreyfus's cause. They wanted to embarrass the conservative government

QUICK REVIEW

Captain Alfred Dreyfus (1859–1935)

- December 22, 1894: Found guilty of espionage
- Conviction stirred near-hysterical public debate
- 1906: Civilian court voids his conviction

THE AGE OF NATION-STATES   **CHAPTER 22**   **549**

The prosecution of Captain Alfred Dreyfus, who is shown here standing on the right at his military trial, provoked the most serious crisis of the Third Republic.

© Bettman/CORBIS

by proving it had denied Dreyfus his rights as a citizen of the republic, and they wanted to humble the military by showing it had offered up Dreyfus to protect guilty parties in its own ranks. In August 1898, further evidence of forged material came to light, and the officer responsible committed suicide in jail. A second military tribunal was convened, and when it still refused to acquit Dreyfus, the president of France stepped in and pardoned him. In 1906, a civilian court voided his convictions.

The Dreyfus case had long-lasting political repercussions. It drew Dreyfus's supporters, the parties on the left, closer together. It forced conservatives onto the defensive, for they had persecuted an innocent man, falsified evidence to protect their own, and embraced violent anti-Semitism. Repercussions from the Dreyfus affair continued to divide the Third Republic until France's defeat by Germany early in World War II (1940).

THE HABSBURG EMPIRE

WHAT PROBLEMS did the Habsburg Empire face?

The Habsburgs responded to the revolts of 1848 to 1849 by reasserting absolutism, a policy that created problems for their empire and the rest of Europe. In an age characterized by the growth of national states, liberal institutions, and industrialism, the Habsburg domains remained dynastic, absolutist, and agrarian. Emperor Francis Joseph (r. 1848–1916) was honest and hard working but unimaginative. He reacted to events more than creatively managing them.

During the 1850s, his ministers used an army and bureaucracy composed largely of German-speaking Austrians to impose a centralized administration on the empire. It abolished internal tariffs and gave the Roman Catholic Church control over education. National groups, such as the Croats and Slovaks, who had helped the empire defeat the Hungarian rebels of 1848, got nothing in recognition of their loyalty, and attempts were made to control Hungary by dividing it into military districts. All of this provoked resentment and opposition, and all it took was some setbacks in foreign affairs to trigger the empire's fall.

Austria's refusal to support Russia in the Crimean War led Russia to withdraw the support, which it had provided for half a century, for Austria's position

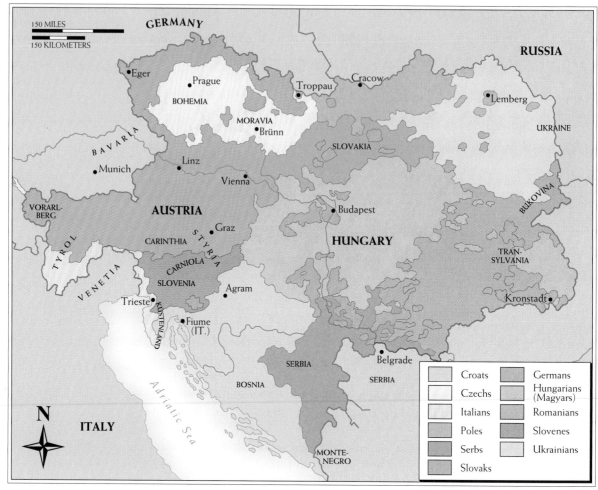

MAP 22–3

Nationalities Within the Habsburg Empire   The patchwork appearance reflects the unusual problem of the numerous ethnic groups that the Habsburgs could not, of course, meld into a modern national state. Only the Magyars were recognized in 1867, leaving nationalist Czechs, Slovaks, and the others chronically dissatisfied.

WHY WAS ethnic diversity in the Habsburg Empire an impediment to building a strong national state?

in Hungary. By 1859, the loss of this prop and of Italian territory to Piedmont necessitated radical changes in the empire's domestic policy. For seven years, Austria's leaders struggled to construct a viable system of government for the empire. (See Map 22–3.)

FORMATION OF THE DUAL MONARCHY

In 1860, Francis Joseph issued the October Diploma. It proposed a federated government for the states and provinces of the empire and vested authority in an imperial parliament and local diets dominated by the landed classes. When Hungary's Magyar nobility opposed the plan, the emperor issued the February Patent (1861). It established a bicameral imperial parliament (the *Reichsrat*), with an upper chamber appointed by the emperor and an indirectly elected lower chamber. However, it stated that government ministers were to report to the emperor, not the *Reichsrat*. It did not guarantee civil liberties. It said that armies could be levied and taxes raised without parliamentary consent, and when the *Reichsrat* was not in session, it allowed the emperor to rule by decree. Although the Magyars again refused to cooperate, the February Patent established the system that governed the empire for six years and Austria until World War I.

Secret negotiations between the emperor and the Magyars produced no concrete result until Prussia's defeat of Austria in 1866. The Prussian triumph reduced Austria's influence in Germany and forced Francis Joseph to come to terms with the Magyars. The *Ausgleich* (compromise) of 1867 established a dual monarchy. Austria and Hungary acknowledged one ruler and shared a few ministries (foreign affairs, defense, and finance), but otherwise they functioned as separate states. Sixty parliamentary delegates from each kingdom met annually to discuss mutual interests, and once a decade Austria and Hungary renegotiated their trade relationship. This cumbersome machinery, unique in European history, reconciled the Magyars to Habsburg rule by giving them the free hand they had long wanted in Hungary.

UNREST OF NATIONALITIES

By acceding to the nationalistic desires of the Hungarians, the Compromise of 1867 increased tensions within the empire, for it allowed German-speaking Austrians and Hungarian Magyars to dominate other ethnic groups. Because the Hungarians had been granted a government on their own terms, other peoples believed the time had come for them to receive similar privileges.

The group that most insistently demanded recognition of their homeland as a separate kingdom (like Hungary) were the Czechs of Bohemia. Francis Joseph was willing to oblige them, but the Magyars objected. They feared this would force them to make similar concessions to minority factions in Hungary. German residents of Bohemia also opposed the plan, for they were convinced it would lead to the Czech language being imposed on them. For over twenty years the emperor placated the Czechs with generous patronage, but the voices of the Czech nationalists became increasingly strident throughout the 1890s. In 1897, Francis Joseph recognized Czech and German as equal official languages. Angry Germans in the Austrian *Reichsrat* protested by disrupting its meetings, and the Czechs responded by doing the same. Their actions paralyzed the *Reichsrat* and forced the emperor to rule by decree. By 1914, constitutional government had come to an end in Austria. It survived in Hungary, but only because it guaranteed the Magyars political supremacy over other nationalities.

As nationalism grew stronger during the last quarter of the nineteenth century, lines between groups were more clearly drawn. Language was believed to be the most important attribute defining a nation, but racial ideologies, which claimed there was a genetic basis for ethnic identities, also found favor. Austria's dominant population was German speaking and loyal to the emperor, but a significant number of Austrians yearned to be part of Bismarck's united Germany. Their nationalism caused them to hold the non-German subjects of the empire in contempt, and many were anti-Semites. These prejudices infected the mind of an Austrian who led Germany in the twentieth century: Adolf Hitler.

Strife among the diverse nationalistic factions within the Habsburg Empire rendered central and eastern Europe politically unstable. Conflicts involved both foreign and domestic policies, for nationalists wanted self-determination within the empire and unification with similar ethnic groups outside the empire. Ukrainians, Romanians, Italians, and Bosnians within the empire aspired to ties with Russia, Romania, Italy, Serbia, or a yet to be created south Slavic (Yugoslav) state. The nationalist

HISTORY'S VOICES

LORD ACTON CONDEMNS NATIONALISM

he English historian Lord Acton (1834–1902) was an important observer of contemporary events, and he was one of the first commentators to recognize the political dangers posed by nationalism.

WHAT THREATS did Acton believe that nationalism posed?

By making the State and the nation commensurate with each other in theory, it [nationalism] reduces practically to a subject condition all other nationalities that may be within the boundary. It cannot admit them to an equality with the ruling nation which constitutes the State, because the State would then cease to be national, which would be a contradiction of the principle of its existence. According, therefore, to the degree of humanity and civilization in that dominant body which claims all the rights of the community,

the inferior races are exterminated, or reduced to servitude, or outlawed, or put in a condition of dependence. . . .

A State which is incompetent to satisfy different races condemns itself; a State which labors to neutralize, to absorb, or to expel them, destroys its own vitality; a State which does not include them is destitute of the chief basis of self-government. The theory of nationality, therefore, is a retrograde step in history. . . .

[N]ationality does not aim either at liberty or prosperity, both of which it sacrifices to the imperative necessity of making the nation the mold and measure of the State. Its course will be marked with material as well as moral ruin, in order that a new invention may prevail over the works of God and the interests of mankind.

From John Emerich Edward Dalbert-Acton, *First Baron Acton, Essays in the History of Liberty*, ed. by J. Rufus Fears (Indianapolis: Liberty Classics, 1985), pp. 431–433.

---

unrest within the late-nineteenth-century Austrian Empire and its neighboring states helped bring on World War I, World War II, and the subsequent bloodshed in the former Yugoslavia. (See "History's Voices: Lord Acton Condemns Nationalism.")

WHAT REFORMS did Alexander II institute in Russia?

RUSSIA: EMANCIPATION AND REVOLUTIONARY STIRRINGS

Russia changed remarkably during the second half of the nineteenth century because foreign policy reversals (particularly loss of the Crimean War and the humiliation of the Treaty of Paris) compelled the Russian government to reconsider its domestic policies.

REFORMS OF ALEXANDER II

Nicholas I's son and heir, Alexander II (r. 1855–1881), was well trained for his duties as tsar, and he had a clear sense of the problems confronting Russia. The debacle of the Crimean War made reform both necessary and possible, and Alexander II seized the opportunity this gave him to attempt the most extensive restructuring of Russia's institutions since the days of Peter the Great.

Abolition of Serfdom The profound cultural gap that separated Russia from the rest of Europe was nowhere more apparent than in the survival of serfdom, an institution that other European states had long abandoned. The only Western countries that still tolerated involuntary servitude in the mid–nineteenth century were Russia, Brazil, and parts of the United States.

In March 1856, following the conclusion of the Crimean War, Alexander II announced his intention to abolish serfdom. The tsar noted that serfdom was economically inefficient and a constant source of social unrest, and he insisted it prevented Russia from effectively exploiting its human and natural resources. For more than five years government commissions wrestled with the problem of how to implement the tsar's wish. Finally, in February 1861—over opposition from nobles and landlords—Alexander issued the emancipation statute.

The serfs were disappointed by the tsar's legislation, for freedom did not bring them ownership of the land they worked. They were required to purchase (with payments spread out over a period of forty-nine years) plots that were often too small to support them. Their payments were to be made to the government to reimburse it for what it spent to reimburse landlords for the losses the emancipation decree inflicted on their estates. The procedures imposed on the peasants for paying their debts (and interest charges) were so complicated and the benefits so limited that many serfs believed emancipation was yet to come. Poor harvests worsened a bad situation by making it impossible for many peasants to keep up with the government's payment schedule. They fell increasingly behind, until a widespread revolutionary upheaval in 1905 persuaded the government to cancel the remaining debt.

Reform of Local Government and the Judicial System   The abolition of serfdom required the reorganization of local government and the judicial system, for village communes replaced landlords as the authorities charged with keeping peace among the peasants. The nobles assumed larger roles in other aspects of local administration. They sat on the provincial and county *zemstvos* (assemblies) that oversaw such things as bridge and road repair, education, and agricultural improvement. The arrangement was not very successful, for the work of the councils was never adequately funded.

In 1864, Alexander addressed abuses and inequities in the judiciary and introduced Russia to important western European legal principles: equality before the law, impartial hearings, uniform procedures, judicial independence, and trial by jury. His judges were not truly independent, however, for the tsar could change the sentences they handed out. Also, certain offenses (such as those involving the press) were not tried before a jury. Nonetheless, the new courts improved the efficiency and honesty of law enforcement.

Military Reform   Russia maintained the largest army on the Continent. To keep it at full strength, recruitment quotas were imposed on villages and serfs were seized from their homes and impressed into service. Common soldiers rarely saw their families again, for they remained on active duty for twenty-five years and suffered harsh treatment.

The poor performance of the Russian army in the Crimean War prompted Alexander's military reforms. He reduced terms of service to fifteen years and slightly relaxed discipline. In 1874, the enlistment period was lowered to six years of active duty followed by nine years in the reserves.

Repression in Poland   In 1863, a failed attempt by Polish nationalists to end Russian dominance of their homeland led Alexander to attempt the "Russification" of Poland. In 1864, he punished the politically restive Polish nobles by emancipating their serfs, and he imposed Russian law, language, and administration throughout Poland. Poland was treated as a Russian province until the end of World War I.

Tsar Alexander II (r. 1855–1881) was assassinated on March 1, 1881. The assassins first threw a bomb that wounded several Imperial guards. When the tsar stopped his carriage to see the wounded, the assassins threw a second bomb, that killed him.

Bildarchiv Preussischer Kulturbesitz

Alexander II rejected any reform proposals that curtailed autocracy, and the reforms he implemented earned him little gratitude from his subjects. The serfs felt their emancipation was incomplete. The nobles and the wealthier, educated segments of society resented his refusal to give them a meaningful role in government. Alexander II was called the Tsar Liberator, but the freedoms he granted did not make him popular. An attempt was made on his life in 1866, and in its wake he became ever more close minded and reactionary. As Russia developed into a police state, the reforming tsar's repressive government inflamed political radicals.

REVOLUTIONARIES

One of the most prominent critics of the tsarist regime was a Russian exile, Alexander Herzen (1812–1870). His newspaper, *The Bell*, helped inspire students, who were disenchanted with the pace of reform in Russia, with enthusiasm for a movement called *populism*. It embraced the communal life of Russian peasants as a model for rebuilding Russian society. In the early 1870s, hundreds of idealistic young Russians, male and female, headed into the countryside. They planned to live with the peasants, gain their trust, and prepare them for the role they were expected to play in the coming revolution. The bewildered and distrustful peasants turned most of them over to the police. Almost two hundred were tried during the winter of 1877–1878. Most were acquitted or given light sentences, for the authorities hoped a display of mercy would diminish sympathy for the naive young revolutionaries. The tsar was urged to pardon the ringleaders, but he refused and made it known that he favored heavy penalties for anyone involved in revolutionary activity. This prompted some radicals to resort to terrorism and directly assault his regime. They were encouraged when, in January 1878, a jury acquitted Vera Zasulich, the would-be assassin of the military governor of Saint Petersburg. Her intended victim's reputation for brutality was seen as a mitigating factor that swayed the verdict in her favor.

In 1879, the most radical of the revolutionary organizations, *Land and Freedom*, split. The faction that hoped to transform Russia by educating the peasants soon dissolved. The other, *The People's Will*, favored the violent overthrow of the

21.7
Anarchism: Michael Bakunin

23.4
John Stuart Mill: from *The Subjection of Women*

autocracy, and it plotted to kill the tsar. Several assassination attempts failed, but on March 1, 1881, Alexander II was killed by a bomb tossed at his carriage. Four men and two women were convicted of involvement in the plot and sentenced to death.

The assassins' act brought Alexander III (r. 1881–1894) to the throne, a tsar who represented all that the revolutionaries saw as inherently evil in auto-cratic government. Alexander set about reversing his father's reforms. He fa-vored government by centralized bureaucracy, not local councils (the *zemstvos*). He built up the secret police, and he increased press censorship. The legacy of reactionary policies he bequeathed to his son, Nicholas II (r. 1894–1917), has-tened the destruction of Russia's monarchy.

GREAT BRITAIN: TOWARD DEMOCRACY

Great Britain was Europe's primary example of a confident liberal state endowed with stable political institutions and equipped to meet for-eign challenges and resolve domestic tensions. Several factors con-tributed to its success. Parliament admitted new groups and interests to the political process. The general prosperity Britain enjoyed in the third quarter of the century eased social pressures, and all classes in British society shared a belief in competitive individualism.

THE SECOND REFORM ACT (1867)

During the early 1860s, pressure built to broaden the franchise. In 1866, a Liber-al ministry introduced a reform bill, but it was defeated. A conservative ministry, which was led in the House of Commons by Benjamin Disraeli (1804–1881), then took office and surprised everyone by proposing to expand the electorate even more than the Liberals had previously suggested. Disraeli's motive for near-ly making Britain a democracy was political self-interest. He believed reform was inevitable and the Conservatives' best strategy was to take credit for it. He ex-pected grateful voters of the working class to support Conservative candidates if those candidates showed themselves responsive to social issues, and he thought the growing suburban middle class would become increasingly conservative. He was by and large correct. The Conservative Party dominated British politics for much of the twentieth century.

GLADSTONE'S GREAT MINISTRY (1868–1874)

The voters in the election of 1868 disappointed Disraeli by choosing a prime minister whose term in office (1868–1874) marked the culmination of British liberalism. William Gladstone (1809–1898) opened the in-stitutions that had been the preserve of the aris-tocracy and the Anglican church to people from all classes and of all faiths. In 1870, competitive examinations replaced patronage appointments as the route to civil service jobs. That same year the Education Act established state-supported el-ementary schools. In 1871, the practice of pur-chasing officers' commissions in the army was abolished, and admission to the faculties of Ox-ford and Cambridge University was no longer limited to members of the Anglican church. In 1872, the Ballot Act introduced the secret ballot.

HOW DID liberal democracy develop in Great Britain?

In a House of Commons debate, William Ewart Gladstone, standing on the right, is attacking Benjamin Disraeli, who sits with legs crossed and arms folded. Gladstone served in the British Parliament from the 1830s through the 1890s. Four times the Liberal Party prime minister, he was responsible for guiding major reforms through Parliament. Disraeli, regarded as the founder of modern British conservatism, served as prime minister from 1874 to 1880.

Image Works/Mary Evans Picture Library Ltd.

Consolidation of States (1854–1900)

1854–1856	The Crimean War
1855	Alexander II becomes tsar
1859	Piedmont and France fight Austria
1860	Garibaldi invades southern Italy
1861	Austria issues the February Patent Proclamation of the Kingdom of Italy (March 17) Russia abolishes serfdom
1862	Bismarck becomes prime minister of Prussia
1863	Russia suppresses the Polish Rebellion
1864	Danish-Prussian War
1866	Austro-Prussian War; Venetia ceded to Italy
1867	North German Confederation formed Formation of the Dual Monarchy: Hungary and Austria Britain's Second Reform Act
1868	Gladstone becomes prime minister of Britain
1870	Franco-Prussian War begins (July 19); Third Republic proclaimed in France (September 4); Italian state annexes Rome (October 2)
1871	The German Empire proclaimed (January 18); Paris Commune (March 28–May 28); Treaty of Frankfurt between France and Germany (May 1)
1872	Introduction of the secret ballot in Britain
1874	Disraeli becomes prime minister of Britain
1880	Gladstone's second ministry
1881	Alexander II assassinated; Alexander III succeeds
1884	Britain's Third Reform Act
1886	Lord Salisbury becomes prime minister of Britain
1892	Gladstone's third ministry
1894	Nicholas II becomes tsar

All of these reforms were typically liberal in that they ended abuses without destroying existing institutions and cleared the way for all citizens to compete on the grounds of ability and merit. They mitigated the danger an illiterate citizenry poses to a democratic state, and they fostered loyalty to the nation by addressing sources of discontent. (See "Encountering the Past: The Arrival of Penny Postage.")

DISRAELI IN OFFICE (1874–1880)

Disraeli succeeded Gladstone as prime minister in 1874. The two men had stood on different sides of most issues for over a quarter century. Whereas Gladstone trusted to individualism, free trade, and competition to solve social problems, Disraeli believed paternalistic legislation and state action were needed to protect the weak. Disraeli talked much but had few specific programs or ideas. The significant social legislation proposed by his ministry was the work of his home secretary, Richard Cross (1823–1914). The Public Health Act and the Artisans' Dwelling Act (both 1875) improved conditions for the working classes, expanded government protection for trade unions, and empowered laborers to fight for additional reforms.

THE IRISH QUESTION

From the late 1860s onward, Irish nationalists sought **home rule**—by which they meant Irish control of local government. Gladstone responded with two major pieces of legislation. In 1869, he disestablished the Anglican church in Ireland so Ireland's Roman Catholics were not taxed to support Protestant clergy. In 1870, a land act provided compensation for Irish tenants who had been evicted and loans for those who wished to purchase the land they rented. The Irish question, however, continued to fester throughout the 1870s. Land ownership was at the heart of the problem. An Irish Land League agitated for change and intimidated landlords, many of whom were English. In 1881, Gladstone strengthened tenant rights but also passed the Coercion Act, a set of regulations designed to restore law and order to Ireland.

By 1885, Charles Stewart Parnell (1846–1891) had persuaded eighty-five Irish members of the House of Commons to work together as a tightly disciplined party. In the election of 1885 their solid voting bloc had the power to decide whether the English Liberals or Conservatives would take office. Gladstone's support for home rule persuaded Parnell to help him form a Liberal ministry, but the home rule issue split the Liberal Party. In 1886, some Liberals joined the Conservatives to defeat Gladstone's Home Rule Bill.

Gladstone's Conservative successor, Lord Salisbury (1830–1903), employed a mix of public works, administrative reform, and coercion to try to reconcile the

home rule Government of a country or locality by its own citizens.

ENCOUNTERING THE PAST

THE ARRIVAL OF PENNY POSTAGE

*C*ommunication systems help draw nations together and are essential to the functioning of popular government. Thus the inexpensive postal system was one of the nineteenth century's more significant innovations, and the British government led the way in its development.

Early postal systems charged by weight and distance to delivery, and the receiver, not the sender, was liable for the cost of delivery. High postage made newspapers expensive and encouraged inventive strategies for avoiding payment. In 1837, an English reformer, Rowland Hill (1795–1879), proposed a simple new system. He suggested low uniform rates for each category of mail (letters, newspapers, etc.) regardless of distance and charged the sender with paying the postage. A system known as the Uniform Penny Post was launched in 1840 and became an instant success. By 1849, it was delivering 329 million items annually. Low cost meant almost everyone could afford to send letters, and the postal service provided a huge number of new jobs in the public sector. In 1874, an international treaty, the Universal Postal Union, guaranteed that postage paid in a sender's nation would assure delivery anywhere in the world.

Hill also proposed the self-adhesive postage stamp—a small receipt pasted to the cover of an item to indicate that delivery costs had been paid. The first stamp bore only the simple legend, "Postage One Penny." Governments soon began to print more elaborate stamps from engraved plates and frequently to alter their design to frustrate forgers. As the number of stamps and postal systems multiplied, the hobby of stamp collecting was born.

WHAT POSTAGE innovations did Rowland Hill introduce? What were their effects on society?

With the new British postal system, the volume of mail vastly increased as did the number of postal workers involved in sorting and delivering it.

Image Works/Mary Evans Picture Library Ltd.

Irish to English government. In 1892, Gladstone returned to power and proposed a second Home Rule Bill, which passed the House of Commons but was defeated in the House of Lords. In 1903, the Conservatives completed the transfer of land to ownership by former tenants, and Ireland became a country of small farms. In 1914, a Liberal ministry took advantage of limitations imposed on the upper house (the House of Lords Act of 1911) to pass the third Home Rule Bill, but its implementation was suspended for the duration of World War I.

The political divisions the "Irish question" created made it difficult for the government to resolve other issues. By the turn of the century, frustration with the inability of the two established parties to enact reforms created an opportunity for a third group, the Labour Party, to attract a significant following and enter British politics.

IMAGE KEY

for pages 536–537

a. Proclamation of the German Empire in the Hall of Mirrors, Versailles, France, January 18, 1871

b. Italian Nationalist and patriot, Giuseppe Garibaldi, the central figure in the story of Italian independence

c. William Ewart Gladstone cartoon from *Vanity Fair*

d. General view of the delegates to the Congress of Paris seated at a table during peace discussions

e. Engraved, seated portrait of Abdul Hamid II (1842–1918), last Sultan of Turkey, 1876–1909 (deposed), known as "The Great Assassin" who ordered the Armenian Massacre of 1894–96

f. Franz von Lenbach (1836–1904) "Prince Otto von Bismark in uniform with Prussian helmet." Canvas. Kunsthistorisches Museum, Gemaeldegalerie, Vienna, Austria. Photograph © Erich Lessing/Art Resource, NY

g. Tsar Alexander II (r. 1855–1881) was assassinated on March 1, 1881. The assassins first threw a bomb that wounded several Imperial guards. When the Tsar stopped his carriage to see the wounded, the assassins threw a second bomb, that killed him

h. Relief Map of Italy

i. The coronation of Francis Joseph of Hungary

j. During the Crimean War, Florence Nightingale of Great Britain organized nursing care for the wounded

SUMMARY

The Crimean War (1854–1856) Russia's attempts to expand its influence over the Ottoman Empire resulted in the Crimean War. France and Britain were hardly natural allies of the Ottomans, but because they did not want Russian power to grow in a region where they had extensive naval and commercial interest, they declared war on Russia in March 1854. The war was a debacle for all parties, made all the more embarrassing by the presence of journalists and photographers who recorded the ineptness on all sides. The Russian mistakes were worse than the British and French mistakes, and the March 1856 Treaty of Paris required Russia to give up territories and claims. Russia lost the image of invincibility that the nation had earned by defeating Napoleon. The Concert of Europe, too, was a casualty of the war: More powers now wanted to change the status quo than were willing to fight to defend it. Instability and adventurism in foreign policy characterized the next twenty-five years in Europe.

Reforms in the Ottoman Empire During the Tanzimat era, the Ottoman Empire underwent significant reforms. European-educated imperial bureaucrats encouraged the sultan to allow administrative councils to draw up decrees that would be issued by the sultan. Under the *Hatt-i Sharif*, in 1839, and the *Hatt-i Hümayun*, in 1856, the economy was liberalized, corruption reduced, and all Ottoman subjects were granted civic equality regardless of religion. The rights of non-Muslims and foreigners were spelled out. Christian missionaries opened schools and operated printing presses. The imperial government sought to copy European legal and military institutions and the secular values of liberalism. Local leaders undertook their own reforms while tension and opposition prevented the Ottoman Empire from gaining strength and stability. In the late 1870s, the Ottoman Empire lost most of its European holdings in the Balkan wars. In 1876, reformers took even bolder steps, but a backlash set in. The empire collapsed after entering World War I on the side of the Central Powers.

Italian Unification Nationalists of various persuasions wanted to unify Italy. The romantic republicans started with secret societies after the Congress of Vienna. Later, Mazzini and Garibaldi publicized the republican cause and mounted guerrilla campaigns. They were opposed by moderate Italians. Count Camillo Cavour rejected republicanism and embraced Enlightenment ideals. He was a monarchist who believed economic ties would foster Italian desire for unification. He encouraged trade, railway construction, and agricultural improvement. In 1855, he entered Piedmont into the Crimean War, in order to win French sympathy. In 1858, Cavour and Napoleon III plotted to incite a war against Austria that they could win. In 1859, French and Piedmontese forces defeated the Austrians in most of northern Italy; soon thereafter, a large group of Italian provinces united with Piedmont. Meanwhile, Garibaldi was uniting southern Italy by force. The Italian kingdom was created in 1860, under Piedmontese rule. Cavour died soon afterward, leaving the problems of northern and southern Italian economic and cultural incompatibility unsolved. "Unredeemed" areas still remained under Austrian control, fostering hostilities that determined Italian alliances in World War I.

German Unification Germany was unified under Prussia, and specifically under the conservative guidance of prime minister Otto von Bismarck. German unification, a nationalist and liberal goal, was achieved through the expansion of Prussia's military monarchy. By 1871, the strongest state on the Continent had one of the most conservative governments. Bismarck, a Junker, had diplomatic and legislative experience when he became prime minister in 1862. Through complex diplomacy, he joined Austria in war against Denmark in 1864, then turned against Austria in 1866. Prussia won both conflicts, and in the process cut the Habsburgs out of German affairs. In 1867, the North German Confederation was organized under a constitution that looked liberal but kept real power in the hands of the Prussian monarchy. Another complex round of diplomacy and warfare, this time involving the Spanish monarchy and French pride, resulted in an important German victory at the Battle of Sedan in September 1870, and the proclamation of the German Empire in January 1871.

France: From Liberal Empire to the Third Republic Napoleon III began his rule in 1851 as an authoritarian. Around 1860, his rule entered a liberal phase, in which he endorsed free trade, loosened political controls and, in 1870, agreed to a liberal constitution. Although these measures widened his domestic support, his foreign policy continued to be disastrous. The Second Empire ended at the Battle of Sedan in September 1870, when Napoleon III was captured by the Germans. France declared the Third Republic and was ready to sue, but Paris continued to resist Prussian siege until January 1871. The National Assembly was dominated by monarchists, although they could not agree on a monarch. Paris, meanwhile, attempted to govern itself independently under the Paris Commune, but the army surrounded the city in April and invaded in late May. In 1875, the National Assembly created a republican legislative system, which survived subsequent scandals and attempts to impose authoritarian control. The Dreyfus affair in the 1890s presented the Third Republic with its greatest trauma. Captain Alfred Dreyfus, who was Jewish, was convicted by a military court for passing secrets to the German army. The evidence against him was forged, but the military court's refusal to reverse the conviction created a rallying cry for leftist groups.

The Habsburg Empire From 1848 until it collapsed, the Habsburg Empire caused problems. Francis Joseph used various mechanisms to attempt to preserve the empire, but in the end he failed. When Austria failed to assist Russia in the Crimean War, it lost a valuable ally. In 1859, Austria was defeated by France and Piedmont. In 1860 and 1861, Francis Joseph attempted to organize the empire's government, but the Magyars resisted. The February Patent of 1861 was the basis of government in Austria proper until World War I. In 1866, Austria was defeated by the Prussians, and in 1867, Francis Joseph compromised with the Magyars to create the dual monarchy, Austria-Hungary. But the Compromise of 1867 fed the hopes of other nationalists, at a time when language and race were being used to draw the boundaries of national and ethnic groups more sharply than ever before. Nationalist unrest within the Austro-Hungarian Empire posed problems for its neighbors and indeed all of Europe, and indeed still poses problems in central and eastern Europe today.

Russia: Emancipation and Revolutionary Stirrings When Alexander II took the throne in Russia in 1855, he set out to impose reforms from the top. He abolished serfdom, but the mechanisms he used for emancipation were a huge disappointment. When emancipation finally came in 1861, serfs were not given free title to their land. They had to pay the government over a period of forty-nine years before they would get title. Many peasants could not afford the payments, but the debts were not cancelled until 1906. Local government, the judicial system, and the military were more satisfactorily reformed. But as his reforms failed to earn him new loyalty, and after Polish nationalists rebelled in 1863, Alexander turned increasingly to repression. This only fueled demands for radical change. In the 1870s, students started a revolutionary movement called populism. When the tsar suggested that students deserved heavier sentences than they had gotten, the revolutionaries started to attack the regime directly. In 1881, a member of the radical society The People's Will assassinated Alexander II. His son Alexander III ruled more repressively until 1894, when Nicholas II took the throne.

Great Britain: Toward Democracy Great Britain experienced difficulties and domestic conflicts during this period but was able to deal with them through the political institutions of the liberal state. Conservative Benjamin Disraeli shepherded the Second Reform Act in 1867. Voting rights were expanded, with the number of eligible voters growing by over a million. William Gladstone was elected prime minister in 1868, and over the next six years access to government institutions was widened to include members of all classes and religions. The paternalistic Disraeli returned to the prime minister's office in 1874 and instituted public health measures, among others. The largest question of the 1880s was Irish home rule. Land ownership in Ireland was the most politicized question. Charles Stewart Parnell organized Irish members of Parliament to lobby for this, and the Irish Party decided the 1885 election in favor of the Liberal Party. Home rule passed the House of Commons repeatedly but was only able to overcome the veto of the House of Lords in 1914.

REVIEW QUESTIONS

1. Why was it so difficult to unify Italy? What were Garibaldi's contributions to Italian unification? What was Otto von Bismarck's plan for unifying Germany? What effect did the unification of Germany have on the rest of Europe?

2. How did France's Second Empire (under Napoleon III) become its Third Republic? What made the Paris Commune a legend throughout Europe? What effect did the Dreyfus affair have on the politics of the Third Republic?

3. What reforms did Tsar Alexander II institute? Can he accurately be called a "visionary" reformer?

4. How did the politics of the British Liberal and Conservative parties evolve in the period from 1860 to 1890? How did British politicians handle the "Irish question"? Are there similarities between England's situation with Ireland and the Austrian Empire's struggles with its nationalities?

KEY TERMS

home rule   (p. 556)

  For additional study resources for this chapter, go to:
www.prenhall.com/kagan3/chapter22

23

The Building of European Supremacy
Society and Politics to World War I

CHAPTER HIGHLIGHTS

Population Trends and Migration
Europeans made up about 20 percent of the world's population in 1900. In the second half of the nineteenth century, Europeans migrated to the Americas, Australia, and South Africa in great numbers.

The Second Industrial Revolution The Second Industrial Revolution expanded production of steel, chemicals, electricity, and oil. New industries and new applications of industrial products were developed. European economies slowed in the last quarter of the nineteenth century.

The Middle Classes in Ascendancy An increasingly diverse middle class dominated the second half of the nineteenth century. Tensions and anxieties marked relations among the groups composing the middle class.

Late Nineteenth-Century Urban Life The proportion of Europeans living in cities increased dramatically in the late-nineteenth century. The cities themselves underwent significant changes including urban redevelopment, the development of suburbs, improved sanitation, and housing reform.

Varieties of Late Nineteenth-Century Women's Experiences Women's lives varied with social rank, but women of all classes were economically dependent on and legally inferior to men. Women were saddled with legal, economic, and educational handicaps. The Second Industrial Revolution created new employment patterns for women. Feminists pushed for expanded rights for women.

Jewish Emancipation Jews gained a tenuous hold on full citizenship in the Habsburg Empire, France, Italy, and Germany. Russia's tradition of harsh discrimination against Jews continued until World War I. Although prejudice did not disappear, the situation for Jews in western Europe improved after 1848.

Labor, Socialism, and Politics to World War I Factory workers began to outnumber artisans and skilled workers. After the failed revolutions of 1848, Europe's workers changed tactics and embraced new institutions and ideologies, including trade unions, democratic political parties, and socialism.

CHAPTER QUESTIONS

WHAT WERE the reasons for European migration in the late nineteenth century?

HOW DID the Second Industrial Revolution transform European life?

HOW DID European middle classes develop?

WHAT FORCES altered European urban life?

WHAT WAS life like for women in late ninteenth-century Europe?

WHAT WERE the major characteristics of Jewish emancipation?

WHAT LED to the development of European labor politics and socialism?

What a Woman may be, and yet not have the Vote

MAYOR	NURSE	MOTHER	DOCTOR or TEACHER	FACTORY HAND

CHAPTER OUTLINE

- Population Trends and Migration
- The Second Industrial Revolution
- The Middle Classes in Ascendancy
- Late Nineteenth-Century Urban Life
- Varieties of Late Nineteenth-Century Women's Experiences
- Jewish Emancipation
- Labor, Socialism, and Politics to World War I

What a Man may have been, & yet not lose the Vote

CONVICT	LUNATIC	Proprietor of white Slaves	Unfit for Service	DRUNKARD

IMAGE KEY
Image Key for pages 562–563 is on page 586.

The growth of industrialism between 1860 and 1914 increased Europe's productive capacity to unprecedented levels. As goods and capital flowed out of Europe and across the globe, Europe's political, economic, and social institutions assumed many of their current characteristics. Nation-states with centralized bureaucracies, large electorates, and competing political parties appeared. Huge corporate structures dominated the business world. Labor organized trade unions. The number of white-collar workers increased. Urban life predominated. Socialism became a major political force. Foundations were laid for welfare states and for vast military establishments—and tax burdens increased to support them.

Europeans, confident in their prosperity, failed to realize how dependent they were on the resources and markets of the wider world. Their assumption that European supremacy was natural and enduring was challenged as the twentieth century unfolded.

POPULATION TRENDS AND MIGRATION

WHAT WERE the reasons for European migration in the late nineteenth century?

In 1900, Europe was home to about 20 percent of the world's people—a greater proportion than ever before or since. Its population rose from about 266 million in 1850, to 401 million in 1900, to 447 million in 1910. Thereafter, growth declined or stabilized in advanced nations and began to increase in less developed countries.

Europe's population was not only large; it exhibited unprecedented mobility in the second half of the nineteenth century. Emancipation removed legal blocks to migration of peasants. Railways, steamships, and better roads increased access to transportation. Offers of cheap land and better wages, which accompanied economic development in Europe, North America, Latin America, and Australia, provided motivation for people to relocate.

Europeans left their continent in record numbers—more than 50 million between 1846 and 1932. Most went to the United States, Canada, Australia, South Africa, Brazil, or Argentina. At midcentury, Great Britain (especially Ireland), Germany, and Scandinavia produced the most emigrants. After 1885, peoples from southern and eastern Europe dominated. The exodus solved some of Europe's domestic problems and contributed, along with trade and industry, to the Europeanization of the world. Not since the sixteenth century had Europe's civilization made such an impact on other cultures. (See Map 23–1.)

THE SECOND INDUSTRIAL REVOLUTION

HOW DID the Second Industrial Revolution transform European life?

The first Industrial Revolution centered on textiles, iron, and applications of steam power. The **Second Industrial Revolution**, which began after 1850, expanded production of steel, chemicals, electricity, and oil.

NEW INDUSTRIES

In the 1850s, an English engineer, Henry Bessemer (1830–1898), discovered a process for manufacturing large quantities of steel cheaply. Production in Great Britain, Belgium, France, and Germany rose from 125,000 tons in 1860 to 32,020,000 tons in 1913. The chemical industry also came of age. The Solway process of alkali production allowed more chemical by-products to be recovered. New dyestuffs and plastics were also developed. Scientific research played an important role in the growth of the chemical industry, and chemists established the modern world's alliance between science and industrial development, with Germany taking the lead.

Second Industrial Revolution
Started after 1850, it expanded the production of steel, chemicals, electricity, and oil.

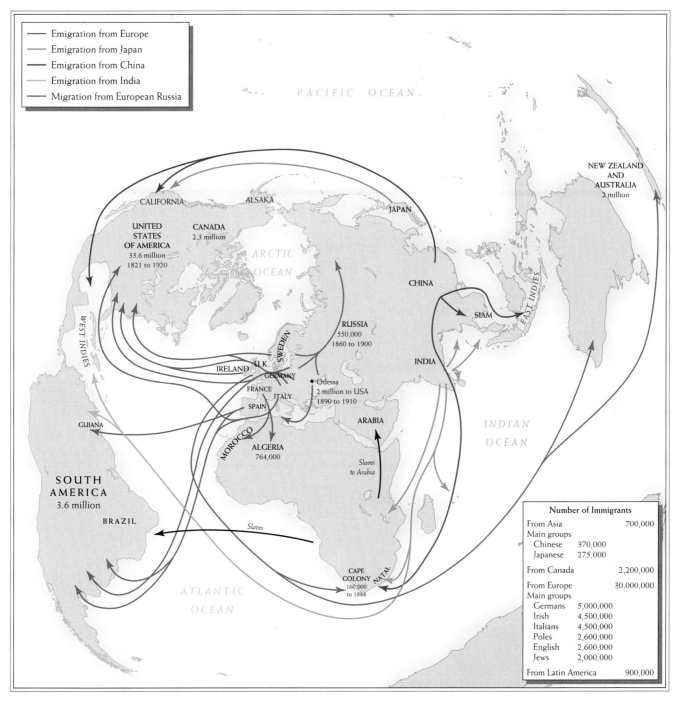

MAP 23–1
Patterns of Global Migration, 1840–1900   Emigration was a global process by the late-nineteenth century. But more immigrants went to the United States than to every other nation combined.

WHAT CHANGES enabled the migration of millions of people in the late nineteenth century?

The application of electrical energy to production had the greatest impact on industry and daily life. Electricity was the most versatile power ever discovered. Because it could be delivered almost anywhere, it opened more places for factory construction and improved the efficiency of production. Great Britain built the first major public power plant in 1881. Electricity quickly spread across Europe, and it soon began to be marketed to homes. (See Map 23–2.)

MAP EXPLORATION

Interactive map: To explore this map further, go to **http://www.prenhall.com/kagan3/map23.2**

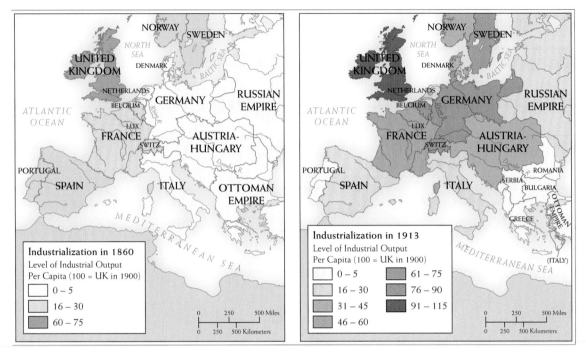

Industrialization in 1860
Level of Industrial Output
Per Capita (100 = UK in 1900)
- 0 – 5
- 16 – 30
- 60 – 75

Industrialization in 1913
Level of Industrial Output
Per Capita (100 = UK in 1900)
- 0 – 5
- 16 – 30
- 31 – 45
- 46 – 60
- 61 – 75
- 76 – 90
- 91 – 115
(ITALY)

MAP 23–2

European Industrialization, 1860–1913   In 1860, Britain was far more industrialized than other European countries. But in the following half century, industrial output rose significantly, if unevenly, across much of western Europe, especially in the new German Empire. The Balkan states and the Ottoman Empire, however, remained economically backward.

WHY DID Britain and Germany take the lead in the Second Industrial Revolution?

The invention and commercialization of automobiles soon led to auto races in Europe and North America. Here Henri Fournier, the winner of the 1901 Paris to Berlin Motor Car Race, sits in his winning racing car manufactured by the Paris-based auto firm of Emile and Louis Mors.

Hulton Archive/Getty Images

The internal combustion engine was invented in 1886. A year later Gottlieb Daimler (1834–1900), a German engineer, put it on wheels and created the automobile. The car remained a novelty until 1909, when Henry Ford (1863–1947), an American entrepreneur, developed production techniques that made autos cheap enough for ordinary people to purchase.

By the turn of the century, the automobile and new industrial and chemical uses for petroleum had created the first significant demand for oil and the first great oil companies: Standard Oil of the United States, British Shell Oil, and Royal Dutch. Then, as now, Europe depended largely on imported supplies.

ECONOMIC DIFFICULTIES

Industry and agriculture boomed from 1850 to 1873, but in the last quarter of the nineteenth century economies slowed. Bad weather and foreign competition created problems for European farmers that motivated much of the immigration of the period. Many of those who left Europe during these years came from rural areas or from countries where industrialization was least advanced. Several large banks failed in 1873. The rate of capital investment slowed, and some industries stagnated for about twenty years. Overall, however, standards of living in industrialized nations improved during the second half of the nineteenth century. Real wages generally held firm or rose. Many workers still lived and labored in abysmal conditions, and there were pockets of *unemployment* (a word that was coined at this time). Labor unrest promoted the growth of trade unions and socialist political parties.

By the end of the nineteenth century, increasing consumer demand had revived the economy. Lower food prices freed everyone to spend more on other kinds of consumer goods. New industries produced new products, and urbanization created larger markets. New sales and distribution techniques (department stores, chain stores, packaging, mail-order catalogs, and advertising) stimulated consumer demand. Imperialism also guaranteed new consumers for Europe's products in Europe's foreign colonies.

THE MIDDLE CLASSES IN ASCENDANCY

The sixty years that led up to World War I were dominated by the middle class. The London Great Exhibition of 1851 (housed in a huge solarium called the Crystal Palace) was a monument to the material comforts that industrialization provided for middle-class life. The middle class constituted the largest group of consumers, and it set standards of taste. The prosperity enjoyed by middle-class people prompted them to defend the status quo and lessened the enthusiasm some had previously shown for revolutionary politics. Property owners, wealthy and modest, worried, whenever issues of social equality and political rights were debated, that socialists and other working-class groups might try to dispossess them.

SOCIAL DISTINCTIONS WITHIN THE MIDDLE CLASSES

The middle class had never been perfectly homogeneous, and during the nineteenth century it grew increasingly diverse. In the lead were a few hundred families, the owners and managers of great businesses who could afford to live in a splendor beyond the reach of many aristocrats. Behind them were the comfortable small entrepreneurs and professionals—people who could afford education, vacations, and private homes furnished with pianos, pictures, books, and journals. A similar lifestyle was enjoyed by people with smaller holdings or lesser educations but respected nonmanual employment (shopkeepers, schoolteachers, and librarians). The wholly new element in

Events in the Formation of the Early Twentieth Century

Year	Event
1848	Britain's Public Health Act
1851	France's Melun Act
1857	Bessemer steel manufacturing process invented
1864	Meeting of the First International
1869	John Stuart Mill publishes *The Subjection of Women*
1875	German Social Democratic Party founded
1876	Telephone invented
1879	Electric light bulb invented
1882	England's Married Woman's Property Act
1884	Britain's Fabian Society founded
1887	Automobile invented
1889	Establishment of the Second International
1895	Invention of wireless telegraphy
1900	Lenin leaves Russia
1902	Formation of the British Labour Party
1903	British Women's Social and Political Union founded Lenin creates the Bolsheviks The Wright brothers begin the age of aviation
1904–1905	Russo-Japanese War
1905	Saint Petersburg's Bloody Sunday Russia's October Manifesto
1907	Norway, first nation to grant women the vote
1909	Henry Ford begins mass production of automobiles
1910	British suffragettes adopt radical tactics
1911	Stolypin assassinated
1914	World War I begins
1918	Some British women acquire the vote
1918	Constitution of the Weimar Republic gives women the vote
1928	British women acquire same voting rights as men

HOW DID European middle classes develop?

ENCOUNTERING THE PAST

BICYCLES: TRANSPORTATION, FREEDOM, AND SPORT

Bicycles, the first mass-produced affordable machines for individual travel, took Western nations by storm between 1880 and 1900. The unprecedented freedom to travel that they gave men and (significantly) women had an immense impact on society.

The bicycle was invented in Germany about 1817, but the early models were clumsy, dangerous, and uncomfortable. They were made of wood, had to be pushed, and riders could not control their speed. Metal frames, solid rubber tires, and chain drives did not appear until the 1870s. In the 1880s, John Boyd Dunlop, an Irish physician, invented the pneumatic tire and France's Michelin brothers the inner tube. By the 1890s, the modern "safety bicycle" was in mass production.

Bicycles enabled people to commute from homes located farther from their workplaces, and bicycles provided new opportunities for recreation and sport. Special clothing was designed for cyclists. "Bloomers," ample trousers worn under skirts, preserved the modesty of female riders. (Feminists hailed the mobility the bicycle provided as a major contribution to women's liberation.) Cycling clubs appeared in the early twentieth century, and the first travel guides were published for cycling tourists. The Michelin tire company's famous series of *Guides*

Michelin was initiated in 1900 to promote cycling—and consumption of tires. Bicycle racing soon became a competitive sport. It was featured in the first modern Olympic Games in 1896, and in 1903, the first Tour de France was held.

WHAT EXPLAINS the bicycle's huge popularity in the late nineteenth century?

The bicycle helped liberate women's lives, but as this poster suggests, it also was associated with glamour and fashion.
© Archievo Iconogralico, S.A./CORBIS

---

society was the white-collar worker of the lower middle class or **petite bourgeoisie** (the secretary, retail clerk, or lower-level bureaucrat). Many of these people had working-class origins. Some belonged to unions, but all had middle-class aspirations and consciously distanced themselves from the lower classes. They pursued educational opportunities and career advancement (especially for their children), and they spent a considerable portion of their disposable income on consumer goods in order to keep up a middle-class appearance. (See "Encountering the Past: Bicycles: Transportation, Freedom, and Sport.")

Significant tensions and anxieties marked relations among the groups composing the middle class. Small shopkeepers resented competition from the department stores and mail-order-catalog distribution systems owned by the great capitalist merchants. (See "History's Voices: Paris Department Stores Expand Their Business.") Professions grew overcrowded, and those who struggled into

petite bourgeoisie New lower middle class made up of white-collar workers such as secretaries, retail clerks, and lower-level bureaucrats.

OVERVIEW   GROWTH OF MAJOR EUROPEAN CITIES (FIGURES IN THOUSANDS)

	1850	1880	1910
Berlin	419	1,122	2,071
Birmingham	233	437	840
Frankfurt	65	137	415
London	2,685	4,470	7,256
Madrid	281	398	600
Moscow	365	748	1,533
Paris	1,053	2,269	2,888
Rome	175	300	542
Saint Petersburg	485	877	1,962
Vienna	444	1,104	2,031
Warsaw	160	339	872

the middle class feared being forced out by economic hard times. Nonetheless, during the decades leading up to World War I, the middle class had sufficient cohesion to set society's values and goals.

LATE NINETEENTH-CENTURY URBAN LIFE

Between 1850 and 1911, the portion of France's population living in cities increased from 25 to 44 percent. In Germany, the shift was from 30 to 60 percent, and other western European countries experienced similarly dramatic urban growth. Migrants to cities from rural areas were uprooted from traditional social support systems and condemned to poor housing, anonymity, and, often, unemployment. Different ethnic groups found it difficult to get along when thrown together—particularly when they had to compete for jobs. The migration of thousands of Russian Jews to western Europe's cities prompted an outbreak of anti-Semitism that became a factor in the politics of the latter part of the century.

WHAT FORCES altered European urban life?

THE REDESIGN OF CITIES

Migration to cities increased demands on their infrastructures and transformed patterns of urban life. During the second half of the century, governments redesigned many European cities. Urban residents moved to the peripheries of cities, and central areas, where large numbers of people from all social classes had customarily lived, were rebuilt as business districts with government offices, large retail stores, and theaters.

The New Paris   The rebuilding of Paris was Europe's greatest urban redevelopment project. Like most European cities, Paris had evolved with little or no planning. Lavish public buildings and squalid hovels were jumbled together. Streets were narrow, crooked, and crowded. The River Seine, which ran through the center

A major feature of the reconstruction of mid-nineteenth-century Paris under the Emperor Napoleon III was a vast new sewer system to provide for drainage in the city. Sewer workmen could travel the length of the structure on small rail cars. Even today tourists still may visit parts of the mid-city Paris sewer system.

Nadar/Getty Images

of Paris, was little more than an open sewer and an obstacle to traffic. In 1850, the government did not even have a complete, accurate map of Paris. This was particularly worrisome, for the city's streets provided battlegrounds for uprisings that, as recently as 1848, toppled French governments.

Napoleon III initiated the redesign of Paris and appointed Georges Haussmann "prefect of the Seine" (from 1853 to 1870) to oversee the city's reconstruction. Whole districts were destroyed to make room for broad boulevards and streets. The wide vistas were beautiful and, from the government's point of view, functional. They allowed quick deployment of troops, and they eliminated narrow passages that rioters might barricade. The project was politically astute for a second reason. It created thousands of government-funded jobs and employment in the private industries that supported public works projects.

Work on Paris continued under the Third Republic. Many department stores, office complexes, and apartment buildings for the middle class were constructed. By the late 1870s, mechanical trams were operating. In 1895, construction of the *métro* (subway) began, and new railway stations were erected toward the close of the century. These improvements in transportation linked the refurbished central city to its expanding suburbs.

Development of Suburbs Redesign of cities displaced many of their residents and raised land values and rents. As both the middle classes and the working class sought alternative housing, suburbs sprawled around cities. They housed families whose breadwinners used the new transportation systems to commute to the town center or urban factories. European suburbs, unlike those that appeared in the United States, often consisted of apartment buildings or closely huddled private houses with small lawns and gardens. Suburban life meant that for hundreds of thousands of Europeans, home and work were more physically separated than ever before.

URBAN SANITATION

The growing conservatism of the middle classes stiffened government's resolve to maintain public order. This led to improvements in health and housing for the poor, for it was believed the well-being of the middle class and the stability of political systems depended on easing the misery of poverty.

Impact of Cholera The great cholera epidemics of the 1830s and 1840s drove this lesson home. Many common deadly diseases touched only the poor, but cholera struck all classes. Before the development of the bacterial theory of disease late in the century, physicians and sanitary reformers believed cholera and other illnesses were spread through infection from airborne miasmas. Miasmas were associated with foul odors and were believed to arise from filth. The best way to improve urban health, therefore, was to rid cities of dangerous, foul-smelling air by cleaning them up.

New Water and Sewer Systems During the 1840s, physicians and government officials began to publicize the dangers posed by human overcrowding and industrial wastes. The solution to the health hazard was said to be new water and sewer systems that would improve cleanliness. Construction of these facilities was slow, and some major urban areas did not have good water until after the turn of the century. The Parisian sewer system was one of the most famous parts of Haussmann's rebuilding program. Wherever such sanitary facilities were installed, the mortality rate dropped considerably.

Expanded Government Involvement in Public Health   Concern for public health led to an expansion of governmental power on various levels. Britain's Public Health Act (1848), France's Melun Act (1851), various laws in the still-disunited German states, and additional later legislation introduced new restraints on private life and enterprise. Medical officers and building inspectors were allowed to enter homes and other structures in the name of public health. Private property could be condemned for posing health hazards. Private land could be excavated for the construction of sewers and water mains, and building codes increasingly restrained the activities of private contractors. At the close of the century, acceptance of the bacterial theory of disease (thanks to the work of Louis Pasteur in France, Robert Koch in Germany, and Joseph Lister in Britain) increased concern for sanitation and encouraged even greater government intervention in the lives of citizens.

HOUSING REFORM AND MIDDLE-CLASS VALUES

The wretched dwellings of the poor were monuments to bad sanitation, and they were viewed as health hazards for the general public. Middle-class reformers and bureaucrats were shocked by reports describing the domestic arrangements of the lower classes and worried by suggestions that revolutions, such as those of 1848, could be caused by the pressures of overcrowded housing. Social activists proposed housing reform as a solution to all kinds of medical, moral, and political problems. Decent housing was expected to foster good family life and create healthy, moral, happy, and politically stable communities. The opportunity to purchase a home was also expected to motivate members of the working class to accumulate capital by adopting the thrifty habits of the middle classes.

The goal of housing reform was to make it possible for the working class to enjoy something resembling middle-class family life. At the minimum, this required a dwelling of several rooms with a private entrance and a toilet. Private philanthropists were the first to attack the problem of housing the poor. Companies operating on low profit margins or making low-interest loans encouraged construction of housing for the poor. Firms such as the German Krupp armaments manufacturers tried to provide themselves with a contented, healthy, and stable work force by constructing model communities for their employees.

By the mid–1880s, migration into cities had made housing a political issue. In 1885, England lowered the interest rates for the construction of inexpensive housing, and soon thereafter, government authorities began public housing projects. Similar action, initiated by local municipalities, followed in Germany, and in 1894, France made inexpensive credit available for constructing housing for the poor. By 1914, the housing problem had been generally acknowledged to exist if not yet adequately addressed.

VARIETIES OF LATE NINETEENTH-CENTURY WOMEN'S EXPERIENCES

*L*ike men, women in the late nineteenth century led lives that reflected their social ranks. Yet within each rank, the experience of women was distinct from that of men. Women, no matter what their class, were always economically dependent and legally inferior.

QUICK REVIEW

Improved Conditions in Cities
- Cholera epidemics spurred action
- New awareness of the value of modern water and sewer systems
- Expanded involvement of government in public health

WHAT WAS life like for women in late-nineteenth-century Europe?

WOMEN'S SOCIAL DISABILITIES

Virtually all European women were handicapped with respect to property rights, family law, and education. However, by the end of the century, improvements had been made in each of these areas.

Women and Property   In most European countries, until the last quarter of the century, married women of all classes could not own property in their own names. At marriage, any property a woman owned, inherited, or earned came under the control of her husband. She had no independent standing before the law, and her legal identity was subsumed in his. The theft of her purse, for instance, was treated as a crime against him.

Because European society was based on private property and wage earning, the law seriously disadvantaged women. However, reform of women's property rights came very slowly. The Married Woman's Property Act of 1882 allowed wives in Britain to own property as individuals, but a French married woman could not even open a savings account in her own name until 1895. She could not retain possession of her own wages until 1907. In 1900, Germany allowed a wife to take a job without her husband's permission, but except for her wages, her husband retained control of most of her property. Similar laws prevailed elsewhere in Europe.

Family Law   Divorce was difficult to obtain, and most nations did not permit termination of a marriage by mutual consent. Expensive court trials were required, and these were beyond the means of women who had no control over their own property. From 1816 to 1884, French law recognized no grounds for divorce. Thereafter, divorces were granted primarily for acts of cruelty and injury that could be proven in court. In Germany, only adultery or serious mistreatment were recognized as reasons for divorce. In England, divorce required an act of Parliament, but after 1857 it could be gained (with difficulty) through the Court of Matrimonial Causes. Adultery was the usual cause for granting a divorce in Britain, but everywhere on the Continent a sexual double standard prevailed. A husband's extramarital sexual relations were tolerated much more than a wife's.

Legal codes required wives to obey their husbands, and the Napoleonic Code and the remnants of Roman law still in effect throughout Europe treated women as lifelong minors. In cases of divorce and separation, husbands were usually given custody of children, and the authority of fathers over children was extensive. A father could take children away from their mother and give them to someone else for rearing. Only a father, in most countries, could permit a daughter to marry, and in some countries he could force his daughter to wed the man of his choice.

The sexual and reproductive rights of women were seldom discussed in the nineteenth century. Both contraception and abortion were illegal well into the twentieth century, and laws punishing rape worked to a woman's disadvantage. Wherever victims turned for help, be it to physicians or lawyers, they confronted a world controlled by men.

Educational Barriers   Throughout the nineteenth century, women had less access to education than men. Most were given only enough schooling to permit them to do their duties as wives and mothers. Not surprisingly, therefore, there were more illiterate women than men, and the absence of a system of private or public secondary education prevented women from acquiring the qualifications needed to enter universities.

QUICK REVIEW

Divorce
- Difficult to obtain and beyond the means of most women
- French law recognized no grounds for divorce between 1816 and 1884
- German law recognized only adultery or serious mistreatment as grounds
- Until 1857 divorce in England required an act of Parliament

University and professional educations were closed to women until at least the third quarter of the century. The University of Zurich admitted women in the 1860s. Women's colleges were founded at Oxford and Cambridge during the last quarter of the nineteenth century, but women who passed examinations at those universities were not awarded degrees until 1920 (at Oxford) and 1921 (at Cambridge). Women were not admitted to lectures at the Sorbonne in Paris until 1880. Universities and medical schools in the Austrian Empire did not allow women to matriculate until the end of the century, and Prussian universities did not admit women until after 1900. Russian women did not attend universities before 1914, but they could study at other degree-granting institutions. Italian universities were more open to female students and instructors than comparable institutions elsewhere.

Restriction of a woman's access to secondary and university education was justified as a defense of her traditional gender roles and a way to shield her from political radicalism. There was one career, however, that provided an exception to the general assumption that women needed little education. Because elementary teaching was associated with child rearing, it was thought of as a female job. It provided a haven for intellectually inclined women, but the schools that trained women for this work were considered inferior to universities.

A few women did enter the professions (primarily medicine), but most nations refused to allow women to practice law until after World War I. Many of the American women who founded or taught in the first women's colleges in the United States had to go to Europe to acquire their educations. Female pioneers in these fields faced grave social obstacles, personal humiliation, and outright bigotry. They and their male allies called into question an article of middle-class faith, namely, that males and females had distinctly separate spheres of activity. Women were often so acculturated to their roles that they were reluctant to campaign for their own liberation. Many of them feared that their family responsibilities were incompatible with feminism.

NEW EMPLOYMENT PATTERNS FOR WOMEN

The Second Industrial Revolution featured two developments that profoundly affected the economic lives of women. The first was an expansion of the types of employment available apart from the better paying learned professions. The second was a reduction in the number of married women in the work force.

Availability of New Jobs   Opportunities for the kinds of industrial occupations that women had filled in the middle of the nineteenth century (especially in textile and garment making) diminished, but expansion of governmental bureaucracies, large-scale business organizations, and retail stores increased demand for women workers. Government-mandated compulsory education increased the need for elementary schoolteachers, and new inventions, such as typewriters and telephones, created jobs for women. These jobs paid low wages, for they required low-level skills. Society also assumed, despite often knowing better, that women did not need a living wage. They were supposed to be lifelong dependents supported by fathers or husbands. A woman could rarely find an adequately paying job or earn as much as a man for comparable work. Men were paid more, for they were assumed to have primary responsibility for maintaining women and children.

Withdrawal from the Labor Force   Most of the women filling the new service positions were young and unmarried. After marriage, or certainly after the birth of a child, a woman usually withdrew from the labor force. She either did not

---

QUICK REVIEW

Women's Work

- Opportunities in factories diminished
- Expansion of governmental bureaucracies, large-scale business organizations, and retail stores increased demand for women workers
- Compulsory education increased demand for elementary schoolteachers
- New technologies created new jobs for women

Shown are women working in the London Central Telephone Exchange. The invention of the telephone opened new employment opportunities for women.

Image Works/Mary Evans Picture Library Ltd.

work for wages or worked at something that could be done at home. Employers often limited openings to unmarried women who did not have family responsibilities that might interfere with work schedules.

Many changes discouraged married women from working outside their homes. Rising wages for males and shrinking family sizes diminished the need for a wife's second income. Improving health conditions helped more men live longer and reduced the number of widows forced back to work. Working children stayed home longer, and their contributions to the family's wage pool obviated the necessity for their mothers to seek employment outside the home. The cultural dominance of the middle-class lifestyle—which defined the wifely role as full-time homemaker—also created social expectations that eased women out of the workforce. The more prosperous a working-class family became, the less suitable it seemed for its women to be earning money.

WORKING-CLASS WOMEN

The assumption that a woman's proper work pertained to the home degraded the economic situation for women who had to work outside their homes. Because their wages were expected merely to supplement those of their husbands, they were treated as casual workers who could be hired and fired according to the whims of the moment.

POVERTY AND PROSTITUTION

23.5
George Bernard Shaw: Act III from *Mrs. Warren's Profession*

Most nineteenth-century cities had a surplus of working women who had to support themselves. Economic vulnerability and poverty drove many of them into prostitution. Prostitution had always been a way for very poor women to earn money, but in the late nineteenth century it was closely related to the difficulty women had making their way in an overcrowded female labor force. On the Continent, prostitution was often legalized and regulated by male governmental officials. Great Britain preferred to ignore its existence.

Most prostitutes were active on the streets for a very few years, usually from their late teens to about age twenty-five. Thereafter, they moved into the regular work force or married. Very poor women, who were recent immigrants from nearby rural areas, were most likely to become prostitutes. Their trade flourished best in cities with large army garrisons or naval ports or, like London, large transient populations. Fewer prostitutes worked in manufacturing towns where there were more opportunities for steady employment and where community life was more stable.

WOMEN OF THE MIDDLE CLASS

A vast social gap separated working-class women from their middle-class counterparts. Middle-class women served society's increasing preoccupation with domestic comfort as their fathers' and husbands' incomes permitted. Their purchases fed a rapid growth in consumerism in the late nineteenth and early twentieth centuries. They and their numerous domestic servants moved into fashionable houses newly constructed in the rapidly expanding suburbs. They filled their homes with manufactured items—clothing, china, furniture, carpets, drapery, wallpaper, and prints. They enjoyed the improvements that sanitation made in urban life and the new conveniences provided by electrical power.

The Cult of Domesticity   During the first half of the nineteenth century, a middle-class husband expected his spouse to be involved in his business. She often handled his accounts and correspondence and may have had little to do with rearing their children, a task assigned to nurses and governesses. By the end of the century, however, things had changed. Middle-class women, if at all possible, were confined to the roles of wives and mothers and did not work for wages. They enjoyed domestic comfort—even luxury—but at the cost of circumscribed lives, ambitions, and intellects. Their duties reflected society's belief that the home was a man's retreat from the stresses of the marketplace. Scores of women's journals urged wives to make their homes comfortable, peaceful and private oases where their husbands could find refuge from the pressures of the male world.

Marriages were usually arranged and spouses chosen for economic reasons. Romantic attractions were considered a threat to social stability. Middle-class women married young and, because the rearing of children had become their chief task, began to have babies immediately. Women received no training for any roles other than those of dutiful daughter, faithful wife, and nurturing mother. Within the home, however, a middle-class woman had weighty duties. She was in charge of a household that could have a large staff of servants. She oversaw all domestic management and child care. She handled most purchases for her family—which led to much advertising being directed toward women. Her initiative was, however, strictly limited. A woman's conspicuous idleness was important as a symbol of first her father's and then her husband's worldly success.

Religious and Charitable Activities   Churches promoted the cult of domesticity, for it viewed religion as a suitable activity for women. Women were expected to attend public worship frequently, to provide religious instruction for their children, and to see that their families observed domestic religious disciplines and rituals. Women were encouraged to pray daily and internalize the aspects of Christian faith that stressed meekness and passivity.

Middle-class women were also expected to do charitable work, which was thought of as an extension of an innate female gift for nurturing. Middle-class women oversaw clubs for poor youth, societies to protect impoverished young women, and schools for infants. They visited and relieved the poor, for their charity was supposed to inspire the poor to emulate their sterling characters. Such work gave women opportunities to expand their sphere of activity, and by the end of the century, some women were doing social work for private, ecclesiastical, and governmental organizations.

Sexuality and Family Size   Recent studies have called into question older theories about sexual repression in the nineteenth century. Diaries, letters, and early sex surveys suggest that middle-class husbands and wives were not sexually inhibited. Much of the era's anxiety about sexuality stemmed from the risks of childbirth, not disapproval of sex.

A major change in the sexual behavior of married people took place during the second half of the century. The children of the middle class became more expensive to rear as social expectations rose, and many couples wanted to limit the number of their offspring so they could sustain a comfortable standard of living. New contraceptive devices became available, and family sizes declined as their use won acceptance by the middle class.

THE RISE OF POLITICAL FEMINISM

Liberal reforms did not automatically benefit women, particularly in the political arena. Liberal leaders feared that women would be unduly susceptible to the religious influences that conservatives would try to use to manipulate their votes. Conservatives, in contrast, were opposed to the break with tradition that they would have had to make to put this theory to the test.

Obstacles to Achieving Equality Women themselves were often reluctant to support feminist causes or particular feminist organizations. For some, other movements (such as a struggle for national independence) took precedence over the campaign for women's rights. Feminists disagreed about which improvements in women's conditions to pursue first and what kind of tactics to use in pursuing reforms. With the exception of England, it was often difficult for working-class and middle-class women to cooperate. The fact that early feminist statements were often linked with unorthodox opinions about sexuality, family life, and property ownership also made it difficult for feminism to enlist widespread public support. Everywhere in Europe, including Britain, the feminist cause was badly divided over both goals and tactics.

Despite these obstacles, liberal societies and laws provided feminists with some useful intellectual tools. As early as 1792, Mary Wollstonecraft (*A Vindication of the Rights of Woman*) made a case for woman's liberation based on the arguments contemporary revolutionaries used to claim political privileges for men. The work of John Stuart Mill (1806–1873) and his wife and collaborator, Harriet Taylor (1804–1858), came to fruition in 1869 with the publication of *The Subjection of Women*. They critiqued woman's place in European society from the perspective of the liberals' rationales for opposing tyranny. Socialists often (but by no means always) indicted capitalist societies for their treatment of women.

Votes for Women in Britain The most effective of the European women's movements were those of Great Britain. Millicent Fawcett (1847–1929) founded a moderate National Union of Women's Suffrage Societies that, by 1908, could stage rallies numbering up to half a million women. Fawcett's husband was an economist who had served as a Liberal Party cabinet minister, and her tactics were those of English Liberals. She believed Parliament would give women votes when women convinced Parliament they would use their political power responsibly.

Emmeline Pankhurst (1858–1928) advocated a much more radical approach. Her husband, who died near the close of the century, fought for labor and for Irish home rule. Irish nationalists used disruptive tactics to promote their cause, and early labor leaders also had confrontations with police over the right to hold meetings. In 1903, Pankhurst and her daughters, Christabel and Sylvia, founded the Women's Social and Political Union. Derisively dubbed **suffragettes**, they spent years lobbying for votes for women. Having failed to move the government by 1910, they resorted to violent action. They organized marches on

23.2
Women Without Power
Change the System

suffragettes Derisive name for members of the Women's Social and Political Union, who lobbied for votes for women.

Parliament and committed arson, broke windows, and sabotaged postal boxes. The Liberal government of Herbert Asquith imprisoned demonstrators, force-fed those who staged hunger strikes in jail, and steadfastly refused women the franchise. When some British women finally won the vote in 1918, the deciding factor was their country's gratitude for their contributions to its victorious struggle in World War I.

Political Feminism on the Continent   Norwegian women were able to vote on national issues by 1907, but the rest of the Continent lagged far behind them and behind the pace set by Britain's feminists. When Hubertine Auclert (1848–1914) began campaigning for votes for French women in the 1880s, she was virtually alone. Almost all French feminists opposed violence in any form, and they never succeeded in organizing mass rallies. Their leaders believed the vote could be achieved by appeal through legal channels. In 1919, the French Chamber of Deputies passed a bill granting the vote to women, but the French Senate defeated it in 1922. French women were not enfranchised until after World War II.

Political feminism was even more underdeveloped in Germany. German law specifically barred women from taking part in politics, but because no one in the German Empire enjoyed many political rights, German women were not particularly sensitive to their situation. Demands for women's rights were viewed as attempts to subvert the state and society. The Union of German Women's Organizations (BDFK), founded in 1894, was primarily concerned with improving social condition, access to education, and various legal protections for women. By 1902, however, it was calling for women to be granted the vote. The German Social Democratic Party endorsed women's suffrage, but the party was so disdained by the German authorities and Germany's Roman Catholics that the support it offered increased opposition to suffrage proposals. German women received the vote in 1919 in the constitution the Weimar Republic adopted to deal with the consequences of defeat abroad and revolution at home.

JEWISH EMANCIPATION

*U*ntil the late eighteenth century, Europe's Jews generally lived apart from Christians in ghettos or villages, and they were regarded as resident aliens, not citizens. The ideals of the Enlightenment called this into question and inspired some reforms.

DIFFERING DEGREES OF CITIZENSHIP

In 1782, Joseph II put Jews in the Habsburg Empire more or less on the same legal footing as Christians. The National Assembly of France recognized Jews as citizens in 1789, and, during the turmoil of the Napoleonic wars, Jews and Christians mixed as approximate equals in Italy and Germany. Steps toward the political emancipation of Jews, however, were subject to repeal whenever governments changed.

Russia had a tradition of harsh discrimination against Jews that continued until World War I. The Russian government undermined Jewish community life, limited publication of Jewish books, restricted areas where Jews might live, required internal passports for Jews, banned Jews from forms of state service, and excluded Jews from many institutions of higher education. The police and others waged *pogroms* (mob assaults aimed at disrupting Jewish communities). Hundreds of thousands of Jews fled Russia and eastern Europe for western Europe and the United States. As immigrants, they continued to be victims of personal prejudices, but their legal position was more secure.

WHAT WERE the major characteristics of Jewish emancipation?

Department stores, such as Bon Marche in Paris, sold wide selections of consumer goods under one roof. These modern stores increased the economic pressure on small traditional merchants who specialized in selling only one kind of good.

Image Works/Mary Evans Picture Library Ltd.

WHAT LED to the development of European labor politics and socialism?

---

anti-Semitism Prejudice against Jews often displayed through hostility.

BROADENED OPPORTUNITIES

The situation for Jews in western Europe improved following the revolutions of 1848. Germany, Italy, the Low Countries, and Scandinavia granted them full citizenship. In 1858, they won the right to be elected to Great Britain's Parliament, and in 1867, Austria-Hungary granted them full legal rights. Jews entered politics and won high office. Politically, they tended to be liberals or, especially in eastern Europe, socialists.

From 1850 to 1880, there was little overt prejudice against Jews, and many entered professions and occupations previously closed to them. They participated fully in literary and cultural life and became leaders in science and education. The process of their acculturation was encouraged when prohibitions against intermarriages were repealed during the last quarter of the century.

Prejudice against Jews did not disappear, however. Anti-Semites openly accused Jewish bankers and financial interests of causing the economic stagnation of the 1870s, and in the 1880s, organized **anti-Semitism** erupted in Germany and France. This motivated some Jewish leaders, the Zionists, to call for the establishment of an independent Jewish nation, but most Jews believed the revival of old prejudices would be temporary and the liberal legal protections they had acquired over the course of the century would protect them. The events of the 1930s and 1940s proved them disastrously wrong.

LABOR, SOCIALISM, AND POLITICS TO WORLD WAR I

*I*ndustrial expansion during the late nineteenth century increased the size and changed the nature of the urban proletariat. For the first time, factory wage earners began to outnumber artisans and highly skilled workers. Europe's laborers had always had to look to themselves to improve their lot, and after the failed revolutions of 1848, they changed their strategy. They stopped rioting in the streets and trying to revive paternalistic guild systems, and they embraced new institutions and ideologies—trade unions, democratic political parties, and socialism.

TRADE UNIONISM

Trade unionism flourished during the second half of the century as governments began to recognize the right of workers to organize. Unions were legalized in Great Britain in 1871 and allowed to picket in 1875. As Napoleon III's power waned, weak labor associations formed, and France's Third Republic legalized unions in 1884. Resistance to unionization in Germany faded after 1890. At midcentury, unions focused primarily on organizing skilled workers, but by the close of the century, unskilled industrial workers were also being unionized. They created large unions numbering thousands of members that met intense opposition from employers, and the majority of workers in Europe was still not organized as World War I approached.

DEMOCRACY AND POLITICAL PARTIES

With the exception of Russia, all the major European states had established broad-based, if not democratic, electoral systems by the late nineteenth century. Great Britain passed its second voting reform act in 1867 and its third in 1884.

Bismarck decreed universal male suffrage for the German Empire in 1871. The French Chamber of Deputies was democratically elected. Universal male suffrage was adopted in Switzerland in 1879, in Spain in 1890, in Belgium in 1893, in the Netherlands in 1896, in Norway in 1898, and in Italy in 1912.

The broadened franchise fundamentally changed politics, for politicians could no longer ignore workers and workers no longer had to go outside institutions of government to seek redress of their grievances. Instead of staging riots to pressure the authorities, workers could hold them accountable at the ballot box. The narrow electorate that formerly dominated governments consisted of people of property who knew what they had at stake in politics. They were a fairly cohesive group that did not require much party organization. The expansion of the electorate, however, brought many voters into the political process whose level of political awareness and interest was low. The modern political party was created to mobilize this new electoral force.

The democratization of politics and the increasing political awareness of workers promised to help socialists challenge the traditional ruling classes. Socialists parties, however, divided over the issue of whether democratic processes or revolutions were needed to improve the lot of the working class.

MARX AND THE FIRST INTERNATIONAL

In 1864, a group of British and French trade unionists founded the International Working Men's Association (or simply the First International). It encompassed a vast array of radical political types. Although Karl Marx believed the capitalist system was too powerful to be peacefully reformed, his inaugural address to the International approved efforts by labor to work with existing political and economic processes. His private doubts about prospects for reform were not made public until after his death.

The violence associated with the doomed Paris Commune of 1871, which Marx had praised as a genuine proletarian movement, cast a pall over socialism. France suppressed socialist activities, and British trade unionists, who received legal protections in 1871, wanted to avoid being associated with supporters of the Commune. Faced with declining interest, the First International held its last European congress in 1873, and it dissolved in 1876. Although it was short lived, the First International had a major impact on the future of European socialism. Throughout the late 1860s, it gathered statistics, kept labor groups informed of mutual problems, provided a forum for the debate of socialist doctrine, made extravagant claims for its own influence on contemporary events, and helped Marxism triumph over other brands of socialism. The apparently scientific character of Marxism made it attractive to an age that was enthralled with scientific progress.

GREAT BRITAIN: FABIANISM AND EARLY WELFARE PROGRAMS

Neither Marxism nor any other form of socialism made much progress in Great Britain, the most advanced industrial society of the day. British trade unions usually supported Liberal Party candidates. In 1892, Keir Hardie became the first independent working man to be elected to Parliament, but the socialist Independent Labour Party, founded a year later, attracted little support.

Labor took little part in politics until the House of Lords removed the legal protection accorded union funds (the Taff Vale decision) in 1901. The Trades Union Congress responded by launching the Labour Party, and in the election of 1906 the new party sent twenty-nine members to Parliament. British trade

Because many major financial institutions of nineteenth-century Europe were owned by wealthy Jewish families, anti-Semitic political figures often blamed them for economic hard times. The most famous such family was the Rothschilds, who controlled banks in several countries. The head of the London branch was Lionel Rothschild (1808–1879). He was elected to Parliament several times, but was not seated because he would not take the required Christian oath. After the requirement of that oath was abolished in 1858, he sat in Parliament from 1858 to 1874.

Getty Images Inc.–Hulton Archive Photos

21.5
Karl Marx and
Friedrich Engles: *The
Communist Manifesto*

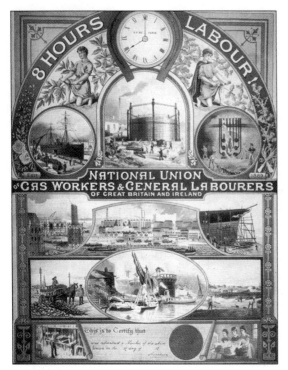

Trade unions continued to grow in late-century Great Britain. The effort to curb the unions eventually led to the formation of the Labour Party. The British unions often had quite elaborate membership certificates, such as this one for the National Union of Gas Workers and General Labourers of Great Britain and Ireland.

The Granger Collection

unionists were not yet socialists, but they were becoming more militant. In the years leading up to the war, there were scores of strikes which the government was forced to mediate.

British socialism was primarily the preserve of non-Marxist intellectuals. Britain's most influential socialist organization was the Fabian Society. Founded in 1884, it took its name from Quintus Fabius Maximus, a Roman general famous for defending Rome by refusing to confront Hannibal in the Second Punic War. The name indicated the society's gradualist approach to social reform. Its leading members, Sidney (1859–1947) and Beatrice (1858–1943) Webb, H. G. Wells (1866–1946), Graham Wallas (1858–1932), and George Bernard Shaw (1856–1950), hoped to convince Britain of the rational wisdom of socialism. They believed collective ownership could solve the problems of industry and that the expansion of state ownership and control of production facilities could be achieved gradually, peacefully, and democratically.

The British government and the major political parties responded slowly to pressures from labor. In 1903, Joseph Chamberlain (1836–1914) split the Conservative Party by proposing to raise tariffs on imports to finance social reforms. After 1906, the Liberal Party, led by Sir Henry Campbell-Bannerman (1836–1908) and after 1908 by Herbert Asquith (1852–1928), pursued a two-pronged policy. Fearful of losing seats in Parliament to the new Labour Party, it restored protections for unions. Then, beginning in 1909 and guided by Chancellor of the Exchequer David Lloyd George (1863–1945), a Liberal ministry enacted a broad program of social legislation. This included establishment of labor exchanges, regulation of sweatshop trades (tailoring and lace making), and the National Insurance Act (1911), which provided unemployment benefits and health care.

Proposals to finance these programs created conflict between the House of Commons and the Conservative-dominated House of Lords. In 1911, the Parliament Act gave the Commons the power to override the legislative veto of the upper chamber, but passage of taxes to support social programs (which were not yet enough to content labor) meant that Britain, the birthplace of nineteenth-century liberal laissez-faire ideology, was expanding the state's role in the lives of its citizens.

FRANCE: "OPPORTUNISM" REJECTED

At the turn of the century, Jean Jaurès (1859–1914) and Jules Guesde (1845–1922) led opposing factions of French socialists. Guesde repudiated Jaurès's group for attempting to work with France's governing ministries. He insisted that socialists could not cooperate with a bourgeois government they were dedicated to overthrowing. The Dreyfus affair brought the socialists' quarrel to a head when, in 1899, Prime Minister René Waldeck-Rousseau (1846–1904) tried to unite Dreyfus's supporters by persuading a socialist, Alexander Millerand (1859–1943), to accept a post in the French cabinet.

Millerand's cooperation with the government was part of a political strategy that socialists termed *opportunism*. In 1904, the Amsterdam Congress of the Second International, which had been founded in 1889 to coordinate various national socialist parties and trade unions, condemned opportunism and ordered France's socialists to form a single party. Jaurès acquiesced, and by 1914, the Socialist Party held the largest bloc of seats in the Chamber of Deputies. Socialists

HISTORY'S VOICES

PARIS DEPARTMENT STORES EXPAND THEIR BUSINESS

*T*he department store became a major retailing institution in the late nineteenth century and was one of the reasons for expanded consumer demand. E. Levasseur's 1907 description follows the growth of such stores in Paris and explains why they exerted such economic power. Note how many of their sales techniques stores still use today.

WHAT KINDS of people might have benefited from the jobs available in these stores? Why might these stores have hurt small retailers?

It was in the reign of Louis Philippe (r. 1830–1848) that department stores for fashion goods and dresses . . . began to be distinguished. The type was already one of other notable developments of the Second Empire; it became one of the most important ones of the Third Republic. These stores have increased in number and several of them have become extremely large. Combining in their different departments all articles of clothing, toilet articles, furniture and many other ranges of goods, it is their special object so to combine all commodities as to attract and satisfy customers who will find conveniently together an assortment of a mass of articles corresponding to all their various needs. They attract customers by permanent display, by free entry into the shops, by periodic exhibitions, by special sales, by fixed prices, and by their ability to deliver the goods purchased to customers' homes, in Paris and to the provinces. Turning themselves into direct intermediaries between the producer and the customer, even producing sometimes some of their articles in their own workshops, buying at lowest prices because of their large orders and because they are in a position to profit from bargains, working with large sums, and selling to most of their customers for cash only, they can transmit these benefits in lowered selling prices. They can even decide to sell at a loss, as an advertisement or to get rid of out-of-date fashions.

The success of these department stores is only possible thanks to the volume of their business, and this volume needs considerable capital and a very large turnover. Now capital, having become abundant, is freely combined nowadays in large enterprises. . . . [T]he large urban agglomerations, the ease with which goods can be transported by the railways, the diffusion of some comforts to strata below the middle classes, have all favoured these developments. . . .

According to the tax records of 1891, these stores in Paris, numbering 12, employed 1,708 persons and rated their site values at 2,159,000 francs; the largest had then 542 employees. These same stores had, in 1901, 9,784 employees; one of them over 2,000 and another over 1,600; their site value was doubled.

Sidney Pollard and Colin Holmes, *Documents of European Economic History*, Vol. 3 (London: Edward Arnold, 1972), pp. 95–96.

did not, however, serve in a French cabinet until appointed by the Popular Front Government in 1936.

French workers tended to vote socialist, but their unions, unlike those in Great Britain, avoided direct political action. The Confédération Générale du Travail, founded in 1895, saw itself as an alternative to socialist parties. Its leaders embraced the doctrines of syndicalism that Georges Sorel (1847–1922) expounded in *Reflections on Violence* (1908). They believed workers should use the general strike, not the political process, to push for reform, and their strikes often conflicted with efforts by the socialists to use the machinery of the state on behalf of workers. Strikes, some of which the government violently suppressed, were common between 1905 and 1914.

GERMANY: SOCIAL DEMOCRATS AND REVISIONISM

The Marxist-dominated German Social Democratic Party, or SPD, was consistently hostile to all nonsocialist governments. The SPD emerged in 1875 in response to the work of Ferdinand Lasalle (1825–1864), a labor agitator who wanted to win a role for the working class in German politics. Because Marxists who opposed reformist politics—particularly Wilhelm Liebknecht (1826–1900) and August Bebel (1840–1913)—helped organize the party, it was, from the start, divided between those who advocated reform and those who trusted only in revolution.

Bismarck's Repression of the SPD　Bismarck, the "Iron Chancellor," opposed socialism. No socialists were involved in an 1878 assassination attempt on William I, but Bismarck used the event to steer laws through the *Reichstag* that suppressed the activities of the SPD. His legislation proved politically counterproductive, however. From the early 1880s onward, the SPD steadily polled increasing numbers of votes in elections to the *Reichstag*.

When repressive laws failed to wean German workers away from socialism, Bismarck resorted to social welfare legislation that provided a paternalistic, conservative alternative to socialism. In 1883, the German Empire instituted health insurance. A year later, it created accident insurance. In 1889, Bismarck sponsored a plan for old-age and disability pensions. These programs were funded by contributions from both workers and employers, and as a state-run system of social security, they did not pose any threat to ownership of property or established political leadership. Germany was the first major industrial nation to create this kind of welfare program.

The Erfurt Program　After Bismarck's forced resignation, Emperor William II (r. 1888–1918) tried to win support from the working class by allowing the antisocialist legislation to expire. The lifting of the repressive laws, which had at any rate never prevented members of the SPD from sitting in the *Reichstag*, forced the party to ponder what attitude it ought to take toward the German Empire.

The SPD's stand, the Erfurt Program of 1891, was formulated by Bebel and by Karl Kautsky (1854–1938). In good Marxist fashion, the party declared its faith in the imminent doom of capitalism and the necessity of socialist ownership of the means of production, but it pledged to pursue these goals through legal political participation, not revolution. Theoretically the SPD was opposed to the German Empire, but in practice it worked with it.

The SPD's dilemma prompted significant rethinking of the orthodox Marxist critique of capitalism in prominent socialist circles. Eduard Bernstein (1850–1932), a socialist thinker who had been exposed to Fabianism in Great Britain, questioned Marx's confident assumption that the inadequacies of capitalism made revolution inevitable. In *Evolutionary Socialism* (1899), Bernstein pointed to recent developments that did not support orthodox Marxist predictions—primarily, a rising standard of living in Europe and sales of stocks that broadened ownership of capitalist industry. These factors increased the size of the middle class instead of forcing it, as Marx had predicted, into the ranks of the proletariat. Moreover, the extension of the franchise to the working class meant that revolution might not be necessary to achieve social change.

The Debate over Revisionism　German socialists generally condemned Bernstein's doctrines (which were dubbed "revisionism"), but the SPD pursued a course of action consistent with Bernstein's views. Trade union members were prospering and did not want revolution, and SPD leaders did not want to provoke the kind of persecution they had experienced under Bismarck. Subsequently, by working for electoral gains, membership expansion, and short-term reform, the SPD succeeded in becoming one of the most important political organizations in imperial Germany.

RUSSIA: INDUSTRIAL DEVELOPMENT AND THE BIRTH OF BOLSHEVISM

During the last decade of the nineteenth century, Russia entered the industrial age and encountered many of the problems that more advanced nations had experienced fifty or seventy-five years earlier. Alexander III (r. 1881–1894) and his successor, Nicholas II (r. 1894–1917), believed Russia had to industrialize if it hoped to maintain its international influence. Sergei Witte (1849–1915), a finance minister appointed in 1892, was given the job of overseeing the process. He was the epitome of the nineteenth-century modernizer. He favored planned economic development, protective tariffs, high taxes, the gold standard, efficient management, and the development of heavy industries.

In this photograph taken in 1895, Lenin sits at the table among a group of other young Russian radicals from Saint Petersburg.

CORBIS/Bettmann

In Russia, as elsewhere, industrialism created considerable social discontent. Landowners resented the profits foreign investors took out of the country. Peasants objected to being taxed to fund industrial development that did not improve their lives, and a small but significant industrial proletariat protested abysmal working conditions.

Emancipation of the serfs in 1861 failed to improve agricultural productivity in Russia. Redemption payments, excessive taxes, and falling grain prices hobbled peasant farmers. Many held land communally as a *mir* (village) and farmed it inefficiently. Many had too little land to support themselves and had to work for the nobility or the *kulaks* (prosperous peasant farmers). To make matters worse, Russia's population increased from 50 million to 103 million between 1860 and 1914.

Social discontent fueled formation of new political parties. The Social Revolutionary Party, founded in 1901, adopted the Populists' agenda of the 1870s. It opposed industrialization and advocated an idealized version of the communal life of the Russian peasantry. In 1903, the liberal/Constitutional Democratic Party (the Cadets) was formed to work for the establishment of a new regime that governed through ministries, guaranteed civil liberties, and promoted progressive economic policies—all under the supervision of a parliament. A socialist Social Democratic Party appeared in 1898, but its leaders were soon driven into exile.

Lenin's Early Thought and Career   Russia had a small working class and no representative institutions. Its socialists, therefore, unlike socialists elsewhere, despaired of working through established political channels. Revolution seemed their only option, and this inclined them to a brand of Marxism developed by two exiles: Gregory Plekhanov (1857–1918) and his disciple Vladimir Illich Ulyanov (1870–1924), or Lenin.

Lenin's father was a high-ranking bureaucrat whose elder son was executed in 1887 for plotting against Alexander III. In 1893, Lenin, while studying in Saint Petersburg, became involved with revolutionary factory workers. He was arrested in 1895 and sent to Siberia. In 1900, he left Russia and spent most of the next

On Bloody Sunday, January 22, 1905, troops of Tsar Nicholas II fired on a peaceful procession of workers who sought to present a petition for better working and living conditions at the Winter Palace in St. Petersburg. This event all but destroyed any chance of reconciliation between the tsarist government and the Russian working class.

Bildarchiv Preussischer Kulturbesitz

Bolsheviks ("majority") Lenin's turn-of-the-century Russian faction favoring a party of elite professionals who would provide the working class with centralized leadership.

Mensheviks ("minority") Turn-of-the-century Russian faction that wanted to create a party with a large mass membership (like Germany's SPD).

seventeen years in Switzerland in the company of exiled Russian Social Democrats.

Unlike the backward-looking Social Revolutionaries, the Social Democrats were Marxists and modernizers. They favored industrial development and believed Russia needed a large proletariat to spark its revolution. Like other socialist groups, they split over the issue of whether to reform the system or overthrow it. Lenin, in *What Is to Be Done?* (1902), condemned any accommodation resembling the practice of the German SPD. He maintained that the working class would not spontaneously develop revolutionary consciousness. Only a small, tightly organized, elite party could sustain adequate revolutionary fervor and resist penetration by police spies. He rejected Kautsky's claim that revolution was inevitable and Bernstein's faith that it would arrive democratically. For Lenin, the social transformation Marx predicted would be the work of a small number of professional revolutionaries, not the proletariat.

In 1903, at its London Congress, the Russian Social Democratic Party split. Lenin emerged the leader of a very slim majority of its members, a faction calling itself the **Bolsheviks** ("majority") in opposition to the more moderate **Mensheviks** ("minority"). The Mensheviks wanted to create a party with a large mass membership (like Germany's SPD), but the Bolsheviks believed parties of this kind were insufficiently radical. They favored a party of elite professionals who would provide the working class with centralized leadership. In 1912, the Bolsheviks established their own organization.

In 1905, Lenin published a plan for initiating revolution in Russia: *Two Tactics of Social Democracy in the Bourgeois-Democratic Revolution.* He fully grasped the profound discontent in the Russian countryside and proposed to overthrow the tsarist regime with an alliance between workers and peasants. In November 1917, his Bolsheviks seized power, but only after others had toppled the government.

The Revolution of 1905 and Its Aftermath   Industrialization, not Lenin, was the source of Tsar Nicholas II's problems. In 1903, he dismissed Witte from office. In 1904, he declared war on Japan, hoping to generate a wave of patriotism. Instead, Russia was defeated, and a political crisis ensued. On "Bloody Sunday" (January 22, 1905), the tsar's troops fired into a crowd of workers in Saint Petersburg who were trying to present a petition to the tsar asking him to improve industrial conditions. The incident marked the point at which vast numbers of ordinary Russians decided they could no longer trust the tsar and his government, and it sparked revolutionary disturbances throughout Russia. Sailors mutinied, peasants rebelled, students staged strikes, the tsar's uncle was assassinated, the liberal Constitutional Democratic Party demanded political reform, and Social Revolutionaries and Social Democrats stirred up urban workers. Early in October 1905, strikes broke out in Saint Petersburg, and groups of workers called *soviets* took control of the city.

Nicholas tried to calm things by issuing the October Manifesto, a pledge to institute constitutional government. Early in 1906, he announced elections for a bicameral representative body, the Duma, but he retained control over ministerial appointments, financial policy, the military, and foreign affairs. When the April elections returned a very radical assembly, the tsar chose a new adviser, P. A. Stolypin (1862–1911). Four months later, Stolypin persuaded him to dissolve the Duma, and a new assembly, which was elected in February 1907, lasted only into June. The government finally won the election of the kind of pliable assembly it wanted in late 1907 by limiting the franchise. With the seating of this third Duma, Nicholas II appeared to have recaptured much of the ground he had conceded, and Stolypin set about repressing rebellion and rallying support from property owners. In November 1906, the government canceled payments for land that peasants still owed under the terms of the Emancipation Act of 1861, and it urged peasants to abandon the communal *mirs* and farm individual holdings. This action, combined with a program offering instruction in farming methods, helped stimulate agricultural production. Moderates approved of the land measures, and many people were eager to compromise with the government to avoid further revolutionary disturbances.

The unpopular Stolypin was assassinated in 1911, and Nicholas failed to find a competent adviser to replace him. The situation at court was complicated by the increasing influence of Grigory Efimovich Rasputin (c. 1871–1916), a strange, uncouth monk who claimed to be able to heal the tsar's hemophilic heir. As social malcontents demanded and conservatives rejected further liberal reforms, the situation deteriorated, and the tsar again began to hope that a bold move on the diplomatic front might rally the popular support he so desperately needed. World War I was about to begin.

SUMMARY

Population Trends and Migration Europeans made up approximately 20 percent of the world's population around 1900, more than they have at any time before or since. Soon thereafter, birth and death rates stabilized or declined in developed regions, but continued to increase elsewhere. In the second half of the nineteenth century, Europeans emigrated in huge numbers. Many went to the Americas, Australia, and South Africa. At midcentury, most of them came from Great Britain, Germany, and Scandinavia; after 1885, more came from southern and eastern Europe.

The Second Industrial Revolution The Second Industrial Revolution was dominated by Germany. At the turn of the century, the emergence of an industrial Germany was the most significant aspect of political and economic life in Europe. The steel industry produced over 32 million tons of steel by 1913. The chemical industry depended on scientific research, and Germany was the first country to attempt to facilitate the flow of information between research and industry. Electrical energy was widely applied, and the automobile had been invented. Economic advances slowed in the final quarter of the century, although the standard of living in most industrial nations continued to grow slowly. Unemployment and poverty contributed to the appeal of trade unions and socialist political parties. Consumer goods were an important aspect of the urban lifestyle.

The Middle Classes in Ascendancy The middle classes set the values and goals for most of society between the middle of the nineteenth century and World War I. In reaction to the 1848 revolutions, the middle classes put aside revolution in favor of preserving their status and possessions. The middle classes diversified: A few families gained wealth exceeding that of the aristocracy; small entrepreneurs and professionals earned enough to purchase private homes, education for their children, and vacations; secretaries, retail workers, and low-level bureaucrats made up the white-collar workers (the petite bourgeoisie), who were close to the working class but deliberately adopted middle-class behaviors and consumption patterns. Tensions existed among these middle-class groups.

IMAGE KEY

for pages 562–563

a. Sir George Clausen (RA) (1852-1944) "Schoolgirls, Haverstock Hill," signed and dated 1880, oil on canvas, 20 1/2 x 30 3/8 in. (52 x 77.2 cm), Yale Center for British Art/Paul Mellon Collection, USA/Bridgeman Art Library (B1985.10.1). Courtesy of the Estate of Sir George Clausen

b. Wooden high bike

c. Oxford Street, London, England

d. Construction of Eiffel Tower

e. Old-fashioned telephone

f. Pierre Auguste Renoir (1841–1919). La Loge. Courtauld Institute Galleries, London, Great Britain. Scala/Art Resource, New York

g. Women working at a telephone exchange

h. Poster denouncing the absurdity of denying the vote to women

i. Italian immigrant family at Ellis Island, New York, 1905

j. British union membership certificate, 1889

Late Nineteenth-Century Urban Life Urbanization increased in the late nineteenth century. Between 1850 and 1910, the population of many major European cities doubled or tripled. There were social, political, economic, environmental, and health consequences of this growth. Governments led the redesign of the central portions of many cities. Parisian streets were widened, for aesthetic and practical reasons. Public works projects created many jobs. Displaced city dwellers often moved to suburbs. Health and housing for the poor came to be seen as prerequisites for safety and security for the middle classes. The cholera epidemics of the early nineteenth century led to concerns in public health and sanitation. Governments gained new powers to intervene in citizens' lives in the name of public health. Working-class housing conditions also became a subject of medical, moral, and political concern to middle-class reformers and bureaucrats. Philanthropies, businesses, and government offered economic incentives to build housing for the poor, trying to create working-class homes and facilitate middle-class family life.

Varieties of Late Nineteenth-Century Women's Experiences Like men, women's experiences reflected their class. But women of all ranks faced disabilities in property rights, family law, and education. The degree of disability diminished in the late nineteenth century. Men controlled their wives' property in Europe until late in the century. Family law often required a woman's obedience to her husband; sexual double standards prevailed; divorce was difficult; and contraception and abortion were illegal. Women's education was minimal and inferior. Teaching was one of the few career paths open to women. The Second Industrial Revolution opened more jobs to women, but the jobs were often low skilled and almost inevitably low paying. Working-class women often labored in sweatshops that lacked job security; some became prostitutes. Middle-class women were usually wives and mothers and discouraged from employment. The "cult of domesticity" made women and their roles within the home a symbol of the success of their father or husband. Women in Britain ("suffragettes"), France, Germany, and elsewhere lobbied for the right to vote, but nowhere did they gain it until after the turn of the century.

Jewish Emancipation Political liberalism facilitated the emancipation of European Jews, to varying degrees and at various speeds in different nations. In the late eighteenth century and the first half of the nineteenth century, Jews gained rights approximating those of other citizens in most western European states. In Russia, traditional discrimination persisted. After the revolutions of 1848, the situation for most European Jews improved, with further political and citizenship rights being granted to Jews in most of western Europe. Even Jews in Austria-Hungary gained full legal rights in 1867. Institutionalized prejudice seemed to have dissipated in western Europe, although certainly not in Russia and only sporadically in eastern Europe. Anti-Semitism grew in the 1870s and 1880s, though, largely as a by-product of economic stagnation. Jewish leaders had faith in liberal government structures to protect their rights.

Labor, Socialism, and Politics to World War I With industrial expansion, the size of the urban proletariat grew. New institutions and ideologies had replaced riots as the way by which workers expressed their will. Unions grew in the second half of the century, but most workers were still not unionized. Broader-based political systems everywhere except Russia brought with them organized mass political parties. Socialist parties divided on whether change would come through reform or revolution. Marx publicly endorsed reform. In Great Britain, trade unionism was allied with the Liberal Party and then the Labour Party. The Fabian Society was Britain's most significant socialist group, and it was gradualist and non-Marxist. In France, socialist parties quarreled among themselves; labor unions favored strikes over political participation. The German Social Democratic Party kept Marxist socialism alive through the turn of the century. In Russia, socialism was almost by definition revolutionary. In 1903, Lenin forced a split in the Russian Social Democratic Party over whether the party should strive for mass membership (the "Menshevik" position) or be limited to elite professional revolutionaries (Lenin's "Bolshevik" position). In 1905, Lenin wrote that the proletariat and the peasantry should unite in revolution in Russia. His formula would prove successful in 1917. Meanwhile, the Bloody Sunday massacre of January 1905 led to upheaval. By October 1905, worker groups called soviets controlled Saint Petersburg, and tsar Nicholas II promised constitutional government. By 1907, however, Nicholas II had dissolved two sessions of the Duma, the new representative legislature, and had taken back most of his powers.

REVIEW QUESTIONS

1. How was European society transformed by the Second Industrial Revolution? What were living conditions like in European cities during the late nineteenth century? Why were European cities redesigned during this period? How were they redesigned?

2. What was the status of European women in the second half of the nineteenth century? Why did they grow discontented with their lot? What tactics did they use in effecting change? What forms did the emancipation of Jews take in the nineteenth century?

3. What was the status of the proletariat in 1860? Had it improved by 1914? What caused the growth in trade unions and organized mass political parties? What were the differences among socialist parties?

4. How important was industrialism in Russia? Were the tsars wise to attempt to modernize their country? How did Lenin's view of socialism differ from that of the socialists in western Europe?

KEY TERMS

anti-Semitism   (p. 578)
Bolsheviks   (p. 584)
Mensheviks   (p. 584)

petite bourgeoisie   (p. 568)
Second Industrial Revolution   (p. 564)

suffragettes   (p. 576)

 For additional study resources for this chapter, go to:
www.prenhall.com/kagan3/chapter23

Visualizing The Past...

Industrialization

HOW DID the advent of industrialization in the nineteenth and early twentieth centuries shape the art of countries that industrialized? Did artists view industrialization as a negative or a positive force?

The industrial revolution began in Britain in the eighteenth century. By the mid–nineteenth century, factories, coal-fired machines, and railroads had spread throughout western Europe, and also the eastern portion of the United States. By the later nineteenth century, industrialization and railroad building advanced in the United States, and also in Japan, which had become the most industrialized non-Western power in the world by the 1930s. Industry was understood to be about power, not only the power machines generated and artists celebrated, but also the power of political and military domination.

Power loom weaving of cotton cloth in a textile mill; colored engraving, 1834. Industrialization began in the cloth industry because cloth was the most important manufactured product in the world from ancient times to the dawn of the modern era. Early factory owners often employed women, whose labor came cheaper than that of men. Factory women worked long hours and were subject to close supervision designed to ensure their morals would not suffer in the factory setting.
The Granger Collection ▼

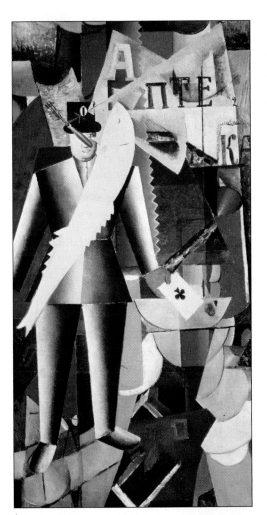

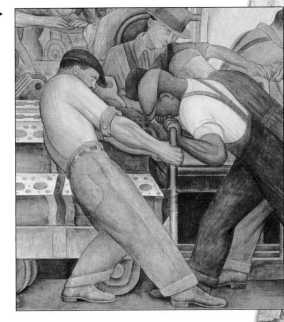

Diego Rivera, *Detroit Industry*, 1933. As industrialization spread from the cloth industry to all forms of manufacture, it became an increasingly masculine enterprise, both because it became a mainstay of male employment in the West but also because its association with power and war meant it was imagined as largely masculine. In this image we see strong, upright American men at work manufacturing the premier symbol of American industry: the automobile.

Diego Rivera (1886–1957). "Detroit Industry". North Wall, 1933. © 2003 Banco de Mexico Diego Rivera & Frida Kahlo Museums Trust. Av. Cinco de Mayo No. 2, Col. Centro, Del. Cuauhtemoc 06059. Mexico, D.F. Reproduction authorized by the Instituto Nacional de Bellas Artes y Literatura. Photograph © 2001 The Detroit Institute of Arts

Kazimir Malevich, *The Aviator*, 1914. Technology seemed to those who experienced industrialization to speed life up to a dizzying rate. Although some found the new emphasis on speed and motion that accompanied industry disorienting, many in the early twentieth century celebrated it, and none more than the futurists. Futurism began in Italy, where it is closely associated with the rise of fascism, which also celebrated speed and power. Cubo-futurism, which this image illustrated, was a Russian creation, product of the advent of industrialization in Russia, and influenced by both cubism and the new photographic techniques emerging in this period.

Malevich, Kazimir (1878–1935). *The Aviator*, 1914. Oil on canvas, 125 × 65 cm. © Scala/Art Resource, NY

George Grosz, *Untitled*, 1920. Artists did not always celebrate industrialization, and especially after World War I, when Europeans became painfully aware of the terrible uses to which industrial technology could be put, images of industry and modern urban society often became more disparaging. Many of the works of George Grosz, an expressionist painter, were harshly critical of the modern, bourgeois industrialized world. Here we see an individual in an urban setting, devoid of identity and no more human than the surrounding industry.

George Grosz (1893–1959). Untitled, 1920. ©Estate of George Grosz/Licensed by VAGA, NY. Photograph © Erich Lessing/Art Resource NY

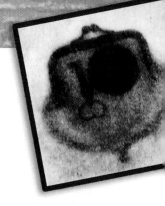

24

The Birth of Modern European Thought

CHAPTER HIGHLIGHTS

The New Reading Public Government funding of public education began in the late 1860s. By 1900, literacy rates in northern Europe had reached 85 percent. The amount of reading material available expanded to meet the demand of the new mass reading public.

Science at Midcentury During the first half of the nineteenth century, science gained ground as the model for all human knowledge. Comte's positivism helped establish the belief that all knowledge should be of the kind common to the natural sciences. Darwin's theory of evolution was misapplied to human ethics by social Darwinists.

Christianity and the Church under Siege The nineteenth century was a challenging period for organized religion. Many intellectuals left the faith and nation-states with liberal governments curtailed the church's influence. A larger and more mobile population put pressure on traditional ecclesiastical organizations. Nonetheless, churches were able to find new followers among the masses.

Toward a Twentieth-Century Frame of Mind New concepts challenged the presuppositions of mid nineteenth-century science, rationalism, liberalism, and bourgeois morality. Scientists, writers, and philosophers all contributed to the development of modernism. Nietzsche and Freud challenged the primacy of reason in human behavior. Late nineteenth-century racists claimed to have discovered a scientific foundation for their beliefs. Resurgent anti-Semitism led to the birth of Zionism.

Women and Modern Thought Women's social roles remained largely unchanged and the scientific community, as a whole, continued to hold a conservative and hostile view of women. Feminist groups worked to gain voting rights for women and to question traditional notions of sexual morality and the family.

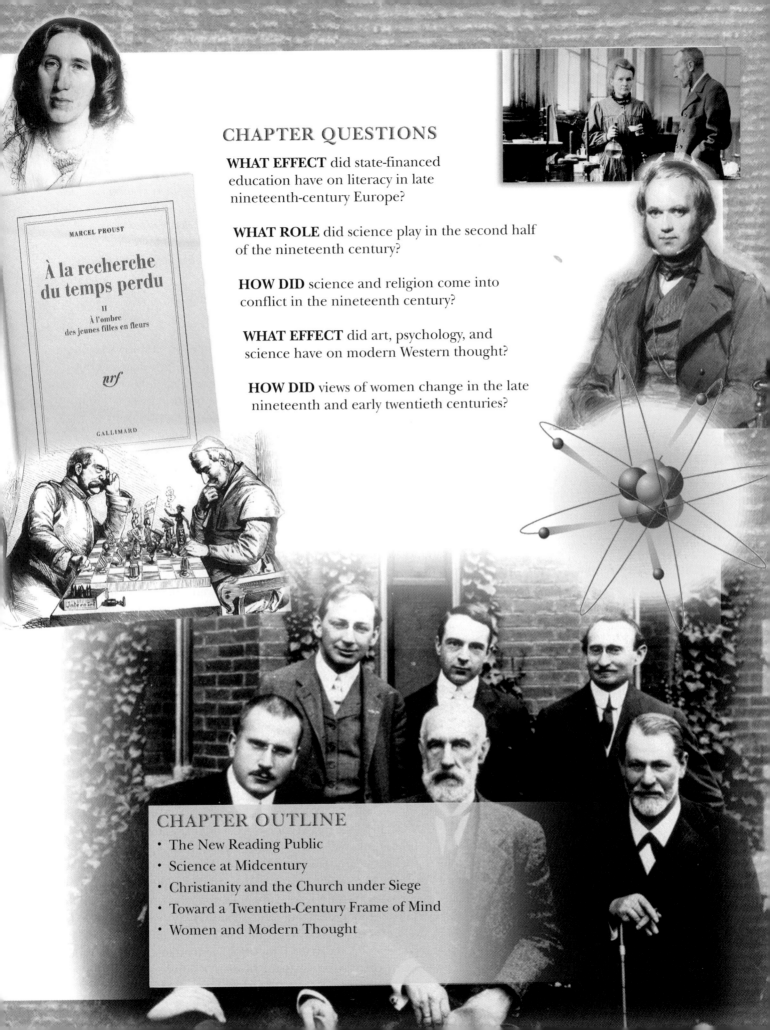

CHAPTER QUESTIONS

WHAT EFFECT did state-financed education have on literacy in late nineteenth-century Europe?

WHAT ROLE did science play in the second half of the nineteenth century?

HOW DID science and religion come into conflict in the nineteenth century?

WHAT EFFECT did art, psychology, and science have on modern Western thought?

HOW DID views of women change in the late nineteenth and early twentieth centuries?

MARCEL PROUST

À la recherche du temps perdu

II
À l'ombre
des jeunes filles en fleurs

nrf

GALLIMARD

CHAPTER OUTLINE

- The New Reading Public
- Science at Midcentury
- Christianity and the Church under Siege
- Toward a Twentieth-Century Frame of Mind
- Women and Modern Thought

IMAGE KEY

Image Key for pages 590–591 is on page 612.

The political systems, industrialized economies, and middle-class lifestyles that emerged in the late nineteenth century were accompanied by intellectual developments that shaped a "modern" mind. The new intellectual orientation was rooted in the Enlightenment (which contributed confidence in reason and science and a tolerant, cosmopolitan outlook) and the romantic movement (which fostered respect for feeling, imagination, artistic insight, and the value of individuals). Most of the West's traditional assumptions about nature, religion, and social life were subjected to radical reexamination. As a result, at the turn of the century European intellectuals were more daring than ever before but less certain about where their work might lead. Fading confidence in the reliability of traditional points of view helped some disadvantaged groups, such as women, win liberating social reforms.

WHAT EFFECT did state-financed education have on literacy in late nineteenth-century Europe?

THE NEW READING PUBLIC

ADVANCES IN PRIMARY EDUCATION

Fifty percent of Europeans were illiterate in 1850, and many of those who could read and write did so poorly. State-financed education changed that, and during the next half century Europe developed its first mass reading public.

In 1868, Hungary led the way in promoting literacy by providing public elementary education. Britain did so in 1870, Switzerland in 1874, Italy in 1877, and France between 1878 and 1881. Prussia's superior educational system was extended in various ways throughout the German Empire after 1871. By 1900, the literacy rate in Britain, France, Belgium, the Netherlands, Germany, and Scandinavia was 85 percent. Italy, Spain, Russia, Austria-Hungary, and the Balkans achieved rates of 30 to 60 percent.

The educational crusade embodied the Enlightenment rationalist faith that right knowledge leads to right action. Both liberals and conservatives believed literacy would enable newly enfranchised voters to use political power responsibly and help the poor to help themselves by making them a more productive labor force. It was certainly the case that once the masses were given a taste of education and realized its benefits, demands for schooling increased. Having already established primary schools, the major nations began to provide secondary education during the World War I era. A generation later, broader access to university instruction was under development.

READING MATERIAL FOR THE MASS AUDIENCE

Advances in technology lowered publication costs just as the expanding literate population developed an appetite for new kinds of reading materials. The number of monthly and quarterly journals designed for particular groups of subscribers increased. Cheap mass-circulation newspapers, such as *Le Petit Journal* of Paris and the *Daily Mail* and *Daily Express* of London, flourished.

Many of the new readers were marginally literate and relatively unsophisticated, and the publications marketed to them were often mediocre. Newspapers, in particular, exploited stories of sensational crimes and political scandals and carried pages of advertising that made extravagant, unsubstantiated claims. Despite the low level of public taste, the new literacy was the intellectual equivalent of the railroad and the steamship. It made it possible for the masses to explore new intellectual territory and to take the initiative in improving skills and deepening understandings. Governments and political leaders quickly discovered the power of newspaper editorials to influence voters.

Public education became widespread in Europe during the second half of the nineteenth century and women came to dominate the profession of schoolteaching, especially at the elementary level. This 1905 photograph shows English schoolchildren going through morning drills.

© Hulton-Deutsch Collection/CORBIS

OVERVIEW   DEVELOPMENT IN SCIENCE, PSYCHOLOGY, SOCIOLOGY, AND FICTION

Discipline	Year	Development
Science	1830s	Comte's positivism says all knowledge should be knowledge common to the physical sciences
	1859	Darwin's theory of evolution by natural selection disputes creationism
	1895	Roentgen announces the discovery of X-rays
Psychology	1900	Freud, the founder of psychoanalysis, publishes *The Interpretation of Dreams*
	early 1900s	Jung, student of Freud, theorizes that the subconscious is inherited from ancestors
	mid-1900s	Horney and Klein attempt to establish a psychoanalytic basis for feminism
Sociology	1850s	Gobineau presents first arguments that race is the major determinant of human history
	1870s	Nationalism becomes a well-organized mass movement equating nationality with race
	1900	Weber traces capitalism to religious doctrines of Puritanism
Fiction	1856	*Madame Bovary* by Flaubert signals the advent of realism
	1870	Verne modernizes popular science fiction
	1920s	Woolf becomes a chief proponent of modernism

SCIENCE AT MIDCENTURY

*T*he link between science and technology in the Second Industrial Revolution made the public more aware of science than ever before, and during the first half of the nineteenth century science gained ground as the model for all human knowledge. Newton's view of the universe as a rational system operating according to mechanical principles remained dominant.

COMTE, POSITIVISM, AND THE PRESTIGE OF SCIENCE

Auguste Comte (1798–1857), building on the Enlightenment's faith, claimed that science was the culmination of human intellectual development. In *The Positive Philosophy* (1830–1842), Comte argued that human understanding evolved in three stages: the theological (where natural events are credited to the action of spiritual beings), the metaphysical (where abstract principles, not personified entities, are thought to control nature), and the positive (where natural phenomena are explained by referring them to each other, not to unobservable forces). Comte believed physical science had entered the positive stage first and that other fields would eventually follow. Comte's philosophy, **positivism**, helped establish the belief that all knowledge should be the kind of knowledge common to the natural sciences. Comte is also remembered as the father of sociology, for he predicted that laws, such as those of physics, would be found to explain social behavior.

During the third quarter of the century, talk emerged of a religion of science that would explain all nature without resorting to supernaturalism. Men such

WHAT ROLE did science play in the second half of the nineteenth century?

24.4
Auguste Comte: from *The Age of Ideology*

positivism Comte's philosophy that all knowledge should be the kind of knowledge common to the physical sciences.

ENCOUNTERING THE PAST

THE BIRTH OF SCIENCE FICTION

During the Renaissance, Europe's fantasy writers set their stories in exotic foreign lands. In the seventeenth century, the moon became a favorite locale, and during the nineteenth century authors turned to outer space and the earth's unexplored deep seas and interior. Modern popular science fiction begins with the work of Jules Verne (1828–1905), who wrote serialized stories for magazines. Verne prided himself on scientific accuracy, and he set his tales in his own age—giving his readers a sense of experiencing real adventures. His most enduring novel is Twenty Thousand Leagues under the Sea (1870), the story of Captain Nemo's submarine Nautilus.

English author H. G. Wells (1866–1946) helped establish many of the conventions of science fiction. *The Time Machine* (1895) explored the conundrum of time travel. *The Island of Dr. Moreau* (1896) described the consequences of inhuman medical experimentation, and *The War of the Worlds* (1898) raised the possibility of invasion from outer space.

The stories of Verne and Wells appeared in cheap illustrated magazines with mass circulation and helped establish science fiction as a fixture of popular culture. As new entertainment media appeared (radio, movies, and then television), their works were repeatedly dramatized. A radio play by Orson Wells (1915–1985) in 1938 based on Wells's *The War of the Worlds* was so realistic that many Americans mistook it for a news report of a Martian landing in New Jersey.

WHY DID science fiction suddenly become popular with the masses in the late nineteenth century? What is the reason for its enduring popularity?

Captain Nemo's submarine confronts a giant octopus in Verne's *Twenty Thousand Leagues under the Sea.*
© Bettman/CORBIS

as Thomas Henry Huxley (1825–1895) in Britain and Ernst Haeckel (1834–1919) in Germany interpreted scientific advances for the general public, proclaiming their belief that science held the answer to all the questions of life. They advocated government support for scientific research and the inclusion of science in the curricula of schools and universities. (See "Encountering the Past: The Birth of Science Fiction.")

DARWIN'S THEORY OF NATURAL SELECTION

In 1859, Charles Darwin (1809–1882) published *The Origin of Species*, the equivalent in biology of Newton's contribution to physics and Copernicus's to cosmology. Darwin's work has been much misunderstood. He did not originate the concept of evolution, which had been discussed widely before his time. His contribution was the principle of natural selection, a theory proposing a mechanical process to explain how evolution operated. Working independently, his contemporary, Alfred Russel Wallace (1823–1913), came up with the same idea.

Building on one of Malthus's insights, Darwin and Wallace contended that more organisms come into existence than can survive in their environment. Those that have a unique trait that gives them a marginal advantage in the struggle for existence change the nature of their species by reproducing more successfully than their competitors. Because the fittest survive to pass on their unique characteristics, a mechanistic process of **natural selection**, not divine choice, shapes the design of living things. Neither Darwin nor anyone else at the time could explain the origin of the chance variations that gave certain individuals advantages over others of their species. Only after 1900, when work on heredity by an Austrian monk named Gregor Mendel (1822–1884) began to circulate, did the mystery of those variations begin to be unraveled.

The theory of evolution by natural selection removed a need for a guiding purpose in nature. It explained a species' traits as the result of its past struggles with the environment, not a deity's plan for its destiny. It called into question a literal interpretation of the biblical narrative of creation and undermined the deistic argument for God as the author of a rationally designed universe. No God was needed if the universe had no design. And if there was no design, no fixity—if nature was nothing but flux and change, might not the same thing be true of society, values, customs, and beliefs? What did "truth" mean in such a world?

In 1871, Darwin published *The Descent of Man* and spelled out the implications of natural selection for the human species. He contended that not only the human frame but human conscience and religious intuition evolved quite naturally as part of a survival strategy. No God was needed to provide an image for humanity. Not since Copernicus had removed the earth from the center of the universe had human pride received so sharp a blow. With so much at stake, Darwin's theories were slow to win support. By the end of the nineteenth century, scientists generally endorsed evolution, but acceptance of natural selection waited until the 1920s and 1930s, when modern genetics began to solve some of the puzzles Darwin's theory created.

SCIENCE AND ETHICS

Debates about Darwin's theories inevitably raised questions about their implications for society. The phrase "survival of the fittest," which Darwin used, was coined earlier by classical economists to summarize their argument for the benefits of a competitive marketplace. After Darwin, some thinkers suggested it might also apply to other fields of human endeavor.

British philosopher Herbert Spencer (1820–1903) made evolution a basis for a theory of ethics. He advocated individualism and asserted that competition is essential if society is to progress. The strong have a kind of ethical imperative to subdue the weak, for attempts to spare the weak only serve (by perpetuating their inferior traits) to undermine the species. Spencer's arguments were used to justify neglect of the poor and the working class, exploitation of colonial peoples, and aggressive competition among nations.

Spenser's **social Darwinism** came close to claiming that might makes right, but Thomas Henry Huxley (1825–1895), a vigorous defender of Darwin's ideas, had a different view of their ethical implications. He argued that struggle in physical nature is not the same as the struggle within human nature—that the process of evolution in the physical world is at odds with the development of ethical awareness in human beings. Nature only shows people how they should not behave.

natural selection   Darwin and Wallace's theory that those species with a unique trait that gives them a marginal advantage in the struggle for existence change the nature of their species by reproducing more successfully than their competitors; the fittest survive to pass on their unique characteristics.

social Darwinism   Spencer's argument (coming close to claiming that might makes right) used to justify neglect of the poor and the working class, exploitation of colonial peoples, and aggressive competition among nations.

HOW DID science and religion come into conflict in the nineteenth century?

CHRISTIANITY AND THE CHURCH UNDER SIEGE

Given the intellectual attitudes that were in the ascendancy, the nineteenth century was a challenging era for organized Christianity. Many intellectuals left the faith, and nation-states with liberal governments curtailed the church's influence. The expansion and migration of population and the growth of cities stressed traditional ecclesiastical organization. Despite all this, however, churches, both Protestant and Catholic, made considerable headway among the masses.

INTELLECTUAL SKEPTICISM

The *philosophes* of the Enlightenment had delighted in pointing out contradictions in the Bible, and the historical scholarship of the nineteenth century brought intellectual rigor to the critical analysis of sacred texts.

History   In 1835, David Friedrich Strauss (1808–1874) published a *Life of Jesus* that questioned whether the Bible contains any genuinely historical information about Jesus. Strauss explained the story of Jesus as a myth spawned by the aspirations of the people of first-century Palestine.

During the second half of the century, Julius Wellhausen (1844–1918) in Germany, Ernst Renan (1823–1892) in France, and William Robertson Smith (1847–1894) in Great Britain showed how human authors had written and revised various books of the Bible and shaped them to reflect the nature of the societies in which these authors had lived. They claimed that the Bible, like the Homeric epics, issued from the concerns of primitive human communities. The doubt these scholars cast on the literal truth of the Bible as a text dictated by God caused a crisis of faith for many literate individuals.

Science   Enlightenment theologians had tried to ground the Christian religion in science, but the scientific discoveries of the nineteenth century had the effect of undermining faith. Darwin's theory cast doubt on the doctrine of creation. Anthropologists, psychologists, and sociologists suggested that religious feelings are nothing but natural phenomena. The geology of Charles Lyell (1797–1875) demonstrated that the earth was much older than the biblical records implied, and by finding natural causes for floods, mountains, and valleys, Lyell removed the miraculous hand of God from the physical processes shaping the earth.

Morality   Questions about Christianity's worth as a moral force accompanied doubts about its historical validity and congruence with science. The colorful behavior of some biblical figures, particularly from the Old Testament, had long embarrassed Christians, but now even the Bible's image of God was criticized. Liberals considered the Old Testament depiction of God as a whimsical, vindictive deity to be unworthy of the progressive, tolerant, rational values they associated with divinity. The New Testament's view of God as a being who, for his own satisfaction, demanded the sacrifice of the world's only perfect man also cast God in what liberals considered to be a troubling moral light.

During the last quarter of the century, an attack of a different kind was made on Christian ethics by Friedrich Nietzsche (1844–1900), a German philosopher. He dismissed Christianity as a religion for sheep—a glorification of weakness instead of the vigor of full-blooded human life. He criticized Christianity for demanding debilitating sacrifices of the flesh and spirit and not encouraging heroic living.

Theological skepticism was confined largely to the upper levels of educated society, but it cost Christianity much of its intellectual respectability. Fewer educated people were attracted to the clerical profession, and many individuals were content to lead their lives with little or no reference to organized Christianity. Direct attacks on faith were not the only explanation for this. The increasing secularism of Western and particularly urban societies was also harmful to faith. Cities expanded faster than ecclesiastical institutions, and whole generations of the urban poor grew up with little or no experience of the church or training in Christian doctrine.

CONFLICT BETWEEN CHURCH AND STATE

For centuries, religious orders or denominations had run most of Europe's schools. The governments of the major nations of the late nineteenth century, however, were secular organizations. Their suspicion and resentment of the church produce a heated debate about religious education in the last quarter of the century.

Great Britain Great Britain's Education Act of 1870 provided for the construction of state-supported schools run by elected school boards in places where religious organizations had failed to provide satisfactory educational opportunities. Intense hostility among competing religious groups created problems in some regions, but these groups cooperated in opposing educational reforms that increased the costs of their schools. In 1902, another Education Act attempted to ensure the quality of all schools by providing state support for, and by imposing the same educational standards on, both religious and nonreligious institutions.

France The church-state conflict in Britain was far less intense than in France. France had a dual system of Catholic and public schools, but the Falloux Law of 1850 mandated Catholic religious instruction (under the tutelage of a local priest) in public schools. Increasing hostility between the Third Republic and the conservative clergy of the French Catholic Church led to the enactment, between 1878 and 1886, of educational reforms sponsored by Jules Ferry (1832–1893). The Ferry laws increased the number of public schools, replaced their religious instruction with civic training, and barred members of religious orders from their faculties. After the Dreyfus affair, the radical government of Pierre Waldeck-Rousseau (1846–1904) punished the French clergy for their reactionary politics by suppressing the religious orders, and in 1905, church and state were separated in France by termination of the Napoleonic Concordat.

Germany and the *Kulturkampf* The most extreme example of church-state conflict was the *Kulturkampf* ("cultural struggle") that Bismarck waged in Germany during the 1870s. When Germany was unified, its Catholic hierarchy wanted its constitution to guarantee freedom for its churches. Bismarck originally left this issue to be decided by each federal state, but he soon concluded that the Roman Catholic Church and the Catholic Center Party posed a threat to the unity of the German Empire. In 1870 and 1871, he brought Prussia's educational system under state management and prohibited clergy (both Catholic and Protestant) from overseeing schools.

Bismarck's secularization of education was the first stage in a concerted attack on the freedom of the Catholic Church in Germany. The May Laws of 1873 (which applied to Prussia but not to the German Empire at large) transferred to the state the disciplinary power over the clergy previously exercised by the pope and the church. Priests were required to be educated in Germany, to pass state examinations, and to seek state ratification for their

Kulturkampf ("cultural struggle") An extreme church-state conflict waged by Bismarck in Germany during the 1870s in response to a perceived threat to German political unity from the Roman Catholic Church.

The conflict between church and state disrupted German politics during the 1870s. This cartoon shows Bismarck and Pope Pius IX attempting to checkmate each other in a game of chess.

Bildarchiv Preussischer Kulturbesitz

appointments to church offices. When many of the clergy resisted, Bismarck resorted to force. In 1876, he arrested or drove from Prussia all the Catholic bishops. This action was the greatest blunder of his career, for such persecution created martyrs and only increased resistance. By the end of the 1870s, the chancellor had won state control of education and established civil laws governing marriage, but at the price of provoking enduring resentment of the German state among Catholics.

AREAS OF RELIGIOUS REVIVAL

The intense hostility of religion's enemies was partly a response to its persistent vitality. The second half of the nineteenth century witnessed the final push to Christianize Europe. In Great Britain, both the Anglican church and the nonconformist denominations grew considerably. In Ireland, the 1870s saw a widespread Catholic devotional revival. France's defeat by Prussia triggered mass pilgrimages by penitents who believed their sins had caused their country's defeat, and the famous cult of the miracle of Lourdes grew during these years. The evangelical programs of all denominations were well organized, well led, and well financed. They focused particular attention on the urban poor, and when they fell short, it was not from want of effort but because Europe's population outstripped their resources.

THE ROMAN CATHOLIC CHURCH AND THE MODERN WORLD

The papacy struggled to chart a course through the turmoil of a period marked by both skepticism and religious revival. The liberal sympathies of Pope Pius IX (r. 1846–1878) vanished on the night in November 1848, when he was forced to flee the revolution that tried to make Rome a republic. The campaign for Italian unification further embittered him and contributed to his determination to wage a counteroffensive against liberalism. In 1864, he issued the *Syllabus of Errors*, a condemnation of modern thought that declared the Roman Catholic faith was incompatible with contemporary science, philosophy, and politics. Pius was helpless to prevent the new Italian state from stripping the papacy of all its territory, save for the Vatican City in Rome, and he concluded that the Roman Catholic church, having lost political and temporal power, could sustain itself in the modern world of nation-states only by exalting the pope's spiritual authority. In 1869, he summoned the First Vatican Council, and a year later, despite opposition from numerous bishops, he promulgated the doctrine of **papal infallibility**. Its assertion that the pope's pronouncements on matters of faith and morals could not be questioned was the most sweeping claim ever made for the monarchical authority of the papacy.

Leo XIII (r. 1878–1903), Pius IX's successor, tried to be more accommodating of the modern age and to address its great social questions. Like Thomas Aquinas (1225–1274), Leo believed the claims of faith and reason could be reconciled. His encyclicals of 1885 and 1890 justified Catholic participation in the politics of liberal states. His most important encyclical, *Rerum Novarum* (1891), defended the legitimacy of private property, religious education, and church authority over marriage law. It condemned socialism and Marxism but affirmed the right of workers to organize unions and demand just treatment from employers. He supported legal protections for labor and urged states to pursue goals that benefited all their citizens. He recommended a model derived from medieval corporate social institutions as an alternative to both socialism and unrestrained capitalism. Leo XIII's endorse-

23.1
The Church Weighs In:
Rerum Novarum

papal infallibility Assertion that the pope's pronouncements on matters of faith and morals could not be questioned.

ment of Catholic participation in politics led to the establishment of democratic Catholic parties and Catholic trade unions across Europe.

Pius X (r. 1903–1914) urged resistance to modern modes of thought and return to traditional devotional life. Between 1903 and 1907, he worked to oppose Catholic modernism, a movement that wanted to win acceptance within the church of scientific biblical criticism. In 1910, he ordered all priests to take an oath to oppose modernism, and the struggle between Catholicism and modern thought resumed.

ISLAM AND LATE NINETEENTH-CENTURY EUROPEAN THOUGHT

The few Europeans who wrote about Islam in the late nineteenth century subjected it to the same kind of scientific critique their contemporaries were applying to Judaism and Christianity. They explained it simply as a historical phenomenon, the natural product of a particular culture. Ernest Renan (1823–1892), the influential French scholar, linked it with Judaism as a manifestation of ancient Semitic mentality and dismissed it as a close-minded faith that blocked the development of science. Renan's view was opposed by Jamal al-din Al-Afghani (1839–1897), an Egyptian intellectual. He pointed out that Christian societies had a six-hundred-year head start on the Muslim world and maintained that Islam would eventually produce cultures as modern as Europe's.

European racism and denigration of nonwhite peoples affected attitudes toward the Arab world, and Christian missionaries confirmed these prejudices by blaming Islam for promoting economic backwardness, mistreating women, and condoning slavery. Missionaries made few converts among Muslims, but the schools and hospitals they established helped educate some young Arabs in Western science and medicine. Many of their students became political leaders in the Middle East.

The decaying Ottoman Empire's interest in Western scientific education and technology met with a variety of responses from religious thinkers. The Salafiyya movement maintained there was no inherent contradiction between science and Islam, but that Islam should modernize itself without directly imitating Europe. The Salafi originally wanted to reconcile Islam with the modern world, but the effect of their teaching in the twentieth century was to persuade Muslims to oppose Western influences. Other Islamic groups—the Mahdist in Sudan, the Sanussiya in Libya, and the Wahhabi in the Arabian peninsula—simply rejected the West and modern thought. They sprang up in regions where the presence of Europeans was least felt. Interest in the West was stronger in places that were, by 1900, controlled by Western powers: Morocco, Algeria, Egypt, Tunisia, and Turkey.

TOWARD A TWENTIETH-CENTURY FRAME OF MIND

During the last quarter of the nineteenth and the first decade of the twentieth century, the kind of fundamental reassessment that Darwin's work necessitated in biology began in other disciplines. New concepts challenged the presuppositions of mid nineteenth-century science, rationalism, liberalism, and bourgeois morality.

WHAT EFFECT did art, psychology, and science have on modern Western thought?

Marie Curie (1869–1934) and Pierre Curie (1859–1906) were two of the most important figures in the advance of physics and chemistry. Marie was born in Poland but worked in France for most of her life. She is credited with the discovery of radium, for which she was awarded the Nobel Prize in Chemistry in 1911.

Ullstein Bild, Berlin. The Granger Collection, New York

SCIENCE: THE REVOLUTION IN PHYSICS

In the late 1870s, some scientists began to question the realist assumptions that underlay traditional science. They warned that Newtonian physics' mechanistic model—a universe of solid atoms moving in absolute time and space—was only a model, not a definitive description of reality. Ernst Mach (1838–1916), in *The Science of Mechanics* (1883), urged scientists to think of their concepts as reports of their sensations as observers, not literal descriptions of the world. All that investigators can know, he warned, is how their senses respond to the world. They cannot get beyond their sensations to the physical realities themselves. Henri Poincaré (1854–1912), a French scientist, agreed. He claimed that scientific concepts were hypothetical constructs, not literal descriptions of the true state of nature. By World War I, few scientists believed any longer that they could discover absolute "truth." Their more modest task was to record observations and devise useful hypothetical or symbolic models of natural phenomena.

X-Rays and Radiation   Laboratory work soon confirmed the provisional nature of scientific knowledge. In December 1895, Wilhelm Roentgen (1845–1923) announced the discovery of X-rays, a form of energy that penetrates various opaque materials. When major steps in the exploration of radioactivity followed within months of the publication of his paper, the comfortably "complete" explanation nineteenth-century physicists thought they had for the world vanished.

In 1896, Henri Becquerel (1852–1908), building on Roentgen's work, discovered that uranium emits a form of energy resembling the X-ray. A year later, J. J. Thomson (1856–1940) of Cambridge University's Cavendish Laboratory hypothesized the existence of the electron, and the interior of the supposedly indivisible atom suddenly became a new frontier for exploration. In 1902, Ernest Rutherford (1871–1937), Thomson's assistant, suggested that radiation is caused by the disintegration of the atoms of certain materials and speculated that immense stores of energy are present within atoms.

Theories of Quantum Energy, Relativity, and Uncertainty   The discovery of radioactivity was followed by revolutionary theories that made the certainties trusted by the previous generation of physicists problematic. In 1900, Max Planck (1858–1947) articulated a quantum theory of energy, which describes energy as a series of discrete quantities or packets rather than a continuous stream. In 1905, Albert Einstein (1879–1955) published his first epoch-making papers on relativity. He contended that time and space constitute a continuum whose measurement depends as much on the observer as on the entities being measured. In 1927, Werner Heisenberg (1901–1976) articulated the uncertainty principle. He postulated that the behavior of subatomic particles is a matter of statistical probability—that it cannot be traced with the certainty of a cause-and-effect encounter between solid objects. The mathematical complexity that substantiates the theories of modern physics makes it impossible for most people to comprehend most scientific work, but the impact that science (applied as technology) has on daily life has made scientists the best supported and most respected group among Western intellectuals.

LITERATURE: REALISM AND NATURALISM

Between 1850 and 1914, the moral certainties of learned and middle-class Europeans underwent modifications no less radical than their concepts of the physical universe. This owed much to the **realist** and **naturalist** authors who tried to describe human behavior with scientific objectivity. They rejected the romantic idealization of nature, poverty, love, and polite society, and portrayed the hypocrisy, the physical and psychic brutality, and the dullness that underlay bourgeois life.

In the preceding generation, writers such as Charles Dickens (1812–1870) and Honoré de Balzac (1799–1850) had vividly depicted the cruelty and misery created by the single-minded pursuit of money in industrialized societies, and George Eliot (born Mary Ann Evans, 1819–1880) had accustomed readers to expect realistic detailed descriptions of scenes and characters. There had always been room, however, in the works of authors of this period for imagination, fancy, and hope that the world could be improved by human effort and the application of Christian values. The major figures of late-century realism, however, were less optimistic. They saw human beings as animals, subject to passions, to Marx's materialistic determinism, and to the pressures of Darwin's struggle for survival. They suggested that society itself perpetuated evil.

Flaubert and Zola   The novel that signaled the advent of realism was *Madame Bovary* (1856) by Gustave Flaubert (1821–1880). It is a story of colorless provincial life and a woman's hapless search for love within and beyond marriage. It views human existence as devoid of heroism, purpose, or even civility.

Emile Zola (1840–1902) developed a rationale for literary realism. He claimed that human events are as much the products of determinism as events in the physical world and that, therefore, writers should observe and describe the characters and actions in their novels in the same way that scientists record the course of laboratory experiments. Zola suggested that literature model itself on medical texts such as Claude Bernard's (1813–1878) *An Introduction to the Study of Experimental Medicine* (1865).

Ibsen and Shaw   The Norwegian playwright Henrik Ibsen (1828–1906) wrote stark, unsentimental dramas depicting crises in domestic life. He peeked beneath the cloak of respectability that the middle-class morality of his generation tried to drape over the family. His most famous play, *A Doll's House* (1879), describes the developing self-awareness of Nora, the spouse of a narrow-minded middle-class man who denies his wife any independence. The play ends as she comprehends her situation and leaves her husband, slamming the door behind her. In *Ghosts* (1881), a respectable middle-class woman deals with the shame and guilt of having passed syphilis, unknowingly contracted from her husband, to her son.

George Bernard Shaw (1856–1950), an Irish playwright who spent most of his life in England, was one of Ibsen's greatest admirers and imitators. His *Mrs. Warren's Profession* (1893) was long censored in England for its blunt treatment of prostitution. In *Arms and the Man* (1894) and *Man and Superman* (1903), Shaw heaped scorn on the romantic era's idealization of love and war, and in *Androcles and the Lion* (1913), he pilloried Christianity. Shaw made sure no one missed the points of his plays by attaching long prefaces to them to spell out the social criticism they intended.

Advocates of realism believed that literature has a serious mission. By portraying reality and the commonplace, by dissecting the "real" world and refusing to let public opinion dictate what they wrote, they hoped to change the common perception of the good life. By forcing audiences to consider unmentionable things, they tried to strip away the veneer of hypocrisy that prevented discussion

QUICK REVIEW

Leading Realists
- Gustave Flaubert (1821–1880)
- Emile Zola (1840–1902)
- Henrik Ibsen (1828–1906)
- George Bernard Shaw (1856–1950)

realists   Authors who tried to describe human behavior with scientific objectivity, rejecting the romantic idealization of nature, poverty, love, and polite society, and portraying the hypocrisy, physical and psychic brutality, and the dullness that underlay bourgeois life.

naturalists   Authors who tried to portray nature and human life without sentimentality.

Virginia Woolf, a member of the Bloomsbury Group whose members were the chief proponents of modernism in England.

Hulton Archive Photos/Getty Images, Inc.

modernism Movement of the 1870s criticizing middle-class society and traditional morality.

Keynesian economics Economic theories and programs ascribed to John M. Keynes and his followers advocating government monetary and fiscal policies that increase employment and spending.

Impressionism Focuses on social life and leisured activities of the urban middle and lower-middle classes, a fascination with light, color, and representation of momentary experience of social life or of landscape.

of important issues. They wanted to compel the public to confront reality by destroying all social and moral illusions. Few of the realist writers who so vividly described society's problems had any solutions to suggest for them, however. They destroyed old values and offered no new ones.

MODERNISM IN LITERATURE

In the 1870s, a multifaceted movement called **modernism** affected all the arts. Like realism, modernism criticized middle-class society and traditional morality. But modernism was less interested in social reform than pure aesthetics—artistic experience for its own sake. The chief proponents of modernism in England were the members of the Bloomsbury Group: authors Virginia (1882–1941) and Leonard Woolf (1880–1969), artists Vanessa Bell (1879–1961) and Duncan Grant (1885–1978), historian and literary critic Lytton Strachey (1880–1932), and economist John Maynard Keynes (1883–1946). Bloomsbury was determined to expose the inadequacy of what it regarded as "Victorian" values, particularly an allegedly repressive Victorian sexual morality.

Strachey, in *Eminent Victorians*, produced a series of biographical sketches less to write history than to heap contempt on famous Victorians. Grant and Bell followed the lead of modernist continental artists. **Keynesian economics** challenged nineteenth-century economic theory. No one, however, charted the changing sensibilities of the time with more care and eloquence than Virginia Woolf. Her novels *Mrs. Dalloway* (1925) and *To the Lighthouse* (1927) portrayed a world that had lost most of the social and moral certainties of the nineteenth century.

The work of Marcel Proust (1871–1922) is a monument to the modernist literary movement on the Continent. His seven-volume novel, *In Search of Time Past* (issued from 1913 to 1927), explored memory using a stream-of-consciousness narrative. He concentrated on a single experience or object and then allowed his mind to wander through all the thoughts it evoked. In a series of novels (including *Buddenbrooks* in 1924 and *The Magic Mountain* in 1927), Germany's Thomas Mann (1875–1955) explored the social experience of middle-class Germans as they attempted to come to terms with the intellectual heritage of the nineteenth century. *Ulysses* (1922), a book of stunning originality by James Joyce (1882–1941), an Irish author who spent much of his life on the Continent, wholly transformed the novel and the structure of the paragraph.

Literary modernism flourished in the atmosphere of turmoil and social dislocation created by World War I, and the war destroyed many of the political and social systems modernism opposed. After war's appalling violence, it became much harder for artists to shock their audiences.

THE COMING OF MODERN ART

At the end of the nineteenth century, new departures in Western art transformed painting and later sculpture in a revolutionary manner that has continued to the present day.

Impressionism The development of **Impressionism**, a style of painting that contemporaries considered to be curious and artistically shocking, arose primarily in Paris. This style, instead of portraying religious, mythological, and historical themes, depicted modern life itself, with a focus on the social life and leisured activities of the urban middle and lower-middle classes. Many of these artists were fascinated with light, color, and the representation of momentary, largely unfocused, visual experience of social life or of landscape.

Edouard Manet (1832–1883), *A Bar at the Folies-Bergère*, 1882.

Edouard Manet (1832–1883), "A Bar at the Folies-Bergère," 1882. Oil on canvas, 96 × 130 cm. Signed dated. Courtauld gift 1932. Courtauld Institute Gallery, London

The Impressionists, who included Edouard Manet (1837–1883), Claude Monet (1840–1926), Camille Pissaro (1830–1903), Pierre-Auguste Renoir (1841–1919), and Edgar Degas (1834–1917), recorded Parisians attending cafés, dance halls, concerts, picnics, horse races, boating excursions, and beach parties. The sites included in these paintings allowed people of different classes to mix socially in their leisure activity.

In the painting *A Bar at the Folies-Bergère* of 1882, whose setting was a popular, large, and expensive concert hall, Manet depicted a young barmaid standing behind a table, with interior light that appears to be coming from the newly invented electric light bulbs. The table, with its bottles, fruit, vase, and flowers, constitutes a formal still-life composition, but also shows objects of commercial consumption—the music hall with a trapeze artist and the audience—not a traditional still life.

The painting leaves one questioning the meaning and expression of the barmaid. The restlessness of the establishment does not register on her face. This may reflect the anonymity of social encounters in modern urban life, or it may be that the barmaid, who like so many such Parisian women, might have had to supplement her meager wages through prostitution, is portrayed like the liquor and fruit: just another object of commerce.

Post-Impressionism   By the 1880s, the Impressionists had an enormous impact on contemporary art. Their movement developed into another style, called **Post-Impressionism**, which focused more on form and structure than on the effort to record the impression of the moment. The major painters of this style were Georges Seurat, Paul Cezanne, Vincent Van Gogh, and Paul Gauguin.

Seurat (1859–1891), who is counted among the first Post-Impressionists because he viewed himself as bringing the new painting of modern life back in touch with earlier artistic traditions, extensively read contemporary scientific works about light, color, and vision. These studies led to a technique known as pointillism, which used small dots or points of paint. Though laborious, the goal

Post-Impressionism Focuses more on form and structure to bring painting of modern life back in touch with earlier artistic traditions.

Georges Braque, *Violin and Palette*
(Violon et Palette), 1909–1910, is
representative of the autonomous
realm of art itself.

Cubism Autonomous realm of
art with no purpose beyond itself.
Includes as many different perspectives, angles, or views of the
object as possible.

was to decompose colors into their basic units, leaving it to the viewer to mix
those dots through the viewer's own perception.

Seurat's work implicitly included social commentary, as in his 1884 painting *A Sunday on La Grande Jatte*, situated on the Grande Jatte, an island in the
Seine where Parisians would gather on Sundays. A boatman indicates a brooding
working-class presence amid the largely middle-class figures, all of whom resemble mechanical mannequins who stand bored and perhaps puzzled by their situation of comfort, leisure, and ease.

Reacting to the Impressionists' fascination with light, Paul Cezanne
(1839–1906) brought form and solidity back into his paintings of still life and of
the Provence landscape. Paul Gauguin (1848–1903) portrayed peoples of the
South Pacific. The art of Africa and of the Pacific gave artists subject matter un-
related to the long-standing Western artistic tradition.

Cubism For over 500 years, Western painting, including Impressionism and
Post-Impressionism, sought to reproduce the appearance of reality. The single
most important new departure in early twentieth-century Western art was
Cubism, a term first coined to describe the paintings of Pablo Picasso
(1881–1973) and Georges Braque (1882–1963). The Cubist painters sought to
redirect the artistic portrayal of reality in the same manner that modernists in literature had reshaped the portrayal of social and moral experience, and that the
new physics had reconceptualized nature itself.

Beginning in 1907, Picasso and Braque rejected the idea of a painting con-
stituting a window onto the real world. Rather, they saw painting as an autonomous realm of art itself with no purpose beyond itself. They represented
only two dimensions in their art, yet attempted to include at one time on a single
surface as many different perspectives, angles, or views of the object painted as
possible. "Reality" was the construction of their experience of multiple perceptions. Braque's still life *Violin and Palette* (1909 and 1910), a well-known Cubist
work, was created with this artistic outlook. It depicts a violin, a palette, and a
musical score from various perspectives, but none of the shapes and parts actually reproduces a recognizable object. The elements have an existence completely
separate from the subjects that inspired the painting.

24.5
Friedrich Nietzsche:
from *The Age of Ideology*

FRIEDRICH NIETZSCHE AND THE REVOLT AGAINST REASON

The legacy of the Enlightenment had been supreme confidence in the power of reason, but, during the second half of the nineteenth century, philosophers focused on reason's limitations. Friedrich Nietzsche (1844–1900), a German philologist, was the most inflammatory of these thinkers. In *The Birth of Tragedy* (1872), Nietzsche claimed that the nonrational aspects of human nature are as important and noble as the rational. He insisted that instinct and ecstasy are vital functions and that to limit the human to the rational is to diminish it. In Nietzsche's view, the strength that produces heroes and great artists springs from something beyond reason. In later works, such as the prose poem *Thus Spake Zarathustra* (1883), Nietzsche criticized democracy and Christianity for empowering the mediocrity of the sheeplike masses. He proclaimed the death of God and the rise of the *übermensch* (the "Overman"), the embodiment of a heroic humanity free to seek its own fulfillment without illusions. The term was often misunderstood as a reference to a superman or superrace, but Nietzsche was no racist or anti-Semite. He idealized a heroism he associated with the Greeks of the Homeric age, a people who had not been exposed to the emasculating influences of Christianity and bourgeois morality.

Two of Nietzsche's most profound works, *Beyond Good and Evil* (1886) and *The Genealogy of Morals* (1887), explore the idea that morality is a human convention that has no grounding in external reality. Good and evil, he claimed, do not exist on their own. They are human projections onto the world. Human beings have to forge from their own inner will the truth and values that are to exist in their world. Nietzsche did not condemn morality, but he challenged people to ponder its worth and purpose. He urged them to reject Christianity, utilitarianism, and middle-class respectability because he believed these things are life denying. He insisted that people could, if they wanted, create a new moral order based on the life-affirming values of pride, assertiveness, and strength.

THE BIRTH OF PSYCHOANALYSIS

All the major figures of late nineteenth-century science, art, and philosophy were driven to probe beneath the surfaces of things—of atoms, of reason, of codes of respectability, and of human relationships. Their work dispelled smugness and complacency, but it also undercut self-confidence. Such was the effect of psychoanalysis.

Development of Freud's Theories   Sigmund Freud (1856–1939), the founder of psychoanalysis, was trained as a physician, and in 1886, he opened a medical practice in Vienna. He worked there until driven out by the Nazis in 1938. Freud early developed an interest in psychic disorders. In 1885, he went to Paris to observe Jean-Martin Charcot's (1825–1893) use of hypnosis to treat hysteria, and in 1895, he collaborated with another Viennese physician, Josef Breuer (1842–1925), on *Studies in Hysteria*.

In the mid–1890s, however, Freud abandoned hypnosis in favor of encouraging his patients to talk freely and spontaneously about themselves. He discovered that they repeatedly associated their neurotic symptoms with experiences going back to childhood. Freud also noted that his patients' problems were often connected with sex, and for a time he speculated that childhood sexual abuse might be the source of mental illness. By 1897, Freud had moved beyond this view to a theory of universal infantile sexuality that scandalized many of his contemporaries. He claimed that human beings are sexual creatures from birth, that

In 1909 Freud and his then-devoted disciple Carl Jung visited Clark University in Worcester, Massachusetts, during Freud's only trip to the United States. Here Freud sits on the right holding a cane; Jung is sitting on the far left.

Clark University/Special Collections/Archives

sexual drives do not emerge at puberty but exist in infants. This cast doubt on the innocence of childhood and forced people to face up to issues of sexuality and mental health that, in his day, they preferred not to discuss.

In 1900, Freud published his most important book, *The Interpretation of Dreams.* It combined his theory of infantile sexuality with another idea, the psychic significance of dreams. As a rationalist, Freud believed that apparently irrational phenomena, such as dreams, must have rational, scientific explanations. He theorized that dreams express unconscious wishes, desires, and drives that waking consciousness suppresses. While awake, the mind censors certain thoughts fundamental to an individual's psychological makeup, but during sleep it expresses them cloaked in symbols. Freud claimed that these unconscious drives and desires help to explain conscious behaviors.

In his later works Freud emphasized the importance of what transpires in the mind below the level of consciousness. He saw the mind as an arena for a struggle among three entities: the **id**, the **ego**, and the **superego**. The id consists of innate, amoral, irrational drives for sexual gratification, aggression, and sensual pleasure. The superego internalizes the moral imperatives that society and culture impose on the personality. The ego mediates between the impulsive id and the self-denying superego. Personality, as expressed in everyday behavior, is the product of the ego's efforts to repress impulses of the id and satisfy the demands of the external world embodied in the superego.

Freud never claimed that humankind ought to liberate the id and free itself of all repression. He believed that excessive repression leads to mental disorders, but he said civilization and the survival of humankind are impossible without some repression of sexuality and aggression. Freud described human beings as attaining rationality, not as being inevitably endowed with it. He wanted civilization to prevail, but he warned that the maintenance of civilized behavior requires an immense sacrifice of instinctual drives. He also suggested that previously unsuspected obstacles lay in the way of achieving rationality, and he was pessimistic about civilization's prospects.

Divisions in the Psychoanalytic Movement By 1910, Freud was attracting many followers, and some of them eventually broke with him to develop theories of their own. Chief among these was Carl Jung (1875–1961), a Swiss whom Freud regarded as his most promising student. Freud was firmly rooted in the rationalism of the Enlightenment, but Jung shared the religious mysticism of the romantics. He questioned the primacy of sexual drives in the formation of human personality and mental disorders and claimed that the subconscious is a soul formed by personal experiences and collective memories inherited from one's ancestors. He believed modern people are largely alienated from these useful collective memories.

Although the psychoanalytic movement had fragmented by the 1920s, it had tremendous influence and affected work in psychology, sociology, anthropology, religious studies, history, and literary theory. The explanations psychoanalysis offered for human behavior have been questioned and the theory's future is uncertain, but there is no doubt about the contribution it made to the development of the modern mind.

id Among Freud's three entities of the mind, the *id* consists of innate, amoral, irrational drives for sexual gratification, aggression, and sensual pleasure.

ego Among Freud's three entities of the mind, the *ego* mediates between the impulsive id and the self-denying superego.

superego Among Freud's three entities of the mind, the *superego* internalizes the moral imperatives that society and culture impose on the personality.

RETREAT FROM RATIONALISM IN POLITICS

Nineteenth-century liberals and socialists had great faith in the fundamental rationality of human beings. They thought that if given votes and properly educated, people would see to their own rational self-interest. By 1900, however, this view was under attack, and questions were being raised about the rationality of politics and human behavior.

Weber   German sociologist Max Weber (1864–1920) regarded the development of rational social orders as humanity's greatest achievement. Where Marx saw capitalism as the driving force in modern society, Weber saw bureaucratization. Bureaucratization is the process whereby labor is divided in an organized community and individuals acquire a sense of personal identity by finding roles for themselves in large systems. Unlike Marx, Weber believed that noneconomic factors account for history's major developments. Weber's *The Protestant Ethic and the Spirit of Capitalism* (1905) traced capitalism itself to the ascetic religious doctrines of Puritanism. The Puritans, he argued, achieved worldly success not because they sought it for its own sake but because of the disciplines they imposed on themselves to assure themselves that they were God's elect.

Theorists of Collective Behavior   Many of Weber's colleagues were less sanguine about human rationality than he was. Gustave Le Bon (1841–1931) was a psychologist of mob behavior who pointed out that reason's power fades when people gather in crowds. In *Reflections on Violence* (1908), Georges Sorel (1847–1922) argued that people are motivated less by reason than by collectively shared ideals. Emile Durkheim (1858–1917) and Graham Wallas (1858–1932) insisted that instinct, habit, and affections have more power than reason to motivate human social behavior. All of these theorists suggested that when people make political decisions, they operate not as rational individuals but as defenders of the groups that give them their senses of identity.

RACISM

The power of social collectives to overwhelm reason and to sacrifice the individual to the group manifests itself in theories of race. **Racism** has a long history, but the prestige enjoyed by biology and the sciences in general provided the racists of the late nineteenth century with what they claimed were objective, material grounds for their belief that some peoples are innately superior to others.

Gobineau   Count Arthur de Gobineau (1816–1882), a reactionary French diplomat, presented the first detailed arguments for the popular belief that race is the major determinant of human history. His four-volume *Essay on the Inequality of the Human Races* (1853–1854) blamed the weaknesses of Western civilization on the degeneration of an original white European race, the Aryans. Linguists of the late eighteenth century had noted similarities among most European languages and Sanskrit and explained them by postulating the existence of a forgotten mother tongue once spoken by an Aryan race. Gobineau claimed that intermarriage with inferior yellow and black peoples had weakened modern Europeans by diluting their superior Aryan blood.

Chamberlain   Gobineau's essay had little influence initially, but racial thinking was encouraged by trends in nineteenth-century science. Anthropologists and explorers adapted Darwin's theory of the survival of the fittest to explain cultural differences, and in 1899 Houston Stewart Chamberlain (1855–1927) published

racism   Belief that some peoples are innately superior to others.

HISTORY'S VOICES

H. S. CHAMBERLAIN EXALTS THE ROLE OF RACE

Houston Steward Chamberlain's Foundations of the Nineteenth Century (1899) *was a major influence on the Nazi Party and fascism. It claimed that racial mixing weakens people physically and morally and that people confident in their racial purity could act with extreme self-confidence and arrogance.*

WHAT DOES Chamberlain mean by "race"? How does it function, as opposed to character or environment, as a determinant of behavior?

The man who belongs to a distinct, pure race, never loses the sense of it. The guardian angel of his lineage is ever at his side, supporting him where he loses his foothold, warning him like the Socratic Daemon where he is in danger of going astray, compelling obedience, and forcing him to undertakings which, deeming them impossible, he would never have dared to attempt. Weak and erring like all that is human, a man of this stamp recognizes himself, as others recognize him, by the sureness of his character, and by the fact that his actions are marked by a certain simple and peculiar greatness, which finds its explanation in his distinctly typical and super-personal qualities. Race lifts a man above himself; it endows him with extraordinary—I might almost say supernatural—powers, so entirely does it distinguish him from the individual who springs from the chaotic jumble of peoples drawn from all parts of the world: and should this man of pure origin be perchance gifted above his fellows, the fact of Race strengthens and elevates him on every hand, and he becomes a genius towering over the rest of mankind, not because he has been thrown upon the earth like a flaming meteor by a freak of nature, but because he soars heavenward like some strong and stately tree, nourished by thousands and thousands of roots—no solitary individual, but the living sum of untold souls striving for the same goal.

From Houston Steward Chamberlain, *Foundations of the Nineteenth Century*, Vol. I., trans. by John Lees (London: John Lane, 1912), p. 269.

Foundations of the Nineteenth Century. It integrated information drawn from many different fields and advanced a theory of biological determinism. Where Gobineau had assumed that the "degeneration" of the human race was irreversible, Chamberlain suggested that careful attention to genetics might enable scientists to breed a new super race. Chamberlain's work had alarming political implications, for he accused the Jews of being the major threat to Europe's racial regeneration. His opinion was shared by Paul de Lagarde (1827–1891) and Julius Langbehn (1851–1907), who both declared the Jews to be a racial and cultural threat to Germany. By linking racism with nationalism, they set Europe on a perilous path. (See "History's Voices: H. S. Chamberlain Exalts the Role of Race.")

Late-Century Nationalism Nationalism had begun as a movement among scholars and liberals who cherished national languages and wanted the map of Europe to acknowledge ethnic identities. From the 1870s onward, however, nationalism became a well-financed, well-organized mass movement that equated nationality with race. It opposed the internationalism advocated by liberals and socialists and favored homogeneous states that commanded unquestioned loyalty from all their citizens. Nationalism even became a kind of secular religion evangelized by state-supported schools. It promoted major conflicts in the early twentieth century, and it has experienced a resurgence following the collapse of communism in the 1990s.

Racial theory encouraged Europeans to impose harsh, condescending treatment on the colonial peoples they governed in the late nineteenth and early twentieth centuries. White Westerners' assumptions of permanent racial superiority affected their attitude not only toward colonists but toward peoples of color who were their fellow citizens.

ANTI-SEMITISM AND THE BIRTH OF ZIONISM

The rationalism of the Enlightenment helped dispel some of Europe's traditional religious prejudice against Jews, and in the first half of the nineteenth century, Jews won political rights and social acceptance in Britain, France, and Germany. During the last third of the century, however, economic pressures created by rampant capitalism revived anti-Semitism, particularly among members of the lower middle class.

Anti-Semitic Politics   Anti-Semitic crusades led in Austria by the head of the Christian Socialist Party Karl Lueger (1844–1910), in Germany by ultraconservative Lutheran chaplain Adolf Stoecker (1835–1909), and in France by the prosecutors of Captain Dreyfus convinced many Jews that cultural assimilation could not guarantee their security. Their racist enemies insisted that the problem with Jews was not objectionable conduct that could be unlearned but the ineradicable defects of inferior blood. If Jews were unacceptable as citizens of European nations, their only safety lay in establishing a nation of their own—or so argued Theodor Herzl (1860–1904), founder of the **Zionist** movement.

Herzl's Response   In 1896, Herzl's *The Jewish State* made a plea for an independent Jewish nation where the Jews of the world would be assured of the rights that should have been theirs in the liberal states of Europe. Herzl, an Austro-Hungarian, directed his appeal to the impoverished Jews of eastern Europe's ghettos and western Europe's slums. His version of Zionism linked opposition to anti-Semitism with socialism.

WOMEN AND MODERN THOUGHT

*M*any of the new ideas advanced in the late nineteenth century seemed to confirm old stereotypes that represented women as weaker and less able than men. Whatever changes science wrought in understandings of gender, significant reorganization of the home and alterations of male-female relationships were not expected to be among them.

ANTI-FEMINISM IN LATE-CENTURY THOUGHT

Late Victorian biologists and anthropologists tended to lump women with non-white races as inferior members of the human family. T. H. Huxley, Darwin's defender and a popularizer of scientific theories, toured giving lectures on what he claimed was scientific evidence for female inferiority. Karl Vogt (1817–1895), a prominent German anthropologist, held similar views. Darwin repeated their ideas in *The Descent of Man*. He and Huxley both thought that women's opportunities for education should be improved, but neither man advocated admitting women to the scientific community. Male scientists insisted that codes of decency prohibited women from discussing certain subjects, and many claimed that women's limited intellects would depress the level of debate in learned societies.

Freud and his followers were trained as medical doctors at a time when medical education assumed the inferiority of women, and many of Freud's theories were developed using case histories of female patients. Some critics maintain

HOW DID views of women change in the late nineteenth and early twentieth centuries?

Zionism   Movement based on the theory that if Jews were unacceptable as citizens of European nations, their only safety lay in establishing a nation of their own.

Josephine Butler (1828–1906) was an English reformer who campaigned relentlessly to repeal the Contagious Diseases Acts.

Getty Images Inc.—Hulton Archive Photos

that Freud portrayed women as incomplete human beings, flawed males who were destined for mental problems. He claimed that without motherhood (particularly the nurturing of sons) they remained unfulfilled. Distinguished female psychoanalysts, such as Karen Horney (1885–1952) and Melanie Klein (1882–1960), challenged Freud's ideas and attempted to establish a psychoanalytic basis for feminism, but the psychoanalytic profession and academic psychology remained dominated by men. Psychology's influence on child-rearing practices ironically gave men power in the one area of social activity that had always been dominated by women.

Virtually all the early sociologists held conservative views of marriage, the family, child rearing, and divorce. Auguste Comte, drawing on Rousseau, portrayed women as biologically and intellectually inferior to men. Herbert Spencer advocated improving women's lot while accepting as fact their inability to be men's equals. Emile Durkheim described women as creatures motivated by feeling more than intellect. Max Weber favored improving social conditions for women, but not changing their social roles.

NEW DIRECTIONS IN FEMINISM

At the close of the nineteenth century, feminist thought revived in Europe and began to raise issues that would not be more fully and successfully explored until after World War II. Many women's organizations concentrated on achieving the vote for women, but consciousness was growing of a broader need to redefine women's relationships to men and society at large—primarily to challenge the double standard of sexual morality and the traditional male-dominated family.

Sexual Morality and the Family Demands for women's rights often began with campaigns to abolish prostitution, a fate to which poverty drove many lower-class women. Between 1864 and 1886, the English Parliament passed the Contagious Diseases Acts. It gave police in cities with naval or military bases the power to force women suspected of prostitution to undergo examination for venereal disease. Without legal recourse, those infected were locked up for months in special hospitals. These laws angered middle-class women, for they literally assigned control over women's bodies to men—as customers, physicians, and police. By denying poor women the freedoms and protections all men enjoyed in English society, they implied that all women were less than fully human. Also, they decreed no penalties for prostitutes' customers. The purpose of these laws was, after all, the protection of these men. A campaign waged by Josephine Butler (1828–1906), head of the Ladies' National Association for the Repeal of the Contagious Diseases Acts, caused these laws to be suspended in 1883 and repealed in 1886. The English experience was replicated by other countries that struggled with the issue of police regulation of prostitution. During the 1890s, the General Austrian Women's Association, led by Auguste Ficke (1833–1916), fought the introduction of legalized prostitution. In Germany, women's groups divided between those who wanted to penalize prostitutes and those who saw prostitutes as victims of male society.

By opposing laws that punished prostitutes and let their customers go free, feminist groups were challenging society's sexual double standard and, by extension, the traditional relationship of men and women in marriage. Virtually all turn-of-the-century feminists advocated greater sexual freedom for women and access to contraception. The prevailing social Darwinism of the era worked in favor of birth control movements, for it could be claimed that limiting the number of children enabled families to compete more successfully in providing for their offspring.

Women Defining Their Own Lives   The European feminist movement hoped to end male-dominated society and create a world in which women could determine their own destinies as freely as men. Many feminists were attracted to socialism, for they assumed a classless society would liberate women. Socialist parties, however, tended to have male leaders (such as Lenin and Stalin), and although they supported attempts to improve women's economic situation, they had no tolerance for feminist calls for changes in family life and sexual codes.

Feminists in literary circles attained the clearest insights into the problems confronting women. Distinguished female writers functioned more or less on an equal plane with men, and this led some of them to wonder if simple equality was the real issue. Virginia Woolf's *A Room of One's Own* (1929) is a fundamental text for twentieth-century literary feminism. It describes the difficulties facing gifted women who want to be taken seriously as intellectuals, and it argues that a woman who wishes to write requires complete independence—an income and a room of her own. Woolf created a new stance for feminist writers by challenging the idea that women should write like men. She insisted that all writers, male as well as female, should be able to share the sensitivities of both sexes and ponder the validity of standard definitions of gender.

By World War I, feminism in Europe had become linked in the popular mind with socialism, political radicalism, and attacks on traditional morality and gender roles. Consequently, when extremely conservative political movements appeared in the years between the world wars, feminism faced stiffened opposition—even in communist societies.

SUMMARY

The New Reading Public   Governments started funding education in the late 1860s. Liberals and conservatives shared the Enlightenment belief that new voters needed more information to exercise their rights properly and thus maintain the political order. By 1900, 85 percent or more of the population of Britain, France, Belgium, the Netherlands, Germany, and Scandinavia could read. (Literacy rates in Italy, Spain, Russia, Austria-Hungary, and the Balkans were about 40 to 70 percent.) This created a mass reading public. New reading material proliferated. Much of it was of low quality, but the sheer numbers of readers allowed an unprecedented popularization of knowledge.

Science at Midcentury   In the mid–nineteenth century, many considered science the model for all forms of human understanding. Educated people believed the physical world was rational, mechanical, and predictable and that science described nature as it really was. French and German universities provided institutional bases for science; the word *scientist* was widely used by century's end. Comte developed positivism. Sociology is based on his belief that positive knowledge, the kind obtained by physical science, is possible in other areas, including social behavior. Darwin proposed natural selection as the mechanism for evolution. Darwin explained humans as products of the struggle for survival. Philosophers and economists also applied the idea of survival of the fittest to their fields. Spencer wrote of competition as an ethical imperative. Huxley countered that evolution determines only physical development, not moral behavior.

Christianity and the Church under Siege   Protestant and Catholic churches remained popular, despite urban growth that outstripped their capacity, attacks

IMAGE KEY

for pages 590–591

a. "Professor Darwin, 'This is the ape of form'". Love's Labour's Lost, Act V, Scene II, Charles Darwin (1809–72) as an ape, 1861, (colour litho) by English School (19th century)

b. One of Darwin's notebooks

c., d. Finches from the Galapagos

e. Curie's radiograph of key and coin in coin purse

f. 1905 photograph shows English schoolchildren going through morning drills

g. George Eliot, the pen name of the novelist Marian Evans (1819–1880)

h. Cover of Proust's book, "Remembrance of Things Past"

i. The conflict between church and state disrupted German politics during the 1870s. In this contemporary cartoon Bismarck and Pope Pius IX seek to checkmate each other in a game of chess

j. Freud and Friends, 1909

k. Marie Curie with her husband Pierre Curie in Laboratory

l. Charles Darwin, painted by George Richmond in 1840

m. Model of the atom

on church influence by the secular nation-state, and a rejection of faith by many European intellectuals. Nineteenth-century historical scholarship challenged the validity of the Bible. Science and moral reasoning also posed challenges to Christian faith. The secular state and the church clashed over many issues, particularly education. In Great Britain, France, and Germany, the government limited religious roles in education. But Christian churches were still strong enough to fight back. Different popes had different ideas about the Catholic Church's best response to modernism, but all aggressively engaged it. The small group of scholars of Islam in Europe applied scientific and naturalistic forms of inquiry to the Islamic faith and the Qur'an. Christians held anti-Islamic attitudes, although missionary families in Islamic areas were more sympathetic. In the Ottoman Empire, political leaders called for Westernized scientific education and technology, but religious leaders had more varied responses to Western ideas.

Toward a Twentieth-Century Frame of Mind At the turn of the century, new ideas of physical reality, human nature, and society challenged the beliefs of earlier science, rationalism, liberalism, and bourgeois morality. New scientific discoveries pointed to the inadequacy of the mechanistic models of the physical world. Einstein's theories of relativity and Heisenberg's uncertainty principle opened the doors to new ways of understanding the material world. Middle-class morality was also thrown into disarray; realist and naturalist authors adopted objective, "scientific" stances. Modernism was critical of bourgeois morality, but endorsed an aesthetic ideal of beauty and experimentation with form. In literature and art, modernism was interested in artistic experience for its own sake. Keynesian economics challenged nineteenth-century economic theory. Freud's psychoanalysis explored areas of the human mind that had not yet been imagined. He used romanticism and Enlightenment rationality. Weber built a model of social behavior that countered Marx by emphasizing noneconomic factors in social development. Racism was used to explain the history and characteristics of large groups. Racial thinking and biological determinism linked with anti-Semitism and aggressive nationalism in a poisonous strand of political theory. The Zionist movement was an important Jewish response to anti-Semitism.

Women and Modern Thought Women's social roles remained largely static. A distinct strain of misogyny became evident in fiction and painting at the end of the nineteenth century. The scientific community, too, held a conservative and hostile view of women. Racial thinking often placed women on a lower plane than men of the same race. Biological thinking led social scientists to reinforce so-called traditional roles for women. Feminist groups worked to gain voting rights for women. They also questioned the double standard of sexual morality and the male domination of the family. Often they approached these issues through challenges to prostitution laws, which punished female prostitutes but not their customers. Some advocated contraception. Others argued that women should be free to develop their personalities; still others joined socialist movements and worked to incorporate a change for the role of women into the socialist agenda. Virginia Woolf articulated a vision of men and women both becoming aware of the full range of identities within each individual.

REVIEW QUESTIONS

1. What were some of the major changes in scientific outlook that occurred between 1850 and 1914? What advances took place in physics? What was the theory of natural selection proposed by Darwin and Wallace? Why did Christianity come under attack in the late nineteenth century? What form did the attack take?

2. How were changes in society reflected in the literature of the late nineteenth century? What was the significance of the explosion of literacy and literary material? What was literary *realism*? How did literary *modernism* differ from realism?

3. How did Nietzsche and Freud challenge traditional middle-class and religious morality? How do you account for the fear and hostility many late nineteenth-century intellectuals displayed toward women? What were some of the social and political issues that especially affected women in the late nineteenth and early twentieth centuries? What new directions did feminism take?

4. What forms did racism take in the late nineteenth century? How did it become associated with anti-Semitism? What was Zionism? Why did Herzl develop it?

KEY TERMS

Cubism   (p. 604)

ego   (p. 606)

id   (p. 606)

Impressionism   (p. 602)

Keynesian economics   (p. 602)

Kulturkampf   (p. 597)

modernism   (p. 602)

naturalists   (p. 601)

natural selection   (p. 595)

papal infallibility   (p. 598)

positivism   (p. 593)

Post-Impressionism   (p. 603)

racism   (p. 607)

realists   (p. 601)

social Darwinism   (p. 595)

superego   (p. 606)

Zionist   (p. 609)

 For additional study resources for this chapter, go to:
www.prenhall.com/kagan3/chapter24

25 Imperialism, Alliances, and War

CHAPTER HIGHLIGHTS

Expansion of European Power and the New Imperialism European progress in science, technology, industry, and agriculture made a new wave of global expansion possible. A variety of motives underlay the new imperialism. By 1890 almost all of Africa had been parceled out among European countries.

Emergence of the German Empire and the Alliance Systems (1873–1890) Under Bismarck's leadership, a united and powerful Germany attempted to preserve the balance of power. A shifting series of alliances culminated in alliances between Germany and Austria and between Russia, Britain, and France.

World War I Ottoman weakness contributed to instability in the Balkans and conflict between European nations over the fate of that region. The assassination of Archduke Francis Ferdinand triggered a chain reaction that culminated in general war. The war in the West soon became a bloody stalemate. In the East, Russia quickly lost ground to the forces of the Central Powers. America entered the war in 1917 tipping the balance toward the Allies.

The Russian Revolution Military and domestic failings led to the fall of the Tsar's government and the creation of a provisional government. Lenin and the Bolsheviks toppled the provisional government and took control of Russia. Russia withdraw from the war and soon descended into civil war. By 1921 the civil war was over and Lenin was in firm control.

The End of World War I American intervention prevented the Germans from gaining an advantage from Russia's surrender. A final German offensive failed, a civilian government was installed, and Germany signed an armistice acknowledging its defeat.

The Settlement at Paris President Wilson's Fourteen Points met resistance from America's European allies and from Wilson's political opponents at home. The final peace settlement redrew the map of Europe, forced Germany to disarm and pay reparations, and created the League of Nations. The Treaty of Versailles created as many problems as it solved.

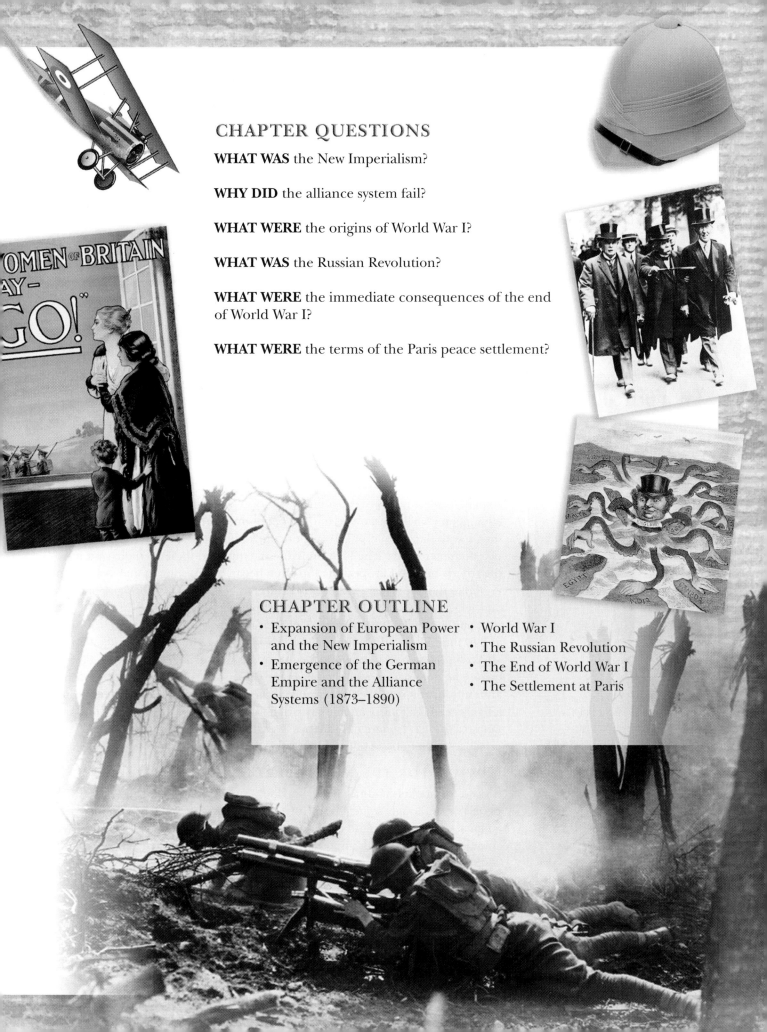

CHAPTER QUESTIONS

WHAT WAS the New Imperialism?

WHY DID the alliance system fail?

WHAT WERE the origins of World War I?

WHAT WAS the Russian Revolution?

WHAT WERE the immediate consequences of the end of World War I?

WHAT WERE the terms of the Paris peace settlement?

CHAPTER OUTLINE

- Expansion of European Power and the New Imperialism
- Emergence of the German Empire and the Alliance Systems (1873–1890)
- World War I
- The Russian Revolution
- The End of World War I
- The Settlement at Paris

IMAGE KEY
Image Key for pages 614–615 is on page 643.

WHAT WAS the New Imperialism?

France's imperialism always reflected its sense of unique cultural superiority, and the French liked to think of themselves as benevolently sharing it with the colonial people they ruled. This magazine cover from 1911 shows the symbol of France bringing civilization, peace, and prosperity to Morocco.

The Granger Collection

25.2
Manifesto for the Society for German Colonization

imperialism Policy of expanding a nation's power by seeking hegemony over alien peoples.

During the second half of the nineteenth century, Europe wielded unprecedented worldwide influence. Massive immigration turned North and South America, Australia, and New Zealand into extensions of the European nations that were, at the time, dividing up Africa into colonies and dictating terms to the countries of Asia. Europe's dominance created a single world economy that might have increased general prosperity, but competition among the great powers led instead to a terrible war that undermined Europe's strength and global influence. The peace settlement that followed humiliated Germany and provoked its desire for revenge. The United States also made the fateful decision to withdraw into disdainful isolation from world affairs.

EXPANSION OF EUROPEAN POWER AND THE NEW IMPERIALISM

Europe's power was based on the progress it made during the nineteenth century in science, technology, industry, agriculture, transportation, communications, and military weaponry. These advancements enabled Europeans (and Americans) to impose their wills on peoples many times their number. The growth of nation-states, a Western phenomenon, also gave Europeans the means to exploit their advantages to maximum effect. Confidence in the superiority of their civilization made them energetic, self-righteous expansionists.

THE NEW IMPERIALISM

Imperialism is a policy of expanding a nation's power by seeking hegemony over alien peoples. The earliest form of imperialism involved seizing land and resettling it with the conqueror's people or controlling trade to exploit the resources of a dominated area. The New Imperialism employed these methods and introduced new ones. A European nation often began by investing capital in a foreign region to develop its mines and agriculture, to build railroads, bridges, harbors, and telegraph systems. These ventures employed large numbers of native peoples, and European states safeguarded their investments by financing local rulers and by intimidating them into making favorable concessions that fundamentally altered indigenous economies and cultures. If these arrangements proved inadequate, the dominant power would assume direct control. Sometimes this meant annexation, or it could result in protectorate status whereby a local ruler became a figurehead for European military occupation. A European state might also establish a foreign "sphere of influence" in which it enjoyed commercial and legal privileges without overt political control.

MOTIVES FOR THE NEW IMPERIALISM

A need for markets and raw materials does not adequately explain the New Imperialism. Although some European businessmen and politicians hoped that colonial expansion might cure the economic depression of 1873 to 1896, colonies were usually not important markets for imperial nations. It is not even certain that colonialism was profitable. Some individuals and companies made a great deal of money from some ventures, but they had minimal influence on the policies of their nations. Economic interests were involved, but an adequate explanation for the New Imperialism requires consideration of other motives.

Advocates of imperialism justified it in various ways. Some argued that European nations had a duty to extend the benefits of their superior civilization to allegedly backward peoples. Churches demanded that governments furnish political

MAP EXPLORATION

Interactive map: To explore this map further, go to **http://www.prenhall.com/kagan3/map25.1**

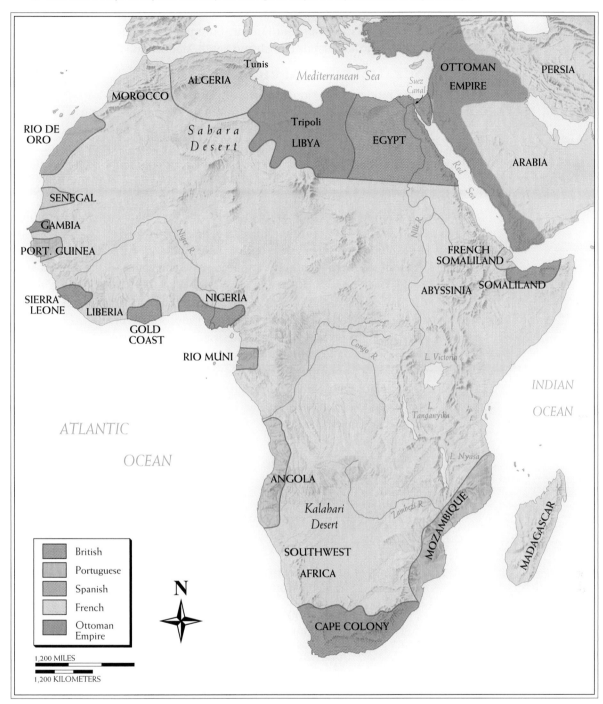

MAP 25–1

Imperial Expansion in Africa to 1880   Until the 1880s, few European countries held colonies in Africa, mostly on its fringes.

FOR WHAT purposes did European countries control parts of Africa before 1880?

and military support for their missionaries. Some politicians (particularly in Germany) hoped that imperialism would deflect public interest from domestic problems. Joseph Chamberlain (1836–1914), Britain's colonial secretary from 1895 to 1903, argued that Britain might finance a program of domestic reform and welfare from the profits of empire, but most of Britain's imperial expansion was complete by the time he proposed this. Some social reformers hoped to use colonies to relieve population pressures in Europe, but most emigrants went to places not controlled by their homelands (North and South America and Australia).

THE SCRAMBLE FOR AFRICA

All of these motives were on display in the late nineteenth century when European imperial powers expanded their economic and political control of Africa. During this so-called "Scramble for Africa," from the late 1870s to about 1900, the European powers sought to maximize their control of African territory and raw materials. Motivated by economic and political competition, and rationalized on religious and cultural grounds, the imperial powers eventually divided almost the entire continent among themselves. Over the long term, European control forcibly integrated African societies into the modern world economy, and new social, economic, and political structures developed.

For centuries, European slave-trading bases had dotted the African coastline, but few Europeans had penetrated the interior. This changed in the late 1870s. (See Map 25–1.) The Congress of Vienna's prohibition of the Atlantic slave trade in 1815, the consequent naval patrols enforcing that decision, and the abolition of slavery in the Americas in the nineteenth century meant that Africa was no longer a source of slave labor (except for Arab slave traders who exported slaves from Central and East Africa to the Muslim world until at least the 1890s). Africa henceforth became important as a supplier of raw materials, such as ivory, rubber, minerals, diamonds, and gold. With fierce competition for territory, German chancellor Otto von Bismarck convened a conference in Berlin in 1884–1885 to regulate the European takeover of African land. (See Map 25–2.) Each European power administered its new possessions in different ways. They justified their rule as necessary for the civilizing mission—that is, bringing civilization to "backward" natives.

North Africa   In North Africa, which was still technically part of the Ottoman Empire, European powers used economic penetration (investments and loans), diplomatic pressure, and force to secure their interest. France took control of Algeria in 1830, Tunisia in the early 1880s, and Morocco between 1901 and 1912. Italy seized Libya in 1911–1912, and Britain took control of Egypt, so that Europeans controlled all of North Africa by 1914.

Egypt   Egypt was an unusual case. For most of the nineteenth century it had been a semi-independent province of the Ottoman Empire under the hereditary rule of a Muslim dynasty. The Khedives, as these rulers were titled, had tried to modernize Egypt by building new harbors, roads, and a European-style army. In so doing, they fell into debt with European creditors. The Suez Canal, which opened in 1869 and was built by French engineers with European capital, connected the Mediterranean and Red Seas. Although the canal reduced shipping distance from India to Britain from 12,000 miles to 7,000 miles, lowered shipping costs, and made many goods more affordable, Egypt itself benefited little from it. The Khedive went bankrupt in 1876 and sold to Britain most of his shares in the company that ran the canal.

In this way, Britain came to control the canal as well as Egypt, even though Egypt never became an official part of the British Empire. Egyptians were heavily

Linking Asia and Europe, the opening of the Suez Canal in 1869 was a major engineering achievement. It also became a major international waterway benefiting all maritime states by reducing the distance from London to Bombay by half.

Key Color/Index Stock Imagery, Inc.

MAP EXPLORATION

Interactive map: To explore this map further, go to **http://www.prenhall.com/kagan3/map25.2**

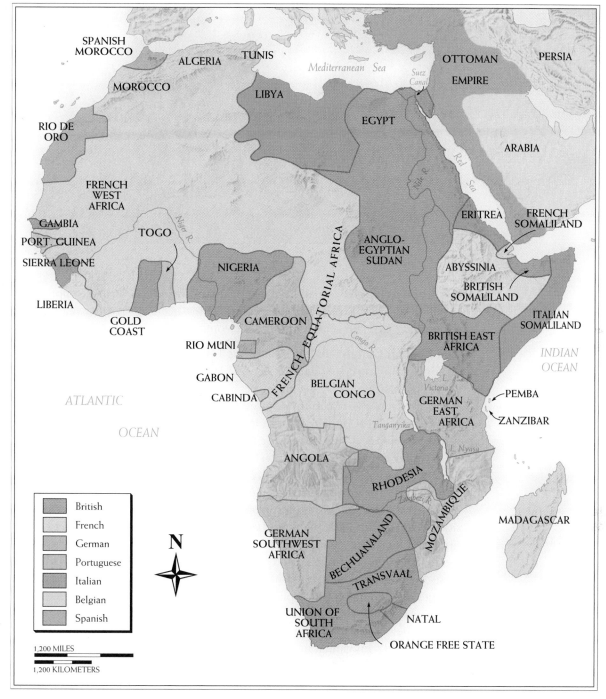

MAP 25–2

Partition of Africa, 1880–1914   Before 1880, the European presence in Africa was largely the remains of early exploration by old imperialists and did not penetrate the heart of the continent. By 1914, the occupying powers included most large European states; only Liberia and Abyssinia remained independent.

WHICH EUROPEAN country had the most African colonies?

Elephant tusks in Central Africa. Ivory was a prized possession used for decorative purposes and jewelry.

Caravan with Ivory, French Congo, (now the Republic of the Congo). Robert Visser (1882–1894). c. 1890–1900, postcard, collotype. Publisher unknown, c. 1900. Postcard 1912. Image No. EEPA 1985–140792. Eliot Elisofon Photographic Archives. National Museum of African Art, Smithsonian Institute

taxed, and its farmers owned little or no land. Although the British suppressed a rebellion in 1881, Britain had to contend with a growing Egyptian nationalism that would eventually seize control of the country in the 1950s.

The Belgian Congo In the 1880s, King Leopold II of Belgium (r. 1865–1909) acquired as his own personal property the lands drained by the vast Congo River and its tributaries. The Belgian government itself had no interest in colonies, therefore Leopold—no doubt inspired by the great wealth that the neighboring Netherlands had accumulated in its long history of colonial trade—used his own wealth and political guile to acquire the Congo territory.

Under the guise of humanitarian concerns, in 1876 Leopold gathered explorers, geographers, and antislavery reformers in Brussels and formed the International African Association. He then recruited Henry Morton Stanley (1841–1904), the famous explorer of Africa, to travel through the Congo and sign "treaties" with local rulers on Leopold's behalf. These rulers in fact had no idea what they were signing, but Leopold won diplomatic recognition for these treaties and thus acquired a colony seventy times the size of Belgium. To the larger, strong European states, allowing Leopold to take this vast territory had the advantage of keeping all other powers out. Leopold eventually bequeathed what became known as the Congo Free State to the Belgian government, after it gave him an interest-free loan to pay for his activities in the Congo.

Leopold's humanitarian public relations masked economic exploitation of the most brutal kind. His administration used slave labor, intimidation, torture, mutilation, and mass murder to extract rubber and ivory from the Congo. Leopold's crimes were exposed amidst international outcry, thanks in great part to the African-American reporter George Washington Williams (1849–1891) and the English journalists E. D. Morel (1873–1924) and Roger Casement (1864–1916). The cruelties in the Congo became the basis for Joseph Conrad's classic novel *Heart of Darkness* (1902) and were recorded in photographs, eyewitness accounts, and newspaper articles, and by an official Belgian commission. According to the most reliable estimates, Leopold's administration cut Congo's population in half in about thirty years, killing millions through murder, exploitation, starvation, and disease.

Southern Africa   South Africa's fertile land and natural resources made it very appealing. The Afrikaners or Boers, descendants of seventeenth- and eighteenth-century Dutch settlers, had long inhabited the area, and the British started to settle there after Britain took over from the Dutch during the Napoleonic Wars.

The Zulu, Shona, and Ndebele peoples resisted British expansion, but eventually the British established colonies in what is now South Africa, Botswana, Zambia, and Zimbabwe. In 1910, after a series of bloody wars with the white Afrikaners, the British formed the Union of South Africa, which remained under the British Empire but guaranteed the Afrikaners the right to rule. Africans and people of mixed race were forbidden to own land, denied the right to vote, and excluded from positions of power. The white elite eventually enforced a policy of Apartheid—"separateness"—that segregated the country and provided the basis for oppression, racial tensions, and economic exploitation.

Asia and the United States

In Asia, Japan's emergence frightened the other powers that were interested in China. The Russians feared any threat to the railroad it was building to the Pacific through Manchuria. With France and Germany, the Russians applied diplomatic pressure that forced Japan out of the Liaotung Peninsula and its harbor, Port Arthur. The United States, fearing that economic opportunities in China would be closed to it, in 1899 proposed the Open Door Policy, which opposed foreign annexations in China and established equal terms in China for all foreign entrepreneurs.

The United States had only recently emerged as a force in international affairs. Since the late eighteenth century, it had gained and consolidated its independence and expanded to the Pacific Ocean. The Monroe Doctrine of 1823 had, in effect, made the entire Western Hemisphere an American protectorate. Cuba's attempt to gain independence from Spain sparked the new U.S. involvement in international affairs. Sympathy for the Cuban cause as well as economic interests persuaded the United States to fight Spain.

With the U.S. victory in the Spanish-American War of 1898, the United States gained varying degrees of control over Cuba, Puerto Rico, the Philippine Islands, Guam, and part of Samoa in the Pacific. The United States annexed Hawaii in 1898, five years after an American-backed coup had overthrown the native Hawaiian monarchy. These developments made the United States an imperial and Pacific power. By the turn of the century, most of the world had come under the control of the industrialized West.

Emergence of the German Empire and the Alliance Systems (1873–1890)

WHY DID the alliance system fail?

By defeating Austria and France and uniting Germany in 1871, Prussia revolutionized the political situation in Europe. The appearance of a vast new nation of great and growing population, wealth, industrial capacity, and military might endangered the balance of power that had existed in Europe since 1815 and the Congress of Vienna. Britain and Russia remained formidable, but Austria, which was struggling to control various nationalistic movements among its subjects, was in decline. France's prestige had been damaged by the Franco-Prussian War and the loss of Alsace-Lorraine to Germany, and it was no longer the dominant nation in western Europe.

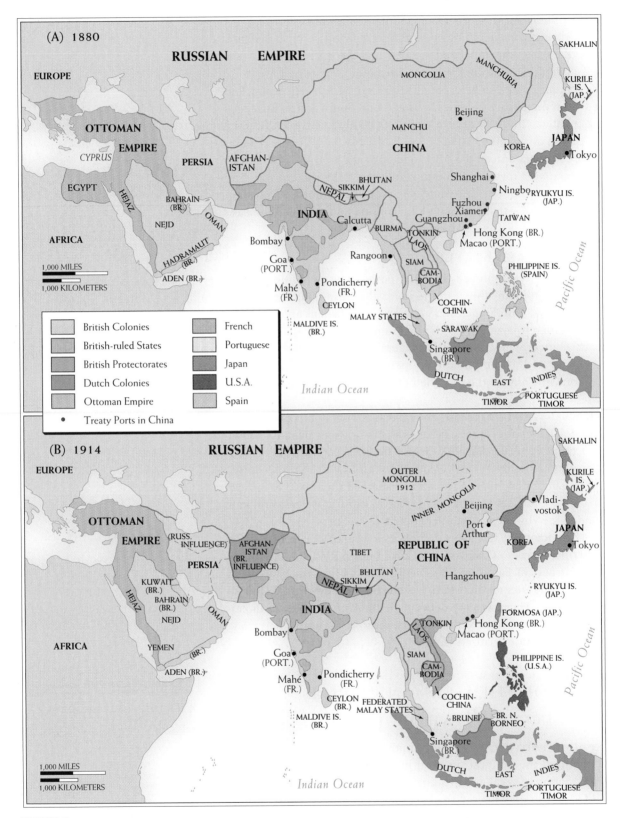

MAP 25–3

Asia, 1880–1914 As in Africa, the decades before World War I saw imperialism spread widely and rapidly in Asia. Two new powers, Japan and the United States, joined the British, French, and Dutch in extending control both to islands and to the mainland and in exploiting an enfeebled China.

WHY DID the emergence of Japan as a great power frighten European nations?

Southern Africa South Africa's fertile land and natural resources made it very appealing. The Afrikaners or Boers, descendants of seventeenth- and eighteenth-century Dutch settlers, had long inhabited the area, and the British started to settle there after Britain took over from the Dutch during the Napoleonic Wars.

The Zulu, Shona, and Ndebele peoples resisted British expansion, but eventually the British established colonies in what is now South Africa, Botswana, Zambia, and Zimbabwe. In 1910, after a series of bloody wars with the white Afrikaners, the British formed the Union of South Africa, which remained under the British Empire but guaranteed the Afrikaners the right to rule. Africans and people of mixed race were forbidden to own land, denied the right to vote, and excluded from positions of power. The white elite eventually enforced a policy of Apartheid—"separateness"—that segregated the country and provided the basis for oppression, racial tensions, and economic exploitation.

ASIA AND THE UNITED STATES

In Asia, Japan's emergence frightened the other powers that were interested in China. The Russians feared any threat to the railroad it was building to the Pacific through Manchuria. With France and Germany, the Russians applied diplomatic pressure that forced Japan out of the Liaotung Peninsula and its harbor, Port Arthur. The United States, fearing that economic opportunities in China would be closed to it, in 1899 proposed the Open Door Policy, which opposed foreign annexations in China and established equal terms in China for all foreign entrepreneurs.

The United States had only recently emerged as a force in international affairs. Since the late eighteenth century, it had gained and consolidated its independence and expanded to the Pacific Ocean. The Monroe Doctrine of 1823 had, in effect, made the entire Western Hemisphere an American protectorate. Cuba's attempt to gain independence from Spain sparked the new U.S. involvement in international affairs. Sympathy for the Cuban cause as well as economic interests persuaded the United States to fight Spain.

With the U.S. victory in the Spanish-American War of 1898, the United States gained varying degrees of control over Cuba, Puerto Rico, the Philippine Islands, Guam, and part of Samoa in the Pacific. The United States annexed Hawaii in 1898, five years after an American-backed coup had overthrown the native Hawaiian monarchy. These developments made the United States an imperial and Pacific power. By the turn of the century, most of the world had come under the control of the industrialized West.

EMERGENCE OF THE GERMAN EMPIRE AND THE ALLIANCE SYSTEMS (1873–1890)

WHY DID the alliance system fail?

*B*y defeating Austria and France and uniting Germany in 1871, Prussia revolutionized the political situation in Europe. The appearance of a vast new nation of great and growing population, wealth, industrial capacity, and military might endangered the balance of power that had existed in Europe since 1815 and the Congress of Vienna. Britain and Russia remained formidable, but Austria, which was struggling to control various nationalistic movements among its subjects, was in decline. France's prestige had been damaged by the Franco-Prussian War and the loss of Alsace-Lorraine to Germany, and it was no longer the dominant nation in western Europe.

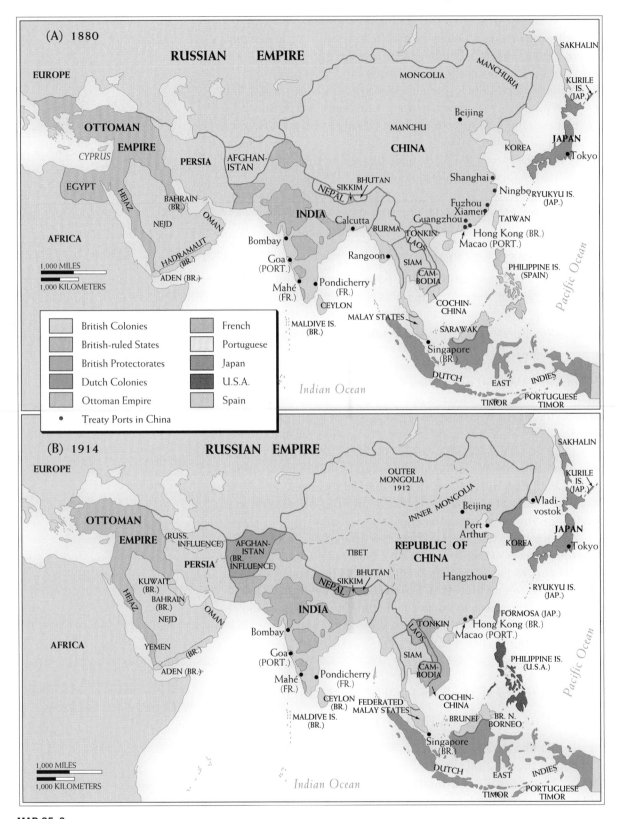

MAP 25–3

Asia, 1880–1914 As in Africa, the decades before World War I saw imperialism spread widely and rapidly in Asia. Two new powers, Japan and the United States, joined the British, French, and Dutch in extending control both to islands and to the mainland and in exploiting an enfeebled China.

WHY DID the emergence of Japan as a great power frighten European nations?

BISMARCK'S LEADERSHIP (1873–1890)

Bismarck wanted to avoid provoking a conflict that might undo his achievements, and following Germany's expansion and unification in 1871, he declared it wanted no more territory. He tried to placate France while simultaneously seeking treaties with Austria and Russia to isolate France in case his efforts failed. However, the Three Emperors' League he formed in 1873 collapsed in 1875, when the Russo-Turkish War pitted Russia against Austria in the Balkans.

The tottering Ottoman Empire was an invitation to disorder in the Balkans, but it survived because the European powers could not agree on how to divide it up. When Slavs in Bosnia and Herzegovina revolted against Turkish rule and Slavs in Serbia and Montenegro came to their aid, rebellion spread to Bulgaria and brought Russia into the fray. The Ottoman Empire quickly sued for peace, and Russia triumphed. It liberated Slavs in the Balkans from Ottoman control, annexed territory, and won a large monetary indemnity. These actions, however, alarmed other nations. Austria feared growth of Russian influence in the Balkans. The British worried that Russia might seize the Dardanelles, alter the European balance of power, and even imperil Britain's control of the Suez Canal.

The Congress of Berlin   Britain and Austria forced Russia to agree to an international conference to review the terms of the Treaty of San Stefano, which had ended its war with the Ottomans. Bismarck's insistence that Germany had no territorial aspirations made him an acceptable international arbiter, and in June–July 1878, he presided over a congress that met in Berlin. Bismarck dubbed himself an "honest broker," and he earned the title.

Bismarck's chief aim was to prevent Germany from being drawn into a war between Austria and an increasingly aggressive Russia. The congress dealt a blow to Russia by depriving its client state, Bulgaria, of two-thirds of its territory and of access to the Aegean Sea. The great powers also compensated themselves for the lands they allowed Russia to keep. Austria-Hungary was authorized to "occupy and administer" Bosnia and Herzegovina, which remained formally under Ottoman rule. Britain took Cyprus, and France was encouraged to occupy Tunisia.

Although Germany asked for nothing, its role in the congress earned it Russia's resentment. The Balkan states were also annoyed. Romania wanted Bessarabia, which Russia kept; Bulgaria wanted the borders originally granted it by the Treaty of San Stefano; and Greece wanted a share in the Ottoman spoils. Serbia and Montenegro deeply resented Austria's occupation of Bosnia and Herzegovina, as did many of the natives of those provinces. These lingering south Slavic issues and the estrangement between Russia and Germany threatened Europe's peace.

German Alliances with Russia and Austria   Russia's hostility drove Germany closer to Austria. In 1879, Germany and Austria signed a secret treaty (the Dual Alliance) and agreed to come to each other's aid if either were attacked by Russia. Each also pledged to stay out of the other's conflicts with other nations. The treaty remained in force until 1918 and became the anchor of Germany's international policy. In retrospect, it may have been an error, for it linked Germany's fortunes with those of the troubled Austro-Hungarian Empire and isolated the Russians, who responded by seeking new alliances in the West.

Bismarck never allowed the alliance to drag Germany into Austria's Balkan quarrels. He also made it clear to the Austrians that the alliance was purely defensive

Bismarck and the young Kaiser William II meet in 1888. The two disagreed over many issues, and in 1890 William dismissed the aged chancellor.

German Information Center

QUICK REVIEW

Congress of Berlin (1878)
- Convened to review the terms of the Treaty of San Stefano between Russia and the Ottoman Empire
- Bismarck acted as the impartial arbiter
- Russian concessions created animosity in Russia against Germany

HISTORY'S VOICES

BISMARCK EXPLAINS HIS FOREIGN POLICY

German Chancellor Otto von Bismarck guided German foreign policy from the empire's establishment in 1871 until his dismissal from office in 1890. The following passage from his memoirs, written in his retirement, sets forth his intentions in creating the system of alliances that is credited with preserving peace among the great powers from 1871 to 1914.

WHAT WAS the form and purpose of Bismarck's system of alliances?

The Triple Alliance which I originally sought to conclude after the peace of Frankfurt, and about which I had already sounded Vienna and St. Petersburg, from Meaux, in September 1870, was an alliance of the three emperors with the further idea of bringing into it monarchical Italy. It was designed for the struggle which, as I feared, was before us; between the two European tendencies which Napoleon called Republican and Cossack, and which I, according to our present ideas, should designate on the one side as the system of order on a monarchical basis, and on the other as the social republic to the level of which the antimonarchical development is wont to sink, either slowly or by leaps and bounds, until the conditions thus created become intolerable, and the disappointed populace are ready for a violent return to monarchical institutions in a Cæsarean form. I consider that the task of escaping from this *circulus vitiosus*, or, if possible, of sparing the present generation and their children an entrance into it, ought to be more closely incumbent on the strong existing monarchies, those monarchies which still have a vigorous life, than any rivalry over the fragments of nations which people the Balkan peninsula. If the monarchical governments have no understanding of the necessity for holding together in the interests of political and social order, but make themselves subservient to the chauvinistic impulses of their subjects, I fear that the international revolutionary and social struggles which will have to be fought out will be all the more dangerous, and take such a form that the victory on the part of monarchical order will be more difficult. Since 1871 I have sought for the most certain assurance against those struggles in the alliance of the three emperors, and also in the effort to impart to the monarchical principle in Italy a firm support in that alliance.

Otto von Bismarck, *Reflections and Reminiscences*, ed. by Theodore S. Hamerow (New York: Harper Torchbooks, 1968), pp. 236–237.

---

and Germany would never be a party to an attack on Russia. Bismarck believed monarchical, reactionary Russia would not seek ties with republican France or democratic Britain. In fact, he expected news of the Austro-German negotiations to frighten Russia into reconciling with Germany.

In this he was correct. By 1881, he had renewed the Three Emperors' League on a firmer basis. Germany, Austria, and Russia pledged neutrality if any of them were attacked by a fourth power. Austria was allowed to annex Bosnia-Herzegovina and promised to help close the Dardanelles to all nations if war came. The league allayed German fears of a Franco-Russian alliance and Russian fears of an Austro-German alliance. It secured Russia from British bids to win Austria's support for the British fleet to enter the Black Sea, and it hoped to keep peace in the Balkans between Austria and Russia. (See "History's Voices: Bismark Explains His Foreign Policy.")

The Triple Alliance In 1882, Italy, which wanted to diminish threats to its security from France, crowned Bismarck's triumph by asking to join the Dual Alliance. This move, by giving Germany treaties with three of the great powers and friendly relations with Great Britain, isolated and neutralized France. Bismarck now, however, faced the challenge of maintaining the complicated system of secret treaties in the face of rivalries among his allies. He succeeded until a change in the German monarchy upset things.

In 1888, Kaiser William II (r. 1888–1918) came to the German throne. At age twenty-nine, he was ambitious, impetuous, imperious, and a believer in the divine right of kings. An injury at birth left him with a physical defect (a withered left arm) for which he overcompensated by vigorous athletic activity, military bearing, and embarrassingly bombastic rhetoric. Like many Germans of his generation, William II believed Germany was destined to lead Europe. At the least, he wanted Britain, under the rule of his grandmother Queen Victoria, to acknowledge Germany its equal. To win a "place in the sun" for Germany, he coveted a navy and colonies like Britain's. This desire, of course, ran counter to Bismarck's strategy of curtailing Germany's expansion to preserve peace on the Continent. When Bismarck opposed William's attempts to build up the German navy, William used a disagreement over domestic policy to dismiss him (1890).

Bismarck had secured Germany and earned it respect as the guardian of peace in Europe. Germany could not have exercised its leadership role without its great military power, but use of this power required consummate statesmanship, restraint, and a clear understanding of the nation's true self-interest—all of which the young kaiser lacked.

Forging of the Triple Entente (1890–1907)

Franco-Russian Alliance   Bismarck's retirement led to the immediate collapse of his system of alliances. His successor, General Leo von Caprivi (1831–1899), doubted his ability to manage Bismarck's complicated policy and hoped to secure Germany by the simpler strategy of drawing closer to Britain. Britain, however, remained aloof, and Germany's maneuvers alienated Russia. Fearing diplomatic isolation and needing foreign investment, the Russians turned to the French. The French, who were even more isolated than the Russians, were delighted to join forces with anyone who promised to help them against Germany. In 1894, despite their inconsistent political philosophies, France and Russia formed a defensive alliance against Germany.

Britain and Germany   Britain held the key to the international situation, and initially it was disposed to favor Germany. Colonial rivalries pitted the British against the Russians in Central Asia and against the French in Africa. Britain had also long opposed Russian control of Constantinople and the Dardanelles and French dominance of the Low Countries. However, despite all this and despite Britain's long history of friendly relations with Germany, within a decade of William II's accession most Britons had come to think of Germany as the chief threat to their national security. They were alarmed by the foreign and naval policies to which Germany was driven by William II's envy of Britain's colonial empire and fleet. At first the emperor tried to win the British over to the Triple Alliance. When Britain chose instead to maintain its "splendid isolation," his strategy changed. He decided to demonstrate Germany's importance as an ally by making trouble for Britain. Germany blocked British attempts to build a railroad from Capetown to Cairo. It openly sympathized with the Boers of South Africa, who were fighting British expansion, and in 1898, William began to implement his plans to build a great German navy. He ordered construction of nineteen battleships. Two years later, he doubled that number.

The architect of the new navy was Admiral Alfred von Tirpitz (1849–1930). He claimed that Germany's intent was to build a fleet not to defeat Britain but, if necessary, to do sufficient damage to the British navy to end its dominance of the seas. The plan was absurd, for the British had greater financial resources than the Germans and could add enough new ships to maintain their advantage over Germany. The main achievement of the policy was to waste German resources by challenging Britain to an arms race.

Initially, Britain was not unduly concerned, but the steady growth of the German navy gradually persuaded the British to abandon their isolationism. Widespread international disapproval of Britain's Boer War (1899–1902)—an unequal struggle in which the great empire crushed a rebellion by South African farmers—also helped convince Britain that it needed some treaties of friendship. Between 1898 and 1901, Joseph Chamberlain, the colonial secretary, made several overtures to Germany. The Germans, however, were confident that a British alliance with France or Russia was impossible, and they spurned him in hopes of extracting more concessions.

The Entente Cordiale The first breach of Britain's isolation came in 1902 when Britain allied with Japan to defend its interests in the Far East from Russia. Britain next overcame its traditional antagonism to France and established the Entente Cordiale (1904). It was not a formal treaty with military provisions but an effort to coordinate the two countries' colonial ambitions. Britain gave France a free hand in Morocco in return for French recognition of British control of Egypt. The Entente Cordiale was a long step toward the alignment of Britain with one of Germany's great potential enemies.

Britain's new relationship with France was surprising, but even more so was Britain's emerging sympathy for Russia. A humiliating defeat in the Russo-Japanese War (1904–1905) and the cost of putting down a revolution sparked by that war had sufficiently weakened Russia to dispel Britain's fears of Russian expansion. Britain's concern now was to prevent Russia from drifting into the German orbit.

The First Moroccan Crisis At this point, Germany tested the new relationship between Britain and France. In March 1905, William II landed at Tangier, made a speech in favor of Moroccan independence, and implied that Germany had a role in determining Morocco's destiny. By challenging France in this way, Germany hoped to reveal the weakness of France and Britain's commitment to France. The Germans demanded an international conference to resolve the issue—a forum for a more dramatic demonstration of their power.

At the conference, which met at Algeciras, Spain, in 1906, the Germans overplayed their hand. Austria sided with Germany, but Spain, Italy, and the United States voted with Britain and France. The Germans received trivial concessions, and France's position in Morocco was confirmed. German bullying had succeeded only in driving Britain and France closer together. Sir Edward Grey, the British foreign secretary, authorized the British and French general staffs to discuss what they might do if Germany attacked France. By 1914, French and British military and naval planning had become so integrated that the two countries were effectively, if not formally, allied.

British Agreement with Russia As Britain grew closer to France, it also grew closer to Russia, France's ally. Germany's expanding navy and its ambitions in the Middle East (highlighted by a proposal for a railroad connecting Berlin to Baghdad) prompted Britain to conclude an agreement with Russia (1907) much like

QUICK REVIEW

First Moroccan Crisis
- March 1905: William II implies Germany has a role in furthering Moroccan independence
- Germany hoped to weaken relationship between France and Great Britain
- 1906: Conference in Algeciras confirms France's claims in Morocco

the Entente Cordiale. It resolved Russo-British disputes in Central Asia and promised wider cooperation. A Triple Entente, an informal, but powerful, association of Britain, France, and Russia, was gradually forming to oppose the Triple Alliance of Germany, Austria-Hungary, and Italy. Given that Italy was an unreliable ally, Germany and Austria-Hungary increasingly feared encirclement.

The equilibrium that Bismarck had worked so hard to establish in Europe began to disintegrate. Britain ceased to help Austria block Russia's ambitions in the Balkans, and Germany was unwilling to restrain Austria for fear of alienating its most important ally. The new alliances had increased the risk of conflict and made the Balkans a flashpoint. Thanks to William II and his ministers, Bismarck's nightmare of a two-front war with France and Russia was in danger of becoming a reality and becoming even more horrible than Bismark had imagined, for it now promised to involve Britain.

WORLD WAR I

THE ROAD TO WAR (1908–1914)

WHAT WERE the origins of World War I?

The Ottoman Empire was weak, but it held a vital corridor of land running across the Balkan peninsula from Constantinople to the Adriatic. The technically Ottoman, but functionally autonomous, states of Romania, Serbia, and Bulgaria lay to the corridor's north and Greece to its south. The lands on the Adriatic coast north of Serbia belonged to the Austro-Hungarian Empire. They included Croatia and Slovenia and, since 1878, an "occupied and administered" Bosnia and Herzegovina.

Except for the Greeks and the Romanians, most of the inhabitants of the Balkans spoke variants of the same Slavic language and felt a kinship with one another that had been strengthened by centuries of foreign domination—Austrian, Hungarian, and Turkish. The nationalistic movements that swept across Europe in the late nineteenth century fanned their desires for independence, and their more radical leaders longed to unify the south Slavic (Yugoslav) peoples. Serbia was to become the center of a new nation that would liberate all the Austrian Empire's Slavic provinces, especially Bosnia. Serbia dreamed of uniting the Slavs as Piedmont had united the Italians and Prussia the Germans.

The Bosnian Crisis   In 1908, the "Young Turks," a group of modernizing reformers, engineered a takeover of the Ottoman Empire. Austria and Russia had hopes of partitioning that empire, and they were alarmed the revolutionaries might succeed in restoring it. To prevent that, Russia consented to Austria's annexation of Bosnia and Herzegovina in return for Austria's support in opening the Dardanelles to Russian warships. Austria announced the annexation but did nothing for Russia when the British and French agreed to help the Turks maintain their hold on the Dardanelles. The Russians were humiliated, for they, a Slavic nation, could not support their "little brothers," the Slavic Serbs who believed Bosnia belonged to them, not Austria.

The Germans were upset that the Austrians had given them no warning before seizing Bosnia. As Austria's chief ally, the coup strained Germany's relations with Russia. Germany was so dependent on the Dual Alliance, however, that it had to allow its foreign policy to be made in Vienna. The Triple Entente was similarly strained, for the refusal of Britain and France to allow Russia to move into the Dardanelles meant they had to acquiesce to some future Russian demand if they wanted to retain Russia's friendship.

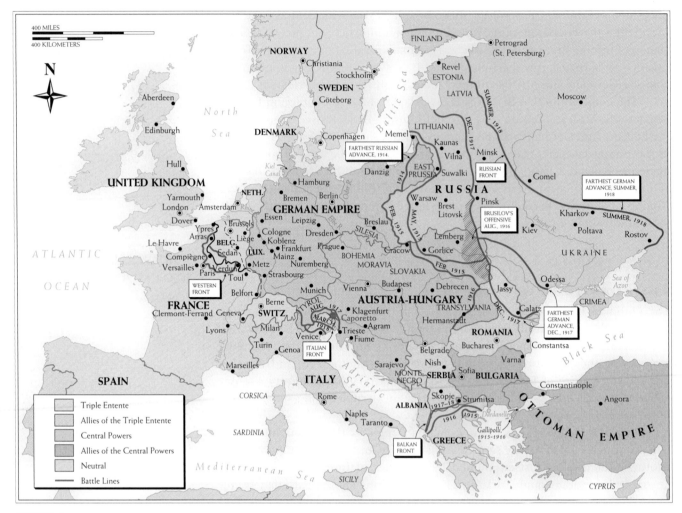

MAP 25–4

World War I in Europe Despite the importance of military action in the Far East, in the Arab world, and at sea, the main theaters of activity in World War I were in the European areas.

WHICH EUROPEAN countries saw the most military action in World War I?

The Second Moroccan Crisis In 1911, a second crisis involving Morocco drove France and Britain closer together. When France sent an army to Morocco to put down a rebellion, Germany sent a gunboat named the *Panther* to the Moroccan port of Agadir—allegedly to protect German residents. The British, anticipating the worst, wrongly believed the Germans meant to seize Agadir and thus acquire a naval base on the Atlantic. In 1907, Germany had built its first "dreadnought," a version of a new type of battleship that Britain had launched in 1906. In 1908, Germany had passed still another naval law to accelerate development of its fleet. When negotiations failed to persuade the Germans to slow naval construction, Britain concluded that the security of its island kingdom was at stake.

The Moroccan dispute was resolved when France yielded some insignificant bits of the Congo in exchange for German recognition of Morocco as a French protectorate. The chief effect of the crisis was to increase Britain's fear of Germany and forge stronger links between Britain and France. Although there was no formal treaty, the growing German navy and the threat to Agadir turned the Entente Cordiale into a de facto alliance.

War in the Balkans   The second Moroccan crisis provoked another crisis in the Balkans. Italy wanted to take Libya from the Turks to enhance its status as a colonial power, but it feared that recognition of the French protectorate in Morocco would encourage France to grab Libya before Italy could. Italy, therefore, promptly attacked the Ottoman Empire to force the Turks to cede it control over Libya and some islands in the Aegean. This encouraged the Balkan states to rise up against the Ottomans, and in 1912, Bulgaria, Greece, Montenegro, and Serbia jointly defeated the Turks. The victors in this First Balkan War quarreled over division of Macedonia, and in 1913, a Second Balkan War gave Turkey and others a chance to strip Bulgaria of much of what it had won in 1878 and 1912.

The First Balkan War alarmed the Austrians, who were determined to prevent the Serbs from seizing Albania and gaining a port on the Adriatic. When the Russians backed the Serbs, Britain sponsored an international conference to resolve the matter (1913). It called for an independent kingdom of Albania. Austria, however, felt humiliated by the airing of Serbia's demands, and the Serbs defied the agreement by staying in Albania until Austria forced them to withdraw.

The Serbs returned to Albania in September 1913, in the wake of the Second Balkan War, and Austria issued an ultimatum. Serbia again withdrew, but many Austrians favored an all-out attack on Serbia to end once and for all the threat it posed to their empire. Russia, however, was committed—in the name of Pan-Slavic solidarity—to helping the Serbs. Britain, France, Italy, and Germany cooperated in restraining both parties, but both sides feared that by holding back they might appear too reluctant to help their friends.

The crisis of 1913 influenced the response the European nations made to the events of 1914 that finally precipitated world war. Russia's allies, having urged it to back down in 1908 and 1913, were reluctant to restrain it again, and the Austrians, having discovered that the threat of force produced better results than international conferences, lost interest in negotiating.

Sarajevo and the Outbreak of War (June–August 1914)

The Assassination   On June 28, 1914, a young Bosnian nationalist shot and killed the heirs to the Austrian throne, Archduke Francis Ferdinand and his wife, as they drove through the Bosnian capital of Sarajevo. The assassin was a member of a terrorist organization called Union or Death (popularly known as the Black Hand). The chief of intelligence on the general staff of Serbia's army had helped plan the crime. His role was not known at the time, but the glee with which the Serbian press reported the event led many Europeans to assume Serbian officials had been involved.

Germany and Austria's Response   The assassination was condemned everywhere in Europe except in Serbia. This persuaded the Austrians, who saw military action against Serbia as a solution to their empire's Slavic problem, that the time had come to declare war. Conrad von Hötzendorf (1852–1925), chief of the

Above: **The Austrian archduke** Francis Ferdinand and his wife photographed in Sarajevo on June 28, 1914. Later in the day the royal couple were assassinated by young revolutionaries trained and supplied in Serbia, igniting the crisis that led to World War I. *Below:* Moments after the assassination the Austrian police captured one of the assassins.

Brown Brothers

Austrian general staff, urged attack, but Count Stefan Tisza (1861–1918), who represented the Hungarian side of the Dual Monarchy, resisted. Count Leopold von Berchtold (1863–1942), the foreign minister, knew German help would be needed to sway the Hungarians and that German support would be required in the likely event Russia intervened to protect Serbia. The ultimate decision, therefore, was Berlin's.

Kaiser William and Chancellor Theobald von Bethmann-Hollweg (1856–1921) readily promised German support for an attack on Serbia and urged the Austrians to move swiftly while the other powers were still angry. The Austrians hoped Germany's protection would discourage intervention by other states and allow them to fight Serbia alone. They were, however, prepared to risk a general European conflict. The Germans, too, recognized the risk of a broader war but believed they could contain the fight. The German decision to support Austria made war difficult if not impossible to avoid, but no evidence indicates that Germany had long been plotting a war. The subsequent conduct of its leaders suggests they were reacting to events, not implementing a master plan.

The kaiser and his chancellor made the fateful commitment to Austria without consulting their advisers. William II was motivated by violent passions. He had been the archduke's friend, and he was outraged by an attack on royalty. Bethmann-Hollweg, the chancellor, was less emotionally involved, but he was reluctant flatly to oppose the emperor and to appear soft to his country's military establishment. Moreover, he, like many other Germans, feared for the future. The time had come to take a "calculated risk." Russia was recovering its strength. The Triple Entente was growing more powerful, and Austria was Germany's only reliable ally. Although it was dangerous to support Austria, it might have been even more dangerous not to. If Austria failed to crush Serbia, Slavic nationalism could disrupt the empire and invite Russian intervention and expansion.

Bethmann-Hollweg hoped the Austrians would strike swiftly and present the powers with a fait accompli. He believed fear of Germany would keep Russia from becoming involved, but if not, he was prepared for war with France and Russia. If it came to that, he convinced himself he could persuade Britain to remain neutral—despite the fact that Germany was continuing to provoke Britain with its naval arms race.

The Austrians did not act quickly, and the Serbians returned so soft and conciliatory an answer to the ultimatum meant to provoke war that even the mercurial German emperor concluded there were no longer grounds for hostilities. The Austrians, however, were determined not to turn back. On July 28, they declared war on Serbia, even though their army could not be mobilized before mid-August.

The Triple Entente's Response   The Russians responded angrily to Austria's treatment of Serbia. Conservative elements within the Russian government opposed war, for they feared it would lead to revolution. Russian nationalists, Pan-Slavs, and the majority of the politically conscious classes, however, demanded action. The government ordered a partial military mobilization in the hope this would dissuade Austria from attacking Serbia. Mobilization of any kind was dangerous, however, for it was generally seen as an act of war. Russia's mobilization especially alarmed the German general staff, for Germany's strategy, the Schlieffen Plan, called for an attack on France before Russia could organize itself to enter the war. Germany concluded, therefore, that it had to ready its forces, and perceptions of military necessity began to escalate pressures on all nations.

OVERVIEW   RELATIVE STRENGTHS OF COMBATANTS IN WORLD WAR I

	Population (Total)	Soldiers Potentially Available	Military Expenditures (1913–1914)
Great Britain	45,000,000	711,000	$250,000,000
France	40,000,000	1,250,000	$185,000,000
Italy	35,000,000	750,000	$50,000,000
Russia	164,000,000	1,200,000	$335,000,000
Belgium	7,500,000	180,000	$13,750,000
Romania	7,500,000	420,000	$15,000,000
Greece	5,000,000	120,000	$3,750,000
Serbia	5,000,000	195,000	$5,250,000
Montenegro	500,000		
United States	92,000,000	150,000	$150,000,000
Germany	65,000,000	2,200,000	$300,000,000
Austria-Hungary	50,000,000	810,000	$110,000,000
Ottoman Empire	20,000,000	360,000	$40,000,000
Bulgaria	4,500,000	340,000	$5,500,000

France and Britain were not eager for war. France's president and prime minister were on their way home from a visit to Russia when the crisis flared on July 24. Had they been in Paris, they might have tried to restrain the Russians. France's ambassador to Russia, however, gave the Russians the same assurances that Germany had given the Austrians, and the Austrians, smarting from the humiliation of the London Conference of 1913, rejected a British proposal for another conference. Germany privately supported Austria while making conciliatory public statements to court British neutrality. Soon, however, Bethmann-Hollweg realized what he should have known from the first. If Germany attacked France, Britain would fight. On July 30, Austria ordered mobilization against Russia, and Germany's sham appeals for Austrian restraint suddenly became sincere. By then, however, it was too late for Austria to retreat without massive loss of face.

Bethmann-Hollweg resisted enormous pressure to call up the army, not because he hoped to avoid war but because he wanted Russia to act first and appear to be the aggressor. This was necessary to rally the German people to support the war. Minutes before Germany was set to initiate mobilization, news arrived that Russia had begun to move. The Schlieffen Plan was promptly put into effect, and on August 1, the Germans occupied Luxembourg. An invasion of Belgium two days later violated Belgian neutrality, which Britain had promised to protect in a treaty of 1839. This action turned the British people against Germany, and when Germany invaded France, Britain entered the war (August 4). As Sir Edward Grey, the British foreign secretary, put it, the lights were going out all over Europe.

When they came on again, Europe was a different place. Debate continues today on the causes for the "Great War," but common opinion holds it was Germany's ambition (fanned by Kaiser William II) that did most to upset the status quo.

STRATEGIES AND STALEMATE (1914–1917)

There was jubilation throughout Europe at the decision to fight, for it released the tensions that the repeated crises of recent years had raised. No general war had been fought since Napoleon's day, and few people anticipated the horrors of modern combat. The dominant memory was of Bismarck's swift, decisive campaigns whose costs were light and rewards great. Both sides expected to take the offensive, force a battle on favorable ground, and win a quick victory. The Allies (the Triple Entente nations) had superior numbers and financial resources and command of the sea. The Central Powers (Germany and Austria) had the advantages of internal lines of communication and of launching the first attack.

Germany's war plan had been developed a decade earlier by Count Alfred von Schlieffen (1833–1913), chief of the German general staff from 1891 to 1906. It called for the German army to outflank the French defenses by sweeping through Belgium to the English Channel. Then the army was to wheel to the south and east, envelop the French, and crush them against German fortresses in Lorraine. The key to the plan lay in making the right wing of the advancing German army immensely strong while deliberately weakening the left along France's frontier. The weakness of the left was meant to draw the French into attacking there while the war was decided by the German right. In the east, the Germans planned simply to hold off the Russians until France fell.

French troops advance on the Western Front. This scene of trench warfare characterizes the twentieth century's first great international conflict. The trenches were protected by barbed wire and machine guns, which gave defenders the advantage.

Hulton/Corbis-Bettmann

The campaign was expected to produce victory in six weeks, but the German commander, Helmuth von Moltke (1848–1916), lacked the courage fully to implement Schlieffen's plan by risking Germany's frontier and depending entirely on the strength of his right wing. Moltke added divisions to the left wing and even weakened the Russian front to get them. His hesitant strategy and mistakes by his commanders in the field caused the Schlieffen Plan to fail—narrowly.

The War in the West   The French, like the Germans, put their faith in an offensive but with less reason than the Germans. They badly underestimated the numbers and effectiveness of the German reserves and overestimated the importance of the courage and spirit of their own troops. Courage and spirit could not prevail against machine guns and heavy artillery. The French attack on Germany's western frontier failed totally, but defeat proved to be better than partial success. It freed troops for use against the main German army and helped the French and British stop the German advance on Paris at the Battle of the Marne (September 1914). (See Map 25–5.)

Thereafter, the war in the West bogged down. The opposing sides dug in behind a wall of trenches and barbed wire that stretched from the North Sea to

Switzerland. Strategically placed machine-gun nests made assaults difficult and dangerous, but both sides repeatedly launched massive attacks preceded by artillery bombardments of unprecedented force. Assaults that cost hundreds of thousands of lives produced advances of mere hundreds of yards. The use of poison gas increased casualties but not victories. In 1916, the British invented the tank as an effective counter to the machine gun, but the Allied command was slow to develop offensive strategies for its use. For three years, the western front shifted only a few miles in either direction.

The War in the East   The war began auspiciously for the Allies on the eastern front. The Russians advanced into Austrian territory and inflicted heavy casualties, but Russian incompetence and German energy reversed these gains. A junior German officer, Erich Ludendorff (1865–1937), under the command of the elderly General Paul von Hindenburg (1847–1934), destroyed or captured an entire Russian army at the Battle of Tannenberg and defeated another one at the Masurian Lakes. In 1915, the Central Powers drove into the Baltic states and Russian Poland and inflicted over 2 million casualties in a single year.

As the battle lines hardened, both sides sought support. In 1916, Romania joined the Allies but was quickly defeated and forced out of the war. Turkey, which was hostile to Russia, and Bulgaria (Serbia's enemy) joined the Central Powers. In the Far East, Japan honored its alliance with Britain by overrunning the German colonies in China and the Pacific—and using the opportunity to improve its position in China. Both sides in the war bid for Italy's support, which the Allies won by promising the Italians spoils from Austria's empire. In a secret treaty of 1915, the Allies agreed to give Italy most of *Italia Irredenta* (the South Tyrol, Trieste, and some of the Dalmatian Islands), colonies in Africa, and a share of the Turkish Empire, and by the spring of 1915, Italy was engaging Austria's armies. Italy's attack weakened Austria and forced the Germans to divide their troops, but Italy's help failed to achieve much of significance for the Allies.

Each side tried to stir up trouble for the other by appealing to nationalistic movements in its opponent's territory. The Germans supported the Irish against Britain, the Flemings against Belgium, and the Poles and the Ukrainians against Russia. They tried to persuade the Turks to lead a Muslim uprising against the British in Egypt and India and against the French in North Africa. The Allies had greater success appealing to nationalists who wanted to break free from the Austrian Empire: Czechs, Slovaks, southern Slavs, and Poles. A movement for Arab independence from Turkey, which was coordinated by Colonel T. E. Lawrence (1888–1935) "of Arabia," was especially important later in the war.

In 1915, Winston Churchill (1874–1965), first lord of the British admiralty, suggested a plan to break the deadlock on the western front. He proposed an attack on the Dardanelles and Constantinople. The plan was to knock Turkey out of the war, relieve the Balkan front, and ease communications with Russia—all at minimal risk. Thanks to British naval superiority and the element of surprise, a naval action alone was deemed sufficient to force the straits and capture the city.

MAP EXPLORATION
Interactive map: To explore this map further, go to
http://www.prenhall.com/kagan3/map25.5

MAP 25–5
The Western Front, 1914–1918   This map shows the crucial Western Front in detail.

WHAT FACTORS made the war on the Western Front one of position rather than of movement?

26.2
Siegfried Sassoon: *They*

If it failed, the fleet could escape with little loss. Success, however, depended on timing, speed, and daring leadership, and the attackers had none of these. Troops were landed, and as Turkish resistance continued, more were added. Before the project was abandoned, the Allies had lost almost 150,000 men and diverted three times that number from more useful occupations.

Return to the West   In 1916, both sides turned their attentions back to the western front. General Erich von Falkenhayn (1861–1922), who had succeeded Moltke in September 1914, attacked the French stronghold of Verdun. His goal was not to take the fortress but to inflict enormous casualties on the French, who had to defend their post against superior firepower from several directions. The French, however, held Verdun with comparatively few men and inflicted almost as many casualties as they suffered. Verdun's commander, Henri Pétain (1856–1951), became a national hero.

The Allies' initiative was a major offensive along the River Somme. Aided by a Russian attack in the East that drew off some German strength and by an enormous artillery bombardment, the Allies hoped to break through the German line, but once again, enormous casualties on both sides yielded no decisive advantage for anyone.

The War at Sea   As the war dragged on, control of the sea became increasingly important. The British ignored international laws that protected ships carrying peaceful cargo and imposed a strict blockade to starve out their enemies. The Germans responded with submarine warfare. By threatening all shipping, they hoped in their turn to starve Britain. These strategies angered neutrals—especially the United States, which ferried extensive trade across the Atlantic.

In 1915, the British liner *Lusitania* was torpedoed by a German submarine, and among its 1,200 drowned passengers were 118 Americans. President Woodrow Wilson (1856–1924) warned Germany that a repetition of this tragedy would have grave consequences, and the Germans tried to avoid incidents that might bring America into the war. Consequently, the German fleet, which had cost so much money and caused so many problems for Europe's diplomats, played no significant part in the war. Its only battle was fought at Jutland in the spring of 1916 and resulted in a standoff that confirmed British domination of the surface of the sea.

America Enters the War   In December 1916, Woodrow Wilson tried to mediate a peace. Neither side, however, was willing to renounce aims the other found unacceptable, and the war seemed likely to continue until exhaustion felled one or both. Two events early in 1917 altered the situation. On February 1, the Germans resumed unrestricted submarine warfare. This prompted the United States to break off diplomatic relations and, on April 6, to declare war on the Central Powers. The decision to enter the war had been made easier by an unexpected development in March. Wilson rallied support for the war as an idealistic crusade "to make the world safe for democracy," which made it difficult for him to join an alliance that included autocratic tsarist Russia. In March 1917, however, a revolution overthrew the tsarist regime.

THE RUSSIAN REVOLUTION

WHAT WAS the Russian Revolution?

*R*ussia's March Revolution was neither planned nor led by any political faction. It resulted from the collapse of the monarchy's ability to govern. Tsar Nicholas II was weak and incompetent, and the demands the war put on the resources of his country and government were too

great. Mismanagement of military and domestic problems caused massive casualties, widespread hunger, strikes by workers, confusion in the army, and peasant uprising. In 1916, the tsar alienated all political factions by adjourning the Duma, Russia's parliament, and announcing his intent to rule alone.

THE PROVISIONAL GOVERNMENT

Strikes and worker demonstrations erupted in Petrograd (Saint Petersburg) early in March 1917. The ill-disciplined troops stationed in the city refused to obey orders to fire on the demonstrators, and on March 15, the tsar acknowledged his inability to control the situation and abdicated. The Duma reconvened to form a provisional government dominated by Constitutional Democrats (Cadets) with western sympathies.

Various groups of socialists, including both Social Revolutionaries and Social Democrats of the Menshevik wing, organized *soviets*, councils of workers and soldiers that had no connection with the Duma's provisional government. The Mensheviks, who were orthodox Marxists, believed Russia had to pass through a bourgeois stage of development before the revolution of the proletariat could begin. So they were willing for the time being to cooperate with the Constitutional Democrats in forming a liberal regime. The provisional government was doomed, however, by its decision to continue the war against Germany, for this perpetuated the suffering and discontent that had brought down the tsar. When Russia's last offensive collapsed in the summer of 1917, military discipline disintegrated, and the masses turned against the government.

LENIN AND THE BOLSHEVIKS

The Bolshevik wing of the Social Democratic Party was opposed to Russia's provisional government, and the Germans seized on the opportunity this gave them to undermine their Russian opponents. The Germans smuggled V. I. Lenin, a brilliant Bolshevik leader, in a sealed train from Switzerland across Germany to Petrograd.

Women munitions workers in England. World War I demanded more from the civilian populations than had previous wars, resulting in important social changes. The demands of the munitions industries and a shortage of men (so many of whom were in uniform) brought many women out of traditional roles at home and into factories and other war-related work.

Getty Images Inc.—Hulton Archive Photos

Lenin saw an opportunity to realize the Marxist dream of striking up a political alliance between workers and peasants (using the Bolshevik-controlled *soviets*). However, the failure of a coup he attempted following 1917's failed military offensive forced him to flee to Finland and resulted in the imprisonment of his chief collaborator, Leon Trotsky (1877–1940). An equally unsuccessful right-wing countercoup gave the Bolsheviks a second chance, and Trotsky and Lenin again took charge. On November 6, Trotsky, who led the powerful Petrograd *soviet*, staged an armed assault on the provisional government, and almost as much to their own astonishment as to that of the rest of the world, the Bolsheviks became Russia's rulers.

THE COMMUNIST DICTATORSHIP

In an election that had been called for late November to select a Constituent Assembly, the Social Revolutionaries won a large majority over the Bolsheviks. The assembly convened in January, but it met for only a day before the Bolsheviks' Red Army dispersed it. All other political parties ceased to function, and the Bolshevik government nationalized land ownership and turned it over to peasant proprietors. Factory workers were put in charge of their plants. The Bolsheviks also repudiated the debts of the tsarist government and seized the banks and the church's property.

Russia's new government signed an armistice with Germany in December 1917, and on March 3, 1918, the Treaty of Brest-Litovsk surrendered Russia's claims to Poland, the Baltic states, and Ukraine. Some territory in the Transcaucasus region was ceded to Turkey, and Russia agreed to pay a heavy war indemnity. The price for peace was terribly high, but Lenin had no choice. Russia was incapable of fighting on, and the Bolsheviks needed time to consolidate their power. Lenin was unconcerned, for he believed the war and Russia's example would soon spark communist revolutions throughout Europe.

There was resistance to the Bolshevik takeover in Russia, and it led to a civil war between the Red Russians who supported the revolution and the White Russians who opposed it. Although the Bolsheviks murdered the tsar and his family in the summer of 1918, the White Russians continued to fight. By 1921, however, Trotsky's Red Army had suppressed domestic opposition and established Lenin in firm control.

THE END OF WORLD WAR I

WHAT WERE the immediate consequences of the end of World War I?

The collapse of Russia and the Treaty of Brest-Litovsk freed Germany to concentrate its forces on the western front. This might have tipped the balance decisively in Germany's favor had not America intervened. It took about a year for American troops to arrive in significant numbers, however, and in the interim the bloody struggle continued. A disastrous Allied offensive on the western front prompted a mutiny in the French army, and a victory of the Austrians over the Italians threatened the loss of Italy.

GERMANY'S LAST OFFENSIVE

In 1918, Germany decided to gamble everything on one last offensive. Its army again advanced as far as the Marne, where a lack of reserves and exhaustion caused it to bog down. The Allies, bolstered by the arrival of American troops, launched a powerful counteroffensive, and when the Austrian fronts in the Balkans and Italy collapsed, the German high command realized the end was imminent.

Ludendorff was determined that peace should be made before the German army was thoroughly defeated and civilians should take responsibility for ending the war. President Wilson refused to deal with any German government but a democracy that claimed to speak for the German people. Consequently, Ludendorff had Prince Max of Baden establish such a government and sue for peace on the basis of the **Fourteen Points** that President Wilson had articulated as America's goals in the war. These idealistic principles included self-determination for nationalities, open diplomacy, freedom of the seas, disarmament, and establishment of a league of nations to keep the peace.

THE ARMISTICE

The disintegration of the German army forced William II to abdicate on November 9, 1918. The Social Democratic Party then proclaimed a republic and blocked formation of a soviet government by a Leninist faction. Two days later Germany signed the armistice. The German people were not aware of the dimensions of their defeat, for no foreign soldiers occupied their homeland. Most expected a mild settlement, and many refused to believe Germany had been beaten. They thought it had been tricked by its enemies and betrayed at home by republicans and socialists.

There was little cause for either side to rejoice. Battle casualties had produced 4 million dead and 8.3 million wounded for the Central Powers and 5.4 million dead and 7 million wounded for their opponents. Millions more civilian deaths were directly and indirectly attributable to the war. The economic and financial resources of the European states had been badly strained, and the old international order was destroyed. Russia had become a Bolshevik dictatorship bent on fomenting world revolution. Germany was in chaos. The Austro-Hungarian, Russian, and Turkish Empires were disintegrating into gaggles of small states. Europe's hold on its overseas colonies had weakened, and the United States was beginning to intervene in European affairs in a major way. Europe was no longer the center of the world, and its nineteenth-century optimism—its confidence in the inevitability of progress through reason, science, and technology—had succumbed to profound disillusionment. Worst of all, it is widely agreed that World War I was mother to World War II and most of the horrors that were to plague the rest of the twentieth century.

Significant Dates from the Era Culminating in World War I

1871	Creation of the German Empire
1873	The Three Emperors' League
1875	The Russo-Turkish War
1879	The Dual Alliance (Germany and Austria)
1882	The Triple Alliance (Germany, Austria, and Italy)
1888	William II becomes the German emperor (kaiser)
1890	Bismarck is dismissed
1894	The Franco-Russian alliance
1898	Germany begins to build a battleship navy
1899–1902	Boer War
1902	The British alliance with Japan
1904	The Entente Cordiale (Britain and France)
1904–1905	The Russo-Japanese War
1905	The first Moroccan crisis
1908–1909	The Bosnian crisis
1911	The second Moroccan crisis
1912–1913	The First and Second Balkan Wars
1914	(August) Germans attack in the West (August–September) First Battle of the Marne (September) Battles of Tannenberg and the Masurian Lakes
1915	(April) Dardanelles campaign (May) Germans sink British ship *Lusitania*
1916	(February) Germans attack Verdun (May–June) Battle of Jutland
1917	(February) Germans declare unrestricted submarine warfare (March) Russian Revolution (April) United States enters war (November) Bolsheviks seize power
1918	(March) Treaty of Brest-Litovsk; German offensive in the West (November) Armistice

THE END OF THE OTTOMAN EMPIRE

The Young Turks, who had seized control of the Ottoman government in 1909, were pro-German, and in November 1914, they brought their country into the war on Germany's side. A few initial successes were followed by a string of defeats at the hands of the Russians, the British, and the Arabs. Hussein (1856–1931), the *sherif* (emir) of the holy city of Mecca, pushed the Ottomans back as far as the oil fields of Mosul in northern Iraq, and by October 30, 1918, Turkey had exited the war. The Ottoman government stood by helplessly as an Allied fleet landed troops and occupied Istanbul.

The peace treaty, which was signed in Paris in 1920, dismembered the Ottoman Empire. Britain and France took control of regions with largely Arab populations. Britain created the state of Iraq and declared Palestine a British **mandate** (a territory under the aegis of the League of Nations but actually ruled as a colony). Syria and Lebanon became French mandates. A Greek invasion of Asia Minor in 1919 rallied the Turks behind a young general, Mustafa Kemal (1881–1938), who took the name Ataturk, "Father of the Turks." He defeated the Greeks, abolished the Ottoman sultanate, deposed the last caliph, and founded the republic of Turkey. Turkey escaped dominance by either Europe or a Muslim religious faction and became a strong, secular nation. The Arab lands were not so fortunate. They were divided up into artificial states that had little coherence, and after World War II forced a weakened Britain and France to retreat from the Middle East, the region's instability became tragically apparent.

THE SETTLEMENT AT PARIS

Representatives of the victorious states gathered at Versailles early in 1919. The "Big Four" were Wilson of the United States, David Lloyd George (1863–1945) of Britain, Georges Clemenceau (1841–1929) of France, and Vittorio Emanuele Orlando (1860–1952) of Italy. Japan also took an important part in the discussions.

At Versailles, as in Vienna in 1815, diplomats faced the challenge of restoring world order after a long, costly war. The delegates to the Congress of Vienna, however, enjoyed advantages not available to their successors at Versailles. They could confine their attention to Europe, ignore public opinion, and draw a new map for Europe that reflected the realities of power and reasonable compromises. The negotiators at Versailles in 1919, in contrast, represented democratic governments accountable to public opinion, and surging nationalistic sentiments meant that Europe's many ethnic groups would refuse to acquiesce if the great powers presumed to distribute them about the map. Compromises were also difficult, for propaganda (much of it American) had turned World War I into a moral crusade. (See "Encountering the Past: War Propaganda and the Movies—Charlie Chaplin.")

Wilson's idealistic **Fourteen Points** granted each nationality a right to self-determination, but Europe's map could not be redrawn to provide every ethnic group with its own homeland. Wilson also had to contend with the many secret treaties that had been made before and during the war. Britain and France had promised their citizens that Germany would be made to pay for the war. Russia had been promised Turkish territory in return for recognizing France's claim to Alsace-Lorraine and Britain's control of Egypt. Romania had been promised Transylvania at the expense of Hungary. Italy and Serbia had competing claims to the islands and shores of the Adriatic. The British had raised Arab hopes for

---

WHAT WERE the terms of the Paris peace settlement?

Fourteen Points President Woodrow Wilson's idealistic principles articulated as America's goals in World War I, including self-determination for nationalities, open diplomacy, freedom of the seas, disarmament, and establishment of a league of nations to keep the peace.

mandate Territory under the aegis of the League of Nations but actually ruled as a colony.

an independent Arab state carved out of the Ottoman Empire—despite the Balfour Declaration (1917), which supported Zionist calls for a Jewish homeland in Palestine. Both these plans conflicted with an Anglo-French agreement to divide up the Middle East.

The national interests of the Allies doomed Wilson's dream of a "peace without victors." France wanted permanently to weaken Germany. Italy wanted control of *Italia Irredenta*. Britain had imperialistic objectives. Japan had aspirations in Asia, and the United States insisted on freedom of the seas and on the Monroe Doctrine. The peacemakers of 1919 were dealing with a world in turmoil. Fear of Germany was intense, and Bolshevism was a new source of anxiety. Communist governments appeared in Bavaria and Hungary, and there was a communist uprising, led by the "Spartacus group," in Berlin. (See Map 25–6.)

The Allies promoted Arab efforts to secure independence from Turkey in an effort to remove Turkey from the war. Delegates to the peace conference of 1919 in Paris included British colonel T. E. Lawrence, who helped lead the rebellion, and representatives from the Middle Eastern region. Prince Feisal, the third son of King Hussein, stands in the foreground of this picture; Colonel T. E. Lawrence is in the middle row, second from the right; and Brigadier General Nuri Pasha Said of Baghdad is second from the left.

CORBIS/Bettmann

THE PEACE

Liberals and idealists who hoped the delegates to Versailles would choose a better way and create a new kind of international order were disillusioned. The notion of a peace without victors was jettisoned when the Soviet Union (as Russia was then called) and Germany were excluded from the peace conference. Terms were dictated to the Germans, and the principle of national self-determination was frequently and unavoidably violated. Wilson, who received undeserved adulation on his arrival at the conference, gradually became the object of equally undeserved scorn.

The League of Nations   Wilson made unpalatable compromises in the hope that injustices could be corrected by a new international organization he insisted on establishing, the League of Nations. The league was not an international government but a group of sovereign states, which agreed to consult and submit differences to arbitration. The league had no army, but it planned to enforce its edicts by economic sanctions and military interventions sponsored by its members. It could not act, however, without the unanimous consent of a council with permanent seats for Britain, France, Italy, the United States, and Japan, and temporary seats for four other states. The exclusion of Germany and the Soviet Union from the league undermined its claim to evenhandedness.

The league placed colonial peoples under the "tutelage" of one or another of the great powers, which were supposed to prepare colonies for independence. This provision had no teeth, and expectations were not fulfilled. Disarmament agreements were equally ineffective. Members of the league retained full national sovereignty and were motivated by their separate interests.

Germany   Although Germany had been unified for less than fifty years, no one seems to have thought of undoing Bismarck's work and splitting it up. To protect France against a resurgent Germany, France received Alsace-Lorraine and the right to work the coal mines of the Saar for fifteen years. Also, a belt of land

26.4
Woodrow Wilson: *Speech on the Fourteen Points*

MAP 25–6

World War I Peace Settlement in Europe and the Middle East   The map of central and eastern Europe, as well as that of the Middle East, underwent drastic revision after World War I. The enormous territorial losses suffered by Germany, Austria-Hungary, the Ottoman Empire, Bulgaria, and Russia were the other side of the coin represented by gains for France, Italy, Greece, and Romania and by the appearance or reappearance of at least eight new independent states from Finland in the north to Yugoslavia in the south. The mandate system for former Ottoman territories outside Turkey proper laid foundations for several new, mostly Arab, states in the Middle East. In Africa, the mandate system placed the former German colonies under British, French, and South African rule.

HOW DID the peace settlement affect the territorial makeup of Europe?

ENCOUNTERING THE PAST

WAR PROPAGANDA AND THE MOVIES—CHARLIE CHAPLIN

*T*he huge expenditure of life and treasure required to conduct the war would not have been tolerated by the masses had governments on both sides not used propaganda to convince their people of its necessity. Propagandists demonized opponents and represented the homefront as totally committed to a noble, even holy, cause. The propagandists of World War I initially relied on newspaper articles and pamphlets to get their message across, but they soon developed powerful visual media—posters, cartoons, caricatures, and (by the middle war years) films. These were equally effective with persons of every age, class, and level of education, and they had great emotional impact.

Movies graphically represented the enemy as horrible or ridiculous and one's own people as noble, brave, and self-sacrificing. Both sides in the Great War produced films that were immensely popular with their people. The Germans considered films so important as morale boosters that they issued special rations of scarce fuel to theaters to keep them functioning through the brutal winter of 1917–1918. Germany did not, however, produce an actor of the status of the British-American comedian, Charlie Chaplin (1889–1977). Chaplin came to America in 1914 to work in vaudeville, and he was a noted film star by the time the war broke out. His most famous character was a tragicomic tramp figure who had many adventures in many movies. Chaplin's major wartime success was *Shoulder Arms* (1918), a farce in which a lone American soldier single-handedly captures a unit of bumbling Germans and the kaiser himself.

WHAT IS the purpose of military propaganda? Can films hurt as well as help war efforts?

Charlie Chaplin in *Shoulder Arms.*
© Sunset Boulevard/Corbis Sygma

---

extending from France's frontier fifty kilometers east of the Rhine was declared a demilitarized zone, and Allied troops were to be stationed west of the Rhine for fifteen years. Britain and the United States promised to defend France if it were again attacked by Germany, and Germany was to be permanently disarmed.

The East   Poland was reestablished and connected to the sea by a corridor that cut East Prussia off from the rest of Germany. The Austro-Hungarian Empire was broken up into five small successor states. Most of its German-speaking people were gathered into the republic of Austria, cut off from the Germans of Bohemia, and forbidden to unite with Germany. The Magyars retained a much-reduced kingdom of Hungary. The Czechs of Bohemia and Moravia joined with

Slovaks and Ruthenians to form Czechoslovakia, which was also home to Poles, Magyars, and several million unhappy Germans. The southern Slavs formed the Kingdom of Serbs, Croats, and Slovenes (Yugoslavia). Italy gained the Trentino and Trieste. Romania acquired Transylvania from Hungary and Bessarabia from Russia. Bulgaria lost territory to Greece, Romania, and Yugoslavia. Finland, Estonia, Latvia, and Lithuania established their independence from Russia. Britain, France, Belgium, and South Africa divided Germany's African colonies among themselves. Its Pacific possessions went to Australia, New Zealand, and Japan. In theory, the "advanced nations" were to govern their various mandates in the interests of native peoples until the latter were ready to govern themselves, but twenty years after the signing of the Versailles treaty, not one had been granted independence.

Reparations   The most controversial part of the peace settlement dealt with reparations the Allies demanded from Germany to reimburse them for the costs of the war. The Americans suggested a figure between $15 billion and $25 billion, an amount Germany could pay. France and Britain, however, had debts of their own to the United States and wanted Germany to pay everything—including pensions to veterans and their dependents. Realistically, it was obvious that Germany could not pay such a huge sum, whatever it might be, and it was decided Germany should pay $5 billion annually until 1921, when a final figure would be set that would have to be paid off in another thirty years. To justify these demands, the Allies declared the Germans were solely responsible for the war.

The Germans, of course, bitterly resented the charge and the blight on their economic future. They had already lost territories containing badly needed natural resources, and now they were presented with an apparently unlimited reparations bill. Germany's prime minister, Philipp Scheidmann (1865–1939), described the treaty as the imprisonment of the German people, but he had no recourse but to accept it. The Weimar government that ruled Germany until 1933 never overcame the stigma of signing the Treaty of Versailles.

EVALUATING THE PEACE

Few peace settlements have been as severely criticized as the one that ended World War I. Both the defeated and the victorious parties found it wanting. But many criticisms of the Treaty of Versailles are unjustified. It did not dismember or ruin Germany, which grew increasingly prosperous in the years leading up to the worldwide depression of the 1930s. The terms the Germans imposed on Russia at Brest-Litovsk (and Germany's plans for Europe, had it won) were far harsher than anything imposed on it at Versailles. The peace Versailles decreed was, however, not likely to last. Dismemberment of the Austro-Hungarian Empire was economically disastrous for central Europe, for it separated raw materials from manufacturing areas and producers from markets. Realignments of national borders also exacerbated ethnic conflicts. The Germans, who believed they had been cheated rather than defeated, remained unreconciled to the outcome of the war, and the Allies' position was not enhanced by rhetoric that professed allegiance to a higher morality than that which had guided the writing of the treaty.

The great weakness of Versailles was its failure to acknowledge reality. Germany and Russia were obviously destined to play important roles in Europe's future, but they were excluded from the League of Nations. The treaty also established no machinery to enforce its terms. It was, therefore, neither conciliatory enough nor harsh enough to create a stable world order.

Summary

Expansion of European Power and the New Imperialism

By the turn of the century, most of the world was under the control of the industrialized west. In the early twentieth century, economic motives were proposed to explain the new imperialism; Lenin famously held this view. But investment did not follow colonization in any consistent way, all the powers relied on vital raw materials from areas they did not control, and colonies were only occasionally demonstrably profitable. The new imperialism was motivated by economic and political competition and rationalized on religious and cultural grounds. In the scramble for Africa, the British sought to control the Suez Canal in order to secure the India trade. Britain coveted southern Africa's natural resources, and the Belgian King exploited the Congo for his own personal designs. Bismarck saw African protectorates as a way to improve Germany's status in relation to France and Britain. Intra-European rivalries also influenced colonial ventures in other parts of the world. Japan emerged as a great power that European nations felt obliged to contain. The United States participated extensively in imperial ventures in the Pacific.

Emergence of the German Empire and the Alliance Systems (1873–1890)

Prussia's military power and unification of Germany upset the balance of power created at the Congress of Vienna. From 1871 until his dismissal by Kaiser William II in 1890, Bismarck acted as an "honest broker" for peace in Europe. He entered Germany into multiple alliances, some of them secret, in a successful effort to maintain a balance of power in Europe. The Dual Alliance with Austria was an anchor of German policy until 1918; Germany under Bismarck's leadership was also at least intermittently allied with Russia and Italy. Bismarck's system of alliances collapsed soon after he left office. Caprivi's incompetence and Kaiser William II's arrogance made an enemy of Britain, which proceeded to enter relationships with France and Russia, creating the Triple Entente. Germany's Triple Alliance (with Austria and Italy) was weak and unstable by comparison.

World War I The 1908 Bosnian crisis, the second Moroccan crisis in 1911, and the First and Second Balkan Wars solidified Europe's alliances and antagonisms, and left many of the powers believing they could not afford to repeat various "mistakes" they had made in facing these crises. When the heir to the Austrian throne was assassinated in Sarajevo, Bosnia, only Austria wanted to go to war, and it was restrained by Hungary. But as the crisis dragged on throughout the summer, all the other European powers came to feel they must go to war. Both the Triple Entente (Britain, France, and Russia) and the Central Powers (essentially, Austria and Germany) had reasonable expectations of quick victory. Both sides bungled their strategies, and neither side understood how to take the offensive against machine guns. The land war dragged on with massive casualties and minimal results. On the sea, Germany's fleet served little purpose except, eventually, to help bring the United States into the war against the Central Powers. U.S. entry into the war came only after the Russian Revolution had overthrown the tsar.

IMAGE KEY
for pages 614–615

a. Red triplane
b. German East Africa bill
c., d., e., f., g., h., i. Badges with arms of First World War allies, and dice showing flags of various countries
j. "Gassed" by John Singer Sargent
k. British biplane
l. Women of Britain Say - "Go!" recruitment poster by E.V. Kealey
m. A British machine gun crew in action on the western front
n. British pith helmet, khaki VillageHatShop.com/PithHelmets.com
o. Lloyd George, Georges Clemenceau, and Woodrow Wilson
p. "The Devilfish in Egyptian Waters:" an American cartoon from 1882 depicting John Bull (England) as the octopus of imperialism grabbing land on every continent

The Russian Revolution Public opinion had supported Russia's entry into World War I, but the government of Nicholas II was incapable of managing a viable war effort. Nicholas II tried to deal with widespread discontent by adjourning parliament (the Duma) and ruling alone, but that strategy also failed. On March 15, 1917, Russia's last tsar abdicated. The Duma reconvened and formed a provisional government; the provisional government continued the war against Germany. Socialist factions formed *soviets*, councils of workers and soldiers; they did not support the provisional government. The Bolsheviks worked against the provisional government. The Germans helped Lenin get from his Swiss exile to Petrograd. The Bolsheviks attempted a coup in the summer of 1917. In November 1917, a second Bolshevik coup took control. When Bolsheviks failed to win a majority of seats in the new Constituent Assembly, the Red Army dispersed the legislature. The Bolsheviks nationalized land, factories, banks, and church property; they repudiated the tsarist government's debt; and they withdrew from the war. The Treaty of Brest-Litovsk imposed harsh terms on Russia, but Lenin had to sign. It took the Bolsheviks until 1921 to overcome domestic resistance and a civil war against the White Russians.

The End of World War I German victory on the eastern front was balanced by the U.S. entry into the war. Germany's last offensive was a fiasco. Kaiser William II abdicated on November 9, 1918, and a republican, socialist-led government signed the armistice on November 11. Most Germans, however, had been prevented from learning the extent of the German army's losses, so the terms of the peace settlement came as an unpleasant surprise; later, the political myth that leftists at home had betrayed the nation became a rallying cry for the right. The Great War was over, at a cost of millions of soldiers' lives and millions of civilians' lives. Europe was transformed forever: The German, Austro-Hungarian, Russian, and Ottoman Empires were all dissolved; the United States became a factor in European affairs; and the nineteenth-century belief in the inevitability of progress was shattered. The Ottoman Empire was dismembered by a treaty between Turkey and the Allies in 1920. Britain and France controlled swaths of the Arab world; Ataturk established the independent republic of Turkey in 1923.

The Settlement at Paris The Treaty of Versailles was a failure because it was not mild enough to win long-term acceptance by all parties, but it was also not harsh enough to make another war impossible. The victorious Big Four represented constitutional democracies and had to respond to public opinion. In Europe, nationalism reached the status of a secular religion, and Wilson's Fourteen Points had raised unrealistically idealistic expectations; a comprehensive resolution of Europe's nationalist controversies was impossible. Previous agreements and secret treaties could not all be honored and were sometimes mutually exclusive. All the powers feared the spread of communism; France in particular feared a rearmed Germany. The League of Nations was meant to remedy the inevitable shortcomings of the peace settlement, but it had no military power to back claims; when the United States failed to ratify the treaty, it also destroyed the league's viability. The most problematic aspect of the treaty was the harshness of its terms toward Germany. The exclusion of Russia from the settlement and the League of Nations reflected a Big Four failure to face realities of European politics.

REVIEW QUESTIONS

1. To what areas of the world did Europe extend its power after 1870? How did the New Imperialism (after 1870) compare with previous imperialistic movements? What role in the world did Bismarck envision for the new Germany after 1871? What was Bismarck's attitude toward colonies?

2. Why, at the turn of the century, did Britain abandon its policy of "splendid isolation"? How did developments in the Balkans lead to the outbreak of World War I? Did Germany want a general war?

3. Why did Germany lose World War I? What were the benefits and drawbacks of the Treaty of Versailles? Could it have secured lasting peace in Europe?

4. How did Lenin establish the Bolsheviks in control of Russia? What role did Trotsky play?

KEY TERMS

Fourteen Points   (p. 638)   **imperialism**   (p. 616)   **mandate**   (p. 638)

   For additional study resources for this chapter, go to:
www.prenhall.com/kagan3/chapter25

26 Political Experiments of the 1920s

CHAPTER HIGHLIGHTS

Political and Economic Factors after the Paris Settlement Following World War I, Europeans conducted numerous experiments in government. Many countries embraced liberal democracy. World War I changed the global economic environment, creating challenges for European governments. Labor enjoyed improved status and closer relations with government.

The Soviet Experiment Begins Once the Russian civil war was over, War Communism gave way to Lenin's New Economic Policy. After Lenin's death, Stalin and Trotsky struggled for power, with Stalin emerging victorious. The Third International was intended to win endorsement of Lenin's version of socialism by all socialist parties everywhere. The Bolsheviks passed laws that had significant implications for women's lives.

The Fascist Experiment in Italy Fear of Bolshevism led to the rise of fascism in Italy. Mussolini exploited postwar turmoil to rise to power and, once in power, took steps to consolidate his position.

Joyless Victors The political climate in France and Britain was not nearly as volatile as it was in Russia and Italy. France strove to increase its security. Britain struggled to come to terms with the postwar global economy.

Trials of the Successor States in Eastern Europe The Treaty of Versailles created new states in Eastern Europe. The right to self-determination was expected to guarantee popular support for the new governments, but economic and ethnic pressures threatened political stability throughout the region.

The Weimar Republic in Germany The Weimar Republic was responsible for the implementation of the Paris settlement. Economic problems and a lack of broad popular support weakened the republic. It is in this context that Hitler assumed the leadership of the Nazi Party. Gustav Stresemann took steps to stem inflation and renegotiate reparations. The Locarno Agreements raised hopes for long-term peace in Europe.

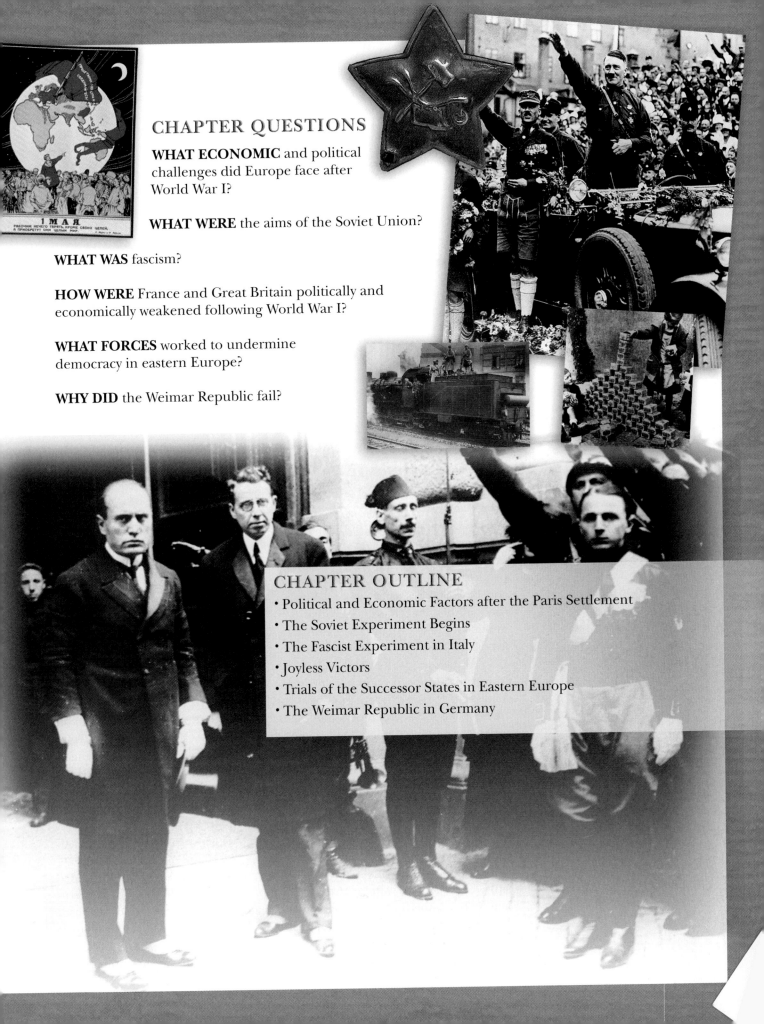

CHAPTER QUESTIONS

WHAT ECONOMIC and political challenges did Europe face after World War I?

WHAT WERE the aims of the Soviet Union?

WHAT WAS fascism?

HOW WERE France and Great Britain politically and economically weakened following World War I?

WHAT FORCES worked to undermine democracy in eastern Europe?

WHY DID the Weimar Republic fail?

CHAPTER OUTLINE

• Political and Economic Factors after the Paris Settlement
• The Soviet Experiment Begins
• The Fascist Experiment in Italy
• Joyless Victors
• Trials of the Successor States in Eastern Europe
• The Weimar Republic in Germany

IMAGE KEY

Image Key for pages 646–647 is on page 666.

WHAT ECONOMIC and political challenges did Europe face after World War I?

The economic and military provisions of the Paris (or Versailles) peace treaties caused problems throughout Europe that created support for the brutally authoritarian, territorially aggressive governments that aspired to dominate Europe in the 1930s and 1940s. These regimes were not inevitable. They were responses to failures to secure democratic systems, stable international relations, and economic prosperity.

POLITICAL AND ECONOMIC FACTORS AFTER THE PARIS SETTLEMENT

Following World War I, Europeans conducted numerous experiments in government. Many countries embraced liberal democracy, and for the first time in Europe's history the politicians found themselves accountable to mass electorates. Too often, however, nations lacked the will and the political skill to make their new systems of government work.

DEMANDS FOR REVISION OF THE PARIS SETTLEMENT

Throughout the 1920s, politicians discovered they could win votes by appealing to nationalistic ambitions and resentments created by the Paris peace treaties. Germans felt humiliated. Various national groups in the successor states of eastern Europe believed they had been treated unjustly, and the French claimed the provisions of the treaty favoring the Allies were not being adequately enforced.

POSTWAR ECONOMIC PROBLEMS

All Europeans dreamed of a return to the prosperity of the prewar years, but it proved impossible to turn back the clock and restore what American president Warren Harding termed "normalcy" to economic life. During the Great War, Europeans had turned the vast power they had acquired in the nineteenth century against themselves and had damaged the foundations of their civilization. Britain had lost more than 750,000 men. France and Germany had sacrificed 1,385,000 and 1,808,000, respectively—and Russia no fewer than 1,700,000 soldiers. Hundreds of thousands more from other nations had been killed and many millions wounded. These casualties represented a waste of human lives and talents and a loss of the producers and consumers essential to a thriving economy.

At the start of the war, Europe was the world's financial and credit center. At its end, European states were deeply in debt to each other and to the United States. The Paris settlement imposed heavy reparation payments on the defeated parties. The Bolsheviks repudiated the debt of the tsarist government, much of which was owed to France. The United States did not seek any reparations from Germany, but it did demand repayment of the loans it had made to its allies. Reparations and debt structures meant no nation any longer had complete control of its own economy. Furthermore, the lack of any means for negotiating international economic cooperation encouraged individual states to believe they had to pursue selfish, nationalistic strategies if they hoped to recover.

Market and trade conditions after the war no longer resembled those that had prevailed before 1914. In addition to the unprecedented loss of life, Europe's infrastructure (transportation systems, mines, industries, etc.) had been damaged or destroyed. Russia all but withdrew from the European economy. The division of eastern and central Europe into a multitude of small states broke up a trade region that had been unified by Germany and Austria-Hungary, and the new political boundaries separated raw materials from the factories that used them. Railway systems were split among nations, and customs barriers appeared where none had been before.

OVERVIEW   TOTAL CASUALTIES IN THE FIRST WORLD WAR

Country	Dead	Wounded
France	1,398,000	2,000,000
Belgium	38,000	44,700
Italy	578,000	947,000
British Empire	921,000	2,090,000
Romania	250,000	120,000
Serbia	278,000	133,000
Greece	26,000	21,000
Russia	1,811,000	1,450,000
Bulgaria	88,000	152,000
Germany	2,037,000	4,207,000
Austria-Hungary	1,100,000	3,620,000
Turkey	804,000	400,000
United States	114,000	206,000

Patterns of international trade also changed. The United States had become less dependent on European production and had begun to compete with Europe's industries. Decline and slowed postwar growth in Europe's colonies and former colonies further lessened demand for European goods. The combatants had financed the war by selling many of their foreign investments. This diminished Europe's power over the world economy and allowed the United States and Japan to penetrate markets in Latin America and Asia that European producers and traders had previously dominated.

NEW ROLES FOR GOVERNMENT AND LABOR

In every country, labor unions had supported wartime production, and workers had cooperated with their governments. Their loyalty had been rewarded with higher wages and admission of their union leaders to government councils. The links established between organized labor and various national governments dispelled the aura of internationalism that had characterized the prewar labor movement, but these ties also made it impossible for governments ever again to ignore labor's demands. The improvement in labor's status was one of the more significant political changes wrought by the war. The middle class reacted to it by becoming increasingly conservative.

THE SOVIET EXPERIMENT BEGINS

Russia's Bolshevik Revolution established the most durable of the authoritarian governments that arose in the wake of World War I. The Soviet Union's Communist Party (the greatest single influence on twentieth-century European history) retained power from 1917 through 1991.

WHAT WERE the aims of the Soviet Union?

It was, however, neither a party of the masses nor a nationalistic movement. In its early days, its membership rarely exceeded 1 percent of the Russian population, and for years it had to contend with widespread domestic opposition.

Communists believed Russia's revolution was not just an event in Russia's history but the dawning of a new epoch in the history of humanity. The Soviet Union's leaders believed they had a duty to export communism, and opposition to their efforts shaped the foreign policies of other Western nations for most of the century.

WAR COMMUNISM

The Red Army, led by Leon Trotsky (1879–1940), gradually eliminated the domestic and foreign troops that tried to overthrow Russia's communist government. The White Russians, who opposed the communists, failed to organize themselves adequately, and they received too little help from the Allies. The threat they posed, however, helped the Bolsheviks justify authoritarian government. Lenin declared the Bolshevik Party a "dictatorship of the proletariat." He thoroughly centralized political and economic administration so all major decisions were made at the top. His economic policy, War Communism, called for government takeover of the banks, the transportation system, and heavy industries. The state also confiscated grain from peasants to feed its soldiers and urban workers. Any resistance to its decrees was vigorously suppressed.

War Communism helped the Red Army triumph and the revolution survive, but it increased domestic opposition to the Bolsheviks (who in 1920 numbered only about 600,000). Many Russians balked at the sacrifices the central party bureaucrats demanded, and the alliance of workers and peasants, which the Bolsheviks claimed to represent, began to break down. In 1920 and 1921, there were large strikes at many factories, peasants resisted the requisition of their grain, and in March 1921, the Baltic fleet mutinied at Kronstadt. The Red Army crushed the revolt with grave loss of life.

THE NEW ECONOMIC POLICY

Faced with difficult conditions, Lenin made a strategic retreat and in March 1921 declared the New Economic Policy (NEP). It permitted private economic enterprises except in banking, heavy industry, transportation, and international commerce. The NEP was designed to court the peasants (whom Lenin believed held the key to the success of the revolution) by allowing them to sell their surplus grain on the open market. This pacified the countryside and created a more secure food supply for cities. Free enterprise flourished in light industry and domestic retail trade as well, but there were virtually no consumer goods for entrepreneurs to buy with the money they made. By 1927, the NEP had restored industrial production to its 1913 level, but it had also turned Russia into a land of discontented small family farmers, private shop owners, and businesspeople.

STALIN VERSUS TROTSKY

The NEP was hotly debated within the Politburo, the Communist Party's governing committee. Some members saw it as a surrender to capitalism and, therefore, a betrayal of Marxist principles. Lenin managed to preserve party unity, but in 1922 he suffered a stroke that led to his death in 1924. Two factions contended to succeed him in leadership of the party—one led by Trotsky and the other by Joseph Stalin (1879–1953), the party's general secretary since 1922. Lenin had voiced reservations about both men but was especially critical of Stalin. Stalin, however, managed the party's day-to-day business and had used his post to build a large following.

Trotsky's Position   Trotsky's and Stalin's fight for control of the party was cast as a dispute about Russia's strategy for industrialization and the future of the communist revolutionary movement. Trotsky represented a left wing that wanted to collectivize agriculture and make the peasants pay for Russia's industrial development. He also insisted that the revolution's success in Russia depended on similar revolutions occurring elsewhere, for Russia needed the help of sympathetic nations to expand its economy. When he sensed his side was losing ground, he became a late convert to principles of free speech and demanded that party members be allowed to criticize government and party policies.

Leon Trotsky led the Bolshevik Army to victory over the opponents of the Russian Revolution. He and Stalin later quarreled over the direction of the revolution. Trotsky lost the struggle with Stalin, who later ordered his execution.

Underwood & Underwood/CORBIS/Bettmann

Stalin's Rise   Stalin came from a poor family and had not, unlike previous Bolshevik leaders, spent time in western Europe. He was much less intellectual and internationalist in his outlook than they, and he was much more brutal. As commissar of nationalities, his treatment of the recalcitrant groups that remained within Russia after the revolution had shocked Lenin (although not enough for Lenin to dismiss him). His service as the party's general secretary—a post many of his colleagues disdained as a mere clerical position—gave him opportunities to build a power base within the party's bureaucracy. He was not a brilliant writer or an effective public speaker, but he was a master of the crucial details of party structure. He used his power over admission to the party and promotion within it to great effect in his fights with other leaders.

In the mid–1920s, a right-wing faction arose in the party and took control of the party's official paper *Pravda* (*Truth*). Given the uncertain economic outlook at this time, it recommended continuing Lenin's NEP. That is, it wanted relatively slow industrialization, decentralized economic planning, and toleration for modest free enterprises and small private farms. Stalin found it expedient to side with this group, and in 1924, he endorsed (in opposition to Trotsky) the doctrine of "socialism in one country." By stating that socialism could succeed in Russia without support from revolutions elsewhere, it effectively nationalized the international Marxist movement.

Stalin cunningly used his control of the Central Committee to marginalize Trotsky and his supporters, and by 1927, Trotsky had been expelled from the party and exiled to Siberia. In 1929, he left Russia for Mexico, where he was murdered in 1940—presumably by Stalin's agents. Stalin emerged in unchallenged control of the Soviet state, but it remained to be seen what he would do with it.

THE THIRD INTERNATIONAL

The Bolshevik Revolution posed a challenge to the socialist parties in western Europe. Most of them were Marxist, but not revolutionary. They believed the lot of the proletariat would be improved gradually by evolutionary means, and they were willing to take part in parliamentary government. The Bolsheviks rejected this and demanded that Europe's social democrats rethink their place in the world of international socialism.

In 1919, Soviet communists organized the Third International (or Comintern). Its purpose was to win endorsement of Lenin's version of socialism by all socialist parties everywhere. In 1920, Comintern imposed the Twenty-One Conditions on its members. The "conditions" required acknowledgment of Moscow's leadership, rejection of revisionist socialism, repudiation of earlier socialist leaders, and adoption of the Communist Party name. The intent was to put an end to democratic socialism's accommodation of gradual reform and parliamentary government.

QUICK REVIEW

Stalin's Rise to Power

- Sided with the opposition to Trotsky in the 1920s
- Used control of the Central Committee to marginalize Trotsky and his supporters
- Emerged from struggle with Trotsky with unchallenged control of the Soviet state

QUICK REVIEW

The Third International (Comintern)

- Organized by Soviet communists in 1919
- Intended to win endorsement of Lenin's version of socialism by all socialists
- Imposed the Twenty-One Conditions on its members

HISTORY'S VOICES

ALEXANDRA KOLLONTAI DEMANDS A NEW FAMILY LIFE

lexandra Kollontai (1872–1952), one of Stalin's supporters, expressed the extreme political left's hopes for the utopian changes in family life that the Russian Revolution would bring about as communism spread and transformed every aspect of society. Her writing spawned groundless rumors that radical experiments with sex and family life were taking place in the Soviet Union.

WHAT MIGHT the costs and benefits be of the kind of communal family life that Kollontai thought communism would engender?

The family is ceasing to be a necessity of the State, as it was in the past; on the contrary, it is worse than useless, since it needlessly holds back the female workers from more productive and far more serious work. . . . But on the ruins of the former family we shall soon see a new form rising which will involve altogether different relations between men and women, and which will be a union of affection and comradeship, a union of two equal members of the Communist society, both of them free, both of them independent, both of them workers. . . . The woman in the Com-

munist city no longer depends on her husband but on her work. It is not her husband but her robust arms which will support her. There will be no more anxiety as to the fate of her children. The State of the Workers will assume responsibility for these. . . .

Henceforth the worker-mother, who is conscious of her social function, will rise to a point where she no longer differentiates between yours and mine; she must remember that there are henceforth only our children, those of the Communist State, the common possession of all workers.

The Worker's State has need of a new form of relation between the sexes. The narrow and exclusive affection of the mother for her own children must expand until it embraces all the children of the great proletarian family. In place of the indissoluble marriage based on the servitude of woman, we shall see rise the free union, fortified by the love and mutual respect of the two members of the Workers' State, equal in their rights and in their obligations.

From Alexandra Kollontai, *Communism and the Family*, as reprinted in Rudolf Schlesinger, ed. and trans., *The Family in the USSR* (London: Routledge and Kegan Paul, 1949), pp. 67–69. Reprinted by permission of Taylor & Francis Books, Ltd.

Debate about the conditions split socialist ranks and led to the rise of separate communist and social democratic parties in many European countries. Communist parties adopted the Russian model and took orders from Moscow. Social democratic parties retained their independence and used the strategies of liberal parliamentary politics to pursue reform. During the 1920s and early 1930s, communists and socialists fought each other more intensely than they opposed either capitalists or political conservatives.

Comintern unintentionally helped recruit support for fascist and Nazi parties. It is difficult to exaggerate the fear that Soviet rhetoric and Communist Party activity aroused in Europe in the 1920s and 1930s, and conservative and right-wing political groups profited from the mass anxiety. The communist parties that were active in Western nations gave right-wing politicians a convenient target. They could justly accuse communists of seeking to overthrow the governments of their respective homelands, and they could cast suspicion on democratic socialist parties as allies of communist insurgents. The divisions that existed in Europe's leftist political parties hampered their ability to defend their position and oppose extreme right-wing groups.

WOMEN AND THE FAMILY IN THE EARLY SOVIET UNION

Communism regarded the traditional family as imbued with capitalist values that were at odds with the kind of social and economic equality it aspired to create. A few of the early Russian revolutionaries envisioned a utopian future of sexual freedom, total equality between spouses, and families based not on economic need, but solely on love and comradeship. These views were not widespread, but they provided a target for German Nazis and Italian fascists, who posed as defenders of traditional gender roles and family values. (See "History's Voices: Alexandra Kollontai Demands a New Family Life.")

Family Legislation from Reform to Repression   The laws the Bolsheviks passed after taking power in 1917 had significant implications for women's lives. Divorce became easier. Marriage became a civil, not a religious, institution. Children born in and outside of wedlock were guaranteed the same rights. Abortion was legalized, and protections were provided for women in the workplace. Women voted and were given high posts in the Communist Party, but they had little effect on the communist government.

The economic, political, and social confusion that accompanied the revolution disrupted family life. Domestic violence was a problem. The number of abandoned children increased, and the new divorce laws made it easy to break up families. Women were given educational and employment opportunities. However, those who worked outside the home were still expected to do housework, and no significant assistance with child care was provided. Women were paid less than men, and the chronic shortage of consumer goods imposed special burdens on them. They were the ones who were expected to stand in long lines to make purchases and to find ways for their families to scrape by.

THE FASCIST EXPERIMENT IN ITALY

Fear of Bolshevism led to the rise of **fascism** in Italy—the first western European experiment with political authoritarianism. *Fascism* comes from *Fasci di Combattimento*, the "Bands of Combat" founded in Milan by Benito Mussolini (1883–1945) in 1919. A number of the right-wing dictatorships that appeared in Europe between the wars have been loosely labeled *fascist*, but it is hard to give the word a precise definition. Most fascist states were antidemocratic, anti-Marxist, antiparliamentary, often anti-Semitic, and usually intensely nationalistic. They opposed the spread of Bolshevism and claimed to want to make the world safe for the small property owners of the middle class. Fascists rejected parliamentary politics, for they believed political parties sacrificed national interests to achieve petty individual objectives. By uniting citizens in pursuit of some great national project, fascists hoped to transcend Marxism's class conflicts and liberalism's party struggles. Fascist governments were usually single-party dictatorships that used terrorism and police surveillance to guarantee absolute loyalty to the state. The Communist Party that led the Soviet Union was small, but fascist states were supported by mass political movements.

THE RISE OF MUSSOLINI

Mussolini recruited his first followers from Italy's war veterans, many of whom believed the Paris peace conference had cheated Italy of territory it deserved. These people also suffered economically from the effects of postwar inflation, and they feared the spread of socialism.

28.6
Socialist Marriage to Motherhood for the Fatherland

WHAT WAS fascism?

fascism   System of extreme right-wing dictatorial government.

Benito Mussolini became famous for bombastic public speeches delivered in settings surrounded by his fascist followers and military supporters.

AP Wide World Photos

Mussolini, a blacksmith's son, worked as a schoolteacher and a day laborer before entering politics. He was initially attracted to socialism, and by 1912, he was editing a socialist newspaper, *Avanti* (*Forward*). In 1914, he broke with the socialists and established his own paper, *Il Popolo d'Italia* (*The People of Italy*). He supported Italy's entry into the war on the side of the Allies, served in the army, and was wounded. By 1919, he had become simply one among many politicians, and his *Fasci* organization was only one of many small groups that jockeyed for position in Italy. Mussolini was a gifted opportunist, however, and he changed his ideas and principles to suit every new occasion. He considered action more important than ideology, and his chief objective was survival.

Postwar Political Turmoil   Postwar Italian politics was a muddle. The Italian Parliament had virtually ceased to function during the war, and many Italians were disillusioned with their leaders, whom they believed had failed to win Italy its fair share at the Paris peace conference. In 1919, a band of Italian nationalists, headed by author Gabriele D'Annunzio (1863–1938), showed how a private military force might succeed when government did not. It seized the city of Fiume (Rijeka), possession of which the government had failed to obtain in the Versailles treaty.

Between 1919 and 1921, Italy experienced considerable internal turmoil. There were industrial strikes. Workers occupied factories. Peasants seized uncultivated land from large estates, and the nation's parliament demonstrated no capacity for dealing with the situation. The government was dominated by two parties that both claimed to represent the working and agrarian classes: a Socialist Party and a new Catholic Popular Party. The refusal of the two factions to cooperate deadlocked Parliament, and many Italians feared the social upheaval and political paralysis would bring on a communist revolution.

Early Fascist Organization   Mussolini initially favored the workers who seized factories and land. However, he reversed himself when he realized that Italians of the upper and middle classes were more concerned about order than vague concepts of social justice. He and his fascists stepped in and took charge wherever the government failed to act. They formed local squads of terrorists who disrupted Socialist Party meetings, beat up socialist leaders, and intimidated their supporters. They attacked strikers and farm workers and protected strikebreakers. Conservative land and factory owners were grateful for the work of the fascist squads, and government officials and courts simply ignored their crimes. By early 1922, intimidation had won fascists control of local governments across most of northern Italy, and in 1921, Italian voters sent Mussolini and thirty-four of his followers to the national Chamber of Deputies.

March on Rome   In October 1922, the Fascists, dressed in their characteristic black shirts, began a march on Rome. King Victor Emmanuel III (r. 1900–1946), who feared the consequences of a confrontation, ensured a fascist seizure of power by refusing to authorize intervention by the army. The cabinet resigned in protest, and on October 29, the king asked Mussolini to become prime minister. The next day Mussolini took the train from Milan to Rome, and by the time his marchers arrived, he was the head of the government.

Although Mussolini technically had acquired office by legal means, his appointment was the result of months of terrorist intimidation. His party did not hold a majority of votes in the government, and politicians of opposing parties, whose ineptitude had given Mussolini his chance, were not alarmed. Many of his opponents assumed his ministry, like others since 1919, would be brief. They failed to comprehend what he was.

THE FASCISTS IN POWER

Mussolini owed his success to the impotence of his rivals, his effective use of his office, his power over the masses, and his sheer ruthlessness. He employed propaganda to great effect to build a cult of personality. His intelligence and oratorical skill enabled him to hold his own with large crowds and prominent individuals, and many responsible Italians credited him with saving Italy from Bolshevism. On November 23, 1922, the king and Parliament commissioned him to restore order and granted him dictatorial authority for one year. Mussolini used this opportunity to put fascists in as many offices as possible.

28.2
Benito Mussolini: from *The Political and Social Doctrine of Fascism*

Repression of Opposition   In 1924, Mussolini had Parliament change the election law to end the confusion created by a succession of weak coalition governments. Previously, the number of seats a party held in the Chamber of Deputies reflected the portion of the popular vote it had won. The new election law gave the party that had the largest popular vote (if at least 25 percent) two-thirds of the total seats. In the election of 1924, the fascists took control of the Chamber of Deputies and used their majority to end parliamentary government and authorize Mussolini to rule by decree. In 1926, all other political parties were dissolved, and Italy became a single-party dictatorship.

Dominance of the government did not diminish the fascists' reliance on violence and terror. Fascists ran the police force, and fascist terrorist squads became a government militia. Late in 1924, fascist thugs murdered Giacomo Matteotti (1885–1924), a prominent socialist member of Parliament who had criticized Mussolini and exposed the criminality of the fascist movement. Most opposition deputies withdrew from the Chamber of Deputies in protest, but their departure only gave Mussolini a freer hand. Many respectable Italians tolerated and even admired Mussolini, for they believed he had saved them from Bolshevism. Any who dared to oppose him were exiled or killed.

Accord with the Vatican   The armies that had unified Italy in the 1860s had seized territory claimed by the papacy and opened a rift between church and state. Mussolini lent respectability to his authoritarian regime by healing the long-standing breach. The Lateran Accord, signed in February 1929, recognized the pope as the temporal ruler of Vatican City and provided compensation for confiscated papal lands. It recognized Catholicism as Italy's official religion, exempted church property from taxation, and gave the church jurisdiction over marriage.

MOTHERHOOD FOR THE NATION IN FASCIST ITALY

The fascist government wanted to increase Italy's birthrate. Therefore, it encouraged women to have more children and stay home to rear them. It provided maternity leaves for working women, insurance, subsidies for large families, and information on child rearing. It outlawed contraception and abortion and suppressed information about sexuality that might help women limit family size. Modest government benefits for mothers and children increased their dependence on the state, for such support was vital at a time when wages were low.

Despite government promotion of female domesticity, women constituted a quarter of Italy's work force—a percentage second only to Sweden. The fascists dealt with this by handicapping women workers. Women were kept in lower skilled jobs and discouraged from competing with men. By law only 10 percent of a company's employees could be women. By 1940, Italian women were doing more low-skilled and part-time work than before the fascists came to power. The number of female domestic servants decreased throughout western Europe but increased in Italy.

JOYLESS VICTORS

Compared with Russia and Italy, the political situation in France and Great Britain seems tame. Neither experienced a revolution or the rise of an authoritarian government, but both were troubled democracies.

FRANCE: THE SEARCH FOR SECURITY

In the wake of World War I, as in the case of earlier conflicts, the French electorate chose doggedly conservative governments dominated by military officers. These governments were opposed to social reform and preoccupied by fears of Germany's resurgence and the spread of Russian communism. The 1920s in France were marked by frequently changing ministries and aimless domestic policies. Between the end of World War I and January 1933, France was governed by no fewer than twenty-seven different cabinets.

New Alliances For five years following the Paris settlement, France's policy was to keep Germany weak by enforcing clauses in the Versailles treaty and by building a system of eastern alliances to replace France's prewar tie with Russia. In 1920 and 1921, three eastern states that stood to lose from any revision of the Versailles treaty (Czechoslovakia, Romania, and Yugoslavia) formed the Little Entente. France allied with them and with Poland, whose independence also depended on the Paris settlement. This new system of eastern pacts was far weaker than the old Franco-Russian alliance, for the small states were no match for Russia and were neither united nor reliable. Poland and Romania were more worried about Russia than France's enemy, Germany, and if Germany threatened any one of them, it was unlikely the others would come to its aid.

Despite their weakness, France's alliances worried Germany and the Soviet Union. In 1922, while the European states were holding an economic conference at Genoa, the Russians and the Germans met at nearby Rapallo. Although the treaty they negotiated on this occasion had no secret political or military clauses, the Germans agreed to help train the Russian army—an offer of assistance that provided German soldiers with an opportunity to improve their skills in the use of tanks and planes. The treaty raised suspicions about Germany's intentions and prompted France to take action.

Quest for Reparations Early in 1923, the Allies declared Germany in technical default of its reparations payments, and Raymond Poincaré (1860–1934), France's prime minister, decided to teach the Germans a lesson. On January 11, 1923, he sent a French army to occupy the Ruhr mining and manufacturing district and hold it until the reparations were paid. The German government responded by ordering a general strike, which Poincaré countered by recruiting French civilians to run the mines and railroads. Germany ultimately paid, but so did France. France's heavy-handed policy alienated the British and generated sympathy for Germany. The cost of the Ruhr occupation also sparked inflation that hurt the economies of both France and Germany.

HOW WERE France and Great Britain politically and economically weakened following World War I?

In 1924, Poincaré's conservative ministry yielded to a coalition of leftist parties, the *Cartel des Gauches*, led by Edouard Herriot (1872–1957). The new cabinet recognized the Soviet Union and adopted a more conciliatory policy toward Germany. Aristide Briand (1862–1932), foreign minister for the remainder of the decade, championed the League of Nations and urged the French not to think their military power gave them the ability to dominate foreign affairs throughout Europe. In 1926, a sharp fall in the value of the franc returned Poincaré and the conservatives to office, and for the rest of the 1920s, conservatives remained in power. France's economy flourished until 1931, a longer period of prosperity than enjoyed by its contemporaries.

GREAT BRITAIN: ECONOMIC CONFUSION

World War I changed Britain's politics but not its political system. In 1918, Parliament increased the electorate by extending the vote to men at age twenty-one and to women at age thirty. (It was ten more years before women won equal treatment.) The war helped dispel the radical image of the Labour Party, for the war effort was directed by a coalition cabinet that included Labour alongside Liberal and Conservative ministers. Liberal prime minister Herbert Asquith (1852–1928) had presided over the cabinet until 1916, when disagreements over management of the war caused him to be ousted by fellow Liberal David Lloyd George (1863–1945). Lloyd George decided to maintain coalition government until the tasks of peacemaking and domestic reconstruction were finished.

The British economy was depressed throughout the 1920s. Unemployment never dipped below 10 percent and often hovered near 11 percent. At least a million people were always without work. Government assistance to the unemployed and to widows and orphans increased, but there was no expansion of the number of jobs available. From 1922 onward, life on the dole with little hope of employment became the fate of thousands of poor British families.

The First Labour Government   In December 1923, King George V (r. 1910–1936) asked Ramsay MacDonald (1866–1937) to form the first Labour ministry in British history. The Labour Party had a socialistic platform, but it was democratic and distinctly opposed to revolution. MacDonald's version of socialism owed little, if anything, to Marx. He wanted social reform but not nationalization of industry. He also understood the most important task facing his government was proving to the British people that the Labour Party was responsible. His nine months in office achieved that goal, and the respect he won for Labour undercut support for the Liberal Party. The Liberal Party continued to exist, but the bulk of its voters drifted into the Conservative or Labour camps.

The General Strike of 1926   The Labour government fell in the autumn of 1924, and the Conservatives governed until 1929. The stagnant economy remained the nation's chief concern. Business and political leaders believed all would be well if they could restore prewar conditions of trade. This, they believed, required a return to the gold standard in 1925. However, by setting the conversion rate for the pound too high against other currencies, they raised the price of British goods to foreign customers. The managers of Britain's industries then tried to restore the competitiveness of their products on the world market by cutting wages to lower production costs.

Trouble first erupted in the coal industry, which was inefficient and poorly managed and had a long history of unruly labor relations. Negotiations broke down, and the coal miners went on strike. Sympathetic workers in other industries supported them with a general strike that lasted for nine days in May 1926. In the end the workers capitulated, for high levels of unemployment weakened the bargaining positions of their unions. After the strike, the government courted labor by erecting new housing and reforming the poor laws. Despite the economic difficulties of these years, the standard of living of most British workers, including those receiving government assistance, improved.

Empire World War I modified Britain's role as an imperial power. The right of self-determination, which Britain had claimed to be defending during the war, made it difficult to oppose liberation movements in its colonies.

The growing popularity of Mohandas Gandhi's (1869–1948) Congress Party forced the British to consider eventually granting self-government to India. During the 1920s, India acquired the right to impose tariffs that favored its industries rather than British manufacturers, and the access of British textile producers to the Indian market was limited.

Ireland In 1914, the Irish Home Rule Bill had passed Parliament, but its implementation was postponed until after the war. When the war dragged on, Irish nationalists decided they could not wait. On Easter Monday 1916, they rose up in Dublin. Theirs was the only revolt staged by a national group against any government in wartime. The British suppressed it within a week but made a grave tactical blunder by executing its leaders. This turned the Irish rebels into martyrs and shifted leadership of the nationalist cause from the Irish Party in Parliament to an extremist group, *Sinn Fein* ("Ourselves Alone"). In the election of 1918, the Sinn Fein Party won all but four of the Irish parliamentary seats outside Ulster (Northern Ireland). The Sinn Fein representatives refused to join the Parliament at Westminster, proclaimed themselves the *Dail Eireann* (Irish Parliament), and on January 21, 1919, declared Ireland's independence. The military wing of the party established the Irish Republican Army (IRA) and waged a vicious guerrilla war against the British army.

In December 1921, secret negotiations produced a treaty establishing the Irish Free State as one of the dominions of the British Commonwealth. The six counties of Ulster were granted home rule and allowed to remain part of what was now called the United Kingdom of Great Britain and Northern Ireland. No sooner had the treaty been signed, however, than a new civil war broke out. Diehards insisted on a totally independent republic. The second civil war continued until 1923. In 1933, the Dail Eireann abolished the oath of allegiance to the British monarch, and the Irish Free State professed neutrality during World War II. In 1949, it declared itself the wholly independent republic of Eire.

TRIALS OF THE SUCCESSOR STATES IN EASTERN EUROPE

WHAT FORCES worked to undermine democracy in eastern Europe?

*I*t had been an article of faith among nineteenth-century liberals sympathetic to nationalism that only good could come from the demise of Austria-Hungary, the restoration of Poland, and the establishment of nation-states throughout eastern Europe. The right to self-determination was expected to guarantee popular support for the new states and make them buffers against the westward spread of Bolshevism. From the beginning, however, they were in trouble, for none of them had strong economies, such as France and Germany had developed in the course of the nineteenth century.

ECONOMIC AND ETHNIC PRESSURES

The collapse of the empires that had long restrained eastern Europe's many ethnic groups freed those groups to demand political self-determination. Majorities in the populations of the new countries refused to compromise with minorities lest they undermine the identities of their new nations, and many minorities wanted independence or union with a nation other than the one that claimed them. In the period between the world wars, all of these states (except Czechoslovakia) succumbed to authoritarian governments.

POLAND: DEMOCRACY TO MILITARY RULE

Poland had been divided up by its neighbors and expunged from the map late in the eighteenth century. Woodrow Wilson's Fourteen Points had urged its restoration, but it disappointed its liberal backers. The Poles' sense of national identity was too weak to overcome differences of class, region, and economic self-interest. Sections of the new Poland had been governed for over a century by Germany, Russia, and Austria. Each had its own laws, administration, economy, and history of experience with electoral institutions. A vast number of tiny political parties made it difficult to form a stable parliament, and the constitution gave the executive too little power. In 1926, a military takeover by Marshal Josef Pilsudski (1857–1935) ended the confusion, and after he died, a group of his officers dominated Poland's government.

Marshal Josef Pilsudski governed Poland from 1926 to 1935.

Hulton Archive/Getty Images

CZECHOSLOVAKIA: SUCCESSFUL DEMOCRATIC EXPERIMENT

Czechoslovakia had unique advantages (a strong industrial base, a substantial middle class, and a tradition of liberal values), and it was the only central European nation to avoid self-imposed authoritarian rule. During the war, Czechs and Slovaks had learned to work together, and in the person of Thomas Masaryk (1850–1937) they had a gifted leader of immense integrity and fairness. He gave his country a chance to become a viable modern nation. There were, however, tensions between Czechs and Slovaks, and other groups (Poles, Magyars, and especially the Germans of the Sudetenland, which the Paris peace settlement included in Czechoslovakia) were also discontent. The parliamentary government's efforts to deal with these factions was doomed when German nationalists in the Sudetenland turned to the Nazi leader, Adolf Hitler, for help. In 1938, the great powers met at Munich and agreed to appease Hitler by dividing Czechoslovakia. They then stood by as he occupied much of the country and gave parts of it to Poland and Hungary.

HUNGARY: TURMOIL AND AUTHORITARIANISM

Hungary's defeat in the First World War cost it land, but Hungary achieved a goal it had long sought: separation from Austria. In 1919, Béla Kun (1886–1937), a communist, established a short-lived Hungarian Soviet Republic. The Allies reacted by authorizing an invasion by Romania to remove the communists. Kun's government collapsed, thousands of Hungarians were executed or imprisoned, and Hungary's landowners established a regency government headed (until 1944) by Admiral Miklós Horthy (1868–1957).

AUSTRIA: POLITICAL TURMOIL AND NAZI CONQUEST

Austria's economy barely functioned, but union with Germany, which would have created a more viable economic unit, was prohibited by the Paris settlement. Throughout the 1920s, the leftist Social Democrats and the conservative Christian Socialists contended for power. Both groups built small armies with which to terrorize their opponents and impress their followers.

In 1933, a Christian Socialist, Engelbert Dollfuss (1892–1934), became chancellor. He tried to steer a course between the Social Democrats and the newly emerging Nazi Party. In 1934, he outlawed all political parties except the Christian Socialists, the agrarians, and the paramilitary groups that composed his "Fatherland Front." He was shot later that year during a Nazi coup attempt that failed. Kurt von Schuschnigg (1897–1977), his successor, presided over Austria until Hitler annexed it in 1938.

SOUTHEASTERN EUROPE: ROYAL DICTATORSHIPS

Yugoslavia had been established in 1917 as the Kingdom of the Serbs, Croats, and Slovenes. Serbs dominated its government in the period between the wars and clashed violently with the Croats. The Croats tended to be Roman Catholic, better educated, and accustomed to reasonably uncorrupt government, whereas the Serbs were Orthodox, somewhat less well educated, and regarded (by the Croats) as corrupt administrators. Each group had parts of the country it dominated and isolated enclaves elsewhere it was determined to defend. Other ethnic factions (particularly the Slovenes and the Muslims of Bosnia-Herzegovina) played the Serbs and the Croats off against each other. All of the political parties (except a small Communist Party) represented ethnic groups. None stood for the nation as a whole. In 1929, King Alexander I (r. 1921–1934), a Serb, tried to impose order by outlawing political parties, jailing popular politicians, and establishing a dictatorial monarchy. He was assassinated in 1934, but authoritarian rule was continued by the regency government appointed for his son.

Royal dictatorships appeared elsewhere in the Balkans. King Carol II (r. 1930–1940) of Romania and King Boris III (r. 1918–1943) of Bulgaria tried to control rival ethnic groups and prevent seizure of power by extremist movements. Greece's parliamentary monarchy was plagued by coups and calls for a republic until General John Metaxas (1871–1941) instituted a military dictatorship in 1936.

THE WEIMAR REPUBLIC IN GERMANY

WHY DID the Weimar Republic fail?

The **Weimar Republic**, which took its name from the city in which its constitution was proclaimed in August 1919, embodied the hopes of German liberals. It was headed by the Social Democrats, the party that came to power after the abdication of Kaiser William II (November 1918). The republic's acceptance of the terms of the Versailles Treaty spared Germany from invasion, but that won it little gratitude from the German people. They blamed the republic for the humiliations and economic hardships imposed by the treaty.

The republic was responsible for implementing the Paris settlement, and throughout the 1920s this connection made it an easy target for the nationalists and the military factions whose policies had caused the war. All of Germany's politicians wanted to revise the treaty, but they differed about the means. The degree of loyalty they felt to the Weimar constitution depended on the extent to which they wanted to alter the Paris settlement.

Weimar Republic German republic that came to power in 1918 embodying the hopes of German liberals.

CONSTITUTIONAL FLAWS

The Weimar constitution was in many ways an enlightened document. It guaranteed civil liberties and provided for universal suffrage and direct election of the Reichstag and the president. However, the Weimar Republic had crucial structural flaws that allowed its liberal institutions to be overthrown. A system of proportional representation made it easy for small parties to win seats in the Reichstag. Ministers were responsible to the Reichstag, but the republic's president could appoint or remove its chancellor. In an emergency the president could declare a temporary dictatorship.

LACK OF BROAD POPULAR SUPPORT

The Weimar Republic had not been established by a popular revolution, and it failed to inspire loyalty in many Germans. Some would have preferred a constitutional monarchy. Civil servants, schoolteachers, and judges, who had previously been the kaiser's devoted agents, distrusted the Social Democrats who dominated republican politics. The officer corps, which profoundly resented the military provisions of the Paris treaty, perpetuated the myth that the German army had surrendered only because it had been stabbed in the back by civilians—particularly by those who had founded the republic.

In March 1920, the right-wing *Kapp Putsch* ("armed insurrection") erupted in Berlin. Led by a civil servant and supported by army officers, the coup failed but only after the government had fled the city and German workers had staged a general strike. When workers in the Ruhr also struck later that month, the government sent in troops. Throughout the early 1920s, there were numerous assassinations or attempted assassinations of important republican leaders, and in May 1921, the Allies humiliated the republic by threatening Germany with occupation unless it agreed to pay a preposterous reparations bill of 132 billion gold marks.

INVASION OF THE RUHR AND INFLATION

Borrowing by nations to finance the war and their deficit spending after the war fueled a disastrous rate of inflation. As government bonds came due, printing presses poured forth paper money to redeem them. Economic decline accelerated after German workers struck to counter France's invasion of the Ruhr in January 1923. By November 1923, an American dollar was worth more than 800 million German marks. German money was literally not worth the paper it was printed on. Stores refused to sell goods, and farmers withheld produce from market.

The great inflation of 1923 devastated the lives of many Germans. Middle-class savings, pensions, and insurance policies were wiped out along with all investments in government bonds. The ease with which debts and mortgages could be paid off triggered speculation in land, real estate, and industry that made fortunes for a few. Union contracts helped workers keep up with rising prices, and farmers and grocery store owners could resort to barter. Many members of the middle and lower middle classes were devastated, however, and their desire for security at almost any cost played into Hitler's hands.

The French invasion of the German Ruhr began a crisis that brought strikes and rampant inflation in Germany. Here French troops have commandeered a German locomotive during one of the strikes.

UPI/CORBIS/Bettmann

HITLER'S EARLY CAREER

Adolf Hitler (1889–1945), the son of a minor Austrian customs official, originally hoped to become an artist. As a young man living in Vienna, he was supported by his widowed mother, an Austrian orphan's allowance, postcards he painted, and

In 1923, Germany suffered from cataclysmic inflation. Paper money became worthless and children used packets of it as building blocks.

Bettmann/Hulton Deutsch/CORBIS/Bettmann

Nazis Members of the National Socialist German Workers' Party that formed in 1920 and supported a mythical Aryan race alleged to be the source of the purest German lineage.

Mein Kampf (*My Struggle*) Strategy dictated by Adolf Hitler during his period of imprisonment in 1923 outlining his political views.

work as a day laborer. In Vienna he also became acquainted with the anti-Semitic ideology of Mayor Karl Lueger's (1844–1910) Christian Social Party.

Hitler served in the German army during World War I. He was wounded, promoted to corporal, and awarded the Iron Cross for bravery. The war gave him his first sense of purpose. He became a rabid German nationalist, an extreme anti-Semite, and an opponent of Marxism (which he associated with Jews). Hitler settled in Munich after his discharge and joined a small political party that in 1920 adopted the name National Socialist German Workers' Party. Its members were more efficiently referred to as the **Nazis**. They paraded under a red and white banner with a black swastika, an ancient symbol of a mythical Aryan race that was alleged to be the source of the purest German lineage. The party's platform (the Twenty-Five Points) called for repudiation of the Versailles Treaty, unification of Austria and Germany, exclusion of Jews from German citizenship, agrarian reform, prohibition of land speculation, confiscation of war profits, state administration of giant economic cartels, and replacement of department stores with small retail shops.

Originally, the Nazis tried to compete with Marxist political parties for workers' votes by supporting nationalization of industries, but when this tactic failed, they began to redefine socialism. They ceased to advocate state ownership of the means of production and insisted instead that all economic enterprises simply be subordinated to the needs of the state. The Nazi Party grew by appealing to every economic group that was under pressure in postwar Germany and by tailoring their message to different audiences. Economically beleaguered war veterans were particularly responsive to their appeals.

Soon after the promulgation of the Twenty-Five Points, Captain Ernst Roehm (1887–1934) created a paramilitary organization to serve the party, the *Sturmabteilung* (Storm Troopers)—the SA, or the "brown shirts," as they were known from the uniform they adopted in the mid-1920s. Until the Nazis won control of the government, the SA was their chief instrument for intimidating socialists, communists, and other opponents. Private armies, such as the SA, skirted the Versailles Treaty's prohibition against rearmament by the German state. The Weimar Republic, forbidden to have an army of its own, had no way to control the paramilitary organizations set up by competing political groups.

On November 9, 1923, Hitler and a band of followers attempted to launch a *Putsch* at a meeting in a beer hall in Munich. Local authorities crushed the coup. Sixteen Nazis were killed, and Hitler was arrested and tried for treason. The trial gave him a national forum for airing his opinions about the Weimar Republic, the Versailles Treaty, the Jews, and the weakened condition of Germany, his adopted homeland. He was sentenced to five years in prison but paroled after a few months. He used his period of confinement to devise a strategy for winning political power by legal methods and to dictate *Mein Kampf* (*My Struggle*), a book outlining his political views. Hitler never swerved from his core beliefs. Among these was a conviction that Germany had to expand eastward to acquire adequate "living space." Hitler was still only a regional politician when he emerged from prison but he was convinced he was destined to restore Germany to greatness. (See "Encountering the Past: The Coming of Radio: The BBC.")

ENCOUNTERING THE PAST

THE COMING OF RADIO: THE BBC

The mass political movements that flourished during the period between the world wars owed much to new media—particularly to radio, the first form of mass electronic communication. Radio (or wireless telegraphy) was developed by Guglielmo Marconi (1874–1937) in the 1890s. The Marconi Company, established in Great Britain in 1897, was soon followed by many others, and in 1920, the first American commercial station (KADA) began to broadcast from Pittsburgh.

In 1922, Britain's government granted a monopoly of the airwaves to the BBC, the British Broadcasting Company. There were no commercials on the BBC. Its programing was funded by licenses radio owners purchased. The original mission of the BBC was to use the power of radio to elevate the level of cultural life in Britain. (To ensure a proper sense of decorum, early broadcasters even wore formal dress even though their audiences could not see them.) The BBC programmed news, classical music, and serious drama. Within a few years, however, it also bent to popular taste and added light music, sports, and vaudeville acts. In 1924, radio enabled George V (r. 1910–1936) to become the first British sovereign ever to address his nation as a whole.

The audience for radio was democratic, but most European and Asian governments have tried to control the airways. The BBC strove to be above politics, but the authoritarian governments that ruled in Europe from the 1920s onward used their control of radio to advance their self-serving political agendas.

HOW DID the philosophy and mission of the BBC differ from those of American commercial radio stations?

In 1932, King George V (r. 1910–1936) delivered the first royal Christmas address over the BBC to the British people.

© Hulton-Deutsch Collection/CORBIS

THE STRESEMANN YEARS

Gustav Stresemann (1878–1929), who became chancellor of the Weimar Republic in August 1923, energized its government. He helped crush Hitler's abortive *Putsch* and various small communist disturbances. He abandoned the expensive policy of passive resistance in the Ruhr, and with the aid of a banker named Hjalmar Schacht (1877–1970) he created a new German currency. Germany's economic prospects improved in 1924, when the Allies agreed to the Dawes Plan (named for American banker Charles Dawes). It lowered Germany's annual reparation payments and pegged their amount to fluctuations in the German economy. After the last French troops left the Ruhr in 1925, foreign capital began to flow into Germany, and the employment situation improved. (See Map 26–1.) That year, the election to the presidency of field

MAP EXPLORATION

Interactive map: To explore this map further, go to
http://www.prenhall.com/kagan3/map26.1

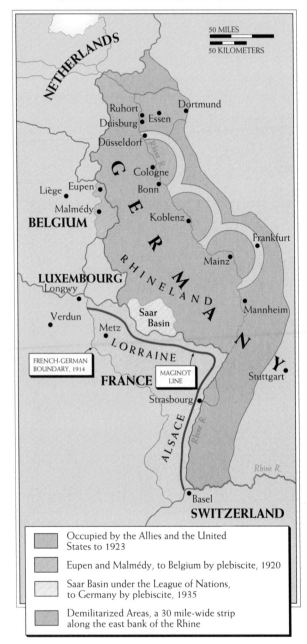

Occupied by the Allies and the United
States to 1923

Eupen and Malmédy, to Belgium by plebiscite, 1920

Saar Basin under the League of Nations,
to Germany by plebiscite, 1935

Demilitarized Areas, a 30 mile-wide strip
along the east bank of the Rhine

MAP 26–1

Germany's Western Frontier The French-Belgian-German border area between the two world wars was sensitive. Despite efforts to restrain tensions, there were persistent difficulties related to the Ruhr, Rhineland, Saar, and Eupen-Malmédy regions that required strong defenses.

WHY WERE the territorial divisions between France, Germany, and Belgium unsatisfactory?

marshal Paul von Hindenburg (1847–1934), a monarchist and war hero, suggested conservatives were becoming reconciled to the republic.

In late November 1923, Stresemann resigned as chancellor to become foreign minister. In this role, he sought both to fulfill and to revise provisions of the Paris settlement. His goal was to recover German-speaking territories lost to Poland and Czechoslovakia and unite Germany and Austria. He hoped a policy of accommodation would restore the respectability and economic stability Germany needed to win acceptance by the community of nations.

LOCARNO

In a spirit of conciliation, foreign secretaries Austen Chamberlain (1863–1937) for Britain and Aristide Briand for France accepted Stresemann's proposal for a fresh start. This led to the Locarno Agreements of October 1925. The border the Versailles Treaty had established between France and Germany was accepted. No agreement was reached about Germany's eastern frontier, but the Germans committed themselves to arbitration with Poland and Czechoslovakia. France supported Germany's admission to the League of Nations and agreed to withdraw from the Rhineland five years ahead of schedule (in 1930).

The Locarno Agreements raised hopes across Europe. Chamberlain and Dawes received the Nobel Peace Prize in 1925 and Briand and Stresemann in 1926. In 1928, the leading European nations, Japan, and the United States signed the Kellogg-Briand Pact, which renounced "war as an instrument of national policy." There were, however, no grounds for the era's extreme optimism. France had merely acknowledged it could not coerce Germany without help, and Britain had signaled its unwillingness to enforce the Paris settlement of Germany's disputed eastern frontiers. Many people in France and Germany were also opposed to conciliation. This became clear in 1929, when the Dawes Plan ran out and was replaced by the Young Plan (named for American businessman Owen D. Young). The Young Plan lowered reparation payments, limited the term for making payments, and removed outside supervision of Germany, but there was an intense outcry in Germany against the continuation of any reparations.

The Germans were far from reconciled to their situation, but another war was not inevitable. With the help of American loans, Europe was recovering its prosperity. A growing economy and further diplomatic accommodations might have rallied the German people behind the Weimar Republic, but the Great Depression of the 1930s sent Europe down quite a different path.

SUMMARY

Political and Economic Factors after the Paris Settlement
Political and economic structures were weak in many European nations, either because the nations themselves were new or because older patterns had been disrupted by World War I. Liberalization of democracy in many countries meant more people—including women—had the vote. Mass electorates expressed their economic and social anxieties, their nationalistic ambitions, and their concerns about the Paris peace treaties at the voting booth, and politicians had to listen. Europe as a whole had lost its global financial dominance, and each nation of Europe had lost its financial independence. Trade relationships were disrupted by the establishment of new states (and often, new tariffs) and the loss to war of transportation and production facilities. The United States and Japan made inroads into global markets that had been dominated by Europe.

The Soviet Experiment Begins The presence of a ruling Communist Party in Europe from 1917 to 1991 significantly influenced the Europe's political history during this period. Communist leaders tended to view the revolution in Russia as an exportable event. Trotsky led the Red Army to victory over the White Russians. Lenin and the Bolsheviks imposed centralized control over almost all aspects of life, but workers, peasants, and soldiers were all expressing strong discontent by 1921. Lenin responded with the New Economic Policy. In 1922, Lenin suffered a stroke. Trotsky and Stalin competed for control of the party; Stalin won. Comintern policy split Europe's socialist parties, allowing the rise of conservative and right-wing groups. Communist rhetoric supported a radical reorganization of family life and women's roles. In reality, most women's daily lives were constrained by the same forces that Western feminists were free to fight against, and Russian women had the added burden of living in a society that suffered from shortages of housing and goods.

The Fascist Experiment in Italy Mussolini's fascist movement was the first to gain power in western Europe in response to fears of the spread of Bolshevism. Fascist movements opposed more than they stood for, but all were nationalistic and based on mass political parties. Ultranationalist D'Annunzio was the first to use nongovernmental military force for political ends in Italy; soon, fascist terror squads under Mussolini's leadership were disrupting Socialist Party meetings. In October 1922, after he and his followers had marched on Rome, Mussolini was legally appointed prime minister. By 1926, he had made Italy into a single-party dictatorship. He used propaganda to build a cult of personality. He used violence and terror to consolidate power; he also made peace between the Italian state and the Vatican with the Lateran Accord in 1929. The fascist government discouraged women from working and encouraged large families.

Joyless Victors Although France and Great Britain avoided revolution or dictatorship, both countries experienced political turmoil after the war. France

Major Political Events of the 1920s

Year		Event
1919	(August)	Weimar Republic's constitution
1920		Kapp *Putsch*
1921	(March)	Lenin's New Economic Policy
	(December)	The Irish Free State recognized
1922	(April)	Treaty of Rapallo
	(October)	Mussolini assumes power
1923	(January)	France occupies the Ruhr
	(November)	Hitler's Beer Hall *Putsch*
	(December)	First Labour Party government in Britain
1924		Death of Lenin
1925		Locarno Agreements
1926		General strike in Britain
1928		Kellogg-Briand Pact
1929	(January)	Trotsky expelled from the Soviet Union
	(February)	Lateran Accord

IMAGE KEY

for pages 646–647

a. Soviet portrait of Lenin as a heroic revolutionary

b. BBC-Marconi AXBT ribbon microphone with cover

c. Leon Trotsky directing his soldiers

d. German five-hundred million mark note

e. Russian propaganda poster celebrating 1st May: "You have nothing to lose but your chains, but the world will soon be yours" Musuem of the Revolution, Moscow, Russia/Bridgeman Art Library, London

f. Benito Mussolini (left) during the Fascist march on Rome, 1922

g. Red Army cap badge, 1919

h. During a Nazi Party rally in Nuremberg in 1927, Adolf Hitler stops his motorcade to receive the applause of the surrounding crowd

i. French soldiers of Engineer Corps man and guard German locomotive during Ruhr crisis strike

j. The German inflation of 1923 made paper money virtually worthless. Here children play with wads of bank notes as if they were blocks

sought security first and foremost and elected conservatives more often than not. France formed new alliances as part of its effort to ensure Europe's adherence to the terms of the Paris settlement. In 1923, when Germany defaulted on reparations payments, France occupied the Ruhr, a German industrial district that bordered France. This cost France, in direct expenses and in the loss of stature that this pointless overreaction brought to the nation. In the late 1920s, France achieved a longer period of economic prosperity than any other nation in that era. In Britain, voting rights expanded. The economy was depressed throughout the 1920s, and unemployment was often near 11 percent. Lloyd George was the last Liberal prime minister; after 1923, Labour and the Conservative Party dominated British politics. The nationwide general strike of 1926 was a milestone in the British labor movement, although it won labor no concessions at the time. Ireland's Easter Monday, 1916, nationalist uprising was suppressed, but in 1919, Ireland declared independence and was recognized as a dominion of the British Commonwealth in 1921; in 1949, the island state minus the six counties of Ulster became the wholly independent republic of Eire.

Trials of the Successor States in Eastern Europe Parliamentary governments floundered in most of the eastern European states set up after the dissolution of the Austro-Hungarian Empire. They lacked the economic base and the history of the gradual expansion of liberal democracy that helped provide stability in Great Britain and France. The new states were not financially independent; they were poor and rural nations in an industrialized world. Each state had at least one minority ethnic group living within its new borders. With the exception of Czechoslovakia, all wound up under authoritarian rule. Poland particularly disappointed European liberals, because its recreation had been a celebrated cause among them.

The Weimar Republic in Germany The Social Democratic leadership of the Weimar Republic was unfairly blamed for accepting the terms of the Versailles Treaty, when in fact the Allies had offered no choice in the matter. All political groups in Germany wanted to revise the treaty, although they all disagreed about how and to what extent to do so. The enlightened Weimar constitution carried the seeds of its own destruction, because it allowed its liberal institutions to be overthrown. Extremism from both the left and the right, often accompanied by violence, threatened the republic throughout its existence. In 1920, the National Socialist German Workers' Party, or Nazis, started to make a name for itself in Munich. The Nazis were rabidly anti-Semitic and nationalist; they issued a platform, the Twenty-Five Points, denouncing Versailles, Jews, and Germany's separation from Austria, among other things; otherwise, they were basically opportunistic, tailoring their message to what their audience wanted to hear. Hitler started to gain his notoriety within this group. Reparations and the work stoppages in the Ruhr after French occupation led to cataclysmic inflation, with disastrous consequences for many middle-class Germans. In 1923, Stresemann took steps to stem inflation and renegotiate reparations. Hindenberg became president in 1925 as the economy improved.

The October 1925 Locarno Agreements confirmed Germany's western borders while leaving the status of the eastern frontier vague. All the signatories to the agreements could feel good about themselves. The return to prosperity was helping reconcile Germans to their government.

REVIEW QUESTIONS

1. How did the Bolshevik Revolution pose a challenge to the rest of Europe? Why did Lenin institute the New Economic Policy? How did Lenin's policies lead to divisions among Western socialist parties? How did Joseph Stalin come to power?

2. What is fascism? How did the fascists succeed in obtaining power in Italy? How did Mussolini's right-wing fascist dictatorship compare with Stalin's left-wing communist dictatorship?

3. Why were Britain and France "joyless victors" after World War I? How did World War I change British politics? What foreign policy problems did France face after the signing of the Versailles Treaty? Was the invasion of the Ruhr wise? Should France have signed the Locarno pact?

4. Why did all but one of the successor states in eastern and central Europe fail to establish viable democracies? Could the Weimar Republic have taken root in Germany, or was its failure inevitable? Why did the Versailles Treaty loom so large as an issue in Germany's domestic politics?

KEY TERMS

fascism   (p. 653)   Nazis   (p. 662)   Weimar Republic   (p. 660)
Mein Kampf   (p. 662)

 For additional study resources for this chapter, go to:
   www.prenhall.com/kagan3/chapter26

27

Europe and the Great Depression of the 1930s

CHAPTER HIGHLIGHTS

Toward the Great Depression Three factors heightened the severity and duration of the Great Depression: The financial problems caused by World War I and the subsequent peace settlement, a crisis in production and distribution of goods, and the failure of the United States and Europe to cooperate on economic policy. The governments of the late 1920s and early 1930s were ill equipped to deal with the problems the depression created.

Confronting the Great Depression in the Democracies Britain's National Government devised a program to fight the depression. These policies had some success and Britain's political system was never really challenged. France's Great Depression started later but lasted longer than Britain's. Right-wing groups rose to challenge the legitimate government. Socialist-Communist cooperation brought the Popular Front to power. By the late 1930s France was politically fragmented.

Germany: The Nazi Seizure of Power The Nazis rose from obscurity by exploiting the fears created by the depression. In 1933 Hitler was appointed chancellor and, subsequently, used the excuse of the Reichstag fire to claim dictatorial power. Hitler turned Germany into a police state, boring down most heavily on Germany's Jews. Hitler called on German women to preserve racial purity. His success in dealing with the depression won support for his regime.

Italy: Fascist Economics Italian Fascists sought to steer a middle course between socialism and a liberal laissez-faire economic system. Under their policy of corporatism, major industries were organized as syndicates of labor and management. After 1930, industrial syndicates were further organized into entities called corporations.

Stalin's Soviet Union: Central Economic Planning, Collectivism, and Party Purges Stalin launched a series of Five-Year Plans to achieve the rapid industrialization of the Soviet Union. The collectivization of agriculture resulted in food shortages, starvation, and the displacement of 2 million people. Resistance to collectivization was widespread. Soviet cities grew rapidly in the 1930s. Many outside observers were impressed with Stalin's apparent accomplishments. During the Great Purges, millions of Soviet citizens were executed, imprisoned, or exiled.

CHAPTER QUESTIONS

WHAT FACTORS led to the Great Depression?

WHAT EFFECT did the Great Depression have on Great Britain and France?

HOW DID the Nazis affect German politics and society?

HOW DID Mussolini transform the Italian economy?

WHAT INDUSTRIAL advances did the Soviet Union make in the 1930s?

CHAPTER OUTLINE
- Toward the Great Depression
- Confronting the Great Depression in the Democracies
- Germany: The Nazi Seizure of Power
- Italy: Fascist Economics
- Stalin's Soviet Union: Central Economic Planning, Collectivization, and Party Purges

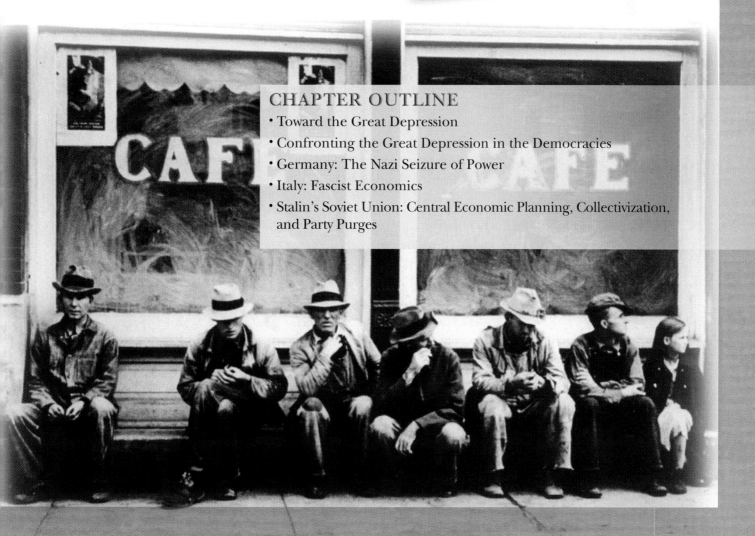

IMAGE KEY

Image Key for pages 668–669 is on page 684.

WHAT FACTORS led to the

Great Depression?

Europe did not share the economic boom that made the 1920s a "roaring" decade for the United States, because the economies of the European nations did not fully recover from World War I. The Great Depression that began when the boom ended in 1929 was the most severe slump ever experienced by capitalist nations. Business and political leaders despaired at the failure of the market's mechanisms to restore prosperity, and Marxists rejoiced that the downfall of capitalism was at hand.

Toward the Great Depression

Three situations heightened the severity and duration of the Great Depression: the financial difficulties created by World War I and the subsequent peace settlement, a crisis in production and distribution of goods on the world market, and the failure of the United States and its European trading partners to cooperate.

The Financial Tailspin

The debts European nations incurred during World War I inflated their currencies, and the demand for consumer and industrial goods that the return of peacetime unleashed drove prices still higher. Price and wage increases subsided after 1921, but nations found it difficult to maintain the value of their currencies. The German financial disaster of 1923 and its specter of uncontrolled inflation explain why most governments refused, when the depression struck, to try to stimulate their economies by running budget deficits.

Reparations and War Debts   French and American politics relating to reparation payments and international war-debt settlements complicated the international economic scene. France had paid reparations following its defeats in 1815 and 1871, and as a victor in World War I, it felt entitled to reparations to finance its postwar recovery. The United States was no less insistent on repayment of the loans it had made to its allies, who were also indebted to one another. Most of the Allies wanted Germany to assume the burden of paying off their obligations.

Reparations and war debts hindered business expansion and international trade by consuming investment capital. The volatile economic situation also encouraged currency speculation that siphoned off more of the capital needed to fund productive enterprises. Governments fought back by placing controls on their currencies, and they imposed high tariffs to curtail importation of foreign goods and prevent unfavorable balances of trade that cost them the money they needed to pay their war debts. These policies contributed to a financial muddle that hurt trade, production, and employment.

American Investments   In 1924, the Dawes Plan renegotiated the sums demanded from Germany as reparations and smoothed debt repayments to the United States. The private American capital that then began to flow to Europe (especially to Germany) created a short burst of prosperity for Europeans. In 1928, however, the booming New York stock market began to siphon money away from European investments, and virtually unregulated financial speculation led to Wall Street's crash in October 1929. The crash produced a banking crisis, for U.S. banks had lent their customers large amounts of money to invest in the stock market. The crash made repayment of these loans impossible and caused banks to fail. Little American capital remained for investment in Europe or elsewhere. Credit of all kinds grew scarce, and renewal of loans already made to Europeans became difficult.

The End of Reparations   The shortage of American loans contributed to a financial crisis in Europe. In May 1931, a major bank, the Viennese Kreditanstalt, collapsed. Government intervention saved Germany's banking system, but Germany could not make its next scheduled reparation payment. In June 1931, the American president, Herbert Hoover, announced a one-year moratorium on payments on all international debts. This struck a blow to France, for its economy depended on German reparations. France, however, had little choice but to consent, for Germany's economy had all but collapsed. In the summer of 1932, the Lausanne Conference terminated all reparations. Debts owed the United States were settled either through small token payments or declarations of default. This decision, however, was not enough to restore stability.

Problems in Agricultural Commodities

Turmoil in the financial markets was accompanied by a downturn in production and trade. In the 1920s, Europe's capacity to produce goods began to exceed demand. Overproduction forced factory closings and increased unemployment. Something similar happened in the agricultural sector of the economy. Improved methods of farming, new crop species, expanded tillage, and better transportation flooded the world market with grain and dropped wheat prices to record low levels. Consumers benefited at first, but the collapse in grain prices meant lower incomes for Europe's farmers at a time when higher wages for industrial workers were driving up the cost of the goods they needed. Farmers curtailed purchases and began to have difficulty paying off mortgages and annual business loans.

Countries tried to protect their domestic grain markets by imposing tariffs on imports, but tariffs disrupted trade and may have made the situation worse. As production outstripped demand and prices plummeted, governments tried to sustain farmers by buying up agricultural commodities. Government-held reserves soon rose to record levels, and farmers in underdeveloped nations in Asia, Africa, and Latin America could not compete in the world market and make enough money to buy the products of Europe's industries.

The unemployment that had persisted in Great Britain and Germany was a sign domestic markets in those countries were already weakening in the 1920s, and economic turmoil in international markets hit all of Europe's industries hard, for they all depended on foreign customers. Domestic demand shrank even more as governments whose tax bases were declining reduced spending to avoid mounting debt. All these factors worked together to deepen and extend the Great Depression.

Depression and Government Policy

During the Great Depression, people with work always well outnumbered the unemployed, and there was some economic expansion—particularly in new industries, such as automobiles, radios, synthetics, and providers of various kinds of services. The general downturn, however, made everyone feel insecure, and people in nearly all walks of life lived in fear that it was only a matter of time before they too faced poverty or reduced circumstances.

The governments of the late 1920s and the early 1930s were not well prepared to deal with these problems. Orthodox economic theory called for them to cut spending to prevent inflation and to wait for market mechanisms to regulate the economy and restore prosperity. In 1936, John Maynard Keynes's (1883–1946) *General Theory of Employment, Interest, and Money* challenged this view by arguing that governments could spend their way out of the depression. By then, Europe's governments were already responding (as never before) to calls from their electorates for economic intervention.

HISTORY'S VOICES

JOHN MAYNARD KEYNES CALLS FOR GOVERNMENT INVESTMENT TO CREATE EMPLOYMENT

Since the nineteenth century, most economists believed that given enough time, capitalistic economies would recover on their own from economic crises and unemployment. Consequently, when the Great Depression struck the worldwide economy, the governments of Western Europe and the United States initially undertook relatively modest actions to address it. Socialists, of course, had long advocated government intervention. In 1936, however, John Maynard Keynes, a prominent British economist who was not a socialist, published The General Theory of Employment, Interest and Money. Keynes believed that the Great Depression demonstrated that economic crises could be so severe that government spending would be needed to generate new economic activity to revive employment and lift the economy out of depression. Keynes's book did not influence many policies during the Great Depression, but after World War II, many Western governments devised economic policies along the lines he advocated.

WHY DOES he call government spending the "socialisation of investment"? How much of his argument is analytical? How much political?

In some respects the foregoing theory is moderately conservative in its implications. For whilst it indicates the vital importance of establishing certain central controls in matters which are now left [mainly in] the individual initiative, there are wide fields of activity which are unaffected. The State will have to exercise a guiding influence on the propensity to consume partly through its scheme of taxation, partly by fixing the rate of interest, and partly, perhaps, in other ways. Furthermore, it

seems unlikely that the influence of banking policy on the rate of interest will be sufficient by itself to determine an optimum rate of investment. I conceive, therefore, that a somewhat comprehensive socialisation of investment will prove the only means of securing an approximation to full employment; though this need not exclude all manner of compromises and of devices by which public authority will co-operate with private initiative. But beyond this, no obvious case is made out for a system of State Socialism which would embrace most of the economic life of the community. It is not the ownership of the instruments of production which it is important for the State to assume. If the State is able to determine the aggregate amount of resources devoted to augmenting the instruments and the basic rate of reward to those who [execute] them, it will have accomplished all that is necessary. . . .

To put the matter concretely, I see no reason to suppose that the existing system seriously misemploys the factors of production which are in use. There are, of course, errors of foresight; but these would not be avoided by centralizing decisions. When 9,000,000 men are employed out of 10,00,000 willing and able to work, there is no evidence that the labour of these 9,000,000 men is misdirected. The complaint against the present system is not that these 9,000,000 men ought to be employed on different tasks, but that tasks should be available for the remaining 1,000,000 men. It is in determining the volume, not the direction, of actual employment that the existing system has broken down.

John Maynard Keynes, *The General Theory of Employment, Interest and Money* (London: Macmillan & Co., Ltd., 1960) pp. 377–78, 379.

WHAT EFFECT did the Great Depression have on Great Britain and France?

CONFRONTING THE GREAT DEPRESSION IN THE DEMOCRACIES

The Great Depression ended the business-as-usual attitude that had characterized politics in Great Britain and France during the late 1920s. The relative success of Britain's response bolstered confidence in democracy. The social and political hostility that emerged from France's actions undercut faith in republican institutions.

OVERVIEW   CAPITALIST, FASCIST, AND COMMUNIST ECONOMIC SYSTEMS

Capitalism	• Private ownership of the means of production • Personal profit can be acquired through investment of capital • Limited government intervention in the economy • Free market, based on supply and demand
Fascism	• Seeks to steer a course between socialism and a liberal laissez-faire system • Corporatism organizes major industries as syndicates of labor and management • Subsidized shipping and protective tariffs are among efforts to become self-sufficient
Communism	• Central planning sets goals for production and coordinates manufacturing • Focuses on development of heavy industries and infrastructure, not consumer goods • Strictly controlled labor force

GREAT BRITAIN: THE NATIONAL GOVERNMENT

In 1929, a second minority Labour government, headed by Ramsay MacDonald, took office. As the number of Britain's unemployed passed 2.5 million in 1931, the ministry split over what to do. MacDonald believed the budget should be slashed, government salaries reduced, and unemployment benefits cut. This was a bleak program for a Labour government. When many of its ministers opposed the prime minister's plan, he requested the resignation of his entire cabinet. MacDonald requested a meeting with King George V, at which he was expected to announce the fall of his government. However, instead of resigning, he agreed to form a coalition cabinet (the National Government) representing Labour, Conservatives, and Liberals. The appearance of political consensus this created helped the government impose unpleasant measures.

The National Government devised three programs to fight the depression. First, it tried to balance its budget by raising taxes, cutting benefits to the unemployed and the elderly, and lowering government salaries. Second, it took Britain off the gold standard and let the value of the pound fall about 30 percent. (This was expected to stimulate exports by lowering the price of British goods abroad.) The third of the government's measures was the Import Duties Bill. It required that importers of goods from places outside the British empire pay an ad valorem tariff—a charge of 10 percent of the value of each item brought into the country. In sum, MacDonald's government abandoned the hallmarks of a century of British commercial policy: the gold standard and free trade.

The National Government's program had some success, and Great Britain avoided the banking crises that hit other countries. Government efforts to keep interest rates down encouraged borrowing for home mortgages and fostered the largest private housing boom in British history. This created demands for goods that helped related industries. In 1934, Britain became the first nation to restore and exceed its 1929 level of production, and by 1937, the number of its unemployed had fallen to below 1.5 million.

Britain's economy was stagnant at the start of the Great Depression and remained so after the crisis had passed, but Britain's political system was never seriously challenged. Unemployed workers demonstrated, but social insurance

In what was known as the "Jarrow Crusade," during the autumn of 1936 a group of approximately 200 protesters marched from the town of Jarrow in northeastern England to London to demonstrate their need for employment and the plight of their town, where the previous year the shipyard had been closed.

Getty Images, Inc./Hulton Archive Photos

kept them from becoming too desperate. The National Government placated the populace by seeming to steer a middle course between the extremes of both the Labour and the Conservative parties.

FRANCE: THE POPULAR FRONT

France's Great Depression began later but lasted longer than Britain's. The economic slide did not affect the French economy until 1931. The government raised tariffs to protect French goods and French agriculture. This sustained the domestic market but did little to combat industrial stagnation. Wages went down, but unemployment was not a major problem. Rarely were more than 500,000 French workers without jobs. Relations between labor and management were nonetheless tense.

The first political fallout from the Great Depression was the election of a second Radical coalition government in 1932. The earlier Radical government's policies had led to rampant inflation in 1924. The new government pursued a deflationary policy, but in the same year it took office, the German reparation payments so important to the French economy stopped. An economic crisis developed, and the political situation became increasingly volatile.

Right-Wing Violence   In addition to the legitimate government represented by the Chamber of Deputies, right-wing groups with authoritarian tendencies won a footing on the political stage. These included *Action Française,* which had been founded before World War I in the wake of the Dreyfus affair, and a veterans' organization, *Croix de Feu* ("Cross of Fire"). More than 2 million people joined these and similar groups. Some advocated monarchy. Others wanted military rule. All opposed parliamentary government, socialism, and communism. Their eagerness to end party politics and mobilize the populace behind efforts to aggrandize the nation suggests a certain sympathy with the spirit of the fascists and Nazis.

On February 6, 1934, right-wing groups staged a large demonstration in Paris. Violence erupted when the crowd attempted to march on the Chamber of Deputies. Fourteen demonstrators were killed and scores injured. This was the largest disturbance in Paris since the Commune of 1871, and it brought down the Radical ministry. A national coalition government composed of all living former premiers took its place, but the demonstration's most important outcome was to alert left-wing parties to the possibility that a right-wing coup might well succeed in France.

Socialist-Communist Cooperation   Between 1934 and 1936, the French left worked at making peace within its own ranks. In 1920, the Comintern had split French left Socialists from French Communists. Stalin's fear of Hitler and desire for allies, however, moderated the communists' stance and opened the way for closer cooperation with socialists. In July 1935, the left-wing parties united to form the Popular Front, and in the election of 1936, they won a majority in the Chamber of Deputies. For the first time in France's history, Socialists formed a cabinet. Léon Blum (1872–1950), who assumed the premiership on June 5, was a Jewish intellectual and humanitarian who believed socialism was compatible with democratic, parliamentary government.

Before the Popular Front came to power, strikes had begun to spread throughout French industry, and Blum's government was immediately challenged by spontaneous work stoppages. Over 500,000 workers staged sit-ins at their factories. These were the most widespread labor disturbances in the history of the Third Republic, and they alarmed a conservative business community that had already been frightened by the Popular Front's electoral victory. Blum moved swiftly. On June 8, he announced an accord that restructured relations between labor and management. Wages were raised 7 to 15 percent, depending on the job involved. Employers were required to recognize unions and accept collective bargaining. The forty-hour week was established, and workers got annual two-week paid vacations. Blum hoped better labor-management relations would reduce worker hostility to France's social and political institutions and help the economy by increasing domestic consumer demand.

Blum raised the salaries of civil servants, instituted a program of public works, provided government loans to small industries, increased spending on armaments, and nationalized some armament industries. A National Wheat Board was set up to manage the production and sale of grain. International monetary pressure forced Blum to devalue the franc in the autumn of 1936 and again in the spring of 1937. This enraged the conservative banking and business communities, and in March 1937, they pressured the ministry to end Blum's reform program. The following June, Blum resigned. The Popular Front ministry held on until April 1938, when it was replaced by a Radical ministry under Daladier.

French industrial production did not return to 1929 levels until 1939, and citizens from all walks of life had reason to wonder if the republic was worth preserving. Business leaders accused it of being inefficient and too subject to socialist pressures. The left remained divided, and the right hated republics in principle. When the time came to defend the republic in 1940, too many French citizens had lost faith in it.

GERMANY: THE NAZI SEIZURE OF POWER

HOW DID the Nazis affect German politics and society?

Germany's Nazi (National Socialist) Party was the most important of the political organizations to emerge from the turmoil of the Great Depression. In the late 1920s, the Nazis were a small group that could not seriously contend for power in the Weimar Republic. The change in their political fortunes was wrought by their successful exploitation of fears created by the depression.

DEPRESSION AND POLITICAL DEADLOCK

27.4
The Depression:
Germany's Unemployed

The prosperity of Weimar Germany was undermined when supplies of foreign investment capital dried up in 1928, and subsequent disputes over economic policy broke up its coalition of center parties and Social Democrats. Social Democrats wanted to spend more on unemployment insurance and social programs; conservative parties, frightened by memories of 1923's rampant inflation, insisted on cuts to balance the budget. President von Hindenburg turned to Chancellor Heinrich Brüning (1885–1970) for help in breaking the deadlock in the Reichstag. Brüning governed by using the emergency presidential decrees that Article 48 of the Weimar constitution authorized. The Weimar Republic became an authoritarian regime, for divisions among parties prevented Parliament from overriding his orders.

As unemployment rose (from 2,258,000 in March 1930 to over 6 million in March 1932) and as government succumbed to gridlock, the desperate masses were drawn to extremist movements. In the election of 1928, the Nazis had won only 12 Reichstag seats and the Communists 54, but by 1930 the Nazis held 107 seats and the Communists 77. The Nazis built their power by campaigning for office while simultaneously employing terror and intimidation. Unemployed men hastened to join the Storm Troopers, and the SA grew from 100,000 in 1930 to almost 1 million in 1933. Its vicious attacks on the Nazis' opponents destroyed decency and civility in political life. The Nazis staged mass rallies resembling religious revivals, and their appeal to the pride and frustration of the German nation won them the support of the masses, intellectuals, and leaders of business, the military, and the media.

HITLER COMES TO POWER

Brüning survived in the chancellor's office for two years, but the lagging economy made him politically vulnerable. In 1932, Hitler decided the moment was right to challenge Hindenburg for the presidency, and he got 30.1 percent of the vote. This was enough to force a runoff, and in the second election, he polled 36.8 percent. Hindenburg retained the presidency, but he decided to replace Brüning as chancellor. Franz von Papen (1878–1969), whom he appointed, was one of a small group of extremely conservative advisers on whom the 83-year-old president had become dependent. Given the continuing paralysis in the Reichstag, these men virtually controlled the government.

The Nazis were the only party with mass support. Papen, therefore, wanted to win Hitler's cooperation, but he did not want to give him any real power. He hoped to convince Hitler that the Nazis could not succeed without the help of the Hindenburg circle. He removed the ban on Nazi meetings that Brüning had imposed and called a Reichstag election for July 1932. When the Nazis won 230 seats (37.2 percent of the vote), Hitler demanded the chancellor's office. Hindenburg refused and tried to deplete the Nazis' finances by calling another election. The Nazis lost 34 seats, and their popular vote dipped to 33.1 percent.

In November 1932, Papen resigned, and his successor, General Kurt von Schleicher (1882–1934), tried to head off civil war between the left and the right by building a broad-based coalition of conservatives and trade unionists. This alarmed Hindenburg's advisers, who did not trust Schleicher's motives, and they persuaded Hindenburg that Hitler was the lesser evil. On January 30, 1933, Hitler was appointed chancellor and Papen returned as vice chancellor. It was assumed that Papen and a cabinet filled with conservatives would be able to keep Hitler under control. Hitler's attainment of the chancellorship was not inevitable. He did not come to office on the tide of history, according to Nazi legend, but rose through the blunders of conservative German politicians.

Because Hitler had obtained office legally, the civil service, the courts, and the other agencies of government could support him in good conscience. He headed a rigidly disciplined party structure, and he was a master of techniques of mass propaganda. (See "Encountering the Past: Cinema of the Political Left and Right.") He knew how to touch the raw nerves of the electorate, and he won support across the social spectrum—not just from the lower middle class. In some rural areas and small towns, Roman Catholic voters opposed him, but his following was strong among farmers, war veterans, and the young whose hopes for the future were dimmed by the Great Depression. Hitler promised them protection from communists and socialists, an end to petty party squabbles, effective government, and an inspiring nationalist vision of a strong, restored Germany.

Some people have assumed that Hitler owed much of his success to support from big business, but little evidence indicates that contributions from business leaders made a crucial difference to the Nazi campaign. Hitler's followers were often suspicious of business and giant capitalism. They wanted a simpler world in which small property owners would be safe from the consolidation of resources in a few hands that resulted from both socialism and capitalism. The Nazis won out over other conservative nationalistic parties because they better addressed the fears of the majority of ordinary German people.

28.3
Adolf Hitler, from *Mein Kampf*

ENCOUNTERING THE PAST

CINEMA OF THE POLITICAL LEFT AND RIGHT

Before television, cinema was the most powerful medium for political propaganda, and brilliant directors served authoritarian regimes of both the left and the right. Sergei Eisenstein (1898–1948) made films for the Soviet Union that, despite their propagandistic content, are acknowledged masterpieces. The Battleship Potemkin, his most famous work, depicts a mutiny aboard a warship during the Russian revolution. It portrays the working class as the hero of the story and of history itself. Two other historical epics, Alexander Nevsky (a medieval Russian prince who defeated German invaders) and Ivan the Terrible (a sixteenth-century despotic tsar), managed remarkably to meet the highest artistic standards and promote reflection on contemporary events—all while pleasing Stalin.

Nazi Germany's great artistic resource was a female documentary filmmaker, Leni Riefenstahl (1902–2003). After the Nazis took power in 1933, Hitler commissioned her to make documentaries extolling his Third Reich. She produced two dazzling films: Triumph of the Will (1934), a record of a Nazi Party rally, and Olympia (1938), based on the Olympic Games held in Berlin in 1936. Her innovative, dramatic techniques made her films classics of twentieth-century cinema—and made them perfect vehicles for conveying the theatricality of the Nazi regime. Despite the support her films gave Hitler, she defended herself as a "pure" artist who (as some scientists have also argued) cannot be held responsible for the use others made of her work.

WHY WERE authoritarian regimes so interested in the cinema? Are artists ethically responsible for the effects of their art?

Leni Riefenstahl filming the 1936 Olympic Games in Berlin with Hitler on the reviewing stand.
© Bettmann/CORBIS

HITLER'S CONSOLIDATION OF POWER

Once in office, Hitler quickly consolidated control by winning full legal authority, crushing alternative political groups, and purging rivals within his own party. The act of a terrorist gave him the opportunity he needed to complete consolidation of his power.

Reichstag Fire   On February 27, 1933, a mentally ill Dutch communist set fire to Berlin's Reichstag building. The Nazis claimed the fire was a prelude to a communist assault on the government, and under Article 48 of the Weimar constitution, Hitler issued an emergency decree suspending civil liberties. The decree remained in effect for as long as Hitler ruled Germany.

The Enabling Act   In early March 1933, there was another Reichstag election. The Nazis received only 43.9 percent of the vote (288 seats), but by evicting Communist deputies and using the fire to intimidate the Reichstag's politicians, Hitler was able to push through the legislation he wanted. On March 23, 1933, the Reichstag passed the Enabling Act. It authorized Hitler to rule by decree and removed all legal limits on his power. Thanks to the act, Hitler never had to bother repealing or amending the Weimar constitution.

The Reichstag fire in 1933 provided Hitler with an excuse to consolidate his power.

Bildarchiv Preussischer Kulturbesitz

Anti-Jewish Policies. Soon after seizing power, the Nazi government began harassing German Jewish businesses. Non-Jewish German citizens were urged not to buy merchandise from shops owned by Jews.

Art Resource/Bildarchiv Preussischer Kulturbesitz

28.8
Leader of the Nazi Women's Organization

Hitler knew he and his party had not been swept into office by destiny. He had worked to get where he was, and he worked to protect his position. He outlawed or undermined any German institution that might have become a rallying point for his opponents. In early May 1933, the Nazi Party, acting like a branch of government, seized the offices, banks, and newspapers of the free trade unions and arrested their leaders. In July of that year, the National Socialists were declared the only legal party in Germany. The Nazis then moved against the governments of the individual federal states in Germany, and by the end of 1933, all their opponents had been silenced.

Internal Nazi Party Purges Hitler's final step was to consolidate his hold on the Nazi Party. His strongest potential rival was Ernst Roehm (1887–1934), commander of the SA and its 1 million soldiers. On June 30, 1934, Hitler ordered the murders of Roehm and key SA officers. By July 2, more than one hundred SA leaders had been killed, including the former chancellor General Kurt von Schleicher and his wife. The regular German army, the only institution that might have prevented the slaughter, was delighted by the destruction of the leadership of a group it saw as trespassing on its territory. Hitler completed his triumph on August 2, 1934, when Hindenburg's death cleared the way for him to claim the offices of both chancellor and president and become sole ruler of Germany and the Nazi Party.

THE POLICE STATE AND ANTI-SEMITISM

Terror had brought the Nazis to power, and once in office, Hitler moved quickly to turn Germany into a police state.

SS Organization The SS, the *Schutzstaffel* ("protective force") that kept Germany under police surveillance, originated in the mid-1920s as Hitler's bodyguard. It was a smaller, but more elite, paramilitary organization than the SA. In 1933, it had about 52,000 members. It carried out Hitler's bloody purge of the Nazi Party in 1934, and by 1936, its leader, Heinrich Himmler (1900–1945), was second only to Hitler.

Attack on Jews Hitler's police state bore down most heavily on Germany's Jews, for anti-Semitism was a key plank in the Nazi program. Nazi anti-Semitism was motivated by biological theories of race rooted in late-nineteenth-century science, not religion.

There were three stages in the Nazi attack on the Jews. In 1933, shortly after assuming power, the Nazis excluded Jews from the civil service and tried, ineffectively, to persuade the public to boycott Jewish businesses. In 1935, a series of measures (the Nuremberg Laws) robbed Jews of rights of citizenship. Professions and key occupations were closed to them. Marriage and sexual intercourse between them and non-Jews were prohibited, and an elaborate attempt was made to establish a legal standard for deciding who was and who was not a Jew. The third assault on the Jews began in November 1938, when Jewish businesses were outlawed. Under orders from the Nazi Party, thousands of Jewish stores and synagogues were sacked on what came to be known as *Kristallnacht* ("glass night," from the sound of breaking windows). The Nazis did everything possible to persuade the masses that Germany had to be "cleansed" of everyone who was not a descendant of the "master race," the legendary Aryans.

The Final Solution In 1941, after the war broke out, Hitler decided to solve the problem of what to do with Europe's Jews by exterminating them. His efficient murder machinery destroyed some 6 million Jews, mostly from eastern Europe. (See Chapter 28.)

RACIAL IDEOLOGY AND THE LIVES OF WOMEN

Mussolini wanted to increase Italy's population; Hitler wanted to "purify" Germany's. Responsibility for preserving German racial purity fell heavily on the women, who were called on to produce strong sons and daughters for the fatherland. Childbearing was declared the female equivalent of the service men rendered the state on the battlefield. Only women judged racially sound were encouraged to have children. Jewish women were especially targeted for death to prevent them from perpetuating their kind, and Germans who were judged undesirable for one reason or another were sterilized or forced to have abortions. The Nazi state offered loans, tax breaks, and child-support allowances to families it believed should have children. Payments were made to men to attract them to fatherhood.

Emphasis on motherhood did not lead to a prejudice against women who worked outside the home. The Nazis understood the necessity for women to work in the depression era. They protected their jobs, and the number of female workers increased in Germany during the Nazi era. Women were, however, urged to seek jobs that suited their female "natures" (farm work, teaching, nursing, social service, and domestic service). As nurturers of the young, they were thought to have special responsibility for instilling patriotism and German cultural values in their children. As housewives, they were to use their financial power to support German products and businesses and boycott Jews.

Young women among an enthusiastic crowd extend the Nazi salute at a party rally in 1938. Nazi ideology encouraged women to favor traditional domestic roles over employment in the workplace and to bear many children. The onset of the war, however, forced the government to recruit women workers.

Bildarchiv Preussischer Kulturbesitz

NAZI ECONOMIC POLICY

Hitler was more effective than any other European leader at dealing with economic problems, and his success promoted loyalty to his tyrannical regime. His strategy for engineering economic recovery was to create jobs by mobilizing his nation for aggressive military action. To this end, he sacrificed political and civil liberties, destroyed trade unions, limited private use of capital, and ignored consumer demand.

Hitler endorsed private property and capitalism but subordinated all economic enterprises to the needs of the state. He instituted a massive program of public works and spending, much of which was related to rearmament. Workers were often assigned jobs rather than being allowed freely to choose them. The government handled labor disputes through compulsory arbitration, and it enrolled workers and employers in the "Labor Front," a propaganda campaign that fostered worker loyalty to the state.

In 1935, Germany renounced the military provisions of the Versailles Treaty and began openly to rearm. In 1936, Hitler charged Hermann Göring (1893–1946), head of the air force, with development of a Four-Year Plan that would prepare Germany—economically as well as militarily—for war. This restored full employment while pandering to the desire of the German people to avenge their humiliation following World War I.

ITALY: FASCIST ECONOMICS

*I*taly's fascists relied on discipline more than economic policy and creativity to solve their country's problems. During the 1920s, Mussolini undertook vast public works, such as draining the Pontine Marshes near Rome. His government subsidized the shipping industry and introduced protective tariffs in a desperate effort to make Italy self-sufficient. Mussolini was, however, unable to stave off the effects of the Great Depression, and throughout Italy production, exports, and wages declined.

SYNDICATES

The Fascists sought to steer an economic course between socialism and a liberal laissez-faire system. Their policy, called **corporatism**, organized major industries as syndicates of labor and management. These syndicates were supposed to promote

HOW DID Mussolini transform the Italian economy?

corporatism Fascist policy organizing major industries as syndicates of labor and management devised to steer an economic course between socialism and a liberal laissez-faire system.

cooperation in designing a planned economy. The government stepped in when necessary to settle labor disputes, but labor and management were urged to look beyond their private interests to the greater goal of productivity for the nation.

CORPORATIONS

After 1930, industrial syndicates were further organized into entities called *corporations*. A corporation united all the people who contributed anything—from raw materials through finished products and distribution—to producing a particular product. Twenty-two corporations encompassed Italy's whole economy. In 1938, Mussolini replaced the Chamber of Deputies with a Chamber of Corporations. Instead of increasing production, however, this vast organizational framework spawned bureaucracy and corruption.

Italy's experiment with corporatism did not last long. In 1935, Italy, like Germany, began to restructure its economy to support military mobilization. When Italy revealed its imperialistic intentions by declaring war on Ethiopia, all the League of Nations did was to impose ineffective economic sanctions. This emboldened Mussolini to press on. To fund his military, he increased taxes and extracted forced loans from the Italian people by compelling purchase of government bonds. Wages fell, and as international tensions mounted, the state increased its control over the economy. Fascism brought order to Italy, but not prosperity.

STALIN'S SOVIET UNION: CENTRAL ECONOMIC PLANNING, COLLECTIVIZATION, AND PARTY PURGES

WHAT INDUSTRIAL advances did the Soviet Union make in the 1930s?

*W*hile Western capitalist systems suffered through the Great Depression, the Soviet Union made great economic progress–but at the cost, or degradation, of millions of lives.

THE DECISION FOR RAPID INDUSTRIALIZATION

Lenin's New Economic Policy (NEP), which encouraged private enterprise among farmers to ensure production of food for urban workers, remained in effect until 1927. By that year, it had helped restore industrial production to 1913's prewar level, but Stalin decided to abandon it and to push for more rapid industrialization. His intent was to strengthen Russia by quickly overtaking the productive capacity of its enemies, the capitalist nations.

Stalin created a series of Five-Year Plans overseen by *Gosplan*, the State Planning Commission. Their focus was not on consumer goods, but on developing heavy industries and building up the country's infrastructure. This was to be achieved by massive central planning that set goals for production and coordinated every step in the manufacturing process. Stalin's strategy promoted the growth of huge centralized agencies that often worked at cross-purposes. Workers were increasingly regimented and compelled to live in deplorable conditions that were worse than anything Marx and Engels had decried in the nineteenth century. Russia maintained full employment of its people throughout the depression but forced them to accept an astoundingly low standard of living and a total loss of political liberty. To elicit their cooperation, the government and the Communist Party built a huge propaganda machine to laud the five-year plans, the heroism of devoted workers, and the alleged success of the system.

By the close of the 1930s, the results of the three five-year plans were truly impressive. Russia's economy grew more rapidly than that of any other Western nation during any comparable time period. By conservative Western estimates, Soviet industrial production rose about 400 percent between 1928 and 1940. Industries that had not previously existed in Russia began to challenge and, in some cases, surpass counterparts elsewhere. Large new industrial cities had been built and populated, but the social and human costs of this development were appalling.

THE COLLECTIVIZATION OF AGRICULTURE

Agricultural productivity had always been a core problem for the emerging Soviet economy. Under the NEP the government purchased a certain amount of grain at prices it set itself. The remaining grain was then supposed to be sold at higher market-determined prices. Many peasant farmers of all degrees of wealth tried to circumvent this system by keeping grain off the market in the hope that its price would rise. The scarcity of available consumer goods further encouraged hoarding. The Soviet government, however, needed grain immediately to feed its expanding urban workforce and to pay for imports. In 1928 and 1929, the state was faced with urban food shortages and social unrest.

Stalin used intimidation and propaganda to support his drive to collectivize Soviet agriculture. Communist Party agitators led groups of peasants, such as these shown above, to demand the seizure of the farms worked by the better-off and more successful farmers known as kulaks.

AP/Wide World Photos

Stalin therefore decided to reverse the NEP agricultural policies. Soviet communist economists and party officials asserted that traditional peasant holdings were too small to reach needed productivity levels. They also claimed that a class enemy—relatively prosperous peasants known as kulaks, numbering less than five percent of the rural population—was responsible for the hoarding and for what they regarded as speculation in the grain trade. The kulaks were often the most productive and efficient farmers. With these two ideas in mind, Stalin decided to collectivize agriculture by forcibly replacing private peasant farms with huge state-owned and state-run farms called collectives. This policy would put the Communist Party in control of the farm sector, free up peasant labor for industry, and enable production and distribution for export.

The collectivization program was vaguely defined, yet it unleashed unprecedented violence as the government announced its intention to eliminate the kulaks as a class. "Dekulakization" ended up targeting anyone accused of being a kulak, which usually meant any peasants who resisted collectivization and were therefore regarded as counterrevolutionary.

Soldiers led by Party officials and army officers led the initial campaign of dekulakization and collectivization. The removal of kulaks from villages and coercion of peasants onto collective farms provoked enormous rural turmoil and violence. In March 1930, Stalin called a brief halt to the process, justifying the slowdown on the grounds of "dizziness from success." However, after that year's harvest was secured, collectivization was renewed with vehemence.

Peasants were determined to keep their land and, faced with confiscation of their livestock, slaughtered millions of horses, cattle, and other animals between 1929 and 1933. Resisters were killed outright. Others starved to death after all their grain had been removed by force. Over two million peasants were deported to distant areas of the Soviet Union or to prison camps where many died from disease, exposure, and malnutrition. Those who survived struggled on, and their children were treated as class enemies.

The ideologically atheist Communist Party also targeted rural priests of the Russian Orthodox Church. The Party had long opposed religion, but collectivization brought more systematic persecution. Between 1926 and 1937, the number of priests recorded in the Soviet census dropped by more than one-half. Jewish rabbis, Catholic priests, Protestant ministers, and Mulsim mullahs received the same harsh treatment.

QUICK REVIEW

Collectivization
- 1929: Stalin orders collectivization of Soviet agriculture
- Stalin responded to resistance by targeting kulaks for elimination
- Collectivization failed to solve the Soviet Union's food supply problem

Poster concerning the First Five-Year Plan (1928–1932) with a photograph of Joseph Stalin (1879–1953). The poster declares: "By the end of the Five-Year Plan, the basis of the USSR's collectivization must be completed."

1932 (colour litho) by Klutchis (fl.1932). Deutsches Plakat Museum, Essen, Germany/Archives Charmet/The Bridgeman Art Library

By 1937, over 90 percent of Soviet grain production had been collectivized. Producers on collective farms could not decide what to produce, nor could they determine prices. Motor-Tractor Stations run by Party officials supplied seed and equipment for several collectives in a region, oversaw the collection and sale of grain, and determined payments that the farmers eventually received. By the middle of the 1930s, the government allowed farmers to till small household plots for their own families or for local sale. These plots, so well tended on a private basis, would become an important part of Soviet agricultural production.

Stalin and the Communist Party had won the battle for control of grain fields at the cost of millions of peasant lives, but they had not solved the problem of producing enough food. That problem would plague the Soviet Union until its collapse in 1991, and it remains a problem for its successor states.

FLIGHT TO THE SOVIET CITIES

Collectivism drove hordes of people from the countryside into cities. Between 1928 and 1932, approximately 12 million made the transition—a migration unprecedented in European history. Many more males than females made the move, and the loss of their support greatly impoverished the disproportionate numbers of women and elderly who were left behind in the countryside. Major cities grew rapidly, and between 1939 and 1980, the proportion of the Soviet population living on the land was halved (falling from two-thirds to one-third).

URBAN CONSUMER SHORTAGES

Cities grew so rapidly that housing and infrastructure could not keep up. Transport systems were too small. Major cities still lacked sewer systems in the 1930s. Newer cities had no paved streets, electric lighting, or running water. Workers lived in barracks and families jammed into tiny apartments in buildings where they shared kitchens, toilets, and baths. The most basic consumer goods (food, clothing, and shoes) were in chronic short supply, and Russians grew accustomed to standing in line for bread. In the 1930s, they consumed less food annually than they had in the years prior to the revolution. The elite of the Communist Party were exempt from all this. Special well-stocked stores were provided for them.

Shortages and inadequate facilities fostered urban crime and spread disease, and the Soviet people relied on ingenuity to survive. They raised food on tiny plots, bartered with one another, stole from the state, and traded on a black market. They suffered and coped in the faith that their sacrifices were building a glorious socialist future—a future that never came.

FOREIGN REACTIONS AND REPERCUSSIONS

Many foreigners were naively enthusiastic about the Soviet economic experiment, for while the capitalist world languished, the Soviet economy grew at a pace never realized in the West. These observers ignored the shortages in consumer goods, the poor housing, and the social cost of the Soviet achievement. The full extent of human suffering and loss during those years will probably never be known, but it far exceeded the price of Europe's nineteenth-century industrialization that had so appalled Marx and Engels.

The internal upheaval created by collectivization and industrialization and the fear that Russia might be left alone to face aggression by Nazi Germany prompted Stalin to make a shift in foreign policy in 1934. He reversed the Comintern rule established by Lenin in 1919 (one of the Twenty-One Conditions) and allowed communist parties in other countries to cooperate with noncommunists in fighting Nazism and fascism.

THE PURGES

Stalin's programs aroused political opposition. In 1929, he forced Nikolai Bukharin, a fervent supporter of the NEP, off the Politburo. Not much is known about continuing resistance at lower levels in the party, but by 1933, Stalin was afraid he was losing control. Whether the threat to him was real or imagined, it resulted in the **Great Purges**, one of the most mysterious and horrendous political events of the twentieth century.

Sergei Kirov (1888–1934), a member of the Politburo, was assassinated on December 1, 1934, and in the wake of his murder, thousands of people were arrested. Many others were expelled from the party and sent to labor camps. At the time, it was believed Kirov had been killed by opponents of the regime, for Stalin accused many of his victims of complicity in the crime. However, Stalin himself may have ordered Kirov's assassination to remove a potential rival. The documentary evidence is inconclusive, but there is no doubt about the use Stalin made of Kirov's death.

Between 1936 and 1938, a series of spectacular show trials took place in Moscow. High Soviet leaders confessed to political crimes they had not committed and were convicted and executed. Other party members were tried in private and shot. Many people received no trials at all, and no one can explain why some were executed while others were sent to labor camps and still others left unmolested. After the civilian party members had been purged, prosecutors turned their attention to the army. Officers, including war heroes, were shot. Hundreds of thousands of members of the party were expelled, and applicants for membership were removed from the rolls. The exact numbers of executions, imprisonments, and expulsions are unknown, but they ran into the millions.

Two things may help explain the purges. One was a power struggle between factions within the Communist Party. The central Moscow leadership used the purges to enhance its control over the lower levels of the party in the far-flung regions of the Soviet Union. They also gave Stalin an excuse to eliminate members of the party elite whom he distrusted. Lower-ranking officials of the party followed his example, and accusations, imprisonments, and executions multiplied at a great rate.

The second motive for the purges may have been Stalin's determination to create a new party structure that was totally loyal to him. The purges weeded out the "old Bolsheviks" of the October Revolution who knew how far Stalin was departing from Lenin's policies. The newcomers who replaced them in the party's leadership knew only the world that Stalin had made.

SUMMARY

Toward the Great Depression   The severity and length of the Great Depression have three interrelated causes: the financial crisis caused by the Great War and the Paris peace settlement; the global crisis in the production and distribution of goods,

Significant Dates from the Era of the Great Depression

1928	Russia's First Five-Year Plan Nazis win first seats in the Reichstag
1929	(October) Wall Street crash Britain's second Labour government Collectivization of Russian agriculture
1931	(May) Collapse of Kreditanstalt in Vienna Britain goes off the gold standard
1932	Lausanne Conference ends reparations (April 10) Hindenburg defeats Hitler for presidency
1933–1934	Stavisky Affair in France
1933	(January 30) Hitler appointed chancellor (February 27) Reichstag fire (March 23) Enabling Act passed (July 14) Nazis declared Germany's only legal party
1934	(June 30) Murder of SA leadership (August 2) Death of von Hindenburg (December 1) Assassination of Kirov
1935	Passage of Nuremberg Laws
1936	Stalin begins the Great Purge (June 5) Popular Front government in France under Blum
1937	Neville Chamberlain becomes British prime minister
1938	Radical ministry in France (November 9) *Kristallnacht*

Great Purges   The arrests, trials, Communist Party expulsions, and executions—beginning with the assassination of Politburo member Sergei Kirov in December 1934—that mainly targeted Party officials and reached its climax from 1936 to 1938.

IMAGE KEY
for pages 668–669

a. Volkswagen on German Reich Stamp, 1939
b. Hitler's mastery of the techniques of mass politics and propaganda—including huge staged rallies like this one in 1938—was an important factor in his rise to power
c. Olympic Games 1936 Poster
d. "Symbol of Work" Poster depicting two workers above a tractor and silo, stands in Russia, USSR. 1930–1934
e. Tractor
f. Unemployed coal miner at Wigan, England, late 1930s
g. A row of men in overalls, and one girl, sit in front of an out-of-business cafe with soaped windows, during the Great Depression, United States
h. The official Soviet portrayal of the collectivization of agriculture. Collective farmers, most of them women, on their way to work. The banner denounces kulaks, the stratum of wealthy peasants
i. Rise of Nazi Germany: Thousands of German troops listen as Hitler speaks at the Nuremberg Rally of 1936

especially after 1929; and the failure of western European and U.S. governments to respond appropriately to these conditions. European governments had an overriding fear of inflation. The Allies depended on payments from Germany to subsidize their economies and pay their own debts to the United States; the German economy, in turn, had become dependent on U.S. private investment in the mid–1920s. When the U.S. stock market collapsed in 1929, U.S. loans to Europe dried up, and the German economy nearly collapsed. Reparations were canceled in 1933. Meanwhile, production and trade faced their own difficulties, including agricultural overproduction; farmers could no longer afford to purchase industrial products, so the manufacture of consumer goods stagnated; this led to a reduction in demand for coal, iron, and textiles, crippling those industries as well. Economic theory held that governments should cut spending in these circumstances, in order to avoid inflation. Governments did experiment with other forms of intervention, though, and these influenced the politics of the period.

Confronting the Great Depression in the Democracies The political responses to the Depression were very different in Great Britain and France, and yielded different results. In Britain, Ramsay MacDonald's National Government was a sell-out by the Labour leader to the Conservative party. Industrial production increased beyond 1929 levels by 1934, and the housing market boomed. Unemployment persisted, however, with nearly 1.5 million unemployed in 1937. Most British citizens remained confident in their government, and radical politics held little appeal. In France, the depression came later and lasted longer. Right-wing political groups grew, as did political bitterness, incivility, and violence. A right-wing political demonstration in Paris in 1934 resulted in fourteen deaths and many injuries. Leftist groups made alliances in the face of right-wing threats and formed the Popular Front in 1935. Leon Blum became premier of a Popular Front government in 1936. Blum instituted progressive labor policies and made other moves that alienated the banking and business communities, leading Blum to resign in 1937. A Radical ministry came to power in 1938. French industrial production did not regain 1929 levels until 1939. Many French citizens lost faith in the Republic, and in republican principles.

Germany: The Nazi Seizure of Power In the late 1920s, the Nazis were visible on the Weimar political scene, but had little influence. The effects of the depression allowed them to seize power. In the early 1930s, unemployment soared—as did membership in the Nazi Storm Troopers (SA). President von Hindenburg appointed Hitler chancellor of Germany in January 1933, hoping to control him. But Hitler and the Nazis had a broad base of support, because they combined an understanding of the electorate's social and economic insecurities with an inspirational nationalism. Hitler consolidated his power by capturing full legal authority, crushing alternative political groups, and purging the Nazi Party of rivals. In March 1933, the Enabling Act allowed Hitler to rule by decree. By the end of 1933, the Nazis had disabled all institutions that might oppose Hitler. Through violence and intimidation, the Nazis created a terrorist police state. The Nuremberg Laws and *Kristallnacht* marked the escalation of official anti-Semitism, which culminated in the Final Solution. Nazi racial ideology called for selective breeding. They encouraged or discouraged women to reproduce, depending on their ethnic and health characteristics, and women were given responsibilities in transmitting the approved culture. Hitler's economic policies achieved great successes. Rearmament and other war preparations spurred economic growth.

Italy: Fascist Economics In the 1920s, Mussolini used massive public works projects, subsidies, and tariffs to attempt to stimulate the economy. The fascists sought a middle course between socialism and liberal laissez-faire capitalism, in a policy known as corporatism. Private ownership was preserved, but industries were organized into syndicates representing labor and management, both of which were supposed to maximize productivity for the sake of the nation rather than pursuing their own class interests. After 1930, industrial syndicates were replaced by bodies called corporations, which grouped industries by production area. Neither form of organization increased productivity, but they did foster bureaucracy and corruption. With Italy's 1935 invasion of Ethiopia, the economy was mobilized for war. Taxes rose while wages and the standard of living declined.

Stalin's Soviet Union: Central Economic Planning, Collectivization, and Party Purges
Stalin implemented a plan for rapid industrialization, which led to tremendous economic growth through the 1930s but cost millions of lives. Starting in 1928, a succession of five-year plans set production goals, and the State Planning Commission organized the economy to meet those goals. Huge new factories were built, and millions of workers were employed. Between 1928 and 1940, Soviet industrial production rose a mind-boggling 400 percent. Meanwhile, in 1929, Stalin had ordered the collectivization of agriculture, so production could be increased under state control and restive peasants could be transformed into obedient industrial laborers in the new factories. The elimination of the *kulak* class was part of the program. Religious leaders became targets of the state. Millions of peasants migrated to the cities, where housing, food, clothing, and consumer goods were in short supply. Stalin retained his grip on power through the Great Purges and the "show trials" of the mid to late 1930s.

REVIEW QUESTIONS

1. What caused the Great Depression of the 1930s? Why was it more severe and longer lasting than previous depressions? Could it have been avoided?

2. How successful, respectively, were Britain's National Government and France's Popular Front in dealing with their nations' economic problems? How did the Great Depression affect Germany?

3. How did Hitler rise to power between 1929 and 1934? What were Hitler's economic policies? How does his economic program compare with the economic policies put in place in Britain, Italy, and France? Why were some nations more successful than others in addressing the Great Depression?

4. What are the characteristics of a police state? How did Hitler, Mussolini, and Stalin use terror to achieve their goals? What were the particular characteristics of Nazi racial policy? What caused the purges in the Soviet Union? What groups were the special targets of the purges? Why?

KEY TERMS

corporatism   (p. 679)   **Great Purges**   (p. 683)

 For additional study resources for this chapter, go to:
www.prenhall.com/kagan3/chapter27

Visualizing The Past...

Imperialism and Race in Modern Art

HOW HAVE the experiences of imperialism and race influenced modern and contemporary art, in both style and technique?

The second half of the nineteenth century witnessed the "second wave" of European imperialism. The United States and Japan also participated in the frenzy of the industrialized powers to obtain the labor and natural resources of other regions. The colonizers focused their attention on regions such as China, the African interior, and the Pacific Islands, which were not yet firmly ensconced in older colonial empires.

The colonial experience had an important legacy in Western art, in terms of providing artistic themes, but also in the influence of Western techniques in painting and sculpture on indigenous artists. The result was often a fruitful and imaginative blending of styles and techniques that in turn have greatly influenced Western artists.

This painting, called *Las Castas* (Human Races) from eighteenth-century Mexico shows the importance of race to Spanish colonial culture. Each image depicts a family from the different "racial" groups as colonial Mexicans understood them. Thus there are not only the main categories of European, African, and Native American, but also various mixed race families.

Human Races (Las Castas), 18th century, oil on canvas, 1.04 x 1.48 m. Museo Nacional del Virreinato, Tepotzotlan, Mexico. Schalkwijk/Art Resource, NY

▲

This painting by the well-known African-American painter **William H. Johnson** of the 1920s American artistic movement known as the "Harlem Renaissance," is called *Moon over Harlem.* The African-American artists of the 1920s such as Johnson created honest, moving images of race relations and the experiences of African Americans in American society. Again we see that race and power, here symbolized by the police, were at the heart of cultural identity in modern Western society.

©Smithsonian American Art Museum, Washington, DC/Art Resource, NY

Jose Clemente Orozco, ▶
Cortés y la Malintzin (1926), fresco. By the twentieth century, Mexico had become primarily a *mestizo,* or mixed race, society. Race remains, however, a central issue in Mexicans' understanding of their past and present national identity. Orozco, in his fresco of the great Spanish conquistador Hernan Cortes and Cortes's Indian translator and concubine, la Malintzin, deals with themes of race, conquest, and gender in a much less idealized way than Gauguin. Both the style and theme of this work reflect the often uneasy but creative mixing of Western and Indian genes and culture that characterizes Mexico's *mestizo* society.

Fundacion Jose Clemente Orozco, Photograph Angel Hurtado, Art Museum of the Americas, OAS/©Orozco Valladeres Family. Reproduction authorized by the Instituto Nacional de Bellas Artes

Paul Gauguin, *Where do we come from? What are we? Where are we going?* (1897), oil on canvas. Gauguin was one of the last French impressionist painters of the late nineteenth century. Like many European colonists, he imagined the people of French Tahiti as a kind of "noble savage" among whom he would find the primitive, spiritually pure lifestyle he sought. Race thus is central to his depiction of the Tahitians, but always in an idealized vision of peace and simplicity.

Paul Gaugin (French 1848–1903), "Wher Do We Come From? What Are We? Where Are We Going To?" Museum of Fine Arts, Boston, MA/A.K.G., Berlin/SuperStock

▼

POLITICS & GOVERNMENT

1939	World War II begins
1941	Japan attacks Pearl Harbor, U.S. enters war
1942	Battle of Stalingrad
1944	Normandy invasion
1945	Yalta Conference; Germany surrenders; atomic bombs dropped on Japan; Japan surrenders; United Nations founded
1946	Churchill gives Iron Curtain speech
1947	Truman Doctrine
1948	Communist takeover in Czechoslovakia and Hungary; State of Israel proclaimed
1948–1949	Berlin blockade
1949	NATO founded; East and West Germany emerge as separate states

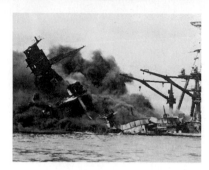

◄ USS Arizona, Pearl Harbor

1950–1953	Korean War
1953	Death of Stalin
1954	French defeat at Dien Bien Phu
1955	Warsaw Pact founded
1956	Khrushchev denounces Stalin; Polish Communist Party crisis; Suez crisis; Soviet invasion of Hungary

◄ Jewish children at Auschwitz, Poland

Joseph Stalin ►

SOCIETY & ECONOMY

1945–1951	Attlee ministry establishes the Welfare State in Great Britain
1947	Marshall Plan to rebuild Europe instituted
1949	Europe divided into Eastern and Western blocs

Churchill, Roosevelt, ► Stalin at Yalta.

1950s and 1960s	Increase in agricultural production
1957	European Economic Community founded

RELIGION & CULTURE

1940	Koestler, *Darkness at Noon*
1942	Lewis, *The Screwtape Letters*
1943	Sartre, *Being and Nothingness*
1947	Camus, *The Plague*; Gramsci, *Letters from Prison*
1949	de Beauvoir, *The Second Sex*; Crossman, *The God That Failed*

1958	Pasternak forbidden to accept Nobel Prize for *Dr. Zhivago*; John XXIII becomes pope
1960s	The Beatles take world by storm

◄ The Beatles

◄ Albert Camus

1960	Khruschev aborts Geneva summit
1961	Berlin Wall erected
1962	Cuban Missile Crisis
1963	Test Ban Treaty
1963–1973	Major U.S. involvement in Vietnam
1964–1982	Brezhnev era in Soviet Union
1967	Six Days' War between Israel and Arab states
1968	Soviet invasion of Czechoslovakia
1973	Yom Kippur War between Israel and Egypt
1975	Helsinki Accords
1978	Camp David Accords; Solidarity founded in Poland
1979–1988	Soviet troops in Afghanistan

1981–1983	Martial law in Poland
1985	Gorbachev comes to power in the Soviet Union
1989	Revolutions sweep across Eastern Europe
1990	German reunification; Yugoslavia breaks up
1991	Persian Gulf War; civil war in former Yugoslavia; August coup in Moscow; Gorbachev resigns; Soviet Union dissolved
1992–1999	Ascendancy of Yeltsin in Russia
1995	Bosnia recognized as independent
1997	Hong Kong returns to China
1999	NATO military campaign against Serbia
2000	Putin elected president of Russia
2001	U.S. attacked by terrorists
2003	U.S. invades Iraq

Russian ▶ troops, Afghanistan

▲ *Persian Gulf War*

▲ *Hong Kong*

1960s	Rapid growth of student population in universities; migration of workers from Eastern and southern to northern and Western Europe; migration of non-European workers to northern and Western Europe
1972	Club of Rome founded
1973–1974	Arab oil embargo

1980s and 1990s	Internal migration from Eastern to Western Europe; racial and ethnic tensions in Western Europe
1990s	Changes in Eastern Europe and Soviet Union open way for economic growth and new trade relations across Europe

◀ *Gasoline shortage, 1973*

Berlin Wall opens ▶ November, 1989

1962–1965	Second Vatican Council
1963	Solzhenitsyn, *One Day in the Life of Ivan Denisovich;* Robinson, *Honest to God*
1968	Student rebellion in Paris
1974	Solzhenitsyn expelled from Soviet Union
1978	John Paul II becomes pope

1980s	Growth of the environmental movement
1990s	Expanding influence of Roman Catholic Church in independent Eastern Europe
1990s	Feminists continue the critical tradition of Western culture
1990s	Era of the Internet opens

Alexander ▶ Solzhenitsyn

Internet use ▶ explodes in China

28 World War II

CHAPTER HIGHLIGHTS

Again the Road to War (1933–1939) Once in power, Hitler took steps to rearm Germany and prepare for war. The polarization of Europe into democratic and fascist states was made clear by the Spanish Civil War. In 1938 the *Anschluss* united Germany and Austria. At the Munich conference, Chamberlain gave in to German demands that the Sudetenland become part of Germany. The Nazi-Soviet Pact provided for the division of Poland between Germany and the Soviet Union.

World War II (1939–1945) Germany's rapid conquest of Europe left Britain isolated, but the defiant British refused to surrender. Germany launched an invasion of the Soviet Union in June 1941. Hitler intended to "impose a new order" on Europe. In December 1941, the Japanese entered the war. Allied successes in the Pacific, Africa, Sicily, and Italy, combined with German setbacks in the Soviet Union, turned the tide of war. D-day spelled the beginning of the end for Germany. The atomic bomb was used to force a Japanese surrender in August 1945.

Racism and the Holocaust The application of Hitler's racial doctrines brought devastation and death to millions. Hitler and his followers carried out a deliberate plan to exterminate all of Europe's Jews. Polish anti-Semitism contributed the vulnerability of Poland's Jews to the Nazi assault.

The Domestic Fronts The Nazis attempted to enlist the entire German population in the war effort. Until 1944, the French resistance movement remained small. Many people, particularly conservatives and rightists, collaborated with the Nazis. Britain's civilian population made critical contributions to the war effort. No nation suffered greater losses in World War II than the Soviet Union, but the nation emerged from the war more powerful and more unified than it had ever been before.

Preparations for Peace A split between the Soviet Union and the other allies soon emerged. Meetings at Yalta and Potsdam set the stage for long-term Soviet occupation of Eastern Europe and the Cold War.

CHAPTER QUESTIONS

WHAT WERE the origins of World War II?

HOW WAS World War II a "total" war?

WHAT WAS the Holocaust?

WHAT IMPACT did World War II have on European society?

HOW DID the Allies prepare for a postwar Europe?

CHAPTER OUTLINE

• Again the Road to War (1933–1939)
• World War II (1939–1945)
• Racism and the Holocaust
• The Domestic Fronts
• Preparations for Peace

IMAGE KEY

Image Key for pages 690–691 is on page 716.

WHAT WERE the origins of World War II?

Idealistic survivors of the First World War hoped it would be "the war to end all wars," but only twenty years after its conclusion a second and even more terrible global conflict erupted. In Europe and Asia, democracies fought for their lives against militaristic, nationalistic, authoritarian, and totalitarian states. Their victory did not establish world peace but marked the start of an era of Cold War during which the European states were subordinated to the Soviet Union and the United States.

AGAIN THE ROAD TO WAR (1933–1939)

World War I and the Versailles Treaty contributed only marginally to the worldwide economic depression of the 1930s, but the war reparations that fueled inflation in Germany in 1923 enabled Adolf Hitler to make a plausible case for the peace settlement as the root of Germany's ills. The Nazi Party succeeded by appealing to German nationalism and attending to Germany's social problems. After Hitler became chancellor in January 1933, Germany's foreign policy also focused on these issues.

HITLER'S GOALS

Hitler's thoughts centered on race from his first published manifesto, *Mein Kampf* (*My Struggle*), the book he wrote in jail in 1924, to his suicide in his underground bunker in Berlin in 1945. He considered the *Volk* (the German people) to be a race, and he was determined to extend Germany's boundaries to take in all the Germanic parts of the old Habsburg Empire, including Austria. He believed a virile, growing Germany would need even more *Lebensraum* ("living space"), which necessitated conquering Poland and Ukraine, lands occupied by Slavs—a "race" Hitler considered fit only for servitude. The Jews, another "race" the Nazis regarded as inferior, were to be removed completely from German territory. Hitler's book and subsequent policy statements developed no blueprint for action. He owed his success less to planning than to his gifts as an improviser. He kept his goals clearly in sight and exploited opportunities as they arose.

The League of Nations Fails When Hitler came to office in 1933, Germany was far too weak to take the land he wanted. It had first to negate the Versailles Treaty's prohibitions against rearmament and rebuild its army. Hitler rightly judged this entailed little risk for Germany. In September 1931, Japan had invaded Manchuria, and China had appealed to the League of Nations for help. A British diplomat, the earl of Lytton (1876–1951), wrote a report condemning the Japanese action, but the league failed to do anything about it. Japan simply withdrew from the league and continued to occupy Manchuria. The league's manifest weakness convinced Hitler it was safe to rearm Germany, and, as he expected, his decision was condemned but unopposed.

Germany Rearms In October 1933, Hitler pointed out that Europe's major powers had not honored the promises they made at Versailles to disarm, and he withdrew Germany from an international disarmament conference and from the League of Nations. The following January, Germany signed a nonaggression pact with Poland, an old enemy on its eastern frontier that France had hoped would prevent it from risking another war along its western border with France. In March 1935, Hitler formally renounced the disarmament provisions of the Versailles Treaty, established a German air force, and reinstated conscription to raise an army of 500,000 men.

Lebensraum German for "living space."

France and Britain, having reneged on promises to disarm, were not in a strong position to object, so they resorted to intimidation. In June 1935, they joined with Mussolini in the Stresa Front and pledged to cooperate in using force to maintain the status quo. This came to nothing. Britain was desperate to maintain its superiority at sea, and it sacrificed France's security by making a separate treaty with Hitler that allowed him to build a German fleet 35 percent as large as Britain's. Italy's ambitions in Africa caused additional friction among the Allies, and their general inability to work together gave Hitler a free hand.

Ethiopian Emperor Haile Selassie in 1936, as he delivered an address before the League of Nations. In the speech, he urged the body to save his country from invading Italian forces.

ITALY ATTACKS ETHIOPIA

Mussolini attacked Ethiopia in October 1935. His plan was to distract the Italians from their domestic problems by fostering fantasies of returning to the glory days of the ancient Roman Empire. The limp response by the League of Nations to his act of imperialist aggression advertised its impotence and the timidity of the Allies. The French and British governments had hoped to offset Germany's growing power by courting Mussolini, but his aggression so outraged their citizens that they had at least to make a show of protesting. For the first time, the League of Nations agreed to impose sanctions on a nation. No arms were to be shipped to Italy and no loans, credits, or trade provided that might assist Mussolini's government. Britain and France, however, refused to go so far as to embargo oil, the one action that could have prevented Italy's victory (and seriously alienated Mussolini). Britain's decision to allow Italy's military vessels to use the Suez Canal totally discredited the commitment of the league to collective security. It also failed to prevent Mussolini from defecting to Hitler's camp. By November 1, 1936, there was talk of a Rome-Berlin **Axis**.

REMILITARIZATION OF THE RHINELAND

The Ethiopian affair diminished Hitler's respect for the Western powers, and on March 7, 1936, he probed their resolve by sending a small armed force into the demilitarized Rhineland. This breached the Versailles Treaty and the Locarno Agreements and removed a key guarantee of French security. France and Britain had every right to resist. Yet neither power did anything but register a feeble protest with the League of Nations. British opinion was opposed to backing France, and the French would not act alone. Memories of the horrors of World War I were still strong, and both countries had to contend with widespread pacifist sentiment. In retrospect, it is clear the Allies lost a great opportunity to stop Hitler before he became a serious menace. His move into the Rhineland was opposed by his generals. Its failure might have led to his overthrow or at least prevented German expansion to the east. The Germans themselves later admitted that the French army could easily have routed the tiny force they sent into the Rhineland.

A rearmed Germany with a defensible western frontier changed the diplomatic game in Europe and prompted the Allies to devise a policy of **appeasement**. It was based on the belief that Germany' grievances were real and Hitler's goals limited. Governments were strongly pressured by the masses to preserve peace, and firmer policies would have necessitated the kind of arms buildup that British leaders particularly hoped to avoid. They feared the cost of such a move and remembered an arms race had led to World War I. While Germany armed, Britain simply hoped for the best, and France huddled behind a newly constructed defensive wall, the Maginot Line.

Axis   Forces (opposed to the Allies) joined together in Europe, including Germany and Italy, before and during World War II.

appeasement   Allied policy of making concessions to Germany based on the belief that Germany's grievances were real and Hitler's goals limited.

Picasso's surrealist painting depicts the horror of the terror bombing of the Basque town of Guernica, which General Francisco Franco's Nationalists—allies of Nazi Germany—attacked during the Spanish Civil War.

Pablo Picasso, "Guernica" 1937, Oil on canvas. 11'5 1/2 x 25'5 3/4. Museo Nacional Centro de Arte Reina Sofia/© 2005 Estate of Pablo Picasso/Artists Rights Society (ARS), New York

THE SPANISH CIVIL WAR

The polarization of Europe between democracies and fascist states became clear after civil war erupted in Spain in 1936. The Spanish monarchy had collapsed in 1931, and Spain had become a democratic republic. The republic's program of moderate reform, however, antagonized landowners, the Catholic Church, nationalists, and conservatives—and failed to satisfy peasants, workers, Catalan separatists, or radicals. In February 1936, the Spanish Popular Front (a coalition of moderate republicans, communists, and anarchists) triumphed at the polls, but losers in the election, especially the Falangists (Spain's fascists), refused to accept defeat. In July, an army led by General Francisco Franco (1892–1975) invaded from bases in Spanish Morocco and began a civil war that lasted almost three years. The conflict turned Spain into a practice arena for World War II. Germany and Italy sent troops, airplanes, and supplies to Franco, and the Soviet Union aided the republicans—as did many American and European volunteers.

The civil war brought Germany and Italy closer together and led to the Rome-Berlin Axis Pact of 1936. The Axis powers were joined that year by Japan in the Anti-Comintern Pact, an alliance formed, ostensibly, to oppose international communism. Western Europe (particularly France) was eager to prevent Spain from falling into the hands of a fascist regime allied with Germany and Italy, but the policy of appeasement continued. Although international law permitted the sale of munitions to Spain's legitimate republican government, France and Britain forbade the export of war materials to either side, and the United States declared neutrality. A half a million lives were lost before Spain succumbed to Franco early in 1939.

AUSTRIA AND CZECHOSLOVAKIA

In 1934, Nazis had assassinated Austria's prime minister and tried to seize power. The coup failed, however, for Mussolini, who was not yet allied with Hitler, quickly moved an army to the Austrian border and intimidated Germany into backing down. By 1938, Hitler and Mussolini had become friends, and the way was clear for the Nazis to make a second bid for Austria. The Austrian chancellor, Kurt Schuschnigg (1897–1977), refused to yield to German threats and announced the Austrian people would decide the question of union with Germany for themselves. He scheduled a plebiscite for March 13. Hitler sent his army into Austria on March 12 and entered Vienna amid the cheers of Austrian sympathizers. This ***Anschluss*** (union of Germany and Austria) was a clear violation of the Versailles Treaty, but despite the fact that German expansion was not likely to stop with Austria, no nation stepped forward to oppose it.

Anschluss Union of Germany and Austria.

Czechoslovakia, France's ally, was now surrounded on three sides by German territory. Hitler was affronted by the very existence of a democratic Czechoslovakia, for the nation had been created partly as a check on Germany. About 3.5 million Germans lived as an unhappy minority in Czechoslovakia's Sudetenland, and Hitler claimed he had to intervene in Czech affairs to protect them. The Czechs tried to stave him off by making concessions, but Hitler increased his demands to force a confrontation that would end with Czechoslovakia's destruction.

In May 1938, the Czechs reacted to rumors of a pending invasion by mobilizing their army. France, Britain, and Russia warned Germany they would defend the Czechs, and Hitler, who was not yet prepared to move, denied he had designs on Czechoslovakia. The public humiliation infuriated him, however, and he put his troops on alert. This frightened France and Britain. Britain's prime minister, Neville Chamberlain (1869–1940), was willing to agree to almost anything to prevent war, and he pressed the Czechs to make further concessions.

On September 12, 1938, Hitler made a speech at a Nazi Party rally in Nuremberg that prompted rioting in the Sudetenland. The Czechs reacted by declaring martial law, and Germany seemed poised to intervene. Between September 15 and 29, Chamberlain made three flights to Germany to negotiate with Hitler, and on September 15, Chamberlain forced the Czechs (who were defenseless without the support of their Western allies) to separate the Sudetenland from Czechoslovakia. A week later, Hitler insisted on being allowed to occupy the Sudetenland.

MUNICH

At the last moment and at Chamberlain's request, Mussolini proposed an international conference to resolve the issue. The meeting took place in Munich on September 29, and it granted Hitler almost everything he wanted. (See Map 28–1.) The Sudetenland became part of Germany. It was recognized that this deprived the Czechs of the ability to defend themselves, but Hitler insisted he had no further territorial ambitions. Chamberlain returned to England to announce that he had made a "peace with honor."

The Munich conference showed Europe how fear of war can bring on war. By giving Germany a part of Czechoslovakia, it encouraged Poland and Hungary to lay claims to other bits of that nation and its Slovak residents to demand a separate state of their own. On March 15, 1939, Hitler swept all this aside by breaking his promise and occupying Prague. If the French and the British had attacked Germany from the west while the Czechs fought in the east, Hitler might have been stopped. A war begun in October 1938 would at least have forced him to fight before he had promises of neutrality and material assistance from the Soviet Union and before he gained control of the resources of eastern Europe.

Poland became Germany's next target. In the spring of 1939, Hitler demanded that Poland restore the formerly German city of Danzig and allow a railroad and a highway through the Polish Corridor to connect East Prussia with the rest of Germany. The Poles refused, and on March 31, Chamberlain announced a Franco-British guarantee of Polish independence. Hitler did not take him seriously. He knew Britain and France were not prepared materially or psychologically for war and had no means of getting effective help to the Poles. To defend Poland, England and France needed the assistance of Russia, which was unlikely.

Agreement at Munich. On September 29–30, 1938, Hitler met with the leaders of Britain and France at Munich to decide the fate of Czechoslovakia. The Allied leaders abandoned the small democratic nation in a vain attempt to appease Hitler and avoid war. Hitler sits in the center of the picture. To his right is British Prime Minister Neville Chamberlain.

Ullstein Bild, Berlin. The Granger Collection, New York

MAP EXPLORATION

Interactive map: To explore this map further, go to **http://www.prenhall.com/kagan3/map28.1**

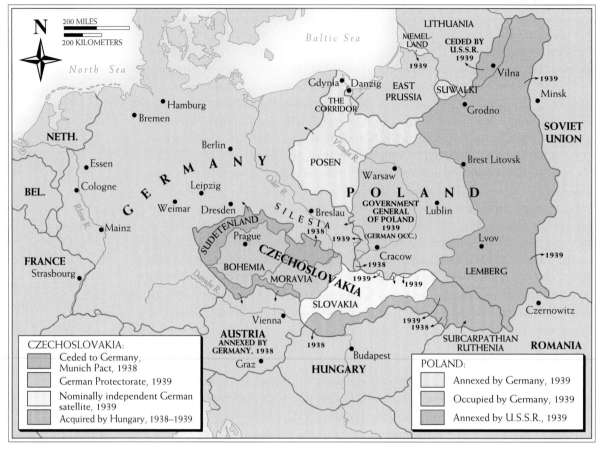

MAP 28–1

Partitions of Czechoslovakia and Poland, 1938–1939 The immediate background of World War II is found in the complex international drama unfolding on Germany's eastern frontier in 1938 and 1939. Germany's expansion inevitably meant the victimization of Austria, Czechoslovakia, and Poland. With the failure of the Western powers' appeasement policy and the signing of a German-Soviet pact, the stage for the war was set.

HOW DID appeasement ultimately lead to war?

The French and the British opposed communism, and Stalin's purge of the Red Army raised doubts about Russia's military effectiveness. The Russian army could also not help Poland without being given permission to enter Poland and Romania, and history made both nations reluctant to agree to this.

THE NAZI-SOVIET PACT

The Russians feared, quite rightly, that the Western powers meant them to bear the burden of a war with Germany alone. Consequently, they opened negotiations with Hitler, and on August 23, 1939, a Nazi-Soviet nonaggression pact was announced. It contained secret provisions that divided Poland between the two powers and allowed Russia to occupy the Baltic states and Bessarabia. The West had offered the Russians danger without prospect of gain, and Hitler had countered with an offer of gain without prospect of danger. Stalin was not about to allow ideological disputes to interfere with rational self-interest. Communist parties in the West followed his lead and reversed themselves. They ceased to advocate resistance to Hitler and called for peace. On September 1, 1939, however, the Germans invaded Poland, and two days later, Britain and France declared war on Germany.

WORLD WAR II (1939–1945)

THE GERMAN CONQUEST OF EUROPE

Using a new military strategy called *blitzkrieg* ("lightning warfare"), in which airplanes supported fast-moving armored columns, Germany quickly defeated Poland. The speed of the German victory astonished the Russians, who hastened to grab parts of Poland for themselves before Hitler took it all. Stalin's territorial gains enabled him to encircle the Baltic countries. He sent in the Red Army, and by 1940, Estonia, Latvia, and Lithuania had become puppet states within the Union of Soviet Socialist Republics, the USSR. In June 1940, the Russians forced Romania to cede Bessarabia, and in November of that year they invaded Finland. The Finns resisted fiercely for six months but finally yielded territory to Russia in exchange for guarantees of independence. Russia's expansionism and the poor performance of its army in Finland may help to explain why Hitler, in June 1941 (just twenty-two months after conclusion of the Nazi-Soviet pact), invaded Russia.

While Hitler and Stalin were occupied swallowing Poland and the Baltic states, France remained entrenched behind the Maginot Line and Britain hastily rearmed. In April 1940, without warning, the Germans attacked and quickly subdued Denmark and Norway. This secured Hitler's northern front, and a month later he struck at Belgium, the Netherlands, and Luxembourg. The Dutch surrendered in a few days and the Belgians, despite French and British aid, less than two weeks later. The British and French armies in Belgium fled to the English Channel and gathered on the beaches at Dunkirk. Hundreds of heroic Britons manning small boats rescued over 200,000 British and 100,000 French soldiers, but losses of men and equipment were high.

France's Maginot Line ran from Switzerland to Belgium. The French had expected the Belgians to continue it along their part of the German border, but when France failed to oppose Hitler's remilitarization of the Rhineland in 1936, the Belgians lost faith in France as an ally and declared neutrality. Hitler's conquest of Belgium opened the way for his army to sweep around the Maginot Line, France's primary defense. The French army was poorly led by aged generals who did not understand tanks and planes, and it soon collapsed. This created an opportunity for Mussolini, who, on June 10, invaded southern France. Less than a week later, a new French government headed by the elderly hero of the Battle of Verdun, Marshal Henri Philippe Pétain (1856–1951), asked for an armistice. Hitler had accomplished in two months what the Germans of World War I had failed to achieve in four years of hard fighting.

THE BATTLE OF BRITAIN

The fall of France left Britain isolated, and Hitler expected this would induce the British to come to terms. Britain, he suggested, could retain its empire in exchange for granting him a free hand on the Continent. If there was any chance the British would agree to this, it disappeared when Winston Churchill (1874–1965) replaced Chamberlain as prime minister in May 1940. Churchill had been an early critic of Hitler, the Nazis, and the policy of appeasement. His sense of history, his confidence in Britain, and his hatred of tyranny made compromise with Hitler impossible.

HOW WAS World War II a "total" war?

29.2
Winston Churchill: *"The Finest Hour"*—House of Commons, June 18

The situation looked hopeless for Britain. Hitler and his allies, including the Soviet Union, controlled all of Europe. Japan was advancing in Asia, and the United States was awash in isolationist sentiment and determined to remain neutral. Churchill, however, used his skill as an orator and an author to inspire his people with the courage and determination to fight. He also established a close relationship with the American president, Franklin D. Roosevelt (1882–1945). Roosevelt found ways to help Britain despite strong opposition in Congress. In 1940 and 1941, America, although still officially neutral, traded Britain military supplies and badly needed warships for leases on British naval bases. The United States also convoyed ships across the Atlantic to help Britain survive.

As weeks passed and Britain remained defiant, Hitler was forced to contemplate invasion. That required control of the air. The first strikes by the **Luftwaffe**, the German air force, were on airfields in southeastern England in August 1940. If Germany had stuck with this strategy, it might have won control of the air and cleared the way for its army to invade Britain. In early September, however, the Luftwaffe chose to avenge British bombing raids on German cities by switching its attention to London. For two months, London was bombed nightly. Much of the city was destroyed, and about 15,000 people were killed.

Strategists who had argued that victory could be achieved through air power alone were proved wrong. Casualties were much less than expected, and Britain's morale was not shattered. The bombings united the British people and made them more resolute, and they were encouraged by the heavy losses the Royal Air Force (RAF) inflicted on the Luftwaffe. With the help of a new invention called *radar* and an excellent system of communications, the British Spitfire and Hurricane fighter planes destroyed more than twice as many German aircraft as the RAF lost. The Battle of Britain was won in the air, and Hitler's defeat forced him to abandon his plans for invading Britain.

THE GERMAN ATTACK ON RUSSIA

Hitler claimed the conquest of Ukraine was necessary to provide *Lebensraum* ("living space") for the German people, and in December 1940, while his bombardment of England was still underway, he ordered his generals to prepare to invade Russia by May 15, 1941. He may have thought a quick victory in the East would undermine Britain's will to fight. Operation Barbarossa (the code name for the attack on Russia) intended to defeat Russia before winter set in. Success required an early start, but Hitler's Italian ally delayed him.

After Mussolini's invasion of France turned into a fiasco, the dictator had attacked the British in Egypt in hopes of redeeming his military reputation. He also invaded Greece from an Albanian base he had seized in 1939. When the British counterattacked in North Africa, drove the Italians back into Libya, and helped the Greeks push into Albania, Hitler had to come to the aid of his Italian ally. He sent General Erwin Rommel (1891–1944), "the Desert Fox," to Africa and an army to Greece to crush resistance and occupy Yugoslavia. These tactics delayed the start of his Russian campaign by a crucial six weeks. (See Map 28–2.)

Operation Barbarossa, which was finally launched on June 22, 1941, almost succeeded. Despite a later claim by the Russians that the Nazi-Soviet pact was a diversion intended to give them time to prepare for war with Germany, Hitler took them by surprise. Stalin had not fortified his frontier, and Hitler's attack so panicked him he failed to orchestrate an orderly retreat for his army. In the first two days of the campaign, 2,000 Russian planes were destroyed while still on the ground, and by November, Hitler had advanced farther into Russia than

Luftwaffe The German air force.

MAP 28–2

Axis Europe, 1941   On the eve of the German invasion of the Soviet Union, a German-Italian Axis bestrode most of Europe by annexation, occupation, or alliance—from Norway and Finland in the north to Greece in the south, and from Poland to France. Britain, the Soviet Union, a number of insurgent groups, and, finally, America, had before them the long struggle of conquering this "fortress Europe" of the Axis.

GIVEN THE diversity of cultures within the Axis, what were its prospects for maintaining order and stability in Europe over the long term?

Napoleon had in 1812. The German army reached the gates of Leningrad, the outskirts of Moscow, and the Don River. Of the 4.5 million troops with which the Russians had begun the fight, they had lost 2.5 million, and of their 15,000 tanks, only 700 were left. Germany's victory seemed imminent.

The Germans failed, however, to deliver a decisive blow. The Nazi general staff wanted to concentrate on taking Moscow before winter. Although this had not worked for Napoleon, it might have worked now, for Moscow had become the hub of Russia's transportation system. Control of the railroads would have enabled the Germans to supply themselves and disrupt life for the Russians.

Hitler chose, instead, to divert a large part of his army to the south. By the time he was ready for an offensive near Moscow, it was too late. Winter set in and devastated the German soldiers, who lacked appropriate clothing and equipment. Stalin used the respite this gave him to construct defenses for Moscow and to bring in additional troops from Siberia. When the Russians counterattacked, the Germans began to have Napoleon's nightmares.

HITLER'S PLANS FOR EUROPE

Hitler often spoke of the "new order" that the Nazi's **Third Reich** would establish in Europe. The two earlier Reichs (empires) were those of Charlemagne in the ninth century and Bismarck in the nineteenth century. Hitler claimed his Reich, unlike theirs, would last for a thousand years. He seems to have had no coherent plan for governing either Germany or Europe, however. He relied on intuition and pragmatism to patch together administrations for the lands he conquered. Some were annexed by Germany. Some were administered by German officials. Some remained nominally independent under puppet governments.

Hitler's regime was probably unmatched in history for its studied use of terror and its active cultivation of inhumanity. The *Lebensraum* he sought for Germans was to be obtained by dispossessing peoples he deemed inferior. In Poland, German colonists evicted Poles from their land or used them as cheap labor. A similar fate on a grander scale was planned for Russia. The Russians were to be driven into central Asia and Siberia and kept in check by frontier colonies inhabited by German war veterans. European Russia was then to be resettled by Germans.

In addition to colonization, cultural germanization was to be employed to build the Reich. People who were racially akin to the Germans (the Scandinavians, the Dutch, and the Swiss) were to be reeducated, purged of dissenting elements, and absorbed into the German nation. Selected individuals from lesser races might also be assimilated. For example, a half-million Ukrainian girls were to be dispatched to Germany as servants and potential wives for German men. (About 15,000 were actually sent.)

Hitler plundered wherever he conquered. He stripped eastern Europe of everything useful, including entire industries. Russia and Poland had only land to offer, but the western European nations the Germans occupied had richer economies. They were forced to support the German armies of occupation at a rate several times above real costs. Germans used the excess income to buy up everything they wanted and deprived defeated populations even of necessities. The Nazis frankly admitted their eagerness to exploit, to enslave, and to destroy. These activities were part of their vision of German glory.

JAPAN AND THE UNITED STATES ENTER THE WAR

The assistance that Roosevelt gave Britain would have justified a German declaration of war, but Hitler held back, hoping America would remain aloof from the European conflict. Isolationist sentiment might, indeed, have kept the United States out of the war in the Atlantic if war had not been forced on the Americans in the Pacific.

Japan's conquest of Manchuria in 1931 raised questions in the United States about Japan's ultimate objectives. When fighting broke out in Europe and the Japanese accelerated their drive to dominate Asia, relations between Japan and the United States worsened. The Japanese allied with Germany and Italy, entered into a treaty of neutrality with the Soviet Union, exploited France's weakness by moving into Indochina, continued their war in China, and planned to

Third Reich Hitler's regime of Nazis.

take Malaya and the East Indies from Britain and the Netherlands. The United States was the only country standing in their way.

The Americans had delayed cutting off supplies of oil and other materials to Japan for fear of provoking an attack on Southeast Asia and Indonesia. When Japan occupied Indochina in July 1941, however, the United States froze Japanese assets and cut off oil shipments. The British and Dutch did the same. The Japanese concluded that to continue the development of their empire, they had to acquire Indonesia for its oil and Malaya for its rubber and tin.

A pro-war faction led by General Hideki Tojo (1885–1948) came to power in Japan in October 1941. A little over a month later, on Sunday morning, December 7, 1941, while Japan's representatives in Washington were discussing a settlement, Japan launched an air attack on America's chief naval base in the Pacific, Hawaii's Pearl Harbor. The Americans were taken totally by surprise. They lost much of their fleet and many airplanes, and for the time being, their ability to wage war in the Pacific was negated. A day later, the United States and Britain declared war on Japan, and three days later, Germany and Italy declared war on the United States.

The Japanese swiftly captured Guam, Wake Island, and the Philippines. By the spring of 1942, they had won control of Hong Kong, Malaya, Burma, Indonesia, and the Southwest Pacific as far as New Guinea. As they prepared to invade Australia, the Germans nearly reached the Caspian Sea in a drive toward Russia's oil fields. In Africa, Rommel closed in on the Suez Canal and pushed the British back to El Alamein, only seventy miles from Alexandria. The German submarines that roamed the Atlantic also made it difficult for Britain's allies to keep it supplied and come to its aid.

The successful Japanese attack on the American base at Pearl Harbor in Hawaii on December 7, 1941, together with simultaneous attacks on other Pacific bases, brought the United States into war against the Axis powers. This picture shows the battleships USS *West Virginia* and USS *Tennessee* in flames as a small boat rescues a man from the water.

U.S. Army Photograph

THE TIDE TURNS

The future looked bleak, but more than twenty nations from around the world joined forces to oppose the Axis powers. Great Britain, the Soviet Union, and the United States took the lead. The Russians accepted all the aid they could get, but they did not trust their allies. They demanded that the democracies relieve pressure on them by opening a "second front" against Germany on the mainland of Europe.

The potential power of the United States was enormous, but it was not yet prepared to contribute to an invasion of Europe. Conscription had been introduced in 1940, but the American army was tiny, inexperienced, and ill equipped. American industry was not geared for war, and German submarines made the Atlantic unsafe for conveying troops to Europe. Not until 1944 would conditions be right for an invasion. In the meantime, however, some developments augured doom for the Axis.

In the spring of 1942, the Allies won their first victory in the Pacific, a battle in the Coral Sea. The damage inflicted on the Japanese navy diminished the likelihood that Japan would invade Australia. A month later, the United States defeated Japan in a fierce air and naval battle off Midway Island. This minimized the risk of another assault on Hawaii and did enough damage to halt Japan's advance. American Marines then landed on Guadalcanal in the Solomon Islands and began to reverse the momentum of the war. The fight in the Pacific was far from over, but Japan was sufficiently contained to allow the Allies to concentrate on Europe.

QUICK REVIEW

The Path to War
- 1931: Japan conquers Manchuria
- July 1941: in response to Japanese occupation of Indonesia, the United States freezes Japanese assets and cuts off oil shipments
- December 7, 1941: Japan launches a surprise attack on Pearl Harbor

In the battle of Stalingrad, Russian troops contested every street and building. Although the city was all but destroyed in the fighting and Russian casualties were enormous, the German army in the east never recovered from the defeat it suffered there.

Hulton Archives/Getty Images, Inc.

Allied troops landed in Normandy on D-Day, June 6, 1944. This photograph, taken two days later, shows long lines of men and equipment moving inland from the beach to reinforce the troops leading the invasion.

Hulton Archives Photos/Getty Images, Inc.

Allied Landings in Africa, Sicily, and Italy British field marshal Bernard Montgomery (1887–1976) stopped Rommel at El Alamein and began to drive the Germans back. In November 1942, an Allied force landed in French North Africa, and the American general, Dwight D. Eisenhower (1890–1969), pushed eastward through Morocco and Algeria. By crushing the Germans between them in Tunisia, the British and American armies won control of the Mediterranean and opened the way for an invasion of Europe from the south.

In July and August 1943, the Allies occupied Sicily and drove Mussolini from power. A new Italian government, led by Marshal Pietro Badoglio (1871–1956), joined the Allies, but Italy did not prove as easy to occupy as the Allies had hoped. Hitler deployed the German army to hold Italy despite the fact that the fierce fighting strained Germany's thinning resources.

Battle of Stalingrad The Russian campaign also heated up in the summer of 1942. The Germans launched offensives on all fronts. Stalingrad, on the Volga, was a key point on the flank of the German army, and Hitler was as determined to take it as Stalin was to defend it. The Battle of Stalingrad raged for months. More Russians died in this one campaign than Americans in the entire war. In the end, Russia prevailed, but Hitler overruled his generals and refused to retreat—sacrificing an entire German army. (See Map 28–3.)

Stalingrad was the turning point in the war for Russia. America provided some material help, but it was mostly increased production from Russian industries that had been moved to or built up in the safe central and eastern regions of the USSR that allowed the Soviets to win the upper hand. As Germany's resources dwindled, Russia's armies advanced inexorably westward.

Strategic Bombing In 1943, the industrial might of the United States began to tell. New technology and tactics greatly reduced the submarine menace, and American and British air forces began a massive bombardment of Germany that continued night and day. Americans preferred the visibility of day missions, for they favored a strategy of "precision bombing" aimed at military and industrial targets. The British believed precision bombing was impossible. They opted to fly at night for maximum security and tried to undercut German morale by indiscriminate "area bombing." Neither approach was very effective until 1944, when the Americans improved the accuracy of their missions and introduced long-range fighters to protect their bombers.

By 1945, the skies were virtually cleared of German planes, and the Allies could bomb at will. Attacks on industrial targets helped shorten the war, but bombing to spread terror also continued—even though it seems to have had little effect. An air raid on Dresden in February 1945 was especially savage. It was much debated within the British government at the time, and it continues to raise moral questions. Whatever else the aerial war over Germany accomplished, it took a heavy toll of the German air force and diverted resources from other military purposes. (See "Encountering the Past: Rosie the Riveter and American Women in the War Effort.")

THE DEFEAT OF NAZI GERMANY

On June 6, 1944 (D-day), American, British, and Canadian troops under the Allied commander Dwight D. Eisenhower landed on the heavily fortified coast of Normandy. Despite

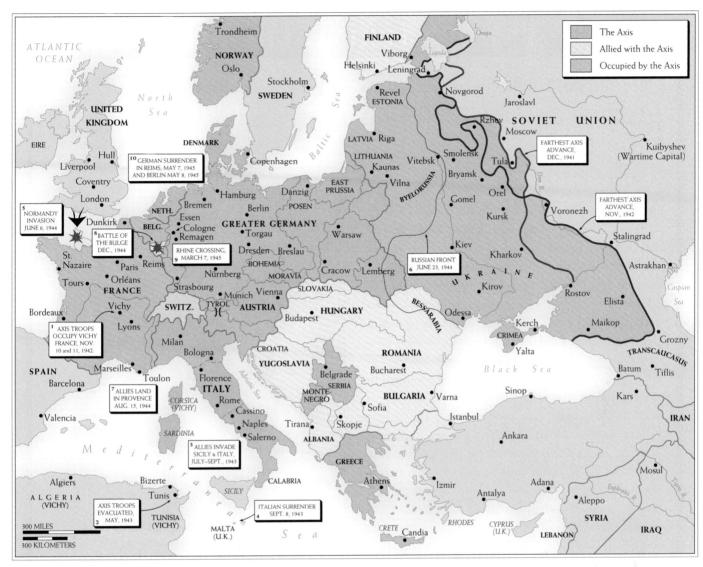

MAP 28–3
Defeat of the Axis in Europe, 1942–1945   Here are some of the major steps in the progress toward Allied victory against Axis Europe. From the south through Italy, the west through France, and the east through Russia, the Allies gradually conquered the Continent to bring the war in Europe to a close.

ON WHICH of these three fronts–southern, western, or eastern–was World War II fought the longest?

the fact that the German coastal defenses were very strong and amphibious assaults are especially vulnerable to wind and weather, the Allies established a beachhead and began to advance. In mid-August they landed in southern France, and within a few weeks France was liberated.

The Battle of the Bulge   In December, the Germans launched a counterattack through Belgium's Ardennes Forest and dented the Allied line—making a "bulge" that gave the battle its name. The Allies suffered heavy losses, but the Battle of the Bulge was Germany's last western offensive. The Allies recovered their momentum and crossed the Rhine in March 1945. As German resistance crumbled, no German in this war, unlike the first one, could doubt that his or her country was being defeated militarily.

QUICK REVIEW

Key Battles
- June 6, 1944 (D-day): Allied forces land in Normandy
- December 1944: Germans inflict heavy losses at the Battle of the Bulge but fail to halt Allies' advance
- May 1945: Soviet troops capture Berlin

ENCOUNTERING THE PAST

ROSIE THE RIVETER AND AMERICAN WOMEN IN THE WAR EFFORT

The huge productive capacity of American industry was essential to Allied victory in the war, and American women helped sustain it. Before the start of the war and despite the unprecedented number of women the Great Depression had forced to seek employment, society was still hostile to the idea of women working outside their homes. World War II changed that. The work force lost millions of men to the military, and women were needed to take their places.

Factories proliferated to produce the vast amounts of equipment needed for the war, and they eagerly recruited workers from groups they had previously spurned: African Americans from the rural south and women. President Roosevelt in a speech in October 1942 observed, "In some communities employers dislike to hire women. In others they are reluctant to hire Negroes. We can no longer afford to indulge such prejudice."

For some women, patriotism was more important than pay. Their jobs provided them with a way to support their male friends and relatives on the battlefield. A popular song told the story of "Rosie the Riveter," a young woman who made aircraft to protect her Marine boyfriend. A painting by Norman Rockwell for the cover of the *Saturday Evening Post* depicted her holding her rivet gun and resting her foot on a copy of Hitler's *Mein Kampf.*

HOW DID the war change attitudes about the place of women and minorities in American society?

Rosie the Riveter was one of the best known symbols of the U.S. war effort in World War II.

Printed by permission of the Norman Rockwell Family Agency. Copyright © 1943 the Norman Rockwell Family Entities

---

The Capture of Berlin In the east, the Russians overcame fierce German resistance and advanced swiftly on Berlin. The Allies refused any terms but unconditional surrender, which may have encouraged the Germans to fight on as long as possible. Finally, on May 1, 1945, Hitler committed suicide in an underground bunker in Berlin, and the Russians, with the consent of their allies, occupied the city. Instead of the millennium Hitler had promised, the Third Reich lasted a mere twelve years.

FALL OF THE JAPANESE EMPIRE

The war in Europe ended on May 8, 1945, and by then victory over Japan was also in sight. The longer the war lasted, the more American superiority in industrial production and population began to tell.

Americans Recapture the Pacific Islands In 1943, the American forces, which were still relatively small, began a campaign of "island hopping." Its goal was not to recapture every island Japan held but to gain strategic sites along the

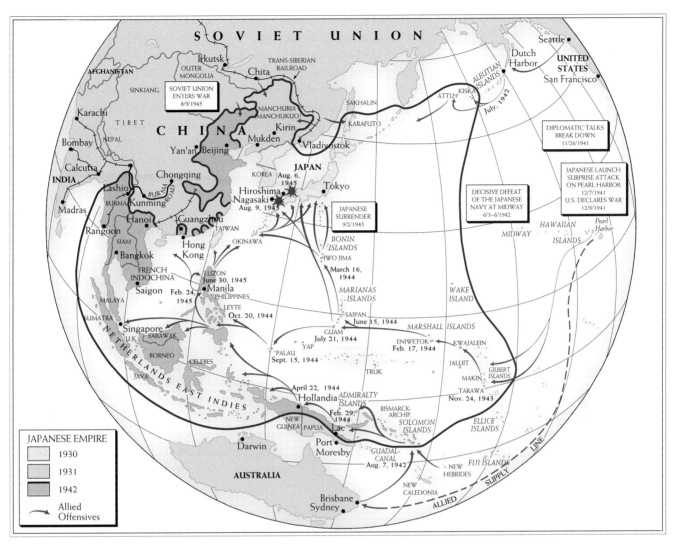

MAP 28–4

World War II in the Pacific   As in Europe, the Pacific war involved Allied recapture of areas that had been quickly taken earlier by the enemy. The enormous area represented by the map shows the initial expansion of Japanese holdings to cover half the Pacific and its islands, as well as huge sections of eastern Asia, and the long struggle to push the Japanese back to their homeland and defeat them.

COULD THE territories that Japan seized at the start of the war have become a coherent empire?

enemy's supply line. Starting from the Solomon Islands, the Americans moved northeast toward Japan. In June 1944, they took the Mariana Islands from which bombing raids could be launched on the Philippines, China, and Japan itself. The capture of the Philippines in October forced the Japanese fleet to retreat to its home waters. In 1945, Iwo Jima and Okinawa fell, giving the Americans more bases for bombers that devastated Japan's industries and navy. (See Map 28–4.)

The Atomic Bomb   When the Japanese government, which was dominated by a military clique, refused to surrender, the Americans made plans to assault the Japanese mainland. A million American casualties and even greater Japanese losses were anticipated, but at this point science provided the Americans with another option. A secret program had been in progress since the start of the war. Staffed in part by refugee scientists who fled Hitler, it was set up to explore military uses for atomic energy.

On August 6, 1945, an American plane dropped an atomic bomb on the Japanese city of Hiroshima. More than 70,000 of the city's 200,000 residents were killed. Two days later, the Soviet Union declared war on Japan and invaded Manchuria, and the next day a second atomic bomb destroyed Nagasaki. The Japanese cabinet wanted to fight on, but unprecedented intervention by Japan's Emperor Hirohito (r. 1926–1989), who by tradition took no part in politics, forced the generals to offer terms on August 14. The Allies insisted on unconditional surrender, but Harry S Truman (1884–1972)—who became president after Franklin D. Roosevelt died in office on April 12, 1945—agreed to Japan's request to keep its emperor. The war ended with the signing of a treaty aboard the USS *Missouri* in Tokyo Bay on September 2, 1945.

Some analysts claim the bombings were not needed to defeat Japan and their real purpose was to frighten the Russians into respecting America after the war. Others have suggested the decision to use the bomb was almost automatic once the nation had committed to its development. At the time, however, the choice was simple. The bomb promised to end the war swiftly and bring a halt to the loss of American lives. Its employment was conscious, not automatic, and it required no ulterior motive.

THE COST OF WAR

World War II was the most terrible war in history. About 15 million military personnel died and at least as many civilians. Deaths from disease, hunger, and other causes indirectly linked to war raise the number of its victims to 40 million. Most of Europe and significant parts of Asia were devastated.

At so terrible a cost, the war bought little peace of mind, for it inaugurated the Atomic Age with the concomitant knowledge that another conflict could extinguish humanity. Human survival depended on achieving a stable peace, but even as the fighting ended, tensions among the victors made prospects for a lasting peace doubtful.

RACISM AND THE HOLOCAUST

WHAT WAS the Holocaust?

*T*he worst abuses of Nazi power sprang not from military or economic necessity but from Hitler's racial doctrines. They categorized several groups of people in eastern Europe as *Untermenschen* ("subhumans"). In parts of Poland, Germans entirely exterminated the Slavic upper and professional classes. Polish schools and churches were closed. The Slavic birthrate was kept down by limiting the right to marry, and harsh living conditions took their toll on the Slavic population. Conditions were even worse for Russia's Slavs. Hitler planned his Russian campaign as a war of extermination and charged Heinrich Himmler, head of the SS, with figuring out how to eliminate 30 million Slavs so Germans might occupy their land. Six million Russian prisoners of war and deported civilian workers may have died under Nazi rule.

Hitler had a special fate in mind for Jews. He intended to make Europe *Judenrein* ("purified of Jews"). At first, he thought he might send them to the African island of Madagascar, but he ultimately decided extermination, the "final solution," was preferable. The Nazis built camps in Germany and Poland where sophisticated technology was employed to kill and dispose of the corpses of millions of men, women, and children with maximum efficiency. The Jews of eastern Europe bore the brunt of this, but Nazis and collaborators shipped Jews from all over Europe to the death camps. Before the war ended, perhaps 6 million of them were killed. Only about a million European Jews survived, most in pitiable condition.

THE DESTRUCTION OF THE POLISH JEWISH COMMUNITY

Prior to the war, Poland, where Jews accounted for 10 percent of the population, was home to Europe's largest Jewish community. Enduring prejudices kept Jews confined to villages and urban neighborhoods of their own, and Polish Jews did not benefit from the emancipation movements that swept western Europe during the nineteenth century. (See Chapter 23.) They scraped by as a poverty-ridden lower class whose dress, language, and culture made them highly visible and suspect in what was an increasingly nationalistic Roman Catholic country.

POLISH ANTI-SEMITISM BETWEEN THE WARS

After Poland's restoration following World War I, Polish leaders were divided over the role of Jews in Polish national life. Josef Pilsudski (1867–1935), who dominated the interwar era, favored including Jews within the civic definition of the nation, and the constitution allowed Jews to participate in Polish political life. Yet, especially after Pilsudski's death, the Polish government, supported by spokesmen for the Polish Roman Catholic Church, pursued policies that were anti-Semitic. The government nationalized industries and discriminated against the employment of Jews in state monopolies and the civil service. It made it difficult for Jews to keep the Sabbath without losing their jobs, and it encouraged people to boycott Jewish shops and businesses. Poles generally refused to recognize as Polish even those Jews who adopted Poland's language, dress, and culture. Many Jews acquiesced to their treatment as outsiders as their fate and viewed assimilation as modernization, not a bid for social acceptance. Poland's constitution guaranteed them political rights, but they were split up into political factions that could not agree on a common strategy for bettering their condition. When World War II broke out in 1939, they were extremely vulnerable.

29.6
Notes from the Warsaw Ghetto

MAP 28–5

The Holocaust The Nazi policy of ethnic cleansing—targeting Jews, Gypsies, political dissidents, and "social deviants"—began with imprisoning them in concentration camps, but by 1943 the *Endlösung*, or *Final Solution*, called for the systematic extermination of "undesirables."

HOW IMPORTANT were the logistics of rail transportation to the Final Solution?

THE NAZI ASSAULT ON THE JEWS OF POLAND

It was the Nazis who tried to destroy the Polish Jewish community and European Jewish communities that fell under German control. Occupation of Poland gave the Nazis control over what they considered to be the chief

Roundup of Warsaw Jews. World War II resulted in the near-total destruction of the Jews of Europe, victims of the Holocaust spawned by Hitler's racial theories of the superiority and inferiority of particular ethnic groups. Hitler placed special emphasis on the need to exterminate the Jews, to whom he attributed particular wickedness. This picture shows a roundup of Jews in Warsaw, where there was a large Jewish population, ultimately on their way to concentration or death camps.

© Hulton-Deutsch Collection/CORBIS

breeding ground for world Jewry. Their first plan was to herd all of Europe's Jews into the Lublin region of Poland. In early 1940, they began to relocate Jews to walled and guarded ghettos that would keep them separate from other Poles. They confiscated the property of the Jews they sent to the ghettos and used the ghettos as a source of cheap contract labor for German industries. The urban ghettos of Lodz and Warsaw each had populations of several hundred thousand. Twenty percent of their residents died from disease and malnourishment. Tens of thousands more Jews died as the Germans advanced into Russia.

In the second half of 1941, the Nazis decided to exterminate the Jews of Europe. Jews were shipped by rail to infamous death camps in Poland: Kulmhof, Belzen, Sobibor, Treblinka, Birkenau, and Auschwitz. The slaughter continued from 1941 to 1944. Only 10 percent of Poland's Jewish population made it through the war, and at its end many of the survivors emigrated to Israel. Europe's largest Jewish community virtually disappeared.

EXPLANATIONS OF THE HOLOCAUST

Students of the Holocaust have debated whether it was a unique aberration or an expression of perennial, abiding human wickedness. They have examined it in light of the massacres carried out by twentieth-century communist regimes (which killed many more people than Hitler), and they have speculated about how much responsibility to assign Hitler and the German people. It is clear that the effectiveness of the campaign to exterminate the Jews owed much to the persistence of anti-Semitism in Christianity and Western culture. This medieval religious prejudice was strengthened in the nineteenth and twentieth centuries by pseudoscientific racial theories. Nationalism, utopian visions of a perfect world created by scientific social engineering, influential media, and the technological power of the modern state all helped persuade people to cooperate with the Nazi death machine. Human beings still have much to learn about themselves from the study of the Holocaust. (See "History's Voices: Mass Murder at Belsen,")

WHAT IMPACT did World War II have on European society?

THE DOMESTIC FRONTS

GERMANY: FROM APPARENT VICTORY TO DEFEAT

Hitler had expected the techniques of the *Blitzkrieg* to win him a quick victory that would not affect social and economic life in Germany, and for the first two years of the war, few sacrifices were required from the German people. Spending continued on domestic projects, and food was plentiful. Conditions changed as the assault on the Soviet Union bogged down. Food imports from the east declined, and Germany had to mobilize for total war.

In 1942, Germany began a push to increase its army and military production. Albert Speer (1905–1981), minister for armaments and munitions, diverted industries from production of consumer goods to military supplies. The output of military products tripled between 1942 and 1944, but productivity declined as a growing labor shortage forced the government to start drafting workers. Shortages of everyday products became serious, and the German worker's standard of living fell. Prices and wages were controlled, and food rationing was implemented in April 1942. The Nazis confiscated food from occupied countries and tried to preserve their home front by passing its suffering on to others.

By 1943, labor was also in short supply. Teenagers, retired men, and increasing numbers of women were recruited into the work force. The Germans closed retail businesses, raised the age for women eligible for compulsory service, shifted non-German domestic workers to wartime industries, closed theaters, moved artists and entertainers into military service, and reduced basic public services such as mail and railways. Thousands of people from conquered lands were sent to do forced labor in Germany.

Women had a special place in Hitler's war effort. Propaganda depicted them as mothers and wives who loyally sent sons and husbands off to war. The wartime activities assigned to them were said to be natural extensions of their maternal roles. As air raid wardens, they protected their families. As factory workers, they equipped their men on the front lines. As farm laborers, they provided food for soldier sons and husbands. As housewives, their frugal management conserved supplies needed to win the war. And, most important, as chaste wives and daughters, they guarded the purity of the German race.

Hitler and other Germans genuinely believed a lack of support from the home front had led to Germany's defeat in World War I, and they devised a propaganda campaign of unique intensity to make sure this did not happen again. Propaganda Minister Josef Goebbels (1897–1945) used radio and cinema to boost the Nazi cause at home, and the same mass media were employed to control occupied lands. The ministry broadcast exaggerated claims of Nazi victories, and when Germany's armies were finally checked on the battlefield, propaganda stiffened resistance by spreading alarm about the consequences of defeat. Allied bombing raids that, after May 1943, devastated one German city after another may actually have played into the hands of the Nazis by seeming to confirm the Nazi propagandists' claims that Germany's enemies were ruthless.

The war effort increased the power of the Nazi Party by bringing everything in Germany under its control. There was virtually no serious opposition to Hitler during the war. In 1944, when a few army officers tried to assassinate him, their failed attempt elicited few signs of popular approval. The utter defeat of the Nazis and the consequent devastation of Germany was to effect a radical change in the nation.

FRANCE: DEFEAT, COLLABORATION, AND RESISTANCE

The truce the French agreed to on June 22, 1940, gave the invading German army the right to occupy more than half of France, including the Atlantic and English Channel coasts. To prevent the French from turning their fleet over to Britain and continuing to fight in North Africa, Hitler left southern France unoccupied until November 1942. Marshal Pétain set up a dictatorial regime in the city of Vichy and tried to preserve some autonomy by closely collaborating with the Germans.

Many conservatives and extreme rightists hoped the Vichy government would end what they considered to be the corrupting influences of liberalism. The Roman Catholic Church supported Pétain, who restored religious instruction in state schools and increased financial support for Catholic institutions. Vichy also endorsed the church's social views—making divorce difficult and subsidizing large families. The Vichy regime promoted intense, chauvinistic nationalism and long-standing prejudices against foreigners working in France. Its chief victims were France's Jews. Even before 1942, when Hitler undertook his "final solution," the French were evicting Jews from posts in government, education, and

HISTORY'S VOICES

MASS MURDER IN A NAZI DEATH CAMP

Hitler's calculated plan to wipe out Europe's Jews, along with millions of other people he considered undesirable for racial and other reasons, was not widely known during the war. Many people were reluctant to believe leaks about these secret operations. Kurt Gerstein, a colonel in the SS, unlike most people involved and at great risk to himself, tried to tell the world what was taking place. The following is an account of what he saw occur in the death camp at Belzec in the Lublin district of Poland in 1942.

WHY DID many Germans take part in exterminating millions of men, women, and children? Why did so conscientious a man as Colonel Gerstein not resist?

A train arrived from Lemberg [Lvov]. There were forty-five cars containing 6,700 people, 1,450 of whom were already dead. Through the gratings on the windows, children could be seen peering out, terribly pale and frightened, their eyes filled with mortal dread. . . . The train entered the station, and two hundred Ukrainians wrenched open the doors and drove the people out of the carriages with their leather whips. Instructions came through a large loudspeaker telling them to remove all their clothing, artificial limbs, glasses, etc. They were to hand over all objects of value at the counter. . . . Shoes were to be carefully tied together, for otherwise no one would ever again have been able to find shoes belonging to each other in a pile that was a good eighty feet high. Then the women and girls were sent to the barber who, with two or three strokes of his scissors, cut off all their hair and dropped it into potato sacks. "That's for some special purpose or other on U-Boats, for packing or something like that," I was told by an SS-Unterscharfuhrer. . . .

Then the column moved off. Headed by an extremely pretty young girl, they walked along the avenue, all naked, men, women, and children, with artificial limbs removed. I myself was stationed up on the ramp between the [gas] chambers with Captain Wirth.

Mothers with babies at their breasts came up, hesitated, and entered the chambers of death. At the corner stood a burly SS man with a priest-like voice. "Nothing at all is going to happen to you!" he told the poor wretches. "All you have to do when you get into

publishing. In 1941, the Germans began to intern the Jews who lived in occupied France, and in the spring of 1942, they started to deport them. Over 60,000 were ultimately sent to extermination camps in eastern Europe. The Vichy government had no part in these decisions, but it did not protest them.

A few French fled to Britain after their homeland surrendered to the Nazis. Under the leadership of General Charles de Gaulle (1890–1969), they organized the French National Committee of Liberation, the Free French. The Vichy government retained control of French North Africa and France's navy until the end of 1942, but the Free French established a base in central Africa and waged propaganda offensives from London. A serious resistance movement did not develop in France until late in 1942, and it remained small. Less than 5 percent of the adult French population joined it.

In early 1944, when it became clear the Allies were winning, the resistance movement grew much larger. General de Gaulle, from his base in London, urged the French to fight their conquerors and the Vichy administration. On August 9, 1944, the Committee of National Liberation repudiated the Vichy government, and French soldiers joined the Allies in liberating Paris. On October 21, 1945, France voted to end the Third Republic and adopt a new constitution—the

the chambers is to breathe in deeply. That stretches the lungs. Inhaling is necessary to prevent disease and epidemics." When asked what would be done with them, he replied: "Well, of course, the men will have to work building houses and roads, but the women won't need to work. They can do housework or help in the kitchen, but only if they want to." For some of these poor creatures, this was a small ray of hope that was enough to make them walk the few steps to the chambers without resistance. Most of them knew what was going on. The smell told them what their fate was to be. They went up the small flight of steps and saw everything. Mothers with their babies clasped to their breasts, small children, adults, men, women, all naked; they hesitated, but they entered the chambers of death, thrust forward by the others behind them or by the leather whips of the SS [Storm Troopers]. Most went in without a word. . . . Many were saying prayers. I prayed with them. I pressed myself into a corner and cried aloud to my God and theirs. How gladly I should have gone into the chambers with them; how gladly I should have died with them. Then they would have found an SS officer in uniform in their gas chambers; they would have believed it was an accident and the story would have been buried and forgotten. But I could not do that yet. First, I had to make known what

I had seen here. The chambers were filling up. Fill them up well—that was Captain Wirth's order. The people were treading on each other's feet. There were 700–800 of them in an area of 270 square feet, in 1,590 cubic feet of space. The SS crushed them together as tightly as they possibly could. The doors closed. Meanwhile, the rest waited out in the open, all naked. "It's done exactly the same way in winter," I was told. "But they may catch their death!" I said. "That's what they're here for," an SS man said. . . . The Diesel exhaust gases were intended to kill those unfortunates. But the engine was not working. . . . The people in the gas chambers waited, in vain. I heard them weeping, sobbing. . . . After 2 hours and 49 minutes, measured by my stop watch, the Diesel started. Up to that moment, men and women had been shut up alive in those four chambers, four times 750 people in four times 1,590 cubic feet of space. Another twenty-five minutes dragged by. Many of those inside were already dead. They could be seen through the small window when the electric light went on for a moment and lit up the inside of the chamber. After twenty-eight minutes, few were left alive. At the end of thirty-two minutes, all were dead.

From Saul Friedlaender, *Pius XII and the Third Reich: A Documentation* (New York: Alfred A. Knopf, 1966, pp. 126–128).

Fourth Republic. Bitter quarrels over who did what during the occupation divided the French for decades.

GREAT BRITAIN: ORGANIZATION FOR VICTORY

On May 22, 1940, the British Parliament gave the government emergency powers, and it instituted compulsory military service, food rationing, and economic controls. All Britain's political parties joined in support of a government led by Winston Churchill.

The nation's most pressing military need was for airplanes to fight the Battle of Britain. Lord Beaverbrook, one of Britain's most important newspaper publishers, oversaw their production, and to find materials a massive campaign to reclaim scrap metal was launched. This was the first of many appeals to support the war effort to which the civilian population enthusiastically responded. Factory hours were extended. Large numbers of women entered the work force, and unemployment disappeared. By the end of 1941, Britain's production surpassed Germany's.

Germany's air raids provided the British people with dramatic war experiences in 1940 and 1941. Thousands were killed and many left homeless. Families

Winston Churchill walks through the rubble-strewn streets of London after the city experienced a night of German bombing. Despite many casualties and widespread devastation, the German bombing of London did not break British morale or prevent the city from functioning.

UPI/CORBIS/Bettmann

sent their children to the countryside for safety. Gas masks were issued to city dwellers, who sought shelter from the bombs in London's subways. Hitler needed most of his air force on the Russian front after the spring of 1941, but he managed to continue some bombing of Britain. Bombs killed more than 30,000 Britons before the war ended, but Allied bombers inflicted worse on the Germans. In Germany, as in England, however, bombing failed to break people's spirits and seems to have increased their determination to resist. The British people made many sacrifices. Transportation facilities strained to carry enough coal to heat homes and fuel factories. Food and clothing were in short supply, and the government imposed strict rationing. Every scrap of land was farmed, increasing tillage by almost 4 million acres. The scarcity of gasoline nearly ended the use of private vehicles.

Like the Germans, the British used propaganda to further the war effort. The British Broadcasting Company (BBC) urged resistance to the Nazis in programs transmitted abroad in all European languages. At home, radio serials and Churchill's famous speeches helped bring the nation together.

THE SOVIET UNION: "THE GREAT PATRIOTIC WAR"

No nation suffered greater losses of life and property during the war than the Soviet Union. About 16 million of its people were killed, and vast numbers of its soldiers suffered imprisonment. Hundreds of cities and towns and well over half the nation's industrial and transportation facilities were devastated. Thousands of Soviets became forced laborers in German factories, and Germany confiscated the Soviet Union's grain, mineral resources, and oil.

In the decade leading up to the war, Stalin had made the Soviet Union a highly centralized state that was permanently on something resembling a wartime footing. Stalin, however, had worried that the army might come to rival the Communist Party, and the purges he carried out in the late 1930s eliminated many of its officers. As the war continued, the army did acquire a degree of independence, and generals ceased to be subservient to party commissars. The military remained under Stalin's control, however, and constrained by the nature of Soviet government and society.

Soviet propaganda differed from that of other nations. The government was not confident in the loyalty of its citizens, so it confiscated radios to prevent German and British propaganda from reaching the populace. The government communicated with people in urban areas over loudspeakers, not radios, and it appealed to patriotism more than Marxist class theory to marshal support for the war. Stalin even made peace with the Russian Orthodox Church in an effort to win support at home and improve the image of the Soviet Union in parts of eastern Europe where the church was strong.

The German army advanced so quickly that thousands of Soviet soldiers were stranded behind German lines. This enabled an active resistance movement to develop quickly in the western Soviet Union. Many soldiers were captured and shipped to Germany as prisoners of war, but others escaped and became guerrilla fighters. In addition to causing trouble for the Germans, these partisans helped keep peasants, who resented the Soviet government's policy of collectivization, from collaborating with the enemy. As the Soviet army moved westward at the end of the war, the partisans rejoined the regular units.

Stalin had entered the war reluctantly, but he emerged from it a major winner. The Soviet Union established itself as a world power second only to the United States, and the feelings of patriotism and self-sacrifice the war inspired in Russia's people rallied them in support of Stalin and the Communist Party.

PREPARATIONS FOR PEACE

The split that quickly developed between the Soviet Union and its allies came as no surprise. The Soviet Union was dedicated to the overthrow of capitalist nations, and those nations were no less open about their hostility to communism. Only the emergency of the war had forced them to put their ideological differences aside—temporarily.

Cooperation against a common enemy and effective propaganda did improve attitudes toward the Soviets in the West, but Churchill was determined to block the Soviets' advance into Europe. Roosevelt's hope that the Allies could work together after the war had faded by 1945, and anticipation of a mutually satisfactory peace settlement upheld by continued cooperation was quickly disappointed.

THE ATLANTIC CHARTER

In August 1941, before the Americans went to war, Roosevelt and Churchill met on a ship off Newfoundland and negotiated the Atlantic Charter. It was intended, in the spirit of Wilson's Fourteen Points, to provide a theoretical basis for the peace they sought. The alliance that Russia, the United States, and Britain entered into on January 1942 was quite different. It was purely military and consciously ignored significant political issues.

TEHRAN: AGREEMENT ON A SECOND FRONT

The leaders of the USSR, Britain, and the United States (the so-called Big Three) first met in Tehran, the capital of Iran, in 1943. Britain and the United States agreed to open a second front in France, and Stalin promised to join the war against Japan once Germany had been defeated. The most important decision reached at Tehran was the choice of Europe's west coast rather than the Mediterranean as the place to begin the Allied offensive. Britain and the United States failed at the time to realize this might lead to Soviet forces occupying eastern Europe. In 1943, the Russians were still fighting far behind their own frontiers, and immediate military objectives overrode all long-range considerations.

By 1944, the situation had changed. In August, Soviet armies reached Warsaw. Its people expected imminent liberation and rose up against the Germans,

Significant Dates from the Era Culminating in World War II

1919	(June) The Versailles Treaty
1931	(Spring) Onset of the Great Depression in Europe
1933	(January) Hitler comes to power
1935	(March) Hitler renounces disarmament (October) Mussolini attacks Ethiopia
1936	(March) Germany remilitarizes the Rhineland (July) Outbreak of the Spanish Civil War (October) Formation of the Rome-Berlin Axis
1938	(March) *Anschluss* with Austria (September) Munich Conference; partition of Czechoslovakia
1939	(August) The Nazi-Soviet pact (September) Germany and the Soviet Union invade Poland; Britain and France declare war on Germany (November) The Soviet Union invades Finland
1940	(April) Germany invades Denmark and Norway (May) Germany invades Belgium, the Netherlands, Luxembourg, and France (June) Fall of France (August) Battle of Britain begins
1941	(June) Germany invades the Soviet Union (July) Japan takes Indochina (December) Japan attacks Pearl Harbor; United States enters the war
1942	(June) Battle of Midway
1942	(November) Battle of Stalingrad begins; Allies land in North Africa
1943	(February–August) Allies take Sicily, land in Italy
1944	(June) Allies land in Normandy
1945	(May) Germany surrenders (August) Atomic bombs dropped on Hiroshima and Nagasaki (September) Japan surrenders

HOW DID the Allies prepare for a postwar Europe?

but the Russians turned south into the Balkans and left the Poles to be annihilated. The Russians realized the dreams of centuries of expansionist tsars by occupying Romania and Hungary. Churchill was alarmed, and in October he went to Moscow to meet with Stalin. They agreed to split up the Balkans. The Soviets were to have Romania and Bulgaria. The West was to control Greece, and both were to share influence equally in Yugoslavia and Hungary.

Germany The Americans were reluctant to agree to enforce spheres of influence of this kind, but the three powers easily agreed on plans for Germany. It was to be disarmed, denazified, and divided into four zones of occupation (one for each of the Big Three and France). Churchill balked at Stalin's demand for $20 billion in reparations and the requisition of forced labor, especially when Stalin claimed half of all this for Russia.

Eastern Europe The settlement of Eastern Europe was a thorny problem. Everyone agreed that the Soviet Union deserved friendly neighbors, but the Western allies wanted those neighbors to be independent and democratic. Western leaders did not want Eastern Europe to come under Russian domination, but Stalin knew that independent, freely elected governments in Poland and Romania could not be counted on to be friendly to Russia. Stalin ignored the Polish government-in-exile in London and set up a puppet government in Poland. Fearing the Allies would betray him by making a separate peace with Germany, he made conciliatory promises to win Allied approval for this coup. He added some people friendly to the West to Poland's government and signed a Declaration on Liberated Europe. It promised self-determination and free democratic elections for all liberated states. Once the war was over, Stalin ignored these agreements.

YALTA

The Big Three held their next meeting at Yalta in the Crimea in February 1945. Western armies had yet to cross the Rhine, but the Soviets were within a hundred miles of Berlin. Roosevelt, faced with the prospect of invading Japan with heavy losses, was eager to bring the Russians into the Pacific war. To encourage their participation, he and Churchill made extensive concessions to Russia in Sakhalin, the Kurile islands, Korea, and Manchuria. Roosevelt suspected Churchill of maneuvering to maintain the British Empire by establishing British spheres of influence. He objected to these as invitations to the Russians to do the same and as sources of future conflicts. Roosevelt, like Wilson, pinned hopes for peace on establishment of an international organization of sovereign states. Soviet support for this seemed well worth the concessions Stalin asked him to make.

In February 1945 Churchill, Roosevelt, and Stalin met at Yalta in the Crimea to plan for the organization of Europe after the end of the war. The Big Three are seated. Standing behind are Lord Leathers, Anthony Eden, Edward Stettinius, Alexander Cadogan, V. M. Molotov, and Averill Harriman.

POTSDAM

The Big Three met for the last time in the Berlin suburb of Potsdam in July 1945. President Truman replaced Roosevelt (who had died in office), and Clement Attlee (1883–1967), leader of the Labour Party, replaced Churchill, whom he had defeated in an election. Previous agreements were reaffirmed, but progress on new issues was slow. Russia's western frontier was moved far into what had been Poland and German East Prussia. Poland was compensated by a grant of authority over the

OVERVIEW   NEGOTIATIONS AMONG THE ALLIES

August 1941	Churchill and Roosevelt meet off Newfoundland to sign Atlantic Charter	Provides basis for the alliance between Britain and the United States.
October 1943	American, British, and Soviet foreign ministers meet in Moscow	Allies reaffirm to fight until the enemy surrenders and to continue cooperating after the war.
November 1943	Churchill, Roosevelt, and Stalin meet at Tehran	Britain and the United States agree to open a second front in France; Stalin promises to join war in Japan after Germany is defeated, and Allied offensive begins on Europe's west coast.
October 1944	Churchill meets with Stalin in Moscow	Agree to share power in the Balkans, with Soviet predominance in Romania and Bulgaria, Western predominance in Greece, and equality of influence in Yugoslavia and Hungary.
February 1945	Churchill, Roosevelt, and Stalin meet at Yalta	Concessions are made to Stalin concerning the settlement of eastern Europe.
July 1945	Attlee, Stalin, and Truman meet at Potsdam	Polish border moved a hundred miles west to accommodate the Soviet Union; Germany divided into occupational zones; and a Council of Foreign Ministers is established to draft peace treaties for Germany's allies.

rest of East Prussia and Germany east of the Oder-Neisse River line. This, in effect, accommodated the Soviet Union by moving Poland about a hundred miles into Germany. A Council of Foreign Ministers was created to negotiate peace terms with Germany's allies, and Germany was divided into occupation zones.

Potsdam left much unresolved, and the war was slow to come to an official end. Italy, Romania, Hungary, Bulgaria, and Finland did not sign peace treaties until February 1947. The Russians rejected the treaty that the United States made with Japan in 1951 and signed their own agreement with the Japanese in 1956. Germany was not completely reunited until 1990.

SUMMARY

Again the Road to War (1933–1939) Hitler and the Nazi Party came to power in Germany through relentless discipline. They were consistent in their nationalism, in their attention to social and economic anxieties faced by Germans, and in their insistence that all of Germany's problems flowed from the Paris peace settlement. Hitler's racial theories and his goal of uniting all German people into one nation drove Nazi Germany's foreign policy. Germany started rebuilding its military in the mid–1930s. Neither the Allies nor the League of Nations took steps to oppose German rearmament. In 1936, Hitler remilitarized the Rhineland; the Western powers responded with appeasement. The 1938 *Anschluss* unified Germany and Austria. Hitler's next target was Czechoslovakia. The British prime minister worked hard to avoid the inevitable, but his policy of appeasing Hitler not only failed to save Czechoslovakia, but also earned him history's disapprobation for further encouraging Hitler's aggression. Hitler occupied Prague in 1939. Chamberlain announced Britain and France would guarantee the independence of the country that Germany intended to dismember next, Poland.

IMAGE KEY

for pages 690–691

a. Atom bomb

b. Nazi party membership book with a photograph of the member, dated and stamped July 15, 1937

c. Children behind a barbed wire fence at the Nazi concentration camp at Auschwitz, southwest Poland

d. "She's a WOW" Poster by Adolph Treidler, 1942

e. "United We Are Strong" Allied War Poster

f. Firemen on the roof of Canon Street Station looking towards St. Paul's Cathedral

g. Churchill, Roosevelt, and Stalin at the Yalta Peace Conference

h. "This is Nazi Brutality:" American World War II poster, 1942, by Ben Shahn

i. Japanese World War II poster for aircraft identification: Curtis P-40 Warhawk ca. 1933–1941

In August 1939, Germany and the Soviet Union signed the nonaggression pact that allowed them to divide Poland between themselves; on September 1, 1939, Germans invaded Poland; and on September 3, Britain and France declared war on Germany.

World War II (1939–1945) World War II was global, and for the combatants in Europe it was total: Civilians died in numbers equal to soldiers, and all aspects of economic, social, and political life were shaped by the war. In June 1940, the Germans occupied France. Churchill, the newly elected prime minister in Britain, was all that stood between Hitler and continental domination. The Luftwaffe's nightly bombing raids on London in the fall of 1940 were Hitler's first significant wartime blunder: They resulted in substantial losses for the Luftwaffe and stiffened British resistance. Operation Barbarossa was his second. The Germans were defeated by the Russian winter and by the heroism of Stalin's army in the Battle of Stalingrad. Hitler intended for his Third Reich to Germanize, colonize, and plunder the rest of Europe. His hopes for keeping the United States out of the war were dashed when Japan bombed Pearl Harbor on December 7, 1941. The United States waited until it was on its way to victory in the Pacific before turning to the war in North Africa, and then Europe. In 1943, the United States and Britain began a massive aerial bombardment campaign against Germany. D-Day, June 6, 1944, marked the beginning of the Allied land offensive in France, which resulted in the fall of Berlin in May and Allied victory in Europe. Japan fought on until Emperor Hirohito forced the government to surrender in August 1945, after the United States had dropped atomic bombs on Hiroshima and Nagasaki.

Racism and the Holocaust Hitler's racial doctrines resulted in brutality against Jews, Slavs, and other peoples. Approximately 6 million Jews were killed in the Holocaust. Jews made up 10 percent of Poland's prewar population, mostly poor and living in separate communities. The government, church, and society in general were anti-Semitic. Nonetheless, Polish Jews were numerous and included many religious, cultural, and political leaders; they were a prime target for the Nazis. In early 1940, Nazis relocated many Polish Jews to sealed ghettos, where 20 percent of the population died of disease and malnourishment. When Germany invaded the Soviet Union in 1941, Nazi propaganda connected Jews and Bolsheviks, and soon the Nazis adopted the policy of exterminating Jews. By 1945, 90 percent of Poland's pre-1939 population of Jews had been killed.

The Domestic Fronts On the home front, civilians were organized for war to a greater extent than in any previous conflict. In Germany, the economy was redirected to wartime production. Consumer goods became scarce. Women were given many roles in the German war effort. Nazi propaganda permeated society, and there was virtually no popular resistance. Much of Germany's physical and political infrastructure was destroyed by the end of the war. In France, the Vichy government was supported by the church and conservatives. All of Britain's political parties had joined in a national government under Churchill. For most of the population, the standard of living improved during the war, leading some to conclude that active government involvement in the society was a positive force. The Great Patriotic War was most destructive in the Soviet Union, where 16 million people were killed. Stalin won further centralization of authority, and the Soviet Union emerged from the war as a great power, second only to the United States.

Preparations for Peace   The fundamental differences between the Soviet Union and the other Allies had been dormant during the fight against Nazi Germany, but they reemerged with a vengeance as soon as the war was over. In 1941, Roosevelt and Churchill had agreed on the Atlantic Charter. The Big Three had entered a purely military alliance in January 1942. At the first meeting between Roosevelt, Churchill, and Stalin, in Tehran in 1943, the three agreed the United States and Britain would open the second front against Germany from the Atlantic coast; this had far-reaching consequences for the geography of the postwar Soviet sphere of influence. By the time the Big Three met again, in February 1945 at Yalta, the situation on the ground was far different. The Soviet Army occupied much of Eastern Europe already. Churchill and Roosevelt ceded much to Stalin; Roosevelt also pressed for a united-nations organization that would help ensure the eventual peace. The final Big Three meeting, at Potsdam in July 1945, gave Russia much of Poland, and Poland a sizable piece of Germany. The seeds of future dissension were sown.

REVIEW QUESTIONS

1. What were Hitler's foreign policy aims? Why did Britain and France adopt a policy of appeasement? Did it buy the West valuable time to prepare for war?

2. How was Hitler able to defeat France so easily in 1940? Why was his air war against Britain a failure? Why did he invade Russia? Why did the invasion ultimately fail?

3. Why did Japan attack the United States at Pearl Harbor? What was the significance of American intervention in the war? Did President Truman make the right decision when he ordered the atomic bombs dropped on Japan?

4. What impact did World War II have on the civilian population of Europe? What impact did the "Great Patriotic War" have on the people of the Soviet Union? What was Hitler's "final solution" for Europe's Jewish population?

KEY TERMS

Anschluss   (p. 694)   **Axis**   (p. 693)   **Luftwaffe**   (p. 698)
appeasement   (p. 693)   *Lebensraum*   (p. 692)   **Third Reich**   (p. 700)

 For additional study resources for this chapter, go to:
www.prenhall.com/kagan3/chapter28

29 The Cold War Era and the Emergence of a New Europe

CHAPTER HIGHLIGHTS

The Emergence of the Cold War The Cold War division between the United States and the USSR was rooted in basic differences in ideology and interests. The United States pursued a policy of containment. In 1949 the United States and its allies formed NATO. The USSR responded with the formation of the Warsaw Pact in 1955. The creation of Israel in 1948 brought the Cold War to the Middle East. The Korean conflict was an expression of the policy of containment.

The Khrushchev Era in the Soviet Union The Khrushchev era witnessed a retreat from Stalinism, but not from authoritarianism. Khrushchev wanted to reform the Soviet Union, but was unwilling to challenge the dominance of the Communist Party. The events of 1956 in Egypt, Poland, and Hungary solidified the position of the United States and the Soviet Union as superpowers. The Cuban missile crisis of 1962 brought the superpowers to the brink of nuclear war.

Later Cold War Confrontations United States and Soviet tensions continued to simmer in the late 1950s. In August 1961 the Berlin Wall was erected and in 1966 the Cuban missile crisis brought the Cold War to the Americas.

The Brezhnev Era Brezhnev crushed Czechoslovakia's "Prague Spring" of 1968. His Brezhnev Doctrine asserted the Soviet Union's right to intervene in the domestic politics of communist countries. Brezhnev pursued a policy of détente with the United States. The invasion of Afghanistan was a disaster for the Soviet Union.

Decolonization: The European Retreat from Empire One of the most significant postwar developments was the decolonization movement. Eighty new independent nations emerged after 1945. The Cold War complicated the process of decolonization.

The Turmoil of French Decolonization France felt a need to retain its colonies to reestablish its status as a great power. The effort to do so led to bloody conflicts in Algeria and Vietnam. The United States was drawn into Vietnam after the French withdrew.

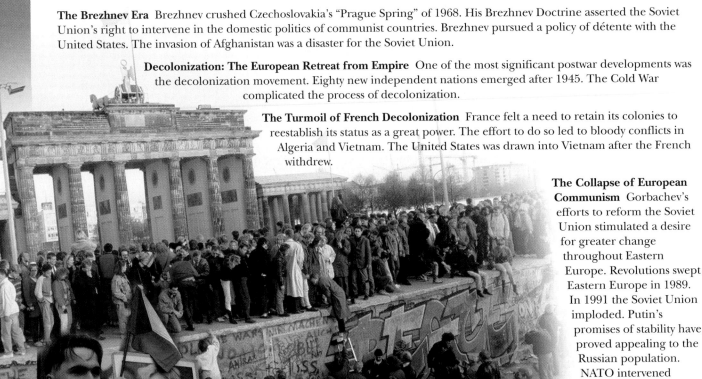

The Collapse of European Communism Gorbachev's efforts to reform the Soviet Union stimulated a desire for greater change throughout Eastern Europe. Revolutions swept Eastern Europe in 1989. In 1991 the Soviet Union imploded. Putin's promises of stability have proved appealing to the Russian population. NATO intervened repeatedly in the former Yugoslavia.

The Rise of Radical Political Islamism Radical Islamism arose primarily in reaction to the secular Arab nationalism that developed in countries like Egypt and Syria in the 1920s and 1930s. Events in Iran and Afghanistan fueled the rise of radical political Islamism. After the withdrawal of the Soviet Union from Afghanistan, the United States became the target of groups like Al Qaeda.

A Transformed West The attacks of September 11, 2001, transformed and redirected U.S. foreign policy. Subsequent U.S. policies, particularly its prosecution of the Iraq War, created a division between the United States and many Europeans. Despite recent problems, the relationship between the United States and Europe will survive.

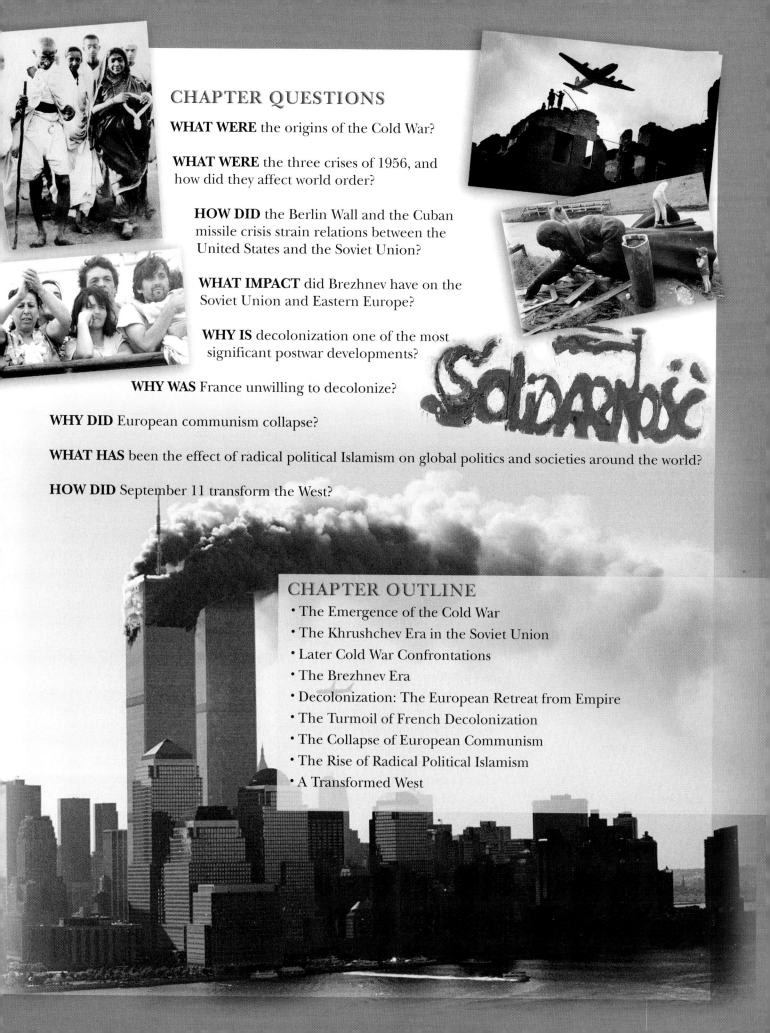

CHAPTER QUESTIONS

WHAT WERE the origins of the Cold War?

WHAT WERE the three crises of 1956, and how did they affect world order?

HOW DID the Berlin Wall and the Cuban missile crisis strain relations between the United States and the Soviet Union?

WHAT IMPACT did Brezhnev have on the Soviet Union and Eastern Europe?

WHY IS decolonization one of the most significant postwar developments?

WHY WAS France unwilling to decolonize?

WHY DID European communism collapse?

WHAT HAS been the effect of radical political Islamism on global politics and societies around the world?

HOW DID September 11 transform the West?

CHAPTER OUTLINE

- The Emergence of the Cold War
- The Khrushchev Era in the Soviet Union
- Later Cold War Confrontations
- The Brezhnev Era
- Decolonization: The European Retreat from Empire
- The Turmoil of French Decolonization
- The Collapse of European Communism
- The Rise of Radical Political Islamism
- A Transformed West

IMAGE KEY

Image Key for pages 718-719 is on page 744.

*Since the end of World War II, two often interrelated sets of international political relation-ships shaped world events: the **Cold War** between the United States and the Soviet Union and the process of decolonization, whereby the peoples of lands dominated by European nations and later by the United States rejected that domination.*

From 1945 until the collapse of communist regimes in Eastern Europe between 1989 and 1991, the simmering conflict of the Cold War dominated global politics and threatened the peace of Europe. Decolonization rapidly became enmeshed with the Cold War, as the rivalry of the two nuclear-armed superpowers expanded into a contest for dominance in the postcolonial world, aggravating local conflicts on every continent.

Since the collapse of the Soviet Union in 1991, the United States has remained the world's single superpower. Symbolically identified as embodying modern values of Western Civilization, the United States has replaced Europe as the object of anti-Western resistance. A notable result of this new situation is the clash between the United States and radical political Islamism. As the era of European and American colonial dominance came to an end, the reciprocal nature of the relationship between the West and the rest of the global community has intensified.

WHAT WERE the origins of the Cold War?

THE EMERGENCE OF THE COLD WAR

Basic differences of ideology and self-interest divided the United States and the USSR. At the end of World War II, the Soviet Union's expanding influence in central Europe, the Balkans, and the Middle East was consistent with the policies of the earlier tsarist governments. In the past, Britain had blocked Russian moves in these regions, but now only the United States was strong enough to contain the Soviets. It made no attempt to push the Soviets back, however, and began to withdraw its troops from Europe. Within a year of the war's end, the United States had reduced its forces in Europe from 3.5 million to 500,000.

The American plan for peace reflected American principles and served American interests. Politically, the United States supported self-determination, autonomy, and democracy. Economically, it favored free trade, freedom of the seas, and unrestrained investment opportunities. As the strongest industrialized power remaining in the world, the United States had much to gain from the kind of international order it envisioned.

The USSR believed it had to extend its borders and dominate the formerly independent states of Eastern Europe to guarantee its security and obtain compensation for its fearful losses in the war. The Soviets saw American opposition to their expansion as a threat to their legitimate national interests and claims, whereas the United States viewed the activities of communist parties in countries friendly to the United States as evidence of a Moscow-led plot for the worldwide subversion of capitalism and democracy. Not long after the war's end, the former allies became mutually and openly hostile. In February 1946, Stalin and his foreign minister, Vyacheslav Molotov (1890–1986), declared the Western democracies enemies of the Soviets, and a month later Churchill, in a speech in Fulton, Missouri, announced that an "Iron Curtain" had descended on Europe, dividing a free and democratic West from a totalitarian East.

CONTAINMENT IN AMERICAN FOREIGN POLICY

In 1947, **containment** became the American foreign policy strategy for countering the communist threat. The plan was to resist the spread of Soviet influence until internal difficulties caused the collapse of the Soviet Union. This ultimately succeeded but it forced the United States to make the kinds of military and financial commitments abroad that it had traditionally avoided.

Cold War Period between the end of World War II (1945) and the collapse of the Soviet Union (1991) in which U.S. and Soviet relations were tense, seemingly moments away from actual war at any time during these years.

containment American foreign policy strategy (beginning in 1947) for countering the communist threat and resisting the spread of Soviet influence.

The Truman Doctrine   In a speech to Congress on March 12, 1947, President Truman set forth what came to be called the Truman Doctrine. It affirmed America's willingness to support all free peoples who wanted to resist subjugation by armed minorities or takeovers by foreign powers. Truman had in mind Greece and Turkey, which were struggling to fend off communist aggressors, but his statement implied America's willingness to help others who were similarly besieged anywhere in the world.

The Marshall Plan   Following the war, Western Europe faced poverty and hunger, but the United States undercut the appeal that communist solutions might have had for desperate electorates by instituting the European Recovery Program—the **Marshall Plan**. (George C. Marshall, the American secretary of state, introduced it.) America provided extensive economic aid to the European states, conditional only on their working together for their mutual benefit. The Soviet Union and its clients were invited to apply for help. Czechoslovakia and Finland wanted to, and Poland and Hungary expressed interest, but the Soviets forbade them to take part for fear that American aid would draw them out of its orbit. The Marshall Plan was a great success. It stimulated tremendous economic growth in postwar Europe that sapped the strength of communist parties in the West.

SOVIET DOMINATION OF EASTERN EUROPE

The West believed communism was inherently aggressive and the policy of containment was therefore justified. From the Soviet perspective, however, the West's efforts at containment looked like attacks on Russia's legitimate interests in Eastern Europe. Tsarist Russia had governed Poland for over a century and had, at the request of the Austrian Empire, intervened in Hungary in 1848 to put down a revolution. Russia had a long-standing interest in the area around the Black Sea, and European powers had, after all, invaded Russia once in the nineteenth century (under Napoleon) and twice in the twentieth. Given this history and the extraordinary losses the Russian people suffered in World War II, it is not surprising that Soviet leaders believed they needed Eastern European satellites to protect their frontiers.

Behind the Iron Curtain that separated Russia's allies from the West, Stalin replaced multiparty governments with thoroughly communist regimes that were completely under his control. In the autumn of 1947, he called a meeting in Warsaw of all communist parties around the world. There, the former Comintern was reborn as Cominform (the Communist Information Bureau), an organization dedicated to spreading revolutionary communism throughout the world. Communist leaders in the West who favored working within the political systems of their states were replaced by hard-liners dedicated to sabotage.

In February 1948, Stalin brutally asserted his new policy. Communists expelled the democratic members of what had been a coalition government in Prague and murdered Jan Masaryk (1886–1948), Czechoslovakia's foreign minister and son of its founder, Thomas Masaryk (1850–1937). President Edvard Benes (1884–1948) was forced to resign, and Czechoslovakia was brought under Soviet rule. The Soviet Union forced subject governments in Eastern Europe to adopt Stalinist policies—one-party political systems, close military cooperation with the Soviet Union, collectivization of agriculture, Communist Party domination of universities and schools, and suppression of religion.

THE POSTWAR DIVISION OF GERMANY

Soviet actions in Eastern Europe made the United States determined to pursue its own course with respect to Germany.

Marshall Plan   The U.S. European Recovery Program introduced by George C. Marshall, American secretary of state, whereby America provided extensive economic aid to the European states, conditional only on their working together for their mutual benefit.

Disagreements over Germany The Allies had no clear plan for dealing with Germany after its surrender. Churchill worried that dismembering Germany would encourage further Soviet expansion, but the Allied armies chose to divide it into separate occupation zones. The Soviets quickly stripped the factories in their eastern zone and then laid claim to all the industrial equipment left in Germany as reparations for their losses in the war. The Western powers refused to agree to this, for the United States did not want to assume financial responsibility for Germany or cause resentment that communist politicians might exploit. It proposed instead to help Germany become self-sufficient by rebuilding its industries. This alarmed the Soviets, who quite reasonably feared German resurgence.

Berlin Blockade In 1948, when the Western powers issued a constitution and currency for the western sectors of Germany, the Soviets protested and withdrew from the joint Allied Control Commission. Berlin, which was under the jurisdiction of all four powers despite being well within the Soviet zone, immediately became a point of contention. The Soviets feared that foreign currencies circulating in Berlin would undercut their own, and they decided to seal the city off by closing the railroads and highways that connected it with West Germany. Their hope was to drive the other occupying armies out of Berlin.

The West countered the Berlin blockade by a nearly year-long airlift of supplies. In May 1949, the Soviets yielded and restored access to Berlin. The incident, however, hastened the separation of Germany into two states. In September 1949, West Germany became the Federal Republic of Germany (FRG), and a month later, the eastern region became the German Democratic Republic (GDR). Berlin remained a divided city isolated inside the communist GDR.

NATO AND THE WARSAW PACT

The USSR became increasingly isolated as the Marshall Plan promoted greater cooperation among the Western nations. In March 1948, Belgium, the Netherlands, Luxembourg, France, and Britain agreed to cooperate economically and militarily, and in April 1949, they joined Italy, Denmark, Norway, Portugal, Iceland, Canada, and the United States in a mutual defense pact, the North Atlantic Treaty Organization (**NATO**). West Germany, Greece, and Turkey soon signed on. NATO committed the United States, for the first time in its history, to the defense of allies outside the Western Hemisphere.

In 1949, the states of Eastern Europe formed the Council of Mutual Assistance (COMECON) to integrate their economies. Unlike NATO, the eastern alliance was controlled by its superpower member, the Soviet Union. The **Warsaw Pact** of May 1955, a mutual defense agreement among Albania, Bulgaria, Czechoslovakia, East Germany, Hungary, Poland, Romania, and the Soviet Union, merely recognized what already existed. The formal division of Europe between two mutually antagonistic alliance systems defined the sides in the Cold War but did not limit their confrontation to the European arena. (See Map 29–1.)

THE CREATION OF THE STATE OF ISRAEL

Following World War I, Great Britain had become the dominant power in the Middle East, but after World War II nationalists who wanted self-determination for their homelands began to challenge the British. The postcolonial struggles that resulted invited interventions by both sides in the Cold War.

British Balfour Declaration Crises in the Middle East centered on relations between Jews and Arabs. In 1897, Theodore Herzl, founder of the Zionist move-

The Allied airlift in action during the Berlin Blockade, which took place from June 1948 until Stalin lifted it in May 1949. Every day during the blockade Western planes supplied the city.

Art Resource/Bildarchiv Preussischer Kulturbesitz

NATO North Atlantic Treaty Organization, a mutual defense pact.

Warsaw Pact Mutual defense agreement among Albania, Bulgaria, Czechoslovakia, East Germany, Hungary, Poland, Romania, and the Soviet Union.

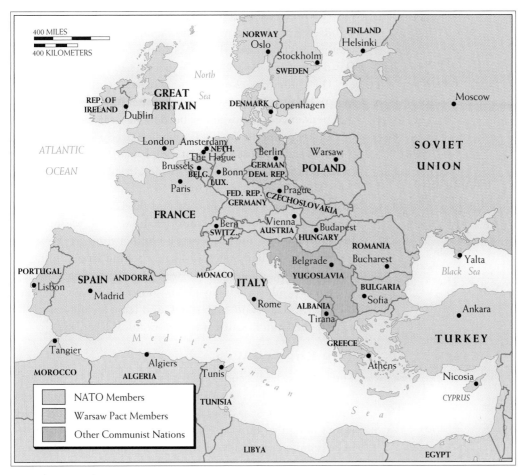

MAP 29–1

Major Cold War European Alliance Systems   The North Atlantic Treaty Organization, which includes both Canada and the United States, stretches as far east as Turkey. By contrast, the Warsaw Pact nations were the contiguous communist states of Eastern Europe, with the Soviet Union, of course, as the dominant member.

TERRITORIALLY, WAS NATO or the Warsaw Pact the stronger alliance?

ment, had campaigned for the creation of a homeland for the world's Jews, and in 1917, the Balfour Declaration promised British support for the eventual establishment of a Jewish state in Palestine. Between the world wars, thousands of Jews, mainly from Europe, emigrated to the British mandate of Palestine, and Britain tried unsuccessfully to mediate the frequent clashes that took place between the native Arabs and the Jewish settlers.

The UN Resolution   The Nazi persecution of Jews rallied support for the Zionist ideal of a Jewish state in Palestine, and following the war the Allies concluded that Jewish refugees from Nazi concentration camps had a sort of moral claim on the international community. In 1947, the British referred the problem of working out a relationship between Palestinian Arabs and Jews to the United Nations, and over opposition from some Arab groups, the United Nations suggested dividing Palestine between Jews and Arabs. The Palestinian Arabs resented the influx of newcomers who displaced many of them from their lands and turned them into refugees.

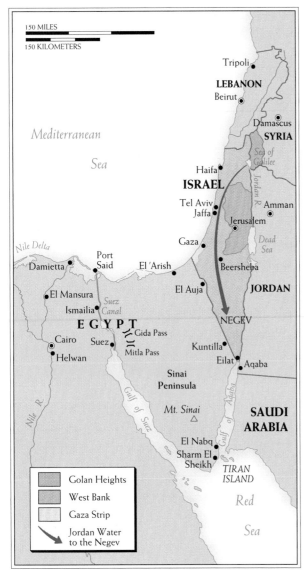

MAP 29–2

Israel and Its Neighbors in 1949　The territories gained by Israel in 1949 did not secure peace in the region. In fact, the disposition of those lands and the Arab refugees who live there have constituted the core of the region's unresolved problems to the present day.

WHAT CHALLENGES does Israel face in terms of territory and self-defense?

Israel Declares Independence　In May 1948, the British withdrew from Palestine and the *Yishuv* (the Palestinian Jewish Community) declared the establishment of the state of Israel. David Ben-Gurion (1886–1973) became its first prime minister. The United States quickly recognized the new nation. During 1948 and 1949, Israel fought the Arabs to defend its independence and pushed its borders beyond the limits set by the United Nations. By 1949, it had secured its existence, but the Arab states refused to grant it diplomatic recognition. The peace it established was only an armed truce. (See Map 29–2.)

Many Israelis had emigrated from Europe, and Israel had strong Western support. Europe and the United States are dependent on oil from Arab countries, however. It was not long, therefore, before the Arab-Israeli conflict drew in the superpowers. The United States was firmly behind Israel, so the Soviet Union ingratiated itself with the Arab states. Israel's existence would become a major source of conflict between the United States and Arab states, and later, a chief complaint against the United States of radical political Islamists.

THE KOREAN WAR

The Japanese had occupied Korea in 1910 and held it until 1945. Following their defeat in World War II, however, they withdrew, and the United States and the Soviet Union agreed to divide Korea along the thirty-eighth parallel. The nation was supposed to be reunited eventually, but by 1948, its halves had coalesced as separate states: the Democratic People's Republic of Korea in the north and the Republic of Korea in the south. The Soviet Union backed the former and the United States the latter.

In late June 1950, North Korea invaded the south, and the United States persuaded the United Nations to authorize international intervention. Great Britain, Turkey, and Australia joined the United States in providing support for what was termed a UN police action to halt North Korean aggression. The United States viewed the Korean conflict as a vital part of its effort to contain the spread of communism.

Late in 1950, UN forces, driving up the Korean peninsula, neared the Chinese border, and China intervened on behalf of the North Koreans. China had been governed since 1949 by a communist regime under Mao Tse-tung (1893–1976), and U.S. policymakers leapt to the conclusion that Mao was simply executing orders from Moscow. No one at the time knew of the tensions that existed between the USSR and China. The Chinese initially pushed the UN forces back, but eventually the war bogged down, and on June 16, 1953, an armistice was signed restoring the thirty-eighth parallel as the border between North and South Korea. The American government claimed success for its policy of containment. The conflict had turned the Cold War into a global struggle, however, and committed the United States to maintaining troops in Korea to the present day.

The formation of NATO and the police action in Korea capped the first round of the Cold War. It ended in 1953 with Stalin's death and the Korean armistice, and for a while tensions appeared to ease. Early in 1955, the Soviets withdrew their army of occupation from Austria, and it became a neutral country. Later that year, France, Great Britain, the Soviet Union, and the United States met in Geneva to discuss nuclear weapons and the future of Germany. There were public displays of friendliness. However, the meeting produced few substantial agreements, and the polemics of the Cold War soon resumed.

THE KHRUSHCHEV ERA IN THE SOVIET UNION

N o nation suffered greater losses during World War II than the Soviet Union, whose people hoped their sacrifices would win them a freer, more comfortable future. In this they were disappointed, for Stalin tolerated few modifications of the regime he had created during the war. He continued to centralize authority, purge opponents, and favor heavy industry over production of consumer goods.

Following Stalin's death (March 6, 1953), the presidium (the renamed politburo) governed the USSR corporately, but power gradually devolved on the party secretary, Nikita Khrushchev (1894–1971). He formally became premier in 1956, but he never acquired Stalin's extraordinary power.

KHRUSHCHEV'S DOMESTIC POLICIES

The Khrushchev era (1956–1964) retreated from Stalinism but not from authoritarianism. Khrushchev wanted to reform the Soviet system but only in ways that did not threaten the dominance of the Communist Party. He permitted intellectuals somewhat greater freedom of expression. He forbade Boris Pasternak (1890–1960), author of *Dr. Zhivago,* to accept the Nobel Prize for Literature in 1958, but in 1963 he allowed publication of Aleksandr Solzhenitsyn's (b. 1918) *One Day in the Life of Ivan Denisovich,* a novel critical of conditions in Russia. Khrushchev tried to improve production of consumer goods and allowed some modest decentralization of economic planning. He recognized that collectivization had not produced an agricultural system capable of feeding his people, and he removed many restrictions on private farming and made hundreds of thousands of additional acres available for wheat cultivation. Initially, grain production set records, but poor farming techniques resulted in soil erosion and soon led to declining yields. The Soviet Union had to resort to importing vast quantities of grain from the West.

The Secret Speech of 1956   In February 1956, at the Twentieth Congress of the Communist Party, Khrushchev broke with Soviet tradition and denounced Stalin in a secret speech, which was soon published abroad. This produced shock and consternation in party circles, but opened the way for limited internal criticism of the Soviet system and gradual removal from government of the stauncher Stalinists. Communist leaders in Eastern Europe took Khrushchev's speech as a sign they could retreat, if not from communism, from the Stalinist policies that had been required of them since the late 1940s. This produced a series of crises that made 1956 one of the key years in the Cold War.

THE THREE CRISES OF 1956

The Suez Intervention   In 1952, Gamal Abdel Nasser (1918–1970) won control of Egypt's government, and in July 1956, he ended the hold that Anglo-French interests had on the Suez Canal. Britain and France feared Egypt's nationalization of the canal threatened their access to Persian Gulf oil. When war broke out between Egypt and Israel later in 1956, Britain and France eagerly intervened. Israel quickly seized the

WHAT WERE the three crises of 1956, and how did they affect world order?

30.1
Nikita S. Khrushchev: *Address to the Twentieth Party Congress*

Sinai, and France and Britain hastened to reoccupy the canal zone—claiming it had to do so to separate the combatants. The operation succeeded militarily but foundered on the shoals of diplomacy. The United States refused to support their venture, and the Soviet Union vigorously protested on behalf of its Arab allies. The Anglo-French forces had to withdraw and return control of the canal to Egypt, and a year later Israel evacuated the Sinai and the Gaza Strip. The Suez incident proved that without U.S. support, the nations of Western Europe could no longer use military force to impose their wills on others. It also showed how the United States and the Soviet Union could prevent widening conflicts by restraining their allies.

Polish Efforts Toward Independent Action Overly optimistic assumptions about the implications of Khrushchev's speech attacking Stalin led to important developments in Eastern Europe. In 1956, a few months after the delivery of the speech, resentment of the rigidly disciplined communist regime had prompted a workers' uprising that forced the resignations of hard-line Stalinist officials and brought Wladyslaw Gomulka (1905–1982) to power in Poland. Gomulka, a communist whom Stalin had imprisoned, was acceptable to the Polish communists and the Soviets. He assured the latter he would continue Poland's membership in the Warsaw Pact, and he promised the former an end to the collectivization of Polish agriculture and an improvement in relations between the government and the Roman Catholic Church. Gomulka's compromise seemed to suggest the Soviets were willing to allow Poland to chart its own course under the leadership of its Communist Party. This prompted another country to seek similar autonomy.

The Hungarian Uprising In late October 1956, demonstrations in Budapest in support of Poland escalated into street fighting. The Hungarian Communist Party appointed a new ministry headed by former premier Imre Nagy (1896–1958), a communist who wanted Soviet troops withdrawn from Hungary. Nagy also wanted to take Hungary out of the Warsaw Pact and declare neutrality. This was wholly unacceptable to the Soviets, who invaded, deposed (and subsequently executed) Nagy, and made Janos Kadar (1912–1989) premier.

The events of 1956 in the Middle East and Eastern Europe taught the nations of Europe what they could expect from the Cold War era. The Western European states could chart their own courses when dealing with each other, but the superpowers prevented them from taking independent action on the broader international scene. The Eastern European countries had no autonomy in either the domestic or the international spheres.

LATER COLD WAR CONFRONTATIONS

*A*fter 1956, the Soviets felt more secure politically, and in 1957, their successful launch of Earth's first satellite (*Sputnik*) confirmed their belief they had achieved technological superiority over the West. They were therefore more willing to contemplate "peaceful coexistence" with the United States, and in 1958, the two powers entered into negotiations to limit testing of nuclear weapons. By 1959, tensions had eased enough for several Western leaders to visit Moscow and for Khrushchev to tour the United States. A summit meeting was scheduled for May 1960. However, just before the Paris Summit Conference was to convene, the Soviets shot down an American U-2 aircraft that was flying reconnaissance over their territory. President Eisenhower accepted responsibility for ordering the surveillance but refused to apologize to the Soviets. Khrushchev retaliated by scuttling the summit. This rehabilitated his image with the leaders of communist China, who feared the Soviet Union was softening its attitude toward the capitalist world.

QUICK REVIEW

Polish-Soviet Relations
- 1956: Wladyslaw Gomulka comes to power in Poland
- Gomulka confirmed Poland's membership in Warsaw Pact, promised an end to collectivization, and improved relations with the Catholic Church
- Compromise prompted Hungary to seek greater autonomy

HOW DID the Berlin Wall and the Cuban missile crisis strain relations between the United States and the Soviet Union?

THE BERLIN WALL

The abortive Paris conference inaugurated the most difficult period in the Cold War. In 1961 the newly elected American president, John F. Kennedy, and Premier Khrushchev met in Vienna, with inconclusive results. Throughout that year thousands of refugees from East Germany had also been crossing into West Berlin, to the chagrin and economic detriment of the East. In August 1961, the East Germans, with Soviet approval, erected the Cold War's starkest symbol, a concrete wall dividing East from West Berlin. Despite speeches and symbolic support from the West, the wall halted the flow of refugees and brought the U.S. commitment to West Germany into doubt.

THE CUBAN MISSILE CRISIS

The most dangerous event of the Cold War was the Cuban missile crisis of 1962. In 1957, Fidel Castro (b. 1926) launched a revolution that in 1959 turned Cuba, an island nation less than a hundred miles from the United States, into a communist country and a Soviet ally. This greatly alarmed the United States, and its worst fears were realized in 1962 when Khrushchev decided to build bases for nuclear missiles in Cuba. America responded with a blockade and a demand for their removal. After a tense week of exchanging threats, the Soviets backed down. Khrushchev's retreat weakened his support at home and raised doubt among non-European communist states about the Soviet Union's reliability as an ally. The People's Republic of China seized the opportunity to increase its influence in international communist circles, and the Soviet military concluded it had to undertake a major buildup to ensure its power as a deterrent to America. In 1963, international tensions eased somewhat when the United States and the Soviet Union concluded a Nuclear Test Ban Treaty.

Cuban Missile Crisis of 1962. The American ambassador to the United Nations displayed photographs to persuade the world of the threat to the United States less than one hundred miles from its own shores.

© CORBIS

QUICK REVIEW

The Cuban Missile Crisis

- 1959: Fidel Castro comes to power as a result of the Cuban revolution
- 1962: Khrushchev orders construction of missile bases in Cuba
- Tense negotiations resulted in the Soviets backing down and removing the missiles

THE BREZHNEV ERA

Many Soviet Communist Party members feared Khrushchev had tried to do too much too soon and done it too poorly. On October 16, 1964, he was forced to resign. Khrushchev was replaced by Alexei Kosygin (1904–1980) and then Leonid Brezhnev (1906–1982).

1968: THE INVASION OF CZECHOSLOVAKIA

Although the Soviet Union had demonstrated in Poland and Hungary in 1956 that it would not tolerate independent action by its Eastern European neighbors, in 1968, Alexander Dubcek (1921–1992) inaugurated the "Prague Spring," an attempt to liberalize communism in Czechoslovakia. When he expanded freedom of discussion and other intellectual rights (at a time when such things were being curtailed in the USSR), the Soviets responded by invading Czechoslovakia and replacing him with leaders more to their liking. Brezhnev also articulated the **Brezhnev Doctrine**, which asserted the Soviet Union's right to intervene in the domestic politics of communist countries. The invasion of Czechoslovakia proved, however, to be the last major Soviet military action in Europe spawned by the Cold War.

THE UNITED STATES AND DÉTENTE

Brezhnev tried to reach an accommodation with the United States while continuing to extend Soviet influence. He sided with North Vietnam in its war with the United States, but his support was limited. He and President Nixon endorsed a

WHAT IMPACT did Brezhnev have on the Soviet Union and Eastern Europe?

Brezhnev Doctrine   Asserted the right of the Soviet Union to intervene in domestic politics of communist countries.

In the summer of 1968, Soviet tanks rolled into Czechoslovakia, ending that country's experiment in liberalized communism. This picture shows defiant flag-waving Czechs on a truck rolling past a Soviet tank in the immediate aftermath of the invasion.

Hulton Archive Photos/Getty Images, Inc.

QUICK REVIEW

Détente

- Brezhnev sought accommodation with the U.S. while continuing to extend Soviet influence
- Brezhnev and President Nixon agreed to a policy of détente that increased trade and reduced deployment of strategic arms
- 1975: U.S. and Soviet Union sign the Helsinki Accords

détente   Relaxation of tensions between the United States and Soviet Union that involved increased trade and reduced deployment of strategic arms.

---

policy called **détente** ("relaxation") that involved increased trade and reduced deployment of strategic arms. In 1975, Gerald Ford, Nixon's successor, joined the Soviet Union in signing the Helsinki Accords. These recognized the Soviet sphere of influence in Eastern Europe but also acknowledged that both nations had a duty to respect human rights. President Jimmy Carter's (1977–1981) insistence that the Soviet Union live up to these commitments led to a cooling of relations between the two countries during his term in office.

The Soviet Union did not abandon its activist foreign policy to pursue détente. It poured resources into conflicts in Angola, Mozambique, Ethiopia, Nicaragua, and Vietnam. It provided arms to Arab enemies of Israel, and to restore its prestige after the Cuban missile crisis it built the largest armed force in the world and achieved virtual nuclear parity with the United States.

THE INVASION OF AFGHANISTAN

It is not clear why the Brezhnev government, at the height of its power, felt compelled to invade Afghanistan, but the decision had long-range consequences for the future of both the Soviet Union and the United States. The U.S. Senate protested by refusing to ratify a second Strategic Arms Limitation Agreement and placing an embargo on American grain shipments to the Soviet Union. It also boycotted the 1980 Olympic Games in Moscow and sent aid to the Afghan rebels. China joined the United States in condemning the invasion.

The Soviet forces could not defeat the Afghan guerrilla fighters who, as the war dragged on, slaughtered about 2,000 Soviet troops annually. The morale and prestige of the Soviet army plummeted, and the conflict was as demoralizing for the Soviet Union as the Vietnam War had been for the United States.

COMMUNISM AND SOLIDARITY IN POLAND

At a time when the increasingly rigid Soviet government was becoming preoccupied by its war in Afghanistan, its authority was challenged by developments in Poland. After the crisis of 1956, Poland's governing Communist Party had succumbed to Soviet domination. The result had been chronic mismanagement of the economy and persistent food shortages. In 1978, the election to the papacy of an outspoken Polish opponent of communism, Karol Wojtyla, focused international attention on Poland. The new pope, John Paul II, received a tumultuous welcome when he visited his homeland in 1979.

In July of the following year, the Polish government sparked hundreds of protest strikes by raising the price of meat. On August 14, workers occupied the Lenin shipyard at Gdansk, and the strike spread rapidly to other facilities connected with the shipbuilding industry. The strikers' leader, Lech Walesa (b. 1944), refused to negotiate through the old government-controlled unions, and the strike did not end until the government allowed the workers to establish an independent union, which they called Solidarity. During the summer of 1981, remarkable changes took place within the Polish Communist Party. For the first time ever in a European communist state, secret elections for a party congress were held. Poland continued to be governed by a single party, but that party permitted real debate. This extraordinary experiment ended late in 1981, when General

Wojciech Jaruzelski (b. 1923) became party head and declared martial law. He arrested several of Solidarity's leaders and imposed martial law until late in 1983. None of this helped Poland solve its economic problems.

RELATIONS WITH THE REAGAN ADMINISTRATION

Early in his first term, American president Ronald Reagan (1981–1989) adopted a new strategy for opposing communism. He relaxed America's grain embargo and muted calls for human rights, but he intensified Cold War rhetoric, increased military spending, slowed arms limitation talks, deployed a major new missile system in Europe, and proposed a new Strategic Arms Defense Initiative. This program, which the press dubbed "Star Wars," aimed at developing a high-technology, space-based defense system to protect the United States from nuclear attack. The Star Wars proposal and the Reagan defense buildup forced the Soviet Union to increase military expenditures when it could ill afford to do so. The economic problems this created contributed to the collapse of the Soviet regime, but there were no signs during Reagan's first term that such a situation was in the offing.

Meanwhile, during the Cold War, extraordinary events had been occuring in Asia and Africa.

The Polish trade union "Solidarity" in 1989 successfully forced the Polish communist government to hold free elections. In June of that year Solidarity, whose members here are collecting funds for their campaign, won overwhelmingly.

Bernard Bisson/CORBIS/Bettmann

DECOLONIZATION: THE EUROPEAN RETREAT FROM EMPIRE

One of the most significant postwar developments was the decolonization movement that engineered the retreat of the European nations from their empires. In 1945, about one-third of the world's population was under colonial rule. Since then more than eighty new independent nations have emerged from these territories and claimed membership in the United Nations. Decolonization was a direct result of World War II, which forced the European powers to recall their armies from their colonies, and indigenous nationalist movements that claimed the rights of self-determination for which wars were fought in Europe.

The United States and the United Nations both opposed colonialism, but the Cold War complicated the process of decolonization. The USSR and the United States both opposed the old colonial empires but wanted to create alliances and spheres of influence that would advance their respective national objectives.

WHY IS decolonization one of the most significant postwar developments?

MAJOR AREAS OF COLONIAL WITHDRAWAL

Decolonization was a worldwide phenomenon that extended through the second half of the twentieth century. The Dutch were forced from Indonesia in 1949. In 1960, Belgium surrendered the Belgian Congo. In 1974 and 1975, Portuguese Mozambique and Angola were liberated. All-white rule ended in Rhodesia in 1979 and in South Africa in 1994. The most dramatic events, however, were those that attended the dissolution of the two largest empires—those of Britain and France. (See Map 29–3.)

INDIA

British domination of India dated from the middle of the eighteenth century. Britain retained control of India for about two centuries by playing hostile ethnic factions against one another. In 1885, the Hindu element in India's population organized the Indian National Congress, and in 1887, the Muslims established

MAP EXPLORATION

Interactive map: To explore this map further, go to **http://www.prenhall.com/kagan3/map29.3**

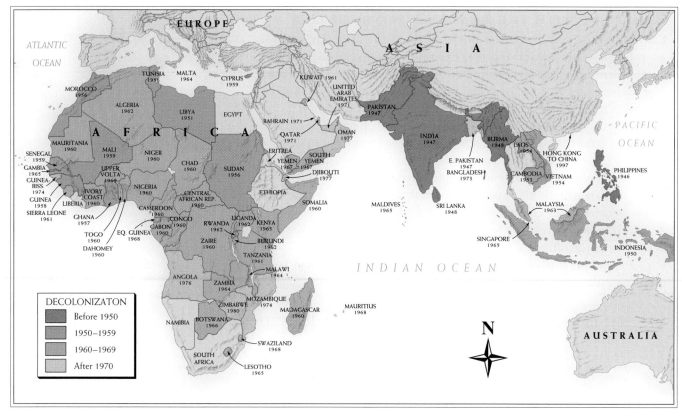

MAP 29–3

Decolonization Since World War II The Western powers' rapid retreat from imperialism after World War II is graphically shown on this outline map covering half the globe—from West Africa to the Southwest Pacific.

WHAT PATTERNS are noticeable about when South Asian, Southeast Asian, and African countries gained their independence?

the Muslim League. The two groups initially attempted to cooperate in efforts to liberalize British policies, but the Muslim preference was for separation and the creation of an independent Muslim nation.

Indian nationalism began to build after World War I and found a remarkable leader in Mohandas Gandhi (1869–1948). He studied law in Britain and absorbed the principles of Western liberal politics. The concept of passive resistance, which he found in the works of the American Henry David Thoreau (1817–1862), inspired the effective strategy he used to liberate his homeland.

Gandhi returned to India in 1915, after studying in Britain and working for over twenty years in South Africa, and he began to organize a campaign of passive resistance to British rule. He was repeatedly jailed, but the hunger strikes he staged in prison drew a great deal of attention and embarrassed the British government. Finally, in 1947, the British, losing their taste for the struggle, agreed to leave India. Gandhi's startling success encouraged anticolonialists elsewhere to adopt his methods, and Martin Luther King, Jr. (1929–1968) applied them to the successful civil rights struggle in the United States in the 1960s. (See "History's Voices: Gandhi Explains His Doctrine of Nonviolence.")

Gandhi's Congress Party drove the British from India, but it failed to create a single, united nation. Gandhi urged religious tolerance. Hostility between Hindus

HISTORY'S VOICES

GANDHI EXPLAINS HIS DOCTRINE OF NONVIOLENCE

*G*andhi wrote the following description of non-violent methods for effecting political change during World War II, but he did not attack the use of violence in international relations. Nazi racism and Japanese imperialism posed too great a danger to colonial peoples of color.

WHAT STRENGTHS and what limitations of non-violent campaigns does Gandhi's description suggest?

I do believe that, where there is only a choice between cowardice and violence, I would advise violence. . . .

But I believe that non-violence is infinitely superior to violence. . . .

Non-violence is the law of our species as violence is the law of the brute . . . [which] knows no law but that of physical might. The dignity of man requires obedience to a higher law—to the strength of the spirit. . . .

Non-violence in its dynamic condition means conscious suffering. It does not mean meek submission to the will of the evil-doer, but it means the pitting of one's whole soul against the will of the tyrant. . . .

I have not the capacity for preaching universal non-violence to the country. I preach, therefore, non-violence restricted strictly for the purpose of winning our freedom. . . . But my incapacity must not be mistaken for that of the doctrine of non-violence. . . . My heart grasps it. But I have not yet the attainments of preaching universal non-violence with effect. . . .

[T]he non-violence of my conception is a more active more real fighting against wickedness than retaliation whose very nature is to increase wickedness. I contemplate a mental, and therefore a moral, opposition to immoralities. I seek entirely to blunt the edge of the tyrant's sword, not by putting up against it a sharper-edged weapon, but by disappointing his expectations that I should be offering physical resistance.

M. K. Gandhi, *Non-Violence in Peace and War* (Ahmedabad: Navajivan Publishing House, 1942) as quoted in Ronald Duncan, ed., *Gandhi: Selected Writings* (New York: Harper & Row, 1971), pp. 48, 49, 52–53, 54–55.

and Muslims was deeply rooted, however, and the Muslim League, led by Ali Jinnah (1876–1948), wanted a separate Muslim state. As the British retreated, sectarian warfare erupted. Gandhi was assassinated, and hundreds of thousands died in the process of dividing the country into the separate states of India and Pakistan. In 1971, East Pakistan declared its independence as the state of Bangladesh. Conflict between India and Pakistan in the disputed region of Kashmir continues to produce armed clashes. In many places decolonization has been followed by the outbreak of bloody ethnic conflicts.

FURTHER BRITISH RETREAT FROM EMPIRE

The surrender of India marked the start of Britain's rather carefully engineered retreat from empire. The need for investment in Britain's Asian and African colonies in the 1940s and 1950s alerted the government and public to the costs of empire and diminished support for it. As the British retreated, however, they tried to leave behind institutions that would support representative self-government. Burma and Sri Lanka (Ceylon) became independent in 1948 and Ghana and Nigeria in 1957 and 1960, respectively. Militant nationalist movements drove the British from Malta, Cyprus, and the Middle East. The subsequent history of the African states has generally been marred by political instability and poverty, but the Asian countries have been relatively stable and have achieved remarkable economic growth.

Ghandi led Indian resistance to British colonial rule. Part of his appeal was the simplicity of his life and dress.
CORBIS/Bettmann

THE TURMOIL OF FRENCH DECOLONIZATION

Britain, a victor in World War II, acknowledged the inevitable and retreated relatively gracefully from empire. France, however, had been humiliated by the Nazi invasion and by the necessity of depending on the Allies for liberation. It felt it needed to retain its colonies to reestablish its status as a great power. The effort to do so led to bloody conflicts in Algeria and in Vietnam (where the United States intervened).

FRANCE AND ALGERIA

MAP EXPLORATION

Interactive map: To explore this map further, go to
http://www.prenhall.com/kagan3/map29.4

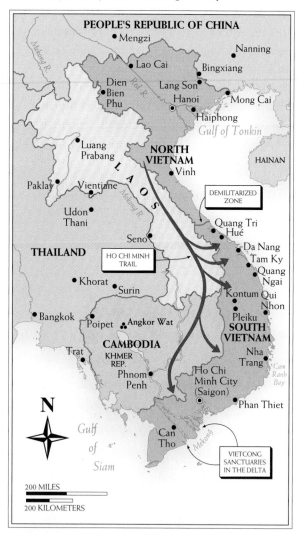

MAP 29–4

Vietnam and its Southeast Asian Neighbors The map identifies important locations associated with the war in Vietnam.

France had conquered Algeria in 1830, in a futile attempt to rally popular support for the monarchy of Charles X. In 1848, France extended its own system of government to Algeria, and the North African country began to attract immigrants from Europe. By World War I, about 20 percent of its population was European. The voting structure gave French settlers as much power as the Arab Muslim majority, and Arabs were excluded from administrative posts. The Free French army occupied Algeria in 1942 but did not alter conditions for the colony. In 1945, a violent clash erupted between Muslims and French settlers at a postwar victory celebration. The French government suppressed it with considerable loss of Arab life, but the event launched an Algerian nationalist movement that demanded Algerian independence. The political compromises France offered failed to satisfy the National Liberation Front (FLN), and in 1954, civil war erupted. It dragged on until 1962. As news spread of the atrocities both sides were committing, the war deeply divided the French public. Many opposed the conflict, but the government insisted that Algeria was an integral part of France. Over a million European settlers lived in Algeria, and the French army (having failed in World War II) refused to consider backing down.

General Charles de Gaulle, former commander of the Free French forces, finally resolved the conflict. He returned to political life, founded the Fifth French Republic, and organized a strategic retreat from Algeria. There were bombings, assassination attempts, and threats of military coups, but in 1962, a national referendum overwhelmingly approved independence for Algeria. Hundreds of thousands of settlers—and the Muslims who had sided with them—then fled to France to avoid reprisals from the FLN. This established a large, and largely unwelcome, Muslim population in France.

FRANCE AND VIETNAM

The French had occupied Indochina (Laos, Cambodia, and Vietnam) between 1857 and 1893. By 1930, they were confronting a nascent nationalist movement led by Ho Chi Minh (1892–1969), head of the Indochina Communist Party. During World War II, Ho Chi Minh elevated his status as a national leader by opposing the Japanese, who occupied Indochina, and the pro-Vichy French colonial administration that collaborated with the Japanese.

In September 1945, Ho Chi Minh declared the independence of Vietnam under the Viet Minh, a coalition of nationalists dominated by the communists. In 1946, France and the Viet Minh declared an armistice, but full-fledged war broke out a year later. The United States paid little attention to France's activities in Vietnam until 1949, when neighboring China became a communist state. This turned France's struggle with Ho Chi Minh into a front in the Cold War. At the time, the United States was not prepared to intervene militarily and only offered the French financial support. In 1954, however, the Viet Minh overran the French military stronghold, Dien Bien Phu, and the French government decided to end a campaign that had become unpopular with its electorate. A truce was achieved by dividing the country. The Viet Minh took the north, and the French retained the south. Elections to choose a government to reunite the country were scheduled for 1956. (See Map 29–4.)

VIETNAM DRAWN INTO THE COLD WAR

The United States, feared that the truce and proposed election risked the spread of communism, and in September 1954, it organized SEATO (the Southeast Asia Treaty Organization: the United States, Great Britain, France, Australia, New Zealand, Thailand, Pakistan, and the Philippines). The United States assumed the government of North Vietnam, like that of North Korea, was a communist puppet, and it became concerned when the French began to withdraw their troops from the south and fights erupted among Vietnamese political factions. The United States stepped in at that point and backed Ngo Dinh Diem (1901–1963), a noncommunist nationalist. He proclaimed the Republic of Vietnam and cancelled the elections planned for 1956. Within a few years, a communist National Liberation Front had appeared to oppose him, and North Vietnam supported its military wing, the Viet Cong. Diem's response was to become increasingly isolated and repressive.

DIRECT U.S. INVOLVEMENT

The Eisenhower and Kennedy administrations supported Diem while trying to reform his government. The American military presence in the country grew rapidly—from 600 in 1961 to 16,000 in 1963. On November 1, 1963, Diem fell to a military coup, which involved the United States, and the Americans turned to Nguyen Van Thieu (1923–2001) to form a new government that, it was hoped, would enjoy greater popular support. Thieu remained in power from 1966 to 1975.

President Lyndon Johnson (1908–1973) greatly expanded America's military commitments in Vietnam, and in 1964, he began to bomb the north. Bombardments continued until 1973, and the number of American soldiers stationed in Vietnam grew to more than 500,000. In 1969, President Richard Nixon (1913–1994) declared a policy of *Vietnamization* and began to withdraw American troops and turn the war over to the South Vietnamese army. A cease-fire was arranged in January 1973, and America withdrew its troops. Two years later, the Viet Cong overran the south and reunited the country under the control of a communist government seated in Hanoi.

The war did major damage to U.S. prestige. It distracted the American government from commitments elsewhere and deeply divided the American people. To some it seemed America had become an ambitious, aggressive, and cruel power that wanted to prolong colonialism. The country's experience in Vietnam continues to cast a long shadow over its foreign policy.

U.S. armed forces patrol in Vietnam. At the war's peak, more than 500,000 American troops were stationed in South Vietnam. The United States struggled in Vietnam for more than a decade, seriously threatening its commitment to Western Europe.

C. Simonpietri/CORBIS/Sygma

WHY DID European
communism collapse?

The Collapse of European Communism

The end of Soviet influence in Eastern Europe and the collapse of the Soviet Union are the most important events of the second half of the twentieth century. The most common cause of a government's fall is a military defeat or a domestic revolution, but the Soviet Union essentially imploded from within.

Gorbachev Attempts to Reform the Soviet Union

Brezhnev died in 1982. His immediate successors, Yuri Andropov (1914–1984) and Constantin Chernenko (1911–1985), died within thirteen months of each other and cleared the way for a reformer, Mikhail S. Gorbachev (b. 1931), to rise to power. Gorbachev inherited an administration whose authority was being undercut by a stagnating economy, corruption, and a lingering war in Afghanistan. Impatient with the inefficiencies of the Soviet system and disappointed in the Communist Party's failure to be true to its socialist ideals, Gorbachev tried to reform the Soviet system and save it. However, his policy changes unleashed forces that overwhelmed the USSR.

Economic *Perestroika*   Gorbachev's primary goal was to raise his country's standard of living by means of ***perestroika*** ("restructuring"). Among other things, *perestroika* entailed reducing the roles of centralized economic ministries. When a strike by Siberian coal miners in July 1989 threatened the Russian economy, Gorbachev acceded to their demands for better wages and more political liberty, and by 1990, he was abandoning Marxist ideology, promoting private ownership of property, and embracing a freer market economy.

Gorbachev's model may have been Lenin's New Economic Policy of the early 1920s, but in the Soviet context his program was genuinely radical in its criticism of centralized planning and its attack on the inefficiency of the party bureaucracy. However, when it proved not to be radical enough to halt the continuing decline of the Soviet economy, he tried to compensate for its failure by pursuing bold political reforms.

Glasnost   Gorbachev's policy, ***glasnost*** ("openness"), opened the way for unprecedented public discussion and criticism of Soviet history and the Communist Party. Censorship was relaxed. Dissidents were released from prison. The reputations of some of the figures whom Stalin had purged were rehabilitated. Workers were allowed to criticize the government's economic policies, and real debate took place at the Communist Party congress in 1988.

The Soviet Union was a vast empire composed of subject peoples who had been conquered either by the tsars or by Stalin, and *glasnost* gave these minorities a chance to express their discontent with Soviet rule. Gorbachev badly underestimated the extent of this internal unrest, as became clear as he advanced from *glasnost* to political *perestroika*. In 1988, he issued a new constitution that permitted real campaigning for seats in the Congress of People's Deputies. The result was the election of numerous dissidents.

1989: Revolution in Eastern Europe

Solidarity Reemerges in Poland   In the early 1980s, Poland's government relaxed martial law and released imprisoned members of the Solidarity labor union. In 1988, when a spate of new strikes erupted, the communist government of General Jaruzelski lost the upper hand. Solidarity was legalized, and the government was forced to negotiate with its founder, Lech Walesa. Jaruzelski

QUICK REVIEW

Defense and the Soviet Economy
- Gorbachev wanted to reduce spending on the military
- Cutbacks caused economic problems in an economy that was based on supplying the military
- Reduction of army and withdrawal from Eastern Europe prompted some Soviet republics to create their own armies

perestroika   ("restructuring") Means by which Gorbachev wished to raise his country's standard of living.

glasnost   ("openness") Gorbachev's policy of opening the way for unprecedented public discussion and criticism of Soviet history and the Communist Party. Censorship was relaxed and dissidents were released from prison.

promised free elections to a parliament that would be granted greater authority, and in the elections of 1989 the communists lost overwhelmingly to Solidarity candidates. No communist leader could form a coalition, so Jaruzelski turned to Solidarity's representatives for help, and for the first time since 1945, a non-communist prime minister governed Poland. Gorbachev approved his appointment.

Toward Hungarian Independence   Throughout 1989, one Soviet-dominated Eastern European state after another moved toward independence. Early in that year, Hungary opened its border with Austria. This created a breach in the Iron Curtain through which thousands of East Germans emigrated to the West. Janos Kadar, the president of the Hungarian Communist Party, whom the Soviets had installed following their intervention in 1956, was also deposed, and the party changed its name to the Socialist Party. Opposition parties were permitted to organize, and free elections were promised.

President Ronald Reagan and Communist Party General Secretary Mikhail Gorbachev confer at a summit meeting in December 1989.

AP Wide World Photos

German Reunification   In the autumn of 1989, mass protest demonstrations were staged in several East German cities, and the Soviet Union informed the East German Communist Party that it would not intervene to suppress them. The East German government then resigned, and in November a new government ordered the opening of the Berlin Wall. Tens of thousands of East Berliners crossed into the western sector to visit relatives and to shop. Suddenly, the way was open for the reunification of Germany, a development, which by February 1990, was viewed as inevitable by the United States, Great Britain, France, and the Soviet Union.

30.6
The Wall in My Backyard.

Revolutions in Czechoslovakia and Romania   The breach in the Berlin Wall was followed by a revolution in Czechoslovakia. In December 1989, popular pressure forced Czechoslovakia's communist government to apologize for the Soviet invasion of 1968 and to resign. A new parliament was seated, and Václav Havel (b. 1936), a well-known playwright and long-term opponent of the communist regime, was elected president.

The only violent revolution to take place in 1989 was Romania's. In mid-December, forces loyal to President Nicolae Ceausescu (1918–1989), who had controlled the country since 1965, fired on crowds of protesters. Bucharest was soon in full revolt, and when Ceausescu and his wife attempted to flee, they were captured, tried, and shot.

The Soviet Stance on Revolutionary Developments   None of the revolutions of 1989 would have succeeded if the Soviet Union had not refused to intervene militarily to prop up the old-line communist governments and parties of Eastern Europe. In October 1989, however, Gorbachev formally renounced the Brezhnev Doctrine and left the peoples of Eastern Europe free, for the first time since the end of World War II, to forge their own political destinies. Thousands took to the streets to denounce domination by the Communist Party and to call for democracy. The Soviet army was compelled to organize a hasty withdrawal from Eastern Europe, and the poverty to which its troops returned at home contributed to a further decline of its influence and morale.

The peaceful character of the Eastern European revolutions may have owed something to the horror with much of the world reacted in the spring of 1989, when China violently suppressed prodemocracy protesters in Beijing's

German youth breach the Berlin Wall in November 1989, an act that days earlier would have been unthinkable and deadly; the breach of the wall was the most symbolic moment in the collapse of European communism.

R. Bossu/Sygma/CORBIS

Significant Dates from the Era of the Cold War

1945	Yalta Conference; founding of the United Nations
1946	Churchill's Iron Curtain speech
1947	(March) Truman Doctrine (June) Announcement of Marshall Plan
1948	Communist takeovers in Czechoslovakia and Hungary; State of Israel proclaimed
1948–1949	Berlin Blockade
1949	NATO founded; East and West Germany emerge as separate states
1950–1953	Korean conflict
1953	Death of Stalin
1955	Warsaw Pact founded; Austria established as a neutral state
1956	(February) Khrushchev's secret speech denouncing Stalin (October) Suez crisis and the Hungarian uprising
1957	*Sputnik* launched
1961	Berlin Wall erected
1962	Cuban missile crisis
1963	Test Ban Treaty (Soviet Union and the United States)
1964	Gulf of Tonkin Resolution; America in Vietnam
1967	Six Days' War, Arab-Israeli conflict
1968	Soviet invasion of Czechoslovakia
1972	Strategic Arms Limitation Treaty
1973	Yom Kippur War
1975	Saigon falls to North Vietnam; Helsinki Accords
1978	Camp David Accords
1979	Soviet invasion of Afghanistan
1981	Solidarity founded in Poland
1982	Israel invades Lebanon; death of Brezhnev
1985	Israel withdraws from Lebanon
1987	Arab uprising on the West Bank commences
1988	PLO accepts Israel's right to exist
1993	Israel and PLO agree to phase out self-rule in the West Bank and Gaza
1995	Israeli prime minister Rabin assassinated

Tiananmen Square. The Communist Party officials of Eastern Europe and the Soviet Union clearly decided at some point in 1989 that they could not risk offending world opinion by similar actions.

THE COLLAPSE OF THE SOVIET UNION

Gorbachev ended support for the communist governments of Eastern Europe because he believed the Soviet Union could no longer afford the expense of propping up their regimes. He also could not endorse repressive measures abroad that were inconsistent with the political reforms he was proposing at home.

Renunciation of Communist Political Monopoly
Early in 1990, Gorbachev proposed to the Communist Party's Central Committee that it relinquish the party's monopoly of power. After intense debate, it concurred. Gorbachev did not want to abandon communism (at least not socialism), but he did want to open the political process to competition. He was determined, however, to preserve the Soviet Union as a strong state with a powerful central government.

New Political Forces By 1990, Gorbachev was facing challenges from three sources. People who passed for conservatives in the Soviet context wanted to use traditional Soviet control mechanisms to manage the country's economic stagnation and social turmoil. In 1991, Gorbachev added some of these people to his government to help him deal with opposition from a second group. Its leader, Boris Yeltsin, wanted a faster transition to a market economy and a more democratic form of government. In 1990, Yeltsin became president of the Russian Republic, the largest and most important of the Soviet Union's constituent states, which gave him a powerful base from which to challenge Gorbachev.

The third source of difficulty for Gorbachev was the increasing regional unrest in some of the Soviet Union's republics. This situation was not new, and in the past the military and Communist Party had successfully suppressed it. Initially, the strongest outcries came from the three Baltic republics: Estonia, Latvia, and Lithuania. They had been independent until the eve of World War II. Stalin had annexed them after the Soviet-German Nonaggression Pact assured him that Hitler would not stand in his way. During 1989 and 1990, the parliaments of the Baltic republics sought increased independence from the Soviet Union, and Lithuania declared full independence. Gorbachev turned to the army for help in dealing with this and the unrest developing in the Soviet Islamic republics of central Asia. Riots broke out in Azerbaijan and Tadzhikistan. Throughout 1990 and 1991,

Gorbachev tried to work out new constitutional arrangements that would reconcile the republics to the central government, and the failure of his effort, more than anything else, may explain the Soviet Union's rapid collapse.

The August 1991 Coup   In August 1991, the conservative forces that Gorbachev had brought into the government attempted a coup. Armed forces occupied Moscow, and Gorbachev was placed under house arrest while vacationing in the Crimea. On the day of the coup, Boris Yeltsin climbed onto a tank in front of the Russian Parliament building, denounced the reactionaries, and called on the world to support democracy in the Soviet Union. The coup collapsed within two days, and what may have been the largest demonstration in Russia's history erupted in Moscow to celebrate its failure. Gorbachev returned to Moscow, humiliated and victimized by people he had brought into his government. The Communist Party was compromised by its role in the coup, and its political influence faded as Yeltsin's following increased. Constitutional ties between the central government and various republics were revised, and on December 25, 1991, Gorbachev resigned, the Soviet Union ceased to exist, and the Commonwealth of Independent States came into being. (See Map 29–5.)

The Russian Revolution had seemed to validate Marxism, and Russia had worked hard to spread Marxist doctrines around the world. The failure of the communist political systems and economies has discredited Marxism, however, and thrust socialism on the defensive.

THE YELTSIN DECADE AND PUTIN

As president of Russia, Boris Yeltsin headed the largest, most powerful state in the new commonwealth. Initially, he enjoyed great popularity in Russia and throughout the commonwealth, but by 1993, he was facing serious economic and political problems. Opposition to Yeltsin, personally and to his programs, developed in the Russian parliament, which was heavily populated by former communists. Relations between the parliament and the president reached an impasse, and in September 1993, Yeltsin suspended parliament. It, in turn, deposed him and tried to provoke a popular uprising against him. The military, however, backed Yeltsin, surrounded the parliament building with troops, and on October 4, 1993 used tanks to crush proparliament rioters who rampaged through Moscow.

This consolidated Yeltsin's position, and all the major Western powers, which were deeply concerned by the turmoil in Russia, declared their support for him. In December 1993, Russians elected a new parliament and approved a new constitution that granted the president extensive powers. In 1994, however, a war erupted between the central government and the Islamic province of Chechnya in the Caucasus, where the Russian government has been unable to regain firm control.

During the mid–1990s, former state-owned industries were privatized in an effort to dismantle the Soviet state and economy. This complicated process involved much corruption and opportunism and created a small group of enormously wealthy individuals, referred to in the press as "the oligarchs," even as the general Russian economy remained stagnant. In 1998, Russia defaulted on its international debt payments, leading to an economic downturn. Amidst further political unrest and his own declining health, Yeltsin resigned the presidency just as the new century opened. Vladimir Putin (b. 1952) succeeded him.

Putin renewed the war against the rebels in Chechnya, resulting in heavy casualties, enormous destruction in Chechnya, but also a strengthened political position for Putin in Russia. After the September 2001 terrorist attacks on the United States. Putin supported the American assault on Afghanistan, largely out

MAP 29–5

The Commonwealth of Independent States   In December 1991 the Soviet Union broke up into its fifteen constituent republics. Eleven of these were loosely joined in the Commonwealth of Independent States. Also shown is the autonomous region of Chechnya, which has waged two bloody wars with Russia in the last decade.

WHAT DOES the breakup of the Soviet Union say about nationalism in the modern era?

of fears that Islamic extremism would spread beyond Chechnya to the largely Muslim nations bordering Russia in Central Asia and the Caucasus.

The Chechen war spawned a terrorist attack in September 2004 in Beslan, a Russian town located in the Northern Caucasus. On the opening day of the school year, a group of Chechens captured an elementary school and held approximately 1,200 students, teachers, and parents hostage for several days. About 330 hostages were killed when government troops stormed the school and the Chechens set off bombs. Such events, as well as Putin's determination that the central government will dominate Russia's economy and political life, help drive Putin's efforts to concentrate power by diminishing local autonomy and moving against leading oligarchs.

Russia remains more democratic than at any time under the Soviet system, but the economy continues to stagnate, corruption and violent crime are rife, its social and educational systems are in decay, life expectancy for men and women is dropping, and the population is projected to decline in the twenty-first century. (See "Encountering the Past: Rock Music and Political Protest.")

ENCOUNTERING THE PAST

ROCK MUSIC AND POLITICAL PROTEST

T he political scene in many parts of the modern world has been powerfully influenced by the rock music pioneered in the United States in the 1950s by African American, working-class, and folk musicians. In America it served as a vehicle for protesting the Vietnam war and for demanding civil rights. Europeans also took it up and set their own stamp on it. Britain's Beatles were the most successful of the early European rock bands, but the lyrics of their songs were minimally political.

Rock music acquired its hard edge as social commentary in the 1970s with the appearance of punk rock groups with provocative names such as the Sex Pistols. Pluralistic Western societies took its antiestablishment message in stride, but in Eastern Europe and the Soviet Union, it was literally revolutionary. During the 1970s and 1980s, it offered social and political critics a major outlet. Rock stars were celebrated for their personal heroism in openly attacking communist governments, and their music expressed and spread the disaffection that contributed to the collapse of communist regimes throughout Eastern Europe.

WHAT IS the source of the mass appeal of rock music? Why did it become antiestablishment? How did it undermine communism?

The Russian rock group "Dynamic" performs in Moscow in 1987.
R. Poderni/TASS/Sovfoto/Eastfoto

THE COLLAPSE OF YUGOSLAVIA AND CIVIL WAR

Yugoslavia was created after World War I by combining six national groups: Serbs, Croats, Slovenes, Montenegrins, Macedonians, and Bosnians. They have quarreled for centuries, and each has staked historical claims to a particular region: Serbia, Croatia, Slovenia, Montenegro, Macedonia, and Bosnia-Herzegovina. These districts, which were separate republics within Yugoslavia, have mixed populations. Many Serbs, for instance, live outside Serbia.

Yugoslavia's first communist leader, Marshal Tito (1892–1980), was independent from Stalin and master of his own foreign policy. He muted ethnic differences by complex power-sharing arrangements and a cult of personality that idolized his leadership. After his death, however, economic problems undermined Yugoslavia's central government, and civil war erupted.

In the late 1980s, the old ethnic differences flared up. Nationalist leaders came to power—most notably Slobodan Milosevic (b. 1941) in Serbia and Franjo Tudjman (b. 1922) in Croatia. The Serbs contended that Serbia did not have adequate influence within the Yugoslav federation and Serbs living elsewhere in Yugoslavia suffered discrimination (especially from Croats). The Croats and Slovenes added to the tension by pushing hard for rapid movement toward a market economy. During the summer of 1990, in the wake of the upheaval in the former Soviet bloc, Slovenia and Croatia seceded from Yugoslavia and were recognized as sovereign states by the European Community.

Destruction of Sarajevo. An elderly parishioner walks through the ruins of St. Mary's Roman Catholic Church in Sarajevo. The church was destroyed by Serb shelling in May 1992.

Reuters/CORBIS/Bettmann

From this point on, violence escalated. Serbia was dedicated to maintaining a united Yugoslavian state under Serbian control. Croatia was equally determined to secure independence. When Serbs in Croatia asked for protection, the Serbian army attacked Croatia, and in June 1991, the two republics went to war. The struggle took a new turn in 1992, when Croatian and Serbian forces decided to divide Bosnia-Herzegovina. The Muslims in Bosnia were caught between the opposing parties, and the Serbs, in particular, began a process of "ethnic cleansing," a euphemism for the murder or dispossession of large numbers of Bosnian Muslims. Unremitting Serbian bombardment of Sarajevo, the capital of Bosnia-Herzegovina, brought the Yugoslavian civil war to the attention of the world, and the United Nations tried, unsuccessfully, to mediate an end to the conflict.

Early in 1990, the bombing of a marketplace in Sarajevo prompted NATO to threaten retaliation against Serbian military positions if the Serbs did not withdraw their artillery from Sarajevo. In 1995, NATO's air strikes finally persuaded the leaders of the warring factions to meet in Dayton, Ohio, to work out a peace agreement. The terms of the complex agreement have been enforced by NATO troops including Americans.

Toward the end of the 1990s, Serbian attempts to drive ethnic Albanians from the province of Kosovo again drew NATO into Yugoslavian affairs. NATO responded with an air campaign that was the largest military operation in Europe since the end of World War II. Within the year a revolution had overthrown the government of Slobodan Milosevic, and the former Serbian leader was handed over to the International War Crimes Tribunal at the Hague, where his trial has dragged on without a verdict.

THE RISE OF RADICAL POLITICAL ISLAMISM

The tragic events of September 11, 2001, signaled the birth of a new kind of political world—one in which the United States, the nations of Europe, and the Russian Federation are endangered by terrorist attacks mounted by non-state-based organizations. These organizations serve ideologies associated with *radical Islam,* a significant but by no means dominant movement within the Muslim world. They were born in the context of decolonization and can be traced back to the 1930s. For many years, however, they had little impact on Middle Eastern politics. The events of September 11, and those following from them, have transformad American foreign policy toward the Middle East, and have also changed European relations with the United States.

ARAB NATIONALISM

Radical Islamism was a reaction against the secular Arab nationalism that developed in countries like Egypt and Syria in the 1920s and 1930s. The nationalists believed their countries could become strong and independent only if they modernized by adopting the technologies and political institutions of the West. The radical Islamists disagreed and wanted societies based on a rigorous interpretation of Islam.

Many of the Arab nationalist leaders of the Cold War era were sympathetic with socialism and the Soviet Union, but socialism and overtly atheitic communism were Western ideologies that deeply offended devout Arab elements in the populations of Muslim countries. Oil further complicated the situations that the Middle Eastern governments, most of which were authoritarian regimes, strove to manage. Some countries

WHAT HAS been the effect of radical political Islamism on global politics and societies around the world?

1979	Iranian Revolution
1979	Russian invasion of Afghanistan
1981	Assassination of President Anwar Sadat
1991	Persian Gulf War
1993	Bombing of the World Trade Center in New York City
1996	Bombing of U.S. army barracks in Saudi Arabia
1998	Bombing of U.S. embassies in East Africa
2000	Bombing of USS *Cole* in the Yemeni port of Aden
2001	September 11 terrorist attacks on American soil

became rich and influential. Others remained poor and weak. Most shared wealth very unequally, and their prosperous middle and upper classes paid little attention to the plight of the poor. A few, such as Saudi Arabia, tried to modernize their infrastructures while clinging to a rigorist, puritanical form of Islam (*Wahhabism*).

THE IRANIAN REVOLUTION

The Iranian Revolution of 1979 was pivotal moment in the history of the Middle East. Ayatollah Ruhollah Khomeini (1902–1989) persuaded the middle and lower classes of a major nation to cooperate in overthrowing a modernizing government supported by the United States. He then established a theocracy with a distinctly Islamic, nationalistic mission. His new Iranian constitution gave clergy, acting on behalf of God, the final word on everything. For the first time, one of the modern Middle East's great states had a religiously dominated government.

The Iranian Revolution challenged the Arab secular nationalists of Egypt, Saudi Arabia, and Algeria, who had failed to attend to the needs of their countries' underclasses. The older generation had embraced nationalism as a way of opposing Europe's colonial powers, but a younger generation, which had failed to prosper under their leadership, now reacted against nationalism. They saw the Islamic Revolution as the beginning of a movement that would spread across boundaries and transform the whole Islamic world.

The Iranian Revolution was driven by what is commonly called Islamic *fundamentalism* but is more accurately described as Muslim *reformism*. It sought to establish a reformed or pure Islam as a contemporary way of life. This lifestyle entailed personal piety and strict religious practices, and for some it implied government by Islamic law—the Shari'a. The Iranian example frightened the conservative Arab governments, for they saw it as raising religious issues that challenged their legitimacy. They began to pay more attention to their own religious authorities, particularly after a member of the radical Muslim Brotherhood assassinated Egypt's president, Anwar Sadat, in 1981.

AFGHANISTAN AND RADICAL ISLAMISM

Russia's invasion of Afghanistan in 1979 added Cold War complicatons to Islamist politics. The Soviet Union's desire to impose a Western, atheistic communist government on Afghanistan was obviously offensive to Muslim religious

Fall of Saddam Hussein's statue in 2003.

Markus Matzel/Das Fotoarchiv/Peter Arnold, Inc.

leaders, and they opposed it by declaring a *jihad*. The term means *struggle,* but it is commonly interpreted as a call for religious war. It gave the nationalistic Afghan resistance movement a universalistic, religious character that persuaded thousands of fundamentalist Muslims to go to Afghanistan to help drive out the Soviets. The United States supported this as a development favoring its side in the Cold War. The conservative Arab states saw it as a useful outlet for the energies of their own religious extremists. When it succeeded in 1989, Muslim fundamentalists saw it as a victory over an impious Western power.

The Taliban and Al Qaeda   The Soviet retreat created a political vacuum in Afghanistan that lasted for almost a decade. By 1998, however, rigorist Muslims called the *Taliban* had taken control of the country. They imposed a harsh version of Islamic law that oppressed women and punished criminals with mutilations and public executions. The Taliban provided refuge for *Al Qaeda* ("Base"), the Muslim terrorist training camps that produced the men who attacked the United States on September 11, 2001. Their ideology was forged in Pakistan's Islamic schools, the *madrasas*. These schools taught a version of reformed Islam that rejected liberal and nationalistic secular values, repudiated Western civilization and culture, and promoted hatred of Israel and the United States.

Jihad Against the United States   The success of the *jihad* in Afghanistan against the Soviet Union emboldened the Muslim extremists to take on the other great Western power, the United States, and the event that precipitated Al Qaeda's action was the Persian Gulf War of 1991. When Saddam Hussein of Iraq sought to seize control of the tiny, oil-rich state of Kuwait, conservative Arab governments were eager to cooperate with the United States to defeat him. Saudi Arabia provided the United States with military bases for the campaign. Osama Bin Laden, an extremist Islamic leader from Saudi Arabia, interpreted this as a Western assault on Islam's most sacred territory, the homeland of the Prophet Muhammad, and the Gulf War added to a long list of grievances the Islamists cherished against America. Some of their religious leaders declared a *jihad* to defeat the new "Crusaders," and through the 1990s a number of places and persons associated with the United States became targets for terrorist attacks.

A TRANSFORMED WEST

HOW DID September 11 transform the West?

*T*he tragedies of September 11 redirected American foreign policy, for they prompted President George W. Bush to declare a "war on terrorism" and depart from long-standing tradition by announcing a policy of preemptive strikes and interventions to disarm potential enemies.

The United States invaded Afghanistan late in 2001 and quickly overthrew the Taliban. Al Qaeda's bases, but not its leaders, were destroyed. They survive dispersed and in hiding. The Bush administration then focused its attention on Saddam Hussein's government in Iraq. Contrary to expectations, Saddam's defeat in the 1991 war had not led to his overthrow, and he was suspected of continuing to develop weapons of mass destruction. The American authorities claimed that preemptive action was needed to prevent these weapons from falling into the hands of terrorists. The inspectors that the United Nations charged with finding and destroying Iraq's facilities for producing such weapons were expelled from the country in 1998.

jihad   A struggle; interpreted as a call for religious war.

The Bush administration was convinced the government of Saddam Hussein had to be removed, and Britain supported its efforts in the United Nations to win passage of a resolution threatening Iraq with military force if it did not voluntarily disarm. When threats of vetoes from France and Russia doomed this effort, the United States and Great Britain invaded in March 2003 and overthrew Iraq's government. The war was vigorously opposed by France, Germany, and Russia and has created strains among traditional allies that suggest that a new era in international relations is dawning.

On March 11, 2004, Al Qaeda terrorists killed at least 190 people in train bombings in Madrid, Spain—the largest terrorit act against civilians in Europe since World War II. Timed just before Spanish elections, the attack and its aftermath influenced European political processes: The Spanish government, which had supported the American invasion of Iraq, unexpectedly lost the election, and the new government withdrew Spanish troops from Iraq.

The Iraq War and the bloody insurgency that has followed it remain controversial. Coalition forces found no weapons of mass destruction in Iraq, the alleged existence of which was a major pretext for launching the war. American and British government commissions criticized the intelligence information used to justify the invasion. More than 2,000 American troops and thousands of Iraqis have been killed.

In 2004, however, President Bush was reelected, and in January 2005, thousands of Iraqis braved threats as they voted in the first meaningful elections in Iraq since the 1950s. In May 2005, British Prime Minister Tony Blair's government was reelected, albeit with a reduced parliamentary majority.

Europeans and Americans differ in their values and political vision, yet the long-term relationship between Europe and the United States will no doubt survive. It is more than likely that events beyond the Euro-Atlantic community, particularly the wider conflict between the West and radical political Islam, will determine U.S.-European relations, just as the division between a democratic West and communist East once did in the past.

On July 7, 2005, a series of bombs rocked the London transport system with the loss of over 50 lives. This photo shows the remains of a London bus on which a suicide bomber took more than a dozen lives near Russell Square, London.

Sion Touhig/CORBIS/Bettmann

Summary

The Emergence of the Cold War The Cold War was based on the fundamental opposition between the ideologies of the Soviet Union and the Western democracies. An "Iron Curtain" separated Western Europe from the satellite states of the USSR. Germany was divided, and in 1949 most nations of Western Europe joined the United States, Canada, and the island states of the Atlantic to form NATO. The Soviet Union responded in 1955 with the Warsaw Pact. Israel's independence in 1948, and the Arab response brought the Cold War to the Middle East. The Korean conflict (1950–1953) was motivated by the West's policy of containing the spread of communism.

The Khrushchev Era in the Soviet Union Stalin strengthened his hold over the Soviet Union during World War II. Nikhita Khrushchev, who succeeded him in 1953, was less powerful. He allowed more intellectual and economic freedom but preserved the Communist Party's dominance. In 1956, the war that followed Egyptian president Nasser's nationalization of the Suez Canal prompted the United States to curtail intervention by the Western European powers in affairs beyond Europe. The USSR permitted modest political reforms in Poland, as long as Poland remained a member of the Warsaw Pact, but in Hungary, it toppled an independent communist government.

IMAGE KEY

for pages 718–719

a. The opening of the Berlin Wall in November, 1989, symbolized the collaspe of the Communist governments in Eastern Europe

b. On the day after the elections, a boy holds a Czech flag and a poster of victorious presidential candidate Vaclav Havel. Prague, Czechoslovakia. December 30, 1989

c. A 20 Euro banknote is presented to the press by the European Central Bank in Paris, August 30, 2001

d. Mahatma Ghandi, leader of the Indian Civil disobedience revolt, as he marched to the shore at Dandi, to collect salt in violation of the law

e. Albanian Refugees Arrive in Italy

f. The second hijacked plane is seen about to hit the second tower of the World Trade Center, September 11, 2001

g. Civilians atop bombed-out ruins of buildings watching American C-54 cargo plane fly overhead during Allied airlift to bring food and supplies to besieged citizens of Soviet controlled Berlin

h. Toppled statue of Lenin

i. May Day Posters in various languages hang below Solidarity graffiti in New York. November 1981, New York, USA

Later Cold War Confrontations Tensions continued to simmer between the United States and the USSR in the late 1950s. In August 1961 the Berlin Wall was erected, and in 1966 the Cuban missile crisis brought the Cold War to the Americas. In 1968 the USSR invaded Czechoslovakia to suppress the Prague Spring.

The Brezhnev Era Brezhnev led the Soviet Union from 1964 to 1982. In 1968 the USSR invaded Czechoslovakia to suppress the Prague Spring, in the last major Soviet military action in Europe of the Cold War. The Helsinki Accords recognized the Soviet sphere of influence in Eastern Europe, but protected human rights. By the early 1980s, Soviet armed forces were the largest in the world, and the USSR's nuclear arsenal nearly equaled that of the United States. The Soviet invasion of Afghanistan in 1979 sapped much of that strength. In July 1980 a shipyard workers' strike at Gdansk in Poland created Solidarity, an independent union. The Soviets responded by increasing their own military spending, a tactic that accelerated the end of the regime.

Decolonization: The European Retreat from Empire World War II accelerated the decolonization process. Mohandas Gandhi utilized Western liberal ideas and the passive resistance strategy of Henry David Thoreau to gain Indian independence in 1947. Britain generally succeeded in establishing representative self-governments in its former colonies.

The Turmoil of French Decolonization France ended its colonial era more slowly and painfully than did Britain. In Algeria nationalists demanded civic equality and fought a civil war until 1962, when a referendum ordered by President Charles de Gaulle approved Algerian independence. In Vietnam Ho Chi Minh fought for independence from France, but in 1955, when the French began to withdraw from South Vietnam, the United States entered the Vietnam War. Many Europeans, Americans, and others questioned U. S. motives and goals.

The Challenges of Western European Unification Economic unification was easier for European nations than military or political union. In 1951 six nations formed the European Coal and Steel Community, which in 1957 became the European Economic Community or the Common Market. In 1973 membership was increased, and in 1998 the EEC created a free-trade zone. In 1999 a common currency was decreed, and the EEC was renamed the European Union. Its euro became the currency of most of Western Europe in 2001. In 2004, the European Union admitted ten more member nations, but discord spread over the details of a constitution designed to regulate relations among members.

The Collapse of European Communism Gorbachev took power in 1985 and attempted to reform the Soviet system, but his reforms set off a cascade of consequences. Revolutions swept Eastern Europe in 1989. Poland elected a Solidarity government, Hungary opened its borders with Austria and promised free elections, and East Germany opened the Berlin Wall. By late 1990, Gorbachev had allied with conservatives, and Yeltsin became the spokesman for a rival group that wanted to move quickly to a market economy and greater democratization. Gorbachev left office, and on December 25, 1991, the Commonwealth of Independent States replaced the Soviet Union, with Boris Yeltsin as president of the Russian Federation. Vladimir Putin succeeded Yeltsin in January 2000 and has presided over a continuing war in Chechnya and persistent social, economic, and demographic problems. Yugoslavian communism also collapsed. NATO intervened to stop the shelling of Sarajevo in 1994 and 1995, and U.S.-led diplomacy resulted in the 1995 Dayton peace accords. A few years later, NATO intervened again, this time in Kosovo.

The Rise of Radical Political Islamism Radical Islamism is a reaction to early twentieth-century Arab secular nationalism. Most nationalist leaders of Muslim countries satisfied their religious critics by giving them some control over social institutions, but the Iranian Revolution of 1979 subjected a major state to Islamist domination. Afghanistan in 1998 was taken over by the Muslim-led Taliban, and radical Pakistani-educated Muslims targeted the United States after the 1991 Persian Gulf War, which they saw as an assault on the Muslim Holy Land.

A Transformed West Terrorist attacks incuding those September 11, 2001, targeted the United States for its military and economic strength and its Western values. The U.S. military response against Afghanistan was widely supported by Europe, but only Great Britain has supported the Bush administration's actions against Iraq. Despite lack of support by the United Nations, the invasion or Iraq succeeded in removing the government of Saddam Hussein after only three weeks of fighting.

REVIEW QUESTIONS

1. How did Europe come to be dominated by the United States and the Soviet Union after 1945? How would you define the policy of containment? What were some of the global events in the period from 1945 to 1982 that were influenced by this American policy?

2. Why did the nations of Europe give up their empires? How did the United States become involved in Vietnam?

3. What internal political pressures did the Soviet Union experience in the 1970s and early 1980s? How did Gorbachev's reforms contribute to the collapse of the Soviet Union?

4. What were the major events in Eastern Europe that contributed to the collapse of communism? What was Poland's role in this process?

5. How has radical political Islam developed? How has it been affected by the invasion of Afghanistan and recent military conflicts in the Middle East?

KEY TERMS

Brezhnev Doctrine (p. 727)   *glasnost* (p. 734)   **NATO** (p. 722)
Cold War (p. 720)   *jihad* (p. 742)   *perestroika* (p. 734)
containment (p. 720)   **Marshall Plan** (p. 721)   **Warsaw Pact** (p. 722)
détente (p. 728)

  For additional study resources for this chapter, go to:
www.prenhall.com/kagan3/chapter29

30 The West at the Dawn of the Twenty-First Century

CHAPTER HIGHLIGHTS

The Twentieth-Century Movement of Peoples World War II created millions of refugees. The Soviets relocated peoples of various nationalities. Between 1945 and 1960 millions of people left Europe voluntarily. The need for an influx of laborers contributed to the growth of Europe's Muslim population. Europe's birthrate has declined in the last quarter century.

Toward a Welfare State Society Christian democratic parties introduced postwar welfare policies. Attitudes toward the welfare state have fluctuated with the European economy. Critics charge that the welfare state has put too heavy a burden on young workers and has limited Europe's economic growth.

New Patterns in Work and Expectations of Women The feminist movement in Europe is less well organized than in America, but it is an influential force. Since World War II, there has been a sharp increase in the number of women working outside the home. The collapse of communist regimes has created special problems for women in Eastern Europe.

Transformations in Knowledge and Culture A proliferation of educational institutions made learning available to a larger and more diverse student body and exposed more people to intellectual movements, such as socialism and existentialism, that challenge traditional beliefs and institutions. Since World War II, Europe has been strongly influenced by America. Environmental groups have achieved considerable political power. The cold war and the memory of the horrors of World War II had an important impact on European art.

The Christian Heritage Despite a number of challenges, Europe's Christian churches still exercise considerable influence. Karl Barth and Paul Tillich articulated important approaches to Christian theology. The Roman Catholic Church has gone through an important period of reform and expansion.

Late Twentieth-Century Technology: The Arrival of the Computer The computer has had a profound effect on European life. The military played a key role in the development of the computer. The advent of desktop computers has given the power of computers to many, but not all, Europeans.

The Challenges of European Unification Western Europe took unprecedented steps toward economic cooperation and unity in the second half of the twentieth century. Increased economic interdependence and the expansion of the European Union have created tensions within the EU.

CHAPTER QUESTIONS

HOW HAS migration changed the face of Europe?

WHAT EFFECT did the Great Depression and World War II have on the way Europeans viewed welfare?

HOW DID the status of women in business, politics, and the professions change in Europe in the second half of the twentieth century?

HOW WAS cultural and intellectual life transformed in Europe during the twentieth century?

WHAT KIND of artistic styles arose in the mid- and late twentieth century?

HOW HAS the Christian heritage of the West been affected by events of the twentieth century?

WHAT IMPACT has the computer had on twentieth-century society?

WHAT LED to Western European unification following World War II?

CHAPTER OUTLINE

- The Twentieth-Century Movement of Peoples
- Toward a Welfare State Society
- New Patterns in Work and Expectations of Women
- Transformations in Knowledge and Culture
- Art Since World War II
- The Christian Heritage
- Late Twentieth-Century Technology: The Arrival of the Computer
- The Challenges of European Unification

IMAGE KEY

Image Key for pages 746–747 is on page 764.

HOW HAS migration changed the face of Europe?

During the second half of the twentieth century, the Cold War influenced life in the West—for individuals as well as states. It closed vast areas to travel and sealed off most of Eastern Europe from the era's material and technological advances. It did not, however, impede the developments that remarkably transformed the Western European countries and the United States. They achieved unprecedented prosperity and technological progress. Europe also took unprecedented steps toward economic cooperation and political union.

THE TWENTIETH-CENTURY MOVEMENT OF PEOPLES

The economic transformation of Europe that followed World War II provoked a great deal of voluntary migration. The most pervasive trend was the movement of people from the country to the city. In Western Europe today, about 75 percent of the population lives in an urban setting.

Much involuntary migration also reshaped societies in the West. The relocations of peasants by the Soviets and of Jews by the Germans are well known, but millions of Germans, Hungarians, Poles, Ukrainians, Bulgarians, Serbs, Finns, Chechens, Armenians, Greeks, Turks, and Bosnian Muslims were also displaced. These movements were extensive enough in some places to change nationalities. The Polish city of Gdansk, for instance, was once the German city of Danzig.

DISPLACEMENT THROUGH WAR

World War II created a vast flood of refugees numbering in the tens of millions. Bombing and fighting destroyed cities and drove people from their homes. The Nazis brought hundreds of thousands of foreign workers into Germany to staff their wartime industries. Hundreds of thousands of soldiers, who were taken as prisoners of war, were sent to remote camps. Shifting political borders forced some ethnic groups to relocate, and after the war, anti-German feeling in Poland, Czechoslovakia, and Hungary compelled the German minorities residing in these places (about 12 million people) to flee to Germany. The Soviets also relocated hordes of peoples of various nationalities.

MIGRATION

Between 1945 and 1960, about half a million Europeans left Europe each year, the largest outflow of people since the economic difficulties of the 1920s. Decolonization, however, drew many non-European natives from former colonies to Europe, which has caused serious ethnic tensions and generated support for right-wing movements with racist ideologies. In 2002, Jean-Marie Le Pen (b. 1928) appealed to the antagonism French workers felt for immigrants from North Africa and won enough support to become one of two candidates in a runoff election for France's presidency. He lost to Jacques Chirac (b. 1932), but his campaign revealed a deep current of racism in French society. Similar movements have sprung up in Britain, Germany, Austria, Italy, the Netherlands, and Denmark. Some of the most serious conflicts involve Europe's growing Muslim population.

THE NEW MUSLIM POPULATION

For centuries, Europeans paid little attention to Islam, but that began to change in the 1960s as a consequence of Muslim immigration. After World War II, a need for laborers to help rebuild their economies induced Western European nations to welcome "guest workers" from Muslim countries. Turks migrated to

Germany, Pakistanis to Britain, and Algerians to France. Decolonization and the pursuit of a better life added to the flow and mix of Muslim immigrants during the waning years of the twentieth century, and even nations that had always had rather homogeneous populations (Italy, Spain, Sweden, Denmark, and the Netherlands) acquired significant Muslim minorities.

Europeans and the guest workers themselves initially assumed these newcomers would eventually return to their homelands. Unlike the United States, few European countries had any experience with large-scale immigration, and most of them made it difficult for immigrants to assimilate. Muslims established separate, self-contained communities and perpetuated languages and cultures that sharply differentiated them from their European neighbors. Their failure to assimilate and their generally low levels of education have hurt them as the number of unskilled jobs they have traditionally filled has declined. They have become easy targets for right-wing politicians, who blame them for social problems and economic difficulties. Their situation attracts some of them to the militant religious movements that have sprung up in many parts of the Muslim world. Some were implicated in the September 11, 2001, attack on the United States.

The European Muslim population is diverse. It is drawn from many different countries, classes, and Islamic traditions. European Muslims hardly present a united front, but their widespread poverty and chronic unemployment make them a source of anxiety for governments that have yet to agree on how to relate to them.

Muslim women wear headscarves in France. The presence of foreign-born Muslims whose labor is necessary for the prosperity of the European economy is a major issue in contemporary Europe. Many of these Muslims, such as these women, live in self-contained communities.

Figaro Magazine/Torregano/Getty Images, Inc.—Liaison

EUROPEAN POPULATION TRENDS

During the past quarter century, European birthrates have declined to the point where Europeans are no longer having enough children to replace themselves. Women in the United States bear an average of 2.1 children, whereas those in Europe average 1.4 or less. No adequate explanation has been found for this trend, but given current tendencies to restrict immigration, as Europeans age and retire, Europe will experience a shortage of workers. Its internal market will shrink, and its influence will diminish along with its share of world population.

TOWARD A WELFARE STATE SOCIETY

*A*fter World War II, most of the nations of Western Europe endorsed principles of liberal democracy. (The exceptions were Portugal and Spain, where dictatorships survived into the mid–1970s.) The experience of the Great Depression and the events leading up to the war had made it clear that stable democracies need sound social and economic bases as well as political structures. Most Europeans concluded, therefore, that one of the duties of government was to ensure economic prosperity and social security. This was the only way to stave off the kind of turmoil that fostered tyranny, war, and the prospect of communism.

WHAT EFFECT did the Great Depression and World War II have on the way Europeans viewed welfare?

CHRISTIAN DEMOCRATIC PARTIES

Except for the Labour Party in Britain, democratic socialist parties did not prosper in Europe during the Cold War. Most states were governed by coalitions headed by various **Christian Democratic parties**. These were a new development

Christian Democratic parties
Postwar parties that welcomed non-Catholic members and fought for democracy, social reform, and economic growth.

Margaret Thatcher, a shopkeeper's daughter who became the first female prime minister of Great Britain, served in that office from May 1979 through November 1990. Known as the "Iron Lady" of British politics, she led the Conservative Party to three electoral victories and carried out extensive restructuring of the British government and economy.

AP Wide Wold Photos

QUICK REVIEW

The Welfare State

• Great Britain was the first European nation to create a welfare state

• France and Germany followed Britain's lead in the 1970s

• European attitudes toward the welfare state have fluctuated with the European economy

---

in postwar politics. They were largely Roman Catholic, but they differed from the Catholic parties that had thrived from the late nineteenth century through the 1930s. Those had been conservative groups held together more by their opposition to communism than by any positive programs of their own. The postwar Christian Democratic parties welcomed non-Catholic members and fought for democracy, social reform, and economic growth.

THE CREATION OF WELFARE STATES

The Great Depression, unemployment's contribution to the rise of authoritarian states, and the mobilization required to fight World War II changed how many Europeans thought about social welfare. After the war, their governments began to spend more on social welfare than on the military—a choice made possible by the protection that NATO and the United States provided.

History offered European two models for the welfare state—one German and one British. In the 1880s, Bismarck had introduced some forms of social insurance to Germany as part of a strategy to undercut the Social Democratic Party's appeal for the masses. By granting German workers some security, he sapped their motivation to agitate for political reform. In Britain, where the working class already had extensive political privileges, social insurance tended to be provided only for the very poor. There was a consensus in both countries that workers should be insured to help them with problems created by disease, injury, and old age, but unemployment was not considered a dilemma that governments should address. People higher up on the social scale could generally look out for themselves, and they viewed unemployment as a short-term problem that workers often created for themselves.

After World War II, the belief spread that social insurance against predictable risks was a right that should be accorded all citizens. Universal coverage obviously appealed to socialists, but even conservatives thought it was a good idea. They assumed that by providing medical care, old-age pensions, and other benefits they could diminish popular pressure for more radical redistributions of income from the rich to the poor.

Great Britain was the first European nation to create a welfare state. The Labour Party laid the groundwork for it during the ministry (1945–1951) of Clement Attlee (1883–1967). The centerpiece of Attlee's program was the National Health Service. In the 1970s, France and Germany followed Britain's example and passed similar health-care legislation. The environment of the Cold War encouraged the institution of additional welfare programs, particularly unemployment insurance. Communist nations promised their people extensive social security and full employment, and capitalist states believed that to block the spread of communism they had to offer their citizens competitive deals. As it turned out, however, the communists always promised more than they could deliver.

RESISTANCE TO THE EXPANSION OF THE WELFARE STATE

Western European attitudes toward the welfare state have fluctuated with the European economy. While Europe was recovering from the war and experiencing economic growth, Europeans trusted government intervention to promote national economies. In the 1970s, however, an era of inflation, slow growth, and high rates of unemployment set in. It persisted through the 1990s and diminished faith in government management. Support built for a free market that (within limits) regulates itself.

The most influential political figure in reasserting the importance of markets and resisting the power of labor unions was Margaret Thatcher (b. 1925) of

HISTORY'S VOICES

MARGARET THATCHER ASSERTS THE NEED FOR INDIVIDUAL RESPONSIBILITY

No single European political figure so challenged and criticized the assumptions of the welfare state and of state intervention in general than Margaret Thatcher, British Prime Minister from 1979 to 1990. Known as the "Iron Lady," Mrs. Thatcher repeatedly demanded that people take individual responsibility rather than rely on state-sponsored support. Yet her administration did not dismantle the key structures of the British welfare state.

HOW AND WHY does Mrs. Thatcher contend that there is no such thing as society? Does she criticize all that government aid to citizens? How does she emphasize the reciprocal character of social relationships? How does she argue in favor of personal and private charity to aid persons in need?

I think we have gone through a period when too many children and people have been given to understand "I have a problem, it is the Government's job to cope with it!" or "I have a problem, I will go and get a grant to cope with it! "I am homeless, the Government must house me!" and so they are casting their problems on society and who is society? There is no such thing! There are individual men and women . . . there are families and no government can do anything except through people and people look to themselves first. It is our duty to look after ourselves and then also to help look after our neighbor, and life is a reciprocal business and people have got the entitlements too much in mind without the obligations, because there is no such thing as an entitlement unless someone has first met an obligation and it is, I think, one of the tragedies in which many of the benefits we give, which were meant to reassure people that if they were sick or ill there was a safety net and there was help, that many of the benefits which were meant to help people who were unfortunate—"It is all right. We joined together and we have these insurance schemes to look after it." That was the objective . . . But it went too far. If children have a problem, it is society that is at fault. There is no such thing as society. There is living tapestry of men and women and people and the beauty of that tapestry and the quality of our lives will depend upon how much each of us is prepared to take responsibility for ourselves and each of us prepared to turn round and help, by our own efforts, those who are unfortunate.

This extract derives from a transcript of the original interview rather than the published text. Reprinted with permission from margaretthatcher.org, the official website of the Margaret Thatcher Foundation.

the British Conservative Party, who served as Prime Minister from 1979 to 1990. She cut taxes, sought to curb inflation, and privatized many industries that Labour Party governments had nationalized. Thatcher reduced trade union power amidst bitter confrontations. She was determined to make the British economy more efficient and competitive. Over time, the Labour Party itself accepted some of her policies. (See "History's Voices: Margaret Thatcher Asserts the Need for Individual Responsibility.")

Critics have also challenged the belief that governments owe their citizens all the benefits promised by Europe's costly welfare states. The welfare burden is only bearable when the number of employed, younger workers (whose taxes pay the bills) is much greater than the number of older people (who draw the benefits). Europe's aging population and high unemployment rates have created fiscal problems that have forced governments across the Continent (including those of the left) to limit the growth of the welfare state and curtail some of its benefits. The golden age of welfare states appears to have passed, and new approaches may be needed to deal with issues of social welfare.

Simone de Beauvoir, here with her companion, the philosopher Jean-Paul Sartre, was the major feminist writer in postwar Europe.

Keystone_Paris/Getty Images Inc./Hulton Archive Photos

NEW PATTERNS IN WORK AND EXPECTATIONS OF WOMEN

Although the decades following World War II witnessed changes that enabled more women than ever before to obtain positions of leadership in business, politics, and the professions, traditional patterns of family and economic life have persisted and have perpetuated gender inequality in European societies.

FEMINISM

The feminist movement in Europe is less well organized than in America, but it is an influential force. After the collapse of communism undercut confidence in socialism, feminist and environmentalist groups assumed chief responsibility for critiquing the European way of life. Feminism is one of the major manifestations of Western civilization's characteristic inclination to self-criticism.

Prior to World War II, the goal of feminists was to win legal and civil equality with men. Early feminists concentrated on campaigning for specific political rights, but since the war, the feminist agenda has broadened. The more radical European feminists claim that society, as currently organized, inherently represses women, and they charge political parties on both the left and the right with failure to address women's issues.

The most influential feminist thinker of the postwar period was the French intellectual Simone de Beauvoir (1908–1986). In *The Second Sex* (1949) she documented the differences it made in life to be born female or male. Although she enjoyed privileges as a member of the French intellectual elite, she and other feminist commentators explained how gender roles handicapped women of all classes. They pointed out that divorce and family law favor men and certain social problems (spousal abuse, for instance) are of particular concern to women.

The emphasis on the right of women to control their own lives may be the most important feature of recent European feminism. Earlier feminism sought, and largely gained, legal and civil equality with men. Current feminism pursues issues that are particular to women, their personal independence and fulfillment.

MORE MARRIED WOMEN IN THE WORK FORCE

One aspect of women's lives that has changed significantly is the sharp increase in the number of married women who work outside the home. Because of low birthrates in the 1930s, few young single women were available for employment after World War II. As married women replaced them in the job market, consumer conveniences and alterations in work schedules made it easier for them to work outside their homes. Primary responsibility for the care of children, however, still limits many women to part-time employment.

Unlike earlier periods in history, children in the modern West are no longer expected to contribute substantially to their families' support. If a family needs more income than one parent can provide, the other seeks work while their children spend years in compulsory education. Many mothers also choose to work outside their homes for reasons of personal fulfillment, not economic necessity.

NEW WORK PATTERNS

Careers and wage-paying jobs occupy a much larger part of a woman's life in the twentieth century than they did in the nineteenth. Single women used to drop out of the work force following marriage, but this is no longer the case. A married woman may temporarily leave her employment to care for a very young child, but quickly turn that child over to a child-care provider and return to her job. Lengthening life spans have also made work outside the home more important to women. Women used to die relatively young, and most of their time was dedicated to bearing and rearing children. Modern women, however, can anticipate many years of vigorous life after their children are grown. Work, therefore, has taken on new significance for them. Career ambitions persuade some women to limit the size of their families, to postpone childbearing, or to forgo it altogether. The age at which women begin to bear children has risen to the early twenties in Eastern Europe and to the late twenties in Western Europe.

WOMEN IN THE NEW EASTERN EUROPE

The collapse of the communist regimes has created special problems for women in Eastern Europe. Under communism well over 50 percent of them were in the work force, and they enjoyed social equality and many government-financed benefits. There were no "women's movements" in these countries, for communist authorities were suspicious of all independent associations.

The governments that have replaced the communists face serious economic challenges, and they have shown little concern for how their policies impact the lives of women. Many of the health and welfare programs that benefit women and children face cutbacks, and in order to be competitive with free-market economies, the states of Eastern Europe will probably shorten the lengthy maternity leaves to which female workers were formally entitled. Women will also probably find themselves more poorly paid than men, and during economic downturns they may be subject to earlier layoffs and later rehires.

TRANSFORMATIONS IN KNOWLEDGE AND CULTURE

Cultural and intellectual life were transformed in Europe during the twentieth century. A proliferation of educational institutions made learning available to a wider and more diverse student body than ever before, which has acquainted more people with intellectual movements that challenge traditional beliefs and institutions. Europe's Christian religion has struggled to adapt to this and remain relevant.

COMMUNISM AND WESTERN EUROPE

Following the Russian Revolution, the socialist movement in western Europe split between independent democratic socialist parties and Soviet-dominated communist parties that supported the agenda of the Third International. Throughout the 1920s and 1930s, these groups were generally opposed to each other.

The Intellectuals   During the 1930s, the Great Depression caused liberal democracies to flounder and right-wing regimes to spring up. Some people saw communism as offering the best defense for humane, liberal values. Many of Europe's students and intellectuals affiliated with the Communist Party and visited the Soviet Union. For some, communism almost became a religion, and they were willing to ignore or justify Stalin's terrorism.

Four events contributed to the gradual disillusionment of many European intellectuals with Soviet communism: the purges of the late 1930s, the Spanish Civil War (1936–1939), the alliance between Russia and Germany in 1939, and the Soviet invasion of Hungary in 1956. Disappointment with the Soviet Union did not,

HOW WAS cultural and intellectual life transformed in Europe during the twentieth century?

QUICK REVIEW

Factors Leading to Disillusionment
- Purges of the 1930s
- Spanish Civil War
- Alliance between Russia and Germany in 1939
- Soviet invasion of Hungary in 1956

however, necessarily entail a loss of confidence in communism itself. Some social critics pinned their hopes for the realization of their vision for society on non-Soviet communist governments, such as Yugoslavia or, in the late 1950s, China.

Some people hoped a uniquely European form of communism would evolve and that communist parties would take control democratically. During the 1930s, the abstract, philosophical writings of the "young Marx" were published. These essays, which preceded the *Communist Manifesto* of 1848, made Marx look more like a humanist than a revolutionary. They suggested that one could be a Marxist without condoning revolution or supporting the Soviet Union. Given the collapse of the Soviet Union and of Eastern Europe's communist governments, the future of European Marxism and of its influence on European intellectual life is uncertain.

EXISTENTIALISM

The intellectual movement that best characterizes mid twentieth-century European thought is **existentialism**. It was not a unified movement, for existentialist philosophers disagreed on major issues. All, however, wanted to continue the nineteenth century's revolt against rationalism.

Roots in Nietzsche and Kierkegaard   The forerunners of existentialism were Friedrich Nietzsche (see Chapter 24) and Søren Kierkegaard (1813–1855), a Danish author who received little attention until after World War I. Both men rejected the dominant Hegelian philosophy of their day and its confidence that life could be explained in abstract, rational terms. Kierkegaard critiqued expressions of this shallow optimism in organized religion. In *Fear and Trembling* (1843), *Either/Or* (1843), and *Concluding Unscientific Postscript,* (1846) he argued that Christian truth could not be captured by creeds, doctrines, and churches. Truth can be comprehended, he insisted, only by passionate engagement with life's challenges.

The intellectual and ethical crises created by World War I brought Kierkegaard's thought to the fore and revived interest in Nietzsche's critique of reason. The war raised doubts about the ability of human beings to control their destinies and to make historical progress. Its destructiveness undercut faith in the redemptive power of reason, for the war's most terrible weapons were the products of rational technology. One of the casualties of war was the nineteenth century's sunny faith in orderly human development.

Questioning of Rationalism   There were two Germans among the major existential writers—Martin Heidegger (1889–1976) and Karl Jaspers (1883–1969)— and two Frenchmen—Jean-Paul Sartre (1905–1980) and Albert Camus (1913–1960). Although they disagreed about many things, they all, in one way or another, questioned the primacy of reason and science in the quest to comprehend the human situation. The Enlightenment tradition claimed that rational analysis—the division of human experience into its component parts—produced understanding. The existentialists, however, maintained that the human condition was greater than the sum of its parts and could only be grasped as a whole. The romantics of the early nineteenth century, who had more gently questioned reason, believed truth could be grounded in imagination and intuition, but the existentialists focused on the obliterating extremes of human experience: death, dread, fear, and anxiety. They claimed that faced with such threats to their existence, human beings must formulate ethical values for themselves. Traditional religion, rational philosophy, intuition, or social customs cannot help a person who stares into the abyss. At such a time, each individual must exercise the dreadful freedom to create value for himself or herself.

27.2
Jean-Paul Sartre:
Existentialism

existentialism   Maintains that the human condition is greater than the sum of its parts and can only be grouped as whole.

Existentialism, like communism, was very much a response to the mood that existed in Europe before and immediately after World War II. During the 1960s, however, the turmoil created by the Vietnam War and the youth revolution redirected the intellectual interests of Europeans.

EXPANSION OF THE UNIVERSITY POPULATION AND STUDENT REBELLION

At the turn of the twentieth century, no more than a few thousand people were enrolled in universities in any major European country, but by the 1980s, that figure had risen to hundreds of thousands. Higher education is now available (although less in Europe than in the United States) to people from a wide variety of social and economic backgrounds and, for the first time, to significant numbers of women.

In 1968 a student rebellion in Paris threatened to bring down the government of Charles de Gaulle. This was only one example of the explosion of student activity that rocked the West in the late 1960s.

© Bettmann/CORBIS

One unexpected result of the ballooning population of students and intellectuals was a rebellious student movement that began in the United States in the early 1960s and then spread to Europe and other parts of the world. It rejected middle-class values, sexual mores, and traditional family life, but it drew much of its energy from opposition to the war in Vietnam. It was, therefore, usually associated with antimilitarism and a radical critique of American politics. In Eastern Europe, however, it targeted the Soviet Union and communist governments.

The student rebellion reached its peak in 1968, when American students demonstrated against U.S. involvement in Vietnam, French students at the Sorbonne in Paris attacked the government of Charles de Gaulle, and Czech students called for a more liberal form of socialism. Each of these protest movements failed to achieve its immediate objective, and in the early 1970s, interest in the student rebellion faded. European students continued to oppose nuclear weapons (particularly the basing of American missiles in Europe), but they abandoned the kinds of disruptive behaviors associated with the 1960s.

THE AMERICANIZATION OF EUROPE

During the past half century, Western Europe has been enormously influenced by the United States. Following World War II, the Marshall Plan rebuilt Europe's economy and NATO provided its defense. Both these programs were American initiatives. Hundreds of thousands of Americans have also spent time in Europe—as soldiers, students, businesspeople, and tourists.

Europeans much discuss and frequently lament the "Americanization" of their culture. The shopping centers and supermarkets that Americans pioneered are displacing Europe's traditional sales districts. American television programs and movies are readily available everywhere. Fast-food restaurants, such as McDonald's, line the streets of European cities from Dublin to Moscow, and American clothing styles (especially blue jeans) are wildly popular throughout Europe. Thanks to the influence of the media and the power of American corporations, American English also seems to be emerging as the common language for Europe's business and academic communities.

A CONSUMER SOCIETY

During the past half century, the economy of Western Europe has differentiated itself from that of Eastern Europe by its emphasis on the manufacture of consumer goods. The Soviet bloc's economic planners concentrated on capital investments and the military. Consequently, people in communist countries experienced a decline in the quantity and quality of food and consumer items.

QUICK REVIEW

Western Europe's Consumer Society
- Western Europe's economy emphasized consumer goods in the second half of the twentieth century
- Soviet bloc economies focused on capital investments and the military
- Discrepancy in Western and Eastern European standards of living caused resentment in the East

ENCOUNTERING THE PAST

TOYS FROM EUROPE CONQUER THE UNITED STATES

Europeans often complain about American influences on their culture, but European products have also shaped life in America. At least one European toy, the LEGO building block, has had an effect on childhood comparable to that of the American Disney Corporation's cartoon characters.

In 1932, Ole Kirk Christiansen founded a company in Denmark to manufacture household goods and wooden toys. The toys did so well, that in 1934 the company adopted the name LEGO (from Danish, Leg godt, "Play well"). The first LEGO building block sets were produced in 1955. The ingenious interlocking design of the LEGO block allowed children to build all kinds of things, and the sets were a hit when they went on sale in the United States in 1961. Subsequent editions were improved by the addition of new forms (such as wheels) that allowed children even freer range for their imaginations.

In 1968, the LEGO Company followed the lead of the Disney organization and began to open amusement parks with rides that resembled large LEGO toys. By the 1990s, it had become the largest toy manufacturer in Europe, and LEGO blocks were estab-lished as staples of popular culture. Museums now house structures made from them, and contests are held at which their builders compete. Some management gurus have even urged business executives to play with LEGO blocks to clarify their thinking.

WHY HAS the influence of LEGO on America been less controversial than that of American fast-food chains on Europe?

Children across the world play with LEGO toys.
Tom Prettyman/PhotoEdit Inc.

Since the early 1950s, Europeans have seen their food supply steadily improve, and they have enjoyed an expanding array of consumer goods and services: automobiles, household appliances, entertainments, clothing, "disposable" conveniences, and vacations—all the appurtenances of the leisured lifestyle.

This development has had dramatic political repercussions. Through the limited number of radios, television, movies, and videos available to them, Eastern Europeans gradually became aware of the discrepancy between their circumstances and those of Westerners. They intuited the link between consumerism and democracy, between free societies and free markets. Although excessive consumerism has been deplored by Western commentators and Christian moralists, it helped generate the mass discontent that brought down Eastern Europe's communist governments. (See "Encountering the Past: Toys from Europe Conquer the United States.")

ENVIRONMENTALISM

The shortage of consumer goods in the West after World War II created a demand that fueled economic expansion through the 1960s. At the time, the public paid scant attention to the ethical implications of growth and its effect on the environment. Concern for the environment emerged, however, in the 1970s, and by the 1980s, an environmental movement with real political clout was underway. Among the most important of the politically active environmental groups were the Club of Rome (founded in 1972) and the German Greens. In 1979, the Greens formed a political party that quickly appealed to a significant number of German voters. Non-European governments and UN agencies also began to take up environmental issues.

Several developments focused the public's attention on the environment. The 1973–1974 Arab oil embargo alerted Europeans to the extent to which their lifestyle depended on imports of natural resources that were in limited supply. At the same time, the dire environmental consequences of three decades of economic expansion were becoming impossible to ignore. Industrial pollution was eliminating fish from major river systems, and acid rain was killing forests. The Cold War's nuclear threat and descriptions of the nightmares that would follow accidents at nuclear reactors also began to have an effect on voters.

The German **Green movement** recruited many of its members from the radical student groups of the late 1960s. It was anticapitalistic and condemned the business community for promoting pollution. It was peace oriented and opposed to nuclear armaments. Unlike the earlier student groups, however, the Greens opted to compete in the electoral process rather than employ mass demonstrations to agitate for changes in government policies. The Greens have had modest success, winning seats in the German parliament and on some local councils.

The 1986 meltdown of nuclear reactors at Chernobyl in the Soviet Union raised environmental issues that no government in Europe could ignore. Many deaths and injuries occurred, and the Soviet authorities had to relocate tens of thousands of people. Clouds of radioactive fallout spread across Europe, posing a widespread threat to human health and food supplies. Chernobyl demonstrated how environmental issues transcend national borders, and it prompted action by governments in both the East and the West. Environmental groups now command a significant share of votes, and as the European Economic Community solidifies, it will likely impose environmental regulations on business and industry. The nations of Eastern Europe face a particularly daunting challenge. The industrial development of the communist era created major environmental degradation that they must address while simultaneously trying to catch up economically with their Western neighbors.

ART SINCE WORLD WAR II

lthough brief coverage of the expansive, varied world of Western art since World War II is impossible, it is useful to note how the Second World War, as well as the Cold War, influenced artistic trends.

CULTURAL DIVISIONS AND THE COLD WAR

The Soviet painter Tatjiana Yablonskaya's (b. 1917) sun-strewn *Bread* (1949) and the American Jackson Pollock's (1912–1956) abstract *One* (Number 31, 1950) were painted only one year apart, yet they are starkly different. Their styles of realism and abstraction mirror the cultural divisions of the Cold War.

Bread is a monumental example of **socialist realism**, the official doctrine of Soviet art and literature that sought to create figurative, traditional, optimistic, and easily intelligible scenes of a bold socialist future of prosperity and solidarity. Socialist realism was the dominant Soviet model beginning in 1934 and spread throughout Eastern Europe until the late 1950s when Nikita Khrushchev liberalized Soviet cultural policy.

WHAT KIND of artistic styles arose in the mid and late twentieth century?

Green movement Made up, in part, of members from the radical student groups of the 1960s, this movement was anticapitalistic, peace oriented, in opposition of nuclear arms, and condemned business for producing pollution. Unlike earlier student groups, though, the Greens opted to compete in the electoral process.

socialist realism Doctrine of Soviet art and literature that sought to create figurative, traditional, optimistic, and easily intelligible scenes of a bold socialist future of prosperity and solidarity.

Tatjiana Yablonskaya, *Bread*, 1949.

Ria Novosti/Sovfoto/Eastfoto

The Copenhagen Opera House opened in Copenhagen, Denmark, in 2005. The structure has come to symbolize free enterprise in the European Union because its full cost was covered by private, rather than government, funding.

AP Wide World Photos

Whiteread's *Nameless Library* in Vienna commemorates the thousands of Austrian Jews killed in the Nazi Holocaust.

Rachel Whiteread, "Untitled (Library)," 1999. Dental plastere, polystyrene, fiberboard and steel, 112-$\frac{1}{2}$ × 210-$\frac{5}{8}$ inches. Hirshhorn Museum and Sculpture Garden, Smithsonian Institution, Joseph H. Hirshhorn Purchase Fund, 2000. Photo: Lee Stalsworth

HOW HAS the Christian heritage of the West been affected by events of the twentieth century?

Pollock's *One* (Number 31, 1950) is completely different and embodies American postwar cultural freedom. Flinging paint from sticks and brushes onto his floor-bound canvas, Pollock freed his lines from representing any figure or outline. His exuberant "drip" paintings are a tangle of visual energy. Skeptical viewers question the merits of such abstract art, yet it is the antithesis of the official style of socialist realism.

New York City—not Paris—emerged as the international center of modern art after World War II, a position it retains today. New York is the home of growing collections of twentieth-century art and dozens of European artists who had fled from the Nazis. The United States, and New York in particular, influenced cultural developments throughout the world.

MEMORY OF THE HOLOCAUST

The work of British sculptor Rachel Whiteread (b. 1963), one of today's leading European artists, illustrates how European art is breaking out of the modernist contours set in the early twentieth century. Whiteread's art returns to familiar forms, even as it compels viewers to see these forms in new ways. It is associated with the minimalist movement, which, through understatement, removes as many features as possible from the object being portrayed, while still retaining the object's form and the viewer's interest. Whiteread's art is austere yet expresses melancholy and loss.

Whiteread's recent work includes large sculptures such as a cast of the interior space of an entire house that was about to be torn down in London. She left the work untitled, but it became known as *House*. The sculpture represents an interior that is solid yet temporary. In fact, the sculpture itself was razed, like the actual house itself, as part of an urban redevelopment plan.

Her most important public work is *Nameless Library*, the Judenplatz Holocaust Memorial in Vienna, which commemorates the deaths of 65,000 Austrian Jews under the Nazis. Resembling a vast haunting tomb, the concrete work shows an outline of books whose spines are turned inward, forever unable to be opened or read. They symbolize the loss both of Jewish contributions to culture and of Jewish lives in the Holocaust.

THE CHRISTIAN HERITAGE

Christianity has been hard pressed during the twentieth century. Material prosperity, political ideologies, environmentalism, gender politics, and simple indifference have replaced religious faith for many people. Europe's Christian churches, however, still exercise considerable influence. In Germany during World War II, churches were among the few institutions not wholly subdued by the Nazis. In Poland and elsewhere in Eastern Europe after the war, the Roman Catholic Church kept opposition to communism alive, and religious affiliation still provides a basis for Christian democratic parties in Western Europe. The thought that Westerners have given to serious issues, such as colonial exploitation, nuclear weapons, human rights, and ethics, owes much to their churches.

NEO-ORTHODOXY

The rational optimism that characterized intellectual life in the nineteenth century encouraged liberal theologians of that era to deemphasize sin and portray human nature as not far removed from divinity. The horror of World War I destroyed illusions about human perfectability and produced "neo-Orthodox" theologians who reminded Christians of the power of evil and the human predilection for self-destructive behavior.

Karl Barth (1886–1968), a Swiss pastor and theologian, was among the most influential of the new neo-Orthodox thinkers. In *A Commentary on the Epistle to the Romans* (1919), he described Christian faith as springing from a sense of God's transcendence and humanity's utter dependence. Barth described God as "wholly other," as a reality encountered in the extreme moments of life when people are forced to confront their insufficiencies. Barth was in a sense returning to the Protestant theology of the Reformation era, but viewing it through Kierkegaard's existentialist philosophy.

LIBERAL THEOLOGY

Neo-Orthodoxy provided an alternative to, but did not replace, the liberal tradition in Christian theology. Liberalism's major spokesman was Paul Tillich (1886–1965), a German American. Where Barth emphasized the gulf between God and humanity, Tillich believed the divine was to be found at work in human nature and culture. A similar critique of supernaturalism as a basis for Christian faith is found in Rudolf Bultmann's (1884–1976) brilliant analysis of the development of the Christian Scriptures. *Honest to God* (1963), a book by Anglican bishop John Robinson, popularized Bultmann's work for lay audiences, and another British liberal Christian, the literary scholar C. S. Lewis (1878–1963), attracted millions of readers with amusing and accessible explications of doctrine (notably, *The Screwtape Letters*). In recent years, however, Europe has produced few important Protestant thinkers.

ROMAN CATHOLIC REFORM

The most significant postwar developments for institutionalized Christianity have involved the Roman Catholic Church. In 1959, Pope John XXIII (r. 1958–1963) called the Twenty-First Ecumenical Council, popularly known as Vatican II. By 1965, the council had carried out the most extensive reform of Catholicism that has taken place, some would say, since the sixteenth century. Catholic liturgy was rewritten, and the mass was offered to the people in their own languages instead of Latin. The papacy authorized freer interactions with other Christian denominations, granted bishops more power, and appointed cardinals from former European colonies to make the church more representative of the world.

Throughout his pontificate John Paul II continued a close relationship with his native Poland, to which he made several visits. The earliest of these was important in demonstrating the authority of the church against Polish communist authorities. Shown here in his Polish visit of June, 1999, the Pope would celebrate mass before several hundred thousand Poles after the collapse of communism, which had occurred a decade earlier.

AP Wide World Photos

Although Pope John and his successors have endorsed some liberal reforms, they have rejected others. They have retained celibacy vows for priests, prohibited contraception, and opposed ordination for women. These doctrines have caused resentment among some laity, led to defection of some clergy, and hampered recruitment of men for the priesthood. The prohibition of contraception has widely been ignored in the West.

In 1978, Karol Wojtyla (1920–2005), the archbishop of Cracow, ascended the papal throne and took the name John Paul II. Although he was the youngest pope to be elected in more than a century, he defended traditional doctrines, stressed the authority of the papacy, and curtailed doctrinal and liturgical experimentation. His strong opposition to communism, however, helped rally the popular forces that brought down Eastern Europe's communist governments,

QUICK REVIEW

Pope John Paul II

- 1978: Karol Wojtyla, archbishop of Cracow, becomes Pope John Paul II
- Defended traditional doctrines, stressed papal authority, and opposed doctrinal and liturgical experimentation
- Worked hard to promote church in non-Western nations

WHAT IMPACT has the computer had on twentieth-century society?

and he worked hard to promote the church in the non-Western world. He campaigned for social justice but limited the political activities of priests.

Roman Catholicism's expansion beyond Europe and North America is contributing to the transformation of Christianity as a world religion. Practice of the faith declined in Europe during the twentieth century but grew rapidly in Africa and Latin America. Within a few years, over half of all Christians will live in the Southern Hemisphere. Cardinals from that part of the world nearly constitute a majority in the College of Cardinals that selects the popes.

The German Cardinal Joseph Ratzinger (b. 1927) became pope in 2005, taking the name Benedict XVI. He is expected to continue the conservative theological and cultural policies of John Paul II.

LATE TWENTIETH-CENTURY TECHNOLOGY: THE ARRIVAL OF THE COMPUTER

During the twentieth century, American technologies, like American popular culture, freely crossed international borders and contributed to the impact that the United States has had on Europe. No single American technological achievement, however, promises to exert a greater influence on life in Europe and elsewhere than the computer.

THE DEMAND FOR CALCULATING MACHINES

In the seventeenth century, Blaise Pascal (1623–1662) and other thinkers associated with the scientific revolution began to experiment with machines that would ease the labor of mathematical calculation. Demand for such inventions increased during the nineteenth century as the expanding responsibilities of nation-states necessitated the collection and management of vast amounts of data. The growth of industry and commercial enterprises added to the market for calculating devices, which the development of complex electrical circuitry finally made possible. Other inventions dependent on electricity (the telephone, telegraph, and wireless) further increased the need for machines to organize large databases and manage customer accounts. By the late 1920s, companies like National Cash Register, Remington Rand, and International Business Machines Corporation had begun to manufacture a variety of such machines.

The earliest computers were very large. Here in a 1946 photograph J. Presper Eckert and J.W. Mauchly stand by the Electronic Numerical Integrator and Computer (ENIAC), which was dedicated at the University of Pennsylvania Moore School of Electrical Engineering.

CORBIS/Bettmann

EARLY COMPUTER TECHNOLOGY

The military did much to spur the development of calculator technology. Following World War I and during World War II, the major powers developed bombers and long-range guns that depended on precise ballistic calculations. The first machine that might legitimately be considered a digital computer, ENIAC (Electronic Numerical Integrator and Computer), was designed and built at the University of Pennsylvania in 1946. It was an enormous piece of equipment that utilized 1,500 electric relays, 18,000 vacuum tubes, and thousands of punch cards.

THE DEVELOPMENT OF DESKTOP COMPUTERS

The invention of the **transistor** in the 1950s revolutionized electronics by miniaturizing circuitry and making the vacuum tube obsolete. This reduced the size of computers, but throughout the 1950s and 1960s, they still had to be programmed with difficult "languages" by persons expertly trained to use them.

transistor Miniaturized electronics circuitry making the vacuum tube obsolete.

In the 1960s, computing technology was transformed yet again. Direction for the control of a computer was transferred to a bitmap covering the screen of its monitor, and in 1964 the "mouse" was invented to ease the movement of the cursor around the computer's screen. The bitmap on the screen hid a complicated computer language behind simple images that a user could manipulate with the mouse. This innovation made it possible for people who were not elaborately trained experts to learn to operate computers. The invention of the microchip—the heart of current computers—by a California start-up company called Intel Corporation imbeded a microprocessor in each computer that freed it from linkage to a mainframe. Xerox Corporation was the first to devise a small computer controlled by a mouse, but the machine was not a commercial success. By 1982, IBM (International Business Machines Corporation) had also produced a small computer, but in marketing its invention it lagged behind a company called Apple Computer Corporation. In 1984, the Apple engineers adapted the Xerox design to create the Macintosh, a highly accessible computer that would fit on a desktop in a home or office. IBM then reengineered its machine and produced the PC (Personal Computer). By the mid–1980s, ordinary people, for a modest cost, could acquire computers that were more powerful than the great mainframes of the 1950s and 1960s. As these computers became increasingly common, everyday life was radically transformed.

Computers are potentially democratizing, but access to them has defined old distinctions between "have" and "have-not" societies in new ways. Computers, for good and ill, give their users the ability to do things that nonusers cannot do. People who do not have the opportunity to master them are severely handicapped as they try to make their way in the world's increasingly computerized economies. Nations whose governments and businesses are not fully integrated into the world of computers will compete at a serious disadvantage. The possession of computers and the ability to use them is, in many arenas, the key to the future.

THE CHALLENGES OF EUROPEAN UNIFICATION

*P*ostwar Europe's greatest political success story is the progress it has made toward political and economic cooperation. This was driven by American encouragement, fear of Soviet expansion, and awareness of Europe's declining influence in the global arena.

WHAT LED to Western European unification following World War II?

POSTWAR COOPERATION

Economic cooperation offered the easiest route to European unification, for it entailed little loss of political sovereignty and produced material benefits that won popular support for pan-European programs. In 1951, France, West Germany, Italy, and the "Benelux" countries (Belgium, the Netherlands, and Luxembourg) initiated a new era of economic cooperation among European states by organizing the European Coal and Steel Community. Its success allayed the doubts about the benefits of economic integration that had been harbored by politicians and business leaders.

THE EUROPEAN ECONOMIC COMMUNITY

The diplomatic isolation of France and Britain that followed their unsuccessful Suez intervention persuaded many politicians that unified action was needed if Europe hoped to retain independence of the superpowers. In 1957, the six members of the Coal and Steel Community signed the Treaty of Rome and formed a new organization, the **European Economic Community (EEC)**. The

European Economic Community (EEC) European nations as members of the "Common Market" pledging to eliminate traiffs, guarantee unimpeded flow of capital and labor, and establish uniform wage scales and social benefits.

members of the Common Market, as the EEC soon came to be called, pledged to eliminate tariffs, guarantee unimpeded flow of capital and labor, and establish uniform wage scales and social benefits.

The Common Market was stunningly successful. By 1968, well ahead of schedule, all tariffs affecting trade among its six members had been abolished. As trade increased and blocks to migration of workers were removed, other countries began to copy the community or consider joining it. In 1959, Britain, Denmark, Norway, Sweden, Switzerland, Austria, and Portugal formed the European Free Trade Area, and by 1961, Great Britain had decided to seek Common Market membership. Twice, in 1963 and 1967, France, under de Gaulle, vetoed British membership, claiming Britain was too closely tied to the United States to support the EEC whole-heartedly. In 1973, Great Britain, Ireland, and Denmark were finally admitted, but in the late 1970s the growth of the EEC slowed. Norway and Sweden, whose economies were relatively strong, declined to join. In 1982, Spain, Portugal, and Greece applied for membership and were eventually admitted, but sharp disagreements and a sense of stagnation began to characterize the EEC.

THE EUROPEAN UNION

Early in 1988, the leaders of the EEC announced a decision that ended a decade of drift. They set 1992 as the year in which their community would become a free trade zone. In 1991, the Treaty of Maastricht endorsed a common currency and a central bank. Some member states staged referendums seeking their citizens' ratification of the treaty. The Danes rejected it, and its narrow passage in France and Great Britain made clear it could not be enforced without winning wider popular support. In 1993, the EEC was renamed the **European Union (EU)**. Its most notable achievement has been the launching of the **euro** in 1999, which by 2002 had become the single circulating currency in most of Western Europe. In May 2004, the European Union added ten new nations, bringing its membership to twenty-five. (See Map 30–1.) Although membership indicated that a nation had achieved economic stability and genuinely democratic institutions, several new member states from the former Soviet bloc are relatively poor and will require much economic support from the Union.

On Friday May 27, 2005, two days before the vote on France's referendum on the EU constitution, a woman stands between a "yes" and a "no" campaign poster in a street of Rennes, western France.

AP Wide World Photos

DISCORD OVER THE UNION

European integration may have reached its high point during the expansion in 2004, when leaders of the member nations adopted a new constitutional treaty for the Union. Known as the **European Constitution**, this treaty is a long, complicated document that would have transferred considerable decision-making authority from governments of the individual states to the Union's central institutions mostly located in Brussels, Luxembourg, and Strasbourg. Either through parliamentary vote or national referendum, all members had to ratify the constitution to put it into effect.

Many in the European elite were surprised in the spring of 2005 when referendums in France and the Netherlands heavily defeated the treaty. As a result Britain, always lukewarm about integration, postponed its referendum and support for the treaty, and support in other nations declined.

Several factors appear to have brought about this crisis for the European Union. First, European political elites have presided over a growing gap between themselves and the voting public. Second, voting against the treaty was a way to protest against the

European Union (EU)   Formerly the European Economic Community (EEC), renamed in 1993.

euro   Launched in 1999 by the EU, a single currency circulating in most of Western Europe.

European Constitution   Treaty that would transfer considerable decision-making authority from governments of the individual states to the Union's central institutions.

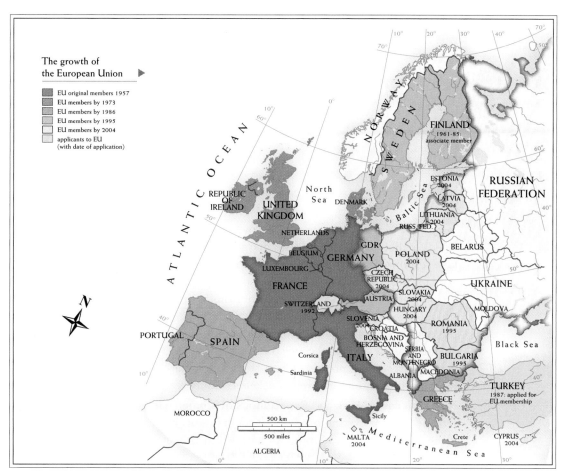

MAP 30–1

The Growth of the European Union   The six-member EEC that was established in 1957 added three members in 1973, and three more in the 1980s. The fall of the Berlin Wall in 1989 and the end of the Cold War led to further EU enlargement into Eastern Europe.

GIVEN THE political, social, historical, and demographic differences among its member states, how successful will EU enlargement and integration be?

stagnating Western European economy and high unemployment. Third, many smaller member states have felt that France and Germany have taken them for granted. Fourth, some nations believe their former national currencies were converted into Euros at an economic disadvantage. Fifth, many people are increasingly reluctant to cede national sovereignty to the central bureaucracy.

Finally, the issue of Turkey's admission as a member state has provided more reason for skeptics to oppose integration. By admitting Turkey, Europe would have to integrate a population larger and poorer than any other member state, placing enormous social and economic burdens on the other states. Furthermore, even though Turkey's government has consistently been adamantly secular, the overwhelmingly Muslim population of Turkey worries Europeans who are concerned about the political, economic, and social implications of Europe's already significant Muslim population.

It is unlikely that European integration will be halted or reversed, but the future development of the European Union will likely occur much more slowly. Member states will have to carry out complicated negotiations and endure bitter debates over social and economic policies.

IMAGE KEY
for pages 746–747

a. A gas mask

b. Many people stand around a huge Euro symbol in a park in Frankfurt's banking district in Germany, Friday, January 1, 1999

c. Jose Bove supporter. June 30, 2000

d. Dolly, the world's first cloned sheep

e. Cellular phone

f. Ayatollah Khomeini addressing an enthusiastic crowd

g. Osman Yagli and his family. Yagli is one of the 30,000 Turkish "Guest Workers" living in West Berlin

h. Multi-ethnic group of three pre-K girls plays with large Lego blocks outside at preschool

i. Computer mouse

j. Pope John Paul II and Cuban President Fidel Castro

k. Cherie Blair during the conference for women lawyers of Great Britain

SUMMARY

The Twentieth-Century Movement of Peoples Significant numbers of people relocated in Europe during the twentieth century. Millions of Europeans also emigrated, European colonials returned from overseas, and non-European peoples migrated to the former colonial powers. Europe's immigrant Muslim communities are often segregated, poorly assimilated, and discriminated against. The declining European birthrate will undoubtedly have profound consequences for future developments.

Toward a Welfare State Society After World War II, most Western European nations endorsed principles of liberal democracy, and many Europeans wanted their governments to take responsibility for ensuring prosperity and social security. Christian Democratic parties took the lead in introducing new policies. A Labour Party ministry introduced universal health care in Britain in 1945, and welfare legislation spread across Western Europe. Through the postwar reconstruction period and the quarter century that followed many Europeans endorsed government management of the economy. Since then, confidence in free markets has grown, and some social welfare programs have been scaled back. Margaret Thatcher was the foremost proponent of a freer market economy.

New Patterns in Work and Expectations of Women Gender inequality persists in Europe, despite expanding economic and political roles for women. Recent feminism has focused on helping women as individuals take control of their lives. European women now have fewer children and more time to develop careers. Abortion has been widely available. Women in Eastern Europe are adapting to free-market, democratic systems.

Transformations in Knowledge and Culture Most Western European intellectuals have become disillusioned with Soviet communism. Interest in Existentialism, a philosophy that questions rationalism, has been encouraged by distrust of the pride in rational achievement that has produced so much suffering and warfare. Social concerns prompted student rebellions in the 1960s, and the economic and military influence of the United States has threatened European culture.

Art Since World War II The Second World War and the Cold War influenced art in the twentieth century. Socialist realism was the dominant official form of art in the Soviet Union and communist bloc, while abstract art, like that of Jackson Pollock, reflected postwar cultural freedom in the West. Minimalist art returns to familiar forms while it compels new ways of viewing the objects being portrayed.

The Christian Heritage Christian churches have continued to be influential even in an increasingly secularized Europe. The Roman Catholic Church changed significantly under Pope John XXIII, but subsequent papacies have been more traditionalist and have furthered the spread of Christianity as a world religion.

Late Twentieth-Century Technology: The Arrival of the Computer Most of the development work for computers was done in the United States and Britain. Calculating machines started to become available in the 1920s. The U.S. Army used the first digital computer, ENIAC, for ballistics computations starting in 1946. By the 1980s, IBM and Apple Computer Corporation were producing desktop computers.

The Challenges of European Unification Economic unification was easier for European nations than military or political union. In 1951 six nations formed the European Coal and Steel Community, which in 1957 became the European Economic Community or the Common Market. In 1973 membership was increased, and in 1998 the EEC created a free-trade zone. In 1999 a common currency was decreed, and the EEC was renamed the European Union. Its euro became the currency of most of Western Europe in 2001. In 2004, the European Union admitted ten more member nations, but discord spread over the details of a constitution designed to regulate relations among members.

REVIEW QUESTIONS

1. How did migration affect twentieth-century social life in Europe? In what ways was Europe "Americanized" in the second half of the century?

2. How and why did European attitudes toward the welfare state and free-market economics change from the end of World War II to the dawn of the twenty-first century?

3. How did women's social and economic roles change in the second half of the twentieth century? What problems have new patterns of work created for women?

4. How did the pursuit and diffusion of knowledge change during the twentieth century? In what sense was existentialism a response to the crises of the twentieth century?

5. What kind of artistic styles arose in the mid and late twentieth century and how did World War II and the Cold War influence those styles?

6. How did western Christian theology develop in the twentieth century? What changes are computers most likely to bring?

7. How did the nations of Western Europe move toward economic and political unity? What challenges face further European integration?

KEY TERMS

Christian Democratic parties   (p. 749)   **European Union**   (p. 762)   **socialist realism**   (p. 757)
Euro   (p. 762)   **existentialism**   (p. 754)   **transistor**   (p. 760)
European Constitution   (p. 762)   **Green movement**   (p. 757)
European Economic Community
   (EEC)   (p. 761)

   For additional study resources for this chapter, go to:
www.prenhall.com/kagan3/chapter30

Visualizing The Past...

Identity and Nationalism in Contemporary Europe

HOW HAS nationalism and identity affected the recent political history of Europe?

The resounding defeat of the referendum on a European Constitution by the voters of France in the summer of 2005 highlights the inherent conflict between the vision of a united Europe and the desire for increased national, ethnic, and linguistic autonomy. While the success of the euro has become a ubiquitous symbol of European unity, equally significant developments across the continent reveal the complicated relationship between identity and nationhood.

▲
Devolution

While the political history of Europe of the last twenty years has witnessed the dramatic breakup of the Soviet Union, the disintegration of Yugoslavia, and the splintering of Czechoslovakia into two countries, "devolution"—the transfer of power from central governments to local units–has made an equally significant impact in Belgium, Germany, Spain, Italy, and the United Kingdom. In September 1997 the people of Scotland, by an overwhelming majority, voted in favor of a separatist Scottish parliament. The parliament can legislate on a range of domestic issues, such as education and health, and has the power to modify the basic rate of income tax. Though Scotland remains an integral part of the United Kingdom, as evidenced in this photograph by the presence of the Queen of England at the opening of the Scottish parliament, its citizens enjoy a high degree of autonomy.

Donald McLeod-POOL/AP Wide World Photos

Revolution ▶

The breakup of the Soviet Union in the early 1990s did not end the desire among the peoples of Eastern Europe for freedom and self expression. In November 2003, the people of Georgia, frustrated by years of corruption and poor government, protested the rigging of elections by then president Eduard Shevardnadze and deposed him in a bloodless "rose revolution." Here, Georgian children, dressed in national costume, and waving the new flag of Georgia, chant anti-Shevardnadze slogans (photo a). Georgia's revolution inspired the "orange revolution" that swept Ukraine in late 2004 and early 2005 in which then president Alexander Lukashenko, a pro-Russian leader accused of falsifying elections, was ousted by supporters of the Western-backed Victor Yuschenko (photo b).

(a) Sergei Supinsky/Agence France Presse/Getty Images

(b) AP Wide World Photos

◀ **Making History**

In September 2005, Angela Merkel, the leader of the Christian Democratic Union party in Germany, narrowly defeated Gerhard Schroeder to become the first woman chancellor of Germany. Merkel, who grew up in East Germany, also became the first person from the former Communist state to lead Germany. Her historic victory thus marks a new era in German politics, which has long been dominated by men and by power brokers from the much more prosperous western half of the country.
AP Wide World Photos

Europe in Transition 1300–1750

1300–1648   1648–1781

POLITICS AND GOVERNMENT

1309–1377 Popes reside in Avignon
1337–1453 Hundred Years' War
1356 *Golden Bull* creates German electoral college
1455–1485 Wars of the Roses in England
1519 Charles V crowned Holy Roman Emperor
1555 Peace of Augsburg recognizes the legal principle, *cuius regio, eius religio*
1558–1603 Reign of Elizabeth I of England
1572 Saint Bartholomew's Day Massacre
1588 English defeat of Spanish Armada
1598 Edict of Nantes gives Huguenots religious and civil rights
1624–1642 Era of Richelieu in France
1642 Outbreak of civil war in England

1648 Peace of Westphalia
1649–1652 The *Fronde* in France
1649 Charles I executed
1660 Charles II restored to the English throne
1661–1715 Louis XIV's years of personal rule
1682–1725 Reign of Peter the Great
1685 Louis XIV revokes Edict of Nantes
1688 "Glorious Revolution" in Britain
1700–1721 Great Northern War between Sweden and Russia
1701–1714 War of Spanish Succession
1740–1748 War of the Austrian Succession
1756–1763 Seven Years' War
1772 First Partition of Poland
1776 American Declaration of Independence

SOCIETY AND ECONOMY

1347–1350 Peak of Black Death
1450 Johann Gutenberg invents printing with movable type
1492 Christopher Columbus encounters the Americas
1498 Vasco da Gama reaches India
1519–1522 Ferdinand Magellan circumnavigates the Earth
1525 German Peasants' Revolt
1540 Spanish open silver mines in Peru, Bolivia, and Mexico
1550–1600 The great witch panics
1600–1700 Period of greatest Dutch economic prosperity
1607 English settle Jamestown, Virginia
1608 French settle Quebec
1618–1648 Thirty Years' War devastates German economy

1619 African slaves first bought at Jamestown, Virginia
1661–1683 Colbert seeks to stimulate French economic growth
1719 Mississippi Bubble in France
1750s Agricultural Revolution in Britain
1763 Britain becomes dominant in India
1763–1789 Enlightened absolutist rulers seek to spur economic growth
1765 James Hargreaves's spinning jenny
1769 Richard Arkwright's waterframe

RELIGION AND CULTURE

1300–1325 Dante Alghieri writes *Divine Comedy*
1302 Boniface VIII issues bull *Unam Sanctam*
1375–1527 The Renaissance in Italy
1378–1417 The Great Schism
1390–1430 Christine de Pisan writes in defense of women
1492 Expulsion of Jews from Spain
1513 Niccolo Machiavelli, *The Prince*
1516 Thomas More, *Utopia*
1517 Martin Luther's *Ninety-five Theses*
1534 Henry VIII declared head of English Church
1540 Jesuit order founded
1541 John Calvin becomes Geneva's reformer
1543 Copernicus, *On the Revolutions of the Heavenly Spheres*
1545–1563 Council of Trent

1549 English *Book of Common Prayer*
1609 Kepler, *The New Astronomy*
1632 Galileo, *Dialogue on the Two Chief Systems of the World*
1637 Descartes, *Discourse on Method*
1651 Hobbes, *Leviathan*
1687 Newton, *Principia Mathematica*
1689 English Toleration Act
1690 Locke, *Essay Concerning Human Understanding*
1748 Montesquieu, *Spirit of the Laws*
1751 First volume Diderot's *Encyclopedia*
1762 Rousseau, *Social Contract* and *Émile*
1763 Voltaire, *Treatise on Tolerance*
1774 Goethe, *The Sorrows of Young Werther*
1776 Smith, *Wealth of Nations*
1781 Kant, *Critique of Pure Reason*

Enlightenment and Revolution 1700-1850

1713–1824

1809–1848

POLITICS AND GOVERNMENT

1713 Treaty of Utrecht	**1804** Napoleonic Code; Napoleon crowned emperor
1713–1740 Frederick William I builds Prussian military	**1805** Third Coalition formed against France, battles of Trafalgar and Austerlitz
1720–1740 Walpole in England, Fleury in France	**1806** Napoleon establishes the Continental System
1740–1748 War of the Austrian Succession	**1808** Spanish resistance to Napoleon stiffens
1756–1763 Seven Years' War	**1812** Napoleon invades Russia; meets defeat
1772 First Partition of Poland	**1814** Congress of Vienna opens
1775–1783 American Revolution	**1815** Napoleon defeated at Waterloo
1789 Gathering of the Estates General at Versailles; fall of the Bastille, Declaration of the Rights of Man and Citizen	**1821** Greek Revolution begins
1793 Louis XVI executed, Second Partition of Poland	**1825** Decembrist Revolt in Russia
1793–1794 Reign of Terror	**1829** Catholic Emancipation Act in Great Britain
1795 Third Partition of Poland	**1830** Revolution in France, Belgium, and Poland, Serbia gains independence
1799 Napoleon named First Consul in France	**1832** Great Reform Bill in Britain
	1848 Revolutions sweep across Europe

SOCIETY AND ECONOMY

1733 James Kay's flying shuttle	**1810** Abolition of serfdom in Prussia
1750s Agricultural Revolution in Britain	**1825** Stockton and Darlington Railway opens
1763 British establish dominance in India	**1828–1850** First European police departments
1763–1789 Enlightened absolutist rulers seek to spur economic growth	**1833** English Factory Act to protect children
1765 James Hargreaves's spinning jenny	**1834** German Zollverein established
1769 Richard Arkwright's waterframe	**1846** Corn Laws repealed in Britain
1773–1775 Pugachev's Rebellion	**1848** Serfdom abolished in Austria and Hungary
1787 Edmund Cartwright's power loom	
1789–1802 Revolutionary legislation restructures French political and economic life	
1794–1824 Wars of independence in Latin America break the colonial system	

RELIGION AND CULTURE

1721 Montesquieu, *Persian Letters*	**1790** Civil Constitution of the Clergy; Burke, *Reflections on the Revolution in France*
1733 Voltaire, *Letters on the English*	**1792** Wollstonecraft, *Vindication of the Rights of Woman*
1738 Voltaire, *Elements of the Philosophy of Newton*	**1802** Napoleon, *Concordat with the Papacy*
1739 Wesley begins field preaching	**1806** Hegel, *Phenomenology of Mind*
1748 Hume, *Inquiry into Human Nature*	**1807** Fichte, *Addresses to the German Nation*
1748 Montesquieu, *Spirit of the Laws*	**1808** Goethe, *Faust*, Part I
1751 First volume of Diderot's *Encyclopedia*	**1817** Ricardo, *Principles of Political Economy*
1762 Rousseau, *The Social Contract* and *Émile*	**1819** Byron, *Don Juan*
1763 Voltaire, *Treatise on Tolerance*	**1829** Catholic Emancipation Act in Great Britain
1774 Goethe, *The Sorrows of Young Werther*	**1830–1842** Comte, *The Positive Philosophy*
1776 Smith, *Wealth of Nations*	**1830** Lyell, *Principles of Geology*
1779 Lessing, *Nathan the Wise*	**1843** Kierkegaard, *Fear and Trembling*
1781 Joseph II adopts toleration in Austria	**1848** Marx and Engels, *Communist Manifesto*
1781 Kant, *The Critique of Pure Reason*	

STUDY IN TIME

A Chronological Survey of Western Civilization

The Middle Ages 476 C.E.–1300 C.E.

476 C.E.–843 C.E.

850 C.E.–1275 C.E.

POLITICS AND GOVERNMENT

330	Constantinople becomes new capital of Roman Empire
410	Visigoths sack Rome
451–453	Attila the Hun invades Italy
455	Vandals overrun Rome
476	Odovacer deposes the last Western emperor
489–493	Theodoric's Ostrogoth kingdom established in Italy
527–565	Reign of Justinian
568	Lombard invasion of Italy
632–733	Muslim expansion and conquests
732	Charles Martel defeats Muslims at Poitiers
768–814	Reign of Charlemagne
843	Treaty of Verdun partitions Carolingian empire

918	Saxon Henry I becomes first non-Frankish king in Germany
987	Capetians succeed Carolingians in France
1066	Battle of Hastings (Norman Conquest of England)
1071	Seljuk Turks defeat Byzantine armies at Manzikert
1099	Jerusalem falls to Crusaders
1152	Frederick I Barbarossa first Hohenstaufen emperor
1187	Saladin reconquers Jerusalem from West
1204	Fourth Crusade captures Constantinople
1214	Philip II Augustus defeats English and German armies at Bouvines
1215	*Magna Carta*
1240	Mongols dominate Russia
1250	Death of Frederick II (end of Hohenstaufen dynasty)
1257	German princes establish electoral college to elect emperor

SOCIETY AND ECONOMY

400	Cities and trade begin to decline in the West; Germanic (barbarian) tribes settle in the West
533–534	*Corpus juris civilis* compiled by Justinian
632–733	Muslims disrupt western Mediterranean trade
700	Agrarian society centered around the manor predominates in the West
700–800	Moldboard plow and three-field system in use
700	Islam enters its Golden Age
800	Byzantium enters its Golden Age
800	Introduction of collar harness

850	Muslims occupy parts of Spain
880s	Vikings penetrate central Europe
900	Introduction of the horseshoe
900–1100	Rise of towns, guilds, and urban culture in West
1086	*Domesday Book*
1130	Gothic architecture begins to displace Romanesque
1200	Shift from dues to rent tenancy on manors

RELIGION AND CULTURE

312	Constantine embraces Christianity
325	Council of Nicaea
395	Christianity becomes the official religion of the Roman Empire
413–426	Saint Augustine writes *City of God*
451	Council of Chalcedon
496	The Franks embrace Christianity
529	Saint Benedict founds monastery at Monte Cassino
537	Byzantine Church of Hagia Sophia completed
590–604	Pope Gregory the Great
622	Muhammad's flight from Mecca (Hegira)
725–787	Iconoclastic Controversy in East
ca. 775	*Donation of Constantine*
782	Alcuin of York runs Charlemagne's palace school
800	Beginning of Carolingian Renaissance

910	Benedictine monastery of Cluny founded
980s	Orthodox Christianity penetrates Russia
1054	Schism between Eastern and Western churches
1075	Pope Gregory VII condemns lay investiture
1095	Pope Urban II preaches the First Crusade
1122	Concordat of Worms ends investiture controversy
1158	First European university founded in Bologna
1210	Franciscan order founded
1216	Dominican order founded
1265	Thomas Aquinas's *Summa Theologica* begun
ca. 1275	*Romance of the Rose*

Toward the Modern World 1850–1939

1850–1900

1900–1939

POLITICS AND GOVERNMENT

1854–1856 Crimean War
1861 Proclamation of the Kingdom of Italy
1867 Austro-Hungarian Dual Monarchy founded
1869 Suez Canal completed
1870 Franco-Prussian War; French Republic proclaimed
1871 German Empire proclaimed; Paris Commune
1880s Britain establishes Protectorate in Egypt
1882 Italy, Germany, Austria form Triple Alliance
1894 Dreyfus convicted in France; Nicholas II becomes tsar of Russia
1898 Germany begins to build a battleship navy
1904 Britain and France in Entente Cordiale
1908–1909 Bosnian crisis

1911 Second Moroccan crisis
1912 Third Irish Home Rule Bill passed
1912–1913 First and Second Balkan Wars
1914–1918 World War I
1917 Russian Revolution; Bolsheviks seize power
1919 Paris Peace Conference; Weimar constitution proclaimed in Germany
1922 Mussolini takes power in Italy
1923 France invades the Ruhr; Hitler's Beer Hall *Putsch*; first Labour government in Britain
1931 National Government formed in Great Britain
1933 Hitler appointed chancellor of Germany
1935 Nuremburg Laws; Italy invades Ethiopia
1936 Popular Front in France; purge trials in the Soviet Union; Spanish Civil War begins
1938 Munich Conference; *Kristallnacht* in Germany
1939 Germany invades Poland, starts World War II

SOCIETY AND ECONOMY

1850–1910 Height of European outward migration
1853–1870 Haussmann redesigns Paris
1857 Bessemer steelmaking process
1861 Serfdom abolished in Russia
1870 Education Act and first Irish Land Act, Britain
1875 Public Health and Artisan Dwelling Acts, Britain
1881 Second Irish Land Act
1886 Daimler invents internal combustion engine
1894 Union of German Women's Organizations founded
1901 National Council of French Women founded
1903 Third Irish Land Act; British Women's Social and Political Union founded; Wright brothers fly the first airplane

1906 Land redemption payments canceled for Russian peasants
1907 Women vote on national issues in Norway
1918 Vote granted to some British women
1921 Soviet Union begins New Economic Policy
1923 Rampant inflation in Germany
1926 General strike in Great Britain
1928 Britain extends full franchise to women
1928–1933 First Five-Year Plan and agricultural collectivization in the Soviet Union
1929 Wall Street crash
1932 Lausanne Conference ends German reparations
mid-1930s Nazis stimulate German economy through public works and defense spending

RELIGION AND CULTURE

1850–1880 Jewish emancipation in much of Europe
1853–1854 Gobineau, *Essay on the Inequality of the Human Races*
1857 Flaubert, *Madame Bovary*
1859 Darwin, *On the Origin of Species*
1864 Pius IX, *Syllabus of Errors*
1867 Mill, *The Subjection of Women*
1871 Darwin, *The Descent of Man*; Religious tests abolished at Oxford and Cambridge
1872 Nietzsche, *The Birth of Tragedy*
1873–1876 Bismarck's *Kulturkampf*
1879 Ibsen, *A Doll's House*
1880s Growing anti-Semitism in Europe
1880 Zola, *Nana*
1883 Nietzsche, *Thus Spake Zarathustra*
1892 Ibsen, *The Master Builder*
1896 Herzl, *The Jewish State*
1899 Bernstein, *Evolutionary Socialism*

1900 Freud, *The Interpretation of Dreams*; Key, *The Century of the Child*
1902 Lenin, *What Is to Be Done?*
1905 Weber, *The Protestant Ethic and the Spirit of Capitalism*; Termination of the Napoleonic Concordat in France
1910 Pope Pius X requires anti-Modernist oath
1920 Keynes, *Economic Consequences of the Peace*
1922 Joyce, *Ulysses*
1924 Hitler, *Mein Kampf*
1929 Woolf, *A Room of One's Own*
1936 Keynes, *General Theory of Employment, Interest, and Money*
1937 Orwell, *Road to Wigan Pier*
1938 Sartre, *Nausea*

Global Conflict, Cold War, and New Directions 1939–2005

1939–1980

1980–2005

POLITICS AND GOVERNMENT

1939 World War II begins
1941 Japan attacks Pearl Harbor, U.S. enters war
1942 Battle of Stalingrad
1945 Yalta Conference; Germany surrenders; atomic bombs dropped on Japan; Japan surrenders; United Nations founded
1947 Truman Doctrine
1948 Communist takeover in Czechoslovakia and Hungary; State of Israel proclaimed
1949 NATO founded; East and West Germany emerge as separate states
1950–1953 Korean War
1954 French defeat at Dien Bien Phu
1955 Warsaw Pact founded

1956 Khrushchev denounces Stalin; Suez crisis; Soviet invasion of Hungary
1961 Berlin Wall erected
1962 Cuban Missile Crisis
1963–1973 Major U.S. involvement in Vietnam
1968 Soviet invasion of Czechoslovakia
1975 Helsinki Accords
1979–1988 Soviet troops in Afghanistan
1985 Gorbachev comes to power in the Soviet Union
1989 Revolutions sweep across Eastern Europe
1990 German reunification; Yugoslavia breaks up
1991 Persian Gulf War; Soviet Union dissolved
2001 U.S. attacked by terrorists
2003 U.S. invades Iraq
2005 Angela Merkl becomes first female chancellor in German history

SOCIETY AND ECONOMY

1945–1951 Attlee ministry establishes the Welfare State in Great Britain
1947 Marshall Plan to rebuild Europe instituted
1949 Europe divided into Eastern and Western blocs
1957 European Economic Community founded
1960s Rapid growth of student population in universities; migration of workers from eastern and southern to northern and western Europe; migration of non-European workers to northern and western Europe
1972 Club of Rome founded
1973–1974 Arab oil embargo

1980s and 1990s Internal migration from Eastern to Western Europe; racial and ethnic tensions in Western Europe
1990s Changes in Eastern Europe and Soviet Union open way for economic growth and new trade relations across Europe

RELIGION AND CULTURE

1940 Koestler, *Darkness at Noon*
1943 Sartre, *Being and Nothingness*
1947 Camus, *The Plague*; Gramsci, *Letters from Prison*
1949 de Beauvoir, *The Second Sex*; Crossman, *The God That Failed*
1958 Pasternak forbidden to accept Nobel Prize for *Dr. Zhivago*; John XXIII becomes pope
1960s The Beatles take world by storm
1962–1965 Second Vatican Council
1963 Solzhenitsyn, *One Day in the Life of Ivan Denisovich*
1968 Student rebellion in Paris
1974 Solzhenitsyn expelled from Soviet Union

1978 John Paul II becomes pope
1980s Growth of the environmental movement
1990s Expanding influence of Roman Catholic Church in independent Eastern Europe
1990s Feminists continue the critical tradition of Western culture
1990s Era of the Internet begins
2005 Benedict XVI becomes pope

The Foundations of Western Civilization
in the Ancient World 1,000,000 B.C.E.–400 C.E.

1,000,000 B.C.E.–539 B.C.E.	750 B.C.E.–275 B.C.E.	431 B.C.E.–312 B.C.E.	46 B.C.E.–400 C.E.

POLITICS AND GOVERNMENT

2700–2200 B.C.E. Egyptian Old Kingdom	**612–539 B.C.E.** Neo-Babylonian (Chaldean) Empire	**338 B.C.E.** Philip of Macedon conquers Greece	**46–44 B.C.E.** Caesar's dictatorship
ca. 2370 B.C.E. Sargon established Akkadian Empire	**594 B.C.E.** Solon's constitutional reforms, Athens	**336–323 B.C.E.** Reign of Alexander III (the Great)	**43 B.C.E.** Second Triumvirate
2052–1786 B.C.E. Egyptian Middle Kingdom	**586 B.C.E.** Destruction of Jerusalem; fall of Judah (southern kingdom); Babylonian Captivity	**330 B.C.E.** Fall of Persepolis; end Achaemenid rule in Persia	**31 B.C.E.** Octavian and Agrippa defeat Anthony at Actium
1792–1750 B.C.E. Reign of Hammurabi; height of Old Babylonian Kingdom; publication of Code of Hammurabi	**559–530 B.C.E.** Reign of Cyrus the Great in Persia	**323–301 B.C.E.** Ptolemaic Kingdom (Egypt), Seleucid Kingdom (Syria), and Antigonid Dynasty (Macedon) founded	**27 B.C.E.–14 C.E.** Reign of Augustus
ca. 1700 B.C.E. Hyksos' Invasion of Egypt	**546 B.C.E.** Persia conquers Lydian Empire of Croesus, including Greek cities of Asia Minor	**287 B.C.E.** Laws passed by Plebeian Assembly made binding on all Romans; end of Struggle of the Orders	**14–68 C.E.** Reigns of Julio-Claudian Emperors
1575–1087 B.C.E. Egyptian New Kingdom (or Empire)	**539 B.C.E.** Persia conquers Babylonia; temple at Jerusalem restored; exiles return from Babylonia	**264–241 B.C.E.** First Punic War	**69–96 C.E.** Reigns of Flavian Emperors
ca. 1400–1200 B.C.E. Height of Hittite Empire	**521–485 B.C.E.** Reign of Darius in Persia	**218–202 B.C.E.** Second Punic War	**96–180 C.E.** Reigns of "Good Emperors"
ca. 1400–1200 B.C.E. Height of Mycenaean power	**509 B.C.E.** Kings expelled from Rome; Republic founded	**215–168 B.C.E.** Rome establishes rule over Hellenistic world	**284–305 C.E.** Reign of Diocletian; reform and division of Roman Empire
ca. 1100–615 B.C.E. Assyrian Empire	**508 B.C.E.** Clisthenes founds Athenian democracy	**133 B.C.E.** Tribunate of Tiberius Gracchus	**306–337 C.E.** Reign of Constantine
ca. 800–400 B.C.E. Height of Etruscan culture in Italy	**490 B.C.E.** Battle of Marathon	**123–122 B.C.E.** Tribunate of Gaius Gracchus	**330 C.E.** Constantinople new capital of Roman Empire
ca. 700–500 B.C.E. Rise and decline of tyranny in Greece	**480–479 B.C.E.** Xerxes invades Greece	**60 B.C.E.** First Triumvirate	**376 C.E.** Visigoths enter Roman Empire
	431–404 B.C.E. Great Peloponnesian War		
	392 B.C.E. Romans defeat Etruscans		
	362 B.C.E. Battle of Mantinea; end of Theban hegemony		

SOCIETY AND ECONOMY

ca. 1,000,000–10,000 B.C.E. Paleolithic Age	**ca. 750–700 B.C.E.** Rise of *Polis* in Greece	**431–400 B.C.E.** Peloponnesian War casualties cause decline in size of lower class in Athens, with relative increase in importance of upper and middle classes	**ca. 150–400 C.E.** Decline of slavery and growth of tenant farming and serfdom in Roman Empire
ca. 8,000 B.C.E. Earliest Neolithic settlements	**ca. 750–600 B.C.E.** Great age of Greek colonization	**ca. 300 B.C.E.–150 C.E.** Growth of international trade and development of large cities in Hellenistic/Roman world	**ca. 250–400 C.E.** *Coloni* (Roman tenant farmers) increasingly tied to the land
ca. 3500 B.C.E. Earliest Sumerian settlements			
ca. 3000 B.C.E. First urban settlements in Egypt and Mesopotamia; Bronze Age begins in Mesopotamia and Egypt			
ca. 2900–1150 B.C.E. Bronze Age Minoan society on Crete; Helladic society on Greek mainland			
ca. 2000 B.C.E. Hittites arrive in Asia Minor			
ca. 1200 B.C.E. Hebrews arrive in Palestine			
ca. 1100–750 B.C.E. Greek "Dark Ages"			

RELIGION AND CULTURE

ca. 30,000–6000 B.C.E. Paleolithic art	**ca. 500–400 B.C.E.** Great age of Athenian tragedy	**106–43 B.C.E.** Life of Cicero	**325 C.E.** Council of Nicaea
ca. 3000 B.C.E. Invention of writing	**469–399 B.C.E.** Life of Socrates	**70–19 B.C.E.** Life of Vergil	**348–420 C.E.** Life of St. Jerome
ca. 3000 B.C.E. Temples to gods in Mesopotamia; development of ziggurat temple architecture	**ca. 450–385 B.C.E.** Great age of Athenian comedy	**65–8 B.C.E.** Life of Horace	**354–430 C.E.** Life of St. Augustine
2700–2200 B.C.E. Building of pyramids for Egyptian god-kings, development of hieroglypic writing in Egypt	**448–432 B.C.E.** Periclean building program on Athenian acropolis	**59 B.C.E.–17 C.E.** Life of Livy	**395 C.E.** Christianity becomes official religion of Roman Empire
ca. 1900 B.C.E. Traditional date for Hebrew patriarch Abraham	**429–347 B.C.E.** Life of Plato	**43 B.C.E.–18 C.E.** Life of Ovid	
ca. 750 B.C.E. Hebrew prophets teach monotheism	**ca. 400 B.C.E.** Thucydides' history of the Peloponnesian War	**9 B.C.E.** Ara Pacis dedicated at Rome	
ca. 750 B.C.E. Traditional date for Homer	**384–322 B.C.E.** Life of Aristotle	**ca. 4 B.C.E.** Birth of Jesus of Nazareth	
ca. 750 B.C.E. Greeks adapt Semitic script and invent the Greek alphabet	**342–271 B.C.E.** Life of Epicurus	**ca. 30 C.E.** Crucifixion of Jesus	
ca. 570 B.C.E. Birth of Greek philosphy in Ionia	**335–263 B.C.E.** Life of Zeno the Stoic	**64 C.E.** Christians persecuted by Nero	
539 B.C.E. Restoration of temple in Jerusalem; return of exiles	**ca. 287–212 B.C.E.** Life of Archimedes of Syracuse	**ca. 70–100 C.E.** Gospels written	
	ca. 275 B.C.E. Founding of museum and library make Alexandria the center of Greek intellectual life	**ca. 150 C.E.** Ptolemy of Alexandria establishes canonical geocentric model of the universe	
		303 C.E. Persecution of Christians by Diocletian	
		312 C.E. Constantine converts to Christianity	

absolutism Government by a ruler with absolute authority.

Academy School founded by Plato in Athens to train statesmen and citizens.

Acropolis At the center of the city of Athens, the most famous example of a citadel.

Act of Supremacy Act of 1534 proclaiming Henry VIII "the only supreme head on earth of the Church of England."

agape Common meal, or "love feast," that was the central ritual of the church in early Christianity.

agora Place for markets and political assemblies.

Ahura Mazda The chief deity of Zoroastrianism, the native religion of Persia. Ahura Mazda is the creator of the world, the source of light, and the embodiment of good.

Albigensians Heretical sect that advocated a simple, pious way of life following the example set by Jesus and the Apostles, but rejecting key Christian doctrines.

Anabaptists ("rebaptizers") The most important of several groups of Protestants forming more radical organizations that sought a more rapid and thorough restoration of the "primitive Christianity" described in the New Testament.

anarchists Those who opposed any cooperation with industry or government.

anti-Semitism Prejudice against Jews often displayed through hostility.

Anschluss Union of Germany and Austria.

apostolic succession Special powers that were passed down from one generation of bishops to another.

appeasement Allied policy of making concessions to Germany based on the belief that Germany's grievances were real and Hitler's goals limited.

Aramaic Semitic language spoken widely throughout the Middle East in antiquity.

Arianism Belief that Christ was the first of God the Father's creations and the being through whom the Father created all other things.

Areopagus Council heading Athens's government comprised of a group of nobles that annually chose the city's nine *archons*, the magistrates who administered the *polis*.

arete The highest virtue in Homeric society: the manliness, courage, and excellence that equipped a hero to acquire and defend honor.

aristocratic resurgence Eighteenth-century resurgence of nobles that mantained the exclusiveness of noble rank, made it difficult to obtain, reserved powerful posts to nobles, and protected nobles from taxation.

Attica Region (about 1,000 square miles) that Athens dominated.

Augsburg Confession Moderate Protestant creed endorsed by the Schmalkaldic League (a defensive alliance of Lutherans).

Augustus ("revered") Name by which the Senate hailed Octavian for his restoration of the republic.

Avignon Papacy Period from 1309 to 1377 when the papal court was situated in Avignon, France, and gained a reputation for greed and worldly corruption.

Axis Forces (opposed to the Allies) joined together in Europe, including Germany and Italy, before and during World War II.

banalities Monopolies maintained by landowners giving them the right to demand that tenants pay to grind all their grain in the landowner's mill and bake all their bread in his oven.

baroque Artistic and architectural Styles that were naturalistic rather than idealized to involve observer on an emotional level through dramatic portrayals.

Beguines Sisterhoods of pious, self-supporting single women.

Black Death Virulent plague that struck in Sicily in 1347 and spread through Europe. It discolored the bodies of its victims. By the early fifteenth century, the plague may have reduced the population of western Europe by two-fifths.

Bolsheviks ("majority") Lenin's turn-of-the-century Russian faction favoring a party of elite professionals who would provide the working class with centralized leadership.

boyars Wealthy landowners among the freemen in late medieval Russia.

Brezhnev Doctrine Asserted the right of the Soviet Union to intervene in domestic politics of communist countries.

Bronze Age (3100–1200 B.C.E.) Began with the increasing importance of metal that also ended the Stone Ages.

Caesaropapism Emperor acting as if he were pope as well as caesar.

caliphate Office of the leader of the Muslim community.

categorical imperative Kant's view that all human beings possess an innate sense of moral duty, an inner command to act in every situation as one would have other people act in that same situation.

catholic ("universal") As in "universal" majority of Christians.

censors Men of unimpeachable reputation, chosen to carry the responsibility for enrolling, keeping track of, and determining the status and tax liability of each citizen.

Chartism The London Working Men's Association's 1838 proposal for political reform featuring the Six Points.

Christian Democratic parties Postwar parties that welcomed non-Catholic members and fought for democracy, social reform, and economic growth.

civilization Stage in the evolution of organized society that has among its characteristics urbanism, long-distance trade, writing systems, and accelerated technological and social development.

Cold War Period between the end of World War II (1945) and the collapse of the Soviet Union (1991) in which U.S. and Soviet relations were tense, seemingly moments away from actual war at any time during these years.

coloni Tenant farmers who were bound to the lands they worked.

condottieri   Military brokers from whom one could hire a mercenary army.

Congregationalists   The more extreme Puritans who believed every congregation ought to be autonomous, a law unto itself controlled by neither bishops nor presbyterian assemblies.

conquistadores   "Conquerors"

conservatism   Form of political thought that, in mid-nineteenth-century Europe, promoted legitimate monarchies, landed aristocracies, and established churches.

Consulate   A republican facade for one-man government by Napoleon.

consuls   Elected magistrates from patrician families chosen annually to lead the army, oversee the state religion, and sit as judges.

containment   American foreign policy strategy (beginning in 1947) for countering the communist threat and resisting the spread of Soviet influence.

Convention   The newly elected French body that met on September 21, 1792, whose first act was to declare France a republic—a nation governed by an elected assembly without a king.

corporatism   Fascist policy organizing major industries as syndicates of labor and management devised to steer an economic course between socialism and a liberal laissez-faire system.

Counter-Reformation   A reorganization of the Catholic Church that equipped it to meet the challenges posed by the Protestant Reformation.

Creole   Merchants, landowners, and professional people of Spanish descent.

Crusades   Campaigns authorized by the church to combat heresies and rival faiths.

Cubism   Autonomous realm of art with no purpose beyond itself. Includes as many different perspectives, angles, or views of the object as possible.

culture   Way of life invented by a group and passed on by teaching.

cuneiform   Developed by the Sumerians as the very first writing system ever used, it used several thousand characters, some of which stood for words and some for sounds.

deism   The *philosophes'* theology. A rational religion, a faith without fanaticism and intolerance that acknowledged the sovereign authority of reason.

Delian League   Pact joined in 478 B.C.E. by Athenians and other Greeks to continue the war with Persia.

détente   Relaxation of tensions between the United States and Soviet Union that involved increased trade and reduced deployment of strategic arms.

"divine right of kings"   The belief that God appoints kings and that kings are accountable only to God for how they use their power.

domestic system of textile production   Means by which urban merchants obtained their wares. They bought wool or other unfinished fiber for distribution to peasant workers who took it home, spun it into thread, wove it into cloth, and returned the finished product to the merchants for sale.

ego   Among Freud's three entities of the mind, the *ego* mediates between the impulsive id and the self-denying superego.

émigrés   French aristocrats and enemies of the revolution who fled to countries on France's borders and set up bases for counterrevolutionary activities.

encomienda   Legal grant of the right to the labor of a specific number of Indians for a particular period of time. This was used as a Spanish strategy for exploiting the labor of the natives.

Epicureans   People who believed the proper pursuit of humankind is undisturbed withdrawal from the world.

equestrians   Men rich enough to qualify for cavalry service.

Estates General   Assembly of representatives from France's propertied classes.

eucharist   ("thanksgiving") Celebration of the Lord's Supper in which bread and wine were blessed and consumed.

euro   Launched in 1999 by the EU, a single currency circulating in most of Western Europe.

European Constitution   Treaty that would transfer considerable decision-making authority from governments of the individual states to the Union's central institutions.

European Economic Community (EEC)   European nations as members of the "Common Market" pledging to eliminate traiffs, guarantee unimpeded flow of capital and labor, and establish uniform wage scales and social benefits.

European Union (EU)   Formerly the European Economic Community (EEC), renamed in 1993.

existentialism   Maintains that the human condition is greater than the sum of its parts and can only be grouped as whole.

fascism   System of extreme right-wing dictatorial government.

fiefs   ("Lands") Granted to cavalry men to fund their equipment and service.

Fourteen Points   President Woodrow Wilson's idealistic principles articulated as America's goals in World War I, including self- determination for nationalities, open diplomacy, freedom of the seas, disarmament, and establishment of a league of nations to keep the peace.

Fronde   Widespread rebellions in France between 1649 and 1652 (named after a slingshot used by street ruffians) aimed at reversing the drift toward absolute monarchy and preserving local autonomy.

Gallican Liberties   The French Roman Catholic Church's ecclesiastical independence of papal authority in Rome.

Gaul   Area that is now modern France.

ghettos   Separate districts in cities and entire villages in the countryside where Jews lived apart from Christians in eighteenth- century Europe.

glasnost ("openness") Gorbachev's policy of opening the way for unprecedented public discussion and criticism of Soviet history and the Communist Party. Censorship was relaxed and dissidents were released from prison.

"Glorious Revolution" Parliament's bloodless 1688 declaration of a vacant throne and proclamation that William and Mary were its heirs.

Golden Bull Arrangements agreed to by the Holy Roman Emperor and the major German territorial rulers in 1356 that helped stabilize Germany.

Great Purges The arrests, trials, Communist Party expulsions, and executions—beginning with the assassination of Politburo member Sergei Kirov in December 1934—that mainly targeted Party officials and reached its climax from 1936 to 1938.

Green movement Made up, in part, of members from the radical student groups of the 1960s, this movement was anticapitalistic, peace oriented, in opposition of nuclear arms, and condemned business for producing pollution. Unlike earlier student groups, though, the Greens opted to compete in the electoral process.

hacienda Large landed estate that characterized most Spanish colonies.

Hegira Forced flight of Muhammad and his followers to Medina, 240 miles north of Mecca. This event marks the beginning of the Islamic calendar.

Hellenistic Term that describes the cosmopolitan civilization, established under the Macedonians, that combined aspects of Greek and Middle Eastern cultures.

Helots Slaves to the Spartans that revolted and nearly destroyed Sparta in 650 B.C.E.

heretics "Takers" of contrary positions, namely in Christianity.

hieroglyphs ("sacred carving") Greek name for Egyptian writing. The writing was often used to engrave holy texts on monuments.

Holy Roman Empire The domain of the German monarchs who revived the use of the Roman imperial title during the Middle Ages.

home rule Government of a country or locality by its own citizens.

hoplite A true infantry soldier that began to dominate the battlefield in the late eighth century B.C.E.

Homo sapiens Our own species, which dates back roughly 200,000 years.

hubris Arrogance produced by excessive wealth or good fortune.

Huguenots French Protestants, named after Besançon Hugues, the leader of the revolt that won Geneva its freedom at that time.

humanitas Wide-ranging intellectual curiosity and habits of critical thinking that are the goals of liberal education.

iconoclasm Opposition to the use of images in Christian worship.

id Among Freud's three entities of the mind, the *id* consists of innate, amoral, irrational drives for sexual gratification, aggression, and sensual pleasure.

Iliad Homer's poem narrates a dispute between Agamemnon the king and his warrior Achilles, whose honor is wounded and then avenged.

imperator "Commander in chief."

imperialism Policy of expanding a nation's power by seeking hegemony over alien peoples.

imperium Right held by a Roman king to enforce commands by fines, arrests, and corporal and capital punishment.

Impressionism Focuses on social life and leisured activities of the urban middle and lower- middle classes, a fascination with light, color, and representation of momentary experience of social life or of landscape.

indulgence Remission of the obligation to perform a "work of satisfaction" for a sin.

Industrial Revolution Term coined by early nineteenth-century observers to describe the changes that the spreading use of powered machinery made in society and economics.

Inquisition Formal ecclesiastical court dedicated to discovering and punishing heresy.

Intolerable Acts Series of laws passed by Parliament in 1774 that closed the port of Boston, reorganized the government of Massachusetts, quartered soldiers in private homes, and transferred trials of customs officials accused of crimes to England.

Ionia Western coast of Asia Minor.

Islam New religion appearing in Arabia in the sixth century in response to the work of the Prophet Muhammad.

Jacobins The best organized of the political clubs, they embraced the most radical of the Enlightenment's political theories, and they wanted a republic, not a constitutional monarchy.

Jacquerie (From "Jacques Bonhomme," a peasant caricature) Name given to the series of bloody rebellions that desperate French peasants waged beginning in 1358.

Jansenism Appearing in the 1630s, it followed the teachings of St. Augustine, who stressed the role divine grace played in human salvation.

jihad A struggle; interpreted as a call for religious war.

Junkers (Prussian nobles) They were allowed to demand absolute obedience from the serfs on their estates in exchange for their support of the Hohenzollerns.

jus gentium Law of all peoples as opposed to the law that reflected only Roman practice.

jus naturale Law of nature that enshrined the principles of divine reason that Cicero and the Stoics believed governed the universe.

Ka'ba One of Arabia's holiest shrines located in Mecca, the birthplace of Muhammad.

Keynesian economics   Economic theories and programs ascribed to John M. Keynes and his followers advocating government monetary and fiscal policies that increase employment and spending.

Kulturkampf   ("cultural struggle") An extreme church-state conflict waged by Bismarck in Germany during the 1870s in response to a perceived threat to German political unity from the Roman Catholic Church.

laissez-faire   Policy of noninterference, especially the policy of government noninterference in economic affairs or business.

latifundia   Great estates that produced capital-intensive cash crops for the international market.

Latium   Region located in present-day Italy that included the small town of Rome.

Lebensraum   German for "living space."

levée en masse   Order for total military mobilization of both men and property.

Lower Egypt   The Nile's 100-mile deep, triangularly shaped delta.

Luftwaffe   The German air force.

Lyceum   School founded by Aristotle in Athens that focused on the gathering and analysis of data from all fields of knowledge.

Magna Carta   ("Great Charter") Document spelling out limitations on royal authority agreed to by John in 1215. It created foundation for modern English law.

Magna Graecia   ("Great Greece") The areas in southern Italy and Sicily where many Greek colonies were established.

mandate   Territory under the aegis of the League of Nations but actually ruled as a colony.

mannerism   Reaction against the simplicity, symmetry, and idealism of High Renaissance art. It made room for the strange, even the abnormal, and gave free reign to the subjectivity of the artist. The name reflects a tendency by artists to employ "mannered" ("affected") techniques—distortions that expressed individual perceptions and feelings.

manor   Communal farm considered to be early medieval Europe's chief economic institution.

manor   A self-sufficient rural community that was a fundamental institution of medieval life.

Marshall Plan   The U.S. European Recovery Program introduced by George C. Marshall, American secretary of state, whereby America provided extensive economic aid to the European states, conditional only on their working together for their mutual benefit.

Marxism   Socialist movement begun by Karl Marx in the mid–nineteenth century that differed from competing socialist views primarily in its claim to a scientific foundation and in its insistence on reform through revolution.

Mein Kampf   (*My Struggle*) Strategy dictated by Adolf Hitler during his period of imprisonment in 1923 outlining his political views.

Mensheviks   ("minority") Turn-of-the-century Russian faction that wanted to create a party with a large mass membership (like Germany's SPD).

mercantilism   Economic theory in which governments heavily regulated trade and promoted empires in order to increase national wealth.

Messiah   Redeemer who would vindicate faith and establish the kingdom of God on earth.

Methodism   Movement begun in England by John Wesley, an Oxford-educated Anglican priest, the first major religion to embody romanticism. It emphasized religion as a "method" for living more than a set of doctrines.

millets   Communities of the officially recognized religions that governed portions of the Ottoman Empire.

Minoan   Civilization of Crete (2100–1150 B.C.E.), and the Aegean's first civilization, named for a legendary king on the island.

modernism   Movement of the 1870s criticizing middle-class society and traditional morality.

Monophysites   Believers in a single, immortal nature of Christ; not both eternal God and mortal man in one and the same person.

monotheism   Having faith in a single God.

Mycenaean   Civilization occupying mainland Greece during the Late Helladic era (1580–1150 B.C.E.).

nationalism   The belief that the people who share an ethnic identity (language, culture, and history) should also be recognized as having a right to a government and political identity of their own.

NATO   North Atlantic Treaty Organization, a mutual defense pact.

natural selection   Darwin and Wallace's theory that those species with a unique trait that gives them a marginal advantage in the struggle for existence change the nature of their species by reproducing more successfully than their competitors; the fittest survive to pass on their unique characteristics.

naturalists   Authors who tried to portray nature and human life without sentimentality.

Nazis   Members of the National Socialist German Workers' Party that formed in 1920 and supported a mythical Aryan race alleged to be the source of the purest German lineage.

neo-gothic   Style that idealized nature and portrayed it in all its power.

Neoclassicism   Style that embodied a return to figurative and architectural models drawn from the Renaissance and the ancient world.

Neolithic   "New stone" age, dating back 10,000 years to when people living in some parts of the Middle East made advances in the production of stone tools and shifted from hunting and gathering to agriculture.

nomes   Egyptian districts ruled by regional governors who were called nomarchs.

Odyssey Homer's epic poem tells of the wanderings of the hero Odysseus.

Old Regime Eighteenth-century era marked by absolutist monarchies, agrarian economies, tradition, hierarchy, corporateness, and privilege.

optimates ("the best men") Opponents of Tiberius and defenders of the traditional prerogatives of the Senate.

orthodox ("correct") As in "correct" faith in Christianity.

Ottoman Empire The authority Instanbul's Ottoman Turkish sultan exercised over the Balkans, the Middle East, and North Africa from the end of the Middle Ages to World War I.

Paleolithic Greek for "old stone"; the earliest period in cultural development that began with the first use of stone tools about a million years ago and continued until about 10,000 B.C.E.

Panhellenic (All Greek) Sense of cultural identity that all Greeks felt in common with one other.

papal infallibility Assertion that the pope's pronouncements on matters of faith and morals could not be questioned.

Papal States Central part of Italy where Pope Stephen II became the secular ruler when confirmed by the Franks in 755.

parlements Regional courts allowed considerable latitude by Louis XIV to deal with local issues.

parliamentary monarchy English rule by a monarch with some parliamentary guidance or input.

patricians Upper class of Roman families that originally monopolized all political authority. Only they could serve as priests, senators, and magistrates.

Peloponnesian Wars Series of wars between Athens and Sparta beginning in 460 B.C.E.

Peloponnesus Southern half of the Greek peninsula.

perestroika ("restructuring") Means by which Gorbachev wished to raise his country's standard of living.

petite bourgeoisie New lower middle class made up of white- collar workers such as secretaries, retail clerks, and lower-level bureaucrats.

phalanx Tight military formation of men eight or more ranks deep.

pharaoh The god-kings of ancient Egypt.

Pharisee Member of a Jewish sect known for strict adherence to the Jewish law.

Phoenicians Seafaring people (Canaanites and Syrians) who scattered trading colonies from one end of the Mediterranean to the other.

plebeians Commoner class of Roman families, usually families of small farmers, laborers, and artisans who were early clients of the patricians.

polytheists Name given to those who worship many gods and/or goddesses.

politique Ruler or person in a position of power who puts the success and well-being of his or her state above all else.

populares Politicians who followed Tiberius's example of politics and governing.

positivism Comte's philosophy that all knowledge should be the kind of knowledge common to the physical sciences.

Post-Impressionism Focuses more on form and structure to bring painting of modern life back in touch with earlier artistic traditions.

Pragmatic Sanction Document recognizing Charles VI's daughter Maria Theresa as his heir.

Presbyterians Puritans who favored a national church of semiautonomous congregations governed by representative presbyteries.

proconsulships Extension of terms for consuls who had important work to finish.

Ptolemaic system Astronomical theory, named after Greek astronomer Ptolemy, that assumed Earth was the center point of a ball-shaped universe composed of concentric layers of rotating crystalline spheres to which the heavenly bodies were attached.

Puritans English Protestants who wanted simpler forms of church ceremony and strictness and gravity in personal behavior.

Qur'an Sacred book comprised of a collection of the revealed texts that God had chosen Muhammad to convey.

racism Belief that some peoples are innately superior to others.

realists Authors who tried to describe human behavior with scientific objectivity, rejecting the romantic idealization of nature, poverty, love, and polite society, and portraying the hypocrisy, physical and psychic brutality, and the dullness that underlay bourgeois life.

regular clergy Those clergy living under a *regula*, the rule of a monastic order.

Reign of Terror Extreme measures employed by the French government in an effort to protect the revolution.

Rococo Style that embraced lavish, often lighthearted decoration with an emphasis on pastel colors and the play of light.

romanticism Reaction against the rationalism and scientism of the Enlightenment, insisting on the importance of human feelings, intuition, and imagination as supplements for reason in the human quest to understand the world.

sans-culottes Parisians (shopkeepers, artisans, wage earners, and factory workers who had been ignored by the Old Regime) who, along with radical Jacobins, began the second revolution in France.

Scholasticism Method of study associated with the medieval university.

scientific revolution The emergence in the sixteenth century of rational and empirical methods of research that challenged traditional thought and promoted the rise of science and technology.

Second Industrial Revolution Started after 1850, it expanded the production of steel, chemicals, electricity, and oil.

secular clergy Clergy, such as bishops and priests, who lived and worked among the laity in the *saeculum* ("world").

Sejm Central legislative body to which the Polish nobles belonged.

September Massacres The execution ordered by the Paris Commune of approximately 1,200 aristocrats, priests, and common criminals who, because they were being held in city jails, were assumed to be counterrevolutionaries.

serf Peasant bound to the land he worked.

Shi'a The "party" of Ali. They believed Ali and his descendants were Muhammad's only rightful successors.

social Darwinism Spencer's argument (coming close to claiming that might makes right) used to justify neglect of the poor and the working class, exploitation of colonial peoples, and aggressive competition among nations.

socialist realism Doctrine of Soviet art and literature that sought to create figurative, traditional, optimistic, and easily intelligible scenes of a bold socialist future of prosperity and solidarity.

spinning jenny Invented by James Hargreaves in 1765, this machine spun sixteen spindles of thread simultaneously.

Stoics People who sought freedom from passion and harmony with nature.

***studia humanitas* (humanism)** Scholarship of the Renaissance that championed the study of Latin and Greek classics and Christian church fathers as an end in itself and as a guide to reforming society. Some claim it is an un-Christian philosophy emphasizing human dignity, individualism, and secular values.

Sturm and Drang ("Storm and Stress") Movement in German romantic literature that emphasized feeling and emotion.

suffragettes Derisive name for members of the Women's Social and Political Union, who lobbied for votes for women.

Sunnis Followers of the *sunna*, "tradition." They emphasize loyalty to the fundamental principles of Islam.

superego Among Freud's three entities of the mind, the *superego* internalizes the moral imperatives that society and culture impose on the personality.

symposium A men's drinking party at the center of aristocratic social life in archaic Greece.

Table of Ranks Issued by Peter the Great to draw nobles into state service, it made rank in the bureaucracy or military, not lineage, the determinant of an individual's social status.

tabula rasa (a blank page) John Locke's *An Essay Concerning Human Understanding* (1690) theorized that at birth the human mind is a tabula rasa.

ten lost tribes Israelites who were scattered and lost to history when the northern kingdom of Israel fell to the Assyrians in 722 B.C.E.

tetrarchy Coalition of four men, each of whom was responsible for a different part of the empire, established by Diocletian.

Thermidorian Reaction Tempering of revolutionary fervor that led to the establishment of a new constitutional regime.

Third Estate Members of the commercial and professional middle classes, or everyone but the clergy (the First Estate) and the nobility (the Second Estate).

Third Reich Hitler's regime of Nazis.

three-field system Developed by medieval farmers, a system in which three fields were utilized during different growing seasons to limit the amount of nonproductive plowing and to restore soil fertility through crop rotation.

transistor Miniaturized electronics circuitry making the vacuum tube obsolete.

transubstantiation Christian doctrine which holds that, at the moment of priestly consecration, the bread and wine of the Lord's Supper become the body and blood of Christ.

tribunes Officials elected by the plebeian tribal assembly given the power to protect plebeians from abuse by patrician magistrates.

ulema ("Persons with correct knowledge") Scholarly elite leading Islam.

Upper Egypt Narrow valley extending 650 miles from Aswan to the border of Lower Egypt.

Utilitarianism Maintained that people should always pursue the course that promotes the greatest happiness for the greatest number.

utopian socialists Early critics of industrialism whose visionary programs often involved plans to establish ideal societies based on noncapitalistic values.

vassal A person granted an estate or cash payments in return for rendering services to a lord.

Vulgate Latin translation of the Bible that became the standard text for the Catholic Church.

Warsaw Pact Mutual defense agreement among Albania, Bulgaria, Czechoslovakia, East Germany, Hungary, Poland, Romania, and the Soviet Union.

water frame Invented in 1769 by Richard Arkwright, this water-powered device produced a 100 percent cotton fabric rather than the standard earlier blend of cotton and linen.

Weimar Republic German republic that came to power in 1918 embodying the hopes of German liberals.

Zionism Movement based on the theory that if Jews were unacceptable as citizens of European nations, their only safety lay in establishing a nation of their own.

Chapter 1

ALLDRED, C. *The Egyptians* (1998). Probably the best one-volume study.

BRYCE, T. *The Kingdom of the Hittites* (1998). A fine new survey.

EHRENBERG, M. *Women in Prehistory* (1989). An account of the role of women in early times.

HALLO W. W. and SIMPSON W. K. *The Ancient Near East: A History*, rev. ed. (1998). A fine survey of ancient Egypt and Mesopotamia.

KAMM, A. *The Israelites: An Introduction* (1999). A good brief, accessible account.

POSTGATE, J. N. *Early Mesopotamia* (1992). An excellent study of Mesopotamian economy and society from the earliest times to about 1500 B.C.E.

RUDGLEY, R. *The Lost Civilizations of the Stone Age* (1999). A bold thesis asserting that many features of civilization existed during the Stone Age.

SAGGS, H. W. F. *The Might that Was Assyria* (1984). A history of one of the ancient world's great empires.

SANDARS, N. K. *The Sea Peoples* (1985). A lively account of the peoples who disrupted the Mediterranean's civilized states in the thirteenth century B.C.E.

SNELL, D. C. *Life in the Ancient Near East, 3100–332 B.C.E.* (1997). A social history focusing on culture and daily life.

Chapter 2

BURKERT, W. *The Orientalizing Revolution: Near Eastern Influence on Greek Culture in the Early Archaic Age* (1992). A study of the eastern impact on Greek literature and religion in the years 750 to 650 B.C.E.

CHADWICK, J. *The Mycenaean World* (1976). A readable account by a man who helped decipher Mycenaean writing.

DREWS, R. *The Coming of the Greeks.* (1988). A fine study of the arrival of the Greeks as part of the Indo-European migration.

FINLEY, M. I. *World of Odysseus*, 2nd. ed. (1978). A fascinating attempt to reconstruct Homeric society.

HANSON, V. D. *The Western Way of War* (1989). A brilliant description of the hoplite phalanx and its influence on Greek society.

HANSON, V. D. *The Other Greeks* (1995). A revolutionary account of the invention of the family farm by the Greeks and the role of agrarianism in the *polis*.

MANVILLE, P. B. *The Origins of Citizenship in Ancient Athens* (1990). An examination of the concept of citizenship in Solon's generation.

OSBORNE, R. *Greece in the Making, 1200–479 B.C.* (1996). An up-to-date illustrated account of early Greek history.

PRICE, S. *Religions of the Ancient Greeks* (1999). A fine discussion of the religious practices of the Athenians.

THOMAS, C. G. and CONANT, C. *Citadel to City-State: The Transformation of Greece, 1200–700 B.C.E.* (1999). A good account of Greece's emergence from the dark ages into the world of the *polis*.

YOUNG, D. C. *The Olympic Myth of Greek Athletics* (1984). A lively challenge to the orthodox view that Greek athletes were amateurs.

Chapter 3

BURKERT, W. *Greek Religion* (1985). A fine general study.

CARTLEDGE, P. *Spartan Reflections* (2001). A collection of valuable essays by a leading scholar of ancient Sparta.

CAWKWELL, *Philip of Macedon* (1978). A brief but learned account of Philip's career.

COOK, J. M. *The Persian Empire* (1983). A solid history that makes good use of archaeological evidence.

FOX, J. R. L. *Alexander the Great* (1973). An imaginative account that does more justice to the Persian side of the problem than is usual.

GARLAND, R. *Daily Life of the Ancient Greeks* (1998). A good account of the way the Greeks lived.

GREEN, P. *From Alexander to Actium* (1990). A brilliant new synthesis of the Hellenistic period.

HAMILTON, C. D. *Agesilaus and the Failure of Spartan Hegemony* (1991). An excellent biography of the king who was the central figure in Sparta during its era of domination.

HAMMOND, N. G. L. *The Genius of Alexander the Great* (1998). A new biography by the dean of ancient Macedonian studies.

KAGAN, D. *Pericles of Athens and the Birth of Athenian Democracy* (1991). An account of the life and times of the great Athenian statesman.

KAGAN, D. *The Outbreak of the Peloponnesian War* (1969). A study of the period from the foundation of the Delian League to the coming of the Peloponnesian War that argues that war could have been avoided.

PATTERSON, C. B. *The Family in Greek History* (1998). An interesting interpretation of the relationship between family and state in ancient Greece.

POLLITT, J. J. *Art and Experience in Classical Greece* (1972). A scholarly and entertaining study of the relationship between art and history.

POLLITT, J. J. *Art in the Hellenistic Age* (1986). An extraordinary analysis that places the art in its historical and intellectual context.

STRAUSS, B. S. *Athens after the Peloponnesian War* (1987). An excellent discussion of Athens' recovery and history in the 4th century B.C.E.

Chapter 4

BAUMAN, R. A. *Women and Politics in Ancient Rome* (1992). A useful study of women's role in Roman public life.

BOARDMAN, J., GRIFFIN, J. and MURRAY, O. *The Oxford History of the Roman World* (1990). An encyclopedic approach to the varieties of the Roman experience.

CORNELL, T. J. *The Beginnings of Rome: Italy and Rome from the Bronze Age to the Punic Wars* (1995). A fine new study of early Rome.

DAVID, J-M. *The Roman Conquest of Italy* (1997). A good analysis of how Rome united Italy.

GRUEN, E. S. *The Hellenistic World and the Coming of Rome* (1984). An explanation of Rome's conquest of the eastern Mediterranean.

LANCEL, S. *Carthage, a History* (1995). A good account of Rome's great competitor.

MEIR, C. *Caesar* (1995). A recent scholarly biography of Rome's great dictator.

MILLAR, F. G. B. *The Crowd in Rome in the Late Republic* (1999). A challenge to the interpretation that only aristocrats counted in the Roman Republic.

MITCHELL, T. N. *Cicero, the Senior Statesman* (1991). An intelligent study of Cicero's later career.

SCULLARD, H. H. A History of the Roman World 753–146 B.C.E., 4th ed. (1980). An unusually fine narrative history with useful critical notes.

WILLIAMS, G. *The Nature of Roman Poetry* (1970). An unusually graceful and perceptive literary study.

Chapter 5

BARNES, T. *The New Empire of Diocletian and Constantine* (1982). A study of the character of the late empire.

BIRLEY, A. R. *Hadrian the Restless Emperor* (1997). A biography of an important emperor.

BROWN, P. *The Rise of Western Christendom: Triumph and Diversity, 200–1000* (1996). A vivid picture of the spread of Christianity by a master of the field.

FERRILL, A. *Caligula: Emperor of Rome* (1991). A biography of the monstrous young emperor.

GALINSKY, G. *Augustan Culture* (1996). A work that integrates art, literature, and politics.

JOHNSTON, D. *Roman Law in Context* (2000). A work that places Rome's law in the context of its economy and society.

KAGAN, D. ed., *The End of the Roman Empire: Decline or Transformation?* 3rd edition (1992). A collection of essays discussing the problem of the decline and fall of the Roman Empire.

LENDON, J. *Empire of Honour: The Art of Government in the Roman World* (1997). A brilliant study that reveals how an aristocratic code of honor led the upper classes to cooperate in Roman rule.

MILLAR, F. G. B. *The Roman Near East, 31 B.C.–A.D. 337* (1993). A valuable study of Rome's relations with an important part of its empire.

RUDICH, V. *Political Dissidence under Nero: The Price of Dissimulation* (1993). A fine exposition of the lives and thoughts of political dissidents in the early empire.

SYME, R. *The Roman Revolution* (1960). A major study of Augustus, his supporters, and their rise to power.

Chapter 6

ARMSTRONG, K. *Muhammad; A Biography of the Prophet* (1992). Substantial popular biography.

BARRACLOUGH, G. *The Origins of Modern Germany* (1963). Originally published in 1946 and still the best survey of medieval Germany.

BARTLETT, R. *The Making of Modern Europe* (1993). How migration and colonization created Europe.

COLLINS, R. *Charlemagne* (1998). Latest biography.

HOURANI, A. *A History of the Arab Peoples* (1991). Comprehensive with overviews of the origins and early history of Islam.

LEWIS, B. *The Middle East: A Brief History of the Last 2000 Years* (1995). Authoritative overview.

MCKITTERICK, R. *Carolingian Culture: Emulation and Innovation* (1994). The culture from which western Europe was born.

NORRIS, J. J. *Byzantium: The Decline and Fall* (1995).

SAWYER, P. *Kings and Vikings: Scandinavia and Europe A.D. 700–1100* (1994). Raiding Vikings and their impact on Europe.

Chapter 7

BALDWIN, J. W. *The Government of Philip Augustus* (1986). An important scholarly work.

FLANAGAN, S. *Hildegard of Bingen, 1098–1179: A Visionary Life* (1998). Latest biography.

HALLAM, E. M. *Capetian France, 987–1328* (1980). Very good on politics and heretics.

HAMBLY, G. R. G. ed., *Women in the Medieval Islamic World* (1998). Elite women from Mamluk and Ottoman court records.

HOLT, J. C. *Magna Carta*, 2nd ed. (1992). Succeeding generations interpret the famous document.

LEYSER, K. *Medieval Germany and Its Neighbors, 900–1250* (1982). Basic and authoritative.

RICHARD, J. *Saint Louis: Crusader King of France* (1992).

RILEY-SMITH, J. *The Oxford Illustrated History of the Crusades* (1992). Sweeping account.

Chapter 8

ARIÈS, P. *Centuries of Childhood: A Social History of Family Life* (1962). Pioneer effort on the subject.

BALDWIN, J. W. *The Scholastic Culture of the Middle Ages: 1000–1300* (1971). Best brief synthesis available.

CLANCHY, M. T. *Abelard: A Medieval Life* (1998). The biography of famous philosopher and seducer of Héloise.

HANAWALT, B. A. *Growing Up in Medieval London* (1993). Positive portrayal of parental and societal treatment of children.

HASKINS, C. H. *The Rise of Universities* (1972). A short, minor classic.

HOPKINS, A. *Knights* (1990). Europe's warriors and models.

LOPEZ, R. *The Commercial Revolution of the Middle Ages* (1971). A master's brief survey.

MÂLE, E. *The Gothic Image: Religious Art in France in the Thirteenth Century* (1913). An enduring classic.

OZMENT, S. *Ancestors: The Loving Family in Old Europe* (2001). A sympathetic look at families past.

SHAHAR, S. *The Fourth Estate: A History of Women in the Middle Ages* (1983). A comprehensive survey, making clear the great variety of women's work.

Chapter 9

ALLMAND, C. *The Hundred Years' War: England and France at War, c. 1300–ca. 1450* (1988). Good overview of the war's development and consequences.

BACKSCHEIDER, P. R. ET AL. (eds.) *A Journal of the Plague Year* (1992). Black death at ground level.

GILLETT, E. H. ET AL. *Life and Times of John Huss: The Bohemian Reformation of the Fifteenth Century* (2001). The latest biography.

KAHN, R. ET AL. *Secret History of the Mongols: The Origins of Chingis Kahn* (1998).

OZMENT, S. *The Age of Reform, 1250–1550* (1980). Highlights of late medieval intellectual and religious history.

PERROY, E. *The Hundred Years' War*, trans. by W. B. Wells (1965). Still the most comprehensive one-volume account.

RENOVARD, Y. *The Avignon Papacy 1305–1403*, trans. by D. Bethell (1970). The standard narrative account.

ZIEGLER, P. *The Black Death* (1969). Highly readable account.

Chapter 10

BARON, H. *The Crisis of the Early Italian Renaissance*, vols. 1 and 2 (1966). A major work, setting forth the civic dimension of Italian humanism.

BURCKHARDT, J. *The Civilization of the Renaissance in Italy* (1867). The old classic that still has as many defenders as detractors.

CONRAD, R. E. *Children of God's Fire: A Documentary History of Black Slavery in Brazil* (1983). Not for the squeamish.

EISENSTEIN, E. L. *The Printing Press as an Agent of Change: Communications and Cultural Transformations in Early Modern Europe*, 2 vols. (1979). Bold, stimulating account of the centrality of printing to all progress in the period.

HERLIHY, D. and KLAPISCH-ZUBER, C. *The Tuscans and Their Families* (1985). Important work based on unique demographic data.

KRISTELLER, P. O. *Renaissance Thought: The Classic, Scholastic, and Humanist Strains* (1961). A master shows the many sides of Renaissance thought.

MARTINES, L. *Power and Imagination: City States in Renaissance Italy* (1980). Stimulating account of cultural and political history.

PANOFSKY, E. *Meaning in the Visual Arts* (1955). Eloquent treatment of Renaissance art.

PARRY, J. H. *The Age of Reconnaissance* (1964). A comprehensive account of exploration in the years 1450 to 1650.

SKINNER, Q. *The Foundations of Modern Political Thought; I: The Renaissance* (1978). Broad survey, including every known political theorist.

VEZZOSI, A. *Leonardo da Vinci, Renaissance Man* (1996). Updated biography.

WHEATCROFT, A. *The Habsburgs* (1995). The dynasty that ruled the center of late medieval and early modern Europe.

Chapter 11

BLOOM, H. *Shakespeare: The Invention of the Human* (1998). A modern master's complete analysis of the greatest writer in the English language.

DURAN, M. *Cervantes* (1974). Detailed biography.

EVENNETT, H. O. *The Spirit of the Counter Reformation* (1968). Essay on the continuity of Catholic reform and its independence from the Protestant Reformation.

GREGORY, B. S. *Salvation at Stake: Christian Martyrdom in Early Modern Europe* (1999). Massive can't-put-down study covering a wide spectrum.

JOHNSTON, P. and SCRIBNER, R. W. *The Reformation in Germany and Switzerland* (1993). Reformation from the bottom up.

OBERMAN, H. A. *Luther: Man Between God and the Devil* (1989). Perhaps the best account of Luther's life, by a Dutch master.

O'MALLEY, J. *The First Jesuits* (1993). Extremely detailed account of the creation of the Society of Jesus and its original purposes.

OZMENT, S. *The Age of Reform, 1250–1550: An Intellectual and Religious History of Late Medieval and Reformation Europe* (1980). A broad survey of major religious ideas and beliefs.

OZMENT, S. *Flesh and Spirit: Private Life in Early Modern Germany* (1999). Family life from courtship and marriage to the sending of a new generation into the world.

STARKEY, D. *Elizabeth: The Struggle for the Throne* (2000).

STARKEY, D. *The Reign of Henry VIII* (1985). Portrayal of the king as in control of neither his life nor his court.

WENDEL, F. *Calvin: The Origins and Development of His Religious Thought*, trans. by Philip Mairet (1963). The best treatment of Calvin's theology.

WILLIAMS, G. H. *The Radical Reformation* (1962). Broad survey of the varieties of dissent within Protestantism.

WUNDER, H. *He is the Sun, She is the Moon: A History of Women in Early Modern Germany* (1998). A model of gender history.

Chapter 12

BRAUDEL, F. *The Mediterranean and the Mediterranean World in the Age of Philip the Second*, vols. 1 and 2 (1976). Widely acclaimed work of a French master historian.

DUNN, R. *The Age of Religious Wars, 1559–1689* (1979). Excellent brief survey of every major conflict.

GEYL, P. *The Revolt of the Netherlands, 1555–1609* (1958). The authoritative survey.

GUY, J. *Tudor England* (1990). A standard history and good synthesis of recent scholarship.

HAIGH, C. *Elizabeth I* (1988). Elizabeth portrayed as a magnificent politician and propogandist.

LOADES, D. *Mary Tudor* (1989). Authoritative and good storytelling.

MATTINGLY, G. *The Armada* (1959). A masterpiece and resembling a novel in style.

WORMALD, J. *Mary, Queen of Scots: A Study in Failure* (1991). Mary portrayed as a queen who did not understand her country and was out of touch with the times.

Chapter 13

ASHTON, R. *Counter-Revolution: The Second Civil War and Its Origin, 1646–1648* (1995). A major examination of the resumption of civil conflict in England that ended with the abolition of the monarchy.

BEIK, W. *Absolutism and Society in Seventeenth-Century France* (1985). An important study that questions the extent of royal power.

BLACK, J. *Eighteenth Century Europe, 1700–1789* (1990). An excellent survey.

BONNEY, R. *Political Change in France Under Richelieu and Mazarin, 1624–1661* (1978). A careful examination of the manner in which these two cardinals laid the foundation for Louis XIV's absolutism.

BREWER, J. *The Sinews of Power: War, Money and the English State, 1688–1783* (1989). An extremely important study of the financial basis of English power.

BURKE, P. *The Fabrication of Louis XIV* (1992). Examines the manner in which the public image of Louis XIV was forged in art.

BUSHKOVITCH, P. *Peter the Great: The Struggle for Power, 1671–1725* (2001). Replaces all previous studies.

COLLINSON, P. *The Religion of Protestants: The Church in English Society, 1559–1625* (1982). The best recent introduction to Puritanism.

DAVIS, N. *God's Playground*, vol. 1 (1991). Excellent on prepartition Poland.

DOYLE, W. *The Old European Order, 1660–1800* (1992). The most thoughtful treatment of the subject.

INGRAO, C. J. *The Habsburg Monarchy, 1618–1815* (1994). The best recent survey.

ISRAEL, J. I. *The Dutch Republic, Its Rise, Greatness, and Fall, 1477–1806* (1995). The major survey of the subject.

KANN, R. A. and DAVID, Z. V. *The Peoples of the Eastern Habsburg Lands 1526–1918* (1984). A helpful overview of the subject.

MCKAY, D. *The Great Elector: Frederick William of Brandenburg-Prussia* (2001). An account of the origins of Prussian power.

MCKAY, D. and SCOTT, H. M. *The Rise of the Great Powers, 1648–1815* (1983). Now the standard survey.

MONOD, P. K. *The Power of Kings: Monarchy and Religion in Europe, 1589–1715* (1999). An innovative examination of the roots of royal authority.

RUSSELL, C. *The Fall of the English Monarchies* (1991). A major revisionist account.

SCHAMA, S. *A History of Britain: The Wars of the British, 1603–1776* (2001). A highly accessible narrative (originally designed for television) that explores the major themes of British development during this period.

SUGAR, P. F. *Southeastern Europe Under Ottoman Rule, 1354–1804* (1977). An extremely clear presentation.

TREASURE, G. *Louis XIV* (2001). The best, most accessible recent study.

UNDERDOWN, D. *A Freeborn People: Politics and the Nation in Seventeenth-Century England* (1996). A lively reply to C. Russell above.

Chapter 14

ASHCRAFT, R. *Revolutionary Politics and Locke's Two Treatises of Government* (1986). A major study emphasizing the radical side of Locke's thought.

BARRY, J., HESTER, M. and ROBERTS, G. eds. *Witchcraft in Early Modern Europe: Studies in Culture and Belief* (1998). A collection of recent essays.

DEAR, P. *Revolutionizing the Sciences: European Knowledge and Its Ambitions, 1500–1700* (2001). A broad-ranging study of both the ideas and institutions of the new science.

FINOCCHIARO, M. A. *The Galileo Affair: A Documentary History* (1989). A collection of all the relevant documents and introductory commentary.

GAUKROGER, S. *Francis Bacon and the Transformation of Early-Modern Philosophy* (2001). An excellent, accessible introduction.

HARRIS, I. *The Mind of John Locke: A Study of Political Theory in Its Intellectual Setting* (1994). The most comprehensive recent treatment.

HEILBRON, J. A. *The Sun in the Church: Cathedrals as Solar Observatories* (2000). A remarkable study of the manner in which Europe's great church buildings were used to make astronomical observations and calculations.

KUHN, T. S. *The Copernican Revolution* (1957). Remains the leading work on the subject.

LEVACK, B. *The Witch Hunt in Early Modern Europe* (1986). Lucid survey.

PYENSON, L. and SHEETS-PYENSON, S. *Servants of Nature: A History of Scientific Institutions, Enterprises, and Sensibilities* (1999). A history of the settings in which the creation and diffusion of scientific knowledge have occurred.

SHAPIN, S. *The Scientific Revolution* (1996). A readable brief introduction.

THOMAS, K. *Religion and the Decline of Magic* (1971). Provocative, much-acclaimed work focused on popular culture.

TUCK, R. *Philosophy and Government 1572–1651* (1993). A continent-wide survey.

WESTFALL, R. S. *Never at Rest: A Biography of Isaac Newton* (1981). The major study.

Chapter 15

BLUM, J. *Lord and Peasant in Russia from the Ninth to the Nineteenth Century* (1961). Remains a classic discussion.

DEANE, P. *The First Industrial Revolution* (1999). A well-balanced and systematic treatment.

EARLE, P. *The Making of the English Middle Class: Business, Community, and Family Life in London, 1660–1730* (1989). The most careful study of the subject.

HOBSBAWM, E. *Industry and Empire: The Birth of the Industrial Revolution* (1999). A survey by a major historian of the subject.

KERTZER, D. I. and BARBAGLI, M. *The History of the European Family: Family Life in Early Modern Times, 1500–1709* (2001). A series of broad-ranging essays covering the entire continent.

KING, S. and TIMMONS, G. *Making Sense of the Industrial Revolution: English Economy and Society, 1700–1850* (2001). Examines the Industrial Revolution through the social institutions that brought it about and were changed by it.

MANUEL, F. E. *The Broken Staff: Judaism Through Christian Eyes* (1992). An important discussion of Christian interpretations of Judaism.

OVERTON, M. *Agricultural Revolution in England: The Transformation of the Agrarian Economy, 1500–1850* (1996). A highly accessible treatment.

STEARNS, P. *The Industrial Revolution in World History* (1998). An extremely broad interpretive account.

VICKERY, A. *The Gentleman's Daughter: Women's Lives in Georgian England* (1998). A richly documented study.

Chapter 16

BAILYN, B. *The Ideological Origins of the American Revolution* (1967). Remains an important work illustrating the role of English radical thought in the perceptions of the American colonists.

BLACKBURN, R. *The Making of New World Slavery from the Baroque to the Modern, 1492–1800* (1997). An extraordinary work.

BRADING, D. *The First America* (1991). A major study of colonial Latin America.

COLLEY, L. *Britons: Forging the Nation, 1707–1837* (1992). A major work with important discussions of the recovery from the loss of America.

DAVIS, R. *The Rise of the Atlantic Economies* (1973). A major synthesis.

HARMS, R. *The Diligent: A Voyage through the Worlds of the Slave Trade* (2002). A powerful narrative of the voyage of a French slave trader.

MACDONAGH, G. *Frederick the Great* (2001). Now the standard biography.

MAIER, P. *American Scripture: Making the Declaration of Independence* (1997). Replaces previous works on the subject.

McNEIL, J. R. *Atlantic Empires of France and Spain: Louisbourg and Havana, 1700–1763* (1985). An examination of imperial policies in terms of two key overseas outposts.

PAGDEN, A. *Lords of All the World: Ideologies of Empire in Spain, Britain, and France, 1492–1830* (1995). One of the few comparative studies of empire during this period.

THORNTON, J. *Africa and the Africans in the Making of the Atlantic World, 1400–1800*, 2nd ed. (1998). A discussion of the role of Africans in the emergence of the transatlantic economy.

WOOD, G. S. *The Radicalism of the American Revolution* (1991). A major interpretation.

Chapter 17

BEALES, D. *Joseph II: In the Shadow of Maria Theresa, 1741–1780* (1987), The best treatment in English of the early political life of Joseph II.

CHARTIER, R. *The Cultural Origins of the French Revolution* (1991). A wide-ranging discussion of the emergence of the public sphere and the role of books and the book trade during the Enlightenment.

DOCK, T. S. *Women in the Encyclopédie: A Compendium* (1983). An analysis of the articles from the *Encyclopedia* that deal with women.

GAY, P. *The Enlightenment: An Interpretation*, 2 vols. (1966, 1969). A classic.

GOODMAN, D. *The Republic of Letters: A Cultural History of the French Enlightenment* (1994). Concentrates on the role of the salons.

LANDES, J. B. *Women and the Public Sphere in the Age of the French Revolution* (1988). An extended essay on the role of women in public life during the eighteenth century.

LEDONNE, J. P. *The Russian Empire and the World, 1700–1917* (1996). An exploration of the major determinants in Russian expansion from the eighteenth to the early twentieth century.

MACMAHON, D. *Enemies of the Enlightenment: The French Counter-Enlightenment and the Making of Modernity* (2001). A very fine exploration of French writers critical of the philosophes.

DE MADARIAGA, I. *Russia in the Age of Catherine the Great* (1981). The best discussion in English.

RAHE, P. A., CARRITHERS, D. and MOCHER, M. A. *Montesquieu's Science of Politics: Essays on "The Spirit of the Laws"* (2001). An expansive collection of essays on Montesquieu and his relationship to other major thinkers.

ROTHCHILD, E. *Economic Sentiments: Adam Smith, Condorcet, and the Enlightenment* (2001). A sensitive account of Smith's thought and its relationship to the social questions of the day.

SPADAFORA, D. *The Idea of Progress in Eighteenth Century Britain* (1990). A major study that covers many aspects of the Enlightenment in Britain.

STAROBINSKI, J. *Jean-Jacques Rousseau: Transparency and Obstruction* (1971). A classic analysis of Rousseau.

SULLIVAN, R. E. *John Toland and the Deist Controversy: A Study in Adaptation* (1982). An important and informative discussion.

WOLFF, L. *Inventing Eastern Europe: The Map of Civilization on the Mind of the Enlightenment* (1994). A remarkable study of the way in which Enlightenment writers recast the understanding of this part of the continent.

Chapter 18

BAKER, K. M. and LUCAS, C. eds., *The French Revolution and the Creation of Modern Political Culture*, 3 vols. (1987). A splendid collection of important original articles on all aspects of politics during the revolution.

CENSER, J. R. and HUNT, L. *Liberty, Equality, Fraternity: Exploring the French Revolution* (2001). A major survey with numerous documents available through a CD-ROM disk.

COBB, R. *The People's Armies* (1987). The best treatment in English of the revolutionary army.

DOYLE, W. *The French Revolution* (2001). A solid brief introduction.

HIGONNET, P. *Goodness beyond Virtue: Jacobins during the French Revolution* (1998). An outstanding work that clearly relates political values to political actions.

KENNEDY, E. *A Cultural History of the French Revolution* (1989). An important examination of the role of the arts, schools, clubs, and intellectual institutions.

LEVY, D. G., APPLEWHITE, H. B. and JOHNSON, M. D. eds. and trans., *Women in Revolutionary Paris, 1789–1795* (1979). A remarkable collection of documents on the subject.

MELZER, S. E. and RABINE, L. W. eds., *Rebel Daughters: Women and the French Revolution* (1992). A collection of essays exploring various aspects of the role and image of women in the French Revolution.

OZOUF, M. *Festivals and the French Revolution* (1988). A pioneering study of the role of the public festivals in the revolution.

PROCTOR, C. *Women, Equality, and the French Revolution* (1990). An examination of how the ideas of the Enlightenment and the attitudes of revolutionaries affected the legal status of women.

TACKETT, T. *Becoming a Revolutionary: The Deputies of the French National Assembly and the Emergence of a Revolutionary Culture (1789–1790)* (1996). The best study of the early months of the revolution.

VAN KLEY, D. K. *The Religious Origins of the French Revolution: From Calvin to the Civil Constitution, 1560–1791* (1996). Examines the manner in which debates within French Catholicism influenced the coming of the revolution.

Chapter 19

ASPREY, R. *The Rise of Napoleon Bonaparte and the Reign of Napoleon Bonaparte* (2001). an extensive two-volume narrative.

BEISER, F. C. *Enlightenment, Revolution, and Romanticism: The Genesis of Modern German Political Thought, 1790–1800* (1992). The best recent study of the subject.

BENTLEY, G. E. *The Stranger from Paradise: A Biography of William Blake* (2001). Now the standard work.

BOYLE, N. *Goethe* (2001). A challenging two-volume biography.

BROOKNER, A. *Romanticism and Its Discontents* (2001). Exploration of French romanticism by a leading novelist.

BROERS, M. *Europe under Napoleon, 1799–1815* (2002). Examines the subject from the standpoint of those Napoleon conquered.

BROWN, D. B. *Romanticism* (2001). A well-illustrated overview.

CHANDLER, D. G. *The Campaigns of Napoleon* (1966). A good military study.

CHAPMAN, T. *Congress of Vienna: Origins, Processes, and Results* (1998). A clear introduction to the major issues.

JOHNSON, P. *Napoleon* (2002). A brief, thoughtful essay.

LEFEBVRE, G. *Napoleon*, 2 vols., trans. by H. Stockhold (1969). The fullest and finest biography.

McGANN, J. J. and SODERHOLM, J. (eds.), *Byron and Romanticism* (2002). Essays on the poet who most embodied romantic qualities to the people of his time.

MUIR, R. *Tactics and the Experience of Battle in the Age of Napoleon* (1998). A splendid account of the experience of troops in battle.

PINKARD, T. *Hegel: A Biography* (2000). A long but accessible study.

REARDON, B. M. G. *Religion in the Age of Romanticism: Studies in Early Nineteenth-Century Thought* (1985). The best introduction to this important subject.

WOLOCH, I. *Napoleon and His Collaborators: The Making of a Dictatorship* (2001). A key study by one of the major scholars of the subject.

Chapter 20

ANDERSON, B. *Imagined Communities*, rev. ed. (1991). An influential and controversial discussion of nationalism.

ARCHER, C. I., MACLACHLAN, C. M. and BEEZLEY, W. H. (eds.), *The Wars of Independence in Spanish America* (2000). Broad selection of essays based on most recent scholarship.

ATHANASSOGLOU-KALLMYER, N. M. *French Images from the Greek War of Independence, 1821–1830: Art and Politics under the Restoration* (2000). Explores both the Greek War of Independence and French politics.

BERDAHL, M. *The Politics of the Prussian Nobility: The Development of a Conservative Ideology, 1770–1848* (1988). A major examination of German conservative outlooks.

BRIGGS, A. *The Making of Modern England* (1959). Classic survey of English history during the first half of the nineteenth century.

BROCK, M. *The Great Reform Act* (1974). The standard work.

CRAIG, G. A. *The Politics of the Prussian Army, 1640–1945* (1955). A splendid study of the conservative political influence of the army on Prussian development.

FORTESCUE, W. *Revolution and Counter-Revolution in France, 1815–1852* (2002). A helpful brief survey.

HOBSBAWM, E. J. *Nations and Nationalism since 1780: Programme, Myth, Reality*, rev. ed. (1992). The best recent introduction to the subject.

JELAVICH, C. and B. *The Establishment of the Balkan National States, 1804–1920* (1977). A standard, clear introduction.

KROEN, S. *Politics and Theater: The Crisis of Legitimacy in Restoration France, 1815–1830* (2000). Examines how French theater reacted to the climate of changing political regimes.

LEVINGER, M. B. *Enlightened Nationalism: The Transformation of Prussian Political Cultures, 1806–1848* (2002). A major work based on the most recent scholarship.

LYNCH, J. *The Spanish American Revolutions, 1808–1826* (1973). An excellent one-volume treatment.

PALMER, A. *Alexander I: Tsar of War and Peace* (1974). An interesting biography that captures much of the mysterious personality of this ruler.

RIASANOVSKY, N. V. *Nicholas I and Official Nationality in Russia, 1825–1855* (1959). A lucid discussion of the conservative ideology that made Russia the major opponent of liberalism.

RUBINSTEIN, W. D. D. *Britain's Century: A Political and Social History, 1815–1905* (1999). Based on the most recent scholarship.

SHEEHAN, J. *German History, 1770–1866* (1989). A very long work that is now the best available survey of the subject.

Chapter 21

ANDERSON, B. S. and ZINSER, J. P. *A History of Their Own: Women in Europe from Prehistory to the Present*, vol. 2 (1988). A wide-ranging survey.

BERLIN, I. *Karl Marx: His Life and Environment* (1948). A classic introduction.

BROCK, P. *The Slovak National Awakening* (1976). A standard work.

HARRISON, J. F. C. *Quest for the New Moral World: Robert Owen and the Owenites in Britain and America* (1969). The standard work.

HIMMELFARB, G. *The Idea of Poverty: England in the Early Industrial Age* (1984). A major work covering the subject from the time of Adam Smith through 1850.

IGNATIEFF, M. *A Just Measure of Pain: The Penitentiary in the Industrial Revolution, 1750–1850* (1978). An important treatment of early English penal thought and practice.

KERTZER, D. I. and BARBAGLI, M. (eds.), *Family Life in the Long Nineteenth Century, 1789–1913: The History of the European Family* (2002). Wide-ranging collection of essays.

LANDES, D. *The Unbound Prometheus: Technological Change and Industrial Development in Western Europe from 1750 to the Present* (1969). Classic one-volume treatment of technological development in a broad social and economic context.

MERRIMAN, J. M. *The Agony of the Republic: The Repression of the Left in Revolutionary France, 1848–1851* (1978). Study of how the Second French Republic and popular support for it were suppressed.

PERKIN, H. *The Origins of Modern English Society, 1780–1880* (1969). A provocative attempt to look at the society as a whole.

RANDERS-PHERSON, J. D. *Germans and the Revolution of 1848–1849* (2001). An exhaustive treatment of the subject.

SORKIN, D. *The Transformation of German Jewry, 1780–1840* (1987). An examination of the decades of Jewish emancipation in Germany.

THOMPSON, E. P. *The Making of the English Working Class* (1964). A classic work.

WINCH, D. *Riches and Poverty: An Intellectual History of Political Economy in Britain, 1750–1834* (1996). A superb survey from Adam Smith through Thomas Malthus.

Chapter 22

BLACKBOURN, D. *The Long Nineteenth Century: A History of Germany, 1780–1918* (1998). An outstanding survey based on up-to-date scholarship.

BLAKE, R. *Disraeli* (1967). Remains the best biography.

BUCHOLZ, A. *Moltke and the German Wars, 1864–1871* (2001). Explains how Prussian leaders invented many aspects of modern warfare.

CUNNINGHAM, M. *Mexico and the Foreign Policy of Napoleon III* (2001). Explores one of the most controversial subjects in French foreign policy.

EDGERTON, R. B. *Death or Glory: The Legacy of the Crimean War* (2000). Multifaceted study of a badly mismanaged war that transformed many aspects of European domestic politics.

KEE, R. *The Green Flag: A History of Irish Nationalism* (2001). A vast survey.

LIEVAN, D. C. *The Russian Empire and Its Rivals* (2001). Explores the imperial side of Russian government.

MAY, A. J. *The Habsburg Monarchy, 1867–1914* (1951). Narrates in considerable detail and with much sympathy the fate of the dual monarchy.

O'BRIEN, C. C. *Parnell and His Party* (1957). An excellent treatment of the Irish question.

PFLANZE, O. *Bismarck and the Development of Germany*, 3 vols. (1990). A major biography and history of Germany for the period.

PLESSIS, A. *The Rise and Fall of the Second Empire, 1852–1871* (1985). A useful survey of France under Napoleon III.

RIDLEY, J. *Garibaldi* (2001). An extensive biography of a remarkable personality.

SKED, A. *Decline and Fall of the Habsburg Empire, 1815–1918* (2001). A major, accessible survey of a difficult subject.

VENTURI, F. *The Roots of Revolution* (trans. 1960). A major treatment of late nineteenth-century revolutionary movements.

WETZEL, D. *A Duel of Giants: Bismarck, Napoleon III, and the Origins of the Franco-Prussian War* (2001). Broad study based on most recent scholarship.

ZELDIN, T. *France: 1848–1945*, 2 vols. (1973, 1977). Emphasizes the social developments.

Chapter 23

ARONSON, I. M. *Troubled Waters: The Origins of the 1881 Anti-Jewish Pogroms in Russia* (1990). The best discussion of this subject.

ASCHER, A. and STOLYPIN, P. A. *The Search for Stability in Late Imperial Russia* (2000). A broad-ranging biography based on extensive research.

BIRNBAUM, P. *Jewish Destinies: Citizenship, State and Community in Modern France* (2000). Explores the subject from the French Revolution to the present.

HAMILTON, R. F. *Marxism, Revisionism, and Leninism: Explication, Assessment, and Commentary* (2000). A contribution from the perspective of a historically minded sociologist.

HAUSE, S. C. *Women's Suffrage and Social Politics in the French Third Republic* (1984). A wide-ranging examination of the question.

HIMMELFARB, G. *Poverty and Compassion: The Moral Imagination of the Late Victorians* (1991). The best examination of late Victorian social thought.

HOBSBAWM, E. J. *The Age of Empire: 1875–1914* (1987). A stimulating survey that covers cultural as well as political developments.

HOLPEN, T. *The Mid-Victorian Generation, 1846–1886* (1998). The most extensive treatment of the subject.

MALIA, M. *Russia under Western Eyes: From the Bronze Horseman to the Lenin Mausoleum* (2000). A brilliant work recording the manner in which intellectuals in western Europe understood Russia.

MOOSE, G. L. *German Jews Beyond Judaism* (1985). Sensitive essays exploring the relationship of Jews to German culture in the nineteenth and early twentieth centuries.

NORD, P. G. *The Republican Moment: Struggles for Democracy in Nineteenth-Century France* (1996). A major new examination of nineteenth-century French political culture.

PINKNEY, D. H. *Napoleon III and the Rebuilding of Paris* (1958). A classic study.

ROGGER, H. *Jewish Policies and Right-Wing Politics in Imperial Russia* (1986). A very learned examination of Russian anti-Semitism.

SERVICE, R. *Lenin: A Biography* (2002). Based on new sources and will no doubt become the standard biography.

SMITH, B. G. *Ladies of the Leisure Class: The Bourgeoises of Northern France in the Nineteenth Century* (1981). Emphasizes the importance of the reproductive role of women.

STONE, N. *Europe Transformed* (1984). A sweeping survey that emphasizes the difficulties of late-nineteenth-century liberalism.

THORPE, A. *A History of the British Labour Party* (2001). A survey from its inception to the present.

TOSH, J. *A Man's Place: Masculinity and the Middle-Class Home in Victorian England* (1999). A pioneering work.

Chapter 24

ALLEN, C. *The Human Christ: The Search for the Historical Jesus* (1998). A broad survey of the issue for the past two centuries.

BOWLER, P. *Evolution: The History of an Idea* (1989). An outstanding survey of the subject.

BOWLER, P. *Reconciling Science and Religion: The Debate in Early-Twentieth-Century Britain* (2001). A superb survey of the cooperation between religious and scientific writers during the period.

BURROW, J. *The Crisis of Reason: European Thought, 1848–1914* (2000). The best overview available.

COPPA, F. J. *The Modern Papacy since 1789* (1999). A straightforward survey.

DALSIMER, K. *Virginia Wolfe: Becoming a Writer* (2002). A psychoanalytic study.

DESMOND, A. and MOORE, J. *Darwin* (1992). A brilliant biography.

GAY, P. *Freud: A Life for Our Time* (1988). The new standard biography.

HELMSTADTER, R. ed., *Freedom and Religion in the Nineteenth Century* (1997). Major essays on the relationship of church and state.

HOURANI, A. *Arab Though in the Liberal Age 1789–1939* (1967). A classic account, clearly written and accessible to the non-specialist.

KATZ, J. *From Prejudice to Destruction: Anti-Semitism, 1700–1933* (1980). An excellent and far-reaching analysis.

KÖHLER, J. *Zarathustra's Secret: The Interior Life of Friedrich Nietzsche* (2002). A controversial new biography.

LACQUER, W. *A History of Zionism* (1989). The most extensive one-volume treatment.

POLIAKOV, L. *The Aryan Myth: A History of Racist and Nationalist Ideas in Europe* (1971). The best introduction to the problem.

STERN, F. *Einstein's German World* (1999). An exploration of German science from the turn of the century to the rise of Hitler.

TURNER, F. M. *Contesting Cultural Authority: Essays in Victorian Intellectual Life* (1993). Essays that deal with the relationship of science and religion and the problem of faith for intellectuals.

VITAL, D. *A People Apart: The Jews of Europe 1789–1939* (1999). A remarkably broad and deeply researched volume.

WILSON, A. N. *God's Funeral* (1999). Explores the thinkers who contributed to religious doubt during the nineteenth and twentieth centuries.

Chapter 25

BALFOUR, M. *The Kaiser and His Times* (1972). A fine biography of William II.

BOSWORTH, R. *Italy and the Approach of the First World War* (1983). A fine analysis of Italian policy.

FERGUSON, N. *The Pity of War* (1999). An analytic study of important aspects of World War I with controversial interpretations.

FIELDHOUSE, D. K. *The Colonial Experience: A Comparative Study from the Eighteenth Century* (1966). An excellent study.

FISCHER, F. *Germany's Aims in the First World War* (1967). An influential interpretation that stirred an enormous controversy by emphasizing Germany's role in bringing on the war.

HALE, O. J. *The Great Illusion 1900–1914* (1971). A fine survey of the period, especially good on public opinion.

HAYNE, M. B. *The French Foreign Office and the Origins of the First World War* (1993). An examination of the influence on French policy of the professionals in the foreign service.

HERWIG, H. *The First World War: Germany and Austria, 1914–18* (1997). A fine study of the war from the loser's perspective.

KEEGAN, J. *The First World War* (1999). A vivid and readable narrative account.

LANGER, W. L. *European Alliances and Alignments*, 2nd ed. (1966). A splendid diplomatic history of the years 1871 to 1890.

LIEVEN, D. C. B. *Russia and the Origins of the First World War* (1983). A good account of the forces that shaped Russian policy.

STEINER, Z. *Britain and the Origins of the First World War* (1977). A perceptive and informed account of the way British foreign policy was made before the war.

WILLIAMSON, S. R. JR. *Austria-Hungary and the Origins of the First World War* (1991). A valuable study of a complex subject.

Chapter 26

BEREND, I. T. *Decades of Crisis: Central and Eastern Europe before World War II* (2001). The best recent discussion of a remarkably troubled region of the early twentieth century.

BESSEL, R. *Political Violence and the Rise of Nazism: The Storm Troopers in Eastern Germany, 1925–1934* (1984). A study of the uses of violence by the Nazis.

BOSWORTH, R. *Mussolini* (2002). A major new biography.

BULLOCK, A. *Hitler: A Study in Tyranny*, rev. ed. (1964). Remains a classic biography.

FURET, F. *The Passing of an Illusion: The Idea of Communism in the Twentieth Century* (1995). A brilliant account of the manner in which communism shaped politics and thought outside the Soviet Union.

HELD, J. ed., *The Columbia History of Eastern Europe in the Twentieth Century* (1992). Individual essays on each of the nations.

JELAVICH, B. *History of the Balkans,* vol. 2 (1983). The standard work.

KERSHAW, I. *Hitler, 1889–1936: Hubris* (1998). The best treatment of Hitler's early life and rise to power.

LINCOLN, B. *Red Victory: A History of the Russian Civil War* (1989). An excellent narrative account.

MCKIBBIN, R. *Classes and Cultures: England, 1918–1951* (2000). Viewing the era through the lens of class.

POLLARD, J. F. *The Vatican and Italian Fascism 1929–32: A Study in Conflict* (1985). Provides the background to the Lateran Pacts.

STERNHELL, Z. *The Birth of Fascist Ideology: From Cultural Rebellion to Political Revolution* (1994). A controversial examination of the roots of Mussolini's ideology.

TUCKER, R. *Stalin as Revolutionary, 1879–1929: A Study in History and Personality* (1973). A useful and readable account of Stalin's rise to power.

WOHL, R. *The Generation of 1914* (1979). An important work that explores the effect of the war on political and social thought.

Chapter 27

ALLEN, W. S. *The Nazi Seizure of Power: The Experience of a Single German Town, 1930–1935,* rev. ed. (1984). A classic treatment of Nazism in a microcosmic setting.

CHASE, W. *Enemies within the Gates?: The Comintern and Stalinist Repression, 1934–1939* (2001). Examines how Soviet policies destroyed the Comintern.

CONQUEST, R. *The Great Terror: Stalin's Purges of the Thirties* (1968). Remains the most useful treatment of the subject to date.

CONQUEST, R. *The Harvest of Sorrow: Soviet Collectivization and the Terror-Famine* (1986). A study of how Stalin used starvation against his own people.

EICHENGREEN, B. *Golden Fetters: The Gold Standard and the Great Depression, 1919–1939* (1992). A remarkable study of the role of the gold standard in the economic policies of the interwar years.

GELLATELY, R. *Backing Hitler: Consent and Coercion in Nazi Germany* (2001). Controversial study emphasizing widespread support for Hitler.

GETTY, J. A. and NAUMOV, O. V. *The Road to Terror: Stalin and the Self-Destruction of the Bolsheviks, 1933–1939* (1999). A major collection of newly available documents revealing much new information about the purges.

JACKSON, J. *The Politics of Depression in France, 1932–1936* (1985). A detailed examination of the political struggles prior to the Popular Front.

JACKSON, J. *The Popular Front in France: Defending Democracy, 1934–1938* (1988). As extensive treatment.

KERSHAW, I. *Hitler,* 2 vols. (2000). The best biography now available.

KERSHAW, I. *The Nazi Dictatorship: Problems and Perspectives of Interpretation* (2000). A very accessible analysis.

KINDLEBERGER, C. *The World in Depression, 1929–1939* (1973). An account by a leading economist whose analysis is comprehensible to the layperson.

PEUKERT, D. J. K. *Inside Nazi Germany: Conformity, Opposition, and Racism in Everyday Life* (1987). An excellent discussion of life under Nazi rule.

PROCTOR, R. *The Nazi War on Cancer* (2000). A fascinating study.

PULZER, P. *Jews and the German State; The Political History of a Minority, 1848–1933* (1992). A detailed study by a major historian of European minorities.

STEPHENSON, J. *The Nazi Organization of Women* (1981). Examines the attitude and policies of the Nazis toward women.

Chapter 28

ADAMTHWAITE, A. *France and the Coming of the Second World War, 1936–1939* (1977). A careful account making good use of the newly opened French archives.

BARTOV, O. *Mirrors of Destruction: War, Genocide, and Modern Identity* (2000). A collection of remarkably penetrating essays.

BECK, E. R. *Under the Bombs: The German Home Front, 1942–1945* (1986). An interesting examination of a generally unstudied subject.

BOTWINICK, R. S. *A History of the Holocaust,* 2nd ed. (2002). A brief but broad and useful account of the causes, character, and results of the Holocaust.

BROWNING, C. *Ordinary Men* (1993). Examines a single Nazi death squad.

BULLOCK, A. *Hitler: A Study in Tyranny,* rev. ed. (1964). A brilliant biography.

GADDIS, J. L. *We Now Know: Rethinking Cold War History* (1998). A fine account of the early years of the Cold War, making use of new evidence emerging since the collapse of the Soviet Union.

GILBERT, M. *The Holocaust: A History of the Jews of Europe During the Second World War* (1985). The best and most comprehensive treatment.

IRIYE, A. *Pearl Harbor and the Coming of the Pacific War* (1999). Essays on how the Pacific war came about including a selection of documents.

KEEGAN, J. *The Second World War* (1990). A lively and penetrating account by a master military historian.

KNOX, M. *Mussolini Unleashed* (1982). An outstanding study of fascist Italy's policy and strategy in World War II.

MARKS, S. *The Illusion of Peace* (1976). A good discussion of European international relations in the 1920s and early 1930s.

MURRAY, W. and MILLETT, A. R. *A War to Be Won: Fighting the Second World War* (2000). A splendid account of the military operations in the war.

THOMAS, H. *The Spanish Civil War,* 3rd ed. (1986). The best account in English.

WANDYCZ, P. *The Twilight of French Eastern Alliances, 1926–1936* (1988). A well-documented account of the diplomacy of central and eastern Europe in a crucial period.

WEINBERG, G. L. *A World at Arms: A Global History of World War II* (1994). A thorough and excellent narrative account.

Chapter 29

ANSPRENGER, F. *The Dissolution of Colonial Empires* (1989). A broad survey.

BOTTOME, E. *The Balance of Terror: Nuclear Weapons and the Illusions of Security, 1945–1985* (1986). An examination of the role of nuclear weapons in the Cold War climate.

ELLMAN, M. and KONTOROVICH, V. *The Disintegration of the Soviet Economic System* (1992). An overview of the strains that the Soviet Union experienced during the 1980s.

FEIS, H. *From Trust to Terror: The Onset of the Cold War, 1945–1950* (1970). A useful general account.

GADDIS, J. L. *The United States and the Origin of the Cold War, 1941–1947* (1992). A major discussion.

GLENNY, M. *The Balkans, 1804–1999: Nationalism, War and the Great Powers* (1999). A lively narrative by a well-informed journalist.

HITCHCOCK, W. *Struggle for Europe: The Turbulent History of a Divided Continent, 1945–2002* (2003). The best overall narrative now available.

JARAUSCH, K. H. *The Rush to German Unity* (1994). Examines the events and background of the reunification of Germany.

JOHNSON, L. *Central Europe: Enemies and Neighbors and Friends* (1996). Examines the various nations of central Europe with an eye to the recent changes in the region.

KEEP, J. *Last of the Empires: A History of the Soviet Union, 1945–1991* (1995). An outstanding one-volume survey.

MANDELBAUM, M. *The Ideas That Conquered the World: Peace, Democracy, and Free Markets* (2002). An important analysis by a major commentator on international affairs.

MANN, R. *A Grand Delusion: America's Descent into Vietnam* (2001). The best recent narrative.

PAREKH, B. *Ghandi: A Very Short Introduction* (2001). A very useful introduction to Ghandi's ideas.

ULAM, A. *The Communists: The Story of Power and Lost Illusions: 1948–1991* (1992). Narrative of the story of the passage from Soviet Communist strength to collapse.

WALKER, M. *The Cold War and the Making of the Modern World* (1994). A major new survey.

Chapter 30

AMBROSIUS, G. and HUBBARD, W. H. *A Social and Economic History of Twentieth-Century Europe* (1989). An excellent one-volume treatment of the subject.

ANDERSON, B. S. and ZINSSER, J. P. *A History of Their Own: Women in Europe from Prehistory to the Present,* vol. 2 (1998). A broad-ranging survey.

BERNSTEIN, R. *Out of the Blue: The Story of September 11, 2001 from Jihad to Ground Zero* (2002). An excellent account by a gifted journalist.

BRAMWELL, E. *Ecology in the 20th Century: A History* (1989). Traces the environmental movement to its late nineteenth-century origins.

CROSSMAN, R. (ed.), *The God That Failed* (1949). Classic essays by former communist intellectuals.

GOLDSTINE, H. H. *The Computer from Pascal to von Neuman* (1972). A clear history of the technological development of the computer.

JENKINS, P. *The Next Christendom: The Coming of Global Christianity* (2002). A provocative analysis.

KEPEL, G. *Jihad: The Trail of Political Islam* (2002). An extensive treatment by a leading French scholar.

LANDAUER, T. K. *The Trouble with Computers: Usefulness, Usability, and Productivity* (1997). An informed skeptical commentary on the impact of computers.

MALTBY, R. ed., *Passing Parade: A History of Popular Culture in the Twentieth Century* (1989). A collection of essays on a topic just beginning to receive scholarly attention.

MONTEFIORE, G. *Philosophy in France Today* (1983). A good introduction to one of the major centers of contemporary thought.

NAIMARK, N. *Fires of Hatred: Ethnic Cleansing in Twentieth-Century Europe* (2002). A remarkably sensitive treatment of a tragic subject.

VIORST, M. *In the Shadow of the Prophet: The Struggle for the Soul of Islam* (2001). Explores the divisions in contemporary Islam.

Part 1 Timeline, Page xlvii and page 1, top to bottom, left to right: (1) Scala/Art Resource, N.Y./Royal portrait head ("Head of Sargon the Great"). From Nineveh (Kuyunjik). Akkadian, c. 2300–2200 B.C.E. Bronze, h: 12" (30.7 cm). Iraq Museum, Baghdad, Iraq. Scala/Art Resource; (2) Giraudon/Art Resource, N.Y./Stele of Hammurabi—detail of upper part: The sun god dictating his laws to King Hammurabi. Babylonian relief from Susa, c. 1760 B.C. (diorite, height of stele c. 2.1 m, height of relief 71 cm). Louvre, Paris, France. Copyright Giraudon/Art Resource; (3) © Naturhistorisches Museum Wien, Photo: Alice Schumacher; (4) Peter Harper/Dorling Kindersley Media Library/Dorling Kindersley/British Museum; (7) *The She-Wolf Suckling Romulus and Remus*, late 15th–early 16th century. The National Gallery of Art, Washington D.C., the Samuel H. Kress Collection. Photograph © Board of Trustees, National Gallery of Art, Washington, D.C.; (6) The Oriental Institute Museum/Courtesy of the Oriental Institute of the University of Chicago; (7) Museum of Natural History; (8) Gary Cralle; (9) Anderson/Rudolf Lesch Fine Arts Inc.; (10) Ministere de la Culture et des Communications/Ministere de la Culture et de la Communication. Direction Regionale des affaires Culturelles de Rhone–Alpes. Service Regional de l'Archeologie; (11) Alinari Archives, Florence; (12) Robert Frerck/Woodfin Camp & Associates; (13) The Granger Collection.

Part 1, Page 2 and page 3, top to bottom, left to right: (1) Liz McAulay/Dorling Kindersley Media Library/Dorling Kindersley/British Museum; (2) Max Alexander/Dorling Kindersley Media Library; (3) Christopher Rennie/Robert Harding World Imagery; (4) Getty Images Inc.–Hulton Archive Photos; (5) Scala/Art Resource, N.Y./"Battle of Alexander the Great at Issus." Roman mosaic. Museo Archeologico Nazionale, Naples, Italy. Scala/Art Resources; (6) Robert Frerck/Woodfin Camp & Associates; (7) Art Resource, N.Y; (8) Library of Congress; (9) Art Resource, N.Y; (10) Liz McAulay/Dorling Kindersley Media Library/Dorling Kindersley/British Museum; (11) Christopher Rennie/Robert Harding World Imagery.

Chapter 1 a. Seated Scribe from Saqqara, Egypt. 5th Dynasty, © 2510–2460 BCE. Painted limestone, height 21 ft (53 cm). Musee du Louvre, Paris. Bridgeman–Giraudon/Art Resource, NY; b. © Judith Miller/Dorling Kindersley/Ancient Art; c. Robert Frerck/Odyssey Production/Woodfin Camp & Associates; d. © Dorling Kindersley; e. © Judith Miller/Dorling Kindersley/Ancient Art; f. Alan Hills and Barbara Winter © The British Museum; g. British Museum, London, UK/Bridgeman Art Library; i. Belly handled amphora, Kerameikos, Height 1.55 m., National Museum, Athens; j. Victory stele of Naram–Sin, King of Akkad, over the mountain-dwelling Lullubi, Mesopotamian, Akkadian Period, © 2230 BC (pink sandstone). Louvre, Paris, France/The Bridgeman Art Library International Ltd.; l. Stele of the Code of Laws of Hammurabi. © 1792–1750 BCE. Diorite. 225

x 65 cm. Found at Susa. Photo: Ch. Larrieu. Reunion des Muses Nationaux et Ecoli du Louvre, Paris/Art Resource, NY; q. Relief, Israel, 105h–6th Century: Judean exiles carrying provisions. Detal of the Assyrian conquest of the Jewish fortified town of Lachish (battle 701 BC). Part of a relief from the palace of Sennacherib at Niniveh, Mesopotamia (Iraq). British Museum, London, Great Britain. Copyright Erich Lessing/Art Resource, NY.

Chapter 2 b. © Gianni Dagli Orti/CORBIS; e. Framer plughing with oxen. 1st half 6th BCE. Greek terracotta group fromThebes, Boetia. 11 x 22 cm. Inv.: CA 352. Photo: Harve Lewandownski. Louvre, Paris. Reunion des Musees Nationaux/Art Resource, NY; f. Joe Cornish/Dorling Kindersley © Archaeological Receipts Fund (TAP); g. © Roger Wood/CORBIS; h. © Foto Marburg/Art Resource, NY; i. Photograph © Eric Lessing/Art Resource, NY; j. © Gianni Dagli Orti/CORBIS; k. "Hydria (water jug)". Greek, Archaic period, ca. 520 B.C. Athens, Attica, Greece the Priam Painter. Ceramic, black-figure, H: 0.53 cm Diam (with handles): 0.37 cm. William Francis Warden Fund. © 2004 Museum of Fine Arts, Boston. Accession #61.195.

Chapter 3 a. Chas Howson © The British Museum; b. © The British Museum; c. © 2004 Christie's Images, Inc.; d. Nick Nicholls © The British Museum; e. Battle between Alexander the Great and King Dareios. House of the Faun, Pompeii VI 12, 2 Inv. 10020. Museo Archeologico Nazionale, Naples, Italy. Photograph © Erich Lessing/Art Resource, NY; f. Louvre, Dept. des Antiquites Grecques/Romaines, Paris, France. Photograph © Erich Lessing/Art Resource, NY; g. John Serafin/SBG; j. Library of Congress. Chapter opening, b. Meredith Pillon, Greek National Tourism Organization.

Chapter 4 a. Walter S. Clark/Photo Researchers, Inc.; b. Dorling Kindersley Media Library; c. Fotostudio Rapuzzi; d. © Sandro Vannini/CORBIS; f. © Araldo De Luca/CORBIS; h. Nick Nicholls © The British Museum; i. Alinari/Art Resource, NY; j. Portland vase, 3rd c. A.D. Cameo-cut glass. British Museum, London; l. North Wind Picture Archives. Chapter opening, d. Rheinisches Landesmuseum, Trier, Germany. Alinari/Art Resource, NY.

Chapter 5 a. Vatican Museums & Galleries, Vatican City/Superstock; b. Andy Crawford © Hessischen Landesmuseums, Darmstadt, Germany; c. Courtesy David Art Images; d. Scala/Art Resource, NY; f. Roger Wood/Corbis/Bettmann; h. © Burstein Collection/CORBIS; i. Ruggero Vanni/Vanni Archive/Corbis/Bettmann. Page 115, Saturnia, Tellus, Goddess of Earth, Air and Water. Panel from the Ara Pacis. 13–9 BCE. Museum of the Ara Paciis, Rome. Nimatallah/Art Resource, NY.

Part 2, Page 144 and page 145, top to bottom, left to right: (1) Canali Photobank/Justinian, detail. c. 547. Mosaic technique. Canali Photobank, Capriolo, Italy; (2) Gianni Dagli Orti/Corbis/Bettmann/Gianni Dagli Orti/Corbis; (3) The New York Public Library/Art Resource/Picture Collection,

The Branch Libraries, The New York Public Library, Astor, Lenox and Tilden Foundations; (4) Giraudon/Art Resource, N.Y./Bayeus, Musee de l'Eveche. "With special authorization of the City of Bayeux". Giraudon/Art Resource; (5) Corbis/ Bettmann; (6) Marvin Trachtenberg/Marvin Trachtenberg; (7) Unidentified/Dorling Kindersley Media Library; (8) Scala/ Art Resource, N.Y./(c)Scala/Art Resource, NY; (9) Corbis/ Bettmann; (10) Robert W. Madden/National Geographic Image Collection; (11) Gavin Hellier/Robert Harding World Imagery; (12) Foto Marburg/Art Resource, N.Y./Copyright Foto Marburg/Art Resource, NY; (13) Bonaventura Berlinghieri/Art Resource, N.Y.

Chapter 6 a. The New York Public Library/Art Resource, NY; b. © Stapleton Collection/CORBIS; c. © Stapleton Collection/CORBIS; d., f. and j. © Dorling Kindersley; e. Kunsthistorisches Museum, Wien oder KHM, Wien; i. Scala/Art Resource, NY; k. Werner Forman/Art Resource, NY; l. By Permission of the British Library. (1000102.021).

Chapter 7 b. Centre Guillaume Le Conquerant. Detail of the Bayeux Tapestry-XIth century. By special permission of the City of Bayeux; c. Neil Lukas © Dorling Kindersley; d. Geoff Brightling © Dorling Kindersley; f. Image Works/Mary Evans Picture Library Ltd.; i. Photograph © Foto Marburg/Art Resource, NY; j. The Bridgeman Art Library International Ltd./Private Collection/The Bridgeman Art Library, London; k. Alan Williams © Dorling Kindersley

Chapter 8 a. The Granger Collection, New York; b. © Museum of London; c. Art Resource, NY/©Giraudon/Art Resource, NY; d. Bildarkiv Preussischer Kulturbesitz; e. The Art Archive/Picture Desk, Inc./Kobal Collection; f. Corbis/Bettmann.

Part 3, Page 216 and page 217, top to bottom, left to right: (1) Max Alexander/Dorling Kindersley Media Library; (2) Art Resource/Reunion des Musees Nationaux/Reunion des Musees Nationaux/Art Reesource, NY; (3) The Granger Collection/ The Granger Collection, New York; (4) Art Resource, N.Y./Lauros-Giraudon/Art Resource, NY; (5) The Granger Collection; (6) Arthur Hacker, The Cloister of the World./The Bridgeman Art Library; (7) The Bridgeman Art Library International Ltd./Elizabeth I, Armada Portrait, c. 1588 (oil on panel) by George Gower (1540–96) (attr. to). Woburn Abbey, Bedfordshire, UK/Bridgeman Art Library, London/New York; (8) Getty Images Inc.–Hulton Archive Photos; (9) Tim Booth/Dorling Kindersley Media Library; (10) Library of Congress/Courtesy of the Library of Congress; (11) Giraudon/Art Resource, N.Y.

Chapter 9 a. Victoria & Albert Museum, London/Bridgeman Art Library; b. © ARPL/HIP/The Image Works; c. Geoff Dann © Dorling Kindersley, Courtesy of the Wallace Collection, London; e. UNESCO/Ann Ronan Picture Library/The Image Works; g. British Library, London. The Bridgeman Art Library Ltd.; h. Hacker Art Books Inc.

Chapter 10 b. The Granger Collection; c. By Permission of The British Library; d. Scala/Art Resource, NY; f. Vatican Museums and Galleries, Vatican City, Italy/Giraudon/Bridgeman Art Library; g. The Mariners' Museum, Newport News, VA; h. This item is reproduced by permission of The Huntington Library, San Marino, California.

Chapter 11 a. © Scala/Art Resource, NY; b. Musee Unterlinden, Colmar, France/SuperStock; c. Geoff Dann © The British Museum; d. Bildarchiv Preussischer Kulturbesitz/Art Resource, NY; e. National Gallery of Ancient Art, Rome, Italy/Canali PhotoBank, Milan/SuperStock; f. Painting-Flemish-17th cent. Peter Paul Rubens (1577–1640) The Miracle of Saint Ignace Loyola. Oil on canvas (1617–1618). Size: 535 × 395 cm. Cat. 313, Inv. 517 Kunsthist. Museum, Gemaeldegalerie, Vienna, Austria. Art Resource, NY; h. From Max Geisberg, "The German Single-Leaf Woodcut, 1500–1550", edited by Walter L. Strauss. Hacker Art Books, 1974. Used by permission of Hacker Art Books, Inc.

Chapter 12 a. © Dorling Kindersley; b. The Granger Collection; c. Geoff Dann © Dorling Kindersley, Courtesy of the Wallace Collection, London; d. © Dorling Kindersley; e. © Dorling Kindersley; f. Getty Images, Inc. - Liaison; g. Queen Mary I, 1554 (oil on panel) by Sir Anthonis Mor (Antonio Moro) (1517/20 - 76/7). Prado, Madrid, Spain/Bridgeman Art Library; h. Oliver Benn/Getty Images, Inc.; i. The Granger Collection, New York.

Chapter 13 a. Neil Lukas © Dorling Kindersley, Courtesy of l'Etablissement Public du Musee et du Domaine National de Versailles; c. and i. © Judith Miller/Dorling Kindersley/ Mendes Antique Lace and Textiles; e. State Historical Museum, Moscow, Russia/Leonid Bogdanov/SuperStock; j. © Bettmann/CORBIS.

Chapter 14 b. Corbis/Bettmann; c. © Paul Almasy/CORBIS; d. ©James A. Sugar/CORBIS; e. Image Works/Mary Evans Picture Library Ltd.; f. British Library, London, UK/Bridgeman Art Library; g. Philip Spruyt/Corbis/Bettmann; h. Sir Francis Bacon (1561–1626), champion of the inductive method of gaining knowledge. National Portrait Gallery, London; j. Bildarchiv Preubischer Kulturbesitz.

Chapter 15 b. J. B. S. Chardin, "The Washerwoman". Nationalmuseum med Prins Eugens Waldemarsudde. PHOTO: The National Museum of Fine Arts; c. Andrew McRobb © Dorling Kindersley; d. Mike Dunning © Dorling Kindersley, Courtesy of the National Railway Museum, York; f. Geoff Brightling © Dorling Kindersley, Courtesy of the Museum of English Rural Life, The University of Reading; i. © Scala/Art Resource, NY.

Chapter 16 a. © Bettmann/CORBIS; b. Getty Images Inc. - Hulton Archive Photos; c. © Bettmann/CORBIS; d. © National Maritime Museum, London; e. and f. Dave King © Dorling Kindersley; g. © Royalty Free/CORBIS; h. Martin van Meytens: "Kaiserin Maria Theresia mit ihrer Familie auf der SchloBterasse von Schobrunn". Kunsthistorisches Museum, Vienna, Austria; i. North Wind Picture Archives; j. © Dorling Kindersley.

A

G

M

WESTERN CIVILIZATION DOCUMENTS CD-ROM

SINGLE PC LICENSE AGREEMENT AND LIMITED WARRANTY

READ THIS LICENSE CAREFULLY BEFORE OPENING THIS PACKAGE. BY OPENING THIS PACKAGE, YOU ARE AGREEING TO THE TERMS AND CONDITIONS OF THIS LICENSE. IF YOU DO NOT AGREE, DO NOT OPEN THE PACKAGE. PROMPTLY RETURN THE UNOPENED PACKAGE AND ALL ACCOMPANYING ITEMS TO THE PLACE YOU OBTAINED THEM.

1. GRANT OF LICENSE AND OWNERSHIP: THE ENCLOSED COMPUTER PROGRAMS <<AND DATA>> ("SOFTWARE") ARE LICENSED, NOT SOLD, TO YOU BY PEARSON EDUCATION, INC. PUBLISHING AS PEARSON PRENTICE HALL ("WE" OR THE "COMPANY") AND IN CONSIDERATION OF YOUR PURCHASE OR ADOPTION OF THE ACCOMPANYING COMPANY TEXTBOOKS AND/OR OTHER MATERIALS, AND YOUR AGREEMENT TO THESE TERMS. WE RESERVE ANY RIGHTS NOT GRANTED TO YOU. YOU OWN ONLY THE DISK(S) BUT WE AND/OR OUR LICENSORS OWN THE SOFTWARE ITSELF. THIS LICENSE ALLOWS YOU TO USE AND DISPLAY YOUR COPY OF THE SOFTWARE ON A SINGLE COMPUTER (I.E., WITH A SINGLE CPU) AT A SINGLE LOCATION FOR ACADEMIC USE ONLY, SO LONG AS YOU COMPLY WITH THE TERMS OF THIS AGREEMENT. YOU MAY MAKE ONE COPY FOR BACK UP, OR TRANSFER YOUR COPY TO ANOTHER CPU, PROVIDED THAT THE SOFTWARE IS USABLE ON ONLY ONE COMPUTER.

2. RESTRICTIONS: YOU MAY NOT TRANSFER OR DISTRIBUTE THE SOFTWARE OR DOCUMENTATION TO ANYONE ELSE. EXCEPT FOR BACKUP, YOU MAY NOT COPY THE DOCUMENTATION OR THE SOFTWARE. YOU MAY NOT NETWORK THE SOFTWARE OR OTHERWISE USE IT ON MORE THAN ONE COMPUTER OR COMPUTER TERMINAL AT THE SAME TIME. YOU MAY NOT REVERSE ENGINEER, DISASSEMBLE, DECOMPILE, MODIFY, ADAPT, TRANSLATE, OR CREATE DERIVATIVE WORKS BASED ON THE SOFTWARE OR THE DOCUMENTATION. YOU MAY BE HELD LEGALLY RESPONSIBLE FOR ANY COPYING OR COPYRIGHT INFRINGEMENT THAT IS CAUSED BY YOUR FAILURE TO ABIDE BY THE TERMS OF THESE RESTRICTIONS.

3. TERMINATION: THIS LICENSE IS EFFECTIVE UNTIL TERMINATED. THIS LICENSE WILL TERMINATE AUTOMATICALLY WITHOUT NOTICE FROM THE COMPANY IF YOU FAIL TO COMPLY WITH ANY PROVISIONS OR LIMITATIONS OF THIS LICENSE. UPON TERMINATION, YOU SHALL DESTROY THE DOCUMENTATION AND ALL COPIES OF THE SOFTWARE. ALL PROVISIONS OF THIS AGREEMENT AS TO LIMITATION AND DISCLAIMER OF WARRANTIES, LIMITATION OF LIABILITY, REMEDIES OR DAMAGES, AND OUR OWNERSHIP RIGHTS SHALL SURVIVE TERMINATION.

4. LIMITED WARRANTY AND DISCLAIMER OF WARRANTY: COMPANY WARRANTS THAT FOR A PERIOD OF 60 DAYS FROM THE DATE YOU PURCHASE THIS SOFTWARE (OR PURCHASE OR ADOPT THE ACCOMPANYING TEXTBOOK), THE SOFTWARE, WHEN PROPERLY INSTALLED AND USED IN ACCORDANCE WITH THE DOCUMENTATION, WILL OPERATE IN SUBSTANTIAL CONFORMITY WITH THE DESCRIPTION OF THE SOFTWARE SET FORTH IN THE DOCUMENTATION, AND THAT FOR A PERIOD OF 30 DAYS THE DISK(S) ON WHICH THE SOFTWARE IS DELIVERED SHALL BE FREE FROM DEFECTS IN MATERIALS AND WORKMANSHIP UNDER NORMAL USE. THE COMPANY DOES NOT WARRANT THAT THE SOFTWARE WILL MEET YOUR REQUIREMENTS OR THAT THE OPERATION OF THE SOFTWARE WILL BE UNINTERRUPTED OR ERROR-FREE. YOUR ONLY REMEDY AND THE COMPANY'S ONLY OBLIGATION UNDER THESE LIMITED WARRANTIES IS, AT THE COMPANY'S OPTION, RETURN OF THE DISK FOR A REFUND OF ANY AMOUNTS PAID FOR IT BY YOU OR REPLACEMENT OF THE DISK. THIS LIMITED WARRANTY IS THE ONLY WARRANTY PROVIDED BY THE COMPANY AND ITS LICENSORS, AND THE COMPANY AND ITS LICENSORS DISCLAIM ALL OTHER WARRANTIES, EXPRESS OR IMPLIED, INCLUDING WITHOUT LIMITATION, THE IMPLIED WARRANTIES OF MERCHANTABILITY AND FITNESS FOR A PARTICULAR PURPOSE. THE COMPANY DOES NOT WARRANT, GUARANTEE OR MAKE ANY REPRESENTATION REGARDING THE ACCURACY, RELIABILITY, CURRENTNESS, USE, OR RESULTS OF USE, OF THE SOFTWARE.

5. LIMITATION OF REMEDIES AND DAMAGES: IN NO EVENT, SHALL THE COMPANY OR ITS EMPLOYEES, AGENTS, LICENSORS, OR CONTRACTORS BE LIABLE FOR ANY INCIDENTAL, INDIRECT, SPECIAL, OR CONSEQUENTIAL DAMAGES ARISING OUT OF OR IN CONNECTION WITH THIS LICENSE OR THE SOFTWARE, INCLUDING FOR LOSS OF USE, LOSS OF DATA, LOSS OF INCOME OR PROFIT, OR OTHER LOSSES, SUSTAINED AS A RESULT OF INJURY TO ANY PERSON, OR LOSS OF OR DAMAGE TO PROPERTY, OR CLAIMS OF THIRD PARTIES, EVEN IF THE COMPANY OR AN AUTHORIZED REPRESENTATIVE OF THE COMPANY HAS BEEN ADVISED OF THE POSSIBILITY OF SUCH DAMAGES. IN NO EVENT SHALL THE LIABILITY OF THE COMPANY FOR DAMAGES WITH RESPECT TO THE SOFTWARE EXCEED THE AMOUNTS ACTUALLY PAID BY YOU, IF ANY, FOR THE SOFTWARE OR THE ACCOMPANYING TEXTBOOK. BECAUSE SOME JURISDICTIONS DO NOT ALLOW THE LIMITATION OF LIABILITY IN CERTAIN CIRCUMSTANCES, THE ABOVE LIMITATIONS MAY NOT ALWAYS APPLY TO YOU.

6. GENERAL: THIS AGREEMENT SHALL BE CONSTRUED IN ACCORDANCE WITH THE LAWS OF THE UNITED STATES OF AMERICA AND THE STATE OF NEW YORK, APPLICABLE TO CONTRACTS MADE IN NEW YORK, EXCLUDING THE STATE'S LAWS AND POLICIES ON CONFLICTS OF LAW, AND SHALL BENEFIT THE COMPANY, ITS AFFILIATES AND ASSIGNEES. THIS AGREEMENT IS THE COMPLETE AND EXCLUSIVE STATEMENT OF THE AGREEMENT BETWEEN YOU AND THE COMPANY AND SUPERSEDES ALL PROPOSALS OR PRIOR AGREEMENTS, ORAL, OR WRITTEN, AND ANY OTHER COMMUNICATIONS BETWEEN YOU AND THE COMPANY OR ANY REPRESENTATIVE OF THE COMPANY RELATING TO THE SUBJECT MATTER OF THIS AGREEMENT. IF YOU ARE A U.S. GOVERNMENT USER, THIS SOFTWARE IS LICENSED WITH "RESTRICTED RIGHTS" AS SET FORTH IN SUBPARAGRAPHS (A)-(D) OF THE COMMERCIAL COMPUTER-RESTRICTED RIGHTS CLAUSE AT FAR 52.227-19 OR IN SUBPARAGRAPHS (C)(1)(ii) OF THE RIGHTS IN TECHNICAL DATA AND COMPUTER SOFTWARE CLAUSE AT DFARS 252.227-7013, AND SIMILAR CLAUSES, AS APPLICABLE.

SHOULD YOU HAVE ANY QUESTIONS CONCERNING THIS AGREEMENT OR IF YOU WISH TO CONTACT THE COMPANY FOR ANY REASON, PLEASE CONTACT IN WRITING: LEGAL DEPARTMENT, PRENTICE HALL, 1 LAKE STREET, UPPER SADDLE RIVER, NJ 07450 OR CALL PEARSON EDUCATION PRODUCT SUPPORT AT 1-800-677-6337.